Brazil

Nick Selby
Andrew Draffen
Robyn Jones
Chris McAsey
Leonardo Pinheiro

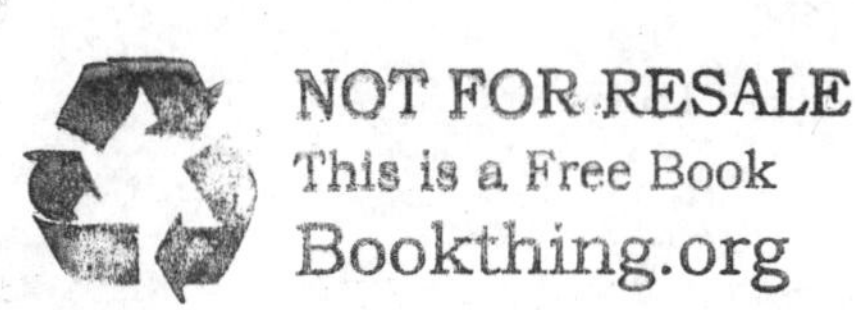

Brazil

4th edition

Published by
Lonely Planet Publications
Head Office: PO Box 617, Hawthorn, Vic 3122, Australia
Branches: 150 Linden Street, Oakland, CA 94607, USA
10a Spring Place, London NW5 3BH, UK
1 rue du Dahomey, 75011 Paris, France

Printed by
The Bookmaker Pty Ltd
Printed in China

Photographs by
Greg Caire
Andrew Draffen
Robyn Jones
Chris McAsey
John Maier, Jr
Guy Moberly
Leonardo Pinheiro

Front cover: A *jacaré* (yacare caiman) in the Pantanal (John Maier, Jr)

First Published
August 1989

This Edition
November 1998

Although the authors and publisher have tried to make the information as accurate as possible, they accept no responsibility for any loss, injury or inconvenience sustained by any person using this book.

National Library of Australia Cataloguing in Publication Data

Brazil

4th ed.
Includes index
ISBN 0 86442 561 9

1. Brazil – Guidebooks. I. Selby, Nick.

918.10464

text & maps © Lonely Planet 1998
photos © photographers as indicated 1998

All rights reserved. No part of this publication may be reproduced, stored in a retrieval system or transmitted in any form by any means, electronic, mechanical, photocopying, recording or otherwise, except brief extracts for the purpose of review, without the written permission of the publisher and copyright owner.

Nick Selby

Nick Selby was born and raised in New York City. Escaping from sound engineering (he worked 'mixing' 'music' on both *As The World Turns* and *Guiding Light* and 'coordinating' sound (huh?) for CBS Sports), Nick moved to Poland in 1990 (wouldn't you have?) and to Russia in 1991, where he wrote *The Visitor's Guide to the New St Petersburg*. Since then he's been travelling and working for LP on a bizarre group of destinations including *Russia*, *St Petersburg*, *Florida*, *Miami*, *Germany* and *Texas*. He lives with his wife, Corinna, in Tarifa, Spain – Europe's southernmost point.

Andrew Draffen

Australian-born Andrew has travelled and worked his way around Australia, Asia, North America and the Caribbean, settling just long enough in Melbourne to complete an arts degree, majoring in history. During his first trip to South America in 1984, Andrew fell in love with both Brazil and his future wife, Stella. They have since toured extensively in Brazil, Europe and Asia, and today travel with their young children, Gabriela and Christopher, whose great-great-grandfather introduced football to Brazil.

Robyn Jones

As a teenager Robyn traded farm life in rural Victoria, Australia for a year as an exchange student in the Brazilian megalopolis of São Paulo. While studying for her degree in architecture she tripped around Australia and Europe. Later she returned to Brazil with Leonardo, to live in Rio de Janeiro for a while and to meet her future in-laws. She worked on the 3rd edition of Lonely Planet's *Brazil* and co-wrote *Fiji*. In between travels Robyn works as an architect in Melbourne, where she lives with Leonardo and their son Alex.

Chris McAsey

After being weeded out of law school, Chris had varying levels of success as kitchenhand, professional footballer and clothing wholesaler. A few years later, he hit the road in a desperate attempt to prolong his youth; travelling, working and studying in western and eastern Europe, Russia, the USA and Japan. He returned to Australia to complete a BA in professional writing and to write a guide to Australia for Japanese people. He now works at Victoria University in Melbourne, Australia.

Leonardo Pinheiro

Leonardo was born and raised in Rio de Janeiro, Brazil. At 15, curious to roam further than Rio city, he jumped on a bus to the north-east coast. From then on he travelled as much as his pocket money and time would allow throughout Brazil. After tertiary studies in Agricultural Science he came to Sydney to do a Master's degree in biotechnology and to check out the Australian surf. He met Robyn, and moved to Melbourne where they live with their baby son Alex. Leonardo has also worked on the 3rd edition of Lonely Planet's *Brazil* and on the 4th edition of *Fiji*. He is currently studying for his PhD in biochemistry.

From the Authors

From Nick Heartfelt thanks to Angela Wilson, and to Jennifer Jackson Martins at EMWP in New York for pre-departure miracles, and Dawn Kelly in Belo Horizonte.

Thanks also to Carlos Alberto A de Moura and PageNet Brasil for keeping me wired through the trip, state tourist officials including Liege Penna (MG); Patricia Servilha (SP); Carla Bastos (Vitória & ES), and all the local tourist offices which gave loads of help. Thank you Doug Trent, Focus Tours; Gary Burniske and George Marshall of The Rainforest Foundation and Carol Goodstein and Michael Goulding of Rainforest Alliance, Roberto Smeraldi at Friends of the Earth Amazônas and Craig Savinton of Kangaroo Tours in São Paulo.

In Tarifa, thanks to my wife Corinna, and to Antony Sharman for computer wonders.

And thanks to Andrew, Chris, Robyn and Leonardo for all their excellent work on both this edition and the last one.

From Andrew Special thanks to my Brazilian family in São Paulo, especially Vera Miller – *a sogra, mais animada da praia*; Iara Costa da Pinto (São Paulo) for her hospitality on many Brazil trips; Ivana and Portuga, *nossa superpadrinhos*; Caralho Malandro (Rio) for all his help and excellent dart-throwing; Mike and Ivandy (Rio), two of Mangueira's finest, Tours Bahia (Salvador), Sanjay Kaul (England), Ian and Monica (USA), Cacau (Tutóia), Dona Mazé (Rio Novo); Martin *Rapaz* Darling (Denmark) – a modern Viking; Edward (Scotland) for his great tips – especially the budget stuff; Frank and Helen Draffen (Australia) for their encouragement and support over the years; and Stella, Gabriela and Christopher D, who make it all worthwhile.

From Chris Thanks to Clodiano and the crew at Epatur, Porto Alegre for the excellent nightlife tour, Vanessa Gouveia Leite (Sebrae, Campo Grande), Neusa Batista for the reviving tea in Brasília, António Carlos Candido (Bonito), Gustavo Nabrzecki (Curitiba), Carmen Bernardes (Canela), Rina, Ray and Jenny (Perth, Australia) for the company in Buenos Aires, and Francisco in Foz do Iguaçu (sorry, I lost your address). At home, special thanks to Paul, Rosemary and Nicole Hearnden, Ross and Jackie McAsey, my Sydney family, James, Fran and Olivia and most of all, my beautiful girls, Gina and Eden.

From Robyn & Leo Special thanks to Leo's family in Rio, especially titia Liane and vovo Laire for their babysitting skills. Thanks to Robyn's family, principally Marj for looking after our bills while we were away. Baby Alex deserves a mention for cooperating *most* of the time and making travelling more interesting!

Thanks also to Leomando de Souza Noronha and Sandra Maria Costa e Lima (Sebrae, Rio Branco do Acre); José de Anchieta Correia and Joseane Araújo (Departamento de Turismo Funcetur, Rondonia), Fláio Carneiro and Chicão Santos (Departamento de Cultura Funcetur, Rondonia); Roselene da Silva Bastos and Tereza Jacqueline Rodrigues Alves (Paratur, Belém); Silvia Helena Ribeiro Ruz and Paulo Moreira Pinto (Bélemtur, Belém); Auda Piani (Assessora de Turismo de Icoaraci); Daniela Cardoso and Lindy Lobato (Santarém Tur); Steven Alexander (Amazon Tours); Ivano Cordeiro, Andre Luiz Albuquerque, Maria Socorro Costa Pinto and Fabiana Ribeiro Leite (Setor de Informaçãoes, Funtur, Manaus); Joelson Bacry (Emantur, Manaus); Gladys (Santa Elena); Robert Chliakhtine (Melbourne).

This Book

The 1st edition of *Brazil* was written by Mitchell Schoen & William Herzberg. The 2nd edition was written by Andrew Draffen, Deanna Swaney & Robert Strauss. The 3rd edition was written by Andrew Draffen, Chris McAsey, Robyn Jones & Leonardo Pinheiro. For this 4th edition, Nick Selby covered the Southeast except Rio de Janeiro city and state, Andrew Draffen covered the Northeast and Rio de Janeiro city and state, Chris McAsey covered the South and Central West and Robyn Jones & Leonardo Pinheiro covered the North.

Thanks to Krzysztof Dydńyski for information on Leticia, Columbian and Peruvian borders and for Santa Elena, Venezuela, taken from Lonely Planet's *South America on a shoestring.*

From the Publisher

The coordinating editor of this book was Helen Yeates. Editing and proofing was done by Craig MacKenzie, Lyn McGaurr, Darren Elder, Katie Cody, Miriam Cannell, Wendy Owen and Bethune Carmichael. Quentin Frayne edited the language section.

Mark Griffiths coordinated the mapping and design of the book with mapping assistance from Jenny Jones, Anthony Phelan, Nick Lynagh-Bannikoff, Ann Jeffree and Jane Hart. Additional illustrations were drawn by Nick. Ada Cheung assisted with layout and indexing and Margie Jung designed the cover. Thanks also to Tim Uden for layout assistance.

Thanks

Many thanks to the travellers who used the last edition and wrote to us with helpful hints, useful advice and interesting anecdotes. Your names appear on page 710.

Warning & Request

Things change – prices go up, schedules change, good places go bad and bad places go bankrupt – nothing stays the same. So, if you find things better or worse, recently opened or long since closed, please tell us and help make the next edition even more accurate and useful.

We value all of the feedback we receive from travellers. Julie Young coordinates a small team who read and acknowledge every letter, postcard and email, and ensure that every morsel of information finds its way to the appropriate authors, editors and publishers.

Everyone who writes to us will find their name in the next edition of the appropriate guide and will also receive a free subscription to our quarterly newsletter, *Planet Talk*. The very best contributions will be rewarded with a free Lonely Planet guide.

Excerpts from your correspondence may appear in new editions of this guide; in *Planet Talk*; or in updates on our Web site – so please let us know if you don't want your letter published or your name acknowledged.

Contents

THE SOUTH 303

THE CENTRAL WEST 359

THE NORTHEAST 409

CEARÁ, PIAUÍ & MARANHÃO 545

THE NORTH 587

PARÁ, AMAPÁ & TOCANTINS 590

AMAZONAS & RORAIMA 633

RONDÔNIA & ACRE 665

LANGUAGE GUIDE 685

GLOSSARY 692

INDEX 698

Map Legend

BOUNDARIES

International Boundary
Provincial Boundary
Disputed Boundary

ROUTES

A25 ..... Freeway, with Route Number
Major Road
Minor Road
Minor Road - Unsealed
City Road
City Street
City Lane
Train Route, with Station
M ..... Metro Route, with Station
Cable Car or Chairlift
Ferry Route
Walking Track

AREA FEATURES

Building
Cemetery
Beach
Market
Park, Gardens
Pedestrian Mall
Reef
Urban Area

HYDROGRAPHIC FEATURES

Canal
Coastline
Creek, River
Lake, Intermittent Lake
Rapids, Waterfalls
Salt Lake
Swamp

SYMBOLS

CAPITAL	National Capital
CAPITAL	Provincial Capital
CITY	City
Town	Town
Village	Village

Place to Stay
Camping Ground
Caravan Park
Hut or Chalet

Place to Eat
Pub or Bar

Airport
Ancient or City Wall
Bank
Beach
Cave
Church
Cliff or Escarpment
Dive Site
Embassy
Golf Course
Hospital
Lighthouse
Lookout
Monument
Mountain or Hill
Museum
National Park

One Way Street
Parking
Pass
Petrol Station
Police Station
Post Office
Ruins
Shopping Centre
Stately Home
Surf Beach
Swimming Pool
Telephone
Temple
Tomb
Tourist Information
Transport
Zoo

Note: not all symbols displayed above appear in this book

Introduction

No country ignites the western imagination as Brazil does. For hundreds of years it has symbolised the great escape into a primordial, tropical paradise. From the mad passion of Carnaval to the enormity of the dark Amazon, Brazil is a country of mythical proportions.

Roughly the size of the USA (excluding Alaska), Brazil is a vast country encompassing nearly half of South America, and bordering most of the continent's other nations – Ecuador and Chile are the exceptions. After 40 years of internal migration and population growth, Brazil is also an urban country; more than two out of every three Brazilians live in a city. São Paulo, with over 17 million inhabitants, is the world's second most populous city.

Brazil's population is clustered along the Atlantic coast and much of the country, including the massive Amazon Basin, remains scarcely populated and inaccessible.

For most, the Brazilian journey begins in Rio de Janeiro. For some it goes no further. One of the world's great cities, Rio has developed a highly advanced culture of pleasure. It revolves around the famous beaches of Copacabana and Ipanema, and is fuelled by the music and dance of samba, the beauty of Corcovado and Pão de Açúcar (Sugar Loaf Mountain), the athleticism of football, the happiness to be found in an ice-cold *cerveja* (beer), the camaraderie of *papo* (chitchat) and the cult of the body-beautiful. This hedonism reaches its climax in the big bang of ecstasy that is Carnaval – four days of revelry and debauchery, unrivalled by any other party on the globe.

Rio de Janeiro state is blessed with some of the country's best beaches: from the world-renowned Búzios to the undeveloped Ilha Grande. Inland, the coastal mountains rise rapidly from under a blanket of lush, green, tropical forest, culminating in spectacular peaks. The mountains are punctuated by colonial cities and national parks that are the venues for Brazil's best hiking and climbing.

The Amazon is the world's largest tropical rainforest, fed by the world's largest river, and home to the richest and most diverse ecosystem on earth – a naturalist's ultimate fantasy! Though it is threatened by rapid and senseless deforestation, the Brazilian Amazon still offers years of exploration for the adventurous traveller.

Brazil's best kept secret – the Pantanal – is south of the Amazon in the centre of the continent. The world's largest wetlands, the Pantanal is home to the greatest concentration of fauna in South America. When the flood waters recede in March, the Pantanal becomes an ornithologist's playground, with over 200 bird species strutting their stuff: macaws, parrots, toucans, rheas and jaburú storks are just a few of the more exotic species to be seen. *Yacare caimans* (alligators), deer, capybaras, anteaters, anacondas, river otters, and the rare jaguar also thrive in the Pantanal, although several of these species are severely threatened by poaching.

The Foz do Iguaçu, at the border of Argentina, Paraguay and Brazil, may be Brazil's most dazzling spectacle. The mighty waterfalls are one of the natural wonders of the world, and are superior, in size and grandeur, to both Niagara and Victoria.

Wherever you go in Brazil, from the standing-room only crowds of Copacabana to the quieter white-sand beaches along the banks of the Amazon, you'll see Brazilians at their beaches playing. The beach is the national passion – everything and everyone goes there. Fortunately, with over 8000km of coastline, there are loads of superb beaches, so you should have no problem finding your own tropical hideaway.

The mixing of races in Brazil – Indian, black and white – is most pronounced in the historic Northeast. Racial diversity and the tenacity of a traditional way of life have created a unique and wonderful civilisation, with much of Brazil's most beautiful music, dance and art, and a series of fascinating 16th and 17th century cities like Recife, Olinda, Fortaleza, São Luís and, of course, Salvador.

Once the capital of Brazil, and one of the richest cities of the New World, Salvador is today the centre of Afro-Brazilian culture. Against a backdrop of 17th century colonial houses, gilded churches and lively beaches, Salvador de Bahia breathes Africa: the rhythms of *afoxé*; the dance of *capoeira*; the spirituality of Candomblé, the Afro-Brazilian religion; and the many colourful pageants and festivals, particularly from December to Carnaval.

Perhaps Brazil is not the paradise on earth that many travellers once imagined, but it is a land of often unimaginable beauty. There are still stretches of unexplored rainforest, islands with pristine tropical beaches, and endless rivers. And there are the people themselves, who delight the visitor with their energy, fantasy and joy.

Facts about the Country

HISTORY

Indian Settlement

It's now accepted that, bar a few Vikings in the north, the pre-Hispanic inhabitants of the Americas arrived from Siberia in waves of migration between about 60,000 and 8000 BC, crossing land now submerged beneath the Bering Strait. The earliest known human traces in Brazil date from about 48,000 BC.

The tribes were highly mobile and, once they crossed into Alaska, they moved south to warmer climates. Eventually, they reached the Amazon Basin in Brazil and spread out from there.

Brazilian Indians never developed an advanced, centralised civilisation like the Inca or Maya. They left little for archaeologists to discover; only some pottery, shell mounds and skeletons. The *sambaquis* (shell mounds) are curious. They are found on the island of Marajó, the home of Brazil's most developed pre-Columbian civilisation, and along the coast in the south. Typically around 2m tall and about 50m long, the mounds are naturally formed by the sea and were used as burial sites and sometimes as dwellings.

The Indian population was quite diverse. At the time of the Portuguese conquest, the Tupi people were most prevalent on the coast and best known to the white conquerors. Most animals, nearly all the rivers and mountains, and many of the towns have Tupi names.

There were an estimated two to five million Indians living in the territory that is now Brazil when the Portuguese first arrived. Today there are fewer than 200,000 living in the hidden jungles of the Brazilian interior.

The Indians were divided into many groups and were primarily hunter-gatherers. The women did most of the work while the men, who were magnificent archers and fishermen, went to war. They lived in long communal huts and every couple of years would pack up the village and move to richer hunting grounds. Music, dance and games played a very important role in their culture. Little surplus was produced and they had very few possessions.

This lifestyle, which came to symbolise the ideal of the noble savage in European minds and inspired many social thinkers such as Rousseau and Defoe, was punctuated by frequent tribal warfare and ritual cannibalism. After battles the captured enemies were ceremonially killed and eaten.

Early Colonisation

In 1500, Pedro Cabral sailed from Lisbon, bound for India, with 13 ships and 1200 men. Following Indies trailblazer Vasco da Gama's directions, his fleet sailed on a south-westerly course in order to exploit the favourable westerly trade winds in the southern hemisphere. The slow sailing ships of the fleet were vulnerable to the strong equatorial current, which took them further west than intended.

Some historians say it was Cabral's secret destination all along, and his official 'discovery' was reported to King João III of Portugal in such matter-of-fact terms that it seems that the existence of Brazil was already well known to mariners. In fact, Portuguese records dating from 1530 suggest that the country had been colonised for more than 40 years.

Cabral landed at present-day Porto Seguro on 22 April. He and his crew were greeted by some of the many Indians living along the coast. Staying only nine days, the Portuguese built a cross and held the first Christian service in the land they dubbed Terra de Vera Cruz (Land of the True Cross). The Indians watched with apparent amazement and then, complying with the exhortations of their guests, knelt before the cross. But it wasn't Catholic ritual that grabbed their attention. It was in fact the construction of the cross. The Indians, living in a Stone Age culture, had never seen iron tools.

Cabral sailed on, leaving behind two convicts to learn the Indians' ways and taking some *pau brasil* (brazil wood) logs, which produces a red dye. Subsequent Portuguese expeditions were disappointed by what they found in Brazil. They had little interest in colonisation; instead they sought the riches of India and Africa where they established trading stations to obtain spices and ivory. But the Indians' Stone Age culture produced nothing for the European market, and the land was heavily forested, barely passable and very wild.

However, the red dye from brazil wood provoked the interest of a few Portuguese merchants and the king granted them the rights to the brazil-wood trade. They began sending a few ships each year to harvest the trees. This trade depended entirely on Indian labour exchanged for metal axes and knives – objects that are still used as peace offerings by Brazilians contacting unknown Indians.

Brazil wood remained the only exportable commodity for the first half of the 16th century. During this time the colony changed its name from Terra de Vera Cruz to Brazil, an act that was later interpreted, as reports of Brazilian godlessness reached superstition-ridden Portugal, as the work of the devil. But the brazil-wood trade, which had never been terribly profitable, was already in jeopardy. The most accessible trees were rapidly depleted. French competition intensified and fighting broke out. The Indians stopped volunteering their labour.

In 1531, King João III sent the first settlers to Brazil. Martim Afonso de Sousa was placed at the head of five ships with a combined crew of 400. After exploring the coastline he chose São Vicente, near the modern port of Santos in São Paulo state, as the first settlement. In 1534, fearing the ambitions of other European countries, the king divided the coast into 12 parallel captaincies. These hereditary estates were given to friends of the *donatários* (Crown) who became lords of their land. Each captaincy comprised 50 leagues (about 300km) of coastline and unlimited territory inland.

The king's scheme was designed to minimise the cost to the Crown while securing the vast coastline through settlement by giving the captaincies to Portuguese nobility. But the wealthy nobles were interested in the riches of Asia, so the captaincies were given to common *fidalgos* (gentry). The settlers who were hampered by the climate, hostility from the Indians and competition from the Dutch and French. One of the donatários, Duarte Coelho, wrote to the king: 'We are obliged to conquer by inches, the land that your Majesty has granted us by leagues'. Four captaincies were never settled and four were destroyed by Indians. Only Pernambuco and São Vicente were profitable.

In 1549 the king sent Tomé de Sousa to be the first governor of Brazil, to centralise authority and to save the few remaining captaincies. Despite the fact that the Indians had recently driven the Portuguese from the area, the king chose the state of Bahia for Sousa to rule from; the Baía de Todos os Santos (Bay of All Saints) was one of Brazil's best bays, as was the land surrounding it.

Ten ships and 1000 settlers arrived safely. On board were Portuguese officials, soldiers, exiled prisoners, New Christians (converted Jews) and the first six Jesuit priests. The great Caramuru, a Portuguese living among the Indians and married to a chief's daughter, selected a spot on high ground for Salvador da Bahia, the new capital of Portuguese Brazil, a position it held until the colonial capital was transferred to Rio de Janeiro in 1763.

The colonists soon discovered that the land and climate were ideal for growing sugar cane. Sugar was coveted by a hungry European market that used it initially for medicinal purposes and as a condiment for almost all foods and even wine. To produce the sugar cane, all the colonists needed were workers. Growing and processing the cane was hard work so the Portuguese attempted to enslave the Indians to work for them.

JOHN MAIER, JR

JOHN MAIER, JR

JOHN MAIER, JR

JOHN MAIER, JR

Faces of Brazil

Brazil
0
200
400 km
Pororoca
The thunderous collision of the Atlantic tide and the mighty Amazon.
Amazonas
Join a jungle tour and venture into the dark Amazon.
Pernambuco
The archipelago of Fernando de Noronha for fantastic scuba diving and snorkelling.
NETHERLANDS ANTILLES
CARIBBEAN SEA
GRENADA
Isla de Margarita
TRINIDAD & TOBAGO
Pico Cristóbal Colon (5775 m)
Maracaibo
Lago de Maracaibo
Caracas
Cucuta
San Cristóbal
Bogotá
VENEZUELA
COLOMBIA
Orinoco
GUYANA
Georgetown
Paramaribo
Cayenne
SURINAME
FRENCH GUIANA
Santa Elena
Boa Vista
GUIANA HIGHLANDS
Serra do Navio
Macapá
ATLANTIC OCEAN
Equator
Branco
Negro
Japurá
Manaus
Rio
Amazonas
Ilha de Marajó
Belém
Salinópolis
Alcântara
São Luís
Parnaíba
Camocim
Sobral
Fortaleza
Rochas
Mossoró
Teresina
Natal
Juazeiro do Norte
Sousa
Picos
João Pessoa
Iquitos
PERU
Leticia
Tabatinga
Fonte Boa
Tefé
Solimões (Amazonas)
Manacapuru
Maués
Santarém
Fordlândia
Imperatriz
Carolina
Caruaru
Recife
São Raimundo Nonato
Juazeiro
Maceió
Jutaí
Yavari
SELVAS
Juruá
Purus
Madeira
Tapajós
Iriri
Xingu
Araguaia
Tocantins
Palmas
Xique-Xique
Estância
Aracaju
Conde
Barreiras
Cruzeiro do Sul
Porto Velho
Rio Branco
Brasiléia
Cobija
Guayaramerín
Guajaá Mirim
Riberalta

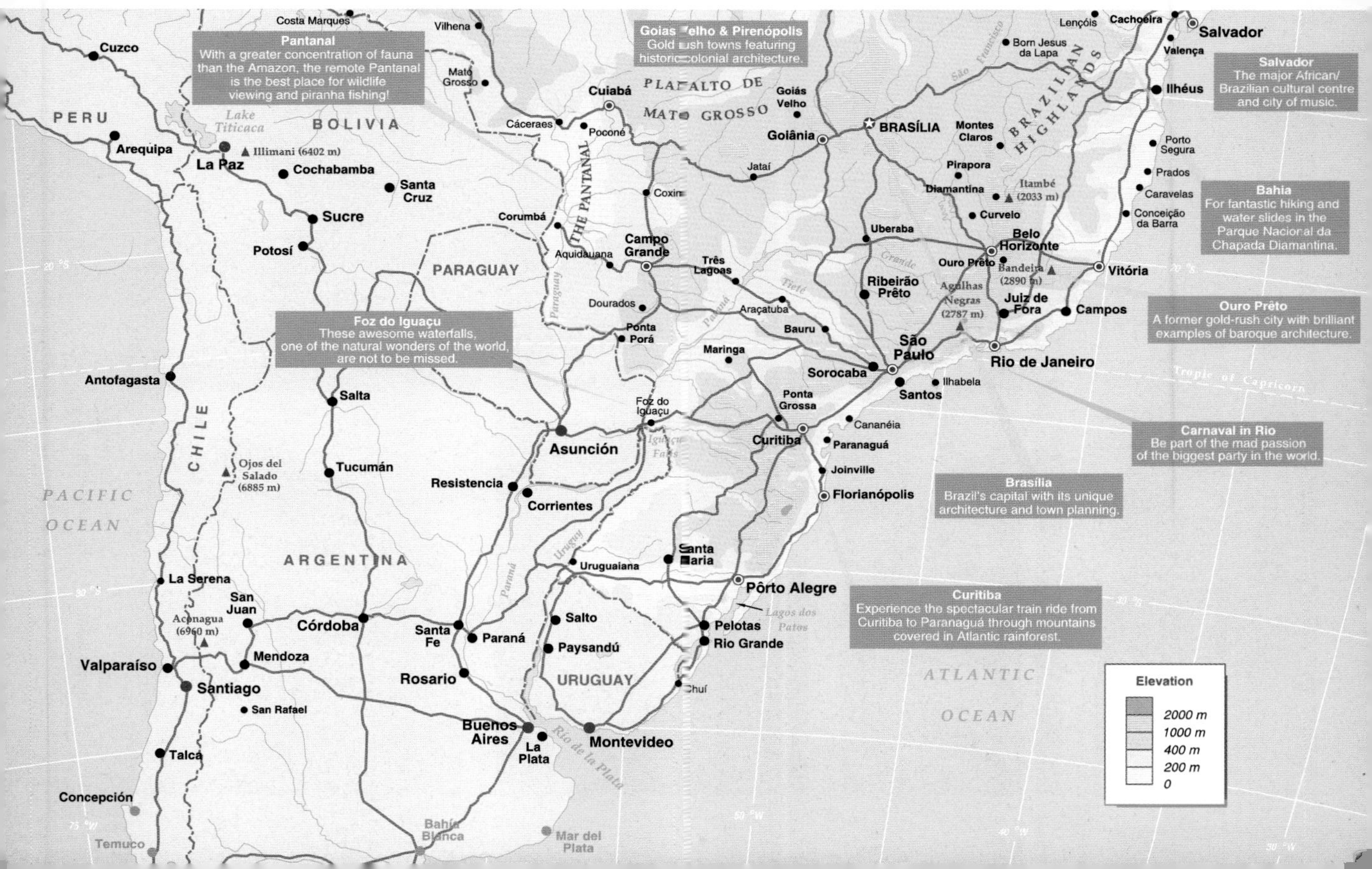
Pantanal
With a greater concentration of fauna than the Amazon, the remote Pantanal is the best place for wildlife viewing and piranha fishing!
Goias Velho & Pirenópolis
Gold rush towns featuring historic colonial architecture.
Salvador
The major African/ Brazilian cultural centre and city of music.
Bahia
For fantastic hiking and water slides in the Parque Nacional da Chapada Diamantina.
Ouro Prêto
A former gold-rush city with brilliant examples of baroque architecture.
Foz do Iguaçu
These awesome waterfalls, one of the natural wonders of the world, are not to be missed.
Carnaval in Rio
Be part of the mad passion of the biggest party in the world.
Brasília
Brazil's capital with its unique architecture and town planning.
Curitiba
Experience the spectacular train ride from Curitiba to Paranaguá through mountains covered in Atlantic rainforest.
Elevation
2000 m
1000 m
400 m
200 m
0
PERU
BOLIVIA
PARAGUAY
CHILE
ARGENTINA
URUGUAY
PACIFIC OCEAN
ATLANTIC OCEAN
PLANALTO DE MATO GROSSO
BRAZILIAN HIGHLANDS
THE PANTANAL
Tropic of Capricorn
Cuzco
Arequipa
La Paz
Lake Titicaca
Illimani (6402 m)
Cochabamba
Santa Cruz
Sucre
Potosí
Costa Marques
Vilhena
Mato Grosso
Cuiabá
Cáceraes
Poconé
Corumbá
Aquidauana
Campo Grande
Coxim
Dourados
Ponta Porã
Goiânia
Goiás Velho
Jataí
BRASÍLIA
Montes Claros
Pirapora
Diamantina
Itambé (2033 m)
Curvelo
Uberaba
Belo Horizonte
Ouro Prêto
Bandeira (2890 m)
Agulhas Negras (2787 m)
Juiz de Fora
Vitória
Campos
Rio de Janeiro
Ribeirão Prêto
Três Lagoas
Araçatuba
Bauru
Maringa
São Paulo
Sorocaba
Santos
Ilhabela
Ponta Grossa
Curitiba
Cananéia
Paranaguá
Joinville
Florianópolis
Foz do Iguaçu
Iguaçu Falls
Asunción
Resistencia
Corrientes
Uruguaiana
Santa Maria
Pôrto Alegre
Lagos dos Patos
Pelotas
Rio Grande
Chuí
Salto
Paysandú
Montevideo
Río de la Plata
Buenos Aires
La Plata
Mar del Plata
Bahía Blanca
Rosario
Santa Fe
Paraná
Córdoba
Salta
Tucumán
Antofagasta
Ojos del Salado (6885 m)
La Serena
San Juan
Aconagua (6960 m)
Mendoza
Valparaíso
Santiago
San Rafael
Talca
Concepción
Temuco
Lençóis
Cachoeira
Salvador
Valença
Ilhéus
Bom Jesus da Lapa
Porto Segura
Prados
Caravelas
Conceição da Barra
São Francisco
Grande
Tietê
Paraná
Paraguay
Uruguay
20°S
30°S
30°W
40°W
50°W
75°W

ANDREW DRAFFEN

ROBYN JONES

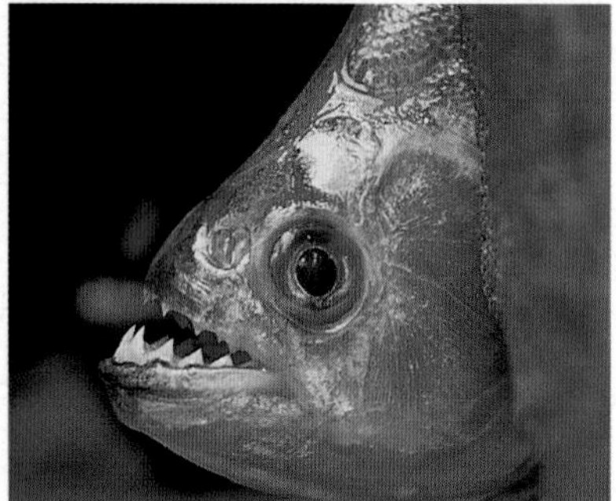
GUY MOBERLY

JOHN MAIER, JR

JOHN MAIER, JR

A	
B	
C	E
D	

A: Jacaré
B: Jaguar skin
C: Piranha
D: Blue Macaws
E: Howler Monkey

Up and down the coast, the Indians' response to the Portuguese was similar. First, they welcomed and offered the strangers food, labour and women in exchange for iron tools and liquor. They then became wary of the whites, who abused their customs and beliefs, and took the best land. Finally, when voluntary labour became slavery and the use of land became wholesale displacement, the Indians fought back and won many battles.

The capture and sale of Indian slaves became Brazil's second largest enterprise. Organised expeditions from São Paulo hunted the Indians into the Brazilian interior, exploring and claiming vast lands for the Portuguese and making fortunes supplying the sugar estates with Indian slaves. These expeditions were called *bandeiras* (flags) after the flag carried by each group, and the men were known as *bandeirantes* (flag-bearers). Their bravery was eclipsed only by their brutality.

The Jesuit priests went to great lengths to save the Indians from the slaughter. They inveighed against the evils of Indian slavery in their sermons, though they said little about black slaves. They pleaded with the king of Portugal and set up *aldeias* (missions) to settle, protect and Christianise the Indians.

Fear of God failed to deter the colonists. The monarchy was ambivalent about Indian slavery and too weak to do anything about it. Most of the Indians not killed by the guns of the bandeirantes or the work on the sugar plantations died from introduced European diseases and the alien life in the missions. Although the Jesuits battled heroically to save the Indians, they merely delayed their destruction. One Brazilian statesman wrote: 'Without the Jesuits, our colonial history would be little more than a chain of nameless atrocities'.

By the end of the 16th century about 30,000 Portuguese settlers and 20,000 black slaves lived in isolated coastal towns surrounded by often hostile Indians. There were about 200 prosperous sugar mills, mostly in Pernambuco and Bahia.

The export economy looked only to Europe, not inland where the forests were dense, the rivers were wild and hostile Indians prevailed. While the legendary gold of El Dorado remained elusive, sugar was extremely lucrative. The sugar trade needed the rich coastal soil and access to European markets. So the Portuguese settled almost exclusively at the mouths of rivers on navigable bays. Wherever sugar-cane grew – mainly Bahia, Pernambuco and Rio – so did the fledgling colony.

Where the captaincy system failed, the sugar trade succeeded. The sparse settlements that would eventually encompass half the continent would continue to be defined by sugar and slavery, even into the 19th century.

Sugar & Slaves

The sugar plantations were self-sufficient economic enclaves. They were geared to large-scale production which required vast tracts of land and specialised processing equipment. This meant a sugar plantation owner needed land, a fair amount of capital and many workers, typically 100 to 150 slaves, both skilled and unskilled.

By the 1550s wealthier sugar barons began to buy African slaves instead of Indians. The Africans were better workers and less susceptible to the European diseases that were killing the Indians faster than the Portuguese guns. Soon tremendous profits were being made by merchants in the slave trade. The infamous triangular trade brought slaves and elephant tusks from Africa, sugar, sugar-cane liquor and tobacco from Brazil, and guns and luxury goods from Europe.

Throughout the 17th century, blacks replaced Indians on the plantations. From 1550 to the abolition of the slave trade in 1850, about 3.5 million African slaves were shipped to Brazil – 38% of the total that came to the New World.

Those who didn't die on the slave ships generally had short and brutal lives. Life on the plantations was hard and tedious with slaves working 15 to 17 hours a day during the busy season. But it was the conditions rather than the amount of work that was largely responsible for the high mortality rate. Disease was rampant and many slaves succumbed to dysentery, typhus, yellow fever, malaria, syphilis, tuberculosis and scurvy.

The plantation owners ruled colonial Brazil. Their control over free whites who worked as sharecroppers was almost total, and over slaves it was absolute. Slaves were dependent on their masters: some were kind, but most were cruel and often sadistic.

Families were routinely broken up and tribal groups mixed to prevent collective rebellion. The culturally sophisticated slaves from Islamic Africa were particularly feared by the white masters.

Resistance to slavery took many forms. The misery of some slaves manifested in *banzo*, the longing for Africa, which culminated in a slow suicide. Documents of the period refer to the desperation of the slaves who starved themselves to death, killed their babies or fled. Sabotage and theft were frequent, as were work slowdowns, stoppages and revolts.

Those who survived life on the plantations sought solace in their African religion and culture, through dance and song. The slaves were given perfunctory indoctrination into Catholicism and, except for the Islamic element, a syncretic religion rapidly emerged. Spiritual elements from many of the African tribes, such as the Yoruba, Bantu and Fon, were preserved and made palatable to the slave masters with a facade of Catholic saints and ritual objects. These are the roots of modern Macumba and Candomblé, prohibited by law until very recently. For further information see the Religion section in this chapter.

Portugal was not an overpopulated country. There was no capitalist revolution and no enclosures, as in England, forcing the peasantry off the land. Consequently, the typical Brazilian settler emigrated by choice with the hope of untold riches. These settlers were notoriously indisposed to work; even poor whites had a slave or two. There was a popular saying that 'the slaves are the hands and the feet of the whites'.

The sugar barons lived on their plantations part-time and escaped to their second houses in the cities, where they often kept mulatto (of mixed black and European parentage) mistresses. The white women led barren, cloistered lives inside the walls of the *casa grande* (big house). Secluded from all but their family and servants, the women married young – usually at 14 or 15 years of age – and often died early.

Sexual relations between masters and slaves were so common that a large mulatto population soon emerged. Off the plantations there was a shortage of white women, so many poorer settlers lived with black and Indian women. Prostitution was prevalent; many of the free mixed-race women could only survive by working as concubines or prostitutes. Brazil was famous for its sexual permissiveness but by the beginning of the 18th century it became known as the land of syphilis (even in the monasteries) and wrought devastation.

The church was tolerant of any coupling that helped populate the colony and many priests had mistresses and illegitimate children. As Gilberto Freyre, Brazil's most famous social scientist, said of the priests: 'a good part if not the majority of them assisted in the work of procreation, and their cooperation was so gratefully accepted that the courts did not arrest or issue warrants for any cleric or friar on the charge of keeping a concubine'.

In the poorer regions of Pará, Maranhão, Ceará and São Paulo, where settlers could not afford black slaves, Indian slaves were more common. Here, interracial sex was more prevalent between whites and Indians and just as tolerated (this is evident in the racial mix in those states today). As in the rest of the colony, sexual relations were rather licentious. As the Bishop of Pará summed up: 'the wretched state of manners in this country puts me in mind of the end that befell the five cities, and makes me think that I am living in the suburbs of Gomorrah, very close indeed, and in the vicinity of Sodom'.

17th Century

The sugar trade made the Portuguese colonisation of Brazil possible. In later years, as Portugal's Asian empire declined, tax revenue from the sugar trade kept the Portuguese ship of state afloat.

Although Spain and Portugal had divided the New World exclusively between themselves with the Treaty of Tordesillas, competing European powers – principally France and Holland – were not deterred from South America. France had successfully operated trading stations in Brazil for many years and had friendly relations with many Indians, who saw the French as a lesser evil than the hated Portuguese.

In 1555 three boatloads of French settlers led by Admiral Nicolas Durand de Villegagnon landed on a small island in Baía de Guanabara. They intended to add a large part of southern Brazil to their empire, which was to be called Antarctic France. After some bloody battles they were finally expelled by the governor general of Brazil, Mem de Sá, in 1567. In a second attempt in 1612 the French took São Luís but were driven out by the Portuguese a few years later.

The Dutch posed a more serious threat to Portuguese Brazil. Dutch merchants had profited from the Brazilian sugar trade for many years, but when Portugal was unified with Spain, the traditional enemy of the Dutch, peaceful trade quickly collapsed. The Dutch set up the Dutch West India Company to gain control of part of Brazil. A large Dutch expedition took Bahia in 1624 but a year later, after bloody and confused fighting, the Portuguese retook the city. They repelled two more attacks in 1627.

The Dutch next conquered Pernambuco in 1630, and from there took control of a major part of the Northeast from Sergipe to Maranhão, which they called New Holland. With their superior sea power the Dutch sailed to Africa and captured part of Portuguese-held Angola to supply slaves for their new colony. In 1637, the Dutch prince, Maurice of Nassau, took over as the governor of New Holland. An enlightened administrator, he was successful in increasing the number of sugar plantations, creating large cattle farms and re-establishing the discipline of his troops and civil administrators. Hospitals and orphanages were founded and freedom of worship was guaranteed in an attempt to win over the local population.

But Nassau was undermined and frustrated by a lack of support from Holland. When he returned home in 1644, the rot set in. The Pernambucan merchants, resenting the Protestant invaders, funded black and Indian soldiers who fought the Dutch on land. The Portuguese governor of Rio de Janeiro and Angola, Salvador de Sá, sailed from Rio and expelled the Dutch from Angola. Finally, when provisions failed to arrive, the Dutch troops mutinied and returned to Europe. A peace treaty was signed in 1654.

Bandeirantes

Throughout the 17th and 18th centuries, bandeirantes from São Paulo continued to march off into the interior to capture Indians. Most bandeirantes, born of Indian mothers and Portuguese fathers, spoke both Tupi-Guaraní and Portuguese. They also learned the survival skills of the Indians and the use of European weaponry, and wore heavily padded cotton jackets that deflected Indian arrows. Travelling light in bands that ranged from a dozen to a couple of hundred, they would go off for months or years at a time, living off the land and plundering Indian villages. By the mid-1600s they had traversed the interior as far as the peaks of the Peruvian Andes and the lowlands of the Amazon forest. These super-human exploits, more than any treaty, secured the huge interior of South America for Portuguese Brazil.

The bandeirantes were ruthlessly effective Indian hunters. The Jesuits, who sought desperately to protect their flock of Indians – who had come to the missions to escape bandeirante attacks – built missions in the remote interior, near the present-day borders with Paraguay and Argentina. Far from São Paulo, the Jesuits hoped that they were beyond the grasp of the bandeirantes. They were wrong, and this was to be their last stand. The Jesuits armed the Indians and desperate battles took place; however, although the bandeirantes were slowed they were never stopped. Finally, with the collusion of the Portuguese and Spanish crowns, the missions fell and the Jesuits were expelled from Brazil in 1759.

Gold

El Dorado and other South American legends of vast deposits of gold and precious stones clouded European minds and spurred on the roving bandeirantes. Despite incessant searching, riches failed to materialise until the 1690s, when bandeirantes discovered a magical lustre in the rivers of the Serra do Espinhaço, Brazil's oldest geological formation, located in an inaccessible and unsettled region inland from Rio de Janeiro.

Soon the gold rush was on. People dropped everything to go to what is now the southern central part of Minas Gerais. Unaware of the hazardous journey, many died on the way. In the orgy to pan, no one bothered to plant, and in the early years terrible famines swept through the gold towns. The price of basic provisions was always outrageous and the majority suffered. But the gold was there – more than seemed possible.

When gold was first discovered, there were no white settlers in the territory of Minas Gerais. By 1710 the population was 30,000 and by the end of the 18th century it was half a million.

For 50 years, until the mines began to decline, Brazilian gold caused major demographic shifts in three continents. Paulistas (inhabitants of São Paulo) left their homes followed by other Brazilians who had failed to strike it rich in commercial agriculture. Some 400,000 Portuguese arrived in Brazil in the 18th century, many headed for the gold fields. Countless slaves were stolen away from Africa, to dig and die in Minas.

Fuelled by competition over scarce mining rights, a Brazilian species of nativism arose. Old-time Brazilians, particularly the combative Paulistas, resented the flood of recent Portuguese immigrants who were cashing in on their gold discoveries. The recent arrivals, numerically superior, loathed the favourable treatment they saw the Paulistas receiving. Gold stakes were more often settled by guns, not by judges, and armed confrontations broke out in 1708. The colonial government was faced with a virtual civil war, which lasted over a year and saw miners carrying pans in one hand and guns in the other, before government intervention slowed the hostilities.

Most of the gold mining was done by black slaves. An estimated third of the two million slaves who reached Brazil in the 18th century went to the gold fields, where their lives were worse than in the sugar fields. Most slave owners put their slaves on an incentive system, allowing the slaves to keep a small percentage of the gold they found. A few slaves who found great quantities of gold were able to buy their own freedom, but for the majority disease and death came quickly.

Wild boom towns arose in the mountain valleys; Sabará, Mariana, São João del Rei, and the greatest, Vila Rica de Ouro Prêto (Rich Town of Black Gold). Wealthy merchants built opulent mansions and employed a class of educated artisans to create some stunning baroque church architecture. But crime, gambling, drinking and prostitution ruled the streets. Portuguese officials provided a sense of European civilisation but the absence of white women led to a large number of mulatto offspring.

Most of Brazil's gold wealth was squandered. A few merchants and miners became incredibly rich and lived on imported European luxury goods. But the gold did little to develop Brazil's economy, create a middle class or better the common worker. Most of the wealth went to Portuguese merchants and the king, until it was ultimately traded for English goods.

By 1750, after a half-century boom, the mining regions were in decline, the migration to the interior was over and coastal Brazil was returning to centre stage.

Apart from some public works and many beautiful churches, the only important legacy of Brazil's gold rush was the shift in population, from the Northeast to the Southeast. Some stayed in Minas Gerais and raised cattle on its rich lands. Many ended up in Rio, and its population and economy grew rapidly as gold and supplies passed through its ports.

19th Century

In 1807 Napoleon's army marched on Lisbon. Two days before the invasion, 40 ships carrying the Portuguese prince regent (later known as Dom João VI) and his entire court of 15,000 had set sail for Brazil under the protection of British warships. When the prince regent arrived in Rio his Brazilian subjects celebrated wildly, dancing in the streets. He immediately took over rule of Brazil from his viceroy.

As foreigners have been doing ever since, Dom João fell in love with Brazil. A great lover of nature, he founded Rio's botanical gardens and introduced the habit of sea bathing to the water-wary inhabitants of Rio. Expected to return to Portugal after Napoleon's Waterloo in 1815, he stayed in Brazil. The following year his mother, mad Queen Dona Maria I, died and Dom João VI became king. He refused to return to Portugal and rule, and declared Rio the capital of the United Kingdom of Portugal, Brazil and the Algarves. Thus Brazil became the only New World colony to ever have a European monarch ruling on its soil.

Five years later he finally relented to political pressures and returned to Portugal, leaving his son, Pedro, in Brazil as prince regent.

According to legend, in 1822, Pedro pulled out his sword and yelled 'Independência ou morte!' (Independence or death), making himself Emperor Dom Pedro I. Portugal was too weak to fight its favourite son, not to mention the British, who had the most to gain from Brazilian independence and would have come to the aid of the Brazilians. The Brazilian Empire was born, attained independence without bloodshed, and Dom Pedro I became the first emperor.

Dom Pedro I only ruled for nine years. From all accounts he was a bumbling incompetent who scandalised even the permissive Brazilians by siring a string of illegitimate children. He was forced to abdicate, paving the way for his five-year-old son to become emperor.

Until Dom Pedro II reached adolescence, Brazil suffered a period of civil war under the rule of a weak triple regency. In 1840, the nation rallied behind the emperor, and his 50 year reign is regarded as the most prosperous period in Brazilian history. He nurtured an increasingly powerful parliamentary system; went to war with Paraguay; interfered in Argentine, Paraguayan and Uruguayan affairs; abolished slavery and encouraged mass immigration. Ultimately, he forged a nation that would do away with the monarchy forever.

In 1889 a military coup supported by the coffee aristocracy and a popular wave of republican sentiment toppled the antiquated Brazilian Empire. The emperor went into exile and died in Paris a couple of years later.

A military clique ruled Brazil for the next four years until elections were held, but because of land and literacy requirements, ignorance and threats, only about 2% of the adult population voted. Little changed, except that power of the military and the coffee growers increased, while it diminished for the sugar barons.

A New Empire

At the beginning of the 19th century there were about three million people in Brazil, not including the Indians, and roughly one million of them were African slaves. In the poorer areas there were fewer black slaves, more poor whites and more Indians.

The central west region – Minas, Goiás, the Mato Grosso – was only settled in isolated pockets where precious metals had been found. The *sertão* (Northeastern interior) was the most settled inland part of the country. Although the arid sertão was unable to sustain much agriculture, cattle could graze and survive. It was a poor business, constantly threatened by drought, but the hardy *sertanejo* (inhabitant of the sertão) – often of mixed Portuguese and Indian extraction – was able to eke out a living.

The south, settled by farmers and their wives from the Portuguese Azores, was economically backward with few settlers who could afford slaves. The Indians had been clustered in the Jesuit missions far to the west to save them from the bandeirantes. The south was, and remains, Brazil's most European region, with a similar physical appearance and cosmopolitan flair.

Slave Revolts & Abolition

Slavery in Brazil was not abolished until 1888, 25 years after the USA and 80 years behind Britain. Resistance to slavery grew throughout the 19th century and the spectre of Haiti – the site of the first successful slave revolt – haunted the Brazilian planters who, as a result, became more brutal towards their slaves.

In Bahia there were several urban insurrections between 1807 and 1835. Most were led by Muslim blacks – both those who were free and those in slavery. The uprising of 1807 in Bahia was carefully planned so that slaves from the sugar plantations would be able to meet up with the city slaves at the entrance to the city and together attack the whites, seize ships and flee to Africa. However, the plot was betrayed and the leaders killed.

The following year, a similar plan was carried out and the blacks were defeated in battle. In Minas Gerais, 15,000 slaves congregated in Ouro Prêto and 6000 in São João do Morro, demanding freedom and a constitution. The last big slave revolt in Bahia was in 1835, and was almost successful.

Slaves fought their oppressors in many ways, and many managed to escape from their masters. *Quilombos* (communities of runaway slaves) scattered throughout the countryside, were common throughout the colonial period. The quilombos ranged from *mocambos* (small groups) hidden in the forests, to the most famous, the great republic of Palmares, which survived through much of the 17th century.

Palmares covered a broad tract of lush tropical forest near the coast of northern Alagoas and southern Pernambuco states. At its height, 20,000 people lived under its protection. Most were black, but there were also Indians, mulattos, *mestiços* (of mixed European and Indian parentage) and bandits. They lived off the land, growing mostly corn. Agriculture was produced collectively and productivity was higher than on the slave plantations.

Palmares was really a collection of semi-independent quilombos united under the rule of one king to fight off the Portuguese forces. Led by Zumbí, who had been a king in Africa, the citizens of Palmares became pioneers of guerrilla warfare and defeated many Portuguese attacks. Fearing Palmares' example, the government desperately tried to crush it. Between 1670 and 1695 the rebel region was attacked (on average) every 15 months, until it finally fell to a force led by Paulista bandeirantes.

Palmares is now the stuff of movies and myths, but there were many quilombos in every state. As abolitionist sentiment grew in the 19th century, the quilombos received more support and ever greater numbers of slaves fled. Only abolition itself in 1888 stopped the quilombos.

Insurrections

With the settlements separated by enormous distances, few transportation or communication links, and an economy oriented toward European markets rather than local ones, the Brazilian nation was weak and lacked a sense of national identity. Throughout the 19th century the Brazilian Empire was plagued by revolts by local ruling elites demanding greater autonomy from the central government, or even fighting to secede. Rio Grande do Sul was torn by a civil war in 1842, called the Farrapos

Lampião

Every country has infamous bad guys somewhere in its history: the US has its western outlaws, the UK has its highwaymen, Australia has its bushrangers and Brazil has its *cangaceiros* (bandits).

At the end of the 19th century, the harsh poverty and social injustice in the drought-plagued sertão of the Northeast caused the formation of gangs of outlaws known as *cangaços*, who attacked towns, *fazendas* (ranches) and army outposts. The most famous cangaceiro was Lampião, who terrorised the sertão for more than 20 years.

Lampião was a cowboy until his parents were killed by a cruel landowner. He and his brothers swore revenge and headed for the sertão to join the roaming bands of outlaws.

Around 1920, two years after he had become a cangaceiro, Lampião became head of his own gang. He gained his nickname, 'the Lamp', because of the bright flashes given off by his rifle when he fought the police. Unlike other cangaço leaders, who were known for their generosity to the suffering people of the sertão, Lampião was renowned for his cruelty.

With his band, which numbered between 15 and 50 men, he roamed the backlands of Pernambuco, Paraíba, Alagoas and Ceará. His fame grew as stories and songs of his deeds spread throughout the Northeast.

In 1929 he met Maria Bonita, who became his lover and the first woman to join the cangaço. For another nine years the cangaço continued to be a thorn in the side of the state and federal governments, who tried many times to bring Lampião to justice. Protected by the frightened populace and scared landowners, the cangaceiros became careless. One night in July 1938, they were surrounded by a group of *polícia militar* from Sergipe. Lampião and Maria Bonita were both killed, along with nine other gang members. Their heads were cut off and for almost 30 years remained on display in the Salvador Medical Institute. They were finally buried in 1969.

The last cangaceiro and surviving member of Lampião's band, Corisco, was killed in 1940, thus ending the cangaços era.

Rebellion. There were insurrections in São Paulo and Minas Gerais, and others swept through the North and Northeast during the 1830s and 1840s.

The bloodiest and most radical was the Cabanagem in the state of Pará. The rebels laid siege to the capital of Belém, appropriating and distributing supplies. They held the city for a year before being defeated by a large government force. The peasants fled to the jungle with the army in pursuit and eventually 40,000 of the state's 100,000 people were killed.

The most serious insurrections, like the Cabanagem, spread to the oppressed peasants and urban poor. The government always struck back and the revolts failed, in part because the upper and middle classes who led them feared the mobilised poor as much as they feared the government.

The 19th century was also a period of messianic popular movements among Brazil's poor. Most of the movements took place in the economically depressed back-lands of the Northeast. Canudos is the most famous of these movements. From 1877 to 1887, Antônio Conselheiro wandered through the back-lands preaching and prophesysing the appearance of the Antichrist and the coming end of the world. He railed against the new republican government, and eventually gathered his followers (who called him the Counsellor) in Canudos, a settlement in the interior of Bahia.

In Canudos, the government sensed dissenting plots to return Brazil to the Portuguese monarchy. Miraculously, the rebels first defeated a force of state police, and then two subsequent attacks by the federal army.

Hysterical demonstrations in the cities demanded that the republic be saved from the rebels. A federal force of 4000 well-supplied soldiers took Canudos after ferocious hand-to-hand fighting that moved from house to house. The military suffered heavy casualties and was disgraced and the federal government embarrassed, but Canudos was wiped out. The military killed every man, woman and child, and then burned the town to the ground to erase it from the nation's memory.

The epic struggle has been memorialised in the masterpiece of Brazilian literature, *Os Sertões* (Rebellion in the Backlands) by Euclides de Cunha. More recently, Mario Vargas Llosa wrote of Canudos in *The War of the End of the World*.

Coffee & Rubber

Popular legend has it that the coffee bean was introduced to Brazil in the early 18th century by Francisco de Mello Palheta, an officer from Maranhão, who went to Cayenne in French Guiana in order to settle a border dispute. He reputedly won the heart of the governor's wife, who put some coffee beans into his cup as a parting gift. On his return to Brazil, he planted them. It was to be another 100 years, however, until coffee rose to become Brazil's new monoculture.

The international sugar market began a rapid decline in the 1820s. The sugar planters had depleted much of their best soil, had failed to modernise and were unable to compete with the newly mechanised sugar mills in the West Indies. As rapidly as sugar exports fell, coffee production rose.

Coffee grew poorly in the harsh northern climate, but flourished on the low mountain slopes of the Paraíba valley from north-east of São Paulo city up to Rio de Janeiro state and along the border with Minas Gerais. As these lands were snatched up, the coffee plantations moved westward into Minas Gerais and western São Paulo.

Coffee production was labour intensive. Because of the large investment needed to employ so many workers, production excluded the small farmer and favoured large enterprises using slave labour. The master-slave sugar plantation system, complete with the big house and slave quarters, was reproduced on the coffee *fazendas* (ranches or farms) of São Paulo and Minas Gerais.

Coffee exports increased rapidly throughout the 19th century and profits soared with the introduction of mechanisation and Brazil's first railways. In 1889 it totalled two-thirds of the country's exports. The modernisation of coffee production also eased the coffee plantations' transition to a free labour force with the end of slavery in 1888. During the next decade 800,000 European immigrants, mostly Italians, came to work on the coffee fazendas. Millions more immigrants – Japanese, German, Spanish and Portuguese – flooded into the cities from 1890 to 1916.

Brazil was still a rural society – only 10% of the population lived in cities in 1890 – but the cities were growing rapidly. São Paulo and Rio in particular were the main beneficiaries of the coffee boom.

In the last decades of the 19th century and the first of the 20th, the Amazon region was the scene of another incredible economic boom. It was *Hevea brasiliensis* (the rubber tree), a native of the American tropics, which was the provider of this good fortune.

Things started to inflate in 1842 with the discovery of the vulcanisation process, which turned rubber into an important industrial material. Demand really increased in 1890, with the invention of the pneumatic tyre and the expansion of the fledgling automobile industry in the USA. The price of rubber skyrocketed, bringing huge wealth

Henry Wickham – Executioner of Amazonas

Henry Alexander Wickham was the man who punctured the Brazilian rubber boom. A classic Victorian character, it's surprising that no film has ever been made about his famous 'seed snatch' from the Amazon.

The idea of establishing rubber plantations in the British colonies in Ceylon, Malaya and the Dutch East Indies was one that had not escaped the crafty British botanists, but they believed that the seeds or seedlings of the *Hevea brasiliensis* would never survive the long journey to England.

In 1876, Wickham, who had been drifting through South America for some time, made a deal with Sir Joseph Hooker at Kew Gardens who assured him he'd get £10 for every 1000 rubber seeds he could provide.

As luck would have it, on 1 March a 1000 tonne liner, the SS *Amazonas*, had its entire cargo stolen from the docks in Manaus. Wickham chartered the ship and instructed the captain to sail at once and meet him in Santarém. Wickham himself went up river by canoe to a spot already chosen for the large numbers of rubber trees that grew there.

For the next week he and his Indian helpers collected seeds by listening for the sharp crack of the exploding seed capsules, which scatter the seeds up to 50m from the tree. He then packed the precious cargo between dried banana leaves and stored them in cane baskets. When he boarded the *Amazonas* in Santarém he had 70,000 rubber tree seeds with him.

As they reached the Brazilian Customs House in Belém, the captain held the ship in the harbour under a full head of steam while Wickham visited the customs officials, declaring: 'All we have here are exceedingly delicate botanical specimens specially designated for delivery to Her Majesty's own Royal Gardens of Kew'.

Immediately on arrival in Le Havre, en route to Liverpool, Wickham jumped ashore and caught a fast boat across the Channel. He finally arrived at Kew Gardens at 3 am, and woke up a surprised Sir Joseph Hooker, who sent a goods train to Liverpool to meet the *Amazonas* and ordered workers to clear the hothouse of its other tropical plants in anticipation of the shipment.

The speed of the whole operation succeeded in bringing live rubber seeds to England, and in August of the same year, the first seedlings were shipped to Ceylon – thus ensuring the collapse of the Brazilian rubber industry.

Wickham was nicknamed the 'Executioner of Amazonas' by the Brazilian rubber barons. He went off to spend his £700 trying to grow tobacco and coffee in northern Queensland, Australia. In 1920 he was knighted by King George V for services to the rubber industry.

and rapid progress to the main Amazonian cities of Belém, Manaus and Iquitos, as well as a large population increase to the region.

Rubber production reached its peak in 1912, when 42,000 tonnes of latex were exported; nearly 40% of Brazilian export revenue.

Then the puncture occurred. Unfortunately for Brazil, in 1876, seeds from the rubber tree had been smuggled out of the Amazon and sent to Kew Gardens in England. The seedlings quickly found their way to the British colonies in South-East Asia, where large rubber plantations were established. These plantations started to yield in 1910 and proved to be extremely efficient. The price of latex plummeted on the world market. The Brazilian rubber boom became a blow out.

Brazil's place in the world economy remained that of an exporter of agricultural commodities and importer of manufactured goods. Some seeds of modernisation had been planted, but there was no economic take-off, no qualitative leap forward. In 1917, after repeated sinkings of Brazilian ships by Germans, Brazil entered WWI on the Allied side. The producţion of foodstuffs during the war years restored a brief period of prosperity, but after the war there were continuing economic crises and local political revolts.

The Vargas Era

Coffee was king until the global economic crisis of 1929 put a big hole in the bottom of the coffee market and badly damaged the Brazilian economy. The coffee growers of São Paulo, who controlled the government, were badly weakened. In opposition to the pro-coffee policies of the government, a liberal alliance formed around the elite of Minas Gerais and Rio Grande do Sul, and nationalist military officers. When their presidential candidate, Getúlio Vargas, lost the 1930 elections, the military took power by force, handing over the reins to Vargas.

Vargas proved to be a gifted political manoeuvrer and was to dominate the political scene for the next 20 years. He skilfully played off one sector of the ruling elite against another, but was careful not to alienate the military. His popular support came from the odd bit of social reform combined with large slabs of demagoguery and nationalism.

In 1937, on the eve of a new election, Vargas sent in the military to shut down congress and took complete control of the country. His regime was inspired by the fascist states of Mussolini and Salazar and he banned political parties, imprisoned political opponents and censored the press. In WWII, Vargas sided with the Allies, but afterwards the contradiction between fighting for democracy in Europe while operating a quasi-fascist state at home was too glaring. Although Vargas was forced to step down by the military, he remained popular.

In 1951 he was legitimately elected president and, with the economic opportunities afforded by the war in Europe, Brazil began its fitful march towards industrialisation and urbanisation. A large network of state corporations, including national petroleum and steel companies, was established, the first minimum wage was set and peasants flocked to the cities for a better life. But Vargas' administration was plagued by corruption. The press, especially a young journalist named Carlos Lacerda, attacked him viciously and the military withdrew their support. In August of the same year, Vargas' bodyguards attempted to murder Lacerda, but instead killed an air force major who was with him. In the resulting scandal, the military demanded Vargas' resignation. He responded melodramatically by shooting himself in the heart. Popular reaction proved extremely sympathetic to the dead president. Anti-government newspapers were burned and the US embassy was attacked. Lacerda was forced into exile, but later returned to become a dynamic governor of Rio.

Late 20th Century

Juscelino Kubitschek, popularly known as JK, was elected president in 1956. His motto was '50 years' progress in five'. His critics responded with '40 years' inflation in four'. The critics were closer to the mark, although industrial production did increase by 80% during Kubitschek's five years.

The dynamic Kubitschek was the first of Brazil's big spenders. Deficit spending and large loans funded roads and hydroelectric projects. Foreign capital was encouraged to invest and Brazil's automotive industry was started. Kubitschek built Brasília, a new capital that was supposed to be the catalyst for development of Brazil's vast interior.

In the 1961 elections, former São Paulo governor Janio Quadros took over the presidency on a wave of public euphoria. He gained 48% of the vote, the highest majority ever. Quadros had huge plans for political reform, but a moralistic streak saw him trying to prohibit the wearing of bathing costumes at beauty contests, bikinis on the beaches and the use of amyl nitrate at Carnaval – an uphill battle indeed. After six months in office he decorated Che Guevara in a public ceremony in Brasília, a move that upset the right-wing military, who started to plot. A few days later Quadros resigned claiming that 'occult forces' were at work.

João 'Jango' Goulart, his vice president and the labour minister under Vargas, took over the presidency. Opposition to Goulart's leftist policies and the fact that he hadn't been elected led to his overthrow by the military in 1964. Within hours of the coup, President Johnson cabled his warmest good wishes. The USA immediately extended diplomatic relations to the military regime and suspicions ran deep that the USA had masterminded the coup.

Much of the middle class welcomed the Revolution of 1964, as it was first called. Brazil's military regime was not as brutal as those of Chile or Argentina; the repression tended to come and go in cycles. But at its worst, around 1968 and 1969, the use of torture and the murder of political opponents were widespread. For almost 20 years political parties were outlawed and freedom of speech was curtailed.

Borrowing heavily from international banks, the generals benefited from the Brazilian economic miracle; year after year in the late 1960s and early 1970s Brazil's economy grew by over 10%. The transformation to an urban and semi-industrialised country accelerated.

Spurred on by the lack of any effective rural land reform, millions came to the cities, and *favelas* (shantytowns) filled the open spaces. The middle class grew, as did the bureaucracy and military.

More mega-projects were undertaken to exploit Brazil's natural resources, to provide quick fixes to underdevelopment and to divert attention from much needed social reforms. The greatest of these was the opening of the Amazon, which has brought great wealth to a few but little to most Brazilians, while helping to turn attention away from the issue of land reform.

The military regime's honeymoon didn't last. Opposition grew in 1968 as students, and then many in the Church – which had been generally supportive of the coup – began to protest against the regime. Inspired by liberation theology, the Church had begun to examine Brazilian misery. Church leaders established communities among the poor to fight for social justice and were appalled by the military's flagrant abuse of human rights, which broke all religious and moral tenets.

In 1980 a militant working-class movement, centred around the São Paulo automotive industry, exploded onto the scene with a series of strikes under the charismatic leadership of Luís Inácio ('Lula') da Silva, the workers' champion.

With the economic miracle petering out and popular opposition picking up steam, the military announced the so-called *abertura* (opening): a slow and cautious process of returning the government to civilian rule.

A presidential election was held in 1985 under an electoral college system designed to ensure the victory of the military's candidate.

Surprisingly, the opposition candidate, Tancredo Neves, was elected. Millions of

Brazilians took to the streets in a spontaneous outburst of joy at the end of military rule. Tragically, Tancredo died of heart failure the day before assuming the presidency and was succeeded by Vice President José Sarney, a relative unknown who had supported the military until 1984.

During Sarney's term the economy was hampered by severe inflation, and by 1990 Brazil had run up a US$25 billion domestic deficit and a US$115 billion foreign debt. However, during this period the congress did manage to hammer out a new, more liberal constitution that guaranteed human rights.

The first democratic presidential election since the military takeover was held in 1989. In a hard-fought campaign, the charismatic Fernando Collor de Mello, ex-Brazilian karate champion and former governor of the small state of Alagoas, narrowly gained victory over the Workers' Party candidate, Lula da Silva. Lula's campaign was not helped by the fact that a few days before the election his ex-lover revealed on national TV that he had offered her money for an abortion 16 years before.

Collor took office promising to reduce inflation and fight corruption, but by the end of 1992, the man who George Bush once said reminded him of Indiana Jones had been removed from office and was being indicted by Federal Police on charges of corruption – accused of being the leader of a gang that used extortion and bribery to suck more than US$1 billion from the economy. Collor joined the long list (11 out of 25) of Brazilian presidents who have left office before the end of their presidential term.

'Collorgate' had a positive side. It proved to the Brazilian people that the constitution of their fragile democracy is capable of removing a corrupt president from office without military interference. Many were disappointed that Collor escaped prison: he was found 'not guilty' of 'passive corruption' by the Supreme Court in December 1994. Pictures of him enjoying his 'retirement' while shopping in New York or skiing in Colorado still appear in the Brazilian newspapers. Collor hasn't shirked the spotlight, and now maintains a Web site (www.visionpoint.com/collor/). Please send comments regarding Brazilian inflation since the publication of this edition to his email address (collor@america.com).

Vice President Itamar Franco became president in December 1992 after Collor's resignation. Considered provincial and unprepared to take office, Franco surprised his critics with an honest and competent administration. His greatest achievement was to begin the long-awaited stabilisation of the economy with the introduction of the Plano Real, the most successful economic plan in a decade.

It was an emotional year for Brazilians in 1994. Grief gripped the country with the death of Formula One hero Ayrton Senna on 1 May, transforming him from living legend into Brazilian sporting god. Two months later, sorrow turned to joy as the Brazilian football team became *tetracampeão*, the first country to win the World Cup four times. Another hero was created in the process: Romário de Souza Faria. Known simply as Romário, the champion Brazilian striker scored six of the 14 goals that took his team to victory.

It was also an election year. Early favourite was Lula, back for a second attempt after losing to Collor. His downfall was the Plano Real, which he criticised early. The architect of the plan, Franco's finance minister Fernando Henrique Cardoso, became known as 'Father of the Real' and rode its success all the way to a landslide victory in the presidential elections in October.

An ex-sociology professor from São Paulo, FHC (as he's known in the press – the people call him Fernando Henrique) is a social democrat, charged with simultaneously encouraging economic progress and growth, while tackling Brazil's social problems.

Through the mid-1990s, Cardoso presided over a Brazil with a stable (if overvalued) currency and record foreign investment.

But economic growth and social justice don't always coincide, especially in a country as volatile as Brazil. With the approach of the

21st century, many lingering problems remain – corruption, violence, urban overcrowding, lack of essential health and education facilities, environmental abuse and dramatic extremes of wealth and poverty.

Brazil has long been known as a land of the future. But the future never seems to arrive.

GEOGRAPHY

Brazil is the world's fifth largest country after Russia, Canada, China and the USA. It borders every country in South America, except Chile and Ecuador, and its 8.5 million sq km occupy almost half the continent. Gigantic Brazil is larger than the USA excluding Alaska, 2½ times the size of India, and larger than Europe (excluding Russia). It spans three time zones and is closer to Africa than it is to Europe or the USA.

As amazing as the size of this enormous expanse is, it's inaccessibile and inhospitable to humans. Much of Brazil is scarcely populated; 36% of the nation's territory is in the Amazon Basin, which, along with the enormous Mato Grosso to its south, has large regions with population densities of less than one person per sq km. Most of this land was not thoroughly explored by Europeans until this century. New mountains, new rivers and new Indian tribes are still being discovered. The Amazon is being rapidly settled, lumbered and depleted.

Geographical Regions

Brazil's geography can be reduced to four primary regions: the long, narrow Atlantic coastal band that stretches from the Uruguayan border to the state of Maranhaõ; the large highlands – called the Planalto Brasileiro, or Central Plateau – which extend over most of Brazil's interior south of the Amazon Basin; and two great depressions – the Amazon Basin, and the Paraguay Basin in the Southeast.

Coastal Band The 7408km coastal band is bordered by the Atlantic Ocean and the coastal mountain ranges that lie between it and the Central Plateau. From Rio Grande do Sul to Bahia the mountains are right on the coast. Sheer mountainsides, called the Great Escarpment, make rivers impossible to navigate. Especially in Rio and Espírito Santo, the *litoral* (coastal region) is rocky and irregular, with many islands, bays and sudden granite peaks, like Pão de Açucar in Rio.

North of Bahia, the coastal lands are flatter and the transition to the highlands more gradual. Rounded hills signal the beginning of the central plateau. There are navigable rivers and the coast is smooth and calm, well protected by offshore reefs.

Planalto Brasileiro The Planalto Brasileiro is an enormous plateau that covers a part of almost every Brazilian state. It is punctuated by several small mountain ranges that reach no more than 3000m – the highest of these are centred in Minas Gerais – and is sliced by several large rivers. The average elevation of the Planalto is only 500m.

From Minas Gerais the Planalto descends slowly to the north. The great Rio São Francisco, called the River of National Unity or more informally Velho Chico, which begins in the mountains of Minas, follows this northerly descent. There are several other rivers slicing through the Planalto. The large tablelands or plains between these river basins are called *chapadões*.

Amazon Basin From the Planalto Brasileiro to the south, the Andes to the west and the Guyana shield to the north, the waters descend to the great depression of the Amazon Basin. In the far west the basin is 1300km wide, to the east, between the Guyana massif and the Planalto Brasileiro, it narrows to less than 100km wide.

There are an estimated 1100 tributaries flowing into the Rio Amazonas, 10 of which carry more water than the Mississippi River. The 6275km Rio Amazonas is the world's largest river. With its tributaries it carries an estimated 20% of the world's fresh water. The Amazon forest contains 30% of the remaining forest in the world.

Paraná-Paranagua Basin In the south, there's the Paraná-Paranagua Basin. This depression, which is not as low-lying as the Amazon, includes the Pantanal and runs into the neighbouring countries of Paraguay and Argentina. It is characterised by open forest, low woods and scrubland. Its two principal rivers, the Rio Paraguai and the Rio Paraná, run south through Paraguay and Argentina.

Political Divisions

For political and administrative purposes, Brazil is generally divided into five regions: the North, the Northeast, the Central West, the Southeast and the South.

North The North is the Amazon forest. It encompasses 42% of Brazil's land and includes the states of Amazonas, Pará, Rondônia, Acre, Tocantins and the territories of Amapá and Roraima. This is Brazil's least populated region and contains most of the country's Indian people. The two major cities are Manaus and Belém, the former on the Rio Negro, and the latter on the Rio Amazonas.

Northeast The Northeast, Brazil's poorest region, has retained much of Brazil's colonial past. It's also the region where the African influence is most evident. It contains 18% of Brazil's area and includes, moving up the coast, the states of Bahia, Sergipe, Alagoas, Pernambuco, Paraíba, Rio Grande do Norte, Ceará, Piauí and Maranhão. These states are divided into the *zona da mata* (bush-land just inside the litoral) and the sertão (the dry interior).

Central West In the old days the Central West was called the *mato grosso* (thick forest). It includes the states of Goiás, Mato Grosso, Mato Grosso do Sul and the federal district of Brasília: 22% of the national territory. Only recently opened to road transport, this is Brazil's fastest growing region.

Southeast The Southeast is developed, urban Brazil. The states of Rio de Janeiro, São Paulo, Minas Gerais and Espírito Santo make up 10% of the national territory but have 43% of the population and contribute 63% of all industrial production.

South In the South, Brazil has more of a European feel, and it comprises the prosperous states of Paraná (the location of the magnificent Foz do Iguaçu), Santa Catarina with its very visible German presence, and Rio Grande do Sul.

CLIMATE

Many travel guides misleadingly suggest a certain sameness to the weather in Brazil. It's true that only the south has extreme seasonal changes as experienced in Europe and the USA, but most of the country does have noticeable seasonal variations in rainfall, temperature and humidity. In general, as you go from north to south, the seasonal changes are more defined.

The Brazilian winter lasts from June to August. While much of the country boasts moderate temperatures all year long, the southern states of Rio Grande do Sul, Santa Catarina, Paraná and São Paulo have average winter temperatures (from June through August) of between 13 and 18°C. There are even a few towns that can get snow, which seems strange to those Brazilians who have never touched the white flakes.

The summer season is from December to February. With many Brazilians on holiday at this time, travel is difficult and expensive, while from Rio to the south the humidity can be oppressive. But it's also the most festive time of year, when Brazilians escape their small, hot apartments and take to the beaches and streets. School holidays, begin sometime in mid-December and go through to Carnaval, usually in late February.

In summer, Rio is hot and humid; temperatures in the high 30°Cs are common and sometimes reach the low 40°Cs. Frequent, short rain cools things off a bit, but its the humidity that makes things uncomfortable. For the rest of the year Rio is cooler with

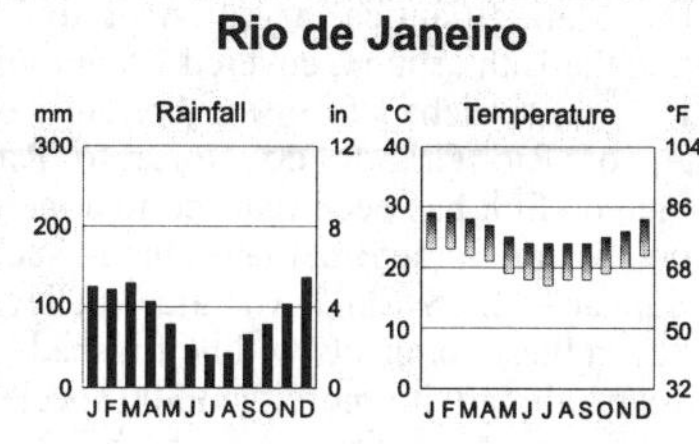

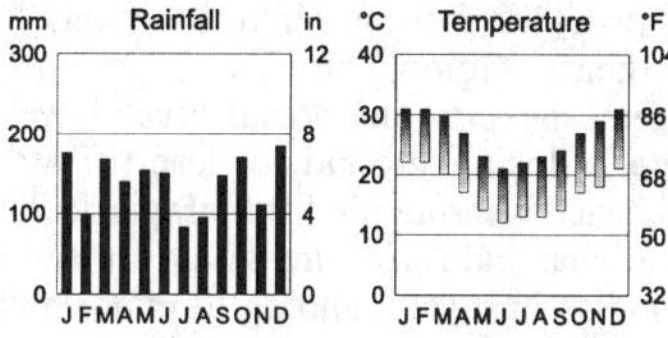

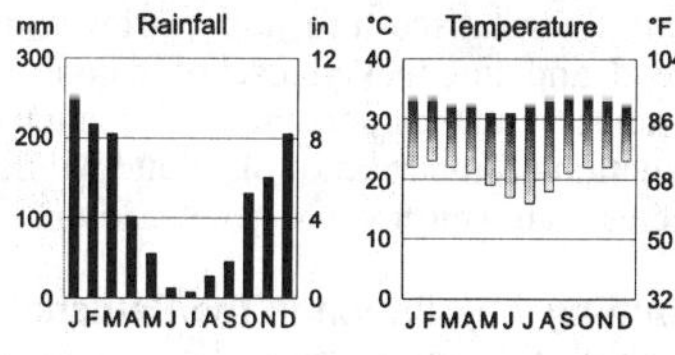

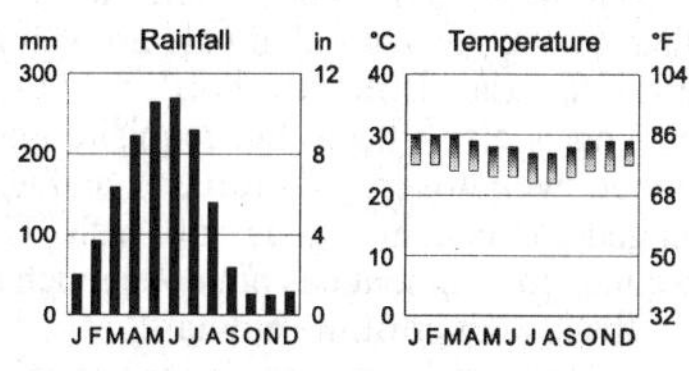

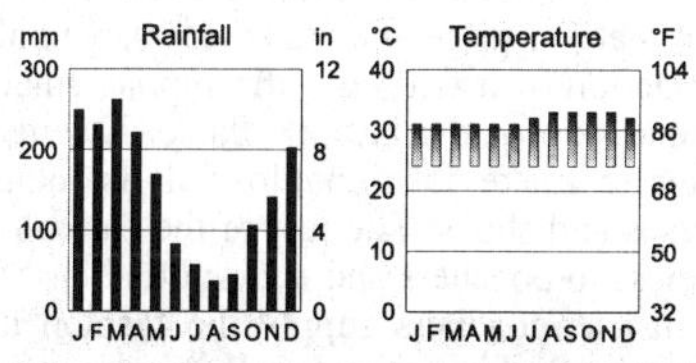

temperatures generally in the mid-20°Cs, sometimes reaching the low 30°Cs. If you are in Rio in the winter and the weather's lousy (the rain can continue for days non-stop), or you want more heat, head to the Northeast.

The Northeast coast gets about as hot as Rio during the summer, but due to a wonderful tropical breeze and less humidity, it's rarely stifling. Generally, from Bahia to Maranhão, temperatures are a bit warmer year-round than in Rio, rarely far from 28°C. All in all, it's hard to imagine a better climate.

The *planalto* (highlands) such as Minas Gerais and Brasília, are usually a few degrees cooler than the coast and not as humid. Here summer rains are frequent, while along the coast the rains tend to come intermittently.

Although there are variations in rainfall throughout Brazil, rain is a year-round affair. The general pattern is for short, tropical rains that come at all times. These rains rarely alter or interfere with travel plans. The sertão is a notable exception – here the rains fall heavily within a few months and periodic droughts devastate the region.

The Amazon Basin receives the most rain in Brazil, and Belém is one of the most rained on cities in the world, but the refreshing showers are usually seen as a godsend. Actually, the Amazon is not nearly as hot as most people presume – the average temperature is 27°C – but it is humid. The hottest part of the basin is between the Rio Solimões and Rio Negro. From June to August the heat tends to decrease a bit.

ECOLOGY & ENVIRONMENT

Brazil faces major environmental challenges, with much of its vast natural wealth constantly under threat. In some ways, it is in the front line in the destruction of the earth and, while international media attention generally focuses on the rape of the Amazon rainforest, there are several other extremely serious environmental issues in Brazil that require equally urgent attention.

In the 1970s, the military government attempted to tame the Amazon with an ambitious plan entitled Plano de Integração National (PNI). Long roads, like the 3000km Transamazônica, were cleared from the jungle and settlers from the Northeast soon followed in the tracks of the bulldozers. The roads were said to be safety valves to ease the social tensions and overpopulation of the drought-stricken Northeast.

Thousands left the Northeast to build homesteads in the newly cleared forest. The majority of these hopeful settlers failed to establish a foothold and either perished or abandoned the land for the favelas of Manaus and Belém.

During the 1980s, the Brazilian government acted as if the forests were an impediment to progress, an asset to be used to pay back the debt incurred during the 20 years of military dictatorship. Encouraged by the International Monetary Fund (IMF) and the World Bank, the Brazilian government provided large incentives to coax multinational timber and mining firms to exploit the Amazon. These gigantic projects were designed to yield short-term profits and pay off the foreign debt regardless of environmental and social consequences. The economic plan was launched with purely extractive goals, and the forests and precious metals were perceived as resources to be exploited at top speed, presumably until they were gone.

Many of the loans for these gigantic projects worsened Brazil's foreign debt, which plagued the economy for more than a decade. Despite increasing criticism at home and abroad, this plan is still being maintained and will eventually exhaust Brazil's resources.

The early 1990s saw a dramatic surge in international and domestic interest in Brazil's ecological progress and environmental attitudes. This was demonstrated by the choice of Brazil as the venue for Eco 92, a mega environmental and ecological bash organised by the United Nations to thrash out appropriate priorities for the environment and economic development.

The Mata Atlântica, a region of forest that, in the 16th century, covered 1.5 million sq km and stretched from the present day states of Rio Grande do Norte to Rio Grande do Sul, has been reduced to a mere 10,000 sq km. Some Brazilian sources, such as Fundação SOS Mata Atlântica, believe that even these remnants will be finished in 15 years, along with more than 300 species of wildlife that are already on the brink of extinction.

The Pantanal is threatened by pollution and poaching (see later in this section). The Northeast region, already experiencing extreme poverty and social breakdown, is literally losing ground to desertification; and beaches throughout Brazil (particularly those near industrial areas) are threatened by indiscriminate dumping of major pollutants or malfunctioning sanitation systems. Further problems involve the burning of huge tracts of land in parks and reserves to clear it for agriculture and cattle; widespread and unchecked use of dangerous pesticides; and the concomitant reduction or extinction of hundreds of plant and wildlife species – an irretrievable genetic loss.

Poaching & Pollution in the Pantanal

Poachers are doing more damage to the Pantanal – where anywhere from 500,000 to two million animals are killed each year – than to the Amazon. Animals are smuggled over the Bolivian border (where poaching is also illegal, but requisite laws are not even tokenly enforced) and exchanged for cocaine, guns and cash. The Brazilian government has not done much to stem the slaughter of the animals.

The slow and fearless *jacaré* (yacare caiman, a crocodilian similar to an alligator) are easily shot at short range. A jacaré skin commands a price of up to US$500, but only a fraction of it is used – the supple, small-scaled skin of the jacaré's flanks is sought after to make fashionable wallets, belts, purses and shoes. The rest of the carcass is useless to poachers and is discarded.

Just as poachers supply the fashion industry with skins, they supply American pet shops with rare tropical fish and birds. While a hyacinth macaw will sell in the USA for US$6000 to US$12,000, a person involved in the early stages of poaching actually receives very little money.

As well as the threat posed by poachers, the delicate environment is also threatened by mercury in gold slurries and ever-expanding farm and ranch lands. Sediments from erosion caused by intensive soya and rice farming flow into the area. Sugar mills and factories that produce *álcool* (sugar-cane fuel) in São Paulo and Mato Grosso dump poisonous waste into rivers that drain into the Pantanal. Scientists have also detected use of the defoliant Thordon, a component of Agent Orange.

Large projects are begun without any environmental impact study. The latest is the proposed construction of a *hidrovia* (aquatic freeway), which would run 3300km from Cáceres through the Pantanal and along the borders of five countries to Neuva Palmira in Uruguay.

As criticism of the project increased, the Brazilian government responded with a 'softly softly' approach, ruling out rock dynamiting, dredging and straightening of river bends from the Pantanal component of the project.

However, with the first stages of work in progress near Cáceres, environmentalists are highly suspicious. Groups continue to fight the project, and have launched a global lobby against further work being carried out until an independent environmental impact study is conducted.

The Fate of the Amazon

The Amazon, a very large, complex and fragile ecosystem – comprising one-tenth of the planet's entire plant and animal species, producing one-fifth of the world's oxygen and containing one-fifth of the world's fresh water – is endangered. Unless things change, the rainforests will be cleared for more ranches and industrial sites, the land will be stripped for mines and the rivers will be dammed for electricity. Already jaguars, caimans, dolphins, monkeys and a host of other wildlife and plant species are threatened with extinction. As in the past, the Indians will die with their forests, and the invaluable, irreplaceable Amazon may be lost forever. In 1995, an area about the size of Belgium was destroyed.

The construction of roads is a prerequisite for exploiting the Amazon. This process was initiated with the construction of the Transamazônica highway in 1970. The ensuing decades saw over US$10 billion thrown into gargantuan projects and schemes offering financial incentives to exploit resources regardless of the effects on the environment. Those involved included the World Bank, the IMF, US and other international banks, and a variety of Brazilian corporations, politicians, and military figures. According to calculations made using Landsat photos, the damming of rivers, burning, and clearing of the forests between 1970 and 1989 destroyed about 400,000 sq km or around 10% of the Amazon forest.

At the end of 1988, Chico Mendes, a rubber-tapper and opponent of rainforest destruction, was assassinated in the town of Xapurí (Acre state) by a local landowner. This sparked an international reaction, which eventually pressured the World Bank and the IMF to declare that they would no longer fund destruction of the rainforest. For further details see the boxed text 'Chico Mendes' in the Rondônia & Acre chapter.

Despite this commitment, it seems there will be no appreciable slackening in the forest destruction. The Perimetral Norte, a highway that is projected to stretch in a huge loop from Macapá (Amapá state) via Boa Vista (Roraima state) all the way to Cruzeiro do Sul (Acre state), is still being touted as a viable project. In the state of Acre, the extension of Hwy BR-364 from Rio Branco to Cruzeiro do Sul is being supported by Japanese finance. Local politician João Toto recently stressed that this road will be 'the salvation of Acre'. The stretch between Rio Branco and Sena Madureira (about 125km) has been completed. The inevitable conclusion is that new highway projects such as these will follow the old pattern of development and open up the Brazilian Amazon to even more destruction.

The military recently claimed in all seriousness that the environmental issues surrounding the Amazon have been exaggerated by foreigners intent on invading the region! Gilberto Mestrinho, thankfully now the ex-governor of Amazonas state, was a proponent (we swear) of 'a chain saw for every family'. Responsible for destroying over 1.5 million sq km of the Brazilian Amazon during his three terms in office, Mestrinho's environmental positions were simply unbelievable: for example, he once said 'I like trees and plants but they are not indispensable. After all, men have lived in space for almost a year without trees ... ').

Much of what is being promised overseas and in Brazil appears to be 'greenspeak', a type of lip service whereby the speaker certifies green intentions for a hazy point in the future without putting these into deeds. In 1996, a law was passed reducing the amount of land that owners could log from 50% of their holdings to 20%. But fines have been near impossible to levy, and of those that have been imposed, over 90% remain unpaid. In 1998, the Brazilian government passed legislation toughening enforcement and creating a category under law known as 'Environmental crimes'. While this grants the Brazilian Environment and Natural Resources Institute (IBAMA) a little more muscle, it's only a little, and landowners, loggers and other developers continue to exploit the Amazon effectively at will.

Exploitation of the Amazon Most biologists doubt that the Amazon can support large-scale agriculture; the lushness of the jungle is deceptive. Apart from volcanic lands and flood plains, which can support continuous growth, the jungle topsoil is thin and infertile; most of it is acidic and contains insufficient calcium, phosphorus and potassium for crops.

Small-scale slash and burn, a traditional agricultural technique adopted by nomadic

JOHN MAIER, JR

Many areas of the Amazon in Rondônia have been destroyed due to dam construction

Indians, seemed to work best at supporting small populations on such fragile lands without ecological compromises. Indians would fell small areas of trees and burn off remaining material. The resulting ash would support a few years of crops: squash, corn, manioc, plantains and beans. After a few seasons, however, the nutrients would be spent and the Indians would move on. The clearings were small in size and number and the land was left fallow long enough for the jungle to recover.

In contrast, modern agricultural techniques are enormous in scale, directed to the production of animal protein rather than vegetable protein, and fail to give the jungle an opportunity to recover. Today, ranchers clear huge areas of land – some cattle ranches are larger than European nations. These lands are never left fallow, so nutrients contained in the biomass of the forest and a thin topsoil are permanently squandered.

Farming and ranching is almost incidental to the deforestation process. Vast tracts of land are bought so that the buyers can speculate for the treasures buried beneath the earth, not those growing on it. Since Brazilian law requires that one-third of the land be put to use, the owners set fire to the land (killing wildlife indiscriminately), plant some grasses and raise cattle. The government then approves the land rights and the important mineral rights are secured.

Effects of Development The Indian tribes in the Brazilian Amazon have borne the brunt of the destruction, which has systematically wiped out their lands and the forest, their sole livelihood. New roads have attracted settlers and *garimpeiros* (wildcat gold miners) into the last refuges of these tribes, which have been virtually wiped out by introduced diseases, violent disputes over land, pollution from mining or the construction of huge dams that simply flood them out of the area. For more details about the Indians see the History and Population & People sections in this chapter.

Giant hydroelectric schemes, such as Balbina (Amazonas state) and Tucuruí (Pará state), are also a source of controversy. In the case of Balbina, a US$750 million project funded by the World Bank, there are doubts as to the usefulness of flooding over 2000 sq km.

Apart from the loss of wildlife and wastage of valuable timber, the possible chemical effects of such large quantities of submerged, decomposing, vegetal matter on the water quality and the surrounding region have not been sufficiently researched. Over 70 major hydroelectric schemes are planned for completion in the Brazilian Amazon by the year 2010.

Thousands of garimpeiros have swarmed into the region to mine the streams and rivers. Unfortunately, their principal mining technique involves the use of mercury separation to extract gold from ore. Large quantities of mercury, a highly poisonous substance, are washed into the water, where they become a major health hazard for local Indians, wildlife and the garimpeiros themselves.

One of the most dramatic and disturbing sights in the forest is the burning of immense tracts to clear the area for agriculture or cattle ranching. While travelling in the region we noticed that many airports – Porto Velho, Cuiabá, Imperatriz, and Açailândia are just a few examples – were regularly closed to air traffic because of the smoke. In broad daylight, we sat outside in semi-gloom (induced by huge clouds of smoke obscuring the sun) at a restaurant in Porto Velho, while a light rain of vegetal ash descended on the tables.

It is quite obvious that no attention whatsoever is being paid to legislation, which restricts the number of fires on any one day; and it would be a Herculean task to enforce such a law.

According to meteorologists, the smoke cloud has already reached Africa and Antarctica. Scientists generally agree that the torching of the forest on such a massive scale contributes to the greenhouse effect, but opinions differ as to how much.

Scientists are becoming increasingly concerned by the regional and global climatic changes caused by massive deforestation. The water cycle which depends fundamentally on transpiration from the forest canopy has been interrupted. Neighbouring lands, such as eastern Pará, are receiving less rainwater than usual, while the spent soils of the surrounding areas and deforested zones are being baked by the sun into desert wastelands.

Perhaps the most devastating long-term effect is the annual loss of thousands of forest species, which disappear into extinction in a process which reduces the genetic pool vital (as a source of foods, medicines and chemicals) for sustaining life on earth.

The Search for Solutions

It is only fair to point out that many of the countries which have criticised Brazil's development of the Amazon were once actively encouraging such development, and have only recently been reminded that their own treatment of the environment was hardly exemplary. The general consensus for the 1990s, however, is that a series of different approaches must be tried to halt and remedy the destruction.

Debt-for-nature swaps, international agreements whereby a portion of a country's external debt is cancelled in exchange for local funding of conservation initiatives, have had underwhelming success. More promising are programmes like the World Bank's Global Environmental Facility (GEF); and the promise by the G7 (through the World Bank) to pump millions of dollars into conservation initiatives in the Amazon. These loans are tied to sustainable management of forests and natural resources, and community participation.

Extractive reserves gained world attention when Chico Mendes, an enthusiastic advocate of these reserves, was assassinated in Acre state. The aim of this concept is to set aside reserves for the sustainable harvesting of brazil nuts, rubber, and other non-timber products. The idea is to use the forest as a renewable resource, without destroying it.

Alternatives are also being researched to stop wasteful clear-cutting of timber. In many cases, huge tracts of forest are wiped out in order to extract only a few commercially valuable tree species, while the rest is considered waste. Different methods are being tried to control the type of timber cut, the size of the area that is logged, and the manner in which forests are harvested – preferably as part of an overall management scheme to retain forests as a sustainable resource.

If any success is to be achieved, these schemes will have to be underpinned with finance and enforcement. Much of what is currently promised in Brazil exists only on paper, and funds have a strange habit of missing their destination or drifting into private accounts. Many of the country's environmental protection units suffer from lack of funds, staff and equipment, and a consequent inability to act. Most environmentalists agree that local communities are in the best position to protect and manage natural resources in the Amazon. Brazil and foreign governments must empower these communities to be the custodians of the Amazon by granting them rights (for land – resources on it and under it) and by training them. Indigenous people in particular, such as the Kayapo, have won battles in which the Brazilian government has granted them ownership over vast areas.

Environmental Movements

The nascent Brazilian conservation movement is beginning to make political inroads, though it is hampered by a general lack of environmental awareness in the country. Environmentalists have demonstrated to industry the benefits of not polluting, and industry is beginning to respond. Nowadays environmental impact studies accompany all major industrial projects, but this does not mean that the companies concerned will feel compelled to act on recommendations made in such studies.

If Brazil's environment is to be preserved it will be through the efforts of groups like these within Brazil and abroad – groups that can educate the public and enlist its support to control consumption of tropical-forest products; to pressure domestic and international banks and institutions to stop financing destructive development projects; and to persuade the Brazilian government to adopt more rational uses for the Amazon.

Ecotourism is also being considered as a powerful tool to encourage countries such as Brazil to earn more from preserving the environment than from destroying it. It is important that the organisations which proclaim an interest in ecotourism prove they are not just jumping onto the 'green' bandwagon, but also actively preserving the environment.

An example of active involvement is the growing pressure exerted by consumers, who can change economic trends on a global scale by simply changing purchasing patterns. Contact the environmental and ecological organisations in the following list for more information about environment and ecology in Brazil. For more details about tour operators, see Organised Tours in the Getting There & Away chapter.

Australia

Friends of the Earth/Aust, Suite 15, 104 Bathurst St, Sydney, NSW 2000 (☎ (02) 9283 2004); 312 Smith St, Collingwood, Vic 3066 (☎ (03) 9419 8700)

Greenpeace Australia Ltd, Level 4, 39 Liverpool St, Sydney, NSW 2000 (☎ 1800 815 151)

Brazil

Friends of the Earth – Amazonia Program, Avenida Brigadeiro Luís Antônio 4442, São Paulo (SP) CEP 01402-002 (☎ (011) 887-9369; fax 884-2795; foeamaz@ibm.net)

SOS Mata Atlântica, Rua Manoel da Nóbrega 456 São Paulo (SP) CEP 04001-001 (☎ (011) 887-1195; fax 885-1680; smata@ax.apc.org)

Instituto Socioambiental (ISA), Avenida Higienópolis 901, São Paulo (SP) CEP 01238-001 (☎ (011) 825-5544; fax 825-7861; jpcapo@ibm.net)

Fundação Vitória Amazônica, Rua R/S casa 7 quadra Q, Morada do Sol/Aleixo, Manaus (AM) CEP 69080-510 (☎ (092) 236-9181)

WWF, SHIS EQ QL 6/8 – cj. E, 2 andar, Brasília (DF) CEP 71620-430 (☎ (061) 248-2899; fax 364-3057; panda@wwf.org.br)

Greenpeace, Rua Pinheiros 240, sala 32, São Paulo (SP) CEP 05422-000 (☎ (011) 3064-8916; fax 282 5500; klshi@dialb.gl3.greenpeace.org)

GAMBÁ, Avenida Juracy Magalhães Jr 768 – Ed. RV Center 1 andar, Salvador (BA) CEP 41940-060 (☎ (071) 240-6822; fax 240-6822; gamba@ax.apc.org)

Amazon NGO Working Group (GTA), Memorial Chico Mendes, Parque da Cidade, Estacionamento 12, Brasília (DF) CEP 70610-300 (☎ (061) 322-3055; fax 321-6333; gta@tba.com.br)

FUNATURA, SCLN 107, Edifício Gemini Center II, Bl B, salas 201/205, Brasília (DF) CEP 70743-520 (☎ (061) 274-5449; fax 274-5324

IMAZON, Caixa Postal 1015, Belém (PA) CEP 66017-000 (☎ (091) 235-4214/235-0122; fax 235-4214; cuhl@ufpa.br)

ISPN, SCLN 202, Bl B, salas 101/104, Brasília (DF) CEP 70832-525 (☎ (061) 321-8085; fax 321-6333)

UK

Friends of the Earth/UK, 26/28 Underwood St, London N17JQ (☎ (0171) 490-1555)

Survival International, 11-15 Emerald St, London WC1N 3QL (☎ (0171) 242 1441)

USA

Rainforest Alliance, 6th Floor, 65 Bleeker St, New York, NY 10012 (☎ (212) 677-1900)

The Rainforest Foundation, 270 Lafayette St, Suite 1107, New York, NY 10012 (☎ (212) 431-9098)

The Rainforest Action Network (RAN), 221 Pine St, No 500, San Francisco, CA 94104 (☎ (415) 398-4404)

The Chico Mendes Fund, Environmental Defense Fund, 257 Park Ave S, New York, NY 10010 (☎ (212) 505-2100)

Conservation International, Suite 200, 2501 M St NW, Washington, DC 20037 (☎ (202) 429-5660)

The Nature Conservancy, 1815 N Lynn St, Arlington, VA 22209 (☎ (703) 841-5300)

Friends of the Earth/USA, Suite 300, 1025 Vermont Ave NW, Washington, DC 20005 (☎ (202) 783-7400)

Greenpeace, 1436 U St NW, Washington, DC 20009 (☎ (202) 462-1177)

Earthwatch, 680 Mt Auburn St (PO Box 9104), Watertown, MA 02272 (☎ (617) 926-8200)

FLORA & FAUNA

The richness and diversity of Brazilian flora and fauna are astounding, and the country ranks first in the world for its variety of primate, amphibian and plant species; third for bird species; and fourth for butterfly and reptile species.

Here is a rough overview of this extraordinary diversity, which, for ease of reference, is divided into general vegetation zones with a few examples of the flora and fauna.

The Pantanal

A vast wetlands area in the centre of South America, the Pantanal is about half the size of France – some 230,000 sq km spread across Brazil, Bolivia and Paraguay.

Less than 100,000 sq km is in Bolivia and Paraguay; the rest is in Brazil, split between the states of Mato Grosso and Mato Grosso do Sul.

The Pantanal – 2000km from the Atlantic Ocean yet only 100m to 200m above sea level – is bounded by higher lands: the mountains of the Serra de Maracaju to the east; the Serra da Bodoquena to the south; the Paraguayan and Bolivian Chaco to the west; and the Serra dos Parecis and the Serra do Roncador to the north. From these highlands the rains flow into the Pantanal to form the Rio Paraguai and its tributaries, which flow south and then east, draining into the Atlantic Ocean between Argentina and Uruguay.

During the rainy season, from October to March, the rivers flood their banks – inundating much of the low-lying Pantanal for half the year and creating *cordilheiras* (patches of dry land). The waters reach their high mark, as much as 3m, in January or February, then recede in March, and flow normally again until the rainy season returns six months later.

This seasonal flooding has made systematic farming impossible and severely limited human incursions into the area. It has also provided an enormously rich feeding ground for wildlife.

The flood waters replenish the soil's nutrients, which would otherwise be very poor due to the excessive drainage. The waters teem with fish, and the ponds provide excellent ecological niches for many animals and plants. Enormous flocks of wading birds gather in rookeries several sq km in size.

When the water recedes later in the dry season the lagoons and marshes dry out and fresh grasses emerge on the savanna (Pantanal vegetation includes savanna, forest and meadows that blend together, often with no clear divisions).

The hawks and jacaré compete for fish in the remaining ponds. The ponds shrink and dry up and the jacaré crawl around for water, sweating it out until the rains return.

The food economy of the diverse and abundant marshland bird life is based on snails, insects and fish. All three abound in the Pantanal and support around 270 bird species including kite and hawk, limpkin, cardinal, heron and egret, woodpecker, ibis and stork, woodrail, kingfisher, cuckoo, hummingbird, parakeet, thornbird, antshrike, wren, jay, blackbird, finch, toucan and macaw.

A mere list doesn't do justice to the colour of a flock of parakeets in flight or the clumsiness of the *tuiuiu* (jabiru stork), the metre-high, black-hooded, scarlet-collared symbol of the Pantanal, nor can it suggest the beauty of *ninha* birds settling like snow in the trees or the speed of a sprinting herd of *ema* (rhea). Keep an ear open for the call of the Southern Lapwing, named *quero-quero* (I want, I want) in Brazil for its sound to Brazilian ears.

Birds are the most frequently seen wildlife, but the Pantanal is also a sanctuary for giant river otters, anaconda and iguana, jaguar, ocelot, cougar, thousands upon thousands of jacaré, pampa and marsh deer, giant and collared anteater, black-and-gold howler monkey, zebu bull and capybara, the world's largest rodents.

Jabiru storks can be spotted in the swampy areas or small lagoons of the Pantanal

The most significant threats to the jaguar are habitat destruction and poaching

The capybara is the most visible mammal in the Pantanal. These rodents have guinea pig faces and bear-like coats. They grow up to 63kg and can be seen waddling in the swampy half of the Transpantaneira, where they feed on aquatic plants. They are equally at home on land or in water and are often seen in family groups of two adults and four or five young, or in large herds.

The two species of anteater in the Pantanal are endangered and not easily seen. The hairy giant anteater roams the dry savanna ground, brush piles and grassy fields in search of the hard termite mounds, which it excavates for 10 to 15 minutes at a time. The lesser anteater, smaller and lighter coloured than the giant, spends most of its time in trees eating ants, termites and larvae. Both are slow, with poor vision, but an excellent sense of smell.

The anteater's strong arms and claws, which keep even the jaguars at bay, offer no protection from the local Pantaneiros, who prize their meat. The killing of anteaters has led to an increase in ants and termites in the last decade, and many absentee landowners now instruct employees to use dangerous pesticides to destroy the mounds, ignoring the fact that these chemicals are then absorbed by cattle and wildlife feeding in the area.

With thousands of jacaré sunning themselves on the edge of each and every body of water, it's hard to believe that they are endangered by poachers (see Poaching & Pollution in the Pantanal earlier in this chapter).

Jacaré feed mainly on fish, and are the primary check on the growth of the piranha population, which has been growing rapidly due to the jacaré slaughter. The size of an adult jacaré is determined by the abundance of food, and varies noticeably: jacaré on the river's edge are often considerably larger than those that feed in small ponds. Although they eat young or injured animals, jacaré rarely attack people or capybara, and many birds mingle with the jacaré in complete peace and harmony.

During the rainy season you must be careful walking in the water. The jacaré are not aggressive and will usually swim away before you get close, but if stepped on, the jacaré will grab the offending leg and roll. This has probably never happened to a tourist, and rarely does a Pantaneiro suffer this unpleasant end, but the odd jacaré attack is used, nonetheless, to justify their slaughter.

Cattle that live side by side with the wildlife graze during the dry season and gather on the little islets that form during the wet season. Amazingly, the cattle live in harmony with the wildlife, as have humans until recently.

Jaguars attack sick or injured cattle, and some eat only their natural prey, capybara and tapir. Some jaguars do go on rampages, killing healthy cattle, and these (and, unfortunately, sometimes others) are then killed by cattle ranchers. Jaguars are also killed for their skins and are threatened with extinction, as are the marsh deer and the giant river otter.

Until recently, Pantaneiros believed that eating jaguar meat boosted masculine qualities like strength and virility, qualities the *zagaeiro* (the traditional hunter of the jaguar) has in abundance. Traditionally using only a *zagara* (a wooden spear with a metal tip) the zagaeiro would chase jaguar up a tree and then taunt the cat until it was ready to leap and attack. At the last moment the zagaeiro would plant the spear in the ground; when the jaguar leapt at the man it would impale itself.

See the Pantanal section in the Mato Grosso chapter for more details about the region.

The Amazon

This is the largest equatorial forest in the world and occupies approximately 42% of Brazil's area.

The rainforest ecosystem is stratified into four layers of plant and animal life. Most of the activity takes place in the canopy layer, 20m to 40m above ground, where plants compete for sunshine and the majority of birds and monkeys live. The dense foliage of the canopy layer blots out the sunlight at lower levels, while a few tall trees poke above the canopy and dominate the forest skyline. A poorly defined middle layer or understorey merges with the canopy from below. Epiphytes hang at this level.

Bushes and saplings up to 5m in height constitute the shrub layer, while the ground layer is composed of ferns, seedlings and herbs – plants adapted to very little light. Ants and termites, the so-called social insects, live here. The *saubas* (leaf-cutter ants) are farmers and use leaves to build underground nests for raising fungus gardens, while army ants swarm through the jungle in huge masses, eating everything in their path. Fungi and bacteria, the decomposers, keep the forest floor clear. It's tidy in comparison to temperate forests.

The forest is not homogeneous; plant species vary with the land and its exposure to water. Plants of the *igapó* (flooded Amazon forest) and flooded lowlands are mostly palms and trees with elevated roots. The valuable hardwoods and the brazil nut tree prefer land that is high and dry. The rubber trees and other plants of the *várzea* (land by the river's edge) have adapted to spending half of the year below water and half the year dry. Then there are the river's aquatic plants like the giant *Vitória regia* water lilies (named after Queen Victoria),

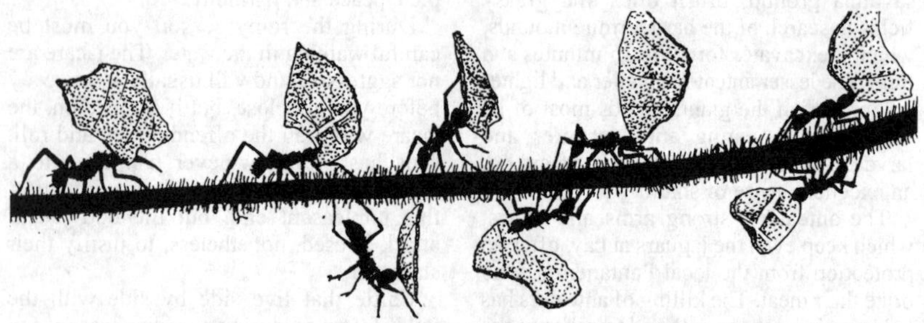

Leaf-cutter ants – sometimes referred to as 'nature's gardeners'

mureru, *camarans* and *manbeca*. There are floating marshes with amphibious grasses, which have earth and aquatic roots, depending on the season and local conditions.

The forest still keeps many of its secrets: to this day major tributaries of the Rio Amazonas are unexplored. Of the estimated 15,000 species of Amazon creatures, thousands of birds and fish and hundreds of mammals have not been classified, and after each foray into the jungle botanists still manage to bring back dozens of unclassified plants.

A cursory sampling of known species of animals– some common, some rare, some virtually extinct – would include the jaguar, tapir, peccary (collared and white-lipped), capybara, spider monkey (black, white-bellied, white-whiskered), howler (black and gold, red, red-handed) sloth (two and three-toed), armadillo (about five species), jacaré, grey and pink river dolphin, manatee and turtle (many species); and various species of snakes such as the boa constrictor and anaconda. Typical bird species include the toucan, parrot, macaw, hummingbird, woodpecker and hawk. Insect life is well represented with over 1800 species of butterfly and more than 200 species of mosquito. Fish species include the piranha, *surubim pintado*, *tucunaré*, *pirarucu*, and electric eels.

Unfortunately, deforestation is taking place on such a vast scale that countless unknown species of animals and plants will be destroyed. We will lose a genetic library that has already given us so much: rubber, manioc, cocoa, anti-malarial drugs, cancer drugs and thousands more medicinal plants.

For more details about the problems facing the Amazon rainforest, see the Ecology & Environment section in this chapter.

Mata Atlântica

The surviving coastal rainforest, known as Mata Atlântica, has been reduced to between 2 and 5% of its original size by sugar-cane farming, logging, coffee cultivation and acid rain. Extending up the Atlantic Coast through Espírito Santo state, where a number of smaller reserves exist, it is fragmented and lots of 'pockets' still exist.

The largest, the Estação Ecológica da Jureia, on the southern coastal escarpment in São Paulo state, owes its survival to the shelving of plans to build a nuclear power plant.

Separated from the Amazon by non-rainforest terrain, the Mata Atlântica is much older (60 million years compared to the Amazon's 40 million) and evolved independently, with only a limited overlap of species. It has an even richer biodiversity than the Amazon, and contains many unique and endangered animals, such as the muriqui (woolly spider monkey, the largest primate in the Americas), brown howler, marmoset and the golden-lion tamarin. Its distinctive flora includes many large trees; brazil wood, iron wood, Bahian jacaranda and cedar, as well as a number of rare tree ferns.

The Mata Atlântica is also home to more than 600 bird species, many of which are unique. These include tinamous and large numbers of the vibrant tanagers. Many species of antbird, hummingbird, flycatcher, woodpecker, tanager and finch are endemic to the Atlantic tropical moist forest biome.

See the Ecology & the Environment section earlier in this chapter for more details.

Mata da Araucaria

The mountainous regions of south-west and southern Brazil were once covered by coniferous forests, which were dominated by the prehistoric-looking araucaria, or parana pine tree. It grows to a height of 30 to 40m, has clear trunks and candelabra-like heads of upturned branches that form flattened crowns. They occur as far north as central Minas Gerais at altitudes above 1200m. Its *pinhões* (seeds) are edible.

The araucaria forests have been decimated by timber cutters are now more scattered, but are much in evidence in the south, where the animal inhabitants include foxes, tree squirrels, skunks, spotted cats and monkeys.

Caatingas

These are dry areas, such as those of the sertão in the Northeast, where vegetation consists mainly of cacti and thorny shrubs that have adapted to lack of water and extreme heat. Much of the wildlife in these areas – anteaters and armadillos for example – has been severely depleted by hunting and habitat destruction. Currently, these areas are being exploited without control. Wood and coal from the *caatingas* (scrub vegetation of the Northeast sertão) are a primary energy source for a large percentage of the region's inhabitants. It's also used to fuel 30% of the Northeast's industries, generates 114,000 jobs directly, and contributes 15% of the income on rural properties. Recent studies show that continuing destruction at its present rate will see the caatingas disappear in Paraíba in 28 years, 40 years in Pernambuco, 50 years in Ceará and 65 years in Rio Grande do Norte. The list of endangered species for the caatingas includes the Spix macaw (of which, as we write, there's only one left alive in the wild), Lear's macaw, and the three-banded armadillo.

Cerrado

These open lands, which also occur in the form of savannas, are usually grassy plains dotted with small trees such as the *mangaba* and *carobeira*. This landscape extends from the borders of Maranhão in the Northeast down through Minas Gerais and as far as the Southwest. Armadillos, foxes and rheas are some of the well-known species in these areas. The *cerrado* are disappearing fast. The use of this land for agricultural purposes, such as soya farming, has reduced available habitat for wildlife, such as the maned wolf and giant anteater, which are native to this region and are now endangered species.

Cruelty to Animals

Brazil has a poor record in its treatment of animals. Stray domestic animals are mistreated and sometimes poisoned. To its shame, the government ignores poaching, smuggling of exotic animals and the murders of manatees and dolphins in the Manaus region for their meat, eyes and genitalia.

In 1998, cockfighting – popular despite being illegal throughout the country – was legalised in Rio de Janeiro city, in contravention of a federal law defining cruelty to animals as a crime.

The World Society for the Protection of Animals began work in Brazil in 1992, and since then has been involved in a number of celebrated fights against cruelty to animals. Most recently it has seriously curtailed the *Farra do Boi*, the Easter week 'celebrations' which involve the torture-killing of several hundred oxen each year in more than 30 communities throughout Santa Catarina. After intense campaigning and a media blitz by WSPA, the Brazilian supreme court banned the practice.

The most important piece of advice WSPA offers travellers is not to handle wild animals that may be thrust at them by locals – many have been taken from their mothers as babies and are mistreated, mishandled, die very early and are soon replaced by other animals obtained the same way.

For more information, contact the Sociedade Mundial de Protecão Animal (WSPA, ☎ (021) 527-7158; fax 286-3940; wspa@world.std.com), Avenida Paulo de Frontin 499, Rio Comprido, Rio de Janeiro, RJ, 20261-240.

NATIONAL PARKS

On a federal and state level, there are 350 parks and ecological stations, ensuring the protection of over 300,000 sq km – roughly 5% of the national territory. Unfortunately, about 70% of the natural reserves exist only on paper, only 33% of them have a minimum infrastructure (warden offices and fences) and only 19.5% have vehicles, equipment, weapons and personnel on an appropriate level. Of all national parks, the government has managed to regulate only 22% of them. To pay out the owners of the land would cost US$1 billion. IBAMA still hasn't expropriated any land, so ranchers continue to use it.

IBAMA makes the distinction between *parques nacionais* (national parks), *reservas biológicas* (biological reserves) and *estações ecológicas* (ecological stations). Only parques nacionais are open to the public for recreational use. Reservas biológicas and estações ecológicas are restricted to researchers and you need permission from IBAMA to visit them.

Despite all this, there are some fantastic parks to see. IBAMA has a minuscule budget that only allows it to publish a small amount of literature in Portuguese and less in English. We have tried to locate and provide as much information as possible in this book. Any feedback from readers regarding visits to these parks would be appreciated.

If you're prepared to rough it a bit and do some camping, you'll experience some spectacular places. Following is a brief overview of Brazil's main national parks, divided into regions for ease of reference. See the regional chapters for more detailed information.

The Southeast

In Rio, the Parque Nacional da Tijuca, surrounded by the city, is a popular day trip and offers magnificent panoramic views. The Parque Nacional do Itatiaia, 155km to the south-east of the city, is a favourite with trekkers and climbers – its big attraction being Agulhas Negras (2787m). Another climbing mecca is the Parque Nacional da Serra dos Órgãos, 86km from Rio. As well as its spectacular peaks it offers some great walks. These last two parks both possess a well-developed tourist infrastructure.

On the border of Rio and São Paulo states, close to Parati, the Parque Nacional da Serra da Bocaina is where the coastal escarpment meets the sea, and the Atlantic rainforest quickly changes to high-altitude araucaria forest as you move up from the coast. There is no infrastructure for tourists.

In Minas Gerais, there are some great parks to visit, including the Parque Nacional de Caparaó in the east of the state, on the border with Espírito Santo. It contains the third highest peak in the country: O Pico da Bandeira (2890m) and you don't have to be a climber to get up there. The tourist infrastructure is well developed, especially for campers. In the south-west of the state, 350km from Belo Horizonte, the Parque Nacional da Serra da Canastra is where the Rio São Francisco begins. The area is very beautiful and contains the spectacular Cascada d'Anta waterfall. The park is also home to many endangered species, such as the maned wolf, giant anteater, pampas deer, giant armadillo and thin-spined porcupine. Camping is permitted.

The Parque Nacional da Serra do Cipó, 100km from Belo Horizonte, is an area full of mountains, waterfalls and open countryside. Its highlands are an arm of the Serra do Espinhaço. The 70m waterfall, Cachoeira da Farofa, and the Canyon das Bandeirinhas are its two principal attractions, but the park contains no tourist infrastructure.

Also in Minas, near its borders with Bahia and Goiás, the Parque Nacional de Grande Sertão Veredas is made up of cerrado, caatinga, *veredas* (swampy plains between hills and rivers), and a few stands of wine palms. Inhabitants of the park include the maned wolf, giant armadillo, banded anteater and rhea. Once again, this is another park with no tourist infrastructure and access is difficult.

The South

In the southern region, the most famous national park is Iguaçu, which contains the falls. Also in Paraná, but near the coast, is the Parque Nacional do Superagui, which consists of the Peças and Superagui islands. Notable attractions of the park include the huge number of wild orchids and the abundant marine life. Created in 1989, it contains no infrastructure for tourists.

Santa Catarina boasts the Parque Nacional de São Joaquim, in the highlands of the Serra do Mar, where it even snows sometimes. As yet, it contains no tourist infrastructure.

Rio Grande do Sul contains one of the most unforgettable parks in Brazil, the Parque Nacional de Aparados da Serra, with its famous Itaimbézinho Canyon. A new visitors centre should be completed by the time this book is published. Camping is permitted inside the park. Close to the town of Rio Grande, in the south of the state, the Parque Nacional da Lagoa do Peixe is an important stopover for many species of migratory birds. It also contains the largest saltwater lagoon in the state. A visitors' centre is still on the drawing board.

The Central West

This region has its share of parks too. Just 10km from the national capital, Brasília, is the Parque Nacional de Brasília, a favourite weekend spot with the city's inhabitants. It contains a visitors centre and a leisure area with natural swimming pools. Parque Nacional da Chapada dos Veadeiros, 200km north of Brasília, in the state of Goiás, contains rare fauna and flora, as well as some spectacular waterfalls and canyons. There is camping close to the park entrance, and a few pousadas (guesthouses) nearby in the small town of São Jorge. In the extreme south-west of the state is the Parque Nacional das Emas. Its main attraction is its abundance of visible wildlife, prevalent during the dry season. Accommodation is

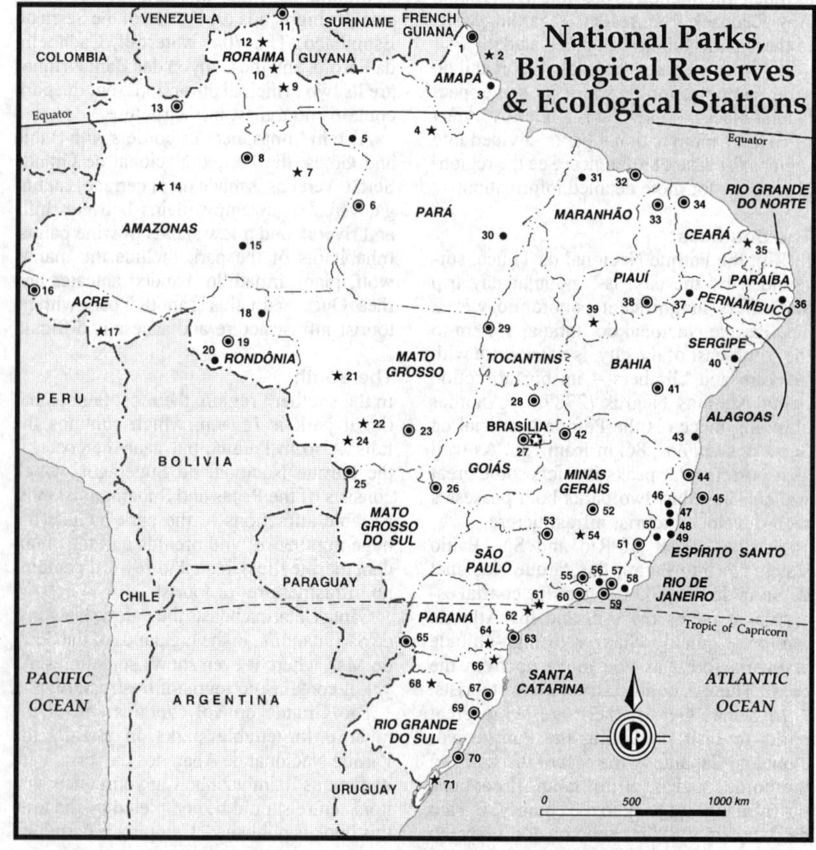

available inside the park, and camping is permitted.

Close to the city of Cuiabá is another popular park, the Parque Nacional da Chapada dos Guimarães, with its waterfalls, huge valleys and strange rock formations. Accommodation inside the park is limited to camping, but there are hotels in the nearby town of the same name.

Halfway between Cuiabá and Corumbá, near the fork of the Paraguai and Cuiabá rivers, the Parque Nacional do Pantanal Matogrossense is deep in the Pantanal and can only be reached by river or by air. Porto

◉ **NATIONAL PARKS**

1 Parque Nacional de Cabo Orange
6 Parque Nacional da Amazônia
8 Parque Nacional do Jaú
11 Parque Nacional de Monte Roraima
13 Parque Nacional do Pico da Neblina
16 Parque Nacional da Serra do Divisor
19 Parque Nacional de Pacaás Novas
23 Parque Nacional da Chapada dos Guimarães
25 Parque Nacional do Pantanal Matogrossense
26 Parque Nacional das Emas
27 Parque Nacional de Brasília
28 Parque Nacional da Chapada dos Veadeiros
29 Parque Nacional do Araguaia
32 Parque Nacional dos Lençóis Maranhenses
33 Parque Nacional de Sete Cidades
34 Parque Nacional de Ubajara
38 Parque Nacional da Serra da Capivara
41 Parque Nacional da Chapada Diamantina
42 Parque Nacional de Grande Sertão Veredas
44 Parque Nacional de Monte Pascoal
45 Parque Nacional Marinho dos Abrolhos
51 Parque Nacional de Caparaó
52 Parque Nacional da Serra do Cipó
53 Parque Nacional da Serra da Canastra
55 Parque Nacional do Itatiaia
57 Parque Nacional da Serra dos Órgãos
59 Parque Nacional da Tijuca
60 Parque Nacional da Serra da Bocaina
63 Parque Nacional do Superagui
65 Parque Nacional do Iguaçu
67 Parque Nacional de São Joaquim
69 Parque Nacional de Aparados da Serra
70 Parque Nacional da Lagoa do Peixe

● **BIOLOGICAL RESERVES**

3 Reserva Biológica do Lago Piratuba
5 Reserva Biológica do Rio Trombetas
15 Reserva Biológica do Abufari
18 Reserva Biológica do Jarú
20 Reserva Biológica do Guaporé
30 Reserva Biológica de Tapirapé
31 Reserva Biológica do Gurupi
36 Reserva Biológica de Saltinho
37 Reserva Biológica de Serra Negra
40 Reserva Biológica de Santa Isabel
43 Reserva Biológica de Una
46 Reserva Biológica do Córrego Grande
47 Reserva Biológica do Córrego do Veado
48 Reserva Biológica de Sooretama
49 Reserva Biológica de Comboios
50 Reserva Biológica Nova Lombardia
56 Reserva Biológica do Tinguá
58 Reserva Biológica do Poço das Antas

★ **ECOLOGICAL STATIONS**

2 Estação Ecológica de Maracá-Jipioca
4 Estação Ecológica do Jari
7 Estação Ecológica de Anavilhanas
9 Estação Ecológica de Niquiã
10 Estação Ecológica de Caracaraí
12 Estação Ecológica da Ilha de Maracá
14 Estação Ecológica de Juami-Japurá
17 Estação Ecológica do Rio Acre
21 Estação Ecológica de Iqué
22 Estação Ecológica da Serra das Araras
24 Estação Ecológica de Taiamã
35 Estação Ecológica de Seridó
39 Estação Ecológica de Uruçui-Una
54 Estação Ecológica de Parapitinga
61 Estação Ecológica de Tupinambás
62 Estação Ecológica dos Tupiniquins
64 Estação Ecológica de Guaraqueçaba
66 Estação Ecológica de Carijós
68 Estação Ecológica de Aracuri/Esmeralda
71 Estação Ecológica do Taim

Jofre, 100km upriver, is the closest you'll get by land. Permission from IBAMA in Cuiabá is required to visit this park. Camping is the only accommodation option here.

The Northeast

In Bahia, the Parque Nacional da Chapada Diamantina has a network of trails offering great hiking to peaks, waterfalls and rivers. See the Bahia chapter for full details about this easily accessible park and the attractive old mining town of Lençóis, which functions as its hub.

Close to the southern border of the state is the Parque Nacional de Monte Pascoal, which contains a variety of ecosystems ranging from Atlantic rainforest to mangrove swamps, beaches and reefs, and rare fauna and flora. A visitors centre is now open and guides are available to take you up the mountain.

Approximately 80km offshore in the extreme south of the state is Parque Nacional Marinho dos Abrolhos, which was designated as Brazil's first marine park in 1983. The attractions are the coral reefs, which can be visited on organised scuba-diving tours; whale-watching, and the bird life on the numerous reefs and islets.

The state of Pernambuco recently incorporated the archipelago of Fernando de Noronha, which lies approximately 525km east of Recife. A section of this archipelago has been designated as the Parque Nacional Marinho de Fernando de Noronha. The attractions here are the exceptionally varied and abundant marine life and bird life. Package tours to the archipelago are available and independent travel is possible. The tourist infrastructure is rapidly being developed.

The state of Ceará contains the Parque Nacional de Ubajara, which is renowned for its limestone caves. Tourist infrastructure is developed, and access to the caves has been re-established with a new cable car replacing the old system destroyed by landslides in 1987.

In the northern region of the state of Piauí is the Parque Nacional de Sete Cidades. The park's interesting set of rock formations resembling *sete cidades* (seven cities) are easily accessible via a hiking trail. Tourist facilities, including transport and accommodation, are established.

In the southern region of the state, the Parque Nacional da Serra da Capivara contains prehistoric sites and rock paintings, which are still being researched. Over 300 sites have been discovered so far, and this park is already considered one of the top prehistoric monuments in South America. Tourism is still limited, since it is difficult to combine ongoing research with public access, but a museum and guided tours are available.

In the state of Maranhão, the Parque Nacional dos Lençóis Maranhenses has a spectacular collection of beaches, mangroves, dunes and fauna. Infrastructure is limited, but transport and basic accommodation are available.

The North

The national parks in the northern region are best known for their diverse types of forests harbouring an astounding variety of fauna and flora. Most of these parks require visitors to obtain permits before arrival. They provide few tourist services, and access normally entails lengthy and difficult travel by plane and/or boat.

The Parque Nacional de Cabo Orange extends along the coastline at the northern tip of Amapá state. This park has retained a diverse variety of wildlife, including rare or endangered species such as the manatee, sea turtle, jaguar, anteater, armadillo and flamingo. At present, there is no tourist infrastructure available for transport or accommodation in the park.

In the state of Pará, the vast forests enclosed by the Parque Nacional da Amazônia are being rapidly eroded by illegal encroachment and destruction. The wildlife here includes a wide variety of rainforest species, but poaching is making rapid inroads into their numbers. And it's difficult to see any change in this situation when only four park guards are responsible for nearly one million hectares. There are limited services for the accommodation and transport of visitors.

The Parque Nacional de Monte Roraima lies on the northern boundary of Roraima state. Established in 1989, this park contains Monte Roraima (2875m), one of Brazil's highest peaks.

In the state of Amazonas, the Parque Nacional do Pico da Neblina adjoins the Venezuelan border and contains Brazil's highest peaks: Pico da Neblina (3014m) and Pico 31 de Março (2992m). Visitors normally require a permit from the IBAMA office in Brasília. No standard tourist infrastructure is established here; however, visitors can arrange access by using a combination of air and river transport.

Brazil's largest national park, Parque Nacional do Jaú, lies in north central Amazonas. Visitors normally require a permit from the IBAMA office in Brasília. As with the Parque Nacional do Pico da Neblina, no standard tourist infrastructure exists, but visitors can arrange access by using a combination of air and river transport.

The Parque Nacional de Pacaás Novas lies close to the town of Ji-Parana in the state of Rondônia. The principal rivers of the state, the Madeira and the Guaporé, both originate within the park, in a region where small communities of indigenous Indians have sought refuge from the massive deforestation and destruction that is still raging through the state. See the chapter on Rondônia for details about visiting the biological reserves of Guaporé and Jaru.

The Parque Nacional da Serra do Divisor lies in the extreme western part of the state of Acre and adjoins the border with Peru. Established in 1989, it has very limited tourist infrastructure.

The Parque Nacional do Araguaia now lies in the recently created state of Tocantins. The park area covers the northern end of the Ilha do Bananal, the world's largest river island, formed by the splitting of the Rio Araguaia. The park has no standard tourist infrastructure, but visitors may be able to make arrangements in Santa Teresinha (Mato Grosso state) or Gurupi (Tocantins).

GOVERNMENT & POLITICS

Brazil slowly returned to democracy in the 1980s. In 1988 a new constitution guaranteed freedom of speech, the right to strike and outlawed the use of torture. It also gave 16 year olds and illiterates the right to vote.

In 1995, Fernando Henrique Cardoso became only the second president elected by popular vote in 32 years to take office. As we went to press, the outcome of Brazilian elections in October 1998, was not known, but Cardoso was running on a platform of economic stability based on the relative strength of the *real* (the Brazilian monetary unit) despite chaos in Asian markets.

The 1988 constitution allows him to choose ministers of state, initiate pieces of legislation and maintain foreign relations. It also names him as commander-in-chief of the armed forces and gives him the power of total veto. These presidential powers are balanced by a bicameral legislature, which consists of a 72-seat senate and a 487-seat chamber of deputies. Presidential elections are held every five years, with congressional elections every four. State government elections are also held every four years, and municipal elections every three years.

Government elections are colourful affairs, regarded by the democracy-starved Brazilians as yet another excuse for a party. Posters cover every available wall space and convoys of cars cruise through the cities creating as much noise as possible in support of their chosen candidate.

Politics remain largely the preserve of the wealthy. In the 1994 elections for state governors and senators, several candidates were forced to drop out because of costs. Inducements to voters are common.

Corruption is still rife at all levels, though not so much at the top since 'Collorgate'.

ECONOMY

Brazil is a land of fantastic economic contrasts. Travelling through the country, you will witness incredibly uneven development. Production techniques that have barely changed from the colonial era dominate many parts of the Northeast and Amazonia, while São Paulo's massive, high-tech automobile, steel, arms and chemical industries successfully compete on the world market.

Since WWII there has been tremendous growth and modernisation, albeit in fits and starts. Today, Brazil's economy is the 10th largest in the world. While it's called a developing country, tremendous development has occurred.

Brazil's rulers, at least since President Kubitschek invented Brasília, have had a penchant for building things big and have been encouraged to do so by the IMF and the World Bank. The government borrowed heavily to finance Brasília's construction between 1957 and 1960. The national debt began to take off exponentially, and a couple of years later inflation followed.

Economic development is slow, but there always seem to be some highly visible mega-projects under way. Many of these are economically ill-advised and some are never completed – the funding dries up, is pocketed by corrupt bureaucrats, or the politician who started it leaves office and the political enemy who takes over decides to abandon

The States of Brazil

the project. Whatever the reason, huge amounts of money are wasted. Utilising the latest technology, much of the new development is capital intensive and few jobs are created – not nearly enough to employ the millions of urban poor who have come from the countryside.

Brazil now has an estimated 64 million workers (a third are women); 17% of people work in agriculture, most as landless peasants, and 12% work in industry. The majority of the rest cannot find decent work and are forced to sell their labour dirt cheap in jobs that are economically unproductive for society and a dead end for the individual.

Cheap labour and underemployment abound in Brazil. Middle-class families commonly hire two or more live-in maids. This contrasts with five-year-old kids, who will never go to school, selling chewing gum or shining shoes. People are hired just to walk dogs, to watch cars or deliver groceries. Large crews of street cleaners work with home-made brooms and hawkers on the beaches sell everything and earn almost nothing. Restaurants seem to have more waiters than customers.

Unlike Mexico or Turkey, the poor in Brazil have no rich neighbours where they can go for jobs. With the exception of some minor agrarian reforms, there is no relief in sight. The *fazendeiros* (estate owners) with their massive land holdings, are very influential with the government. Apart from the occasional token gesture they are unlikely to be interested in parting with their land.

Instead of land reform, the government built roads into the Amazon; the road between Belém and Brasília in 1960 and the Transamazônica and the Cuiabá to Porto Velho roads in the 1970s. The idea was to open up the Amazon to mineral and agricultural development, and to encourage settlement by the rural poor.

The mineral-poor Amazonian soil proved hard for the peasants to farm. After cutting down the forest and opening up the land they were forced off by the hired guns of big cattle ranchers. The settlement of the Amazon continues today, particularly along the strip between Cuiabá, Porto Velho and Rio Branco, where violent boom towns, deforestation and malaria follow in the wake of the settlers.

Over 50% of Brazil's industry is clustered in and around São Paulo. Most important is the car industry. Labour relations with the workers at Volkswagen, General Motors and Ford were managed by a system modelled on fascist Italy: government-approved unions backed by the power of the military state. From 1968 to 1978 the workers were silent and passive, until the day 100 workers at a bus factory went to work and sat down in front of their machines. Within two weeks 78,000 metalworkers were on strike in the São Paulo industrial belt.

The strikes rapidly spread to other industries. There were mass assemblies of workers in soccer stadiums, and the government-sponsored unions were replaced. At the invitation of the Catholic Church, union offices were moved to the cathedral of São Bernardo. Caught by surprise, the corporations and military gave in to substantial wage increases. Both sides prepared for the next time.

In 1980 there was a new wave of better organised strikes, with greater rank-and-file control. Demands were made to democratise the workplace, with shop-floor union representation and factory and safety committees. Many improvements were won, many have since been lost, but the working class had flexed its muscles and no one has forgotten.

Brazilian economists call the 1980s the Lost Decade, wild boom-and-bust cycles decimated the economy. Record-breaking industrial growth fuelled by foreign capital was followed by negative growth and explosive hyperinflation.

Until 1994, the only certainty in the economy was its uncertainty. Then came the Plano Real, an economic plan that stabilised the currency, ended the inflation that had corroded the salaries of the lowest wage earners, and provoked a rise in consumption. Out of the seven plans introduced in the 1980s and 1990s, the Real was the first without shocks or broken contracts. The death of the previous monetary unit, the cruzeiro real, was announced 52 days before the Plano Real introduced a new currency, the *real*. Backed by the record volume of international reserves (achieved after a healthy 4.2% increase in the gross national product in 1993), the *real* began on a one-for-one parity with the US dollar. Then the unthinkable happened: the Brazilian currency became worth more than the dollar.

Brazilians went shopping. In the first three months after the introduction of the plan, economic activity grew by 8%, and industrial sales rose by more than 12%. The gross national product for 1994 grew 5.7%. By the summer of 1995, a new optimism had swept through Brazil. Was this the beginning of the long-awaited economic miracle?

Economic growth has kept the *real* stable, and foreign investment is at record levels – in 1997, the US alone invested US$16 billion. But after the collapse of Asian money markets in 1997, analysts say that Brazil's economy is decidedly shaky.

At the end of 1998 the *real* was overvalued by at *least* 20% – and without constitutional reforms to the pension and civil services and a reduction of insanely high interest rates.

There's no law to prevent the government from printing reais to pay for large budget deficits. If that happens, the inflation dragon of the 1980s will be back.

The Plano Real showed that the economy has great potential. All the ingredients for progress are here: a large labour force, the means of production, transport systems and markets for the products.

The question is whether or not they can be coordinated efficiently. The harsh reality is that seven out of 10 Brazilians still live in poverty.

Social Conditions

The richest 10% of Brazilians control a whopping 54% of the nation's wealth; the poorest 10% have just 0.6% – and the gap is widening. Sixty million live in squalor without proper sanitation, clean water or decent housing. Over 60% of the people who work make less than twice the minimum wage. Unemployment and underemployment are rampant.

Wealthy Brazilians live closed, First World existences in luxurious houses behind high walls protected by armed guards and guard dogs.

In this developing country, 40 million people are malnourished; 25 million live in favelas; 12 million children are abandoned; and more than seven million between the ages of seven and 14 don't attend school. Brazil, with its dreams of greatness, has misery that compares with the poorest countries in Africa and Asia.

As always, these ills hit some groups much harder than others. If you are a woman, a black, an Indian or from the North or Northeast the odds against escaping poverty are high. One third of the women employed in Brazil work as maids and nannies, and most earn less than the minimum wage. Of Brazil's 21 million illiterates, 13 million are black. Life expectancy in the Northeast is 56 years, compared to 66 in the rest of the country.

The Indians are fighting for survival; less than 200,000 remain from an estimated five million when the Portuguese arrived. They still suffer violent attacks from ranchers and gold prospectors laying claim to their land.

The killing of peasant leaders, trade unionists and church workers involved in land disputes and strikes continues.

Though torture has been outlawed by the constitution, reports of death in custody after its use to obtain a confession continue, although there are few eyewitnesses. The killing of criminal suspects by uniformed and off-duty police in 'death-squad' operations, especially in Baixada Fluminense, on the outskirts of Rio de Janeiro, is widely reported.

The federal government is aware of the scale of human-rights violations and the chronic failure to administer justice at state and local levels, but will not accept responsibility for matters it deems beyond its jurisdiction.

For the vast majority, Brazil is, as it has always been, a country of poverty and inequality, where reforms are as elusive as the wind.

POPULATION & PEOPLE

Brazil's population is almost 155 million, making it the world's sixth most populous country. The population has been rising rapidly over the last 45 years, although in the last 10 years it seems to have slowed a little. There were only 14 million Brazilians in 1890, 33 million in 1930, 46 million in 1945, and 71 million in 1960. The population has more than doubled in the last 35 years.

Still, Brazil is one of the least densely populated nations in the world, averaging only 15 people per sq km. The USA, by comparison, averages 25 people per sq km. The population is concentrated along the coastal strip and in the cities. There are around 10 million in the enormous expanses of the North and less than 10 million in the Central West, while there are over 65 million in the Southeast and over 42 million in the Northeast. Brazil also has a young population: half its people are less than 20 years old, 27% under 10.

There are 12 million *abandonados* (children without parents or home). Many are hunted by the so-called 'death squads' made

Sem Terra

The *Movimento dos Trabalhadores Rurais Sem Terra* (MST) – Rural Workers' Landless Movement – is the latest in a long Brazilian tradition of peasant grass roots movements. Arising in 1985 from a Catholic Church group in Rio Grande do Sul, Brazil's southernmost state, the MST has gained momentum and popular support in the last few years as it struggles for land reform using a high media profile and it's trademark invasions of unused farmland.

It has developed into a highly organised network with an ideological mix of the ideas of Nicaraguan Sandinistas, Mexican Zapatistas and liberation theology. Led by the intellectual João Pedro Stedile and the charismatic José Rainha, the movement now claims more than 100,000 members in camps throughout the country (the government argues the figure is more like 40,000).

Land reform has now displaced international concern about the destruction of the Amazon. Official figures show about half of Brazil's farmland is owned by just 2% of landowners, one of the worst land-distribution ratios in the world.

More than 100 people have died in rural violence since the present government took office, the most publicised deaths being the massacre of 19 landless by the polícia militar in Eldorado dos Carajás, Pará, in April 1996.

In a well-publicised, long march on Brasília in April 1997, about 2000 landless, carrying farm tools and revolutionary-looking red flags, converged on the capital to demand land reform and justice for the killers of their dead colleagues.

The government has responded by speeding up its long awaited land reform program, creating a new ministry for agrarian reform, raising taxes on unused land and offering more credit to new settlers, but the MST has called for more radical change.

Ironically, much of the destruction of the Amazon rainforest in the last couple of years is attributable to the landless, who have been clearing the areas they have invaded for cultivation.

Andrew Draffen

up of vigilantes who take it upon themselves to torture and murder the children under the pretence that 'they grow up to become criminals anyway, so why not get rid of them now?' The fate of these children is one of the most pressing social problems facing Brazil.

Now an urban country, 40 years ago Brazil was still a predominantly rural society. Due to internal migration, two-thirds of Brazilians now live in nine large urban areas. Greater São Paulo has over 17 million residents, greater Rio over 10 million.

Some 500 years ago when Pedro Cabral departed Brazil, he left two convicts behind who subsequently married natives. So colonisation through interracial reproduction was how the Portuguese managed to control Brazil. This 'strategy' was pursued, often consciously and semi-officially, for hundreds of years. First with native Indians, then with the black slaves and finally between Indians and blacks, interracial sex thoroughly mixed the three races. There are literally dozens of terms to describe people's various racial compositions and skin tones. Most Brazilians have some combination of European, African, Amerindian, Asian and Middle Eastern ancestry.

Brazil has had several waves of voluntary immigration. After the end of slavery in 1888, millions of Europeans were recruited to work in the coffee fields. The largest contingent was from Italy, but there were also many Portuguese and Spaniards, with smaller groups of Germans and Russians. Japanese immigration began in 1908 and today São Paulo has the largest Japanese community outside of Japan.

Some 50,000 Portuguese came to Brazil from Africa in 1974 and 1975 with the liberation of Portugal's African colonies. During the 1970s many Latin Americans fleeing military dictatorships in Argentina, Chile, Uruguay and Paraguay settled in Brazil.

Indians

The government Indian agency, Fundação Nacional do Indio (FUNAI), has documented 174 different Indian languages and dialects. Customs and belief systems vary widely.

Growing international concern over the destruction of the Amazon rainforest has also highlighted the plight of the Brazilian Indians, who are facing extinction early next century – if not sooner. At present the number of Indians is estimated at less than 200,000. Of the several hundred tribes already identified, most are concentrated in the Amazon region and virtually all Brazilian Indians face a host of problems that threaten to destroy their environment and way of life. An estimated 40 tribes have never been in contact with outsiders. For more details about Indians and their status refer to the History, Ecology & Environment, Indian Art, and Culture sections in this chapter.

Indian Policy During the 20th century, the general thrust of official Brazilian policy towards the Indians and their lands has concentrated on pacification, integration, and dispossession.

In 1910, Marechal Cândido Rondon (1865-1958), who favoured a humane and dignified Indian policy, founded the Serviço de Proteção ao Indio (SPI) to protect the Indians against massacres and land dispossession. Unfortunately, Rondon's good intentions were swept aside and SPI became notorious for corrupt and greedy officialdom, physically eliminating Indians or forcing them off their lands. By the late 1960s, SPI had become the target of fierce national and international criticism.

In 1967, SPI was replaced by FUNAI, which was intended to redress the SPI wrongs. FUNAI was set the ambitious and controversial tasks of protecting Indian reserves, administering the medical and educational needs of the Indians, and contacting and pacifying hitherto unknown tribes.

FUNAI has been criticised for adopting a patronising attitude toward Indians, and for manipulating against Indian interests in favour of other claims to Indian land.

It's difficult to see how this grossly underfunded and understaffed organisation can escape contradictions when it represents the interests of the Indians and simultaneously acts on behalf of the government and military, which have both been expropriating Indian lands for industry and settlement.

Religious organisations, such as Conselho Indígenista Missionário (CIM) and Centro Ecumênico de Documentação e Informação (CEDI) have attempted to right the imbalance, but there appears to be little interest in changing patronising attitudes or giving the Indians a chance to represent their rights as decreed by Brazilian law. The constitution recognises Indian rights to their traditional lands, which cover approximately 87 million hectares (about 10% of Brazil's territory).

FUNAI recently started using a computer network and satellite photographs to monitor the borders of large and remote tracts of land from invading lumber workers and prospectors. The monitoring system covers many of the reservations and posts plus five major parks: Xingu and Aripuanâ parks in Mato Grosso, Araguaia Park on Ilha do Bananal in Tocantins, Tumucumaque Park on the Guyanese border of Pará and the Yanomami Park in Roraima.

Recent Developments During the 1980s, Indian tribes, which had seen their people and lands destroyed by development projects (particularly highway construction) in the 1970s, were stung into independent action to protect themselves.

In 1980, nearly 1000 Xavante Indians, who had tired of FUNAI inactivity, started marking the boundaries of their reserve in Mato Grosso state. When a fierce conflict arose with encroaching ranchers, 31 Xavante leaders paid a surprise visit to the president of FUNAI in Brasília and demanded immediate boundary demarcation. Further pressure was exerted on FUNAI when Txucarramãe Indians killed 11 agricultural workers whom they had caught trespassing on their Xingu reserve and clearing the forest. In 1982, over 200 Indian leaders assembled in Brasília to debate land ownership at the First National Assembly of Indigenous Nations.

Subsequent years saw a spate of hostage takings and confiscations by Indians, who were thereby able to force rapid decisions from the government. As an attempt to deflect criticism and placate public opinion, the government hired and fired FUNAI officials in quick succession; a convenient scapegoat technique (where the name is changed but little else) that continues in the 1990s. In 1989, the First Meeting of the Indigenous Nations of Xingu included a huge cast of Brazilian Indians, foreign environmentalists, and even the rock star Sting. Two Kayapo chiefs, Raoni and Megaron, then accompanied Sting on a world tour to raise funds for the preservation of the Amazon rainforest.

During the 1990s, international attention has focused on the plight of the Yanomami (see the next section). Environmentalists and ecologists who attended Eco 92 pressed for practical changes to benefit the Indians and their environment – nobody wants to be fobbed off with speeches and papers that are simply public relations exercises to be filed and forgotten.

The Yanomami The Yanomami are one of the newly discovered Indian peoples of the Amazon. Until some Yanomami were given metal tools by visitors, all their implements were made of stone, ceramic, animal hides and plants. They are literally a Stone Age people rapidly confronting the 20th century. The plight of the Yanomami has aroused considerable foreign interest, since the problems experienced by the Yanomami are considered typical of those encountered by other Indians in Brazil.

In 1973 the Yanomami had their first contact with westerners; Brazilian air force pilots and religious missionaries. In 1974 and 1975 as Hwys BR-210 (Perimetral Norte) and BR-174 were cut through the Catramani and Ajarani tributaries of the Rio Negro, people from several Yanomami villages mixed with the construction workers and contracted and died from measles, influenza and venereal disease. Over a dozen villages were wiped out.

In 1988, the government instituted an absurd plan to create 19 separate pockets of land for the Yanomami, thereby depriving the Indians of 70% of their territory. Thousands of garimpeiros swarmed into the area and ignored all boundaries. Two years later, growing international and national criticism of the genocide being perpetrated on the Yanomami forced the authorities to declare only a handful of designated zones open for mining. The garimpeiros continued to prospect at random and resisted all efforts, even force, to dislodge them.

In 1991, the Venezuelan government officially recognised the Yanomami territory on the Venezuelan side of the Brazilian border as a special Indian reserve; a few months later President Collor defied opposition and followed suit on the Brazilian side. The Brazilian military continues to oppose the decision and prefers to encourage development and settlement of the border areas as a buffer against possible foreign intrusions.

The Yanomami are a slight people, with Oriental features. Their estimated 18,000 semi-nomadic tribespeople are scattered over 320 villages on either side of the Brazilian-Venezuelan border. They speak one of four related languages: Yanomam, Yanam, Yanomamo and Sanumá.

The centre of each community is the Yano, a large circular structure where each family has its own section facing directly onto an open central area used for communal dance and ceremony. The Yano is built with palm-leaf thatch and timber posts. Each family arranges its own section by slinging hammocks around a fire, which burns constantly and forms the centre of family life.

Inter-tribal visits are an opportunity to eat well – if the hunt has been successful everyone gets to eat monkey, which is a delicacy. Otherwise tapir, wild pig and a variety of insects make up the protein component of the meal, which is balanced with garden fruits, yams, plantains and manioc. The Yanomami also grow cotton and tobacco. Once their garden soils and hunting grounds are exhausted, the village moves on to a new site.

The Yanomami hold elaborate ceremonies and rituals and place great emphasis on inter-tribal alliances. The latter are intended to minimise any feuds or violence, which, as has often happened in the past, can escalate into full-scale wars. Inter-tribal hostility is thought to manifest in disease that comes from evil spirits sent by the shamans (medicine men) of enemy tribes. Disease is cured with various herbs, shaman dances and healing hands. Sometimes the village shaman will enlist the good spirits to fight the evil spirits by using *yakoana* (a hallucinogenic herbal powder).

The Yanomami have some curious practices. When a tribal person dies, the body is hung from a tree until dry, then burned to ashes. The ashes are mixed with bananas, which are then eaten by friends and family of the deceased to incorporate and preserve the spirit. The mourning ritual is elaborate and includes having one member of the tribe assigned to cry for a month (as determined by the phases of the moon, since the Yanomami have no calendar and the only number they have greater than two is 'many'). Friends or allies from other communities will travel three to four days to join the mourning tribe.

These days even such remote tribes are exposed to encroaching civilisation in the shape of clearance roads for the Perimetral Norte, illegal airstrips built by garimpeiros, and FUNAI posts. Despite the latest positive moves from the Brazilian government, the Yanomami lands are not adequately protected against encroachment and dispossession by brute force. More details about providing support for the Yanomami can be obtained from Survival International – for the address refer to the Ecology & Environment section in this chapter.

Further Information There are several governmental and religious organisations that publish information about Brazilian

Indians. *Poratim* is a newsletter published by the Conselho Indígenista Missionário (CIM) (☎ (061) 225-9457), Edifício Venâncio III, Sala 310, Caixa Postal 11.1159, CEP 70084, Brasília (DF). In the past, FUNAI's own publication, *Jornal da Funai*, was produced at the same address as CIM, but future publishing plans are unclear. *Aconteceu* is a biweekly journal (with a strong ecological emphasis) published by the Centro Ecumênico de Documentação e Informação (CEDI) (☎ (021) 224-6713), Rua Santo Amaro, 129, Rio de Janeiro, CEP 22211 (RJ).

There are also various individuals or small groups working on alternative projects for tribes such as the Ticuna and Wapichana. In Amazonas, there's Alírio Mendes Moraes (Ticuna), Coordenação das Organizações Indígenas da Amazônia Brasileira (COIAB) (☎ (092) 624-2511), Avenida Leopoldo Peres, 373, Caixa Postal 3264, Manaus, CEP 69000 (AM). In the same state, education is the emphasis of the Organização Geral dos Professores Ticuna Bilingüe (☎ (092) 415-5494), Avenida Castelo Branco, 594, Projeto Alto Solimões, Benjamin Constant, CEP 69630 (AM). In the state of Roraima, a group has been established by Clovis Ambrósio (Wapichana), Conselho Indígena de Roraima (CIR) (☎ (095) 224-5761), Avenida Sebastião Diniz, 1672 W, Bairro São Vicente, Boa Vista, CEP 69300 (RR).

If you contact any of these organisations, groups or individuals, remember that they operate on minimal budgets, so you should at least pay return postage and material costs in advance. It is also worth pointing out that truth and facts about the Indians are hard to pinpoint, and official information is often presented in a flexible manner to suit the political, financial, or cultural agenda of those involved.

Outside Brazil, one of the most active and reputable organisations providing information on Indian affairs is Survival International, which has campaigned especially hard on behalf of the Yanomami Indians and has members and offices worldwide (for address details see the Ecology & Environment section earlier in this chapter). Survival International members receive a regular newsletter, *Urgent Action Bulletins*, campaign documents, and an annual review.

For suggested reading, see the Books and Maps sections in the Facts for the Visitor chapter.

Visiting a Reservation If you're a physician, anthropologist or sociologist with an genuine scholarly interest, you can make an application to FUNAI for authorisation to visit a reservation.

If you are not a Brazilian citizen you must submit a research proposal together with your curriculum vitae. You also need to include a letter of introduction from your home research institute, a letter from the Brazilian researcher or research institute taking responsibility for you and your work and agreeing to accompany you into the field, as well as a declaration that you speak Portuguese and know Brazilian law, vaccination certificates for yellow fever, typhoid and tetanus and an x-ray to show that you are free from tuberculosis.

All of this documentation must be in Portuguese and be presented initially to the embassy or consulate of your home country in Brazil. The staff there will then send it to the Ministry of Foreign Relations in Brasília, which will in turn forward it to the National Centre for Research (CNPQ). It will take a minimum of 90 days for CNPQ to consider your proposal. If this body agrees to authorise your project, the file is finally passed to the FUNAI office in Rio at the Museu do Índio (Indian Museum) where Professor Neyland further processes it and Dra Claúdia scribbles the final signature.

The procedure is intentionally difficult. It is intended to protect the Indians from the inadvertent spread of diseases to which they have no natural immunity as well as from overexposure to alien cultural ideals. Nevertheless, many applicants make it through all the obstacles, and as many as 60 projects have been approved in one three-month period.

EDUCATION

Education in Brazil is based on class. Public schools are so bad that anyone with the means sends their children to private schools. Almost all university students are from private schools, so very few poor children reach university and the poverty cycle is renewed. Many poor children must work to eat and never attend school. Even for those who are able to go, there aren't enough schools, teachers or desks to go around. Since our last edition, funding for education has been cut by 15%, and austerity measures and the Asian monetary crisis is certain to make matters worse.

The government claims a literacy rate of 80% but according to EDUCAR, the government department for adult education, only 40% of Brazilians old enough to be in the workforce are capable of reading a newspaper with comprehension. The government's definition of 'literate' covers those who can write their names, know the alphabet and sound out a few words. In the workplace, it has become obvious that these people are functionally illiterate.

Only two out of every 10 students make it through elementary school. The remainder drop out to support themselves and their family.

The Brizola government of Rio de Janeiro was one of the first to understand and act upon the connections between poverty, hunger and illiteracy, and set up food programmes in schools. The kids come to school for the food and stay for the lessons. Some schools have classes at night for those children who work during the day.

Mass media has also been used with some success. Since 1972, TV and radio educational programmes have been on the air, concentrating on *primeiro grau* (primary) and *segunda grau* (secondary) students but not exclusively. One course consists of 235 radio and TV programmes, with the objective of qualifying primary teachers. In 1989 Universidade Aberta (Open University), a tertiary education programme, was introduced. You'll often see the workbooks on newsstands.

While these measures are not enough – many primary school students still have only three hours of classes per day – they show that some programmes are successful.

ARTS

Brazilians are among the most musical people on the planet. Wherever you go, you'll find people playing, singing and dancing. Perhaps because of its African roots, Brazilian music is a collective community act, a celebration, a festa.

Brazilian popular music has always been characterised by great diversity. Shaped by the mixing of a variety of musical influences from three different continents, the music of the people is still creating new and original forms.

Thus, *samba canção*, for example, is a mixture of Spanish bolero with the cadences and rhythms of African music. *Bossa nova* was influenced by North American music, particularly jazz, and samba. And the music called *tropicalismo* is a mix of musical influences that arrived in Brazil in the 1960s, including Italian ballads and bossa nova.

Music & Dance

Samba *Tudo dá samba*: everything makes for a samba. The most popular Brazilian rhythm, samba, was first performed at the Rio Carnaval in 1917, though its origins go back much further.

It is intimately linked with African rhythms; notably the Angolan tam-tam, which provided the basis for its music and distinctive dance steps. It caught on quickly after the advent of radio and records and has since become a national symbol. It is the music of the masses.

The 1930s are known as the Golden Age of Samba. By then, samba canção had also evolved, as had *choro*, a romantic, intimate music with a ukulele or guitar as its main instrument, playing off against a recorder or flute.

The most famous 'Brazilian' singer of this period, perhaps of all time, is Portuguese-born Carmen Miranda. A star of many Hollywood musicals of the period, she was known for her fiery, Latin temperament and her 'fruity' costumes. She has since become a cult figure among Rio's gay community, and many of them impersonate her during Carnaval in Rio.

Bossa Nova In the 1950s came bossa nova, and the democratic nature of Brazilian music was altered. Bossa nova was new, modern, intellectual and became internationally popular. The middle class stopped listening to the old interpretations of samba and other regional music like the *forró* of the Northeast.

Bossa nova initiated a new style of playing instruments and singing. The more operatic, florid style of singing was replaced by a quieter, more relaxed sound; remember the soft sound of *The Girl from Ipanema* composed by the late Antônio Carlos (Tom) Jobim and Vinicius Moraes? João Gilberto is the founding father of bossa nova, and leading figures, like Baden Powell and Nara Leão, are still playing in Rio. Another bossa nova voice, who became Brazil's most beloved singer, was Elis Regina.

Bossa nova was associated with the rising middle class of urban, university-educated Brazil. It was a musical response to other modernist movements of the 1950s and 60s such as the Cinema Novo, the Brazilian Modern Architecture of Oscar Niemeyer et al, and other aspects of the cultural life of the nation during the optimistic presidency of Juscelino Kubitschek (1956-60).

Tropicalismo At the end of the 1960s the movement known as tropicalismo burst onto the scene. Tropicalismo provoked a kind of general amnesty for all the forgotten musical traditions of the past. The leading figures – Gilberto Gil, Caetano Veloso, Rita Lee, Macalé, Maria Betânia and Gal Costa – believed that all musical styles were important and relevant. All the styles and traditions in Brazilian music could be freely mixed. This kind of open thinking led to innovations like the introduction of the electric guitar and the sound of electric samba.

Música Popular Brasileira Paralleling these musical movements are several incredibly popular musicians who are hard to categorise: they are simply known as exponents of MPB – Música Popular Brasileira (Popular Brazilian Music).

Chico Buarque de Holanda, who mixes traditional samba with a modern, universal flavour, is immensely popular, as is Paulinho da Viola, a master *sambista* who also bridges the gap between traditional samba and pop music. Jorge Bem comes from a particular black musical tradition of the Rio suburbs, but plays an original pop samba without losing the characteristic black rhythms. Another example is Luís Melodia, who combines the samba rhythms of the Rio hills with more modern forms from the 1970s and 80s, always with beautiful melody.

Milton Nascimento, also from Minas, was elected by readers of *DownBeat* magazine as the number one exponent of world music. He has long been famous in Brazil for his fine voice, stirring anthems and ballads that reflect the spirituality of the Mineiro (someone from Minas).

Brazilian Rock Derived more from English than American rock, this is the least Brazilian of all Brazilian music. It's all the rage with the young. Groups like Titãs, Kid Abelha, Legião Urbana and Plebe Urbana are worth a listen if you like rock music, as is Skank, an up and coming band. Heavy metal bands like Sepultura and Ratos do Porão have huge domestic followings. Sepultura is now famous among head bangers worldwide. Brazilian rap music is also popular with groups like MRN (Movimento e Ritmo Negro) and Racionais MC, with their hard-edged lyrics about life in the favelas.

Regional Music Samba, tropicalismo and bossa nova are all national musical forms, but wherever you go in Brazil you'll hear regional specialities.

The Northeast has perhaps the most regional musical styles and accompanying dances. The most important is the forró, a mix of Northeastern music with Mexican music – maybe introduced via Paraguay – with nuances of the music of the Brazilian frontier region. The forró incorporates the European accordion, the harmonica, and the *zabumba* (an African drum).

Another distinctive type of music is the wonderful Bumba Meu Boi festival sound from São Luís in Maranhão. *Frevo* is a music specific to Recife.

The *trio elétrico*, also called *frevo baiano*, is more of a change in technology than music. It began as a joke when, during Carnaval in Salvador, Dodô, Armandinho and Osmar got on top of a truck and played frevo with electric guitars. The trio elétrico is not necessarily a trio, but it is still the backbone of Salvador's Carnaval, when trucks piled high with speakers with musicians perched on top drive through the city surrounded by dancing mobs. But it wasn't popularised until Caetano Veloso, during the period of tropicalismo, began writing songs about the trio elétrico.

Afoxé is another important type of black music of Brazil. Religious in origin, it is closely tied to Candomblé (Afro-Brazilian religion), and primarily found in Bahia. Afoxé is the most African-sounding music in Brazil and it has been rejuvenated by the strong influence of reggae and the growth of a black-consciousness movement in Bahia.

The influence of Indian music was absorbed and diluted, as was so much of the various Indian cultures in Brazil. In musical terms, several whites have idealised what they thought those influences were. The *carimbó* (music of the Amazon region) where the majority of Indians live today – is influenced primarily by the blacks of the litoral. Maybe the forró is the Brazilian music most influenced by the Indians, via Nordestinos (people from the Northeast) who have occupied a good part of the Amazon region since the end of last century.

Music Trends *Mangue Beat*, from Recife, combines folkloric and regional musical styles with international influences as diverse as hip-hop and tejano. The biggest name to date on the scene, Chico Science, died in an automobile accident in 1997, but other artists, including Mestre Ambrósio and Mundo Livre S/A are exporting well, and mangue beat should catch fire internationally.

Pagode, a type of samba that has existed for some time, has become widely popular. For some of the best pagode, listen to Bezerra da Silva, who was popular in the favelas before ever recording. Pagode, samba, frevo and forró all have corresponding dances – perhaps a reflection of the African influence and the Brazilian use of music as a celebration of communication.

Lambada has become another international success story. Influenced by various Caribbean rhythms like rumba, merengue and salsa, lambada became really popular in Brazil and eventually in Europe and the USA. It even inspired a couple of terrible Hollywood movies.

The most successful lambada artist is Beto Barbosa and her group Kaoma, made up of Brazilian, Argentine and French musicians. Other Brazilian musicians who have recorded lambada tracks include Lulu

Santos, Pepeu Gomes and Moraes Moreira, and even Caetano Veloso.

Also hugely popular is *sertanejo*, a kind of Brazilian country and western music. It has long been a favourite with truck drivers and cowboys, but has only recently entered the mainstream of popular music. Sertanejo is characterised by soaring harmonies and its lyrics about broken hearts, life on the road etc. Some of the popular exponents are: José Rico and Millionario, Chitãozinho and Xororó, and Leandro e Leonardo.

Axé (a samba-inspired, pop/rock/reggae/funk fusion from Salvador) has also become well known thanks to the music of the flamboyant Daniela Mercury.

If you want to have a listen to some Brazilian music before you arrive, the 'Brazil Classics' series, compiled by David Byrne and distributed by Warner Brothers, is a good starting point. These records are readily available, and cover samba and forró, and feature some individuals like Bahian Tom Zé. Bossa nova records are relatively plentiful, especially the Grammy Award-winning collaborations between Brazilian and American artists, like João Gilberto and Stan Getz. *The Rhythm of the Saints*, an album by Paul Simon, was heavily influenced by Brazilian music. It included backing by Milton Nascimento and the popular Grupo Cultural Olodum from Bahia.

Buying Records & Tapes The widest selection of records can be found in the large cities, like São Paulo and Rio. Regional music enthusiasts should check out the selection available at the Museu Folclorico Edson Carneiro in Rio.

Records and tapes (called K7 – 'ka-sette') cost around US$8. Compact discs are also widely available in Brazilian cities, but there are doubts as to their quality compared to 'imported' CDs. They cost around US$15 to $20.

Painting & Sculpture

The first colonial painters were the Jesuit and Benedictine missionaries, who painted their churches and sacred objects in a European baroque style. The Dutch invasion in the north brought with it some important Flemish artists, such as Frans Post, who painted the flora and fauna in their tropical surroundings.

Brazilian baroque art peaked in the 18th century, when the wealth provided by the gold rush allowed talented artists to reach their full potential and create many beautiful works. The acknowledged genius of this period is the sculptor and architect Antônio Francisco Lisboa, better known as Aleijadinho (see the Minas Gerais chapter for details of his life and works).

In the 19th and 20th centuries, Brazilian artists have followed the international trends of neoclassicism, romanticism, impressionism, academicism and modernism.

The best internationally known Brazilian painter is Candido Portinari. Early in his career he made the decision to paint only Brazil and its people. Strongly influenced by the Mexican muralists like Diego Rivera, he managed to fuse native, expressionist influences into a powerful, socially conscious and sophisticated style.

Indian Art In its original form, Indian art was created for religious or utilitarian purposes and was considered part of the Indian way of life.

After first contact with Europeans had been made, Indians were soon visited by traders who perceived their art as valuable items to be acquired by bartering and then sold as curiosities or collectables in Brazil and abroad. Today many Indians produce art items for sale as tourist curios – the income pays their keep on the margin of a society that has destroyed their environment, their way of life, and left no other purpose for their art.

The Indians are renowned for a wide range of artistic handicrafts. The plumage of forest birds is used to create necklaces, bracelets, earrings, headdresses, capes and blankets. Some tribes pluck the original feathers from a bird such as a macaw, and smear the plucked area of the bird's skin with a vegetable dye which changes the colour of the new plumage. Members of some tribes use dyes and tattoos to decorate their bodies.

Ceramic arts were a speciality of the Marajó Indians who flourished long before the arrival of the Portuguese, and today the Carajás tribe in the state of Tocantins is famed for its skilfully painted figurines. Grasses, leaves and bark from the forests are used in highly developed Indian handicrafts such as weaving and basketry. The Kaxinawá tribe in the state of Acre is especially skilled at producing woven bags and baskets to transport or store forest foods. For more details about the Indians of Brazil, refer to the Population & People section in this chapter.

Architecture

There are many examples of outstanding architecture that have been proclaimed by UNESCO as part of the world's cultural heritage.

Representing the colonial period are Olinda, in Pernambuco, and the historic centre of Salvador, which is considered to be the finest example of Portuguese colonial architecture in the world.

The town of Ouro Prêto and Aleijadinho's masterpiece, the church of Bom Jesus de Matzinhos in Congonhas, (in the state of Minas Gerais), represent the golden age of Brazilian baroque architecture.

The remains of the 17th century Jesuit missions in Rio Grande do Sul, on the border between Brazil, Argentina and Paraguay, are notable for the fine woodcarving and masonry of the Guaraní Indians, who achieved their own distinct style.

The central urban plan of the capital, Brasília, also earns a UNESCO rating as a striking example of modern architecture.

Literature

There are a few dozen excellent Brazilian works of fiction translated into English but, sadly, many of today's best writers have not been translated.

In the mid to late 1990s, Brazilians have been buying books in record numbers. Best-selling author Paulo Coelho, whose 11 titles have sold over 7 million books in Brazil alone, is looking at record advances for his new novel *O Monte Cinco*.

Machado de Assis is simply world class. The son of a freed slave, Assis worked as a typesetter and journalist in late 19th century Rio. A tremendous stylist with a great sense of humour, Assis had an understanding of human relations that was subtle and deeply cynical, as the terse titles of books like *Epitaph of a Small Winner* (Avon Bard, 1977) and *Philosopher or Dog* (Avon Bard, 1982) might suggest. He wrote five major novels; a favourite is *Dom Casmurro* (Avon Bard, 1980).

The most famous writer in Brazil is Jorge Amado. Born near Ilhéus, Bahia, in 1912, and a long-time resident of Salvador, Amado has written colourful romances of Bahia's people and places. Strongly influenced by Communism during his early work, Amado's later books are better, although the subjects are lighter. His books are widely translated and easy to obtain. The best are *Gabriela, Clove and Cinnamon* (Avon Bard, 1974), which is set in Ilhéus, and *Dona Flor and her Two Husbands* (Avon Bard, 1977), whose antics occur in Salvador. Amado's *Tent of Miracles* (Avon Bard, 1978) explores racial relations in Brazil and *Pen, Sword and Camisole* (Avon Bard, 1986) laughs its way through the petty worlds of military and academic politics. *The Violent Land* (Avon Bard, 1979) is another of Amado's classics. The three short stories about a group of Bahian characters that make up *Shepherds of the Night* (Avon Bard, 1980) inspired the first visit to Brazil of one of LP's authors.

Without a word to waste, Graciliano Ramos tells of peasant life in the sertão in his best book, *Barren Lives* (University of Texas Press, 1965). The stories are powerful portraits – strong stuff. Autran Dourado's *The Voices of the Dead* (Taplinger, 1981) goes into the inner world of a small town in Minas Gerais. He has penned another couple of books about Minas Gerais, his home state. Read anything you can find by Mário de Andrade, one of Brazil's pre-eminent authors. His comic *Macunaíma* could only take place in Brazil.

Clarice Lispector has several collections of short stories, all of which are excellent. Lídia Fagundes Telles' books contain psychologically rich portraits of women in today's Brazil. Dinah Silveira de Queiroz's *The Women of Brazil* is about a Portuguese girl who goes to 17th century Brazil to meet her betrothed.

Márcio Souza is a modern satirist based in Manaus. His biting humour captures the horror of the Amazon and his imaginative parodies of Brazilian history reveal the stupidity of personal and official endeavours to conquer the rainforest. Both the *Emperor of the Amazon* (Avon Bard, 1980), and *Mad Maria* (English edition by Avalon) shouldn't be missed if you're going to the Amazon, but his latest farce, *The Order of the Day* (Avon Bard, 1986), is disappointing. *The Impostors* (Avon Bard, 1987), by Pablo Vierci, is a humorous novel about Amazon mayhem.

The bizarre and brutal *Zero* (Avon Bard, 1983), by Ignácio de Loyola Brandão, had the honour of being banned by the military government until a national protest helped lift the ban. *The Tower of Glass* (Avon Bard, 1982), by Ivan Ângelo, is all São Paulo: an absurdist look at big-city life where nothing that matters, matters. It's a revealing and important view of modern Brazil, 'where all that's solid melts into air'. João Ubaldo Ribeiro's *Sergeant Getúlio* (Avon Bard, 1980) is a story of a military man in Brazil's Northeast. No book tells better of the sadism, brutality and patriarchy that run through Brazil's history.

SOCIETY & CONDUCT

Traditional Culture

Brazilian culture has been shaped not only by the Portuguese, who gave the country its language and religion, but also by native Indians, black Africans, and other settlers from Europe, the Middle East and Asia.

Although often ignored, denigrated or feared by urban Brazilians, Indian culture has helped shape modern Brazil and its legends, dance and music. Many native foods and beverages, such as tapioca, manioc, potatoes, maté and *guaraná*, have become staples. The Indians also gave the colonisers numerous objects and skills that are now in daily use, such as hammocks, dugout canoes, thatched roofing, and weaving techniques. For more details about the Indians refer to the sections on Indian Art and Population & People earlier in this chapter.

The influence of African culture is also very powerful, especially in the Northeast. The slaves imported by the Portuguese brought their religion, music and cuisine with them, all of which have profoundly influenced Brazilian identity.

All these elements have combined to produce a nation of people well known for their spontaneity, friendliness and lust for life. As you would expect from such a diverse population mix, there are many regional differences and accents.

One of the funniest aspects of this regional diversity is the rivalry between the citizens of Rio and São Paulo. Talk to Paulistas (inhabitants of São Paulo state) and they will tell you that Cariocas (inhabitants of Rio) are hedonistic, frivolous and irresponsible. Cariocas think of Paulistas as materialistic, neurotic workaholics. Both Paulista and Carioca agree that the Nordestinos (Northeasterns), do things more slowly and simply, and are the worst drivers! Mineiros, from the state of Minas Gerais, are considered the thriftiest and most religious of Brazilians – Cariocas claim they're saving up for their tombs!

In Brazil, time is warped. The cities and their 20th century urban inhabitants exist only a short distance from fishermen, cowboys and forest dwellers whose lifestyles have varied little in 300 years. In the forests, the ancient traditions of the native Brazilians remain untouched by TV soap operas – for the time being.

Brazilians have an excellent sense of humour and adore telling 'Portuguese' jokes, just as Americans tell Polish jokes and Australians and Brits tell Irish jokes.

If you manage to get a grasp of the language, listen to Brazilians when a group of them get together on the beach or in a corner bar. If you can get past the fact that they all talk at once, you'll discover that the conversation almost always turns to football, criticism of the government, family matters or the latest twist in a current soap opera.

The Portuguese language, love of football, Carnaval and the sound of samba unify Brazilians. Listen and watch their expressive way of communicating; go to a football game and watch the intensity and variety of emotions, both on the field and in the stands; experience the bacchanalia of Carnaval and attempt to dance the samba and you may begin to understand what it is to be Brazilian.

Kiss Kiss

The standard Brazilian greeting is to kiss members of the opposite sex on each cheek. To get it right, always start by going to *their* right cheek – you lunge to your left. Kiss once, then switch cheeks. If you're close, or wishing luck or marriage on the person you're kissing, throw in a third kiss back on the first cheek (kiss, kiss, kiss).

RELIGION

Officially, Brazil is a Catholic country and claims the largest Catholic population of any country in the world. However, Brazil is also noted for the diversity and syncretism of its many sects and religions, which offer great flexibility to their followers. For example, without much difficulty you can find people from Catholic backgrounds who frequent the church and have no conflict appealing for help at a *terreiro de umbanda* (the house of one of the Afro-Brazilian cults).

Historically, the principal religious influences have been Indian animism, Catholicism and African cults brought by the blacks during the period of slavery. The slaves were prohibited from practising their religions by the colonists in the same way that they were kept from other elements of their culture, such as music and dance, for fear that it would reinforce their group identity. Religious persecution led to religious syncretism. To avoid persecution the slaves gave Catholic names and figures to all their African gods. This was generally done by finding the similarities between the Catholic images and the *orixás* (gods) of Candomblé (see later in this section). Thus, the slaves worshipped their own gods behind the representations of the Catholic saints.

Under the influence of liberalism in the 19th century, Brazilians wrote into their constitution the freedom to worship all religions. But the African cults continued to suffer persecution for many years. Candomblé was seen by the white elites as charlatanism that showed the ignorance of the poorest classes. The spectrum of religious life was gradually broadened by the addition of Indian animism to Afro-Catholic syncretism, and by the increasing fascination of whites with the spiritualism of Kardecism (also described later in this section).

Today Catholicism retains its status as the official religion, but it is declining in popularity. Churches are closing or falling into disrepair due to lack of funds and priests, and attendances at church services are dwindling such an extent that people now merely turn up for the basics: baptism, marriage, and burial. The largest numbers of converts are being attracted to the Afro-Brazilian cults, and spiritist or mystic sects. Nowadays, the intense religious fervour extends across gradations and subdivisions of numerous sects; from purist cults to groups that worship Catholic saints, African deities and the Caboclos of the Indian cults simultaneously.

Note that in this book, we use the abbreviation NS for 'Nossa Senhora' (Our Lady) or 'Nosso Senhor' (Our Lord): eg NS do Pilar.

Afro-Brazilian Cults
These cults do not follow the ideas of major European or Asian religions; neither do they use doctrines to define good and evil. One of the things most shocking to Europeans in their first contact with the African images and rituals was the cult of Exú. This entity was generally represented by combined human and animal images, with a horn and an erect penis. Seeking parallels between their own beliefs and African religions, European Catholics and Puritans identified Exú as the devil. For Africans, however, Exú represents the transition between the material and the spiritual worlds.

In the ritual of Candomblé, Exú acts as a messenger between the gods and human beings. For example, everything related to money, love, and protection against thieves comes under the watchful eye of Exú. Ultimately, Exú's responsibility is the temporal world.

Candomblé This is the most orthodox of the cults brought from Africa by the Nago, Yoruba, and Jeje peoples. Candomblé, an African word denoting a dance in honour of the gods, is a general term for the cult in Bahia. Elsewhere in Brazil the cult is known by different names: in Rio it's Macumba; in Amazonas and Pará it's Babassuê; in Pernambuco and Alagoas it's Xangô; in Rio Grande do Sul it's either Pará or Batuque; and the term Tambor is used in Maranhão. For suggested reading on Candomblé, see the Books section in the Facts for the Visitor chapter.

The Afro-Brazilian rituals are practised in a *casa-de-santo* or *terreiro* directed by a *pai* or *mãe de santo* (literally father or mother of the saint – the Candomblé priest or priestess). This is where the initiation of novices takes place as well as consultations and rituals. The ceremonies are conducted in the Yoruba language. The religious hierarchy and structure is clearly established and consistent from one terreiro to the next. Not all ceremonies are open to the public.

If you attend a Candomblé ceremony, it's best to go as the invited guest of a knowledgeable friend or commercial guide. If your request to visit is declined, you should accept the decision. Some ceremonies are only open to certain members of a terreiro, and there is genuine concern that visitors may not know the customs involved and thereby interrupt the rituals.

Although the rules for Candomblé ceremonies are not rigidly fixed, there are some general points that apply to most of these ceremonies. If in doubt, ask the person who has taken you to the ceremony. Dress for men and women can be casual, but shorts should not be worn. White is the preferred colour; black, purple, and brown should be avoided. Hats should not be worn inside the terreiro; and if you wish to smoke, you should only do so outside.

On arrival at the terreiro, make sure you do not stand blocking the doorway. There's usually someone inside who is responsible for directing people to their seats – men are often seated on the right, women on the left. The seating pattern is important, so make sure you only sit where indicated. Watch respectfully and follow the advice of your friend or guide as to what form of participation is expected of you. Sometimes drinks and food are distributed. Depending on the ritual involved, these may be intended only as offerings, or else for your consumption. In the case of the latter, there's no offence taken if you don't eat or drink what's offered. For a description see the boxed text of 'An Evening of Candomblé' in the Bahia chapter.

According to Candomblé, each person has an orixá (god) that attends from birth and provides protection throughout life. The orixá for each person is identified after a pai or mãe de santo makes successive throws with a handful of *búzios* (shells). In a divination ritual known as *Jogo dos Búzios* (Casting of Shells) the position of the shells is used to interpret your luck, your future and your past relation with the gods.

The Jogo dos Búzios can be traced back to numerology and cabalism. It is a simple version of the Ifa ceremony in which the orixá Ifa is invoked to transmit the words of the deities to the people. The mãe de santo casts 16 seashells on a white towel. She interprets the number and arrangement of face-up and face-down shells to predict the future.

The Jogo dos Búzios is a serious, respected force in Bahia. In 1985 it was used by many politicians to forecast the election results. In Salvador, visitors can consult a mãe de santo for Candomblé-style fortune telling any day of the week, except for Friday and Monday, but Thursday is best.

Like the gods in Classical mythology, each orixá has a personality and particular history. Power struggles and rulership conflicts among the many orixá are part of the history of Candomblé.

Although orixá are divided into male and female types, there are some that can switch from one sex to the other. One example is Logunedé, son of two male gods, Ogun and Oxoss. Another example is Oxumaré, who is male for six months of the year and female for the other months. Oxumaré is represented by the river that runs from the mainland to the sea or by the rainbow. These bisexual gods are generally, but not necessarily, the gods of homosexuals. Candomblé is very accepting of homosexuality and this may explain the foundation of these practices and why they are legitimised by the cult's mythology.

To keep themselves strong and healthy, followers of Candomblé always give food to their respective orixá. In the ritual, Exú is the first to be given food because he is the messenger who contacts the orixá. Exú likes *cachaça* and other alcoholic drinks, cigarettes, cigars, strong perfumes and meat. The offering to the orixá depends on their particular preferences. For example, to please Iemanjá, the goddess of the sea, one should give perfume, white and blue flowers, rice and fried fish. Oxalá, the greatest god, the owner of the sun, eats cooked white corn. Oxúm, god of fresh waters and waterfalls, is famous for his vanity. He should be honoured with earrings, necklaces, mirrors, perfumes, champagne and honey.

Each orixá is worshipped at a particular time and place. For example, Oxósse, who is the god of the forests, should be revered in a forest or park, but Xangô, the god of stone and justice, receives his offering in rocky places.

In Bahia and Rio, followers of Afro-Brazilian cults turn out in huge numbers to attend a series of festivals at the year's end – especially those held during the night of 31 December and on New Year's Day. Millions of Brazilians go to the beach to pay homage to Iemanjá. Flowers, perfumes, fruits and even jewellery are tossed into the sea to please the mother of the waters, or to gain protection and good luck in the new year.

Umbanda Umbanda, or white magic, is a mixture of Candomblé and spiritism. It traces its origins from various sources, but in its present form it is a religion native to Brazil. The African influence is more Angolan/Bantu. The ceremony, conducted in Portuguese, incorporates figures from all of the Brazilian races: *preto velho* (the old black slave) *o caboclo* and other Amerindian deities, *o guerreiro* (the white warrior etc). In comparison to Candomblé, Umbanda is less organised and each pai or mãe de santo modifies the religion.

Quimbanda is the evil counterpart to Umbanda. Its rituals involves lots of blood, animal sacrifice and nasty deeds. The practice of Quimbanda is technically illegal.

Kardecism

During the 19th century, Allan Kardec, the French spiritual master, introduced spiritism to Brazilian whites in a palatable form.

Kardec's teachings, which incorporated some eastern religious ideas into a European framework, are now followed by large numbers of Brazilians. Kardecism emphasises spiritism associated with parlour seances, multiple reincarnations and speaking to the dead. Kardec wrote about his teachings in *The Book of Spirits* and *The Book of Mediums*.

Other Cults

Brasília has become the capital of the new cults. In the Planaltina neighbourhood, visit Tia Neiva and the Vale do Amanhecer, and Eclética de Mestro Yocanan (see the Brasília chapter).

A few of the Indian rites have been popularised among Brazilians without becoming part of Afro-Brazilian cults. Two such cults are União da Vegetal in Brasília, São Paulo and the South; and Santo Daime in Rondônia and Acre. A hallucinogenic drink called *ayahuasca*, made from the root and vine of two plants, *cipó jagube* and *folha chacrona*, has been used for centuries by the indigenous peoples of South America. This drink is central to the practices of these cults, which are otherwise very straight – hierarchy, moral behaviour and dress follow a strict code. The government tolerates the use of ayahuasca in the religious ceremonies of these cults, and tightly controls the production and supply.

The cult of Santo Daime was founded in 1930 in Rio Branco, Acre, by Raimundo Irineu Serra. Today it claims around 10,000 members, including notable Brazilian figures such as the flamboyant singer Ney Matogrosso, the cartoonist Glauco, and the anthropologist Edward Macrae. The cult, led by Luís Felipe Belmonte, has 10 churches and communities in Brazil. The two major communities are Ceú da Mapiá in Amazonas, and Colônia Cinco Mil in Rio Branco, Acre.

Facts for the Visitor

HIGHLIGHTS

Brazil offers much more than Carnaval and Amazon River trips. The following are some suggestions for you to explore and enjoy the country.

Historical Cities & Architecture

A former gold rush boom town, Goiás is filled with 18th century colonial architecture and impressive churches and museums.

The Teatro Amazonas (Manaus), the famous opera house in the middle of the jungle, is a reminder of the opulent lifestyles led by the rubber barons.

The historic colonial gold city of Pirenópolis (Goiás) was placed on the National Heritage register in 1989.Ouro Prêto is the jewel in the crown of a string of spectacular baroque historical cities in Minas Gerais, including Tiradentes, Diamantina and São João del Rei.

Other historic cities include Salvador and Pelourinho, Olinda, and Lençóis.

Museums

Visit the fascinating Museu Emílio Goeldi (Belém) for a study of the peoples and development of Amazonia; check out natural history at Alcântra's Museu Histórico; anthropology and herbal/indigenous medicine at the Museu do Homem do Nordeste, Recife.

For Japanese immigrant history and culture visit the Museum of Japanese Immigration, São Paulo; and, in Rio de Janeiro, there are folk arts and crafts at the Museu Folclorico Edson Carneiro and Museu da República, with arts from the republican period in the Palácio do Catete.

Beaches

The country's most impressive beaches include Prainha (Natal, Rio Grande do Norte); Praia do Santinho (Florianópolis, Santa Catarina), an uncrowded open surf beach backed by sand dunes; and Praia Ponta do Bicho (Ilha do Mel, Paraná), a beautiful sweeping bay with calm water.

Other great beaches include Prejuiças (Lençóis Maranhenses, Maranhão), Pepino and Barra (Rio de Janeiro), and Parati (Rio state). The North also has some beautiful river beaches such as Alter do Chão (Pará), and Algodoal and Salinópolis, at the mouth of the Rio Amazonas.

Festivals

For three days at Cavalhadas (Pirenópolis), the town returns to the Middle Ages, with a series of medieval tournaments and dances.

Other excellent festivals include Carnaval (Olinda); Semana Santa (Goiás Velho), when the main street of the town is lit by hundreds of torches in a procession that reenacts the removal of Christ from the cross and his burial; Círio de Nazaré (Belém); Cavalhadas (Pirenópolis); and New Year's Eve on Copacabana beach (Rio de Janeiro).

Restaurants

The authors' favourites include:

Japanese	Miako (Belém)
African	Casa do Benin (Salvador)
Baiana & Chinese	Pousalegre (Lençóis)
Northeastern	Raizes (Natal)
Sandwiches	Cervantes (Rio de Janeiro)
Gaúcho Cuisine	Tio Flor (Porto Alegre)
Dessert	Colombo (Rio de Janeiro); Café Colonial (Pedra Azul State Park, Espírito Santo) a close runner up.

Accommodation

There are a variety of jungle lodges around Manaus, from floating lodges to towers with suspended walkways through the trees.

Nhundiaquara (Morretes), a colonial building on the banks of the Rio Nhundiaquara, has an open-air dining room. At the Hospedaria do Colégio Caraça (Santa Bárbara, Minas Gerais), you can sleep in a former monastery, eat spectacular natural food and watch the nightly feeding of wolves. The Pousada do Ipê (Goiás Velho) has comfortable *apartamentos* with mountain views set around a shady courtyard; excellent natural food.

The Hotel Solar da Ponte (Tiradentes, Minas Gerais) is a lovingly recreated colonial mansion. In Espírito Santo, the Aroso Baço Hotel, with stunning views of Pedra Azul is a definite winner.

Music & Dance

Carimbo, *boi* and *brega* are regional music styles of the North. There are huge musical parties every Tuesday and Sunday night in Pelourinho (Salvador); head for the *forró* (hot, popular dances) at the Estudantina club (Rio de Janeiro). And don't miss Samba do Enredo at the Rio Carnaval.

Wildlife Viewing

Pantanal Matogrossense: a vast wetlands area, the Pantanal boasts the greatest concentration of fauna in the New World, visible to the most casual observer. The Pantanal supports around 270 bird species including toucans, macaws and parakeets, ibises and storks. There are also river otters and capybara, anaconda, jaguar, ocelot, monkeys, anteaters and swamp deer.

National Parks & Natural Attractions

Parque Nacional da Aparados da Serra contains the famous Canyon do Itaimbézinho, a fantastic narrow canyon with waterfalls and sheer 600 to 720m parallel escarpments. The park is one of the country's last araucária forests.

Foz do Iguaçu, one of the natural wonders of the world, superior in size and grandeur to both Niagara and Victoria; and Parque Nacional da Chapada dos Guimarães, a beautiful region reminiscent of the American Southwest.

The Estação Ecológica de Anavilhanas is a huge arquipélago on the Rio Negro, 100km upriver from Manaus.

The phenomenon of the *pororoca,* the thunderous collision of the Atlantic tide and the Rio Amazonas (Ilha de Marajó and Amapá) occurs at full or new moon.

Religious Experiences

The most intense religious experiences in the country are Candomblé in Bahia, Colônia Cinco Mil in Rio Branco, and, in Brasília, Vale de Amanhecer, a religious community of 2000 mediums who believe that a new civilisation will come with the third millennium – an interesting place to head for on New Years' Eve 1999! At the annual Catholic festival of Círio de Nazaré (Belém) there is an outpouring of devotion for the tiny image of the Virgin.

Sport

In a sports mad country, the best experiences would include Capoeira in Bahia, and football and *futvolei* (foot volleyball) in Rio.

Offbeat Attractions & Activities

Canoeing in flooded forest and *igarapés* (jungle trips around Manaus) is a wonderful experience. Check out dune-buggy rides in Natal and the Ribeirão do Meio water slides (Lençóis). Get your kit off at the nudist beach at Tambaba (João Pessoa), and take a catamaran excursion from São Luís to Alcântara.

In Minas Gerais, hit the hippy-dippy mountainside town of São Tome Das Letras to check out the UFOs; take the half-hour steam train ride between São João del Rei and Tiradentes; and ease your aching tootsies in a hot spa in Caxambu's Parque das Aguas.

And don't miss double hang-gliding in Rio, tubing down the Rio Nhundiaquara (Morretes), the four hour scenic train ride from Curitiba to Paranaguá (Paraná); and get a close-up view of pirahna dental work by pirahna fishing (Mato Grosso do Sul).

SUGGESTED ITINERARIES

The following presents a general idea of some sample itineraries:

One Week

Why only a week? Brazil deserves much more! Pick a city and stay put. Either **Rio de**

Janeiro, the *cidade maravilhosa* or vibrant, exciting **Salvador**. Going anywhere else, unless you've got friends, business or an adventure destination in mind, is a waste of time. In both cities there's lots of music, and both offer short, interesting side trips.

In Rio state, there are four national parks within a few hours of the city for great hiking in the lush Atlantic rainforest; fantastic diving and beaches along the south coast toward the colonial gem, Parati; and Búzios, the beach resort for Rio's beautiful people, is a couple of hours to the north.

Close to Salvador there are some great beaches, and the island of Itaparica, the largest in the Baía de Todos os Santos. The Recôncavo region, with its colonial towns, is also close by.

Two to Three Weeks

An extra couple of weeks means you can move a little more and really start to enjoy Brazil. A Brazil Airpass allows you up to five flights in 21 days, and you can add on extra flights for US$100.

If you don't mind moving around a bit, travel light and have some fun. In 14 to 21 days, your route could include:

Brasília Brasília is such a bizarre place and it is, after all, the capital. It's good for two days maximum, and rent a car – the city was built for driving not walking.

Cuiabá Capital of the western state of Mato Grosso, Cuiabá is the place to fly into for a three or four day Pantanal trip. Make sure you also visit **Chapada dos Guimarães**.

Florianópolis Florianópolis is the capital of the southern state of Santa Catarina, located on the island of Santa Catarina. Rent a car for a couple of days and explore a lovely island with some great beaches.

Fortaleza Fortaleza is a good base for seeing the northern beaches. Buy a hammock and go to the beach, or take a bus and spend a couple of days in the amazing **Jericoacoara dunes**.

Manaus Manaus is the capital of the northern state of Amazonas. Three or four days here could easily include a jungle trip. The city itself has some historical attractions like the opera house and market.

Minas Gerais Belo Horizonte has some great nightlife, and it's a good base from which to explore the colonial towns with their rich baroque churches. **Ouro Prêto** and **Tiradentes** are the most beautiful, but there are others close by, like **Mariana** and **Diamantina**.

Foz do Iguaçu A sight not to be missed in **Paraná**. These falls should be included on any itinerary for a minimum of two days.

Recife There are good beaches here and the colonial town of **Olinda** is next door. You could easily spend two days here.

Rio de Janeiro Rio is a good starting and finishing point for any trip. You could easily spend 14 to 21 days in Rio state and never be bored. Instead of buying an airpass, you could rent a car and tour the state. There's lots of variety, from beaches to mountains.

Salvador Try to spend at least a week here, in what's truly the black Rome. There is so much African heritage here, yet it's so Brazilian too. A must for music lovers.

There are many other cities or towns that you could visit. For instance, **Tabatinga** is a small town on the border with Peru and Colombia. It was an interesting experience, as well as a good way to head back into Peru.

Ninety Days or More

Now you're talkin'. Ninety days is the maximum visa length before you need to leave the country or get an extension (if you need a visa that is). You'll be able to move much slower and get a good feel for the variety that Brazil offers.

Many travellers with this much time will be including Brazil in their itinerary for a tour around South America. We advise you to spend the last part of your tour in Brazil, because once you get here, you won't want to leave!

The classic travel route around Brazil is entering through Paraguay or Bolivia at **Corumbá**, spending some time exploring the **Pantanal**, then moving east through **Foz do Iguaçu**, **São Paulo** and **Rio**, checking out Rio city and state and then moving north into **Bahia**, lying on the beach at one of the hip resorts like **Arraial d'Ajuda**, **Trancoso** or **Morro de São Paulo**. The city of **Salvador** is on this route and it's definitely worth some time.

Most travellers then move through the Northeast region, with its multitude of beaches, before arriving in **Belém** and moving up the **Rio Amazonas** and on to Peru or Colombia.

It's surprising how many travellers choose to end their trip with a 21 day airpass. It's a good way to take in some of the out-of-the-way places you may have missed.

If you have six months for travelling, spend a month in Rio (from the start of February until Carnaval would be ideal). Spend December or January at a hip beach in the Northeast – you'll meet lots of Brazilians on holiday (then you can go and visit them later!).

Spend two weeks in the city of Salvador, three weeks in the Pantanal, another two in the Amazon, three days at Foz do Iguaçu and at least two weeks in Minas Gerais. Travel through the Northeast for a month or so.

Of course, you may want to stop and stay put for a while. That's the best thing about travelling for long periods. You'll have a great time.

PLANNING

When to Go

See the Climate section in the Facts about the Country chapter for details of seasonal factors that may influence your decision on when to visit the country. There are few regions that can't be comfortably visited all year round.

What Kind of Trip

Brazil's diversity means that you can choose exactly the type of trip you'd like; from mountain climbing and caving to hot-air ballooning to an off the beaten track adventure, from Amazon river trips to just lolling about on one of the country's luscious beaches for a month – Brazil just can't disappoint.

Because distances are so great, you'll need to spend some time with this book planning exactly what sort of trip you'd like – every bit of predeparture planning helps you enjoy your time on the ground. See the Suggested Itineraries and Activities sections in this chapter for what Brazil holds in store.

Maps

Given the size of Brazil, it's essential to be armed with decent maps that give a clear idea of scale. It's easy to underestimate distances and the time required for travel, particularly if you plan to visit several regions using roads rather than airports.

In the USA, Maplink (☎ (805) 965-4402), 25 E Mason St, Dept G, Santa Barbara, CA 93101, is an excellent and exhaustive source for maps of Brazil and just about anywhere else in the world. A similarly extensive selection of mapping is available in the UK from Stanfords (☎ (0171) 836-1321), 12-14 Long Acre, London WC2E 9LP.

For general mapping of South America with excellent topographical detail, it's hard to beat the sectional maps published by International Travel Map Productions (Canada). Coverage of Brazil is provided in *South America – South* (1987), *South America – North East* (1989), *South America – North West* (1987) and *Amazon Basin* (1991).

A recommended general reference map is Bartholomew's *Brazil & Bolivia World Travel Map* (1993).

Within Brazil, the maps used by most Brazilian and foreign travellers is published by Quatro Rodas, which also puts out the essential *Quatro Rodas: Guia Brasil*, an annually updated travel guide in Portuguese.

A companion volume is *Guia Rodoviário*, a compact book of maps in ahandy plastic case, which covers individual states and provides useful distance charts.

The city maps provided in *Quatro Rodas: Guia Brasil* help with orientation. It's a question of pot luck if you hunt for maps from tourist offices. If you're after detailed street layout, take a look at the phone books. The telephone companies in many states include excellent city maps either in the *Lista Telefônica* (White Pages) or in the *Páginas Amarelas* (Yellow Pages); and the same companies are also starting to distribute 'shopping maps', which are equally useful.

What to Bring

The happiest travellers are those who can slip all their luggage under their plane seats. Pack light. Backpacks with detachable day-packs make a versatile combination. Travel packs are backpacks that can be converted into more civilised-looking suitcases. They are cleverly compartmentalised, and have internal frames and special padding.

Use small padlocks to secure your pack, particularly if you have to leave it unattended in one of the more down-market hotels. For more details about security, refer to the section on Dangers & Annoyances in this chapter.

What you bring will be determined by what you do. If you're planning a river or jungle trip read the Amazon chapter in advance. If you're travelling cheap, a cotton sheet sleeping-sack will come in handy.

With its warm climate and informal dress standards, you don't need to bring many clothes to Brazil. Except for the South and Minas Gerais, where it gets cold in the winter, the only weather you need to contend with is heat and rain, and whatever you're lacking you can purchase while travelling. Buying clothes is easy and has the added advantage of helping you appear less like a tourist – if you like to stand out in a crowd try wearing Birkenstock sandals and an American-style bathing suit on Brazil's beaches. The only exception is if you wear big sizes, which can be difficult to find, particularly for shoes.

Unlike other basic necessities, clothing is not particularly cheap in Brazil. Shoes are the notable exception. You can get some good deals on leather shoes. Tennis shoes are the norm in Brazil, as are light jeans. Bring a pair of comfortable shorts and a light rain jacket. Bring your smallest bathing suit – men and women – but a *maiô* (Brazilian suit) is easy to find. There are many funny T-shirts that are practical garments to buy along the way, and are also good souvenirs.

You don't need more than a pair of shorts, trousers, a couple of T-shirts, a long-sleeved shirt, bathing suit, towel, underwear, walking shoes, flip flops and some rain gear. Quick-drying, light cotton clothes are the most convenient. Suntan lotion and sun-protection cream are readily available, as are most other toiletries.

Usually, one set of clothes to wear and one to wash is adequate. It's probably a good idea if one set of clothes is presentable or could pass at a good restaurant or club (or to renew your visa at the federal police station). While dress is informal, many Brazilians are very fashion conscious and pay close attention to their own appearance and yours.

For information regarding compiling a basic medical kit, see the Health section in this chapter.

TOURIST OFFICES

Local Tourist Offices

Embratur, the Brazilian Tourist Board, has moved its headquarters to Brasília, but still maintains an office in Rio de Janeiro (☎ 509-6017) at Rua Uruguaiana 174, 8th floor. In Brasília, their address is: Embratur, Setor Comercial Norte, Quadra 2, Bloco G, Brasília, DF, CEP 70710 (☎ (061) 224-9100).

Tourist offices elsewhere in Brazil are generally sponsored by individual states and municipalities. In many places, these offices rely on shoestring budgets that are chopped or maintained according to the whims (or feuds!) of regional and local politicians. Some tourist offices clearly function only as a sinecure for the family and relatives of politicians; others have dedicated and knowledgeable staff who are interested in providing information. Some offices are conveniently placed in the centre of town; others are so far out of range that you'll spend an entire day getting there. Keep your sense of humour, prepare for pot luck and don't expect too much!

Tourist Offices Abroad

Brazilian consulates and embassies are able to provide limited tourist information.

VISAS & DOCUMENTS

The only truly essential documents are your passport and visa, an airline ticket, a yellow World Health Organization health certificate and money.

Passport

By law you must carry a passport with you at all times, but many travellers opt to carry a photocopy (preferably certified) when tripping around town and leave their passport secure at their hotel. It's convenient to have extra passport photos for any documents or visas you might acquire in Brazil.

Tourist Card On entering Brazil, you must fill out a two-part tourist card; immigration officials will keep half, you keep the other. When you leave Brazil, this will be taken by immigration officials. Make sure you don't lose your card while travelling around Brazil, or your departure could be delayed until officials have checked your story. For added security, make a photocopy of your section of the tourist card and keep this in a safe place, separate from your passport.

While researching this edition we crossed the Brazilian border many times. At one stage, while travelling from Brazil to Uruguay, we missed the fact that the requisite part of our tourist card had not been collected on departure. Several weeks later, when we arrived at Ponta Porã on the Paraguay-Brazil border, the immigration authorities explained that we had not technically left Brazil! After considerable cogitation and some friendly banter, the officials asked us to make a certified deposition concerning the details of our 'disappearance'. Then the old cards were doctored, and we were issued with new cards.

Visas

At the time of writing, Brazilian visas were necessary for visitors who were citizens of countries that required visas for visitors from Brazil. Australian Canadian, New Zealand and American citizens required visas; but citizens of the UK, Switzerland, France, Germany, South Africa, Belgium Spain, and Scandinavian countries did not.

Tourist visas are issued by Brazilian diplomatic offices and are valid for arrival in Brazil within 90 days of issue and then for a 90 day stay. They are renewable in Brazil for an additional 90 days.

It should only take about three hours to issue a visa (it's instant in some embassies and consulates). You need a passport valid for at least six months, a single passport photograph (either B&W or colour) and a round-trip ticket or a statement from a travel agent, addressed to the Brazilian diplomatic office, stating that you have the required ticketing. If you only have a one-way ticket they may accept a document from a bank or similar organisation proving that you have sufficient funds to stay and buy a return ticket, but it's probably easier to get a letter from a travel agent stating that you have a round-trip ticket.

Visitors under 18 years of age must submit a notarised letter of authorisation from their parents or a legal guardian.

Visa Extensions These are handled by the Polícia Federal, and they have offices in the major Brazilian cities. You must apply before your visa lapses, or suffer the consequences. Don't leave it until the last minute, either. Go for an extension about 15 days before your current visa expires. The tourist office can tell you where the nearest Polícia Federal office is.

In most cases a visa extension seems to be pretty automatic, but sometimes they'll only give you 60 days. The police may require a ticket out of the country and proof of sufficient funds, but this seems to be entirely at the discretion of the police officer.

When applying for an extension, you will sometimes be told to go to a *papelaria* (stationery shop) and buy a DARF form (US$1). After filling it out, you must then go to a bank and pay a fee of about US$16. You then return to the Polícia Federal with the DARF form stamped by the bank. The extension should then be routinely issued.

If you opt for the maximum 90 day extension and then leave the country before the end of that period, you cannot return until the full 90 days have elapsed. So schedule your dates carefully if you plan to leave and re-enter the country.

Visas for Adjoining Countries The following information is intended as a rough guide only. Visa regulations are notoriously changeable, so check before you travel. For details of the relevant embassies and consulates, refer to individual cities mentioned.

Argentina
: Australians and New Zealanders require visas. Citizens of most Western European countries, Canada and the USA do not. There are Argentine consulates in Porto Alegre, Foz do Iguaçu, Rio, São Paulo and Brasília.

Bolivia
: Citizens of most Western European countries, Canada, the USA, Australia and New Zealand do not require visas. Dutch and French citizens require visas. There are Bolivian consulates in Brasília, Rio, São Paulo, Corumbá, Campo Grande, Manaus and Guajará-Mirim.

Colombia
: Visas are no longer required to enter Colombia, except if you are a Chinese national. There are consulates in Brasília, Manaus, Rio, São Paulo, and Tabatinga.

Guyana
: Most visitors require visas. Guyana has consulates in Brasília and São Paulo.

French Guiana
: Citizens of the USA, Canada and the EU do not require visas. Australians and New Zealanders require visas, which can be obtained at French consulates in Brasília, Belém, Recife, Rio, São Paulo, and Salvador.

Paraguay
: Australians and New Zealanders require visas, EU nationals (except those from Greece and Portugal), Americans and Canadians do not. There are Paraguayan consulates in Brasília, Campo Grande, Corumbá, Curitiba, Foz do Iguaçu, Porto Alegre, Ponta Porã, Rio and São Paulo.

Peru
: Australians, New Zealanders and South Africans require visas. There are Peruvian consulates in Brasília, Manaus, Rio Branco, Belém, Rio and São Paulo.

Suriname
: Visas are not required from UK or Canadian citizens. There is an embassy for Suriname in Brasília.

Uruguay
: Australians and New Zealanders require visas. There are Uruguayan consulates in Brasília, Chuí, Jaguarão, Porto Alegre, Rio and São Paulo.

Venezuela
: All overland travellers require visas. There are Venezuelan consulates in Brasília, Manaus, Belém, Boa Vista, Porto Alegre, Rio and São Paulo.

Onward Tickets

While you can receive your visa to Brazil by showing a letter from a travel agent, on arrival immigration officials may ask to see your onward ticket. If you don't have one you risk being denied entry to the country.

Travel Insurance

A travel insurance policy to cover theft, loss and medical problems is a good idea. The policies handled by STA Travel and other student travel organisations are usually good value. Some policies offer lower and higher medical-expense options; the higher ones are chiefly for countries such as the USA, which has extremely high medical costs. There is a wide variety of policies available so check the small print.

Some policies specifically exclude 'dangerous activities', which can include scuba diving, motorcycling, even trekking. A locally acquired motorcycle licence is not valid under some policies.

You may prefer a policy that pays for medical services directly rather than you having to pay first and claim later. If you have to claim later, make sure you keep all documentation. Some companies ask you to make a phone call back (reverse charges) to a centre in your home country where an immediate assessment of your problem is made.

Check that your chosen policy also covers ambulances or an emergency flight home.

Driving Licence & Permits

Your home driving licence is valid in Brazil, but because local authorities probably won't be familiar with it, you should do them (and yourself) a favour and also carry an International Driver's Permit. IDPs are issued by your national motoring association, which usually cost the equivalent of about US$10.

To rent a car you must be at least 25 years old, have a credit card in your name and a valid driving licence.

Vehicle Documents All vehicles in Brazil must carry the registration and proof of insurance. See the Car & Motorcycle section in the Getting There & Away chapter later in the book for more information.

Hostel Card

A Hostelling International membership card is essential if you plan to stay in the *albergues de juventude* (youth hostels). Most hostels in Brazil will let you in without one, but will charge more. HI cards are available in any hostel for varying fees, usually less than US$20. For information on the growing network of Brazilian youth hostels, contact the head office of the Federação Brasileira dos Albergues de Juventude (FBAJ) (☎ (021) 286-0303; fax 286-5652) in Botafogo, in the hostel at Rua General Dionísio 63.

Student, Youth & Seniors' Cards

The International Student Identity Card (ISIC) is practically useless in Brazil, where in larger cities on good days it might get you a US$0.50 discount to a major museum but usually not even that. If you've got one, bring it, but don't make a special trip to get one for Brazil. Seniors do get more discounts than students, so bring along any seniors' cards you may have.

Photocopies

As a backup for emergencies, make sure that you have photocopies of the following: your passport (including relevant visas), tourist card (provided when entering Brazil), travellers cheque numbers, and airline tickets. For more hints on safety, see the Security section under Dangers & Annoyances later in this chapter.

EMBASSIES & CONSULATES

Brazilian Embassies & Consulates

The Federative Republic of Brazil maintains embassies and consulates in the following countries:

Australia
19 Forster Crescent, Yarralumla, ACT 2600 (☎ (02) 6273-2372)

Canada
450 Wilbrod St, Ottawa, Ontario KIN-6MB(☎ (613) 237-1090)

Chile
Calle Enrique Mac-Iver 225 'Ed Banco Exterior' 15 Piso, Centro, Santiago (☎ (2) 639-8867)

Colombia
Calle 93 NR 14-20, Piso 8, Apartado Aerea 90540, Bogota 8 (☎ (571) 218-0800)

France
34 Cours Albert, 1er, 75008 Paris (☎ 01 2 59 92 50)

Germany
Esplanade 11, Poste 13187, Berlin 15 (☎ (030) 883-1208)

Ireland
Harcourt Centre, Europa House, 5th floor, Harcourt St, Dublin 2 (☎ (1) 475-6000)

Netherlands
Mauritskade 19, 2514 HD, Den Haag (☎ (70) 302-3959)

New Zealand
Level 9, 10 Brandon St, Wellington (☎ (04) 473-3516)

Paraguay
Calle General Diaz C/14 De Mayo NR 521, Edificio Faro Internacional – Tercero Piso, Caixa Postal 1314, Asuncion (☎ (21) 44 8069)

UK
Embassy: 32 Green St, London, W1Y 4AT (☎ (171) 499-0877)
Consulate: 6 St Alban's St, London, SW1Y 4SQ (☎ (171) 930-9055)
USA
Embassy: 3006 Massachusettes Ave, NW, Washington, DC 20008 (☎ (202) 238-2828; fax (202) 238-2818)
Consulates: New York (☎ (212) 757-3080) 531 5th Ave, room 210, New York, NY 10176; Atlanta (☎ (404) 521-0061); Boston (☎ (617) 542-4000); Chicago (☎ (312) 464-0244); Houston (☎ (713) 961-3063/64/65); Los Angeles (☎ (213) 651-2664); Miami (☎ (305) 285-6200); San Francisco (☎ (415) 981-8170)
Venezuala
Centro Gerencial Mohedando, Piso 6, Calle Los Chaguaramos Con Avenida Mohedano, La Castellana 1060, Caracas (☎ (2) 261 7553)

Embassies & Consulates in Brazil

Most countries maintain embassies in Brasília (see that chapter for more information), but many also have offices in Rio and São Paulo, which can take care of most travellers' needs. These include:

Rio de Janeiro

Argentina
Praia de Botafogo 228, 2nd floor, Botafogo (☎ 553-1646; fax 552-4191)
Bolivia
Avenida Rui Barbosa 664, No 101, Flamengo (☎ 551-1796; fax 551-3047)
Canada
Rua Lauro Muller 116, Room 2707, 1104 Botafogo (☎ 542-9297; fax 275-2195)
Chile
Praia do Flamengo 344, 7th floor, Flamengo (☎ 552-5349; fax 553-6371)
Colombia
Praia do Flamengo 284, No 101, Flamengo (☎ 552-6248; fax 552-5449)
Ecuador
Avenida NS de Copacabana 788, 8th floor, Copacabana (☎ 235-6695; fax 255-2245)
France
Avenida Presidente Antônio Carlos 58, 8th floor, Centro (☎ 210-1272; fax 220-4779)
Germany
Rua Presidente Carlos de Campos 417, Laranjeiras (☎ 553-6777; fax 553-0184)
Netherlands
Praia de Botafogo 242, 7th floor, Botafogo (☎ 552-9028; fax 552-8294)
Paraguay
Praia de Botafogo 242, 2nd floor, Botafogo (☎ 553-2294; fax 553-2512)
Peru
Avenida Rui Barbosa 314, 2nd floor, Botafogo (☎ 551-6296; fax 551-9796)
Uruguay
Praia de Botafogo 242, 6th floor, Botafogo (☎ 553-6030; fax 553-6036)
UK
Praia do Flamengo 284, 2nd floor, Flamengo (☎ 553-3223; fax 553-5976)
USA
Avenida Presidente Wilson 147, Centro (☎ 292-7117; fax 262-1402)
Venezuela
Praia de Botafogo 242, 5th floor, Botafogo (☎ 552-6699; fax 551-5248)

São Paulo

Argentina
Avenida Paulista 1106, 9th floor (☎ 284-1355)
Australia
Rua Tenente Negrão 140, 12th floor (☎ 829-6281)
Bolivia
Rua da Eonduras 1147, (☎ 881-1688)
Canada
Avenida Paulista 854, 5th floor (☎ 253-4944)
Chile
Avenida Paulista 1009, 10th floor (☎ 284-2044)
Colombia
Rua Pescioto Commide 996 (☎ 284 0998)
France
Avenida Paulista 1842, 14th floor (☎ 287-9522)
Germany
Avenida Brigadeiro Faria Lima 2092, 12th floor (☎ 814-6644)
Netherlands
Avenida Brigaderio Faria Lima 1779, 3rd floor (☎ 813 0522)
Paraguay
Rua Bandeira Paulista 600, 15th floor (☎ 820-1412)
Peru
Rua Votuverava 350 (☎ 870-1793)
UK
Avenida Paulista 37, 17th floor, (☎ 287-7722)
Uraguay
Alameda Santos 902, 10th floor (☎ 284-0998)
USA
Rua Padre João Manoel 933 (☎ 881-6511)

CUSTOMS

Travellers entering Brazil are allowed to bring in one radio, tape player, typewriter, video and still camera. Personal computers are permitted, but you may be required to fill in a note promising to take it with you when you leave.

Airport customs sometimes use a random check system: after collecting your luggage you pass a post with two buttons; if you have nothing to declare, you push the appropriate button. A green light means walk straight out; a red light means you've been selected for a baggage search. Customs searches at land borders are more thorough, especially if you're coming from Bolivia.

MONEY

Currency

The name of the currency in Brazil has changed five times since 1986. The monetary unit is the *real* (pronounced HAY-ow); the plural is reais (pronounced HAY-ice). It's made up of 100 centavos and as we write is the most overvalued currency since the Ukranian *kupon* was worth something.

The frustratingly similar coins are: one, five, 10, 25 and 50 centavos. There's also a one *real* coin as well as a one *real* note.

Notes are different colours, so there's no mistaking them. As well as the green one *real* note there's a blue/purple five, a red 10, a brown 50 and a blue 100.

Exchange Rates

Exchange rates are written up every day in the major daily papers: *O Globo*, *Jornal do Brasil* and the *Folha de São Paulo*, and are always announced on the evening TV news.

Approximate bank rates as of July 1998 were as follows:

Australia	A$1	=	R$0.70
Canada	C$1	=	R$0.78
France	1FFr	=	R$0.19
Germany	DM1	=	R$0.64
Ireland	I£	=	R$1.66
Japan	¥100	=	R$0.81
New Zealand	NZ$1	=	R$0.59
UK	UK£1	=	R$1.89
USA	US$1	=	R$1.16

Exchanging Money

There are currently three types of exchange rate in Brazil: official (also known as *comercial* or *câmbio livre*), *turismo* and *paralelo*.

With limited exceptions in large cities, the only currency you can exchange is US dollars – your best bet is to carry these.

Until recently, the official rate has always been much lower than the parallel rate. A few years ago, all dollars exchanged at banks were changed at the official rate as were all credit card transactions, making it an extremely unfavourable transaction. However, thanks to a certain amount of deregulation in an attempt to wipe out black-market trading it's now possible to change cash dollars and travellers cheques at banks using the turismo rate, which is only slightly less than the parallel rate.

Since the introduction of the Plano Real (see the History section in the Facts About the Country chapter), the difference between the official and parallel rates has been minimal. Full parallel rates are usually available only at borders and in the larger cities like Rio and São Paulo.

Cash & Travellers Cheques US dollars are easier to trade and are worth a bit more on the parallel market, but travellers cheques are an insurance against loss. Now that they can be exchanged at the turismo rate, they are good value and it's good sense to use them. But they can be hard to change, and unless you change them at a bank that has a deal with the issuer, there's usually a US$10 to $20 per cheque 'transaction fee', so you might prefer to carry a Visa card (see Credit Cards).

American Express is the most recognised travellers cheque, but they charge 1% of the face value of the cheque (on top of the interest your money makes while sitting in their banks). With lost cheques they can sometimes be a little reluctant to give your money back on the spot – *always* the case if you've made a claim in the last year or two.

American Express has offices in Rio de Janeiro, Salvador, Recife, Maceió, Natal,

Fortaleza, Belém, Manaus, Campo Grande, Brasília, Florianópolis, Curitiba, Belo Horizonte and São Paulo. American Express card holders can purchase US-dollar travellers cheques from American Express offices in the large cities.

Thomas Cook, Barclays and Citibank travellers cheques are less widely accepted but you can cash them in large cities. Leave Westpac cheques back in Australia.

Get travellers cheques in US dollars and carry some small denominations for convenience. Have some emergency US cash to use when the banks are closed.

Learn in advance how to get refunds from your travellers cheque company. Leave a copy of the serial numbers somewhere safe (we leave one at home, too), and keep the record of serial numbers separate from your cheques on the road. Keep a close, accurate and current record of your travellers cheque expenditures. This speeds up the refund process. Guard your travellers cheques – they are valuable to thieves even without your counter signature.

ATMs There is a good national network of automatic teller machines (ATMs) throughout Brazil. Bradesco machines are in most cities and most give you cash from a Visa card (if you've activated your four-digit Personal Identification Number, or PIN), as well as from bank cards on the Plus network. Banco do Brasil (which has distinctive red booths in almost every sizeable town) ATMs are increasingly offering this service as well. Citibank ATMs are in major cities and also accept Visa/Plus.

Credit Cards Visa, American Express and MasterCard are accepted by many hotels, restaurants and shops. But it's surprising how many don't accept credit cards, so ask first if you plan to use one.

Visa is the most versatile credit card in Brazil. Visa cash advances are widely available from the Banco Econômico, Banco do Brasil and Bradesco; and even in some small towns which have no other currency exchange facilities.

Many travellers are now using this system instead of travellers cheques or cash (though it's good to carry cash for emergencies). Put your travelling money into your Visa account so it's in credit, and you won't have to worry about getting someone at home to pay your bills. Some banks in the USA, Australia, New Zealand and the UK are now selling Visa Travel Money, a prepaid Visa card similar to a telephone card: your credit limit is the amount you buy the card with, and it's not rechargeable, but accepted like a regular Visa card. They charge a 2% fee of the purchase price of the card, so it's more expensive than travellers cheques but more accessible.

MasterCard holders can pay for many goods and services with their card, but cash advances are difficult.

At present, you get billed at the turismo rate in reais. Sometimes, the hotel, restaurant or store will try to add an extra charge for using the card. It's illegal to do this, and you can make a complaint to the relevant credit card company, which may decide to terminate its contract with the offending establishment. Vote for fair play with your credit card!

New-style credit card coupons do not have carbon paper inserts and offer more protection against misuse. If you sign an old-style coupon, be sure to ask for the carbon inserts and destroy them after use; a worthwhile precaution against duplication.

International Transfers Transferring money from a bank at home to you in Brazil is either cheap and extremely problematic or easy and usuriously expensive. If you have an account in a Brazilian bank, the procedure is straightforward; forward your Brazilian bank's SWIFT address, physical address, ABA routing number and branch number as well as your account number to whoever's sending the money, and (depending on your Brazilian banker's overnight Fed Fund habits) anywhere from 24 to 72 hours later it should be in your Brazilian account. If you don't have an account in Brazil, the best advice is to ask your bank at home for the name of the bank they have a correspondent relationship with in Brazil and ask them for the best possible way to do it.

Shop around. Citibank has branches throughout the world and is a good bet. The Brazilian American Cultural Center (BACC), which has offices in the USA and Brazil, provides a special remittance service for members – for details and the main address of BACC, refer to the Useful Organisations section in this chapter.

The fastest (and most expensive) way to get money to Brazil is through Western Union or Money Gram, the latter is available at selected American Express and Thomas Cook offices throughout the world. Money can be sent within 15 minutes to one of those company's offices, or to one of the thousands of correspondent banks in Brazil the organisation maintains a relationship with. The cost from either service (Money Gram is slightly cheaper) is about 10%.

Black Market Foreigners can buy and sell dollars with little restriction – save your receipts when you buy *real* to ease changing back to dollars.

When banks aren't around, a sort of 'grey market' solution to the exchange problem has popped up in the cities and larger towns in the form of *casas de câmbio* (exchange houses). These generally, and happily, give you the full paralelo amount as opposed to the turismo rate offered at banks. Some will even change travellers cheques.

Changing money on the street – unless you're in an area so remote you're not going to find anyone with which to change money – is a bad idea, and usually unnecessary.

Security

Carry only what you need in pockets, the rest in a pouch inside your clothes – see Dangers & Annoyances for more safety information.

There is a chronic shortage of change all over Brazil, especially in the Northeast. When you change money, ask for lots of small notes – and take very few notes in denominations larger than the equivalent of US$10. *Troco* or *miúdo* (change) is often unobtainable from newsagents, restaurants, street stalls, in taxis, on buses etc.

Although the shortage genuinely exists, it is also commonly used as an excuse to simply retain a fat tip. If you encounter this problem, insist that the seller finds change and hang around until it is procured.

If you want to find out if the seller has change – preferably *before* you purchase – ask *'tem troco?'* (do you have change?). If you want to convey that you don't have change, say *'não tem troco'* (there is no change), which makes it clear that you neither have change nor have been able to find any in the vicinity – thus heading off the seller's inevitable request that you hunt around the vicinity! Sweets are often used instead of small change.

Costs

Short of a currency collapse (which appears inevitable, but you never know) Brazil is no longer even remotely a cheap country. Prices as we write are similar to those in Australia or the south-eastern USA.

The Brazilian currency has taken a roller coaster ride over the last two decades – from our first couple of trips in 1984 and 1985, when budget travel was ridiculously cheap; to 1990, when prices skyrocketed; to the introduction in 1994 of the *real*, which for a time, was worth more than the US dollars.

Since our last edition in 1996, prices have increased dramatically – and that's against the US dollars, not just compensatory rises to keep pace with the falling *real*. We found that in US dollar terms hotel prices had risen by 50%; bus transport doubled; and food rose a bit.

Day to Day Costs If you're travelling on buses every couple of days, staying in hotels for US$20 a night, and eating in restaurants and/or drinking in bars every night, US$40 to $50 a day is a rough estimate of what you would need.

The authors of this edition found that they each spent approximately US$40 to $60 per day including bus transport (not plane transport, which was extra), taxis, train rides and attraction admissions. The authors spent between US$60 and $80 per day in Rio and São Paulo cities.

If you plan to lie on a beach for a month, eating rice, beans and fish every day, US$20 to $30 would be enough.

During the holiday season (December to February) accommodation costs generally increase by around 25 to 30%, sometimes more in popular resorts.

One of our authors, who covered the Pantanal, Foz do Iguaçu, Curitiba-Paranaguá and Florianópolis, found that:

For most of my trip I spent an average of US$58 per day, including accommodation, food and drinks, water, local transport (including the odd taxi), intercity transport and other expenses (maps, local guidebooks, laundry), but not including a few days' car hire.

Chris McAsey

Cutting Costs It's possible to do it for less of course. You can cut costs by travelling outside high season, eating at *por quilo* or *rodizio* restaurants and using the growing network of hostels more. The hostels we checked out were relaxed, and less formal than those in other countries.

The best way to cut costs and improve your trip is to make the extra effort to get off the track to some of the 'forgotten' places, where price rises haven't always caught up. Travellers in Brazil are becoming increasingly concentrated in the major centres now, so the reward for getting out is more worthwhile than ever. Tourism in the smaller towns has dropped off (even in Cuiabá, the guides claim foreign tourism has dropped off 50% in the last three years), so prices are often lower.

Solo Travellers Brazil is not among the kinder destinations for solo travellers. The cost of a single room in a hotel is not much less than for a double, and when you eat, you'll find that most dishes in restaurants are priced for two people.

Tipping

Most services get tipped 10%, and as the people in these services make the minimum wage – which is not enough to live on – you can be sure they need the money. In restaurants the service charge will usually be included in the bill and is mandatory. If a waiter is friendly and helpful you can give more.

Even when it is not included, it's still customary to leave a 10% tip; unless the service is atrocious, the waiter shouldn't be punished for giving you the option. There are many places where tipping is not customary but is a welcome gesture. The local juice stands, bars, coffee corners, street and beach vendors are all tipped on occasion.

Because of the massive level of unemployment, some services that may seem superfluous are customarily tipped anyway. Self-appointed 'parking assistants' are the most notable. It's the definition of extortion, euphemistically called 'tips' (give them US$0.25 to $0.50 on your way *out* of the spot, not in advance). Petrol-station attendants, shoe shiners and barbers are also frequently tipped.

Taxi drivers are not usually tipped. Most people round the price up to the nearest *real*, but tipping is not expected.

Bargaining

'Quem não chora não mama'
(Those who don't cry, don't suckle)

– Brazilian saying to justify bargaining

Bargaining for hotel rooms should become second nature. Before you agree to take a room, ask for a better price. '*Tem desconto?*' (Is there a discount?) and '*Pode fazer um melhor preço?*' (Can you give a better price?) are the phrases to use.

There's often a discount for paying *á vista* (cash) or for staying during the *baixa estação* or *época baixa* (low season) when hotels need guests to cover running costs. It's also possible to reduce the price if you state that you don't want a TV, private bath, or air conditioning. If you're staying longer than a couple of days, ask for a discount. Once a discount has been quoted, make sure it is noted on your bill at the same time – this avoids misunderstandings at a later date. Bargain also in markets and in unmetered taxis.

POST & COMMUNICATIONS

Postal services are pretty good in Brazil. Though sometimes receiving letters is dicey, most mail seems to get through. Air mail letters to the USA and Europe arrive in a week or so. For Australia, allow about two weeks.

Postal Rates

It's about US$1 for an international letter or postcard.

Sending Mail

There are mail boxes on the street but it's safer to go to a post office. Most *correios* (post offices) are open from 9 am to 6 pm Monday to Friday, and Saturday morning. Brazilian postal codes are five numbers followed by three; the first five are the base postal code for the city, the following three the specific location. In this book we list the base postal code for each city.

Receiving Mail

The *posta restante* system seems to function reasonably well and post offices hold mail for 30 days. A reliable alternative for American Express customers is to have mail sent to one of its offices.

Telephone

International Calls To phone Brazil from abroad, dial your international access code, plus 55, plus the city code (omitting the first 0) then the number.

While phoning abroad from Brazil is expensive, the price has been lowered substantially since our last edition and this trend should continue after worldwide deregulation in 1998. To the USA it costs approximately US$1.35 a minute. Prices are 25% lower from 8 pm to 6 am daily and all day Sunday. To Canada, the charge is US$1.70; to the UK and France it's US$1.80 a minute, and to Australia and New Zealand US$2.50 a minute. There are no cheaper times to these last two countries.

Every town has a *posto telefônico* (phone company office) for long-distance calls. Generally you tell them the country code you're dialling and you'll be assigned a booth. Pay when you're finished.

If you're calling direct dial ☎ 00, then the country code, then the area code, then the phone number. So to call New York, you dial ☎ 001-212-phone number. For information on international calls dial ☎ 000333.

Country codes include: UK ☎ 44, USA ☎ 1, Australia ☎ 61, New Zealand ☎ 64, Canada ☎ 1, France ☎ 33, Germany ☎ 49, Argentina ☎ 54, Chile ☎ 56, Peru ☎ 51, Paraguay ☎ 595.

Home Country Direct services are available from any phone for Australia (☎ 000-8061), Canada (☎ 000-8014), France (☎ 000-8033), Germany (☎ 000-8049), Israel (☎ 000-8097), Italy (☎ 000-8039), Japan (☎ 000-8081), the Netherlands (☎ 000-8031), the UK (☎ 000-8044) and the USA (☎ 000-8010 for AT&T, 000-8012 for MCI and 000-8016 for Sprint).

International collect calls *(a cobrar)* can be made from any phone. To get the international operator dial ☎ 000111 or 107 and ask for the *telefonista internacional*. If they don't speak English you could experiment with some of the following phrases:

I would like to make an international call to …
Quero fazer uma ligação internacional para …

I would like to reverse the charges.
Quero fazê-la a cobrar.

I am calling from a public (private) telephone (in Rio de Janeiro).
Estou falando dum telefone público (particular) no Rio de Janeiro.

My name is …
Meu nôme é …

The area code is …
O código é …

The number is …
O número é …

If you're having trouble, reception desks at larger hotels are helpful.

Domestic Calls National long-distance calls can also be made at the local phone company office, unless you're calling collect. All you need is the area code and phone number, and a few dollars. For calling collect within Brazil, dial ☎ 9 – area code – phone number. A recorded message in Portuguese will ask you to say your name and where you're calling from, after the beep. The person at the other end then decides if they will accept the call.

Area codes for the major cities are as follows:

Aracaju	☎ 079
Belém	☎ 091
Belo Horizonte	☎ 031
Boa Vista	☎ 095
Brasília	☎ 061
Campo Grande	☎ 067
Cuiabá	☎ 065
Curitiba	☎ 041
Florianópolis	☎ 0482
Fortaleza	☎ 085
Goiânia	☎ 062
Macapá	☎ 096
Maceió	☎ 082
Manaus	☎ 092
Natal	☎ 084
Porto Alegre	☎ 0512
Porto Velho	☎ 069
Recife	☎ 081
Rio Branco	☎ 068
Rio de Janeiro	☎ 021
Salvador	☎ 071
São Luís	☎ 098
São Paulo	☎ 011
Teresina	☎ 086
Vitória	☎ 027

Local Calls Brazilian public phones are nicknamed *orelhôes* (big ears). Many public phones now use phonecards, which cost R$3 for 32 local calls, R$4 for 50. Older phones use *fichas* (tokens), which can be bought at newsstands, pharmacies etc. They cost less than US$0.05, but it's a good idea to buy a few extra fichas because phones tend to consume them liberally.

To use card phones (which usually also accept fichas), slide the card in, check the readout to see if it's given you proper credit, and dial.

To use coin phones, wait for a dial tone, deposit the ficha and dial your number. Each ficha is generally good for a couple of minutes locally, but the time can vary considerably. When your time is up, you will be disconnected without warning, so it's a good idea to deposit an extra ficha.

To call the operator dial ☎ 100, and for information call ☎ 102.

Phone Books There are several kinds of *lista telefônica* (telephone book) available. In larger cities *assinantes*, list names in alphabetical order; and *endereço*, list street names in alphabetical order followed by house numbers, and the householder's name and phone number. The Brazilian Yellow Pages is the *Páginas Amarelas*.

Phone books for other cities can be found at larger telephone offices. Phone books also usually include excellent city maps.

Fax, Telex & Telegraph

Post offices send and receive telegrams and the larger branches also have fax services. Faxes generally cost US$5 for the first page and US$3 for each additional page to the USA and Canada, US$8/4.50 to Australia and New Zealand, and US$6/4 to the UK.

Email & Internet Access

Internet access is taking off in larger cities, where Internet cafés are becoming more popular, but access is still limited in rural areas. We list Internet cafés where possible in this book.

INTERNET RESOURCES

For the latest up-to-date links in and about Brazil, visit Lonely Planet's Web site (www.lonelyplanet.com.au), which has destination profiles, feature stories, reports from travellers on the road, and much more. You can also visit Lonely Planet on America Online (Keyword: lp), or on the French Minitel system at 3615 lonelyplanet.

Some other major Web sites to get you started are:

lanic.utexas.edu/ilas/brazctr/school.html
: Brazil site at the University of Texas; heaps of links and Real Brazil, an English language journal of Brazilian affairs

www.embratur.gov.br
: Embratur National Tourism Site

www.brasil.emb.nw.dc.us/embing6.htm
: Brazilian embassy, Washington DC; probably the most reliable set of Brazil links around plus constantly updated visa information

www.crl.com/~brazil/address.htm
: Brazilian consulate, San Francisco; listings of addresses and telephone numbers of US and some international Brazilian consular offices

www.wttc.org and www.tnc.org
: Green Globe and The Nature Conservancy; both run Web sites with information about natural history with information and links to the Amazon and ecotourism issues

BOOKS

Most books are published in different editions by various publishers in several countries. As a result, a book might be a hardcover rarity in one country while it's readily available in paperback in another. Fortunately, bookshops and libraries search by title or author, so your local bookshop or library is best placed to advise you on the availability of the recommendations in this section.

Lonely Planet

Lonely Planet publishes an excellent *Brazilian phrasebook* (US$5.95) that covers practically anything you'd ever need to say in Portuguese down here. *South America on a shoestring* (US$29.95) covers all countries on the continent and the Falkland Islands.

Lonely Planet also publishes specialised *Latin American Spanish* (US$5.95) and *Quechua* (US$3.95) phrasebooks (Quechua is spoken widely among the indigenous peoples of Peru and Bolivia); *Trekking in the Patagonian Andes* (US$15.95); and the new Lonely Planet author-tested *Chile & Easter Island travel atlas*.

The French language Lonely Planet Guides de Voyage publish titles for *Brésil* and Central American destinations including *Mexique* and *Cuba*.

Guidebooks

Quatro Rodas publishes the best all-round series of Brazil guides. They're in Portuguese, but keyed in English and extremely easy to follow.

The bigger sellers are readily available at most newsagents and all are available in Brazilian bookshops. The price isn't marked, so you'll have to ask the vendor – generally they cost about US$20 to $30.

The flagship title is *Quatro Rodas: Guia Brasil* (about R$22), which contains a wealth of information about accommodation, restaurants, transport, sights etc. If you buy it in Brazil it comes with an excellent fold-out map of the country. It doesn't cover budget options.

Other titles include *Guia São Paulo Ruas*, and *Guia Rio de Janeiro Ruas*, both superb atlases to São Paulo and Rio. *Guia Rodoviário* is a comprehensive road atlas with excellent country-wide maps as well as main roads into all other Mercosul countries. *Guia de Estradas* is *Guia Rodoviário* on steroids. Then there's the beautiful and pricey *Guia de Praias*, geared towards beach freaks on driving tours with stunning satellite photographs of the country's most wonderful beaches plus information on hotels, camping sites, some maps and fauna and ecological parks and projects.

If you can find it, Quatro Rodas' *Viajar Bem e Barato: O Superguia de Viagens Econômicas*, is an excellent budget travel guide. It covers accommodation from the rock-bottom options *(dormitórios* and the like usually only used by locals) to the better value budget places, even though some of them are a fair hike out of town. There's not much detail on transport, and little on history and cultural highlights.

Travellers planning river trips on their own will find practical advice in *South American River Trips* (Bradt Publications, 1982) and the harder to locate *Up the Creek* by John Harrison (Bradt Publications, 1986).

Backcountry Brazil (Bradt Publications, 1990) provides useful supplementary information if you want to skip the cities.

Travel

Travelers' Tales Brazil (Travelers' Tales Inc, 1998), edited by Lonely Planet author Scott Doggett and Annette Haddad, is a fine anthology of tales of travel and life in Brazil, with submissions from writers including Bill McKibben, Joe Kane, Petru Popescu and Alma Guillermoprieto. It's varied enough to keep you riveted and laughing – great bus reading.

Peter Fleming's *Brazilian Adventure* (Penguin, 1978) is about the young journalist's expedition into Mato Grosso in search of Colonel Fawcett, who had disappeared. At the time this area was the world's last, vast unexplored region. What Fleming found is less important than the telling: written with the humour of the disenchanted Briton. Travel adventures don't get any funnier than this – highly recommended.

Then again, maybe they do get funnier: it's not exactly about Brazil (though he does pass through), but Redmond O'Hanlon's *In Trouble Again* is one of the most hilarious true travel tales ever written – see if you don't squirm as he describes the *candiru* toothpick fish that lodges itself in your … well, just read it and see.

Also not solely about Brazil is Peter Mattheissen's *The Cloud Forest* (Collins Harvill, 1960), an account of his 30,000km journey across the South American wilderness from the Amazon to Tierra del Fuego. It's well worth a read. Mattheissen is a master at describing his environment.

Moritz Thomsen's *The Saddest Pleasure: A Journey on Two Rivers* (Graywolf Press, 1990) is a highly recommended book – skip the sickly introduction – about the author's experiences in South America, including journeys through Brazil and along the Amazon.

Ninety-Two Days by Evelyn Waugh is another screecher, a tale of his trip through Brazil and Guiana that he himself described as a 'warning against travel'.

Running The Amazon by Joe Kane is the story of the 10 men and one woman who in 1986 became the only expedition ever to cover the entire length of the Rio Amazonas, from the Andes to the Atlantic, on foot and in rafts and kayaks.

Guess what *Eat Smart in Brazil: How to Decipher the Menu, Know the Market Foods & Embark on a Tasting Adventure* (Ginkgo Press) is about?

We really enjoyed Paul Rambali's *It's all True – in the Cities and Jungles of Brazil* (William Heinemenn Ltd London, 1993). Rambali, founding editor of *The Face* magazine, writes of his travel experiences in Brazil with many shrewd and humourous insights. Among other things he looks at favela gangsters, street kids, soap operas and neo-evangelism.

In the 19th century, practically every westerner who visited Brazil seems to have written a travelogue, and some, with their keen powers of observation, are quite good. Maria Graham's *Journal of a Voyage to Brazil & Residence there During Part of the Years 1821, 1822, 1823* is as precise as the title suggests. Henry Koster wrote *Travels in Brazil* in 1816; Herbert H Smith wrote *Brazil, the Amazon & the Coast* in 1880.

The Amazon & Indians

The first and last word on the history of the Portuguese colonisation, the warring and the enslavement of the Indians is *Red Gold* (Harvard University Press, 1978) by John Hemming. Hemming has brought Indian history up to date in *Amazon Frontier: The Defeat of the Brazilian Indians* (Harvard University Press, 1987).

Before the Bulldozer: The Nambiquara Indians and the World Bank by David Price (Seven Locks Press) is the story of an anthropologist's attempt to defend a small society from the development of a 1600km highway in western Brazil, partly financed by the World Bank.

Other interesting titles are *The Last Indians: South America's Cultural Heritage* by Fritz Tupp, *Aromeri Brazilian Indian Feather Art* by Norberto Nícola and Sónia

Ferraro, and *Aborigines of the Amazon Rain Forest: The Yanomami* (Time Life Books, 1982) by Robin Hanbury-Tenison. *Amazonia* (1991) by the renowned explorer and photographer Loren McIntyre, records in magnificent photographs the gradual demise of the region and its original inhabitants. To learn more about McIntyre's many journeys in search of the source of the Amazon and his extraordinary psychic experiences with indigenous tribes, pick up a copy of *Amazon Beaming* (1991) by Petru Popescu.

Amazon Watershed, the New Environmental Investigation by George Monbiot tells the story of Brazilian peasants being forced by the military to relocate into the Amazon to make way for massive timber projects along Brazil's northern frontier. It also accuses the USA, UK, IMF and the World Bank of promoting the destruction of the Amazon rainforest.

The works of Márcio Souza (see the Literature section in the Facts about the Country chapter), a skillful Brazilian satirist, are set in the Amazon. Anthropologist Darcy Ribeiro's interesting novel *Maíra* (Random House, 1983) is about the clash between Indian animism and Catholicism.

Alex Shoumatoff has written three excellent books about the Amazon, all of them entertaining combinations of history, myth and travelogue. His latest work, *The World is Burning* (Little Brown, 1990), recounts the Chico Mendes story.

Armchair adventurers will enjoy Spix & Martius' *Travels Brazil*, a three volume chronology of the pair's 3½ year journey from 1817 to 1820. Illustrated with wonderful etchings, it is a biologist's record of customs, social life, ethnology and a description of flora and fauna. You may still be able to find second-hand copies of George Woodcock's *Henry Walter Bates, Naturalist of the Amazons* (Faber & Faber, 1969), a fascinating account of Bates' many years spent in pursuit of plant life during the mid-19th century.

Those interested in *yagé*, the hallucinogenic drug used by certain tribes of the upper Amazon, will find *Wizard of the Upper Amazon – the Story of Manuel Córdova-Rios* (Houghton Mifflin, 1975) and the sequel *Rio Tigre and Beyond* by F Bruce Lamb interesting reading. Speaking of druggie tales, in 1941 Harvard professor Richard Evans Schultes began a 12 year journey into the Amazon during which time he mapped and studied the region and lived among dozens of tribes. *One River: Science, Adventure and Hallucinogenics in the Amazon Basin* is the story of how Schultes sent, in the 1970s, two students back to the region to study … coca!

The Fate of the Forest: Developers, Destroyers, and Defenders of the Amazon (Verso, 1989) by Susanna Hecht & Alexander Cockburn is one of the best analyses of the complex web of destruction, and provides ideas on ways to mend the damage. Arnold Newman's *Tropical Rainforest: A World Survey of Our Most Valuable and Endangered Habitat with a Blueprint for its Survival* is a massive analysis of rainforest destruction and possible strategies for sound forest management. *People of the Tropical Rainforest* (University of California Press & Smithsonian Institute, 1988) is a compilation of writings about the rainforest by experts on the subject. Augusta Dwyer delivers a fierce indictment of corruption and mismanagement in the Amazon in *Into the Amazon: The Struggle for the Amazon*.

Three cheers for *The Rainforest Book* (Living Planet, 1990) by Scott Lewis, a concise analysis of rainforest problems and remedies. It's packed with examples that link consumer behaviour with rainforest development, listings of organisations to contact; and advice on individual involvement. A similar publication compiled by the Seattle Audubon Society and the Puget Consumers Co-operative is the booklet entitled *Rainforests Forever: Consumer Choices to Help Preserve Tropical Rainforests* (1990).

History & Politics

Brazil has a fascinating and fantastic past, but for some reason the good surveys of Brazilian history have yet to be translated into English. So the best way to go, if you want to understand the flow of Brazilian history in English, is via several of the excellent narratives. One exception is *A History of Brazil* by E Bradford Burns (Columbia University Press), an in-depth look at the history of the country up to 1993.

John Hemming's *Red Gold: The Conquest of the Brazilian Indians* follows the colonists and Indians from 1500 to 1760, when millions of Indians were effectively eliminated or pacified. Hemming, a founder of Survival International and eloquent campaigner for Indian rights, has extended his analysis of Indian history in *Amazon Frontier: The Defeat of the Brazilian Indians* (Pan Macmillan).

Caio Prado Junior, Brazil's leading economic historian, presents a descriptive analysis of the legacy of Brazil's colonial past in *The Colonial Background of Modern Brazil*. It's probably the single best interpretation of the colonial period in English. Prado presents a sweeping view of Brazil's lack of development, which he blames on the export-based economy and the social relations of slavery.

Celso Furtado, a leading economist and the current minister of culture, has written a good introductory economic history of the country titled *The Economic Growth of Brazil* (Greenwood, 1984).

Charles R Boxer is from the good old school of British economic history, which took writing seriously. All his books are fine reading and illuminating history. His *Golden Age of Brazil, 1695-1750* (University of California Press, 1962) has an excellent introductory chapter summarising life in 17th century Brazil, and then focuses on the gold rush in Minas Gerais and its consequences on the rest of the colony. Boxer has also written *Salvador de Sá & the Struggle for Brazil & Angola, 1602-1686* and *The Dutch in Brazil, 1624-1654*.

The most famous book on Brazil's colonial period is Gilberto Freyre's *The Masters & the Slaves: A Study in the Development of Brazilian Civilization* (University of California Press, 1986). There's a new paperback edition from the University of California Press, which also publishes Freyre's other works: *The Mansions & the Shanties: The Making of Modern Brazil* (University of California Press, 1986) and *Order & Progress: Brazil from Monarchy to Republic* (University of California Press, 1986).

Freyre's argued that Brazilian slavery was less harsh than in the USA, and through interracial pairing Brazil has avoided the racial problems of the USA. His views contributed to the myth of racial democracy in Brazil and have been severely rebuked by academics over the past 20 years. Still, Freyre's books can be read on many levels, including social history, and there are fascinating comments on folklore, myths and superstition, religion and sexuality.

Emília Viotti da Costa has a collection of well written essays in English that is one of the best treatments of 19th century Brazil. *The Brazilian Empire: Myths & Histories* (University of Chicago Press, 1986) interweaves the ideological and economic components of Brazilian history, and the results are illuminating and suggestive. Her essays, particularly on slavery and the landless poor, explode many of the harmony myths that hide the realities of oppression and poverty.

The English narratives on 20th century Brazilian history are less satisfying. Peter Flynn's *Brazil: A Political Analysis* presents a political history from 1889 to 1977. Thomas Skidmore's *Politics in Brazil, 1930-1964* is good. And Irving L Horowitz covers the Goulart era in *Revolution in Brazil*.

Alfred Stepan has edited a collection of essays called *Authoritarian Brazil: Origins, Policies & Future* (Yale University Press, 1973). These are often heavy with theory, but quite interesting, particularly the essays by Fishlow, Cardoso and Schmitter.

Finally, the unbelievable rebellion in Canudos by the followers of the mystic Antônio Conselheiro has been immortalised in *Rebellion in the Backlands* (University of Chicago Press, 1985), by Euclides da Cunha. Mixing history, geography and philosophy,

Os Sertões (in Portuguese) is considered the masterpiece of Brazilian literature. It's an incredible story about the outcasts of the Northeast, and is a sort of meditation on Brazilian civilisation. The story of the author and the rebellion is told by Mário Vargas Llosa in his novel *The War of the End of the World* (Avon Bard, 1985); entertaining, light reading for the traveller.

For readers who like their history with a dose of fiction, *Brazil* (Simon & Schuster, 1986) by Errol Lincoln Uys, is an interesting novel that traces the history of two Brazilian families from pre-Cabral times to the foundation of Brasília.

General

For a description of Brazilian literature and suggested reading, refer to the Literature section in the Facts about the Country chapter.

Flora & Fauna Guides *Rainforests – A Guide to Tourist and Research Facilities at Selected Tropical Forest Sites in Central and South America*, by James L Castner, is full of information and well worth getting hold of if you want to do some research or even just visit the rainforest.

Margaret Mee's *In Search of the Flowers of the Amazon Forest* is beautifully illustrated, and highly recommended for anyone (not just botanists) interested in the Amazon.

Neotropical Rainforest Mammals: A Field Guide, by Louise Emmons & François Feer, provides colour illustrations to identify mammals of the rainforest. For a reference work, rather than a field guide, you could consult the *World of Wildlife: Animals of South America* (Orbis Publishing, 1975) by F R de la Fuente.

Birders in the Amazon region of Brazil often use field guides for adjacent countries – many species overlap. Amateur interests should be satisfied with titles such as *South American Birds: A Photographic Aid to Identification* (1987) by John S Dunning; or *A Guide to the Birds of Venezuela* by Rodolphe de Schauensee & William Phelps. For a definitive tome, rather than a lightweight guide, you could start with *A Guide to the Birds of South America* (Academy of Natural Science, Philadelphia).

Last, but not least, for some fascinating oddities you should dip into *Ecology of Tropical Rainforests: An Introduction for Eco-Tourists* (Free University Amsterdam, 1990) by Piet van Ipenburg & Rob Boschhuizen. This booklet is packed with intriguing and bizarre scientific minutiae about sloths, bats, the strangling fig etc; and more extraordinary details of rainforest ecology. Available in the UK from J Forrest, 64 Belsize Park, London NW3 4EH; or in the USA from M Doolittle, 32 Amy Rd, Falls Village, CT 06031. All proceeds from sales of this booklet go to the Tambopata Reserve Society, which is funding research in the Tambopata Reserve in the rainforests of south-eastern Peru.

Religion The strength and cultural richness of Candomblé has attracted and inspired a number of perceptive western authors, several of whom were converted. *Orixás*, by Pierre Fatumbi Verger, is a photo book comparing the Brazilian and African religions. *The African Religions of Brazil* (John Hopkins, 1978), by the well-known French anthropologist Roger Bastide, is a scholarly look at the social forces that shaped Candomblé. Ruth Landes' *The City of Women* is about Candomblé in Bahia. For a quick overview in Portuguese, dip into *ABC do Candomblé* by Vasconcelos Maia. Edison Carneiro, a famous student of Candomblé, has written about the subject in *Candomblé da Bahia*. For light reading, try Jorge Amado's novel *Dona Flor and Her Two Husbands*, which is available in English translation.

Other Books Florestan Fernandes' *The Negro in Brazilian Society* was one of the first books to challenge the myth of racial democracy. Thomas Skidmore's *Black into White: Race & Nationality in Brazilian Thought* is an intellectual history of the racial issue.

Carolina Maria de Jesus lived and wrote in the slums of São Paulo. Her book *Child of the Dark* (NAL, 1965) is strong and compelling. It was published in the UK and Australia under the title *Beyond All Pity*. In *The Myth of Marginality: Urban Politics & Poverty in Rio de Janeiro* (University of California Press, 1976) Janice Perlman debunks some of the myths about life in the favelas.

FILMS

English Most movies in the cinemas are screened in their original language with Portuguese subtitles. Brazil gets most of the hits from the USA, including many of the violent Rambo-type films, at around the same time they're released in Europe, or six months or so after US release. Brazilians adore comedians like Woody Allen and the Marx Brothers, though the dubbing of the latter's films raises sometimes hilarious problems with the puns.

Portuguese From the romanticism of *Black Orpheus* to the realism of *Cinema Novo* and Glauber Rocha, Brazil has produced a number of excellent films.

Since the end of the dictatorship there has been a film renaissance. *Pixote*, Hector Babenco's compelling film about young street urchins, won the best film award at Cannes. Many recent Brazilian films are historical, providing special insight into the country.

Carlota Joaquina – Princesa de Brasil (1994), the first film directed by Brazilian actress Carla Camurut, is an hilarious blend of fairytale, satire and historical drama about a Spanish princess married to the Portuguese prince regent (later to become Dom João VI) when the entire Portuguese court fled to Brazil to escape Napoleon.

Rio has many film aficionados and special events. The Cineclub Botafogo is always a good venue. There are special events like the annual film festival in September, and cinema on the beach at Copacabana in the summer. Other film festivals include the Brazilian Film Festival, held in Gramado, Rio Grande do Sul, in August.

NEWSPAPERS & MAGAZINES

Brazil's media industry is concentrated in the hands of a few organisations. The companies that own the two major TV stations, O Globo and Manchete, also control several of the nation's leading newspapers and magazines.

English Rio de Janeiro, São Paulo and Brasília have two daily English newspapers. Both are pricey, about US$2.50 to $3.50 per copy. The best by far is the Latin American edition of the *Miami Herald*, now printed in São Paulo. It isn't cheap, but it's comprehensive and has excellent coverage of Latin America and the American sport scene.

The *International Herald Tribune*, which is also available in other major cities in Brazil, has articles syndicated from the *New York Times* and the *Washington Post*, and far more eurocentric coverage.

Time and *Newsweek* magazines are available throughout Brazil (around US$4 per copy). Their coverage is weak on Latin America and sports. The *Economist* is sold in Rio and São Paulo; it costs about US$6. In the large cities you can find all sorts of imported newspapers and magazines at some newsstands, but they are expensive.

Portuguese *Folha de São Paulo* has slid a bit, but it's still Brazil's finest newspaper. It has excellent coverage of national and international events and has a good guide to entertainment in São Paulo. The Turismo section in the Thursday edition always has a table showing costs of internal flights. It's available in Rio and other major cities.

The *Jornal do Brasil* and *O Globo* are Rio's main daily papers. Both have entertainment listings. *Balcão* is a Rio weekly with only classified advertisements, a good source for buying anything. *O Nacional* is a weekly paper that has some excellent critical columnists. *O Povo* is a popular daily with lots of gory photographs.

The monthly magazine *Viage e Turismo* (R$6) is an excellent source of information, with prices of travel within and from Brazil.

Veja (it means, and is an imitation of, *Time*), is the country's best-selling magazine. It's a good way to practise your Portuguese. *Isto E* has the best political and economic analysis, and reproduces articles from the British *Economist*, but it's not light reading. It also provides good coverage of current events.

Environmental and ecological issues (both national and international) are covered in the glossy monthly magazine, *Terra*. It seems genuine about environmental concerns as well as having some great photos.

Sources of information and literature about Brazilian Indians are given in the Population & People section of the Facts about the Country chapter, and in the Books section of this chapter.

RADIO & TV

English There's precious little English language programming on Brazilian broadcast TV. Major hotels and some bars and restaurants have satellite television, which carry (at the very least) CNN and sometimes other programmes from the USA, including HBO and sports channels.

Portuguese Many of the worst American movies and TV shows are dubbed into Portuguese and shown on Brazilian TV. Brazil's most famous TV hosts, who have to be seen to be believed, are Xuxa, the queen of kiddy titillation, and Faustão. Both are strong statements on the evil of TV. Both are on the tube for countless hours.

Xuxa, living proof that Freud had it right about children's sexuality, has coquettishly danced and sung her way into the hearts of tiny Brazilians everywhere. Her bubblegum pop albums routinely enter the Brazilian top 10, but she doesn't export. Faustão hosts *Domingão de Faustão*, a seemingly endless bump'n'grind variety show on Sunday afternoon.

Sunday night, *Fantastico* is a three hour tabloid news show that lets it all hang out; afterwards, *Sai de Baixo* is a comedy programme. Also on Sunday are highlights of soccer matches played that day.

The most popular programmes on Brazilian TV are the *novelas* (soap operas), followed religiously by many Brazilians. Several programmes have had successful runs on European and Australian TV. The novelas are aired at various times from 6 to 9 pm.

The news is on several times a night but broadcast times vary from place to place. O Globo and Manchete, the two principal national networks, both have pedestrian national news shows. *Aqui Agora* (Here Now) is a sensational news show on SBT that is worth a look, even if you don't understand Portuguese.

Cable TV is making surprising inroads into Brazil bringing the glitz and glamour of programmes like ESPN (the sports network), CNN, RAI (Radio Televisione Italia), and of course, MTV, as well as ads for luxury products to the screens of those who can afford it. Most Brazilian viewers, though, can only afford to consume the images.

PHOTOGRAPHY & VIDEO

Film

You can only get slide film developed in the big cities and it's expensive to buy (around US$20-25 a roll). If you're shooting slides it's best to bring film with you and have it processed back home.

Heat and humidity can ruin film, so remember to keep it in the coolest, driest place available. Use a lead film bag to protect film from airport x-ray machines. This is especially important for the sensitive high-ASA films.

If you must get your film processed in Brazil, have it done at a large lab in Rio or São Paulo. In Rio, Technica Miyazaki (☎ 522-4894), Rua Djalma Ulrich 110, shop 214 in Copacabana (enter through Avenida NS de Copacabana 1063) is recommended for camera repairs.

Equipment

Cameras are expensive and cumbersome objects. They will certainly suffer on the road and they may get broken, lost or stolen. But there are so many good shots out there that you'll kick yourself if you don't bring one along.

Your choice of camera will depend on your photographic requirements. Automatic 35mm rangefinders will suffice for standard portraits and landscapes. But if you want to take general wildlife shots, a 200mm or 300mm zoom lens is essential. A 400mm or 500mm telephoto with a fixed focal length lens is preferred by photographers who are after close-up shots of wildlife.

If you're staying in Rio or another large city and you're nervous about bringing your expensive camera, pick up a readily available disposable camera when you're here.

Useful accessories would include a small flash, a cable release, a polarising filter, a lens-cleaning kit (fluid, tissue and aerosol), plenty of silica-gel packs, and a bean bag or clamp ormonopod. Don't carry a flashy camera bag – use something less likely to attract the attention of thieves; and make sure your equipment is insured.

Photographic equipment and accessories are expensive and you'd be well advised to buy your film and equipment before arrival. However, Kodak and Fuji print film are sold and processed almost everywhere.

Photography

Photography in the rainforest requires careful consideration of the lack of light. You'll have to experiment with a combination of fast film (400 ASA and upwards), a tripod, flash unit, and cable release. When exposed to the humid conditions of the forest for an extended period of time, your cameras and lenses may have their functioning impaired by fungus growth. The standard preventative measure is to keep your photographic gear sealed in bags together with silica-gel packs. Unseal only for use and reseal everything immediately after each photo session.

If you're shooting on beaches, remember to adjust for the glare from water or sand, and keep sand and saltwater away from your equipment.

It's foolish to bring a camera to a beach unless it will be closely guarded – for more advice on camera security see the Dangers & Annoyances section in this chapter.

Video

Brazilian video and television operates on the PAL system. American (NTSC) and French (SECAM) machines and pre-recorded tapes won't play on Brazilian machines and vice versa.

Video cameras are no longer a big deal in Brazil so you won't get any weird stares as you shoot. Some churches charge special admission for video camera operators. Properly used, a video camera can give a fascinating record of your holiday. Often the most interesting things occur when you're actually intent on filming something else.

One good rule to follow for beginners is to try to film in long takes, and don't move the camera around too much. If your camera has a stabiliser, you can use it to obtain good footage while travelling on various means of transport, even on bumpy roads. And remember, you're travelling – don't let the video take over your life and turn your trip into a Cecil B De Mille production.

Finally, remember to follow the same rules regarding people's sensitivities as for a still photography – having a video camera shoved in their face is probably even more annoying and offensive for locals than a still camera. Always ask permission first.

Restrictions

Avoid taking photographs or video in banks or near military bases or other sensitive areas.

Photographing People

Some Candomblé temples do not permit photography. Respect the wishes of the locals and ask permission before taking a photo of them.

Airport Security

The major cities have modern x-ray equipment, which should be safe for most lower speed films, but it's best to use a lead film bag or request a hand search of your camera bag to protect film from airport x-ray machines. This is especially important for the sensitive high-ASA films.

TIME

Brazil has four official time zones, generally and euphemistically depicted on maps as a neat series of lines. In the real world, these lines are subject to administrative convenience. This means that travellers are subject to the vagaries (and inconvenience) of geodesic demarcation, state boundaries, and the euphemistic term that saves the bacon of all officials – *acidentes geográficos* (geographical accidents).

The Brazilian time system rewards unhurried travellers moving short distances – most other travellers have a few tales to tell about connections missed due to temporal ignorance.

Brazilian Standard Time covers the eastern, north-eastern, southern, and south-eastern parts of Brazil, including Brasília, Amapá, Goiás, Tocantins, and a portion of Pará. This zone is 3 hours behind GMT/UTC.

So, barring daylight savings time, when it is noon in Brazil it is: 3 pm in London; 10 am in New York; 7 am in San Francisco; 1 am the next day in Sydney or Melbourne and 11 pm in New Zealand.

Moving westwards, the next time zone covers Roraima, Rondônia, Mato Grosso, Mato Grosso do Sul, part of Pará and all but the far western fringe of Amazonas. This zone is 1 hour behind Brazilian standard time, and 4 hours behind GMT/UTC.

The time zone for the far west covers Acre and the western fringe of Amazonas, which are 2 hours behind Brazilian standard time, and 5 hours behind GMT/UTC.

The island of Fernando de Noronha, far to the east of the Brazilian mainland, has its own time zone, 1 hour ahead of standard Brazilian time, and 2 hours behind GMT/UTC.

Brazilians, by the way, are not noted for their punctuality! Don't be surprised, or angry, if they arrive a couple of hours later than expected. To them it is acceptable, and they always have the most inventive reasons for not arriving on time. If you find yourself arriving late, you might like to blame it on an accident – geographical perhaps?

Four Hours for the Price of Three

Connoisseurs of Brazilian timekeeping will be thrilled to hear that the relationship between time in the rest of the world and within Brazil's time zones, as explained in this chapter, varies. This is because Brazil continues to adopt, in its bizarre fashion, daylight-savings time (which requires clocks to be set one hour ahead in October, and one hour back in March or April), seemingly at will and at random and in sync with no other nation. This creates annual gaps – which can last from one to three weeks – during which it's very difficult to tell if, say, São Paulo is one, two, three or even four hours ahead of, say, New York.

ELECTRICITY

Electrical current is not standardised in Brazil, so it's a good idea to carry a converter if you can't travel without your hair dryer.

In Rio de Janeiro and São Paulo, the current is almost exclusively 110 or 120V, 60Hz AC. Salvador and Manaus have 127V service. Recife, Brasília, Santos and various other cities have 220V service. Check before you plug in.

The most common power points have two round sockets.

WEIGHTS & MEASURES

Brazil uses the metric system. There is a metric conversion table inside the back cover of this book.

The Brazilian system indicates decimals with commas and thousands with points (so a thousand bucks would be written US$1.000,00).

LAUNDRY

Oddly, washing clothes isn't cheap here, at least if you send out. Most Brazilians wash their own clothes or have domestics do it. If you don't wash your own, enquire at your hotel: housekeepers will often wash clothes at home to make a few extra reais. Coin laundries are available in larger cities and generally cost US$3.50 each to wash and to dry.

TOILETS

Brazilians are quite nice about letting you use toilets in restaurant and bars. Public toilets can be found in most cities and towns; there's usually an entrance fee of between US$0.25 and $0.75. There are public toilets at every bus and train station and airport.

HEALTH

Travel health depends on your predeparture preparations, your daily health care while travelling and how you handle any medical problem that develops. While the potential dangers can seem quite frightening, in reality few travellers experience anything more than upset stomachs.

Everyday Health

Normal body temperature is up to 37°C (98.6°F); more than 2°C (4°F) higher indicates a high fever. The normal adult pulse rate is 60 to 100 per minute (children 80 to 100, babies 100 to 140). As a general rule the pulse increases about 20 beats per minute for each 1°C (2°F) rise in fever.

Respiration (breathing) rate is also an indicator of illness. Count the number of breaths per minute: between 12 and 20 is normal for adults and older children (up to 30 for younger children, 40 for babies). People with a high fever or serious respiratory illness breathe more quickly than normal. More than 40 shallow breaths a minute may indicate pneumonia.

Predeparture Planning

Immunisations Plan ahead for getting your vaccinations: some of them require more than one injection, while some vaccinations should not be given in combination. It is recommended you seek medical advice at least six weeks before travel.

Record all vaccinations on an International Health Certificate, available from your doctor or government health department.

Discuss your requirements with your doctor, but vaccinations you should consider for this trip include:

Diphtheria & Tetanus Diphtheria can be a throat infection and tetanus can be a fatal wound infection. Everyone should have these vaccinations. After an initial course of three injections, boosters are necessary every 10 years.

Hepatitis A The most common travel-acquired illness after diarrhoea, hepatitis A can put you out of action for weeks. Havrix 1440 is a vaccination that provides long term immunity (possibly more than 10 years) after an initial injection and a booster at six to 12 months. Gamma globulin is not a vaccination but is ready-made antibody collected from blood donations. It should be given close to departure because, depending on the dose, it only protects for two to six months.

A combined hepatitis A and hepatitis B vaccination, Twinrix, is also available. This combined vaccination is recommended for people wanting protection against both types of viral hepatitis. Three injections over a six month period are required.

Hepatitis B This disease is spread by blood or by sexual activity. Travellers who should consider a hepatitis B vaccination include those visiting countries where there are known to be many carriers, where blood transfusions may not be adequately screened, or where sexual contact is a possibility. It involves three injections, the quickest course being over three weeks with a booster at 12 months.

Meningococcal Meningitis Healthy people carry this disease; it is transmitted like a cold and you can die from it within a few hours. There are many carriers and vaccination is recommended for travellers to Brazil. A single injection will give good protection for three years. The vaccine is not recommended for children under two years because they do not develop satisfactory immunity from it.

Polio Polio is a serious, easily transmitted disease. Everyone should keep up to date with this vaccination. A booster every 10 years maintains immunity.

Rabies Vaccination should be considered by those who will spend a month or longer in a country where rabies is common, especially if they are cycling, handling animals, caving, travelling to remote areas, or for children (who may not report a bite). Pretravel rabies vaccination involves having three injections over 21 to 28 days. If someone who has been vaccinated is bitten or scratched by an animal they will require two booster injections of vaccine, those not vaccinated require more.

Tuberculosis TB risk to travellers is usually very low. For those who will be living with or closely associated with local people in Brazil there is some risk. As most healthy adults do not develop symptoms, a skin test before and after travel to determine whether exposure has occurred may be considered. A vaccination is recommended for children living in these areas for three months or more.

Typhoid This is an important vaccination to have where hygiene is a problem. Available either as an injection or oral capsules.

Yellow Fever Protection lasts 10 years and is recommended for all travel to South America. The states of Acre, Amapá, Amazonas, Goiás, Maranhão, Mato Grosso, Mato Grosso do Sul, Minas Gerais, Pará, Rondônia, Roraima and Tocantins are yellow fever zones. You usually have to go to a special yellow fever vaccination centre. Vaccination poses some risk during pregnancy but if you must travel to a high-risk area it is advisable; also, people allergic to eggs may not be able to have this vaccine. Discuss with your doctor.

Malaria Medication Antimalarial drugs do not prevent you from being infected, but kill the malaria parasites during a stage in their development and significantly reduce the risk of becoming very ill or dying. Expert advice on medication should be sought, as there are many factors to consider including the area to be visited (malaria is endemic in large sections of Brazil but not in others, so check the latest available information), the risk of exposure to malaria-carrying mosquitoes, the side effects of medication, your medical history and whether you are an adult or child or pregnant. Travellers going to isolated areas in high-risk countries might like to carry a treatment dose of medication for use if symptoms occur.

Medical Kit Check List Consider taking a basic medical kit including:

- Aspirin or paracetamol (acetaminophen in the US) – for pain or fever.
- Antihistamine (such as Benadryl) – useful as a decongestant for colds and allergies, to ease the itch from insect bites or stings, and to help prevent motion sickness. Antihistamines may cause sedation and interact with alcohol so care should be taken when using them; take one you know and have used before, if possible.
- Antibiotics – useful if you're travelling well off the beaten track, but they must be prescribed. Carry the prescription with you.
- Loperamide (eg Imodium) or Lomotil for diarrhoea; prochlorperazine (eg Stemetil) or metaclopramide (eg Maxalon) for nausea and vomiting.
- Rehydration mixture – for treatment of severe diarrhoea; particularly important for travelling with children.
- Antiseptic such as povidone-iodine (eg Betadine) – for cuts and grazes.
- Multivitamins – especially for long trips when dietary vitamin intake may be inadequate
- Calamine lotion or aluminium sulphate spray (eg Stingose) – to ease irritation from bites or stings.
- Bandages and Band-Aids.
- Scissors, tweezers and a thermometer (note that mercury thermometers are prohibited by airlines).
- Cold and flu tablets and throat lozenges. Pseudoephedrine hydrochloride (Sudafed) might be useful if flying with a cold to avoid ear damage.
- Insect repellent, sunscreen, lip balm and water purification tablets.
- A couple of syringes, in case you need injections in an area with medical hygiene problems. Ask your doctor for a note explaining why they have been prescribed.

Health Insurance Make sure that you have adequate health insurance. See Travel Insurance in the Visas & Documents section earlier in this chapter.

Travel Health Guides If you are planning to be away or travelling in remote areas for a long period of time, you may like to consider taking a more detailed health guide.

Staying Healthy in Asia, Africa & Latin America by Dirk Schroeder (Moon Publications, 1994) – probably the best all-round guide to carry; it's compact, detailed and well organised.

Travellers' Health by Dr Richard Dawood (Oxford University Press, 1995) – comprehensive, easy to read, authoritative and highly recommended, although it's rather large to lug around.

Where There is No Doctor by David Werner (Macmillan, 1994) – a very detailed guide intended for someone, such as a Peace Corps worker, going to work in an underdeveloped country.

Travel with Children by Maureen Wheeler (Lonely Planet Publications, 1995) – includes advice on travel health for younger children.

There are also a number of excellent travel health sites on the Internet. You can choose from the Lonely Planet home page (www.lonelyplanet.com.au/weblinks/wlprep.htm#hea) to the World Health Organization, the US Center for Diseases Control & Prevention and Stanford University Travel Medicine Service.

Other Preparations Make sure you're healthy before you start travelling. If you are going on a long trip make sure your teeth are OK. If you wear glasses take a spare pair as well as your prescription.

If you require a particular medication, make sure that you take an adequate supply, as it may not be available locally. Take part of the packaging showing the generic name of the drug, rather than the brand, which will make getting replacements easier. It's a good idea to have a legible prescription or letter from your doctor to show that you legally use the medication to avoid any problems.

Basic Rules

Food There is an old colonial adage that goes: 'If you can cook it, boil it or peel it you can eat it … otherwise forget it'. Vegetables and fruit should be washed with purified water or peeled where possible. Beware of ice cream that is sold in the street or anywhere it might have been melted and refrozen; if there's any doubt (eg a power cut in the last day or two) steer well clear. Shellfish such as mussels, oysters and clams should be avoided, as well as undercooked meat, particularly in the form of mince (ground) meat. Steaming does not make shellfish safe for eating.

If a place looks clean and well run and the vendor also looks clean and healthy, then the food is probably safe. In general, places that are packed with travellers or locals will be fine, while empty restaurants are questionable. The food in busy restaurants is cooked and eaten quite quickly with little standing around and is probably not reheated.

Water The number-one rule is *be careful of the water* and especially ice. If you don't know for certain that the water is safe assume the worst. Reputable brands of bottled water or soft drinks are generally fine, although in some places bottles may be refilled with tap water. Only use water from containers with a serrated seal – not tops or corks. Take care with fruit juice, particularly if water may have been added. Milk should be treated with suspicion as it is often unpasteurised, though boiled milk is fine if it is kept hygienically. Tea or coffee should also be OK, since the water should have been boiled.

Water Purification The simplest way of purifying water is to boil it thoroughly. Vigorously boiling should be satisfactory; however, at high altitude water boils at a lower temperature, so germs are less likely to be killed. Boil it for longer in these environments.

Consider purchasing a water filter for a long trip. There are two main kinds of filter. Total filters take out all parasites, bacteria and viruses, and make water safe to drink. They are often expensive, but they can be more cost effective than buying bottled water. Simple filters (which can even be a nylon mesh bag) take out dirt and larger foreign bodies from the water so that chemical solutions work much more effectively; if water is dirty, chemical solutions may not work at all.

It's very important when buying a filter to read the specifications, so that you know exactly what it removes from the water and what it doesn't. Simple filtering will not remove all dangerous organisms, so if you cannot boil water it should be treated with chemicals.

Chlorine tablets (Puritabs, Steritabs or other brand names) will kill many pathogens, but not some parasites like giardia and amoebic cysts. Iodine is more effective in purifying water and is available in tablet form (such as Potable Aqua). Follow the directions carefully and remember that too much iodine can be harmful.

Medical Problems & Treatment

Self-diagnosis and treatment can be risky, so you should always seek medical help. Although we do give drug dosages in this section, they are for emergency use only. Correct diagnosis is vital.

An embassy, consulate or five-star hotel can usually recommend a good place to go for advice. In some places standards of medical attention are so low that for some ailments the best advice is to get on a plane and go somewhere else.

Antibiotics should ideally be administered only under medical supervision. Take only the recommended dose at the prescribed intervals and use the whole course, even if the illness seems to be cured earlier. Stop immediately if there are any serious reactions and don't take at all if you are unsure that it is the correct one. If you are allergic to commonly prescribed antibiotics such as penicillin or sulpha drugs, carry this information (eg on a bracelet).

Environmental Hazards

Fungal Infections Fungal infections occur more commonly in hot weather and are usually found on the scalp, between the toes or fingers, in the groin and on the body (ringworm). You get ringworm (which is a fungal infection, not a worm) from infected animals or other people. Moisture encourages these infections.

To prevent fungal infections wear loose, comfortable clothes, avoid artificial fibres, wash frequently and dry carefully. If you do get an infection, wash the infected area at least daily with a disinfectant or medicated soap and water, and rinse and dry well. Apply an antifungal cream or powder like tolnifate (Tinaderm). Try to expose the infected area to air or sunlight as much as possible and wash all towels and underwear in hot water, change them often and let them dry in the sun.

Heat Exhaustion Dehydration and salt deficiency can cause heat exhaustion. Take time to acclimatise to high temperatures, drink sufficient liquids and do not do anything too physically demanding.

Salt deficiency is characterised by fatigue, lethargy, headaches, giddiness and muscle cramps; salt tablets may help, but adding extra salt to your food is better. Gatorade and other sports drinks are a widely available (but expensive) alternative to salt tablets.

Heatstroke This serious, and occasionally fatal condition can occur if the body's heat-regulating mechanism breaks down and the body temperature rises to dangerous levels. Long, continuous periods of exposure to high temperatures and insufficient fluids can leave you vulnerable to heatstroke.

The symptoms are feeling unwell, not sweating very much (or at all) and a high body temperature (39 to 41°C or 102 to 106°F). Where sweating has ceased the skin becomes flushed and red. Severe, throbbing headaches and lack of coordination will also occur, and the sufferer may become confused or aggressive. Eventually the victim will become delirious or convulse. Hospitalisation is essential, but in the interim get victims out of the sun, remove their clothing, cover them with a wet sheet or towel and then fan continually. Give fluids if they are conscious.

Jet Lag Jet lag is experienced when a person travels by air across more than three time zones (each time zone usually represents a one-hour time difference). It occurs because many of the functions of the human body (such as temperature, pulse rate and emptying of the bladder and bowels) are regulated by internal 24 hour cycles. When we travel long distances rapidly, our bodies take time to adjust to the 'new time' of our destination, and we may experience fatigue, impaired concentration disorientation, anxiety, insomnia, and loss of appetite. These effects will usually be gone within three days of arrival, but try to minimise the impact of jet lag by following these hints.

- Rest for a couple of days prior to departure
- Try to select flight schedules that minimise sleep deprivation; arriving late in the day means you can go to sleep soon after you arrive. For very long flights, try to organise a stopover.
- Avoid excessive eating (which bloats the stomach) and alcohol (which causes dehydration) during the flight. Instead, drink plenty of non-carbonated, non-alcoholic drinks such as fruit juice or water.
- Avoid smoking
- Make yourself comfortable by wearing loose-fitting clothes and perhaps bringing an eye mask and ear plugs to help you sleep.
- Try to sleep at the appropriate time for the time zone you are travelling to.

Motion Sickness Eating lightly before and during a trip will reduce the chances of motion sickness. If you are prone to motion sickness try to find a place that minimises movement – near the wing on aircraft, close to midships on boats, near the centre on buses. Fresh air usually helps; reading and cigarette smoke don't. Commercial motion-sickness preparations, which can cause drowsiness, have to be taken before the trip commences. Ginger (available in capsule form) and peppermint (including mint-flavoured sweets) are natural preventatives.

Prickly Heat Prickly heat is an itchy rash caused by excessive perspiration trapped under the skin. It usually strikes people who have just arrived in a hot climate. Keeping cool, bathing often, drying the skin and using a mild talcum or prickly heat powder or resorting to air-conditioning may help.

Sunburn You can get sunburnt surprisingly quickly, even through cloud. Use a sunscreen, hat, and barrier cream for your nose and lips. Calamine lotion or Stingose are good for mild sunburn. Protect your eyes with good quality sunglasses.

Infectious Diseases

Cholera This is the worst of the watery diarrhoeas and medical help should be sought. Outbreaks of cholera are generally widely reported, so you can avoid such problem areas. *Fluid replacement is the most vital treatment* – the risk of dehydration is severe as you may lose up to 20L a day. If there is a delay in getting to hospital, start taking tetracycline. The adult dose is 250mg four times daily. It is not recommended for children under nine years, nor for pregnant women. Tetracycline may help shorten the illness, but adequate fluids are required to save lives.

Diarrhoea Simple things like a change of water, food or climate can all cause a mild bout of diarrhoea, but a few rushed toilet trips with no other symptoms is not indicative of a major problem.

Dehydration is the main danger with any diarrhoea, particularly in children or the elderly as dehydration can occur quickly. Under all circumstances *fluid replacement* (at least equal to the volume being lost) is the most important thing to remember. Weak black tea with a little sugar, soda water, or soft drinks allowed to go flat and diluted 50% with clean water are all good.

In cases of severe diarrhoea, a rehydrating solution is preferable to replace minerals and salts lost. Commercially available oral rehydration salts (ORS) are very useful; add them to boiled or bottled water. In an emergency you can make up a solution of six teaspoons of sugar and a half teaspoon of salt dissolved in a litre of boiled or bottled water.

You need to drink at least the same volume of fluid that you are losing in bowel movements and vomiting. Urine is the best guide to the adequacy of replacement – if you have small amounts of concentrated urine, you need to increase fluid intake. Keep drinking small amounts often. Stick to a bland diet as you recover.

Lomotil or Imodium can be used to bring relief from the symptoms, although they do not actually cure the problem. Only use these drugs if you do not have access to toilets (eg if you *must* travel). For children under 12 years, Lomotil and Imodium are not recommended. Do not use these drugs if the person has a high fever or is severely dehydrated.

In certain situations antibiotics may be required: diarrhoea with blood or mucous (dysentery), any fever, watery diarrhoea with fever and lethargy, persistent diarrhoea not improving after 48 hours and severe diarrhoea. In these situations gut-paralysing drugs like Imodium or Lomotil should be avoided.

A stool test is necessary to diagnose which kind of dysentery you have, so you should seek medical help urgently. Where this is not possible the recommended drugs for dysentery are norfloxacin 400mg twice daily for three days, or ciprofloxacin 500mg twice daily for five days. These are not recommended for children or pregnant women. The drug of choice for children would be co-trimoxazole (Bactrim, Septrin, Resprim) with dosage dependent on weight. A five day course is given. Ampicillin or amoxycillin may be given in pregnancy, but medical care is necessary.

The onset of amoebic dysentery is more gradual; fever may not be present. It will persist until treated and can recur and cause other health problems.

Giardiasis is another type of diarrhoea. The parasite causing this intestinal disorder is present in contaminated water. The symptoms are stomach cramps, nausea, a bloated stomach, watery, foul-smelling diarrhoea and frequent gas. Giardiasis can appear several weeks after you have been exposed to the parasite. The symptoms may disappear for a few days and then return; this can go on for several weeks. Tinidazole, known as Fasigyn, or metronidazole (Flagyl) are the recommended drugs. Treatment is a 2g single dose of Fasigyn or 250mg of Flagyl three times daily for 5 to 10 days.

Hepatitis Hepatitis is a general term for inflammation of the liver. It is a common disease worldwide. The symptoms are fever, chills, headache, fatigue, feelings of weakness and aches and pains, followed by loss of appetite, nausea, vomiting, abdominal pain, dark urine, light-coloured faeces, jaundiced (yellow) skin and the whites of the eyes may turn yellow.

Hepatitis A is transmitted by contaminated food and drinking water. You should seek medical advice, but there is not much you can do apart from resting, drinking lots of fluids, eating lightly and avoiding fatty foods. People who have had hepatitis should avoid alcohol for some time after the illness, as the liver needs time to recover.

Hepatitis E is transmitted in the same way, it can be very serious in pregnant women.

There are almost 300 million chronic carriers of hepatitis B in the world. It is spread through contact with infected blood, blood products or body fluids, for example through sexual contact, unsterilised needles and blood transfusions, or contact with blood via small breaks in the skin. Other risk situations include having a shave, tattoo, or having your body pierced with contaminated equipment. The symptoms of type B may be more severe and may lead to long-term problems.

Hepatitis D is spread in the same way, but the risk is mainly in shared needles.

Hepatitis C can lead to chronic liver disease. The virus is spread by contact with blood, usually via contaminated transfusions or shared needles. Avoiding these is the only means of prevention.

HIV & AIDS HIV, the Human Immunodeficiency Virus, develops into AIDS, Acquired Immune Deficiency Syndrome, which is a fatal disease. HIV is a major problem in many countries, and Brazil has one of the highest rates of infection in the world. Increasingly, AIDS in Brazil is spread through hetrosexual contact.

Any exposure to blood, blood products or body fluids may put the individual at risk. The disease is often transmitted through sexual contact or dirty needles – vaccinations, acupuncture, tattooing and body piercing can be potentially as dangerous as intravenous drug use. HIV/AIDS can also be spread through infected blood transfusions; some developing countries cannot afford to screen blood used for transfusions.

If you do need an injection, ask to see the syringe unwrapped in front of you, or take a needle and syringe pack with you. Fear of HIV infection should never preclude treatment for serious medical conditions.

Intestinal Worms These parasites are most common in rural, tropical areas. The different worms have different ways of infecting people. Some may be ingested on food, including undercooked meat, and some enter through your skin. Infestations may not show up for some time, and although they are generally not serious, if left untreated some can cause severe health problems later. Consider having a stool test when you return home to check for these and determine the appropriate treatment.

Meningococcal Meningitis This very serious disease attacks the brain and can be fatal. There are recurring epidemics in the Amazon area in Brazil.

A fever, severe headache, sensitivity to light and neck stiffness that prevents forward bending of the head are the first symptoms. There may also be purple patches on the skin. Death can occur within a few hours, so urgent medical treatment is required.

Treatment is large doses of penicillin given intravenously, or chloramphenicol injections.

Sexually Transmitted Diseases Herpes, gonorrhoea, and syphilis are among these diseases; sores, blisters or rashes around the genitals, discharges or pain when urinating are common symptoms. In some STDs, such as wart virus or chlamydia, symptoms may be less marked or not observed at all especially in women. The symptoms of syphilis eventually disappear but the disease continues and can cause severe problems later. While abstinence from sexual contact is the only 100% effective prevention, using condoms is also effective. Antibiotics are used to treat gonorrhoea and syphilis. The different sexually transmitted diseases each require specific antibiotics. There is no cure for herpes or AIDS.

Tuberculosis (TB) TB is a bacterial infection usually transmitted by coughing, but may also be transmitted through consumption of unpasteurised milk. Milk that has been boiled is safe to drink, and the souring of milk to make yoghurt or cheese also kills the bacilli. Travellers are usually not at great risk as close household contact with the infected person is usually required before the disease is passed on.

Typhoid Typhoid is a dangerous gut infection caused by contaminated water and food. Medical help must be sought.

In its early stages sufferers may feel they have a bad cold or flu on the way, as early symptoms are a headache, body aches and a fever that rises a little each day until it is around 40°C (104°F) or more. The victim's pulse is often slow relative to the degree of fever present – unlike a normal fever where the pulse increases. There may also be abdominal pain, vomiting, constipation, or diarrhoea.

In the second week the high fever and slow pulse continue and some pink spots

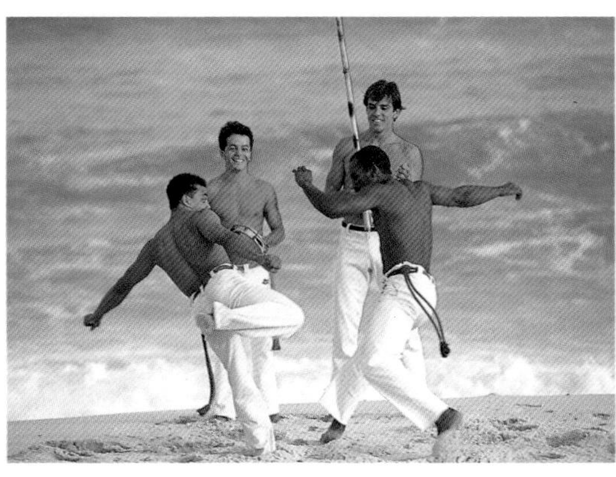

ALL PHOTOS BY JOHN MAIER, JR

A	B
C	D
E	F

A: Aerobics on a Rio beach
B: Beach futvolei
C: Train surfer
D: Waterfall slide
E: Martial art/dance, Capoeira
F: Fitness station on Copacabana beach

ALL PHOTOS BY JOHN MAIER, JR

The Rio Carnaval

may appear on the body; trembling, delirium, weakness, weight loss and dehydration may also occur. Meningitis, perforated bowel, or pneumonia may develop.

The fever should be treated by keeping the victim cool and giving them fluids as dehydration should also be watched for. A 750mg dose of Ciprofloxacin twice a day for 10 days is good for adults.

Chloramphenicol is recommended in many countries. The adult dosage is two 250mg capsules, four times a day. Children aged between eight and 12 years should have half the adult dose; and younger children one-third the adult dose.

Insect-Borne Diseases

Travellers are advised to prevent mosquito bites at all times. The main precautions are:

- wear light coloured clothing
- wear long pants and long sleeved shirts
- use mosquito repellents containing DEET on exposed areas of skin (prolonged overuse of DEET may be harmful, especially to children, but its use is considered preferable to being bitten by infected mosquitoes)
- avoid highly scented perfumes or aftershave
- use a mosquito net impregnated with mosquito repellent (permethrin) – it may be worth taking your own
- impregnating clothes with permethrin effectively deters mosquitoes and other insects

Malaria This serious and potentially fatal disease is spread by mosquito bites. If you are travelling in malaria-infected areas it is extremely important to avoid mosquito bites and to take tablets to prevent this disease. Symptoms range from fever, chills and sweating, abdominal pains, headache, diarrhoea and a vague feeling of ill-health. Seek medical help immediately if malaria is suspected. Untreated malaria can rapidly become more serious and can be fatal.

If medical care is not available, malaria tablets can be used for treatment. You need to use a different malaria tablet to the one you were taking when you contracted malaria. The treatment dosages are mefloquine (two 250mg tablets and a further two six hours later), fansidar (single dose of three tablets). If you were previously taking mefloquine then other alternatives are halofantrine (three doses of two 250mg tablets every six hours) or quinine sulphate (600mg every six hours). There is a greater risk of side-effects with these dosages than in normal use.

Yellow Fever This viral disease is also transmitted by mosquitoes. The initial symptoms are headache, fever, abdominal pain, and vomiting. Seek medical attention urgently and drink lots of fluids.

Typhus Typhus is spread by ticks, mites or lice. It begins with fever, chills, headache

Nutrition

If your food is poor or limited in availability, if you're travelling hard and fast and therefore missing meals, or if you simply lose your appetite, you can soon start to lose weight and place your health at risk.

Make sure your diet is well balanced. Cooked eggs, tofu, beans, lentils and nuts are all safe ways to get protein. Fruit you can peel (bananas, oranges or mandarins for example) is usually safe (though melons can harbour bacteria in their flesh and are best avoided) and a good source of vitamins. Try to eat plenty of grains (including rice) and bread. Remember that although food is generally safer if it is cooked well, overcooked food loses much of its nutritional value. If your diet isn't well balanced or if your food intake is insufficient, it's a good idea to take vitamin and iron pills. Make sure you drink enough – don't rely on feeling thirsty to indicate when you should drink. Not needing to urinate or small amounts of very dark yellow urine are danger signs. Always carry a water bottle with you on long trips. Excessive sweating can lead to loss of salt and therefore muscle cramping. Salt tablets are not a good idea as a preventative, but in places where salt is not used much adding salt to food can help.

and muscle pains followed a few days later by a body rash. There is often a large painful sore at the site of the bite and nearby lymph nodes are swollen and painful. Typhus can be treated under medical supervision. Seek local advice on areas where ticks pose a danger and always check your skin (including hair) carefully for ticks after walking in a danger area such as a tropical forest. A strong insect repellent can help, and serious walkers in tick areas should consider having their boots and trousers impregnated with benzyl benzoate and dibutylphthalate.

Dengue Fever There is no preventative drug available for this mosquito-spread disease, which can be fatal in children. A sudden onset of fever, headaches and severe joint and muscle pains are the first signs before a rash develops. Recovery may be protracted.

Chagas' Disease In remote rural areas of Brazil, this parasitic disease is transmitted by a bug that hides in crevices in the walls and thatched roofs of mud huts and on palm fronds. It bites at night and a hard, violet-coloured swelling appears in about a week. Chagas' disease can be treated in its early stages, but when untreated infection can led to death some years later.

Filariasis This is a mosquito-transmitted parasitic infection. Possible symptoms include fever, pain and swelling of the lymph glands; inflammation of lymph glands; swelling of a limb or the scrotum; skin rashes and blindness. Treatment is available to eliminate the parasites from the body, but some of the damage may not be reversible. Medical advice should be obtained promptly if the infection is suspected.

Leishmaniasis A group of parasitic diseases transmitted by sandfly bites, occurring in many parts of Brazil. Cutaneous leishmaniasis affects the skin, causing ulceration and disfigurement and visceral leishmaniasis affects the internal organs. Seek medical advice as laboratory testing is required for diagnosis and correct treatment. Avoiding sandfly bites is the best precaution. Bites are usually painless, itchy and yet another reason to cover up and apply repellent.

Schistosomiasis Also known as bilharzia, this disease is carried in water by minute worms. They infect certain varieties of freshwater snails found in rivers, streams, lakes and particularly behind dams. The worms multiply and are eventually discharged into the water.

The worm enters through the skin and attaches itself to your intestines or bladder. The first symptom may be a tingling and sometimes a light rash around the area where it entered. Weeks later a high fever may develop. A general feeling of being unwell may be the first symptom, or there may be no symptoms. Once the disease is established abdominal pain and blood in the urine are other signs. The infection often causes no symptoms until the disease is well established (months to years after exposure) and damage to internal organs is irreversible.

Avoiding swimming or bathing in fresh water where bilharzia is present is the main method of preventing the disease. Even deep water can be infected. If you do get wet, dry off quickly and dry your clothes as well.

A blood test is the most reliable test, but the test will not show positive in results until a number of weeks after exposure.

Cuts, Bites & Stings

Bedbugs & Lice Bedbugs live in various places, but particularly in dirty mattresses and bedding, indicated by spots of blood on bedclothes or on the wall. Bedbugs leave itchy bites in neat rows. Calamine lotion or Stingose spray may help the itch.

All lice cause itching and discomfort. They make themselves at home in your hair (head lice), your clothing (body lice) or in your pubic hair (crabs). You catch lice through direct contact with infected people or by sharing combs, clothing and the like.

Powder or shampoo treatment will kill the lice and infected clothing should then be washed in very hot, soapy water and left in the sun to dry.

Rabies Rabies is a fatal viral infection present in many countries. Many animals can be infected (such as dogs, cats, bats and monkeys) and it is their saliva that is infectious. Any bite, scratch or even lick from a warm-blooded, furry animal should be cleaned immediately and thoroughly. Scrub the area with soap and running water, and then apply alcohol or iodine solution. Medical help should be sought promptly to receive a course of injections to prevent the onset of symptoms and death.

Tetanus Tetanus occurs when a wound becomes infected by a germ which lives in soil and in the faeces of horses and other animals. It enters the body via breaks in the skin. All wounds should be cleaned promptly and adequately and an antiseptic cream or solution applied. Use antibiotics if the wound becomes hot, throbs or pus is seen. The first symptom may be discomfort in swallowing, or stiffening of the jaw and neck; this is followed by painful convulsions of the jaw and whole body. The disease can be fatal.

Insect Bites & Stings Bee and wasp stings are usually painful rather than dangerous, however, in people who are allergic to them severe breathing difficulties may occur and require urgent medical care. Calamine lotion or Stingose spray will give relief and ice packs will reduce the pain and swelling.

Cuts & Scratches Wash well and treat any cut with an antiseptic such as povidone-iodine. Where possible avoid bandages and Band-Aids, which can keep wounds wet.

Ticks You should always check all over your body if you have been walking through a potentially tick-infested area, as ticks can cause skin infections and other more serious diseases. If a tick is found, press down around its head with tweezers, grab the head and gently pull upwards. Avoid pulling the rear of the body as this may squeeze the tick's gut contents through the attached mouth parts into the skin, increasing the risk of infection and disease. Smearing chemicals on the tick will not make it let go and is not recommended.

Snakes To minimise your chances of being bitten always wear boots, socks and long trousers when walking through undergrowth where snakes may be present. Don't put your hands into holes and crevices, and be careful when collecting firewood.

Snake bites do not cause instantaneous death and antivenenes are usually available. Immediately wrap the bitten limb tightly, as you would for a sprained ankle, and then attach a splint to immobilise it. Keep the victim still and seek medical help. Applying tourniquets and sucking out the poison are now comprehensively discredited.

If possible, take the dead snake for identification. Don't attempt to catch the snake if there is a possibility of being bitten again.

Women's Health

Gynaecological Problems Sexually transmitted diseases are a major cause of vaginal problems. Symptoms include a smelly discharge, painful intercourse and sometimes a burning sensation when urinating. Male sexual partners must also be treated.

Medical attention should be sought and remember in addition to these diseases HIV or hepatitis B may also be acquired during exposure. Besides abstinence, the best thing is to practise safe sex using condoms.

Use of antibiotics, synthetic underwear, sweating and taking the contraceptive pill can lead to fungal vaginal infections in hot climates. Maintaining good personal hygiene, and loose-fitting clothes and cotton underwear will help to prevent these infections.

Fungal infections, characterised by a rash, itching and a discharge, can be treated with a vinegar or lemon-juice douche, or with yoghurt. Nystatin, miconazole or clotrimazole pessaries or vaginal creams are the usual treatment.

Pregnancy It is not advisable to travel to some places while pregnant because some vaccinations (eg for yellow fever) are not advisable during pregnancy. In addition, certain diseases (eg malaria) are much more serious for the mother and may increase the risk of a stillborn child in pregnancy.

Most miscarriages occur during the first three months of pregnancy. Miscarriage is not uncommon, and can occasionally lead to severe bleeding. The last three months should also be spent within reasonable distance of good medical care. A baby born as early as 24 weeks stands a chance of survival, but only in a good modern hospital.

While pregnant women should avoid all unnecessary medication, vaccinations and malarial prophylactics should still be taken where needed. Additional care should be taken to prevent illness and particular attention should be paid to diet and nutrition. Alcohol and nicotine, for example, should be avoided.

Back Home

Be aware of illness after you return. Take note of odd or persistent symptoms of any kind, get a check-up and remember to give your physician a complete travel history. Most doctors in temperate climes will not suspect unusual tropical diseases. If you have been travelling in malarial areas, have yourself tested for the disease.

WOMEN TRAVELLERS

Attitudes Towards Women

Depending on where they travel in Brazil, women travelling alone will experience a range of responses. In São Paulo, for example, where there are many people of European ancestry, foreign women without travelling companions will scarcely be given a sideways glance. In the more traditional rural areas of the Northeast, where a large percentage of the population is of mixed European, African and Indian origin, blonde-haired and light-skinned women – especially those without male escorts – will certainly arouse curiosity.

Although *machismo* is an undeniable element in the Brazilian social structure, it is manifested less overtly than in Spanish-speaking Latin America. Perhaps because attitudes toward sex and pornography are quite liberal in Brazil, males feel little need to assert their masculinity or prove their prowess in the eyes of peers.

Flirtation – often exaggerated – is a prominent element in Brazilian male/female relations. It goes both ways and is nearly always regarded as amusingly innocent banter; no sense of insult, exploitation – or serious intent – should be assumed.

Safety Precautions

If unwelcome attention is forthcoming, you should be able to stop it by merely expressing disgust or displeasure.

Although most of the country is nearly as safe for women as for men, there are a few caveats that are also likely to apply at home. It's a good idea to keep a low profile in the cities at night and avoid going alone to bars and nightclubs if you'd rather not chance this being misinterpreted.

Similarly, women should not hitch either alone or in groups; and even men or couples should exercise discretion when hitching. Most important, some of the more rough-and-ready areas of the north and west, where there are lots of men but few local women, should be considered off limits to lone female travellers.

What to Wear

Once you've spent an hour in Copacabana or Ipanema, where some women run their errands wearing *fio dental* (the famous skimpy bikini) you'll be aware that in some parts of Brazil, the dress restrictions aren't as strict as in others. What works in Rio will probably not be appropriate in a Northeastern city, or a Piauí backwater. It seems largely a matter of personal taste, but it's still best to blend your clothing in to meet local standards.

GAY & LESBIAN TRAVELLERS

Brazilians are pretty laid back when it comes to most sexual issues, and homosexuality is widely accepted in most larger urban areas. Bisexuality, or at the very least, bisexual sex, is condoned if not winked at. Especially in Rio, Salvador and São Paulo, the gay bars are all-welcome affairs attended by fun loving crowds of heterosexuals, homosexuals and who-gives-a-sexuals – people are far more concerned with dancing and having a good time than determining your sexual preference.

That said, the degree to which you can be out in Brazil varies greatly by region, and in some smaller towns flamboyance is not appreciated.

Organisations

A useful (if commercial) Internet resource is the Rio Gay Guide: ipanema.com/rio/gay/ which lists gay and lesbian friendly hotels and B&Bs in Rio and other areas.

The São Paulo's Gay and Lesbian Centre can be reached on ☎ (011) 221-1900.

The national AIDS helpline can be contacted on ☎ 0800-612-437. There are also AIDS helplines in Rio (☎ (021) 332-0787) and São Paulo (☎ (011) 280-0770).

DISABLED TRAVELLERS

Wheelchair-bound travellers don't have the easiest of times in Brazil, but in the large cities there is a concerted effort to keep people mobile. Problems you'll encounter include immensely crowded public buses. It pays to plan your trip through contact with some of the organisations listed in the next section.

Organisations

There are a number of organisations and tour providers around the world that specialise in the needs of disabled travellers.

In Australia, try *Independent Travellers* (☎ (08) 232 2555; fax (08) 232 6877), 167 Gilles St, Adelaide, SA 5000; and in the UK, *RADAR* (☎ (0171) 250-3222), 250 City Rd, London, or *Mobility International* (☎ (0171) 403-5688).

In the USA, Twin Peaks Press (PO Box 129, Vancouver, WA 98666 (☎ (202) 694-2462, (800) 637-2256) publishes several useful handbooks for disabled travellers, including *Travel for the Disabled* and the *Directory of Travel Agencies for the Disabled*. *Handicapped Travel Newsletter* is a nonprofit publication with good information on travelling around the world and US government legislation. Subscriptions are US$10 annually and can be obtained by writing to PO Drawer 269, Athens, TX 75751 (☎/fax (903) 677-1260). Here are some other useful organisation within the USA:

Access
: PO Box 356, Malverne, NY 11565 (☎ (516) 887-5798) – the Foundation for Accessibility by the Disabled

Info Center for Individuals with Disabilities
: Fort Point Place, 1st Floor, 27-43 Wormwood St, Boston, MA 02210 (☎ (617) 727-5540, TTY 345-9743, (800) 248-3737)

Mobility International USA
: PO Box 3551, Eugene, OR 97403 (☎ /TDD (503) 343-1284; fax (503) 343-6812) – advises disabled travellers on mobility issues, and runs an exchange program

SATH
: 347 5th Ave No 610, New York, NY 10016 (☎ (212) 447-7284) – SATH means Society for the Advancement of Travel for the Handicapped

Moss Rehabilitation Hospital
: 1200 W Tabor Road, Philadelphia, PA 19141-3099 (☎ (215) 456-9600, TTY 456-9602) – offers a travel information service

SENIOR TRAVELLERS

Travellers over 65 years old can expect to receive some discounts at such places as museums and tourist attractions, but nowhere near the level you would at home. In the USA, some national advocacy groups that can help seniors (of any nationality, if you're over 50 years old) in planning their travels are: the American Association of Retired Persons (AARP; ☎ (202) 434-2277, (800) 424-3410), 601 E St NW, Washington, DC 20049; Elderhostel (☎ (617) 426-8056), 75 Federal St, Boston, MA

02110-1941 (for people 55 and older, and their companions; Elderhostel arranges some trips to Brazil); and the National Council of Senior Citizens (☎ (202) 347-8800), 1331 F St NW, Washington, DC 20004.

Grand Circle Travel (☎ (617) 350-7500; fax (617) 350-6206) offers escorted tours and travel information in a variety of formats and distributes a useful free booklet entitled *Going Abroad: 101 Tips for Mature Travelers*. Contact them at 347 Congress St, Boston, MA 02210.

TRAVEL WITH CHILDREN

Brazil's no more easy or difficult than most other countries when it comes to travel with children, though it does have the bonus of all that beach! In major cities, kids can be occupied forever with the museums and attractions. Lonely Planet's *Travel With Children* is an essential resource.

USEFUL ORGANISATIONS

One of the most useful sources for visitors to South America is the South American Explorers Club (☎ (607) 277-0488), 126 Indian Creek Rd, Ithaca, NY 14850, USA. This club provides services, information and support to mountaineers, scientific researchers, explorers and travellers. It also sells a wide range of books, guides, and maps for South America, and publishes a quarterly journal and a mail-order catalogue. If you're travelling elsewhere in South America, the club maintains clubhouses in Ecuador and Peru. Considering the massive package of benefits offered, membership is quite a bargain.

The Brazilian American Cultural Center (BACC) (☎ (212) 730-0515, (800) 222-2746), 16 W 46th St, New York, NY 10036, USA, is a tourism organisation and travel agency which offers its members discounted flights and tours. It also sells discounted air passes and other air tickets for travel within Brazil. Members also receive a monthly newspaper about Brazil and the Brazilian community in the USA, and can send money to South America using BACC's remittance service. BACC also has offices in Rio de Janeiro (☎ (021) 267-3499) and São Paulo (☎ (011) 231-3100).

DANGERS & ANNOYANCES

Security

Brazil receives a lot of bad international press about its violence and high crime rate. Not surprisingly, most official surveys of foreign visitors to Brazil report that concern about safety and security was one of the major reasons for feeling apprehensive about travelling to Brazil. During both this and our last research trip, all authors felt that Brazil's reputation as a violent nation, especially regarding travellers, is exaggerated.

However, as many readers may not have previously experienced the type and extent of crime evident in Brazil (or other Latin American countries), this section has been written in detail to heighten awareness. While it may go on and on about the types of dangers and annoyances that could happen, this is not a compendium of things that will or even *might* happen to you. It is neither necessary nor helpful to become paranoid.

By using a common-sense approach, there are many things travellers can do to reduce the risks.

Predeparture Precautions

If you work on the elements of vulnerability, you can significantly reduce the risks. For starters, take with you only those items that you are prepared to lose or replace. Travel insurance is essential for replacement of valuables and the cost of a good policy is a worthwhile price to pay for minimum disturbance or even abrupt termination of your travel plans. Loss through petty theft or violence is an emotional and stressful experience which can be reduced if you think ahead – the less you have, the less you can lose.

Don't bring jewellery, chains, or expensive watches, and if you have to wear a watch, use a cheapie worth a few dollars and keep it in your pocket.

Be prepared for the worst – make copies of your important records: a photocopy of the data pages of your passport, visa, tourist card (issued on entry to Brazil), travellers cheque numbers, credit card numbers, airline tickets and essential contact addresses. Keep one copy on your person, one copy with your belongings and exchange one with a travelling companion. Leave one at home, too, with someone you can call to have it all faxed to you.

By law you must carry a passport with you at all times, but many travellers opt to carry a photocopy (preferably certified) while they amble about town, and leave the passport locked up somewhere safe. A passport is worth a lot of money to some people, so keep a close eye on it. If you do lose it, the photocopies described above and a copy of your birth certificate usually speed up the issuing of a new passport at embassies and consulates.

Credit cards are useful in emergencies, for cash advances and for regular purchases. Make sure you know the number to call if you lose your credit card and be quick to cancel it if lost or stolen. New credit card coupons do not have carbon paper inserts and offer more protection against misuse. If you sign an old-style coupon, be sure to ask for the carbon inserts and destroy them after use. Similarly, destroy any coupons that have been filled out incorrectly. These are worthwhile precautions against unwanted duplication of your credit card details.

Security Accessories A thick backpack cover or modified canvas sack improves protection against pilfering, planting of drugs and general wear and tear. Double zippers on your daypack can be secured with safety pins, which reduce the ease of access favoured by petty thieves. A medium-size combination lock or padlock is useful to replace the padlock on your hotel door. Rubber wedges are handy to prevent access to doors or windows. To deter thieves operating with razors, you can line the inside of your daypack (and even your backpack) with lightweight wire mesh.

Don't keep all your valuables together: distribute them about your person and baggage to avoid the risk of losing everything in one fell swoop.

Various types of money belt are available to be worn around the waist, neck or shoulder; and leather or cotton material is more comfortable than synthetics. Such belts are only useful if worn *under* clothing – pouches worn outside clothing are easy prey and attract attention. Determined thieves are wise to conventional money belts, and some travellers now also use cloth pouches sewn into trousers or attached inside with safety pins. Other methods include belts with a concealed zipper compartment; and bandages or pouches worn around the leg. Brazilians wear, with an attitude, a leather or vinyl pouch over a shoulder or on the side of their hip.

If you wear glasses, secure them with an elastic strap to deter petty theft.

Finally, the extra pair of eyes provided by a travelling companion are an obvious asset.

Security Precautions in Brazil

There are certain key things you can do to reduce attention from criminals. Your style of dress should be casual and preferably something that blends in – inexpensive clothes bought in Brazil are an obvious choice.

Most travellers carry a daypack. Whether you're in a bus station, restaurant, shop or elsewhere, whenever you have to put your daypack down, *always* put your foot through the strap. It makes things more difficult for furtive fingers or bag-slashers.

If you have a camera with you, never wander around with it dangling over your shoulder or around your neck – keep it out of sight as much as possible. It's also unwise to keep it in a swanky camera bag, which is an obvious target. We sometimes carried a camera in a sturdy plastic bag from a local supermarket.

Get used to keeping small change and a few banknotes in a shirt pocket so you can pay bus tickets and small expenses without extracting large amounts of money, which could quickly attract attention. This easily accessible money is also useful to rapidly appease a mugger. If you carry a wallet, keep it in your front pocket, and don't use it on public transport or in crowded places where it might attract unwelcome attention.

Before arriving in a new place, make sure you have a map or at least a rough idea of the area's orientation. Try to plan your schedule so you don't arrive at night, and do use a taxi if this seems the appropriate way to avoid walking through high-risk areas. A travelling companion is useful, since solo travellers are more easily distracted. Be observant and learn to look like a street-smart local. Walk purposefully.

Cream A perfect example is the 'cream technique', very common throughout the world, as well as in Brazil. The trick commences when you're walking down the street or standing in a public place, and someone surreptitiously sprays a substance on your shoulder, your daypack or anything else connected with you. The substance can be anything from mustard to chocolate or even dog shit. An assistant (young or old, male or female) then taps you on the shoulder and amicably offers to clean off the mess … if you'll just put down your bag for a second. The moment you do this, someone makes off with it in a flash.

The golden rule is to ignore any such attempt or offer, and simply endure your mucky state until you can find a safe place, such as your hotel, where you can wash. Just a couple of hours after arriving in Rio, we experienced an unsuccessful attempt of this kind.

Diversion Another distraction technique involves people working to divert you or literally throw you off balance. This usually happens when you're standing in the street or somewhere busy like a bus station. One or more characters suddenly ask you a question, bump into you or stage an angry discussion or fight around you, and whilst you are off balance or diverted, there'll be an attempt to pick your pockets or grab your gear. Assume that any and all public brawls, arguments, large acrimonious altercations and other colourful street spectacles are conspiracies designed to rob *you* personally and treat them as such.

Money Changing Never change money on the street; ignore the itinerant money-changers who whisper favourable rates into your ear as you pass; and never follow any of these types into a side street for such a transaction. *Never*.

Drugging There have also been some reportings of druggings. The most disturbing news on this front is the tasteless, odourless drug called Rohypnol (generically Flunitrazepam), aka rophies, roofies or 'the date-rape drug'.

Sold legally in some Latin American countries despite its ban in the USA and Europe, Rohypnol is dissolved into alcoholic drinks by sociopathic scumbags and given to victims, who are soon rendered unconscious. Sedation is so deep that rape victims have been known to have absolutely no memory of any crime. Effects, which can occur as quickly as 15 minutes after ingestion, include dizzyness, disorientation, extreme fatigue and memory loss.

In 1997, Rohypnol manufacturer Hoffman-La Roche released a slow-dissolving, colour-releasing tablet, which turns light liquids blue and dark ones murky, but older tablets and generics can remain in the market.

Exercise *extreme* caution when you are offered cocktails, beer, wine, or even soft drinks, cigarettes, sweets etc. If the circumstances make you suspicious or uneasy, the offer can be tactfully refused by claiming stomach or other medical problems.

In the Northeast, male travellers have reported that 'good-time' ladies at beach bars make friendly advances over spiked drinks. The semi-conscious traveller is then accompanied back to his hotel, where the woman explains that she needs the key to help her 'drunken friend' to his room – where she cleans out all his valuables and then makes a quick exit.

Favourite Scams Distraction, here and throughout the world, is a common tactic employed by street thieves. The scams that are popular in Brazil are the same ones popular in New York and Mexico City. These scams are continually being developed, and imported or exported across borders. Keep abreast of new scams by talking to other travellers.

In our experience, theft and security are sources of endless fascination and stories; some are true, some are incredible, and some are taller than Corcovado! If you think that this section is useful and would like to forewarn others about new developments, we'd appreciate your feedback. You might even derive some consolation from letting off steam, and satisfaction by steering other travellers out of the clutches of criminals.

On the Beach Don't bring anything to city beaches apart from just enough money for lunch and drinks. No camera, no bag and no jewellery. Wear your bathing suit and bring a towel. That's it. If you want to photograph the beach, that's OK, but go with a friend, then return the camera to your room before staying on the beach. Don't hang out on deserted city beaches at night. See the Rio city Dangers & Annoyances section for more tips.

On the Street Thieves watch for people leaving hotels, car-rental agencies, American Express offices, tourist sights – places with lots of foreigners. Then they follow their targets. If you notice you are being followed or closely observed, it helps to pause and look straight at the person(s) involved or, if you're not alone, simply point out the person(s) to your companion. This makes it clear that the element of surprise favoured by petty criminals has been lost.

Don't advertise the fact that you're a foreigner by flashing big bills or wearing jewellery. Keep your watch out of sight in your pocket. Don't carry much money in the streets and even less on the municipal buses. Carry just enough money on your person for the evening's entertainment and transport, and keep it discreetly stashed away in a money belt, money sock, secret pocket or shoe.

Always have enough money on hand to appease a mugger (about US$2 to $5). We've heard about Israeli tourists, fresh from military training, foiling attempted muggers, disarming them and breaking all their fingers, but we do not recommend resistance. There have been other reports of tourists shot dead whilst pursuing muggers – an absurd price to pay for the loss of valuables. Don't carry weapons because in many cases this could make matters much worse. In any case, if you've prepared for your trip along the lines mentioned earlier in this section, you'll probably feel happier just letting the unpleasant event pass.

Buses When you take buses, have your change ready before boarding. You are less of a target once you have passed the turnstile, or if you're standing near the conductor. Avoid the super-crowded buses. If you talk out loud, it's easier for thieves to identify you. If you're carrying valuables, take a taxi.

Long-distance bus travel is usually well organised. If you hand over luggage to be placed in the baggage compartment, make sure you receive and keep your receipt. Two or more items can be padlocked together. We always try to take our pack inside and put it on the overhead luggage racks. If you have to place baggage on the roof, secure it with a padlock.

Taxis Although taxi drivers and their tricks with taxi fares can be irritating (see the Getting Around chapter for more details), taxis currently pose minimal problems with outright theft.

When entering or leaving a taxi, it's advisable (particularly for solo travellers) to keep a passenger door open during the loading or unloading of luggage – particularly if this is being done by someone other than the driver. This reduces the ease with which a taxi can drive off with your luggage, leaving you behind! A neater solution for those who travel light is to fit luggage inside the taxi rather than in the boot.

Also, when entering or leaving a taxi, remember to watch your luggage (slip your foot or arm through a strap). Opportunistic thieves are quick to make off with items while you are distracted by price-haggling or baggage arrangement. If you're travelling as a pair (or larger group), it's a good general precaution to always have at least one person remain close to the open passenger door or inside the taxi whenever luggage is still in the taxi.

Immediately question the presence of any shady characters accompanying the driver, and don't hesitate to take another taxi if you feel uneasy. If there are mechanical or orientation problems en route, do not allow yourself to be separated from your luggage. When you arrive at your destination, *never* hand over your luggage to a person who tries to help you out of the car and offers to carry something, unless you are quite positive about their identity. Otherwise, you may watch your luggage disappearing down the street ('May I take your bags? Thanks!').

Boats Passengers on local boats, particularly in northern Brazil, are the target of thieves who take advantage of crowded conditions, long journeys and unsecured baggage – particularly at night. Before boarding, beware of entrusting your baggage to someone wearing an official uniform who requests to see your ticket and even issues a receipt.

We met a German traveller who had done this in Belém, only to return several hours later to find that the official had been bogus, the padlock for the boat's 'storage room' had belonged to the impostor, and the German's backpack had disappeared.

Once on board, make sure you keep all valuables on your person, never flash your money around, and keep your camera out of sight as much as possible. Double zippers on your baggage should be padlocked and a bicycle padlock or chain is useful to secure your baggage to a fixture on the boat. Some travellers use a large eyelet hook and a rope to suspend baggage from the ceiling next to their hammock. Do not assume that cabins have secure access.

It is important that any baggage you are not carrying on your person is secured to the boat. Thieves prefer to rifle through unsecured and unobserved baggage, extract valuables and then simply dump the evidence (your baggage) overboard. This happened to one of us when a daypack was stolen and dumped overboard during a long Amazon trip. The biggest blow was the loss of dozens of rolls of film and personal effects.

Hotels If you consider your hotel to be reliable, place valuables in its safe and get a receipt. Package your valuables in a small, double-zippered bag that can be padlocked, or use a large envelope with a signed seal that will easily show any tampering. Count your money and travellers cheques before and after retrieving them from the safe – this should quickly identify any attempts to extract single bills or cheques that might otherwise go unnoticed.

Check the door, doorframe, and windows of your room for signs of forced entry or unsecured access. If your hotel provides a padlock, it's recommended to use your own combination lock (or padlock) instead. A hotel padlock obviously increases the number of people with access to your room; and there have been reports of criminals holding up hotel receptionists at gunpoint while an accomplice takes the keys and cleans out the rooms. Don't leave your valuables strewn around the room. It's too much of a temptation to cleaners and other hotel staff.

Banks

Brazilian banks have outdone the Italians in the inconvenient entry department by installing revolving doors that contain metal detectors at their entrances. If you have any threatening metal in your pockets when you attempt to enter a bank – say, a foil-wrapped stick of chewing gum – the doors slam shut with Papillonian finality, and you're required to empty your pockets and bags before being awarded entry. It's a pain, but at least there are fewer guns being brought into banks.

Beggars

A disconcerting aspect of travel in Brazil, particularly in the cities of the Northeast, is the constant presence of beggars. With no social-welfare system to sustain them, the elderly, blind, crippled, mentally ill and jobless take to the streets and try to arouse sympathy in any way they can.

Since giving even a pittance to every beggar encountered will be financially impossible for many visitors, everyone has to formulate their own personal idea about what constitutes an appropriately humanitarian response. Some travellers choose to give to only the most pathetic cases or to those enterprising individuals who provide some value for the money, such as by singing or playing a musical instrument. Others simply feel that contributions only serve to fuel the machine that creates beggars and ignore them.

All we can offer on this issue is a couple of guidelines, the rest must be left to your conscience. The physically impaired are always underemployed, and frequently have to fall back on selling lottery tickets and telephone tokens, but they do manage to earn something. The mentally retarded, indigent or the elderly, who would appear to have no other possible means of support, may be especially good candidates. Keep in mind, however, that many families simply set their older members on the pavement with a tin bowl hoping to generate a little extra income. For those who go begging for bones, scraps and leftovers, or others who are truly trying to change their situations, a bowl of soup or a nutritious hot meal will go a long way.

Regarding the numerous children who beg, it's probably best not to give money since it will lead to their exploitation by unscrupulous adults and will give the impression that something can be had for nothing. For a child who appears truly hungry, a piece of fruit or other healthy snack will be greatly appreciated. If such gifts are refused and money is demanded, it should be fairly obvious what's really going on.

Plumbing

Much of the plumbing in Brazil is jerry-built or poorly installed and can pose problems to

Directions

Brazilians, bless 'em, give the worst street directions. To compound the fact that the words for 'opposite' and 'straight ahead' are the same (*en frente*), your destination will invariably be straight ahead, opposite something.

When you first ask, the person will probably claim not to know the place you're asking for. Then, spookily, they'll know it intimately: 'Oh, of course, you want the Credit Lyonnais *private* banking office – say hi to François, would you, and tell him he owes me 50 francs?'

Then they'll begin the directional process. Brazilians indicate straight, right and left by thrusting their arms forward then pointing, with their open hand, palm outward, and pushing their fingertips vaguely in the correct direction.

The biggest nuisance is that there's no correlation of distance to complexity. A shop literally around the corner will receive the same treatment as, say, Paris, France, or a distant suburb reached with a change of bus. Even if your Portuguese is good, the conversation goes on a while.

To clarify, repeat gestures more dramatically and narrate them – 'Do you mean RIGHT at the CORNER'? Pin down distances ('How many metres?'). Use a map when available (but don't be surprised if that doesn't help much in rural areas).

Above all, keep your cool and your sense of humour. Almost all Brazilians try very hard to get you where you're going, usually with a smile and a *tudo bem* thumbs up for luck.

Nick Selby

the uninitiated. Bathtubs are rare outside of expensive tourist hotels, as are hot and cold running water.

However, it is possible to have hot, or at least tepid, showers thanks to a deadly-looking device that attaches to the shower head and electrically heats the water as it passes through. Bare wires dangle from the ceiling or run into the shower head.

The dangling variety indicates that the device is broken, as many are. Don't bother getting undressed until you're sure that it's working.

Most heaters are activated by the flow of water – the less water, the hotter. Others have three temperature settings on the head. It's not a good idea to change the setting while the shower is on.

When the heater is activated, it will emit an electrical humming sound and the lights in the room will dim or go out altogether. This is because the heater requires a great deal of electricity to operate effectively.

Don't touch the water controls again until you've dried off and have your footwear on. This may be tricky, especially if the shower stall is small.

LEGAL MATTERS

Police

If something is stolen from you, you can report it to the police. No big investigation is going to occur but you will get a police report to give to your insurance company. However, the police aren't always to be trusted either. Brazilian police are known to plant drugs and sting gringos for bribes. The bribes are like pyramids: the more people are involved, the bigger the bribe becomes.

Drugs

The military regime had a pathological aversion to drugs and enacted stiff penalties, which are still in force. Drugs provide a perfect excuse for the police to get a fair amount of money from you, and Brazilian prisons are brutal places.

Police checkpoints along the highways stop cars and buses at random. Police along the coastal drive from Rio to São Paulo are notorious for hassling young people and foreigners. Border areas are also very dangerous.

A large amount of cocaine is smuggled out of Bolivia and Peru through Brazil. Be very careful with drugs. If you're going to buy, don't buy from strangers and don't carry anything around with you.

Marijuana Marijuana is plentiful in Brazil, and very illegal. Nevertheless, it's widely used, and, like many things in Brazil, everyone except the military and the police has a rather tolerant attitude towards it.

Bahia seems to have the most open climate. But because of the laws against possession, you won't bump into much unless you know someone or go to an 'in' vacation spot with the young and hip like Arraial d'Ajuda, Morro de São Paulo or Canoa Quebrada, or at more groovy hippie hangouts like São Tome de las Letras in Minas.

Hallucinogens There are some wild hallucinogenic substances in the Amazon. The best known is *Banisteriopsis caapi*, better known as yagé or ayahuasca, which comes from a jungle vine and has ritual uses among certain tribes and cults.

For more details about the cults refer to the Religion section in the Facts about the Country chapter. For further reading on the topic of drugs, refer to the Amazon & Indians section under Books in this chapter.

Coca If you're coming from one of the Andean countries and have been chewing coca leaves, be especially careful to clean out your pack before arriving in Brazil. Here's what happened to a traveller who didn't:

I got out of jail after four days with the help of the consul, and was supposed to stay in Rio for 14 days waiting for trial, but my lawyer found out that the judge wanted to send me to jail so he suggested I leave immediately. The consul gave me a passport and I flew south to Porto Alegre and crossed the border into Uruguay without difficulty before flying home.

My parents were very happy of course, but it cost them a lot of money to get me out. A lady from the consulate in Rio wrote and told me that I'd been sentenced to four years in jail, and it was only 17.7 grams of coca leaves!

I'm glad to be home, safe and in one piece, and I don't have to fight with those disgusting cockroaches! Just think of it – four years in a Brazilian jail! I can't even imagine it but it was so close.

Name withheld for obvious reasons

Cocaine There's a lot of this around, and because of the stiff penalties involved with possession or apparrent possession (a little planted coke goes a long way to locking you up), we advise you to stay away from it in any form.

BUSINESS HOURS

Most shops and government services (eg post offices) are open Monday to Friday from 9 am to 6 pm and Saturday from 9 am to 1 pm. Because many Brazilians have little free time during the week, Saturday morning is usually spent shopping.

Some shops stay open later than 6 pm in the cities and the huge shopping malls often stay open until 10 pm and on Sunday as well.

Banks, always in their own little world, are generally open from 10 am to 4.30 pm. Câmbios often open an hour later, when the daily dollar rates are available. Business hours vary by region and are taken less seriously in remote locations.

PUBLIC HOLIDAYS & SPECIAL EVENTS

Holidays

National holidays fall on the following dates:

1 January
New Year's Day
6 January
Epiphany
February/March (four days before Ash Wednesday)
Carnaval
March/April
Easter & Good Friday
21 April
Tiradentes Day
1 May
May Day
June
Corpus Christi
7 September
Independence Day
12 October
Our Lady of Aparecida Day
2 November
All Souls' Day
15 November
Proclamation Day
25 December
Christmas Day

Most states have several additional local holidays when everyone goes fishing.

Festivals

Major festivals include:

January
Torneio de Repentistas (Olinda, Pernambuco)
Festa de São Lázaro (Salvador, Bahia)
1 January
New Year & Festa de Iemanjá (Rio de Janeiro)
Procissão do Senhor Bom Jesus dos Navegantes (Salvador, Bahia)
1 to 20 January
Folia de Reis (Parati, Rio de Janeiro)
3-6 January
Festa do Reis (Carpina, Pernambuco)
6-15 January
Festa de Santo Amaro (Santo Amaro, Bahia)
Second Sunday in January
Bom Jesus dos Navegantes (Penedo, Alagoas)
Second Thursday in January
Lavagem do Bonfim (Salvador, Bahia)
24 January to 2 February
NS de Nazaré (Nazaré, Bahia)
February
Grande Vaquejada do Nordeste (Natal, Rio Grande do Norte)
2 February
Festa de Iemanjá (Salvador, Bahia)
First Saturday in February
Buscada de Itamaracá (Itamaracá, Pernambuco)
February/March
Lavagem da Igreja de Itapoã (Itapoã, Bahia)
Shrove Tuesday (and the preceding three days to two weeks, depending on the place)
March
Procissão do Encontro (Salvador, Bahia)
After Easter Week (usually April)
Feiras dos Caxixis (Nazaré, Bahia)

Mid-April
Drama da Paixão de Cristo (Brejo da Madre de Deus, Pernambuco)
15 days after Easter (April or May)
Cavalhadas (Pirenópolis, Goiás)
45 days after Easter (between 6 May and 9 June)
Micareta (Feira de Santana, Bahia)
Late May or early June
Festa do Divino Espírito Santo (Parati, Rio de Janeiro)
June
Festas Juninas & Bumba Meu Boi (celebrated throughout June in much of the country, particularly São Luís, Belém and throughout Pernambuco and Rio states)
Festival Folclórico do Amazonas (Manaus, Amazonas)
22-24 June
São João (Cachoeira, Bahia & Campina Grande, Paraíba)
July
Festa do Divino (Diamantina, Minas Gerais)
Regata de Jangadas Dragão do Mar (Fortaleza, Ceará) 17 to 19 July
Missa do Vaqueiro (Serrita, Pernambuco)
Mid-August
Festa da NS de Boa Morte (Cachoeira, Bahia)
15 August
Festa de Iemanjá (Fortaleza, Ceará)
September
Festival de Cirandas (Itamaracá, Pernambuco)
Cavalhada (Caeté, Minas Gerais)
12-13 September
Vaquejada de Surubim (Surubim, Pernambuco)
October (second half)
NS do Rosário (Cachoeira, Bahia)
12 October
Festa de Nossa Senhora Aparecida (Aparecida, São Paulo)
Starting second Sunday in October
Círio de Nazaré (Belém, Pará)
November
NS da Ajuda (Cachoeira, Bahia)
1-2 November
Festa do Padre Cícero (Juazeiro do Norte, Ceará)
4-6 December
Festa de Santa Barbara (Salvador, Bahia)
8 December
Festa de Nossa Senhora da Conceição (Salvador, Bahia)
Festa de Iemanjá (Belém, Pará and João Pessoa, Paraíba)
31 December
Celebração de Fim de Ano & Festa do Iemanjá (Rio de Janeiro)

ACTIVITIES

Hiking

Hiking in Brazil is best during the cooler months of the year – April to October. During the summer, the tropical sun heats the rock to oven temperatures and turns the jungles into steamy saunas.

There are lots of great places to hike in Brazil, both in the national and state parks and along the coastline. Lots of good hikes are mentioned in the appropriate chapters. It's also a good idea to contact some of the climbing clubs (see the Rio city chapter for addresses), who have details of trekking options.

Mountaineering

Climbing in Brazil is also best from April to October. While summer climbing still occurs, it's usually done in the early morning or late afternoon when the sun's rays are not so harsh.

The best thing about rock climbing in Brazil is that one hour you can be on the beach, and the next on a world-class rock climb 300m above a city. Brazil has lots of fantastic rock climbs, ranging from the beginner level to routes yet to be conquered. In Rio de Janeiro, the centre of rock climbing in Brazil, there are 350 documented climbs that can all be reached within 40 minutes from the city centre.

Climbing Vocabulary Although most Brazilians in the clubs know a little English, not everyone does. It helps to know a little Portuguese to smooth the way.

equipment	*equipamento*
bolt	*grampo*
rope	*corda*
carabiner	*mosquetão*
harness	*baudrie*
backpack	*mochila*
webbing	*fita*
chalk powder	*pó de magnésio*
rock	*rocha*
summit	*topo/cume*
crack	*fenda*
route	*via/rota*

a fall	*queda*
to be secured	*estar preso*
a hold	*uma agarra*
to belay	*dar segurança*
to make a stupid mistake and fall	*tomar uma vaca*

Surfing

Surfing in Brazil has become seriously popular recently, and Brazilian professionals are making a splash on the world scene, so long dominated by Americans and Australians.

There are currently five Brazilians in the top 30 in the world, including a 21 year old from Florianópolis.

Surfing is popular all along the coast and there are some excellent waves to be had, especially in the south. The best surf beaches arev at Santa Catarina, and the Brazilian championships are held near Florianópolis at Praia da Joaquina.

In Rio state, Saquarema has the best surf. Búzios and Itacoatiara beach in Niterói are also popular breaks. There's also plenty of surf close to the city of Rio – see the Rio de Janeiro chapter for details. The waves are best in the Brazilian winter (from June to August). The World Pro Tour contest (Kaiser Summer Surf) is held at in October at Barra Beach, Rio.

On other surf beaches, including even those in Espiríto Santo state, with only 1-3m breaks, surfing is still a way of life, and boogie boarding is popular as well. Rentals of boogie boards and surfboards are easy to arrange right on the beach wherever you go.

Surfing Vocabulary Despite their reputation for aggressiveness in the water, once on land Brazilian surfers become very interested in foreign surfers and their travels. They also are reasonably willing to lend their boards if you ask politely.

surfer	*surfista*
wave	*onda*
wind	*vento*
surfboard	*prancha*
boogie board	*body board*
to break	*quebrar*

Are there any waves?
Tem ondas?
Could I borrow your board please?
Pode me emprestar sua prancha por favor?
Let's go surfing.
Vamos pegar ondas.

Windsurfing

Windsurfing is catching on. In Rio you can rent equipment down at Barra da Tijuca. There's windsurfing at Ilhabela and even Santos in São Paulo state, Porto Seguro and Belém, among other places.

Other Water Sports

As you would expect in a place with such a long coastline and so many beach lovers, all water sports are popular. And as you would expect in a place with such a large gap between rich and poor, they're restricted to those who can afford them. What this means to the traveller is that in order to rent the equipment needed to practise any of the above activities you need to go to established resorts.

Sailing is big in Búzios in Rio state and the larger resorts along the coast. Diving doesn't match the Caribbean, but it is worthwhile if you're keen. Angra dos Reis is the best place in Rio state, and Porto Seguro in Bahia has been recommended.

Fishing in the interior of Brazil is fantastic. The Rio Araguaia in Goiás and Tocantins is known as a fishing paradise with a large variety of fish including the pintado, dourado and tucunaré. In the Pantanal, licensed fishing is allowed on the Taquari, Coxim, Aquidauana, Cuiabá and Paraguay rivers. Fishing for piranha is not undertaken by serious anglers, though it's good fun.

Hang-Gliding

It's easy to fly *duplo* in Rio. Go to Pepino beach, where you'll see the gliders landing. Prices vary – if you go alone during the week when it's not busy, someone will take you up (straight up) Pedra Bonita and fly down with you on a glider built for two for US$60 to $80 (see the Rio de Janeiro chapter for more information).

LANGUAGE COURSES

There are lots of ways to learn Portuguese in Brazil. It's easy to arrange tutorial instruction through any of the Brazilian-American institutes where Brazilians go to learn English, or at the IBEU (Instituto Brazil Estados Unidos) in Rio de Janeiro – that city, by the way, offers the most opportunities for classes. However, there will be a language institute in each large city; see the individual chapters for more information.

WORK

Travellers on tourist visas aren't supposed to work in Brazil. The only viable paid work is teaching English in a big city, but you need to be able to speak a bit of Portuguese and allow enough time to get some pupils.

One of the authors taught English in São Paulo for five months a few years ago and found that he was able to earn between US$5 and $10 per hour – a bit less than the going rate, according to teachers we later consulted. Teaching company executives during their lunch hour and taking private pupils at home offer the most lucrative options, but both these take some time to set up. Look in the classifieds under 'Professor de Ingles', or ask around at the English schools.

Volunteer work with welfare organisations is quite easy to find if you're prepared to do some door-knocking. One traveller we met walked up to the front door of a Catholic home for abandoned children in Recife and asked if there was anything he could do. The priests gave him a bed and he spent the next two months helping to cook, getting the children out of jail, telling them stories and breaking up knife fights. He said that it was the highlight of his trip.

ACCOMMODATION

Brazilian accommodation is simple, yet usually clean and reasonably safe. In low seasons you don't need to reserve in hotels in advance, but reservations are absolutely essential during high season and in special event times like Carnaval.

Reservations

If you're staying in middle to high-class hotels, reservations are a good idea in popular tourist centres (especially in Rio) during vacations (July and December to February) and in any vacation mecca (eg Búzios) during weekends. We try to list hotel phone numbers for this purpose, but you can also get them from travel agents and tourist information offices.

Be wary of taxi drivers, particularly in Rio, who know just the hotel for you. You may find yourself being taken to an expensive hotel which pays the cabby a commission.

Another good reason for making a reservation in this class of hotel is that the price may be up to 30% cheaper than the 'rack-rate' you'd get if you just walked in off the street. If your language skills aren't up to it, get a travel agent to do it for you.

To avoid summer crowds, it is not a bad idea to travel during the week and stay put, usually in a city, during the weekends, when the locals are making their pilgrimages away from the cities. This minimises your contact with crowded buses and hotels and gets you into the city for the weekend music and festivities.

Camping

Camping is becoming increasingly popular in Brazil and is a viable alternative for travellers on limited budgets or those who want to explore some of the country's national or state parks.

For detailed information on camping grounds, get the *Guia Quatro Rodas Camping Guide* from most newsstands. The Camping Club of Brazil (Camping Clube do Brasil), Rua Senador Dantas 75, 25th floor, Rio de Janeiro, has 52 sites in 14 states.

Minimum-Impact Camping The following guidelines are recommended for those camping in wilderness or other fragile areas of Brazil:

- Select a well-drained campsite and, especially if it's raining, use some type of waterproof groundsheet to prevent having to dig trenches.
- Along popular routes, set up camp in established sites.
- Biodegradable items may be buried but anything with food residue should be carried out – including cigarette butts – lest it be dug up and scattered by animals.
- Use established toilet facilities if they are available. Otherwise, select a site at least 50m from water sources and bury wastes in a cathole at least several inches deep. If possible, burn the used toilet paper or bury it well.
- Use only biodegradable soap products (you'll probably have to carry them from home) and to avoid thermal pollution, use natural-temperature water where possible. When washing up dishes with hot water, either let it cool to outdoor temperature before pouring it out or dump it in a gravelly, non-vegetated place away from natural water sources.
- Wash dishes and brush your teeth well away from watercourses.
- When building a fire, try to select an established site and keep fires as small as possible. Use only fallen dead wood and when you're finished, make sure ashes are cool and buried before leaving. Again, carry out cigarette butts.

Rental Accommodation

It's possible to rent holiday or short or long-term apartments through a number of sources. Real estate agencies in most large cities will be geared to provide information on rentals by foreigners. The best bet is to speak to other foreigners when you're here to get a better idea of current prices, which vary from city to city. Check in the major newspapers' classified real estate sections for comparison prices. Generally speaking, a flat that runs US$450 per week in Belo Horizonte will cost you two to three times that in Rio or São Paulo.

Hostels

Hostels in Brazil are called *albergues de juventude*, and in the last few years the Brazilian organisers have been trying to get their act together. There are now over 100 hostels and more are planned. Most state capitals and popular tourist areas have at least one. Although quality varies widely, the cost is very reasonable and is regulated by the federation in Brazil.

A night in a hostel will cost from US$7.50 to $16 per person. It's not always necessary to be a member to stay in one, but it'll cost you more if you're not.

Hostelling International cards are accepted, but if you arrive in Brazil without one you can buy guest membership cards for about US$20 from the head office in each state. Booklets listing the hostels and describing how to get there (in Portuguese) are available at these offices and most travel agents.

The head office of the Federação Brasileira dos Albergues de Juventude (FBAJ) (☎ (021) 286-0303; fax (021) 286-5652), is in the Rio suburb of Botafogo, in the hostel at Rua General Dionísio 63. The FBAJ publishes a useful directory of Brazilian hostels, and it's available from most newsstands for US$10.

Pousadas

Most budget travellers stay at a *pousada* (small guesthouse) where a room without a bathroom can go for as little as US$10 per person. These rooms with communal bathrooms down the hall are called *quartos*. Similar rooms with a private bathroom are called *apartamentos*, and cost a couple of dollars more. Not all pousadas are cheap; there are many five-star ones.

Dormitórios

A *dormitório* is dorm-style sleeping with several beds to a room. These are usually the cheapest places in town, often costing as little as R$5 a head per night.

Hotels

Brazil has modern luxury hotels all over the place, and decent ones can cost as little as US$20 to $30 a double per night and, at the other end of the scale, as much as US$100 to $350 per night in Rio and São Paulo. A 10% tax is often added to the bill.

Aparthotels, available in the larger cities, provide the comforts of a good hotel without some of the glitter. They are also a bit cheaper. A good, medium-priced aparthotel should

Motels

Motels are a Brazilian institution and should never be confused with hotels. They have names like Alibi, Ilha do Capri, Motel Sinless, L'Amour and Wet Dreams. Rented by the hour, the motel is the Brazilian solution to the lack of privacy caused by overcrowded living conditions. Used by adults who still live with their parents, kids who want to get away from their parents and couples who want to get away from their kids, they are an integral part of the nation's social fabric, a bedrock of Brazilian morality, and are treated by Brazilians with what most outsiders consider to be incredible nonchalance.

The quality of motels varies, reflecting their popularity with all social classes. Most are out of the city centre, with walled-in garages for anonymity. Rooms have circular vibra-beds with mirrors overhead, adult movies, and room service with a menu full of foods and sometimes sex toys (with instructions).

Most travellers don't spend much time in motels, but they can be quite useful, and a lot of fun if you're travelling as a couple. If you're having trouble finding accommodation, they're not too expensive.

cost somewhere from US$75 per night for a double room.

Most hotels in Brazil are regulated by Embratur, the federal tourism authority. They also rate the quality of hotels from one to five stars. Regulated hotels must have a price list with an Embratur label, which is usually posted on the wall in every room and behind the reception desk. Even so, it still pays to bargain.

It's a good idea to look at a room before deciding to take it. Check the shower for hot water, check the bed, check the lock on the door. Three big sleep killers in Brazil are mosquitoes, heat and, in rural areas, roosters! Fans do wonders for stopping the first two, but you can't do much about the third – and, unfortunately, visualising yourself with your hands around the rooster's neck doesn't help!

Many medium-priced and expensive hotels have safes that are safe to use so long as you get a receipt.

In the off season many hotels have promotional rates. Ask about them. Sometimes good hotels have a few quartos or cheaper rooms that are not advertised. It pays to enquire about these, as they allow you to use all the facilities of the hotel while paying considerably less than the other guests.

For more details about bargaining, refer to the Money section in this chapter.

There are a few games played by hotel clerks to get you into a more expensive room. If you want a single room there are only doubles; if you want a quarto, there are only apartamentos. Don't say yes too quickly – if you feign a desire to look for alternative lodging, they will often remember that there is a cheaper room after all. In reality, some hotels don't have singles. It is generally much cheaper to travel with someone, as rooms for two are nowhere near twice as expensive as rooms for one.

Accommodation in Remote Areas

If you're travelling where there are no hotels – the Amazon or the Northeast – a hammock and a mosquito net are essential. With these basics, and friendly locals, you can get a good night's rest anywhere.

Most fishing villages along the coast have seen an outsider or two and will put you up for the night. If they've seen a few more outsiders, they'll probably charge you a couple of dollars.

FOOD

The hub of the Brazilian diet revolves around *arroz* (white rice), *feijão* (black beans) and *farofel* (manioc flour). It's possible to eat these every day and in some regions it's hard not to. The tasty black beans are typically cooked in bacon. The white rice is often very starchy. Farofel, the staple of the Indians, slaves and Portuguese for hundreds of years, is a hardy root that grows everywhere. It seems to be an acquired taste for foreign palates.

From the rice-bean-farofel group, meals go in one of three directions: *carne* (steak), *galinha* (chicken) and *peixe* (fish). This makes up the typical Brazilian meal and is called *prato feito* (set meal) or *prato do dia* (plate of day) in *lanchonetes* from Xique Xique to Bananal. They are typically enormous meals and incredibly cheap, but after a while they can become a trifle monotonous. If quantity is your thing, you can live like a king.

Meat, chicken and fish is ... well, cooked, and that's about it. Don't get us wrong – it's generally good meat, chicken or fish, but Brazilians don't do much with it.

Steak, big and rare, is the national passion. The best cuts are *filet* and *churrasco*. Chicken is usually grilled, sometimes fried. Fish is generally fried.

In the cities you can get many of the dishes that you like back home. There's also fine dining. For US$7 to $12 you can have a superb Italian, Japanese or Indian dinner in Rio or São Paulo. *Churrascarias* and *rodízios* bring you all the meat you can eat and a variety of other goodies for a fixed price (around US$20 in Rio). They must be tried – vegetarians (those who can stand the carnage) have no problem filling up at the salad bar either. Rodízios are especially good in the South.

Lanchonetes are stand-up fast-food bars where you can order sandwiches and *pasteis* (crumbed hors d'oeuvres).

Restaurantes have more proper sit-down meals. Never order *um almoço* (a lunch) unless you have a big appetite or care to share with a friend – the portions are immense.

Saving Money

The standard fare for budget travellers has long been the *prato feito* (made plate), a large helping of rice, beans, salad and beef, chicken or fish. Now, many restaurants and lanchonetes also offer self-serve, *por quilo* buffets. After you put what you want on the plate, they weigh it, and you pay according to the weight. Most people will only eat around half a kilo, so if you see a sign saying 'self-serve comida por quilo – R$7' or 'R$0.70' (the price per 100g), you'll pay around US$4 for a meal.

Regional Cuisine

Despite much sameness there are regional differences. The cooking in the Northern interior *(comida do sertão)* has a heavy Indian influence, using many unique, traditional tubers and fruits. On the Northeastern coast the cuisine (*comida baiana*) has a distinct African flavour using peppers, spices and the delicious oil of the *dendê* palm tree. The slaves also introduced greater variety in the preparation of meat and fish, and dishes like *vatapá* and *caruru*.

Minas Gerais is the home of *comida mineira*, a heavy but tasty cuisine based on pork, vegetables like *couve* (spinach-like leaf) and *quiabo* (bean-like vegetable); and *tutú*, a kind of refried bean-paste.

In the South, *comida gaúcha* from Rio Grande do Sul revolves around meat, meat and more meat. This cuisine has the most extensive vocabulary for different cuts of meat you're ever likely to hear.

Vegetarians

Vegetarianism is catching on slowly in Brazil, so vegetarian and especially vegan travellers must plan accordingly. Many Brazilian waiters consider 'sin carne' (without meat) to include such 'vegetable' groups as chicken, pork, animal fats and other products, so be very clear when ordering in restaurants. Beware especially the typical black bean dishes, almost always including or flavoured with meat.

Most cities now have vegetarian restaurants that serve salads, casseroles, brown rice etc. With any luck the food might be healthy, but it's rarely tasty.

You'll do very well if you bring along a small cooker and pot, as fresh produce is readily and cheaply available throughout much of the country. Vegans should bring along whatever it is they have for breakfast. If you don't mind a little chanting with your food, remember that Hare Krishna groups usually run vegetarian restaurants, and sometimes they're free.

Breakfast

Breakfast is called *café da manhã*; it's often shortened to *café*, which is also the word for coffee. Served at most hotels (with the possible exception of the very cheapest places), for no extra charge, café includes coffee, steamed milk, fruit, biscuits or bread, maybe cheese and meat, and rarely eggs. If you tire of this, or don't like it in the first place, go into any *padaria* (bakery) or market and buy a good *iogurte* (yoghurt), then get some fruit, which is always abundant and delicious.

Lunch

Lunch is the main meal for Brazilians. Lanchonetes, mentioned earlier, are everywhere. Portions are almost always big enough for two. A good non-meat choice is a *suco* (juice) bar for a natural fruit juice and sandwich. Many places have a self-serve lunch buffet.

Dinner

Dinner doesn't vary much from lunch, unless you go to a better restaurant. Most dishes are intended to be divided between two people, and are priced accordingly (if you can't eat it all ask for a *embalagem* (doggie bag) and give it to someone on the street).

In the cities, Brazilians dine late. Restaurants don't get busy in Rio and São Paulo until 10 pm on weekends. A 10% tip is generally included in the bill. If not it's customary to leave at least 10%.

Most places in Rio will bring you a *couvert* (appetiser), whether you ask or not. This is optional, so you are perfectly within your rights to send it back. The typical couvert is a ridiculously overpriced and tedious basket of bread, crackers, pheasant eggs and a couple of carrot and celery sticks. Most restaurants will still bring bread with your soup at no extra charge.

Overcharging is standard operating procedure in most Rio restaurants. Some places don't even itemise their bills. Don't hesitate to ask the waiter: *'pode discriminar'?* ('can you itemise'?). Also, take your time and count your change – short-changing is very common. It's all part of the game. They good-naturedly overcharge and you can good-naturedly hassle them until the bill is fixed. They're used to it.

Brazilian Dishes

The following are some common Brazilian dishes:

acarajé – this is what the Baianas, Bahian women in flowing white dresses, traditionally sell on street corners throughout Bahia. The Baianas are an unforgettable sight but you're likely to smell their cooking before you see it. It's the wonderful-smelling dendê (palm) oil. Acarajé is made from peeled brown beans, mashed in salt and onions, and then fried in dendê oil. Inside these delicious fried balls is vatapá, dried shrimp, pepper and tomato sauce. Dendê oil is strong stuff. Many stomachs can't handle it, and Americans believe it will cause instant heart disease.

angú – a cake made with very thin cornflour, called fubá, and mixed with water and salt.

barreado – a mixture of meats and spices cooked in a sealed clay pot for 24 hours, served with banana and farofel. The state dish of Paraná.

bobó de camarão – manioc paste cooked and flavoured with dried shrimp, coconut milk and cashew nuts.

camarão á paulista – unshelled fresh shrimp fried in olive oil with lots of garlic and salt.

canja – a big soup made with chicken broth. More often than not a meal in itself.

carangueijada – a kind of crab cooked whole and seasoned.

carne de sol – a tasty, salted meat, grilled and served with beans, rice and vegetables.

caruru – one of the most popular Brazilian dishes brought from Africa, this is made with okra or other vegetables cooked in water. The water is then drained, and onions, salt, shrimp and malagueta peppers are added, mixed and grated together with the okra paste and dendê oil. Traditionally, a sea fish such as garoupa is then added.

casquinha de carangueijo or *siri* – stuffed crab. The meat is prepared with manioc flour.

cozido – any kind of stew, usually with more vegetables than other stew-like Brazilian dishes (eg potatoes, sweet potatoes, carrots and manioc).

dourado – found in fresh water throughout Brazil; a scrumptious fish.
empadão – a tasty meat, vegetable, olive and egg pie. A typical dish of Goiás.
feijoada – the national dish of Brazil, feijoada is a meat stew served with rice and a bowl of beans. It's served throughout the country and there are many variations, depending on what animal happens to be walking through the kitchen while the chefs are at work. Orange peel, peppers and farinha accompany the stew.
frango ao molho pardo – chicken pieces stewed with vegetables and then covered with a seasoned sauce made from the blood of the bird.
moqueca – a kind of sauce or stew and a style of cooking from Bahia. There are many kinds of moqueca: fish, shrimp, oyster, crab or a combination. The moqueca sauce is defined by its heavy use of dendê oil and coconut milk, often with peppers and onions. A moqueca must be cooked in a covered clay pot.
moqueca capixaba – a moqueca from Espírito Santo uses lighter urucum oil instead of dendê oil.
pato no tucupi – roast duck flavoured with garlic and cooked in the tucupi sauce made from the juice of the manioc plant and jambu, a local vegetable. A very popular dish in Pará.
peixada – fish cooked in broth with vegetables and eggs.
peixe a delícia – broiled or grilled fish usually made with bananas and coconut milk. Delicious in Fortaleza.
prato de verão – this dish, which translates literally as summer plate, is served at many suco stands in Rio. Basically, it's a fruit salad.
pirarucu ao forno – pirarucu is the most famous fish from the rivers of Amazônia. It's oven-cooked with lemon and other seasonings.
tacacá – an Indian dish of dried shrimp cooked with pepper, jambu, manioc and much more.
tutu á mineira – a bean paste with toasted bacon and manioc flour, often served with cooked cabbage. A typical dish of Minas Gerais.
vatapá – a seafood dish with a thick sauce made from manioc paste, coconut and dendê oil. Perhaps the most famous Brazilian dish of African origin.
xinxim de galinha – pieces of chicken flavoured with garlic, salt and lemon. Shrimp and dendê oil are often added.

Fruit

Expand your experience of fruit juices and ice creams beyond pineapple and orange; in Brazil you can play blind man's buff with your taste buds. From the savoury nirvana of *graviola* to the confusingly clinical taste of *cupuaçú*, fruits and juices are a major Brazilian highlight. For more details about styles of juices, refer to the following Drinks section.

To get you started, we have included a partial list of Brazilian fruits, particularly those found in Rio. Many of the fruits of the Northeast and Amazon have no English equivalent, so there's no sense in attempting to translate their names: you'll just have to try the exotic tastes of *ingá, abiu, mari-mari, pitanga, taperebá, sorva, pitamba, uxí, pupunha, seriguela, bacuri* and *jambo*. The following taste descriptions are unashamedly subjective: be bold with your choices and enjoy!

abacate – avocado
abacaxí – pineapple
açaí – gritty, forest-berry taste and deep purple colour. This fruit of the açaí palm tree is also used in wines and syrups.
acerola – wonderful cherry flavour. A mega-source of vitamin C.
ameixa – plum, prune
bacaba – Amazonian fruit used in wines and syrups.
betarraba – beetroot
biribá – Amazonian fruit eaten plain.
burití – a palm-tree fruit with a mealy texture and a hint of peach followed by an odd aftertaste. Also used in ice cream and for wine.
cacau – pulp from cocoa pod; tastes wonderfully sweet and creamy. It's nothing like cocoa, which is extracted from the bean.
caja – pear-like taste
cajú – fruit of cashew (the nut is enclosed in an appendage of the fruit). It has a tart taste, like a cross between lemon and pear.
carambola – starfruit, which has a tangy, citrus flavour
cenoura – carrot
cupuaçú – cool taste, strangely clinical. It's best with milk and sugar.
fruto-do-conde – green, sugar-apple fruit, very popular.
gengibre – ginger; commonly drunk as atchim (a mixture of lemon and ginger)
genipapo – tastes like curdled cow piss – not everyone's favourite! Better as a liqueur.
goiaba – guava

graviola – custard apple, which is aromatic and has an exquisite taste
jaca – large fruit of the jackfruit tree
laranja – orange
limão – lemon
mamão – papaya (pawpaw)
manga – mango
mangaba – tart flavour, similar to pear
maracujá – passion fruit
melancia – watermelon
melão – honeydew melon
morango – strawberry
murici – mealy fruit with vague caramel taste
pera – pear
pêssego – peach
pupunha – a fatty, vitamin-rich Amazonian fruit taken with coffee
sapotí – gritty, semi-sweet Worcestershire-sauce taste. Brits may even recognise a hint of Marmite. Rather confusing for a fruit!
tamarindo – pleasantly acidic, plum-like
tangerina – mandarin orange, tangerine
tapereba – gritty texture, the flavour resembles a cross between acerola and sweet potato
uva – grape

DRINKS

Nonalcoholic Drinks

Juices *Sucos* (juices) in Brazil are divine. They vary by region and season (the Amazon has fruits you won't believe). Request them *sem açúcar e gelo* or *natural* if you don't want sugar and ice.

Often you'll get some water mixed into a suco; if you're worried about getting sick ask for a *vitamina*, which is juice with milk. Banana and avocado are also great with milk.

Another way to avoid water is to drink orange juice, which is rarely adulterated and it mixes well with papaya, carrot, and several other fruits. An orange, beet and carrot juice combo is popular in Rio. There is an incredible variety of fruits and combinations. Spend some time experimenting.

Caldo de cana is a tasty juice extracted directly from lengths of sugar cane, usually while you wait. The machine that does the crushing is a noisy, multi-cogged affair that has to be cranked up every time someone wants a drink. Caldo and pasteis are a favourite combination among Brazilians.

Coffee & Tea Brazilians take their coffee as strong as the devil, as hot as hell, and as sweet as love. They call it *cafezinho* and drink it as an espresso-sized coffee without milk and cut with plenty of sugar. The cafezinho is taken often and at all times. It's sold in stand-up bars and dispensed in offices to keep the workers perky. We've known Brazilians to take one to bed with them to go to sleep. If you don't like the sugar, hunt around for a coffee stand that has *espresso*. They're easy to find in cities and large towns. *Café com leite* is coffee with hot milk, usually drunk for breakfast.

Chá, tea, is not nearly as important a drink as coffee, except in the state of Rio Grande do Sul, where the gaúchos drink *maté*, a strong tea drunk through a silver straw from a hollow gourd.

Soft Drinks Soft drinks *(refrigerantes)* are found everywhere and are cheaper than bottled water. Coke is number one, Guaraná is number two, though in some places the reverse is true. Made from the berry of an Amazonian plant, Guaraná tastes as if you've just swallowed a tube of lipstick.

Alcoholic Drinks

'Para que nossas mulheres não fiquem viúva'
(May our wives never be widows)

– Brazilian drinking toast

Cachaça is found everywhere – even in the most miserable frontier shantytowns. Bottled beer usually follows the introduction of electricity to a region. At the pinnacle of Brazilian civilisation is *chopp* (see the following section), which is only found in large and prosperous economic centres with sealed roads and electricity.

Beer Brazilians, like most civilised people, enjoy their beer served icy cold *(bem gelada)*. A *cerveja* is a 600ml bottled beer. Of the common brands, Antártica (say 'ant-OKT-chee-kah') is the best, followed by Brahma (although some Brazilians argue that Brahma is better in Rio), Skol, Kaiser and Malt 90. The best beers are the regional ones, like Bohemia from Petrópolis, Cerpa and Original from Pará, Cerma from Maranhão and the tasty Serramalte from Rio Grande do Sul. Bavaria is a tasty pils, which only comes in 300ml bottles and is found in the more upmarket bars. Caracu is a stout-like beer, also only available in 300ml bottles. Very popular now is Xingu, a sweet black beer from Santa Catarina. Hunt around for it – you won't be sorry. Imported beer is all the rage among Brazilians, but we believe that when in Rio ...

Brazilians gesture for a tall one by horizontally placing the Boy Scout sign (three fingers together) a foot above their drinking tables. A *cervejinha* is 300ml of bottled or canned beer. Cans are more expensive than bottles. Some experts argue that it tastes better from the can – this is a debatable subject and one you'll have to form your own opinion on after researching the matter. If you're buying beer to take away, you'll be charged a hefty deposit for the bottles unless you trade in empties.

Chopp (pronounced 'shope' with a little 'pfff' at the end, 'shope-fff') is a pale blonde pilsener draft, lighter and far superior to canned or bottled beer. In big cities you may even find *chopp escuro*, a kind of light stout. Key phrase: *Moço, mais um chopp!* (Waiter, one more chopp).

Wine Brazilian wine is improving but vile. Forrestier is at the top of a very low heap of vintages. The whites are better than the reds and the Argentine wines are much better than both. Often restaurants that serve wine will offer more Chilean and even American wines than Brazilian ones.

Cachaça *Cachaça*, *pinga* or *aguardente* is a high-proof sugar-cane alcohol produced and drunk throughout the country. It ranges from excrementally cheap to as dear as whisky, and yes, there is a difference in effect (and after-effect!). Cachaça literally means 'booze'. Pinga (which literally means 'drop', though don't say that in some Spanish speaking countries, where it means 'penis') is considered more polite. The production of cachaça is as old as slavery in Brazil. The distilleries grew up with the sugar plantations, first to supply local consumption and then to export to Africa to exchange for slaves.

There are well over 100 brands of cachaça, with differences in taste and quality. A cheap cachaça can cut a hole in the strongest stomach lining. Velho Barreiro, Ypioca, Pitú, Carangueijo, and São Francisco are some of the better labels. Many distilleries will allow you to take a tour and watch the process from raw sugar to rot gut and then sample some of the goodies. The smaller distilleries usually make a much smoother cachaça than the commercial brands.

Other Alcoholic Drinks *Caipirinha* is the Brazilian national drink. The ingredients are simple: cachaça, lime, sugar and crushed ice, but a well-made caipirinha is a work of art. *Caipirosca* is a caipirinha with vodka replacing cachaça. *Caipirissima* is still another variation, with Bacardi rum instead of cachaça.

Batidas are wonderful mixes of cachaça, sugar and fruit juice.

ENTERTAINMENT

Cinemas

There are cinemas in almost every town of any size, except of course, in the more remote locations. Cinemas show mainly American films in the original language with subtitles. Shows run from afternoon to night, and a film usually costs about US$5. Adult movie theatres are commonplace, and there seems to be far less a social stigma about attending here than in other countries. At least, that's what we told ourselves over and over again! Admission is usually about US$2.

Discos

There are major discos in the major cities, as you'd expect. São Paulo and Rio especially have concentrations of clubs, but other cities like Belo Horizonte and Salvador will surprise you with their nightlife. In this book we list selected clubs as well as what's on guides and listings magazines. Club admission in the large cities ranges from US$5 to $20.

Classical, Opera, Theatre & Ballet

While these are limited almost exclusively, and not overly notably, to Rio and São Paulo, there are notable performances at the neoclassical Teatro da Paz in Belém. There are free classical concerts every Sunday morning in São Paulo's Parque do Ibirapuera.

Rock, Jazz & Folk/Traditional Music

The best places to hear live music are the pubs and bars that are in most towns and cities of any size. See the individual chapter listings for venue information. Generally there is a small cover charge for places with live music.

Pubs & Bars

Brazilian pubs and bars are congenial, friendly places, and there's no telling where they'll turn up. Rio and São Paulo have highly competitive, sophisticated drinking spots, and other cities have a strange mix of places. Check individual chapter listings for bars, but also check in local papers and magazines for new venues that open all the time.

SPECTATOR SPORTS

Football

Soccer was introduced to Brazil after a young student from São Paulo, Charles Miller, returned from his studies in England with two footballs and a rule book and began to organise the first league. It quickly became the national passion, and Brazil has since won four World Cups. Brazilians are, to put it mildly, psycho about the game.

No one goes to work on game days, a situation that the government – which is prepared to spend whatever it takes to win the World Cup – laments. When the national team unexpectedly lost to France in the 1998 World Cup, millions cried on the streets and a mass depression gripped the country for weeks.

The fans are insane but they know their football. Each good play is rewarded with superlatives. A fancy dribble past an opponent receives a Spanish bullfight *olé*; a goal results in delirium. And radio and TV announcers stretch the word 'goal' for at *least* 20 seconds (GOOOOOOOOOOOOAL!) an astounding bit of audio even before it's enhanced by a wah-wah reverb effect.

Brazilians play the world's most creative and artistic style of football. You'll see tiny kids playing skilled, rough matches in the streets, on the beaches, just about anywhere.

Matches are played on Sunday and Wednesday. Go to a game. It's an intense spectacle, and one of the most colourful pageants you'll likely ever see.

Volleyball

Surprisingly, volleyball is Brazil's second sport. A natural on the beach, it's also a popular spectator sport on TV. A local variation you'll see on Rio's beaches is volleyball played without the hands (futvolei). It's quite fun to watch but it's bloody hard to play.

Motor Racing

Brazilians love speed. Taxi drivers may give you a hint of it, and since the early 1970s Brazilian drivers have won more Formula One Grand Prix world championships than any other nationality. Emerson Fittipaldi was world champion twice in the 1970s, Nelson Piquet won his third world championship in 1987, and the late great Ayrton Senna took it out three times. The Brazilian Grand Prix traditionally kicks off the Formula One season in Rio around March each year.

SHOPPING

A smart souvenir hunter can do well in Brazil, provided they know a little about Brazilian culture. Most people find the best souvenirs to be music, local crafts and artwork.

Brazilian music (see the Arts section in the Facts about the Country chapter) is sure to evoke your most precious travel memories. The best record stores in the

Pelé

Brazil's most famous international personality is undoubtedly Pelé. He was the centre of attention on Bill Clinton's 1997 visit to Brazil, and by accompanying the Brazilian president on a recent trip to London he made sure the delegation received valuable press attention. Queen Elizabeth even knighted him. He's come a long way.

Born in Três Corações, Minas Gerais on 23 October 1940, Édson Arantes do Nascimento became the greatest soccer player in the world, known to everyone as Pelé.

His public image remains impeccable. He's never smoked, never been photographed with a drink in hand and has NEVER been involved with drugs.

In a 22 year career, the teams in which Pelé played gained 53 titles; three World Cup titles (Sweden in 1958, Chile in 1962 and Mexico in 1970), dual world club championships (with Santos in 1962 and 1963), two South American championships, 11 Paulista state championships and four Rio-São Paulo tournaments.

In 1971, Pelé retired from the Brazilian team and in 1974 he retired from Santos. In 1975 the New York Cosmos coaxed him north to the USA. He played there until 1977, when they won the American championship. He finally retired at the end of that year, after a game between the Cosmos and Santos, in which he played the first half for the Cosmos and the second half with Santos.

In 1363 games (112 for the Brazilian team), he scored 1282 goals. When he scored his 1000th goal in 1969 he dedicated it 'to the children of Brazil'. Pelé called getting the goal 'one of the greatest blessings a man could ever expect to receive from God'.

In 1981 he received the title 'Athlete of the Century' from the French sports daily *L'Équipe*. In Brazil he is known simply as O Rei (The King).

In 1994 Pelé was included in Brazil's new government. He was given the title of *Ministro Extraordinário dos Esportes* – the Extraordinary Minister of Sport. He is no ordinary minister, that's for sure. When Pelé wanted to work as a guest commentator for the Globo network during the 1998 World Cup a small problem arose – government ministers aren't allowed to do such things. Pelé was about to resign, but since 1998 was an election year, the president wouldn't hear of it. He came up with a classic piece of Brazilian *jeito* (way of fixing things). Pelé would resign from the ministry for the duration of the World Cup, and then be re-admitted afterwards!

Andrew Draffen

country are in the big shopping malls of São Paulo.

Although nearly everything can be found in Rio and São Paulo, there is a premium for moving craft and art pieces from the hinterland into the fancy stores of the big cities. The inexpensive exceptions include the weekly hippie fair at Ipanema (see the

Rio de Janeiro city chapter), the ubiquitous FUNAI stores and museum gift shops.

Most of the Indian crafts sold in FUNAI stores are inexpensive, but the quality generally matches the price. Museum gift shops, on the other hand, stock some very worthwhile souvenirs. They are particularly good for prints of local art. The Carmen Miranda museum in Rio sells T-shirts of the great lady herself, complete with her fruit headdress.

Outside the big cities, your best bet for craftwork are artisan fairs, co-operative stores and government-run shops. The Northeast has a rich assortment of artistic items. Salvador and nearby Cachoeira are notable for their rough-hewn wood sculpture. Artisans in Fortaleza and the southern coast of Ceará specialise in fine lace. The interior of Pernambuco, in particular Caruaru, is famous for the wildly imaginative ceramic figurines and the traditional leather hats worn by the *sertanejos*. Functional and decorative hammocks are available in cities throughout the Amazon. These string, mesh or cloth slings are fixtures in most Brazilian homes. They are indispensable for travellers and make fine, portable gifts.

Minas Gerais is most famous for its gemstones. However, if you're in the market for fine jewellery and precious stones, wait until you return to the big cities to make your purchases. Buy from a large and reputable dealer like Amsterdam-Sauer, Roditi or H Stern. Stern is an international dealership based in Ipanema and its reputation for quality and honesty is beyond reproach. It isn't a discount store, but its jewellery is less expensive in Brazil than in its outlets in other parts of the world.

Brazilian leather goods are moderately priced, but the leather isn't particularly supple. The better Brazilian shoes, belts, wallets, purses and luggage are sold in the upmarket shops of Ipanema and Copacabana. Shoes are extremely good value, but much of the best is reserved for export and larger sizes are difficult to find. Quality, cheap, durable, leather soccer balls with hand-stitched panels are sold all over Brazil in sporting-goods stores. Inflated soccer balls should not be put in the cargo hold of a plane.

In an effort to draw industry to the Amazon, the government lifted many tax and tariff restrictions in Manaus. The advantage to tourists in this free-trade zone is minimal unless you are particularly interested in picking up electrical equipment that has been assembled in Brazil.

Finally, here are a few more ideas for the avid souvenir hunter. Coffee-table picture books on Brazil, videotapes of Carnaval and of highlights of the Brazilian national team and Pelé in various World Cup matches are hawked in the streets of Copacabana. Guaraná powder, a stimulant (said to be an aphrodisiac), is sold in health-food stores and chemists around the country. Mounted reprints of old Rio lithographs are sold in Rio's Cinelândia district on the steps of the opera house. The smallest of Brazil's bikinis are sold at Bum-Bum or Kanga shops.

Candomblé stores are a good source of curios, ranging from magical incense guaranteed to bring good fortune and increase sexual allure, wisdom and health, to amulets and ceramic figurines of Afro-Brazilian gods. If you are travelling in Brazil during Carnaval make sure you pick up a copy of the Carnaval edition of *Manchete* magazine.

Getting There & Away

Most travellers start their Brazilian odyssey by flying to Rio, but this is only one of many ways to arrive. Other gateway airports include Recife (popular with German package tourists on their way to one of the many beach resorts catering to their needs), Fortaleza, Salvador and Manaus (capital of the state of Amazonas), and Belém (capital of the state of Pará). Manaus and Belém are both halfway between Rio and Miami.

Brazil also has land borders with every other country in South America except Chile and Ecuador, so while some travellers may be bussing in from Uruguay in the south, others may be arriving via the *trem da morte* (death train) from Bolivia. By river, many travellers take a slow boat down the Amazon from Iquitos in Peru.

However you're travelling, it's worth taking out travel insurance. Work out what you need. You may not want to insure that grotty old army surplus backpack, but everyone should be covered for the worst possible case – an accident, for example, that will require hospital treatment and a flight home. It's a good idea to make a copy of your policy, in case the original is lost. If you are planning to travel for a long time, the insurance may seem very expensive – but if you can't afford it, you certainly won't be able to afford to deal with a medical emergency overseas.

AIR

Cheap deals on air travel are volatile. With some legwork you can usually save a couple of hundred dollars. Check newspapers and discount or Latin American specialist travel agents for good deals.

Airports & Airlines

The most popular international gateway is Aeroporto Galeão in Rio de Janeiro. From there, connecting flights to airports throughout the country leave regularly (be warned that a 1998 fire in Rio's domestic terminal, Aeroporto Santos Dumont, may continue to cause inconvenience; see the Rio de Janeiro City chapter for more information). São Paulo's Aeroporto São Paulo/Guarulhos is probably the second most popular gateway.

Varig, Brazil's international airline, flies to many major cities in the world. From the USA the basic carriers serving Brazil are Varig, Continental Airlines, Delta Airlines, American Airlines, United Airlines and Japan Airlines (JAL) (from the west coast); from the UK, British Airways and Varig; and from Australia, Qantas, and Aerolineas Argentinas.

Buying Tickets

Your plane ticket will probably be the single most expensive item in your budget, and buying it can be an intimidating business. There is likely to be a multitude of airlines and travel agents hoping to separate you from your money, and it is always worth putting aside a few hours to research the current state of the market. Start early; some of the cheapest tickets have to be bought months in advance, and some popular flights sell out early. Talk to other recent travellers – they may be able to stop you making some of the same old mistakes.

Look at the ads in newspapers and magazines (not forgetting the South American press if you have access to it). Consult reference books and watch for special offers, and then phone around travel agents for bargains. (Airlines can supply information on routes and timetables; however, except at times of inter-airline war they do not supply the cheapest tickets.) Find out the fare, the route, the duration of the journey and any restrictions on the ticket. Then sit back and decide which is best for you.

You may discover that those impossibly cheap flights are 'fully booked, but we have another one that costs a bit more ...' Or the flight is on an airline notorious for its poor safety standards and leaves you in the world's least favourite airport mid-journey for 14 hours. Or they claim only to have the last two seats available for Brazil for the whole of July, which they will hold for you for a maximum of two hours. Don't panic – keep ringing around.

Use the fares quoted in this book as a guide only. They are approximate and based on the rates advertised by travel agents at the time of going to press. Quoted airfares do not necessarily constitute a recommendation for the carrier.

If you are travelling from the UK or the USA, you will probably find that the cheapest flights are being advertised by obscure bucket shops whose names haven't yet reached the telephone directory. Many such firms are honest and solvent, but there are a

Air Travel Glossary

Baggage Allowance This will be written on your ticket; you are usually allowed one 20kg item to go in the hold, plus one item of hand luggage. Some airlines which fly transpacific and transatlantic routes allow for two pieces of luggage (there are limits on their dimensions and weight).

Bucket Shops At certain times of the year and/or on certain routes, many airlines fly with empty seats. This isn't profitable and it's more cost-effective for them to fly full, even if that means having to sell a certain number of drastically discounted tickets. They do this by off-loading them onto bucket shops (UK) or consolidators (USA), travel agents who specialise in discounted fares. The agents, in turn, sell them to the public at reduced prices. These tickets are often the cheapest you'll find, but you can't purchase them directly from the airlines. Availability varies widely, so you'll not only have to be flexible in your travel plans, you'll also have to be quick off the mark as soon as an advertisement appears in the press. Bucket-shop agents advertise in newspapers and magazines and there's a lot of competition, so it's a good idea to telephone first to ascertain availability.

Bumped Just because you have a confirmed seat doesn't mean you're going to get on the plane – see Overbooking.

Cancellation Penalties If you have to cancel or change a discount ticket, there may be heavy penalties involved; insurance can sometimes be taken out against these penalties. Some airlines impose penalties on regular tickets as well, particularly against 'no-show' passengers.

Check In Airlines ask you to check in a certain time ahead of the flight departure (usually two hours on international flights). If you fail to check in on time and the flight is overbooked, the airline can cancel your booking and give your seat to somebody else.

Confirmation Having a ticket written out with the flight and date on it doesn't mean you have a seat until the agent has confirmed with the airline that your status is 'OK'. Prior to this confirmation, your status is 'on request'.

Courier Fares Businesses often need to send their urgent documents or freight securely and quickly. They do it through courier companies. These companies hire people to accompany the package through customs and, in return, offer a discount ticket which is sometimes a phenomenal bargain. In effect, what the courier companies do is ship their freight as your luggage on the regular commercial flights. This is a legitimate operation – all freight is completely legal. There are two shortcomings, however: the short turnaround time of the ticket, usually not longer than a month; and the limitation on your luggage allowance. You may be required to surrender all your baggage allowance for the use of the courier company, and be only allowed to take carry-on luggage.

Economy-Class Tickets Economy-class tickets are usually not the cheapest way to go, though they do give you maximum flexibility and they are valid for 12 months. If you don't

few disreputable operators who will take your money and disappear, to reopen elsewhere a month or two later under a new name. If you feel suspicious about a firm, don't give them all the money at once – leave a deposit of 20% or so and pay the balance when you get the ticket. If they insist on cash in advance, go somewhere else. And once you have the ticket, ring the airline to confirm that you are actually booked on the flight.

You may decide to pay more than the rock-bottom fare by opting for the safety of a better-known travel agent. Firms such as STA Travel, who have offices worldwide, Council Travel in the USA or Travel CUTS in Canada are not going to disappear overnight, leaving you clutching a receipt for

use them, most are fully refundable, as are unused sectors of a multiple ticket.

Lost Tickets If you lose your airline ticket, an airline will usually treat it like a travellers cheque and, after enquiries, issue you with a replacement. Legally, however, an airline is entitled to treat it like cash, so if you lose a ticket, it could be forever.

MCO An MCO (Miscellaneous Charges Order) is a voucher for a value of a given amount which resembles an airline ticket and can be used to pay for a specific flight with any IATA (International Air Transport Association) airline. MCOs, which are more flexible than a regular ticket, may satisfy the irritating onward ticket requirement, but some countries are now reluctant to accept them. MCOs are fully refundable if unused.

No-shows No-shows are passengers who fail to show up for their flight for whatever reason. Full-fare no-shows are sometimes entitled to travel on a later flight. The rest of us are penalised (see Cancellation Penalties).

Open Jaw Tickets These are return tickets which allow you to fly to one place but return from another, and travel between the two 'jaws' by any means of transport at your own expense. If available, this can save you backtracking to your arrival point.

Overbooking Airlines hate to fly with empty seats, and since every flight has some passengers who fail to show up (see No-shows), they often book more passengers than they have seats available. Usually the excess passengers balance those who fail to show up, but occasionally somebody gets bumped. If this happens, guess who it is most likely to be? The passengers who check in late.

Reconfirmation You must contact the airline at least 72 hours prior to departure to 'reconfirm' that you intend to be on the flight. If you don't do this, the airline can delete your name from the passenger list and you could lose your seat.

Stand-by This is a discounted ticket where you fly only if there is a seat free at the last moment. Stand-by fares are usually available only at the airport, but sometimes may also be handled by an airline's city office. To give yourself the best possible chance of getting on the flight you want, get there early and have your name placed on the waiting list. It's first come, first served.

Transferred Tickets Airline tickets cannot be transferred from one person to another. Travellers sometimes try to sell the return half of their ticket, but officials can ask you to prove that you are the person named on the ticket. This may not be checked on domestic flights, but on international flights, tickets are usually compared with passports.

Travel Periods Some officially discounted fares vary with the time of year. There is often a low (off-peak) season and a high (peak) season. Sometimes there's an intermediate, or shoulder, season as well. At peak times, when everyone wants to fly, both officially and unofficially discounted fares will be higher, or there may simply be no discounted tickets available. Usually the fare depends on your outward flight – if you depart in the high season and return in the low season, you pay the high-season fare.

a non-existent ticket, and they do offer good prices to most destinations.

Once you have your ticket, write its number down, together with the flight number and other details, and keep the information somewhere separate. If the ticket is lost or stolen, this will help you get a replacement.

It's sensible to buy travel insurance as early as possible. If you buy it the week before you fly, you may find, for example, that you're not covered for delays to your flight caused by industrial action.

Leaving Brazil Currency restrictions on ticket purchases have been discontinued; you can walk into any airline office or travel agency and pay for international tickets in US$, *real* or with a credit card.

To the USA, a Rio or São Paulo to New York flight costs about US$800; Continental and Delta seem to have the lowest fares as we write, including, with the former, an off-season fare from New York to São Paulo of just US$550 return. A Recife-Miami flight is around US$700 one way, and from Rio add another US$100.

To Europe, the cheapest tickets are Rio-London. The cost can be as low as US$950 return.

The best way to Australia is to get a return ticket (from US$1326) and either throw away the return portion or, hell, come on back!

Discount Tickets Discount tickets have restrictions. The most pernicious is the limit on the amount of time you can spend in Brazil. Charter flights often restrict a stay to as little as three weeks. Most other tickets have a 90 day limit. There's usually a premium for tickets valid over 180 days. Although the Transbrasil Airpass is no longer the bargain it once was, it's worth mentioning here that you *must* purchase it outside Brazil. (See the Getting Around chapter for more information.)

If you are planning to stay in Brazil for more than 90 days, cheap airline tickets are a big problem. You are required to buy a return ticket before you will be issued with a visa in the USA, but it's not hard to get around this (see the Visa section in the Facts for the Visitor chapter). Unfortunately, the cost of a one-way ticket is more than half the price of a return economy fare. For example, from Los Angeles to Rio return costs about US$1050 if you buy from the airlines, but you may be able to obtain a discount ticket for as little as US$700 from a specialist travel agent. The fare for a one-way ticket is US$1300, and for a round trip valid for over three months the fare is doubled. Absurd! This means it may be cheaper to buy a discounted return ticket with a 90 day limit, bury the return portion ticket and then buy a ticket in Brazil when you are ready to go home.

If you need a visa to Brazil, and plan to stay more than six months, you have to consider leaving the country to get a new visa. Ask about package deals. We were once able to get a round-trip Aerolineas Argentinas ticket from New York to Buenos Aires with an unlimited stopover in Rio. This gave us a free ride to Buenos Aires to get new visas after several months in Brazil – ask your travel agent about similar deals.

Travellers with Special Needs
If you have special needs of any sort – you've broken a leg, you're vegetarian, travelling in a wheelchair, taking the baby, terrified of flying – you should let the airline know as soon as possible so that they can make arrangements accordingly. You should remind them when you reconfirm your booking (at least 72 hours before departure) and again when you check in at the airport. It may also be worth ringing around the airlines before you make your booking to find out how they can handle your particular needs.

Airports and airlines can be surprisingly helpful, but they do need advance warning. Most international airports will provide escorts from the check-in desk to the plane where needed, and there should be ramps, lifts, accessible toilets and reachable phones. Aircraft toilets, on the other hand, are likely to present a problem; travellers should discuss this with the airline at an early stage and, if necessary, with their doctor.

Guide dogs for the blind will often have to travel in a specially pressurised baggage compartment with other animals, away from their owner, though smaller guide dogs may be admitted to the cabin. All guide dogs will be subject to the same quarantine laws (six months in isolation etc) as any other animal when entering or returning to countries currently free of rabies such as the UK or Australia.

Deaf travellers can ask for airport and in-flight announcements to be written down for them.

Children under two travel for 10% of the standard fare (or free, on some airlines), as long as they don't occupy a seat. They don't get a baggage allowance either. 'Skycots' should be provided by the airline if requested in advance; these will take a child weighing up to about 10 kg. Children between two and 12 can usually occupy a seat for half to two-thirds of the full fare, and they do get a baggage allowance. Push chairs can often be taken as hand luggage.

The USA

The *New York Times*, *LA Times*, *Chicago Tribune* and the *San Francisco Examiner* all produce weekly travel sections in which you'll find any number of travel agents' ads. Council Travel and STA Travel have offices in major cities nationwide. The Brazilian American Cultural Center (BACC ☎ (800) 222-2746, see the section on Useful Organisations in the Facts for the Visitor chapter) offers its members low-priced flights to Brazil.

Also highly recommended is the newsletter *Travel Unlimited* (PO Box 1058, Allston, MA 02134) which publishes details of the cheapest airfares and courier possibilities for destinations all over the world from the USA.

From the USA, major Latin American gateway cities are New York, Los Angeles and Miami. All have basically the same fare structure. Economy fares often have to be purchased two weeks in advance and common restrictions require a minimum stay of two weeks and a maximum of three months. Varig offers this type of return ticket to Rio costing US$836 (ex Miami), US$795 (ex New York) and US$1050 (ex Los Angeles).

Air Bolivia has a Miami-Manaus service and a return ticket, with a two-week advance purchase and a two-week to one-month stay, which costs US$798.

Some of the cheapest flights from Brazil to the USA are charters from Manaus to Miami, the Disneyworld express! Manaus, which lies halfway between Rio and Miami, is a useful gateway city if you plan to make a long circuit around Brazil.

Canada

Travel CUTS has offices in all major cities. The *Toronto Globe & Mail* carries travel agents' ads, and the magazine *Great Expeditions* (PO Box 8000-411, Abbotsford BC V2S 6H1) is useful. Travellers interested in booking flights with Canadian courier companies should obtain a copy of the newsletter published by Travel Unlimited (see the USA section for details).

Australia & New Zealand

Aerolineas Argentinas flies to Brazil over the South Pole once a week (twice during peak periods) via Sydney, Auckland and Buenos Aires to Rio de Janeiro. This ticket is valid for six months. If you shop around, you should be able to pick up a fare for approximately A$1950 from Sydney, a bit more from Melbourne or Brisbane. Aerolineas has some other interesting fares: a Circle Americas fare to South and North America for A$2969; Circle Pacific fares via South America for A$3455; a Two-Continents fare that includes Africa and South America for A$3500; and a Round-the-World (RTW) fare via South America for A$3199 that's valid for one year. It also has some winter specials you should watch for, like a A$1650 fare to Brazil for up to 45 days.

Qantas flies Sydney-Rio de Janeiro via Los Angeles for A$4200. The Los Angeles-Rio leg is on Varig, and a maximum of two stopovers are allowed in the Pacific in places like Honolulu and Tahiti. A Qantas/Varig RTW ticket costs A$3700. United Airlines flies Sydney-Auckland-Los Angeles-New York-Rio for A$2749. South African Airways has a flight to Rio via Johannesburg for A$1329 one way and A$2149 return. The return fares allow for a free side-trip within South Africa (see Africa in this section for more information on Africa-South America fares).

The UK

Look for travel agents' ads in the Sunday papers, the travel magazine *Complete Traveller* and listings magazines such as *TNT* and *Time Out*. Also look out for the free magazines widely available in London – start by looking outside the main train stations.

To initiate your price comparisons, you could contact travel agents such as: Journey Latin America (JLA) (☎ (0181) 747-3108) which publishes a very useful *Flights Bulletin*; Travel Bug (☎ (0161) 721-4000); Trailfinders (☎ (0171) 938-3444); STA (☎ (0171) 361-6262); and South American Experience (☎ (0171) 379-0344). For courier-flight details, contact Polo Express (☎ (0181) 759-5383) or Courier Travel Service (☎ (0171) 351-0300).

The Globetrotters Club (BCM Roving, London WC1N 3XX) publishes *Globe*, a newsletter for members which covers obscure destinations and can help find travelling companions.

Prices for discounted flights between London and Rio start around £300 one way or £500 return – bargain hunters should have little trouble finding even lower prices.

For free (if commercially geared) advice on air travel, call the Air Travel Advisory Bureau (☎ (0171) 636 5000) for London or (☎ (0161) 832 2000) for Manchester.

Continental Europe

The newsletter *Farang* (La Rue 8 á 4261, Braives, Belgium) deals with exotic destinations, as does the magazine *Aventure au Bout du Monde* (116 Rue de Javel, 75015 Paris). From Germany, you can expect to pay about DM1400 return for a basic discounted ticket; check publications like *In München* for cheaper deals.

South Africa

STA (☎ (011) 447-5551) has offices all over the country. Seriously helpful is the Johannesburg Student Union Building Branch at Wits University (☎ (011) 716-3045).

Rennies Travel has a comprehensive network of agencies throughout SA; its main office is on the 11th floor ISM Building, 124 Main St, Johannesburg (☎ (011) 331-5898).

From Johannesburg, Varig and South African Airways fly directly to São Paulo and Rio de Janeiro. A typical discounted return fare is about R3600, and, on Varig, can include another destination within Brazil or to certain other South American destinations like Montevideo. One reader told us a non-discounted return ticket cost her R5000.

Asia

Hong Kong is the discount plane ticket capital of the region. Its bucket shops, however, are at least as unreliable as those of other cities. Ask the advice of other travellers before buying a ticket.

STA Travel, which is reliable, has branches in Hong Kong, Tokyo, Singapore, Bangkok and Kuala Lumpur.

From the orient, the hot tickets are with JAL and Singapore Airlines. JAL flies Tokyo-Los Angeles-Rio de Janeiro-São Paulo, and it often has the best fares to Rio from the west coast of the USA.

LAND

Car & Motorcycle

Anyone planning to take their own vehicle with them needs to check in advance what spares and petrol are likely to be available. Lead-free is not on sale worldwide, and neither is every little part for your car. Brazil has plenty of Volkswagen spares.

Documents Drivers of cars and riders of motorbikes entering Brazil will need the vehicle's registration papers, and their domestic licence. An international driving

ANDREW DRAFFEN

ANDREW DRAFFEN

ANDREW DRAFFEN

Top: View from Pão de Açúcar
Middle: Cable-car ride to Pão de Açúcar
Bottom: View of Pão de Açúcar

ANDREW DRAFFEN

JOHN MAIER, JR

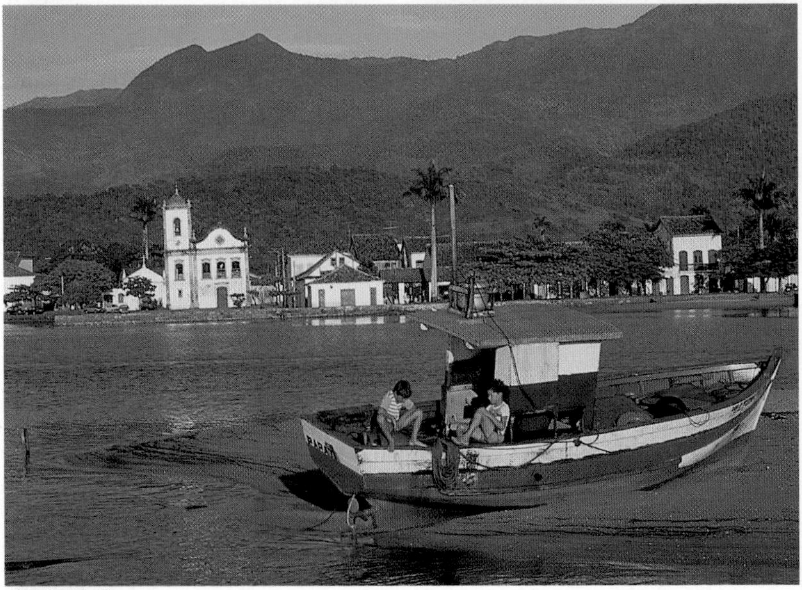

JOHN MAIER, JR

Top Left: Petrópolis
Top Right: A spectacular view from Parati
Bottom: Low tide at Parati

permit is helpful too. You should also carry liability insurance. You may need a *carnet de passage en douane*, which is effectively a passport for the vehicle, and acts as a temporary waiver of import duty. The carnet may need to have listed any more expensive spares that you're planning to carry with you, such as a gearbox. This is necessary when travelling in many countries, including those in South America, and is designed to prevent car-import rackets.

Another document used in South America is the *libreta de pasos por aduana*, a booklet of customs passes. It supposedly takes the place of the carnet, but since the refundable bond for the libreta is only US$100, it doesn't seem much of a deterrent to selling a vehicle.

Some travellers recently reported that the only documents they required were the title of the vehicle and a customs form issued on arrival which must be kept and presented upon departure. Contact your local automobile association for details about all documentation. Remember that it's always better to carry as much documentation as you can.

Bicycle

You don't see many long-distance cyclists in Brazil. Crazy drivers who only respect vehicles larger than themselves, lots of trucks on the main roads spewing out unfiltered exhaust fumes, roads without shoulder room and the constant threat of theft are just some of the reasons for this. We wouldn't recommend long-distance cycling in Brazil. It seems a downright dangerous thing to do.

If you're still determined to tackle Brazil by bike, before you leave home, go over your bike with a fine-toothed comb and fill your repair kit with every imaginable spare. As with cars and motorbikes, you won't necessarily be able to buy that crucial gismo for your machine when it breaks down somewhere in the back of beyond as the sun sets.

Bicycles can travel by air. You can take them to pieces and put them in a bike bag or box, but it's much easier simply to wheel your bike to the check-in desk, where it should be treated as a piece of baggage. You may have to remove the pedals and turn the handlebars sideways so that it takes up less space in the aircraft's hold; check all this with the airline well in advance, preferably before you pay for your ticket.

Argentina

Coming from or going to Argentina, most travellers pass through Foz do Iguaçu (see the Foz do Iguaçu section in the Paraná chapter for more information).

Bolivia

Corumbá Corumbá, opposite the Bolivian border town of Quijarro, is the busiest port of entry along the Bolivia-Brazil border. It has both rail and bus connections from São Paulo, Rio de Janeiro, Cuiabá and southern Brazil.

The train service between Quijarro and Santa Cruz is known as the Death Train, but it's a beautiful ride. Taxis are available between the railhead at Quijarro and the frontier. For further information, see the Corumbá section in the Mato Grosso & Mato Grosso do Sul chapter.

Cáceres From Cáceres, north of Cuiabá, you can cross to San Matías in Bolivia. There are daily buses which do the 4½ hour trip for US$10. Bolivia's Transportes Aereos Militares (TAM) operates flights each way between San Matías and Santa Cruz, Bolivia (via Roboré) on Saturday. During the dry season, there's also a daily bus between the border town of San Matías and San Ignacio de Velasco (in Bolivia's Jesuit missions), where you'll find flights and bus connections to Santa Cruz.

Coming from Bolivia, there are daily *micro* buses (again, only during the dry season) from San Ignacio de Velasco to the border at San Matías, from where you'll find onward transport to Cáceres and Cuiabá.

Guajará-Mirim Another popular crossing is between Guajará-Mirim in Brazil and Guayaramerín, Bolivia, via motorised canoe or motorboat ferry across the Rio Mamoré.

Guayaramerín is connected with Riberalta by a road which should be extended to Cobija/Brasiléia in the near future. At present, there's a dirt track to Cobija which is impassable in the wet season – in the dry, there's a bus once a week. Another long dusty route strikes southward toward Rurrenabaque and La Paz (the capital of the Bolivian Amazon) with a spur to Trinidad. The Madeira to Mamoré railway from Guajará-Mirim to Porto Velho has long since been abandoned, but there are eight bus connections twice daily (during the dry season) between Porto Velho and Guajará-Mirim – a 5½ hour bus ride on the new road.

It's possible to take a six day river trip up the Mamoré to Trinidad, and from there on to Puerto Villarroel near Cochabamba. When the water is high enough to accommodate cargo transport, it's also possible to travel up the Rio Beni from Riberalta at least as far as Rurrenabaque, which is 15 hours by bus from La Paz. Conditions are basic, so be prepared. Alternatively, AeroSur has daily flights from both Guayaramerín and Riberalta, Lloyd Aero Boliviano (LAB) has three flights per week from both Guayaramerín and Riberalta. For further information see the Guajará-Mirim and Guayaramerín sections in the Rondônia & Acre chapter.

Brasiléia In Acre state, in the far west of Brazil, there's a border crossing between Brasiléia and Cobija in Bolivia. You can either take a rowboat ferry across the Rio Acre or a taxi across the international bridge over the Rio Abunã. For more details, see the Brasiléia and Cobija sections in the Amazonas & Roraima chapter.

Colombia

Leticia The Colombian border crossing is at Leticia/Tabatinga. For more information on the Triple Frontier region, refer to the Benjamin Constant, Tabatinga and Leticia sections in the Amazonas & Roraima chapter.

French Guiana

Both Brazilians and foreigners may enter French Guiana from Oiapoque by motorised dugout, but it is reportedly not possible for non-Brazilian passport holders to enter Brazil overland from French Guiana. The obvious corollary is that you shouldn't enter French Guiana at St Georges (the French Guianese town opposite Oiapoque) unless you intend to fly from Cayenne or to re-enter Brazil elsewhere. This route will be feasible during the dry season only. Those who require a French visa should pick it up in Belém. For further information see under Macapá in the Amapá chapter.

Guyana

The border crossing is at Bonfim in Roraima state and is reached via Boa Vista. You may want to save yourself the trouble of a difficult overland passage by flying directly to Georgetown on one of the two weekly Varig/Cruzeiro flights from Boa Vista. See the Boa Vista section in the Amazonas & Roraima chapter for more details.

Paraguay

Foz do Iguaçu/Ciudad del Este and Ponta Porã/Pedro Juan Caballero are the two major border crossings. See the Foz do Iguaçu section in the Paraná chapter and the Ponta Porã section in the Mato Grosso chapter for details.

Iñapari There is another border crossing into Peru at Assis Brasil. From Brasiléia, take a bus 110km west to Assis Brasil where you'll get an exit stamp. Across the Rio Acre from Assis Brasil is the muddy little Peruvian settlement of Iñapari where you must officially check into Peru with the police. For more details, see sections on Brasiléia and Assis Brasil.

Suriname

It isn't possible to enter Suriname overland from Brazil without first passing through either French Guiana or Guyana.

Uruguay

From Uruguay, travellers usually pass through the border town of Chuy/Chuí: Chuy is the Uruguayan town on one side of the main street and Chuí is the Brazilian town on the other side. See the Rio Grande do Sul chapter for details.

There are four other border crossings: at Aceguá; from Rivera to Santana do Livramento; from Artigas to Quaraí; and at Barra do Quaraí near the border with Argentina.

If you're driving from Brazil, you'll need to stop at the Brazilian checkpoint to get an exit stamp and the Uruguayan checkpoint for the Uruguayans to check that you have a Brazilian exit stamp and a Uruguayan visa (if you need one). Buses will stop at the checkpoints.

Venezuela

Santa Elena From Boa Vista (Roraima state) you can cross into Venezuela via the border town of Santa Elena. There's a Venezuelan Consulate in Boa Vista, open Monday to Friday, 8 am to noon. Everyone requires a visa (free for most nationalities) to enter Venezuela overland. You'll need a photo, an onward ticket, sufficient funds, and probably a letter from your embassy, bank and/or employer guaranteeing that you're gainfully employed or financially sound. Further information is included under Boa Vista and Santa Elena in the Amazonas and Roraima chapter.

RIVER

Passenger boat services between Corumbá and Asunción (Paraguay) have been discontinued. Boat transport through the Pantanal is infrequent – enquire at the Porto Geral.

Peru

Islandia & Santa Rosa The main route between Brazil and Peru is along the Amazon from Tabatinga (Brazil) to Iquitos. Some boats leave from Islandia (the Peruvian port village on an island at the junction of the Rio Yauari and the Amazon) and from Santa Rosa a few kilometres further upstream in Peru. For further information on the Triple Frontier region, refer to the Benjamin Constant, Tabatinga and Leticia sections in the Amazonas and Roraima chapter.

DEPARTURE TAXES

Get ready to get angry. Brazilian departure taxes are steep, and in a state of constant flux. At the time of writing, the airport tax for international flights is US$36. But take note that as we researched this edition the Cardoso government introduced austerity measures that would have increased the already extortionate departure fee to, hold on to your hats, US$90! After this announcement was made, dire predictions of tourist fall-off forced the government to reconsider. You pay at the airport if the tax is not included in the price of your ticket – ask when you buy the ticket if it includes departure tax.

ORGANISED TOURS

The following list of organisations and tour agencies provides a sample of the tour options available for independent travellers with special interests.

Brazil

Expeditours (☎ (021) 287-9697; fax 521-4388), Rua Visconde de Pirajá 414 (Room 1010), Rio de Janeiro, is one of the largest ecological tour operators in Brazil. It specialises in the Amazon and Pantanal, but runs many other programs for the special-interest traveller. Expeditours is highly recommended.

Focus Tours (☎ (031) 332-4627), in Belo Horizonte, Minas Gerais (speak to Regina Caldeira in English or Portuguese), runs a variety of tours with a strong emphasis on the environment and ecology; see the section on the USA for more information and the American office details.

The UK

The boom in ecotourism worldwide has prompted the creation of groups and organisations in the UK and elsewhere to monitor the effects of tourism and provide assessments and recommendations for those involved. For more information on ecotours try contacting Tourism Concern (☎ (0171) 753-3330), 277-281 Holloway Rd, London, N7 8HN, or Green Globe

Choosing An Ecotourism Company

'Ecotourism' is the industry buzz word of the 1990s, and many companies around the world claim they're 'professional' and offer 'naturalist' guides. When you choose an ecotourism tour operator, you run the risk of hiring someone who's not really ecologically aware, or just using 'green' words to snare tourists. We asked Doug Trent of Focus Tours how he would pick an ecotour operator (if it weren't his own), and he said to start by asking the operator: 'What aspects of your business do you think qualify it as an ecotour business'?

Look for a portion of the profits going into destination country conservation projects, rubbish removal from sensitive areas, funding conservation and social projects etc. Look for something beyond what you would find with any lodge or tour (eg almost all lodges hire people from the regions where the lodges are found). Do they give them any special training that would allow workers to progress into positions that are more profitable?

Ecotours usually cost considerably more than traditional tourism. Ask a number of questions to determine the nature and level of professionalism of a natural history tour. Here are three broad questions you might ask:

- 'Who are your guides, and what are their qualifications?' Look for professional naturalist qualifications, rather than assuming that someone who lived in the area all their life would know the natural history of the region.
- 'What equipment do your guides use?' Binoculars will be used by all professional guides. A spotting telescope is priceless when an animal is far from the observer. Tape recording and playback equipment is essential to seeing many animals in forest situations. Spotlights are necessary for night and crepuscular wildlife viewing. Appropriate bird and mammal field guides should be on hand.
- 'Can you send a copy of your bird and mammal list for the tour areas?' They should have a tour checklist already prepared with English and Latin names and send you a sample – if they can't, at least with English names, they might not have adequate knowledge of the natural history of a given area.

For more detailed information on ecotour travel, check out Tourism Concern's Community Tourism Web site at www.gn.apc.org/tourismconcern/

(☎ (01223) 890-255; fax 890-258), PO Box 396, Linton, Cambridge, CB1 6UL.

The USA

Focus Tours (☎ (505) 466-4688; focustours@aol.com), 103 Moya Rd, Santa Fe, NM 87505, USA, is rated highly for its dedication to conservation and use of naturalists as guides. Tour members are given the use of telescopes and bird-identification books, and guides also use professional recording equipment to call out otherwise shy animals. Tour destinations include the Pantanal (and Chapada dos Guimarães), Minas Gerais, Amazon, Parque Nacional do Itatiaia and Serra da Canastra. Focus also runs tours to other South American destinations including Argentina, Chile, Bolivia and Paraguay. Its owner, Doug Trent, has been running ecological tours to Brazil since before the word 'ecotourism' was coined, and what he doesn't know about birds isn't worth knowing. Although he has a number of tour agendas, Doug is very flexible, and would be happy to include destinations of special interest to his clients. Doug tells us that on 40% of his tours they spot a jaguar. We haven't met any other tour guides who can claim a figure that high!

Brazilian Views (☎ (212) 472-9539), 201 E 66th St, Suite 21G New York, NY 10021, is a small agency offering a wide range of tailored, special-interest tours based on topics such as horticulture, weaving, bird-watching, arts and crafts, gems and minerals etc.

Victor Emanuel Nature Tours (☎ (800) 328-8368), Box 33008, Austin, TX 78764, specialises in bird-watching trips.

Earthwatch (☎ (617) 926-8200), 680 Mt Auburn St (PO Box 9104), Watertown, MA 02272, organises trips for volunteers to work overseas on scientific and cultural projects with a strong emphasis on protection and preservation of ecology and environment. Other organisations which provide tours with a similar emphasis include Conservation International (☎ (202) 429-5660) and The Nature Conservancy (☎ (703) 841-5300).

For more addresses, see the Environment & Ecology section in the Facts about the Country chapter.

Australia

Inca Tours South America (☎ (02) 4351-2133; fax 4351-2526), 3 Margaret St Wyong, NSW 2259, specialises in travel to South America. Lew Pullbrook, who runs it, has been visiting the continent for years and really knows his way around. Lew organises trips for small or larger groups and he's happy for backpackers to call for a bit of advice.

WARNING

The information in this chapter is particularly vulnerable to change: prices for international travel are volatile, routes are introduced and cancelled, schedules change, special deals come and go, and rules and visa requirements are amended. Airlines and governments seem to take a perverse pleasure in making price structures and regulations as complicated as possible. You should check directly with the airline or a travel agent to make sure you understand how a fare (and ticket you may buy) works. In addition, the travel industry is highly competitive and there are many lurks and perks.

The upshot of this is that you should get opinions, quotes and advice from as many airlines and travel agents as possible before you part with your hard-earned cash. The details given in this chapter should be regarded as pointers and are not a substitute for your own careful, up-to-date research.

Getting Around

AIR

Flying in Brazil is not cheap, but with the seemingly endless expanses of sertão, Amazon and Pantanal between many destinations, the occasional flight can be an absolute necessity. And even if you don't use it, having extra money for flights can add flexibility to your travel plans.

Brazil has three major national carriers and several smaller regional airlines. The biggies are Varig/Cruzeiro, VASP and Transbrasil. Together they cover an extensive network of cities; they don't all go to the same places, but at least one of them goes to every major city. As this edition was being researched, fares were coming down steadily, but they're still expensive. If you plan on doing a bit of flying, check whatever special discounts are available.

Stop Press

As we went to press, a nascent domestic airfare deregulation programme was poised to render all airfares stated here obsolete. This is great news for travellers who could see airfares on major routes drop by 40% or even more. Check with your travel agent before you leave for Brazil or enquire on arrival.

Domestic Air Services

Strange routes, bizarre connections, long lay overs and frequent stops are always a danger on domestic flights. Planes flying along the coast often stop at every city, so if you're going from Rio to Fortaleza it's possible that the plane will stop at Salvador, Maceió, Recife and João Pessoa on the way. Sometimes these outrageously indirect flights are unavoidable, but not always. Some travellers use these flights as an alternative to the airpass. Transbrasil has a flight like this from Belém to Rio, for around US$350, with unlimited stopovers, valid for 6 or 12 months. If you are only travelling the coastal regions, it seems a much better deal.

The smaller domestic airlines include Nordeste, Rio Sul, TABA, Votec and Tam. They mostly use the Bandeirante, a small Brazilian-built prop-plane (which some claim is not too safe) and fly to smaller cities where the major carriers don't go. We used Nordeste to fly to Ilhéus once when we couldn't get a seat on a plane directly to Salvador.

Air Taxi There are also many air-taxi companies, which mostly fly in the Amazon region. These flights are expensive, although the price usually drops if there are more passengers – and sometimes you can bargain.

Military Flights Aeronautica, which flies military transport planes, has been known to give free flights when it has extra space, but you might have to wait a while. First the officers get a seat, then the soldiers, then the civilians. Go to the desk marked 'CAN' in the airport and ask about the next military flight, then show up again two days before scheduled departure time and sign up. It helps to have a letter of introduction from a consulate. Some air bases (eg Santarém) restrict flights to Brazilian nationals, but it's not as rigid as it often appears. The whole process is hit and miss but it's worth a try, particularly in the North in cities like Boa Vista, Macapá, Porto Velho, Manaus, Santarém, Rio Branco, Belém and São Luís.

Domestic Airport Tax At the time of writing, the airport tax for domestic flights ranged from US$12 to $15, but can (and does) change all the time. The exact figure for the appropriate tax can vary slightly, but is usually added to the price of your ticket. If you have an airpass, you'll have to pay it at each airport. Yes, it is a real rip-off.

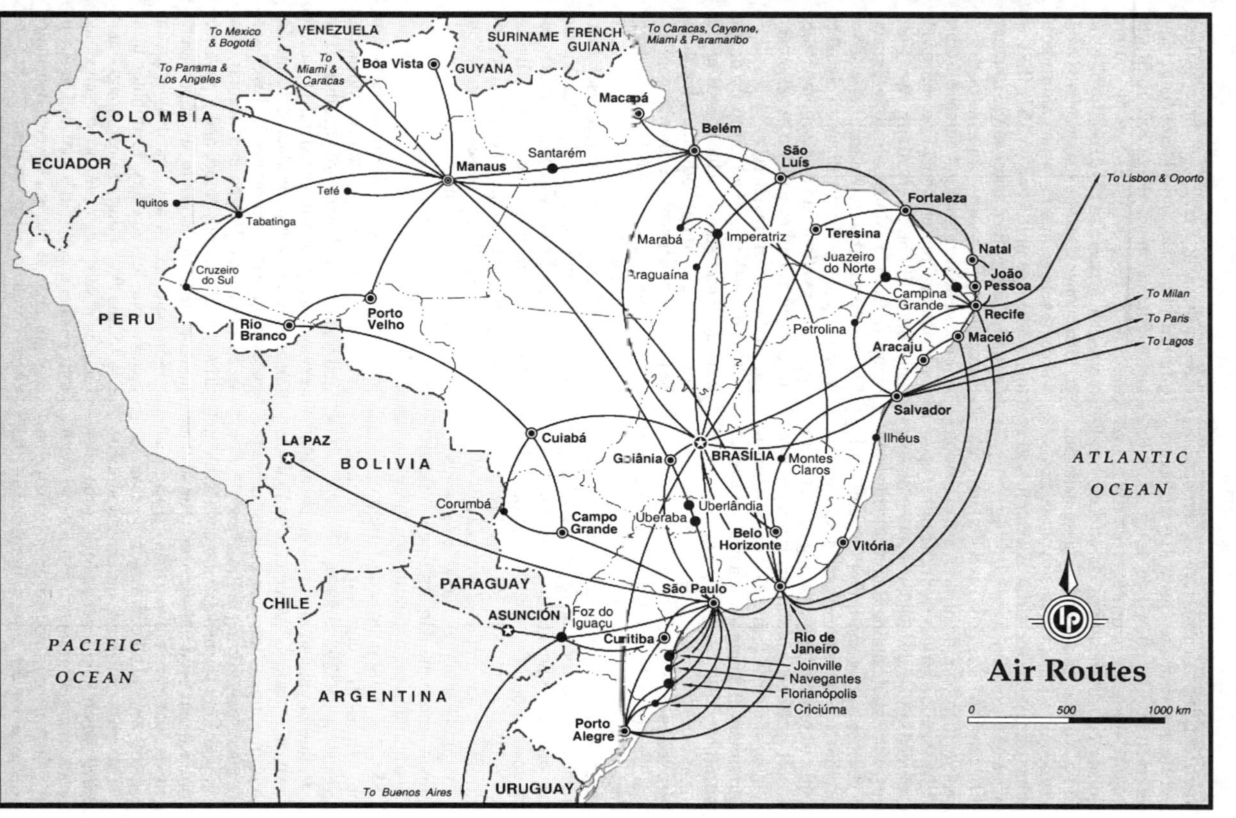
Air Routes
0
500
1000 km
ATLANTIC
OCEAN
PACIFIC
OCEAN
To Mexico & Bogotá
To Panama & Los Angeles
To Miami & Caracas
To Caracas, Cayenne, Miami & Paramaribo
To Lisbon & Oporto
To Milan
To Paris
To Lagos
To Buenos Aires
VENEZUELA
GUYANA
SURINAME
FRENCH GUIANA
COLOMBIA
ECUADOR
PERU
BOLIVIA
PARAGUAY
CHILE
ARGENTINA
URUGUAY
Boa Vista
Macapá
Belém
Manaus
Santarém
Tefé
Iquitos
Tabatinga
Cruzeiro do Sul
Rio Branco
Porto Velho
São Luís
Fortaleza
Teresina
Marabá
Imperatriz
Araguaína
Juazeiro do Norte
Natal
João Pessoa
Campina Grande
Recife
Maceió
Petrolina
Aracaju
Salvador
Ilhéus
LA PAZ
Cuiabá
BRASÍLIA
Montes Claros
Corumbá
Campo Grande
Uberlândia
Uberaba
Belo Horizonte
Vitória
São Paulo
ASUNCIÓN
Foz do Iguaçu
Curitiba
Rio de Janeiro
Joinville
Navegantes
Florianópolis
Criciúma
Porto Alegre

Reservations Air reservations can appear and disappear mysteriously. If you have a reservation it's often necessary to both confirm it and reconfirm it, even if you've already bought the ticket. If you have been told a flight is full, keep trying to make the reservation and perhaps alter your tactics by going directly to the airline's central ticket office or the airport.

Because flying is expensive, it's rarely difficult getting on a flight, with the exception of the vacation periods from December up to Carnaval and July. Make reservations as early as possible during Carnaval! However, if you get caught short, don't assume all is lost. Several times travel agents were unable to get us reservations, assuring us that there wasn't a ticket to Salvador within two months of Carnaval, and we got the reservation simply by going to the airline counter at the airport.

Airpasses

The Transbrasil Brazil Airpass can be a good deal. It now costs from US$490 to $540 depending on the carrier and buys you five flight coupons for five flights anywhere in the country. It's possible to pay US$100 each for an additional four flight coupons, adding up to US$890 to $940 for nine flights. All travel must be completed within 21 days.

Airpasses are also available for areas of limited travel; the Airpass II, covering the Central and South of the country, costs from US$350 to $400 depending on the carrier; the Airpass III, covering the Northeast, costs from US$290 to $340.

Before buying an airpass, you should sit down and work out whether it is really a good investment for your purposes. There are often delays flying in Brazil and it's rare that you don't waste a day in transit. Unless you're intent on a whistle-stop tour of the country, there are only so many flights that you will want to take in two or three weeks.

The pass *must* be purchased outside Brazil, where you'll get an MCO (miscellaneous charges order) in your name with 'Brazil Airpass' stamped on it, which you exchange for an airpass from one of the three airlines in Brazil. All three airlines offer the same deal, and all three fly to most major cities, although Varig/Cruzeiro flies to more cities than the other two. If you are buying an airpass and have specific plans to go to a smaller city, you may want to check with a travel agent to see which airline goes there (for example, only VASP flies to Corumbá, the port of entry to the southern Pantanal).

Airpass holders who get bumped from a flight for any reason should reconfirm all their other flight reservations. We were bumped from a Manaus-Foz do Iguaçu flight once and then found that because we weren't on that particular flight, all our other airpass reservations had been scrubbed from the computer. This experience has also been reported by other travellers.

The airpass cannot be used to fly on the Rio-São Paulo shuttle which lands at the downtown airports of both cities, but it can be used to fly between the international airports of both cities. The MCO is refundable if you don't use it in Brazil.

In New York, the BACC (see Useful Organisations in the Facts for the Visitor chapter) sells its version of an airpass (actually just tickets for up to five flights, which you can't change after booking) for as low as US$300 in low season and about US$500 in high season.

BUS

Except in the Amazon Basin, buses are the primary form of long-distance transportation for the vast majority of Brazilians. Bus services are generally excellent. Departure times are usually strictly adhered to, and the buses are clean, comfortable and well-serviced Mercedes, Volvos and Scanias. The drivers are generally good, and a governor limits their wilder urges to 80km per hour.

All major cities are linked by frequent buses – one leaves every 15 minutes from Rio to São Paulo during peak hours – and there is a surprising number of scheduled long-distance buses. It's rare that you will have to change buses between two major cities, no matter what the distance. See the

Dangers & Annoyances section in the Facts for the Visitor chapter for more information.

'Progress is roads' goes the saying in Brazil. And wherever there is a road in Brazil, no matter what condition it's in, there is a bus that travels it. We will never forget the bus that rescued us on an almost deserted peninsula out near Ponta do Mutá – a place where few people go, and no one seems to have heard of. How we got there is hard to explain, how the bus got there is impossible to explain. The 'road' was more like a wide trail, impassable by normal car and apparently unknown to Brazilian cartographers. But the bus came and eventually delivered us to a humble fishing village of no more than a hundred people.

Bus service varies by region. The South has the most and the best roads. Coastal highways are usually good, at least until São Luís. The Amazon and the sertão are another story. In several areas there the road alternates every few hundred metres between dirt (which is better) and pothole-infested sealed road (which is much worse). This pattern conforms to no obvious geographical or human design, and forces constant speeding up and slowing down.

Road construction has increased tremendously in previously unsettled regions in Brazil. This applies particularly to the Transamazônica highway and the Amazon region where roads have become the cornerstone of government strategies for economic development and military schemes to defend Brazilian borders. But many of these roads are precarious at best. Most are unsealed and are washed out during the rainy season, when buses get stuck and are always being delayed. In the dry season buses are usually scorching hot, dusty and stuffed with people. Bus transportation in the Amazon is always an adventure, teaching a healthy respect for the power and the size of the forest.

Classes

There are two classes of long-distance buses. The ordinary or *comum* is the most common. It's quite comfortable and usually has a toilet on board. The *leito* or *executivo* is Brazil's version of the couchette. Although they usually take as long to reach their destination as a comum and cost twice as much, leitos, which often depart late at night, are exceptionally comfortable. They have spacious, fully reclining seats with blankets and pillows, air-conditioning, and more often than not, a steward serving sandwiches, coffee, soda and água mineral. If you don't mind missing the scenery, a leito bus can get you there in comfort and save you the cost of a hotel room.

With or without toilets, buses generally make pit-stops every three or four hours. These stops are great places to meet other bus passengers, buy bizarre memorabilia and wish you were back home eating a healthy vegetarian quiche.

Reservations

Usually you can go down to the rodoviária and buy a ticket for the next bus out. Where this is difficult, for example in Ouro Prêto, we try to let you know. In general though it's a good idea to buy a ticket at least a few hours in advance, or if it's convenient, the day before departure. On weekends, holidays and from December to February this is always a good idea.

Aside from getting you on the bus, buying a ticket early has a few other advantages. First, it gets you an assigned seat – many common buses fill the aisles with standing passengers. Second, you can ask for a front row seat, with extra leg space, or a window seat with a view (ask for a *janela* or an even-numbered seat).

You don't always have to go to the rodoviária to buy your bus ticket. Selected travel agents in the major cities sell tickets for long-distance buses. This is a great service which can save you a long trip out to an often chaotic rodoviária. The price is the same and the travel agents are more likely to speak some English and are usually less rushed.

Costs

Bus travel throughout Brazil is very cheap (fares work out to about US$3 per hour): for example, the six-hour trip from Rio to São Paulo costs US$18, and the 22 hour trip from Rio to Foz do Iguaçu is US$54.

Driving in Brazil

Last edition, I rented a late-model Volkswagen Gol (the predecessor to the Golf) 1000. In Brazil it's known as the people's car, because it's the cheapest car around.

Road conditions varied from excellent to pretty bad, and we ended up with 10 flat tyres for the trip. Flat tyres are very common in Brazil, and, luckily, there are *borracheiros* (tyre repairers) at frequent intervals along the roads.

The most serious thing that happened was a slight collision that broke a headlight and put a scratch in the rear passenger door of the other car. Since we didn't want to pay for the damage, we got a police statement in Cuiaba. But we still got screwed by the rental car company – it had a clause in very fine print which said that the renter had to pay 70% of the daily rental rate for each day that the car was off the road getting fixed!

Driving in Brazil was an interesting experience. You have to be on the lookout on blind corners, because there's probably a Brazilian coming the other way who's decided to overtake a truck. Car wrecks are piled up at the police checkpoints that dot the highways. We saw some horrible wrecks.

The police we met on the roads were a mixed bunch. At the checkpoint on the São Paulo-Paraná border, a cop pulled us over to look at our papers. He found some bogus problem and told us that there would be a fine. Five minutes later and US$60 poorer, we were on our way. But another time when we got stopped for speeding, the cop was very friendly. He said he didn't want us to give Australians the impression that Brazilian police officers were bastards. Only some of them are it seems.

Andrew Draffen

Bus Terminals (Rodoviárias)

In every big city, and most small ones, there is a central bus terminal *(rodoviária*, pronounced 'HO-do-vee-ah-ree-ya'). The rodoviárias are most frequently on the outskirts of the city. Some are modern, comfortable stations. All have restaurants, newsstands and toilets, and some even have post offices and long-distance telephone facilities. Most importantly, all the long-distance bus companies operate out of the same place, making it easy to find your bus.

Inside the rodoviária you'll find ticket offices for the various bus companies. They usually post bus destinations and schedules in their windows; occasionally they are printed on leaflets; sometimes you just have to get in line and ask the teller for information. This can be difficult if you don't speak much Portuguese and the teller is in a highly agitated state after the 23rd cafezinho or speaks with an accent from the interior of Ceará. The best strategy is probably to have a pen and paper handy and ask the teller to write down what you need to know.

When you find a bus company that goes to your destination, don't assume it's the only one; there are often two or more and the quality may vary.

TRAIN

There are very few railway passenger services in Brazil, despite the fact that there is over 30,000km of track. Most trains only carry cargo.

Passenger services have been scaled down or even discontinued in the last few years, as the national railway company becomes more and more debt-ridden. Enthusiasts should not despair, however, as there are still some great train rides.

The Belo Horizonte-Vitória run is cheaper and far more pleasant than the bus ride. The Curitiba-Paranaguá train that descends the coastal mountain range offers some unforgettable views, as does the steam train that runs from São Paulo to Santos every weekend.

Speaking of steam trains, affectionately known in Brazil as *Maria Fumaças* (Smoking Marys), the 13km run from São João del Rei to Tiradentes in Minas Gerais is great fun. Other pleasant short trips are those from Joinville to the island of São Francisco do Sul, in Santa Catarina, and the ride through the mountains from Campos do Jordão to Santo Antônio do Pinhal (São Paulo), the highest stretch of track in the country.

Probably the train of most interest to travellers is the route from São Paulo to Corumbá, on the Bolivian border. It's no longer possible to take a train for the whole journey. The Bauru (São Paulo) to Campo Grande leg must be done by bus. (See the São Paulo chapter for details.)

CAR & MOTORCYCLE

Car The number of fatalities caused by motor vehicles in Brazil is estimated at 80,000 per year. The roads can be very dangerous, especially the busy highways like the Rio to São Paulo corridor. If you thought the Italians were wild drivers, just wait. This isn't true everywhere, but in general the car owner is king of the road and shows it; other motorists are treated as gate-crashers, pedestrians shown no mercy, and certainly no courtesy.

Especially in Rio, the anarchic side of the Brazilian personality emerges from behind the driver's wheel as lane dividers, one-way streets and footpaths are disregarded and violated. Driving is unpoliced and traffic violations unheard of. One of the most bizarre examples of this we encountered was while being given a lift by police on a highway north of Salvador – after waiting for several hours while every other car barrelled past without a thought of stopping. The police car, running at its top speed of about 140km/h, was passed by several other cars at speeds of over 150km/h. As each car passed, the police simply shook their heads and sighed, *Não respeito* (No respect).

Despite all appearances to the contrary, Brazil does hold to the convention that a red light means 'stop'. In practice, this quaint concept has been modified to mean 'maybe we'll stop, maybe we'll slow down – but if it's night we'll probably do neither'.

Drivers use their horns incessantly, and buses, which have no horns, rev their engines instead. One of the craziest habits is driving at night without headlights. This is done, as far as we can tell, so that the headlights can be flashed to warn approaching vehicles.

Many drivers are racing fans and tend to drive under the influence, pretending they are Formula One drivers. The worst are the Rio bus drivers, or maybe the São Paulo commuters, or maybe the Amazonian truck drivers, or maybe ... we could go on and on. This cult of speed, a close cousin to the cult of machismo, is insatiable; its only positive aspect is that, unlike grandma driving to church on Sunday, these drivers tend to be very alert and rarely fall asleep at the wheel.

Driving at night is hazardous, at least in the Northeast and the interior, where roads are often poor and unreliable. Like malaria, potholes are endemic. Poorly banked turns are the norm.

The Brazilian speed bump industry must be one of the world's largest, and its products are unbelievably huge, too. Always slow down when you enter a town, since many have speed bumps, variously known as *quebra-molas*, *lombadas* (over which your car will *lambada)*, *ondulações* or *sonorizadores*, which you never see until it's too late. Another big danger is the farm trucks with inexperienced drivers carrying workers and cargo to town.

On the bright side, many trucks and buses in the Northeast help you pass at night with their indicators. A flashing right indicator means it's clear to go, a flashing left means that a vehicle is approaching from the opposite direction. Everything happens more slowly in the Northeast, and this holds true for driving too.

Car Rental Renting a car is expensive with prices similar to those in the USA and Europe.

But if you can share the expense with friends it's a great way to explore some of the many remote beaches, fishing villages and back roads of Brazil. Several familiar multinationals dominate the car-rental business in Brazil and getting a car is safe and easy if you have a driver's licence, a credit card and a passport. You should also carry an international driver's licence.

There is little competition between the major rental companies. Prices are usually about the same, although there are occasional promotional deals (the only ones we encountered were during off-season weekends in non-tourist towns). Fiat Unos are the cheapest cars to rent, followed by the Volkswagen Golf, Gol and Chevette (which has a good reputation). Sometimes the rental companies will claim to be out of these cheaper models; if this is the case, don't hesitate to shop around. Also, when you get prices quoted on the phone, make sure they include insurance, which is required. When looking at the contract, pay close attention to any theft clause which appears to load a large percentage of any loss onto the hirer. Another tricky clause we found was that if you have an accident and get a police statement, you don't have to pay for the damage. But you do have to pay 70% of the daily hire for the number of days it takes the rental company to fix the car!

The big companies have offices in most cities; they are always out at the airport and often in the centre of town as well. In the phone book, look under *autolocadoras* or *locadoras de automóveis*. There are usually discounts for weekly and monthly rentals, and no drop-off charges.

Motorcycles Unless you're a competent rider, it's not a good idea to motorcycle around Brazil. There are road laws but no one obeys them, so anything goes. If you do decide to do it, then go for it. Brazil is a beautiful country, but try to keep your eyes on the road.

A road/trail bike is ideal because of it's versatility. Smaller bikes are OK for the cities, but on the Brazilian highways, with heavy truck traffic and pollution, it's wise to have a larger one.

Renting a bike is as expensive as renting a car. If you want to buy a bike, Brazil manufactures its own, but they are expensive. The most powerful we saw was 600cc.

Motorcycles are popular in Brazil, especially in and around the cities. Theft is a big problem; you can't even insure a bike because theft is so common. Most people who ride keep their bike in a guarded place, at least overnight. For the traveller this can be difficult to organise, but if you can manoeuvre around the practical problems, Brazil is a great place to have a motorcycle.

BICYCLE

You don't see many long-distance cyclists in Brazil. We wouldn't recommend cycling there, as conditions are very dangerous. See the Road section in the Getting There & Away chapter for more details.

HITCHING

Hitching is never entirely safe in any country in the world, and we don't recommend it. Travellers who decide to hitch should understand that they are taking a small but potentially serious risk. People who do choose to hitch will be safer if they travel in pairs and let someone know where they are planning to go.

Hitching in Brazil, with the possible exception of the Amazon and Pantanal, is difficult. The phrase for hitching in Portuguese is *carona*, so ask '*pode dar carona*' ('can you give me/us a lift'). The best way to hitch – practically the only way if you want a ride – is to wait at a petrol station or a truck stop and talk to the drivers. But even this can be difficult. A few years back there were several assaults by hitchhikers and the government began to discourage giving rides in public service announcements.

BOAT

Although river travel in Brazil has decreased rapidly due to the construction of a comprehensive road network, it is still possible to travel by boat between some of the river cities of the Rio São Francisco. See the River Travel section in the Bahia chapter.

For information on river travel in the Amazon region, see the North chapters.

LOCAL TRANSPORT

Bus

Local bus services tend to be pretty good in Brazil. Since most Brazilians take the bus to work every day, municipal buses are usually frequent and their network of routes is comprehensive. They are always cheap and crowded.

In most city buses, you get on at the back and exit from the front, though sometimes the reverse is true. Usually there's a money collector sitting at a turnstile, with the price displayed nearby. If you're unsure if it's the right bus, it's easy to hop on the back and ask the money collector if the bus is going to your destination – *você vai para ...?* If it's the wrong bus no one will mind if you hop off, even if the bus has gone a stop or two.

Crime can be a problem on buses. Rather than remain outside the turnstile, it's safer to pay the fare and go through the turnstile. Try to avoid carrying valuables if you can. If you must take valuables with you then keep them well hidden. See the Dangers & Annoyances section in the Facts for the Visitor chapter for more information.

Jumping on a local bus is one of the best ways to get to know a city. With a map and a few dollars you can tour the town and maybe meet some of the locals.

Taxi

Taxi rides are reasonably priced, if not cheap, but you should be aware of various tricks used by some drivers to increase the charges. We encountered some superb, friendly, honest and knowledgeable taxi drivers. However, we also met plenty of rogue cabbies with unsavoury characteristics.

Taxis in the large cities usually have meters with prices which are subject to frequent updates using a *tabela* (price sheet) to convert the price on the meter to a new price. This is OK as long as the meter works and the tabela is legal and current (don't accept photocopies). Unless you are certain about a standard price for a standard trip (and have verified this with the driver) or you have purchased a ticket from a taxi ticket office (described later in this section), you must insist that drivers turn on their meters (no excuses) at the beginning of the ride and show you a valid tabela at the end.

What you see is what you pay – no extras if you've only loaded a couple of pieces of baggage per person or the driver thinks the trip to the town centre has required 'extra' fuel. If the meter doesn't work or the driver won't engage it for whatever reason, then negotiate a fare before getting on board, or find another cab. If you want to get a rough idea about the going rate prior to taking a taxi ride into town, ask a newsagent or an official at the rodoviária, train station or the airport.

As a general rule, Tarifa I (standard tariff) applies from approximately 6 am to 10 pm (Monday to Saturday); Tarifa II (higher tariff) applies outside these hours, on holidays and outside city limits. Sometimes there is a standard charge, typically for the trip between the airport and the city centre. Many airports and rodoviárias now have a system for you to purchase a taxi ticket from a *bilheteria* (ticket office). However, in a few places, the ticket office applies a much higher rate than if you flag a taxi down outside the rodoviária or airport – we've indicated where this is the case.

The same general advice applies to taxis without meters. You must agree on the price beforehand, and make sure there is no doubt about it. Learn the numbers in Portuguese. If the driver hesitates for a long time or starts using fingers instead of talking to you about numbers, you may find the price has been grasped from imagination rather than being the normal rate. You don't want to have an argument at the end of the ride – it's not worth it, even if you win.

If the driver claims to have no change, hold firm and see if this is just a ploy to extract more from you. We often found that change mysteriously appeared out of the driver's pocket when we said we'd be happy to wait in the taxi until change could be found. You can avoid this scenario by carrying change. (More tips can be found under Carrying Money in the Facts for the Visitor chapter.)

If possible, orient yourself before taking a taxi, and keep a map handy in case you find yourself being taken on a wild detour – even following the route on the map during the ride isn't a bad idea, and it's an effective way of orienting yourself. Never use taxi touts – an almost certain rip-off. Deal directly with the taxi driver at the taxi rank, or with the taxi company.

The worst place to get a cab is wherever the tourists are. Don't get a cab near one of the expensive hotels. In Rio, for example, walk a block away from the beach at Copacabana to flag down a cab. Many airports have special airport taxis which are about 50% more expensive than a regular taxi which is probably waiting just around the corner. If you are carrying valuables, however, the special airport taxi, or a radio-taxi can be a worthwhile investment. These are probably the safest taxis on the road.

For more tips on security and taxi travel see the Dangers & Annoyances section in the Facts for the Visitor chapter.

The Southeast

The Southeast

The Southeast region, known in Brazil as the Sudeste, comprises almost 11% of the country's land area and is home to a whopping 44% of Brasileiros – 90% of whom live in cities. The region is made up of the states of Rio de Janeiro, Espírito Santo, São Paulo and Minas Gerais.

Geographically, the Southeast contains the most mountainous areas of the Planalto Atlântico: the Serras da Mantiqueira, do Mar and do Espinaço, making it popular with hikers and climbers.

Most of the region was once covered by the lush Mata Atlântica, but this has been devastated since the arrival of the Portuguese. Inland, Minas Gerais also contains areas of cerrado and caatinga. Two great rivers begin in the mountains of the Southeast: the Paraná, formed by the Paraíba and Grande rivers, and the São Francisco, which begins in the Serra da Canastra in Minas.

The Southeast is the economic powerhouse of Brazil and contains 60% of the country's industry. This wealth attracts migrants from all over Brazil, who flock to the three largest cities of Brazil – São Paulo, Rio de Janeiro and Belo Horizonte – in search of something better.

Attractions of the Southeast include the *cidade maravilhosa* Rio de Janeiro; historic colonial towns (Parati, Ouro Prêto and many others in Minas); national parks (Serra dos Órgãos, Itatiaia and Caparaó); and the people themselves – the hard-working Paulistas (from São Paulo), the fun-loving Cariocas (from Rio), the strong-willed Capixabas (from Espírito Santo) and the spiritual Mineiros (from Minas Gerais).

HIGHLIGHTS

- Double hang-gliding in Rio de Janeiro
- Hiking and diving on Ilha Grande (Rio state)
- A Flamengo-Fluminense football game at Maracanã stadium (Rio de Janeiro)
- The colonial village of Parati (Rio de Janeiro)
- Trekking the old gold route from São Jose Barreiro to Parati (you actually cross the São Paulo-Rio border during this trek)
- Trekking through the Parque Nacional Serra dos Orgãos from Teresópolis to Petrópolis (Rio de Janeiro)
- Cycling from Leblon to Flamengo in Rio on Tuesday evenings with hundreds of other bikers (Rio de Janeiro)
- Brazilian baroque churches in the colonial towns of Minas Gerais
- Hiking in the Parque Nacional de Caparaó on crisp, clear winter days (Minas Gerais)
- The steam train ride from São João del Rei to Tiradentes (Minas Gerais)

Rio de Janeiro City

• *pop 7 million* ✉ *20000-000* ☎ *021*

Rio is the *cidade maravilhosa* (marvellous city). Seven million Cariocas, as the inhabitants are called, are jammed into the world's most beautiful city setting – between ocean and escarpment. This makes Rio one of the most densely populated places on earth. This thick brew of Cariocas pursues pleasure like no other people: beaches and the body beautiful, samba and football, *cerveja* (beer); and *cachaça* (sugar-cane rum).

Rio has its problems, and they are enormous. A third of the people live in the *favelas* (shantytowns) that blanket many of the hillsides. The poor have no schools, no doctors and no jobs. Drug abuse and violence are endemic. Police corruption and brutality are commonplace. Nevertheless, in Rio everything ends with samba – football games, weddings, work, political demonstrations and, of course, a day at the beach. There's a lust for life, and a love of romance, music, dance and talk that seem to distinguish the Cariocas from everyone else. For anyone coming from the efficiency and rationalism of the developed, capitalist world this is potent stuff. The sensuality of Carnaval is the best known expression of this Dionysian spirit, but there are plenty more.

Rio has its glitzy side – the international tourist crowd and the lives of its rich and famous. But happily it's also a good city for the budget traveller. There are plenty of cheap restaurants and hotels. The beaches are free and democratic. There's lots to explore in the city centre and in several other neighbourhoods with their parks and museums. Public transport is fast and easy. And if you can meet some locals – not nearly so hard as in New York, London or Sydney – well, then you're on easy street.

History

Gaspar de Lemos set sail from Portugal for Brazil in May 1501 and entered a huge bay in January 1502. Mistaking the bay for a river, he named it Rio de Janeiro.

It was the French, however, who first settled along the great bay. Like the Portuguese, the French had been harvesting brazil wood along the Brazilian coast, but unlike the Portuguese they hadn't attempted any permanent settlements until Rio de Janeiro.

As the Portuguese colonisation of Brazil began to take hold, the French became concerned that they'd be pushed out of the colony. Three ships of French settlers reached the Baía de Guanabara in 1555. They settled on a small island in the bay and called it Antarctic France.

Almost from the start, the town seemed doomed to failure. It was torn by religious divisions, isolated by harsh treatment of the Indians and demoralised by the puritanical rule of the French leader, Nicolas de Villegagnon. Antarctic France was weak and disheartened when the Portuguese attacked.

A greater threat to the Portuguese were the powerful Tamoio Indians, who had allied with the French. A series of battles occurred, but the Portuguese were better armed and better supplied than the French, whom they finally expelled in 1560. They drove the Tamoio from the region in a series of bloody battles.

The Portuguese set up a fortified town on the Morro Castelo in 1567 to maximise protection from European invasion by sea and Indian attack by land. They named it São Sebastião do Rio de Janeiro, after King Sebastião of Portugal.

The founding 500 Cariocas built a typical Brazilian town: poorly planned, with irregular streets in medieval Portuguese style. By the end of the century the small settlement was, if not exactly prosperous, surviving on the export of brazil wood and sugar cane, and from fishing in the Baía de Guanabara.

MAP 1
Rio de Janeiro
MAGÉ
Ponta do Saco
Ilha do Morro Grande
Rio Estrela
Rio Iguacu
Avenida Presidente Kennedy
Rodovia Washington
BR 40
Sarapui Canal
DUQUE DE CAXIAS
Ilha de Pancaraiba
Ilha de Brocoió
Baía de Guanabara
Ilha de Paquetá
Ilha do Boqueirão
Rio São João de Meriti
Ilha do Governador
Aeroporto Internacional Rio de Janeiro
BR 116
BR 101
Linha Vermelha
Avenida Brasil
CORDOVIL
IRAJÁ
PENHA
Ilha do Engenho
Ponta do Catalão
Avenida Uranos
Serra da Misericordia
Ilha do Fundão
BONSUCESSO
COSMOS
Ponta de Santo Antônio
Automóvel Clube
INHAÚMA
Ponte Presidente Costa e Silva
Ilha da Conceínção
CAJU
Avenida Suburbana
Ponta de Armação
MAP 2
SÃO CRISTOVÃO
Estação Dom Pedro II
ÁGUA SANTA
MÉIER
Quinta da Boa Vista
NITEROI
Aeroporto Santos Dumont
CENTRO
Ilha da Boa Viagem
Serra dos Pretos Forros
Maracanã
Avenida Menezes Cortes
Avenida Conde de Bonfim
Estrada dos Três Rios
ANDARAI
TIJUCA
MAP 3
FLAMENGO
Serra dos Três Rios
Serra da Carioca
Estrada de Jacarepaguá
Excelsior
Pico da Tijuca
Cristo Redentor
CORCOVADO
Corcovado (710m)
PARQUE NACIONAL DA TIJUCA
Avenida Passos
BOTAFOGO
LAGOA
Est do Bom Retiro
ALTO DA BOA VISTA
MAP 5
MAP 4
Ilha da Cotunduba
Avenida Édison
Vista Chinesa
Jardim Botânico
Lagoa Rodrigo de Freitas
COPACABANA
PARQUE NACIONAL DA TIJUCA
GÁVEA
ITANHANGÁ
LEBLON
IPANEMA
Lagoa da Tijuca
SÃO CONRADO
VIDIGAL
PEPINO
BARRA DA TIJUCA
JOÁ
Avenida Sernabetiba
ATLANTIC OCEAN
Ponta do Marisco
Ilha das Palmas
0
2.5
5 km

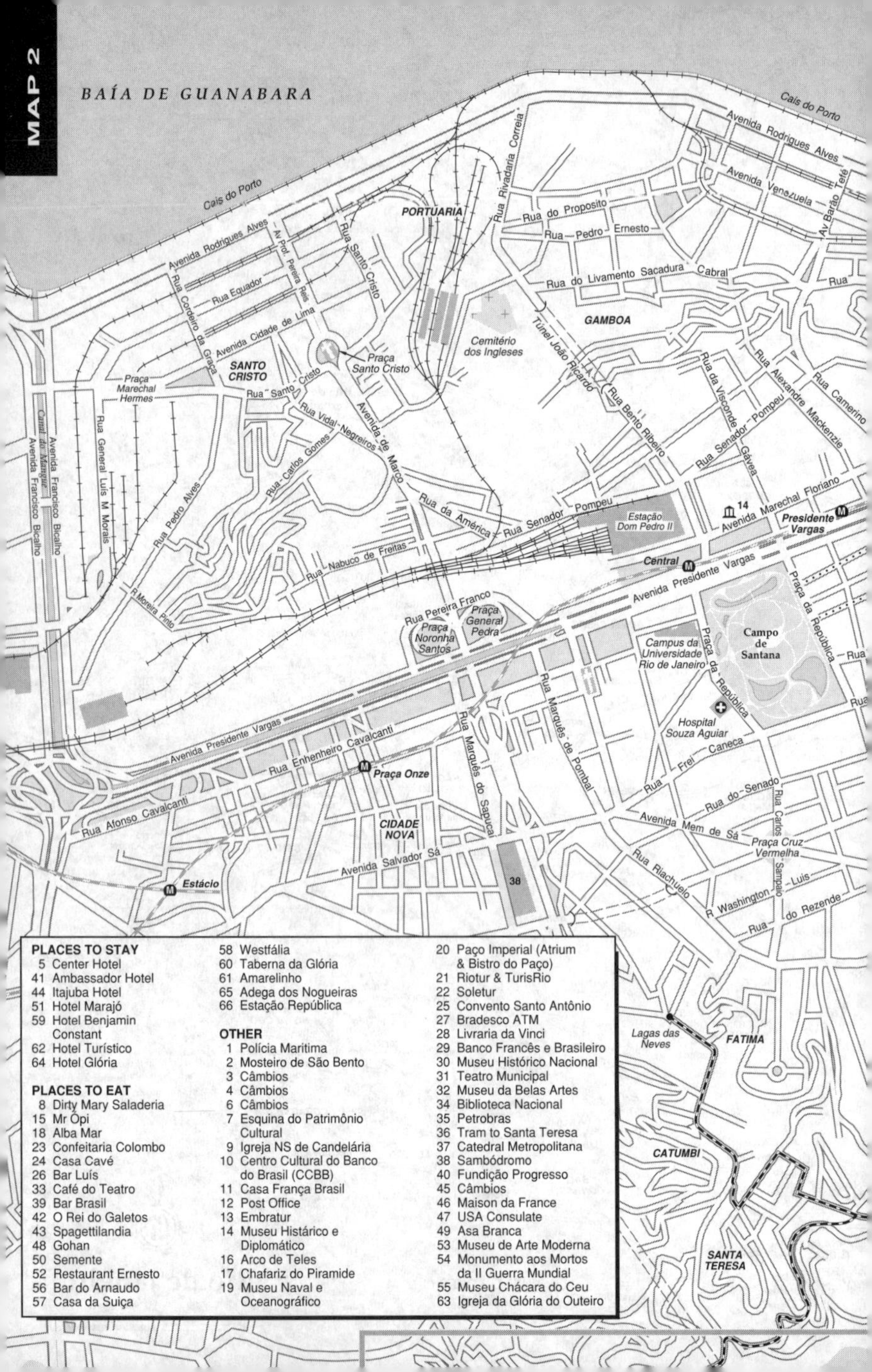

BAÍA DE GUANABARA

PLACES TO STAY
5 Center Hotel
41 Ambassador Hotel
44 Itajuba Hotel
51 Hotel Marajó
59 Hotel Benjamin Constant
62 Hotel Turístico
64 Hotel Glória

PLACES TO EAT
8 Dirty Mary Saladeria
15 Mr Ôpi
18 Alba Mar
23 Confeitaria Colombo
24 Casa Cavé
26 Bar Luís
33 Café do Teatro
39 Bar Brasil
42 O Rei do Galetos
43 Spagettilandia
48 Gohan
50 Semente
52 Restaurant Ernesto
56 Bar do Arnaudo
57 Casa da Suiça
58 Westfália
60 Taberna da Glória
61 Amarelinho
65 Adega dos Nogueiras
66 Estação República

OTHER
1 Polícia Maritima
2 Mosteiro de São Bento
3 Câmbios
4 Câmbios
6 Câmbios
7 Esquina do Patrimônio Cultural
9 Igreja NS de Candelária
10 Centro Cultural do Banco do Brasil (CCBB)
11 Casa França Brasil
12 Post Office
13 Embratur
14 Museu Histárico e Diplomático
16 Arco de Teles
17 Chafariz do Piramide
19 Museu Naval e Oceanográfico
20 Paço Imperial (Atrium & Bistro do Paço)
21 Riotur & TurisRio
22 Soletur
25 Convento Santo Antônio
27 Bradesco ATM
28 Livraria da Vinci
29 Banco Francês e Brasileiro
30 Museu Histórico Nacional
31 Teatro Municipal
32 Museu da Belas Artes
34 Biblioteca Nacional
35 Petrobras
36 Tram to Santa Teresa
37 Catedral Metropolitana
38 Sambódromo
40 Fundição Progresso
45 Câmbios
46 Maison da France
47 USA Consulate
49 Asa Branca
53 Museu de Arte Moderna
54 Monumento aos Mortos da II Guerra Mundial
55 Museu Chácara do Ceu
63 Igreja da Glória do Outeiro

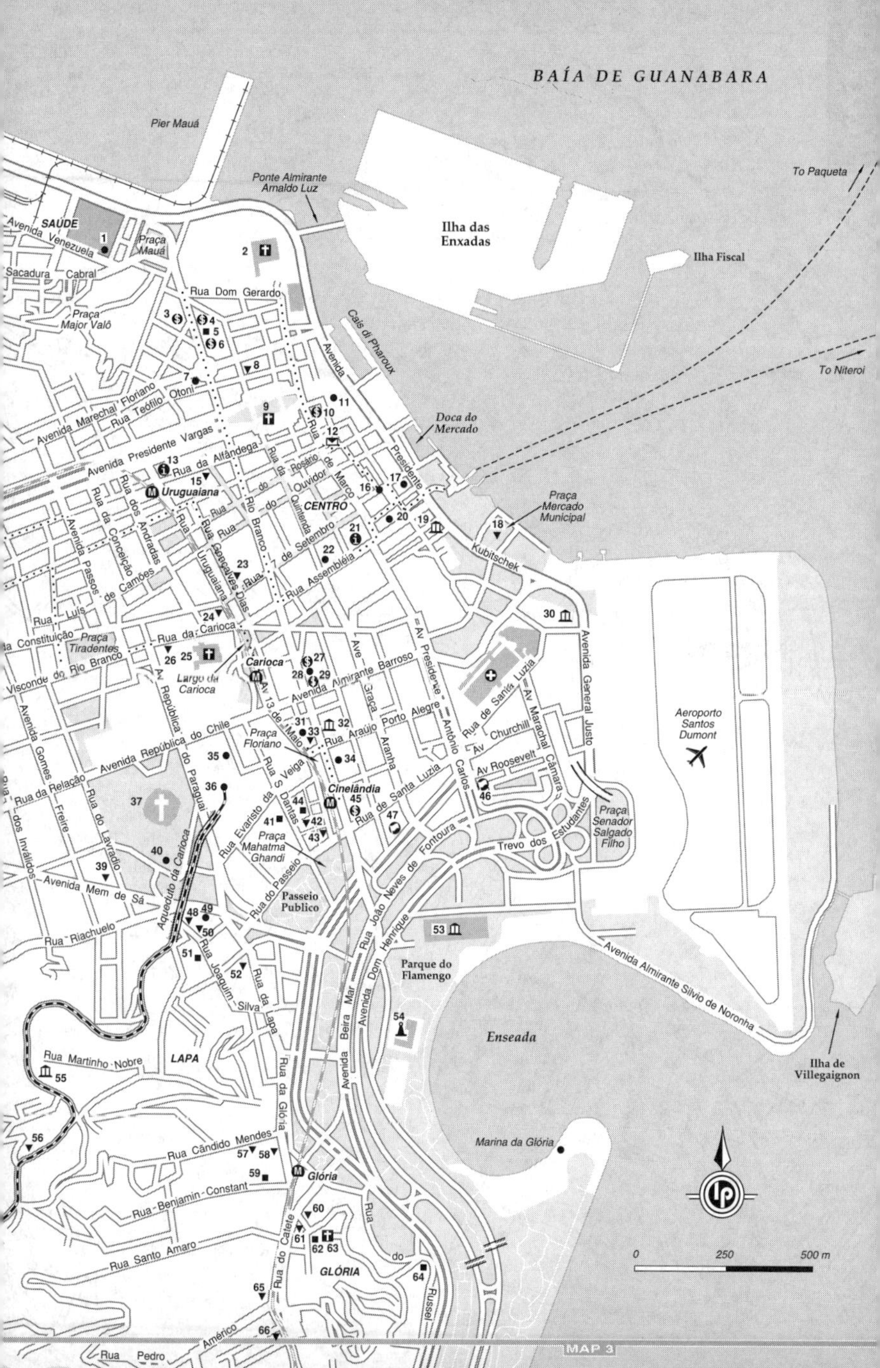

BAÍA DE GUANABARA
Pier Mauá
Ponte Almirante Arnaldo Luz
Ilha das Enxadas
Ilha Fiscal
To Paqueta
To Niteroi
SAÚDE
Avenida Venezuela
Praça Mauá
Sacadura Cabral
Rua Dom Gerardo
Praça Major Valô
Cais di Pharoux
Avenida Presidente Kubitschek
Doca do Mercado
Avenida Marechal Floriano
Rua Teófilo Otoni
Avenida Presidente Vargas
Rua da Alfândega
Uruguaiana
CENTRO
Rua do Ouvidor
Rua do Rosário
Rua do Quitanda
Rua 1º de Marco
Rua 7 de Setembro
Rio Branco
Praça Mercado Municipal
Rua Assembléia
Rua dos Andradas
Rua da Conceição
Avenida Passos
Rua Uruguaiana
Rua Gonçalves Dias
Rua de Camões
Rua Luís
Rua da Constituição
Praça Tiradentes
Rua da Carioca
Visconde do Rio Branco
Largo da Carioca
Carioca
Av 13 de Maio
Avenida Almirante Barroso
Av Presidente Antônio Carlos
Ave Graça Aranha
Rua de Santa Luzia
Av Marachal Câmara
Avenida General Justo
Aeroporto Santos Dumont
Av Churchill
Av Roosevelt
Rua Araújo Porto Alegre
Avenida República do Chile
Praça Floriano
Rua S Dantas
Rua Evaristo da Veiga
Cinelândia
Rua de Santa Luzia
Praça Senador Salgado Filho
Trevo dos Estudantes
Avenida Gomes Freire
Rua da Relação
Rua do Lavradio
Av República do Paraguai
Rua dos Inválidos
Praça Mahatma Ghandi
Aqueduto da Carioca
Avenida Mem de Sá
Rua do Passeio
Passeio Publico
Rua João Neves de Fontoura
Avenida Dom Henrique
Rua Riachuelo
Rua Joaquim Silva
Rua da Lapa
Parque do Flamengo
Avenida Almirante Silvio de Noronha
Avenida Beira Mar
Enseada
Ilha de Villegaignon
Rua Martinho Nobre
LAPA
Rua da Glória
Marina da Glória
Rua Cândido Mendes
Glória
Rua Benjamin Constant
Rua do Catete
Rua do Russel
Rua Santo Amaro
GLÓRIA
Rua Pedro Américo
0
250
500 m
1
2
3
4
5
6
7
8
9
10
11
12
13
15
16
17
18
19
20
21
22
23
24
25
26
27
28
29
30
31
32
33
34
35
36
37
39
40
41
42
43
44
45
46
47
48
49
50
51
52
53
54
55
56
57
58
59
60
61
62
63
64
65
66

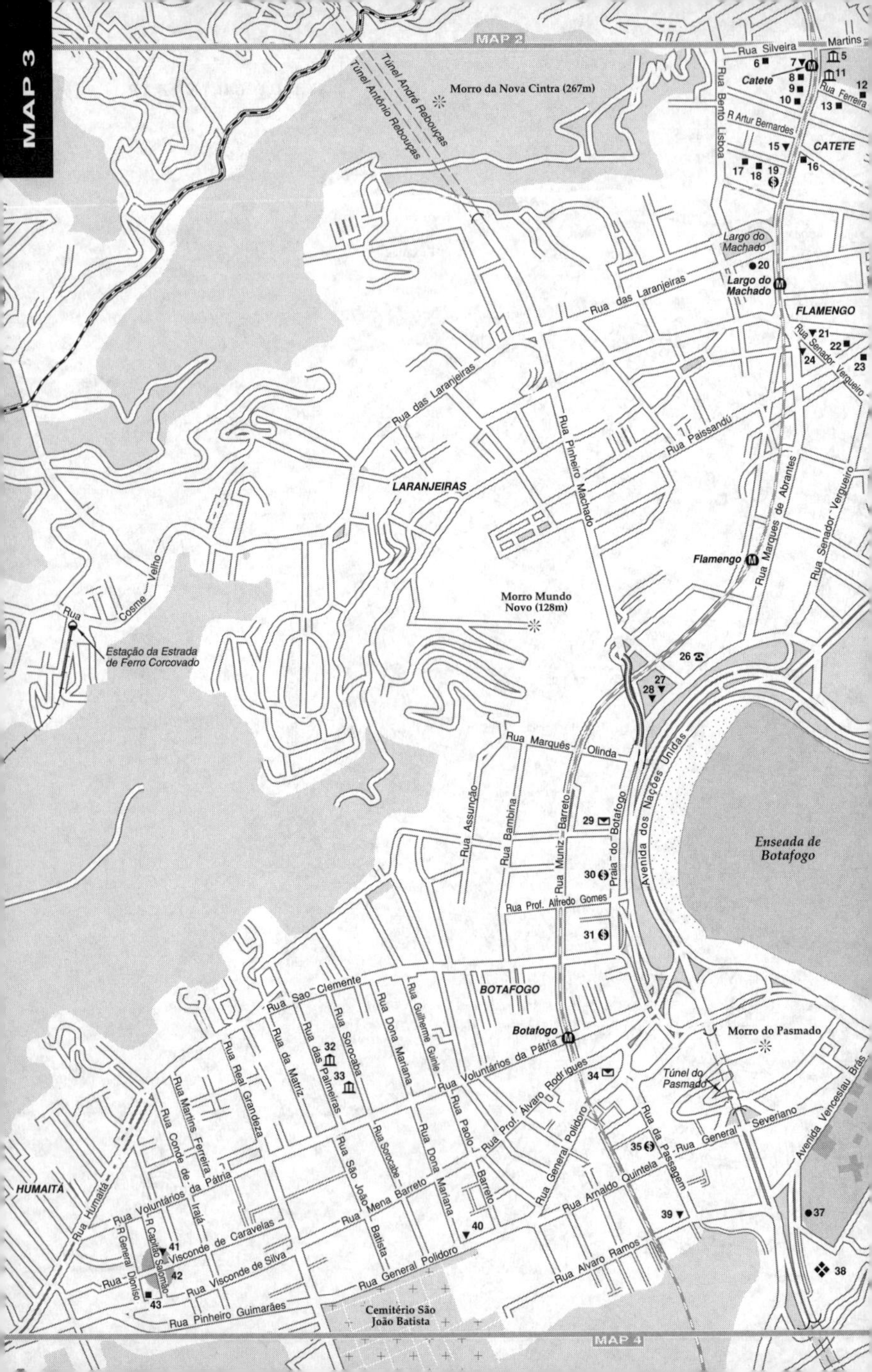
MAP 3
MAP 2
MAP 4
Túnel André Rebouças
Túnel Antônio Rebouças
Morro da Nova Cintra (267m)
Rua Silveira Martins
Catete
Rua Ferreira
R Artur Bernardes
Rua Bento Lisboa
CATETE
Largo do Machado
Largo do Machado
Rua das Laranjeiras
FLAMENGO
Rua Senador Vergueiro
Rua Paissandú
LARANJEIRAS
Rua Pinheiro Machado
Rua Marques de Abrantes
Rua Senador Vergueiro
Flamengo
Morro Mundo Novo (128m)
Rua Cosme Velho
Estação da Estrada de Ferro Corcovado
Rua Marquês Olinda
Avenida dos Nações Unidas
Rua Assunção
Rua Bambina
Rua Muniz Barreto
Praia do Botafogo
Enseada de Botafogo
Rua Prof. Alfredo Gomes
BOTAFOGO
Rua São Clemente
Botafogo
Morro do Pasmado
Túnel do Pasmado
Rua Real Grandeza
Rua da Matriz
Rua das Palmeiras
Rua Sorocaba
Rua Dona Mariana
Rua Guilherme Guinle
Rua Voluntários da Pátria
Rua Prof. Álvaro Rodrigues
Rua General Polidoro
Rua da Passagem
Rua General Severiano
Avenida Venceslau Brás
Rua Martins Ferreira
Rua Conde de Irajá
Rua São João Batista
Rua Sorocabe
Rua Paolo Barreto
Rua Mena Barreto
Rua Arnaldo Quintela
HUMAITÁ
Rua Humaitá
Rua Voluntários da Pátria
R General Dioniso
R Capitão Salomão
Rua Visconde de Caravelas
Rua Visconde de Silva
Rua General Polidoro
Rua Alvaro Ramos
Rua Pinheiro Guimarães
Cemitério São João Batista
5
6
7
8
9
10
11
12
13
15
16
17
18
19
20
21
22
23
24
26
27
28
29
30
31
32
33
34
35
37
38
39
40
41
42
43

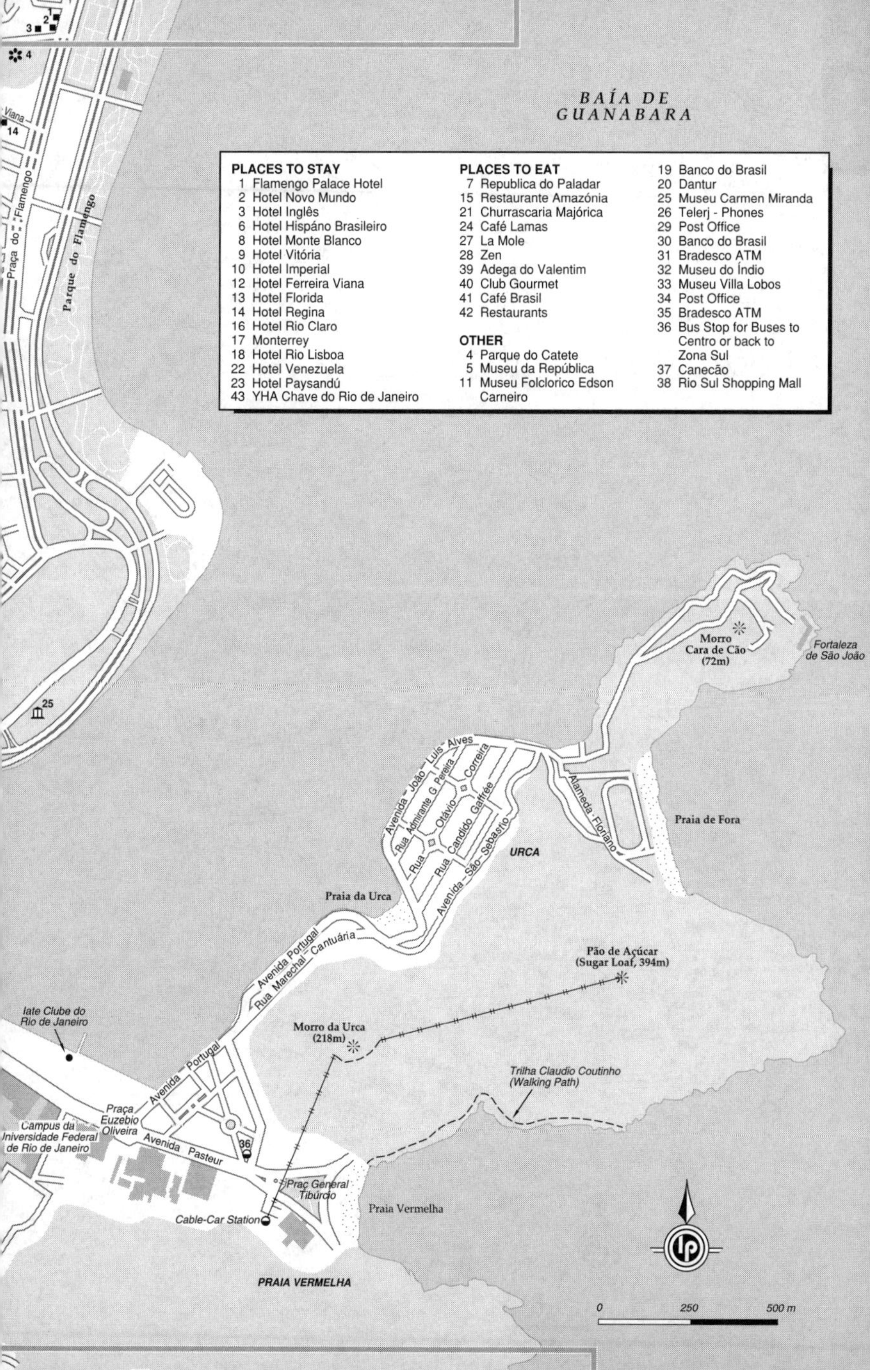

BAÍA DE GUANABARA
PLACES TO STAY
1 Flamengo Palace Hotel
2 Hotel Novo Mundo
3 Hotel Inglês
6 Hotel Hispáno Brasileiro
8 Hotel Monte Blanco
9 Hotel Vitória
10 Hotel Imperial
12 Hotel Ferreira Viana
13 Hotel Florida
14 Hotel Regina
16 Hotel Rio Claro
17 Monterrey
18 Hotel Rio Lisboa
22 Hotel Venezuela
23 Hotel Paysandú
43 YHA Chave do Rio de Janeiro
PLACES TO EAT
7 Republica do Paladar
15 Restaurante Amazónia
21 Churrascaria Majórica
24 Café Lamas
27 La Mole
28 Zen
39 Adega do Valentim
40 Club Gourmet
41 Café Brasil
42 Restaurants
OTHER
4 Parque do Catete
5 Museu da República
11 Museu Folclorico Edson Carneiro
19 Banco do Brasil
20 Dantur
25 Museu Carmen Miranda
26 Telerj - Phones
29 Post Office
30 Banco do Brasil
31 Bradesco ATM
32 Museu do Índio
33 Museu Villa Lobos
34 Post Office
35 Bradesco ATM
36 Bus Stop for Buses to Centro or back to Zona Sul
37 Canecão
38 Rio Sul Shopping Mall
Viana
Praça do Flamengo
Parque do Flamengo
Morro Cara de Cão (72m)
Fortaleza de São João
Avenida João Luis Alves
Rua Admirante G Pereira
Correira
Rua Otávio
Rua Candido Gaffrée
Avenida São Sebasho
Alameda Floriano
Praia de Fora
URCA
Praia da Urca
Avenida Portugal
Rua Marechal Cantuária
Pão de Açúcar (Sugar Loaf, 394m)
Iate Clube do Rio de Janeiro
Morro da Urca (218m)
Trilha Claudio Coutinho (Walking Path)
Praça Euzebio Oliveira
Campus da Universidade Federal de Rio de Janeiro
Avenida Pasteur
Prac General Tibúrcio
Cable-Car Station
Praia Vermelha
PRAIA VERMELHA
0 250 500 m

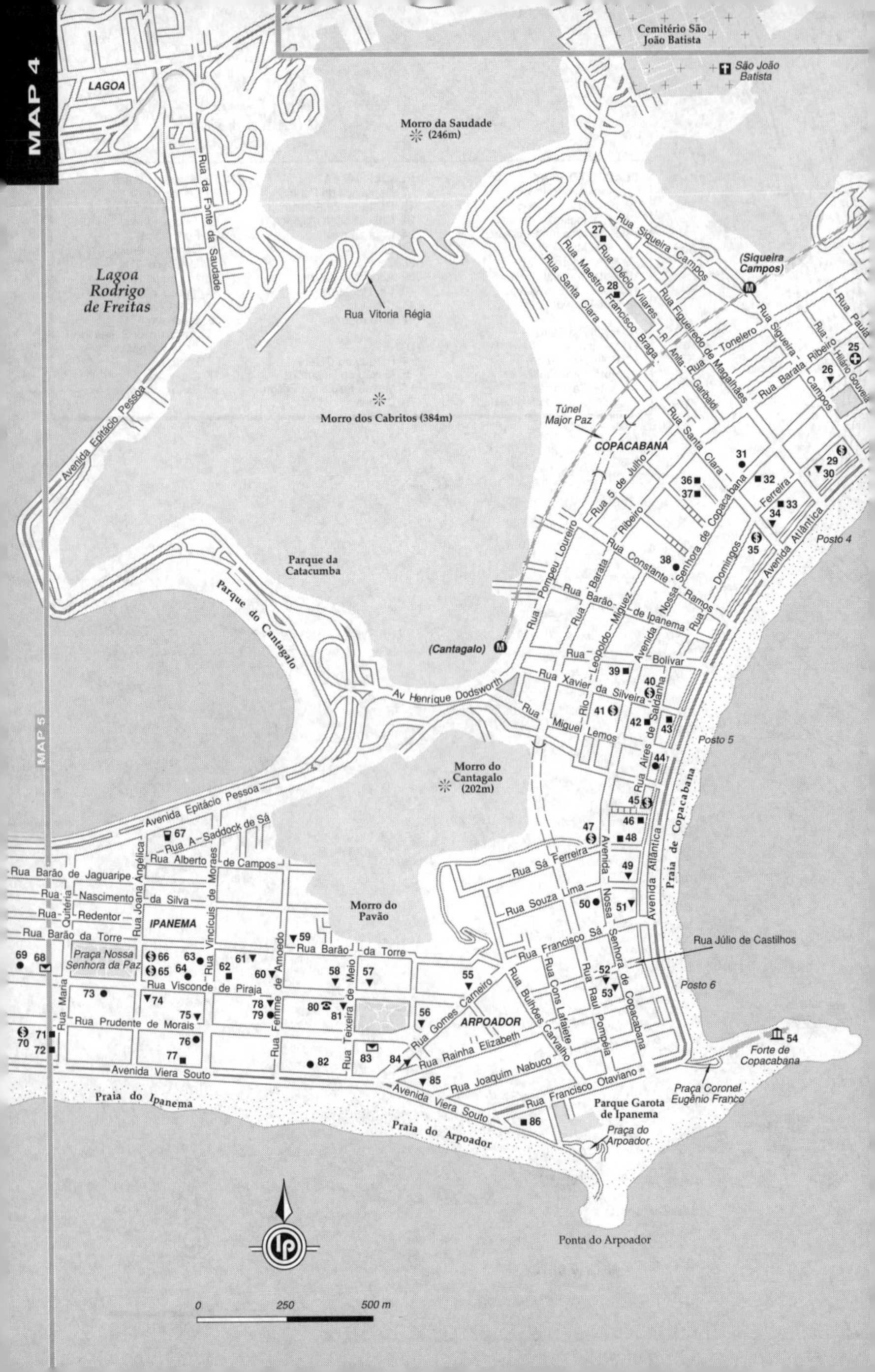

Cemitério São João Batista
São João Batista
LAGOA
Morro da Saudade (246m)
Rua da Fonte da Saudade
Lagoa Rodrigo de Freitas
Rua Vitoria Régia
Avenida Epitácio Pessoa
Morro dos Cabritos (384m)
Rua Siqueira Campos
(Siqueira Campos)
Rua Décio Vilares
Rua Maestro Francisco Braga
Rua Santa Clara
Rua Figueiredo de Magalhães
R. Anita Garibaldi
Rua Tonelero
Rua Barata Ribeiro
Rua Hilário Gouveia
Rua Paula
Túnel Major Paz
COPACABANA
Rua 5 de Julho
Rua Santa Clara
Ferreira
Avenida Nossa Senhora de Copacabana
Rua Domingos
Avenida Atlântica
Posto 4
Parque da Catacumba
Parque do Cantagalo
Rua Pompeu Loureiro
Rua Barata Ribeiro
Rua Constante Ramos
Rua Barão de Ipanema
Rua Leopoldo Miguez
(Cantagalo)
Rua Bolivar
Rua Xavier da Silveira
Av Henrique Dodsworth
Rua Miguel Lemos
Avenida de Saldanha
Rua Aires
Posto 5
Morro do Cantagalo (202m)
Praia de Copacabana
Avenida Epitácio Pessoa
Rua A. Saddock de Sá
Rua Alberto de Campos
Rua Barão de Jaguaripe
Rua Nascimento da Silva
Rua Redentor
Rua Barão da Torre
Rua Quitéria
Rua Joana Angélica
Rua Vinícius de Moraes
IPANEMA
Rua Sá Ferreira
Rua Souza Lima
Morro do Pavão
Rua Francisco Sá
Rua Júlio de Castilhos
Posto 6
Praça Nossa Senhora da Paz
Rua Barão da Torre
Rua Visconde de Pirajá
Rua Maria
Rua Prudente de Morais
Rua Farme de Amoedo
Rua Teixeira de Melo
Rua Gomes Carneiro
ARPOADOR
Rua Bulhões Carvalho
Rua Cons Lafaiete
Rua Raul Pompéia
Avenida Nossa Senhora de Copacabana
Rua Rainha Elizabeth
Rua Joaquim Nabuco
Rua Francisco Otaviano
Avenida Viera Souto
Praia do Ipanema
Praia do Arpoador
Parque Garota de Ipanema
Praça do Arpoador
Praça Coronel Eugênio Franco
Forte de Copacabana
Ponta do Arpoador

25 26 27 28 29 30 31 32 33 34 35 36 37 38 39 40 41 42 43 44 45 46 47 48 49 50 51 52 53 54 55 56 57 58 59 60 61 62 63 64 65 66 67 68 69 70 71 72 73 74 75 76 77 78 79 80 81 82 83 84 85 86

MAP 5

0 250 500 m

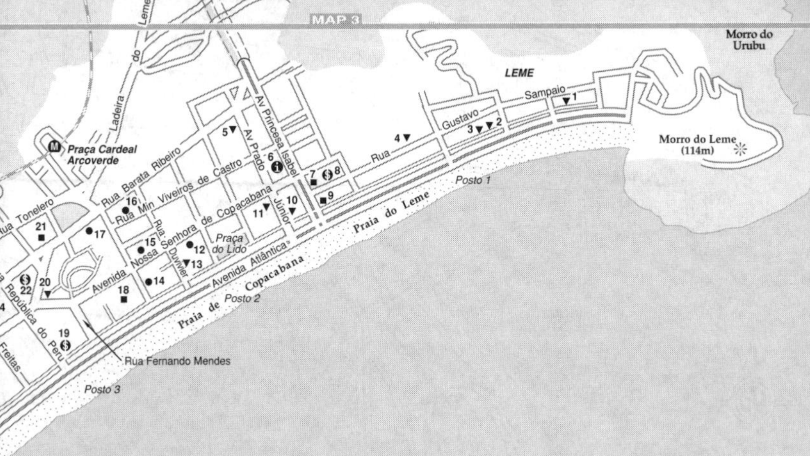

OCEANO

ATLÂNTICO

PLACES TO STAY
- 7 Hotel Acapulco
- 9 Le Meridien
- 18 Copacabana Palace & American Express Office
- 21 Copacabana Hotel Residência
- 23 Apa Hotel
- 27 Hotel Santa Clara
- 28 Copacabana Praia Hostel
- 32 Grande Hotel Canada
- 33 Hotel Toledo
- 36 Pousada Girassol
- 37 Hotel Angrense
- 39 Hotel Copa Linda
- 42 Hotel Biarritz
- 43 Rio Palace Hotel
- 46 Hotel Debret
- 48 Hotel Martinique
- 62 Hotel Vermont
- 71 Ipanema Inn
- 72 Caesar Park Hotel
- 77 Sol Ipanema
- 86 Arpoador Inn

PLACES TO EAT
- 1 Mariús
- 2 Da Brambini
- 3 Sindicato do Chopp
- 4 Restaurant Shirley
- 5 Cervantes
- 10 Mab's
- 11 O Crack dos Galetos
- 13 Quick Galetos
- 20 Traiteurs de France
- 26 La Mole
- 30 Arataca
- 34 Sindicato do Chopp
- 49 Restaurant Lucas
- 51 Sindicato do Chopp
- 52 Copa Rio Galetos
- 53 Lope's Confeitaria
- 55 Arab
- 56 Casa da Feijoada
- 57 Norte Grill & Ming
- 58 Yemanjá
- 59 Pulcinela
- 60 Bar Bofetada & Sindicato do Chopp
- 61 Natural
- 74 Chaika's
- 75 Garota da Ipanema
- 78 Limo's
- 81 Le Bon Jus
- 84 Caffé Felice
- 85 Barril

OTHER
- 6 Riotur
- 8 Bradesco ATMs
- 12 Andesol
- 14 Varig
- 15 VASP
- 16 Laundrette
- 17 Stop Bike
- 19 Câmbios
- 22 Bradesco ATMs
- 24 Telerj
- 25 Galdino Campos Cárdio Copa
- 29 Câmbios
- 31 IBEU
- 35 Bradesco ATMs
- 38 Livraria Siciliana
- 40 Câmbios
- 41 Bradesco ATMs
- 44 Help
- 45 Câmbios
- 47 Câmbios
- 50 Laundrette
- 54 Museu Histórico do Exército
- 63 Toca da Vinícius
- 64 Letras & Expressões
- 65 Banco do Boston
- 66 Banco do Brasil
- 67 Bar Lagoa
- 68 Post Office
- 69 VASP
- 70 Câmbio
- 73 Bum Bum
- 76 Vinicius piano bar
- 79 Laundrette
- 80 Telerj
- 82 Casa da Cultura Laura Alvim
- 83 Post Office

Instituto Nacional de Belas Artes
Parque Lage
JARDIM BOTÂNICO
Rua Fernando Magalhães
Rua Pachaco Leão
Rua Jardim Botânico
Avenida Borges de Medeiros
Jardim Botânico
Ilha Piraqué
Lagoa Rodrigo de Freitas
0 250 500 m
Vaz
Rua Major Rubens
Praça Santos Dumont
Jóquei Clube
Hipódromo da Gávea
Parque Brigadeiro Faria Lima
Rua Marquês de São Vicente
Rua Artur Araipe
GÁVEA
Rua Mário Ribeiro
Praça NS Auxiliadora
Clube de Regatas Flamengo
Padre Leonol-França
Ilha dos Caiçaras
MAP 4
Praça Milton Campos
R Conde de Bernadotte
Avenida Bartolomeu Mitre
R Humberto de Campos
Rua Humberto de Campos
Avenida Visconde de Albuquerque
Rua General Venâncio
Rua General
LEBLON
Rua José Linhares
Rua Cupertino Durão
Rua Carlos Góis
Rua Almirante Guilhem
Avenida Afrânio de Melo Franco
Jardim de Alah
Avenida Epitácio Pessoa
Rua Barão de Jaguaripe
R Nascimento da Silva
Rua Redentor
Rua Barão da Torre
IPANEMA
Rua Henrique Dumont
Rua Aníbal de Medonça
Rua Garcia D'Avila
Rua Maria Quitéria
Praça Espanha
Rua Visconde de Pirajá
Praça Almirante Saldanha Gama
Rua Prudente de Morais
R Paul Redfern
Avenida Viera Souto
Praia do Ipanema
Rua Dias Ferreira
Rua Rainha Guilhermia
Rua Ataulfo de Pavia
Rua Anstolle Espinola
Praça Antero Quental
Rua João Lira
Avenida General San Martin
Artiges
Flores
Urquiza
Avenida Delfim Moreira
Praia do Leblon
Avenida Niemeyer

PLACES TO STAY
9 Hotel San Marco
12 Everest Rio Hotel
15 Hotel Carlton
19 Sheraton Hotel

PLACES TO EAT
1 Claude Troisgras
2 Guímas
8 Pier 510
13 Restaurants & Bars
14 Sabor Saúde
16 Celeiro
17 Restaurant Bozó
18 Antiquaris

OTHER
3 Hipodromo Up
4 Plataforma
5 Academia da Cachaça
6 Tourist Police
7 Scala
10 Museu H Stern
11 Bradesco ATMs

In 1660 the city had a population made up of 3000 Indians, 750 Portuguese and 100 blacks. It grew along the waterfront and what is now Praça 15 de Novembro (often referred to as Praça Quinze). Religious orders came (Jesuits, Franciscans and Benedictines) and built austere closed-in churches.

With its excellent harbour and good lands for sugar cane, Rio became Brazil's third most important settlement (after Salvador de Bahia and Recife-Olinda) in the 17th century. Slaves were imported and sugar plantations thrived. The owners of the sugar estates lived in the protection and comfort of the fortified city.

The gold rush in Minas Gerais at the beginning of the 18th century changed Rio forever. In 1704 the Caminho Novo, a new road to the Minas gold fields, was opened. Gold poured through the ports of Rio until it began to run out half a century later. Much of the gold was used to repay Portuguese debts to the British. Many of the Portuguese immigrants didn't return to Minas, but stayed on in Rio.

Rio was now the prize of Brazil. In 1710 the French, who were at war with Portugal and raiding its colonies, attacked the city. The French were defeated, but a second expedition succeeded and the entire population abandoned the city in the dark of night. The occupying French threatened to level the city unless a sizeable ransom in gold, sugar and cattle was paid. The Portuguese obliged. During the return voyage to an expected heroes' welcome in France, the victors lost two ships in severe storms and most of the gold.

Rio quickly recovered from the setback. Its fortifications were improved, many richly decorated churches were built and by 1763 its population had reached 50,000. With international sugar prices slumping, Rio replaced Salvador de Bahia as the colonial capital in 1763.

In 1808 the entire Portuguese monarchy and court – barely escaping the invasion by Napoleon's armies – arrived in Rio. So the city came to house the court of the Portuguese Empire – or at least what was left of it. With the court came an influx of money and skills that helped build some of the city's lasting monuments, like the palace at the Quinta da Boa Vista and the Jardim Botânico (a pet project of the king). The Portuguese court was followed by talented French exiles, such as the architect Jean de Montigny and the painters Jean Baptiste Debret and Nicolas Antoine Taunay.

The coffee boom in the mountains of São Paulo and Rio revitalised Brazil's economy. Rio took on a new importance as a port and commercial centre, and coffee commerce modernised the city. A telegraph system and gas street lights were installed in 1854. Regular passenger ships began sailing to London in 1845, and to Paris in 1851. A ferry service to Niteroí began in 1862.

At the end of the 19th century the city's population exploded due to European immigration and internal migration (mostly ex-slaves from the declining coffee and sugar regions). In 1872 Rio had 275,000 inhabitants; by 1890 there were about 522,000, a quarter of them foreign-born. By 1900 the population had reached 800,000. The city spread rapidly between the steep hills, bay and ocean. The first tunnel through the mountains to Copacabana was built in 1892 and the Leme Tunnel was completed in 1904. The rich started to move further out, in a pattern that continues today.

The early 1920s to late 1950s was Rio's golden age. It became a romantic, exotic destination for Hollywood celebrities and international high society, who came to play and gamble at the casinos and dance or perform at the nightclubs.

The city remained the political capital of Brazil until 1960, when the capital was moved to Brasília. During that decade, a hotel building boom along the beaches saw the rise of big hotels like the Sheraton, Rio Palace and the Le Meridien. At the same time, the favelas of Rio were becoming overcrowded with immigrants from poverty-stricken areas of the north-east and interior, who swelled the number of urban poor in the city. The 'marvellous city' began to lose its gloss, as urban crime and violence began to increase.

The turning point for Rio came when it was chosen as host city for Eco 92, the United Nations Conference on Environment and Development. In the build-up to the conference, major projects, financed by federal grants, were undertaken to upgrade Rio's roads and restore many old buildings and parks, as well as improve living conditions in the favelas. This trend has continued.

Rio remains the cultural and tourist capital of Brazil. It still sets the fashion and pace for the rest of the nation and should continue to do so for many years to come.

Orientation

Rio is divided into a *zona norte* (north zone) and a *zona sul* (south zone) by the Serra da Carioca, steep mountains that are part of the Parque Nacional da Tijuca. These mountains descend to the edge of the city centre, where the zonas norte and sûl meet. Corcovado, one of these mountain peaks, offers the best way to become familiar with the city's geography – from it you have views of both zones. The statue Cristo Redentor (Christ the Redeemer), with his outstretched arms, gazes down on the Bahia da Guanabara and the landmark Pão de Açúcar (Sugar Loaf). His left arm points toward the zona norte, and his right toward the zona sul suburbs of Copacabana, Ipanema, Leblon and beyond.

Rio is a tale of two cities. The upper and middle classes reside in the zona sul, the lower class, in the zona norte. Favelas cover steep hillsides on both sides of town – Rocinha, Brazil's largest favela with between 150,000 and 300,000 residents, is in Gávea, one of Rio's richest neighbourhoods. Most industry is in the zona norte, as is most of the pollution. The ocean beaches are in the zona sul.

Unless they work in the zona norte, residents of the zona sul rarely go to the other side of the city. The same holds true for travellers, unless they head north to the Maracanã football stadium or the Quinta da Boa Vista, with the national museum, or the international airport on the Ilha do Governador.

Information

Tourist Offices Riotur (Map 2) is the Rio city tourism agency. It operates a tourist information hotline (☎ 542-8080) from 9 am to 5 pm Monday to Friday. The receptionists speak English and more often than not they'll be able to help you.

The main office (☎ 217-7575; fax 531-1872) is at Rua da Assembléia 10, 8th floor, Centro, but the special 'tourist room' (☎ 541-7522) is in Copacabana, at Avenida Princesa Isabel 183. It's open Monday to Friday from 9 am to 6 pm, and has free brochures (in Portuguese and English) and maps.

You can also get the brochures at their information booths at the main rodoviária (open daily from 6 am to 11 pm), Pão de Açúcar (daily from 8 am to 7 pm), the international airport at Galeão (daily from 5 am to 11 pm), Cosme Velho at the Corcovado railway station (daily from 7 am to 7 pm), and sometimes in your hotel.

When arriving in Rio by bus, the Riotur booth at the rodoviária can save you a lot of time by calling around town to find a vacant hotel and making a reservation. The staff only have lists of the mid-range to top-end hotels, but if you give them the phone number of a cheaper one they will be happy to call it. Riotur is also in charge of Carnaval and puts out a special programme during this time.

TurisRio (☎ 531-1922; fax 531-2506) is the Rio state tourism agency. Its office is in the same building as Riotur's main office (metrô stop Carioca), on the 7th floor. Embratur (☎ 509-6017; fax 509-7381) is Brazil's national tourism agency. Their main office is in Brasília, but there's a branch at Rua Uruguaiana 174, on the 8th floor. For the average traveller, neither of these agencies is worth a special trip.

Foreign Consulates See the Facts for the Visitor chapter for consular addresses. Consulates in Rio are open from Monday to Friday.

Visa Extensions If you need to renew your visa, go to the Polícia Marítima building (☎ 291-2142; Map 2) at Avenida Venezuela 2, Centro (near the far end of Avenida Rio Branco). It's open Monday to Friday from 9 am to noon and 1 to 4 pm for visa extensions. Bring a passport, money and airline ticket (if you have one). The fee is around US$16. The process is called *Prorrogação da Vista* (visa extension). First, you need to buy a DARF form from one of the sellers at the front door. They'll give you two copies for US$1. Complete the form (there are samples on the notice board next to the counter), take it upstairs at the Unibanco branch across the road and pay the fee. They'll keep one copy of the DARF. Take the other one back to the Polícia Marítima and they'll stamp the extension in your passport.

Money In the centre of the city, there are several travel agéncies/*casas de câmbio* on Avenida Rio Branco, a couple of blocks before and after the intersection with Avenida Presidente Vargas (see Centro map). Many banks in the city have currency-exchange facilities. They include: the Banco do Brasil, Rua Senador Dantas 105; Banco de Boston, Avenida Rio Branco 110; Citibank, Rua da Assembléia 100 and the Banco Francês e Brasileiro, Avenida Rio Branco 193.

In Copacabana, there is a cluster of casas de câmbio behind the Copacabana Palace Hotel, near the intersection of Avenida NS de Copacabana and Rua Fernando Mendes. Banco do Brasil has a branch at Avenida NS de Copacabana 691-A. Ipanema has several casas de câmbio scattered along Rua Visconde da Pirajá.

At the international airport, it's best to change money at one of the casas de câmbio on the ground floor (arrivals). Their opening hours are 6.30 am to 11 pm. Banco do Brasil, on the 3rd floor, is open 24 hours, but they charge a 3% commission, even for cash.

You can get Visa cash advances at any Banco do Brasil, or from any Bradesco Dia e Noite (Day & Night) ATM. Emergency phone numbers for credit cards are:

American Express	☎ 0800-78-5050
MasterCard	☎ 0800-78-4410
Visa	☎ 292-5394

Post Any mail addressed to Posta Restante, Rio de Janeiro, Brazil, ends up at the post office at Rua Primeiro de Março 64 (Map 2), in the city. They hold mail for 30 days and are reasonably efficient. Post offices usually open from 8 am to 6 pm weekdays and until noon on Saturday.

The American Express agent in Rio is Kontik-Franstur SA (☎ 548-2148; Map 4), Avenida Atlântica 1702, Copacabana CEP 20040, Copacabana, Rio de Janeiro, Brazil. They are pretty reliable.

Telephone International phone calls can be made from these locations in Rio:

Aeroporto Santos Dumont – 6 am to 11 pm
Aeroporto Internacional – 24 hours
Centro, Praça Tiradentes 41 – 24 hours
Copacabana – Avenida NS de Copacabana 540 (upstairs) – 24 hours
Ipanema, Rua Visconde de Pirajá 111 – 6 am to 11 pm
Rodoviária Novo Rio – 24 hours
Méier – Dias da Cruz 182 – 6.30 am to 11 pm

Fax Faxes can be sent from any large post office in Rio. The branch at the International Airport is open 24 hours.

Online Services The one Internet café in Rio is @ Café in Barra Shopping, Avenida das Américas 4666.

Travel Agencies Rio has no shortage of travel agents eager to give advice, book bus and plane tickets and organise tours. They can also save you unnecessary trips to the rodoviária by selling bus tickets in advance. Many agents are brusque and unhelpful but some are quite the opposite, so it's usually worth walking out on type one to find type two.

In Copacabana, try Andesol (☎ 275-4370; fax 541-0748), Avenida NS de Copacabana 209. Eric speaks English, French, German, Spanish and Italian and is very helpful.

Blumar/Brazil Nuts (☎ 511-3636; fax

511-3739), Rua Visconde de Pirajá 260, Ipanema, is also useful. Soletur (☎ 525-5000; fax 267-6846) is one of the big operators, and can arrange tours to anywhere else in Brazil. They have offices in the centre at Rua da Quitanda 20, in Copacabana at Rua Santa Clara 70, and in Ipanema at Rua Visconde de Pirajá 351. Dantur Passagems e Turismo (☎ 205-1144), Largo do Machado 29, shop 41, is useful if you're staying in the Catete/Botafogo/Flamengo area.

Gay and lesbian travellers should contact Ganesh (☎ 350-5520; fax 359-1037), Estrada do Otaviano 598, a travel agency specialising in gay and lesbian tourism. They offer a transfer service from the airport to your hotel for US$15, and can assist and advise you on anything you need in Rio.

Bookshops Finding foreign language (ie English and French) books is difficult outside Rio and São Paulo, so stock up before heading into the interior. Nova Livraria Leonardo da Vinci, in Edifício Marques do Herval (just past Avenida Rio Branco 185; Map 2), is Rio's best bookshop; it's one floor down on the *sobreloja* (mezzanine) level. It has Rio's largest collection of foreign books (including Lonely Planet guides) and knowledgeable staff who, for a tidy sum, will order just about any book you want. It's open 9 am to 7 pm Monday to Friday and 9 am until noon on Saturday.

Each of the Livraria Siciliana chain has a collection of paperbacks in English. They are at Visconde de Pirajá 511, Ipanema, and Avenida NS de Copacabana 830, Copacabana (Map 4).

Ipanema has lots of good bookshops. Livraria Letras & Expressões, Rua Visconde de Pirajá 276, stocks many books in English. It's open 24 hours a day. Livraria Travessa, Rua Visconde de Pirajá 462 has many foreign-language, books. Both these bookshops have groovy little cafés.

Bossa Nova fans should check out Toca da Vinícius in Rua Vinícius de Morais for music and books about the genre.

Many newsstands on Avenida Rio Branco in the Centro, in Copacabana and Ipanema have large selections of foreign newspapers and magazines.

Libraries The Biblioteca Nacional, Avenida Rio Branco 219 (Map 2), is the largest public library in Latin America. It has an archive of nearly six million works and also houses a café and bookshop. Opening hours are Monday to Friday from 9 am to 8 pm and Saturday from 9 am to 3 am.

Founded in 1837, the Real Gabinete Português de Leitura, (Royal Portuguese Reading Cabinet), Rua Luís de Camões, is a beautiful building housing 120,000 volumes. The archive includes many rarities, such as manuscripts by Gonçalves Dias and Machado de Assis. It's open weekdays from 9 am to 5.45 pm.

Instituto Brasil-Estados Unidos (IBEU; ☎ 548-8332) has an English library with a large fiction collection, many books about Brazil in English and a good selection of current magazines from the USA. To borrow books you have to take classes there or buy a membership, but it's cheap. The library is at Avenida NS de Copacabana 690, 3rd floor.

Maison de France (☎ 210-1272; Map 2), Avenida Presidente Antônio Carlos 58, has a library with records, CDs, videos, and 22,000 books – all in French. It's open Tuesday to Friday from 10 am to 5 pm.

Cultural Centres The monthly Riotur guide gives details of current exhibitions at the cultural centres. The Centro Cultural do Banco do Brasil (CCBB), Rua Primeiro do Março 66 (Map 2), is Rio's finest cultural centre. It always has interesting exhibitions and is well worth a look. They often have free lunch time concerts as well. Opening hours are Tuesday to Sunday from noon to 8 pm.

Close by, Casa França Brasil, in the old customs building (Map 2), stages many prominent exhibitions. It's open Tuesday to Sunday from 10 am to 8 pm. The Paço Imperial, Praça 15 de Novembro (Map 2), is an important arts space, and has cafés, a restaurant and bookshop. It's open Tuesday to Sunday from noon to 6 pm. In Ipanema, the Casa da Cultura Laura Alvim, Avenida Viera Souto 176, has a theatre and often puts on interesting exhibitions.

Laundry There are laundrettes in Copacabana at Rua Ministro Viveiros de Castro 194 and Avenida NS de Copacabana 1226 (Map 4). In Catete, English is spoken at the laundrette at Rua Correia Dutra 16-A. In Ipanema there's one on Rua Farme de Amoedo close to the intersection with Rua Visconde de Pirajá (Map 4).

If you don't want to wash your own clothes, enquire at your hotel, as often the housekeepers wash clothes at home to make a few extra reais.

Medical Services In Copacabana, Galdino Campos Cárdio Copa (☎ 255-9966) is a 24 hour medical clinic at Avenida NS de Copacabana 492. They have English and French speaking staff. Cárdio Plus (☎ 521-4899), Rua Visconde de Pirajá, is another 24 hour clinic, but they only speak Portuguese.

24 Hour Pharmacies These include Farmácia Piauí, Avenida Ataulfo de Paiva 1283, Leblon (☎ 274-8448); Rua Barata Ribeiro 646 and Rua Prado Junior 237 in Copacabana (☎ 255-6249); and Praia do Flamengo 224, Flamengo (☎ 284-1548).

Emergency To call emergency telephone numbers in Rio you don't need a phonecard. The numbers include:

Police	☎ 190
Ambulance	☎ 193
Fire	☎ 193

The Tourist Police Office (☎ 511-5112; Map 5), Rua Afrânio de Melo Franco (in front of Scala), Leblon, is open 24 hours. If you are robbed, you should report it to them. Although there won't be a big investigation you will get a police form to give to your insurance company.

Dangers & Annoyances Rio receives a lot of bad international press about its violence, high crime rate, and *balas perdidas* (stray bullets) – but don't let this stop you from coming. Travellers to Rio have as much chance of getting mugged as in any big city, so the same precautions apply here. By following a few common-sense precautions, you're unlikely to suffer anything more than sunburn.

On the Street Dress down and leave your watch and any other jewellery in the hotel room (if you consider it reliable). There are large digital clocks all over Rio if you must know the time – or buy a cheap watch.

Leave all important documents, like passport (carry a photocopy) and travellers cheques, at the hotel. Get used to keeping small change and a few banknotes in a shirt pocket so that you can pay bus tickets and small expenses without extracting large wads which attract attention. Better still, carry only the cash you think you'll need. If you do take your wallet, keep it in your front pocket.

At night, don't walk into any alleys, narrow streets, underpasses or wherever there are trees and bushes that may be used as hiding places. Leaving discos or clubs late at night, get a taxi from the door.

Sightseeing in the centre of town is safer during the week, because it's crowded. On weekends you stand out much more.

Camera If you have a camera with you, keep it out of sight as much as possible. We sometimes carried a camera in a sturdy plastic bag from a local supermarket, or a smaller one in a front pouch. Disposable cameras are widely available in photo shops in Rio – a wise investment.

Buses If you ride the local buses (which are great fun) have your change ready before boarding. Avoid the super-crowded ones. If you talk out loud, it's easier for thieves to identify you. The air-conditioned buses are more expensive, but more secure. Take one from the airport to save a few dollars. If you have valuables (like your backpack with everything in it), take taxis rather than buses.

Beaches The heavy police presence on Copacabana and Ipanema mean the beaches are quite safe – but don't go to sleep. Take only the money you need for snacks and drinks. We found a Carioca's wallet on the beach one evening – it contained his ID card, enough grass for one joint, two bucks and a condom.

The favourite beach rip-off scam (apart from the fast snatch and grab) is where the thieves wait for you to be alone on the beach guarding you and your friend's gear (because you decided to take it in turns to go in the water). One thief approaches from one side and asks you for a light or the time. While you're distracted, the thief's partner grabs your gear from the other side.

Hotels If you consider your hotel to be reliable (as a rough guide in Rio probably any place with three stars or more), place valuables in its safe and get a receipt.

Count money and travellers cheques before and after retrieving them from the safe – this should quickly identify any attempts to extract single bills or cheques.

Don't leave your valuables strewn around the room. It's too much of a temptation to cleaners and other hotel staff.

See the Security Precautions in Brazil section in the Facts for the Visitor chapter for more information.

Credit Cards Keep your credit card in sight at all times. Don't give it to waiters and let them take it away. Don't keep it in the hotel safe. We get letters all the time from readers who are victims of credit-card fraud. We've also been victims ourselves! Rio must be one of the capitals of credit card scams.

Walking Tour (Map 2)

There's more to Rio than beaches. Don't miss exploring some of the city's museums, colonial buildings, churches (of course) and traditional meeting places – restaurants, bars, shops and street corners. The centre of Rio, now a potpourri of the new and old and looking the best it has in years, still has character and life. Many of the places mentioned in the following walking tour are described in more detail in the following sections.

Take a bus or the metrô to **Cinelândia** and find the main square on Avenida Rio Branco, called **Praça Floriano**; it's the heart of Rio today. Towards the bay is the **Praça Mahatma Gandhi**. The monument was a gift from India in 1964. Behind the praça and across the road, the large aeroplane hangar you can see is the **Museu de Arte Moderna**.

Praça Floriano comes to life at lunch time and after work when the outdoor cafés are filled with beer drinkers and samba musicians. The square is Rio's political marketplace. There's daily speech making, literature sales and street theatre. Most city marches and rallies culminate here on the steps of the old **Câmara Municipal**.

Across Avenida Rio Branco is the **Biblioteca Nacional**. Built in 1910 in neoclassic style, it's open to visitors and usually has exhibitions. You'll also find the **Museu Nacional de Belas Artes** in Avenida Rio Branco, housing some of Brazil's best paintings.

The most impressive building on Praça Floriano is the **Teatro Municipal**, home of Rio's opera, orchestra and gargoyles. The theatre was built in 1905 and remodelled in 1934 and shows the influence of the Paris Opéra. The front doors are rarely open, but you can visit the ostentatious Assyrian Room Restaurant & Bar downstairs (entrance on Avenida Rio Branco). Built in the 1930s, it's completely covered in tiles, with beautiful mosaics.

Now do an about-face and head back to the other side of the Teatro Municipal and walk down the pedestrian-only Avenida 13 de Maio (on your left are some of Rio's best suco bars). Cross a street and you're in the **Largo da Carioca**. Up the hill is the recently restored **Convento de Santo**

JOHN MAIER, JR

Teatro Municipal

Antônio. The original church here was started in 1608, making it Rio's oldest. The church's Santo Antônio is an object of great devotion to many Cariocas in search of husbands. The church's sacristy, which dates from 1745, has some beautiful jacarandawood carving and Portuguese blue tiles.

Gazing east at the skyline from the convent, you'll notice the Rubik's-cube-like **Petrobras building**. Behind it is the ultramodern **Catedral Metropolitana** (the inside is cavernous with huge stained-glass windows). If you have time for a side trip, consider heading over to the nearby *bonde* (tram) that goes up to **Santa Teresa**.

Next, find the shops along 19th century Rua da Carioca. The old wine and cheese shop has some of Brazil's best cheese from the Canastra mountains in Minas Gerais. They also have bargains in Portuguese and Spanish wines. Two shops sell fine Brazilian-made instruments, including all the Carnaval rhythm-makers, which make great gifts. There are several good jewellery shops off Rua da Carioca, on Rua Ramalho Ortigão.

At Rua da Carioca 39 is **Bar Luis**, Rio's longest running restaurant. It was opened in 1887 and named Bar Adolf until WWII. For decades, many of Rio's intellectuals have chewed the fat while eating Rio's best German food here.

At the end of the block you'll pass the **Cinema Iris**, which used to be Rio's most elegant theatre (sadly, it's now a porno movie and strip joint), and emerge into the hustle of **Praça Tiradentes**. It's easy to see that this was once a fabulous part of the city. On opposite sides of the square are the **Teatro João Caetano** and the **Teatro Carlos Gomez**, which show plays and dance performances. The narrow streets in this part of town house many old, mostly dilapidated, small buildings. It's well worth exploring along Rua Buenos Aires as far as **Campo de Santana** and then returning along Rua da Alfândega. Campo de Santana is a pleasant park, once the scene – re-enacted in every Brazilian classroom – of the Regent Prince, Dom Pedro, proclaiming Brazil's independence from Portugal in 1822. Have a wander through the park and try to spot some of the agoutis (small, rodent-like animals) that run wild there.

Back near Avenida Rio Branco, at Rua Gonçalves Dias 30, hit the famous **Confeitaria Colombo** for coffee and turn-of-the-century Vienna. Offering succour to shopping-weary matrons since 1894, the Colombo is best for coffee (very strong) and desserts.

From here, cross Avenida Rio Branco, go down Rua da Assembléia, stop at Riotur and TurisRio if you want tourist information, then continue on to **Praça 15 de Novembro**. In the square is the **Pyramid Fountain**, built in 1789, and a **craft market**. Facing the bay, on your right is the **Paço Imperial**, which was the royal palace and the seat of government. It's now an important cultural centre.

On the opposite side of the square is the historic **Arco de Teles**, running between two buildings. Walking through the arch you'll find several restaurants, fishing supply shops and a couple of simple colonial churches. It's a colourful area.

Back at Praça 15 de Novembro, walk across to the **waterfront**, where ferries leave to **Niterói** and **Ilha da Paquetá**. The ferry to Niterói takes only 15 minutes and you never have to wait long. Consider crossing the bay and walking around central Niterói if you have some time (the feel is different from Rio – much more like the rest of Brazil). Even if you return immediately the trip is worth it just for the view.

When you're facing the bay, the **Alba Mar** restaurant is a few hundred metres to your right. It's in a green gazebo overlooking the bay. On Saturday the building is surrounded by the tents of the **Feira de Antiguidades**, a strange and fun hotchpotch of antiques, clothes, foods and other odds and ends.

If you want to extend your walking tour, go back through Arco de Teles and follow the street around toward Rua Primeiro de Março. Walk up along the right-hand side and you'll come to the **Centro Cultural do Banco do Brasil**. Go in and have a look at the building and any of the current exhibitions. Most are free. Then have a look behind the CCBB at the **Casa França-Brasil**. From there, you'll be able to see the **Igreja NS de Candelária**. Have a look inside and then keep going up Rua Primeiro de Março, through the naval area, to Rua Dom Geraldo, the last street before the hill. **Mosteiro de São Bento** is on top of the hill. To get there, go to Rua Dom Geraldo 40 and take the lift to the 5th floor. From Rua Dom Geraldo, head back toward Avenida Rio Branco, and try to imagine that in 1910 it was a tree-lined boulevard, with sidewalk cafés – the Champs Elysées of Rio.

City & Zona Sul

Centro (Map 2) Rio's centre is all business and bustle during the day and absolutely deserted at night and on weekends. It's a working city – the centre of finance and commerce. The numerous high-rise office buildings are filled with workers who pour onto the daytime streets to eat at the many restaurants and shop at the small shops. Lots of essential services for the traveller are in Centro. The main airline offices are here, as are foreign consulates, Brazilian government agencies, money exchange houses, banks and travel agencies.

Centro is the site of the original settlement. Most of the city's important museums and colonial buildings are here. Small enough to explore on foot, the city centre is lively and interesting, and occasionally beautiful (despite the many modern, Bauhaus-inspired buildings).

Two wide avenues cross the centre: Avenida Rio Branco, where buses leave for the zona sul, and Avenida Presidente Vargas, which heads out to the *Sambódromo* and the zona norte. Rio's modern subway follows these two avenues as it burrows under the city. Most banks and airline offices have their headquarters on Avenida Rio Branco.

Cinelândia (Map 2) At the southern edge of the business district, Cinelândia's shops, bars, restaurants and movie theatres are popular day and night. There are some decent hotels here that are reasonably priced. The bars and restaurants get crowded at lunch and after work, when there's often 'happy-hour' samba in the streets. There's a greater mix of Cariocas here than in any other section of the city.

Lapa (Map 2) The area next to the old aqueduct, that connects the Santa Teresa bonde and the city centre, is one of the two main red-light districts in Rio and the scene of many a Brazilian novel. There are also several music clubs, like the *Fundação Progresso* and *Asa Branca*, and some very cheap hotels. Lapa goes to sleep very late on Friday and Saturday.

Santa Teresa (Map 2) This is one of Rio's most unusual and charming neighbourhoods. Situated along the ridge of the hill that rises from the city centre, Santa Teresa has many of Rio's finest colonial homes. In the 1800s

Rio's upper crust lived here and rode the bonde to work in the city. The bonde is still there but the rich moved out long ago.

During the 1960s and 1970s many artists and hippies moved into Santa Teresa's mansions. Just a few metres below them, the favelas grew on the hillsides. Santa Teresa was considered very dangerous for many years. It's still necessary to be cautious here, especially at night.

Catete & Flamengo (Map 3) Moving south along the bay, you'll come to Catete and Flamengo, two areas which have the bulk of inexpensive hotels in Rio. Flamengo was once Rio's finest residential district and the Palácio do Catete housed Brazil's president until 1954, but with the new tunnel to Copacabana the upper classes began moving out in the 1940s. Flamengo is still mostly residential. The apartments are often big and graceful, although a few high-rise offices have recently been built among them. With the exception of the classy waterfront buildings, Flamengo is mostly a middle-class area.

There is less nightlife and fewer restaurants here than in nearby Botafogo or Cinelândia, which are five minutes' away by subway.

Botafogo (Map 3) Botafogo's early development was spurred by the construction of a tram that ran up to the botanical garden linking the bay and the lake. This artery still plays a vital role in Rio's traffic flow and Botafogo's streets are extremely congested. There are several palatial mansions here that housed foreign consulates when Rio was the capital of Brazil. This area has fewer high-rise buildings than much of the rest of Rio.

There are not many hotels in Botafogo but there are lots of good bars and restaurants where the locals go to avoid the tourist glitz and high cost of Copacabana.

Copacabana (Map 4) This is the famous curved beach you know about. Copacabana is the capital of Brazilian tourism. It's possible to spend an entire Brazilian holiday without leaving it, and some people do just that. For pure city excitement, Copacabana is Rio's liveliest theatre. The majority of Rio's medium and expensive hotels are here and they are accompanied by plenty of restaurants, shops and bars. It is also the heart of Rio's recreational sex industry. There are many *boîtes* (bars with strip shows) and prostitutes; anything and everyone is for sale.

What's surprising about Copacabana is all the people who live there. Fronted by beach and backed by steep hills, Copacabana is for the greater part no more than four blocks wide. Crammed into this narrow strip of land are 25,000 people per sq km, one of the highest population densities in the world. Any understanding of the Rio way of life and leisure has to start with the fact that so many people live so close together and so near to the beach.

Only three parallel streets traverse the length of Copacabana. Avenida Atlântica runs along the ocean. Avenida NS de Copacabana, two blocks inland, is one way, running in the direction of the business district. One block further inland, Rua Barata Ribeiro is also one way, in the direction of Ipanema and Leblon. These streets change their names when they reach Ipanema.

From Christmas to Carnaval there are so many foreign tourists in Copacabana that Brazilians who can't afford to travel abroad have been known to go down to Avenida Atlântica along the beach and pretend they are in Paris, Buenos Aires or New York. As always when there are lots of tourists, there are problems. Prices are exorbitant, hotels are full and restaurants get overcrowded. The streets are noisy and hot.

Ipanema & Leblon (Maps 4 & 5) These are two of Rio's most desirable districts. They face the same stretch of beach and are separated by the Jardim de Alah, a canal and adjacent park. They are residential, mostly upper class and becoming more so as rents continue to rise. Most of Rio's better restaurants, bars and nightclubs are in Ipanema and Leblon; there are only a few hotels, although there are a couple of good aparthotels.

Barra da Tijuca (Map 1) Barra is the Miami of Rio – beaches and shopping malls dot the landscape. Like fungi in a rainforest, hundreds of buildings have sprung up wherever there happens to be an open space. Whether condo, restaurant, shopping centre or disco, these big, modern structures are, without exception, monstrosities.

Barra da Tijuca is no longer fashionable with Rio's rich and famous. It's too far from anywhere, suffers huge traffic bottlenecks and a chronic shortage of water. The rich and famous are moving back to Ipanema, Leblon and the traditional Avenida Oswaldo Cruz area of Flamengo. Barra caters to *emergentes*, the nouveau riches from the towns west of Rio.

Beaches

Going to the beach, a ritual and way of life for the Carioca, is Rio's common denominator. People of all walks of life, in all shapes and sizes congregate on the sand. To the casual observer one stretch of sand is the same as any other. Not so. The beach is complex. Different times of the day bring different people. Different stretches of the beach attract different crowds. Before and after work, exercise is the name of the game. Tanning is heaviest before 2 pm. On prime beach days, the fashionable pass the morning out at Barra and the afternoon back at their spot in Ipanema.

Every 20m of coastline is populated by a different group of regulars. For example, Arpoador has more surfers and people from the zona norte. In front of the luxury hotels you'll always find tourists and a security force watching over them.

Swimming isn't recommended at any of the bay beaches because of the sewage and industrial waste that pollutes the water. Work on the long-awaited treatment plants is just beginning.

Flamengo (Map 3) This popular beach is a thin strip of sand on the bay, with a great view. The park and beach were a landfill project. It's within an easy walk of most of the budget hotels in Catete/Flamengo. There's a different class of Carioca here than on the luxurious beaches to the south, and it's fun to watch them play.

Botafogo (Map 3) This small beach is on a calm bay inlet looking out at Pão de Açúcar. The Rio Yacht Club is next door.

Copacabana/Leme (Map 4) One of the world's most famous beaches runs 4.5km in front of one of the world's most densely populated residential areas. There is always something happening on the beach during the day and along the footpaths at night: drinking, singing, eating and all kinds of people checking out the scene; tourists watching Brazilians, Brazilians watching tourists; the poor, from nearby favelas, eyeing the rich, the rich avoiding the poor; prostitutes looking for tricks and johns looking for treats.

From the scalloped beach you can see the granite slabs that surround the entrance to the bay – a magnificent meeting of land and sea. The last kilometre to the east, from Avenida Princesa Isabel to the Leme hill, is called Praia do Leme. When you go to Copacabana, which you must, do as the locals do: take only the essentials with you. The area is now heavily policed, so it's OK to walk around during the evening. Avenida NS de Copacabana is more dangerous; watch out at weekends when the shops are closed and there are few locals around.

Arpoador (Map 4) This small beach is wedged between Copacabana and Ipanema. There's good surfing here, even at night when the beach is lit, and there's a giant rock that juts out into the ocean with a great view.

Ipanema/Leblon (Maps 4 & 5) These two beaches are really one, although the beach narrows on the Leblon side, separated by the canal at Jardim de Alah. Ipanema, like the suburb, is Rio's richest and most chic beach. There isn't quite the frenzy of Copacabana, and the beach is a bit safer and cleaner.

Different parts of the beach attract different crowds. Posto Nine is Garota de Ipanema beach, right off Rua Vinícius de Morais. Today it's also known as the Cemitério dos Elefantes because of the old leftists, hippies and artists who hang out there, but it's also popular with the young and beautiful who like go down there around sunset and smoke a joint. The beach in front of Rua Farme de Amoedo, also called Land of Marlboro, is the gay beach.

Ipanema is an Indian word for 'dangerous, bad waters'. The waves can get big and the undertow is often strong. Be careful, and swim only where the locals are swimming.

Vidigal (Map 5) Under the Sheraton Hotel and the Morro Dois Irmãos, this beach is a mix of the hotel and favela dwellers who were pushed further up the hill to make way for the Sheraton. It's often polluted.

Pepino/São Conrado (Map 1) After the Sheraton there is no beach along the coast for a few kilometres until Pepino beach in São Conrado. You can also take Avenida Niemeyer to the tunnel leading to Barra da Tijuca.

Pepino is a beautiful beach, less crowded than Ipanema. It's where the hang-gliders hang out when they're not hanging up there. Along the beach are two big resort hotels, the Hotel InterContinental and Hotel Nacional. Behind them, nestled into the hillside, is Brazil's biggest favela, Rocinha.

Bus No 546, 547 or 557 goes to Pepino. Don't take valuables, as these are frequent targets of robbers. There is also a São Conrado executivo (No 2016) that goes along Copacabana and Ipanema to Pepino.

Barra da Tijuca (Map 1) The next beach out is Barra. It's 12km long, with clean, green water. The first few kilometres are filled with bars and seafood restaurants. The beautiful people hang out in front of barraca do Pepê. Further out there are only *barracas* (food and drink stalls) on the beach. It's calm on weekdays, and crazy on hot summer weekends.

Beaches Further Out

The beaches further south – Recréio, Prainha, Grumari, Marambaia – are very beautiful and worth exploring but not easily accessible by public transport. They only get busy on weekends when bus lines swell. All have barracas. Prainha, the next beach past Barra, is one of the best surfing beaches in Rio. Grumari is arguably the prettiest beach near the city, and there is a restaurant on the beach where the crabs are good.

To reach these beaches by car you can turn off the Rio-Santos road, Hwy BR-101, at Barra and follow the beach road. If it's a busy weekend, go a few kilometres further and turn left at Estrada Bemvindo Novais, at Recreio dos Bandeirantes or Estrada Vereador.

Pão de Açúcar (Sugar Loaf; Map 3)

Pão de Açúcar, God's gift to the picture-postcard industry, is dazzling. Two cable cars lift you 396m above Rio and the Baía de Guanabara. From here, Rio is undoubtedly the most beautiful city in the world. There are many good times to make the ascent, but sunset on a clear day is the most spectacular. As day becomes night and the city lights start to sparkle down below, the sensation is delightful.

Everyone must go to Pão de Açúcar, but if you can, avoid going from about 10 to 11 am and 2 to 3 pm when most tourist buses are arriving.

The two-stage cable cars (☎ 541-3737) leave about every 30 minutes from Praça General Tibúrcio in Urca. They operate daily from 8 am to 10 pm and cost US$14. On top of the lower hill there's a restaurant/theatre.

To get to Pão de Açúcar take an Urca bus from Centro, Flamengo and Botafogo (No 107); from the zona sul, take No 500, 511 or 512.

Corcovado & Cristo Redentor (Map 1)

Corcovado (Hunchback) is the mountain and *Cristo Redentor* (Christ the Redeemer) is the statue. The mountain rises straight up from the city to 710m. The statue, with its welcoming outstretched arms, stands another 30m high and weighs over 1000 tonnes (a popular song talks about how the Cristo should have his arms closed against his chest because for most who come to Rio the city is harsh and unwelcomely).

The statue was originally conceived as a national monument to celebrate Brazil's 100 years of independence from Portugal. The centenary came and went in 1922 without the money to start construction, but in 1931 the statue was completed by French sculptor Paul Landowski, thanks to some financial assistance from the Vatican.

Corcovado lies within the Parque Nacional da Tijuca. You can get there by car or by taxi, but it's more fun to go up in the cog train – sit on the right-hand side going up for the view. The round trip costs US$15 and leaves from the station at Rua Cosme Velho 513 (Cosme Velho). You can get a taxi there or a Rua Cosme Velho bus – a No 184 or 180 bus from Centro, Gloria and Flamengo, a No 583 from Largo Machado, Copacabana and Ipanema, or a No 584 from Leblon.

During the high season, the trains, which only leave every 30 minutes, can be slow going. Corcovado, and the train, are open from 8.30 am to 6.30 pm. Needless to say, the view from up top is spectacular.

Santa Teresa Bondinho (Map 2)

The *bondinho* (little tram) goes over the Arcos da Lapa (old aqueduct) to Santa Teresa from Avenida República do Chile and Senador Dantas in Centro. Santa Teresa is a beautiful neighbourhood of cobbled streets, hills and old homes. Favelas down the hillsides have made this a high-crime area. Young thieves jump on and off the tram very quickly. Go, but don't take valuables. Public transport stops at midnight, so you'll need a car if you are going anywhere after that time.

There's a small Museu do Bonde (☎ 240-5709) at the central tram station, Rua Professor Lélio Gama 65 with a history of Rio's tramways since 1865, for bonde buffs.

JOHN MAIER, JR

Santa Teresa Bondinho

You may wonder why people choose to hang onto the side of the tram even when there are spare seats. It's because they don't have to pay the 50 cent fare.

Parks & Gardens

Parque Nacional da Tijuca (Map 1)

Tijuca is all that's left of the tropical jungle that once surrounded Rio de Janeiro. In 15 minutes you can go from the concrete jungle of Copacabana to the 33 sq km tropical forest of Parque Nacional da Tijuca. A more rapid and drastic contrast is difficult to imagine. The forest is exuberant green, with beautiful trees, creeks and waterfalls, mountainous terrain and high peaks. It is home to different species of birds and animals including iguanas and monkeys. It also has an excellent trail system, with several good day hikes. Maps are available at the small artisan shop just inside the park entrance.

The heart of the forest is the beautiful Alto da Boa Vista with several waterfalls (including the 35m Cascatinha Taunay), peaks and restaurants.

It's best to go by car, but if you can't, catch a No 221 Alto da Boa Vista bus from Praça 15 or Avenida Getúlio Vargas or the No 233 or 234 Alto da Boa Vista buses from Rodoviária Novo Rio. These buses pass the park entrance. An alternative is to catch the metrô to Saens Penã, then take any Barra da Tijuca bus going to and get off midway at the entrance to the park, close to Alto da Boa Vista.

The best route by car is to take Rua Jardim Botânico two blocks past the botanical garden (heading away from Gávea). Turn left on Rua Lopes Quintas and then follow the Tijuca or Corcovado signs for two quick left turns until you reach the back of the botanical garden, where you go right. Then follow the signs for a quick ascent into the forest and past the Vista Chinesa (get out for a view) and the Mesa do Imperador. Turn right when you seem to come out of the forest on the main road. After a couple of kilometres you'll see the stone columns to the entrance of Alto da Boa Vista on your left. You can also drive up to Alto da Boa Vista by heading out to São Conrado and turning right up the hill at the Parque Nacional da Tijuca signs.

Jardim Botânico (Map 5) The botanical garden was first planted by order of the prince regent Dom João in 1808. There are over 6000 varieties of plants on 141 hectares. Open daily from 9 am to 5 pm, the gardens are quiet and serene on weekdays, but blossoms with families and music on weekends. The row of palms, planted when the garden first opened, and the Amazonas section with the lake containing the huge Vitória Regia water lilies, are some of the highlights. It's not a bad idea to take insect repellent. Entry costs US$2 and they give out a useful map of the gardens with a suggested walking tour.

The garden is at Rua Jardim Botânico 1008. To get there take a Jardim Botânico bus: from Centro, No 170; from the zona sul, No 571, 572, or 594.

Parque Lage (Map 5) This beautiful park, at Rua Jardim Botânico 414, is at the base of Parque Nacional da Tijuca. There are gardens, little lakes and a mansion which now houses the Instituto de Belas Artes – there are often art shows and sometimes performances there. It's a tranquil place, with no sports allowed and a favourite of families with small children. It's open from 9 am to 5 pm. Take a Jardim Botânico bus.

Parque do Flamengo (Map 2) Flamengo is a huge park with loads of fields and a bay for activities and sports. There are three museums here – Museu Carmen Miranda, Museu dos Mortos da Segunda Guerra Mundial and Museu de Arte Moderna.

To get there take a Via Parque do Flamengo bus: from Centro, bus Nos 125 or 132, and from the zona sul, bus Nos 413 or 455.

Parque da Catacumba (Map 4) With high-rise buildings on both sides, Catacumba is on the Morro dos Cabritos, which rises from the Lagoa Rodrigo de Freitas. It was the site of a favela which was destroyed to make the park. A shaded park for walkers only, it's a good place to escape the heat and see some excellent outdoor sculptures. At the top of the hill there is a great view. During summer there are free Sunday afternoon concerts, featuring some of Rio's best musicians, in its outdoor amphitheatre.

Parque da Cidade Up in the hills of Gávea, this park is also calm and cool, and popular with families. Open daily from 7 am to 5 pm, the Museu da Cidade is in the park grounds.

Parque do Catete (Map 3) The grounds of the old presidential palace are now the Parque do Catete, a quiet refuge from the city.

Quinta da Boa Vista (Map 1) Rio's main park and Museu Nacional makes a great Sunday outing, and if you want to make a day out of it, the zoo, Nordeste Fair (see Things to Buy) and Maracanã soccer stadium are all nearby. The park is open daily from 8 am to 7 pm.

Museums

Museu Nacional (Map 1) This museum and its grand imperial entrance are still stately and imposing, and the view from the balcony to the royal palms is majestic. However, the graffitied buildings and unkempt grounds have suffered since the fall of the monarchy. The park is large and busy, and, because it's on the north side of the city, you'll see a good cross-section of Cariocas.

There are many interesting exhibits: dinosaur fossils, sabre-toothed tiger skeletons, beautiful pieces of pre-Columbian ceramics from the littoral and planalto of Peru, a huge meteorite, hundreds of stuffed birds, mammals and fish, gory displays of tropical diseases and exhibits on the peoples of Brazil.

The last of these are the most interesting. Rubber-gatherers and Indians of the Amazon, lace workers and *jangadeiro* (fishermen) of the Northeast, *candomblistas* of Bahia, *gaúchos* of Rio Grande do Sul and *vaqueiros* (cowboys) of the sertão are all given their due. What's interesting about these exhibits is that, with a little bit of effort and a lot of travelling, you can see all of these peoples in the flesh. The Indian exhibit is particularly good – better than that of the FUNAI Museu do Índio.

The museum (☎ 568-8262) is at the Quinta da Boa Vista and is open Tuesday to Sunday from 10 am to 4 pm. Admission is US$3 (free on Thursday). To get there from Centro take the metrô to São Cristóvão or bus No 472 or 474; from the zona sul take bus No 472 or 474 as well.

Museu Nacional de Belas Artes (Map 2) At Avenida Rio Branco 199 is Rio's best fine-art museum. There are over 800 original paintings and sculptures in the collection. The most important gallery is the Galeria de Arte Brasileira, with 20th century classics such as Cândido Portinari's *Café*. There are also galleries with foreign art (not terribly good) and contemporary exhibits.

The museum (☎ 240-0068) is open Tuesday to Friday from 10 am to 6 pm; and Saturday, Sunday and holidays from 2 to 6 pm. Admission is US$1 (free on Sunday) and photography is prohibited. Take any of the city-bound buses and get off near Avenida Rio Branco, or take the metrô to Carioca station.

Museu Histórico Nacional (Map 2) Restored in 1985, this former colonial arsenal is filled with historic relics and interesting displays, one of the best being the re-creation of a colonial pharmacy. The museum (☎ 240-2003) is near the bay at Praça Marechal Âncora. It's open Tuesday to Friday from 10 am to 5.30 pm, weekends from 2 to 6 pm. Admission is US$1 (free on Sunday).

Museu Folclorico Edson Carneiro (Map 3) The small Edson Carneiro museum (☎ 285-0441) should not be missed – especially if you're staying nearby in the Catete/Flamengo area. It has excellent displays of folk art – probably Brazil's richest artistic tradition – a folklore library, and a small craft shop with some wonderful crafts, books and folk records at cheap prices.

The museum is next to the grounds of the Palácio do Catete. The address is Rua do Catete 181, Catete, and it's open Tuesday to Friday from 11 am to 6 pm, and Saturday, Sunday and holidays from 3 to 6 pm. Entry is free.

Museu da República & Palácio do Catete (Map 3) The Museu da República and the Palácio do Catete (☎ 285-6350) at Rua do Catete 153, have been wonderfully restored. Built between 1858 and 1866 and easily distinguished by the bronze eagles on the eaves, the palace was occupied by the president of Brazil from 1896 until 1954, when Getúlio Vargas killed himself here. His bedroom, where it took place, is on display. The museum, which occupies the palace, has a good collection of art and artefacts from the republican period. It's open Tuesday to Friday from noon to 5 pm. Admission is US$2 (free on Wednesday).

Museu do Índio (Map 3) At Rua das Palmeiras 55, Botafogo, the FUNAI Museu do Índio (☎ 286-2097) has a good library with over 25,000 titles, a map and photo collection and a quiet garden. Opening hours are Tuesday to Friday from 10 am to 5 pm and weekends from 1 to 5 pm. Entry is free.

Museu H Stern (Map 5) The headquarters of the famous jeweller H Stern (☎ 259-7442 ext 336), Rua Visconde de Pirajá 490, contains a museum. You may find the 12 minute guided jewellery tour interesting if you're in the neighbourhood. With a coupon you can get a free cab ride to and from the shop and anywhere in the zona sul. It's open Monday to Friday from 8.30 am to 6 pm and Saturday from 8.30 am to 12.30 pm. Entry is free.

Museu Carmen Miranda (Map 3) The small Carmen Miranda Museum (☎ 551-2597) in Parque do Flamengo is across the street from Avenida Rui Barbosa 560 and is open Monday to Friday from 11 am to 5 pm, and Saturday and Sunday from 1 to 5 pm. Carmen, of course, was Hollywood's Brazilian bombshell, although she was actually born in Portugal. She made it to Hollywood in the 1940s and has become a cult figure in Rio. During Carnaval hundreds of men dress up as Carmen Miranda lookalikes. The museum is filled with Carmen memorabilia and paraphernalia, including costumes, T-shirts, posters, postcards, records and a small exhibit. Entry is US$1.

Museu Villa-Lobos (Map 3) This museum (☎ 266-3845) is in a century-old building and is dedicated to the memory of Heitor Villa-Lobos. This great Brazilian composer, regarded as the father of modern Brazilian music, was the first to combine folkloric themes with classic forms. As well as personal items, there's also an extensive sound archive. At Rua Sorocaba 200 in Botafogo, it's open from Monday to Friday from 10 am to 5 pm. Entry is free.

Museu de Arte Moderna (Map 2) The airport hangar-like construction, at the northern end of Parque do Flamengo, is the Modern Art Museum (☎ 210-2188). Construction began in 1954, but for much of the past few years all that has been seen of the museum are its grounds, designed by Brazil's most famous landscape architect, Burle Marx (who landscaped Brasília).

The museum was devastated by a fire in 1978 which consumed 90% of its collection. The museum has worked hard to rebuild its collection, but it still houses only temporary exhibitions. It's open Tuesday to Sunday from noon to 8 pm. The entry fee is US$5.

Museu Naval e Oceanográfico (Map 2) This museum (☎ 533-7626) chronicles the history of the Brazilian navy from the 16th century to the present. It's close to Praça 15 de Novembro and is open from noon to 4.30 pm daily. The entry fee is US$2.

Museu Histórico e Diplomático (Map 2) Housed in the restored Itamaraty Palace which was home to Brazil's presidents from 1889 to 1897, this museum has an impressive collection of art and antiques. Located at Rua Marechal Floriano 196 (a short walk from Presidente Vargas metrô station), the museum has guided tours on Monday, Wednesday and Friday from 1 to 5 pm. To guarantee a tour in English or French, call them on (☎ 253-7961). Entry costs US$2.

Sambódromo & Museu do Carnaval (Map 2) Designed by Oscar Neimeyer and completed in 1984, the Sambódromo also houses the Museu do Carnaval. It contains lots of interesting material relating to the history of Rio's samba schools. It's open Tuesday to Sunday from 11 am to 5 pm and entry is free. Enter through Rua Frei Caneca. Empty sambadromes are like empty stadiums – there's not a lot happening. Entry is free.

Museu Chácara do Céu (Map 2) This delightful museum (☎ 507-1932) at Rua Murtinho Nobre 93, Santa Teresa, occupies part of the old mansion of wealthy industrialist and arts patron Raymundo Ottoni de Castro Maya. It contains art and antiques from his private collection, which he bequeathed to the nation, including works by Monet, Vlaminck, Portinari and Picasso to name a few. The house is surrounded by beautiful gardens and has a great view of Guanabara Bay.

It's open daily (except Tuesday) from noon to 5 pm. Entry is US$5, free on Sunday. To get there, take the No 206 or 214 bus from the Menezes Cortes bus terminal in the Centro to the Curvelo stop. You can take the tram, but don't carry valuables.

Museu Histórico do Exército e Forte de Copacabana (Map 4) Built in 1914, the fort preserves its original characteristics, with walls up to 12m-thick and fortified with Krupp cannons. The museum (☎ 287-2192) displays weapons, but one of the best reasons to visit is the fantastic view of Copacabana. The fort is open from Tuesday to Sunday between 10 am and 4 pm. Entry is US$2.

Museu Casa do Pontal Owned by Frenchman Jaques Van de Beuque, this impressive collection of over 4500 pieces is one of the best folk-art exhibitions in Brazil. Works are grouped according to themes, including music, Carnaval, religion and folklore.

The museum (☎ 437-6278) is located just past Barra at the Estrada do Pontal 3295. It's open on weekends from 9.30 am to 5.30 pm. Admission costs US$8.

Ilha da Paquetá (Map 1)

This island in the Baía de Guanabara was once a very popular tourist spot and is now frequented mostly by families from the zona norte. There are no cars on the island, so transport is by foot, bicycle (there are literally hundreds for rent) and horse-drawn carts. There's a certain dirty decadent charm to the colonial buildings, unassuming beaches and businesses catering to local tourism. Sadly, the bay is too polluted to safely swim in and the place gets very crowded.

Go to Paquetá for the boat ride through the bay and to see Cariocas at play – especially during the Festa de São Roque, which is celebrated over five days in August. Boats leave from near the Praça 15 de Novembro in Centro. The regular ferry takes one hour and costs US$3. The hydrofoil is worth taking, at least one way. It gets to the island in 25 minutes and costs US$8. The ferry service goes from 5.30 am to 10.30 pm, leaving every two to three hours. The hydrofoil leaves every hour on the hour from Rio (8 am to 5 pm) and returns every hour from Paquetá (8 am to 5.30 pm).

Cycling

Cycling is popular with Cariocas. There is a bike path around Lagoa das Freitas, one in Barra da Tijuca, and one on the oceanfront from Ipanema to Leme. This same bike path also goes all the way to Flamengo. If you have a bit of road sense and don't mind mixing it with the traffic, a bike is a fun way to get around the zona sul. On Tuesday nights Riobikers take to the streets. Riobikers started out as a group of cyclists who enjoyed riding in a group. The idea caught on and now every Tuesday night, thousands of bikers take to the road from Leblon to the Museu de Arte Moderna in Aterro do Flamengo. The streets are closed to other traffic after 9 pm and the bikers move off at around 9.30 pm from Leblon.

Stop Bike (☎ 275-7345), in the small arcade at Rua Barata Ribeiro 181, has a few mountain bikes to rent for US$16 a day, and they give good deals if you rent for longer. The woman who runs the shop speaks English. If you just want to cruise the beachfront at Copacabana and Ipanema, bikes can be rented on Sunday and holidays on Avenida Atlântica in front of Rua República do Peru. They cost US$4 per hour.

Golf

Rio has two 18 hole golf courses close to the city: Gávea Golf Club (☎ 322-4141), Estrada da Gávea 800, and Itanhangá Golf Club (☎ 494-2507), Estrada da Barra 2005. The clubs welcome visitors during the week from 7 am to sunset, but on weekends you need to be invited by a member.

Green fees are about US$75 a round, plus club hire of US$25 and caddie hire for US$25.

A cheaper option is Golden Green (☎ 433-3950), which has six tricky par-three holes. It's open daily from 7 am to 7 pm. Cost is US$10 for 18. Club rental is US$15 and cart rental an extra US$12. It's near Barra beach, opposite Posto Seven.

Helicopter Flights

Joy flights over the city can be arranged by Helisight (☎ 511-2141). It has three helipads at strategic, scenic locations: Mirante Dona Marta, just below Cristo Redentor, at Lagoa Rodrigo de Freitas and from Morro da Urca, the first cable-car stop as you go up to the Pão de Açúcar. There are seven different flights to choose from. Five minute flights cost US$40 and a 30 minute flight costs US$140 per person. These flights are a definite 'video opportunity'.

Surfing

In Rio city, surfing is very popular, with the locals ripping the fast, hollow beach breaks. When the surf is good, it gets crowded. Arpoador, between Copacabana and Ipanema, is where most surfers congregate, though there are some fun beach breaks further out in Barra, Grumari, Joá and Prainha (considered by many to be the best surf spot in Rio). Boards can be rented in Rio, but they're so cheap that you'd be crazy not to buy one, especially if you've planned a surfing expedition down the coast. Galeria River (pronounced 'heever'), at Rua Francisco Otaviano 67 in Arpoador, is an arcade full of surf shops.

Hang-Gliding, Para-Gliding and Ultra-Leve

If you weigh less than 80kg (about 180lb) and have US$100 you can do the fantastic – hang-glide off the 510m Pedra Bonita on to Pepino beach in São Conrado. This is one of the giant granite slabs that towers above Rio. No experience is necessary. To arrange a *voo duplo* (double flight) go out to Pepino and the pilots will be waiting on the beach. We're told that the winds are very safe here and the pilots know what they are doing. Guest riders get their bodies put in a kind of pouch that is secured to the kite.

Flight Information Most tandem pilots can mount a camera with flash, wide-angle lens, motor drive and a long cable release on a wing tip to take pictures of you in flight. If you want to take pictures yourself you must realise that take-off and landing pictures are impossible since you can't be encumbered with equipment. Your camera must fit into the velcro pouch in the front of your flight suit. It's a good idea to have the camera strapped around your neck and a lens cover strapped to the lens or you will risk losing the equipment and beaning a Carioca on the head. Flights are usually extremely smooth so it's possible to take stable shots. Photos of the hang-gliders themselves are dramatic, especially when taken from above.

Know your exact weight in kilograms in advance. Ideally your pilot should be heavier than you. If you're heavier than the pilot, he or she will have to use a weight belt and switch to a larger glider. If you're over 80kg you may still be able to fly – it depends on the weight of the pilot. You don't need any experience or special training – anyone from seven to 70 years can do it.

Cautious flights depend on atmospheric conditions. You can usually fly on all but three or four days per month, and conditions during winter are even better. For the experience of a lifetime, it's not that expensive: US$80 for anywhere from 10 to 25 minutes of extreme pleasure. The price includes being picked up and dropped off at your hotel. If you fly early in the day, you have more flexibility with delays.

The best way to arrange a flight is to go right to the far end of Pepino beach on Avenida Prefeito Mendes de Morais, where the fly-boys hang out at the Voo Livre club. Ruy Marra is an excellent tandem-glider pilot and widely regarded as one of the best pilots in Rio. He runs Super Fly Agency (☎ 332-2286) in São Conrado at Estrada das Canoas 1476, casa 2. (Ruy is also the person to see if you're interested in para-gliding.) Also recommended is Carlos Millan (☎ 522-5586), who also runs a tour agency called Rio Aventura, with emphasis on radical sports. The Associação Brasileiro de Voo Livre (☎ 322-0266), offers classes in hang-gliding.

Ultra-leve (ultralight) flights, are more comfortable than hang-gliders, but you have to listen to the motor. The trips leave from the Aeroclube do Jacarepaguá. The Clube Esportivo de Ultra-Leve (☎ 221-6489) has some long-range ultralights that can stay up for over two hours. Fifteen minute flights cost around US$45.

Hiking & Climbing

Excellent hiking is possible surprisingly close to the city. There are three national parks with trail systems in Rio state: Parque Nacional da Tijuca, Parque Nacional da Serra dos Órgãos and Parque Nacional do Itatiaia (see the Rio de Janeiro State chapter for information on these latter two parks).

Clubs For anyone interested in climbing and hiking, Rio's clubs are the best source of information as well as the best meeting place for like-minded people. The clubs meet regularly and welcome visitors. The following clubs are well organised and have bulletin boards listing excursions on the weekends:

Centro Excursionista Brasileiro (CEB)
Avenida Almirante Barroso 2, 8th floor, Centro. It meets on Wednesday and Friday evenings and is geared toward trekking and day hikes. CEB also runs a small restaurant which is open from 6 pm, Monday to Friday, where people meet informally to plan excursions.

Centro Excursionista Rio de Janeiro (CERJ)
Avenida Rio Branco 277/805, Centro. It meets on Tuesday and Thursday evenings. CERJ offers the greatest diversity of activities ranging from hikes to technical climbing.

Clube Excursionista Carioca (CEC)
Rua Hilário de Gouveia 71/206, Copacabana. meets on Wednesday and Friday evenings at 10.30 pm. This club specialises in difficult technical climbing.

Pão de Açúcar (Sugar Loaf; Map 3) On Pão de Açúcar (396m), there are 50 established climbing routes. Climbers are often seen scaling the western face below the cable cars. One of the best hikes is up the back side of Pão de Açúcar. The hike takes 1½ hours and requires climbing experience, because there are two 10 to 15m exposed parts. If you require assistance, talk to the climbing or hiking clubs about organising a guide.

The hike begins on the left-hand side of Praça General Tibúrcio (the same praça where the cable cars are boarded), where a sealed jogging track runs for 1200m along the base of Morro de Tijuca and Pão de Açúcar. At the end of the track pick up the trail on the other side of the cement tank in the tall grass. Follow this trail (always taking the uphill forks) for 100m. At the old foundations, some 30m above the water, the trail ascends steeply for 60m until levelling off on a narrow ridge. From the ridge, the broad eastern flank of Pão de Açúcar is seen. Follow the trail up the far left-hand side ridge.

At the base of the rock the trail deviates slightly to the right for the next 40m until coming to two iron bolts on the smooth exposed rock. This is the first exposed area, and although it can be crossed without ropes, requires agility and alertness. There is nothing to break a fall except the rocks in the ocean, 120m below.

From the second bolt, stay next to the rock slab for the following 6m. To cross the gap between the first rock slab and the next slab it is safer to step up on to the second rock slab rather than continuing along the exposed face. Another 20m higher up there is a third iron bolt, which is a good place to take in the view before tackling the crux of the climb – above the clearly defined path.

At the fourth bolt, the hike becomes a climb for the next 10m. This section is best climbed by finding the holds behind the rock slabs and pulling yourself up. After the sixth and final bolt, the climbing is over. Follow the well-defined path up 200m to the small children's park at the top.

Corcovado (Map 1) Corcovado (710m) offers technically difficult climbs with fantastic views of Pão de Açúcar and Lagoa Rodrigo. Private guides and the clubs are the best means for unravelling its many diverse routes. Well-equipped and experienced climbers can easily climb its eastern face on the route K-2 (rated 5.9).

The climb begins 200m below the summit. To get to the base of the climb, take the train to the top and instead of ascending the stairs to the left, follow the road out of the parking lot for 15 minutes. After the first rocky outcrop on the northern side, descend two more turns in the road. At the second turn there is a cement railing, behind which is a poorly maintained trail.

Follow this trail as it hugs the base of the rock for 200m around to the eastern face of the mountain. Don't get discouraged by the tall grass which obstructs the trail; just keep to the base of the rock. On the eastern face the start of the climb is at the 20m crack in the whitened rock. From there the climb is clearly marked with well-placed bolts to the top, just underneath the statue of Christ.

Tai Chi Chuan

Tai chi enthusiasts might like to join in one of the daily sessions held at Praça NS da Paz in Ipanema or on the beachfront at Arpoador. There are sessions held at sunrise and at 5 pm.

Tennis

The tropical climate of Rio is not ideal for tennis, but if you fancy a game, you can book a court at the InterContinental (☎ 322-2200) or Sheraton (☎ 274-1122). Courts are available for use by non-guests for US$10 an hour. Lob Tênis (☎ 558-2335), Rua Stefan Zweig 290 in Laranjeiras, rents courts for US$25 an hour and opens until midnight. In Barra da Tijuca, there are many tennis centres, including Akxe Sport Club (☎ 325-3232), Avenida Canal de Marapendi 2900 and Rio Sport Center (☎ 325-6644) at Avenida Ayrton Senna 2541.

Walking & Jogging

There are some good walking and jogging paths in the zona sul. If you're staying in the Flamengo-Catete area, Flamengo Park has plenty of space and lots of workout stations. There is 9.5km of cycling, jogging and walking track around Lagoa Rodrigo de Freitas. You can rent bicycles, tricycles or quadricycles at the lake. At the Parque do Cantalago there,. Along the seaside, from Leme to Barra da Tijuca, there's a bike and footpath. On Sunday the road itself is closed to traffic and is full of cyclists, joggers, rollerbladers and prams.

Closed to bikes, but not to walkers and joggers, is the Pista Cládio Coutinho, between the mountains and the sea at Praia Vermelha in Urca. It's open daily from 7 am to 6 pm and is very secure because the army maintains guard posts. People in bathing suits aren't allowed in (unless they're running). It's a nice place to be around sunset.

Language Courses

The Instituto Brasil-Estados Unidos (IBEU; ☎ 548-8332) has a variety of Portuguese language classes that start every month or two. The cost for a four week course that meets three times a week is about US$150. For information stop by Avenida NS de Copacabana 690, on the 5th floor.

Next door to IBEU is a Casa Matos shop which sells the language books for the IBEU courses. It's a good place to pick up a book or dictionaries to study Portuguese on your own. Other places that offer courses include Britannia (☎ 511-0143), with branches in Leblon and Ipanema and Berlitz (☎ 240-6606) in the Centro and Ipanema.

Organised Tours

City Tours Most of the larger tour companies, like Gray Line (☎ 291-1444; fax 259-9862), operate sightseeing tours of Rio. Their brochures are sitting on the reception desks of most hotels. Tours cover the usual tourist destinations and their prices are quite reasonable. A four hour tour to Corcovado and Tijuca costs around US$30.

Unfortunately, many of our readers complain they spend more time on the bus as it picks up passengers from other hotels than the actual tour itself!

For a more personalised tour, there are several excellent independent operators, all of whom will pick you up and drop you off at your hotel. Dolores Leão (☎/fax 220-2043) is a lively guide who speaks English, Spanish, Italian and French. Her buggy tours are highly recommended by many readers. Rio Custom Tours (☎ 274-3217; mobile ☎ 987-4374) is run by Maria Lúcia Yolen. She likes to show that Rio is not all samba, beaches and Corcovado. Some of her tours include the Sunday mass at São Bento, complete with Gregorian chants, a trip to the Casa do Pontal and its excellent folk-art collection, and a tour through Santa Teresa. Also recommended is Pedro Novak (☎/fax 232-9710), who operates jeep tours to a variety of destinations in the city and Rio state.

Historic Rio Tour Run by art historian Professor Carlos Roquette (☎ 322-4872), who speaks English and French as well as Portuguese, these tours bring old Rio to life. Itineraries include a night at the Teatro Municipal, colonial Rio, baroque Rio, imperial Rio and a walking tour of the Centro. Professor Roquette really knows his Rio, and if you have an obscure question, we're sure he would welcome it.

Favela Tour This is one of our favourite tours, and is highly recommended. If you want to visit a favela you'd be crazy to do it on your own. Since large amounts of cocaine are trafficked through them each week, there are lots of young, heavily-armed characters around. The safest alternative is to take one of the favela tours that now operate in Rio. English-speaking Marcelo Armstrong (☎ 322-2727, mobile ☎ 989-0074) is the pioneer of favela tourism. He takes individuals and small groups to visit Rocinha, the largest favela in Rio, and Vila Canoas near São Conrado. The tour visits a school, medical centre and private houses, and you come away with a good idea of how a favela operates. You can take a camera, but ask permission before taking anybody's picture and don't take photos of suspicious or armed characters. Marcelo also conducts a variety of other interesting tours and is a terrific guide.

Villa Riso Colonial Tour Villa Riso in São Conrado, next to the Gávea Golf Club, recreates a colonial *fazenda* (farm), complete with employees wearing colonial gear. The house and gardens date from the early 18th century. A three hour tour includes a buffet lunch (normally a *feijoada* or *churrasco*) and a medley of Brazilian theatrical music. You must make reservations (☎ 322-1444; fax 322-5196). The cost is US$40 and they only open on Sunday.

The Ronnie Biggs Experience Flush with victory after the British government's failed bid to extradite him, Ronnie Biggs – the Great Train Robbery robber and living legend – continues to host barbecues at his hilltop home in Santa Teresa. Preferring groups of 10 or more, Ronnie charges US$60 a head for all you can eat and drink. There're plenty of photo opportunities and you can purchase a T-shirt with the slogan 'I know someone who went to Brazil and met Ronnie Biggs – honest!'. Ronnie is a great raconteur

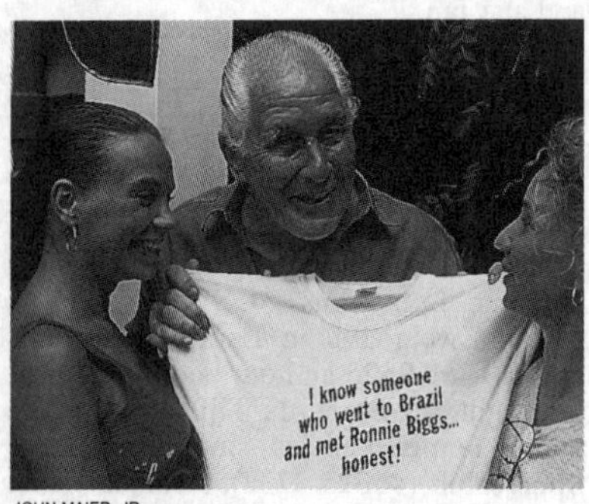

JOHN MAIER, JR

Great train robber Ronnie Biggs has lived in Rio de Janeiro for the past 27 years

and a lot of fun. If you can get a group together, give him a call on (☎ 242-8343). If you can't, give him a call anyway and he might be able to squeeze you in if there's a barbecue already organised.

Ronnie suffered a stroke in early 1998 which affected his speech, so we're not sure if he'll still run the barbecues when he recovers. Call to find out. His son Michael speaks good English.

Carnaval

See the following Carnaval chapter for everything you need to know about Carnaval.

Places to Stay

Rio has a star rating system. Hotels are ranked from one star for the cheapest to five for the most luxurious. There are many hotels unclassified by Embratur (our speciality), but still regulated. Many hotels have a 10% service charge, and will also collect a 5% government room tax. The cheaper places don't seem to bother with this.

So what do the stars mean? Well, a five-star hotel has a pool or two, at least two very good restaurants, a nightclub and bar, gym, sauna and a beauty salon. A four-star hotel has a good restaurant, a sauna and a bar. A three-star hotel may have everything a four-star hotel has, but there's something that downgrades it; the furnishings may be a bit beat-up, cheaper, or a bit sparser. There's a big gap between three-stars and two-stars. A two-star hotel is usually clean and comfortable, but that's about all.

By the way, all hotels with a star rating have air-conditioning in the rooms, though some of the older models are very noisy! They also have a small frigobar (refrigerator) in the rooms; sometimes empty or full of nibbles costing double what they would in the nearby supermarket. Bathrooms have bidets, a sign of the continental influence.

Below one and two stars there are still plenty of decent places to stay if you're travelling on a tight budget and need a safe place to sleep. Air-conditioning is usually optional (if available), but mostly the rooms have fans.

Breakfast is usually included in the room rate. It ranges from sumptuous buffets at the top end to coffee and a bread roll at the budget end. In between there should be fresh juice, good coffee, fresh rolls with a slice of ham and cheese and a couple of pieces of fruit.

Reservations are a good idea, especially if you plan to stay in a mid-range or top-end hotel. You can save up to 30% by booking in advance. If you want to make sure you have an ocean view, request it when you make your reservation. It will cost around 20% more than other rooms. At Carnaval time hotel prices go up and everyone gives dire warnings of there being no places to stay. It's not a good time to arrive without a reservation, but you should be able to find a room somewhere.

Prices we've quoted here in the mid-range and top-end hotels are the rate for a standard room if you walk-in off the street, so you should be able to get the price down a bit by reserving in advance.

Places to Stay – Budget

Camping The camping grounds in Rio are relatively safe but all located outside the centre.

The Camping Clube do Brasil has a camping ground *CCB-10* (☎ 490-3400) at Estrada do Pontal 5900, Recreio dos Bandeirantes, opposite the beach. The price is US$7.50 per person. There are two other camping grounds in Recreio, both with a lot of permanent residents. *Novo Rio* (☎ 437-6518) at Avenida das Américas, Km 18, has a grassy area with plenty of shade. It charges US$12 per person. *Ostal* (☎ 437-8213) at Avenida Sernambetiba 18790, is opposite the beach. It costs US$8 per person.

Hostels Rio has a couple of quite good hostels. The YHA *Chave do Rio de Janeiro* (☎ 286-0303; fax 286-5652) at Rua General Dionísio 63, Botafogo, is a model youth hostel. You'll meet lots of young Brazilians here from all over the country. It gets busy, so you need to make reservations. The only problem with this place is its location, but if you get the hang of the buses quickly, it shouldn't hamper you too much. From the rodoviária, catch a No 170, 172 or 173 bus and ask the driver to let you off at the Largo dos Leões. Go up Rua Voluntários da Pátria until Rua General Dionísio, then turn left. The charge is US$14 for members, a bit more during summer. Non-members pay US$21 and can only stay 24 hours. Non-member student card holders pay US$17. Breakfast is included. Guest memberships for other YHA hostels in Brazil are also sold here for US$20, and the directory for other hostels in Brazil for US$8.

The non-YHA hostel *Copacabana Praia* (☎ 547-5422), is in Copacabana at Rua Tenente Marones de Gusmão 85. Although it's a few blocks from the beach it's still good value. A relaxed and friendly place, it costs US$15 for dormitory beds and US$40 for apartments with a stove and a refrigerator. These apartments will sleep up to four people. Sheet rental costs an extra US$5.

Hotels The best area for budget hotels is around Glória, Catete and Flamengo. This used to be a desirable part of the city and is still quite nice. Many of the places used to be better hotels, so you can get some pleasant rooms at very reasonable prices. These hotels are often full from December to February, so reservations are not a bad idea.

From Glória to Lapa, near the aqueduct, on the edge of the business district, there are several more budget hotels. Generally, these are hardly any cheaper than the hotels further from the city in Catete, but the area is less safe at night. If, however, everything else is booked up you'll see several hotels if you walk along Rua Joaquim Silva (near the Passeio Público), then over to Avenida Mem de Sá, turn up Avenida Gomes Freire and then turn right in to Praça Tiradentes. The *Hotel Marajó* (☎ 224-4134), Rua Joaquim Silva 99 is recommended. Single/double/triple apartamentos cost US$25/28/54. An apartamento with two single beds costs US$36.

Glória (Map 2) The *Hotel Turístico* (☎ 557-7698), Ladeira da Glória 30, is one of Rio's most popular budget hotels, even though their prices are getting a bit high. There are always plenty of gringos staying here. It's across from the Glória metrô station, 30m up the street that emerges between two side-walk restaurants. The rooms are clean and safe, with small balconies. The hotel is often full, but they do take reservations. Single quartos cost US$25 and apartamentos start at US$30/35.

Right near the Glória metrô station, the *Hotel Benjamin Constant*, Rua Benjamin Constant 10, is one of the cheapest places around. The rooms are small and dingy, but the cost is only US$8 per person without breakfast.

Catete (Map 3) The *Hotel Ferreira Viana* (☎ 205-7396), Rua Ferreira Viana 58, has cramped, cheap quartos at US$13.50/23 for singles/doubles with a good hot shower down the hall. Double apartamentos are US$27.

On busy Rua do Catete there are several budget hotels worthy of note. The *Hotel Monte Blanco* (☎ 225-0121), at No 160, a few steps from the Catete metrô stop, is very clean and has air-conditioned apartamentos for US$18/26. Ask for a quiet room in the back; they have round beds and sparkling wall paint. Up the stairs at No 172, the *Hotel Vitória* (☎ 205-5397) has clean apartamentos for US$18/24.

The *Hotel Imperial* (☎ 556-0772; fax 558-5815), No 186, is a funky hotel with car parking. The quality and prices of the rooms vary, starting at US$40/45 for apartamentos. Some of the rooms have air-conditioning. The *Hotel Rio Claro* (☎ 558-5180), a few blocks down at No 233, has musty singles for US$20 and doubles with air-conditioning, TV and hot shower for US$23.

The *Hotel Hispáno Brasileiro* (☎ 265-5990), Rua Silveira Martins 135, has big, clean apartamentos. Singles are US$20 and doubles US$30.

Turn down the quiet Rua Artur Bernardes for a couple more budget hotels: the *Monterrey* (☎ 265-9899) and *Hotel Rio Lisboa*

(☎ 265-9599) are at Nos 39 and 29 respectively. Quartos at the Monterrey go for US$15/20 (US$25 for two single beds) and apartamentos cost US$20/25. At the Rio Lisboa, single quartos cost US$12 and apartamentos are US$16/21. These two are the cheapest places in Catete.

Groups of young Israeli backpackers have been barred from all but three hotels in Catete because they are too noisy and cook in the rooms. Those that still accept them are the Vitória, Monte Blanco and Hispáno Brasileiro.

Flamengo (Map 3) Near the Largo do Machado metrô station, the elegant palm-tree-lined Rua Paissandú has two excellent budget hotels. The *Hotel Venezuela* (☎ 557-7098), No 34, is clean and cosy. All the rooms have double beds, air-conditioning, TV and hot water. Apartamentos cost US$17/30. The *Hotel Paysandú* (☎ 558-7270), at No 23, is a two-star Embratur hotel with quartos for US$18/33 and apartamentos for US$25/40. Both are good value for money.

Copacabana (Map 4) The *Pousada Girassol* (☎ 256-6951), Travessa Angrense 25-A, is a recently renovated pousada, with cheerful, comfortable apartamentos with ceiling fans for US$25/40/50. It's an excellent location and very good value. English is spoken. Next door at No 25, the *Hotel Angrense* (☎/fax 548-0509) has clean and dreary quartos for US$25/40 and apartamentos for US$30/50. Travessa Angrense isn't on most maps but it intersects Avenida NS de Copacabana just past Rua Santa Clara.

Places to Stay – Mid-Range

Centro (Map 2) The three-star *Center Hotel* (☎ 296-6677; fax 233-6781), Avenida Rio Branco 33, provides decent apartamentos for US$47/53 plus a 10% service charge. Their brochure in English includes the information that: 'The Hotel owns individual safe for guests to keep documents and other worthless objects'.

Cinelândia (Map 2) The quiet *Itajuba Hotel* (☎ 210-3163; fax 240-7461), Rua Álvaro Alvim 23, has rooms with refrigerators. Apartamentos are US$33/50. Nearby is the *Ambassador Hotel* (☎ 297-7181; fax 220-4783), Rua Senador Dantas 25, which has parking and a restaurant. They charge US$43/50 and offer a discount for paying cash.

Catete & Flamengo (Map 3) At Rua Ferreira Viana 29, the *Hotel Regina* (☎ 556-1647; fax 285-2999) is a respectable mid-range hotel with a snazzy lobby, clean rooms and hot showers. Apartamentos start at US$40/46. At Rua Silveira Martins 20, the *Hotel Inglês* (☎ 265-9052), is a good two-star hotel where singles/doubles/triples cost US$35/45/57. The three-star *Flamengo Palace* (☎ 557-7552; fax 265-2846), Praia do Flamengo 6, next to the Novo Mundo Hotel, has comfortable apartamentos with a view of the Pão de Açúcar for US$63/71. Rooms without the view are US$54/61. They have a 10% service charge.

Leme (Map 4) The *Hotel Acapulco* (☎ 275-0022), Rua Gustavo Sampaio 854, is a three-star Embratur hotel with apartamentos costing US$50/70. It's one block from the beach, behind the Le Meridien.

Copacabana (Map 4) The *Hotel Santa Clara* (☎ 256-2650; fax 547-4042), Rua Décio Vilares 316, is a delightful mid-range option, with apartamentos starting at US$43/50. A few blocks away, the *Hotel Copa Linda* (☎ 267-3399), has small and basic rooms for US$45 single or double. It's at Avenida NS de Copacabana 956 on the 2nd floor.

There are several hotels that offer more for the money than the two just mentioned. Right nearby, the *Grande Hotel Canada* (☎ 257-1864; fax 255-3705), Avenida NS de Copacabana 687, has apartamentos starting at US$51/61, less in low season. The rooms are modern, with air-conditioning and TV. It's two blocks from the beach in a busy area.

The *Hotel Martinique* (☎ 521-1652; fax 287-7640) combines a perfect location with good rooms at a moderate cost. It's on the quiet Rua Sá Ferreira at No 30, one block from the beach at the far end of Copacabana. Clean, comfortable rooms with air-conditioning start at US$45/60 and they have a few tiny singles for US$30.

Also one block from the beach, is the two-star *Hotel Toledo* (☎ 257-1990; fax 287-7640), Rua Domingos Ferreira 71. The rooms are as fine as many higher priced hotels. Good value apartamentos start at US$54/60 and they also have some tiny singles for US$30. The *Biarritz Hotel* (☎ 522-0542; fax 287-7640) is a small place at Rua Aires Saldanha 54, close to the beach behind the Rio Othon Palace. Apartamentos start at US$54/60 and all rooms have air-conditioning and TV. Also try the *Apa Hotel* (☎ 548-8112; fax 256-3628), three blocks from the beach at Rua República do Peru 305. Rooms here are US$50/55.

If you want to spend more money and stay on the beachfront, the *Hotel Debret* (☎ 522-0132; fax 521-0899), Avenida Atlântica 3564, is a traditional hotel set in a converted apartment building. It has attractive colonial-style furnishings and rooms for US$50/60. Rooms with a sea view are US$75. The entrance is on Rua Almirante Gonçalves.

Ipanema & Leblon (Maps 4 & 5) There are two relatively inexpensive hotels in Ipanema. The *Hotel San Marco* (☎/fax 239-5032) is a couple of blocks from the beach at Rua Visconde de Pirajá 524. Rooms are small but with air-conditioning, TV and refrigerator. Apartamentos start at US$42/46. The *Hotel Vermont* (☎ 521-0057; fax 267-7046), Rua Visconde de Pirajá 254, also has simple rooms at US$60/65.

You can get an ocean-side apartment at the *Arpoador Inn* (☎ 523-0060; fax 511-5094), on Rua Francisco Otaviano. This six floor hotel is the only one in Ipanema or Copacabana that doesn't have a busy street running between your room and the beach. The musty beachfront rooms are more expensive than those facing the street but the view and the roar of the surf makes it all worthwhile. Rooms without the view cost US$52/57, with view US$104/115. The *Ipanema Inn* (☎ 287-6092), Rua Maria Quitéria 27 around the corner from the Caesar Park, may appeal to beach-loving and budget-conscious travellers who don't mind beat-up rooms. TV is an optional extra and the hotel provides umbrellas and towels for the beach. Apartamentos cost US$60/70.

The *Hotel Carlton* (☎ 259-1932; fax 259-3147), Rua João Lira 68, is on a very quiet street, one block from the beach in Leblon. It's a small, friendly hotel, away from the tourist scene. Apartamentos are US$48/52. They also have one, two-room suite for US$85.

Places to Stay – Top End

Catete/Flamengo (Map 3) The *Hotel Flórida* (☎ 556-5242; fax 285-5777), Rua Ferreira Viana 81, is popular with package tour groups. Rooms have private baths with good, hot showers and polished parquet floors. Rooms cost US$74/81. Make your reservations well in advance for stays during the high season.

Behind a beautiful white façade is the five-star *Hotel Glória* (☎ 555-7272; fax 55-7282), Rua do Russel 632. Once a grand 1920s beachfront hotel, the Glória fell off the pace when the tunnel went through to Copacabana and Ipanema. It even lost its beach when the big landfill of 1965 was landscaped into Parque do Flamengo. That didn't stop it from maintaining its status as a fine hotel. It was upgraded and renovated in 1990 and it's easily the best hotel close to the city centre. Favoured by business travellers, package tour groups and politicians, the Glória is a classy place. Rooms start at US$160/220.

Close by is the other top hotel in the area, the *Novo Mundo* (☎ 557-6226; fax 265-2369) at Praia do Flamengo 20. Once a luxury hotel, the Novo Mundo has slipped a little recently, but it provides good service and a great view of Pão de Açúcar for US$102/113.

Leme (Map 4) *Le Meridien* (☎ 275-9922; fax 541-6447), Avenida Atlântica 1020 is modern, luxurious and chic. Popular with Europeans, Le Meridien is home to some fine French restaurants and bars. On New Year's Eve, the hotel turns into a fireworks cascade. Rooms start at US$180/200.

Copacabana (Map 4) Of the many top hotels in Rio, the 1920s style *Copacabana Palace* (☎ 548-7070; fax 235-7330), Avenida Atlântica 1702, is the one favoured by royalty and rock stars. It is truly a symbol of the city. After a massive facelift, it is a modern luxury hotel as well. With a great pool and excellent restaurants, the formal Cipriani and the Pergula, the Copacabana Palace is a wonderful splurge. Standard apartments cost US$290/315, or you might like to try the presidential suite for only US$1350 a night.

The *Rio Palace* (☎ 521-3232; fax 227-1454), Avenida Atlântica 4240, has excellent views and luxurious public areas. It's very popular with US tourists and has a long list of stars who've stayed there. Frank Sinatra sang in the auditorium. The Cassino Atlântico shopping centre is right there and its restaurant, La Pré Catalan, is very good. The pool area has great views. Apartamentos start at US$230/250, but they may offer a 30% discount.

Ipanema (Maps 4 & 5) The *Caesar Park* (☎ 287-3122; fax 521-6000), Avenida Vieira Souto 460, is favoured by ex-dictators, and business people with large expense accounts. Service is impeccable. The feijoada (see the Places to Eat chapter) on Saturdays at the Caesar is legendary. The spectacular breakfast views are also a good start to the day. Security is tight on the beach in front, too. Rooms begin at US$230/250. The imperial suite is a steal at US$3240 a night.

On the beachfront, the four-star *Sol Ipanema* (☎ 523-0095; fax 521-6464), Avenida Vieira Souto 320, is a quiet hotel opposite Posto 9 where the beautiful people go. It supplies towels, chairs and umbrellas. Double rooms start at US$125, but the view is worth an extra US$25. The *Everest Rio Hotel* (☎ 287-8282; fax 521-3198) is a decent five-star place, a block from the beach at Rua Prudente de Morais 1117. Apartamentos start at US$90/100, but they offer a good corporate rate.

Places to Stay – Long Term

A relatively inexpensive option in Copacabana, Ipanema and Leblon is to rent an apartment by the week or the month. There are loads of agencies. Brasleme Imóveis (☎ 542-1347), Rua Barata Ribeiro 92-A, Copacabana, rents apartments for a minimum of three days from US$75. Apartur Imóveis (☎ 287-5797), Rua Visconde de Pirajá 371 S/204, Ipanema, offers similar deals. Also recommended is Yvonne Reimann (☎ 513-0281), who rents self-contained flats to visitors for a week or more. Prices are around US$55 a night for a two-room flat.

If you are interested in renting an apartment, you could look under *temporada* or *apartamentos para aluguel* in any daily newspaper. If you just want a room in someone's house or apartment, look for *vaga* or *quarto*.

Aparthotels There are also residential hotels, or aparthotels, that are often more spacious and less expensive than normal hotels. This has been the fastest growing sector in the hotel industry in the past few years, so there are lots of small, modern apartments available. Prices vary from the mid-range to the top end, and during the low season, large discounts are usually available.

The *Rio Flat Service* (☎ 274-7222; fax 239-8792) has three residential hotels that are more like apartments. All apartments have a living room and a kitchen. Without the frills of fancy hotels, they still have a swimming pool, breakfast and room service. Apartments start at US$100 a night, or US$1850 a month. The *Copacabana Hotel Residência* (☎ 548-7212; fax 235-1828), Rua Barata Ribeiro 222, is similar to the Rio Flat Service. The guide given out by Riotur has a full listing of aparthotels in the various suburbs.

Places to Eat

There's lots of fast food in Rio: you'll see the 'golden arches' all over the place and a local version called *Bob's*. There are other chains around the city, like *La Mole*, which has cheap, decent Italian food and *Sindicato do Chopp*, with several locations in Copacabana and Ipanema. Pizzas are a popular Brazilian fast food, and you'll see plenty of pizzerias. Pizzas are standard menu items in most restaurants. They're a good option for solo travellers.

Traditional Brazilian fast food can be found at the juice bars and the *botecos*. Botecos (often called *botequims)* are Cariocas' local bars. Patrons drop in for a cafezinho and a shot of cachaça before work, and a snack, a caipirinha or a chopp later in the day. Botecos are not known for their cleanliness, but nobody seems to mind – not the Cariocas anyway. The quality of food served by botecos varies but can be good. Try such delights as a coxina de galinha (a savoury chicken wrapped in dough) or a pastel de palmito (a small pastry with palm heart inside).

The plates at the many botecos are big enough to feed two and the price is only US$4 to $5. For something lighter, and probably healthier, you can eat at a suco bar. Most have sandwiches and fruit salads. Make a habit of asking for an *embalagem* (doggie bag) when you don't finish your food. Wrap it and hand it to a street person.

Galetos are small restaurants serving barbecued chicken and steak. It's grilled over the open flame as you sit behind the counter watching it, and Cariocas of all kinds sidle up to the counter and hop into a galeto with the *couvert* of chopped onions, tomato and bread rolls. The whole thing costs around US$5. You'll do plenty of finger lickin'.

Centro (Map 2) *Bar Luis*, Rua da Carioca 39, is a Rio institution that opened in 1887. The city's oldest *cervejaria* (public house), on Rio's oldest street, is a bar-less old dining room serving good German food and dark draft beer at moderate prices. It's open for lunch and dinner until midnight Monday to Saturday .

Café do Teatro, Avenida Epitácio Pessoa 1244, under the Teatro Municipal is a place to recall the good old days. Entering the dark, dramatic Assyrian Room, with its elaborate tile-work and ornate columns, is like walking into a Cecil B De Mille film. The 70-year-old restaurant is where Rio's upper crust used to dine and drink after the theatre; it must be seen to be believed. They serve lunch only and close on Saturday and Sunday. It's somewhat expensive and semi-formal, but don't be deterred – you can have a drink and light snack by the bar, listen to piano music, and breathe in the Assyrian atmosphere.

Confeiteria Colombo, Rua Gonçalves Dias 34, one block from and parallel to Rio Branco, is a big Viennese coffee house/restaurant where you can sit down for a meal, or stand if you're just having a dessert or cake. The Colombo is best for coffee and cake or a snack. Another old-style coffee house is *Casa Cavé* on the corner of Rua 7 de Setembro and Uruguiana. It has good ice cream.

Inside the Paço Imperial at Praça 15 de Novembro, the *Atrium* and the *Bistro do Paço* are both very popular with locals. After lunch you can wander around the exhibitions.

The green gazebo structure near the Niterói ferry is *Alba Mar* (☎ 240-8428), Praça Marechal Âncora 184. It looks out on the Baía de Guanabara and Niterói. Go for the view and the seafood. It stays open from 11.30 am to 10 pm Tuesday to Saturday. Dishes start at US$20 and the peixe brasileira is recommended.

There are lots of self-serve lunch places downtown. A couple of the better ones are *Mr Ôpi*, Rua da Alfândega 91, and *Dirty Mary Saladeria*, Rua Teófilo Otoni 50.

Cinelândia (Map 2) Tucked away in the small streets are lots of cheap lanchonetes and galetos *(O Rei do Galetos* is a good one). *Spagettilandia*, Rua Alvaro Alvim, has decent spaghetti dishes for around US$4.

Lapa & Santa Teresa (Map 2) *Restaurante Ernesto* on the corner of Rua da Lapa and Rua Teotônio Regatas is close to the arch of the viaduct that the bondinho crosses to head up to Santa Teresa. It's a good place to eat if you're going to a show in the city. In Santa Teresa at Rua Almirante Alexandrino 316-B, *Bar do Arnaudo* has the city's best carne do sol. It's closed Monday. A couple of cheap vegetarian places in Lapa are *Semente* and *Gohan*, both on Rua Joaquim Silva.

Glória & Catete (Maps 2 & 3) A couple of good, cheap *por quilo* (self-serve) places are *Estaçao Republica*, on the corner of Rua do Catete and Rua Andrade Pertence, and the one upstairs at Rua do Catete 152.

Westfalia, Rua da Gloria 318, serves good German food. *Taberna da Glória*, Ld do Russel 32A, has friendly service and is good for Brazilian staple dishes, like the Sunday cozido, roast piglet on Thursdays and feijoada on Saturdays. On the other corner of Ladeira da Gloria is *Amarelinho*, an air-conditioned, self-serve lunch place that gets packed at lunch time. *Adega dos Nogueiras*, Rua Pedro Americo, has a wonderful picanha that 'serves three' for around US$10.

Restaurant Amazónia, upstairs at Rua do Catete 234, has good steak and a tasty broiled chicken with creamed-corn sauce, both for about US$12. Avoid the lanchonete downstairs, which has slipped in quality and freshness. For a splurge, eat at the restaurant in the Museu da República, Rua do Catete 153. It has excellent food and a nice, relaxed atmosphere.

Botafogo & Flamengo (Map 3) The popular *Churrascaria Majórica*, Rua Senador Vergueiro 11/15, Flamengo, has good meat, reasonable prices and an interior done in gaúcho kitsch. It's open for lunch and dinner.

Café Lamas has been operating at Rua Marques de Abrantes 18-A in Flamengo, since 1874 and is one of Rio's most renowned eateries. It has a lively and loyal clientele and is open for lunch and dinner with a typical meaty menu and standard prices; try the grilled linguiça, or filet mignon.

In Botafogo, *Café Brasil*, Rua Capitão Salomão 35 is a Brazilian restaurant open from 11.30 am to 1 pm (2 pm on Fridays and Saturdays). Its speciality is *comida mineira* (food from Minas Gerais), eaten for lunch, not dinner.

Adega do Valentim is a highly recommended Portuguese restaurant at Rua da Passagem 176, open from noon till 2 am daily. The baked rabbit with spicy rice is excellent.

Leme (Map 4) *Máriu's* (☎ 542-2393), Avenida Atlântica 290, Leme, has an all-the-meat-you-can-eat deal for US$20. Many people think this is Rio's best *churrascaria*, so be prepared to wait during prime time as they get a big tourist crowd. It's open from 11.30 to 1.30 am.

Restaurante Shirley, Rua Gustavo Sampaio 610-A, has delicious seafood plates from US$12 to $30. Try the mussel vinaigrette appetiser or the octopus and squid in ink.

Copacabana (Map 4) Copacabana is a great place for the budget-conscious traveller to eat. There are botecos and small restaurants on almost every corner.

For cheap grilled chicken, there are lots of galetos in Copacabana. They include *O Crack dos Galetos*, Avenida Prado Junior 63, one block from the beach, and *Quick Galetos*, Rua Duvivier 284, near the Hotel Internacional Rio. *Lope's Confeiteria*, Avenida NS de Copacabana 1334, off Júlio de Castilhos, is an excellent lanchonete with big portions and little prices for typical Brazilian food.

Restaurante Lucas, Avenida Atlântica 3744, is across from Rua Sousa Lima and has reasonably priced German dishes starting at US$10.

Arataca, at Rua Domingues Ferreira 41, is one of several Arataca restaurants in Rio which feature the exotic cuisine of the Amazon. This place is actually a counter-lunch stand and deli, around the corner from one of their regular restaurants, and has the same food for half the price. In addition to regional dishes such as vatapá and pato (duck), they serve real guaraná juice (try it) and delicious sorbets made from Amazonas fruits.

Mab's, Avenida Atlântica (the Copacabana side of Princesa Isabel, across from Le Meridien, has excellent seafood soup in a crock, chock-full of piping hot creepy-crawlies for US$10.

Cervantes is Rio's best sandwich joint and is also a late-night hang-out for a strange and colourful crew. It's on the infamous Avenida Prado Junior, where everyone and everything goes at night. Meat sandwiches come with pineapple (US$5). The steaks and fries are excellent too.

Ipanema (Maps 4 & 5) Some good self-serve lunch places are the friendly *Arab*, Rua Gomes Carneiro 131-A and *Norte Grill*, Rua Visconde da Pirajá 112. Next door, the *Ming* Chinese restaurant also has cheap lunch specials.

If you want to eat a feijoada and it isn't Saturday, go to *Casa da Feijoada*, Rua Prudente de Morais 10-B, any day of the week. They also have delicious home-made sweets for dessert.

Yemanjá, Rua Visconde de Pirajá 128-A, offers good Bahian food at a reasonable price, something which is usually hard to find in Rio. The seafood moquecas are excellent and portions are large enough for two.

Barril, Avenida Vieira Souto 1800, at the beach, is open late into the night. This popular beach café is for people-meeting and watching. After a day at Ipanema beach, you can stroll over to the *Caffé Felice*, Rua Gomes Carneiro 30, for terrific ice cream or a healthy sandwich.

Chaika's, Rua Visconde de Pirajá 321, is open from 8 am to 2 pm. This is where the girl from Ipanema really eats. There's a stand-up fast-food bar, and a restaurant in the back with delicious hamburgers, the sweetest pastries and good cappuccinos (a rarity in Rio). Chaika's stays busy late into the night.

The open-air *Pier 510*, on the corner of Rua Garcia d'Avila and Rua Barão da Torre is a good place for an inexpensive meal. Try the seafood risotto for US$10. It feeds two easily.

Pulcinela, on the corner of Rua Farme de Amoedo and Rua Barã o de Torre is one of Rio's best Italian restaurants. Their couvert is outstanding – you may not want to eat anything else.

Bar Lagoa, Avenida Epitácio 1674, is Rio's oldest bar/restaurant. It doesn't open till 7.30 pm but stays open until 3 am. There's always a good crowd and you can just drink beer, or you can eat a full meal. The food is excellent, the menu typically Brazilian, and the atmosphere great.

Natural, Rua Barão da Torre 171, is a health-food restaurant which has an inexpensive self-serve lunch and dinners.

Le Bon Jus, on the corner of Teixeira de Meio and Visconde de Pirajá, is a good juice and sandwich bar, as is *Limo's*, one block west on the corner of Farme de Amoedo and Visconde de Pirajá. Readers recommend the 'heavenly' sucos.

Garota de Ipanema, Rua Vinícius de Morais 49, has lively open-air dining. There are always a few foreigners checking out the place Tom Jobim and Vinícius de Moraes wrote *The Girl from Ipanema*. A recent Brazilian Playboy survey rated their chopp as the best in Rio – a bold claim indeed, but who could resist a sample after a rap like that? Their petiscos are delicious – try their famous kibes.

Leblon (Map 5) *Sabor Saúde*, Avenida Ataulfo de Paiva 630, is Rio's best health-food emporium and is open daily from 8.30 am to 10.30 pm. They have two natural-food restaurants: downstairs has good meals for US$6 while upstairs is more expensive. There's also a small grocery shop and take-away-food counter.

Celeiro, Rua Dias Ferreira 199, has a fantastic (but expensive) salad bar. It's open from 11.30 am to 5 pm every day except Sunday. Don't let the silly name put you off *Restaurante Bozó*, Rua Dias Ferreira 50 –

the staff are very serious about their food. Try the scrumptious and filling medallions of filet mignon wrapped in bacon and smothered in pepper sauce.

Gávea (Map 5) *Guimas*, José Roberto Macedo Soares 5, is one of our favourite restaurants. It's not cheap, but the prices (US$20 to $30 per person) are fair for the outstanding cuisine you're served.

Guimas offers what many restaurants in Rio lack – creative cooking. Try the pernil de carneiro (lamb with onions) or the Oriental shrimp curry and a Rio salad. The small, but comfortable open-air restaurant opens at 8 pm and gets very crowded later in the evening. If you order one of their boa lembrança specials, you'll receive an attractive ceramic plate.

Parque Nacional da Tijuca (Map 1) *Os Esquilos* is a beautiful colonial restaurant in Alto da Boa Vista. It has a typical Brazilian menu which isn't expensive. It is open Tuesday to Sunday from noon to 7 pm.

Other Areas *Tia Palmira* serves traditional Brazilian food in a great outdoor setting and can be very crowded at weekend lunch times. It's at Caminho do Souza 18, Barra de Guaratiba, and is open from 11 am to 5 pm (closed Mondays).

Lokau is a seafood restaurant in a lovely location overlooking a lagoon. It's at Avenida Sernambetiba 13500, Barra da Tijuca, and is open from noon to 1 am (from noon to 8 pm on Sundays). It can be crowded on weekends.

Cândidos, Rua Barros de Alarcão 352, Pedra de Guaratiba, is a traditional seafood place adored by Cariocas. Try a seafood moqueca. It's open from noon to 9 pm (from noon to 11 pm Saturdays).

Fine Dining Rio is loaded with fancy restaurants which are not all that expensive for the visitor. Here's a list of some of the best:

French

Club Gourmet, Rua General Polidoro 186, Botafogo (☎ 295-3494; Map 3)

Claude Troisgras, Rua Custódio Serrão 62, Jardim Botanico (☎ 537-8582; Map 5)

Traiteurs de France, Avenida NS de Copacabana 386, Copacabana (☎ 548-6440; Map 4)

Italian

Quadrifoglio, Rua JJ Seabra 19, Jardim Botânico (☎ 294-1433)

Osteria Dell'Angolo, Rua Paul Redfern 40, Ipanema (☎ 259-3148)

Japanese

Zen, Praia de Botafogo 228, Botafogo (☎ 533-5060; Map 3)

Polish

A Polonesa, Rua Hilário de Gouveia 116, Copacabana (☎ 547-7378)

Portuguese

Antiquarius, Rua Aristides Espinola 19, Leblon (☎ 294-1049; Map 5)

Swiss

Casa da Suiça, Rua Cândido Mendes 157, Glória (☎ 252-5182; Map 2)

Entertainment

Any night of the week is a good one for going out and joining Cariocas at what they love: singing or dancing. Cariocas love to go out late in the evening, and we haven't met a gringo yet who's complained about Rio's nightlife.

To find out what's going on, pick up the *Jornal do Brasil* at any newsstand and turn to the entertainment section. On Fridays the publication includes an entertainment magazine called *Programa* which lists the week's events. *O Globo* also includes its *Rio Show* magazine on Fridays. For even more listings, check the *Veja Rio* lift-out in the weekly *Veja* magazine. The entertainment sections are easy to figure out, even if you don't speak Portuguese.

Nightlife varies widely by the neighbourhood. Leblon and Ipanema have upmarket, trendy clubs with excellent jazz. Botafogo is the heart of gay Rio. Cinelândia and Lapa in the centre have a lot of samba and pagode. Copacabana is a mixed bag, with some good local hang-outs but also a strong tourist influence with a lot of sex for sale.

Cinemas Most movies in the cinemas are screened in their original language with Portuguese subtitles; consequently there are plenty of films in English. Brazil gets most of the hits from the USA, and also many European films.

For a complete listing of cinemas and current films, look in the daily newspapers. If the titles are written in Portuguese, the English translation is usually underneath. Entry to movies is around US$5.

Discos There are many discos with bright lights and loud music in the big city, but the hip venues change regularly – check out a copy of *Programa*. Many of the discos have stiff dress codes and admission charges, designed in part to deter the many prostitutes who come to meet tourists.

The current favourites are: *Cabaré Kalesa*, Rua Sacadura Cabral 11, (Map 2) at Praça Mauá in the Centro; *Totem*, Rua Almirante Alexandrino 1991, Santa Teresa; *Fundição Progresso*, Rua dos Arcos, (Map 2) in Lapa, and *Hipodromo Up*, Praça Santos Dumont, (Map 5) Gávea. There are many, many more.

Help deserves a special mention here. It calls itself the biggest disco in Latin America and no one seems to doubt it. At Avenida Atlântica 3432 in Copacabana, it's full of 'professional' ladies, and lots of drunken gringos seem to get robbed just outside. That doesn't mean you shouldn't go there – it's definitely an interesting place – but keep the above-mentioned warning in mind.

Theatre There are many fine Brazilian actors and playwrights, but there's not much point going to the theatre if you don't understand Portuguese. If you fancy a look anyway, there's a full listing available in the entertainment sections of the newspapers mentioned in the introduction to this chapter.

Big Shows Rio plays host every week to a different set of national and international stars, as well as holding large rock and jazz festivals each year. There's no central booking system, so tickets need to be purchased from the box office at the venue. Use the concierge at your hotel to get hold of tickets. It's much easier.

The Metropolitan (☎ 283-3773), in Via Parque Shopping in Barra da Tijuca, opened in 1994 and is now the major venue for top international and Brazilian acts, as well as opera, ballet, Broadway musicals and Carnaval balls. For visitors staying in the zona sul, this is a disadvantage for all but the well-heeled, because a taxi from, say, Le Meridien to the Metropolitan and back costs around US$40.

Other more accessible venues include *Canecão* (☎ 295-3044), which still gets the big stars of music, both national and international. It's right next to the giant Rio Sul shopping mall at the entrance to the Copacabana tunnel.

Maracanã (☎ 264-9962) is the venue for the biggest shows in Rio. Frank Sinatra, Sting, Madonna, Paul McCartney and the Rolling Stones have all performed here.

Asa Branca (☎ 224-2342), Avenida Mem de Sá, has samba and pagode shows that aren't staged especially for tourists.

Gay Venues Rio is the gay capital of Latin America, and during Carnaval, thousands fly in from all over the world. Favourite bars in Botafogo include *Bastilha*, Rua das Palmeiras 66; *Dr Smith*, Rua da Passagem 169 and *Tamino*, Rua Arnaldo Quintela 26. In Copacabana try *The Ball*, Rua Raul Pompéia 94. For the latest info on happening places, call Ganesh (☎ 350-5520).

Samba If you want to see and hear samba, you can go to one of the big tourist productions, head to one of the samba school rehearsals, or go to one of the escolas de samba.

The big tourist shows are corny, glitzy, lavish, Vegas-style performances, with plenty of beautiful, topless mulatas who make samba look easy. The most popular is *Plataforma* (☎ 274-4022), Rua Adalberto Ferreira 32 in Leblon. Shows start around 10 pm.

Samba Schools In the samba schools, things start to heat up in October. That's when, after intense lobbying, they finally choose the samba do enredo that their members will defend with blood, sweat and beer in the

Sambódromo. Rehearsals are generally open to the public for watching and joining in the samba. Entry costs only a few dollars, and you can really make a night of it. Check with Riotur or the newspaper for schedules and locations. In order of distance away from the zona sul, the major school are:

São Clemente
  Rua Assunção 63, Botafogo
Estácio de Sá
  Rua Miguel de Frias 35, Cidade Nova (☎ 293-8994)
Salgueiro
  Rua Silva Teles, Andaraí (a popular one to visit because it's not in a favela and relatively close to the Zona Sul)
Unidos de Vila Isabel
  Boulevard 28 de Setembro 355, Vila Isabel
Unidos da Tijuca
  Avenida Francisco Bicalho 47, Centro (☎ 291-2122)
Mangueira
  Rua Visconde de Niterói 1072, Mangueira (☎ 234-4129)
Imperatriz Leopoldinense
  Rua Professor Lacê 235, Ramos (☎ 270-8037)
Império Serrano
  Avenida Ministro Edgard Romero 114, Madureira (☎ 450-1285)
Portela
  Rua Clara Nunes 81, Oswaldo Cruz (☎ 390-0471)
Beija Flor
  Rua Praçinha Wallace Paes Leme 1025, Nilópolis (☎ 293-9294)
Mocidade Independente de Padre Miguel
  Rua Coronel Tamarindo 38, Padre Miguel (☎ 332-5823)

Samba Clubs *Cordão Bola Preta* (☎ 240-8049) is a big dance house with different types of popular music played each night. It has *serestas*, *roda de samba* and *pagode*. The club is right in the centre, on the 3rd floor of Avenida 13 de Maio. The highly recommended *Casa da Mãe Joana* (☎ 580-5613), Rua Sá Cristovão 73, in Sá Cristovão gets packed out on a Friday night. It's probably a good idea to go in a taxi to both these places. When you leave, wait at the entrance for a taxi to pass – don't start wandering around the streets looking for one.

Forró Forró is the popular dance of Brazil's Northeast and there are plenty of Northeasterners in Rio going out dancing every weekend. The accordion-laced forró is easier on foreign ears than most of the current samba. The dancing is a blast and the orchestras really cook. The dance halls are called *gafieiras*, and the two most famous ones are both in Centro: *Estudantina* (☎ 232-1149), on the 1st floor of Praça Tiradentes 79, and *Elite* (☎ 232-3217), on the 1st floor of Rua Frei Caneca 4. They are open Thursday, Friday and Saturday nights until about 4 am. The cover charge is US$5. If you don't fancy going into the city, *Carinhoso* (☎ 287-3579) at Rua Viscondé de Pirajá 22 in Ipanema is the zona sul alternative, but it's pretty tame in comparison.

Jazz In September or October every year, Rio hosts the Free Jazz Festival, which brings together some of the top international jazz greats and their skilful Brazilian counterparts. Big names to attend in the past include George Benson, Ray Charles, Dizzy Gillespie, Stephane Grapelli, Etta James and the Count Basie Orchestra, to name but a few.

At any other time in Rio, fans can hit one of the many jazz venues in the zona sul. The music ranges from hot jazz to the cool bossa nova sounds of popular Brazilian music. *Jazzmania* (☎ 522-2447), Avenida Rainha Elizabete 769, Copacabana, is Rio's most serious jazz venue. It has more international stars than any other club, but also the best of Brazilian jazz. The club is expensive with entry at around US$20 cover on weekends and a little less on weekdays. The music starts about 11 pm and goes late.

Other important venues include *Mistura Fina* (☎ 537-2844), Avenida Borges de Medeiros 3207 in Lagoa and *Vinícius* (☎ 287-1497), Rua Vinícius de Moraes 39. There are plenty of other places to hear jazz and bossa nova. Check the listings in the newspapers mentioned in the introduction to this section.

Bars A great way to meet Cariocas is to check out one of the popular zona sul *baixos*. Baixos are small concentrations of bars and cafés. Hanging around baxio-style means having a chopp at an outdoor table while standing in the street, and just looking and chatting. Cariocas aren't known for their formality and are quite happy to converse with friendly strangers.

Bar Brasil (Map 2) in Lapa is an old bohemian hang-out and is always lively. Some Cariocas who live in the zona sul only come into the centre to go to Bar Brasil. Lapa, along Avenida Mem de Sá, is generally an interesting area to explore at night.

In Copacabana, the beachfront bars are a good place to have a couple of chopps in the early evening, but as the night wears on things get a little seedier, and it might be time to move on. The *Sindicato do Chopp* has two branches in Copacabana (Avenida Atlântica and Rua Santa Clara 18; Map 4). They're popular with locals and get pretty noisy.

In Ipanema, Sindicato do Chopp and *Bar Bofetada* (Map 4), next to each other on Rua Farme de Amoedo, are both always packed with locals, who spill onto the street until the wee hours. There's also a cluster of restaurants and bars on the corner of Rua Prudente de Morais and Rua Paul Redfern.

In Leblon, the *Academia da Cachaça*, Rua Conde de Bernadotte 26 (Map 5), is a popular spot for a few drinks. Their range of cachaça is impressive – some of the good stuff is even smooth!

A real hot spot in the zona sul is Praça Santos Dumont in Gávea. There are lots of bars and people hanging around in the streets drinking and looking at everyone else.

The *Zeppelin Bar*, behind the Sheraton Hotel on Avenida Niemeyer (Map 5), is a quaint bar/restaurant overlooking the ocean. It's medium priced, with great live folk and pop music from Thursday to Sunday night. A very relaxed atmosphere.

Bar Lagoa (already mentioned in Places to Eat) is our favourite bar and a great late-night hang out where the Carioca crowd is loud (Map 4).

Getting a taxi late at night in Lapa or Cinelândia isn't a problem; there is also limited bus service all night long. You can catch buses to the zona sul along the Praça Mahatma Gandhi on Avenida Luis de Vasconcelos.

Gambling Casinos in Brazil were closed in 1946 after a presidential decree outlawed gambling. That hasn't stopped Cariocas, who love to have a flutter on their favourite numbers in the illegal *jogo do bicho*, the thriving numbers game that's been around for more than a century. If you've ever wondered what all those guys with note pads and little tables are doing sitting around all over Rio, now you know. Legal gambling takes the form of lotteries, *raspadinhas* (scratch 'n' win tickets) and betting on sporting events such as football and horse racing. Lately, other types of gambling have also been tolerated – notably, bingo. It may be a sign that in the not-too-distant future casinos will make a comeback.

Anyone who thinks bingo is only played by little old ladies in church halls will get a surprise in Rio. The large, luxurious bingo houses are just like casinos, except the only thing that gets played is bingo! And there's no Brazilian equivalent of bingo chatter of the 'two fat ladies 88' variety either. This is serious gambling and the games are quite quick. Playing bingo is fashionable among Cariocas but we can't seriously advise anyone going to Rio to try it. What would you tell your friends back home? If you do get curious, the two most popular bingo palaces are *Bingo Arpoador*, Rua Francisco Otaviano 35 in Copacabana, and *Scala Bingo*, Avenida Afrânio de Mello Franco 292 in Leblon.

Motels Motels are a unique cultural experience and can be a lot of fun – see the Facts for the Visitor chapter for a basic description of what you can expect. The quality of Rio motels varies, reflecting their popularity with all social classes. Most are out on the approach roads to the city, like Avenida Brasil in the zona norte and Avenida Niemeyer between Leblon and São Conrado.

In Rio, a three-storey suite usually has all the usual motel amenities plus a hot tub on the top floor with skylights that open, and a sauna and bathroom on the 2nd floor. The more expensive ones have touches like Roman fountains gushing away. For the best suites, expect to pay around US$100 for 12 hours – more on weekends. Standard rooms cost quite a bit less, and are a lot of fun too.

Some of the more popular motels are *Sinless* (☎ 322-3944), Avenida Niemeyer 214, and *Shalimar* (☎ 322-3392), next door. *Holiday* (☎ 494-2650) is at Estrada de Furnas 3700 in Barra da Tijuca.

Red-Light The two main red-light areas in Rio are in Lapa, along Rua Mem de Sá, and in Copacabana. Lapa is much seedier than Copacabana, although you need to be wary in both. In Copacabana, Praça do Lido is the centre of the red-light area. There are lots of erotic shows/strip joints on Rua Duvivier *(New Munich* and *Don Juan)*, Rua Belfort Roxo *(Pussy Cat Bar)*, Rua Ronaldo de Carvalho *(Lido* and *Golden Club)* and Avenida Princesa Isabel *Barbarela Boite, New Scotch Boite* and *La Cicciolina)*. The erotic shows often include live sex acts. Cover charge is between US$20 and whatever they think they can squeeze out of you. It usually includes a two-drink minimum.

Spectator Sport

Football Maracanã (Map 1) is Brazil's temple of soccer and a veritable colossus among coliseums. It easily accommodates over 100,000 people and, on occasions – the World Cup Game of 1950 or Pelé's last game – has squeezed in close to 200,000 crazed fans (it's seating has now been reduced). If you like sports, if you want to understand Brazil, or if you just want an intense, quasi-psychedelic experience, then by all means go see a game of *futebol*, preferably a championship game or one between rivals Flamengo (Fla) and Fluminense (Flu).

Brazilian soccer is perhaps the most imaginative and exciting style in the world. Complementing the action on the field is the action in the stands,which are filled with totally fanatical fans who cheer their team on in all sorts of ways: chanting, singing and shouting; waving banners and streamers in team colours; pounding huge samba drums; exploding firecrackers, Roman candles and smoke bombs (in team colours); launching incendiary balloons; throwing toilet paper, beer and even dead chickens – possibly Macumba inspired. The scene, in short, is sheer lunacy.

Obviously, you have to be very careful if you go to Maracanã. Don't wear a watch or jewellery. Don't bring more money than you need for tickets, transport and refreshments. The big question is how to get to and from the game safely.

The big games are held on Sunday at 5 pm year-round. Tourist buses leave from major hotels at 2.30 pm (but they often run a bit late) for 5 pm Sunday games. They cost about US$40, which is an absolute rip-off, but this is a safe and easy way to get to the game. They drop you off and pick you up right in front of the gate and escort you to lower-level seats. Unfortunately, this is not the best perspective for watching the game, but it is the safest because of the overhead covering which protects you from descending objects (like cups full of bodily fluids).

However, you get to the stadium, it's a good idea to buy these lower-level seats, called *cadeira*, instead of the upper-level bleachers, called *arquibancada*. The price is US$8, unless it's a championship game, when it's more.

The metrô is closed on Sunday, and taking a bus or cab can be a hassle. Getting to the stadium isn't too difficult, though: catch a Maracanã bus (from the zona sul, No 434, 464 or 455; from Centro (Praça 15), No 238 or 239) a couple of hours before the game. Returning to your hotel by bus is often a drag – they are very crowded. Taking a cab is a possible alternative, but they can be hard to flag down; the best strategy is to walk a short distance away from the stadium.

Horse Racing There's lots to see at the racetrack (Map 5). The *Jóquei Clube*, which seats 35,000, is on the Gávea side of the Lagoa Rodrigo de Freitas at Praça Santos Dumont 31 (take any of the buses that go to Jardim Botânico). It's a beautiful track, with a great view of the mountains and Corcovado. It's rarely crowded and the fans are great to watch – it's a different slice of Rio life. Racing takes place every Saturday and Sunday afternoon, and Monday and Friday nights.

Beach Sports Surprisingly, volleyball is Brazil's second most popular sport. A natural activity for the beach, it's also a popular spectator sport on TV. A local variation you'll see on Rio's beaches is volleyball played without the hands *(footvolei)*. It's fun to watch but bloody hard to play.

Peteca is a cross between volleyball and badminton, and is played with a peteca, similar to, but a little larger than, a shuttlecock. You'll see them being hawked on the beach. Peteca is a particular favourite with older Cariocas who are getting a bit slow for volleyball.

Usually played on the firm sand at the shoreline, *frescobal* involves two players, each with a wooden racquet, hitting a small rubber ball back and forth as hard as possible. Cariocas make it look easy.

Things to Buy

Most shops are open Monday to Friday from 9 am to 7 pm (some stay open even later). Saturday has half-day shopping, from 9 am to 1 pm. The malls usually open from 10 am to 10 pm, Monday to Friday, and 10 am to 8 pm on weekends.

Pé de Boi This shop sells the traditional artisan handicrafts of Brazil's Northeast and Minas Gerais. There's lots of wood, lace, pottery and prints, and it's not inexpensive. You have to buy closer to the source to get a better price, but if you have some extra dollars – US$10 to $20 at a minimum – these pieces are the best gifts to bring home from Brazil: imaginative and very Brazilian.

Otherwise it's worth a visit just to look around. Ana Maria Chindler, the owner, knows her stuff and is happy to tell you about it. Pé de Boi (☎ 285-4395), Rua Ipiranga 53, Laranjeiras, is open Monday to Friday until 7 pm and on Saturday from 10 am to 1 pm.

Artíndia Inside the Museu do Índio in Botafogo is a tiny craft shop with masks, toys, pots, baskets, musical instruments and weapons for sale at reasonable prices. The museum (☎ 286 2097) is at Rua das Palmeiras 55, Botafogo.

Art Supplies Casa Matos is the big chain. There's a shop in Copacabana at Avenida NS de Copacabana 690. They also have a branch at Largo do Machado. In the centre you could try Papelaria União, Rua do Ouvidor 58, or the Instituto do Patrimônio Histórico e Artístico Nacional (IPHAN) at Avenida Rio Branco 46. They also sell prints of famous Brazilian paintings and poster tubes to carry home some of Rio's best gifts – art prints, giant photos and posters.

Music Casa Oliveira is a beautiful music shop at Rua da Carioca 70 in Centro – Rio's oldest street. It sells a wide variety of instruments, including all the noise makers that fuel the Carnaval *baterias* (rhythm sections), a variety of small mandolin-like string instruments, accordions and electric guitars. These make great presents and it's a fun place to play even if you don't buy.

Shopping Malls Brazilians, like Americans, seem to measure progress by shopping malls. They love to shop at these monsters. Rio Sul was the first mall to maul Rio. There are all kinds of shops. The C&A department store has a good range of clothes and is inexpensive. Rio Sul is right before you enter the Copacabana tunnel in Botafogo. There are free buses from Copacabana. Barra da Tijuca must be the mall capital of Brazil. Barra Shopping, Avenida das Américas, is the big one, on the right as you drive south into Barra and more are under construction. They're hard to miss!

Bathing Suits Since your bathing suit has too much fabric attached to the seams, resign yourself to buying a new one. Bum Bum is the trendsetter of the bikini world, and it knows it. It's not cheap, but you're paying for style not fabric. It's in Ipanema on Rua Visconde de Pirajá in the Forum shopping centre opposite Praça NS da Paz. If you're on a budget, there are plenty of other boutiques that sell bikinis for less money but with just as little fabric.

Hippie Fair This is an arts and crafts fair, with many booths selling jewellery, leather goods, paintings, samba instruments and clothes. There is some awful stuff here and some that's OK. Prices shoot way up during the peak tourist season and the air rings with the sounds of New Yorkers hunting down good buys.

The fair takes place every Sunday at the Praça General Osório in Ipanema. You can find the same items at Praça 15 de Novembro in Centro or at the northern end of Copacabana beach. If you're just beginning to travel in Brazil, skip it.

Nordeste or São Cristóvão Fair The Nordeste Fair is held at the Pavilhão de São Cristóvão on the north side of town every Sunday, starting early and going until about 3 pm. The fair is very Northeastern in character. There are lots of barracas selling meat, beer and cachaça; bands of accordions, guitars and tambourines playing the forró; comedy, capoeira battles and people selling magic potions. It's a great scene.

Of course there's plenty to buy. Apart from food, they have lots of cheap clothes, some good deals on hammocks and a few good nordeste gifts like leather *vaqueiro* (cowboy) hats.

If you're ready for adventure come along the night before the market. This is set-up time and party time. At about 9 or 10 pm the barracas open for dinner and beer. Some vendors are busy setting up, others are already finished. Music and dance starts, and doesn't stop until sunrise. It's great fun so long as you're careful.

Getting There & Away

Air From Rio flights go to all of Brazil and Latin America. Shuttle flights to São Paulo leave from the conveniently located Aeroporto Santos Dumont in the city centre along the bay. Almost all other flights – domestic and national – leave from Aeroporto Galeão.

All three major Brazilian airlines have their main offices in the centre (metrô stop Cinelândia).

You can also walk over to Aeroporto Santos Dumont where they have ticket counters and make reservations from there.

Varig/Cruzeiro (☎ 292-6600 for reservations or ☎ 282-1319 for information) has its main office in Centro at Avenida Rio Branco 277 (☎ 220-3821). There are also offices at Rua Rodolfo Dantas 16 in Copacabana (☎ 541-6343), and Rua Visconde de Pirajá 351, Ipanema (☎ 287-9040). The city office is much more reliable and knowledgeable than the other Varig offices.

VASP (☎ toll free 0800-998277, 24 hours) has a city office at Rua Santa Luzia 735. They also have offices at Aeroporto Santos Dumont (☎ 292-2112), and at Rua Visconde de Pirajá 444 (☎ 292-2112) in Ipanema.

Transbrasil (☎ 297-4422) is in the centre at Rua Santa Luzia 651. The other offices are at Avenida Atlântica 1998 (☎ 236-7475), Copacabana and Aeroporto Santos Dumont (☎ 262-6061).

Nordeste Linhas Aéreas (☎ 220-4366) is at Aeroporto Santos Dumont. It goes to Porto Seguro, Ilhéus and other smaller cities in the Northeast. Rio Sul (☎ 262-6911) does the same for the south and is also at Aeroporto Santos Dumont.

International airlines with offices in Rio include:

Aeroflot
  Avenida NS de Copacabana 249, Copacabana (☎ 275-0440; fax 541-9542)

Aerolineas Argentinas
  Rua da Assembléia 100, 29th floor, Centro (☎ 292-4131; fax 224-4931)

Aero Peru Avenida Nilo Peçanha 505, Centro (☎ 210-3124; fax 262-5065)

Air France
  Avenida Presidente Antônio Carlos 58, 9th floor, Centro (☎ 220-8661; fax 532-1284)

Alitalia
  Avenida Presidente Wilson 231, 21st floor, Centro (☎ 240-7822; fax 240-7493)
Avianca
  Avenida Presidente Wilson 165, No 801 (☎ 220-7697; fax 220-9848)
American Airlines
  Avenida Presidente Wilson 165, 5th floor, Centro (☎ 210-3126; fax 220-1022)
British Airways
  Avenida Rio Branco 108, 21st floor, Centro (☎ 221-0922; fax 242-2889)
Canadian Airlines International
  Rua da Ajuda 35, 29th floor, Centro (☎ 220-5343; fax 220-0855)
Iberia
  Avenida Presidente Antônio Carlos 51, 8th floor, Centro (☎ 282-1336; fax 240-9842)
Japan Air Lines
  Avenida Rio Branco 156, No 2014, Centro (☎ 220-6414; fax 220-6091)
KLM
  Avenida Rio Branco 311A, Centro (☎ 292-7747; fax 240-1595)
Lan Chile
  Rua 7 de Setembro 111, Centro (☎ 220-9722; fax 532-1420)
Lloyd Aero Boliviano
  Avenida Calógeras 30, Centro (☎ 220-9548; fax 533-2835)
Lufthansa
  Avenida Rio Branco 156 D, Centro (☎ 217-6111; fax 262 -1458)
South African
  Avenida Rio Branco 245, 4th floor, Centro (☎ 262-6252; fax 262-6120)
Swissair
  Avenida Rio Branco 108, 10th floor, Centro (☎ 297-5177; fax 224-9205)
United Airlines
  Avenida Presidente Antônio Carlos 51, Centro (☎ 532-1212; fax 262-7786)

Bus From Rio there are buses to everywhere. They all leave from the loud Novo Rio Rodoviária (☎ 291-5151 for information – only Portuguese spoken), Avenida Francisco Bicalho in São Cristóvão, about 20 minutes north of the centre. At the rodoviária you can get information on transport and lodging at the Riotur desk on the ground floor.

Excellent buses leave every 15 minutes or so for São Paulo (six hours). Most major destinations have leito (executive) buses which leave late at night. These are very comfortable. Many travel agents in the city sell bus tickets. It's a good idea to buy a ticket a couple days in advance if you can.

National Bus Destinations & Times

Angra dos Reis	US$11	2¾ hours
Belém	US$146	52 hours
Belo Horizonte	US$22	7 hours
Brasília	US$67	17 hours
Cabo Frio	US$11	3 hours
Curitiba	US$39	12 hours
Florianópolis	US$52	18 hours
Foz do Iguaçu	US$54	21 hours
Goiânia	US$52	18 hours
Ouro Prêto	US$14	7 hours
Parati	US$15	4 hours
Petrópolis	US$5	1½ hours
Porto Alegre	US$68	26 hours
Recife	US$108	38 hours
Salvador	US$75	28 hours
São João del Rei	US$18	5½ hours
Vitória	US$22	8 hours

International Bus Destinations & Times

Asunción	US$60	25 hours
Buenos Aires	US$120	46 hours
Montevideo	US$110	39 hours
Santiago	US$210	74 hours

Getting Around

To/From the Airport All international and nearly all domestic flights use Galeão international airport (GIG), 15km north of the city centre on Ilha do Governador.

Aeroporto Santos Dumont is in the heart of the city on the bay. It's used for the São Paulo shuttle and some flights to a variety of other destinations like Porto Seguro or Belo Horizonte. You can take the same bus as for Galeão airport or get to the city and take a taxi, or simply walk to the airport from Centro.

Bus & Metrô There are two air-conditioned airport bus routes operating from 5.20 to 12.10 am, every 40 minutes to one hour. One route goes to the centre and to Aeroporto Santos Dumont (US$2.50) the other route goes to the city centre and along the beaches of Copacabana, Ipanema, Leblon, Vidigal, São Conrado and Barra (US$5). The driver will stop wherever you ask along the route. On both routes, you can stop at the rodoviária if you want to catch a bus out of

Rio immediately. If you want to catch the metrô, ask the driver to let you off right outside the entrance to Carioca metrô station

You can catch the bus on the first floor (arrivals) of the main terminal, where the bus company – Empresa Real – has an office and waiting room. If you're heading to the airport you can get the bus in front of the major hotels along the beach, but you have to look lively and flag them down. Aeroporto Internacional should be written on the direction sign.

Taxi Taxis from the airport may try to rip you off. The safe course is to take a radio-taxi, for which you pay a set fare at the airport. This is also the most expensive way to go. A yellow-and-blue *comum* (common) taxi is about 20% cheaper if the meter is working and if you pay what is on the fare schedule. A sample fare from the airport to Copacabana is US$20 in a yellow-and-blue taxi versus US$30 in a radio-taxi. If you're entering Brazil for the first time, on a budget, a good compromise is to take a bus to somewhere near your destination and then take a short taxi ride to your hotel.

Sharing a taxi from the airport is a good idea. Taxis will take up to four people. If you're headed to Leblon or Ipanema, the Tunnel Reboucas is more direct than the beach route.

If you want to take a taxi from the rodoviária, there's a booth selling pre-paid tickets next to the Riotur information desk. It's no more expensive than walking out and taking a cab off the rank, in fact, it ensure the drivers don't try to rip you off.

To/From the Rodoviária Local buses leave from the stops outside the rodoviária. Don't try walking into town from there – it's a seedy area.

For Copacabana, the best are bus Nos 127, 128 or 136. The best buses to Ipanema and Leblon are Nos 128, 172 or 173.

For the budget hotels in Catete and Glória, take bus Nos 136 or 172. These run along Praia do Flamengo and Praia do Botafogo. If you want the budget hotel district in Catete, keep an eye out on the right-hand side for the baroque Igreja da Glória, perched up on a hill. Get out and walk over to Rua Catete.

An alternative is to take any bus that goes to the centre on Avenida Rio Branco. Get off near the end of Avenida Rio Branco and hop on the metrô. Get off the metrô at Catete station, which is in the heart of the budget hotel area.

Bus The buses are a real mixture of the good, the bad and the ugly. The good: Rio's buses are fast, frequent, cheap and, because Rio is long and narrow, it's easy to track down the right bus and usually no big deal if you've hopped on the wrong one. The bad: Rio's buses are often crowded, slowed down by traffic and driven by raving maniacs as if they are motorbikes. The ugly: Rio's buses are the scene of many of the city's robberies.

Don't carry any valuables on the buses. Don't advertise being a foreigner, and do have your money ready when you enter the bus. Be particularly cautious if you're boarding a bus in a tourist area. If you feel paranoid about something on the bus, get off and catch another.

In addition to their number, buses have their destinations, including the areas they go through, written on the side. Nine out of 10 buses going south from the centre will go to Copacabana and vice versa. All buses have the price displayed above the head of the money collector. The buses you need to catch for specific destinations are listed under individual sights.

If you're staying in the Catete/Flamengo area and want to get to the beaches by bus, you can either walk to the main roadway along Parque do Flamengo and take any Copacabana bus or you can walk to Largo do Machado and take bus No 570.

Train The train station, Estação Dom Pedro II, is at Praça Cristiano Ottoni on Avenida Presidente Vargas. To get there take the metrô to Central station.

Metrô Rio's excellent subway system is limited to points north of Botafogo and is open from 5 am to 11 pm daily, except Sunday. The two air-conditioned lines are cleaner, faster and cheaper than buses (discounts are offered with multiple tickets).

The main line from Botafogo to Saens Pena has 15 stops, of which the first twelve are: Botafogo, Flamengo, Largo do Machado, Catete, Glória, Cinelândia, Carioca, Uruguiana, Presidente Vargas, Central, Cidade Nova and Estácio, which is common to both lines. At Estácio the lines split: the main line continues west towards the neighbourhood of Andarai, making stops at Afonso Pena, Engenho Velho and Tijuca, and the secondary line goes north towards Maracanã stadium and beyond. The main stops for Centro are Cinelândia and Carioca.

Taxi Rio's taxis are quite reasonably priced, if you're dividing the fare with a friend or two. Taxis are particularly useful late at night and when carrying valuables, but they are not a completely safe and hassle-free ride. First, there have been a few rare cases of people being assaulted and robbed by taxi drivers. Second, and much more common, the drivers have a tendency to exaggerate fares.

Now, what to watch out for: most important, make sure the meter works. If it doesn't, ask to be let out of the cab. The meters have a flag that switches the meter rate; Tariff 1 is from 6 am to 9 pm and Tariff 2 is 9 pm to 6 am. In December, all taxis stay on Tariff 2 (legally – this gives the drivers their Christmas bonus). Make sure meters are cleared before you start (find out the current starting number).

The taxi drivers that hang out near the hotels are sharks. It's worth walking a block to avoid them. Most people don't tip taxi drivers, although it's common to round off the fare to the next *real*.

The meters are weighted towards distance not time. This gives the drivers an incentive to drive quickly (for a head rush tell your driver that you are in a bit of a hurry) and travel by roundabout routes. It's illegal for cabs to take more than four passengers.

The radio-taxis (☎ 260-2022) are 30% more expensive than the ordinary ones, but they will come to you and they are safer.

Car Car rental agencies are at the airport and clustered together on Avenida Princesa Isabel in Copacabana. There doesn't seem to be much price competition between the companies. Prices are not cheap, at about US$70 a day, but they go down a bit in the off season. When they give prices on the phone the agencies usually leave out the cost of insurance, which is mandatory. Most agencies will let you drop off their cars in another city without an extra charge.

Walking For God's sake be careful! Drivers run red lights, run up on footpaths and stop for no one and nothing.

Carnaval

Carnaval, like Mardi Gras, is a holiday which orginated from various pagan spring festivals. These tended to be wild parties during the Middle Ages until tamed in Europe by both the Reformation and the Counter-Reformation versions of Christianity. But not even the heavy hand of the Inquisition could not squelch Carnaval in the Portuguese colony, where it came to acquire Indian costumes and African rhythms.

People speculate that the word carnaval derives from the Latin *carne vale*, 'goodbye meat'. The reasoning goes something like this: for the 40 days of Lent, the nominally Catholic Brazilians give up liver and fillet steaks, not to mention luxuries such as alcohol and pastries. To compensate for the deprivation ahead, they rack up sins in advance in a deliriously carnal blow-out in honour of King Momo, the king of Carnaval.

Every year, wealthy and spaced-out foreigners descend on Rio en masse to get drunk, get high, bag some sun, and exchange exotic diseases. Everyone becomes a little bit unglued at this time of year and there are more car accidents and murders than usual. Some of the leaner and meaner Cariocas can get a little ugly with all the sex, booze and flash of money. Apartment rates and taxi fares triple and quadruple, and some thieves keep in the spirit of the season by robbing in costume.

The excitement of Carnaval builds all year and the pre-Lenten revelry begins well before the official start. A month before Carnaval starts, rehearsals at the *escolas de samba* (samba clubs) are open to visitors on Saturday. The rehearsals are usually in the favelas. They're fun to watch, but go with a Carioca for safety. Corny tourist Carnaval shows are held all year round at Plataforma in Leblon.

The escolas de samba are actually predated by *bandas* (marching bands, amateur equivalents of the escolas de samba), which are now returning to the Carnaval scene as part of the movement to return Carnaval to the streets of Rio. Riotur has all the information in a special Carnaval guide.

Carnaval Balls

Carnaval balls are surreal and erotic events. Breasts were painted, stickered with tattoos, covered with fish-net brassieres, or just left bare. Bottoms were spandexed, G-stringed or mini-skirted.

In one ball at Scala we saw a woman (transsexual?) bare her breasts and offer passers-by a suck, while rickety old ladies were bopping away in skimpy lingerie. A young and geeky rich guy was dancing on tables with whores past their prime, young models and lithe young nymphets, all in various stages of undress.

More action took place on the stages. One stage had a samba band, the other was crushed with young women. They didn't so much dance, as ground their hips and licked their lips to the incessant, hypnotic music and the epileptic flashing of the floor lights. Throngs of sweaty photographers and video crews mashed up to the stage. Everyone played up for the camera, all vying for space and the attention of the photographers. The Vegas-style head-dresses, the pasty-faced bouncers and the rich men in private boxes overlooking the dance floor lent a mafioso feel.

Carnaval is the holiday of the poor. Not that you could tell from the price of the tickets to the balls. Some of them cost more than the monthly minimum wage. There are snooty affairs like the ones at the Copacabana Palace or in Barra at the Metropolitan. Raunchier parties are held in Leblon at Scala, Canecão in Botafogo and Help disco in Copacabana.

Tickets go on sale roughly a fortnight beforehand and the balls are held nightly for the preceding week and all through

Carnaval. Buy a copy of the *Veja* magazine with the *Veja Rio* insert. It has details of all the balls and bandas.

There are three basic laws of Carnaval. One: beautiful, flirtatious and apparently unaccompanied women are either escorted by huge, jealous cachaça-crazed men wielding machetes, or else they are really men dressed up as women. Two: everything costs several times more within the club than outside. And finally: don't bring more money than you're willing to lose – the club bouncers are big, but not all that effective.

Street Carnaval

What do Cariocas do in the afternoon and early evening during Carnaval? They dance in the streets behind *bandas* (marching bands with brass and percussion instruments), which pump out the banda theme song and other Carnaval marching favourites as they move along. To join in the fun, all you need to do is jump in when you see the banda pass. Bandas are one of the most traditional aspects of Carnaval in Rio.

Banda de Ipanema is a traditional banda that parades on the second Saturday before Carnaval, starting from Praça General Osório in Ipanema. It's full of drag queens and party animals. It starts around 5 pm and goes until around 9 pm. The banda also parades again on Carnaval Saturday. Banda Carmen Miranda, with its famous gay icon, is also a lot of fun, not only for gays, but for everyone. It parades through Ipanema streets around 4 pm on the Sunday before Carnaval. There are lots of bandas parading in Copacabana before and during Carnaval, too.

The street parades in Avenida Rio Branco in the Centro and Boulevard 28 de Setembro in Vila Isabel, both on Carnaval Saturday, are really worth checking out. You won't see many other tourists there, but just carry a few dollars in your pocket for beers and a snack, and you'll have nothing to worry about.

JOHN MAIER, JR

Over the top feather headdresses and bare breasts are part of the passing street parade

Tchica-tchica-bum! Carmen Miranda – the Brazilian Bombshell

Carmen Miranda, the flamboyant star of Broadway and Hollywood who made pineapples a fashion statement

Contrary to general perceptions, Carmen Miranda is more than just tutti-frutti headdresses and a gay icon – she remains the greatest Brazilian singing star.

Born in rural Portugal in 1909, Carmen Maria Miranda da Cunha was raised in Rio. An apprentice milliner at 15, the green-eyed beauty who loved to sing was a favourite with customers, and soon she became a national radio and stage star. Her charm, unique way of singing, gently self-deprecating comic touches and rolling eyes captivated everyone.

By 1939, at the zenith of the blockbuster, Ziegfield Folly-inspired musicals, she was dazzling Broadway. One rapt reporter described as her as 'a bejewelled songbird with a serpent's sting'. Another fan recalled that 'she'd arrive at a party and all of a sudden, gold glittered all over the room'.

Carmen then went to Hollywood and made many lighthearted tropical escapades including the Busby Berkeley extravaganza *The Gang's All Here*. At her peak in 1945, she was the highest paid entertainer in the United States.

But when she flew home to Brazil she was snubbed – 'Americanised', sniffed the critics. Carmen forgave, but never forgot the rebuke, and when Hollywood beckoned again, she was gone.

As the star of her fame waned and her private life became unbearable, Carmen became dependant on high doses of uppers and downers, with tragic consequences. This drug cocktail led her into deep depression, even forcing her in desperation to submit to electroshock therapy. She needed to be carried onto the plane for her last trip to Rio in 1954. Journalists who attended the only press conference she gave noticed how much she had aged.

Carmen stayed in her room at the Copacabana Palace for 49 days. On her return to Hollywood, she was again faced with the unremitting demands of a busy schedule, her tyrannical husband, and her continued drug dependency.

A few months later she was dead, felled by a massive heart attack. She was only 46. Peritonitis was given as the medical reason for the fatal seizure, but those closest to Carmen were convinced that she died of a broken heart.

The Brazilian president declared a day of mourning and over a million tearful fans lined the streets of Rio to farewell their idol.

Carmen has become a cult figure among Rio's gay community, and Carnaval sees many of them impersonating her. It's interesting, though, that the small Museu Carmen Miranda in the Parque do Flamengo is visited by more foreign visitors than Cariocas.

Many of Carmen's recordings have recently been repackaged as CD boxed sets, so fans should have no trouble finding them in the music stores.

Samba Parades

In the *sambódromo*, a tiered street designed for samba parades, the Brazilians harness sweat, noise and confusion, and turn it into art. The 16 top level samba schools prepare all year for an hour of glory in the sambódromo.

The best escola is chosen by a hand-picked set of judges on the basis of many components including percussion, the *samba do enredo* (theme song), harmony between percussion, song and dance, choreography, costume, storyline, floats and decorations. The championship is hotly contested, with the winner becoming the pride of both Rio and Brazil.

The parades begin in moderate mayhem, then work themselves up to a higher plane of frenzy. The announcers introduce the escola, the group's colours and the number of wings. Far away the lone voice of the *puxador* starts the samba. Thousands more voices join him, and then the drummers kick in, 200 to 400 per school. The booming drums drive the parade. This samba do enredo is the loudest music you're ever likely to hear in your life. The samba tapes flood the air waves for weeks before the beginning of Carnaval.

From a distance it looks as though it's a single, living organism. It's a throbbing beast – and slowly it comes closer, a pulsing, glittering, Japanese movie monster slime-mould threatening to engulf all of Rio in samba and vibrant, (not to mention vibrating) mulatas.

The parades begin with a special opening wing or *abre alas*, which always displays the name of the school and the theme of the escola. The whole shebang has some sort of unifying message – social commentary, economic criticism or political message, but it's usually lost in the glitz. The abre alas is then followed by the *commissão de frente*, who greet the crowds. The escola thus honours its elderly men for work done over the years.

Next follow the main wings of the escola, the big allegorical floats, the children's wing, the drummers, the celebrities

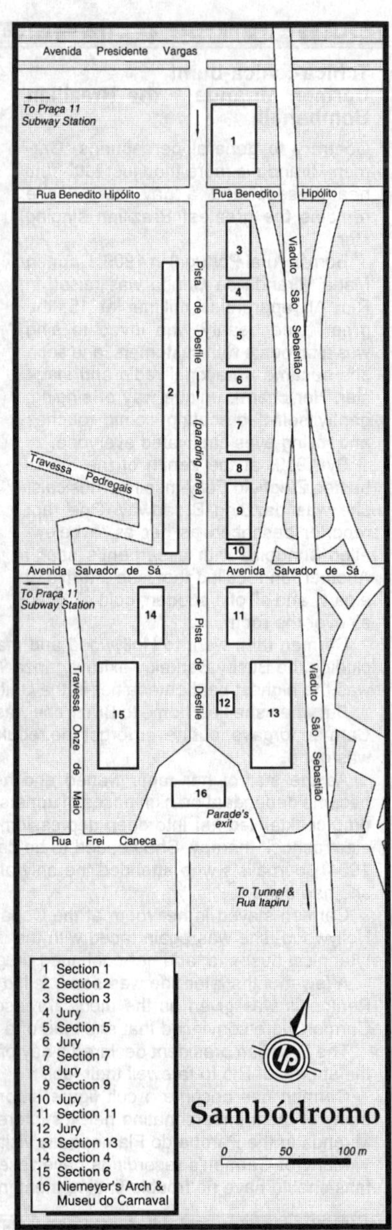

Sambódromo Glossary

alas – literally the 'wings'; these are groups of samba school members responsible for a specific part of the central samba do enredo. Special alas include the *bahianas*, women dressed as bahian 'aunts' in full skirts and turbans. The *abre-ala* of each school is the opening wing or float.

bateria – the drum section. It's the driving beat behind the school's samba. The 'soul' of the school.

carnavalescos – the artistic directors of each school who are responsible for the overall layout and design of the school's theme.

carros allegoricos – the dazzling floats, usually decorated with near-naked mulatas. The floats are pushed along by the school's maintenance crew.

desfile – all the schools are divided up and the most important ones *desfilar* (parade) on the Sunday and Monday night of Carnaval. Each school's desfile is judged on its samba, drum section, master of ceremonies and flag bearer, the floats, the leading commission, costumes, dance coordination and harmony.

destaques – the richest and most elaborate costumes. The heaviest ones usually get a spot on one of the floats.

diretores de harmonia – the school organisers, usually dressed in white or the school colours, who run around yelling and 'pumping up' the wings and making sure that there aren't any gaps in the parade.

enredo – the central theme of each school and the *samba do enredo* is the samba that goes with it. Themes vary tremendously.

passistas – the best samba dancers in the school. They roam the parade in groups or alone, stopping to show their fancy footwork along the way. The women are scantily dressed and the men usually hold tambourines.

puxador – the interpreter of the theme song. He (they're invariably male) works as a guiding voice leading the school's singers at rehearsals and in the parade.

and the bell-shaped Baianas twirling in their elegant hoop skirts. The Baianas honour the history of the parade itself, which was brought to Rio from Salvador de Bahia in 1877.

The *mestre-sala* (dance master) and *porta-bandeira* (flag bearer) waltz and whirl. Celebrities, dancers and tambourine players strut their stuff. The costumes are fabulously lavish: 1.5m feathered head-dresses, long flowing capes sparkling with sequins, rhinestone studded G-strings.

The floats gush neo-baroque silver foil and gold tinsel. Sparkling models sway to the samba, dancing in their private processions. All the while the puxador leads the song, repeating the samba do enredo for the duration of the parade.

Over an hour after it began, the escola makes it past the arch and the judges' stand. There is a few minutes' pause. TV cranes stop bobbing up and down over the Pepsi caps and bibs of the foreign press corps.

Now garbage trucks parade down the runway clearing the way for the next escola. Sanitation workers in orange jump-suits shimmy, dance and sweep, gracefully catch trash thrown from the stands and take their bows. It's their Carnaval, too.

The parade continues on through the night and into the morning, eight more samba schools parade the following day, and the week after, the top eight schools parade once more in the parade of champions.

Tickets

Getting tickets at the legitimate prices can be tough. Many tickets are sold well in advance of the event; check with Riotur about where you can get them, because the official outlet varies from year to year. People queue up for hours and travel agents and scalpers snap up the best seats. Riotur reserves seats in private boxes for tourists for US$200.

If you do happen to buy a ticket from a scalper (no need to worry about looking for them – they'll find you!), make sure you get both the plastic ticket with the magnetic strip and the ticket showing the seat number. The tickets for different days are colour-coded, so double-check the date as well.

But don't fret if you don't get a ticket by either of these means. It is possible to see the show without paying an arm and a leg. The parades last 8 to 10 hours each and no one can or wants to sit through the whole thing. Unless you're an aficionado of an escola that starts early, don't show up at the sambódromo until midnight, three or four hours into the show. This is when you can get tickets at the grandstand for about US$10.

And if you can't make it during Carnaval proper, there's always the cheaper (but less exciting) parade of champions the following week.

If you can possibly avoid it, don't take the bus to or from the sambódromo. It's much safer to take the mêtro, which runs around the clock during Carnaval. This is also gives you a great opportunity to check out the paraders commuting in costume.

By the way, there's nothing to stop you from actually taking part in a Carnaval parade. Most samba schools are happy to have foreigners join one of the alas. All you need is something along the lines of US$200-300 for your costume and you're in. It helps to arrive in Rio a week or two in advance to get this organised. Ask at the hotel how to go about it. It usually takes only a few phone calls and a fitting.

Dates

Dates for the Carnaval parade in coming years are:

1999	14-15 February
2000	5-6 March
2001	24- 25 February
2002	9-10 February
2003	1-2 March

Rio de Janeiro State

The small state of Rio de Janeiro offers much more than just the *cidade maravilhosa* (marvellous city). Within four hours of travel from any point in the state, and often much less, are beaches, mountains and forests that equal any in Brazil. Many of these places offer more intimate settings in which to meet Cariocas, who have known about the natural wonders surrounding the city for years. You won't find virgin sites like in the Northeast – tourism here is fairly developed and prices are higher than in most of Brazil. But if you have only a couple of weeks in Brazil and think that you'll return some day, an itinerary that covers the entire state of Rio would be one of the best possible. For those with all the time in the world, it's easy to pass a month or two here.

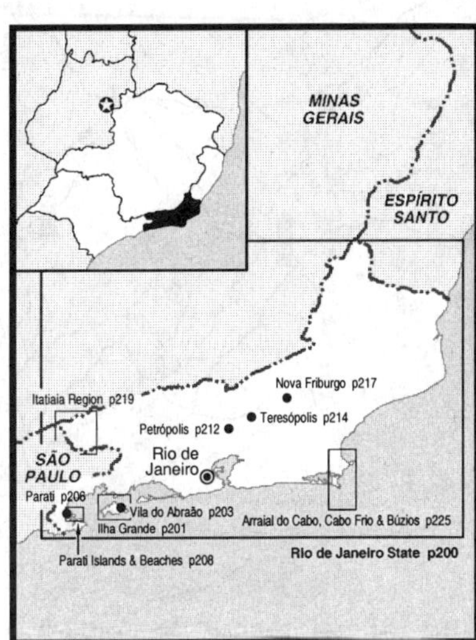

Rio de Janeiro state, which lies just above the Tropic of Capricorn, has an area of 43,919 sq km – about the size of Switzerland – and a population of over 14 million. The littoral is backed by steep mountains which descend into the sea around the border with São Paulo and gradually rise farther inland in the north. This forms a thin strip of land nestled between the lush green mountains and the emerald sea, with beaches that are the most spectacular in Brazil.

Divided by the city of Rio and the giant Baía de Guanabara with 131km of coast and 113 islands, are two coastal regions, each with rather different natural characteristics: the Costa Verde (west) and the Costa do Sol (east).

Along the Costa Verde are hundreds of islands, including Ilha Grande and the Restinga de Marambaia, which make for easy swimming and boating. The calm waters and the natural ports and coves allowed safe passage to the Portuguese ships that came to transport sugar, and later gold, to Europe. They also protected pirates, who found a safe haven on Ilha Grande.

Beaches wait to be explored, particularly farther away from Rio city, where the coastal road stays close to the ocean and the views are spectacular. The most famous spots are Angra dos Reis, Parati and Ilha Grande.

To the east, the mountains begin to rise farther inland. The littoral is filled with lagoons and swamps. Stretching away from the coast are plains which extend about 30km to the mountains. Búzios and Cabo Frio, famous for their beauty and luxury, are only two hours from Rio by car. Saquarema, one of Brazil's best surfing beaches, is even closer.

Driving due north from Rio city, you pass through the city's industrial and motel sections and soon reach a wall of jungled mountains. After the climb, you're in the cool Serra dos Órgãos. The resort cities of Petrópolis and Teresópolis are nearby and many smaller villages offer Cariocas an escape from the tropical summer heat. The fantastic peaks of the Parque Nacional da Serra dos Órgãos, outside Teresópolis, provide superb hiking and climbing opportunities.

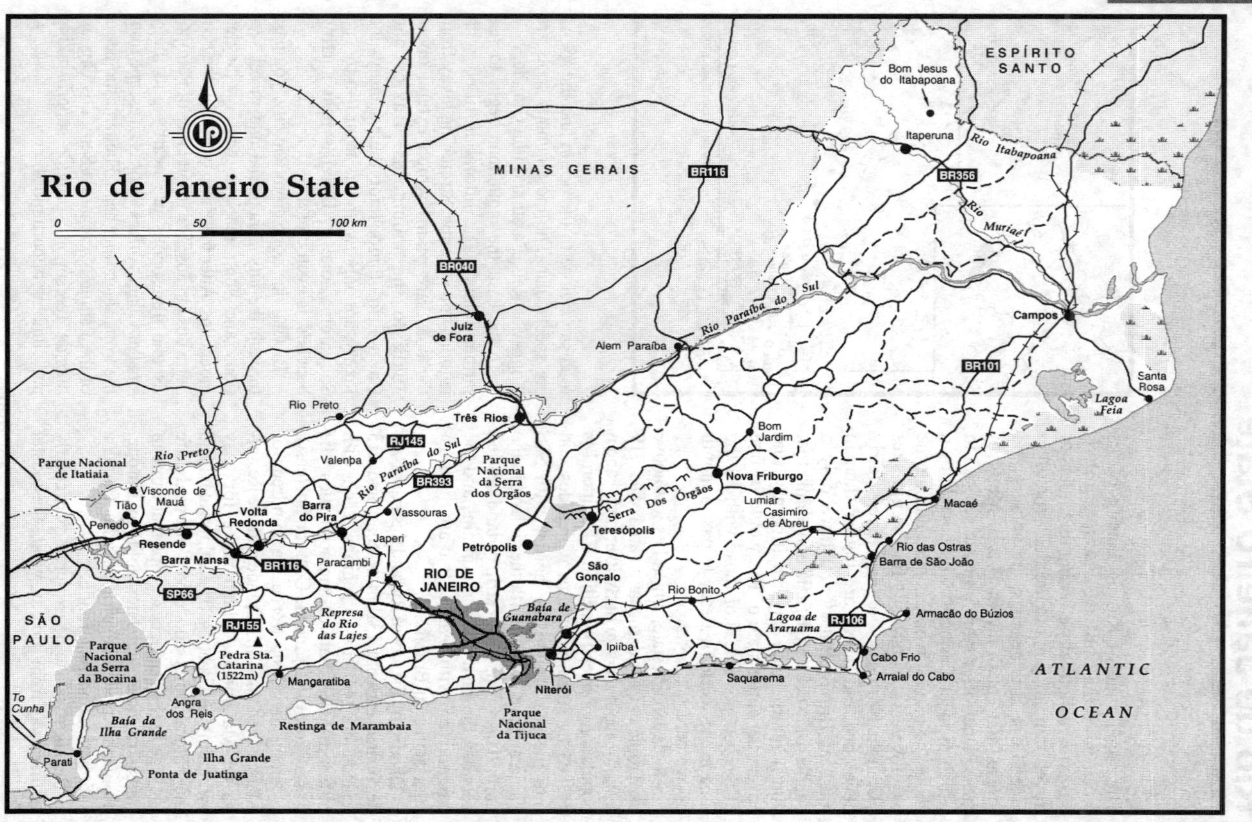
Rio de Janeiro State
0
50
100 km
MINAS GERAIS
ESPÍRITO SANTO
SÃO PAULO
ATLANTIC
OCEAN
Bom Jesus do Itabapoana
Itaperuna
Rio Itabapoana
BR356
Rio Muriaé
BR116
BR040
Juiz de Fora
Rio Paraíba do Sul
Alem Paraíba
Campos
BR101
Santa Rosa
Lagoa Feia
Rio Preto
Três Rios
RJ145
Bom Jardim
Parque Nacional de Itatiaia
Rio Preto
Valenba
Rio Paraíba do Sul
BR393
Parque Nacional da Serra dos Órgãos
Nova Friburgo
Visconde de Mauá
Tião
Penedo
Volta Redonda
Barra do Pira
Vassouras
Serra Dos Órgãos
Lumiar
Casimiro de Abreu
Macaé
Resende
Japeri
Teresópolis
Petrópolis
Rio das Ostras
Barra Mansa
BR116
Paracambi
Barra de São João
RIO DE JANEIRO
São Gonçalo
SP66
Rio Bonito
Represa do Rio das Lajes
Baía de Guanabara
Lagoa de Araruama
RJ106
Armacão do Búzios
RJ155
Pedra Sta. Catarina (1522m)
Ipiíba
Cabo Frio
Parque Nacional da Serra da Bocaina
Mangaratiba
Saquarema
Arraial do Cabo
Niterói
To Cunha
Angra dos Reis
Baía da Ilha Grande
Restinga de Marambaia
Parque Nacional da Tijuca
Parati
Ilha Grande
Ponta de Juatinga

The other mountain region where Cariocas play is the Itatiaia area in the corner of the state that borders São Paulo and Minas Gerais. Getting there takes only four hours, the route passing near the steel city of Volta Redonda.

Indian Names

Many place names in Rio state are derived from Indian words. Among them are:

Araruama – place where the macaw eats
Baré – in the middle of many fish
Cunhambebe – women who speak too much
Grataú – ghost's den
Grumari – a kind of tree
Guanabara – arm of the sea
Guaratiba – place with much sun or place of many holes
Ipanema – place that gives bad luck or place of dangerous sea
Itacuruçá – stone's cross
Itaipu – stone that the sea hits
Itaipuaçu – little Itaipu
Jabaquara – crack in the earth
Jeribá – a kind of coconut palm
Mangaratiba – banana orchard
Maricá – belly
Parati – a kind of fish
Paratininga – dry fish
Sapeca – burned
Saquarema – lagoon without shells
Tijuca – putrid-smelling swamp

West of Rio de Janeiro

ILHA GRANDE

✉ 23990-000 ☎ 021

Ilha Grande is almost all tropical beach and Atlantic rainforest, with only three towns on the island. Freguesia de Santana is a small hamlet with no regular accommodation. Parnaioca has a few homes by a lovely strip of beach near the old prison.

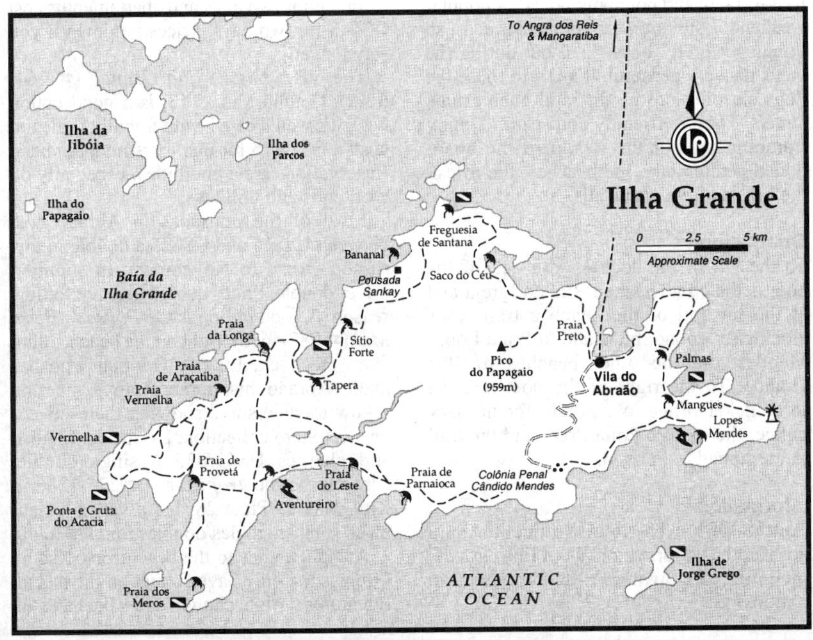

Abraão has plenty of pousadas and camping grounds and ferry connections to Mangaratiba and Angra dos Reis.

If you really want to get away from it all, Ilha Grande may well be the place to go. The options are pretty attractive. You can rent a boat in Abraão and buzz around to Freguesia or Parnaioca. Then there are trails through the lush, steamy forest to various beaches around the island. For instance, it is a 2½ hour trek to Praia Lopes Mendes, which some claim to be the most beautiful beach in Brazil. Praia de Parnaioca also ranks up there. And these are only two of the island's 102 beaches!

Vila do Abraão

Abraão could be a movie set for *Papillon*. It has a gorgeous, palm-studded beachfront of pale, faded homes, and a tidy white church. Not far away are the ruins of an old prison that will still give you the creeps if you go inside.

As a base on Ilha Grande, you can't go past Abraão, and not many do. It's a popular weekend destination for young Cariocas, so things get pretty busy then, but during the week it's very peaceful. It's OK to rouse the dogs sleeping on the dirt and cobblestone streets. They're friendly and seem to enjoy tramping around the island to the abandoned penitentiary, the beaches, the forest, the hills and the waterfalls.

Orientation

To the left of the dock as you get off the boat is the cobblestoned Rua da Igreja and at the far end of the beach a trail leads clockwise around the island to Praia Lopes Mendes and the other beaches of Ilha Grande. To the right of the dock are the ferry ticket office, a pousada for military police, the road to Praia Preta and the trail to the ruined old prison.

Information

Tourist Office The tourist office in Angra dos Reis has information about Ilha Grande, including the available accommodation options.

Money It's better to change money before you get here. The top-end hotels, tourist stores and the Banco do Brasil branch (open summer only) will usually change cash US dollars. Lutz, the German owner of the Pousada Beira Mar, will change and accept travellers cheques.

Places to Stay

Cheap lodging on Ilha Grande is not difficult to find, especially as competition increases. There are now more than 60 pousadas on the island and more are going up.

The cheapest option is to camp. *Camping Renato*, up a small path beside Dona Penha's, has well-drained, secure sites and basic facilities, as well as an on-site café and bar. They charge US$5 per person. Other camping grounds include *Das Palmeiras*, next to Dona Penha's, and *Cerca Viva* (☎ 551-2336), a camping ground and pousada combined, in a secure spot at Rua Getúlio Vargas 351. It rents small on-site tents for US$18/24 for two days. Quartos are US$32 a double for two days and apartamentos cost US$43 for two days. Prices go down if you stay longer.

The YHA hostel, *Ilha Grande* (☎ 264-6147), Getúlio Vargas 13, is a good option here. It's well located, with friendly staff, and costs US$12/15 for members/nonmembers. Reservations are a good idea, especially on weekends and holidays.

Most of the pousadas in Abraão cost between US$15 and US$25 a double in low season (April to November). In summer, prices double. Prices quoted here are for low season. A good option is the *Pousada Beira Mar* (☎ 987-4696), right on the beach, 300m from the dock. Lutz, a German who has made Abraão his home, enjoys meeting fellow travellers and showing them his extensive photo collection. He speaks English and charges US$15/25 a single/double. Close by is the *Tropicana* (☎ 225-1286 in Rio), Rua da Praia 28. It's a very pleasant place and has singles/doubles for US$30/40.

At right angles to the beachfront, Rua da Igreja is the only paved street on the island. It features a white church, a few bars and the

Hotel Mar da Tranquilidade (☎/fax 365-2833). The hotel has charming apartamentos for US$15/25. Around the corner in Rua Getúlio Vargas the *Hotel Alpino* (☎ 987-6501) is in a beautiful garden setting. Chalets are US$30/40 outside the tourist season.

Just before the Alpino is *Penhas*, the house of Dona Penha. It's the first place on the right after Camping das Palmeiras. Dona Penha has gone upmarket in the last few years and her comfortable apartamentos go for US$20/30. A more expensive place close to the dock is *Agua Viva* (☎/fax 986-2519), with ample suites for US$40/50 with air-conditioning, frigobar and cable TV (though why anyone would come to Ilha Grande to watch TV is baffling). Ilha Grande's most stylish hotel is the *Pousada Sankay* (☎ (024)365-4065), 50 minutes away by boat at Enseada do Bananal. Doubles start at US$70.

Places to Eat

Restaurante Lubel is a decent place which serves prato feitos with abundant portions of fresh fish (US$4). It's just around the corner from the church. The three best places to eat in town are: *Bar Casarão da Ilha* which is expensive but serves very high quality seafood; *Restaurant Minha Deusa* with cheap, good home-cooking; and *Bar Restaurant Lua & Mar*, which serves good seafood dishes if you don't mind waiting.

Getting There & Away

Catch a Conerj ferry from either Mangaratiba or Angra dos Reis. From Mangaratiba to Abraão, the ferry leaves weekdays at 8 am and weekends at 9 am. It returns from Abraão daily at 5 pm.

The ferry from Angra dos Reis to Abraão leaves at 3 pm on weekdays and 2.30 pm on weekends, returning from Abraão at 9.30 am

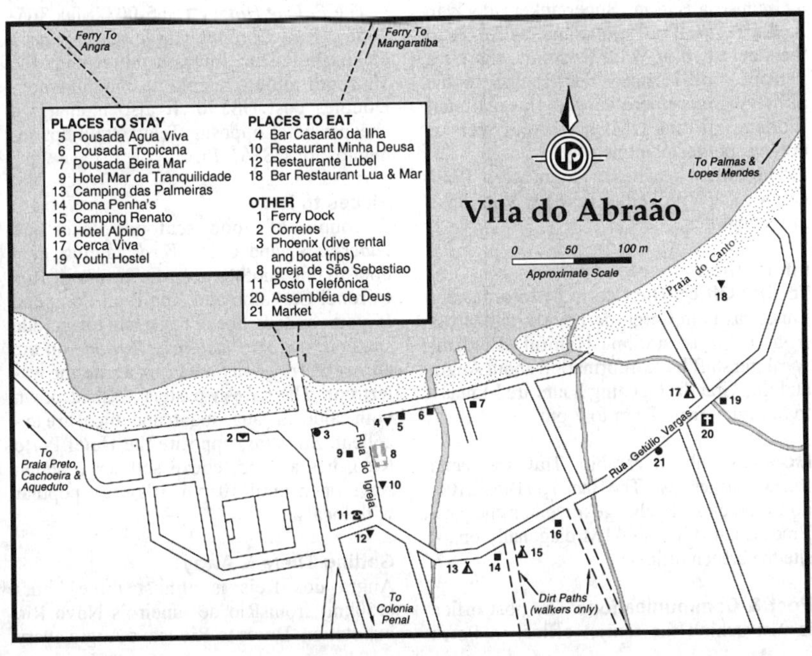

on weekdays and 11 am on weekends. It's a 1½ hour, US$5 ride.

An alternative from Angra is to catch the schooner Santa Isabel, which leaves from the dock behind the Receita Federal building (close to the tourist office) daily at 10 am on weekdays and 9 am on weekends. The same boat returns daily from Abraão at 4 pm. Fare is US$10 one-way.

Boat Trip Phoenix (☎ 987-2369), next to the dock, rents masks and flippers for US$5 a day. It also runs a US$40 day cruise or a two day trip, for US$90, which circumnavigates the island. You can sleep on board or in a simple pousada in Araçatiba for US$8.

ANGRA DOS REIS

• *pop 93,000* ✉ *23900-000* ☎ *024*

Angra dos Reis is a base for nearby islands and beaches, not a tourist attraction in itself. The savage beauty of the tropical, fjord-like coastline along this stretch of Hwy BR-101 has been badly blemished by industrialisation. Supertankers dock in Angra's port, a rail line connects Angra to the steel town of Volta Redonda, there's a Petrobras oil refinery and, thanks to the military government and the International Monetary Fund (IMF), a controversial nuclear power plant nearby.

The closest beaches to Angra are at Praia Grande and Vila Velha. Take the Vila Velha municipal bus.

Information

Tourist Office The Centro de Informações Turísticas is in Largo da Lapa, right across from the bus station. Helpful, English-speaking staff have information about Angra and Ilha Grande. Opening hours are Monday to Saturday from 8 am to 7 pm.

Money Cambisul câmbio, Travessa Santa Luzia, changes cash. The Banco do Brasil, Rua do Comércio, will change travellers cheques. Bradesco also has an ATM diagonally opposite the branch office.

Post & Communications The post office is just behind the tourist office, in Praça Lopes Trovão. Long-distance telephone calls can be made from Telerj, Avenida Raul Pompéia 97.

Places to Stay

A cheapie close to the bus station is *Pousada Angra Antiga*, Rua Arcebispo Santos 162, with basic, clean single/double quartos for US$15/25 without breakfast. If you want a shower in your room, the best budget bet is the central *Porto Rico* (☎ 365-0992), Rua Colonel Carvalho 54. Small, clean apartamentos with fan but without breakfast go for US$20/30. The *Pousada Praia Grande* (☎ 365-0605), Estrada do Contorno 1890, Praia Grande, Angra dos Reis, is on the right-hand side, 200m before the Angra Inn. Take the Vila Velha bus from the rodoviária. The hotel has a nice courtyard and classy doubles for US$40. *Pousada do Jamanta* (☎ 365-1374), Praia do Bonfim, has been recommended. It has doubles for US$20 per person.

The *Palace Hotel* (☎ 365-0032; fax 365-2656), Rua Coronel Carvalho 275, is a clean, three-star Embratur hotel with TV, air-conditioning, telephone and hot water. Doubles cost US$90. It also manages a cheaper hotel opposite Telerj, with apartamentos for US$55/75.

Places to Eat

A couple of good seafood places are *Taberna 33* and *Costa Verde*, almost next door to one another near the corner of Rua Coronel Carvalho and Rua Raul Pompéia. If your budget doesn't stretch to include seafood, there's *Pastelaria Verolme* on the corner of Travessa Santa Luzia near the waterfront. Their fresh pasteis washed down with caldo da cana (sugarcane juice) are excellent. *Barretos*, opposite the Hotel Porto Rico, has a good, cheap self-serve and it stays open until 10 pm. It's very popular with locals.

Getting There & Away

Angra dos Reis is almost three hours (150km) from Rio de Janeiro's Novo Rio bus station. Buses to Rio leave Angra every hour from 4 am to 8.40 pm (US$11). To Parati, there are six local buses a day, the first leaving at 6 am (US$5, two hours).

PARATI

• *pop 28,000* ✉ *23970* ☎ *024*

Oh! Deus, se na terra houvesse um paraíso, não seria muito longe daqui!
(Oh! God, if there were a paradise on earth, it wouldn't be very far from here!)

Amerigo Vespucci

Amerigo was referring to steep, jungled mountains that seem to leap into the sea, a scrambled shoreline with hundreds of islands and jutting peninsulas, and the clear, warm waters of the Baía da Ilha Grande, as calm as an empty aquarium. All this still exists, though no longer in a pristine state, along with one of Brazil's most enchanting towns – the colonial village of Parati, which Amerigo did not get to enjoy.

Parati is both a great colonial relic, well preserved and architecturally unique, and a launching pad to a dazzling section of the Brazilian coastline. The buildings are marked by simple lines that draw the eye to the general rather than the specific, and earthy colours and textures that magnify, through contrast, the natural beauty that envelops the town. So while the individual buildings in Parati may well be beautiful the town, when viewed as a whole, is truly a work of art.

Dozens of secluded beaches are within a couple of hours of Parati by boat or bus. There are good swimming beaches close to town, but the best are along the coast toward São Paulo and out on the bay islands.

One of the most popular spots between Rio and São Paulo, Parati is crowded and lively throughout the summer holidays, brimming with Brazilian and Argentine holiday-makers and good music. That the town is all tourism there is no doubt; there are so many boutiques and ritzy restaurants. But if you get around these obstacles, Parati is a delight, and there are plenty of beaches to accommodate all visitors.

History

Parati was inhabited by the Guianas Indians when Portuguese from the former hereditary province of São Vicente settled here in the early part of the 16th century. With the discovery of gold in Minas Gerais at the end of the 17th century Parati became an obligatory stopover for those coming from Rio de Janeiro as it was the only point where the escarpment of the Serra do Mar could be scaled. The precarious road was an old Guianas Indian trail that cut past the Serra do Facão (today Cunha, São Paulo) to the valley of Paraíba and from there to Pindamonhangaba, Guaratinguetá and then the mines.

Parati became a busy, important port as miners and supplies disembarked for the gold mines and gold was shipped to Europe. The small town prospered and, as always, the wealthy built churches to prove it. There was so much wealth in Parati that in 1711 Captain Francisco do Amaral Gurgel sailed from Parati to save Rio de Janeiro from a threatened French siege by handing over a ransom of 1000 crates of sugar, 200 head of cattle and 610,000 gold cruzados.

Parati's glory days didn't last long. After the 1720s, a new road from Rio to Minas Gerais via the Serra dos Órgãos cut 15 days off the route from Parati and the town started to decline. In the 19th century, the local economy revived with the coffee boom and now, with the recent construction of the road from Rio, the town's coffers are once again being filled. Parati is also renowned for its excellent cachaça.

The town is easy to look around, just stroll on the *pes-de-moleque* (street urchins' feet), the local name for the irregular cobblestone streets, washed clean by the rains and high tides. It's a couple of kilometres off the Rio to Santos highway, at the south-west corner of Rio de Janeiro state. Until 1954 the only access to Parati was by sea. In that year a road was built through the steep Serra do Mar, passing the town of Cunha, 47km inland. In 1960 the coastal road from Rio, 253km away, was extended to Parati and 330km beyond to São Paulo.

Orientation
Parati is small and easy to navigate, but one thing that becomes confusing is street names and house numbers. Many streets have more than one name, which has locals, as well as tourists, thoroughly perplexed. The numbering system seems totally random.

Information
Tourist Office The Centro de Informações Turísticas (☎ 371-1266, ext 218), on Avenida Roberto Silveira, is open daily from 9 am to 9 pm.

Parati Tours (☎/fax 371-1327) is on Avenida Roberto Silveira 11, just before you hit the colonial part of town. It's also useful for information. Its five hour schooner cruises are US$15 (US$20 with lunch). It also rents bicycles (US$2 an hour or US$10 per day).

Money The Banco do Brasil on Avenida Roberto Silveira, changes cash and travellers cheques between 11 am and 2.30 pm. It also does Visa cash advances. There's a Bradesco ATM close to the bus station.

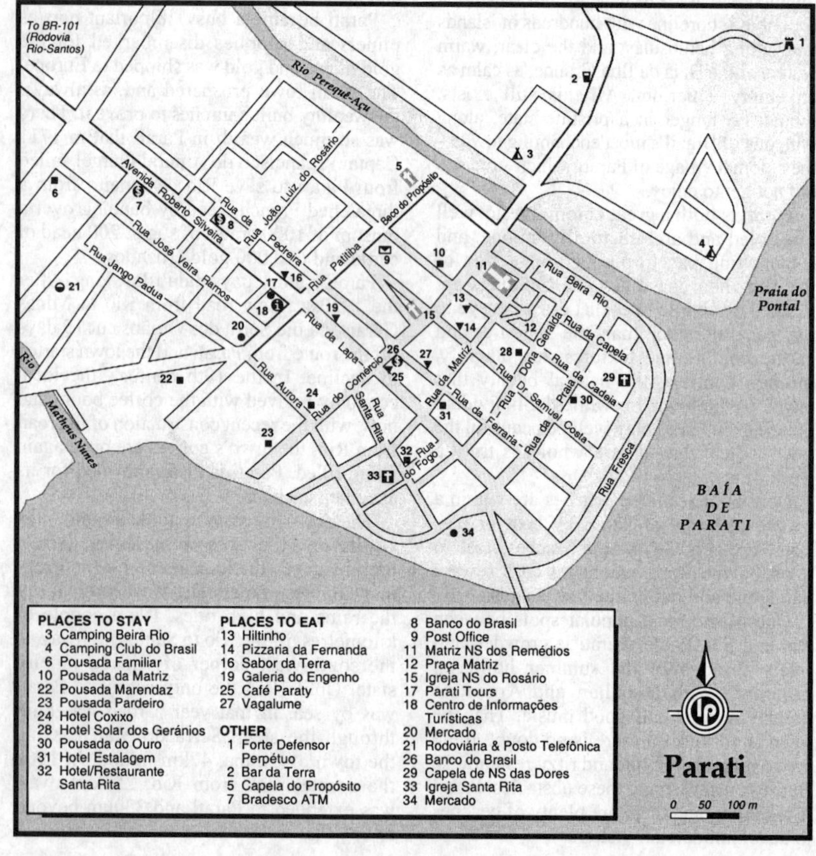

Post & Communications The post office is on the corner of Rua da Cadeia and Beco do Propósito. The Telerj station is at the rodoviária.

Churches

Parati's 18th century prosperity is reflected in its beautiful old homes and churches. Three main churches were used to separate the races – **NS do Rosário** was for slaves, **Santa Rita** for freed mulattos and **NS das Dores** for the white élite.

The **Igreja NS do Rosário e São Benedito dos Homens Pretos** (1725), Rua Dr Samuel Costa, was built by and for slaves. Renovated in 1857, the church has gilded wooden altars dedicated to Our Lady of the Rosary, St Benedict and St John. The pineapple crystals are for prosperity and good luck.

Igreja Santa Rita dos Pardos Libertos (1722), Praça Santa Rita, has a tiny museum of sacred art and some fine woodwork on the doorways and altars. **Capela de NS das Dores** (1800), Rua Dr Pereira, was renovated in 1901. The cemetery is fashioned after the catacombs.

Matriz NS dos Remédios (1787), Praça Mons Hélio Pires, was built on the site of two 17th century churches. Inside, there is art from past and contemporary local artists. According to legend, construction of the church was financed by a pirate treasure hidden on Praia da Trindade.

Forte Defensor Perpétuo

The Forte Defensor Perpétuo was built in 1703 to defend from pirate attacks the gold being exported from Minas Gerais. The fort was rebuilt in 1822, the year of Brazil's independence, and was named after Emperor Dom Pedro I. It's on the Morro da Vila Velha, the hill just past Praia do Pontal, a 20 minute walk north of town. The fort houses the **Casa de Artista e Centro de Artes e Tradições Populares de Parati**.

Islands & Beaches

The closest fine beaches on the coast – **Vermelha**, **Lulas** and **Saco** – are about an hour away by boat (camping is allowed on the beaches). The best island beaches nearby are probably **Araújo** and **Sapeca**, but many of the islands have rocky shores and are private. The mainland beaches tend to be better. These beaches are all small and idyllic; most have barracas (serving beer and fish) and, at most, a handful of beach-goers.

Parati has some 65 islands and 300 beaches in its vicinity. Don't limit yourself to the following list of the most accessible beaches north of town, as there are plenty more. If you do come across any really special beaches and you can bear to share your secret, we'd love to know about them. See the Getting Around section for information on how to get to the less accessible beaches.

Praia do Pontal On the other side of the canal, 10 minutes away on foot, is Parati's city beach. There are several barracas and a lively crowd, but the beach itself is not attractive and the water gets dirty.

Praia do Forte On the side of the hill, hidden by the rocks, Praia do Forte is the cleanest beach within a quick walk of the city. It is relatively secluded and frequented by a youngish crowd.

Praia do Jabaquara Continue on the dirt road north past Praia do Pontal, over the hill, for 2km to Praia do Jabaquara, a big, spacious beach with great views in all directions. There is a small restaurant and a camping ground that's better than those in town. The sea is very shallow, so it's possible to wade way out into the bay.

Special Events

Parati is known for colourful and distinctive festivals. The two most important are the Festa do Divino Espírito Santo, which begins nine days before Pentecostal Sunday, and the NS dos Remédios, on 8 September. The former is planned throughout the year and features all sorts of merrymaking revolving around the *fólios*, musical

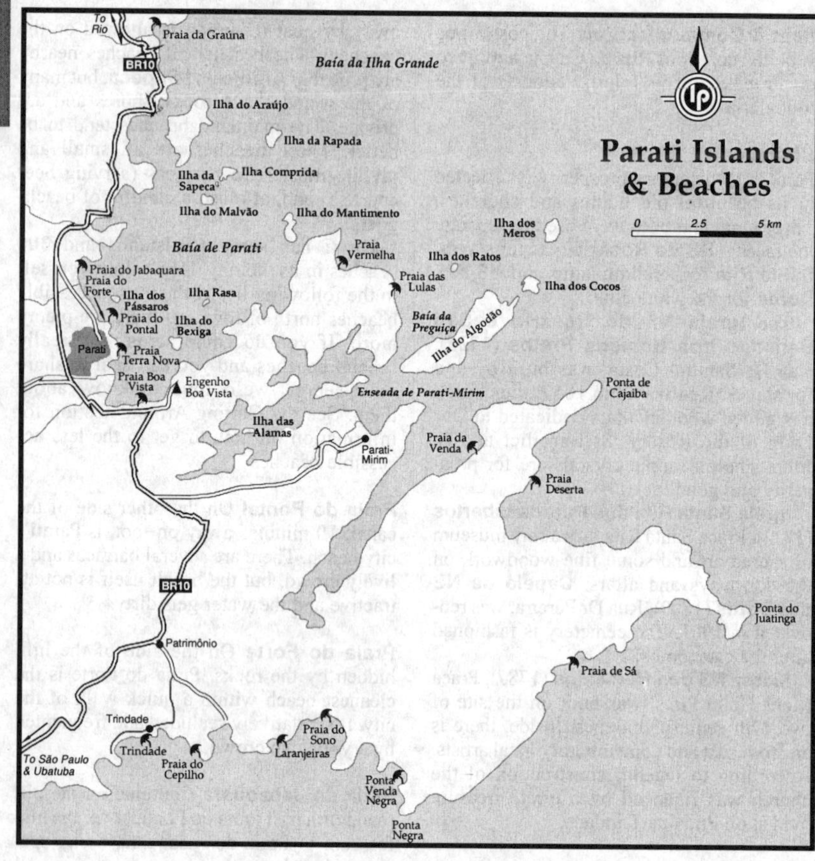

groups that go from door to door singing and joking.

The Festas Juninas, held during the month of June, are filled with dances, including the *xiba* (a circle clog dance) and the *ciranda* (a xiba with guitar accompaniment). The festivals culminate on 29 June with a maritime procession to Ilha do Araújo. Parati is a good option for Carnaval if you want to get out of Rio for a couple of days.

The Parati region produces excellent cachaça, and in 1984 the town council, in its wisdom, inaugurated the annual Festival da Pinga. The pinga party is held over an August weekend.

Places to Stay

Parati has two very different tourist seasons. From December to February hotels get booked up and room prices double, so reservations are a good idea. Many places require the full amount to be paid in advance – usually placed in their bank account in Rio or São Paulo. This is often nonrefundable. The rest of the year, finding accommodation is easy and not expensive, the town is quiet and some of the boutiques and restaurants close for the winter. The prices quoted here are low-season rates.

Places to Stay – Budget There are several camping grounds on the edge of town, just over the bridge.

The *Pouso Familiar* (☎ 371-1475), Rua José Vieira Ramos 262, is close to the bus station and charges US$14/22 a single/double, including a good breakfast. It's a friendly place, run by a Belgian/Brazilian couple Joseph and Lúcia. Joseph speaks English, French, German, Spanish and, of course, Flemish, and is very helpful. The pousada also has laundry facilities.

Another recommended place is the *Pousada Marendaz* (☎ 371-1369), Rua Dr Derly Ellena 9. Run by Rachel and her four sisters, it's more of a family home than a hotel and charges US$10 per person.

The *Hotel Estalagem* (☎ 371-1626), Rua da Matriz, charges US$30/40. Ask for the room upstairs – it has a great view. There's also a restaurant out the back. The *Pousada da Matriz* (☎ 371-1610), Rua Mal Deodoro 334, is well located and has rooms for US$15 per person.

Places to Stay – Mid-Range The *Hotel Solar dos Gerânios* (☎/fax 371-1550), Praça da Matriz (also known as Praça Monsenhor Hélio Pires), is a beautiful old hotel with wood and ceramic sculptures, flat brick and stone, rustic heavy furniture and *azulejos* (Portuguese tiles). Rooms come with hot showers. Singles/doubles start US$15/ 25.

Located in the mountains, 16km from Parati, is the *Hotel Fazenda le Gite d'Indaiatiba* (☎ 371-1327; fax 371-2188). Run by a French guy (if you have any trouble finding the place, ask for the French's hotel – everybody knows it), it has small bungalows in a beautiful setting with a great view. You can go horse riding, trekking or just down to the beach. There's a good library of mostly French books. The cost is US$40 a night for a double during the week, a bit more on weekends. To get there by bus, take the Barra Grande via Grauna and get off at the last stop in Grauna. By car, head toward Rio for 12km, then turn off at the Fazenda Grauna road and follow it for 4km.

Places to Stay – Top End There are three splendid, four-star colonial pousadas in Parati. Owned by a famous Brazilian actor, the *Pousada Pardeiro* (☎ 371-1370; fax 371-1139), Rua do Comércio 74, has a tranquil garden setting, refined service and impeccable decor. This is one of the best pousadas in Brazil, with single/double rooms going for US$80/100.

The *Hotel Coxixo* (☎ 371-1460; fax 371-1568), Rua do Comércio 362, is just a notch below the Pousada Pardeiro, but it has some standard rooms that are a good deal at US$50. The pousada is cosy and colonial, with beautiful gardens and a pool, and the rooms are simple but comfortable and pretty. To get the US$50 doubles, make reservations early; most doubles go for US$70.

The *Pousada do Ouro* (☎ 371-1378; fax 371-1311), Rua da Praia 145, is the kind of place where you can imagine bumping into Mick Jagger, Sonia Braga, or Tom Cruise, especially when you enter the hotel lobby and see photos of them posing in front of the pousada. The hotel has everything – bar, pool and a good restaurant. Doubles cost US$100 to US$120.

Places to Eat

Parati has many pretty restaurants but once your feet touch the cobblestones, prices go up. To beat the inflated prices in the old part of town, try the self-serve at *Sabor da Terra*, Rua Roberto Silveira 80. Also popular is *Bar da Terra*, across the bridge and up the hill on the left-hand side. It also has live music from Thursday to Sunday nights. The best restaurants in the old town include the *Galeria do Engenho*, Rua da Lapa, which serves large and juicy steaks for US$15, and *Vagalume*, Rua da Ferraria. *Hiltinho*, Rua da Cadeia, is more expensive, but there's a good menu and portions are ample. Another recommended restaurant is *Pizzaria da Fernanda*, Rua Dr Samuel Costa, which has tasty pizzas.

Entertainment

Café Parati, a popular hangout on the corner of Rua do Comércio and Rua da Lapa, has become very upmarket. *Bar da Terra* also gets pretty lively. Or just wander the streets and you'll hear some music outside the restaurants by the canal or inside one of the bars.

Getting There & Away

The new rodoviária (☎ 371-1177) is at Parque Imperial, 500m up from the old town.

There are 12 buses daily from Parati to Rio; it's a four hour trip, with the first bus leaving at 2 am and the last at 9.15 pm. Buses leave Rio for Parati at 6 and 9 am, and 12.30, 3, 6.20 and 8 pm. The cost is US$15.

Eighteen buses a day go from Parati to Angra dos Reis, the first leaving at 5 am and the last at 7.20 pm (US$3, two hours). There are three daily buses (at 11 am, 1 and 11.30 pm) for São Paulo (US$14, six hours). Three daily buses go to Ubatuba (at 7 am, noon and 7 pm), and three more go to Cunha.

Getting Around

To visit the less accessible beaches, many tourists take one of the schooners from the docks. Departure times vary with the season, but the information is easy to obtain. Tickets cost US$15 per person, with lunch served on board for an additional US$10. The boats make three beach stops of about 45 minutes each.

A more independent alternative is to rent one of the many small motorboats at the port. For US$15 per hour (more in summer), the skipper will take you where you want to go. Bargaining is difficult, but you can lower the cost by finding travelling companions and renting bigger boats – they hold six to 12 passengers.

If you figure on a one hour boat ride and an hour at the beach, you need a boat for at least three hours. Of course, there are even more beautiful beaches farther away.

The strategy of the boat skippers, since they usually can't return to port for another boatload, is to keep you out as long as possible. So don't be surprised if the first beach you go to is out of beer, or the next beach would be much more pleasant if it had cleaner water. These can be very compelling reasons not to return as scheduled and searching for paradise has a price.

AROUND PARATI

Praia Barra Grande

About 20km up the Rio to Santos highway, Barra Grande is an easy to reach alternative to the beaches in Baía de Parati. There are 11 municipal buses a day leaving from Parati, the first one at 7.10 am.

Praia de Parati-Mirim

For accessibility, cost and beauty, this beach is hard to beat. Parati-Mirim is a small town 27km from Parati. The beach has barracas and houses to rent. From Parati, it's a couple of hours by boat. If you're on a budget, catch a municipal bus, which makes the 40 minute trip for only US$0.70. Get the Parati Mirim bus from the rodoviária at 6.50 am, or 1 or 4.40 pm.

Praia do Sono

Beaches don't get much prettier than this. Past Ponta Negra on the coast going south, about 40km from Parati, Praia do Sono can have rough water and is sometimes difficult to land on. It's a four to five hour boat ride. The much cheaper alternative is to take the Laranjeiras bus from Parati, then get directions in Laranjeiras for the 1½ hour walk to Sono. Buses leave Parati at 5.15 am, and 12.30 and 6.40 pm. There's food but no formal lodging at the beach. Rough camping is permitted.

Praia da Trindade

About 5km before Sono, this is another beauty. It has lots of simple pousadas so you can stay here for a night or two. The beach is accessible by boat, as well as by the same bus as for Praia do Sono. Ask the driver to let you off at the entrance to Trindade. From the bus stop, it's 4km downhill.

Inland

The old gold route, now the road to Cunha (6km), is a magnificent jungle ride up the escarpment. The steep, dirt part of the road gets treacherous in the rain. Catch the Cunha bus in Parati.

Take the Ponte Branca bus from Parati to the Igrejinha da Penha, a small, triple-turreted hillside church. You'll find a 750m forest trail to a beautiful waterfall and water slide. Buses charge US$0.70 for the round trip, and leave at 5.45, 9 and 11.30 am, and 2 and 6 pm.

Fazenda Bananal-Engenho de Murycana is 4km off the Parati to Cunha road, 10km from town. It's a touristy spot with an old sugar mill, a restaurant, a zoo, and free samples of cachaça and batidas.

Parque Nacional da Serra da Bocaina

On the border between Rio and São Paulo, where the mountains of the Serra do Mar meet the sea, is the Parque Nacional da Serra da Bocaina. Rising from sea level to the 2132m **Pico da Boa Vista**, the park contains a mixture of vegetation, from Mata Atlântica to Mata Araucária (pine forests) and windswept grassy plateaus in the higher altitudes.

Wildlife is plentiful and includes a large population of the rare spider monkey, as well as other monkeys such as the howler and ring-tailed. Other animal species include the tree porcupine, sloth, deer, tapir, giant anteater and the otter. Birds found in the park include the harpy and black-hawk eagles and the black-beaked toucan.

Places to Stay The park possesses little tourist infrastructure, but there is an expensive hotel nearby, the *Pousada Vale dos Veados* (☎ 577-1102) on the Estrada da Bocaina at Km 42, which charges US$150 a double with full board. Reservations are necessary. Rough camping is permitted if you're following the old gold trail.

Getting There & Away Travellers going from Parati to Cunha actually pass through the southern end of the park. If you have a car and are driving in from the coast, take the Cunha-Campos Novo road to the park. If you're coming from the Rio-São Paulo Dutra (multilane highway), turn off at Queluz and drive for 37km, passing through the town of Areias and continuing on to São José dos Barreiros, the closest town to the park. In São José, contact MW Trekking (☎/fax (012) 577-1178) on the main square. It's run by José Milton, an enthusiastic guy who speaks English. He has lots of different programmes for trips into the Serra da Bocaina, including a three day trek down the old *trilha de ouro* (gold route) to the coast. Call for details and to make reservations. The trek costs US$140, all inclusive.

The Mountains

PETRÓPOLIS

• *pop 270,000* ✉ *25600-000* ☎ *024*

Petrópolis is a lovely mountain retreat with a decidedly European flavour. It's only 60km from Rio de Janeiro, making it an ideal day trip. This is where the imperial court spent the summer when Rio got too muggy, and it's still the home of the heir to the throne, Princess Isabel's grandson, Dom Pedro de Orleans e Bragança.

Wander around or ride by horse and carriage through the squares and parks, past bridges, canals and old-fashioned street lamps.

Information

Petrotur has a handy information booth on Praça Dom Pedro with brochures and maps. Opening hours are Tuesday to Saturday from 9 am to noon and 2 to 5 pm, Sunday from 9 am to 3 pm.

Walking Tour

This tour is around 4km and takes approximately two hours, including time spent at the attractions. Start at the **Catedral São Pedro de Alcântara**, which houses the **tombs** of Dom Pedro II, Dona Teresa and Princesa Isabel.

As you leave the cathedral, turn right down Rua 13 de Maio and walk a couple of hundred metres past some crummy shops, until you reach the river. Cross over and turn left for the **Palácio Cristal**, an iron and glass structure built in France, then imported in 1879 to serve as hothouse in which to grow orchids. Continue along down Rua Alfredo Pachá. You'll see the Bohemia beer **brewery** on your right. Sorry, no free samples.

Turn left again into Avenida Rui Silvera and go down to Praça Rui Barbosa. Cut across the park to the right, and up towards the pink university building with the floral clock in front. Next door, perched up high, is the **Casa de Santos Dumont**, the interesting summer home of Brazil's diminutive father of aviation and inventor of the wristwatch. It's open Tuesday to Sunday from 9 am to 5 pm. Go in and have a look.

As you leave, turn right and start walking uphill, then turn right at the first street on your right. There's a **sign** advertising the Hotel Margaridas. Keep walking uphill, always taking the right fork, until you reach the **Trono de Fátima**, a 3.5m sculpture of NS de Fátima Madonna, imported from Italy. From here you have a great view of the town and surrounding hills.

Head back down the hill, past the university and through Praça Rui Barbosa (you may want to grab a drink from one of numerous drink stands in the park), then along Avenida Koeller, where you'll pass some fine mansions. Turn right at Avenida Tiradentes and make your way up to Petrópolis' main attraction, the **Museu Imperial**, housed in the perfectly preserved and impeccably appointed palace of Dom Pedro II. One interesting

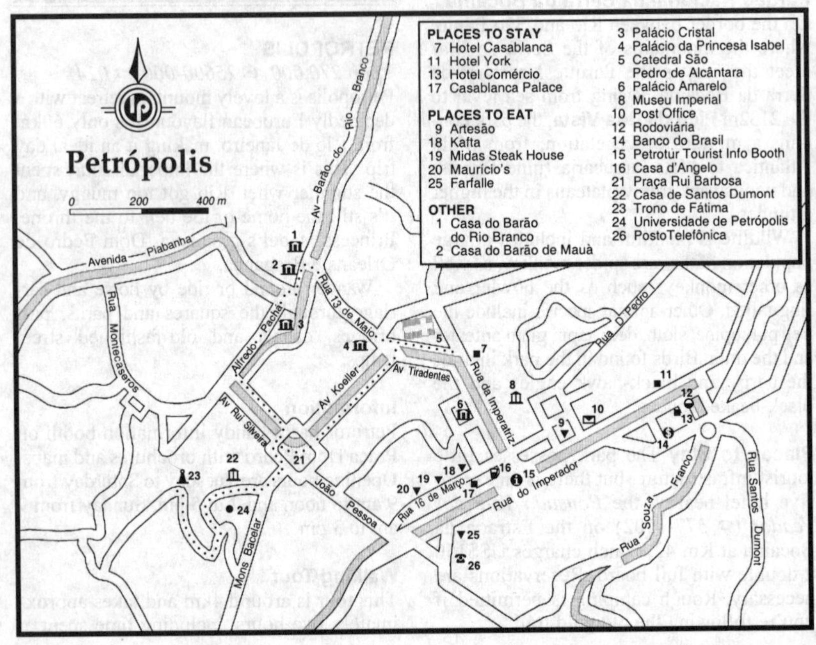

exhibit is the 1.7kg imperial crown, with its 639 diamonds and 77 pearls. The museum is open Tuesday to Sunday from noon to 5.30 pm and entry is US$3.

Places to Stay

The *Hotel Comércio* (☎ 242-3500), Rua Dr Porciúncula 56, is directly across from the rodoviária. Quartos are clean and cheap, US$12/22 for singles/doubles. Apartamentos cost US$20/30.

If you want to spend a bit more, the *Hotel York* (☎ 243-2662; fax 242-8220), Rua do Imperador 78, and the *Casablanca Palace* (☎ 242-0162), Rua 16 de Março 123, have apartamentos for US$50/60. York is closer to the rodoviária.

Hotel Casablanca (☎ 242-6662) is next to the Museu Imperial and has apartamentos for US$75/90. Yes, the two Casablanca hotels are run by the same people.

There are some beautiful top-end hotels around Petrópolis. Elected the most charming in Brazil by *Guia Brasil* in 1995, the *Pousada Alcobaça* (☎ 221-1240), Rua Agostinho Goulão 298, in the suburb of Corrêas, has beautiful gardens crossed by a small river, a pool, a sauna and a tennis court. Doubles go for US$150. The excellent restaurant, which is open to the public, offers main courses for around US$20.

Places to Eat

A couple of good places for a self-serve, por quilo lunch are *Farfalle*, upstairs on the corner of Rua do Imperador and Rua Marechal Deodoro, and *Artesão*, on Rua Imperador near the post office.

Rua 16 de Março has lots of eateries, such as *Kafta*, the Arab restaurant at No 52, *Maurício's* seafood place (at No 154) and the *Midas Steak House* (at No 170).

Entertainment

For a drink in elegant surroundings, try *Casa d'Angelo*, on the corner of Rua do Imperador and Rua da Imperatriz. In the suburb of Itaipava, there are lots of nightspots along the Estrada Bernardo Coutinho. Try *Bar Nucrepe*, at No 12,701.

Getting There & Away

From Rio, buses to Petrópolis leave every half hour from 5.15 am onwards. The trip takes 1½ hours and costs US$5.

VASSOURAS

• *pop 29,000 ✉ 27700-000 ☎ 0244*

Vassouras, a quiet resort 118km north of Rio, was the most important city in the Paraíba valley in the first half of the 19th century. Surrounded by the huge fazendas of the 19th century coffee barons, the town still wears the money they poured into it. They actually were barons, for 18 of them were given titles of nobility by the Portuguese crown. With the abolition of slavery in 1888 and the resulting decline in coffee production, Vassouras' importance diminished, and this preserved the town.

Museu Chácara da Hera

Vassouras' favourite grande dame is the aristocratic heiress Eufrásia, a woman who claimed to be devoted to Vassouras despite having palaces in London, Brussels and Paris. Her former home, the Museu Chácara da Hera, is on Rua Fernandes Junior, and is open Wednesday to Sunday from 11 am to 5 pm.

Fazendas

There are a few old churches in the centre, as well as old buildings of the schools of medicine, philosophy and engineering, but the real attractions of Vassouras are the coffee fazendas. Unfortunately, if you don't have a car you're in for some long hikes. Although the fazendas are protected by the historical preservation institutes, permission must be obtained from the owners before touring the grounds. For more information, ask at the Casa de Cultura, next to the cinema on Praça Barão do Campo Belo.

Nine kilometres from town is the Fazenda Santa Eufrásia, one of the oldest in the area, dating from the end of the 18th century. If you have a car, take the road to the small town of Barão de Vassouras, 5km away. Pass through the town and after 3km you'll see the impressive Fazenda Santa Mônica, situated on the banks of the Rio Paraiba.

The Fazenda Paraiso and the Fazenda Oriente are farther out on the same road.

Places to Stay & Eat

The *Pensão Tia Maria*, just up from the bus station at Rua Domingos de Almeida 134, charges US$15 per person. There are no double beds. Other accommodation options are expensive. The *Mara Palace* (☎ 471-1993; fax 471-2524), Rua Chanceler Dr Raul Fernandes 121, charges between US$48 and US$72 a double. At Avenida Sebastião Manoel Furtado, the *Hotel Parque Santa Amália* (☎/fax 471-1897) charges US$50 for doubles, US$80 with full board.

The *Pensão Tia Maria* and a few other places nearby have reasonable comida caseira. But for top restaurants, you are about a hundred years too late.

Getting There & Away

The bus station is on Praça Juiz Machado Jr. Frequent buses make the 2½ hour trip to Rio (US$6). The first leaves at 6.15 am, with others leaving every 1½ hours after that. The last one is at 8.30 pm.

TERESÓPOLIS

• *pop 126,000* ✉ *25950-000* ☎ *021*

Do as Empress Maria Tereza used to do and escape the steamy summer heat of Rio into the cool mountain retreat of Teresópolis (910m), the highest city in the state, nestled in the strange, organ-pipe rock formations of the Serra dos Órgãos. The road from Rio to Teresópolis first passes the sinuous curves of a padded green jungle then winds and climbs past bald peaks which have poked through the jungle cover to touch the clouds.

The city itself is modern, prosperous and dull. The principal attraction is the landscape and its natural treasures – in particular the strangely shaped peaks of **Pedra do Sino** (2263m), **Pedra do Açu** (2230m), **Agulha do Diabo** (2020m), **Nariz do Frade** (1919m), **Dedo de Deus** (1651m), **Pedra da Ermitage** (1485m) and **Dedo de Nossa Senhora** (1320m).

With so many peaks, it's no wonder that this is the mountain climbing, rock climbing and trekking centre of Brazil. The region has extensive trails and it's possible to trek over the forested mountains to Petrópolis. Unfortunately, the trails are unmarked and off the maps but it's easy and inexpensive to hire a guide at the national park, or go with a group organised by one of the hiking and mountaineering clubs in Rio.

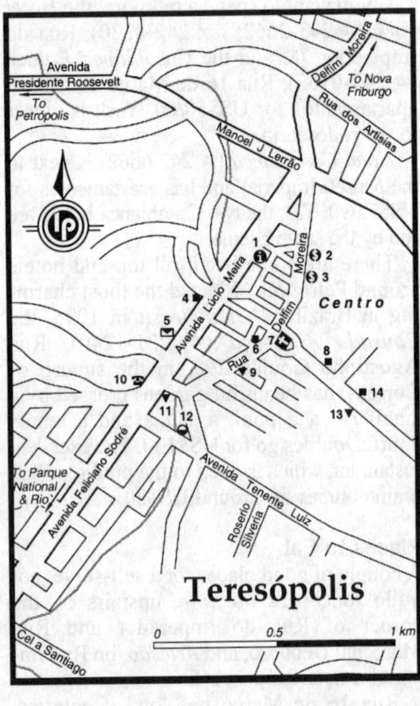

1 Tourist Stand
2 Banco do Brasil
3 Bradesco ATM
4 Hotel Comary
5 Post Office
6 Hotel Avenida
7 Igreja Matriz
8 Várzea Palace Hotel
9 Cheiro de Mato
10 Posto Telefônica
11 Sand's
12 Rodoviária
13 Tempero com Arte
14 Center Hotel

Teresópolis is, however, not simply for alpinists alone: it's a centre for sports lovers of all varieties. There are facilities for volleyball, motocross, and equestrian activities – many of Brazil's finest thoroughbreds are raised here – not to mention football. Teresópolis also bears the distinction of being the training base of Brazil's World Cup squad.

Orientation

Teresópolis is built up along one main street which changes names every few blocks. Starting from the highway to Rio in the Soberbo part of town and continuing north along the Avenida Rotariana (with access to the national park), the road is renamed Avenida Oliveira Botelho, Avenida Alberto Torres, Feliciano Sodré and then Avenida Lúcio Meira. Most of the sites are west of the main drag and up in the hills. The cheap hotels are near the Igreja Matriz de Santa Tereza, Praça Baltazar da Silveira.

Information

Tourist Office The Terminal Turístico tourist office is in Soberbo, at the intersection with the road to Rio. It's open daily from 8 am to 11 pm, and the view of Rio from the office is great. If you're travelling by bus, however, it's a hassle to get to; you can pick up the same maps at the tourist stand on Avenida Lúcio Meira, which is open Monday to Friday from 8.30 am to 5 pm, and weekends from 8.30 am to 1.30 pm.

Post & Communications The post office is on Avenida Lúcio Meira. The Telerj station for long-distance telephone calls is close by.

Parque Nacional da Serra dos Órgãos

The main entrance to the national park is open daily from 8 am to 5 pm (admission US$0.50). The 3.5km walking trail, waterfalls, swimming pools, tended lawns and gardens make this a very pretty park for a picnic. There are some chalets for rent at the park substation, 12km towards Rio from the park entrance. There are also camping sites.

Other Attractions

The **Mulher de Pedra** (Rock Woman) rock formation, 12km from Teresópolis towards Nova Friburgo, really does look like a reclining woman.

Colina dos Mirantes is a good place to view the Serra dos Órgãos range and the city. On clear days you can see as far as the Baía de Guanabara. To get there, take Avenida Feliciano Sodré. The Quebra Frascos, the royal family of the Second Empire, lived in this neighbourhood. The best spot for viewing the **Dedo de Deus peak** is from Soberbo.

Places to Stay – Budget

The cheapest place is the *Hotel Comary* (☎/fax 742-3463), Avenida Almirante Lúcio Meira 467, which has quartos for US$8 without breakfast. Double apartamentos are US$30. Have breakfast at the *padaria* (bakery) next door. The *Várzea Palace Hotel* (☎ 742-0878) is at Rua Prefeito Sebastião Teixeira 41/55, behind the Igreja Matriz. This grand old white building with red trim has been a Teresópolis institution since 1916. Can this really be a budget hotel? Cheap and classy quartos are US$21/30, apartamentos are US$30/45.

Other hotels nearby include the *Center Hotel* (☎ 742-5890), at Sebastião Teixeira 245, which has nice apartamentos for US$54/65. The *Hotel Avenida* (☎/fax 742-2751), Rua Delfim Moreira 439 in front of the Igreja Matriz, has decent apartamentos for US$30/40.

Places to Stay – Top End

The more expensive hotels are out of town. The *Hotel Alpina* (☎/fax 742-5252) at Km 4 on the road to Petrópolis has apartamentos for US$80 a double. There's a golf club across the road.

Along the Teresópolis to Nova Friburgo road are two hotels. Run by the Hare Krishnas, the *Pousada Vrajabhumi* (☎/fax 644-6220) at Km 6 is in the middle of a forest reserve. There are chalets and natural swimming pools, and rates start at US$60 a double (including all meals, which are vegetarian).

The hotel restaurant is open to the public for lunch and dinner. At Km 27, the *Hotel Rosa dos Ventos* (☎ 742-8833; fax 742-8174) is the only Brazilian hotel in the international Relais & Chateaux chain. It has everything except that no one under the age of 16 is permitted to stay here. Daily rates, breakfast and lunch included, are around US$200.

Places to Eat

Restaurante Irene (☎ 742-2901) at Rua Tenente Luís Meireles 1800 in Bom Retiro, basks in its reputation for providing the best *haute cuisine* in Teresópolis. It's expensive and reservations are required.

Cheiro de Mato, Rua Delfim Moreira 140, is a decent vegetarian restaurant. *Tempero com Arte*, opposite the Center Hotel, is a comfy little place serving some good home cooking. *Sand's*, Avenida Almirante Lúcio Meira, near the bus station, has a cheap self-serve lunch spread.

Getting There & Away

The rodoviária is on Rua 1 do Maio, off Avenida Tenente Luiz. Buses to Rio depart every half hour from 5 am to 10 pm (US$6, 1½ hours, 95km). There are seven buses to Petrópolis (from 6 am to 9 pm), and plenty to Novo Friburgo.

Getting Around

To get to the park from the city centre, take the hourly Albequerque Soberbo bus (US$0.60). Its last stop is the Terminal Turístico in Soberbo. An alternative is to take the more frequent Alto bus, and get off at the Praçinha da Alto – a short walk from the park.

NOVA FRIBURGO

• *pop 170,000* ✉ *28600-000* ☎ *024*

During the Napoleonic Wars, Dom João II encouraged immigration to Brazil. At the time, people were starving in Switzerland so, in 1818, 300 families from the Swiss canton of Friburg packed up and headed for Brazil. The passage to Brazil was horrible; many died but enough families survived to settle in the mountains and establish a small village in the New World.

Like Teresópolis and Petrópolis, Nova Friburgo has good hotels and restaurants, as well as many lovely natural attractions: waterfalls, woods, trails, sunny mountain mornings and cool evenings. (It's chilly and rainy during the winter months, from June to August.) The Cónego area is interesting for its Germanic architecture and its apparently perpetually blooming flowers.

Information

Tourist Office The tourist office on Praça Dr Demervel B Moreira is open daily from 8 am to 8 pm. As well as maps, it has a complete list of hotels, including the cheapest, with updated prices.

Post & Communications The post office is opposite Praça Getúlio Vargas. The Telerj office is on Avenida Alberto Braune.

Things to See & Do

Most of the sights are a few kilometres out of town. Scout out the surrounding area from **Morro da Cruz** (1800m). The chairlift station is in the centre of town at Praça Teleférico. The chairlift to Morro da Cruz runs from 9 am to 6 pm on weekends and holidays. **Pico da Caledônia** (2310m) offers fantastic views, and launching sites for hang-gliders. It's a 6km uphill hike, but the view is worth it.

You can hike to **Pedra do Cão Sentado**, explore the **Furnas do Catete** rock formations, or visit the mountain towns of **Bom Jardim** (23km north on Hwy BR-492) or **Lumiar** (25km from Mury and a little bit before the entrance to Friburgo). Hippies, cheap pensions, waterfalls, walking trails and white-water canoe trips abound in Lumiar.

Places to Stay

Primus (☎ 523-2898), up a steep hill on Rua Adolfo Lautz 128, is the best deal in town. Very comfortable apartamentos with everything (including padded toilet seats!) go for US$25/35 with a huge breakfast spread. The views are great and it's nice to watch the birds who come to the feeders

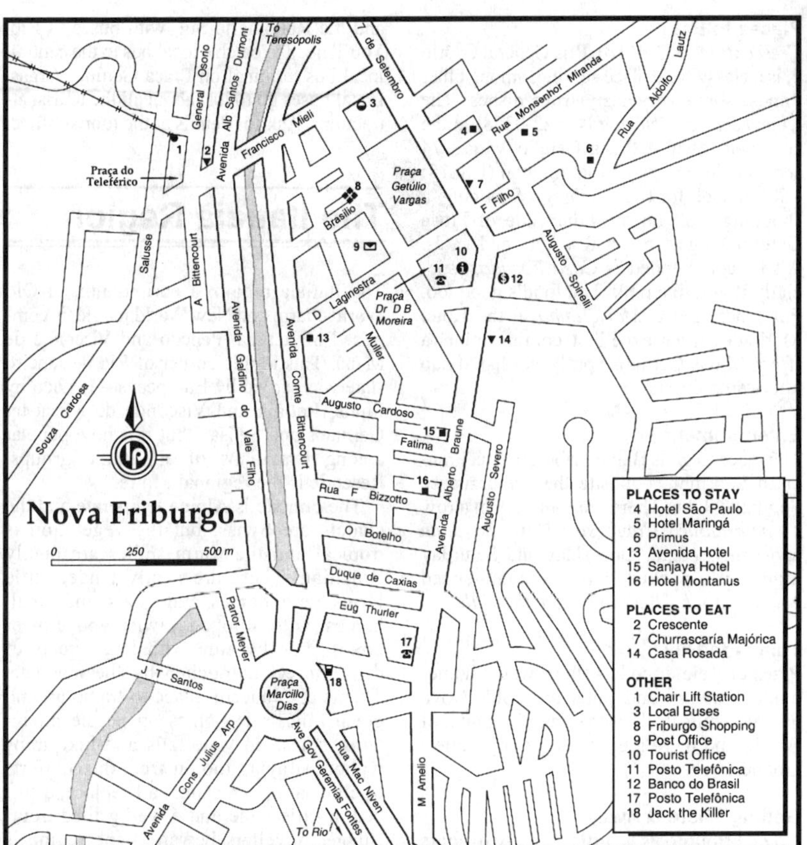

outside. Another good deal is the *Hotel São Paulo* (☎ 522-9135), Rua Monsenhor Miranda 41. In a restored old building, it has a pool and apartamentos for US$31/40. Also recommended is the *Hotel Maringá* (☎ 522-2309), Rua Monsenhor Miranda 110. It has quartos for US$15/25, apartamentos for US$25/35 and a restaurant downstairs. Another good option is the *Hotel Montanus* (☎ 522-1235), Rua Fernando Bizzotto 26, which has simple apartamentos for US$34/42, but you can bargain them down. The *Avenida Hotel* (☎ 522-9772), Rua Dante Laginestra 89, is a bit cheaper, with quartos for US$20/30 and apartamentos for US$33/40.

A good, mid-range place in the centre of town is the *Sanjaya Hotel* (☎ 522-6052), Avenida Alberto Braune 58. It charges US$57/72.

Rates at the top hotels are all for double occupancy and include full board. In town, *Sans Souci* (☎/fax 522-7752), Rua Itajai, charges US$70. The *Hotel Garlipp* (☎/fax 542-1330) is in Mury, 10km out on the road to Niterói, and apartamentos start at US$85.

Places to Eat
Crescente (☎ 523-4616), Rua General Osório 4, is a classy little place serving, among other things, some very tasty trout dishes. The *Churrascaría Majórica* (☎ 522-0358) in the centre of town at Praça Getúlio Vargas 74 serves a decent cut of filet mignon (US$15) – it's enough for two. *Friburgo Shopping,* a shopping mall on the other side of Praça Getúlio Vargas, has a few bars and cafés. Also recommended is *Casa Rosada*, especially if you like pink. The food's good too. For lunch, *Dona Mariquinha* in the Hotel Maringá serves excellent comida mineira (from Minas Gerais). You'll feel like a nap afterwards for sure.

Entertainment
The place to go is Baixo Friburgo, Rua Francisco Sobrinho, opposite the Friburguense Football Clube. There are four bars in a row – *Ancoradouro*, *Campestre*, *Deixo Saudade* and *Frago Legal*. On Friday and Saturday nights, it's packed. Other recommended bars are *Bock's Beer* and *Jack the Killer*.

Things to Buy
Praça do Teleférico has shops where homemade liqueurs and jams are sold. Nova Friburgo bills itself as the lingerie capital of Brazil, and there are lots of factory outlets around town.

Getting There & Away
Nova Friburgo is a little over two hours (US$6) by bus from Rio, via Niterói, on 1001 Lines. The ride is along a picturesque, winding, misty jungle road. From Novo Friburgo, buses to Rio leave every half hour to an hour from 6 am to 9.30 pm. To Teresópolis there are four daily buses, at 7 and 11 am, and 3 and 6 pm (US$5, two hours). If you're heading to the coast, an adventurous trip is to catch a bus to Lumiar and from there catch another to Macaé.

Getting Around
There are two long-distance bus terminals in Novo Friburgo: the Rodoviária Norte, where they depart for Petropolis and Teresópolis, and the Rodoviária Sul, with buses to Rio. You'll need to catch a local bus to the central, local bus terminal on Praça Getúlio Vargas. Local buses go to just about all the tourist attractions. Ask for details at the tourist office.

The Itatiaia Region

The Itatiaia region, a curious mix of Old World charm and New World jungle, is comprised of Itatiaia, Penedo and Visconde de Mauá. This idyllic corner of Rio de Janeiro state was settled by Europeans – Penedo by Finns, Itatiaia and Visconde de Mauá by Germans and Swiss – but it is now popular among Brazilians of all ethnic groups. Resende is the regional centre.

The climate is Alpine temperate and the chalets are Swiss, but the vegetation is tropical and the warm smiles are purely Brazilian. There are neatly tended little farms with horses and goats and small homes with clipped lawns and flower boxes, side by side with large tracts of dense forest untouched by the machete. This is a wonderful place to tramp around green hills, ride ponies up purple mountains, splash in waterfalls and hike trails without straying too far from the comforts of civilisation – a sauna, a fireplace, a soft bed, a little wine and a well-grilled trout! Budget travellers beware – the region is frequented by wealthy Cariocas and Paulistas, so food and accommodation tend to be expensive.

The region lies in the Serra da Mantiqueira's Itatiaia massif, in the north-west corner of Rio de Janeiro, and borders the states of São Paulo and Minas Gerais. The Parque Nacional do Itatiaia is due north of the Serra de Bocaina.

RESENDE
• *pop 94,000* ✉ *27500-000* ☎ *024*

Resende, the largest city in the Itatiaia region, is the transport hub for Penedo and Visconde de Mauá. It has no tourist attractions but is the home of the military academy (Academia Militar das Agulhas Negras) and a university.

Places to Stay

The military and the university may account for the very cheap hotels in the Campos Elízio part of the city. The best is the *Hotel Presidente* (☎ 354-5464), Rua Luis Pistarni 43, with simple but clean single/double quartos for US$15/20. Double apartamentos are US$25. Lodging doesn't come much cheaper in this part of Brazil. Unless you are camping, you are likely to pay at least twice as much in Penedo, Mauá or the national park, but it's worth the extra to stay in those places rather than commute from Resende.

Getting There & Away

Buses from Rio de Janeiro and São Paulo go to and from Resende several times a day. From Resende it's reasonably easy to hitch or catch a taxi or bus to your final destination. The Cidade de Aço line runs 11 buses a day to Resende from Rio, the first leaving at 7 am and the last at 9 pm (US$7, 2½ hours).

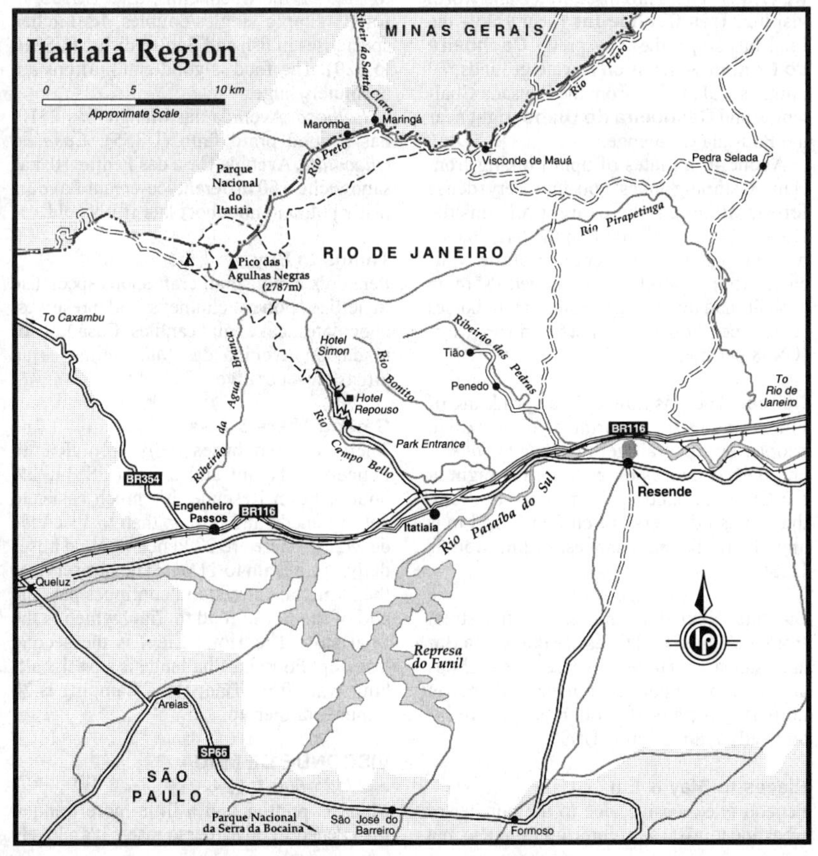

PENEDO

✉ 27500-000 ☎ 024

Finnish immigrants, led by Toivo Uuskallio, settled Penedo in 1929. If the beautiful Scandinavian woodwork doesn't convince you of this, the number of saunas will. The Finns planted citrus groves along the banks of the Rio das Pedras, but when this enterprise failed they turned to preparing Finnish jams and jellies, home-made liqueurs and sauces.

Things to See & Do

Penedo's main attractions are the forest and waterfalls. There are three waterfalls worth visiting: **Três Cachoeiras** (near Tião – the final bus stop), the very pretty **Cachoeira do Roman** which is on private grounds, 10 minutes walk uphill from the Pousada Challenge, and **Cachoeira do Diabo,** right near the Pousada Challenge.

About 40 minutes of uphill hiking from Hans Camping takes you into very dense forest, although there are trails inside. Hopefully you will run into the large bands of big monkeys and steer clear of the wildcats. At the point where Penedo's main asphalt road turns to dirt, you can hire horses (US$5 per hour) or a horse and carriage (US$8 per hour).

Dances There is now only a sprinkling of Finns among the assortment of Brazilian people, but they all get together for *letkiss* and *jenkiss* dances every Saturday night at the Clube Finlandês. From 9 pm to 2 am, the Finnish dancers put on Old World togs and do traditional dances. Admission is US$5.

Saunas Next door and across the street from the Clube Finlandês are the Sauna Bar and Sauna Finlandesa. These sweat shops are open to the public from early afternoon until 10 pm (later if enough people are interested). Admission is US$5.

Places to Stay & Eat

Penedo is expensive, due to the number of weekend tourists who come up from Rio, but the accommodation is well above average, the food is good and daily rates usually include breakfast and lunch. *Hans Camping*, several kilometres up from the last bus stop, charges US$10 per person for camping sites. It has a sauna, a natural swimming pool, a bar and a nearby waterfall.

The *Pousada Challenge* (☎ 351-1389), about 1km up from Tião on the Estrada da Fazendinha, has very clean prefabricated chalets which sleep three. Doubles cost US$70, including breakfast, lunch and use of the pool and sauna.

The *Hotel Lidel* (☎/fax 351-1204), next to Tião on the Cachoeiras, asks US$35/45 for its simple singles/doubles. Its kitchen specialises in fish and Bahian dishes (US$10 to $20). The food is good and portions are absolutely huge.

Palhoça, Avenida das Mangueiras 2510, has a good prato feito (US$5). *Casa do Chocolate*, Avenida Casa das Pedras 10, has sandwiches, 50 different ice-cream flavours if it's hot, and hot chocolate if it's cold.

Things to Buy

Penedo's many small craft shops specialise in jellies, honey, chutneys and preserves, chocolates, cakes and candles. Casa Encabulada, on Avenida das Mangueiras, is an artists' co-operative.

Getting There & Away

There are two buses daily from Rio to Penedo at 11 am and 5 pm (US$11, 2½ hours). From Resende, it's much easier to get to Penedo and Itatiaia than to Visconde de Mauá. There are 22 Penedo-bound buses daily, from 6 am to 11 pm. The bus services the 3km main street and continues past the end of the paved road to Tião, which is the final stop. The Hotel Lidel is the second last stop. Pousada Challenge is a brisk half-hour walk from Tião; Hans Camping is 20 minutes farther up.

VISCONDE DE MAUÁ

✉ 27525-000 ☎ 024

Mauá is prettier and a little more tranquil than Penedo, and harder to reach. It's a lovely place, with streams, tinkling goat bells, cosy chalets and country lanes graced with wildflowers. There are horses for hire by the footbridge (US$4 per hour), but some of them are pretty small.

Orientation

Mauá is actually made up of three small villages a few kilometres apart. The bus stops first at Vila Mauá, the largest village. Vila Maringá, 3km away on the other side of the Rio Preto, is actually in Minas Gerais, and has lots of restaurants and places to stay. At the end of the bus route, 3km farther on, is Vila Maromba which has restaurants and pousadas, but not as many as Maringá. Most travellers stay in Maringá or Maromba. Hitching around here is fairly easy.

Information

There are two places where you can go for tourist information. One is a cabana at the entrance to Vila Mauá where you'll find information about activities and a list of places to stay, though not the cheapest ones. It's open Tuesday to Sunday from 8 am to 8 pm (closed for lunch). The Casa do Turista has similar information. It's 1km farther along the road to Maromba.

Things to See & Do

The **Santa Clara Cachoeira**, the nicest waterfall in the area, is a 40 minute walk from Vila Maromba in Maringá. For a bit of a hike, climb up through the bamboo groves on either side of the falls.

The young and the restless can follow the trail from Maromba to the **Cachoeira Veu de Noiva** in the Parque Nacional do Itatiaia, a full day's hike each way. It's possible to kayak the rapids of the Rio Preto which divides Minas Gerais from Rio. It also has small river beaches and natural pools.

Places to Stay

Most pousadas offer full board with lodging; small signposts at each intersection make them easy to find. If you don't want full board, you can bargain the price down quite a bit.

In Maringá, a handy place to stay is the *Casarão* (☎ 354-3030). It's a hostel, camp ground and regular pousada rolled into one. Small, simple apartamentos with veranda and hammock are US$65 a double with full board. Camping sites are US$5 per person. The hostel costs US$25 per person with full board and treks can also be organised. The bus stops right outside.

The *Hotel Casa Alpininha* (☎/fax 387-1390) is in Maringá on the other side of the river. Doubles cost US$50, including breakfast and lunch. Lots of places in Maringá charge around US$50 a double.

Maromba has a few cheap pousadas next to the bus stop. The *Pousada Sonhador*, on the right-hand side of the church, charges US$15/20 a single/double, including breakfast. It also serves a good prato feito.

Places to Eat

Rua Ponte de Pedestres in Maringá has a couple of good places. *Filho da Truta* has the ubiquitous por quilo and *Chapeau Noir* has home cooking, often with by live music. *Renascer*, also in Maringá, serves trout for US$10. *Casarão* serves comida caseira. The US$10 plate is plenty for two people.

Things to Buy

The Mensageiro dos Ventos is a hippie store which sells T-shirts, embroidered blouses, natural perfumes and soaps. Casa da Chocolate in Maringá has plenty of home-made goodies.

Getting There & Away

The two daily buses from Resende to Visconde de Mauá (US$5, about 2½ hours on a winding dirt road) leave at 4 and 6 pm Monday to Saturday. On Sunday there's one bus at 8 am. Buses leave for Resende at 7.45 and 10 am every day, except Sunday, when a bus leaves at 4pm. From Rio, there are direct buses on Friday night at 7.30 pm and Saturday at 7.30 am. Direct buses to Rio leave on Sunday evening at 4 pm and Monday morning at 8.45 am. The trip takes 4½ hours and the fare is US$10.

Getting Around
If you get sick of walking, Bike Montanha, in Maringá, rents mountain bikes for US$3 an hour.

PARQUE NACIONAL DO ITATIAIA
This national park, established in 1937 to protect 120 sq km of ruggedly beautiful land, contains over 400 species of native birds, as well as monkeys and sloths. It features lakes, rivers, waterfalls, alpine meadows and primary and secondary Atlantic rainforests. Don't let the tropical plants fool you; temperatures drop below freezing in June and, occasionally, Itatiaia even has a few snowy days!

Museum
The park headquarters, the museum and **Lago Azul** (Blue Lake) are 10km in from the Via Dutra highway (BR-116). The museum, open Tuesday to Sunday from 8 am to 4 pm, has glass cases full of stuffed and mounted animals, pinned moths and snakes in jars.

Activities
Mountain and rock climbing, and trekking enthusists will want to pit themselves against the local peaks, cliffs and trails.

Every two weeks, a group scales the **Agulhas Negras** peak. At 2787m, it's the highest in the area. For more information, contact the Grupo Excursionista de Agulhas Negras (☎ 354-2587), and refer to the sections on Hiking and Mountaineering in the Facts for the Visitor chapter.

A walk to the Abroucas refuge, at the base of Agulhas Negras, is a 26km, eight hour trek from the park entrance. The mountain refuge can sleep 24 people and is accessible by car from the Engenheiro Passos to São Lourenço road (near the Minas Gerais and Rio de Janeiro border). Reservations are required. Call the IBAMA in Resende (☎ 352-1461) for maps and advice from the park IBAMA office before setting off.

Simpler hikes include the walk between Hotel Simon and Hotel Repouso (where the painter Guignard lived, worked and left a few of his paintings), and the 20 minute walk from the Sítio Jangada to the Poronga waterfalls.

Places to Stay
Camping is the cheapest option inside the park. There's the camping ground *Aporaoca*, 4km from the main entrance to the park. (When you get to the Gula & Artes store and the ice-cream shop, there's a signpost; the camping ground is 200m up behind.) Sites are US$3 per person.

Sloths eat, sleep, mate and give birth while hanging upside down!

There is a YHA hostel, *Ipê Amarelo* (☎ 352-1232), Rua João Mauricio de Macedo Costa 352, in Campo Alegre, a suburb of Itatiaia. It has bicycles for rent.

The *Pousada do Elefante*, close to the Hotel Simon, is the cheapest hotel in the park. It's basic but well located. It charges US$40 for doubles with three filling but repetitive meals a day. Other hotels are expensive, three-star Embratur affairs with saunas and swimming pools, such as the *Hotel Simon* (☎ 352-1122), which charges US$100 for a double with full board. The *Hotel do Ypê* (☎ 352-1453; fax 352-1166) charges US$75 a double or US$100 to stay in a chalet. Not far from the park entrance, the *Hotel Aldéia da Serra* (☎ 352-1152) is reasonably priced, with chalets for US$50/65, all inclusive.

Getting There & Away

Every 20 minutes on weekdays and every 40 minutes on weekends (from 7 am to 11pm), there is a bus from Resende to the town of Itatiaia. From Praça São José in Itatiaia, take the van with the Hotel Simon sign up to the park. It leaves at 8 and 10 am, noon, and 2, 5 and 7 pm. The ride costs US$3 and you'll also have to pay the park entry fee (US$2) as you go through the main gate. A taxi costs US$15.

East of Rio de Janeiro

SAQUAREMA

• *pop 45,000* ✉ *28990-000* ☎ *024*

After the famous beaches of Rio and Baía de Guanabara, with their high-rise hotels and bars spilling onto the sands, the quiet, clean beaches east of Rio are a welcome change.

Saquarema, 100km from Rio de Janeiro, sits between long stretches of open beach, lagoons and mountains. The town takes unusual pride in the natural beauty of its setting. Polluting industries are forbidden in the municipality, so it's still possible to find sloths and bands of monkeys in the jungles. Motorboats aren't allowed to muck up the lakes and lagoons, which means the water is still pure and fish and shrimp are abundant. The long shoreline of fine, white sand and clean water attracts surfers, sports fishermen and sun worshippers.

Saquarema is a horse-breeding and fruit-growing centre; you can visit the orchards and pick fruit, or hire horses or a jeep and take to the hills.

Ah, but the beaches ... **Boqueirão, Barra Nova** and **Jaconé**, south of town, are long and empty save for a couple of fishing villages. **Praia Itaúna** is 3km north of Saquarema where an annual surfing contest is held during the first two weeks of October.

History

On 17 March 1531, Martim Afonso de Sousa founded a Portuguese settlement here and met with the Tamoio Indian chief Sapuguaçu. Nonplussed by de Sousa's five ships and 400 sailors, Sapuguaçu chose to ally the Tamoios with the French. In 1575 Antônio Salema, then Governor of Rio de Janeiro, decided to break the Tamoio-French alliance and, with an army of over 1000 men, massacred the Indians and their French military advisers.

The next big event in Saquarema's history was the slave revolt of Ipitangas, in which 400 slaves took over the plantation mansion and kicked out their master. For a few days, the slaves held the town and fought against the cavalry which rode out from Niterói. The town pillory, Bandeque's Post (named after the leader of the slave revolt), was in use as recently as the end of the 19th century.

Information

Tourist Office The Secretaria de Turismo at the Prefeitura is quite useless. The best place to go for information is Saquatur Toulouse Lagos Turismo (☎/fax 651-2161) in Pousada Ilhas Gregas, Itaúna. The manager, Conceição, is very helpful. Her husband Luis speaks English and French.

Money There's a Banco do Brasil in town. If it isn't changing money, ask Conceição, at her travel agency.

Post & Communications The post office is close to the bus stop in Praça Oscar de Macedo Soares. The posto telefônico is in Rua Barão da Saquarema.

Special Events

Saquarema hosts the NS de Nazaré mass on 7 and 8 September. It attracts around 150,000 pilgrims, second only to the Nazaré celebrations of Belém.

Places to Stay – Budget

The *Pousada Ilhas Gregas* (☎ 651-1008) is excellent. Only 100m from the beach at Rua do Prado 671 in Itaúna, it has bicycles, a swimming pool, a sauna and a bar/restaurant. It's easy to catch a taxi here from the bus station in Saquarema, but if you feel like a hike, get off the bus at the petrol station 'Sudoeste' and walk for half an hour along Avenida Oceânica, until you get to the centre of Itaúna (where there are lots of beachfront bars and kiosks). Go along Avenida NS de Nazareth and take the second street on the left (Rua das Caravelas), then the first street on your right (Rua do Prado). It charges US$18 per person.

The *Pousada da Mansão* (☎ (021) 259-2100 in Rio), Avenida Oceanica 353, has rooms in the old mansion for US$15/25 a single/double, and there's camping there too. Sonia, who runs the place, speaks English. The *Hotel Saquarema* (☎ 651-2275) right at the bus stop charges US$20 per person, but stay there only as a last resort. It's OK, but there are better places for the same price.

The *Pousada da Titia* (☎ 651-2058), Avenida Salgado Filho 774, is a good alternative, with quartos for US$20 a double and apartamentos for US$30.

Places to Stay – Top End

There are stacks of places charging around US$60 a double. (If you're thinking of staying in one of these places, go and see Conceição at Saquatur. She has brochures and all the latest information. It will save you quite a lot of legwork.) A couple of the popular ones are the *Pousada Pedra d'Agua Maasai* (☎ 651-1092), near Itaúna beach, and the *Pousada Pratagi* (☎ 651-2161), Avenida Salgado Filho 4484.

The *Hotel Fazenda Serra da Castelhana* (☎ 962-0919), Km 4 on the road to Latino Melo, charges US$90 a double with full board and has very good food. It's in the suburb of Palmital.

Places to Eat

There are lots of lanchonetes at Itaúna. You might like to try *Garota da Itaúna*, Avenida Oceânica 165, and the restaurant at the Pousada Pedra d'Agua Maasai, which specialises in seafood dishes.

Getting There & Away

From Rio to Saquarema there are buses leaving every hour from 6.30 am to 8.30 pm. The two hour trip costs US$6. To get to Cabo Frio, take a local bus to Bacaxá. From there, buses to Cabo leave every half hour.

ARRAIAL DO CABO

• *pop 22,000 ✉ 28930-000 ☎ 024*

Arraial do Cabo sits on a square corner of land, with Cabo Frio 10km due north and Praia Grande stretching due west 40km (continuous with Praia Maçambaba). The village of Arraial do Cabo spreads out from the edges of four bays and has beaches that compare with the finest in Búzios but, unlike Búzios, Arraial is a place where people live and work. The saltworks of the Companhia Nacional de Alcalis, north of town, process both salt and *barrília*, a type of phosphate extracted from the salt.

Information

There's no tourist office in Arraial but you don't really need one as the layout is fairly straightforward and the attractions are the beaches. The post office is in Praça Castelo Branco and the Telerj office is next to the Hotel Praia Grande.

ANDREW DRAFFEN

JOHN MAIER, JR

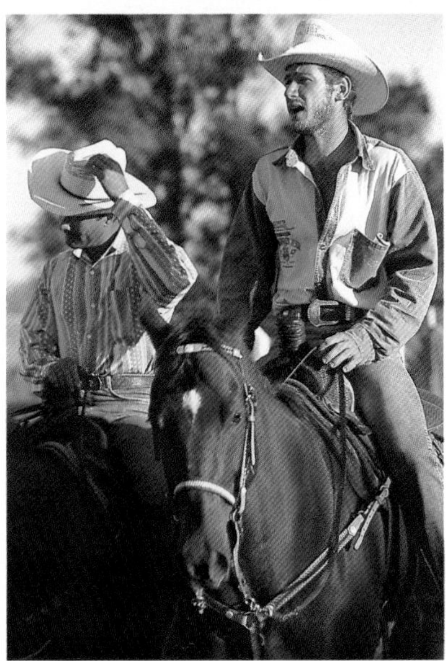

JOHN MAIER, JR

Top: São Paulo's new market,
Bottom Left: Sunbathing in downtown São Paulo
Bottom Right: Vaqueiros, São Paulo state

JOHN MAIER, JR

JOHN MAIER, JR

JOHN MAIER, JR

ANDREW DRAFFEN

Left: German style archicture in Blumenau

Middle: Windmill, Blumenau

Right: Waterfall in Rio Grande do Sul

Bottom: The mighty Foz do Iguaçu

Beaches

'Discovered' many years ago by Amerigo Vespucci, **Praia dos Anjos** has beautiful turquoise water but a little too much boat traffic for comfortable swimming. The favourite beaches in town are **Praia do Forno**, **Praia Brava** and **Praia Grande**. Stretching along a pretty piece of road to Cabo Frio, Praia do Forte has bleached white sand and a backdrop of low scrub, cacti and grasses. The **Museu Oceanográfico** on Praia dos Anjos is open Tuesday to Sunday from 9 am to noon and 1 to 4.30 pm.

The **Gruta Azul** (Blue Cavern) on the far side of Ilha de Cabo Frio, is another beautiful spot. Be alert to the tides as the entrance to the underwater cavern isn't always open.

Places to Stay

Expect prices to rise by 30% in high season. Prices quoted here are for low season.

The Camping Club do Brasil has a camping ground *CCB – RJ05* (☎ 622-1023) at Praia dos Anjos. It charges US$10 per person. The *Hotel Praia Grande* (☎ 622-1369), Rua Dom Pedro 41, is a good cheapie in the centre of town with US$15/30 singles/doubles.

At Praia dos Anjos, the *Porto dos Anjos* (☎ 622-1629), Avenida Luis Correa 8, is a house that's been converted into a pousada. Its double rooms (US$30) have sea views. *Pousada da Prainha* (☎ 622-2512), Rua D 90, is close to Prainha and has simple apartamentos for US$45. Also close to Prainha is *Pousada dos Corais* (☎ 622-2182), Rua E 101, with a pool and air-conditioned apartamentos for US$60 a double. The *Santorini Pousada dos Navegantes* (☎/fax 622-2278), on Praia Grande, is a very pretty resort hotel with a courtyard pool. Its apartamentos cost US$70/80.

Diving Arrail Sub (☎ 622-1149) and Send-Mar (☎ 622-1356) both run diving trips.

Places to Eat

Garrafa de Nansen Restaurante, Rua Santa Cruz 4, is a classy seafood place where you can eat very well for about US$15 per person. Cheaper eats are available at *Meu Cantinho*, in the centre of town at Rua Dom Pedro I, No 18. Its US$10 fish dinners will easily feed two. Pousada da Prainha also has a good self-serve restaurant. The best restaurant in town is *Todos as Prazeres* (☎ 622-2365), Rua José Pinto Macedo near Prainha, with creative dishes such as fish in orange sauce with coconut farofa, and apple and gorgonzola soup.

Getting There & Away

There are five direct buses daily from Rio to Arraial, the first at 7 am and the last at midnight (US$11, three hours). An alternative is to catch one of the frequent buses to Cabo Frio. Then take the municipal bus from Cabo Frio (US$0.60), which loops around Arraial and returns to Cabo Frio every 20 minutes.

Getting Around

Boat Seu João runs a three hour boat trip to Gruta Azul, Praia do Forno, As Prainhas, Boqueirão and Praia Ilha do Farol for US$12 per person. For more information, ask at the Pousada dos Corais.

CABO FRIO

• *pop 102,000* ✉ *28900-000* ☎ *024*

The Cabo Frio district formerly comprised Cabo Frio (the most populous town), Búzios (the wealthy sophisticated resort) and Arraial do Cabo (which has since become independent, politically and economically, because of its salt industry).

History

According to Márcio Verneck, a local historian, Cabo Frio was inhabited at least 5500 years ago. Before the Portuguese arrived, the warring Tamoio and Goitacazes tribes lived here. In 1503 the Portuguese armada, under the command of Amerigo Vespucci, landed at Praia dos Anjos in Arraial do Cabo and 24 men were left behind to start a settlement, one of the first in the Americas. Fantastic reports about this community became the model for Thomas More's *Utopia*.

The economy of the Portuguese settlement was based on the coastal brazil wood, which was felled and shipped back to Europe. Portuguese vessels were at the mercy of Dutch and French corsairs until 1615, when the Portuguese defeated their European foes, founded Santa Helena de Cabo Frio, and took the French-built fort of São Mateus to protect their trade. In time, the Franciscans joined the settlement and built the NS dos Anjos convent. They were followed by the Jesuits at Fazenda Campo Novo. By the 1800s, with the brazil-wood stands completely destroyed, the economy was geared toward fishing and, more recently, tourism, saltworks and chemical industries.

Orientation

Canal do Itajuru links the Lagoa de Araruama to the Atlantic Ocean. Cabo Frio lies to one side of this canal. The town is 2km along Avenida Júlia Kubitschek from the bus station. There's a map of Cabo Frio on the wall of the bus station.

Information

Tourist Office There are tourist information booths at the rodoviária and at Avenida do Contorno, Praia do Forte. They have hotel information, but no English is spoken.

Money There's a Banco do Brasil at Praça Porto Rocha 44 and a Bradesco ATM at Avenida Assunção 904.

Post & Communications The post office is at Largo de Santo Antônio 55, in the centre, and the Telerj office is on Praça Porto Rocha.

Forte São Mateus

This stone fortress, a stronghold against pirates, was built in 1616, and is open from 10 am to 4 pm Tuesday to Sunday. It's at the end of Praia do Forte.

Dunes

There are three sand dune spots in and about Cabo Frio. The dunes of **Praia do Peró**, a super beach for surfing and surf-casting, are 6km north in the direction of Búzios, near Ogivas and after Praia Brava and Praia das Conchas. The **Dama Branca** (White Lady) sand dunes are on the road to Arraial do Cabo. The **Pontal** dunes of Praia do Forte town beach stretch from the fort to Miranda hill.

The dunes can be dangerous because of robberies, so get advice from the locals before heading out to the beaches and dunes.

Places to Stay

Cabo Frio is a bit too built-up, and it's hard to understand why anyone would want to stay here rather than at Arraial do Cabo or Búzios. If you do enjoy staying in crummy beach cities, both the *Camping Club do Brasil* (☎ 643-3124), and *Bosque Club* (☎ 645-0096) on Rua dos Passageiros at No 700 and No 600 respectively have camping sites.

There's a good hostel, the YHA *Praia das Palmeiras* (☎ 643-2866), at Rua Praia das Palmeiras 1. It has a minibus that does trips to Búzios. To get there on foot from the bus station, go up Rua Geraldo de Abreu. After 100m, turn left on Avenida Excelcior (by the canal) and follow it to the shore of the lagoon. The hostel is 50m to the left. In total, the distance is 1.2km.

The cheapest hotels in the Centro are located on Rua José Bonifácio. Try the *Atlântico* (☎ 643-0996; fax 643-0662), at No 31, where basic apartamentos with fan are US$35 per person – 30% less in low season.

There are lots of top-end hotels along the waterfront, but for the money, you'll have a better time in Búzios.

Places to Eat

There are some good eateries around Praça Porto Rocha, in the Centro. *Bacalhauzinho* at No 27 has excellent bacalhau and a nice atmosphere. *New Junior* is close by at No 84 with sidewalk tables and US$5 prato feito. For dessert, try *Confeitaria Branca* at No 15.

Getting There & Away

The old coastal road takes longer than Hwy BR-101 but provides a beautiful, level route winding around foggy green mounds. There are regular buses from Rio de Janeiro and Niterói (US$10, three hours).

Getting Around

To get to Arraial do Cabo from Cabo Frio, catch a local bus from the bus stop just up to the right as you leave the bus station. To get to Búzios, cross the road and catch a bus from the stop on your left. Local buses cost US$0.70.

BÚZIOS

• *pop 12,000* ✉ *28925-000* ☎ *024*

Búzios, a lovely beach resort, is on a peninsula (scalloped by 17 beaches) which juts into the Atlantic. A simple fishing village until the early sixties, when it was 'discovered' by Brigitte Bardot and her Brazilian boyfriend, the village is now littered with boutiques, fine restaurants, fancy villas, bars and posh pousadas. During the holiday season (when the population explodes to 100,000!) prices here are twice those in the rest of Brazil.

Orientation

Búzios is not a single town but rather three settlements on the peninsula – Ossos, Manguinhos and Armação – and one called Rasa, farther north on the mainland.

Ossos (Bones), at the northernmost tip of the peninsula, is the oldest and most attractive. It has a pretty harbour and yacht club, a few hotels and bars, and a tourist stand.

Manguinhos, at the isthmus, is the most commercial; it even has a 24 hour medical clinic.

Armação, in between, has the best restaurants, along with city necessities such as international telephones, a bank, petrol station, post office and a pharmacy.

North-west along the coast is Rasa and the island of Rasa, where Brazil's political dignitaries and the rich relax.

Information

Tourist Office The Secretaria de Turismo (☎ 623-2099), Praça Santos Dumont 111 in Armação, is open weekdays from 8 am to 6 pm and weekends from 8 am to 4 pm. From any newsstand, pick up a copy of *Guia Verão Buzios* (US$4). It has information in English as well as in Portuguese, including a list of places to stay (but not prices).

Money Bradesco has an ATM at Travessa Turíbio de Farias 71 in Armação. Fairtour, close by, operates a câmbio.

Beaches

In general, the southern beaches are trickier to get to, but they're prettier and have better surf. The northern beaches are more sheltered and are closer to the towns.

Working anticlockwise from south of

Maguinhos, the first beaches are **Geribá** and **Ferradurinha** (Little Horseshoe). These are beautiful beaches with good surf, but the Búzios Beach Club has built condos here.

Next on the coast is **Ferradura**, which is large enough for windsurfing, and **Lagoinha**, a rocky beach with rough water. **Praia da Foca** and **Praia do Forno** have colder water than the other beaches. **Praia Olho de Boi** (Bull's Eye) was named after Brazil's first postage stamp. It's a pocket-size beach reached by a little trail from the long, clean beach of **Praia Brava**.

João Fernandinho and **João Fernandes** are both good for snorkelling, as are the topless beaches of **Azedinha** and **Azeda**. **Praia dos Ossos**, **Praia da Armação**, **Praia do Caboclo** and **Praia dos Amores** are pretty to look at, but not for lounging around. **Praia da Tartaruga** is quiet and pretty. **Praia do Gaucho** and **Manguinhos** are town beaches farther along.

Places to Stay

If you want to camp, *Country Camping Club* (☎ 629-1122), Rua Maria Joaquina 895, Praia Rasa, is a good spot but it's a bit out of the way.

Lodging is somewhat on the expensive side, especially in summer, so consider accommodation in Saquarema or Cabo Frio, or rent a house and stay a while. In the low season, however, you should be able to find a room as cheap as those in Cabo Frio or Arraial. Most places charge the same price for singles as they do for doubles. Búzios is a romantic place and solo travellers are unusual. In general, rooms to let are cheaper than pousadas. All accommodation listed has showers and prices include a light breakfast. The high season is December to March and again in July.

The *Pousada Mediterrânea* (☎ 623-2353), Rua João Fernandes 58, is a whitewashed and tiled little hotel. Low-season doubles with a lovely inland view are US$48. The *Zen-Do* across the road is a private home with rooms to let. Yesha Vanicore runs a progressive household and has doubles for US$30 in the low season. Yesha, a friendly lady, speaks English and is an excellent vegetarian cook. The *Pousada la Chimere* (☎/fax 623-1108), Praça Eugênio Harold 36, is a great splurge; it has a lovely courtyard and large, well-appointed rooms with a view over the square. Doubles are US$90 in low season, US$115 in high season.

In Armação, *Estalagem* (☎ 623-1243), Avenida José Bento Ribeiro 156, is right in the middle of all the action. This is where Bardot stayed all those years ago. Its double rooms go for US$40 in low season, and US$70 in high season.

Places to Eat

For good, cheap food, eat grilled fish right on the beaches. Brava, Ferradura and João Fernandes beaches have little thatched-roof fish and beer restaurants.

Most of the better restaurants are in or near Armação. *Restaurante David*, Rua Manoel Turibe de Farias, is good value – an ample US$8 prato feito usually includes shark fillet (cassão) with rice, beans and salad.

For fancier fare, *Le Streghe* (The Witch), Rua das Pedras 201, has great pasta and northern Italian dishes, and obsequious service.

Chez Michou Crêperie, also on Rua das Pedras, is a popular hang-out because of its incredible crepes – any kind you want. The outdoor bar has delicious pinha coladas (US$3).

On Avenida Beira Mar between Ossos and Armação are *Satíricon* (with overpriced Italian seafood) and the *Oriente Express* (a flash Japanese sushi bar and steakhouse).

Entertainment

The centre of action in Búzios is the Rua das Pedras in Armação. And it all starts late – don't even think of getting here before midnight. There are some good bars, restaurants and nightclubs (on weekends and in season), but mostly it seems that everybody just likes walking up and down the street looking at everybody else. The most happening bar in town is *Takatakata*, Avenida José Bento Ribeiro Dantas 144. Kijzer Van Derhoff is a showman as well as a barman, and his fiery concoctions are legendary.

Getting There & Away

From Cabo Frio to Búzios (Ossos), take the municipal bus (a 50 minute, 20km run). There are four direct buses daily from Rio, at 6.30 and 10.15 am, 2.15 and 7.15 pm. The three hour trip costs US$11.

Getting Around

Rent A Bike at Avenida José Bento Ribeiro Dantas 843 and Casa Central Bicicleta at Rua Lúcio Quintanilha 152, both in Armação, have bicycles for hire for around US$20 a day.

The schooner *Queen Lory* makes daily trips from Armação out to Ilha Feia, Tartaruga and João Fernandinho. There is a 2½ hour trip which costs US$15 and a five hour trip for US$20. These trips are good value, especially since caipirinhas, soft drinks, fruit salad and snorkelling gear are included in the price. To make a reservation, ask at your pousada or visit Queen Lory Tours (☎ 623-1179), Rua Angela Diniz 35.

BARRA DE SÃO JOÃO

Barra de São João, not to be confused with São João da Barra (which is farther north up the coast), is an easy-going place set on a narrow spit of land between a small river and the Atlantic. Old, well-preserved colonial homes with azulejos give the town a warm, Portuguese feel, and the village architecture is protected by law. The long, quiet beach is good for surf-casting.

Places to Stay

Don't get the idea that accommodation will be any cheaper here than in Búzios. All the 'simple' pousadas in town charge at least US$30 a double. They include *Pousada Moraes*, Avenida Amaral Peixoto 388, and the *Hotel Brasil*, 100m away and on the opposite side of the road.

Getting There & Away

Barra de São João, 57km from Cabo Frio, is serviced by 10 buses a day.

Espírito Santo

Espírito Santo doesn't exactly leap to the minds of travellers, who usually see the state through bus windows as they ride between Rio de Janeiro and Bahia states. But though parts of the state are heavily industrialised, its beaches offer the chance to really get off the beaten tourist path and experience beach life as the Brazilians do – your fellow beach-goers will likely be from Minas Gerais, southern Bahia or northern Rio state.

Inland, the lush mountainous coffee and strawberry producing regions have interesting towns populated by Italian and German immigrants, ecological reserves and the splendid Pedra Azul State Park.

The coastline ranges from calm blue inlets to good surfing beaches where turbulent water creates a brownish hue. Some of the fishing villages and beaches on the southern coast are very attractive, and to the north, Conceição da Barra and the nearby sand dunes at Itaúnas are worth a visit.

Excellent seafood is available in Espírito Santo; especially noteworthy is the *moqueca capixaba* (see Food in the Facts for the Visitor chapter for more information).

Colonised in the 16th century, Espírito Santo became an armed region to prevent gold from being smuggled out of Minas. Coffee plantations, the prime source of income up until the 1960s, have been superseded by mining and shipping. Vitória is also home to Garota, Brazil's famous (and delicious) chocolate.

VITÓRIA

•pop 267,500 ✉ 29000-000 ☎027

Vitória, the capital, is 521km from Rio de Janeiro and 602km from Porto Seguro, making it a convenient place to break the journey between Rio and Bahia. Founded in 1551, Vitória has little to show of its colonial past. It's a port city; export coffee and timber pass through here, and the port at nearby Tubarão is the outlet for millions of tonnes of iron ore.

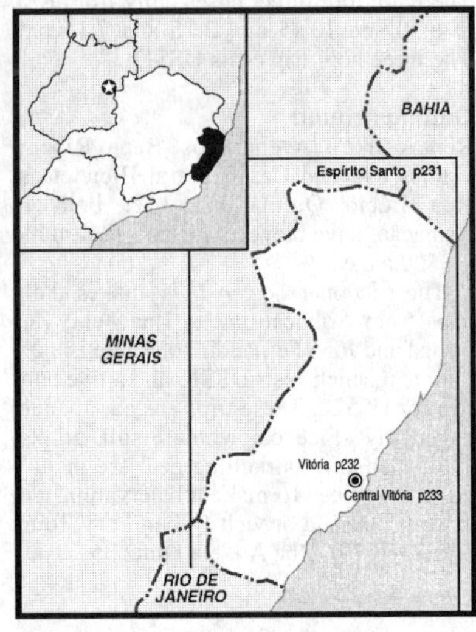

Orientation

The rodoviária is 1km west of town. There are two strips of beach: Praia do Camburí, a 10 minute bus ride north-east of the city, and Praia da Costa, 12km south of town, at Vila Velha.

Information

ADERES (☎/fax 322-8282), the state tourism authority, is at Avenida Vitória 2045, on the 3rd floor of the edificio COHAB (side entrance); it's open weekdays from 9 am to 6 pm. At the rodoviária there's an information booth called CODESP, which opens erratically, and another booth at the airport.

Money The best cash exchange rate can be found at the Escal souvenir shop off Avenida Marechal Mascarenhas opposite the ferry stop. You can change travellers cheques at the Banco do Brasil in Avenida Governador Bley.

Post & Telephone The main post office is in the centre, on Avenida Jerônimo Monteiro, and there's a branch at the rodoviária. There are three posto telefônicos: at the rodoviária, at the airport and on Rua do Rosário, in the centre.

City Centre

The pink **Anchieta Palace**, on Praça João Climaco, is a 16th century former Jesuit college and church. It's now the seat of state government, and the only part you can enter is the **tomb of Padre José de Anchieta** (1534-97) the co-founder of São Paulo and an early missionary who was hailed as the 'Apostle of Brazil'.

Close by is the **Catedral Metropolitana**, with its neogothic exterior and interesting stained-glass windows.

Teatro Carlos Gomes on Praça Costa Pereira is a replica of La Scala in Milan. The **Parque Moscoso** is where Capixabas (as state natives are called) go for a break.

Vila Velha

This was the first place in Espírito Santo to be colonised. The most interesting thing to do here is climb to the **Convento da Penha**, atop the 154m granite Morro da Penha. Even if you don't usually visit convents, the view makes the climb totally worth it. In the week after Easter, thousands of devotees come to this major pilgrimage centre to pay homage to the image of NS de Penha, some even making the climb on their knees.

Praia da Costa, the main Vila Velha beach, is nearby. It has fewer hotels and restaurants than Camburí, but you can swim and body surf.

Praia do Camburí, this 5km stretch of beach (don't swim, it's polluted) is punctuated by restaurants, nightspots and mid-range hotels.

Places to Stay

The HI hostel *Praia da Costa* (☎ 329-3227), Avenida São Paulo 1163, near the beach (see the Vitória map), has beds for US$7.50/12 with/without an HI card. There's a second HI hostel (same prices) at the university campus near the airport (☎ 324-0738); take any local bus to UFES (ooh-FAYZ) and ask for the Correio Nove – new post office – which is opposite the hostel.

There is a row of 'crash-pad' hotels opposite the bus station; the best is *Spala*, at US$15 per person. But the centre is easy to get to, and it's worth the effort to get away from the bus station's uninspiring surroundings.

In the centre are lots of cheap hotels. If you're really hard up head for the marginally

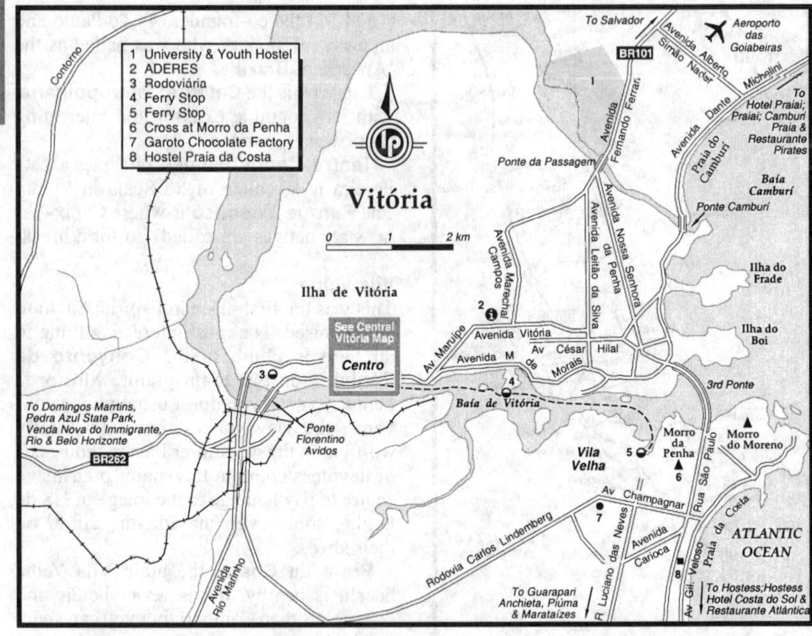

acceptable *Hotel Restaurante Europa*, Rua 7 de Setembro next to Praça Costa Pereira; clean-ish quartos are US$8 a head and apartamentos US$12/20 for singles/doubles. The food in the restaurant is cheap.

The *Hotel Cidade Alta* (no ☎), Rua Pedro Palácios 213, is a superb deal. Spotless quartos cost US$10/15 a single/ double and scrubbed apartamentos are US$15/23; it's cheap, clean and honest.

The *Hotel Prata* (☎ 222-4311), Rua Nestor Gomes 201, near the Anchieta Palace charges US$14/22 (US$9/14 in low season) for musty singles/doubles. You have to be out by 10 am, but the breakfast is good.

The *Cannes Palace Hotel* (☎ 222-1522; fax 222-8061), Avenida Jerônimo Monteiro 111, is more expensive at US$30/50 for singles/doubles – if you're going to spend that sort of money, you may as well be on the beach.

Out at Camburí, the cheapest beachfront place is the *Hotel Praia* (☎ 227-8777) at Avenida Dante Michelini 207 with singles/ doubles for US$35/50. The *Camburí Praia* (☎ 227-1322), Avenida Dante Michelini 1007, costs a few dollars more.

The three-star *Hostess* (☎ 329-2111) at Avenida Antônio Gil Velloso 442 has singles/doubles for US$42/55. Its more expensive sister is the best in Vila Velha, the four-star *Hostess Hotel Costa do Sol* (☎ 329-4000), Avenida Antônio Gil Velloso 1400. It has excellent rooms for US$120 and suites, complete with jacuzzis, from US$174.

Places to Eat

In the centre, the *Sabor Natura Restaurante*, Rua 13 de Maio 90, has a veggie-friendly self-serve lunch for US$7/kg. A good lunch buffet in the centre is the US$10 all-you-can-eat session at the *Cannes Palace Hotel* (see Places to Stay).

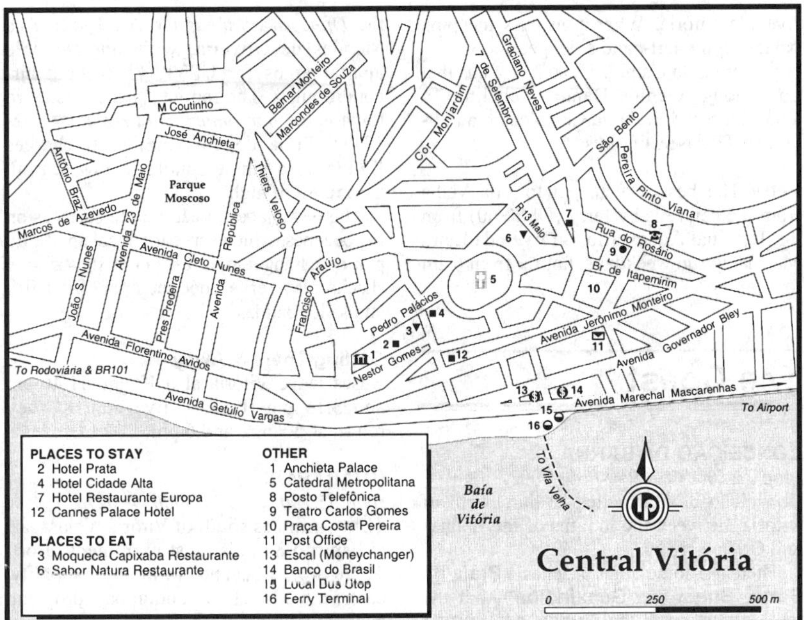

Restaurante Atlântica (☎ 329-2341), Avenida Antonio Gil Veloso 80 in Vila Velha, has excellent moqueca capixaba at US$20 for two, and local seafood dishes from US$8 to US$12. For self-catering travellers, there's a 24 hour deli around the corner from the Hostess Hotel Costa do Sol.

Restaurante Piratas, Avenida Dante Michelini 747, Praia do Camburí, has a good squid vinaigrette for US$8.50, and you can find a good rodízio at *Churrascaria Canoas*, Avenida Dante Michelini 47.

Things to Buy

The Garoto chocolate factory (☎ 320-1200) makes Brazil's best chocolate. Visit the factory store, where the stuff is really cheap and fresh, at Praça Meyerfreund Gloria, off Rodovia Carlos Lindemberg in Vila Velha – take bus No 500 from the city centre.

Getting There & Away

There are nine buses a day to Belo Horizonte (US$23, eight hours). To Ouro Prêto, there's a direct bus at 10.45 pm (US$20, eight hours). To Porto Seguro, there's one daily bus, at 9 am (US$31, nine hours). Eleven buses a day make the eight hour journey to Rio (US$22).

There's also a daily train to Belo Horizonte at 6.30 am; see the Belo Horizonte section in the Minas Gerais state chapter for more information.

Getting Around

To/From the Airport The airport is 10km from the city centre; take the local bus marked aeroporto/rodoviária from/to the centre (US$0.55).

Bus All local buses (US$0.95) run from the various stops outside the rodoviária; the route is written on the side of each bus. For the centre, catch any bus that goes along

Avenida Vitória. When you pass the pink palace on the left-hand side, get out.

For Praia do Camburí, catch any bus that goes along Avenida Dante Michelini. To Vila Velha and Praia da Costa catch an all-yellow TRANSCOL bus.

Ferry The best way to get to Vila Velha from the centre is by ferry (US$0.60) from the Terminal Aquaviário, on Avenida Beira Mar. They run weekdays, hourly from 6 am to 7 pm.

The Coast

CONCEIÇÃO DA BARRA

•pop 23,500 ✉ 29960-000 ☎ 027

Conceição da Barra lies 254km north of Vitória, between the mouths of the Itaúnas and Cricaré rivers.

There are some quiet beaches – **Praia da Barra**, **Bugia** and **Guaxindiba** – but the main attraction is the **Dunas de Itaúnas** 23km north of Conceição da Barra. These 20m to 30m-high dunes of fine sand have engulfed the small village of Vila de Itaúnas – not even the steeple of its church is visible anymore. However, you might spot some turtle researchers from Projeto TAMAR (see the boxed text 'TAMAR Saves Sea Turtles' in the Bahia chapter) who can give you turtle-watching tips. From the dunes you can see the sea, the Rio Itaúnas and the surrounding Atlantic rainforest, and you can even dune-surf. Buses (US$2.50, 20 minutes) run here from Conceição at 9 am, noon and 3 pm.

Places to Stay & Eat

There are plenty of pricey hotels in town so budget travellers should consider a hammock in a fishing hut at Bugia or camping near the dunes.

The *Rustico's Hotel* (☎ 762-1193), Rua Muniz Freire 299, is a simple place with rooms for US$25 – you may be able to bargain the price down if you're alone. Also central is the *Dunas de Itaúnas* (☎ 762-1302), Rua Mendes de Oliveira, with single/double apartamentos for US$30/45 without air-conditioning. The top-end place to stay in town is the *Barramar Praia Hotel* (☎ 762-1311), Praia de Guaxindiba. It charges US$35/40 a single/double in low season, US$50/80 in high.

The best places to eat are the barracas on the beaches, which serve the local speciality puã de caranguejo, a tasty crab stew. These shacks also serve coconut milk, fried fish and killer batidas.

Getting There & Away

Buses leave Vitória at 6.40 and 11.40 am and 3.15 pm (US$14, five hours). They return at 6 am, 2 and 6 pm.

GUARAPARI

•pop 65,500 ✉ 29200-000 ☎ 027

Thirty minutes south of Vitória, Guarapari is Espírito Santo's most prominent resort. There are 23 beaches in the municipality, each with a lovely mountain backdrop and each swarming with Brazilian holiday-makers in the high seasons – it's certainly off the gringo tourist route.

The best beach is **Praia do Morro**, north of the city; there's surfing (2m to 3m-breaks) here and boogie/surf boards can be rented in summer for US$5/10 per half day. However, you should be aware that its so called 'healing' black monazitic sand is in fact highly radioactive!

Orientation & Information

The centre is 500m south of the rodoviária, across the bridge; the beach is 200m further on. The Casa da Cultura 50m east of the bridge, opposite the city market, has city maps and information in Portuguese. The posta telefônico is on Avenida Des Lourival de Almeida, the main waterfront drag.

Places to Stay

Guaracamping (☎ 261-0475), Avenida F, QD 40, is an HI hostel (US$10 with HI card, US$15 without) and camping ground (US$7 per tent). It's two minutes from the bus station but there's no sign; walk west from the rodoviária, cross the main road, take the next left and it's one block down on the right hand corner. This area is known as *Muquiçaba* – mosquito nest – so bring repellent.

There are two good central budget places close to the beach: *Hotel Maryland* (☎/fax 261-0553), Rua Dr Silva Melo 98, has single/double apartamentos for US$25/30. About one and a half blocks away, the *Hotel do Ângelo* (☎/fax 261-0230), Rua Pedro Caetano 254, is a good deal with friendly staff and singles/doubles at US$20/30.

A bit more upmarket and in the same vicinity is the *Solar da Ruth* (☎ 261-1836), Rua Dr Silva Melo 215, a very friendly one-star hotel close to the beach with singles/ doubles for US$30/38, and the *Coronado* (☎ 361-0144; fax 261-1444), a three-star place right on the beach for US$40/46, plus 10% at peak times.

The *Best Western Porto do Sol* (☎ 361-1100; fax 261-2929), Avenida Beira Mar 1, by Praia do Morro, is Guarapari's four-star hotel. Singles/ doubles cost US$100/120 in the high seasons, US$60/80 in low.

Places to Eat

The self-serve restaurant (US$8/kg) at the *Hotel Maryland* is excellent. *Pizzaria do Ângelo* at the Hotel do Ângelo is good and cheap at lunch and unforgivably expensive at dinner. There's pizza and fast food upstairs at the shopping mall on Avenida Dr Roberto Calmon, and fruits and snacks at the kiosks at the west end of Praia do Meio.

Peixada do Irmão, Rua Jacinto de Almeida 72, is highly recommended for seafood.

Getting There & Away

Buses run between Vitória and Guarapari every hour from 6 am to 9 pm (US$3, 1¼ hours). Frequent buses make the 28km trip to Anchieta.

ANCHIETA

•pop 16,000 ✉ 29230-000 ☎ 027

Eighty-eight kilometres south of Vitória, Anchieta's attractions are the 16th century church of **NS de Assunção** and, alongside, the **Museu Padre Anchieta** (free, closed Monday). The church walls, built by local Indians and Padre José de Anchieta, are original. The interesting museum contains relics uncovered during restoration.

Places to Stay & Eat

There're no cheapies, but the nicest is the charming colonial *Anchieta* (☎ 536-1258), 100m south of the bus stop. Airy singles/ doubles cost US$30 or US$35 with TV and double bed.

The *Hotel Porto Velho* (☎ 536-1181), right above the bus stop, has singles/ doubles with TV and refrigerator for US$30/40.

Opposite the post kiosk at the bus stop is a friendly lanchonete with sandwiches and cheap burgers. Popular with locals is the *Varanda*, Rua Costa Pereira 204, which serves good moqueca for US$8 as well as pizzas and steaks. The *Restaurante Peixada do Garcia*, Praia Ubu, 10km north towards Guarapari, is reputedly excellent.

Getting There & Away

To Guarapari, buses (US$1.50) run every 20 to 30 minutes from 6 am to 6.50 pm. To Vitória (US$4.75) they run five times daily.

AROUND ANCHIETA

Iriri

A great, secluded, palm-lined beach with gentle surf is the attraction in Iriri, 10km south of Anchieta. Frequent buses connect it with Piúma, 2km south, so most make it a day trip, but the *Hotel Espadarte* (☎ (027) 534-1151), Rua Padre Anchiete, is worth every penny of the US$43/62 it charges in low season, US$69/99 in high season.

PIÚMA

•pop 10,000 ✉ 29285-000 ☎ 027

The rarest shell in the world, the *Oliva Zelindea*, is occasionally found in Piúma, 100km south of Vitória. Nice beaches and some nearby offshore islands are worth a look.

The coastline is dominated by the 300m, cone-shaped **Monte Aghá**, which is a good place for hang-gliding and climbing.

Islands

Ilha do Gamba, an ecological reserve, is connected to the mainland by a thin isthmus. At low tide, you can walk from there to **Ilha do Meio**, which preserves wild orchids and native trees.

The next island is **Ilha dos Cabritos**, which has a so-so seafood restaurant. Boats run from the first island to the latter two (US$3 to US$5) in summer, otherwise pay a fisherman to take you over.

Beaches

Praia Boca da Barra and Praia Maria Nenen are surf beaches, while Praia Acaiaca has calm water.

Places to Stay

Vila Rica (☎ 520-1753), Rua Feliciano Lopes 23, charges US$17 per head for small, clean apartamentos with fans. It also has a camping ground. So does *Dom Manuel Pousada e Camping* (☎ 520-1370) next to the Solar de Brasilia, which charges US$15/25 for single/double quartos and US$5 per head for camping.

Rooms with a sea view are available at the *Pousada Itaputanga* (☎ 520-1348), Rua Franklin Ferreira de Souza, for US$25 to US$40 a double.

Another nice place is the *Solar de Brasilia* (☎ 520-1521), Avenida Eduardo Rodrigues 15. Singles/doubles are US$20/30 in low season and US$50 in high season. The breakfast is excellent and there's a swimming pool.

The *Coliseu Hotel* (☎ 520-1273), Avenida Beiramar, is right on the water; a super deal at US$25/40.

The flashy *Monte Aghá* (☎ 520-1622; fax 520-1677), Avenida Minas Gerais 20, has doubles with a terrace for US$50, including a bag of Cheetos. Classy, huh?

Places to Eat

Most of Piúma's restaurants are located along the beachfront, on Avenida Beira Mar. *Belabatok* has great seafood and carne do sol. Right next to Belabatok, *d'Angelus* is also very popular, offering a cheap, self-serve lunch for US$7/kg.

Getting There & Away

There are frequent buses that go to Anchieta (US$2) and Marataízes (US$1.80). Four a day go to Vitória (US$6).

AROUND PIÚMA

Marataízes

Twenty-five minutes south of Piúma, Marataízes caters to the working-class mineiro holiday crowd during high summer season. While there's no big attractions here there is an OK stretch of beach and the town is clean.

Getting There & Away

Buses leave for Vitória (US$7.50) daily at 6 and 6.15 am, and 3.10 pm.

Inland

DOMINGOS MARTINS

•pop 27,000 ✉ 29260-000 ☎ 027

Forty-one kilometres west of Vitória, Domingos Martins, also known as Campinho, is a small village settled by Germans in 1847. Dotted with *fachwerk* houses, it's a pleasant mountain retreat with cool fresh air, and it makes a good base for exploring the streams and forests of the mountains.

Kautsky Reserve

Roberto Kautsky is a dedicated botanist who's cultivated over 100 species of orchids at his home (☎ 268-1209) at the south end of town (ask anyone) and on his mountain-side reserve. He'll drive you, free for the asking, to the reserve in his ancient jeep and talk your ear off in German, 'bad English' or Portuguese – people come from miles around and it's a great experience. Show up before noon or from 2 to 6 pm.

Other Attractions

In the centre, the **museum**, on the first floor of the Casa da Cultura, exhibits early settlers' belongings and tools. Farther up the main road, near the main praça and

Lutheran Church, the **Recanto dos Colibris**, at the far end of Avenida Presidente Vargas, is a pretty gathering spot.

Seven kilometres east of town there's a **musical water clock**, decorated with figures of the 12 apostles, in the Hotel Vista Linda (see Places to Stay & Eat).

Places to Stay & Eat

There are pretty views indeed at the *Vista Linda* (☎ 268-1323), Km 35 on Hwy BR-262, with singles/doubles from US$27.50/ 55. The *Campinho*, near the bus stop, has rooms for US$20/37. The *Hotel e Restaurante Imperador* (☎ 268-1115), Rua Duque de Caxias 275, has a pool and sauna; rooms cost US$40/50.

Huge pizzas (US$13) come with free samples of local wines at *Adega Alemã Schwambach* (☎ 268-1423) just inside the city limits. Their Jubuticaba wine is simultaneously sweet and bitter. One litre costs US$4 to US$6. The restaurant in the *Imperador* is also worth a try.

Getting There & Away

Nine buses a day make the 41km trip from Vitória to Domingos Martins (US$3, one hour). Any bus between Vitória and Belo Horizonte stops here on request, too.

AROUND DOMINGOS MARTINS

Parque Estadual da Pedra Azul

Vitória-Belo Horizonte buses also stop at the best reason to come inland: the 500m Pedra Azul, 50km west down Hwy BR-262. The rock, tinted by a blueish moss, is at the centre of Parque Estadual da Pedra Azul (☎ 248-1356). Rangers escort hikers to the rock's nine **natural pools**, about a 1½ hour, moderately difficult hike from the base trail. It's free, but you must book three days in advance.

Climbers with their own equipment can climb the rock – bolts should reach the summit by the time you read this.

Places to Stay & Eat

Serious climbers are permitted to camp in the park, free, but you'll need to prove to the rangers you know what's what. In winter, it gets down near freezing during the day and below freezing at night, so pack wisely.

The area is dotted by fancier resort hotels with horses for hire. The best is right near the park headquarters off Hwy BR-262 at Km 90 – the spectacular, amenity-packed *Aroso Baço Hotel* (☎ 248-1147; fax 248-1180), with beautifully detailed, immaculate singles/doubles from US$120/ 140. Ask for a view of the rock.

Just past the park's main trail-head, 1½ kilometres south of Hwy BR-262, the *Café Colonial* (☎ 248-1124) serves up tea and coffee along with dozens of cakes, cookies and salads – all you want for US$7 per person. It's open weekends and holidays only from 2 to 8 pm.

Ten kilometres west of the park HQ on Hwy BR-262 is the Italian immigrant community of Venda Nova do Imigrante (pop 12,000). *Restaurant Dalla Nina* has lots of pasta dishes for under US$5 and decent steaks. The good *Lanchonette Futura* is worth a try, too.

SANTA TERESA

•pop 30,000 ✉ 29650-000 ☎ 027

Santa Teresa, a small town settled by Italian immigrants, has a cheerful, flowered plaza, a cool, mountain climate and vineyards. Nearby excursions include the valley of Canaã and the Reserva Biológica Nova Lombardia.

Museu Biológico de Professor Melo Leitão

The town's main attraction, this biological museum represents the life's work of Augusto Ruschi, a staunch environmentalist and world-renowned hummingbird expert, who died in 1986 after being poisoned by a frog. The museum also has a small zoo, a butterfly garden, a snake farm, and a large number of orchids and other flora. It's open only on weekends, from noon to 5 pm. Time your visit to Santa Teresa accordingly, as the museum is very interesting.

Places to Stay & Eat
Hotel Pierazzo (☎ 259-1233) Avenida Getúlio Vargas 115, has very nice singles/doubles for US$30/54. Cheaper is *Globo* at Rua Jerônimo Vervloet 190, at US$20 per person.

A few doors down from the Pierazzo and upstairs from a lanchonette is the *Restaurante Zitu's*, which does good pasta.

Getting There & Away
Santa Teresa is 76km away from Vitória. There are seven buses a day that make the journey (US$6, two hours). There are, though, no roads directly linking Domingos Martins with Santa Teresa, which means that the only way of getting there is to backtrack through Vitória.

Minas Gerais

Minas Gerais presents a welcome contrast to the rest of Brazil. While the name means General Mines, the state is packed with exquisite colonial towns, seemingly frozen in another epoch. Their baroque churches and sacred art, mostly sculptures from one of the world's great artists, Aleijadinho, represent over half of Brazil's national monuments.

Nestled in the Serra do Espinhaço mountain range are the *cidades históricas*, historic colonial cities which grew up with the great gold boom. The foothills and streams of these mountains were scoured for gold throughout the 18th century.

Minas also has several hydromineral spa towns in the mountainous south-west corner and a number of prehistoric caves close to the capital, Belo Horizonte.

Ouro Prêto has more of everything – homogeneous baroque architecture, churches, Aleijadinho, museums and fame – than any city in Brazil. It also has more tourists, traffic, boutiques, locals hawking things to visitors and expensive hotels and restaurants.

The best time to visit Minas is between March and August.

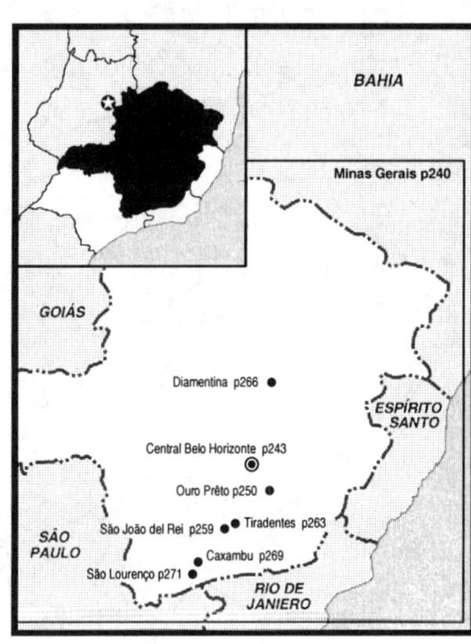

History

Around 1695, bandeirantes (groups of explorers from São Paulo in search of Indian slaves and precious metals) found gold along the banks and in the beds of rivers flowing from Brazil's oldest mountains.

The deposits were called *faisqueiras* (sparkles) because the larger pieces were actually visible – all the miners had to do was pick them up.

Word got out. Brazilians flocked to Minas and Portuguese immigrated to Brazil. These two groups soon fought over land claims in the Guerra dos Emboabas. Slaves were brought from the sugar fields of Bahia and the savannas of Angola, as few whites did their own mining. Until the last quarter of the 18th century, the slaves of Minas Gerais were digging up half the world's gold.

Minas set the gold rush standard –crazy, wild and violent – over 100 years before the Californian and Australian ones. Disease and famine were rampant. The mine towns were known for their licentiousness and prostitutes like the infamous Chica da Silva in Diamantina have been immortalised in the cinema.

Merchants and colonial officials became rich, as did a few gold miners. Gold siphoned off to Portugal ended up feeding England's Industrial Revolution and so the only lasting benefits to come to Brazil were the development of Rio de Janeiro (the main port for the gold) and the creation of the beautiful, church-clad mining cities that dot the hills of Minas Gerais.

Ouro Prêto was the most splendid of these. Vila Rica de Ouro Prêto (Rich Town of Black Gold), as it was known, grew to 100,000 people and became the richest city in the New World.

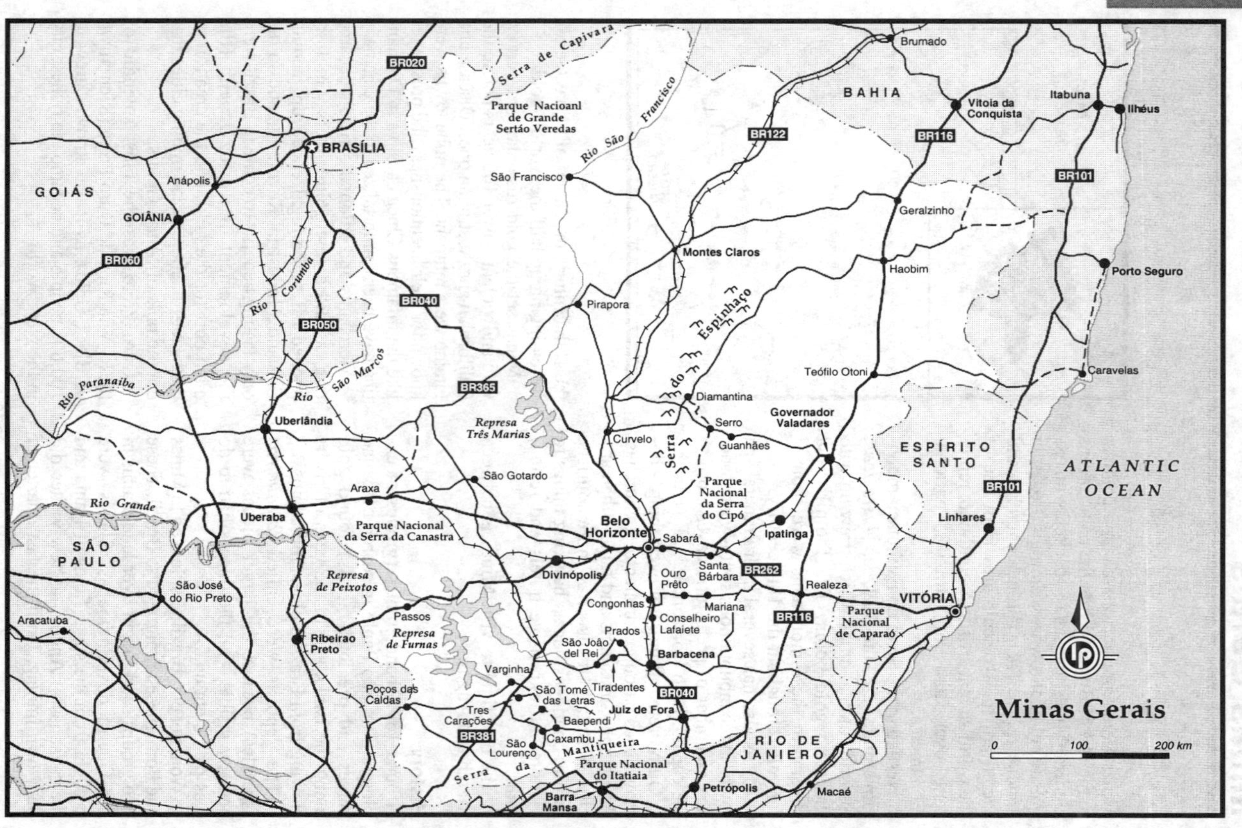
Minas Gerais
0
100
200 km
ATLANTIC OCEAN
BAHIA
ESPÍRITO SANTO
RIO DE JANIERO
SÃO PAULO
GOIÁS
Brumado
Vitoia da Conquista
Itabuna
Ilhéus
Geralzinho
Haobim
Porto Seguro
Teófilo Otoni
Caravelas
Governador Valadares
Linhares
VITÓRIA
Parque Nacional de Caparaó
Realeza
Ipatinga
Macaé
Petrópolis
Guanhães
Serro
Diamantina
Serra do Espinhaço
Montes Claros
Parque Nacional da Serra do Cipó
Sabará
Santa Bárbara
Ouro Prêto
Mariana
Congonhas
Conselheiro Lafaiete
Prados
São João del Rei
Tiradentes
Barbacena
Juiz de Fora
Belo Horizonte
São Tomé das Letras
Baependi
Caxambu
Serra da Mantiqueira
São Lourenço
Parque Nacional do Itatiaia
Barra Mansa
Varginha
Tres Caraçoes
Poços das Caldas
Curvelo
Pirapora
Divinópolis
São Gotardo
Represa Três Marias
Parque Nacional da Serra da Canastra
Passos
Represa de Furnas
Represa de Peixotos
Ribeirao Preto
Araxa
Uberaba
Uberlândia
Rio São Marcos
Rio Corumba
Rio Paranaiba
Rio Grande
Rio São Francisco
São Francisco
Parque Nacioanl de Grande Sertão Veredas
Serra de Capivara
BRASÍLIA
Anápolis
GOIÂNIA
São José do Rio Preto
Aracatuba
BR020
BR122
BR116
BR101
BR060
BR040
BR050
BR365
BR262
BR381

Orientation

Minas is as large as France, part of a vast plateau that crosses Brazil's interior. Rising along the state's southern border with Rio and São Paulo is the Serra da Mantiqueira with some of Brazil's highest peaks.

The major historical cities are clustered in three spots along the Serra do Espinhaço.

São João del Rei, with Tiradentes nearby, is 200km south of Belo Horizonte; Ouro Prêto and Mariana are 100km south-east of it; and Diamantina is 290km north.

Minas has good roads but travel is usually a sinuous affair. Much of the terrain is characterised by hills, deep valleys and plateaus running off the larger mountains.

Climate

Minas is rainy from October to February and dry from March to September. The rainy season is characterised by almost daily downpours but they rarely last for long. Although the climate is warm, it's still much cooler than the heat of Rio.

The dry season is cool and from July to September it can actually get cold. There is often fog during September and October.

Even during the rainy season, travel – with umbrella – is quite practical, with one proviso. From December to February, Ouro Prêto is deluged by tourists, who can be more of a nuisance than the rain.

Northern Minas is less populated. It's an arid land with shrub-like trees that look dead during the dry season but quickly regain their foliage when it rains. The most common tree is the pepper tree *(aroeira)*.

Economy

Minas Gerais wears its name well, producing more iron, tin, diamonds, zinc, quartz and phosphates than any other state in Brazil. It has one of the world's largest reserves of iron.

The state's industrial growth rate has been well above the national average over the past few years, and Minas Gerais should soon surpass Rio de Janeiro as Brazil's second most powerful economy, behind São Paulo.

Minas is also known for its milk and cheese production. The agricultural sector is diverse and strong, with fruit and cattle also important.

BELO HORIZONTE

• *pop 2.2 million* ✉ *30000-000* ☎ *031*

Sprawling Belo Horizonte ('bellow-hree-ZONCH-eh') is the state capital of Mineas Gerias, and Brazil's third largest city.

Most people aren't coming to Belo but rather through it, on their way to Ouro Prêto or Diamantina. But there's more than you'd expect in this vibrantly efficient city and, if you look around, you'll find plenty to keep you busy.

Orientation

Central Belo is a grid 45° off north. The main drag is Avenida Afonso Pena, which runs from the rodoviária at the north-west straight south-east through the centre. There are three pivotal praças: bustling Praça Sete, just south-east of the rodoviária; serene Praça da Liberdade, south of Sete; and, south-east of Liberdade, Praça da Savassi, the centre of Belo nightlife and cafe society.

The train station is at the eastern end of Avenida Amazonas. Belo is a hilly town, so distances on a map can be deceptive.

Information

Tourist Office Belotur (☎ 277-7669), the municipal tourist organisation, puts out an excellent monthly guide in Portuguese, English and French. It lists the main tourist attractions and how to get to them using local buses, includes a city map, flight times, accurate long-distance bus schedules and everything and anything else you wanted to know about Belo Horizonte but didn't know how to ask.

Belotur has booths at Confins airport (open daily from 8 am to 10 pm), at Avenida Afonso Pena 1055 at the north-west corner of Parque Municipal (see later in this section) and at the rodoviária (both are open weekdays from 8 am to 8 pm, to 4 pm on weekends). The staff here speak English and can also supply you with state tourist information.

Turminas (☎ 212-2133; turminas@net.em.com.br), Avenida Bias Forts 50 at Praça da Liberdade, is the state tourism office. It's open Monday to Friday from 12.30 to 6.30 pm.

Radio Favela, 104.5 FM, is an unlicenced station which has operated from a local favela since 1982. There's great music and community information, plus club dates and entertainment news daily.

Money Change money at Banco do Brasil, Rua Rio de Janeiro 750, near Praça Sete. There are lots of other banks and casas de câmbio in the city centre – try Nascente Turismo, at Rua Rio de Janeiro 1101. Casas de câmbio usually open at 11 am.

Post & Communications The main post office is at Avenida Afonso Pena 1270; there's another at the rodoviária. Telemig has telephone posts at Praça Sete, Rua dos Tamoios 311, the rodoviária and at Confins airport.

Online Services Cybernet Café (☎ 261-5166), Avenida Cristóvão Columbo 596 near Savassi, has Web access for US$8/hour.

Praça da Liberdade

This green square is the site of an architectural ensemble with classical government buildings, a Jetsons-like condo, Art-Deco offices and, at the north-west end, the playful postmodern ***Rainha sa Sucata*** (Scrap Queen), home to Turminas.

Parque Municipal

Parque Municipal is an enormous sea of green roughly a 10 minute walk south-east of the rodoviária along Avenida Afonso Pena. It's a great place to shake off the traffic and get your head together. Its highlight is the **Palácio das Artes**, an art gallery and performing arts centre at the south-west corner of the park.

Museu Histórico Abílio Barreto

In an old colonial farmhouse, this newly renovated free museum is all that remains of the town of Curral del Rey, on which Belo was built. There's a photographic archive and other historical bric-a-brac. It's at Rua Bernardo Mascarenhas, Cidade Jardim (bus No 8902 Luxemburgo/Sagrada Familia from Avenida Amazonas), open Tuesday to Sunday from 10 am to 5 pm.

Pampulha

Fans of architect Oscar Niemeyer won't want to miss his creations in the Pampulha district, in the north of the city (bus No 2004 Bandeirantes/Olhos/d'Agua), around a large lake. Others will be disappointed; the area has an unkempt feel about it. There's the **Igreja de São Francisco de Assis**, built in the 1940s, and the **Museu de Arte de Belo Horizonte**, among others.

Places to Stay – Budget

Hostels & Pousadas The *Pousadinha Mineira* (☎ 446-2911; fax 442-4448), Rua Araxá 514, has dormitory rooms for US$7.50 with an HI card, US$11 without one, and it's open from 7 am to midnight. From the rodoviária, follow Avenida Santos Dumont to Rua Rio de Janeiro, then turn left and go up a couple of blocks to Avenida do Contorno. Cross it and follow Rua Varginha up a few blocks to Rua Araxá.

The *Pousada Beagá* (☎ 337-1845; fax 275-3592), Rua Santa Catarina 597, is in the Lourdes district. (From the rodoviária, follow Avenida Paraná to Rua dos Tupis and turn right, then turn left on Rua Santa Catarina). It's open from 7 am to 11 pm.

Hotels The simple, well-kept *Hotel Magnata* (☎ 201-5368), Rua Guarani 124, is an island in the sleaze of the rodoviária's red-light district, with apartamentos for US$24/35 a single/double, but you can get them down to US$21.50/31.50 on slow days. It's strictly *familiar* – no rooms by the hour.

Better deals are had at two other central places: *Hotel Contijo* (☎ 272-1177), Rua Dos Tupinambás 731, with quartos (ask for a clean one until you get it) from US$18/31, apartamentos at US$26/37; and the slightly nicer *Hotel Bragança* (☎ 212-6688), Avenida Paraná 109, with decent rooms for US$30/45.

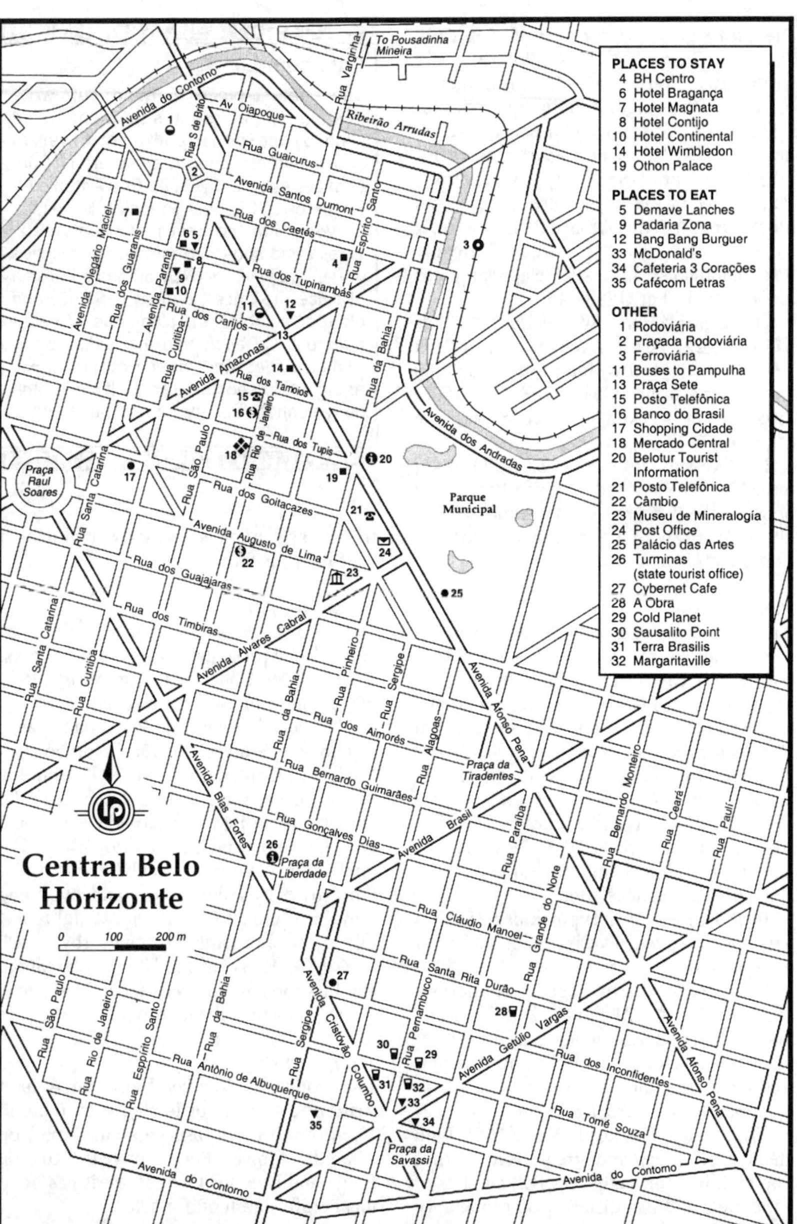
Central Belo Horizonte
PLACES TO STAY
4 BH Centro
6 Hotel Bragança
7 Hotel Magnata
8 Hotel Contijo
10 Hotel Continental
14 Hotel Wimbledon
19 Othon Palace
PLACES TO EAT
5 Demave Lanches
9 Padaria Zona
12 Bang Bang Burguer
33 McDonald's
34 Cafeteria 3 Corações
35 Cafécom Letras
OTHER
1 Rodoviária
2 Praçada Rodoviária
3 Ferroviária
11 Buses to Pampulha
13 Praça Sete
15 Posto Telefônica
16 Banco do Brasil
17 Shopping Cidade
18 Mercado Central
20 Belotur Tourist Information
21 Posto Telefônica
22 Câmbio
23 Museu de Mineralogía
24 Post Office
25 Palácio das Artes
26 Turminas (state tourist office)
27 Cybernet Cafe
28 A Obra
29 Cold Planet
30 Sausalito Point
31 Terra Brasilis
32 Margaritaville
To Pousadinha Mineira
Ribeirão Arrudas
Parque Municipal
Praça Raul Soares
Praça da Tiradentes
Praça da Liberdade
Praça da Savassi
Avenida do Contorno
Av Oiapoque
Rua Guaicurus
Avenida Santos Dumont
Rua dos Caetés
Rua dos Tupinambás
Rua dos Carijós
Avenida Amazonas
Rua dos Tamoios
Rua dos Tupis
Rua dos Goitacazes
Avenida Augusto de Lima
Rua dos Guajajaras
Rua dos Timbiras
Avenida Álvares Cabral
Rua dos Aimorés
Rua Bernardo Guimarães
Rua Gonçalves Dias
Avenida Brasil
Rua Cláudio Manoel
Rua Santa Rita Durão
Avenida Getúlio Vargas
Rua dos Inconfidentes
Rua Tomé Souza
Rua Antônio de Albuquerque
Avenida dos Andradas
Avenida Afonso Pena
Avenida Bias Fortes
Avenida Cristóvão Columbo
Avenida Olegário Maciel
Rua dos Guaranis
Avenida Paraná
Rua Curitiba
Rua São Paulo
Rua Rio de Janeiro
Rua Santa Catarina
Rua S de Brito
Rua Vargihna
Rua Espírito Santo
Rua da Bahia
Rua Pinheiro
Rua Sergipe
Rua Alagoas
Rua Pernambuco
Rua Paraíba
Rua Grande do Norte
Rua Bernardo Monteiro
Rua Ceará
Rua Paulí
0 100 200 m

Places to Stay – Mid-Range & Top End

The *BH Centro* (☎ 222-3390; fax 222-3146), Rua Espírito Santo 284, is a reliable option with single/double quartos for US$24/36 (if it's slow you can talk them down to US$21/32) and apartamentos for US$34/50 (or US$30/44). At Avenida Paraná 241 in the city centre, a couple of blocks from Avenida Afonso Pena, the *Hotel Continental* (☎ 201-7944) is clean, friendly and not too noisy. Fifties-style apartamentos are a good deal at US$28/45.

The central *Hotel Wimbledon* (☎ 222-6160; fax 222-6510), Avenida Afonso Pena 772, is a good deal with a rooftop pool and large rooms from US$122/148, (30%/50% discount on weekdays/weekends for the asking).

The five-star *Othon Palace* (☎ 273-3844; fax 212-2318), Avenida Afonso Pena 1050 opposite the park, has singles/doubles from US$194/214, with a 50% discount for two or more nights.

Places to Eat

At the southern end of Praça da Savassi is the popular *Cafeteria 3 Corações*, good for coffee and cakes. There are lots of lanchonetes and fast-food places clustered around Praça Sete. *Bonanza* meets *ER* at *Bang Bang Burguer*, Rua São Paulo 679 and Avenida Amazonas 322, with waiters in cowboy hats and cooks in surgical masks. *Padaria Zona*, Avenida Parana 163, has super roast chickens at US$3.29 each. The *Demave Lanches* chain has a good outlet at Rua Dos Tupinambas 736.

Torino, at Rua dos Tupinambas 253, has a wood-fired oven, a varied menu and a por quilo lunch.

There are wonderful vegetarian offerings at *Naturalis* (☎ 221-4260), Rua Tome de Souza 689 in Savassi, which has terrific set-lunch specials for about US$6, plus delicious fresh-squeezed juices.

Applause for *Casa Dos Contos* (☎ 222-1070), Rua Rio Grande do Norte 1065, with an arty clientele and great pasta dishes like ravioli al formaggi (US$12) and lots of good meat and fish dishes. Complimentary fritter-like starters get passed out while you wait for your food.

Café com Letras

The coolest place to hang out, write postcards, get great sandwiches and wine by the glass, and meet travellers and expatriate English speakers is *Cafe com Letras* (☎ 225-9973), Rua Antônio Albuquerque 785, near Praça da Savassi.

Along with the best real buffalo mozzarella and sun-dried tomato sandwiches we've had in years (R$5.50 and a bargain at twice the price), crêpes (R$3.50) and other delectables, the place has a Shakespeare & Co bookshop that sells Lonely Planet guides and other English books, and the Clio chocolate shop. It's one-stop conversation, literary fix and decadence.

Entertainment

The *Palácio das Artes* regularly holds concerts, dance presentations and other shows, all for US$6. Check with the tourist office when you're in town for a schedule.

The scene in town is at Praça da Savassi, just down Avenida Cristóvão Columbo from Praça da Liberdade (bus No 2003 from the centre). Chic, flirty hordes descend on the corner of Rua Pernambuco and Rua Tomé de Souza to patronise *Sausalito Point*, *Margaritaville*, *Cold Planet* and *Terra Brasilis*; the crowd fills the streets and everyone joins in. There's live music most nights at *A Obra*, a cool basement place nearby.

Estrella, Rua Curitiba 1275, has great rap and hip-hop parties every second Saturday, with a fun and offbeat crowd.

Things to Buy

The wonderful Sunday **Feira de Arte e Artesano** is open, officially, from 6 am to 1 pm (but it often lasts to about 3 pm) on Avenida Afonso Pena between Rua da Bahia and Rua dos Guajajaras. It has good local crafts and food for sale.

The **Centro de Artesanato Mineiro** (☎ 222-2765), Avenida Afonso Pena 1537, Palácio das Artes (at the edge of the Parque Municipal), is a government store with a varied assortment of mineiro crafts: ceramics, jewellery, tapestries, rugs, quilts and soapstone sculptures. It's open Saturday from 9 am to 8.45 pm and Sunday from 9 am to 1.45 pm.

The **Gem Center**, at Avenida Alvares Cabral 45, is not far from the municipal park. Around 20 reputable gem dealers have small shops in the building.

Getting There & Away

Air There are flights from Belo's two airports to just about anywhere in Brazil and frequent VASP/Cruzeiro/Transbrasil flights link Belo with Rio, Brasilia, Vitória and São Paulo.

City air offices include:

Transbrasil
  Rua dos Tamoios 86 (☎ 274-3533)
Varig/Cruzeiro
  Avenida Olegário Maciel 2251 (☎ 291-9292)
VASP
  Avenida Olegário Maciel 2221, Lourdes (☎ (0800) 99-8277 toll free)

Offices at Confins airport include:

Transbrasil	☎ 689-2475
Varig	☎ 689-2305
VASP	☎ 689-2266

Bus Buses take seven hours to get to Rio (US$22/39 for regular/executivo), 9½ hours to São Paulo (US$25.50/50.50), 12 hours to Brasília (US$24) and around 22 hours to Salvador (US$57); the Salvador bus leaves nightly at 7 pm. Buses take eight hours to Vitória (US$31/51), but the train's cheaper and nicer.

There are 12 buses a day (13 on Sunday) to Ouro Prêto, the first at 7 am and the last at 8.15 pm (9 pm on Sunday). The trip takes 1¾ hours and costs US$6.

There are eight buses a day to Mariana, from 6 am to 11 pm. The two hour trip costs US$4.50. Six buses go daily to Diamantina (US$17.50, 5½ hours), the first at 5.30 am and the last at midnight. Seven go daily to São João del Rei, the first at 6.15 am and the last at 7 pm. From 5 am to 11 pm, buses run to Sabará every 15 minutes; catch them at the local bus section of the rodoviária.

To the mineral spring resorts, there are two buses a day to Caxambu (US$7), at 7.30 am and 9.45 pm; two to São Lourenço (US$8), at 12.30 pm and 11 pm, with an extra 3 pm bus on Friday, and four to Poços das Caldas (US$24).

Train There's a daily train to Vitória (US$11.50/17.50 regular/executivo class; 14 hours) leaving Belo's main train station at 7 am. This train also stops in Santa Bárbara (US$2.40/4.50; three hours; see the Parks section later in this chapter) and Sabará.

Getting Around

To/From the Airports Belo Horizonte has two airports. Most planes use the new international Aeroporto Confins, 40km from the city. The closer, sleepy Aeroporto da Pampulha handles some Rio and São Paulo shuttle flights.

There's a conventional bus (US$6; one hour) to Confins leaving every half hour to an hour between 4.45 am and 10.45 pm. Even though it's not advertised, this bus will stop at Aeroporto da Pampulha on the way to Aeroporto Confins – make sure the driver knows your destination.

An executivo bus (US$11) leaves from Praça Raoul Soares every 45 minutes to an hour between 6 am and 9.45 pm.

AROUND BELO HORIZONTE

Sabará

• *pop 93,000 ✉ 34500-000 ☎ 031*

Sabará stands on the muddy banks of the Rio das Velhas (Old Ladies' River), 25km south-east of Belo. It was the first major gold-mining centre in the state and, at its peak was one of the world's wealthiest towns. This prosperity is reflected in its houses, mansions, churches, statues, fountains and sacred art.

But Sabará is now a poor town dominated by a Belgian metalworks. In the boom years of the early 1700s, when the Rio das Velhas was 15 times wider, slave boats would sail all the way down the Rio São Francisco from Bahia. Sabará produced more gold in one week than the rest of Brazil produced in a year. You can still pan the riverbed for gold flakes, but the nuggets are long gone.

Since it's only half an hour by bus from Belo, Sabará makes an easy and interesting day trip.

Orientation & Information There's an information booth at the entrance to town, but it's useless. The major sights are signposted from Praça Santa Rita anyway.

Churches Most of the churches have small entry fees.

Matriz de NS de Conceição The Portuguese Jesuits, cultural ambassadors of the far-flung Portuguese Empire, were among the first westerners to make contact with the orient. A tangible result is the Matriz de NS de Conceição (1720) on Praça Getúlio Vargas is a fascinating blend of oriental arts and Portuguese baroque – overwhelming with its gold leaf and red Chinese scrolls.

There are even pagodas on some of the church door panels by the sanctuary and several other interesting little details in the church. Floorboards cover the graves of early church members, the gold and silver nuggets nailed on these tablets indicate whether the deceased was rich or poor.

On the ceiling of the church is the patron saint of confessors, John Nepomuceno of 14th century Czechoslovakia, depicted holding his severed tongue. King Wenceslau ordered St Nepumeco's tongue cut out because the saint refused to reveal whether or not the Moldavian queen was faithful. Nepumeco died of his wound, but became very popular posthumously in Czechoslovakian cult circles and, inexplicably, in Minas Gerais during the gold era. Look for the little angel at his side who shushes churchgoers with a finger to his lips.

Igreja de NS do Ó After surviving an attack by his own troops in 1720, Captain Lucas Ribeiro de Almeida built a chapel in thanks to the Virgin Mary. Like NS de Conceição, the chapel has oriental details. It's popular with pregnant women (and those who pray for fertility).

Igreja de NS do Rosário This half-built church on Praça Melo Viana was started and financed by slaves but never finished. It now stands as a memorial to the abolition of slavery in 1888. The church is open daily from 8 am to noon and 2 to 6 pm.

Igreja NS do Carmo Aleijadinho had a lot to do with the decoration of this church on Rua de Carmo. His touch is everywhere, especially in the faces of the statues of São Simão and São João da Cruz.

Other Things to See & Do A testament to the wealth of bygone days, Sabará's elegant opera house, O Teatro Imperial (1770) has crystal lamps and three tiers of seats in carved wood and bamboo cane.

Housed in an old gold foundry (1730), the **Museu do Ouro** (gold museum), Rua da Intendência, contains art and artefacts of Sabará's glory years.

If you're of equestrian bent, Tropa Serrana (☎ 344-8986; mobile ☎ 983-2356), offers spectacular value with its one, two, or five day horse riding treks through the countryside south-east of Belo for US$40/ 80/400, including meals and lodging.

Getting There & Away From Belo, buses leave every 15 minutes from the local section behind the rodoviária. Return buses leave the bus stop on Avenida Victor Fantini; you can also catch one on the road out of town.

Getting Around Túlio Marques Lopes, who's held more jobs than most LP writers, runs the tours. He speaks a bit of English and a smattering of Spanish. Most trips meet at the BH shopping mall but Túlio will pick you up at your hotel if it's central.

The food is excellent, and surprisingly elaborate, consisting of authentic Minerian specialities. Groups of four or more can ride from Belo to Ouro Prêto (five days).

CAVES

Three interesting and popular day trips from Belo Horizonte are to caves within two hours of the city.

Gruta de Maquiné

Gruta de Maquiné (☎ 201-3087), is the most famous, and crowded, of the caves. Its seven huge chambers are well lit to allow guided tours to pass through. Admission is US$4, free for kids under five, and it's open from 8 am to 5 pm. There are cafés at the cave; *Chero's* (☎ 771-7887) has good and cheap comida mineira.

Getting There & Away A bus (US$8.25, 2¼ hours) to the caves departs from Belo Horizonte's rodoviária every day at 8.15 am and returns at 2.45 and 4.20 pm, which gives you ample viewing time.

Gruta da Lapinha

The highlight here (☎ 681-1958) is the Véu da Noiva, a crystal formation in the shape of a bride's veil. Admission is US$4, US$1 for kids under five. Caves are open from 9 am to 4.30 pm.

Getting There & Away A bus (US$4, 45 minutes) leaves Belo's rodoviária every day at 10.15 am and returns at 4 pm.

Gruta Rei do Mato

The Cave of the Forest King (☎ 773-6465) has prehistoric paintings and petroglyphs; admission is US$1.50, free for kids and it's open from 8 am to 7 pm.

Getting There & Away A bus (US$5, 1½ hours) leaves Belo's rodoviária every half hour from 6.30 am, and return buses run until 9.30 pm.

Colonial Towns

CONGONHAS

• *pop 36,000* ✉ *36415-000* ☎ *031*

Little is left of Congonhas' colonial past except the extraordinary *Prophets* of Aleijadinho at the Basílica do Bom Jesus de Matosinhos. While the town is dirty, industrial and commonplace, these dramatic statues are exceptional. They are Aleijadinho's masterpiece and Brazil's most famed work of art. It's worth taking the trouble to get to Congonhas just to see them.

Congonhas is 72km south of Belo Horizonte, 3km off Hwy BR-040. The city grew up with the search for gold in the nearby Rio Maranhão, and the economy today is dominated by iron mining in the surrounding countryside.

The 12 Prophets

Already an old man, sick and crippled, Aleijadinho sculpted the *Prophets* from 1800 to 1805. Symmetrically placed in front of the **Basílica do Bom Jesus de Matosinhos**, each of the prophets from the Old Testament was carved out of one or two blocks of soapstone. Each carries a Latin message: six of them are good, six bad.

Much has been written about these sculptures – their dynamic quality, the sense of movement (much like a Hindu dance or a ballet), how they complement each other and how their arrangement prevents them from being seen in isolation. The poet Carlos Drummond de Andrade wrote that the dramatic faces and gestures are 'magnificent, terrible, grave and tender' and commented on 'the way the statues, of human size, appear to be larger than life as they look down upon the viewer with the sky behind them'.

Before working on the *Prophets*, Aleijadinho carved or supervised his assistants in carving the wooden statues which were placed in the six little **chapels** that represent the Passion of Christ: The Last Supper, Calvary, Imprisonment, Flagellation and

Aleijadinho

The church of São Francisco de Assis, the Carmo church façade, the *Prophets* of Congonhas do Campos and innumerable relics in Mariana, Sabará, Tiradentes and São João del Rei were all carved by Aleijadinho (Antônio Francisco Lisboa).

Brazil's Michelangelo lost the use of his hands and legs at the age of 30 but, with a hammer and chisel strapped to his arms, he advanced art in Brazil from the excesses of the baroque to a finer, more graceful rococo. The Mineiros have reason to be proud of Aleijadinho – he is a figure of international prominence in the history of art. Aleijadinho's angels have his stylistic signature: wavy hair, wide-open eyes and big, round cheeks.

The son of a Portuguese architect and a black slave, Aleijadinho lived from 1730 to 1814 and was buried in the Matriz NS da Conceirção, within 50 paces of his birth site. By federal decree he was declared patron of Brazilian arts in 1973. For many years, Manuel da Costa Ataíde, from nearby Mariana, successfully collaborated with Aleijadinho on many churches. Aleijadinho would sculpt the exterior and a few interior pieces and Ataíde would paint the interior panels. With his secretly concocted vegetable dyes, Ataíde fleshed out much of Aleijadinho's work.

Coronation, Carrying of the Cross and the Crucifixion.

Some of the figures, such as the Roman soldiers, are very crude and clearly done by assistants, while others are finely chiselled. The statues were restored in 1957 by the painter Edson Mota, and the gardens were designed by Burle Marx.

Special Events

Held from 7 to 14 September, the Jubileu do Senhor Bom Jesus do Matosinhos is one of the great religious festivals in Minas Gerais. Each year, approximately 600,000 pilgrims arrive at the church to make promises and do penance, receive blessings and give and receive alms. The Holy Week processions in Congonhas are also famous, especially the dramatisations on Good Friday.

Places to Stay & Eat

If you start early, you can avoid spending a night here – there's nothing here but the *Prophets*. The *Colonial Hotel* (☎ 731-1834) is basic but friendly; it has a pool and it's right across the street from the *Prophets*. Clean quartos cost US$15 per person, apartamentos are US$25/45 a single/double.

Next door, the *Cova do Daniel* restaurant is good, if frayed at the edges.

Getting There & Away

There are six daily buses from Belo Horizonte to Congonhas (US$5.75, 1¾ hours). The last return bus to Belo Horizonte leaves Congonhas at 8.20 pm. Buses leave every 45 minutes for Conselheiro Lafaiete (US$1.45, 30 minutes) from 5.30 am to 6.15 pm.

From there, you can catch buses to Ouro Prêto (US$6.50, 2½ hours) which leave Monday to Friday at 7.05 and 9 am, noon, and 3 and 6 pm; Saturday at 7.05 am, noon 3 and 6 pm; and Sunday at 6 am, 3 and 6 pm.

Try to get to Lafaiete a bit early to make sure you get a bus; if you do miss the last bus, there are a couple of hotels across from the rodoviária.

From Ouro Prêto to Lafaiete, buses leave Monday to Saturday at 5 am and 9 am (no 5am bus Saturday), noon, and 2.50 and 6 pm; on Sunday they leave at 6 am, noon, and 2.40 and 6 pm.

There are also midnight buses from Lafaiete to Rio.

From Congonhas to São João del Rei, catch one of the Belo Horizonte to São João del Rei buses that stop off at Congonhas. There are seven a day, the first at 7.30 am and the last at 8.20 pm.

Getting Around

From the rodoviária, the Basílica bus leaves every half hour and costs US$0.40. It's a 15 minute ride up the hill to the basilica and the *Prophets*. Get off just after the bus passes the church (as it heads downhill) for the best approach and first view of the statues. The same bus returns you to the rodoviária, or you can have the Colonial Hotel staff call you a taxi (US$5).

OURO PRÊTO

• *pop 65,000 ✉ 35400-000 ☎ 031*

Ouro Prêto, in the remote Serra do Espinhaço range, is truly the jewel in the minero crown. The odd-shaped peak of Itacolomy (1752m), 18km from town, which the first bandeirantes to penetrate the region used as a reference point, is the first sign you're approaching the city.

History

According to the Jesuit Antonil, a mulatto servant in the Antônio Rodrigues Arzão expedition went to the rivulet Tripui to quench his thirst and pocketed a few grains of an odd black metal he found in the stream bed. It turned out to be gold, of course, but the exact location of the river was forgotten during the long expedition; only the strange shape of the peaks of Itacolomy were remembered.

In 1698, Antônio Dias de Oliveira rediscovered the area, convinced he had found El Dorado. The mines were the largest deposits of gold in the western hemisphere, and the news and gold fever spread fast. Stories abound of men who acquired fabulous wealth from one day to the next, and others who died of hunger with their pockets full of gold.

Portuguese King Dom João V was quick to claim a royal fifth in tax, and a chain of posts was established to ensure that the crown got its cut. In theory, all gold was brought to these *casas de intendências* to be weighed and turned into bars, and the royal fifth was set aside. Tax shirkers were cast into dungeons or exiled to Africa. One common technique used to avoid the tax was to hide gold powder in hollow images of the saints.

Bitter about the tax, the Paulista miners rebelled unsuccessfully against the Portuguese. Two years later, in 1711, Vila Rica de Ouro Prêto, the present town's predecessor, was founded.

The finest goods from India and England were made available to the simple mining town. The gold bought the services of baroque artisans, who turned the city into an architectural gem. At the height of the gold boom in the mid-18th century, there were 110,000 people (mainly slaves) in Ouro Prêto versus 50,000 in New York and about 20,000 in Rio de Janeiro.

The royal fifth, estimated at 100 tonnes of gold in the 18th century, quickly passed through the hands of the Portuguese court, built up Lisbon and then financed the British Industrial Revolution.

The greed of the Portuguese led to sedition by the inhabitants of Vila Rica (1720). As the boom tapered off, the miners found it increasingly difficult to pay ever-larger gold taxes. In 1789, poets Claudio da Costa and Tomás Antônio Gonzaga, Joaquim José da Silva Xavier (nicknamed Tiradentes, 'tooth-puller', for his dentistry skills) and

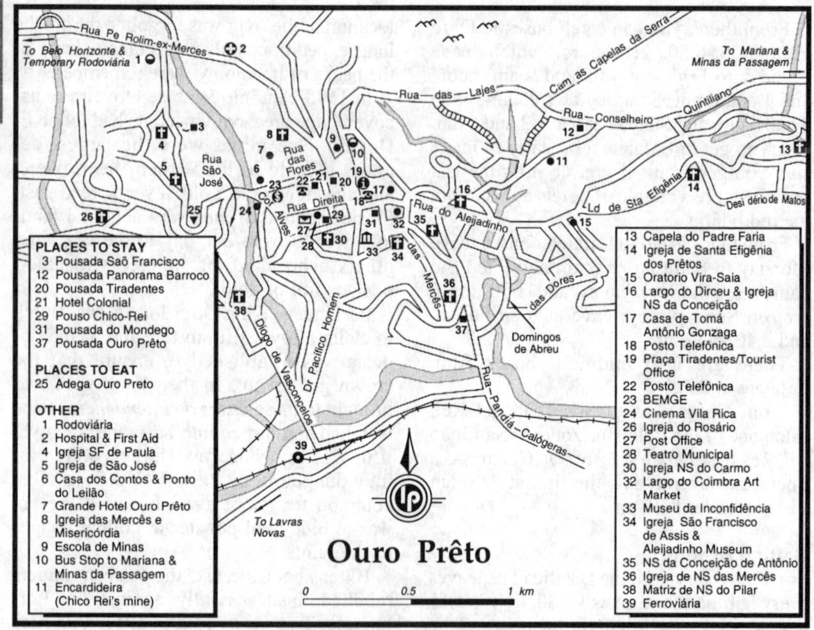

others, full of French revolutionary philosophies, hatched the Inconfidência Mineira.

The rebellion was crushed in its early stages by agents of the crown. Gonzaga was exiled to Mozambique, and Costa did time in prison. Tiradentes, the only man not to deny his role in the conspiracy, was abandoned by his friends, jailed for three years without defence, then drawn and quartered.

By decree of Emperor Dom Pedro I, Vila Rica, capital of Minas Gerais since 1721, became the Imperial City of Ouro Prêto. In 1897, the state capital was shifted from Ouro Prêto to Belo Horizonte. This was the decisive move that preserved Ouro Prêto's colonial flavour.

The former capital assumes the symbolic role of state capital once a year, on 24 June. The city was declared a Brazilian national monument in 1933, and in 1981 UNESCO proclaimed Ouro Prêto a World Cultural Heritage Site.

Climate

The city is 1km above sea level and temperatures vary from 2° to 28°C. Winters are pretty cold. It can be rainy and foggy all year round, but you can expect daily showers in December and January.

Orientation

Praça Tiradentes is the town centre. Ouro Prêto is divided into two parishes. If you stand in Praça Tiradentes facing the Museu da Inconfidência, the parish of Pilar is to the right, the parish of Antônio Dias to the left.

All of Ouro Prêto's streets have at least two names: the official one and the one used by the locals because the other one is too much of a mouthful. Rua Conde Bobadella, the street leading off to the right from Praça Tiradentes as you're facing the Museu da Inconfidência, is commonly known as Rua Direita. Rua Conselheiro Quintiliano is known as Rua das Lajes and Rua Senador

Rocha Lagoa as Rua das Flores. To add to the confusion, the names are rarely posted.

The town is very hilly and the rain-slicked, cobblestone streets are extremely steep. Bring comfortable walking shoes with good tread.

If you plan to spend only one day in Ouro Prêto, make sure it's not a Monday, as almost all the museums and churches are closed then.

Information

Tourist Office The tourist office, Praça Tiradentes 41, is open from 8 am to 6 pm during the week and from 8 am to 5 pm on weekends. English is spoken and staff give out a leaflet which indicates the opening times of the museums and churches; they also sell good maps (US$2) and copies of *Guia de Ouro Prêto*, by Manuel Bandeira, in Portuguese (US$10). *Passeio a Ouro Prêto*, by Lucia Machado de Almeida, has sections in English, French and Portuguese and costs US$22. By the same author is the *Minas Gerais Roteiro Turístico-Cultural das Cidades Historicas* (Embratur-AGGS). Lonely Planet thanks Embratur for permission to use this material when discussing the myths and legends of Ouro Prêto.

Official guides (US$30 for four hour tours, US$54 for four to eight hours) and interpreters (US$42/66) can be booked at the tourist office. Cássio really knows his baroque and speaks excellent English. Beware of unofficial guides as there are some nasty characters hanging around.

The tourist office also organises treks into the surrounding hills and horserides to Itacolomy. The cost is around US$50 for the day. Speak to João, Alexandre or Renaldo a day before you go, to give them enough time to get the horses ready.

Money The BEMGE bank is near the Casa dos Contas. Banco do Brasil is at Rua São José 195, and most of the jewellery stores in town will change cash dollars.

Post & Communications The post office is in Rua Direita, near Praça Tiradentes. The posto telefônica is on the east side of the praça around the corner from the tourist office.

Things to See

Apart from Niemeyer's **Grande Hotel Ouro Prêto** and two other modern monstrosities, no 20th century buildings defile this stunningly beautiful colonial city. Spend a day walking on the cobblestone roads around the dark rock walls of the village admiring its carved fountains, statues and crumbling orange-tiled roofs. Through the mist is a vista of green hills and church steeples.

If you hustle it's possible to see most of the sights in the **Antônio Dias parish** in the morning, lunch in or about **Praça Tiradentes**, and spend the afternoon visiting the **Pilar parish**, the **mineral museum** and the **Inconfidência museum**. But you need, at the least, two days to see the town and its surroundings properly.

Most churches charge admission of around US$2, so pick and choose if you're on a tight budget. Our favourites are, in rough order: **Igreja de São Francisco de Assis** (if you only visit one, make sure it's this one), **Igreja de Santa Efigênia dos Prêtos**, **Matriz de NS do Pilar** and **Capela do Padre Faria**.

Start at about 7.30 am from Praça Tiradentes and walk along Rua das Lajes, the road to Mariana, for a panoramic view of town.

Those after something strenuous can hike to the peak of Itacolomy; it's 18km from Praça Tiradentes. **Parque Itacolomy** is a pleasant excursion, with good walking trails, waterfalls and orchids (the easiest approach is from Mariana).

Capela do Padre Faria Work your way downhill off the road to this chapel. Padre Faria was one of the original bandeirantes, and the chapel (built between 1701 and 1704) is Ouro Prêto's oldest. The chapel is set behind a triple-branched papal cross (1756), the three branches representing the temporal, spiritual and material powers of the Pope. It's the richest chapel in terms of gold and artwork but, due to poor documentation the artists are anonymous. In 1750 the church bell rang for Tiradentes (when his body was taken to Rio); later, it rang once again for the inauguration of Brasília. Note that the angel on the right-hand side of the high altar has butterfly wings. The church is open from 8 am to noon.

Igreja de Santa Efigênia dos Prêtos Descending the Ladeira do Padre Faria back towards town, you'll come to the Igreja de Santa Efigênia dos Prêtos, built between 1742 and 1749 by and for the black slave community. Santa Efigênia, patron saint of the church, was the Queen of Nubia and the featured saints, Santo Antônio do Nolo and São Benedito, are black. The slaves prayed to these images that they wouldn't be crushed in the mines.

The church is Ouro Prêto's poorest in terms of gold and its richest in terms of artwork. The altar is by Aleijadinho's master, Francisco Javier do Briton. Many of the interior panels are by Manuel Rabelo de Souza (see if you can find the painting of Robinson Crusoe), and the exterior image of NS do Rosário is by Aleijadinho himself. The church was financed by gold extracted from Chico-Rei's gold mine, Encardadeira (see the boxed text 'Chico-Rei'). Slaves contributed to the church coffer by washing their gold-flaked hair in baptismal fonts. Others managed to smuggle gold powder under fingernails and inside tooth cavities. The church is open from 8 am to noon.

Oratorio Vira-Saia At the beginning of the 18th century, there was a rash of ghost incidents in the city. Phantoms sprung from the walls near Santa Efigênia church and winged through town, spooking the townspeople. The simple village folk would faint and drop their bags of gold powder, which the bandit-like ghosts would snatch. The terrorised people asked the bishop for permission to build oratories, and the bishop complied. Designed to keep evil spirits at bay, the oratories (glass-encased niches containing images of saints) were built on many street corners.

Not many oratories remain, but there's one on Rua dos Paulistas (also called Bernardo Vasconcelos) and another on Rua Antônio Dias; the most famous one of all is the Oratorio Vira-Saia. Nowadays, these few remaining oratories are used to scare off evil spirits during Holy Week.

The small oratory of Vira-Saia is at the bottom of the Ladeira de Santa Efigênia (also known as Vira-Saia), on the corner with Rua Barão do Ouro Branco. 'Vira-Saia' has two possible meanings: it may originate from the Portuguese *virar* (turn) and *sair*

Chico-Rei

The first abolitionist in Brazil was Chico-Rei, an African tribal king. Amid the frenzy of the gold rush an entire tribe, king and all, was captured in Africa, sent to Brazil and sold to a mine owner in Ouro Prêto.

Chico-Rei worked as the foreman of the slave miners. Working Sundays and holidays, he finally bought his freedom from the slave master, then freed his son Osmar. Together, father and son liberated the entire tribe.

This collective then bought the fabulously wealthy Encardadeira gold mine, and Chico-Rei assumed his royal functions once again, holding court in Vila Rica and celebrating African holidays in traditional costume.

News of this reached the Portuguese king, who immediately prohibited slaves from purchasing their freedom.

Chico-Rei is now a folk hero among Brazilian blacks.

(depart) or, alternatively, comes from *vira-saia*, which means turncoat or traitor.

In the latter part of the 18th century, gold caravans destined for the Portuguese crown were robbed on a regular basis, despite measures to cloak shipments by altering dates and routes. It didn't take long to surmise that it was an inside job. Someone working in the Casa de Fundição was leaking information.

No one suspected that Antônio Francisco Alves – pillar of the community, upstanding citizen, mild-mannered businessman and gentle father – was the brains behind the Vira-Saia bandits who looted the government's gold caravans. After a caravan's route was planned, Alves would steal out to the oratory and turn the image of NS das Almas within the sanctuary to face the direction of the gold traffic.

A reward was posted for the identity of the criminal. Finally a member of Alves' own band, Luis Gibut, turned him in. Gibut was a French Jesuit who fell in love with a beautiful woman, abandoned the order, became a highway bandit and, eventually, the turncoat's turncoat. This same Luis Gibut was responsible for teaching Aleijadinho the misspelled Latin phrases which the artist incorporated into many of his works.

Alves, his wife and his daughters were dragged off into the jungle to meet their fate. Sra Duruta, a good neighbour, came to the rescue and saved Alves, but it was too late for his wife and kids. Alves was one step ahead of the long arm of the law, but he didn't get off scot free. Shortly afterwards, he was plugged by another unnamed vira-saia. The criminal gang continued to do successful robberies without its first chief. Luis Gibut, ex-Jesuit, traitor and poor speller, is probably still doing time in purgatory.

Largo do Dirceu Largo do Dirceu is next, just before you get to the Igreja Matriz NS da Conceição de Antônio Dias. This used to be a popular hangout of the poet Tomás Antônio Gonzaga and his girlfriend and muse, Marília. It figures prominently in *Marília de Dirceu*, the most celebrated poem in the Portuguese language.

Matriz NS da Conceição de Antônio Dias & Around The cathedral of the Antônio Dias parish, Matriz NS da Conceição de Antônio Dias was designed by Aleijadinho's father, Manuel Francisco Lisboa, and built between the years 1727 and 1770. Note the painting of the eagle; its head points downwards, symbolising the domination of the Moors by the Christians. Aleijadinho is buried by the altar of Boa Morte. The cathedral is open from 8 am to noon and 1 to 5 pm.

The Museu do Aleijadinho adjoins the church and has the same hours. Nearby is Encardideira, the abandoned mine of Chico-Rei (ask around for directions). It's dangerous, full of crumbling secret passageways and rumoured to be haunted.

Casa de Tomás Antônio Gonzaga Rua do Ouvidor 9 is the address of Tomás Antônio Gonzaga's house, now the seat of the municipal government. This is where Gonzaga, his poet friend Claudio da Costa (author of *Vila Rica*), Tiradentes and others conspired unsuccessfully to overthrow the Portuguese monarchy. The sad little event came to be known as the Inconfidência Mineira.

Igreja de São Francisco de Assis Across the street from Gonzaga's house is the Igreja de São Francisco de Assis. After the *Prophets* in Congonhas, Aleijadinho's masterpiece, this is the single most important piece of Brazilian colonial art, and it was lovingly restored in 1992. The entire exterior, a radical departure from the military baroque style, was carved by Aleijadinho himself, from the soapstone medallion to the cannon waterspouts and the military (two-bar) cross. The interior was painted by Aleijadinho's long-term partner, Manuel da Costa Ataíde.

The sacristy is said to be haunted by the spirit of an 18th century woman. In the dead of night, her head dissolves into a skull and she screams: 'I'm dying, call Father Carlos'. The church and adjoining Aleijadinho museum are open from 8.20 to 11.45 am and 1.30 to 4.45 pm.

Praça Tiradentes Praça Tiradentes is the centre of town. It's a good place to have lunch, catch your breath by the statue of Tiradentes, or take in some museums before the churches of the Pilar parish open in the afternoon.

The **Museu da Inconfidência**, formerly the old municipal headquarters and jail, is an attractive building built between 1784 and 1854. Used as a prison from 1907 until 1937, the museum contains the Tiradentes' tomb, documents of the Inconfidência Mineira, torture instruments and important works by Ataíde and Aleijadinho. The museum is open from noon to 5.30 pm.

Igreja NS do Carmo The Igreja NS do Carmo was a group effort by the most important artists of the area. Begun in 1766 and completed in 1772, the church features a facade by Aleijadinho. It's open from 8 to 11.30 am and 1 to 5.30 pm.

Casa de Tiradentes The home of Joaquim José da Silva Xavier (Tiradentes) is near the church. After his failed rebellion against the Portuguese which ended with his execution in Rio, Tiradentes' head was paraded around town. His house was demolished and its grounds were salted to ensure that nothing would grow there.

Escola de Minas The Escola de Minas in the old governor's palace in Praça Tiradentes has a very fine museum of metals and mineralogy. It's open from noon to 5 pm Monday to Friday.

Casa dos Contos The Casa dos Contos (Counting House, US$1) is now a public library and art gallery. Claudio da Costa was imprisoned here after participating in the Inconfidência Mineira. It is open from 12.30 to 5 pm. Next door is the **Ponto do Leilão**, where slaves were taken to be tortured.

Matriz de NS do Pilar The Matriz de NS do Pilar is the second most opulent church in Brazil (after Salvador's São Francisco) in terms of gold. It has 434kg of gold and silver and is one of Brazil's finest showcases of artwork. Note the wild bird chandelier holders, the laminated beaten gold, the scrolled church doors, 15 panels of Old and New Testament scenes by Pedro Gomes Chaes, and the hair on Jesus (the real stuff, donated by a penitent worshipper).

Legend has it that the Pilar and Antônio Dias parishes vied for the image of NS dos Passos. In order to settle the argument, the image was loaded onto a horse standing in Praça Tiradentes and rockets were fired to scare the horse; the idea was that the image would belong to the parish to which the horse bolted. Since the horse knew only one path, it galloped straight to the Matriz do Pilar. The church is open from noon to 5 pm.

Teatro Municipal Built in 1769 by João de Souza Lisboa, the Teatro Municipal is the oldest theatre in Minas Gerais and perhaps in Brazil. The theatre is open from 1 to 5.30 pm.

Special Events

Ouro Prêto's Semana Santa (Holy Week) procession, held on the Thursday before Palm Sunday and sporadically until Easter Sunday, is quite a spectacle. The Congado is to Minas what Candomblé is to Bahia and Umbanda is to Rio: the local expression of Afro-Christian syncretism. The major Congado celebrations are for NS do Rosário (on 23 to 25 October, at the Capela do Padre Faria), for the New Year and for 13 May (the anniversary of abolition).

The Cavalhada, held in Amarantina (near Ouro Prêto) during the Festa de São Gonçalo from 17 to 23 September, isn't as grand as the one in Pirenópolis, but is impressive nonetheless. The Cavalhada is a re-enactment of the battles between Christians and Muslims in Iberia.

Carnaval in Ouro Prêto is popular, too, a special feature being the *janela erótica* (erotic window), along Rua Direita, where people dance naked behind a thin curtain.

Places to Stay – Budget

Ouro Prêto is a university town, with schools of pharmacy and biochemistry, mineralogy, geology and engineering. Twenty per cent of housing here is devoted to student lodging, known as *repúblicas*. We don't recommend them, although they are the cheapest places to stay in town; they're closed from Christmas to Carnaval, they're loud, and they stack as many people as possible into rooms, with mattresses on the floor.

The tourist office will ring around to find a vacancy for you, though don't expect it to find cheap places – despite claims to the contrary, it charges more than the hotels directly, so you're better on your own.

The two cheapest places have great views. The best deal in town is the *Pousada São Francisco* (no ☎), Rua Padre José Marcos Penna 202 next to the Igreja de São Francisco de Paula *(not* São Francisco de Assis), which has absolutely spectacular views and seriously friendly staff. Spotless dormitory beds with/without a view are US$10/15 per person; apartamentos are US$20/30 for singles/doubles. There's a communal kitchen and breakfast is included. From the rodoviária, walk 100m down the hill to the church; facing downhill, look for the break in the fence on the left and follow the path down to the pousada. If you pass the church you've missed the turn.

The *Pousada Panorama Barroco* (☎ 551-2582), Rua Conselheiro Quintiliano 722, north-east of the centre, charges US$10 per person in quartos, plus US$4 for breakfast.

Hospedaria Casarão (☎ 551-2056) at Rua Direita 94-B is a family home above a store. There are eight rooms and the cost is US$10 per person.

A fine bet is the *Pousada Ouro Prêto* (☎/fax 551-3081), Largo Musicista José das Anjos Costa (also called das Mercês) 72, right below the Igreja NS das Mercês. It's a friendly place and Gerson, who runs it, speaks English. It, too, has a fantastic view, and all the comforts that delight the traveller. It's US$30/50/60 for single/double/triple apartamentos.

Places to Stay – Mid-Range

There are a number of mid-range hotels close to the centre of town. *Pousada Tiradentes* (☎ 551-2619), Praça Tiradentes 70, opposite the tourist office, is exceptionally good value at US$40/50 for single/double apartamentos in low season, US$75/90 in high. It features Carribean paintwork, huge rooms and friendly staff.

The chilly *Hotel Colonial* (☎ 551-3133) at Travessa Camilo Veloso 26 has single/double apartamentos for US$50/70. The *Pousada Nella Nuno* (☎ 551-3375) at Rua Camilo de Brito 59 has nice double quartos for US$40 and apartamentos for US$55 a double. There's lots of art here as the owner is an artist.

Places to Stay – Top End

The *Pouso Chico-Rei* (☎ 551-1274) at Rua Brigideiro Mosqueira 90 has wonderful doubles completely furnished in antiques (US$65/80 without/with bath).

Pousada do Mondego (☎ 551-2040; fax 551-3094) at Largo do Coimbra 38 is close to Igreja São Francisco de Assis; it's in an 18th century colonial mansion. Singles/doubles start at US$120/136, but you'll pay more if you want the view (starting at US$135/155). This is an excellent top-end choice.

The five-star *Solar NS do Rosário* (☎ 551-4200; fax 551-4288) at Rua Getúlio Vargas 270 even boasts its own mine. Swank singles/doubles go for US$140/160.

Places to Eat

Most of the restaurants are clustered along two streets, Rua Direita and Rua São José. Ouro Prêto is a good place to try some regional cooking. One typical Minas dish is tutu a mineira, a black-bean feijoada with couve (a type of kale). *Restaurante Casa Do Ouvidor* on Rua Direita is the place to try it.

Frango na Brasa Lua Cheia (☎ 551-3143), Rua Direita 151, has fabulous stuff for vegetarians, Asian-influenced recipes and fresh everything. It also has meat dishes, all good except the churrasco, which is vile. It's US$7/kg at lunch and reasonable per plate prices at night.

Another very good bet is *Adega Ouro Prêto* (☎ 551-4171), Ladeira São José 24, near the pousada São Francisco, with good por quilo at lunch (US$7/kg) but more expensive Italian food at night.

Café e Cia at Rua São José 187 has good sandwiches and a great view of the town. It also has a self-serve lunch.

Five of us ate very nicely with a large pizza (US$13.50) at *De Consola's*, a cozy place in the Antonio Diaz section of town; it also has a good wine selection.

Entertainment

The kids hang out in Praça Tiradentes before thronging to *Club Ouro Prêto*, Praça de Sportes, for some slow and steamy dancing. It's open Saturday and Sunday nights from 8 to 11 pm. The rest of the week, especially on Friday and Saturday after 11 pm, there's a lot of spontaneous music in the bars and from buskers along Rua Direita.

Acaso 85, opposite the Hotel Rosario, is a very chic place for drinks, set in a recently rediscovered two-level limestone cellar with a fireplace.

The *Cinema Vila Rica* has first run films in English and kids' films during the day.

Things to Buy

A soapstone quarry in Santa Rita de Ouro Prêto, 28km away, provides endless supplies for attractive carvings, and imitations of Aleijadinho. Woodcarvings, basketwork and unglazed ceramics are sold in the souvenir shops of Praça Tiradentes. Largo do Coimbra, a block east, is a very good weekend art market.

Imperial topaz is found only in this area of Brazil, and there are lots of gem shops around Praça Tiradentes. Casa das Pedras and Grupiara Pedras both sell topaz with a certificate of guarantee.

Getting There & Away

There's frequent service between Belo Horizonte and Ouro Prêto; see the Belo chapter for more information (US$6, 1¾ hours). During peak periods, buy your bus tickets a day in advance – they sell out fast. One bus a day goes to Rio, at 11 pm (US$14, seven hours).

Getting Around

In 1996, a landslide wiped out the main road to town and the Rodoviária was moved about 1km west. In mid-1998, the city was saying that the old rodoviária should be reopened 'very soon'. If it's not (which is likely), from the 'temporary' rodoviária walk east about 500m, around the rickety wooden sidewalk near where the road collapsed, then walk another 250m to the permanent station. In town, you can go everywhere on foot.

AROUND OURO PRÊTO

Minas de Passagem

We get a kick out of this place, probably the best gold mine to visit in the Ouro Prêto region. There's an immense system of tunnels that goes down very deep and then spreads horizontally. Only a fraction of the mine is open to the public, but for most terrestrials, it's enough.

The descent into the mine is made in a rickety antique cable car (though the guide is quick to assure you that the cable itself is new), giving you a first-hand idea of just how dangerous mining can be.

The mine opened in 1719. Until the abolition of slavery, it was worked by black slaves, many of whom died dynamiting into the rock. Even after abolition, the life of the 'free' miner was little improved.

The mandatory guided tour, led by former miners and in English where possible, is short and quite informative. It covers the mine's history and details the work methods used to extract the gold, quartz and other metals. There's a **shrine** to dead miners at the bottom.

The mine (☎ 557-1255) is open Monday to Saturday from 9 am to 5.30 pm, to 4 pm Sunday and the entry fee is a stiff US$15 per person. This is mitigated by the mine's shallow, sparkling clear 2km-wide **subterranean lake**, in which you are free to

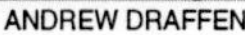

ANDREW DRAFFEN

ANDREW DRAFFEN

ANDREW DRAFFEN

JOHN MAIER, JR

Top Left: Presidential Guard
Middle: Cathedral Brasília

Top Right: Interior of Cathedral Brasília
Bottom: Inside the main chapel, Cathedral Brasília

JOHN MAIER, JR

JOHN MAIER, JR

JOHN MAIER, JR

Top: Bridges of the Pantanal
Bottom Left: Pantanal Sunset
Bottom Right: Wading in the Pantanal

swim. The water's cold, averaging 16° to 18°C, but blue and pure and it's great fun, so bring a bathing suit.

The mine is between Ouro Prêto and Mariana. Take any local bus (US$0.85 from Ouro Prêto, US$0.35 from Mariana) that runs between the two and ask the driver to let you off at Minas de Passagem.

MARIANA

• pop 40,000 ✉ 35420-000 ☎ 031

Founded in 1696, Mariana is a pleasant old mining town with a character unlike its busy neighbour, Ouro Prêto, only 12km away by paved road. Mariana is touristed but not overrun, retaining the high-altitude tranquillity of many of the mining towns.

Information

The tourist terminal (☎ 557-1158), where the bus from Ouro Prêto stops, has an information office which gives away excellent free maps and sells worthless ones for US$3. It also sells Portuguese-language guidebooks.

Things to See

The 18th century churches of **São Pedro dos Clérigos**, **NS da Assunção** and **São Francisco**, and the **Catedral Basílica da Sé**, with its fantastic German organ dating from 1701, are all worthwhile. There are **organ concerts** every Sunday at 12.30 pm (US$6).

The **museum** at Casa Capitular is also worth a look. While walking through the old part of town, you'll come across painters and wood sculptors at work in their studios.

Places to Stay

The *Hotel Central* (☎ 557-1630), Rua Frei Durão 8, is a real budget hotel with quartos for US$15/27 a single/double and apartamentos for US$23/39.

The *Hotel Providência* (☎ 557-1444), Rua Dom Silveiro 233, is an interesting cheapie. Originally the living quarters for the nuns who still run a school next door, it has a chapel (for pious tightwads), and an excellent swimming pool. You have to go through the school to get to it, so don't walk around in your swimming gear or the nuns might have heart attacks. Quartos are US$18/32 and apartamentos are US$22/35 a single/double.

Just around the corner, the *Pousada do Chafariz* (☎ 557-1492), Rua Con Rego 149, has modern rooms with TV and frigobar (but obdurate staff) for US$30/48.

The best hotel in town is the *Pouso da Typographia* (☎ 557-1577; fax 557-1311), Praça Gomes Freire 220. It's worth going in just to see the antique printing presses in the foyer. Singles/doubles cost US$58/81.50, but you can bargain during the week.

Places to Eat

Frango na Brasa Lua Cheia (☎ 557-3232), Rua Dom Viçoso 23, has everything as good as at the branch in Ouro Prêto, at the same prices. Nearby, there are wonderful breads and sweets at *Pão Pão*.

Restaurante Tambaú, near the town square, also has good regional food at reasonable prices, as does *Tempero de Minas*, two doors down from the Pousada do Chafariz. There's surprisingly good self-serve food (US$7/kg) at the bus station.

Getting There & Away

A bus (US$0.85, 35 minutes) leaves Ouro Prêto for Mariana every half hour from the far side of the Escola de Minas.

LAVRAS NOVAS

• pop under 1000 ☎ 031

The very off-the-beaten-track village of Lavras Novas is 22km south of Ouro Prêto. The area around it is stunningly beautiful mountain country, and there are two waterfalls within easy hikes.

The town was founded as a *quilombo*, a refuge of runaway slaves – see the History section in the introductory Facts about the Country chapter for a full explanation.

Today it's a peaceful little town that gets invaded by Mineiro ecotourists during th e holidays, on their way through for climbing, hiking and swimming. The focal point is the **Church of Cristo Redentor**.

Waterfalls

The two closest waterfalls are **Chapada**, 9km west, with natural swimming pools, and **Moinho,** 2km north, which is peaceful and less frequented.

Horse Riding

Carlos rents horses for US$15 to $20 a half day. Ask at any of the pousadas or restaurants and they'll find him.

Places to Stay & Eat

At the east end of town, opposite the church, is *Pensão doa Maria* (☎ 557-2092). It has quartos for US$10/person, and though Maria's nice, you get what you pay for. She's got a restaurant with surprisingly good chicken (US$0.50 per drumstick), and US$3 for the plate of the day. *Pousada Alisson* (☎ 961-1317), run by the folks who operate the *Lavrinhas Restaurant*, both at the west end of town, is a charming and more than spotless pousada with a wood stove and doubles at US$43 to $58 including breakfast and lunch. The restaurant has huge views into the valley and lovely pastries.

At the east end of town, behind the church, is the excellent *Casa Antiga Taberna*, a cozy bar and restaurant with a fireplace, live music and food – the plate of the day is US$5.

Getting There & Away

Local bus services are such that you'll have to spend at least a night here – a bus leaves Praça Tiradente daily at 5.15 pm and returns the following day at 6.45 am. Hitching is possible but difficult; the road is well signed. Start from the road above the abandoned train station at Ouro Prêto's southern end. By car, the dirt road is bumpy and precipitous, the scenery beautiful. After heading south past the old train station, pass the aluminium factory and at the intersection ignore signs to turn left or right. Continue straight across the main road and follow it for 17km.

SÃO JOÃO DEL REI

• pop 74,000 ✉ 36300-000 ☎ 032

São João del Rei is one of Minas Gerais' original gold towns. The old city centre, which is protected by Brazil's Landmarks Commission, features several of the country's finest churches and some fine colonial mansions – one of which belonged to the late and still-popular ex-president Tancredo Neves. It also has a good museum, a variety of other sites and activities and is the gateway for excursions to the stunningly beautiful village of Tiradentes.

The city sits between the Serra de São José and the Serra do Lenheiro, near the southern end of the Serra do Espinhaço.

Orientation

The city is bisected by the Rio Lenheiro, which is traversed by several bridges, including two 18th century stone ones.

São João del Rei is sandwiched between two hills, both of which provide excellent views, particularly at sunset. The rodoviária is a 15 minute walk north-west of the old centre.

Information

Tourist Office The tourist information office (☎ 371-7833), Praça Frei Orlando 90 opposite the São Francisco church, is open from 8 am to 5 pm. Also helpful is the Associação Commercial e Industrial (☎ 371-7377), Avenida Hermilio Alves 272, near the theatre. French speakers can find those of that ilk at the Alliance Françaises (☎ 981-1462) at Rua Padre José Maria Xavier 66a.

Money Change cash and travellers cheques at the BEMGE bank, Avenida Presidente Tancredo Neves 213. Banco do Brasil on Avenida Hermilio Alves has a Visa/Plus ATM.

Post & Communications The post office is on Avenida Tiradentes. There are telephone posts on Avenida Presidente Tancredo Neves and at the rodoviária.

Churches

Floodlights illuminate the churches each night and give them a fantastic appearance.

Igreja de São Francisco de Assis This exquisite baroque church (1774) is one of

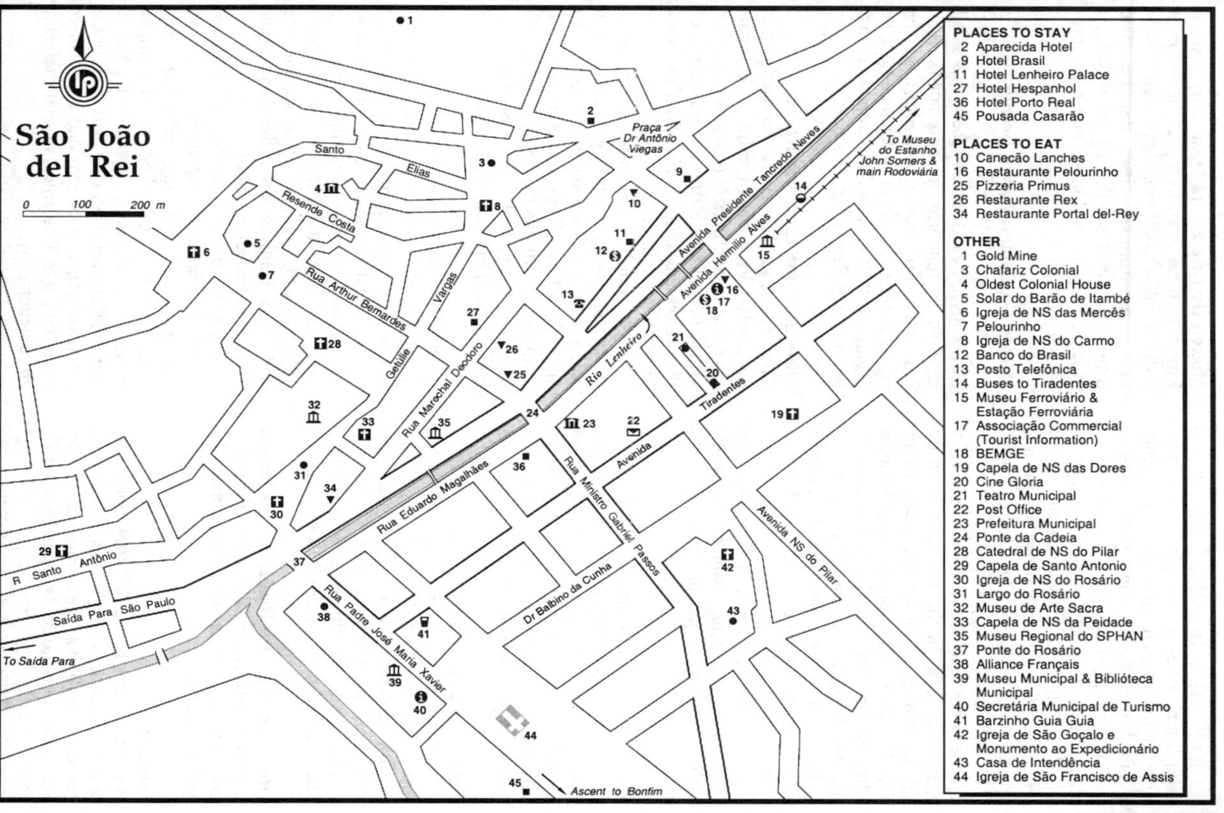
São João del Rei
0 100 200 m
PLACES TO STAY
2 Aparecida Hotel
9 Hotel Brasil
11 Hotel Lenheiro Palace
27 Hotel Hespanhol
36 Hotel Porto Real
45 Pousada Casarão
PLACES TO EAT
10 Canecão Lanches
16 Restaurante Pelourinho
25 Pizzeria Primus
26 Restaurante Rex
34 Restaurante Portal del-Rey
OTHER
1 Gold Mine
3 Chafariz Colonial
4 Oldest Colonial House
5 Solar do Barão de Itambé
6 Igreja de NS das Mercês
7 Pelourinho
8 Igreja de NS do Carmo
12 Banco do Brasil
13 Posto Telefônica
14 Buses to Tiradentes
15 Museu Ferroviário & Estação Ferroviária
17 Associação Commercial (Tourist Information)
18 BEMGE
19 Capela de NS das Dores
20 Cine Gloria
21 Teatro Municipal
22 Post Office
23 Prefeitura Municipal
24 Ponte da Cadeia
28 Catedral de NS do Pilar
29 Capela de Santo Antonio
30 Igreja de NS do Rosário
31 Largo do Rosário
32 Museu de Arte Sacra
33 Capela de NS da Peidade
35 Museu Regional do SPHAN
37 Ponte do Rosário
38 Alliance Français
39 Museu Municipal & Biblióteca Municipal
40 Secretária Municipal de Turismo
41 Barzinho Guia Guia
42 Igreja de São Goçalo e Monumento ao Expedicionário
43 Casa de Intendência
44 Igreja de São Francisco de Assis
Santo
Elias
Resende Costa
Praça Dr Antônio Viegas
To Museu do Estanho John Somers & main Rodoviária
Avenida Presidente Tancredo Neves
Avenida Hermilio Alves
Rua Arthur Bernardes
Vargas
Getúlio
Rua Marechal Deodoro
Rio Lenheiro
Tiradentes
Avenida
Rua Ministro Gabriel Passos
Avenida NS do Pilar
Rua Eduardo Magalhães
Dr Balbino da Cunha
Rua Padre José Maria Xavier
R Santo Antônio
Saída Para São Paulo
To Saída Para
Ascent to Bonfim

our favourites in Brazil. It looks out on a palm-lined, lyre-shaped plaza. The best view of the church set against the palms and the hills is from behind it, up the hill.

This was Aleijadinho's first complete project, but much of his plan was not realised. Still, the exterior, with an Aleijadinho sculpture of the ***Immaculate Virgin*** and several angels, is one of the finest in Minas.

Records are sketchy; Aleijadinho probably did the main altar, but his work was completely changed. In the second altar to the left, there is an image of ***São João Evangelista*** which is the work of Aleijadinho, as is the ***Santo Antônio***. There's particularly fine woodwork in the rear of the church.

Tancredo Neves, who led Brazil from military rule, is buried in the church graveyard.

The church is open from 8 am to noon. On Sunday, the local Coalhada (all-white) orchestra and choir perform at the 9.15 am mass.

Igreja de NS do Carmo Begun in 1732, this church was also designed by Aleijadinho, who did the frontispiece and sculpture around the door. In the second sacristy is a famous unfinished sculpture of Christ. The church is open from 8 to 11 am and 4 to 7 pm.

Catedral de NS do Pilar Begun in 1721, this church has exuberant gold altars and fine Portuguese tiles. The mulatta Rapadura orchestra and choir accompany the 7 pm mass here on Wednesday. On Thursday and Friday, the Coalhada takes their place. The church is open from 8 to 11 am.

Igreja de NS do Rosário This simple church (1719) was built to honour the patron saint who was protector of the slaves. It's open from 8 to 10 am.

Museums

Museu Regional do SPHAN One of the best museums in Minas Gerais, this colonial mansion (1859) was under renovation when we visited but should be open by the time you read this.

Museu de Arte Sacra Open daily (except Monday) from 9 am to 5 pm, the museum (US$1) has a small but impressive collection of art from the city's churches. The drops of blood on the figure of Christ mourned by Mary Magdalene are represented by rubies.

Museu do Estanho John Somers This is a pewter factory with a display and store owned by an Englishman (there is a small English community in São João). The museum is north-west of the centre along the river, past the rodoviária, at Avenida Leite de Castro 1150. It is open daily from 9 am to 5 pm, to 4 pm Sunday and it's free.

Mina de Ouro-Tancredo Neves

This former gold mine is a thin wedge that descends 53m through solid rock. Apart from the adrenalin rush of when you enter, you'll get an interesting demonstration of the regional mining techniques. It's all very impressive, and free.

If you don't mind walking through a pretty depressing favela to get there, put on some decent walking shoes and follow the signs from town till you reach a steep hill. Walk up the hill into the favela and turn left along the footpath. The mine is right there, behind the 'Exportak' sign.

Maria Fumaça Train

Chugging along at 25km/h on the steam-powered *Maria Fumaça*, along a picturesque 13km stretch of track from São João to Tiradentes, makes a great half-hour train ride. The line has operated nonstop since 1881 with the same Baldwin locomotives and, since being restored, the 76cm-gauge track is in perfect condition.

The train runs only on Friday, Saturday, Sunday and holidays, leaving São João at 10 am and 2.15 pm and returning from Tiradentes at 1.20 and 5 pm. The single/return trip (including admission to the Museu Ferroviário) costs US$6.60/13.20, kids under 10 US$6.60. It gets crowded so be there early. Going to Tiradentes, sit on the left side for a better view.

If you're only going to Tiradentes for the day and need more time than the return train allows, you can easily take a later bus back to São João.

Museu Ferroviário The expertly renovated railway museum (US$1 or free with a train ticket), housed inside the train station, contains a wealth of artefacts and information about the steam train era of the late 19th century. Walk down the track to the large rotunda that looks like a colosseum – this is where the trains are kept and it's the best part of the museum, which is open Tuesday to Sunday from 9.30 to 11.30 am and 1.30 to 5 pm.

Special Events

Someone's always celebrating something in Saõ João. The list of festivals just goes on and on – 15 religious and 10 secular on one calendar – so stop by the tourist office for a schedule of events.

Locals boast, credibly, that their **Carnaval** is the best in Minas Gerais. The **Semana da Inconfidência**, from 15 to 21 April, celebrates Brazil's first independence movement and the hometown boys who led it.

Another important festival is the **Inverno Cultural**, during July, with lots of theatre, concerts and dances.

Places to Stay – Budget

There is a good stock of inexpensive hotels in the old section of the city, right where you want to be. The once-grand *Hotel Brasil* (☎ 371-2804), Avenida Presidente Tancredo Neves 395, facing the river, is a real bargain at US$10 per person, US$15 in apartamentos.

Another good cheapie option is the *Aparecida Hotel* (☎ 371-2540), Praça Dr Antônio Viegas 13, with quartos for US$10 per person and apartamentos for US$20/30 a single/double.

The *Hotel Hespanhol* (☎ 371-7677), Rua Marechal Deodoro 131, offers clean and relatively spacious quartos for US$15/29 a single/double and apartamentos for US$30/48.

Places to Stay – Top End

Up the hill behind the Igreja de São Francisco is the lovely *Pousada Casarão* (☎ 371-7447) at Rua Ribeiro Bastos 94. Like many of Minas' elegant mansions turned pousadas, this place is exquisite, and it has a small swimming pool. The rooms cost US$49.50/66 for singles/doubles.

The *Hotel Lenheiro Palace* (☎/fax 371-8155) facing the river at Avenida Presidente Tancredo Neves 257 has charm and style for US$60/85 a single/double.

The *Hotel Porto Real* (☎/fax 371-7000), Avenida Eduardo Magalhães 254, is São João's modern, four-star place. Nice pool and bar area and friendly staff. It has singles/doubles for US$90/120.

Places to Eat

Canecão Lanches, Praça Dr Antônio Viegas, is a great lauchonete and super cheap juice bar – a huge mixed fruit milkshake is US$0.80. It has sandwiches and snacks, too.

Pizzeria Primus, Rua Arthur Bernardes 97, has good pizza – try the primus special, US$5.50. Of the town's self-serve places, three stand out: *Restaurante Portal del-Rey*, Praça Severiano Resende, is good if you get there around noon – before the wood-burning warmer over-cooks all the food (US$7.50/kg); *Restaurante Pelourinho*, next to the Associação Commercial e Industrial, has very good food at US$6.90/kg and great deserts; and *Restaurante Rex*, Rua Marechal Deodoro 124, is a bit dear at US$8/kg.

For regional cooking, try *Quinto do Ouro*, Avenida 7 de Setembro 80, or *Gruta Mineira*, Rua Marechal Deodoro.

Entertainment

The music of Minas is extremely good and different from anything else you've ever heard. Try the *Teatro Municipal* for weekend concerts. *Cabana da Espanhola*, Avenida 31 de Março, has live music Thursday to Sunday. Another central place to try is *Feitiço Mineiro*, near the Catedral do Pilar; it has live music on Friday and Saturday nights.

Cine Gloria screens first-ish run movies nightly.

Barzinha Guli Guli and *Cabanha Zotti*, Avenida Tiradentes near the tourist office, are lively late-night places for beer and light meals.

Getting There & Away

Bus See the Tiradentes section for more information. Direct buses for São João leave Rio (US$18 to $21, depending on time, 5½ hours) daily at 9 am, and 4 and 11 pm. The return bus leaves at 8.30 am, noon and 4 pm and midnight Monday to Saturday, and at 4, 10 and 11.30 pm on Sunday. There are also frequent buses to Juiz de Fora, where you can transfer to a São João or Rio bus.

From São João to Belo Horizonte (US$11, 3½ hours), there are seven buses a day. From Monday to Friday, the first bus leaves at 6 am and the last at 6.30 pm. There are extra buses on Sunday night, until 10 pm. This is also the bus to Congonhas (US$6.25, two hours).

To get to Ouro Prêto, catch a bus to Conselheiro Lafaiete (two per day, US$7.75, 2½ hours); there are more frequent Lafaiete buses at Congonhas. From there, catch buses to Ouro Prêto (for schedules, see the Congonhas section).

Train For details of the picturesque train ride to Tiradentes, see the earlier section on the *Maria Fumaça* train.

Getting Around

Bus Local buses get you to the rodoviária in 10 minutes. They leave from the small bus stop in front of the train station. To get to the centre from the rodoviária, catch any yellow bus (US$0.50) from the bus stop to your left as you walk out (in front of the butcher), not from the more obvious one directly in front.

Taxi From the rodoviária, you have two taxi options – traditional taxis (US$6) or the cool and totally cheap motorbike taxi (☎ 371-5278). The information booth at the rodoviária will call one if you ask. The price to the centre is only US$1! Drivers are safe and carry a helmet (use it) for the passenger.

TIRADENTES

• *pop 10,500* ✉ *36325-000* ☎ *032*

They don't make towns any prettier than Tiradentes. 10km down the valley from São João del Rei, its gold-era rival, colonial Tiradentes sits on a hill below a mountain. With few signs of change over the last two centuries, the town has that magic quality of another age – and for some odd reason, that's a very good feeling.

Originally called Arrail da Ponta do Morro (Hamlet on a Hilltop), Tiradentes was renamed to honour the martyred hero of the Inconfidência (see History in the Ouro Prêto section), who was born at a nearby farm.

The town's colonial buildings run up a hillside, where they culminate in the beautiful **Igreja Matriz de Santo Antônio**.

If you stand between the church's Aleijadinho frontispiece and famous sundial, there is a colourful view of the terracotta-tiled colonial houses, the green valley, and the towering wall of stone formed by the Serra de São José.

Information

The Secretária de Turismo (☎ 355-1212) is at Rua Resende Costa 71, the only three-storey building in town. Staff have maps and other useful information. The post office is in the same building.

The best source of English-language information is John Parsons, an Englishman, who owns the Solar da Ponte hotel. If you call in advance he'll give you all you need to know about the town's excellent hiking and riding opportunities, even if you don't stay at his hotel.

Igreja Matriz de Santo Antônio

Named for the town's patron saint, this church is built on the site of another church. Commenced in 1710 and restored in 1983, it is one of Brazil's most beautiful. There are two bell towers and a frontispiece by Aleijadinho. It is one of the last that he completed. Leandro Gonçalves Chaves made the sundial in front of the church in 1785.

The all-gold interior is rich in Old Testament symbolism. There is a painting by João Batista illustrating the miracle of Santo

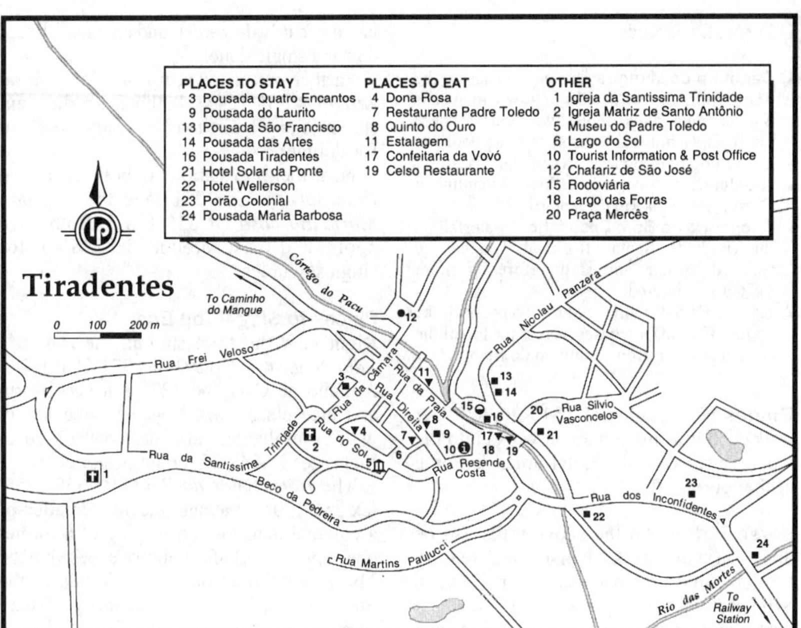

Antônio making a donkey kneel before the Pope. There is also a polychrome organ which was built in Portugal and brought to Tiradentes by donkey in 1798. Ask about performances.

The church is open from 8 am to 5 pm, but usually closes for lunch between noon and 1 pm.

Museu do Padre Toledo

This museum is dedicated to another hero of the Inconfidência, Padre Toledo, who lived in this 18-room house where the Inconfidêntes first met. The museum features regional antiques and documents from the 18th century.

Igreja da Santissima Trindade

After a short walk along Rua da Santissima Trindade, you arrive at this simple pilgrimage church. Dating from 1810, it was built on the site of a small chapel where Tiradentes chose the triangle (symbolising the holy trinity) as the symbol on the flag for the new nation.

Chafariz de São José

Constructed in 1749 by the town council, this beautiful fountain has three sections: one for drinking, one for washing clothes and one for watering horses. The water comes from Mãe d'Agua via an old stone pipeline.

Serra de São José

At the foot of these mountains there is a 1km-wide stretch of protected Atlantic rainforest, and you can hike through several trails. The most popular and simple is to **Mãe d'Agua**, the source of the spring at Chafariz de São José. From Chafariz, follow the trail back for about 25 minutes. It is lush with moss and plants and the waters are clear and fresh.

Other walks include:

- **Caminho do Mangue** This walk heads up the Serra from the west side of town to Aguas Santas, and takes about two hours. There you'll find a mineral water swimming pool and a very good Portuguese-owned churasscara
- **A Calçada** A stretch of the old road that linked Ouro Prêto with Rio de Janeiro
- **Cachoeira do Bom Despacho** A waterfall on the Tiradentes-Santa Cruz road. This can be reached by car, and is therefore far more visited and littered
- **Round Robin** A fine six hour walk would be up to A Calçada, then west across the top of the serra and down from Caminho do Mangue

Guides For guides (US$10 to $20 per walk) and information about walks into the mountains, ask at the Hotel Solar da Ponte or the tourist office.

Horse Riding All the above trails can be done on horseback. Horses are readily available in the town and cost from US$6 to $10 per hour with a guide. John Parsons at the Solar da Ponte is offering a five day ride from Tiradentes to Ouro Prêto and two day rides to an 18th century farmhouse; prices are on request and depend on the size of your group.

Places to Stay

Tiradentes has lots of good but expensive pousadas and only a few cheap places. If you can't find anything within your budget, ask around for homes to stay in, or commute from São João del Rei. Try to avoid staying here on the weekend, as it gets crowded and the prices quoted below can double.

Places to Stay – Budget & Mid-Range

The *Pousada do Laurito* is the best cheapie in town, with a good central location and singles/doubles for US$18/27. Next to the bus station, the *Pousada Tiradentes* (☎ 355-1232) has a certain amount of charm and costs US$18/35 a single/double. The *Hotel Wellerson* (☎ 355-1226) also has singles/doubles for US$16/26. The *Pousada Quatro Encantos* near the Santo Antônio church has a great little garden and charges US$35/45 for a single/double.

Farther out of town, try the *Pousada da Terra* (☎ 355-1243), 800m from the train station along a dirt road. It charges US$40 for doubles.

Near the train station are both the *Porão Colonial* (☎ 355-1251) and the *Pousada Maria Barbosa* (☎ 355-1227). Both have pools and cost around US$28/40 for singles/doubles.

Places to Stay – Top End

Right near the train station, the *Pousada Villa Real,* (☎ 355-1292; fax 371-2866), Rua Antônio de Carvalho 127, is a very warm and nice place owned by the same family which runs the Pousada Casarão in São João. It charges US$49/60 for singles/doubles.

The *Hotel Solar da Ponte* (☎ 355-1255; fax 355-1201) is a magnificent recreation of a colonial mansion, on the site of a former one, and one of the country's best hotels. The first building on the south side of the little stone bridge, it's marked by a small sign.

The rooms are simple and beautifully decorated. There's a salon, pool and sauna and afternoon tea is included in the US$97/153 price; there's a 20% discount in low season and a four day minimum during Carnaval.

Places to Eat

The *Restaurante Padre Toledo* has excellent bife acebolada (beef with onions). *Estalagem* does a mean feijão com lombo (beans with pork). Try *Dona Rosa* for some regional specialities. *Quinto do Ouro* is the town's most upmarket restaurant, with both regional and international dishes. On the main square, *Celso Restaurante* has good food at reasonable prices. For dessert, stroll up to *Confeitaria da Vovó* for coffee and cake.

Things to Buy

Tiradentes has surprisingly good antiques, woodwork and silver jewellery. The antique stores sell furniture, clocks, china and even chandeliers.

Getting There & Away

Tiradentes is 20 minutes from São João del Rei. The best approach is the wonderful train trip mentioned earlier in this section, but buses come and go between São João and Tiradentes every 40 minutes. From São João, the first and last buses leave for Tiradentes at 5.50 am and 5.45 pm on weekdays, 7 am and 5.45 pm on Saturday and 8.15 am and 10 pm on Sunday. From Tiradentes, the last bus back to São João del Rei leaves at 6.20 pm from Monday to Saturday and at 8.30 pm on Sunday.

DIAMANTINA

• pop 46,000 ✉ 39100-000 ☎ 038

One of Brazil's prettiest and least visited colonial gems, Diamantina boomed when diamonds were discovered in the 1720s, after the gold finds in Minas. The diamonds petered out, but because of its isolation, Diamantina is a well preserved colonial city, with fine mansions and excellent hiking in the surrounding mountains.

The centre, apart from the relatively new cathedral and a couple of incongruous traffic lights, hasn't changed for hundreds of years. Most of the churches and historical houses remain closed, but it doesn't matter much – the exteriors are more interesting anyway.

Diamantina is 5½ hours north of Belo Horizonte. After you pass the town of Curvelo (Minas' geographical centre), the stark landscape of northern Minas, with its rocky outcrops and barren highlands, is a sharp contrast to the lush hills in the south. Diamantina also is the birthplace of Juscelino Kubitschek, former Brazilian president and the founder of Brasília.

Information

Tourist Office The tourist office (☎ 531-1636), Praça Antônio Eulálio 53, hands out a guide in Portuguese which includes a map. It also has keys to most of the tourist attractions, many of which seem to be undergoing restoration indefinitely.

Money Banco do Brasil in the main praça has a Visa/Plus ATM, but neither it nor the BEMGE bank changes money. Head to Mauricinho, in the little shop behind the BEMGE bank, for parallel rates on US dollars in cash.

Post & Communications The post office is just west of Praça Antônio Eulálio. The posto telefônica is on the south-west end of the main square.

Casa da Chica da Silva

This colonial mansion on Praça Lobo de Mesquita was the home of diamond contractor João Fernandes de Oliveira and his mistress and former slave, Chica da Silva. It's empty at the moment, but from the outside it's possible to get an idea of the lifestyle of the extravagant mulatta. The huge colonial door leads to her private chapel.

Igreja de NS do Carmo

This is the most opulent church in Diamantina, and it's worth having a look inside. Constructed between 1760 and 1765, this church had its tower built at the rear – lest the bells should awaken Chica da Silva. The organ was made in Diamantina and wrought in gold and there are rich, golden carvings.

Igreja de NS do Rosário dod Pretos

This is the oldest church in town, dating from 1731. Very interesting here is the tree that has grown through a wooden cross.

Museu do Diamante

Just west of Praça JK is the house of Padre Rolim, one of the Inconfidêntes. It's now a museum (US$1) with furniture, coins, instruments of torture and other relics of the diamond days. It's open from noon to 5.30 pm Tuesday to Sunday.

Mercado Municipal

Built by the army in 1835, the market, in Praça Barão Guaicuí, was in use until only a couple of years ago. Its wooden arches inspired Niemeyer's design for the presidential palace in Brasília.

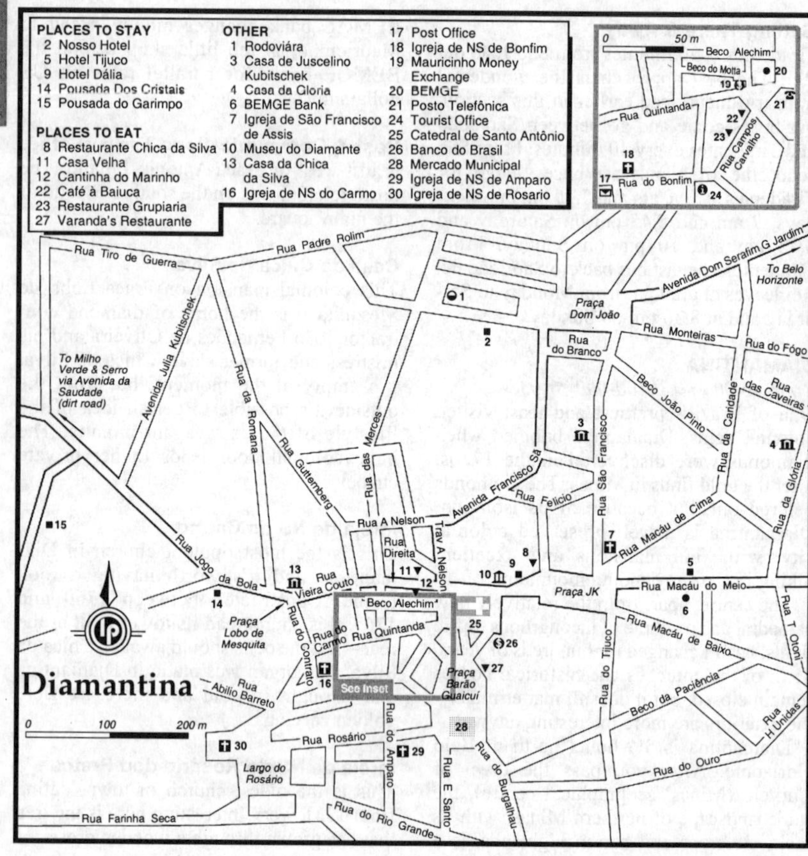

Casa da Glória

Consisting of two houses on opposite sides of Rua da Glória connected by an enclosed, 2nd storey passageway, Casa da Glória was originally the residence of the diamond supervisors and also the official palace of the first bishop of Diamantina. Today, appropriately, the building houses the Institute of Geology.

Casa de Juscelino Kubitschek

This small house at Rua São Francisco 241 reflects the simple upbringing of the former president, whose grandparents were poor Czech immigrants. Kubitschek himself believed that his early life in Diamantina influenced him greatly. There are some good photos of JK along the staircase in the Hotel Tijuco.

Hikes

While you are here, walk a couple of kilometres down the Caminho dos Escravos (built by slaves) to the **Serra da Jacuba**. There are **waterfalls** at Toca, 5km south of town along Hwy BR-259.

Places to Stay

The *Nosso Hotel* (☎ 531-1565) opposite the bus terminal is the cheapest at US$8 per person, but it looks like a place where Huggy Bear would send Starsky and Hutch to rap with a snitch, and it's a long uphill walk from the centre.

Romantic cheapies can be had at the charming *Pousada Dos Cristais* (☎ 531-2897), Rua Jogo de Bola 53, with clean quartos (with separate but private bath) for US$15/person and apartamentos from US$20/35.

The quaintly eclectic *Hotel Dália* (☎ 531-1477; fax 531-3526) at Praça JK 25 is another good deal, a nice old building next door to the Museu do Diamante. It has single/double quartos that cost US$20/35 and apartamentos that go for US$30/45.

The top-end hotels are *Hotel Tijuco* (☎ 581-1022), Rua Macáu do Meio 211, a Niemeyer erection (US$45/65 for singles/doubles), and the *Pousada do Garimpo* (☎ 531-2523), a tasteful place at the west end of town at Avenida da Saudade 265 (US$54/72 without view, US$60/78 with). There's a pool and sauna.

Places to Eat

Café à Baiuca just off the main square is a favourite local place for coffee and cakes. Down the road, *Restaurante Grupiaria*, Rua Campos Carvalho 12, is a popular place with good mineiro dishes which, as in most restaurants in town, sell for US$13 to $16 for two, half that for one.

Cantinha do Marinho upstairs on Rua Direita at the main square has a buffet lunch for US$5 per plate including a drink. At dinner try the lombo com Feijão tropiero (US$9).

Good if you're on a date is the *Restaurante Chica da Silva* (☎ 531-3059), Praça JK 27, behind the Hotel Dalia, with excellent meat and chicken dishes at moderate prices. And very nice indeed is *Casa Velha* (☎ 531-3538), upstairs at Rua Direita 106 opposite Cantinha do Marinho, with a terrific por quilo lunch (US$8/kg) and very good Miniero food at dinner.

Getting There & Away

Buses (US$17.50, five hours) leave Belo Horizonte for Diamantina daily at 5.30, 9 and 11.30 am, 2.30 and 6.30 pm and midnight. Buses return to Belo Horizonte Monday to Friday at 1, 6 and 10.45 am, noon, and 3.30 and 6 pm; on Saturday at 6 and 10.45 am, noon, and 3.30 and 6 pm; and on Sunday at 1 and 6 am, noon, and 3.30 and 6 pm and midnight.

Mineral Spa Towns

The southern spa towns of Minas are well developed health resorts whose excellent mineral springs have various therapeutic applications. Been travelling hard and fast? Recovering from a tropical disease? Sick of seemingly idyllic beaches? Overdosing on baroque? If the answer to any of these questions is yes, the spa towns await you.

CAXAMBU

• *pop 23,000* ✉ *37440-000* ☎ *035*

Caxambu is a tranquil resort for the middle class and the elderly who come here to escape the heat of Rio and the madness of Carnaval. Some couples have been coming every summer for 30 years or more.

The springs were first tapped in 1870. Realising the curative properties of the waters, medical practitioners flocked to the town. In 1886, Dr Policarpo Viotti founded the Caxambu water company (nationalised in 1905).

Caxambu water was celebrated on the international water circuit, winning gold medals long before Perrier hit Manhattan singles bars. It took the gold medal in Rome's Victor Emmanuel III Exposition of 1903, and another in the St Louis International Fair of 1904, then the Diploma of Honour in the University of Brussels Exposition of 1910.

These water Olympics were discontinued during WWI, and Caxambu's history was uneventful until 1981, when Supergasbras (no relation to lingerie manufacturer WonderBra) and Superagua, private firms, took over the government concession. Caxambu water is sold throughout Brazil.

Information

Tourist Office Obtain maps and other information from the helpful tourist office in Praça Conego José de Castilho Moreira (☎ 341-3977), next to the rodoviária, open Monday to Friday from 8.30 am to 6 pm.

Money The local Banco do Brasil, apparently, is too busy to deign to change your money – try the larger hotels. Forget travellers cheques.

Post & Communications The post office is on Avenida Camilo Soares, next to the Hotel Gloria. The posto telefônica is at Rua Major Penha 265.

Parque das Aguas

The Parque das Aguas is a rheumatic's Disneyland; people come to take the waters, smell the sulphur, compare liver spots, watch the geyser spout, rest in the shade by the canal and walk in the lovely gardens.

Liver problems? Go to the Dona Leopoldina **magnesium fountain**. Skin disorders? Take the **sulphur baths** of Tereza Cristina. Itchy trigger finger? Hit the **rifle range**! VD? The **Duque de Saxe fountain** helps calm the bacteria that cause syphilis. And there's much, more, from kidney stone cures to stomach ailment alleviators, and from eyebaths to anaemia fixers.

The park is open daily from 7 am to 6 pm, and admission to the grounds is US$2. Separate fees are required for most activities, including the pools (US$5, US$3 for kids), and for the **chairlift** (US$3) to the top of Morro Cristo.

Other Attractions

At 800m above sea level, there is an image of Jesus on top of the **Morro Cristo** hill. On Rua Princesa Isabela is the **Igreja de Santa Isabel da Hungria**, built by the princess after she had conceived thanks to the miraculous waters of Caxambu.

Horse-and-buggy tours into the countryside from the park entrance (1½ hours) range from US$20 to $26 for two. The standard tour includes the **Fabrica de Doce** and the **Chacarra Rosallan**, an old farm with a flower orchard and fruit grove famous for its home-made fruit liqueurs: jaboticaba and tangerine. A city buggy tour is US$18.

The Fabrica de Doce has locally-produced honey (US$5), liqueurs (US$2) and preserves (US$4).

There's **yoga**, **massage** and **tarot readings** on offer south of town at Chácara das Rosas in Bairro Campo do Meio; see Places to Stay, below.

Places to Stay

Caxambu is geared to prosperous travellers, but if you're here outside peak holiday times you can get some good deals. Most hotel prices include all meals.

The *Hotel São José* (☎ 341-3133), Rua Major Penha 264, is an apartment hotel with TVs, big double beds and hot showers. Single/double apartamentos are US$25/50 (with breakfast only).

It's seriously pleasant at the *Chácara das Rosas* (☎ 341-3499), Km 93 on Hwy BR-354 (the hourly Emisa bus to Campo do Meio stops here), a pousada with lush grounds and comfortable rooms for US$25/50 in low season, US$40/80 in high season. Shiatsu massage here costs about US$30, and there's a holistic spa.

The *Hotel Marques* (☎ 341-1013) at Rua Oliveira Mafra 223 has singles/doubles for US$30/60. Next door, rooms at the *Alex Hotel* (☎ 341-1331) are US$50/70.

The *Hotel Caxambu* (☎ 341-3300), Rua Major Penha 145, is another lovely place right in the centre of town with a pool, playground and a good restaurant; standard rooms are US$80/100 (US$55/65 breakfast only), and luxury rooms from US$100/120.

The *Palace Hotel* (☎ 341-1044), Rua Dr Viotti 567, is a good top end deal in a place that looks like something out of *Bananas*. With full board the prices are US$70/85 for

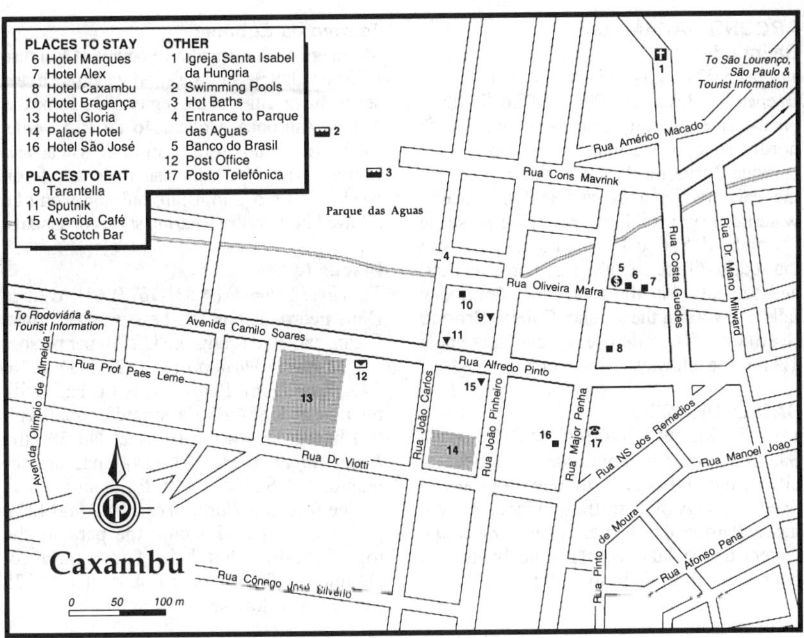

singles/doubles. There's a huge pool out back with great slides.

Absolute top of the line is the magnificent *Hotel Gloria* (☎ 341-1233), Avenida Camilo Soares 590, a posh resort complex with a range of activities for the leisure set. Rooms complete with TV, bath, bar, telephone and three meals a day are US$150/170. Facilities include a large gym with indoor basketball court, tennis (clay courts in the park), a physical rehabilitation centre and a sauna.

Places to Eat

Superb pastries, pies and juices are at *Avenida Café* (☎ 341-4363), Avenida Camilo Soares 648, near the park entrance. Upstairs, the *Avenida Café & Scotch Bar* (same ☎), does a fusion of well prepared Brazilian and Italian dishes with main courses ranging from US$7 to $12.

Sputnik, on Avenida Camilo Soares, close to the park, is a good lanchonete for a snack.

Tarantella (pronounced like the spider) near the park entrance at Rua João Pinheiro 326 has the best pasta and pizza in town.

La Forelle (☎ 341-1961) on Hwy BR-354 3km south of town is an interesting, if pricey, restaurant run by a Brazilian-Dane which specialises – as the name suggests – in trout and salmon dishes. It also serves excellent fondue. Good fish, reasonable service, but crap wine list. You'll drop at least US$55 for dinner for two with wine.

Getting There & Away

There are two daily buses from Belo Horizonte (see that section for details). Seven daily buses (US$2.30) make the 49km trip between Caxambu and São Lourenço on a winding, wooded road. There are two direct buses a day to São Paulo (US$15.50, 6½ hours) at 12.50 and 7.50 am, and two to Rio (US$13, 5½ hours), at 8 am and midnight, and an extra bus on Sunday at 4 pm.

AROUND CAXAMBU

Baependi

• *pop 17,000* ✉ *37443-000* ☎ *035*

Baependi ('Baya-PENCH') is a small village on the river of the same name about 6km north-east of Caxambu. Its treasure is the baroque **Santa Maria Cathedral** (1752), but the real attraction is the river and the peaceful waterfall 13km south of town. Hire horses in Caxambu (US$6 to $10 per hour; check with the tourist office for a list of horse owners) and set out; skip the first, more developed falls in favour of the second, **Caixao Branco (Gamarra)**. The ride is easy and takes about 1½ hours each way. Bring a picnic.

SÃO LOURENÇO

• *pop 31,000* ✉ *37470-000* ☎ *035*

São Lourenço, south of Caxambu, is another city of mineral waters, though more developed, smoggy and traffic-clogged. It, too, has a Parque das Aguas, boasting healing waters and a lake with paddle boats. It's open daily from 8 am to 5.20 pm.

Information

Tourist Office In front of the Parque das Aguas, the tourist office is open every day from 8 to 11 am and 1 to 6 pm. Bored staff have a list of hotels and a map of the attractions.

Money Local banks don't exchange but surprisingly good rates can be had from the cashier at the Hotel Brasil.

Post & Communications The post office is on Rua Dr Olavo Gomes Pinto. The posto telefônica is at Rua Coronel José Justino 647.

Laundry It's US$3.50 each to wash and dry at Lav & Serve, Rua Coronel José Justino 678.

Circuito das Aguas

Taxis and vans that congregate at Avenida Getúlio Vargas offer half-day tours of the Circuito das Aguas (Water Circuit) for US$25 to $40 per person; it's best to organise it the day before. The tours normally visit Caxambu, Baependi, Cambuquira, Lambari and Passo Quatro.

Templo da Euboise

Members of the Brazilian Society of Euboise believe that a new civilisation will arise in the seven magic cities of the region: São Tomé das Letras, Aiuruoca, Conceição do Rio Verde, Itanhandu, Pouso Alto, Carmo de Minas and Maria da Fe. You can visit their temple on weekends from 2 to 4 pm, but you won't be allowed in if you're wearing shorts or sandals.

Places to Stay

The *Hotel Colombo* (☎ 331-1577), 611 Avenida Dom Pedro II, has the best price in town. Clean, carpeted rooms are US$10 per person.

The *Hotel Miranda* (☎ 332-3111) at No 545 Rua Dom Pedro II isn't bad with quartos at US$40/50 a single/double with full board. Down the street at No 587 the *Hotel Imperial* (☎ 331-1144) has apartamentos at US$46/70 with full board.

The four-star *Hotel Brasil* (☎ 331-1422), Rua João Lage 87 facing the park, is the top-of-the-line hotel in São Lourenço. Doubles with full board start at US$175 (less 30% in low season).

Places to Eat

Pick up some incredible home-made cheeses – marinated mozzarella or smoked provolone – for less than US$6/kg at *Laticinios Julimani*, Avenida Dom Pedro II 696.

Most of the restaurants in town can't compete with the food in the hotels. But *Restaurante Namaste* just across from the park entrance has a great and generous set-price lunch at US$6. It's open from 9.30 am to 4 pm daily, except Tuesday. There's also a good health-food restaurant inside the park itself.

Getting There & Away

There are seven buses daily to Caxambu (US$2.30, 45 minutes), and six to both Rio (US$11, five hours) and São Paulo (US$12, six hours).

AROUND SÁO LORENÇO

Poços Das Caldas

There are day trips from Sáo Lorenço to this city, built on the crater of an extinct volcano.

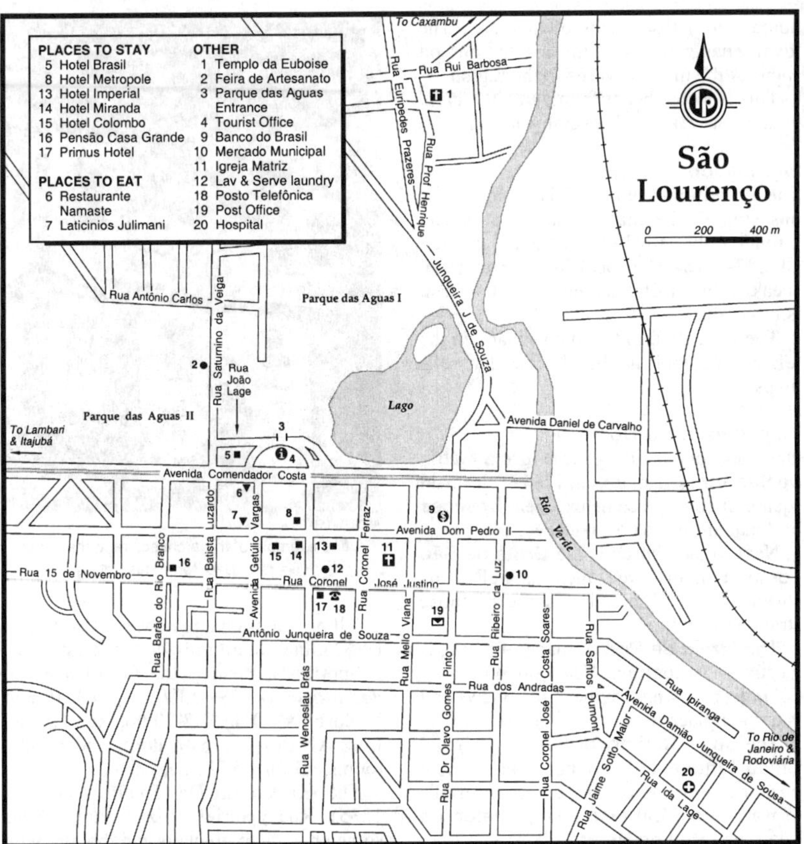

A mineral spring town, it was settled by glass blowers from the island of Murano, near Venice. There are full-day tours to Poços das Caldas from Sào Lorenço for US$50 per person which leave from in front of the Parque de Aqua at 7 am. Check with the tourist office to see if they're still running.

SÃO TOMÉ DAS LETRAS

• pop 6000 ✉ 37418-000 ☎ 035

São Tomé das Letras is a charming village at 1300m about sea level. If you're into mysticism or superstition, or just looking for a cheap, fun and idyllic place to rest up for a few days, this is the place .

Considered by local mystics to be one of the seven sacred cities of the world, the town is filled with kif-carrying hippies, stories of flying saucers and visiting extraterrestrials, a cave that is really the entrance to a subterranean passageway to Macchu Picchu in Peru ... and then there are the *weird* stories.

Most of the town's churches and buildings are old and made (actually sort of home-made) from slabs of quartzite. The town's name refers to the inscriptions on some of the many caverns in the region.

This is also a beautiful mountain region, with great walks and several waterfalls.

Information

The Prefeitura Municipal is opposite the bus stop in the main square, but it can provide only verbal information. Fernando (☎ 237-1218), the local head of tourism, speaks a bit of English and his enthusiasm is infectious.

There's a shop in the main square, to the left as you look at the church, that sells maps.

Things to See & Do

One non-stone building is the **Igreja Matriz de São Tomé**, dating from 1785, in the main square. It contains some excellent **frescoes** by Joaquim José da Natividade.

Next to the church is the **Gruta de São Tomé**, a small cave which, as well as its shrine to São Tomé, has some of those strange inscriptions.

The **Igreja de Pedra**, made of stone, is worth a photograph. The lookout, only 500m from town, provides great views and is a good place to watch the sun set or rise.

The caves, **Carimbado** (3km away) and **Chico Taquara** (3.5km), both contain more puzzling inscriptions. The popular waterfalls to walk to are **Euboise** (3km), **Prefeitura** (7km) and **Véu de Noiva** (12km).

Special Events

In August, the Festas de Agosto attract lots of pilgrims and the Mystic Festival, from late December to early January, attracts students and teachers of mysticism – it's a scene.

Places to Stay

The run-down *Pousada Mahã-Mantra* (☎ 989-5563), 10m behind the stone church, is the cheapest cot in town at US$5 per person without breakfast; camping, nearby at *Gruta do Leão*, which is supposedly stocked with enchanted water, is US$3 per person.

ANDREW DRAFFEN

A fine example of the architecture in the stone village of São Tome das Letras

All pousadas charge between US$15 and US$25, but not all provide breakfast.

Spotlessly clean is the *Pousada Reino dos Magos* (☎ 237-1300, or book in São Paulo on ☎ (011) 842-7908), Rua Gabriel Luiz Alvarez 27, with dorm and private rooms, all for US$15 per person.

The *Hospedaria Dos Sonhos I* (☎ 237-1235), Rua Gabriel Luiz Alvarez 28, is somewhat nicer than its neighbour, with private rooms for US$17 per person with breakfast. It's nicer even than the *Hospedaria Dos Sonhos II* (same ☎), under the same management and with similar prices, right near the stone church.

Others in town include *Pousada Arco Iris*, Rua Armando Duplessis Vilela, popular with travellers, and the *Pousada Serra Branca*, right up the road, with apartamentos for US$25 per person.

Places to Eat

Ximan (☎ 236-1345), Rua Camilo Rios 12, has awesome hot foods and salads for US$7/kg. *Bar do Gê* at Rua Gabriel Luiz

Alves 28 is another surprisingly good restaurant. The bar *All Days of Peace and Music Woodstock*, in Rua Camilo Rios, is a good place to meet people who've seen UFOs.

Things to Buy

There are lovely people selling inexpensive, locally made clothing and folkcraft at Nõ Cego (☎ 237 1201), Rua Capitão Pedro José Martins.

Getting There & Away

A direct daily bus from São Paulo was slated to start after this book went to press, stopping in the city of Três Corações (which happens to be Pelé's birthplace and has a statue of him), 38km to the west. Buses from Três Corações (US$2.75) leave Monday and Saturday at 6 and 11 am and 3.30 pm, and on Sunday at 7 am and 2 pm. The road should be sealed by the time you read this.

From Caxambu, buses to Três Corações (US$5, 1½ hours) leave six times a day from 6.30 am to 8.45 pm.

There are several buses a day from São João del Rei to Três Corações (US$4.50, 2¼ hours).

Hitching from Três Corações is possible, but not at all easy. To try it, cross the river next to the bus station and turn into the first street on the right – the one with the train track down the middle. About 50m down on the left-hand side, there's a bus stop. Take the B Ventura bus to its final destination and stick out the thumb.

Parks

PARQUE NATURAL DO CARAÇA

The Santa Bárbara region, 105km east of Belo Horizonte, is one of the most beautiful mountain retreats around. The Caraça Natural Park occupies a transition area between Mata Atlântica and wild mountain vegetation. The 11,000 hectare park (admission US$5) includes several mountains, including **Pico do Sol** (2070m), **Alto do Inficcionada** (2068m), **Morro do Piçarrão** (1839m), **Pico da Conceição** (1803m) and **Pico da Trindade** (1908m). The hillsides are lined with easily accessible hiking trails and creeks that form waterfalls and natural swimming pools.

The town of Santa Bárbara itself (pop 25,000, ☎ area code 031) has a collection of lovely baroque colonial churches, including the **Igreja Matriz do Santo Antônio**, **Igreja de Nossa Senhora das Mercês** and, 26km outside the town, the area's main attraction, the **Hospedaria do Colégio Caraça**.

The working neogothic style church was once a monastery, though it has been converted to a highly recommended pousada and guesthouse (☎ (031) 837-2698). Staff offer very friendly advice on walks into the surrounding countryside and tips on hikes and treks, and prayers are not required! A highlight is when staff feed a relatively tame pack of wolves, which gather round each night for the feeding.

Accommodation runs from bare-boned quartos (US$25 per person) to swank private doubles with bath from US$70 to $90. There's a restaurant on the premises that serves awesome and cheap comida mineira – all ingredients are grown locally. You need to book on weekends, as the place gets packed with escapees from Belo taking in the air.

In Santa Bárbara itself, other accommodation is available at the *Hotel Karaiba* (☎ (031) 832-1501), Praça Pio XII 281, with quartos from US$18 to $32 per person.

Getting There & Away

The Belo-Vitória train stops in Santa Bárbara and there are five to 10 buses a day from Belo Horizonte (US$7, 2½ hours). From Santa Bárbara, a taxi to the Hospedaria do Colégio Caraça will cost US$35 plus the US$5 admission to the Natural Park.

PARQUE NACIONAL DE CAPARAÓ

This 25,000 hectare park is popular with climbers and hikers from all over Brazil. The panoramic views are superb, taking in the Caparaó valley that divides Minas Gerais and Espírito Santo. Caparaó contains the highest mountains in southern Brazil, including the third highest peak in the country, **Pico da Bandeira** (2890m). Other peaks include **Cristal** (2798m) and **Calçado** (2766m). All three can be reached via a good network of trails that exist within the park. Climbing gear isn't necessary.

Despite being ravaged by fire in 1988 and by human interference for the last 300 years, the park has a few lush remnants of Mata Atlântica, mostly in Vale Verde, a small valley split by the Rio Caparaó.

Wildlife in the park is not exactly plentiful, but there are still some opossums, agoutis and spider monkeys to be seen. Bird life includes various eagles, parrots and hummingbirds.

Between November and January there's lots of rain and it's too cloudy for good views. The best time to visit the park is between June and August – although these are the coldest months, the days are clear. Bring warm clothes!

The park is open daily from 7 am to 5 pm and costs US$3 to enter. Make sure you pick up a map.

Places to Stay

It's possible to camp inside the park. There are two official campsites: *Tronqueira*, 8km from the park entrance, and *Terreirão*, a further 4.5km away, halfway to the summit of Pico da Bandeira.

Camping costs US$5 a night, but it's a good idea to reserve a site about a week before you arrive by ringing IBAMA (☎ (032) 747-2555).

If you don't have a tent, the nearest place to stay is the *Caparaó Parque Hotel* (☎ 747-2559), a short walk from the park entrance. It's a pleasant, friendly place, but a bit on the expensive side, with singles/doubles for US$47/77. The *Pousada Clube do Bezerra* (☎ 747-2628) nearby has much cheaper rooms from US$20 to $40. If that's too steep, ask around for a room to rent in Alto do Caparaó, the village closest to the park.

Getting There & Away

Caparaó can be reached via Belo Horizonte, or from Vitória, in Espírito Santo. You'll need to catch a bus to the town of Manhumirim, and then another local bus to Alto do Caparaó, a further 25km away.

Unfortunately, the bus timetables work against the budget traveller. There are two buses a day to Manhumirim from both Belo Horizonte and Vitória. From Belo, they leave at 10 am and 5 pm, from Vitória at 9.30 am and 3.30 pm. The trip from either direction takes around five hours. The problem is that there are only two local buses a day to Alto do Caparaó, at 8 am and noon. To avoid staying in Manhumirim, catch one of the many buses going to Presidente Soares and ask to be dropped off at the Caparaó turn-off, then hitch the rest of the way.

Alternatively, if you can afford it, take a taxi from Manhumirim to Alto do Caparaó (US$35 to $50, depending on the mood of the driver and your own bargaining ability).

PARQUE NACIONAL DA SERRA DO CIPÓ

Formed by mountains, rivers, waterfalls and open grasslands, the Parque Nacional da Serra do Cipó, about 100km north-east of Belo, is one of Minas' most beautiful. Its highlands, together with an arm of the Serra do Espinhaço, divide the water basins of the São Francisco and Doce rivers. The park contains no infrastructure for tourism.

Most of the park's vegetation is cerrado and grassy highlands, but the small river valleys are lush and ferny and contain a number of unique orchids. Fauna include the maned wolf, tamarin monkey, banded anteater, tree hedgehog, otter, jaguar and there are large numbers of bats. Bird life includes woodpeckers, blackbirds and hummingbirds. The park is also home to a small, brightly coloured frog which secretes deadly toxins from its skin. Brazilians call it *sapo-de-pijama* (the pyjama-frog).

Other attractions of the park include the 70m waterfall **Cachoeira da Farofa**, and the **Canyon das Bandeirantes**, named after the early adventurers from São Paulo who used the area as a natural road to the north in their search for riches.

Camping

Camping Véu da Noiva is 3km from the Rio do Cipó and has spaces for trailers and tents, plus hot showers and two restaurants and two natural swimming pools. Book and get more information from the Associação Cristã de Moços de Minas Gerais (☎ (031) 337-3200), Rua Martim Carvalho, Santo Agostinho. One reader wrote about his camping experience:

Take the bus about 20km past the hotel near the Rio do Cipó and ask the driver to let you off at the 4WD road to the right, just past the stone bridges. Follow the track for about 5km until it becomes a footpath through the bushes. After 3-4km you get to a small, very dry plateau where you'll be completely alone and have a superb view over the canyons to both sides.

There are waterfalls and pools down in the river which are very nice to swim in. There is marvellous vegetation and nasty beasties, including snakes, giant spiders and scorpions. When you return to Belo Horizonte, make sure you make a short stop just past the Rio do Cipó. There's a great pub opposite the hotel, about 50m to the right. It's actually an old watermill, the mood is great and the owner speaks English. It's worth a visit!

Geert Van de Wiele

Getting There & Away

From Belo, take a bus to Lagoa Santa, then another bus to Conceição do Mato Dentro. The road from Conceição do Mato Dentro passes next to the park and Cardeal Mota, the nearest town.

São Paulo State

São Paulo is South America's richest state – the industrial engine that powers the Brazilian economy. Thirty of Brazil's 50 largest companies are in São Paulo, as is 50% of the nation's industry. The state contains South America's largest city, São Paulo, a megalopolis with 17 million inhabitants. One in every nine Brazilians lives in São Paulo City.

The state's beaches are good and make a nice break if you're meandering your way up to Rio. And charming Campos do Jordão is a great weekend getaway any time of year.

São Paulo City

• *pop 17-20 million* ✉ *01000-000* ☎ *011*
Brazil's most cosmopolitan and modern city, São Paulo is home to immigrants and ethnic neighbourhoods. Millions of Italians came here at the end of the 19th century, millions of Japanese arrived this century, and millions of Brazilians from the countryside and from the Northeast are still pouring in.

This diversity and industrial development has produced Brazil's largest, most cultured and best educated middle class. Paulistanos (inhabitants of the city; inhabitants of the state are called Paulistas) call their city Sampa and, despite constantly complaining about street violence, traffic problems and pollution, they wouldn't dream of living anywhere else.

São Paulo is on a high plateau; cold in the Brazilian winter and smoggy-hot in the summer. It can be an intimidating place, but if you know someone who can show you around or if you just like big cities it's worth a visit. At its best it offers the excitement and nightlife of one of the world's great cities.

History

Founded in 1554 when a group of Jesuit priests led by Manoel da Nóbrega and José de Anchieta arrived at the Piratininga plateau, São Paulo remained a backwater for many years.

By the early 17th century, it had a few churches and a small village. The growing Indian slave trade saw the town become a headquarters for the bandeirantes – the slave-trading pioneers who, in their treks into the Brazilian interior, explored much unknown territory. For them, the Treaty of Tordesilhas, which divided South America between Spain and Portugal, was nothing more than a line on a map and they were largely responsible for expanding the boundaries of Portuguese territory.

By the 18th century, the bandeirantes had turned their attention to mineral exploration and had discovered gold mines in Minas Gerais, Goiás and Mato Grosso. São Paulo was used as a stopover by the increasing

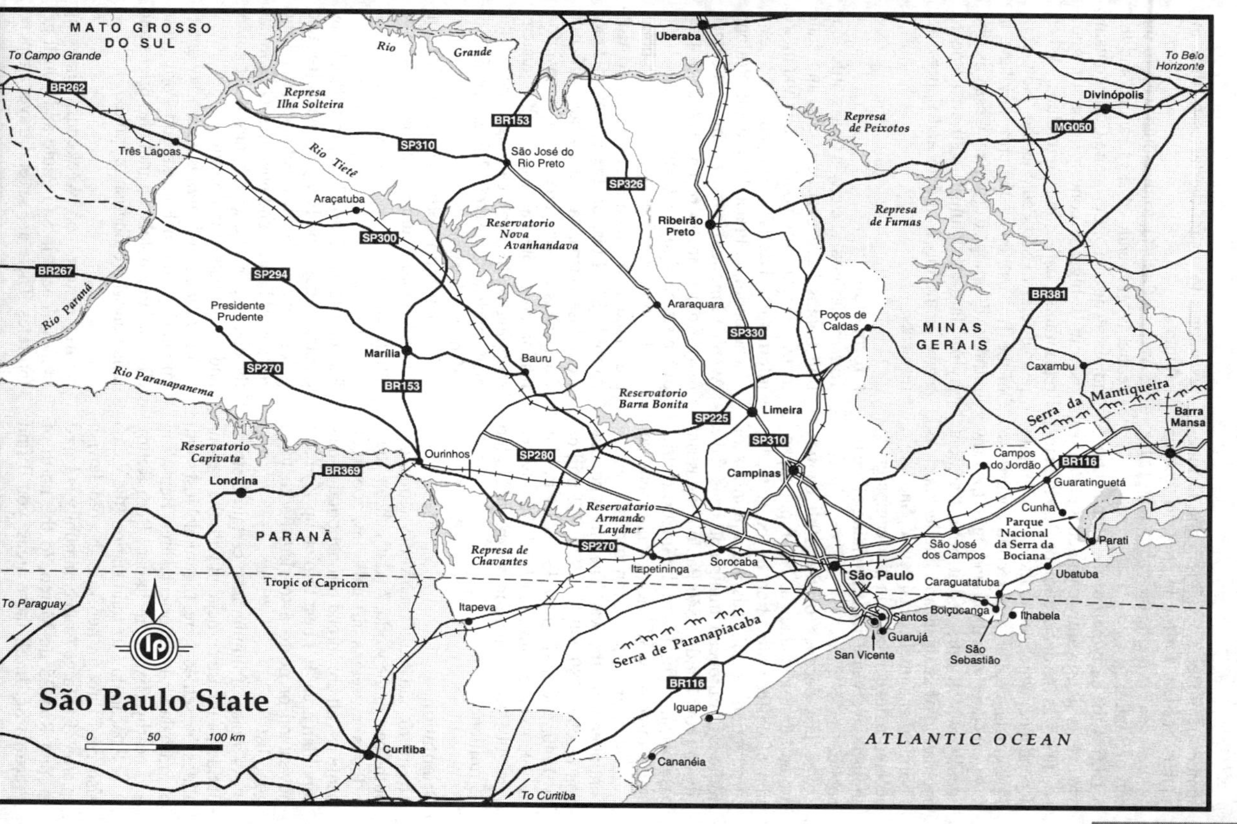
São Paulo State
MATO GROSSO DO SUL
MINAS GERAIS
PARANÁ
ATLANTIC OCEAN
Tropic of Capricorn
To Campo Grande
To Belo Horizonte
To Paraguay
To Curitiba
Divinópolis
Uberaba
Ribeirão Preto
Araraquara
Limeira
Campinas
Poços de Caldas
Caxambu
Barra Mansa
Serra da Mantiqueira
Campos do Jordão
Guaratinguetá
Cunha
Parati
Parque Nacional da Serra da Bociana
Ubatuba
Ilhabela
São Sebastião
Caraguatatuba
Boiçucanga
São José dos Campos
São Paulo
Santos
Guarujá
San Vicente
Sorocaba
Itapetininga
Serra de Paranapiacaba
Iguape
Cananéia
Itapeva
Curitiba
Londrina
Ourinhos
Bauru
Marília
Presidente Prudente
Araçatuba
Três Lagoas
São José do Rio Preto
Represa de Peixotos
Represa de Furnas
Reservatorio Barra Bonita
Reservatorio Armando Laydner
Reservatorio Nova Avanhandava
Represa de Chavantes
Reservatorio Capivata
Represa Ilha Solteira
Rio Grande
Rio Tietê
Rio Paranapanema
Rio Paraná
BR262
BR267
SP294
SP270
SP300
SP310
BR153
SP326
BR369
SP280
SP225
SP330
MG050
BR381
BR116
0
50
100 km

number of pioneers, explorers and fortune-hunters heading for the interior, as well as by sugar dealers taking their shipments to the port of Santos.

During the early part of the 19th century, two events significantly changed São Paulo. The first was the declaration of Brazilian independence, which led to the city becoming a provincial capital. The second occurred a few years later with the founding of the Law Faculty which attracted a new, transient population of students and intellectuals. As a political and intellectual centre, São Paulo became a leader both in the campaign to abolish slavery and in the founding of the republic.

The last decades of the 19th century brought dramatic change. The rapid expansion of coffee cultivation in the state, the construction of railroads and the influx of millions of European immigrants caused the city to grow rapidly. São Paulo's industrial base began to form, and the import restrictions caused by WWI meant rapid industrial expansion and population growth, which continued after the war. The city's population reached 580,000 by 1920, 1.2 million by 1940, two million by 1950, 3.1 million by 1960 and 5.2 million by 1970. By the year 2005, the population is expected to top 25 million.

Orientation

The metrô, São Paulo's subway system, is one of the best in the world. And it's cheap, too.

Parks, museums, art galleries, zoos, you name it – all are spread throughout the metropolitan area. It's best to pick up *Veja* at a newsstand or go to a tourism booth for a good list.

As a city of immigrants, certain districts of São Paulo are associated with the nationalities that settled there. Liberdade, just south of Praça da Sé, is the oriental area. Bela Vista and nearby Bixiga are Italian. Bom Retiro, near Estação da Luz train station (the metrô also runs through here), is the old Jewish quarter. The large Arab community is based around Rua 25 de Março, to the north of Praça da Sé. In all these areas, you'll find restaurants to match the tastes of their inhabitants.

Avenida Paulista, to the south-west of the centre, is an avenue of skyscrapers, and the adjoining district of Cerqueira César contains the city's highest concentration of good restaurants, cafés and nightclubs. When people refer to São Paulo as the 'New York of the Tropics', this is the area they have in mind. Adjoining Cerqueira César is the stylish Jardims Paulista district, home to many of the city's middle and upper-class residents.

Information

Tourist Offices The city's tourist information booths have excellent city and state maps. They are also good for bus and metrô information. English is spoken.

The booth on Praça da República (along Avenida Ipiranga) is most helpful; it's open daily from 9 am to 6 pm. There's a post office attached to this booth.

Other tourist offices open the same hours are found at: Avenida Paulista, near MASP; Avenida São Luís, on the corner of Praça Dom José Gaspar; and a 24 hour office at Congonhas airport. There is also an information booth out the front of the Iguatemi shopping centre. You can also contact the main tourism office (☎ 267-2122, ext 627, or 640 on weekends).

The state tourist office (☎ 239-0087) is at Praça Antônio Prado 9 in the deco Banespa building.

Publications The *Guia São Paulo* by Quatro Rodas is probably the best all-round guide to the city, with street maps, hotel and restaurant listings and bus lines. *O Guia* has the clearest presentation of any street guide, and it also lists tourist points.

São Paulo this Month is a monthly entertainment guide in English and Portuguese (free at large hotels). It includes prices and tells you where English is spoken.

Money Except on weekends, changing money is easy in São Paulo and you'll get top rates. There are several travel agencies

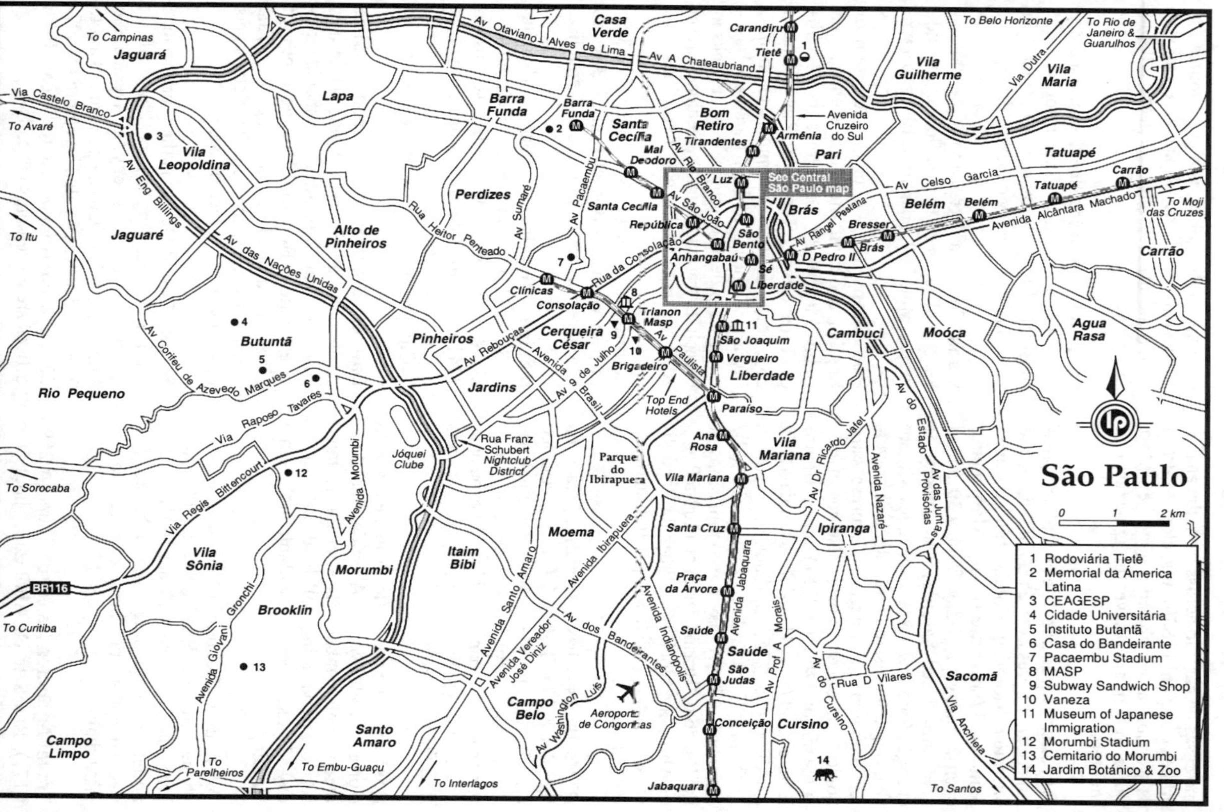
São Paulo
0
1
2 km
1 Rodoviária Tietê
2 Memorial da América Latina
3 CEAGESP
4 Cidade Universitária
5 Instituto Butantã
6 Casa do Bandeirante
7 Pacaembu Stadium
8 MASP
9 Subway Sandwich Shop
10 Vaneza
11 Museum of Japanese Immigration
12 Morumbi Stadium
13 Cemitario do Morumbi
14 Jardim Botânico & Zoo
See Central São Paulo map
To Campinas
To Avaré
To Itu
To Sorocaba
To Curitiba
To Parelheiros
To Embu-Guaçu
To Interlagos
To Santos
To Belo Horizonte
To Rio de Janeiro & Guarulhos
To Moji das Cruzes
Jaguará
Lapa
Barra Funda
Casa Verde
Santa Cecília
Bom Retiro
Vila Guilherme
Vila Maria
Vila Leopoldina
Jaguaré
Alto de Pinheiros
Perdizes
Pari
Tatuapé
Belém
Brás
Carrão
Butuntã
Rio Pequeno
Pinheiros
Cerqueira César
Jardins
Liberdade
Cambuci
Moóca
Agua Rasa
Vila Mariana
Parque do Ibirapuera
Moema
Ipiranga
Vila Sônia
Brooklin
Morumbi
Itaim Bibi
Campo Belo
Saúde
Cursino
Sacomã
Santo Amaro
Campo Limpo
Jóquei Clube
Rua Franz Schubert Nightclub District
Top End Hotels
Aeroporto de Congonhas
Av Otaviano Alves de Lima
Av A Chateaubriand
Via Castelo Branco
Av Eng Billings
Av das Nações Unidas
Rua Heitor Penteado
Av Sumaré
Av Pacaembu
Rua da Consolação
Av Rebouças
Avenida 9 de Julho
Av Brasil
Av Paulista
Av Corifeu de Azevedo Marques
Via Raposo Tavares
Via Regis Bittencourt
Avenida Morumbi
Avenida Giovani Gronchi
Avenida Santo Amaro
Avenida Vereador José Diniz
Av dos Bandeirantes
Avenida Ibirapuera
Avenida Indianópolis
Av Washington Luís
Avenida Jabaquara
Av Prof A Morais
Av do Cursino
Rua D Vilares
Av Dr Ricardo Jafet
Avenida Nazaré
Av do Estado
Av das Juntas Provisórias
Via Anchieta
Av Rio Branco
Av São João
Avenida Cruzeiro do Sul
Av Celso Garcia
Av Rangel Pestana
Avenida Alcântara Machado
Via Dutra
Carandiru
Tietê
Armênia
Tirandentes
Luz
São Bento
República
Anhangabaú
Sé
Liberdade
D Pedro II
Brás
Bresser
Belém
Tatuapé
Carrão
Barra Funda
Mal Deodoro
Santa Cecília
Clínicas
Consolação
Trianon Masp
Brigadeiro
São Joaquim
Vergueiro
Paraíso
Ana Rosa
Vila Mariana
Santa Cruz
Praça da Árvore
Saúde
São Judas
Conceição
Jabaquara
BR116

and casas de câmbio across from the airline offices on Avenida São Luís, close to Praça da República, which are a good bet. Most banks in this area have foreign-exchange counters.

Travellers Cheques The central branch of American Express (☎ 251-3383) is at the Sheraton Mofarrej Hotel, Rua Alameda Santos 1437, near the Trianon-Masp metrô, open Monday to Friday from 9.30 am to 5.30 pm, closed Saturday and Sunday. It changes American Express cheques without charging commission and sells US$ travellers cheques to American Express card holders. American Express also has offices at the airport (☎ 6445-3351), and at Centro Empresarial (☎ 3741-8478), Avenida Maria Coelho Aguiar 215, 8th Floor.

Thomas Cook and other cheques can be changed (only by paying commission) at the Banco do Brasil branch at 1202-5 Rua 7 de Abril, one block from Praça da República, which charges US$11 per transaction – not per cheque.

ATMs Banespa has a branch at Praça da República 295. The Itaú Caixa Eletrônico branch opposite the Teatro Municipal has ATMs that accept MasterCard and Cirrus bank cards. Citibank machines, like the ones at Avenida Paulista 1111, accept Visa and Plus bank cards.

Post The main post office is in the Praça do Correio, right where Avenida São João meets Anhangabaú. The posta restante service, downstairs, will hold mail for 30 days. Fax services are available in the same building.

Telephone The Telesp long-distance telephone office is at Rua 7 de Abril, 200m from Praça da República. Cabinet 16 has a 120V outlet and data plug for notebooks. São Paulo telephone numbers can have seven or eight digits.

Travel Agencies Kangaroo Tours (☎ 259-0177), Rua Sete De Abril 235, about 50m from metrô República, is a great source for good deals on domestic and international flights and airpasses. See Craig, and tell him LP sent ya!

Foreign Consulates See the introductory Facts for the Visitor chapter for specific consular office information. Consulates in São Paulo are open Monday to Friday.

Visas For visa extensions, the Polícia Federal office is on the 1st floor at Avenida Prestes Maia 700, open from 10 am to 4 pm.

Bookshops There's an OK selection of English books at the Book Centre, Rua Gabus Mendes 29, near Praça da República. Litec Livros Técnicos, Rua Timbiras 257, has English computer textbooks. Livraria Francesa at Rua Barão de Itapetininga 275 deals exclusively with books in French. Livraria Cultura at Avenida Paulista 2073 has quite a wide variety of titles.

Laundry There's a coin laundry (US$3.50 each to wash and dry) at Rua Consolaçaõ 825, five minutes from Praça da República.

Medical Services Einstein Hospital (☎ 845-1233), Avenida Albert Einstein 627, in the south-west corner of the city (bus No 7241 to Jardin Columbo) is one of the best in Latin America.

City pharmacies are open seven days.

Dangers & Annoyances Reports of crime in the city have increased, and while it is still safer than Rio, travellers should exercise caution. Be careful in the centre at night, and around the cheap hotels in Rua Santa Efigênia. Watch out for pickpockets on buses and on Praça da Sé.

Tourist Police Deatur is the tourist police service and has English-speaking staff. It has two offices in the city: at Avenida São Luís 115 (☎ 214-0209), open from 8 am to 8 pm, and at Rua 15 de Novembro (☎ 607-8332), open from 8 am to 7 pm. Both offices are closed on weekends.

Walking Tour

The triangle formed by Praça da Sé, Estação da Luz metrô station and Praça da República contains the old centre of São Paulo, and it's certainly worth having a look round this area.

A good place to start is the **Mercado Municipal** at Rua da Cantareira 306. Dating from 1933, this lively area used to be the city's wholesale market, until the CEAGESP (a huge new market) was built. Check out the German-made, stained-glass windows with their agricultural themes.

Not far from the market is Praça da Sé, the geographical centre of the city, and the **Catedral**, which was completed in 1954. There are a lot of buskers here, but don't bring any valuables, because there are also lots of pickpockets and bag snatchers.

Close by is the **Pátio do Colégio**, where the city was founded in 1554 by the Jesuits José de Anchieta and Manoel da Nóbrega. The church and college have been reconstructed in colonial style.

A couple of blocks from Praça da Sé, in the Largo São Francisco, is the **Law Faculty** of the University of São Paulo. The nearby bars are local student hang-outs, especially **Bar & Restaurante Itamaraty**.

Up Rua Libero Badaró and across the **Viaduto do Chá** (the bridge over the Vale do Anhangabaú) is the **Teatro Municipal**, the pride of the city. It's baroque with art nouveau elements. The area between here and Avenida Ipiranga is pedestrians-only and busy during the day. There are plenty of clothing, shoe, book and record shops, travel agencies, photo places and lunch counters.

A Dead King

Ayrton Senna da Silva, 34, was the third-highest paid athlete in the world in 1993, earning US$18.5 million. To Brazilians he was a living legend, their triple champion and living proof that Brazilians could take on the world and win. Then, on 1 May 1994 during the Italian Grand Prix at the Imola circuit in San Marino, tragedy struck.

The race itself began badly: Pedro Lamy in a Lotus and JJ Lehto of Benetton collided at the start and two of Lamy's tyres hit four spectators. In the pits, one of the tyres from the Minardi driven by Michele Alboreto flew off and injured six people.

Then, at 9.13 am Brazilian time, Senna's Williams left the track on Tamburello curve at 300 km/h and smashed against the wall. It was transmitted live on TV and the scene traumatised the whole of Brazil. The champion was dead.

Senna was awarded a state funeral with full honours. His Brazilian fans turned out in huge numbers to pay their respects. When the plane carrying his body arrived in São Paulo, 250,000 fans waited in sorrow. The service was attended by 110,000 mourners and 250,000 followed their idol to Morumbi cemetery.

In Brazil, Ayrton Senna is now worshipped as a sporting god. To visit Morumbi, southwest of the city centre, take bus No 7241 Jardim Columbo from Praça da República.

Up on Avenida Ipiranga, on the corner of Avenida São Luís, is the tallest building in town, the 41-storey **Edifício Itália**. There's a restaurant and piano bar at the top, as well as a viewing terrace. Strictly speaking, you're supposed to be a customer to go there; if you're not, act like one. The best time to go up is right on sunset. This is the only time you'll ever get to see the horizon and, as the sun goes down over the nearby hills and the city lights start to sparkle, you could almost convince yourself that São Paulo is beautiful.

Next to the Itália is another one of the city's landmarks, **Edifício Copan**, with its famous curve – another architectural project by Oscar Niemeyer.

Along Avenida Ipiranga, just past Praça da República, is the intersection with Avenida São João. When people get nostalgic about the city (yes, some do), this is the place they write songs about. **Bar Brahma**, on the corner, is a classic bar where you may want to go and try to compose yourself.

The area between here and the Estação da Luz gradually deteriorates. Rua Santa Efigênia is where Paulistanos go for cheap electronic goods, and the area between here and the station is known as ***boca do lixo*** (garbage mouth!) – a red-light area with striptease shows, and desperate characters after dark.

Museum of Art

The Museu de Arte de São Paulo (MASP; ☎ 251-5644), Avenida Paulista 1578 (metrô to Paraiso station, then change for Trianon-Masp), has Latin America's best collection of western art in its ugliest building, including the work of many French impressionists. There are also a few great Brazilian paintings; Cândido Portinari's work alone is worth the trip. There are also temporary exhibits, and a pleasant cafeteria on the 1st floor.

Admission is US$8 for adults, US$4 for students, free for those under 10 or over 60. It's open Tuesday to Sunday from 11 am to 6 pm (to 8 pm on Thursday, when it's also free). Go early, as the light can be very bad late in the day.

Outside, on Sunday, there is the **Feira de Antiguidades do MASP**, a market held from 9 am to 5 pm, full of old odds and ends, big and small.

For a bit of relaxation after the museum, visit the small park – a tropical oasis amid the mountains of concrete – across Avenida Paulista.

Parque do Ibirapuera

There's lots to do in this park, and many people doing it on weekends. Take the metrô to Santa Cruz and then bus No 775-C Jardim Maria Sampião, or bus No 5121 Santo Amaro from Praça da República. The large edifice across the street from the park is the São Paulo state legislature. Just outside the park, at the end of Avenida Brasil, is Victor Brecheret's huge monument *Bandeiras*, built in memory of the pioneers of the city.

Inside the park is the **Museu de Arte Moderna** (☎ 549-9688), the oldest museum of modern art in the country with a huge collection of works from the 1930s to the 1970s. There's also a **planetarium** (☎ 575-5206) with sessions daily; plus other assorted monuments including a Japanese pavilion and, in the Bienal building, several museums.

Museu de Arte Contemporânea

This museum has many of the big names in modern art and a good collection of modern Brazilian artists. It's housed, at least part of it, in the Bienal building, which also has a couple of enormous exhibition halls. The rest of the collection is at the Cidade Universitária, which is open Tuesday to Sunday from 1 to 6 pm.

The Bienal international art exhibition is also worth a mention. It's the largest in Brazil and if you happen to be in town when it's on, don't miss it. It takes place every second (even) year.

Museu Aeronautica & Museu de Folclore

These two museums were closed during 1997-98 for renovation and their conbined future is unclear.

Museum De Arte Sacra & Jardim da Luz
The best of Brazil's many museums of sacred-art is at Avenida Tiradentes 676. Take the metrô to Tiradentes. The museum is open Tuesday to Sunday from 1 to 5 pm. Two blocks down Avenida Tiradentes is the **Jardim da Luz** and an old British-built metrô station, Estação da Luz.

Museum of Japanese Immigration
This fascinating museum (☎ 279-5465,), Rua São Joaquim 381, three blocks downhill (east) from the São Joaquim metrô station, has exhibitions on the growth of the Japanese community from the arrival in Santos of the first 781 settlers aboard the *Kasato-Maru* in 1908, through to today. It's open Tuesday to Sunday from 1.30 to 5.30 pm. Entry is US$2.

Museu Lasar Segall
Lasar Segall was a great Lithuanian expressionist artist (1891-1957) who made Brazil his home and became leader of its modern movement in the 1920s. In addition to displaying his work, the museum (☎ 574-7322) gets some very good exhibitions. It's a fair way from the centre at Afonso Celso 362, Vila Mariana (metrô: Santa Cruz), and is open Tuesday to Sunday from 2.30 to 6.30 pm.

Fundção Maria Luisa & Oscar Americano
Also a long way from the centre at Avenida Morumbi 3700 in posh Morumbi (bus No 7241 Jardim Colombo from Praça da República), is this modern Brazilian home (☎ 842-0077), set in beautifully landscaped surroundings. It contains imperial antiques, and eight oils by Dutch artist Frans Post, painted in Olinda. It's open Tuesday to Friday from 11 am to 5 pm (Saturday and Sunday from 10 am) and is a great place to come for afternoon tea.

Butantã Snake Farm
One of the most popular tourist sights in town, the Instituto Butantã (☎ 813-7222) keeps over 1000 serpents from which it milks venom for the production of anti-venin to treat snake and spider bites as well as for vaccines against a number of diseases, including typhoid fever, typhus and diphtheria. Its two museums are both open Tuesday to Sunday from 9 am to 5 pm. Admission for both is US$1.25. The farm is in a very nice park, good for picnics, at the edge of the Cidade Universitária (bus No 702-U Butantã-USP from Praça da República).

Casa do Bandeirante
Not far from the snake farm this typical pioneer's abode, with a sugar mill, ox cart and farm implements, is interesting if you're in the area. It's in Praça Monteiro Lobato, and is open Tuesday to Sunday between 9 am and 5 pm.

Memorial da Ámerica Latina
Near Barra Funda metrô station at Rua Mario de Andrade 664 this group of buildings is another Niemeyer creation. Outside is a 7m cement hand. Inside are the **Centre of Latin American studies**, an auditorium with free concerts, and various handicraft exhibits. Portinari's painting *Tiradentes* hangs in the Salão de Atos and huge panels by Carybé and Poty represent the people of South America.

Organised Tours
The city runs three four-hour city tours on Sunday, each costing US$15. The Verde (9.30 am to 2.30 pm) hits parks and gardens; the Cultural (10 am to 2 pm) visits museums; and Histórico (1.30 to 5.30 pm) tours old houses and monuments. Get tickets and information at the tourist offices, or call ☎ 6971-5000.

Places to Stay
São Paulo has plenty of hotels, and they come in groups, which makes it easy to find one that suits your style. Prices tend to be reasonable. Many give weekend discounts of 20%. Rooms are hardest to find midweek and for the mid-range and top-end hotels, it's best to reserve a week in advance.

Places to Stay – Budget Down and out in São Paulo is done in an area between the Estação da Luz and the Praça da República.

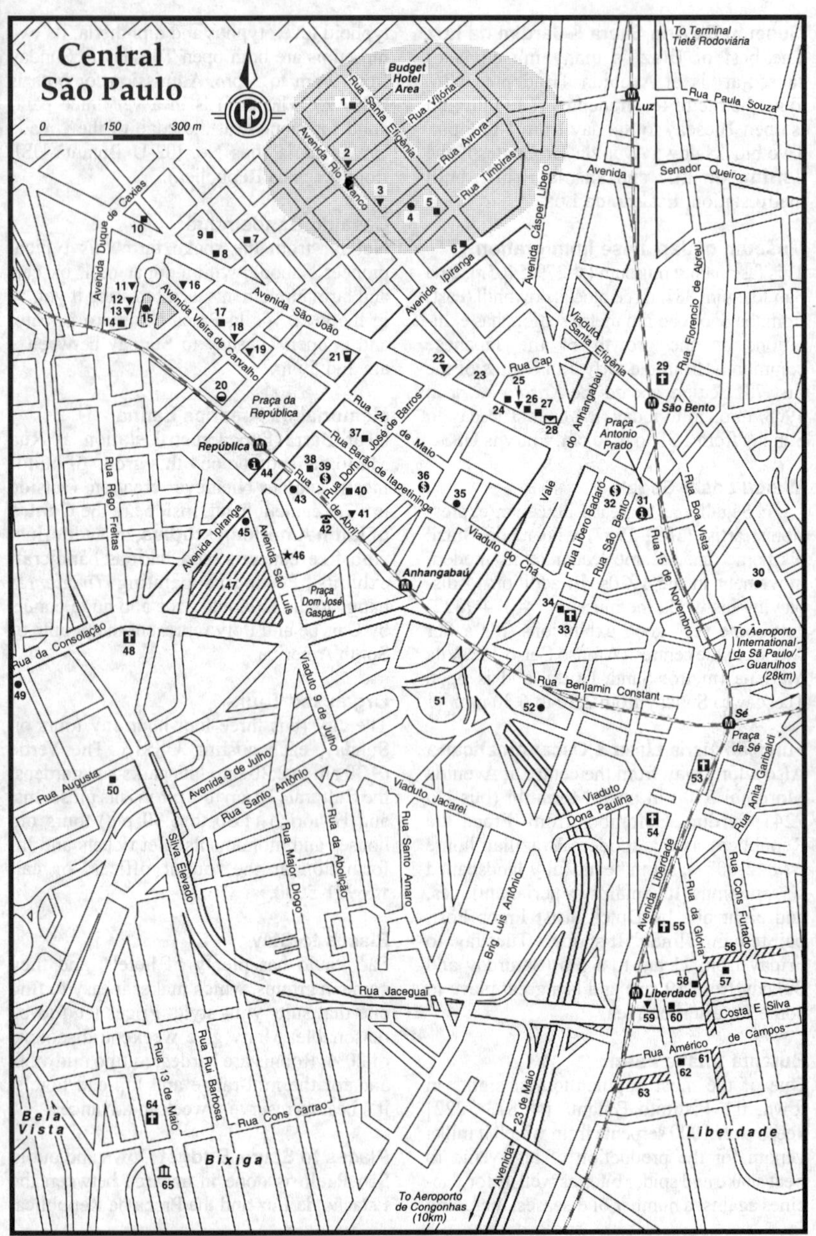
Central São Paulo
0
150
300 m
Budget Hotel Area
To Terminal Tietê Rodoviária
Luz
Rua Paula Souza
Avenida Senador Queiroz
Rua Santa Efigênia
Rua Vitória
Avenida Rio Branco
Rua Aurora
Rua Timbiras
Avenida Cásper Libero
Avenida Duque de Caxias
Avenida Ipiranga
Avenida São João
Avenida Vieira de Carvalho
Viaduto Santa Efigênia
Rua Florencio de Abreu
Rua Cap
Praça da República
República
Rua 24 de Maio
Rua Dom José de Barros
Rua Barão de Itapetininga
Rua 7 de Abril
Rua Dom
Vale do Anhangabaú
São Bento
Praça Antonio Prado
Rua Rego Freitas
Avenida Ipiranga
Avenida São Luís
Viaduto do Chá
Rua Libero Badaró
Rua São Bento
Rua 15 de Novembro
Rua Boa Vista
Anhangabaú
Praça Dom José Gaspar
Rua da Consolação
Viaduto 9 de Julho
To Aeroporto International da Sã Paulo/ Guarulhos (28km)
Rua Benjamin Constant
Sé
Praça da Sé
Rua Anita Garibaldi
Rua Augusta
Avenida 9 de Julho
Rua Santo Antônio
Viaduto Jacarei
Viaduto Dona Paulina
Rua Major Diogo
Rua da Abolição
Rua Santo Amaro
Silva Elevado
Brig Luís Antônio
Avenida Liberdade
Rua da Glória
Rua Cons Furtado
Liberdade
Costa E Silva
de Campos
Rua Jaceguai
Rua Américo
Rua 13 de Maio
Rua Rui Barbosa
Rua Cons Carrao
Avenida 23 de Maio
Bela Vista
Bixiga
Liberdade
To Aeroporto de Congonhas (10km)
1
2
3
4
5
6
7
8
9
10
11
12
13
14
15
16
17
18
19
20
21
22
23
24
25
26
27
28
29
30
31
32
33
34
35
36
37
38
39
40
41
42
43
44
45
46
47
48
49
50
51
52
53
54
55
56
57
58
59
60
61
62
63
64
65

PLACES TO STAY
1 Galeâo Hotel
5 Pauliceía Hotel
6 San Remo Hotel
7 Hotel Artemis
8 Hotel Riviera
9 Hotel Manchete
10 Hotel Atlântica
14 Hotel Esplanada
17 Hotel Itamarati
24 Municipal Palace
26 Britannia Hotel
27 Hotel Central
34 Othon Palace Hotel
37 Hotel Joamar
38 Hotel Sâo Sebastiâo
40 Hotel Rivoli
50 Grand Hotel Ca'd'Oro Hotel & Ca'd'Oro Restaurant
56 Cheap Hotels
57 Ikeda Hotel
58 Hotel Isei
60 Osaka Plaza
61 Cheap Hotels
62 Banri

PLACES TO EAT
2 Lanches Aliados
3 Pâo de Açucar (supermarket)
11 Churrascaria Novilho de Prata
12 Churrascaria Carre
13 La Casserole
16 Arroz de Ouro (macrobiotic)
18 Baby-Beef Rubaiyat
19 Casa Ricardo
22 Ponto Chic
25 Bar e Restaurante Leâo
41 Viva Melhor
59 Sunday Street Fair Food Stalls
63 Japanese Restaurants

OTHER
4 Litec Livros Técnicos
15 Mercado de Flores
20 Buses to Airports
21 Bar Brahma
23 Largo de Paissandu
28 Post Office
29 Mosteiro Sâo Bento
30 Patío do Colégio
31 State Tourist Information
32 Moneychangers
33 Igreja de Santo Antônio
35 Teatro Municipal
36 Itaú ATM Centre
39 Banco Do Brasil
42 Telesp (Telephones)
43 Book Centre
44 Tourist Information Booth
45 Edifício Itália
46 Deatur Tourist Police
47 Airlines, Travel Agencies & Money Exchange
48 Igreja NS de Cons olaçâo
49 Coin Laundry
51 Praça da Bandiera Local Bus Terminal
52 Law Faculty
53 Catedral
54 Igreja Sâo Gonçalo
55 Igreja das Almas
64 Igreja NS Achiropita
65 Museu Memórias do Bixiga

There are dozens of budget and below-budget hotels on Rua dos Andradas and Rua Santa Efigênia and the streets that intersect them from Avenida Ipiranga to Avenida Duque de Caxias. The area is safe during the day but seedy at night. There's a lot of prostitution in this district and some of the hotels here cater specifically to this high-turnover clientele. These are often the sleaziest places, and the management will usually indicate that you're not welcome.

There are several cheap places on Santa Efigênia. The *Pauliceía Hotel* (☎ 220-9733), Rua Timbiras 216 (on the corner of Rua Santa Efigênia), is a good deal, and is clean and safe. A single quarto goes for US$15 and a double for US$26. Apartamentos cost US$20/30 a single/double. The *San Remo Hotel* (☎ 229-6845), Rua Santa Efigênia 163, is a bit better, with quartos for US$22/29 and apartamentos for US$31/40 a single/double. The friendly *Galeão Hotel* (☎ 220-8211), Rua dos Gusmões 394, is good value. It's really a mid-range hotel (apartamentos start at US$28), but has cheapish quartos – US$20/30.

A step up in style and price are the hotels in the pedestrian part of Avenida São João, between the post office and Largo de Paissandu, where there are three relatively cheap places – the *Hotel Municipal Palace* (☎ 228-7833) at No 354; the *Britannia Hotel* (☎ 222-9244) at No 300; and the *Hotel Central* (☎ 222-3044) at No 288. The first has fine and clean quartos from US$23 per person (listed as US$29 but you can bargain) and single/double apartamentos from US$37/50. The second and third have single/double quartos for US$30/45 and apartamentos for US$40/55.

Liberdade An alternative to staying in the central district is to head over to Liberdade, the Japanese, Chinese and Korean area. The metrô stops very close to the hotels, and it's quieter, safer and more interesting at night. You can also pig out on cheap Japanese food. There are several less expensive hotels as you walk downhill from the metrô station at Praça da Liberdade (there's an information booth here that can give directions).

The really friendly *Ikeda Hotel* (☎ 278-5853), Rua dos Estudantes 134, has single/double quartos from US$21/38, apartamentos (in a separate building) with singles/ doubles/triples for US$32/60/75. The inconspicuous *Hotel Isei* (☎ 278-6646), Rua de Glória 290, has singles/ doubles for US$30/38, apartamentos from US$38/53.

Places to Stay – Mid-Range There are loads of mid-range hotels on the streets around Praça da República. They come in clusters, by price, along certain streets.

In the pedestrian streets close to Praça da República are a few places worth a mention. A stone's throw from the tourist booth, the *Hotel São Sebastião* (☎ 257-4988), Rua 7 de Abril 364, has single/double quartos for US$28/38 and apartamentos for US$38/64. Around the corner *Hotel Rivoli* (☎ 231-5633), Rua Dom José de Barros 28, has apartamentos and quartos for the same price. A nice little place a bit further down the street at No 187 is *Hotel Joamar* (☎ 221-3611), with apartamentos for US$39/51 a single/double.

On the other side of Praça da República is Avenida Vieira de Carvalho, a dignified, quiet street with a couple of favourites and some very expensive hotels. The *Hotel Itamarati* (☎ 222-4133; fax 222-1878), No 150 close to the bus stop, is a well-kept old place, with clean rooms and helpful management. Single/double quartos are US$31/44 and apartamentos US$40/53.

Across from the Estação da Luz, the *Hotel Florida* (☎ 220-2811), is a good place in a crummy location, with singles/doubles for US$46/64.

There are three big hotels to choose from on the 700 block of Avenida Ipiranga: *Plaza Maraba Hotel* (☎ 220-7811), with singles/ doubles for US$45/71; the *Terminus* (☎ 222-2266), with singles/doubles for US$49/71; and the *Excelsior* (☎ 222-0377), the best and most expensive of the three, with singles/ doubles for US$100/130.

Liberdade More expensive places in Liberdade include the *Banri* (☎ 270-8877; fax 278-9225), Rua Galvão Bueno 209, where singles/doubles start at US$48/64. The *Osaka Plaza* (☎ 270-1311; fax 270-1788), right across the street from the metrô, has all the modern amenities, with doubles starting at US$70/99, and a three-person suite for US$133.

Around Avenida Paulista There are no real bargains here; the two-star *Pamplona Palace* (☎ 285-5301), Rua Pamplona 851, is the closest you'll get; singles/doubles go for US$37/49. The seriously friendly *Hospedaria Mantovani* (☎ 889-8624), Rua Eliseu Guilherme 269, is a large house that's been converted into a small hotel. It's very clean and well kept, with double apartamentos for US$68.

Places to Stay – Top End As in Rio, the residential hotels all offer excellent deals. The *Augusta Park Hotel* (☎ 255-5722; fax 256-2381), Rua Augusta 922, Consolação, is a fine option with singles/doubles from US$100/120.

The well located *Trianon Residence* (☎ 283-0066; fax 283-0181) near Avenida Paulista, Alameda Casa Branca 363, Cerqueira César, has rooms from US$148/ 165. In the centre the Soviet-looking *Othon Palace* (☎ 239-3277), Rua Líbero Badaró 190, has decent singles/doubles starting at US$125/155.

There are good hotels on Avenida Cásper Líbero, a quiet street for the centre. The *Marian Palace* (☎ 228-8433) has singles/ doubles starting at US$135/153. Down the block the *Planalto* (☎ 227-7311) offers the same amenities for more, at US$142/285. The *Best Western São Paulo Centre* (☎ 228-

6033; fax 229-0959), Largo Santa Efigênia 40, is an old beauty; singles/doubles start at US$97/115.

São Paulo's luxury hotels include the *Maksoud Plaza* (☎ 253-4411; fax 253-4544), Alameda Campinas 150, Bela Vista, with single/double rooms for US$325/360; the magnificent *Grand Hotel Ca'd'Oro* (☎ 236-4300; fax 236-4311), Rua Augusta 129; and the *São Paulo Hilton* (☎ 256-0033; fax 257-3137), Avenida Ipiranga 165, with singles/doubles going for US$244/254. The *Sheraton Mofarrej* (☎ 284-5544) at Alameda Santos 1437 is the most expensive place in town: US$350/395 for singles/doubles.

Places to Eat

The best reason to visit São Paulo is to eat. Because of the city's ethnic diversity, you can find every kind of cuisine at reasonable prices. There are also a million cheap lanchonetes, pizzerias and great churrascarias and some of the best Italian and Japanese food that you'll find outside those countries.

Paulistanos love to dine out, and they leave late. Although restaurants open earlier, most don't fill up until 9 or 10 pm on weekdays, and later on weekends when many stay open until 2 or 3 am.

The places mentioned in this section are the more traditional ones. That they've been around for a long time is a recommendation in itself, since Paulistanos are very particular diners. The selection given is limited to areas easily reached by public transport. If you have a car or don't mind grabbing a taxi, there are hundreds of other eateries to choose from. The best listing of good restaurants is in the São Paulo lift-out section of the weekly *Veja* magazine.

City Centre There are a few inexpensive places several notches above the rest. *Ponto Chic* is a friendly, informal restaurant, but the best reason to go is the famous Brazilian sandwich, the bauru, which Ponto Chic invented many moons ago. The bauru (US$8) consists of beef, tomato, pickle and a mix of melted cheeses, served on French bread. Not only is it popular in urban and backland Brazil, it is also served in Paris. Ponto Chic is only a few blocks from the Praça da República, at Largo Paissandu 27 and is open until 4 am.

Another winner is the *Lanches Aliados* on the corner of Avenida Rio Branco and Rua Vitória. It's a cheap and cheerful lunch spot with excellent food and friendly service. The *Casa Ricardo* features 20 different sandwiches and is reasonably priced. Open until 7 pm, it's at Avenida Vieira de Carvalho 48. The *Mel* at Rua Araújo 75 has some excellent and cheap natural and vegetarian lunches. There's a good café on the 1st floor of the Bienal Building.

If it's lean meat you seek, *Baby-Beef Rubaiyat* has three churrascarias: the one in the centre (☎ 222-8333) is at Avenida Vieira de Carvalho 116. Also in Avenida Vieira de Carvalho, *Carlino* (☎ 223-1603) at No 154 is a reasonably cheap Italian restaurant that's been there for over a century. There are lots more restaurants further up on Largo do Arouche.

The *Bar e Restaurante Leão* at Avenida São João 320 has all-you-can-eat Italian meals and a salad bar, at reasonable prices. *Ca'd'Oro* (☎ 236-4300) in the Grand Hotel Ca'd'Oro is considered one of the best. It's very expensive; a jacket and reservations are recommended.

Bela Vista & Bixiga Loaded with Italian restaurants and bars, these two districts offer some of the best places in the city at night. On Rua Avanhandava, in Bela Vista, there are two very good and very Italian restaurants. *Il Cacciatore* (☎ 256-1390), Rua Santo Antônio 855, and *Famiglia Mancini* (☎ 256-4320), Rua Avanhandava 81, have large selections of pasta and wine and stay crowded until very late with the after-theatre crowd. They are both moderately priced – US$8 to $10 buys a large plate of pasta.

In Bixiga, Rua 13 de Maio has stacks of Italian restaurants. *Cantina e Pizzeria Lazzarella* (☎ 288-1995), No 589, is full of Brazil kitsch. It's festive, the food is good and large plates of pasta cost about US$10. *Roperto* (☎ 288-2573), No 634, is another good Italian place, and *Speranza* (☎ 288-8502), No 1004, is one of the best pizzerias around. If you're after a snack after the MASP, try the *Subway* sandwich shop right opposite, or the amazing salad bar at *Vaneza* (☎ 289-9708), Avenida Paulista 1217.

Cerqueira César There are lots of restaurants and bars in the area bounded by Avenida Paulista, Rua da Consolação, Rua Estados Unidas and Alameda Ministro Rocha Azevedo. Most are fairly expensive, but there are quite a few reasonable ones. A good sandwich place is the very traditional *Frevo*, Rua Oscar Freire 603. If you want to be really Paulistano, order one of the beirute á modas and a chopp. Waiters calling for a chopp yell for a rabo de peixe (fish tail). *Baguette*, Rua da Consolação 2426, in front of the cinema, is another sandwich and beer place, open 24 hours and packed at 3 am.

Almanara (☎ 853-6916), Rua Oscar Freire 523, is a traditional place that serves good Arab food. The churrascarias *Wessel Grill* (☎ 280-9107), Rua Bela Cintra 1855, *Rodeio* (☎ 883-2322), Rua Haddock Lobo 1498, and *Esplanada Grill* (☎ 881-3199), Rua Haddock Lobo 1682, are all excellent but expensive.

Sushi Guen, Avenida Brig Luis Antonio 2367, is a reasonably priced Japanese place.

There are a few French restaurants in the area, but nothing cheap. If bucks aren't a worry, try the famous soufflés at *Marcel* (☎ 3064-3089), Rua da Consolação 3555.

There are several fine and reasonably priced Italian restaurants. *L'Osteria do Piero* (☎ 853-1082), Alameda Franca 1509, is a local favourite, with rotating specials, closed Monday. *Babbo Giovanni* (☎ 853-3678), Rua Bela Cintra 2305, has good, cheap pizza.

For a big splurge, many think *Massimo* (☎ 248-0311) at Alameda Santos 1826 is the city's best Italian restaurant. *Z Deli*, Alameda Lorena 1214, is a hugely popular Jewish deli. Vegetarians won't feel left out in this area; there's a healthy fixed menu at *Cheiro Verde* (☎ 289-6853), Rua Peixoto Gomide 1214, and *Sattva*, Rua da Consolação 3140, has some imaginative vegetarian dishes.

Liberdade Liberdade has lots of inexpensive oriental restaurants and spectacular food at the Sunday street fair, when stalls at the southern side of Praça da Liberdade have gyoza (US$1.50), sukiyaki (US$5) and much more.

There are several good Japanese restaurants to choose from on Rua Tomás Gonzaga. *Gombe* at No 22 is always full. It has great sushi and sashimi and excellent sukiyaki. Other favourites include *Kaburá* (☎ 277-2918), Rua Galvão Bueno 346, and *Diego*, Praça Almeda Junior 25, with its strong, Okinawan dishes. *Sushi-Yassu* (☎ 279-6622), Rua Tomás Gonzaga 98, is the most famous, and the most expensive – about US$15 a meal (closed Monday).

Self-Catering Pão de Açúcar is a well-stocked supermarket, right in the centre on Avenida Rio Branco, that accepts Visa, MasterCard and American Express cards. The Asian markets in Liberdade are open on Sunday, when most other city supermarkets are closed.

Entertainment

São Paulo's nightlife approaches the excitement, diversity and intensity of New York's. Everyone is out playing until the wee hours and you can get stuck in traffic snarls at 3 am! To enjoy it, all you need is money (plenty) and transport. The best list of events is found in the weekly *Veja* magazine (US$4), which also lists restaurants, bars, museums, fairs etc. Another good source is the *Illustrada* section of the *Folha de São Paulo*.

Classical There's a steady stream of opera and classical concerts in the Teatro Municipal, check there or at the tourist office to get tickets. There are free classical concerts every Sunday at 11 am in Parque do Ibirapuera.

Clubs Cover charges for clubs range from US$10 to $20. The best street for clubs and such is Rua Franz Schubert, south-west of the centre; from Terminal Bandeiras (see

Getting Around later in this section) take bus No 6291 Brooklin to the corner of Avenida Cidade Jardim and Rua Franz Schubert. The biggest here is *Kremlin* (☎ 816-3747), Rua Franz Schubert 193, with techno, oldies and an older crowd. Others include *Saga*, *Limelight* (☎ 816-3411) with a younger crowd and plenty of techno; and *Arccadia*.

The bars and restaurants along Rua 13 de Maio in Bixiga also hum at night. They attract a young crowd, so prices are reasonable, and you can go there and plan out a full evening in one neighbourhood. The biggest bar is *Café Piu-Piu*, No 134, which has music every night, except Monday: jazz, rock, and a sequin-shirted, 20-gallon-hatted band that plays American country music. *Café do Bixiga*, No 76, is a traditional bar that stays open late.

Bela Vista is another good area for nightlife. There's lots happening and it's central, though the clubs are not as close together as those in Bixiga. *Spazio Pirandello*, Rua Augusta 311, is always lively – the crowd includes both gay and straight clientele. There's art on the walls and a bookshop downstairs.

Bars *Bar Brahma* on the corner of Rua São João and Avenida Ipiranga in the heart of the central hotel district, is the city's oldest drinking establishment. From 7 pm to midnight, the antique surroundings host equally dated live music. The best tables are upstairs. It's friendly and relaxing and a popular after-work hang-out for many Paulistano professionals.

The *Riviera Restaurant & Bar* on the corner of Rua Consolacão and Avenida Paulista, takes you right back to the seedy 1940s. It's inexpensive and unassuming – a good place to go with a friend. If you want to speak some English, try *Finnegan's Pub* (☎ 852-3232), Rua Cristiano Viana 358, Pinheiros. Paulistanos know it as a gringo bar, and it gets lively. The *Paris Café* is a hangout by the university.

Gay & Lesbian São Paulo has a lively gay scene, and the straight/gay mix in gay places is pretty good. A popular club is *Corintho*, Alameda dos Imarés 64, with live shows starting at 11 pm Wednesday to Sunday.

In Jardim Paulista *Clube Massivo* (☎ 883-7505), Alameda Itu 1548, has a good mix of straight, gay and lesbian, as does techno-heavy *Samantha Santa*, Frei Caneca 916, in Cerqueira César.

Live Music The classic is *Bourbon Street Music Club* (☎ 542-1927), Rua dos Chanés 127, Moema, with jazz and Dixieland; *Santana Samba*, Avenida Cruzeiro do Sul 3454, Santana, with rap and other black music; and there's samba nightly at *Mistura Brasileira*, Rua Alfreres de Magalhães 103, Santana.

Things to Buy

Shopping is almost as important to Paulistanos as eating out. Those who can afford it like to shop in one of the many large malls that dot the city. For the traveller, these malls don't hold much interest – prices tend to be higher than those in the centre of town. However, if you're a big fan of malls, you'll find a list of addresses in the *São Paulo this Month* guide.

More interesting are the many markets and fairs that take place around town, especially on weekends. The most popular is at Praça da República, Sunday from 8 am to 2 pm. It's a great place for people-watching (and getting pickpocketed). Offerings include Brazilian precious stones, leather gear, woodcarvings, handmade laces and paintings. Some of the painters, especially the native artists, are excellent.

Liberdade, the oriental district, has a big street fair all day on Sunday and is only five minutes from the centre by metrô. The fair surrounds the metrô station.

A couple of markets worth a look are the Mercado Municipal (see Walking Tour) and the CEAGESP market (on Avenida Doutor Gastão Vidigal, in the district of Jaguaré). The huge CEAGESP market is the centre of food distribution for the whole city, and is quite a sight. The best time to go is Tuesday to Friday from 7 am to noon, when there's a flower market as well. On other days, it just has lots and lots of fresh produce.

Another excellent market takes place every weekend in Embu, 28km from São Paulo. It's renowned for its rustic furniture, ceramics, paintings and leather items, and you'll find things here from all over Brazil. If you can't make it to the fair on the weekend, it's still worth coming during the week, as most of the artists have permanent shops and there are stacks of handicrafts stores. While there, have a look at the old Jesuit church in the main square; it contains a small sacred-art museum, and the first organ made in Brazil.

Getting There & Away

Air From São Paulo's three airports (see Getting Around for details), there are flights to everywhere in Brazil and to many of the world's major cities. São Paulo is the Brazilian hub for Continental Airlines and thus the first stop for many arriving from the USA.

Before buying a domestic ticket, be sure to check which airport the flight departs from and how many stops it makes (flights to coastal cities often make several stops along the way).

The São Paulo to Rio shuttle flies every half hour (or less) from Congonhas airport into Santos Dumont, in central Rio. The flight takes less than an hour and you can usually go to the airport, buy a ticket (US$300) and be on a plane within the hour. Most of the major airlines have offices on Avenida São Luís, near the Praça da República. They include:

Varig/Cruzeiro
(☎ 231-9400) Rua da Consolação 362
Transbrasil
(☎ 231-1529) Avenida São Luís 250
VASP
(☎ 220-3622) Praça da República 343
Aerolineas Argentinas
(☎ 214-4233) Rua Araújo 216, 6th floor.

Bus The Terminal Tietê rodoviária (☎ 235-0322) is easy to reach – just get off at the Tietê metrô station, which is adjacent to and connected with it. It's an enormous building, but easily navigated. The information desk in the middle of the main concourse has Portuguese-speaking staff.

Bus tickets are sold on the 1st floor, except for the Rio shuttle, which has its ticket offices on the ground floor at the rear of the building. Buses leave for destinations throughout Brazil, and there are also buses to major cities in Argentina, Paraguay, Chile and Uruguay from the booths at the south end of the terminal – turn left from the metrô.

All the following buses leave from the Terminal Tietê. Frequent buses traverse the 429km of the Via Dutra highway to Rio, taking six hours. The cost is US$18 for the regular bus and US$34 for the leito. There are also buses travelling to Brasília (US$46, 14 hours), Belém (US$137, 46 hours), Belo Horizonte (US$25.50, 9½ hours), Foz do Iguaçu (US$49, 15 hours), Cuiabá (US$62, 13 hours), Porto Velho (US$126; 46 hours), Campo Grande (US$62, 13 hours), Salvador (US$85, 32 hours), Curitiba (US$10, six hours) and Florianópolis (US$20, 12 hours).

Buses to Santos, Guarujá and São Vicente leave every five minutes from a separate bus station at the end of the southern metrô line (Jabaquara station). It's a one hour trip.

If you're staying outside the city centre, find out whether there's a local bus station nearby at which buses stop on their way out of town. For example, several southbound buses stop at Itapemirim Turismo (☎ 212-5402), Avenida Valdemira Feirrara 130, near the Cidade Universitária, on their way to Florianópolis, Curitiba etc. If you catch the bus here, it saves an hour's drive into the city and an hour's ride back.

Train The Estação da Luz metrô station also services what's left of the long-distance train routes to Bauru (from where you can get a bus to Campo Grande). Long-distance routes have been severely cut back in recent times, so it'll pay to check the following information. The information booth (☎ 225-0040) at Luz station has all the details.

You can't get a direct train to Campo Grande or Corumbá from São Paulo – you have to take the train or bus from São Paulo to Bauru, then catch a bus to Campo Grande and then get another train to Corumbá. Trains go to Bauru every day at 8 am, noon, and 4 and 11 pm. Buses from Bauru to Campo Grande leave at 4.30 pm. For connections from Campo Grande to Corumbá and Bolivia, see the Campo Grande Getting There & Away section in the Mato Grosso & Mato Grosso do Sul chapter.

Getting Around

To/From the Airport São Paulo has three airports. Congonhas (☎ 536-3555) serves Rio and other local destinations. It is the closest – 14km south of the city centre. Radio taxis at the front of the terminal charge about US$38 to the centre; *comums* (regular taxis) will cost about US$25.

For buses to the centre, walk out of the terminal and then to your right, where you'll see a busy street with a pedestrian overpass. Head to the overpass but don't cross; you should see a crowd of people waiting for the buses along the street, or ask for the bus to Terminal Bandeiras. The trip takes about an hour and the last bus leaves at around 1 am.

Aeroporto São Paulo/Guarulhos (☎ 6445-2945), São Paulo's international airport, is 30km east of the city. There's an Airport Services bus that goes to Praça da República, Terminal Tietê rodoviária and Congonhas airport. It costs US$10 and leaves from the stop just in front of the arrivals terminal. Another bus (also US$10) does a circuit of 11 four and five-star hotels in the Jardims Paulista area and the centre. From here to the centre, a comum taxi will cost US$30 and a radio-taxi US$46.

To the airport, you can catch Airport Services buses from Praça da República, Terminal Tietê rodoviária and Congonhas airport. Alternatively, take a metrô to Bresser and at the small bus terminal there grab a shuttle bus (US$1.50, 30 minutes).

If possible, avoid the Aeroporto Viracopos (☎ (019) 725-5000), 97km from the city, near Campinas. A taxi from here into town will cost about US$75 to $100.

Metrô A combination of metrô and walking is the best way to see the city. The metrô is cheap, clean, safe and fast. It's open from 5 am to midnight. The most useful ticket is the *multiplo 10*, 10 rides for US$10. A single ride costs US$1.25, or two for US$2.

There are currently three metrô lines, two of which intersect at Praça da Sé. The third runs along Avenida Paulista from Paraiso station. See the main São Paulo map for more information.

Bus Buses are slow, crowded during rush hours and not too safe. The tourist information booths are excellent sources of information about buses. Bus transfer points are at Praça da República and bustling Terminal Bandeiras, where you catch buses to far-flung destinations within the city.

Taxi Both the comum and radio-taxi services are metered; flagfall is US$4 and it's about US$2 per kilometre. Radio-taxis (☎ 251-1733) cost 30 to 50% more than the comum and will pick you up anywhere in the city.

The Paulista Coast

UBATUBA

• *pop 50,000* ✉ *11680-000* ☎ *012*

The Ubatuba litoral is a stunning stretch of beach along the northern São Paulo coast. The pre-eminent beach resort for well-to-do Paulistanos, it has elegant beach homes and hotels, especially south of the town of Ubatuba. To the north, all the way to Parati, the beaches are wilder, cleaner and often deserted. There are few hotels, but plenty of campsites.

Most travellers don't go to Ubatuba unless they want to escape São Paulo for the weekend or are driving along the Rio-Santos coastal road.

While the beaches are top-notch, they're rather expensive, get crowded in summer and retain little of the fishing culture that animates so many Brazilian coastal towns.

Information

There's a tourist office shack where Rua Professor Thomaz Galhardo hits the bay. It's open from 8 am to 6 pm, with helpful staff and a useful map.

Banco do Brasil has a branch on the corner of Rua Dona Maria Alves and Rua Carvalho. The post office is on Rua Dona Maria Alves, and the posto telefônico is at Rua Professor Thomaz Galhardo 81.

Beaches

Within the district of Ubatuba, there are some 74 beaches and 15 islands. Even if you don't have wheels, there's a fine beach a couple of kilometres south of town, with barracas and some surfing. Other recommended beaches south of Ubatuba include **Enseada** (8km away), **Flamengo** (12km), **do Lázaro** and **Domingas Dias** (15km). The big, loud party scene is 6km south at **Praia Grande**.

North of town, the beaches are hidden away down the steep hillside. They're harder to find, but good for boogie-boarding and surfing and well worth the effort. The best are: **Vermelha do Norte** (9km north), **Itamambuca** (15km), where the river meets the sea; **Promirim** (23km) and **Ubatumirim** (33km).

Port

The port is at Praia de Saco da Rebeira, 12km south of Ubatuba. You can book daily cruises (3½ hours, US$25) into the Baía da Enseada and out to the Ilha Anchieta.

Special Events

On 29 June, Ubatuba celebrates the **Festa de São Pedro Pescador** with a big maritime procession.

Places to Stay

If you don't have a car, the more expensive centre is the most convenient place to stay because you can catch local buses to some of the beaches. We don't recommend the cheapest option, *Jangadeiro Hotel* (☎ 432-1365), Avenida Abreu Sodré 111. Singles/doubles cost only US$10/15, but room keys are identical, it's filthy and management is reprehensible. It's on Praia do Perequê, a 15 minute walk from the centre. There's a camping ground nearby at Avenida Leovegildo dias Viera 1854, Itaguá.

Much better are the pricey hotels within a couple of blocks of the bus station, including the *Hotel Xareu* (☎ 432-1525), Rua Jordão Homem da Costa 413; *Hotel São Nicolau* (☎/fax 432-3310), Rua Conceição 213; and the excellent *Parque Atlântico* (☎ 432-1336), Rua Conceição 185. All charge US$30/40 a single/double in low season, US$70/80 at peak times.

The *Ubatuba Palace* (☎ 432-1500), Cel Domiciano 500, is the city's finest hotel and singles/doubles cost US$60/70.

Places to Eat

Buchneiros, Rua Conceição 61, is a pizzeria (US$9 to $16) with a huge wood burning oven. On the waterfront near the centre, *Cantina Perequim*, Rua Guarani 385 (☎ 432-1354), is an Italian restaurant that's popular with locals.

Gauchão at Rua Guarani 378 is the best churrascaria in town. *Kilo & Cia* is in the centro at Rua Dona Maria Alves 393; it has a good self-serve lunch. *Gaivota* at Avenida Leovegildo dias Viera 240 offers a varied menu and is popular with locals.

Getting There & Away

Bus There are two bus stations in Ubatuba, less than two blocks apart. The main rodoviária is on Rua Professor Thomaz Galhardo, between Rua Hans Staden and Rua Cunhambebe. The Reunidas bus company, which also runs buses to Rio and São Paulo, has a ticket office in a lanchonete on the corner of Rua Professor Thomaz Galhardo and Rua Coronel Domiciano.

To São Paulo (US$12, four hours), there are eight buses daily, the first leaving at 12.30 pm and the last at 6.30 pm. Buses to

Parati (US$3.50, 1½ hours) leave at 9.40 am, and 5 and 9.40 pm. There are frequent buses to Rio (US$15, five hours).

For Saõ Sebastão, get a local bus to Caraguátatuba (US$1.85, 40 minutes) then change in front of the main rodoviária for a Saõ Sebastão bus.

Car Ubatuba is 72km south-west of Parati on the sealed coastal road – a 1½ hour drive at a reasonable speed. Rio is 310km (five hours) away. Heading south along the coast from Ubatuba, you reach Caraguátatuba (54km away), São Sebastião and Ilhabela (75km), and Santos (205km). After Caraguátatuba, the road begins to deteriorate and an unending procession of speed bumps rear their ugly heads.

São Paulo is 240km from Ubatuba. By far the fastest route is to turn off the coastal road onto Hwy SP-099 at Caraguátatuba, then climb the escarpment until you meet the Rio-São Paulo highway, BR-116, at São José dos Campos. This is a beautiful, rapid ascent, and the road is in good condition.

SÃO SEBASTIÃO

• *pop 33,000* ✉ *11600-000* ☎ *012*

The coastal town of São Sebastião faces the Ilha de São Sebastião (popularly known as Ilhabela), a 15 minute ferry trip across the channel. Huge oil tankers anchor in the calm canal between the island and mainland, waiting to unload at São Sebastião. Most visitors stay here because they can't find lodging at Ilhabela or to enjoy the canal's excellent windsurfing conditions.

Information

The tourist office (☎ 452-2544), Avenida Dr Altino Arantes 174, on the waterfront, is open Monday to Saturday from 8 am to 6 pm and Sunday from noon to 6 pm. The Banco do Brasil at Rua Duque de Caxais 20 has a Visa/Plus ATM.

Places to Stay

The *Hotel Roma* (☎ 452-1016), Praça Major João Fernandes 174, has simple doubles from US$25. The *Pousada da Sesmaria* (☎ 452-2437), Rua São Gonçalo 190 near the centre has singles/doubles from US$23/30.

The best place in town is the lovely and spotless *Pousada da Ana Doce* (☎ 452-1615), Rua Expedicionários Brasilieros 196, with singles/doubles from US$40/50, higher whenever possible.

Places to Eat

Along the waterfront you'll find several good fish restaurants, including *Super Flipper* and, next door, *El Greco*; both have main courses from about US$12.

Getting There & Away

The rodoviária at Praça da Amizade 10 has a regular service to São Paulo (US$13), Rio (US$14), Santos (US$10) and Boiçucanga (US$2).

The Rio-Santos highway is slow going between São Sebastião and Santos. A much quicker route to São Paulo (200km) is through Caraguátatuba, despite a zillion speed bumps along the coastal road.

ILHABELA

• *pop 13,000 (winter); 100,000 (summer)* ✉ *11630-000* ☎ *012*

With an area of 340 sq km, Ilhabela is the biggest island along the Brazilian coast. The island's volcanic origin is evident in its steeply rising peaks, which are covered by dense, tropical jungle. There are 360 waterfalls, and the flatlands are filled with sugar cane plantations. The island is known for its excellent jungle hiking and its fine cachaça.

Although Ilhabela is a beautiful place, visiting it can be a drag. During summer, the island is besieged by Paulistas. Besides the threat to the environment, the crowds create all sorts of logistical difficulties: hotels fill up, waits of two to three hours for the car ferry are common, and prices soar. The bugs are murder, especially the little bloodsuckers known as *borrachudos*. Use plenty of insect repellent at all times.

The time to go to Ilhabela is on weekdays in the low season. Once you arrive, the name of the game is to get away from the west coast, which faces the mainland and where almost all human activity is concentrated. To get to the other side of the island requires either a car, taxi (☎ 974-1046), a boat trip or a good strong pair of hiking legs.

Information

The Secretária de Turismo de Ilhabela (☎ 472-2200) is at the old airstrip, Campo de Aviação. It has a complete list of hotels, pousadas, chalets and camping grounds. The post office and the ticket office for buses to São Paulo are in the same street.

There's a tourist information post (☎ 472-8557) of limited usefulness at the roundabout 200m from the ferry dock, in the district of Barra Velha. It's open every day from 9 am to noon and 2 to 6 pm.

Colonial Buildings

Vila Ilhabela has quite a few well-preserved colonial buildings, including the slave-built **Igreja NS da Ajuda** (dating from 1532), the **Fazenda Engenho d'Agua** (1582) in Itaquanduba and **Fazenda Santa Carmen** (at Feiticeira beach).

Beaches

There are more than 50 beaches on the island, but most of them are hard to reach and are accessible only by boat or on foot.

Of the sheltered beaches on the island's north side, **Praia Pedra do Sino** and **Praia Jabaquara** are recommended. On the east side, where the surf is stronger, try **Praia dos Castelhanos** (good camping and surf), **Praia do Gato** and **Praia da Figueira**.

Waterfalls

Two kilometres inland from Perequê beach, **Cachoeira das Tocas** is made up of various small waterfalls with accompanying deep pools and water slides. It costs US$4 to get in, which includes insect repellent. It's a great place to go if you're sick of the beach. **Cachoeira de Água Branca**, in the middle of the jungle, is another waterfall to check out. Access is from Veloso beach.

Pico São Sebastião

The 1379m peak of São Sebastião, in the district of Barra Velha, provides a great view – definitely worth it if you're feeling energetic.

Activities

Paulistas on holiday like their toys. As a consequence you can rent almost anything here: powerboats, yachts, kayaks, jet-skis, windsurfers, motorbikes, dune buggies, bicycles, tennis courts, helicopters and diving gear are just some of the alternatives.

Places to Stay

Reservations are a good idea, especially on weekends. Many choose to stay in São Sebastião, where hotels are cheaper.

Near the ferry terminal is the lovely *Pousada Caravela* (☎ 472-8295), Rua Carlos Rizzini 70, with two-room suites for US$40/50 a single/double in low season, US$60/70 in high season.

Near the beach, the *Pousada dos Hibiscos* (☎ 472-1375), Avenida Pedro Paula de Morais 714, has singles/doubles for US$45/70. It's 800m from town. Also close to town and similarly priced is the *Costa Azul* (☎ 472-1365), Rua Francisco Gomes da Silva Prado 71.

If you plan on staying for a few days, self-contained chalets are a reasonably priced option. *Chalé Praia Grande* (☎ 472-1017) in the southern part of the island is the cheapest, at US$26 per day. There are lots of camping grounds near Barra Velha, where the ferry stops, and just a bit further south, at Praia do Curral.

There is certainly no lack of top-end hotels on the island; the tourist office has a list.

Places to Eat

At the roundabout near the tourist office is a good self-serve ice cream place, and for self-catering, hit the *Ihla da Princesa supermarket*, Avenida Princesa Isabel 2467, Barra Velha. In Vila Ilhabela itself, there are a few good, cheap lanchonetes: two in the pedestrian mall and a couple on Rua da

Padroeira. *Cheiro Verde* at Rua da Padroeira 109 has a good prato feito for US$5, while *Convés* at No 139 has tasty sandwiches. Right on the pier at *Pier Pizza* you can have a tasty chopp and watch the fishermen pull in the swordfish.

A bit further from Vila is *Deck*, at Avenida Almirante Tamandaré 805, a popular seafood restaurant. *Recanto da Samba*, on the waterfront, is a great place to have a beer and stare at the mainland.

Getting There & Away

The ferry (15 minutes) between São Sebastião and Ilhabela runs frequently from 5.30 am to midnight (and often until much later in summer). Cars cost US$8, motorcycles US$4, pedestrians US$2 if you board the pedestrian-only ferry to the right of the car ferry entrance, or free (hint) if you ... well, sorta just (wink) *walk* onto the car ferry.

BOIÇUCANGA

• *pop 5000* ☎ *012*

A laid-back surfer town, charming Boiçucanga is well serviced by simple hotels and decent restaurants. While the surf here isn't as good as at nearby Maresias and Camburi, there are friendly people and some good walks into the Mata Atlântica (Atlantic rainforest).

Information

A good source of information here is José Mauro B Pinto y Silva, who runs a tourist information service called Amart (☎ 465-1276), Avenida Walkir Vergani 319. An English-speaking budget traveller, José is a friendly guy who can help you out with just about anything, including cheap places to stay, surf, windsurf and information on treks into the forest.

Beaches

There are some great beaches along this stretch of coastline, all accessible by bus. Both **Maresias,** 7km north, and **Camburi,** 5km south, are great surf beaches. **Barra do Sahy** has calmer water.

Islands

There are many nearby offshore islands you can visit (one called Alcatraz), either by renting a kayak (about US$10/hour on the beaches) or by arranging for José Benedito dos Santos (☎ 975-1879) or Lili (☎ 975-3732) to drop you off in the morning and pick you up at night. You can't camp. Trips average US$10 each way per person.

Places to Stay

There are camping grounds at all the beaches and they are a good, cheap accommodation option. In Boiçucanga, *Camping do Vovô Kido* (☎ 465-1157), has tent sites for US$10 perperson and very simple (bed-in-a-box) quartos for US$15 per person.

Cheaper hotels in Boiçucanga include the *Dani* (☎ 465-1299), Avenida Walkir Vergani 455, with singles/doubles for US$25/35, and *Pousada Boiçucanga* at No 522 with dorm beds for US$15.

It's cheaper to stay in Boiçucanga but wealthier surfers stay in Maresias. There's a hostel here (☎ 965-1561), Rua da Sudelpa 111, 1km from the beach. Another option is *Hotel Villa'l Mare* (☎ 974-5676), near the beach, which has singles/doubles from US$35/50, higher at peak times. English is spoken.

At Camburi, just off the main road, an enjoyable top-end place to stay is the *Pousada das Praias* on the old Hwy SP-55 (Antiga SP-55) at No 22. During the week, doubles go for US$80, but on weekends the price goes up to US$100.

Places to Eat

The *Big Pão* bakery, right off the beach, has good snacks and is open 24 hours. Near the beach, *Sinhá Moça* (☎ 974-2355) has a good US$5 lunch buffet and *Cantina & Pizzeria Ibarape* (☎ 465-1211) has good pizza, chicken and drinks.

Getting There & Away

Buses run along the coast from about 6 am to about 8 pm. The 'bus station' is the camper van at the north end of town. Schedules are unpredictable.

GUARUJÁ

• *pop 220,500 ✉ 11400-000 ☎ 013*

Horrible Guarujá, 87km from São Paulo, is the state's biggest beach resort. We said big, not nice; it's a crowded, urban beach that's popular because it happens to be the closest one to São Paulo. The tourist information office at the bus station here is tended by an armed *and* unhelpful person. The condo-crammed beachfront has plenty of hotels, restaurants, boutiques etc. There's surfing along **Tombo Beach**.

Places to Stay & Eat

The best budget bet is the *Pensão Europa* (☎ 386-6879), Rua Rio de Janeiro 193, one block from Praia das Pitangueiras, with simple singles/doubles at US$20/30. Farther along the same street at No 131 is *Hotel Rio Guaruja* (☎ 386-6081), a small and popular place with singles/doubles for US$35/50. A São Paulo-based reader recommended the *Pousada MiraMar* (☎ 354-1453) at Rua Antônio Marques 328, two blocks from Tombo Beach. There are many other, more expensive places.

Stacks of restaurants and bars line the waterfront. *Nutris* (☎ 355-4612), Avenida Leomil 538, is a good self-serve place.

Getting There & Away

The rodoviária is just outside town. From there, catch local bus No 1 or 15 (US$1) to the beach. Buses to São Paulo leave every half hour, the US$8.50 trip taking just over an hour. You'll pass through Cubatão, one of the most polluted places in the world. Depressed? Just think – it used to look even worse.

SANTOS

• *pop 420,000 ✉ 11000-000 ☎ 013*

The largest and busiest port in Latin America, Santos was founded in 1535 by Brás Cubas. The city has seen better days and, as a destination for travellers, it holds little interest. Only the façades remain of many of the grand 19th century houses built by wealthy coffee merchants, and the local beaches are polluted.

Information

There are tourist information booths at Praia do Gonzaga (☎ 284-2377) and the rodoviária. If you need to change money, try Casa Branco, in the centre, at Praça da República 29.

Places to Stay & Eat

The waterfront, along Avenida Presidente Wilson, is the place to head for cheaper hotels and lots of restaurants, but the expense account crowd has showed up in force. The *Maracanã Santos* (☎ 237-4030) at No 172 is good value with singles/doubles from $30/60. The *Hotel Gonzaga* (☎ 234-1411) at No 36 is also a decent cheapie. Businessfolk cram the very nice *Mendez Plaza Hotel* (☎ 289-4243), Avenida Floriano Peixoto 42, which has posh singles/doubles from US$130/160. There's good pizza at *Zi Tereza* (☎ 284-4832), Avenida Ana Costa 449, in the centre.

Getting There & Away

The rodoviária is right in the centre at Praça dos Andradas 45. Frequent buses go to São Paulo, 72km away.

IGUAPE

• *pop 26,500 ✉ 11920-000 ☎ 013*

Iguape was founded in 1538, making it one of the oldest towns in Brazil.

Information

Tourist information is available from the prefeitura, Rua 15 de Novembro 272. It's open on weekdays from 8 to 11 am and 1 to 5 pm.

Things to See

The town attractions are the **Museu de Arte Sacra** (in the Igreja do Rosário) and the **Mirante do Morro do Espia** (a lookout with a good view of the port and surrounding area). There are also several beaches. **Ilha Comprida**, with a 74km stretch of beach, is a five minute ferry ride away.

Places to Stay & Eat

In the centre, *De Martis* (☎ 841-1325), Rua

Major Rebello 258, is the best deal with singles/doubles for US$26/30. The friendly *Solar Colonial* (☎ 841-1591) is good, too, with clean rooms from US$32/45. On Ilha Comprida, the *Alpha* (☎ 842-1270), Rua São Lourenço 14, has apartamentos for US$50 for up to four people.

Eating in Iguape means seafood, seafood and more seafood. Try *Gaivota* and *Arrastão*, both on the seafront at Ilha Comprida, or *Panela Velha* (☎ 841-1869), Rua 15 de Novembro 190, with main courses from US$12 to $20.

Getting There & Away

Four buses a day, the first at 6 am and the last at 8 pm, make the trip to São Paulo. For Cananéia, take a bus to Pariquero and switch from there, or hitch along the beach on Ilha Comprida.

CANANÉIA

• pop 10,000 ✉ 11990-000 ☎ 013

Founded in 1531, Cananéia is considered the oldest city in Brazil, and was the first port of call of Martim Afonso de Sousa's fleet of Portuguese settlers.

Beaches

Ilha Comprida is only 10 minutes away by boat. To the south are the popular beaches of **Prainha** and **Ipanema**, with a waterfall, and, a two hour boat ride away, **Ilha do Cardoso**, an ecological reserve with some nice, deserted places.

Other Attractions

There's not a lot to do in Cananéia itself, and the colonial buildings are in poor shape. For the hard-up there's a **marine museum**, Rua Professor Besnard 133, or you could walk 1km up **Morro de São João** for a good view of the surrounding islands.

Places to Stay

The *Recanto do Sol* (☎ 851-1162), Rua Pedro Lobo 271, has reasonable singles/doubles for US$25/40. The *Beira-Mar* (☎ 851-1115), Avenida Beira-Mar 219, is a bit better for doubles; rooms are US$25/35. The *Hotel Coqueiro* (☎ 851-1255), Avenida Independência 542, has doubles for US$35 to $50, and a swimming pool.

Places to Eat

Cananéia is renowned for its oysters. The town also has a couple of excellent Japanese restaurants: *Naguissa* (☎ 851-1382), Rua Teotônio Vilela 38, does fish specialities from March to November. The *Bom Abrigo*, on Avenida Luís Wilson Barbosa, is open for dinner only (closed on Tuesday).

Getting There & Away

A direct bus leaves Cananéia for São Paulo at 4.30 pm.

CAMPOS DO JORDÃO

• pop 45,000 ✉ postcode 12460-000 ☎ 012

Nestled in the Serra da Mantiqueira, three hours by bus from São Paulo, is Campos do Jordão. It's a highly popular weekend mountain getaway for wealthier Paulistas who like to feel the cold and show off their leather outerwear. Campos looks very much like a southern German town – hills, woodsmoke, *fachwerk* houses and picture postcard views.

Restaurants and hotels keep up their end of this illusion by serving *glühwein*, holding an Oktoberfest, maintaining exorbitant prices, serving bland, heavy food and being pikers with the soap – *Bayern ist hier*!

But Campos' popularity is based on its undeniable prettiness – which, depending on your views, is either utterly sweet or indescribably twee.

At 1700m, Campos is a good place from which to check out some of the last remaining virgin *araucária* (Parana pine) forests, and to hike to the top of some high peak, with spectacular views of the Paraíba valley and of the coastal mountain range, the Serra do Mar. The railway line which connects Campos with Santo Antônio do Pinhal is the highest in Brazil.

Orientation

Campos is made up of three main districts: Abernéssia (the oldest), Jaguaribe (where the rodoviária is located) and Capivari, the centre. The three districts are connected by a tram line *(suburbio)* that's an attraction in itself.

Information

Tourist Office The main tourist office (☎ 263-1531) is in Capivari at the tram stop in the old train station. Tamara speaks English, and friendly staff will find you the cheapest place in town if you ask them. There's also an office at the gateway to the valley, on the main road into town just before Abernéssia.

They're both open daily from 8.30 am to 5 pm (to 6.30 pm in the July peak period).

Money There's a Banco do Brasil in Abernéssia, but you should be able to change cash dollars at some of the boutiques in Capivari.

Post & Telephone There's a posto telefônico in Abernéssia, in front of the tram stop, and another in Capivari near the church. The post office is also in Abernéssia, on Avenida Dr Januário Miraglia.

Things to See & Do

The Horto Florestal state park (US$2) is 14km east from Capivari. It contains the largest araucária reserve in the state, and there are some fine walks. Staff at the reception desk (☎ 263-1414, near the trout farm) hand out maps.

Another spot that deserves a visit is the **Pico do Itapeva**, 15km away. From 2030m, it's possible to see almost all of the Paraíba valley, with its industrial cities and the Rio Paraíba.

Close to Capivari is a chairlift (minifério, US$5) to the top of the 1700m **Morro do Elefante**, which has a good view of the town.

The **Palácio Boa Vista** (☎ 262-2966), 3.5km from Abernéssia, is the state governor's summer residence, and contains many antiques. It's open on Wednesday, Thursday and on weekends and holidays from 10 am to noon and 2 to 5 pm, entry is US$5.

The 19km **electric train ride** (US$15, 2½ hour round trip) from Campos to Santo Antônio do Pinhal is one of the country's best. It allows a 30 minute stopover in Santo Antônio – bring your own snack or you will be at the mercy of vendors. The train leaves Campos Tuesday to Friday at 2 pm, and Saturday, Sunday and holidays at 9.30 and 10 am and 1.30 and 2 pm. For the best views, sit on the right-hand side when leaving Campos.

Places to Stay

July is peak tourist period in Campos, when prices double or even triple.

Camping & Hostels The *Camping Clube do Brasil* (☎ 263-1130) has a camping ground 10km east of Capivari. It costs US$20 per person for nonmembers, US$7.50 for members – see Accommodation in Facts for the Visitor for more information.

The *Albuerge da Juvente* (☎ 262-3986), Avenida Irineu Gonçalves da Silva 255, in Jaguaribe behind the Mantiqueria bus garage, has dormitory beds for US$10/15, members/nonmembers, including breakfast.

Pousadas & Hotels A US$10 taxi ride from Capivari is *Pous da Recanto* (☎ 262-4224), Rua Professor Raul Pedroza de Moraes 74, opposite the convent on the way out to the Palacio Boa Vista. It has rooms for US$25 per person with breakfast.

The *Pousada so Donde* (☎ 263-3635), Avenida Victor Godlinho 440, in Jaguaribe, charges US$45 on weekdays, US$65 on weekends.

Looming over the city is the Stalin-esque *Parque Hotel* (☎ 263-1044), with big, draughty rooms from US$68/85.

The *Nevada Hotel* (☎ 263-1611) includes all meals in its price of US$120 a double.

The oldest and most stylish place to stay is the *Toriba* (☎ 262-1566) on Avenida Ernesto Diedericksen 4km from Abernéssia. Its single/double rooms go for US$108/146. There's also an ashram nearby; see Around Campos do Jordão at the end of this chapter.

Places to Eat

The local speciality is *pinhãou* (pine nuts) fried in butter or served with rice. For quick snacks, hit *Batata Quente e Cia* in Capivari.

The *Keller Haus*, Avenida Emilio Ribas 478, in Capivari, is a fairly good and reasonably priced German place; *Baden-Baden* at Rua Djalma Forjaz 93 also does German food, but it's pricier. Nearby, in the Boulevard Geneve mall, there's a mock English pub, the *Royal Flag*, upstairs in the watchtower, with live music or videos in high season at 9.30 pm nightly. There's an expensive but decent Japanese restaurant, *Namako,* in the Aspen Mall.

Getting There & Away

Bus From São Paulo to Campos, there are seven buses daily, the first at 6 am and the last at 6.15 pm. From Campos to São Paulo, there are also seven buses a day, from 6 am to 6.20 pm. The trip costs US$13.30.

To Ubatuba, take a bus (US$4) to Taubate (every two hours from 6 am to 8 pm) and change for the bus (US$9.50) to Ubatuba.

Train For details of the train ride to Santo Antônio do Pinhal, see Things to See & Do earlier in this section.

Getting Around

The tram (US$0.50) runs about every half hour between 7.15 am and 6.05 pm, and gets very crowded.

Local buses run out to the state park and to the camping ground. Take the Horto Florestal bus to its final stop.

Mountain bikes can be rented in Capivari from Machina do Tempo (☎ 262-5000), Boulevard Geneve shopping mall, for US$10/hour, US$66/day.

Horses are available (about US$10/hour) at Centro Hipico Tarundu – check with the tourist office.

AROUND CAMPOS DO JORDÃO

Creole's Cave

Gruta dos Crioulos was used as a hideout by slaves escaping from the surrounding fazendas. It's 7km from Jaguaribé on the road to Pedra do Baú, which is a huge, 1950m rectangular granite block. To get to the top you have to walk 2km north and climb 600 steps carved into the rock. It's 25km from Campos.

Krsna Shakti Ashram

There's a beautiful ashram (☎ 263-3168, or in São Paulo ☎ (011) 259-8968), 30km north of Campos, which offers access to lovely mountainside waterfalls, river and natural mineral water pools, plus all meals, yoga classes and meditation, for US$250 per person per day (you can negotiate). You don't have to meditate to stay there!

You can also come up just for dinner in the vegetarian dining room, by prior arrangement. People there speak English and German. Karina at Idade da Pedra (☎ 263-2085) in the Cadij Plaza mall in Campos lives at the ashram and can give you more information.

Access is by car, but you can be picked up in Campos.

The South

The South

The Southern region, known in Brazil as Região Sul, includes the states of Paraná, Santa Catarina and Rio Grande do Sul. It covers almost 7% of the country's land area and contains 24 million inhabitants – just over 15% of Brazil's population. Most of these people are descendants of the German, Italian, Swiss and Eastern European immigrants who settled the region in the latter half of the 19th century. They have kept their customs, language and architecture alive, so you'll see painted wooden houses with steep roofs and onion-spire churches, and find small towns where Portuguese is still the second language.

Geographically, Paraná, Santa Catarina and the northern part of Rio Grande do Sul are dominated by *planaltos* (tablelands). Near the coast, the Planalto Atlântico is formed of granite, while the Planalto Meridional in the interior is formed of volcanic basalt, with rich, red soil known as *terra roxa*. In the southern interior of Rio Grande do Sul are the *pampas* (grassy plains). Along the coast there are three large saltwater lagoons: Patos, Mirim and Mangueira.

With the exception of the north of Paraná, the climate is subtropical, and the vegetation varies from Mata Atlântica remnants on the Paraná and Santa Catarina coast to the almost-extinct Mata Araucária and pine forests of the Planalto Meridional. Snow is not uncommon on the Planalto Meridional during winter.

The region's economy has changed dramatically in the last 35 years. Where huge herds of cattle were once driven across the pampas by *gaúchos* (cowboys), there are now endless fields of soya beans – much of which goes to feed European cattle. Heavy industry, encouraged by cheap electricity from the Itaipu dam, has transformed the South into Brazil's second-most developed region.

Sulistas (Southerners) especially the gaúchos from Rio Grande do Sul are proud of their differences from other Brazilians and periodically entertain the idea of separatism. Sulistas are willing partners in Mercosul, with increasing ties to the economies of Uruguay and Argentina.

HIGHLIGHTS

- Iguaçu Falls – one of the natural wonders of the world (Paraná)
- The spectacular train ride from Curitiba to Paranaguá through mountains covered in Atlantic rainforest (Paraná)
- Riding tyre tubes down the Rio Nhundiaquara near Morretes (Paraná)
- Saturday night forro on Ilha do Mel (Paraná)
- The beaches and surf of Ilha da Santa Catarina (Santa Catarina)
- The sound and light show at the ruins of the São Miguel mission (Rio Grande do Sul)
- Itaimbézinho Canyon at the Parque Nacional de Aparados da Serra (Rio Grande do Sul)
- The region's primeval araucária tree

Paraná

CURITIBA

• *pop 1,480,000* ✉ *80000-000* ☎ *041*

Curitiba, the capital of Paraná, is one of Brazil's urban success stories. As happened in many of Brazil's cities, thousands began to flood into Curitiba in the 1940s. With only 140,000 residents in 1940, the city has since grown tenfold, to almost 1.5 million people today.

Yet, with the assistance of a vibrant local and state economy, Curitiba has managed to modernise in a relatively sane manner – historic buildings have been preserved, a handful of streets have been closed to cars and there are many parks, gardens and wide boulevards.

Surprisingly, a progressive mayor has instituted several incentives, including lower bus prices, to get people out of their cars – and the strategy worked. Traffic congestion was reduced, and today it's easier to get around in Curitiba than in most cities in Brazil. Drivers even stop at red lights, pedestrians can cross streets without blood-type identification bracelets, and although we haven't actually researched it, we'll bet that Curitiba's divorce, heart attack, murder and dog-abandonment rates are all down.

The local Curitibanos are mostly descended from Italian, German and Polish immigrants. There is a large university population which gives the city a young feel and a good music scene.

At 900m above sea level, Curitiba is on top of the great escarpment along the route from Rio Grande do Sul to São Paulo. Due to this location, it flourished briefly as a pit stop for *gaúchos* and their cattle until a better road was built on an alternative route. Curitiba quickly went back to sleep. It wasn't until the tremendous growth of the coffee plantations in northern Paraná, at the beginning of the 20th century, that the modern city of Curitiba began to take shape.

Like the gaúchos of old, most visitors are just passing through. The highway from São Paulo (400km) to Florianópolis (300km) and Porto Alegre (710km) intersects Curitiba, and it's also the turn-off for the train to Paranaguá and the bus to Foz do Iguaçu.

There's not much in Curitiba for the visitor, but it's still possible to pass a pleasant day in a park or museum waiting for your bus or train to leave. It's a fairly easy city to walk around, so if you have errands to do or clothes to buy, this is a good place for it.

Information

Tourist Office The Departmento de Turismo (☎ 352-4021) is at Rua da Gloria 362, 3rd floor. English is spoken. There's a handy new information booth in Rua 24 Horas with maps and some good glossy brochures. Other information booths are at the airport and in the Galeria Schaffer on Rua das Flores.

Foreign Consulates The following South American countries have consulates in Curitiba:

Chile
  Rua Marechal Deodoro 235, 1st floor (☎ 225-1369)
Paraguay
  Rua Voluntários da Pátria 400, 5th floor (☎ 222-9226)
Peru
  Avenida Getúlio Vargas 3767 (☎ 242-5819)
Uruguay
  Rua Emiliano Perneta 297, 9th floor (☎ 232-0436)

Many other countries also have consulates in Curitiba. They include:

Austria
  Rua Cândido Hartmann 570, 28th floor (☎ 336-1166)
France
  Rua Ubaldino do Amaral 927 (☎ 264-5358)
Germany
  Avenida João Gualberto 1237 (☎ 252-4244)
Italy
  Rua Marechal Deodoro 630, 21st floor (☎ 222-6066)
Japan
  Rua Marechal Deodoro 630, 18th floor (☎ 224-3861)
Netherlands
  Rua Marechal Floriano Peixoto 96, 17th floor (☎ 222-0097)
Switzerland
  Rua Marechal Floriano Peixoto 228, 11th floor (☎ 223-7553)
UK
  Rua Presidente Faria 51, 7th floor (☎ 322-1202)

Money The Banco do Brasil branch at Praça Tiradentes 410 changes money and has Visa automatic tellers. Many travel agencies double as *casas de câmbio* (money exchange houses). A central one is Triangulo Tourismo (☎ 233-0311), Praça Osório 213.

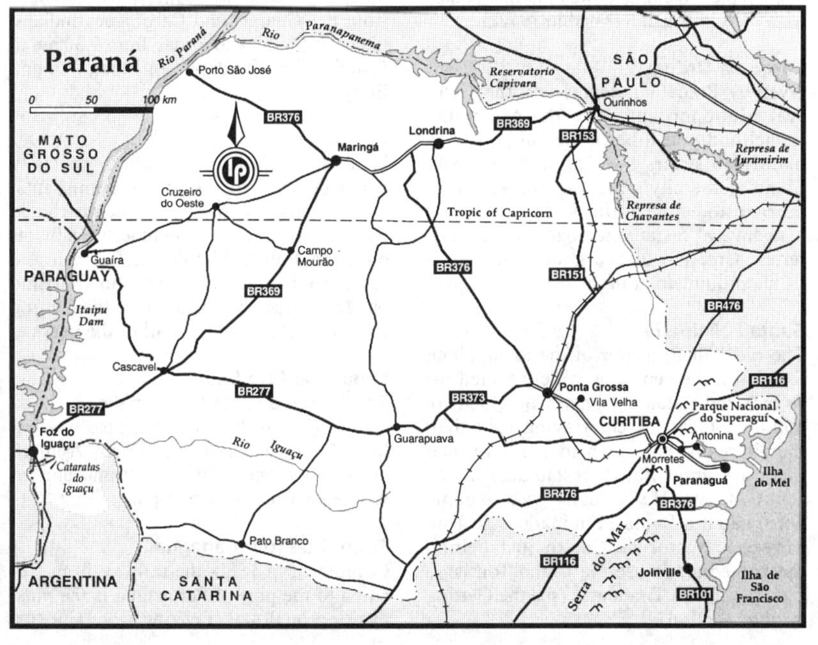

Post & Telephone You'll find the main post office is at Rua 15 de Novembro 700, near Praça Santos Andrade. Telepar, the phone company, is at Rua Visconde de Nácar 1388.

Bookshops English language books are available at Livraria-Curitiba, Rua Voluntários da Pátria 205 (Praça Santos Andrade). The newsagent in Rua 24 Horas has a good range of magazines.

Passeio Público

Take a stroll in the Passeio Público on Avenida Presidente Carlos Cavalcanti, where Curitibanos have relaxed since 1886. There's a lake and a small zoo. The park complex is closed Monday.

Rua 15 de Novembro

Known locally as Rua das Flores since 1720, when it was already the main commercial boulevard, it's good for walking, shopping and people-watching. It was the first pedestrian mall in Brazil, created in 1972.

Largo da Ordem

Over by Praça Tiradentes and the Catedral Metropolitana, take the pedestrian tunnel and you'll be in the cobblestoned historic quarter, the Largo da Ordem. Some of the city's historic edifices have been restored beautifully, and there are also several restaurants, bars and art galleries here. It's also a good place for a drink and music at night.

Santa Felicidade

The old Italian quarter of the town, about 8km from the centre, is widely touted for its bars and restaurants, many of which are monuments of kitsch. Having said that, there's really not much to see here, and there are good Italian restaurants in the centre of town. If you really want to come here, catch a Santa Felicidade bus from Travessa Nestor de Castro just behind the cathedral, or use the Linho Tourismo bus from Praça Tiradentes (see the Getting Around section).

Rua 24 Horas

This is a covered arcade about 100m long, with gift shops, restaurants and bars that open – you guessed it – 24 hours a day. It's a popular addition to the city, and very crowded around 3 am.

Estação Plaza Show

This huge new complex on Avenida 7 de Setembro has bars, restaurants, a dance club, live music venue and cinemas. After 6 pm, entry to the centre costs US$3. The complex also houses the Museu Ferroviária, the old train station that has recently been restored.

Museu Paranaense

The Museu Paranaense at Praça Generoso Marques is in an Art Nouveau building that used to house the municipal government. It's worth a visit just to check out the building itself. Chronicling the history of the state of Paraná, the museum has a hotchpotch of objects and a collection of artefacts from the Guaraní and Caigangues Indians. It's open Monday to Friday from 9.30 am to 5.30 pm and Saturday from 10 am to 4 pm. Entry is free.

Parks

Parks are a Curitiba speciality, especially parks devoted to the area's immigrants. These parks consist of reconstructed houses and replicas of churches used by pioneering Polish, Ukrainian, German and Japanese immigrants. The Linho Tourismo bus from Praça Tiradentes (see the Getting Around section) stops at all of the parks.

Museu de Arte Sacra

The Museu de Arte Sacra in the Igreja da Ordem (Largo da Ordem) is also worth a look. It's open Tuesday to Friday from 10 am to noon and 1.30 to 6.30 pm, and on weekends from 9 am to 1 pm.

Train Ride to Paranaguá

Completed in 1880, the railway from Curitiba to the port of Paranaguá is the most exciting in Brazil. Leaving from Curitiba at an altitude of 900m, the train descends a steep mountainside to the coastal lowlands. The 110km track goes through 13 tunnels and crosses 67 bridges. The view below is sublime and, depending on the cloud formations and tone of the sunlight, often surreal: threatening mountain canyons, tropical lowlands and the vast, blue Atlantic.

When you arrive in Paranaguá four hours later, you will have seen the world change rapidly and radically: the climate is hot and muggy, and often rainy in the winter; the land is flat and low until it hits the wall of mountain; the vegetation is short, lush and uniform; and the people are sturdy, with strong Indian features and faces defined by years by the sea.

There is a *trem* (regular train) and a *litorina* (tourist train), both of which run from Curitiba to Paranaguá, stopping in Morretes along the way, and then back to Curitiba. The trem leaves Curitiba Tuesday to Sunday at 8 am and returns from Paranaguá at 4 pm. Tickets cost US$15 one way and US$20 return, which includes a snack and drink for the trip.

The air-conditioned litorina runs only on Saturday and Sunday. It leaves Curitiba at 9 am and starts back from Paranaguá at 3 pm. Tickets cost US$30 one way and US$40 return. It's full of tourists, and has a recorded description of the sights in Portuguese, English, Spanish and French.

Both trains take about four hours each way, but this may vary according to how many stops have to be made to clear the tracks. For the best view on the way down to the coast, sit on the left-hand side.

Getting tickets for the trem is not difficult during the week except during January and other holiday periods. They can be bought at the station in the morning. Buying tickets on weekends may be more tricky – if you arrive in Curitiba late on Friday and want to take the train the next day, you should go to the station at about 6 am. Even if tickets for both trains are sold out, don't take the bus yet. Some of the local travel agencies seem to buy a few extra tickets for the litorina in case they get customers for a tour; if they don't, they come to the train station to sell the extra tickets. So hang about and ask around – you may get lucky.

It's a good idea to check the latest schedule when you arrive. Tickets are sold at the *ferroviária* (train station) behind the *rodoviária* (bus station). For information, contact the ticket office in Curitiba (☎ 323-4007).

THE SOUTH

Places to Stay – Budget

There's a YHA youth hostel (☎ 233-2746) at Rua Padre Agostinho 645, in the suburb of Mercês. Catch the Campina do Siqueira – Capão do Imbui bus, which heads to Campina do Siqueira from outside the rodoviária. Get off at Praça 29 de Março and walk two blocks along Rua Desembargador Molta, to its intersection with Rua Padre Agostinho.

If you're leaving town the next day, there are three cheap hotels in a row on Avenida Presidente Afonso Camargo, just across from the *rodoferroviária* (bus and train station). At No 355, the clean and friendly *Hotel Maia* (☎ 264-1684) has single/double quartos for US$15/25, with breakfast included. Next door, at No 367, the *Hotel Imperio* (☎ 264-3373) charges the same prices. Right alongside is *Hotel Cristo Rei*, the cheapest of the bunch, with fairly dingy quartos for US$10/20, but you don't get breakfast. A better value cheapie is *City Hotel* (☎ 264-3366), one block away at Rua Francisco Torres 816. Clean quartos cost US$10/17, but breakfast isn't included here either.

Hotel Itamarati (☎ 222-9063) is a good place to head for, close to the rodoviária at Rua Tibagi 950. Quartos cost US$18/30, including an excellent breakfast.

If you're staying a few days, or want to be close to the bars and restaurants around Largo da Ordem, the *Golden Hotel* (☎ 323-3603), Rua Tobias de Macado 26, is excellent value. *Apartamentos* (rooms with bathrooms) cost US$15/22, which includes a good breakfast that can be eaten overlooking Praça Tiradentes.

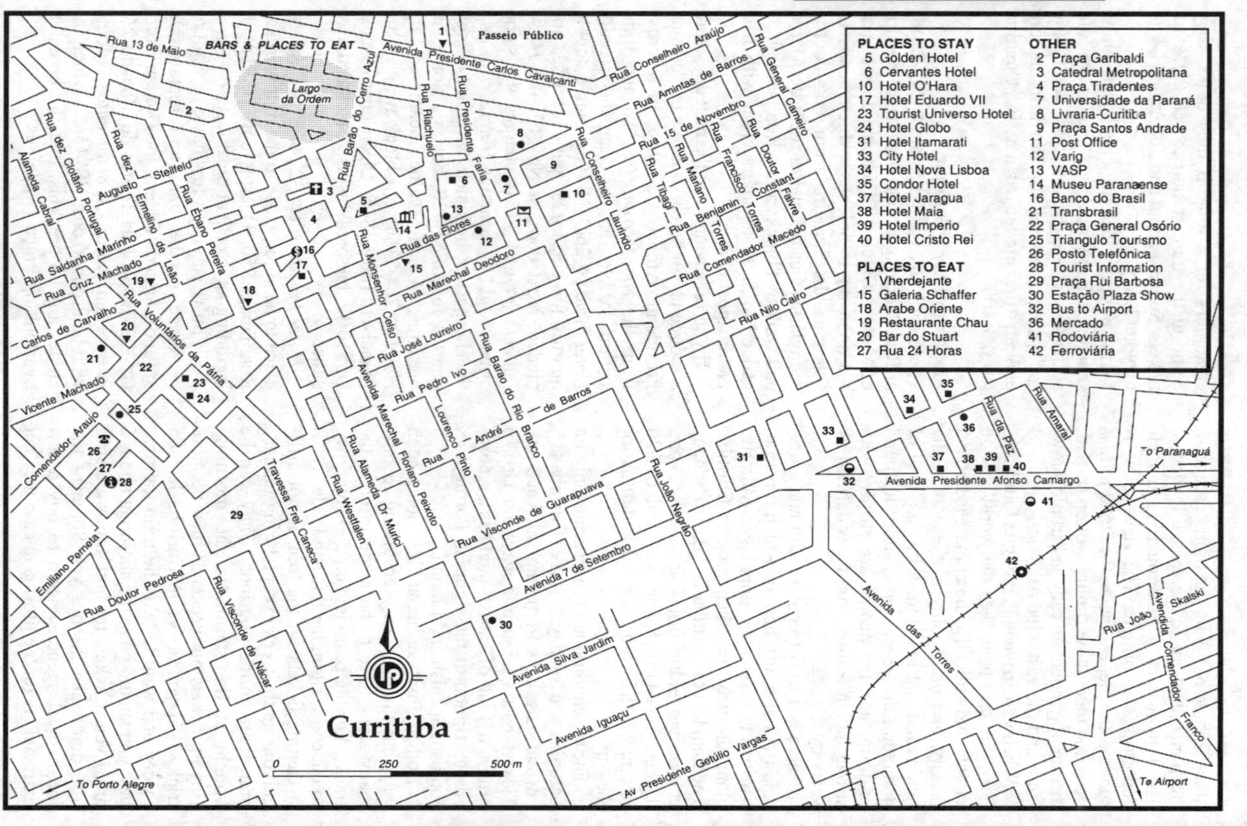
Curitiba
PLACES TO STAY
5 Golden Hotel
6 Cervantes Hotel
10 Hotel O'Hara
17 Hotel Eduardo VII
23 Tourist Universo Hotel
24 Hotel Globo
31 Hotel Itamarati
33 City Hotel
34 Hotel Nova Lisboa
35 Condor Hotel
37 Hotel Jaragua
38 Hotel Maia
39 Hotel Imperio
40 Hotel Cristo Rei
PLACES TO EAT
1 Vhrdejante
15 Galeria Schaffer
18 Arabe Oriente
19 Restaurante Chau
20 Bar do Stuart
27 Rua 24 Horas
OTHER
2 Praça Garibaldi
3 Catedral Metropolitana
4 Praça Tiradentes
7 Universidade da Paraná
8 Livraria-Curitiba
9 Praça Santos Andrade
11 Post Office
12 Varig
13 VASP
14 Museu Paranaense
16 Banco do Brasil
21 Transbrasil
22 Praça General Osório
25 Triangulo Tourismo
26 Posto Telefônica
28 Tourist Information
29 Praça Rui Barbosa
30 Estação Plaza Show
32 Bus to Airport
36 Mercado
41 Rodoviária
42 Ferroviária
BARS & PLACES TO EAT
Passeio Público
Largo da Ordem
Rua 13 de Maio
Avenida Presidente Carlos Cavalcanti
Rua Conselheiro Araújo
Rua Amintas de Barros
Rua General Carneiro
Rua Barão do Cerro Azul
Rua Riachuelo
Rua Presidente Faria
Rua 15 de Novembro
Rua Conselheiro Laurindo
Rua Tibagi
Rua Mariano Torres
Rua Francisco Torres
Rua Doutor Faivre
Rua Benjamin Constant
Rua Comendador Macedo
Rua Nilo Cairo
Rua das Flores
Rua Marechal Deodoro
Rua Monsenhor Celso
Rua José Loureiro
Rua Pedro Ivo
Rua Barao do Rio Branco
Rua André de Barros
Rua Lourenço Pinto
Avenida Marechal Floriano Peixoto
Rua Alameda Dr Murici
Rua Westfalen
Travessa Frei Caneca
Rua Visconde de Guarapuava
Avenida 7 de Setembro
Rua João Negrão
Rua Visconde de Nácar
Rua Doutor Pedrosa
Emiliano Perneta
Rua dez Stellfeld
Rua Ébano Pereira
Augusto Ermelino de Leão
Rua dez Clotário Portugal
Alameda Cabral
Rua Saldanha Marinho
Rua Cruz Machado
Rua Voluntários da Pátria
Carlos de Carvalho
Vicente Machado
Comendador Araujo
Rua Amaral
Rua da Paz
Avenida Presidente Afonso Camargo
Avenida das Torres
Avenida Comendador Franco
Rua João Skalski
Avenida Silva Jardim
Avenida Iguaçu
Av Presidente Getúlio Vargas
To Paranaguá
To Airport
To Porto Alegre
0
250
500 m

Places to Stay – Mid-Range

Near the rodoferroviária, the *Hotel Nova Lisboa* (☎ 264-1944), Avenida 7 de Setembro 1948, is a clean, bright place with single/double apartamentos for US$30/45. A bit more expensive is the *Condor Hotel* (☎ 262-0322), a few doors up at Avenida 7 de Setembro 1866. Single/double rooms with bath cost US$40/57.

In the centre, *Cervantes Hotel* (222-9593), Travessa Alfredo Bufren 35, has old-world charm and comfortable apartamentos with TV and fridge for US$26/48. *Hotel O'Hara* (☎ 232-6044), in a colonial building at Rua 15 de Novembro 770, opposite Praça Santos Andrade, has singles/ doubles for US$39/55. Also central is the *Hotel Globo* (☎ 323-1233), Rua Senador Alencar Guimarães 71, very close to Praça General Osório. Comfortable singles/ doubles are US$40/50.

Places to Stay – Top End

A top-end hotel across from the rodoferroviária is the *Hotel Jaragua* (☎ 322-4341; fax 323-1593), Avenida Presidente Afonso Camargo 279, which charges US$87/109 for singles/doubles.

In the centre of town, at Rua Cândido de Leão 15, close to Praça Tiradentes, the *Hotel Eduardo V11* (☎ 322-6767) is the colonialists' choice. Singles/doubles go for US$60/80. Post-modernists will prefer *Tourist Universo Hotel* (☎ 322-0099), Praça Osório 63, where singles/doubles start at US$75/96.

Places to Eat

Rua das Flores has some classic *confeitarias* (confectionery shops). *Schaffer* in the Galeria Schaffer at No 424 was founded in 1918 and is famous for its coffee and cakes. On the 2nd floor, *Alfândego* is a great place for a por quilo lunch eaten overlooking the pedestrian mall. Also in the city centre is the *Arabe Oriente*, 1st floor, Rua Ébano Pereira 26. Open daily for lunch and dinner, it has big portions and good food.

On Rua 24 Horas there are several places: *Le Lasagne* serves five types of lasagne, while *Le Mignon* serves a varied menu, with cheap 'chef's suggestions'.

There are several medium-priced outdoor restaurants in the Largo da Ordem area – walk around, look at menus and see what looks best. Readers have recommended *No Kafe Fest* and *Schwarzwald* (for its roast duck). The latter is also a popular student hangout in the evening.

The *Vherdejante* vegetarian restaurant has fish dishes and good self-serve, fixed-price lunches. It's at Rua Presidente Faria 481, in front of the Passeio Público. You can also get a por quilo Chinese lunch at *Restaurante Chau*, at Rua Carlos de Carvalho 50.

Bar do Stuart, Praça General Osório 427, is an upmarket bar with good small meals. It's open daily until midnight. In Santa Felicidade, *Famiglia Fandanelli*, Rua Manoel Ribas 5667, is handy for travellers because the Santa Felicidade bus stops in front. Its agnoletti vicenza has to be tasted to be believed – a combination of white grapes, almonds, pasta and a thick, cheese sauce, which is 'É uma delícia'.

Entertainment

Curitiba has an active live music and club scene. For the latest on what's happening, pick up a copy of *Sexta Basica*, a weekly mag with listings of live music, dance clubs, bars and theatre.

Around the Largo da Ordem and nearby Praça Garibaldi, there are several bars and live music venues including *Schwardwald*, *Alambique*, *Firefox* and *Academia do Chopp*.

Baixo Batel is a vaguely defined nightlife district centred around Alameda Dom Pedro II and Praça Espanha. Some of the popular bars include *Alles Bier*, Avenida Vicente Machado 866, and *Montego Bay*, on the corner of Rua Coronel Dulcídio and Alameda Dom Pedro II. For live indie music, try *Bar do DCE* on Rua Imaculada Conceicão; for blues, head to *Mississipi Blues*, Praça Espanha 27; and for axé and pagoda, check out *Zimbabwe*, Avenida Iguaçu 2074, Agua Verde.

Things to Buy

The Feira de Arte e Artisano, held in Praça Garibaldi on Sunday from 9 am to 2 pm, offers an excellent variety of arts and crafts for sale.

Getting There & Away

Air There are flights from Curitiba to all major cities in Brazil.

Bus From the rodoviária there are many daily buses to São Paulo (US$19, six hours) and Rio (US$39, 12 hours), and to all major cities to the south. There are 13 buses a day to Foz do Iguaçu: the first leaves at 6.45 am and the last, a *leito* (overnight express), at 11.45 pm. The price is US$33 for a regular bus and US$64 for a leito. There are frequent buses to Joinville (US$6, two hours) and Florianópolis (US$15, 4½ hours).

From Curitiba you can also get direct buses to Asunción (US$37, 14 hours), Buenos Aires (US$82, 30 hours) and Santiago (US$122, 50 hours).

If you miss the train, there are plenty of buses to Morretes, Antonina and Paranaguá. Try to get a bus that goes along the Estrada da Graciosa, the old pioneer road completed around 1873. The trip isn't as stunning as the train ride but it's still pretty. It takes just over 1½ hours to get to Paranaguá.

Train See the Train Ride to Paranaguá section earlier in this chapter. Steam-train rides to Lapa, an historic city 70km away, have been discontinued.

Getting Around

To/From the Airport Alfonso Pena airport (☎ 381-1515) is 17km from the city (US$25 by taxi, more at night). An Aeroporto bus (US$0.75) leaves about every half an hour from outside the Hotel Promenade, on the corner of Avenida 7 de Setembro and Rua Mariano Torres, near the rodoferroviária.

Bus You can walk to most places of interest, but if you're footsore, there's an excellent local bus network. Destinations are well marked and fares are US$0.40. The main bus terminals are on Praça Tiradentes, Praça General Osório and Praça Rui Barbosa.

Particularly useful is the white Circular Centro minibus. It does regular circuits of the city, stopping at the Passeio Público, Praça Tiradentes, Praça Santos Andrade near the university, and outside the rodoviária. Look for the bus stop with the white top.

A great way to see many of the sights that you wouldn't see just walking around the city is on the Linha Turismo bus, which does a two hour tour of the city's main attractions. It departs from Praça Tiradentes, in front of the cathedral, Tuesday to Sunday every half an hour between 9 am and 5.30 pm. You can get off the bus at any of the attractions and hop on the next white Linha Turismo bus that passes. At each stop there is a timetable posted. It costs US$6 for four tickets (allowing you to get on and off at four stops).

AROUND CURITIBA

Vila Velha

An interesting day trip is a visit to the 'stone city' of Vila Velha, 93km from Curitiba on the road to Foz do Iguaçu. Here you'll find an interesting collection of sandstone pillars created by millions of years of erosion. There's also a place to swim and an elevator ride into a crater lake.

To get there, catch a *semi-direto* (semi-direct) bus to Ponta Grossa from the rodoviária and ask to be let out at Vila Velha. The entrance is about a 2km walk from where the bus drops you. Unless you camp, there's nowhere to stay in the park, so make sure you get the last bus back, which you can flag down along the road at around 3.45 pm.

MORRETES

• *pop 15,000* ✉ *83350-000* ☎ *041*

Founded in 1721 on the banks of the Rio Nhundiaquara, Morretes is a tranquil little colonial town in the midst of the lush coastal vegetation zone. It's a good place to relax, swim in the river and take some walks in the nearby state park.

Several buses and the train stop at Morretes on the way to Antonina and Paranaguá. If you like the feel of the place, just hop off – the spectacular part of the train ride is over anyway. The town itself is very small and easy to get around.

Marumbi State Park

The park offers some great hikes, and is very popular with Curitibanos, who get off the train and hike down the old pioneer trails that were the only connections between the coast and the Paranaense highland in the 17th and 18th centuries. The two best walks are the Graciosa trail, which passes close to the Estrada da Graciosa, and the Itupava trail. Views from both are fantastic.

To get to the park from Morretes, catch a bus to São João de Graciosa. It's a couple of kilometres from there to the park entrance, where you can pick up a trail map. Don't forget to take some insect repellent!

Rio Nhundiaquara

This river served as the first connection between the coast and the highlands. Now, one of the best things to do on it is hire a truck inner tube from the guy who runs the service station and go 'tubing' (in Portuguese *bóia*, or *cross*). The guy who rents the tubes will also take you upriver and drop you off. It takes about four hours to float back down. See Dona Gloria at the Hotel Nhundiaquara for more details.

Cascatinha

Five kilometres from Morretes on the Rio Marumbi is Cascatinha, a large lake that is a good place to swim and/or camp.

Places to Stay

There are three hotels in Morretes. The *Hotel Nhundiaquara* (☎ 462-1228) is the best place to stay. It's right on the river at Rua General Carreiro 13. The owner, Dona Gloria, is really helpful. She charges US$10/18 for quartos, and US$17/28 for single/double apartamentos, with breakfast included. Being next to a fast-flowing river, it's also free from mosquitoes!

The *Hotel Bom Jesus* (☎ 462-1282), Rua 15 de Novembro, is a bit cheaper. Boxy quartos cost US$10/15, but breakfast isn't included. The most expensive hotel in town is the *Porto Real Palace* (☎ 462-1344), Rua Visconde de Branco 85, with singles/doubles for US$27/44. The new red carpet is blindingly bright, but everything else is fading fast.

Places to Eat

The speciality of the region is a filling dish called barreado, a delicious mixture of meats and spices cooked in a sealed clay pot for 24 hours. Originally it was cooked during Carnaval, to give the revellers a huge protein fix, but today it's considered the state dish. Quite a few new restaurants have sprung up along the riverfront in the last few years serving barreado and seafood.

Your Money & Your Boots

The old Jesuit trails from Curitiba to the coast run through beautiful stretches of Mata Atlântica, the rainforest that once covered all of the Brazilian coast. You can get information on the trails at any of the local hiking and sporting goods stores in Curitiba. Try Casa da Montanhista, in Shopping Italia, on Rua Marechal Deodoro in the centre.

Unfortunately, I've heard from Brazilian friends that there have been some assaults on these trails recently, at least in areas outside Marumbi state park. The armed robbers took everything, including hiking boots and coats. It's safe to hike and rock climb inside the park, and information about both is easy to get. The rock climbing in the park is on old techno routes; outside the park (in the assault zone!) it's freeclimbing.

Johanne Schulz

Most only open for lunch, so don't plan on doing anything strenuous in the afternoon!

On Largo Dr Jose Pereira along the riverfront, *Serra do Mar* serves a huge combination barreado/seafood meal for US$10: it's enough for two. It's one of the few restaurants open for dinner as well. Across the street *Restaurante Casarão*, an upmarket place with a balcony overlooking the river, serves barreado for US$9 per person. Just across the bridge, on the other side of the river, *Restaurante Madalozo* has a barreado and seafood rodízio (smorgasbord) lunch for US$10 per person. The restaurant at the Hotel Nhundiaquara is the original and possibly the best – it's been serving barreado for 50 years and you can get a half-serve for US$6. Readers have also recommended *Restaurante Europa*.

ANTONINA

• *pop 18,500* ✉ *83370-000* ☎ *041*

Antonina is 14km east of Morretes and 75km east of Curitiba on the Baía de Paranaguá. Similar to Morretes, Antonina is old and peaceful. Its first settlers panned for gold in the river. The fine church in the centre, the Igreja de NS do Pilar, was started in 1715 and rebuilt in 1927. Its festival is held on 15 August.

The beaches along the bay are muddy, but there are good views of the Baía de Paranaguá. Frequent direct buses link Antonina to Curitiba and Paranaguá, but unfortunately, trains no longer stop here.

Places to Stay

There are four hotels in town, but none could be considered a bargain. The best value is *Hotel Monte Castelo* (☎ 432-1163) on the main square at Praça Coronel Macedo 46. It's run by a friendly young couple and has quartos for US$10/20 for singles/doubles and apartamentos for US$15/30. The *Hotel Luz* (☎ 432-1787), Rua Comendador Araújo 189, charges the same prices, but it's a bit of a hike to the water. *Christina Hotel* (☎ 432-1533), Rua 15 de Novembro, has basic apartamentos for US$20/30 a single/double.

The *Regency Capela Antonina* (☎ 432-1357), Praça Coronel Macedo 208, could be worth a splurge. Comfortable apartamentos start at US$38/48 a single/double – rooms at the front have breezy balconies with views of the bay. There's a seafood restaurant attached.

Places to Eat

Restaurante Albatroz, just below the church at Travessa Marques do Herval 14, is a friendly restaurant/bar with seafood dishes for around US$20 for two. There's a great view of the bay from the upstairs room. Near the bus station on Rua 15 de Novembro is *Restaurante Maré Alta,* a rustic little place – the house special is carrocel de frutas do mar for US$10 per person. The little joint at Rua Doutor Carlos da Costa 173 has the best lunch deal – a home-cooked buffet for US$3.90.

PARANAGUÁ

• *pop 115,500* ✉ *83200-000* ☎ *041*

The train ride from Curitiba isn't the only reason to go to Paranaguá. It's a colourful city, with an old section near the waterfront that has a feeling of tropical decadence. There are several churches, a very good museum and other colonial buildings that are worth a look. Paranaguá is also the place from which you leave for Ilha do Mel and the mediocre beaches of Paraná.

One of Brazil's major ports, Paranaguá is 30km from the sea, on the Baía de Paranaguá. Goods from a vast inland area are shipped through here. The primary exports have been gold, mate, Madeira and coffee, and are now corn, soy, cotton and vegetable oils.

Paranaguá's old section is small enough to wander around without a set itinerary. Without much effort, you can see most of Paranaguá's colonial buildings, churches, waterfront bars and various markets in a couple of hours.

Information

The main tourist information office is along the waterfront on Rua General Carneiro. Staff are helpful and have maps of the region. It's closed on Monday. There's another office inside the train station open from noon to 4 pm.

If you need to change money, try Tassi Turismo on Rua Faria Sobrinho. For Visa withdrawals, the Banco do Brasil is at Largo Conselheiro Alcindino 103.

Museu de Arqueológico e Etnologia

Don't miss it! Many Brazilian museums are disappointing; this one is not. Housed in a beautifully restored Jesuit school that was built from 1736 to 1755 (the Jesuits didn't get to use the school for long, as they were expelled from Brazil in 1759), the museum has many Indian artefacts, primitive and folk art, and some fascinating old tools and wooden machines.

The museum is at Rua 15 de Novembro 567 (near the waterfront). It's open Tuesday to Sunday from noon to 5 pm. Entry costs US$1.

Churches

The city's churches are simple, unlike baroque churches. The **Igreja de NS do Rosário** is the city's oldest. Also worth visiting are the **Igreja São Francisco das Chagas** (1741), **Igreja de São Benedito** (1784) and **Igreja de NS do Rocio** (1813).

Waterfront

Down by the waterfront, you'll find the new and old municipal **mercados** (markets), and depending on the time and day, both can be quite lively. Nearby is a bridge that leads to the Ilha dos Valadares. There are 8500 people on the island, mostly fishermen and mostly poor. During festivals, they dance the Paraná fandango: a hybrid dance that combines the Spanish fandango and the dances of the Carijó Indians.

Boats for Ilha do Mel and Guaraqueçaba leave from the jetty opposite the tourist

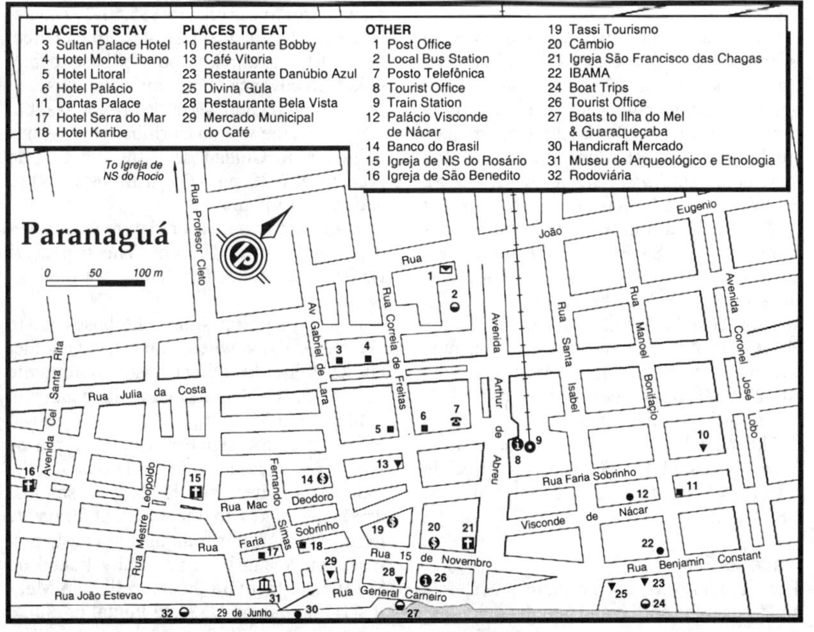

office on Rua General Carneiro (see Getting There & Away in this section). A tourist boat that explores the river leaves from Praça Manoel Ricardo, just below the Restaurante Danúbio Azul. There are no regular departure times; ask around at the jetty. The tour costs US$5 per person and lasts 1½ hours.

Places to Stay

There are some cheap places near the waterfront and rodoviária; the area has character, but it's almost deserted at night. *Hotel Karibe* (☎ 423-4377), Rua Fernando Simas 86, is a friendly place housed in a colonial building. Bright quartos cost US$10/20 for singles/doubles with a good breakfast; comfortable apartamentos with air-conditioning and fridge go for US$20/28. Around the corner at Rua 15 de Novembro 588, *Hotel Serra do Mar* (☎ 422-8904) is also good value. Clean but dark double apartamentos cost US$20; upstairs, brighter doubles with air-conditioning cost US$25.

Closer to the train station, a good cheapie is the *Hotel Litoral* (☎ 423-1734), Rua Correia de Freitas 65. Large rooms open onto a sunny courtyard. Single/double quartos go for US$10/12 and apartamentos are US$12/15. Just round the corner, the more upmarket *Hotel Palácio* (☎ 422-5655), Rua de Correia Freitas 66, has quartos for US$13.50/22 a single/double and apartamentos from US$18/30. In the same area, the *Sultan Palace Hotel* (☎ 423-1044), Rua Julia da Costa 230, has character. Clean quartos cost US$10/20 and apartamentos US$17/30. Ask for a room with a balcony. Nearby, the bland *Hotel Monte Libano* (☎ 423-3571) has singles/doubles for US$31/42. It's at Rua Julia da Costa 152.

The best hotel in town is the *Dantas Palace* (☎ 423-1555), Rua Visconde de Nácar 740, where singles/doubles start at US$71/93.

Place to Eat

The *Café Vitoria*, on the main praça, is a good place for coffee and people-watching.

There are some good por quilo restaurants around town for lunch. *Divina Gula*, on the corner of Rua Benjamin Constant and Rua Santa Isabel, is always packed with locals, as is *Restaurante Bobby*, Rua Faria Sobrinho 750. The *Mercado Municipal do Café* is also good for lunch. It's been restored, and contains five small cafés serving cheap seafood and snacks.

For dinner, *Restaurante Bela Vista*, on Rua General Carneiro, serves a seafood prato feito (plate of the day) for US$5.50, and you can eat outside along the waterfront. *Restaurante Danúbio Azul* has seafood upstairs, beer and pizza downstairs. Big seafood dishes for around US$14 should be enough for two. The restaurant is open daily for lunch and dinner. It's down at Rua 15 de Novembro 95, with an excellent view of the waterfront.

Getting There & Away

Bus All out-of-town buses leave from the rodoviária on the waterfront. The first of many buses to Curitiba (US$5.50, 1½ hours) leaves at 6 am, the last at 11 pm. Direct buses fill up quickly, so it's best to buy tickets in advance. There are many buses to both Antonina and Morretes, if you want to stop off on the way to Curitiba. There is one daily bus to Cuidad del Este (for Foz do Iguaçu) at 6.30 pm. The trip costs US$30 and takes 14 hours.

There are two buses a day to Guaraqueçaba, at 9 am and 2 pm. The trip costs US$9.50 and takes five hours, but the boat is quicker.

If you're going south, 12 buses go to Guaratuba daily, where you can get another bus to Joinville. Direct buses to Joinville (US$6.50, three hours) leave Paranaguá at 7.40 am and 3.45 pm.

To get to the beaches, catch a Praia de Leste or a Pontal do Sul bus at the rodoviária. There are 11 daily buses that drive the 30km to the coast at Praia de Leste, then go north along the coast, past Ipanema, Shangri-lá and finally Pontal do Sul (where there are boats to Ilha do Mel). It's 1½ hours and US$1 to Pontal do Sul.

Train The train returns to Curitiba daily at 4 pm. On weekends, the litoral train returns at 3 pm (see the Train Ride to Paranaguá section in Curitiba earlier this chapter).

Boat There are now daily boats to Ilha do Mel from Paranaguá but it's a good idea to check the latest schedule at the tourist office on Rua General Carneiro. During summer, two boats leave the jetty opposite the tourist office for Ilha do Mel every weekday at 3 pm, and at 10 am on Saturday. The *Jean Carlos* (US$5, 1½ hours) goes to Praia dos Encantadas, and the *Proverbio II* (US$6, two hours) sails to Nova Brasília.

If you want access to Parque Nacional do Superagui, there is also a daily boat to Guaraqueçaba at noon. The trip takes around three hours.

ILHA DO MEL

• pop 1000 ☎ 041

Ilha do Mel, an oddly shaped island at the mouth of the Baía de Paranaguá, wasn't discovered by the Portuguese until the 18th century. In 1767, to secure the bay and its safe harbours from French and Spanish incursions, King Dom José I ordered a fort built. Since then, not too much has happened. The few people on the island were ordered out during WWII, in the name of national defence. Most significantly, the island is now part of the Patrimônio Nacional, which has prevented it from being turned into more cheesecake for the rich.

The island is popular in the summer because of its excellent beaches, scenic walks and relative isolation. Its undoing might be that it's becoming too popular. However, it is administered by the Instituto de Terras e Cartografia Florestal (ITCF), which intends to preserve the island more or less as it is.

Unfortunately, it can't stop the sea from making changes. Erosion has almost opened a channel at Nova Brasília, which eventually could cut the island in two. You'll see lots of houses crumbling into the sea as you walk from Nova Brasília to the fort.

From January to Carnaval, and during Easter, the island is very popular with a young party crowd, but there's still a lot of beach, and always room for an extra hammock. If you're travelling up or down the coast, it's crazy not to visit the island at least for a day. Many people end up staying much longer.

Orientation

The island has two parts, connected by the beach at Nova Brasília, where most of the locals live. The bigger part is an ecological station, thick with vegetation and little visited, except for Praia da Fortaleza. On the ocean side are the best beaches – Praia da Fora, Praia do Miguel and Praia Ponta do Bicho. All are reached by a trail that traverses the beaches and coves, and the steep hills that divide them. The bay side is muddy and covered with vegetation.

Boats from Paranaguá and Pontal do Sul arrive at either Nova Brasília or Praia dos Encantadas. Brasília and nearby Praia do Farol are the surfers' favourite hang-outs because they're close to Praia Grande. They're also closer to the fort, which is definitely worth a look. Encantadas, on the south-western side of the island, is a bit smaller, but more crowded during summer than Brasília. Out of season, Ilha do Mel is a very tranquil place.

The entire island can be walked around in eight hours, but by far the best walking is along the ocean side (east), from the southern tip of the island up to the fort. A warning: the stretch from Praia Grande to Praia da Fora should only be done at low tide, especially when the surf is big. Take some strong footwear for rock hopping or cliff scaling. *Bichos de pé* (small parasites) are prevalent elsewhere on the island, so keep something on your feet when you're off the beach.

Beaches

The best beaches face the ocean toward the east. **Praia Grande** is a 20 minute walk from Nova Brasília and a two hour walk from Praia dos Encantadas. According to local surfers, it has the best waves in Paraná, especially in winter. **Praia da Fora**, close to

Praia dos Encantadas, also has good waves and a few barracas. **Praia Ponta do Bicho**, just past the fort, is a beautiful sweeping bay with calmer water.

Other Attractions

Points of interest include the **Grutas das Encantadas**, small caves at the southern tip (Ponta Encantada) where, legend has it, beautiful mermaids enchant all who come near them. The fort, **Fortaleza de NS dos Prazeres**, was built in 1769 to guard the bay at Praia da Fortaleza. From inside the fort, a trail leads up to the WWII gun emplacements and a magnificent view of the whole area. The **Farol das Conchas** lighthouse, built in 1872 on the orders of Dom Pedro II, stands at the island's easterly point, at Praia do Farol. The fishermen on the island regularly catch hammerhead sharks, which they call 'formula ones'.

Special Events

Ilha do Mel goes crazy during Carnaval. Book accommodation well ahead, or bring a tent or hammock. Towards the end of

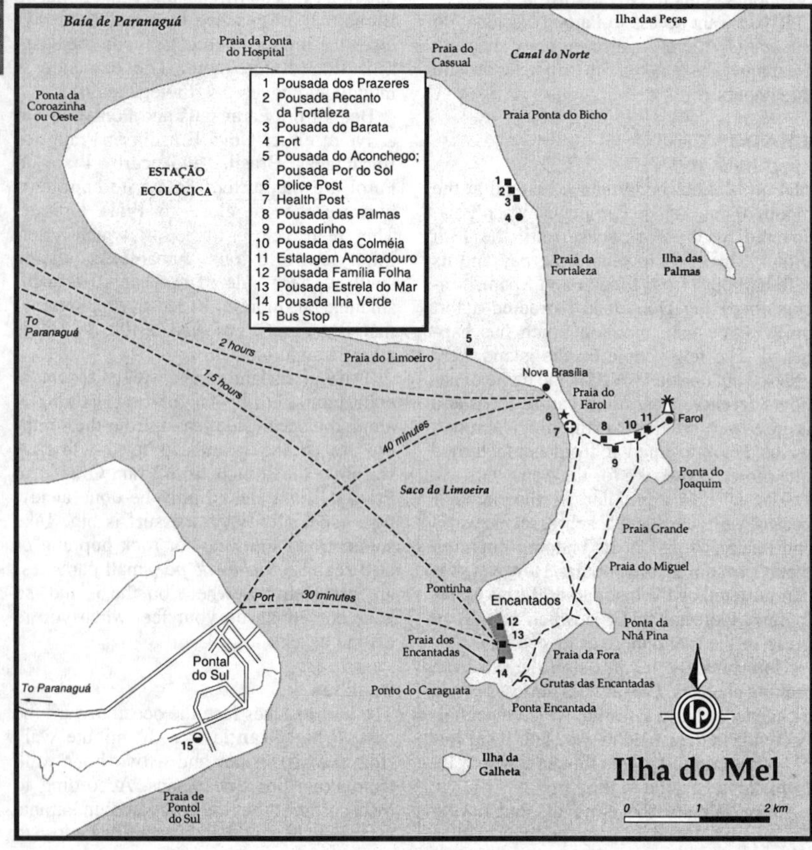

November, the Garajagan Surf Open is held – accompanied by some serious all-night partying.

Places to Stay

If you happen to arrive on the island on a holiday weekend or at another peak time, rooms will be hard to find, but you rent space to sling a hammock. There are plenty of designated camping areas: just about every second backyard in Praia dos Encantadas, two in Nova Brasília and one at Praia do Farol. All have electricity and water and cost US$3 per person. You're not supposed to camp outside these areas. Watch out for the tides if you decide to crash out on the beach.

There are pousadas at Nova Brasília, Praia da Fortaleza, Praia do Farol and Praia dos Encantadas.

The biggest concentration of places is at Praia do Farol, along the track to the right from Nova Brasília. The prices quoted here increase around 20 to 50% in the high season. The *Pousadinho* (☎ 978-3662) is highly recommended. Low-season prices are US$30 for a double quarto, with breakfast included. Staff speak French, English and Italian. Across the track, *Pousada Tropical* (☎ 423-3526) has basic quartos for US$12 per person. Out towards the lighthouse, *Estalagem Ancoradouro* (☎ 356-2195) is a quiet place with quartos for US$23 per person, including breakfast and dinner. Nearby, *Pousada das Colméia* (☎ 242-0867) has a shady balcony and quartos for US$15 per person. Other good pousadas in the area include *Pousada Valentin* (☎ 457-9089) and *Pousada das Palmas*.

On the bay side towards Praia do Limoeiro, *Pousada do Aconchego* (☎ 978-3648) and *Pousada Por do Sol* (☎ 457-9036) have bed and board deals for around US$35 per person.

During summer, Praia da Fortaleza is a good option if you want to escape the crowds. There are three pousadas close together on the lovely beach just past the fort. There is only one restaurant at Fortaleza, so accommodation includes meals. Closest to the fort, *Pousada do Barata* (☎ 978-3795) has small quartos for US$25 per person, with all meals included. Nearby, *Pousada Recanto da Fortaleza* (☎ 978-1367) has quartos for US$30 per person, including breakfast and dinner. Last along the beach, *Pousada dos Prazeres* (☎ 978-3221) is a friendly place with rooms for US$30 per person, with all meals provided.

At Praia dos Encantadas, there are several beachfront pousadas. To the left of the pier as you come off the boat, the new *Pousada Estrela do Mar* (☎ 991-9296) is good value. Spotless quartos cost US$15/30 for singles/doubles, with a good breakfast included. Further along the beach, *Pousada Família Folha* (☎ 978-4504) is run by the vivacious Elvira. Small bunk rooms cost US$10 per person, with breakfast included. To the right of the pier, Pousada da Tia Maria (☎ 978-3352) has clean and comfortable apartamentos for US$15/20. Nearby, Ilha Verde (☎ 978-2829) has quartos for US$20 per person and double apartamentos for US$50 in a pleasant garden setting. The owner, Christina, raves about the beautiful sunsets on the doorstep.

Places to Eat

There are barracas with food and drinks at Nova Brasília, Praia dos Encantadas and Praia da Fora. At Brasília, the *Davi* restaurant, just past the health post, has a prato feito for US$3.50. Nearby, *Toca do Abutre* serves tasty seafood dishes for US$7 – the stroganoff de camarão is excellent. On Praia do Farol, *Catarina's* is a shady place for lunch with good seafood pancakes, juices and delicious cakes.

At Praia dos Encantadas, there are two good beachfront cafés next to each other: *Delírios* and *Forró do Zorro*. They both serve much the same thing – seafood. You'd be crazy to eat anything else on Ilha do Mel anyway. Just back from the beach, *Waimea Café* serves a seafood prato feito for US$3.

Entertainment

On Friday and Saturday nights, you'll find music, *forró* (music of the Northeast) and the odd beach festa. At Brasília, *Toca do*

Abutre occasionally has live music on weekends. On the bay side towards Praia do Limoeiro, *Toca da Coelho* is a beach bar and dance club on weekends, in summer at least. At Encantadas, *Bar e Restaurante Linhado do Equador* has live music on weekends.

Getting There & Away

Boats for Nova Brasília and Praia dos Encantadas leave from Paranaguá at 3 pm every weekday, and at 10 am on Saturday. The boats return from Ilha do Mel to Paranaguá at 8 am on weekdays and 4 pm on Sunday.

From Pontal do Sul, there are at least two boats daily (more in summer) to both Nova Brasília and Encantadas at 2.50 pm and 4.30 pm. They return to Pontal do Sul at 4 pm and 5.30 pm. The trip takes about 40 minutes and costs US$3. Check at the tourist information office in Paranaguá for the latest schedule.

Getting Around

If there are a few of you or if you have lots of luggage, it might be worth hiring a small cart to transport your stuff to a pousada. Look for them when you get off the boat. Water taxis for up to four people cost US$8 to Praia do Farol, US$15 to the fort and US$12 to Praia Grande. If you get sick of walking, mountain bikes can be rented at Nova Brasília (US$5 an hour).

PARANÁ BEACHES

Descending the Serra do Mar from Curitiba, you get a good view of the Paraná coast. The broad beach runs uninterrupted from Pontal do Sul to Caiobá. With the notable exception of Ilha do Mel, these are unspectacular beaches, hot and humid in the summer and too cold in the winter. There's plenty of camping and numerous seafood barracas, and each town has a few hotels. Unfortunately, the condominium blight is spreading.

Praia de Leste is a small, unattractive town with a couple of hotels and is the closest beach to Paranaguá, a bit more than half an hour away. The beach is open and windy, and there are some beach breaks for surfing.

Pontal do Sul is the end of the line, where you can get boats to Ilha do Mel. In between are summer homes and lots of open, unused beaches.

PARQUE NACIONAL DO SUPERAGUÍ

Comprised of the Superaguí and Peças islands in the Baía de Paranaguá, this marine park was created in 1989. It is renowned for its mangroves and salt-marshes and also contains a great variety of orchids, dolphins, jaguars and parrots, threatened with extinction as the Mata Atlântica (coastal rainforest) shrinks.

The principal island of the park, the Ilha do Superaguí, is the most visited. Boats disembark at Vila Superaguí, a fishing settlement with a population of about 350. There is a small pousada (*Pousada Carioca*, charging US$15 per person), a basic restaurant and some small general stores. Some of the families rent out rooms in their simple, wooden houses.

To help maintain the environment, all visitors should call in to the IBAMA checkpoint. It's about 2km from the village, but there's only one ranger for the whole island and he's not always at the post.

Beaches away from Vila are deserted. The longest is Praia a Deserta, a 20km-long strip of fine, white sand. The water is calm, but swimmers need to watch out for the stinging jellyfish that appear when the water gets warm.

There are no regular boats to Ilha do Superaguí. The closest town to Superaguí is Guaraqueçaba, which is accessible by bus from Curitiba and by bus and boat from Paranaguá. The boat leaves Paranaguá daily at noon and takes around three hours. It returns from Guaraqueçaba to Paranaguá daily at 5 am.

In Guaraqueçaba, boats anchor in front of the old mercado municipal, and it's possible to meet men from the island and negotiate a ride to the island. You can identify their boats by the words 'S.AGUI' painted on the bow or stern. How much they charge you for the ride depends on how plentiful the fish were and the price of diesel.

The trip is interesting, as the boat passes through mangroves and provides a great view of one of the world's best-preserved saltwater lagoons. It takes about 2½ hours, depending on sea conditions.

If you get stuck in Guaraqueçaba, there are a couple of pousadas. Try *Pousada Mata Atlanticâ* (☎ 482-1220), on Rua Dr Ramos Siquera, next to the old mercado, or *Pousada Iasa* (☎ 482-1291), at Rua Inácio Barboso Pinto 53.

For more information about the park, visit IBAMA in Paranaguá (on the corner of Rua Benjamin Constant and Rua Manoel Bonifaço), or if you are in Guaraqueçaba, telephone IBAMA on ☎ (041) 482-1262.

BAÍA DE PARANAGUÁ ISLANDS

There are several other islands in the Baía de Paranaguá that can be visited, but you'll have to do some scraping around to get there, as there are no regular boat services.

The **Ilha dos Currais** is known for its bird life and the **Ilha da Cotinga** for its mysterious inscriptions and ruins.

FOZ DO IGUAÇU

• *pop 230,000* ✉ *85850-000* ☎ *045*

Arising in the coastal mountains of Paraná and Santa Catarina (the Serra do Mar) at the modest elevation of 1300m, the Rio Iguaçu snakes west for 600km, pausing behind the Foz do Areia Cruz Machado and Salto Santiago dams and picking up a few dozen tributaries along the way. It widens majestically and sweeps around a magnificent forest stage before plunging and crashing in tiered falls. The 275 falls are over 3km wide and 80m high, which makes them wider than Victoria, higher than Niagara and more beautiful than either. Neither words nor photographs do them justice: they must be seen and heard. They're what the Romantic poets had in mind when they spoke of the awesome and sublime.

Thousands of years before they were 'discovered' by whites, the falls were a holy burial place for the Tupi-Guaraní and Paraguas tribes. Spaniard Don Alvar Nuñes, also known as Cabeza de Vaca (presumably because of his stubbornness), happened upon the falls in 1541 in the course of his journey from Santa Catarina, on the coast, to Asunción. He named the falls the Saltos de Santa Maria, but this name fell into disuse and the Tupi-Guaraní name of Iguaçu (Great Waters) was readopted. No agreement has been made on spelling – in Brazil it's Iguaçu, in Argentina Iguazú and in Paraguay Iguassu. In 1986 the international commission of UNESCO declared the region (along with the Pantanal) a World Heritage Site.

Foz do Iguaçu went through a frenzied period while the Itaipu dam was under construction and the population increased from 35,000 to 190,000. It's settled down since then, but can still be a dangerous place, particularly at night, when you should avoid the riverfront area. Ciudad del Este (in Paraguay) is pretty shabby, while Puerto Iguazú (in Argentina) is much more mellow.

Orientation

The falls are roughly 20km east of the junction of the Paraná and Iguaçu rivers, which form the tripartite Paraguayan, Brazilian and Argentine border (marked by obelisks).

The Ponte Presidente Tancredo Neves bridges the Rio Iguaçu and connects Brazil to Argentina. The Rio Paraná, the Paraguayan border, is spanned by the Ponte da Amizade; 15km upstream is Itaipu, the world's largest hydroelectric project.

The falls are unequally divided between Brazil and Argentina, with Argentina taking the larger portion. To see them properly you should visit both sides – the Brazilian park for the overview and the Argentine park for a close-up look. Travellers should allow at least two days to see the falls; more if you want to visit Ciudad del Este or the Itaipu dam.

The best time of the year to see the falls is between August and November. If you come during the May to July flood season, you may not be able to approach the swollen waters on the catwalks. It's always wet at the falls. This area gets over 2m of rain annually, and the falls create a lot of moisture. Lighting for photography is best in the morning on the Brazilian side and in the late afternoon on the Argentine side.

Information

Tourist Office Foztur maintains five information booths with up-to-date information: maps, lists of hotels with a one-star and up rating, restaurants and bus timetables. Staff are very helpful and most speak English. Some also speak Italian, Spanish and German. There are booths at Rua Barão do Rio Branco, in the city (open from 8 am to 10 pm), at the rodoviária (open from 6 am to 6 pm), at the airport (open from 9 am until the last plane), on the Paraguayan border (open from 8 am to 8 pm), and at the entrance to the city, on Hwy BR-27 (open from 7 am to 6 pm).

Teletur (☎ 1516) maintains a 24 hour information service with English-speaking operators.

Money The Banco do Brasil on Avenida

Brasil changes money and has Visa ATMs. It charges around US$10 to change travellers cheques. There are dozens of casas de câmbio all over town, but not many change travellers cheques. Readers have recommended Caribe Tourismo at the airport; it will change travellers cheques without charging a commission.

Post & Telephone The post office is on Praça Getúlio Vargas. International telephone calls can be made at Rua Marechal Floriano Peixoto 1222, and on the corner of Rua Rebouças and Rua Almirante Barroso.

Visas Visitors who spend the day outside Brazil will not require visas or exit stamps, but you should carry your passport with you in case of border checks. Travellers who intend to stay longer must go through all the formalities.

Local buses don't always stop at the borders, and some readers have later been hit with hefty fines when leaving Argentina and Paraguay for not having the appropriate exit/entry cards. If you are travelling on to Argentina or Paraguay, make sure you ask the bus driver to stop so you can get your exit/entry card at the border.

The Argentine consulate (☎ 574-2969) can be found at Travessa Eduardo Branchi 26. It's open Monday to Friday from 9.30 am to 2 pm. The Paraguayan consulate (☎ 523-2898), Rua Bartolomeu de Gusmão 738, is open on weekdays from 8.30 am to 4.30 pm. Brazil has a consulate in Puerto Iguazú (☎ 572-1348), Avenida Guaraní 70, open on weekdays from 8 am to 2 pm. In Paraguay, the Brazilian consulate (☎ 616-2308) is at Rua Pay Perez 337, on the corner of Pamplliega. It's open from 8 am to noon.

The Falls – Brazilian side

Although the Brazilian side has a smaller chunk of the falls, the Brazilians have the Grand View across the churning lower Rio Iguaçu to the raging falls. The Brazilian park is larger, with 1550 sq km of rainforest, but the Argentine forest is in better shape.

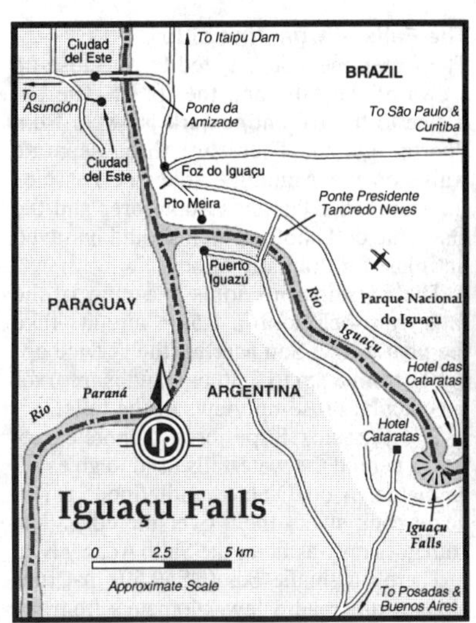

Walk to the observation tower by the Floriano falls, then over to Santa Maria falls. The walkway gives you an even better view of the Garganta do Diablo (Devil's Throat) and an invigorating cold shower.

If you have the cash, you can treat yourself to a helicopter ride over the waterfalls, but there's a campaign to stop the flights because of environmental concerns. According to some readers, this has forced the pilots to fly at higher altitudes, which detracts from the experience. For US$50, you get seven minutes in the air. The choppers will take up to three passengers, but it's best to sit by the edge of the bubble. Helisul Taxi Aereo (☎ 523-1190) operates from just outside the park entrance. Travellers flying into Foz or Puerto Iguazú with accommodating weather and pilots can see the falls from the air.

You can catch a boat (US$30 per person) to the Garganta do Diablo from the boat ramp 3km back along the road to Foz – the bus can drop you there on the way in or out. Sometimes the boat operators have an odd sense of humour – they'll cut the engine and float to the edge of the falls.

The Falls – Argentine side

The Argentine side is noted for its close-up views of the falls and the forest. The entrance to the Argentine park is 18km from Puerto Iguazú. There are three separate walks on the Argentine side: the Passeios Inferiores, the Passeios Superiores and the Garganta do Diablo, which should be saved until last for dramatic effect.

The Passeios Inferiores is a view of the falls from below on a 1.5km circuit. Take the boat to Isla San Martin (the service operates from 8 am to 5.30 pm, and is free) for spectacular close-up views of the falls.

The Passeios Superiores' concrete catwalks behind the waterfalls used to go as far as Garganta do Diablo, until floods a few years back swept them over the edge. The path goes only as far as the Salto Adán y Eva.

There's a shuttle bus (US$0.50) that runs along a dirt road a few kilometres from the park entrance to Puerto Canoas. From here you can take a hair-raising boat ride out to Garganta do Diablo (US$4), where 13,000 cubic metres of water per second plunge 90m in 14 falls, arranged around a tight little pocket.

The view at the precipice is hypnotising. Visitors will be treated to a multisensory experience: roaring falls, huge rainbow arcs, drenching mist and, in the distance, parrots and hawks cruising over deep, green forest. Watch for the swifts, which drop like rocks into the misty abyss, catch insects in midair, shoot back up, and dart behind the falls to perch on the cliffs.

Forest Tour (Argentina)

There's more to the 550 sq km Argentine park than just waterfalls. If you intend to do a forest tour, do it on the Argentine side; they do a better job of protecting their parklands than the Brazilians, and there are guides at the visitor centre in the park. If you can, arrange the tour the evening before, and pick up a wildlife list to study. Try to arrive at before 7 am or in the late afternoon, the best times to spot birds and wildlife.

If possible, go in a small group and bring binoculars and a tape recorder (to record the sounds of the forest). You'll see fantastic butterflies (they congregate around pools of urine and on sweaty handrails to sip the salty fluid), parrots, parakeets, woodpeckers, hummingbirds, lizards, 3cm-long ants, beautifully coloured spiders, and all sorts of orchids, lianas and vines.

There are four species of toucan in the park. Their long beaks are deceptive, they're actually so light and spongy that the birds are back-heavy and therefore clumsy fliers. The toucans eat fruit, eggs, chicks, and leaves of the amba *(Cecropia adenopus)* tree. Amba

The Green Toucan is a noisy and gregarious bird with a well-developed sense of curiosity

leaves are also used to make a medicinal tea that is good for coughs.

Other creatures in the park include monkeys, deer, sloths, anteaters, racoons, jaguars, tapirs, caimans and armadillos, but as in other tropical rainforests, large animals are not very abundant and tend to be nocturnal. On our last research trip, the forest tour to Macuco had been suspended after a ranger's son was killed by a jaguar.

The foliage is lush and lovely: 2000 species of plants stacked in six different layers, from forest-floor grasses, ferns and bushes to low, middle and high tree canopies. The forest cover, in addition to harbouring a wide variety of animals and insects, protects the soil from erosion, maintains humidity and moderates temperatures. Tarzan vines, lianas and epiphytes connect and blur the distinction between the forest levels.

Itaipu Dam

How did Brazil ever manage to run up such a huge foreign debt? Part of the answer is by engaging in mammoth projects like Itaipu, the world's largest hydroelectric works. The US$18 billion joint Brazilian-Paraguayan venture has the capacity to generate 12.6 million kilowatts – enough electricity to supply the energy needs of Paraguay and southern Brazil. The concrete used in this dam could have paved a two-lane highway from Moscow to Lisbon.

Fortunately, the dam will not affect the flow of water in Iguaçu, as the Paraná and Iguaçu rivers meet downstream of the falls. The Itaipu dam has, however, destroyed Sete Quedas (the world's largest waterfall, with 30 times the water spilled by Iguaçu) and created a 1400 sq km lake. Local weather patterns and populations of plants and animals have been affected, and the complete environmental repercussions of these changes will not be felt for decades.

Guided tours of the Itaipu dam are given six times a day from Monday to Saturday at 8, 9 and 10 am, and 2, 3 and 4 pm. The one hour tours are free of charge. The Itaipu dam is 19km from Foz.

Ciudad del Este (Paraguay)

Across the Ponte da Amizade, at Ciudad del Este, you can play roulette or baccarat at the Casino de Leste, or purchase up to US$150 of duty-free imported goods (no great deals), or some nifty Paraguayan lacework and leather goods.

Special Events

The Pesca ao Dourado (Dourado Fishing Contest) takes place in the first two weeks of October.

Places to Stay – Budget

Camping *Camping Clube do Brasil* (☎ 574-1310) is the closest camping ground to the falls. Just before the entrance to the park, there's a dirt road to the left. The camping ground is 600m along this track. Camping costs US$12 per person, and there's a restaurant and swimming pool. Closer to Foz, *Internacional* (☎ 572-1813) is in a well-treed area with a swimming hole. Camping costs US$8 per person. It's on the right-hand side of Avenida dos Cataratas, 3km out of Foz on the road to the falls.

Hotels The best place for budget travellers is the *Pousada Evelina* (☎/fax 574-3817), Rua Irlan Kalichewski 171, 3.5km out of Foz on the way to the falls. Scrupulously clean apartamentos cost US$12 per person, including a good breakfast. English, French and Spanish are spoken here, and there are easy connections to the centre and both sides of the falls. To get there from the rodoviária, take either a Jd Copacabana or J das Flores bus and ask to get off at Supermacado Chemin. Walk down the hill towards the city and turn left at the third street.

There's a YHA youth hostel, *Albergue da Juventude Paudimar* (☎ 574-5503), 11km from town on Rodovia das Cataratas, also on the way to the falls.

There is a cluster of cheap hotels around Rua Rebouças in the centre, but the area is pretty seedy in the evenings. *Hotel Senhor do Bonfim* (☎ 572-1849), in a small dead-end street off Rua Almirante Barroso, charges US$6 per person for clean quartos. There's no sign; it's the last building on the right. Nearby, at Rua Rebouças 809, the *Minas Foz Hotel* (☎ 574-5208) has basic apartamentos for US$10 per person, not including breakfast. The rooms facing the street are the best. A few doors away at No 829, *Trento Hotel* (☎ 574-5111) has fairly dingy apartamentos for US$10/15 for singles/doubles.

At Rua Rebouças 335, the *Vale Verde* (☎ 574-2925) is rather grungy, but the lady who runs the place is helpful. She charges US$5 per person, no breakfast. *Pousada da Laura* (☎ 574-3628), Rua Naipi 629, is safe and friendly. English, French and Spanish are spoken. Run-down apartamentos out the back cost US$10 per person, with breakfast included. Better rooms inside the house cost US$12 per person.

Places to Stay – Mid-Range

You can negotiate discounts at all of these hotels outside the high season. Our favourite is the *Hotel Del Rey* (☎ 523-2027), Rua Tarobá 1020. Large and very comfortable rooms with air-conditioning and fridge cost US$25/35, with breakfast included. The hotel has a pool and is close to the local bus terminal. *Ilha do Capri* (☎ 523-1685), Rua Barão do Rio Branco 409, is getting a bit jaded, but it's still good value. Singles/doubles go for US$40/55.

The *Imperial Hotel* (☎ 523-1299), Avenida Brasil 168, is better value, with apartamentos for US$20/30 a single/double. The rooms in front get a bit noisy. The *Hotel Diplomata* (☎ 523-1615), Avenida Brasil 678, has a pool and charges US$30/50 for singles/doubles.

Places to Stay – Top End

If you're travelling on someone else's money, or really want to splash out, the classiest place is the *Hotel das Cataratas* (☎ 523-2266; fax 574-1688), right next to the waterfalls. Singles/doubles cost US$190/228 (30% less in the low season), but, hey, at least you'll save on park entrance fees and bus fares!

Places to Eat

Restaurants come and go quickly in Foz. New por quilo and buffet joints pop up all the time, and only a few of the more expensive restaurants are well established. Fast food is big news – the city recently got its first McDonald's, and kids were wearing 'Foz tem McDonald's' (Foz has McDonald's) T-shirts around town. Seems the city's finally on the map!

For lunch, *Maria & Maria's Confeitaria* is good for pies, sandwiches and pastries. It's at two locations: No 495 and No 1285 Avenida Brasil. *Ver o Verde*, Rua Edmundo de Barros 111, has a vegetarian buffet lunch for US$5.50. *Andreolli's*, Rua Jorge Sanways 681, is better value; for US$2, you can fill up on fresh salads and vegetables and chomp into some meat if you're that way inclined.

The best and most upmarket churrascaria (restaurant featuring meat) in town is at *Búfalo Branco*, Rua Rebouças 530. It costs US$14 per person. At the other end, *Tropicana*, Avenida Juscelino Kubitschek 198, is a popular student hang-out with rodízio for US$3.80 and pizza from US$5. Next door, *Nissei* looks like a fast-food place, but is really an expensive Japanese restaurant. There's a nightly US$5 special, though, and the Monday yakisakana (a whole fish with rice and Japanese vegetables) is good value.

Santino Pezzi, on Rua Almirante Barroso, has an airy terrace above the street and good pasta dishes from US$8. The *Bier Garten*, on the corner of Avenida Jorge Schimmelpfeng and Rua Marechal Deodoro da Fonseca, serves a good variety of pizza, steaks and chopp (draught beer). It's in a good setting, and gets crowded at night.

Entertainment

There are a couple of big dance clubs in Foz, but most have a minimum drink charge of US$10-15. Try *Tass Tass*, on the corner of Avenida Jorge Schimmelpfeng and Avenida Marechal Floriano Peixoto, or *Pathyo*, on the corner of Rua Almirante Barroso and Rua Jorge Sanways.

Klaus Club, on Avenida Costa e Silva, has live music and a dance club on separate floors. *Uti Bar*, Rua Edmundo da Barros 1044, is a more sophisticated bar/venue for older cats.

Getting There & Away

Air There are frequent flights from Foz do Iguaçu to Asunción, Buenos Aires, Rio and São Paulo. On Avenida Brasil, VASP (☎ 523-2212) is at No 845, Transbrasil (☎ 574-3836) at No 1225, and Varig (☎ 523-2111) at Avenida Brasil 821.

In Puerto Iguazú, Aerolineas Argentinas (☎ 20168), Aguirre 295, offers three daily services to Buenos Aires' Aeroparque from US$130. Lapa (☎ 20214), Avenida Perito Moreno 184, next to the Hotel Libertador, also has daily flights for US$115.

Bus All long-distance buses arrive at and depart from the international bus station, 6km from the centre of town.

The trip from Foz do Iguaçu to Curitiba is 635km, (US$33, 9½ hours); there are 14 buses a day. Eight buses a day make the 14 hour trip to São Paulo (US$42). To Rio, there are six a day (US$54, 21 hours).

There are hourly buses from Ciudad del Este to Asunción (US$13, 5½ hours), and one daily to Pedro Juan Caballero at 11.30 pm for access to Mato Grosso do Sul (US$25, 7 hours). Ten buses a day run from Puerto Iguazú to Buenos Aires (US$45, 18 hours).

Getting Around

To/From the Airport Catch a P Nacional bus (US$0.70, 30 minutes). They run every 22 minutes from 5.30 am to 7 pm and then every hour until 12.40 pm. A taxi is US$20.

To/From the Rodoviária To get to the centre, walk down the hill to the local bus stop and catch any Centro bus. They run every 15 minutes from 5.30 am to 1.15 am.

Bus All local buses leave from the urban bus terminal on Avenida Juscelino Kubitschek.

The Brazilian Falls Catch a Cataratas bus (US$1.30) to get to the Brazilian side of the falls. On weekdays, buses run every hour, the first bus leaving the terminal at 8 am and the last at 6 pm. Buses return to the city on the hour; the last bus leaves the falls at 6 pm. On weekends, buses leave the terminal every 40 minutes from 8 am until 6 pm. The last bus leaves the falls at 6 pm.

At the entrance to the park, you'll have to get out and pay the US$6 entry fee. The bus will wait while you do this.

If you want to do both sides of the falls in one day, get off the bus back to Foz where the road turns off to Puerto Iguazú (ask the conductor to let you know). Follow the road sign to Argentina – there's a bus stop 100m along the road where you can pick up a bus to Puerto Iguazú.

The Argentine Falls In Foz, catch a Puerto Iguazú bus to the Argentine side of the falls. Buses start running at 7 am and leave every 13 minutes (on Sunday, every 50 minutes) until 8.50 pm. The fare is US$2. At the bus station in Puerto Iguazú, transfer to an El Pratico bus.

You can pay for everything in one go at the bus station: the bus fares to and from the park, the bus to and from Puerto Canoas, entry to the park and the boat ride to Garganta do Diablo. You can pay in Argentine pesos, Brazilian reais or US dollars: the bus costs US$4, park entry US$5, and the boat at Puerto Canoa out to the Garganta do Diablo US$4.

From Monday to Friday, the bus leaves every 45 minutes from 6.40 am to 8.15 pm, but not at 1 pm (which is siesta time). On weekends, it runs every two hours from 7 am to 5 pm.

Itaipu From the local bus stop opposite the urban terminal in Foz, take a Conjunto C or Vila C bus heading to Itaipu. There's one every 20 minutes from 5.30 am to 11 pm, but Itaipu closes for visits after 4 pm. The last bus stop is at the Ecomuseu (worth a look), about 400m from the Itaipu visitor centre.

Ciudad del Este From the urban terminal in Foz, buses for Ciudad del Este start at 7 am and leave every 10 minutes.

Santa Catarina

Unlike most immigrants to Brazil, the Germans and Italians who settled in Santa Catarina in the 19th century owned their small family-run farms. This European and use has produced a far more egalitaxrian distribution of wealth than in most of Brazil, and many of the state's 4.5 million people still own their rich farmland.

Combined with some healthy small-scale industry, this has created one of Brazil's most prosperous states. The relative affluence and efficient services give the state the feel of Europe rather than of Brazil – at least in the highlands, which are green and pastoral. But if Santa Catarina is reminiscent of Switzerland, it's less because of geography than sedate middle-class consumerism.

You'll rarely find the kind of primitive fishing villages that predominate in the Northeast. Most travellers don't come to Santa Catarina for foreign culture – they come for the beaches.

There's no doubt that the beaches are beautiful: there are wide surf beaches with some of Brazil's best surfing, and Caribbean-like bays with clear, clean turquoise water. The water is warm during the summer months, and there are plenty of calm beaches for swimming. The currents can be very dangerous in places, so be careful.

Many of Santa Catarina's beaches have become fashionable vacation spots for well-to-do Paulistas, Curitibanos and Argentines; during the January-February holiday season, the beaches and hotels are jammed. Several little Copacabanas have sprouted up in towns such as Camboriú, and this growth is rapidly changing the coastline.

Santa Catarina is consistently hot during the summer. In winter, the wind along the coast picks up considerably, although it never gets too cold. The best months to go, unless you like crowds, are March, April, November and December.

Compared with other parts of Brazil, this is a polite and proper place. You may be excluded from a bar if you're not wearing a shirt, and shorts are the briefest attire acceptable on intercity buses – no swim suits. What's so unusual about this Brazilian state is that these rules are respected.

JOINVILLE

• pop 400,000 ✉ 89200-000 ☎ 047

Imagine a city where blondes stroll through town on clean, well-lit streets, perusing Bavarian-façaded shops full of modern western appliances, parks and houses with well-manicured lawns, flower festivals, and a central park in which children play at night: a city that is polite and efficient. Now here's the hard part: imagine this city is in Brazil.

Santa Catarina's second largest city, Joinville (pronounced 'jovial') is described as 'an industrial city'. The industry, however, is outside the pleasant inner city, which is quite habitable and seems like the kind of place to raise a family. For the traveller, Joinville is relaxed, if unexciting.

The views around the town are beautiful, particularly where the highway traverses the lush coastal mountains. The drive north up to Guaratuba is stunning.

Orientation
The city centre is small, with most shops and services concentrated around Rua 15 de Novembro and Rua Princesa Isabel.

Information
Tourist Office There is a tourist office (☎ 433-1511) on Praça Nereu Ramos, open from 9 am to 6 pm Monday to Sunday. It offers maps and brochures and the staff speak German and a little English.

Money Bradesco, on Rua 15 de Novembro behind the local bus terminal has Visa ATMs. Casa Roweder Câmbio e Tourismo, Rua do Principe 158, changes travellers cheques.

Post & Telephone The post office is on Rua Princesa Isabel. Make phone calls from the *telefônica* across the road.

Museu Nacional da Imigração
Housed in the old palace (built in 1870) at Rua Rio Branco 229, the Museu Nacional da Imigração is full of objects used by the pioneers of the state. It's open from 9 am to 6 pm Tuesday to Friday.

Alameda das Palmeiras
In front of the Museu Nacional is an impressive, palm-lined walkway. These Imperial palms are over a century old. Don't miss the rare 'dual' palm. It's the second palm on the right as you face away from the museum.

Museu Arqueológico do Sambaqui
At Rua Dona Francisca 600, this museum is an exposition of the Sambaqui Indian lifestyle. It's worth a visit on a rainy day. The museum is open Tuesday to Sunday from 9 am to noon and 2 to 6 pm.

Museu de Arte de Joinville
This interesting museum is set in lovely gardens and houses works by local artists. There's a small restaurant attached. It's at Rua 15 de Novembro 1400, and is open Tuesday to Sunday from 10 am to 8 pm.

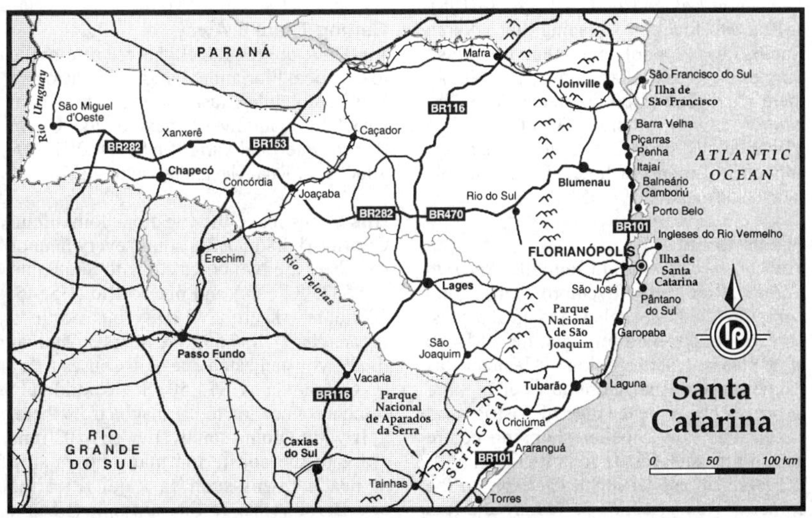

THE SOUTH

Mirante

A high tower on top of the Morro da Boa Vista, this is a good place from which to get your bearings. It also provides a 360° view of Joinville, and you can see the Baía da Babitonga and São Francisco do Sul.

Special Events

In the second half of July, Joinville hosts the largest dance festival in Latin America.

Places to Stay – Budget

The central *Hotel Ideal* (☎ 422-3660), Rua Jerônimo Coelho 98, has single/double quartos for US$15/20 and apartamentos for US$20/30. A bit further, at Rua 15 de Novembro 801, *Hotel Mattes* (☎ 433-2447) has quartos for US$16/28 and comfortable apartamentos for US$22/34. Next door, *Hotel Mendes* is a bit cheaper.

Places to Stay – Mid-Range

The *Hotel Príncipe* (☎ 433-4555) is centrally located at Rua Jerônimo Coelho 27. It's clean, has friendly staff, and a very good breakfast. Singles/doubles start at US$27/40.

Places to Stay – Top End

The *Colón Palace Hotel* (☎/fax 433-6188), at Rua São Joaquim 80 facing Praça Nereu Ramos, has a pool and great breakfast. Singles/doubles cost around US$64/80, but there are discounts on weekends. The *Tannenhof Othon* (☎/fax 433-8011), Rua Visconde de Taunay 340, is Joinville's best and most expensive hotel. Single/double rooms start at US$79/105.

Places to Eat

You can eat very well in Joinville. *Recanto Natural*, Rua 15 de Novembro 78, has good por quilo lunches of salads and meat dishes. *La Cascina* has a buffet lunch for US$4.50 in a pleasant setting along Alameda das Palmeiras. On Rua Jerônimo Coelho, *Café Expresso* has a great range of pastries and cakes. The new Mueller shopping centre has all the usual fast food in its food hall.

For cheap eats at night, *Chaplin*, on the corner of Rua Visconde de Taunay and Rua Pedro Lobo, is a small student bar with prato feito for US$3 and live acoustic music. *Expresso* is a popular upmarket bar/restaurant nearby on Avenida Juscelino Kubitschek. Its speciality is 'beirutes', a fairly bland imitation of a Lebanese kebab. The chopp (draught beer) is good, though.

Joinville boasts good German and Italian food and is a major chocolate producer. The *Bierkeller*, Rua 15 de Novembro 497, has the city's best-value German food. Prices start at US$10 per meal, but there are cheaper specials for around US$6.50.

If you like pizza, *Mama Mia* at Rua Rio Branco 193 does it 42 ways. They're wood fired and start at US$10. Good pasta dishes start at US$7 – ask for a half-serve if you're dining solo. Committed carnivores should head next door to *Neu Fidler*, where steak is prepared in one of 14 ways; prices range from US$10 for two people. Further down the street at Rua Rio Branco 299, *Pinheiro* has the city's best fish, but it's expensive.

Things to Buy

If you're in town on the second Saturday of the month, check out the artisan fair in Praça Nereu Ramos.

Getting There & Away

Air There are regular flights from Joinville to Curitiba, Florianópolis, Brasília, Rio and São Paulo. InterBrasil (☎ 422-6060) is at Rua São Joaquim 70, next to the Colón Palace Hotel, and Varig/Rio Sul (☎ 0800-99-7000) is at Rua Alexandre Dohler 277.

Bus Buses make the trip from Joinville to Curitiba (US$6.50, 2½ hours) every hour or so. There are two buses a day to São Paulo (US$32, 9 hours) and one to Rio (US$45, 13 hours). There is a daily bus north to Paranaguá (US$6.50, 3½ hours). Alternatively, you can catch one of six buses a day to Guaratuba (US$4.50, 1½ hours) and catch a connection to Paranaguá from there.

If you're going south, Hwy BR-101 runs close to the coast, and many buses stop at beach towns such as Itajaí, Piçarras and Barra Velha. To Florianópolis (US$14,

2½ hours), there are 15 buses a day – four of them are express. The *semi-diretos* (semi-direct), run via Itajaí and Balneário Camboriú, leaving every two to three hours. Ten buses a day run to Blumenau (US$9.50, 2½ hours), and three go to Porto Alegre (US$21, 9hours) and Foz do Iguaçu (US$34, 12 hours).

The closest beaches on Ilha de São Francisco (US$4.80, 1¼ hours). There are plenty of buses, especially on weekends – the first leaves at 6.30 am and the last at 8.20 pm.

Boat A day trip by boat to Ilha de São Francisco leaves from the Barco Principal on the Rio Cachoeira at 10 am, returning at 5 pm. The trip cost US$15 per person (including lunch).

Getting Around

The airport is 12km from the city, and the rodoviária is 2km out. Buses to Praça da Bandeira eave every 20 minutes from a stop at the side of the airport terminal.

Car Locasul (☎ 433-9393) and Hertz (☎ 433-4141) rent cars for around US$72 per day – more if you want to return the car in another city.

THE SOUTH

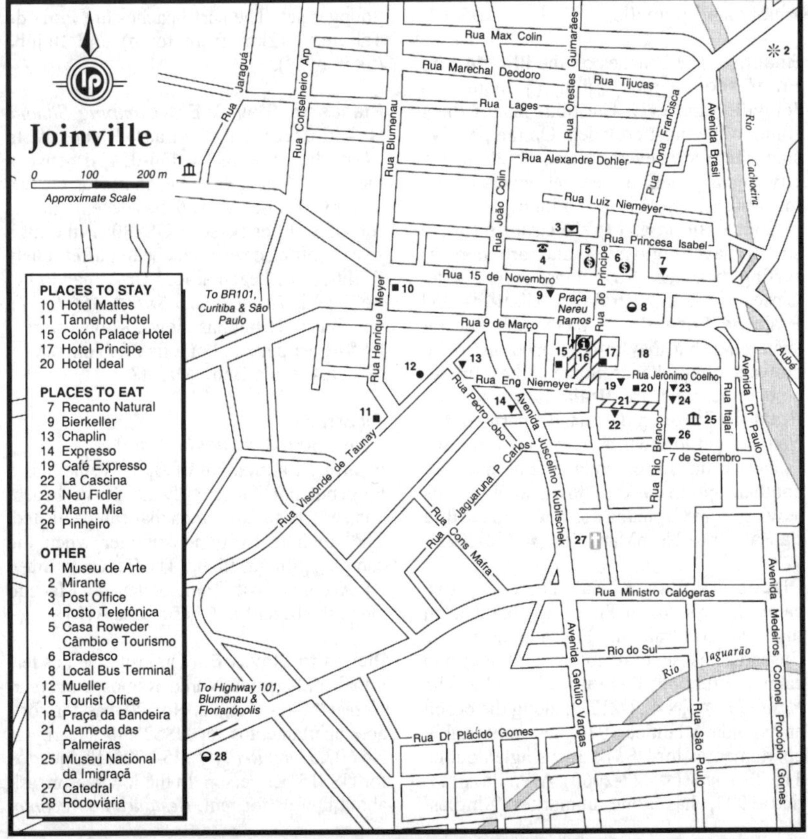

JOINVILLE TO FLORIANÓPOLIS

This stretch of coast has many beautiful beaches, but it's being developed rapidly and without controls. In general, the more famous a beach, the more developed and ugly it is. Balneário Camboriú, the area's best-known beach town, is an excellent example.

São Francisco do Sul

• *pop 28,000* ✉ *89240-000* ☎ *047*

This historic city's island setting was 'discovered' way back in 1504 by the Frenchman Binot Paulmier de Goneville, but the city itself wasn't settled until the middle of the next century. It became the port of entry for the German immigrants who settled the land around Joinville.

Beaches The beaches on the **Ilha de São Francisco** are good, but their proximity to Joinville (and even Curitiba) makes them some of the most crowded. On the positive side, there are several cheap hotels in the city, and a variety of beaches accessible by local buses. There is also a lot of surfing.

Both **Prainha** and **Praia Grande** (to the south) have big waves and are popular surfing beaches. Swimming is not safe. Closer to the city, **Praia da Ubatuba** and **Praia de Enseada** are pretty, and safe for swimming, but they're developed and often crowded on weekends. Some of the more secluded beaches are **Praia Itaguaçu** and **Praia do Forte** on the island's northern tip. You can get to them by local bus from São Francisco do Sul or Praia de Enseada. For another option, ask in town about boats leaving from Capitania dos Portos to the **Ilha da Paz**, or call SubMarine on (☎ 442-2022).

Places to Stay & Eat There are two camping grounds at Praia da Ubatuba, on the road to Praia de Enseada. Praia de Enseada has several hotels, and you can catch a direct bus there from Joinville. The *Enseada* (☎/fax 422-2122), along the beach at Avenida Atlântica 1074, has comfortable apartamentos for US$18/30 a single/double. The *Turismar* (☎ 422-2060), Avenida Atlântica 1923, has gone upmarket. Singles/doubles start at US$30/50. There's a restaurant attached. For seafood, try *Restaurante Panorâmico* on the 2nd floor at Avenida Atlântica 1288, then finish yourself off at *Paviloche*, the icecream buffet below. In São Francisco do Sul, the *Kontiki* (☎ 442-0232), Rua Camacho 33, across from the waterfront, is reasonable; it charges US$18 per person.

Barra Velha

• *pop 13,500* ✉ *88390-000* ☎ *047*

If driving south from Joinville on the Hwy BR-101, this is the first point where the road meets the sea. About 4km to the south of town, Praia do Grant is popular with the younger set. The surf beaches are Praia do Tabuleiro (2km from town) and Itajuba (5km away).

Places to Stay & Eat *Camping Simone* (☎ 456-0226) is at Rua Lauro Ramos 69. In town, the *Mirante* (☎ 456-0343), between the rodoviária and the beach at Rua Governador Celso Ramos 106, has decent quartos for US$10 per person (US$30 in the high season). It also serves a cheap buffet lunch. Right on the beach at Rua Dr Armando Petrelli 17 is *Hotel Bela Vista* (☎ 456-0267), which is ugly but has views. Rooms start at US$12 per person. For a fine fish dinner, try *Siri* at Avenida Beira Mar 48.

Piçarras

• *pop 9500* ✉ *88380-000* ☎ *047*

Piçarras, 14km south of Barra Velha, has a long but not particularly attractive beach, and several small islands that can be visited. The town is lively in summer when the camping grounds fill up. The Banco do Brasil on Avenida Jose Temisotcles de Macedo along the beachfront, has a Visa ATM.

Places to Stay & Eat Opposite the bus terminal on Avenida Nureu Ramos, *Itacolomi Hotel* (☎ 345-0466), at No 670, has comfortable apartamentos for US$25/40. Nearby at No 607, *Hotel Real* (☎ 345-0706) has quartos for US$15 per person. In the low season, ask about houses for rent. *Restaurante Recanto*, a few doors from the bus station, has a breezy terrace and a seafood prato feito for US$3. For fine seafood dining, try *Restaurante do Maneco* at Avenida Nereu Ramos 299.

Getting There & Away There are two small bus terminals in Piçarras: Avenida Nureu Ramos (intercity and local buses), and on Avenida Getúlio Vargas, closer to Hwy BR-101 (buses to Joinville and Curitiba).

Penha

• *pop 15,500* ✉ *88385-000* ☎ *047*

Penha is a fishing town, and the nicest place to stay on this part of the coast. Only 6km from Piçarras, the ocean is calm at the tree-lined town beaches, Praia da Armação and Prainha. The beaches to the south are less crowded. From Praia da Armação, you can rent a boat to the nearby islands of Itacolomi and Feia. Ask at the pier; the going rate is about US$40 for 3 hours for up to five people.

Places to Stay & Eat There are lots of camping grounds near the main beach and some good hotels and seafood restaurants on Praia da Armação. The friendly *Hotel Itapocoroí* (☎ 345-5015) charges US$20/30 a single/double for comfortable apartamentos. Nearby, *Costamar Praia Hotel* (☎ 345-6861) charges the same prices (the rooms on the top floor have great views). Good beach-side restaurants include *Sabor Marinho*, in front of the Hotel Itapocoroí, and *Petisqueira do Alírio*, 100m down the beach.

Getting There & Away Intercity buses don't stop in Penha. From Piçarras, take a local Circular or Navagantes bus to Penha.

Itajaí

At the turn-off to Blumenau, Itajaí is an important port for the Itajaí valley. However, there's not much here to interest the traveller and the best beaches are out of town. Plenty of buses come and go from Itajaí.

Balneário Camboriú

This little Copacabana, with its sharp hills dropping into the sea, nightclubs with 'professional companions' and an ocean boulevard named Avenida Atlântica, is out of control. In summer, the population increases tenfold.

Balneário Camboriú is Santa Catarina's most expensive town. Here you can meet well-heeled Argentines, Paraguayans and Paulistas who spend their summers in beach-hugging high-rise buildings.

Roughly 6km south of the city along Hwy BR-101, the Museu Arqueológico e Oceanográfico (open daily from 9 am to 6 pm) is worth visiting, and there's a nude beach (a rarity in Brazil) at Praia do Pinho, 13km south of the city.

Porto Belo

• *pop 7800* ✉ *88210-000* ☎ *047*

The beaches around Porto Belo are the last good continental beaches before Ilha de Santa Catarina. **Praia de Bombas** (3km away) and **Praia Bombinhas** (7km from town) are the prettiest beaches around. For a great walk, head out to Ponta do Lobo, 12km from Praia Bombinhas. From Rua Manoel Felipe da Silva in Porto Belo, you can get a boat to the islands of Arvorerdo and João da Cunha. Both have fine beaches.

Places to Stay & Eat Both Praia de Bombas and Praia Bombinhas have *barracas* and camping grounds and are relatively uncrowded. At Praia de Bombas, *Pousada do Costão* (☎ 369-1402) has apartamentos with cooking facilities for US$35 a double. At Bombinhas, *Pousada Bombinhas* (☎ 369-1448) has singles/doubles for US$15/30. *Pousada Retiro dos Padres* (☎ 369-1467) at the end of Retiro dos Padres, and *Pousada Águas Claras* (☎ 326-7799) at No 329, Rua 420, are recommended mid-range options. On Avenida Governador Celso Ramos in Porto Belo, *La Ponte* at No 1988 and *Petiscão* at No 2170 both have tasty seafood.

Getting There & Away

There are 10 buses a day to Porto Belo (US$3, 40 minutes) from Balneário Camboriú. Semi-direto buses from Florianópolis and Joinville stop at Camboriú.

THE SOUTH

BLUMENAU

• *pop 230,000* ✉ *89000-000* ☎ *047*

Blumenau is 60km inland from Itajaí. Nestled in the Vale do Itajaí on the Rio Itajaí, Blumenau and its environs were settled largely by German immigrants in the second half of the 19th century. The area is serene, but the city is busy and promotes its German culture with the commercial flair of Walt Disney.

Information

Tourist Office There's an information booth in the centre, on the corner of Rua Nereu Ramos and Rua 15 de Novembro. Staff speak German, and have useful maps and information about other towns in the Itajaí.

Money The Bradesco branch at Rua 15 de Novembro 849 has Visa ATMs.

Post & Communications The post office is on Rua Padre Jacobs. The telephone office is at Rua 15 de Novembro 710 – it's just a small doorway off the street, so keep your eyes peeled.

Special Events

Blumenau hosts an increasingly popular Oktoberfest, from the first Friday in October.

Places to Stay

Hotel Herman (☎ 322-4370), Rua Floriano Peixoto 213, has single/double quartos for US$14/22 and apartamentos for US$20/36, including breakfast. The manager loves a chance to practise his German. Close by is the *City Hotel* (☎ 322-2205), Rua Ângelo Dias 263. Singles/doubles start at US$14/24. Readers have also recommended the *youth hostel* (☎ 323-4332), Rua São Paulo 2457.

Moving up the price scale, the rather grand *Hotel Gloria* (☎ 322-1988), Rua 7 de Setembro 954, has quartos for US$25/45 and apartamentos for US$35/60. Nearby at Rua Padre Jacobs 45, the *Hotel Garden Terrace* (☎ 326-3544) is Blumenau's fanciest sleepery. Rooms start at US$110/150.

The Beat of a Different Drum

The people of Blumenau arc largely the descendants of German immigrants who settled in the south of Brazil in the second half of the 19th century. Blue eyed, blonde and fair skinned, they are proud of their differences from other Brazilians and have kept their customs, language and architecture alive.

Tourists from all over Brazil come to experience this outpost of German culture, which reaches a peak during the first week of October, when the town hosts Brazil's biggest Oktoberfest. The party starts off in traditional fashion, with folk dancing displays by lederhosen-clad Blumenauns, folk songs, bratwurst and beer. But as the night wears on and the normally sedate southerners get a few *cervejas* under their belts, the party undergoes a change of direction.

Musicians have been flown over from Germany, but the brass and accordions are put away, and the sounds of samba and *frevo* take over. The good old German knees-up is abandoned, and the bump and grind of the black north-east fires the party on until the early hours of the morning.

Chris McAsey

Places to Eat

Some of cheaper hotels don't provide breakfast, so the best place to head is the *Cafehaus Gloria*, in the Hotel Gloria. Its US$5.50 café colonial is excellent.

Gruta Azul, Rua Rudolfo Freygang 8, has a lovely balcony overlooking the river, good German food and a harp player in the evening, if you're feeling romantic. Prices are reasonable for two, but watch out for the 'optional' appetisers. For Chinese food, try *Restaurante Chinês* on the corner of Rua 15 de Novembro and Avenida Rio Branco. You could try snacking at one of the chopperias near the Rua República Argentina bridge – the *Tunga* has pizza, chopp and live

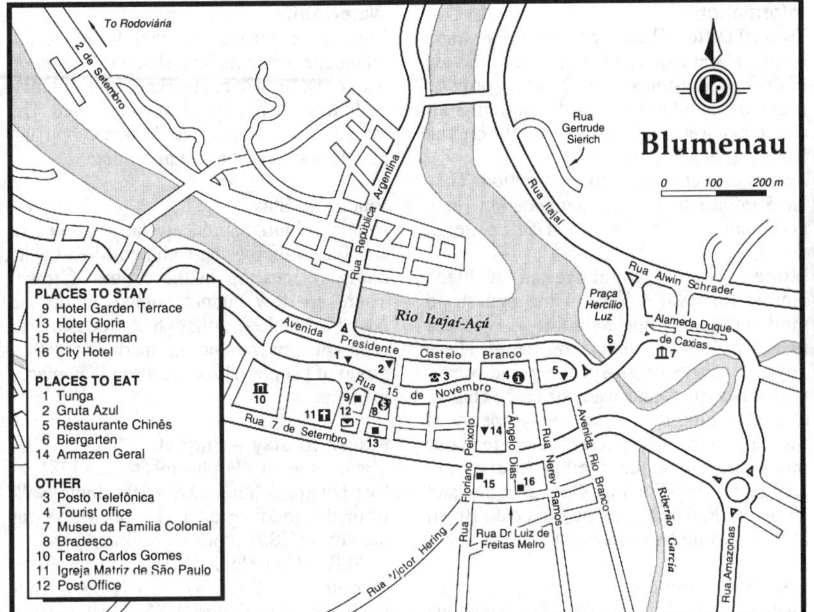

music. The *Biergarten* on Praça Hercílio Luz is another good spot for a beer and snack overlooking the river. *Armazen Geral*, Rua Floriano Peixoto 55, is where members of the 'young and blonde' meet and graze.

Getting There & Away

You can buy bus tickets in advance at the agencies around the corner of Rua Padre Jacobs and Rua 7 de Setembro. There are about 20 buses a day to Florianópolis from Blumenau. The direct buses (US$11, 2½ hours) leave at 8 am, noon, and 3 and 5.45 pm. Semi-diretos buses stop at Itajaí, Balneário Camboriú and Itapema, and take three hours. There are 15 buses a day to Joinville (US$9.50, 2½ hours), and eight to Curitiba (US$12, 4½ hours).

Getting Around

From inside the rodoviária, there are hourly buses to the city. Otherwise, walk out of the rodoviária to the far side of Avenida 2 de Setembro and take a Fortaleza or Troncal bus (US$0.75) to Rua 7 de Setembro in the centre. A taxi costs US$8.

FLORIANÓPOLIS

• *pop 275,000* ✉ *88000-000* ☎ *048*

Florianópolis, the state capital, fans out from the spot where the coast and the large Ilha de Santa Catarina almost connect. The two sides of the city are joined by two bridges, including Brazil's longest steel suspension bridge. The mainland part of the city has the industry, but the central section is on the island, facing the Baía Sul. Over the hill, on the northern shore, is a long row of luxury high-rises and modern restaurants.

The city is modern, but the island side, where you'll probably spend your time, has a small-city feel. It's easy to get around on foot, and there are regular public buses to the island's beautiful beaches.

Information

Tourist Office There are handy information booths at the rodoviária and next to the old *alfândega* (customs house). They provide maps, transport and hotel information. Staff can make reservations for hotels on the island. Spanish is spoken.

Lots of touts wait at the bus station. They have information on accommodation (they get commission of course), and can be useful.

Money There's an active street black market for cash dollars in the pedestrian mall on Rua Felipe Schmidt – even the tourist office will direct you there! These guys, mostly Spanish-speaking and armed with calculators and wads of cash, change at the top rate. It's all done very openly. If the situation has altered, change your money at a casa de câmbio (money-exchange house). For travellers cheques and Visa withdrawals, go to the Banco do Brasil at Praça 15 de Novembro 20.

Post & Communications The post office faces Praça 15 de Novembro. The telephone office is on the corner of Rua Dumont and Rua Visconde de Ouro Prêto.

Praça 15 de Novembro & Around

While you'll probably want to get out to the beaches as soon as possible, it's worth wandering around the city for a look at some of the colonial buildings.

From Praça 15 de Novembro and its 100-year-old **fig tree**, cross Rua Arcipestre to the pink **Palácio Cruz e Souza**. It's the state museum, but the most interesting things to see are the ornate parquetry floors and the outrageous 19th century ceilings. Entry is US$1. It's open Tuesday to Friday from 10 am to 7 pm, and on weekends from 1.30 pm to 7 pm.

On the high point of the praça is the **Catedral Metropolitana**; it was remodelled this century, so not much from the colonial era remains. The least-remodelled colonial church is the **Igreja de NS do Rosário**, further up from the cathedral on Rua Guilherme.

Waterfront

Back down on the old waterfront are the alfândega (customs house) and the *mercado municipal* (municipal market), both colonial buildings that have been well preserved. The market is a good place to drink a chopp and people-watch in the late afternoon.

Places to Stay

Hotels in Florianópolis are fairly expensive and fill up during the summer. Most of the budget places are in the centre of town. There are few budget hotels out on the island's beaches, although it's possible to economise by renting an apartment with a group of people. There are also many places to camp.

Places to Stay – Budget

There's a good YHA hostel (☎ 222-3781) at Rua Duarte Schutel 227, a 10 minute walk from the rodoviária. It charges US$8 for members (US$1 more for nonmembers).

At Rua Conselheiro Mafra 324, the *Hotel Cruzeiro* (☎ 222-0675) is seedy but friendly. Basic quartos cost US$10 per person. On the next parallel street you'll find the *Hotel Cacique* (☎ 222-5359), Rua Felipe Schmidt 423, popular with travellers and touts alike; it's good and often full. It has quartos for US$15/25 a single/double (if you bargain), and a few apartamentos for US$21/35. Breakfast is not included.

Another good place is the *Felippe Hotel* (☎ 222-4122), Rua João Pinto 26. It charges US$15 per person, with breakfast.

Places to Stay – Mid-Range

What this city lacks is a decent mid-range hotel in the centre of town. If you find one, please let us know. The *Hotel Valerim Centre* (☎ 222-1100), Rua Felipe Schmidt 554, has overpriced apartamentos for US$34/45 a single/double.

Places to Stay – Top End

On Avenida Hercílio Luz, you'll find two places that are reasonable value. At No 652, the *Hotel Genesis* (☎ 224-5388; fax 224-5890) has singles/doubles for US$70/100.

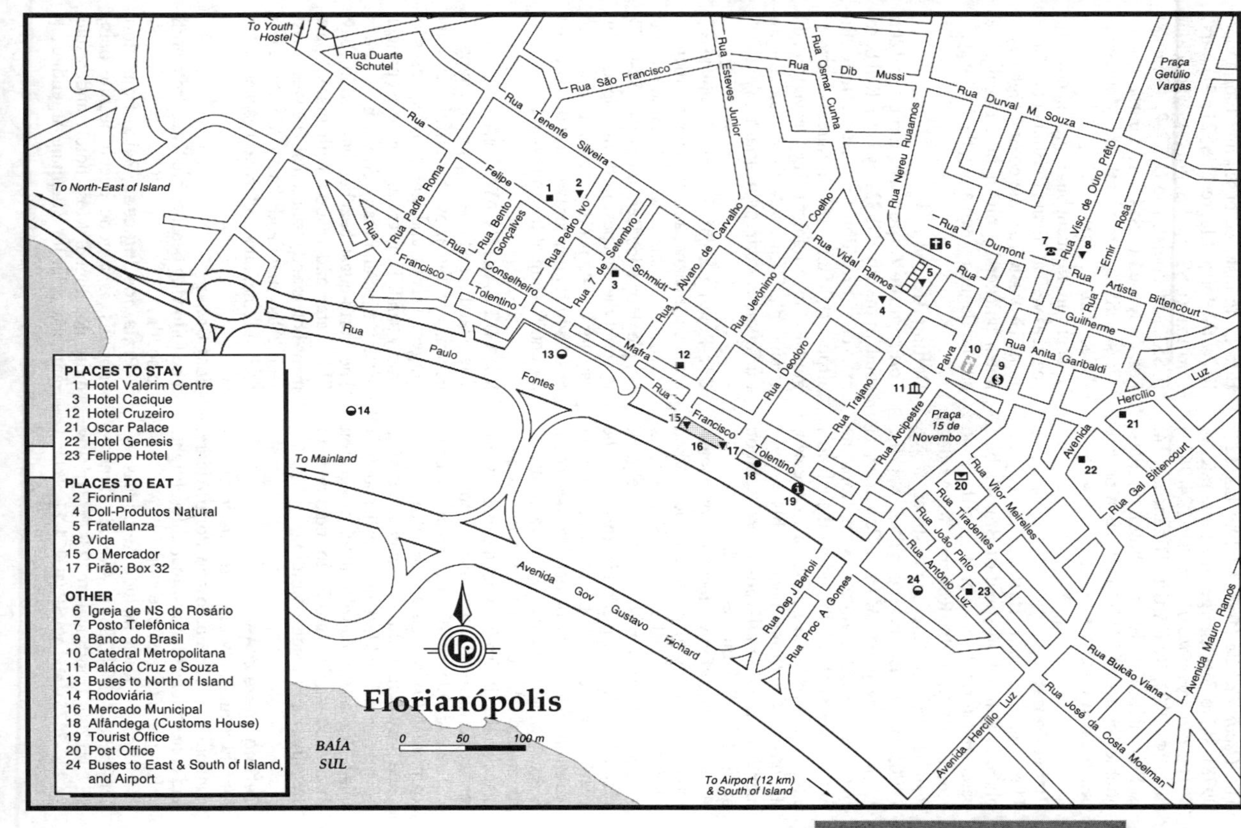
Florianópolis
BAÍA SUL
0 50 100 m
To Youth Hostel
To North-East of Island
To Mainland
To Airport (12 km) & South of Island
Praça Getúlio Vargas
Praça 15 de Novembro
Rua Duarte Schutel
Rua São Francisco
Rua Esteves Junior
Rua Osmar Cunha
Rua Dib Mussi
Rua Nereu Ruaamos
Rua Durval M Souza
Rua Visc de Ouro Prêto
Rua Emir Rosa
Rua Artista Bittencourt
Rua Tenente Silveira
Rua Felipe Schmidt
Rua Vidal Ramos
Rua Dumont
Rua Padre Roma
Rua Bento Gonçalves
Rua Pedro Ivo
Rua 7 de Setembro
Rua Álvaro de Carvalho
Coelho
Rua Jerônimo
Rua Deodoro
Rua Trajano
Rua Arcipestre Paiva
Rua Anita Garibaldi
Rua Guilherme
Rua Conselheiro Mafra
Rua Francisco Tolentino
Rua Paulo Fontes
Avenida Gov Gustavo Richard
Rua Vitor Meirelles
Rua Tiradentes
Rua João Pinto
Rua Antônio Luz
Rua Proc A Gomes
Rua Dep J Bertoli
Avenida Hercílio Luz
Rua Gal Bittencourt
Avenida Mauro Ramos
Rua Bulcão Viana
Rua José da Costa Moelman
PLACES TO STAY
1 Hotel Valerim Centre
3 Hotel Cacique
12 Hotel Cruzeiro
21 Oscar Palace
22 Hotel Genesis
23 Felippe Hotel
PLACES TO EAT
2 Fiorinni
4 Doll-Produtos Natural
5 Fratellanza
8 Vida
15 O Mercador
17 Pirão; Box 32
OTHER
6 Igreja de NS do Rosário
7 Posto Telefônica
9 Banco do Brasil
10 Catedral Metropolitana
11 Palácio Cruz e Souza
13 Buses to North of Island
14 Rodoviária
16 Mercado Municipal
18 Alfândega (Customs House)
19 Tourist Office
20 Post Office
24 Buses to East & South of Island, and Airport

The *Oscar Palace* (☎ 222-0099; fax 222-0978), at No 760, charges the same rate.

The *Florianópolis Palace* (☎ 224-9633; fax 224-2233), Rua Artista Bittencourt 14, is Florianópolis' five-star hotel. Singles/doubles cost US$131/143. It has a private beach out at Canasvieiras.

Places to Eat

The *Macarronada Italiana* is a great place to splurge on some of Brazil's best pasta and formal service. It's on the Baía Norte, at Avenida Rubens de Arruda Ramos 196. On the same street at No 1990, *Sushimasa* is expensive, but the sushi is very good. *Martim-Pescador*, at Beco do Surfista, about 18km from the city, serves seafood, including the island's excellent shrimp. In Lagoa da Conceicão, *Arante do Canto* has been highly recommended; it has an all-you-can-eat seafood buffet for US$8 on weekends.

In the centre of town, there are some interesting restaurants to try in the old market. *Pirão* has seafood dishes from US$6, and *Box 32* and *O Mercador* both have some great seafood snacks. The market is crowded in the evening, but can get a bit seedy as the night wears on. *Fratellanza*, on Estrada do Rosario, is an elegant restaurant with seafood dishes for around US$16 for two. *Fiorinni*, a quiet place on Rua Pedro Ivo with a small outdoor terrace, has fish and meat dishes from US$6.

There are plenty of cheap *lanchonetes* in town, many of which are health-food oriented – try *Doll-Produtos Natural* for vegie burgers or a breakfast of muesli and fruit salad. Vegetarians can also lunch at *Vida*, on Rua Visconde de Ouro Prêto, next door to the Alliance Française building.

Getting There & Away

Air There are daily direct flights from Florianópolis to São Paulo and Porto Alegre, and connections to most other cities. Flights to Rio make at least one stop.

Airlines in town include Aerolineas Argentinas (☎ 224-7835), Avenida Tenente Silveira 200, Transbrasil (☎ 223-7777), Varig (☎ 223-7475), and VASP (☎ 224-1122).

Bus Long-distance buses link Florianópolis with Porto Alegre (US$21, 7 hours), Curitiba (US$15, 4½ hours), São Paulo (US$32, 11 hours), Rio (US$52, 18 hours), Foz do Iguaçu (US$41, 16 hours), Buenos Aires (US$70, 26 hours) and Montevideo (US$56, 20 hours).

There are frequent buses up and down the coast, as well as inland to Blumenau. Travel along Hwy BR-101, the coastal highway, is much quicker by direct bus. Local buses can be flagged down along the highway.

Getting Around

To/From the Airport The airport is 12km south of the city (US$22 by taxi). Red buses marked Correador Sudoeste run to the airport (US$0.60, 45 minutes) every 15 minutes until midnight. They leave from the second platform away from Rua António Luz at the eastern rodoviária.

Car Renting a car is a good way to get around the island, and it's not too expensive if you split the cost with three or four people. Barcellos Rent a Car (☎ 982-0173) is about the cheapest in town. Cloves rents cars for US$45 per day including insurance, or US$40 per day for two days or more. Ask around for him at the rodoviária.

ILHA DE SANTA CATARINA

The island's east-coast beaches, facing the ocean, are the most beautiful, with the biggest waves and greatest expanses of empty sand. They are also the most popular for day trips and many do not have hotels. The north-coast beaches have calm, bay-like water and resorts with many apartment-hotels and restaurants. The west coast, facing the mainland, has a Mediterranean feel and small, unspectacular beaches.

East Coast

The following beaches are listed from north to south.

Praia dos Ingleses, 34km from Florianópolis, is a good beach despite being quite developed. Most hotels and restaurants here cater for Brazilian, Argentine and

Uruguayan tourists. *Sol & Mar* (☎ 269-1271) has the best-value accommodation in town. It's right on the beach, and has doubles for US$30.

Praia do Santinho has one of the island's most beautiful beaches and one good *pousada*. The coast road ends here, which keeps the traffic and crowds down, although there are some resort developments under construction at the southern end of the beach. *Pousada do Santinho* (☎ 269-2836) is highly recommended. Large, comfortable apartamentos with views cost US$25/36 for singles/doubles, with a big breakfast included. The hotel's restaurant serves good seafood meals, and there's a juice bar as well. The Ingleses bus from Florianópolis stops right at the door.

The island's longest beach, **Praia do Moçambique** (or Praia Grande), is 14km long and undeveloped. A pine forest hides it from the road (SC-406) that runs a couple of kilometres inland from it. The camping here is good. The closest accommodation is at **Rio Vermelho**, close to the lagoa on SC-406. There are a couple of pousadas along the main road, including the basic *Pousada Chácara Passiflora* (☎ 269-1638), and the more upmarket *Pousada Ryo Vermelho* (☎ 269-1337), in a quiet bush setting 400m off SC-406.

Barra da Lagoa, a big, curved beach at the end of Praia do Moçambique, is a short bus trip from Florianópolis. It's still home to indigenous fishermen, descended from the original Azorean colonists. Although there are more hotels and restaurants here than anywhere on the east coast (except Praia dos Ingleses), they aren't modern eyesores. There are plenty of houses for rent. A good place to stay is the *Gaivota* (☎ 232-3253), run by a friendly family. Try to get a front room. Small singles/doubles cost US$15/20 with breakfast included. A few doors away, *Lanchonete Barba Branco* serves great seafood pasteis. Further along the bay at Rua Angelina Joaquim dos Santos 300, *Pousada 32* (☎ 232-3232) has two-room flats for four people at US$70.

Praia Mole is a beautiful stretch of beach, with one hotel, the four-star *Cabanas da Praia Mole* (☎ 232-0231; fax 232-0482). Rooms cost around US$166/200. The beach is very hip in summer – there's plenty of opportunity for people-watching and noshing at the beach barracas.

Praia da Joaquina hosts the Brazilian surfing championship in January and is the busiest beach on the island. The surf pumps, but the beachfront is pretty barren. There are a few restaurants overlooking the beach. You might want to try dune-surfing on the Joaquina dunes – you can hire a board there. The *Joaquina Beach Hotel* (☎ 232-0059) has doubles for US$50. *Hotel Cris* (☎ 232-0380; fax 232-0075) is cheaper: doubles cost US$35 (US$95 in the high season). About 1km back along the approach road, *Pousada Felicidade da Ilha*, run by Dona França, has apartamentos with cooking facilities for US$15/25. Close by, *Pousada Bizkaia* (☎ 232-0273) has doubles for US$30. There is a shady restaurant attached.

The three main beaches to the south are more remote, and quite spectacular. **Praia do Campeche** has a few barracas, and the beach is long enough for everyone to find a private patch of sand. The only place to stay is the upmarket *Pousada São Sebastião* (☎ 237-4066), around 2km from the main beach.

Praia da Armação is similarly undeveloped. As at Campeche, the current is often strong.

Pântano do Sul, at the end of the sealed road, is a small fishing village with a couple of restaurants. The mountains close in on the sea, which is calm and protected. The *Pousada Sol da Costa* (☎/fax 222-5071) is a tranquil place on the beach at Costa de Dentro, about 4km past Pântano do Sul. Double apartamentos with cooking facilities start at US$20 and the owner, Valdir, speaks English.

To get there, take the Costa de Dentro bus from Florianópolis. If you're driving, turn right just before entering the village of Pântano do Sul, then continue on past the newly developed Praia das Açores until you reach Costa de Dentro.

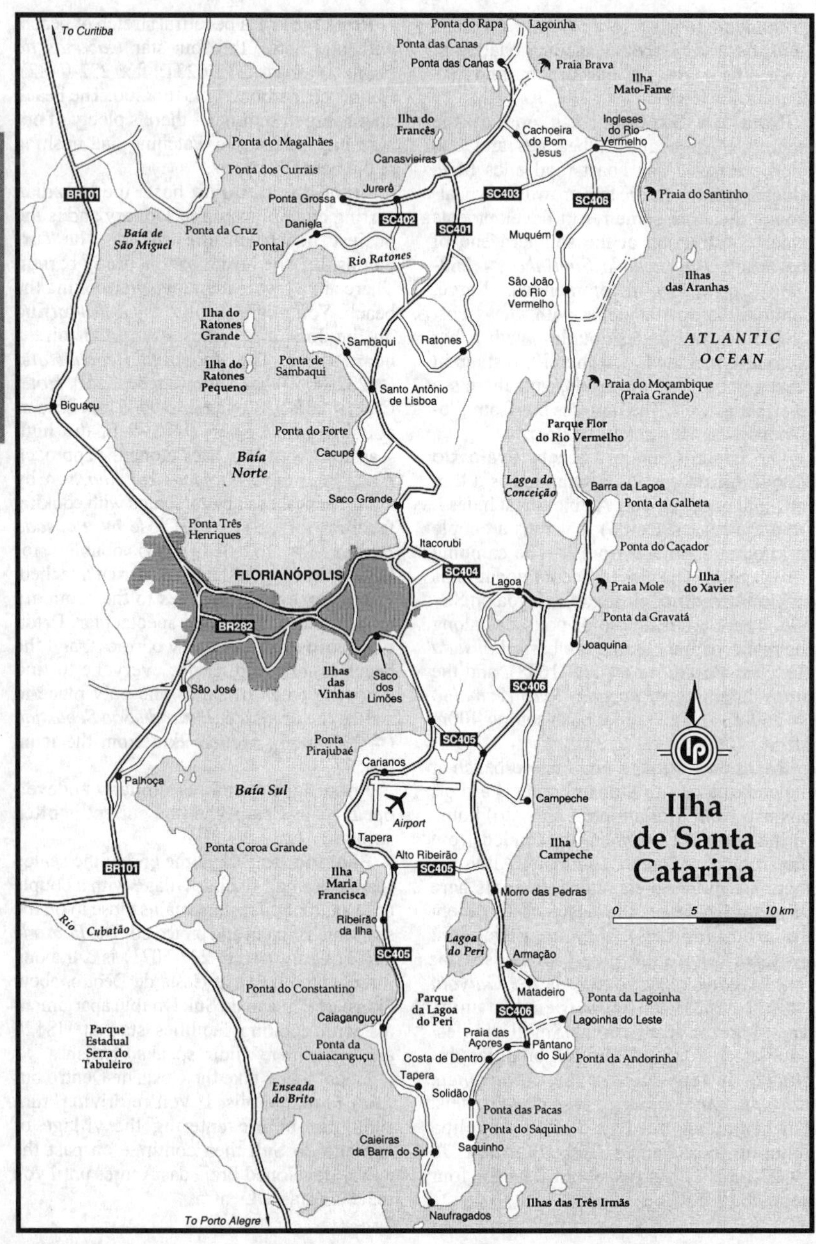
To Curitiba
Ponta do Rapa
Lagoinha
Ponta das Canas
Ponta das Canas
Praia Brava
Ilha Mato-Fame
Ilha do Francês
Cachoeira do Bom Jesus
Ingleses do Rio Vermelho
Ponta do Magalhães
Ponta dos Currais
Canasvieiras
BR101
Jurerê
SC403
Ponta Grossa
SC406
Praia do Santinho
SC402
SC401
Daniela
Baía de São Miguel
Ponta da Cruz
Muquém
Pontal
Rio Ratones
São João do Rio Vermelho
Ilhas das Aranhas
Ilha do Ratones Grande
Sambaqui
Ratones
ATLANTIC OCEAN
Ilha do Ratones Pequeno
Ponta de Sambaqui
Santo Antônio de Lisboa
Praia do Moçambique (Praia Grande)
Biguaçu
Parque Flor do Rio Vermelho
Ponta do Forte
Cacupé
Baía Norte
Lagoa da Conceição
Barra da Lagoa
Saco Grande
Ponta da Galheta
Ponta Três Henriques
Itacorubi
Ponta do Caçador
FLORIANÓPOLIS
SC404
Lagoa
Ilha do Xavier
Praia Mole
BR282
Ponta da Gravatá
Joaquina
Ilhas das Vinhas
Saco dos Limões
São José
SC406
SC405
Ponta Pirajubaé
Carianos
Palhoça
Baía Sul
Campeche
Airport
Ilha de Santa Catarina
Tapera
Ilha Campeche
Ponta Coroa Grande
Alto Ribeirão
BR101
SC405
Ilha Maria Francisca
Morro das Pedras
0
5
10 km
Ribeirão da Ilha
Rio Cubatão
Lagoa do Peri
SC405
Armação
Matadeiro
Ponta do Constantino
Parque da Lagoa do Peri
Ponta da Lagoinha
SC406
Lagoinha do Leste
Caiaganguçu
Parque Estadual Serra do Tabuleiro
Praia das Açores
Pântano do Sul
Ponta da Cuaiacanguçu
Costa de Dentro
Ponta da Andorinha
Tapera
Enseada do Brito
Solidão
Ponta das Pacas
Ponta do Saquinho
Saquinho
Caieiras da Barra do Sul
Ilhas das Três Irmãs
Naufragados
To Porto Alegre

The area is one of the best places on the island for observing birds and other wildlife. There are some great walks along the hilly trails from either Armação or Pântano do Sul.

North Coast

The north coast is the most developed coast on the island, and the beaches are narrow; however, the sea here is calm and warm.

Canasvieiras has many (mostly expensive) apartments and holiday homes, and during summer it also boasts nightlife. It's one of the busiest beach towns on the island, and plenty more construction has been planned.

There's a YHA youth hostel (☎ 223-1692) at Rua Dr João de Oliveira 100 and a few apartment-hotels that are affordable for groups of three or four. *Hotel Residêncial Locabana* (☎ 266-0400), five minutes from the beach at Avenida das Nações 525, has two-room flats with cooking facilities for US$25. The *Canasbeach Hotel* (☎ 266-1227), one block from the beach at Avenida Madre Maria Villac 1150, has comfortable double apartamentos for US$50.

A few kilometres west, **Jurerê** is similar, but a bit quieter. Out at Praia do Forte are the ruins of the **Fortaleza de São José da Ponta Grossa**, built in 1750. Jurerê has two top-end hotels, including the *Jurerê Praia Hotel* (☎ 282-1108; fax 282-1644).

West Coast

If you want to explore the west coast, **Sambaqui**, north of Florianópolis, makes a charming and peaceful base. There are a handful of barracas, and on weekends there are usually some beach-goers in the area. After the town and the barracas, keep walking along the road to some tiny, secluded beaches with good views.

On the south-west coast, the old colonial town of **Ribeirão da Ilha** has an impressive little church, the **Igreja NS da Lapa**.

The Interior

It's not just the beaches: the whole island is beautiful. **Lagoa da Conceição** is the most famous region in the interior, but it gets busy, even during the week. The views of the lagoon, surrounding peaks and sand dunes make for some great walks or boat rides. Boats can be hired right next to the bridge. A typical price is US$20 for two hours, but the boats can take up to 10 people.

One of the cheaper places to stay is the *Chales do Canto* (☎ 232-0471), Rua Laurindo Januário da Silveira 2212. Small chalets for up to four people cost US$35. At *Hotel Cabanas Ilha da Magia* (☎ 232-0468), right next to the spot on the lake where you hire boats, cosy (or pokey, depending on how claustrophobic you are) cabanas for two people cost US$30. The bus can drop you right outside.

If you're heading south by car from Lagoa, the turn-off is unmarked. Take the road on the left just before the bridge, or you'll be back in Florianópolis before you know it. On the way down south, the turn-off to Lagoa do Peri is at Morro das Pedras. The lake is fun to explore.

Getting Around

Local buses serve all of the island's beach towns, but the schedule changes with the season, so check the times at the tourist office or at the central rodoviária in Florianópolis. During summer, additional microbuses leave from the centre and go directly to the beaches. These microbuses take surfboards; regular buses don't.

The buses for the east and south of the island (including Lagoa and Joaquina) leave from the local bus terminal in front of Rua Antônio Luz. Buses for the north leave from the local bus terminal close to the rodoviária. Buses, with their destinations clearly marked, include services for Sambaqui, Lagoa da Conceição, Rio Vermelho, Moçambique, Campeche, Barra da Lagoa, Canasvieiras (Jurerê), Pântano do Sul, Costa de Dentro, and Ingleses (which continues on to Praia do Santinho).

The island is one of those places where a one day car rental is a good idea (see the Florianópolis Getting Around section).

With a car, you can check out most of the island and pick a beach to settle on. Alternatively, try one of the bus tours offered by the travel agencies. Itaguatur (☎ 241-0333) has a good one, costing US$15 for an eight hour tour.

Scuna-Sul (☎ 224-1806) has a range of boat excursions around the island. A three hour Baía Norte cruise on a big sailing boat costs US$15.

SOUTH OF FLORIANÓPOLIS

Garopaba

• *pop 11,800 ✉ 88495-000 ☎ 048*

The first beach town south of Florianópolis, Garopaba, is 95km away, including a 15km drive from the Hwy BR-101. The beaches are good, but the town hasn't been overrun by tourists and you can still see fishermen at work. Garopaba is the base for Mormaii Surfwear, which sponsors a big surfing contest in August. Praia do Silveira, 3km away, has good surf, and Siriú (11km) has large sand dunes.

Places to Stay For a cheap sleep, there are lots of camping grounds on Praia Garopaba. Or ask around for rooms in houses. One block back from the beach at Rua Marques Guimarães 81, *Lobo Hotel* (☎ 254-3129) is a friendly, family-run place with apartamentos for US$12/20 for singles/doubles, including breakfast. *Pousada da Praia* (☎ 254-3334), Avenida dos Pescadores 121, is pretty bland, but it's well situated on the beach front. Apartamentos here cost US$20/25.

Places to Eat *Viva Mar*, next to the church on Praça Governor Ivo Silveira, serves good seafood. For a cheaper seafood feed, try the buffet at *Champagne*, Avenida dos Pescadores 51, along the beachfront.

Getting There & Away There are 14 buses a day to Garopaba from Florianópolis (US$6.50, two hours). There are two bus agencies in town: buses to the south, including Porto Alegre, leave from Praça Governor Ivo Silveira. Buses to the north, including Florianópolis, leave from Rua Antônio Claudine de Sousa, one block from the beach.

There are more regular intercity buses leaving from Imbituba on Hwy BR-101, or from the bus terminal in Araçatuba, a suburb of Imbituba. Many of the buses to Porto Alegre stop at Laguna and Tubarão.

Laguna

• *pop 44,000 ✉ 88790-000 ☎ 048*

Laguna has an active fishing industry and is the centre of tourism for the southern coast. Situated on the line that once divided the Americas between Spain and Portugal in the Treaty of Tordesillas in 1494, it's an historic city, settled by Paulistas in the 1670s. Laguna was occupied by the farrapos soldiers and declared a republic in 1839 in the Guerra dos Farrapos, which was fought between republicans and monarchists.

Information Banco do Brasil and Bradesco, both on Rua Cons Jerônimo Coelho, have Visa ATMs.

Museums If it's raining, have a look at **Museu Anita Garibaldi** on Praça República Juliana. It honours the Brazilian wife of the Italian leader and is open from 8 am to noon and 2 to 6 pm. Entry is US$2. The **Casa de Anita Garibaldi**, on Praça Vidal Ramos, contains some of her personal possessions and is open the same hours.

Beaches The best beaches are out at **Farol de Santa Marta**, 18km from the city plus a 10 minute ferry ride. It's a laid back place and there are beautiful dunes. You can camp or ask about rooms to rent in houses. There are two mid-range pousadas, the *Jurika* (☎ 986-4000) and *Pousada Farol de Santa Marta* (☎ 986-1257). Both have doubles for around US$50.

Mar Grosso, the city beach, is lined with concrete high-rise hotels and restaurants, but the beach itself is OK.

Places to Stay & Eat Hotels in Laguna seem to be closed a lot of the time. Your best bets are the *Hotel Recanto* (☎ 644-0902), on the waterfront at Rua Avenida Engenho Colombo Salles 108, and *Hotel Beira Mar* (☎ 644-0260), 100m away on the same street. In Mar Grosso, there's a youth hostel (☎ 644-0015) at Avenida João Pinho 530. The *Ondão* (☎ 647-0940), on Avenida Rio Grande do Sul, has grungy singles/doubles for US$12/ 20. Seafood is the order of the day. In Mar Grosso, try *Arrastão*, Avenida Senador Galotti 629, or *Spettus*, at No 418.

Getting There & Away There are plenty of buses going north to Florianópolis. If you're travelling south to beach towns in Rio Grande do Sul, take a bus to Vila São João (US$6.50, four hours), where you can pick up a connecting bus to Torres.

Getting Around Buses run to Farol de Santa Marta from Laguna daily except Sunday, leaving from the rodoviária and the 'Balsa' (where the ferry crosses the lagoon), about 3km from town. Grab a timetable from the Zannattatur agency at the rodoviária.

South of Laguna

Further south are the coal-mining towns of Tubarão and Criciúma. Unless you want to go to the mineral baths, there's no reason to stay in either. Both are serviced by regular buses along the coastal route. From Tubarão you can get to several mineral baths, including Termas do Gravatal (20km), Termas da Gurada (12km) and those on the Rio do Pouso (19km).

The radioactive mineral waters found here are said to heal rheumatism, ulcers and a variety of other ailments. Unfortunately, none of the hotels around the termas is inexpensive. There is camping, however, or you can come up from Tubarão for the day.

SÃO JOAQUIM

• *pop 22,000* ✉ *88600-000* ☎ *049*

São Joaquim is Brazil's highest city, at 1355m. Not many foreigner travellers come to Brazil for snow, but if they did, this is the place. The mountains are scenic in winter.

Bom Jardim da Serra

Bom Jardim da Serra, in the middle of the Serra do Rio do Rastro, is a hair-raising but beautiful 45km drive from São Joaquim. The **Parque Nacional de São Joaquim** is here. It's completely undeveloped, so if you want to explore, contact Ibama in Florianópolis (☎ (048) 224-6077) or in Urubici, 56km from São Joaquim (☎ (049) 278-4002), or ask about hiring a local guide.

Places to Stay

One of the cheapest places to stay around here is the *Minuano* (☎ 233-0656). Double chalets cost US$35. It's at Rua Urubici 230, next to the Parque da Maçá. The *Nevada* (☎ 233-0259), Rua Manoel Joaquim Pinto 190, has singles/doubles for US$20/40.

An alternative is the *Fazenda Santa Rita* (☎ 232-0170). It's close to the national park, 31km on the São Joaquim to Bom Jardim da Serra road. Visitors can ride horses, swim in the river or walk on nearby nature trails. The fee is US$45 per person.

Places to Eat

For a good churrasco lunch, try the *Schilichting* at Rua Aristides Cassão 117. *Casa da Pedra*, Praça Cesário Amarante 360, has a rodízio de pizza for US$5.

Getting There & Away

There's a daily bus from Florianópolis to São Joaquim at 6.15 pm.

Rio Grande do Sul

PORTO ALEGRE

• pop 1.3 million ✉ 90000-000 ☎ 051

Porto Alegre, Brazil's sixth biggest city, lies on the eastern bank of the Rio Guaíba at the point where its waters empty into the huge Lagoa dos Patos. This lively modern city makes a living from its freshwater port and commerce. Settled by the Portuguese in 1755 to keep the Spanish out, Porto Alegre was never a centre of colonial Brazil; it's mainly a product of the 20th century, which is when many of the German and Italian immigrants arrived here.

Although many travellers just pass through Porto Alegre, it's an easy place in which to spend a few days. There are some interesting museums and impressive neoclassical buildings, as well as some good restaurants and nightlife, and the friendly *gaúcho* (cowboy) hospitality.

Information

Don't forget that Porto Alegre has distinct seasonal weather changes: it gets very hot in summer (30 to 40°C) and you need a good jacket in winter. City beaches are too polluted for swimming, but the once popular Ipanema beach has some good bars and cafés.

Tourist Office Epatur (☎ 225-4744), the tourist information agency for the city, is at Travessa do Carmo 84. To get there, walk south on Avenida Borges de Medeiros, then turn left into Avenida Loureiro da Silva. Walk about 100m and you'll see the office on the right-hand side. It has excellent maps of the city and English is spoken. It's open Monday to Friday from 9 am to 6 pm. Epatur also has information booths at the rodoviária, which is open every day from 7 am to 7 pm; in the *prefeitura* (city hall) on Praça 15 de Novembro; and at the airport.

Setur (☎ 224-4784) has information about both city and state. It's close to Epatur at Avenida Borges de Medeiros 1501, 10th floor. The office is open Monday to Friday from 8.30 am to noon, and 1.30 to 6 pm.

Foreign Consulates The following South American countries are represented by consulates in Port Alegre:

Argentina
: Rua Prof Annes Dias 112, 1st floor (☎ 224-6799)

Paraguay
: Rua Quintino Bocaiuva 554, room 302 (☎ 346-1314)

Uruguay
: Rua Siqueira Campos 1171, 6th floor (☎ 224-3499)

Other countries with consulates in Porto Alegre include Germany, Austria, Denmark, Spain, France, UK, Italy, Japan, The Netherlands, Sweden and Switzerland. Epatur, the city tourist information agency, can give you a complete list of addresses and telephone numbers.

Money There are lots of *casas de câmbio* (money-exchange houses) in Porto Alegre. Try Prontur, Avenida Borges de Medeiros 445, or Aerotur, Rua dos Andradas 1137. The Banco do Brasil at Avenida Uruguai 195 has a câmbio and Visa ATMs. For 24 hour Visa withdrawals, Bradesco is at Rua Vigário José Inácio 494, but this area can be seedy at night.

Post & Telephone The post office is at Rua Siqueira Campos 1100. Make telephone calls from CRT, Avenida Borges de Medeiros 512, on the corner of Avenida Salgado Filho.

Museu Histórico Júlio de Castilhos Near the cathedral at Rua Duque de Caixas 1231, this interesting museum contains diverse objects concerning the history of the state: such as special moustache cups, a pair of giant's shoes and a very intricate wooden chair. It's open from 9 am to 5 pm Tuesday to Friday, and from 1 to 5 pm on weekends.

Museu de Arte do Rio Grande do Sul In the Praça da Alfândega, this museum has a good collection of works by gaúcho artists. It is open from 10 am to 7 pm Tuesday to Sunday.

Mercado Público

Constructed in 1869, the *mercado* (market) is a lively one, and lots of stalls sell the unique tea-drinking equipment of the gaúchos: the *cuia* (gourd) and *bomba* (silver straw).

Parque Farroupilha

This big, central park (also known as Parque da Redenção) is a good place to see gaúchos at play. If you're due for some exercise, why not rent a bicycle here. On Sunday morning, the Brique da Redenção (a market/fair) fills up a corner of the park with antiques, leather goods and music.

Centro de Tradição Gaúcho

If you're really interested in gaúcho traditions, check out this institute at Rua Guilherme Schell 60, in Santo Antônio.

Morro Santa Teresa

Porto Alegre is renowned for its stunning sunsets which reflect off the waters of the Rio Guaíba. A good place to watch one is Morro Santa Teresa, 6km from the city centre. This 131m hill provides good views of the city and the river but the area is a bit hairy after dark. On the way up there, have a look at Porto Alegre's unusual high-rise cemetery.

To get to Morro Santa Teresa, catch a Nova Santa Teresa bus from Rua Uruguai in the Centro.

River Cruises

The *Cisne Branco* operates tourist cruises on the river, passing many of the uninhabited islands in the river delta. There is a range of trips from 'happy hour' cruises (US$10) to three hour dinner cruises (US$28). The sunset cruises are popular. The boat leaves from the waterfront at the. end of Rua Caldas Júnior, Centro. Timetables change frequently so ask for a schedule at the tourist office.

Places to Stay – Budget

The *Hotel Ritz* (☎ 225-3423), Avenida André da Rocha 225, is Porto Alegre's youth hostel. It's well located close to the centre of town. English and Spanish are spoken.

The *Hotel Uruguai* (☎ 228-7864), Rua Dr Flores 371, is a secure and cheap place to stay. Single/double quartos cost US$9/18, and apartamentos cost US$11/22. Nearby at Avenida Vigarió José Inácio 644 the very friendly *Hotel Palácio* (☎ 225-3467) is popular with travellers. Large quartos cost US$20/30 a single/double, and apartamentos go for US$28/36.

Over on Rua Andrade Neves there are a few hotels (and some good bars and places to eat). The *Hotel Marechal* (☎ 228-3076) is a bit grungy, but it's often full. Quartos cost US$10 per person.

An interesting place to stay is the *Hotel Praça Matriz* (☎ 225-5772), which is in an ornate old building right on Praça da Matriz, at Largo João Amorim de Albequerque 72. Comfortable apartamentos with TV and fridge cost US$25/35.

Places to Stay – Mid-Range

On Rua Andrade Neves there are two good mid-range options. *Hotel Lancaster* (☎ 224-4737) has single/double apartamentos for US$35/50. The entrance to the hotel is at Travessa Eng Acelino de Cavalho 67. The *Metrópole* (☎ 226-1800), Rua Andrade Neves 59, has bright but smallish apartamentos for US$32/44. The *Hotel Santa Catarina* (☎ 224-9044) at Rua General Vitorino 240 has standard apartamentos for US$37/52.

Places to Stay – Top End

The grand *City Hotel* (☎ 224-2988), Rua Dr José Montaury 20, has rooms starting at US$72/90. The *Lido* (☎ 226-8233; fax 226-8009), Rua Gen Andrade Neves 150, is another elegant top-end alternative. Singles/doubles cost US$75/89.

Places to Eat

The city abounds in *churrascarias* (restaurants featuring barbecued meat): the steaks here are very tender, so it's a good place to get your iron level up. On the flip side (Porto Alegrenses love contrasts) there's

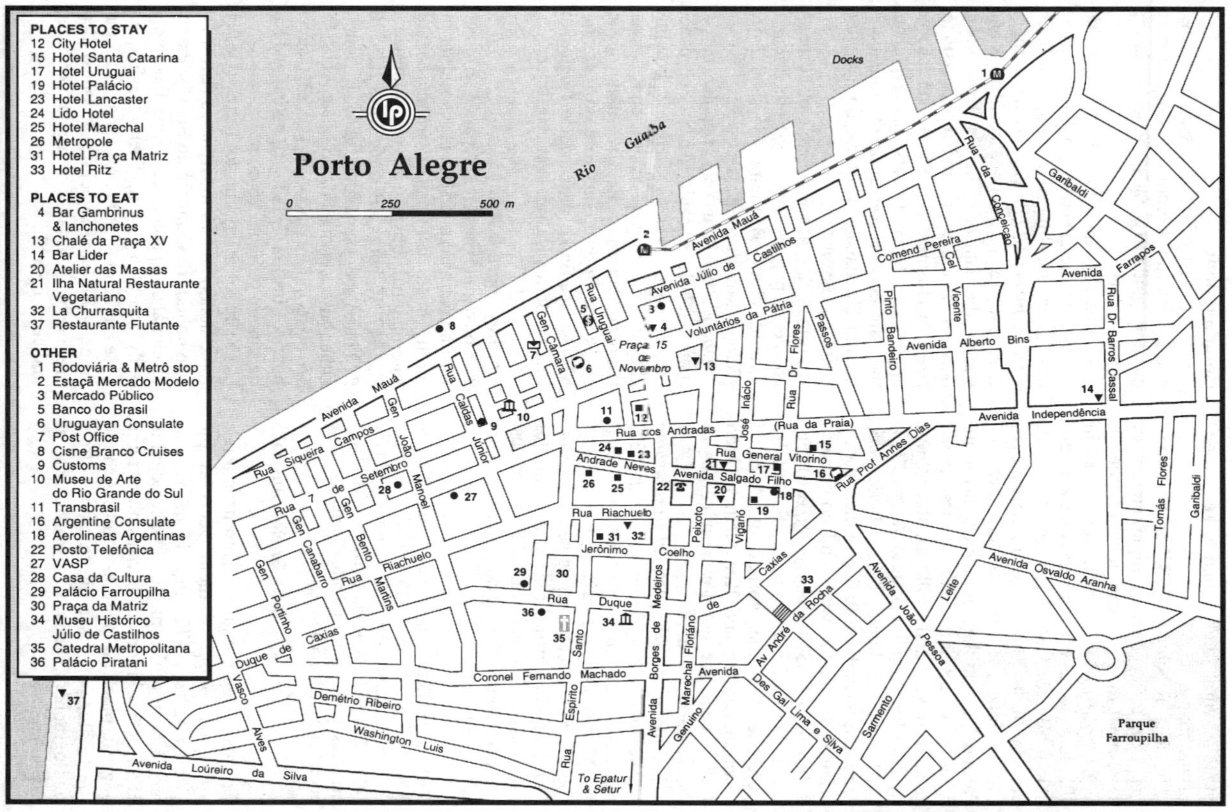
Porto Alegre
0 250 500 m
PLACES TO STAY
12 City Hotel
15 Hotel Santa Catarina
17 Hotel Uruguai
19 Hotel Palácio
23 Hotel Lancaster
24 Lido Hotel
25 Hotel Marechal
26 Metropole
31 Hotel Pra ça Matriz
33 Hotel Ritz
PLACES TO EAT
4 Bar Gambrinus & lanchonetes
13 Chalé da Praça XV
14 Bar Lider
20 Atelier das Massas
21 Ilha Natural Restaurante Vegetariano
32 La Churrasquita
37 Restaurante Flutante
OTHER
1 Rodoviária & Metrô stop
2 Estaçã Mercado Modelo
3 Mercado Público
5 Banco do Brasil
6 Uruguayan Consulate
7 Post Office
8 Cisne Branco Cruises
9 Customs
10 Museu de Arte do Rio Grande do Sul
11 Transbrasil
16 Argentine Consulate
18 Aerolineas Argentinas
22 Posto Telefônica
27 VASP
28 Casa da Cultura
29 Palácio Farroupilha
30 Praça da Matriz
34 Museu Histórico Júlio de Castilhos
35 Catedral Metropolitana
36 Palácio Piratani

enough natural food around to keep vegetarians happy.

At Rua Riachuelo 1331 is *La Churrasquita*, a vegetarian's nightmare, with more meat than you can poke a barbecue fork at. *Bar Lider*, Avenida Independência 408, is a casual bar/restaurant serving delicious filé for US$13 (enough for two). *Bar do Beto*, Rua Venâncio Aires 876, Cidade Baixa (near the southern corner of Parque Farroupilha), is a local favourite for juicy steaks and salads. For traditional gaúcho cooking and a folkloric floor show, try *Tio Flor*, Avenida Getúlio Vargas 1700.

At Rua Riachuelo 1482, *Atelier das Massas* is an ambient Italian restaurant with original art on the walls and good pasta dishes from US$10 (enough for two). For vegetarian food with an Indian flavour, try *Ocidente*, on the corner of Avenida Osvaldo Aranha and Rua General João Telles, near the north-eastern corner of Parque Farroupilha.

For lunch, the *Ilha Natural Restaurante Vegetariano*, Rua General Vitorino 35, packs the locals in for a vegetarian buffet. The Mercado Público has a central food hall and a bunch of cafés on its perimeter. *Bar Gambrinus* is a rustic little place famous for its tainha fish filled with shrimp, or just wander around the market and see what takes your fancy.

Caffeine addicts should check out *Café á Brasileira*, Rua Uruguai 310, or *Café Anglais*, in the Galéria Pedro Barcellos, Rua dos Andradas 1438. *Cafe Haiti*, Avenida Otavio Rocha 151, is the oldest espresso bar in Porto Alegre, and has a good buffet restaurant upstairs.

Mark Groves, Australia

One real Alegre tradition is to have a late afternoon *chopp* (draught beer) at the *Chalé da Praça XV*, Praça 15 de Novembro, in front of the market. Constructed in 1885, it's a landmark bar/restaurant and a great place to people-watch. Around the Chalé, you'll see old-fashioned street photographers, known in Portuguese as *lambe-lambes*.

Entertainment

From a tourist office, newsstand or large hotel, pick up a copy of *Programa*, a monthly guide to what's happening in the city and state.

At Rua dos Andrades 736, the *Casa da Cultura* is the place to go for art-house movies and local theatre. On the 7th floor, *Café Concerto Majestic* has an outdoor terrace where you can have a cold drink and watch the sunset. There's free music between 7 and 9 pm and the occasional street performer. A US$5 cover charge applies after 9 pm. Locals also rave about the sunsets at *Restaurante Flutuante*, behind the Espaço Cultural do Trabalho Usina do Gasômetro.

Porto Alegre has an active club scene. A couple of popular gay clubs are *Enigma*, Avenida Pinto Bandeira 485, and *Doce Vicio*, at Rua Vieira de Castro 32.

Dado Bier is a very popular bar at Avenida Nilo Peçanha 3228. For dance music, bowl over to *Strike*, a bowling alley/dance club (yep, really!) on Rua Cristiano do Patricínio. For live indie music, check out *Opinão*, Rua José do Patricínio 834, Cidade Baixo, or *Garagem Magica*, on Rua Dr Barros Cassal, near Bar Lider.

Getting There & Away

The busy rodoviária has separate terminals for international/interstate buses and for intercity buses within Rio Grande do Sul. International buses run to Montevideo (US$47, 12 hours), Buenos Aires (US$76, 22 hours) and Asunción (US$48, 15 hours). Other buses service Foz do Iguaçu (US$45, 16 hours), Florianópolis (US$21, seven hours), Curitiba (US$25, 10 hours) and Rio de Janeiro (US$68, 26 hours).

Ten buses a day run to Torres (US$11, three hours) and 10 to Gramado (US$7.50, two hours). To Cambará do Sul (for Parque Nacional de Aparados da Serra), there's one daily bus at 6.15 am. There are frequent buses to Pelotas and Rio Grande. To Santo Angelo (for São Miguel das Missões) there are five buses a day. The trip takes 6 hours and costs US$27.50.

Getting Around

Porto Alegre has a one-line metrô that the locals call Trensurb. It has 15 stations, but the only useful ones for visitors are the central station by the port (Estação Mercado Modelo), the rodoviária (the next stop) and the airport (three stops further on). A ride costs US$0.50.

SERRA GAÚCHA

North of Porto Alegre, you quickly begin to climb into the Serra Gaúcha. The bus ride is beautiful, as are the mountain towns of Gramado and Canela. Settled first by Germans (in 1824) and later by Italians (in the 1870s), the region is as close to the Alps as Brazil gets. It's known as the Região das Hortênsias (Hydrangea Region). Both Gramado and Canela are popular resorts and are often crowded with Porto Alegrenses, particularly when it's hot in the big city. There are plenty of hotels and restaurants, especially in Gramado, and many have a German influence.

Hikers abound in the mountains here. In winter there are occasional snowfalls and in spring the hills are blanketed with flowers. The best spot is the Parque Estadual do Caracol, reached by local bus from Canela.

Gramado

• *pop 25,200* ✉ *95670-000* ☎ *054*

This popular mountain resort promotes itself as 'Naturally European' and is a favourite with well-to-do Argentines, Uruguayans, Paulistas and gaúchos. It has lots of cosy restaurants, manicured gardens and expensive, Swiss-style chalet/hotels.

Information There's a useful Centro de Informações in the centre of town on Praça Major Nicoletti. It's open from 9 am to 8 pm. The Banco do Brasil on Rua Garibaldi has a câmbio and Visa ATMs.

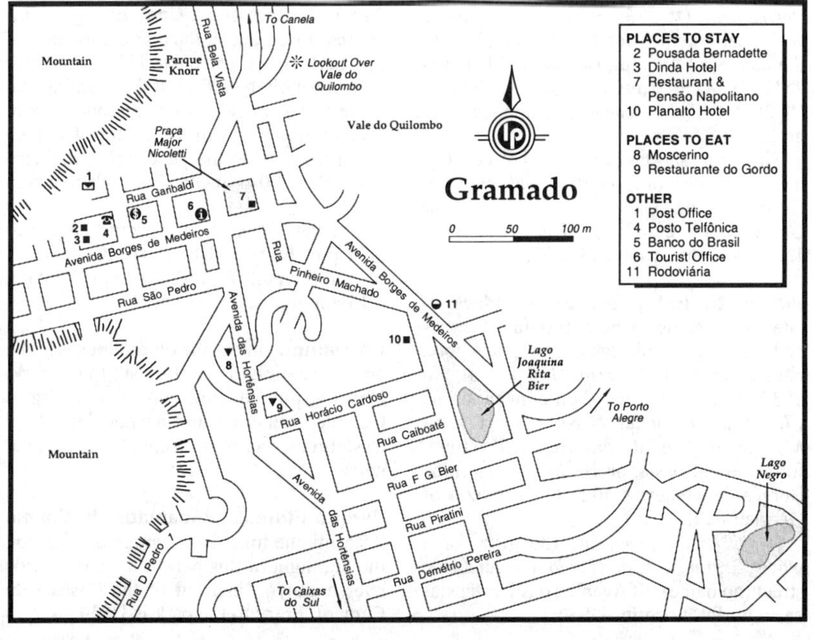

Parks Well-kept parks close to town include the Lago Negro, Rua 25 de Julho 175, and the Parque Knorr at the end of Rua Bela Vista. The Lago Negro park has a small lake, while the Parque Knorr has good views of the spectacular Vale do Quilombo. There's also the Lago Joaquina Rita Bier, a lake surrounded by hydrangeas at Rua Leopoldo Rosenfeldt.

Special Events Each year, usually in August, Gramado hosts the Brazilian Film Festival. It's a big event which attracts the jet set.

Places to Stay There's no cheap accommodation in Gramado. The *Hotel Planalto* (☎ 286-1210), Avenida Borges de Medeiros 2001 near the rodoviária, has one of the best deals in town. Single/double apartamentos cost US$37/44. The *Dinda Hotel* (☎/fax 286-2810), Rua Augusto Zatti 160, has apartamentos for US$30/60 a single/double. At No 200 on the same street, *Pousada Bernardette* (☎ 286-1569) is a new place with apartamentos for US$40/60. Close to the centre, at Avenida Borges de Medeiros 2512, the *Restaurant & Pensão Napolitano* (☎ 286-1847) is a cheaper option – rooms go for US$20/35.

There's no shortage of top-end places. The best ones are out on the road between Gramado and Canela. The *Villa Bella Gramado* (☎ 286-2688), Rua Villa Bella 125, has rooms from US$74/97.

Places to Eat Every second place in Gramado seems to be a restaurant, especially along Avenida das Hortênsias. A good churrascaria is *Recanto Gaúcho*, at No 5532. Fondue lovers should head to *Le Chalet de la Fondue* at No 1297. Try the *Moscerino*, Avenida das Hortensias 1095, for excellent pasta, or *Tio Muller*, Avenida Borges de Medeiros 4029 for a rodízio of German food.

If you want to escape the glitz for a while, *Restaurante do Gordo* in a quiet side street (no name) off Avenida das Hortênsias has a buffet lunch for US$4.

Getting There & Away The rodoviária is close to the centre at Avenida Borges de Mendeiros 2100. There are frequent buses to Porto Alegre (US$7.50, two hours). Local buses from the rodoviária make the 15 minute trip to Canela.

Canela

• *pop 30,800* ✉ *95680-000* ☎ *054*

Canela is the best jumping-off point for some great hikes and bicycle rides in the area. There are cheaper hotels here than in Gramado, so budget travellers should make this their base.

Information The tourist office (☎ 282-1287; canela@via-rs.com.br) is located on Praça João Correa and is very helpful. It has good maps of the region and a list of recommended agencies for half-day tours of the main attractions (US$25 per person), and for rafting trips and mountain-bike adventures.

Parque Estadual do Caracol Eight kilometres from Canela, the major attraction of this park is a spectacular 130m waterfall. It's incredibly beautiful in the morning sun – the water sparkles as it cascades down. Two kilometres from the centre of Canela along the road to the park is the 'Pinheiro Grosso', a 700-year-old 42m-high araucária pine.

The park is open daily from 8.30 am to 6.30 pm. Entry is US$3. The Caricol bus runs to the park from Praça João Correa at 8.15 am, noon and 5.30 pm.

Castelinho One of the oldest houses in the area, Castelinho is on the road to the park. Now a pioneer museum containing a German restaurant and a chocolate shop, Castelinho was built without using metal nails.

Parque Floresta Encantada de Canela A 45 minute hike from Parque do Caracol, the highlight of this park is a chair-lift ride over a canyon in front of the Cascata do Caracol. Entry to the park is US$4.

Parque da Ferradura A 7km hike from the Parque do Caracol entrance brings you to Ferradura, a stunning 400m horseshoe-shaped canyon formed by the Rio Santa Cruz. The park is open daily from 8.30 am to 5.30 pm. Entry is US$3.50.

Parque das Sequoias Just 2.5km from town, this park was created in the 1940s by Curt Menz, a botanist who cultivated more than 70 different tree species with seeds from around the world. The plantation occupies 10 hectares, and the rest of the park (25 hectares) is native forest. Entry is US$2. The park has lots of trails and a pousada. To get there, walk behind the Catedral da Pedra in town and follow the signs.

Morros Pelado, Queimado & Dedão These hills provide stunning views of the Vale do Quilombo, and on clear days you can see the coast. Reached via the road to the Parque das Sequoias, they're 5, 5.5 and 6.5km from Canela respectively.

Special Events In mid-October, Canela hosts an international theatre festival. In the last week of May, 80,000 pilgrims arrive in town to celebrate the Festa de NS de Caravaggio. A highlight of the festival is a 6km procession from the Igreja Matrix to the Parque do Saiqui.

Both Canela and Gramado go Christmas crazy. The towns compete to see which can create the most extravagant Christmas decorations. Canela's Sonho de Natal festival starts in the middle of November!

Places to Stay Camping is available at *Camping Sesi* (☎ 282-1311), 2.5km from town at Rua Francisco Bertolucci 504. The youth hostel, *Pousada do Viajante* (☎ 282-2017), is at Rua Ernesto Urban 132, near the new rodoviária.

The *Hotel Turis* (☎ 282-2774), Avenida Osvaldo Aranha 223, has recently changed management and is now a hostel for local students, but travellers might still be welcome if there's room. The *Hotel Bela Vista* (☎ 282-1327), Rua Osvaldo Aranha 160, has quartos for US$20/30. The *Vila Vecchia* (☎ 282-1051), Rua Melvin Jones 137, has comfortable apartamentos with TV and fridge for US$40 a double.

THE SOUTH

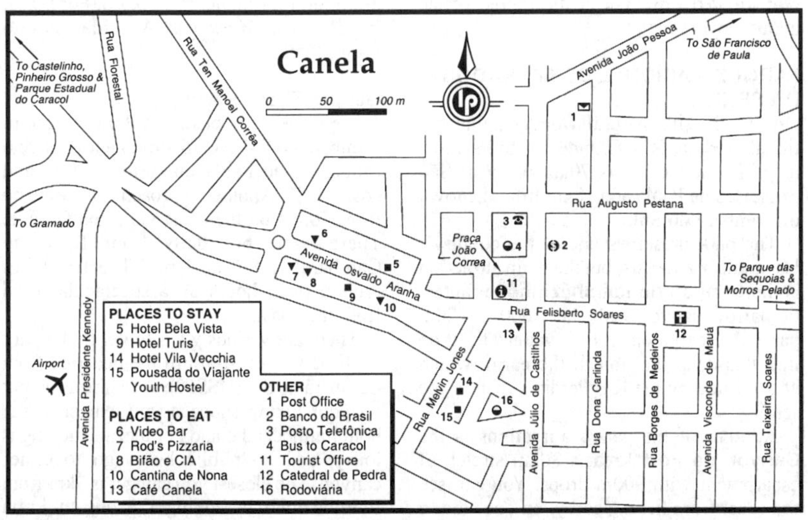

The *Pousada das Sequoias* (☎ 282-1373) in the park of the same name is 2km from the centre. It has small chalets in picturesque surroundings for US$35/50.

The best top-end place to stay is the *Laje de Pedra* (☎ 282-4300), 3km from the centre, on Avenida Presidente Kennedy. It has great views of the Vale do Quilombo. Rooms start at US$110/160.

Places to Eat Highly recommended is *Cantina de Nono*, Avenida Osvaldo Aranha 161. A plate of its comida caseira costs US$5. Say *hola* to Norbert, the friendly Chilean waiter. Big meat-eaters will enjoy *Bifão e Cia*, on the same street at No 301. For rodízio pizza, head to *Rod's Pizzaria* at No 497. For lunch, the restaurant in the Parque do Caracol has a varied menu, and prato feito for US$6. For music and snacks at night, check out *Video Bar* or *Cafe Canela*, both on Avenida Osvaldo Aranha.

Getting There & Away There are frequent buses from Canela to Porto Alegre via Gramado. There are also buses to São Francisco de Paula (US$1.75, one hour), for connections to Cambará do Sul.

Getting Around Ask at the tourist office about bicycle rental.

PARQUE NACIONAL DE APARADOS DA SERRA

One of Brazil's natural wonders, this national park is Rio Grande do Sul's most magnificent area. It is 70km north of São Francisco de Paula and 18km from the town of Cambará do Sul.

The park preserves one of the country's last araucária forests, but the main attraction is the **Canyon do Itaimbézinho**, a fantastic narrow canyon with sheer 600 to 720m parallel escarpments. Two waterfalls drop into this deep incision in the earth, which was formed by the Rio Perdiz's rush to the sea.

Another of the park's attractions is the **Canyon da Fortaleza**, a 30km stretch of escarpment with 900m drops. You can see the coast from here. Nearby, on one side of the canyon, is the **Pedra do Segredo**, a 5m monolith with a very small base. It's 23km from Cambará, but unfortunately in a different direction from Itaimbézinho.

Information

A new IBAMA visitor centre (☎ 251-1305) at Itaimbézinho should be completed by the time this book is published. It will be open from 9 am to 5 pm daily.

Places to Stay & Eat

Camping is a good option in this area. There are good spots near the old Paradouro Hotel in the park and near the Fortaleza canyon.

Cambará do Sul has three cheap hotels on Avenida Getúlio Vargas: the *Pousada Fortaleza*, 300m to the left as you face the city square from the bus station, the *Hotel São Jorge* (☎ 251-1295), 50m to the right, and *Pousada Sabrina* (☎ 251-1147) at No 586. They all charge around US$10 per person. Three kilometres from town on the road to Ouro Verde, *Pousada Corucacas* (☎ 251-1128) is a working farm, with horse riding and fishing. Rooms cost US$25/50.

Pousada Sabrina has an attached restaurant serving rodízio for lunch (US$7) and prato feito for dinner (US$5.50). For pizza, try *Pizzaria Mariza* at Avenida Getúlio Vargas 650.

Getting There & Away

There's one daily bus from Porto Alegre to Cambará do Sul at 6.15 am. The trip via São Francisco de Paula takes four hours and costs US$8. Another approach is to come up from Torres on the coast via Praia Grande. There's one bus daily from Torres to Cambará do Sul at 4 pm. The trip takes around three hours on a spectacular road from the coast.

There are various ways to get to the park itself. If you can't afford the taxi ride from Cambará do Sul (US$50), or to hire a car, put on your hiking shoes if you expect to see both Itaimbézinho and Fortaleza. Hitching is lousy, and no public buses go to either canyon. The closest you can get is 3km from Itaimbézinho by taking the bus to Praia

Grande. Ask the driver to drop you off at the park entrance.

LITORAL GAÚCHO

The Litoral Gaúcho is a 500km strip along the state of Rio Grande do Sul – from Torres on the border with Santa Catarina to Barra do Chuí at the Uruguayan border. Of all Brazil's coastline, this stretch is the least distinguished. The beaches are really one long beach uninterrupted by geographical variations – wide open, with little vegetation and occasional dunes. The sea here is choppier and the water less translucent than in Santa Catarina.

In winter, currents from the Antarctic bring cold, hard winds to the coast. Bathing suits disappear, as do most people. Most hotels shut down in March, and the summer beach season doesn't return until November, with the arrival of the northern winds.

The three resort towns on the north coast are Torres, Capão da Canoa and Tramandaí. They all fill up in summer with Porto Alegrenses, Uruguayans and Argentines: this is not a place to get away from it all. There are some cheaper hotels, but the flavour is more weekend resort than fishing village.

Torres

• *pop 25,800* ✉ *95560-000* ☎ *051*

Torres, 205km from Porto Alegre, is well known for its fine beaches and the beautiful basalt-rock formations along the coast. This is good country in which to walk and explore, and is especially worthwhile if you can get here early or late in the season, when the crowds have thinned out.

Information There's a really good tourist office on the corner of Avenida Barão do Rio Branco and Rua General Osório. It publishes a list of hotels, including the cheapest ones, and a good city map.

There are a few casas de câmbio in town. Try Selautur, Avenida Beira do Rio Branco 10. For travellers cheques and Visa withdrawals, Banco do Brasil is at Avenida Barão do Rio Branco 236.

Boat Trip Boats to the ecological reserve on Ilha dos Lobos leave from Ponte Pênsil on the Rio Mampituba in summer. To get to the jetty, walk to the end of Rua Benjamin Constant and turn left. The trip costs US$5 per person.

Places to Stay Torres has plenty of camping grounds and a surprising number of reasonably priced hotels. If you're here in the low season, make sure you get a discount.

The cheapest hotel in Torres is the *Hotel Medusa* (☎ 664-2378), Rua Benjamin Constant 828. Small but clean singles/doubles cost US$10/15. At Avenida José Bonifácio 382, *Hotel Costa Azul* (☎ 664-3291) is a friendly family-run place one block from the rodoviária. Comfortable apartamentos go for US$18/28. Close to the beach on the corner of Rua Júlio de Castilhos and Rua Borges de Medeiros, *Pousada Brisa do Mar* (☎ 664-2019) is a good mid-range option. Well-appointed apartamentos cost US$25/40.

Places to Eat At last count there were more than 35 restaurants in Torres. For seafood, *Mariscão*, Avenida Beira Mar 145, is recommended. For churrasco, *Bom Gosto*, Avenida Barão do Rio Branco 242, is excellent. A tasty pizza is served by *Ravena* at No 117.

Getting There & Away There are hourly buses to Porto Alegre (US$11, three hours), and one daily bus to Cambará do Sul, at 4 pm.

Capão da Canoa

• *pop 25,500* ✉ *95555-000* ☎ *051*

This smaller resort, 140km from Porto Alegre, lacks the glamour of Torres. Its best known beach is Praia de Atlântida, 3km from town. The beach is big and broad, and the lagoons are popular spots for windsurfing.

Places to Stay As in Torres, there are several camping grounds here. For less expensive lodging, try the *Brasiltur* (☎ 664-1753) at Rua Lamônaco 11, which has basic quartos for US$12 per person. The *Karina* (☎ 664-3341) at Avenida Barão do Rio Branco 711 has quartos for US$15 per person. Three kilometres away on Atlântida beach, the *Atlântida* (☎ 665-2032) at Avenida Central 310 is the most expensive hotel in Capão, with rooms starting at US$50/60 for singles/doubles.

Places to Eat Lots of the restaurants here close down over winter. For seafood, try the *Taberna Don Ciccilo*, Rua Guaracy 1826. *Catarinense* on Avenida José Bonifácio has a prato feito for US$3.50.

JESUIT MISSIONS

Soon after the discovery of the New World, the Portuguese and Spanish kings authorised Catholic orders to create missions to convert the natives into Catholic subjects of the crown and the state. The most successful of these orders were the Jesuits, who established a series of missions in a region which spanned parts of Paraguay, Brazil and Argentina. In effect, it was a nation within the colonies, a nation which, at its height in the 1720s, claimed 30 mission villages inhabited by over 150,000 Guaraní Indians. Buenos Aires was merely a village at this time.

ANDREW DRAFFEN

Statue at São Miguel das Missões

Unlike those established elsewhere, these missions succeeded in introducing western culture without destroying the Indian people, their culture or the Tupi-Guaraní language.

In 1608, Hernandarias, governor of the Spanish province of Paraguay, ordered the local leader of the Jesuits, Fray Diego de Torres, to send missionaries to convert the infidels, and so in 1609, the first mission was founded. Preferring indoctrination by the Jesuits to serfdom on Spanish estates or slavery at the hands of the Portuguese, the Indians were rapidly recruited into a chain of missions. The missions covered a vast region of land that encompassed much of the present-day Brazilian states of Paraná, Santa Catarina and Rio Grande do Sul as well as portions of Paraguay and northern Argentina.

The Jesuit territory was too large to defend, and the Portuguese *bandeirantes* (bands of Paulistas who explored the Brazilian interior while searching for gold and Indians to enslave) found the missionary settlements easy pickings for slave raids. Thousands of Indians were captured, reducing the 13 missions of Guayra (Brazilian territory) to two. Fear of the bandeirante slavers caused these two missions to be abandoned, and the Indians and Jesuits marched westward and founded San Ignacio Miní (1632), having lost many people in the rapids of the Paraná. The missions north of Iguaçu were decimated by attacks from hostile Indian tribes and were forced to relocate south.

Between 1631 and 1638, activity was concentrated in 30 missions which the mission Indians were able to defend. In one of the bloodiest fights, the battle of Mbororé, the Indians beat back the slavers and secured their lands north of San Javier.

The missions were miniature cities built around a central church, and included baptisteries, libraries, dormitories for the Indian converts and the priests, and cemeteries. They became centres of culture and intellect as well as of religion. An odd mix of European Baroque and native Guaraní arts, music and painting developed. Indian scholars created a written form of Tupi-Guaraní and, from 1704, published several works in Tupi-Guaraní, using one of the earliest printing presses in South America.

As the missions grew, the Jesuit nation became more independent of Rome and relations with the Vatican became strained. The missions became an embarrassment to the Iberian kings, and finally, in 1777, the Portuguese minister Marques de Pombal convinced Carlos III to expel the Jesuits from Spanish lands. Thus ended, in the opinion of many historians, a grand 160 year experiment in socialism, where wealth was equally divided and religion, intellect and the arts flourished – a utopian island of progress in an age of monarchies and institutionalised slavery. Administration of the mission villages passed into the hands of the colonial government. The communities continued until the early 1800s, when they were destroyed by revolutionary wars of independence, then abandoned.

Today, there are 30 ruined Jesuit missions: seven lie in Brazil (in the north-western part of Rio Grande do Sul), eight are in the southern region of Itapuá, Paraguay, and the remaining 15 are in Argentina. Of these 15 Argentine missions, 11 lie in the province of Missiones.

Brazilian Missions

In Santo Angelo, the municipal tourist office (☎ (055) 313-1600) is on Praça Pinheiro Machado. Close by, Missiotur (☎ (055) 312-4055) in the Hotel Santo Angelo Turis on Rua Antonio Manoel, organises tours of the mission. There's a 24 hour Visa ATM at Bradesco on Avenida Brasil.

São Miguel das Missões This mission, 58km from Santo Angelo, is the most interesting of the Brazilian missions. Every evening at 8.30 pm there's a sound and light show. Entry is just US$2, or US$1 for students.

Also nearby are the missions of São João Batista (on the way to São Miguel) and São Lourenço das Missões (10km from São João Batista).

Paraguayan Missions

The most important mission to see is Trinidad, 25km from Encarnación. The red-stone ruins are fascinating.

Argentine Missions

In Argentina, don't miss San Ignacio Miní, 60km from Posadas on Ruta Nacional 12, where there's a sound and light show every night. Of lesser stature is Santa Maria la Mayor, 111km away from Posadas on Ruta 110. It's possible to cut across the province of Missiones to San Javier (Ruta 4), crossing by barge to Brazil at Puerto Xavier, or further south at Santo Tome, and taking a ferry across the Rio Uruguay to São Borja, Brazil.

The border at Uruguaiana, 180km south of São Borja, is more commonly used. Buses operate to Buenos Aires, Santiago do Chile and Montevideo. The Argentine consulate (☎ (055) 412-1925) is at Rua Santana 2496, 2nd floor, while the Uruguayan consulate (☎ (055) 412-1514) is at Rua Duque de Caixas 1606.

There's an excellent information office (☎ (01) 322-0686) for the Argentine missions in Buenos Aires at Avenida Santa Fé 989. In Posadas, there's an information office (☎ (0752) 22-977) at Avenida Colón 1985.

Places to Stay & Eat

In Brazil, Santo Angelo has several hotels, but it's great to stay out at São Miguel to see the sound and light show. The missions were always placed on high points in the countryside, so there's a great view. The *Hotel Barichello* (☎ (055) 381-1104) is the only place to stay. Singles cost US$18 and doubles with a shower are US$28. It's a good place to eat, too.

In Paraguay, Encarnación has some cheap, modest hotels and restaurants.

Across the Rio Paraná from Encarnación is the capital of the Argentine province of Posadas. Everything is more expensive, but the food is better and the lodging (there are 25 hotels to choose from) is fancier.

Getting There & Away

Air There are daily flights from São Paulo and Porto Alegre to Santo Angelo with Varig/RioSul. In Santo Angelo, Varig (☎ (055) 312-2465) is on Avenida Brasil, near the corner of Rua Forrencio de Abreu.

Bus There are five buses a day from Porto Alegre to Santo Angelo (US$27.50, seven hours).

To access the Argentine missions, there are 15 daily buses from Puerto Iguazu at Foz do Iguaçu to San Ignácio (Pesos 20, five hours). These buses continue to Posadas. Use Encarnación as a base for visiting the missions of Paraguay. From the Paraguayan border town of Cuidad del Este, opposite Foz do Iguaçu, there are daily buses to Encarnación, 320km south.

Getting Around

It's possible to rent a car from the three base cities, but driving a rental car over borders is difficult. In Santo Angelo, try Localiza (☎ (055) 312-5353) or Sulmive (☎ (055) 312-1000).

PELOTAS

• *pop 305,000* ✉ *96000-000* ☎ *0532*

Pelotas, 251km south of Porto Alegre, was a major port in the 19th century for the export of dried beef, and home to a sizeable British community. The wealth generated is still reflected in some grand, neoclassical mansions around the main square, Praça General Osório. Today the town is an important industrial centre, and much of its canned vegetables, fruits and sweets is exported.

There's really no reason to stay in Pelotas, but if you're waiting for a bus connection and have time to spare, it's worth checking out.

If awards were given for the 'Most Imaginative Use of Concrete', then the bus station in Pelotas would be a major contender. The rubber spiral walkways to the 2nd floor are a spinout, too!

Money The Banco do Brasil on the corner of Rua General Osório and Rua Lagoa da Costa has a Visa ATM.

Places to Stay & Eat

The *Palace Hotel* (☎ 22-2223), Rua 7 de Setembro 354, is the best value. It's a bright, friendly place with quartos for US$13.50/21 a single/double, and apartamentos for US$21/29. The *Rex Hotel* (☎ 22-1163), Praça Coronel Osório 205, has fairly dingy quartos for US$15/25.

There's a very popular por quilo joint, the *Palandar*, at Rua Marechal Floriano 12. At Rua 7 de Setembro 306, the *Bavaria* serves good German food. Pelotas is renowned for its sweets, which can be sampled right next door at *Otto Especialidades*. The Palace Hotel has a good churrascaria.

Getting There & Away

Pelotas is a transport hub. There are regular buses to Uruguay and buses to Porto Alegre every half an hour.

RIO GRANDE

• *pop 178,500* ✉ *96200-000* ☎ *0532*

Once an important cattle centre, Rio Grande lies near the mouth of the Lagoa dos Patos, Brazil's biggest lagoon. To the north, the coast along the lagoa is lightly inhabited. There's a dirt road along this stretch, which is connected with Rio Grande by a small ferry. This active but little visited port city is more interesting than Pelotas if you want to break your journey in this area.

Information

A useful map is available from travel agencies or big hotels, such as the Charrua. Pampasul is a central câmbio along the shopping mall, at Rua General Bacelar 426. For Visa withdrawals, Bradesco is at Rua Floriano Peixoto 196. International telephone calls can be made from the phone booths on Praça Dr Pio, next to the post office.

Catedral de São Pedro

The oldest church in the state, this cathedral was erected by the Portuguese colonists. Baroque in style, it's classified as part of the Patrimônio Histórico. It's on Praça Dr Pio, in the centre. Homesick Australians might want to sniff around the massive *Eucalyptus globulus* tree in the middle of the square, which was planted in 1877.

Museu Oceanográphico

This interesting museum 2km from the centre on Avenida Perimetral, is the most complete of its type in Latin America. It has a large shell collection, and skeletons of whales and dolphins. It's open daily from 9 to 11 am and 2 to 5 pm.

Museu da Cidade

The Museu da Cidade is in the old customs house which Dom Pedro II ordered built on Rua Richuelo along the waterfront. It's open on weekdays from 9 am to noon and 2 to 5 pm and on Sunday from 1 to 5 pm.

São José do Norte

Boats leave the terminal on the waterfront every 30 minutes for the trip across the Lagoa dos Patos to the fishing village of São José do Norte. This is a nice trip to do around sunset. The last boat back to Rio Grande leaves at 10 pm. The round trip costs US$1.50.

Places to Stay

There are a few cheap hotels in Rio Grande, but the one to head for is the *Paris Hotel* (☎ 31-3866) in a 19th century building at Rua Marechal Floriano 112. It's seen better days, but its courtyard is an excellent place in which to sit and contemplate the glory days of the city. Single/double quartos cost US$13/18, and apartamentos US$19/25. It's a US$5 taxi ride from the rodoviária. One block away at Rua General Bacellar 159 is *São Luiz Hotel*, which has basic quartos for US$6 per person.

Moving up in price, the *Hotel Europa* (☎/fax 31-3933) is at Rua General Netto 165, opposite Praça Tamandaré. Rooms cost US$39/52 but a 20% discount applies in the low season. The top hotel in town is the *Charrua Hotel* (☎/fax 31-3833), Rua Duque de Caixas 53, opposite Praça Xavier Ferreira. Singles/doubles cost US$47/58.

Places to Eat

Restaurante Marcos, Avenida Silva Paes 400, has lots of seafood and meat dishes from US$10 for two people. There are a few good restaurants a block away on Rua Luiz Lorea. At No 363, *Caçarola* has a rodízio for US$5, and there's Chinese food at *China-Brasil* at No 385. For lunch, *Armazem Macrobiotica*, Rua General Bacelar 218, has a vegetarian buffet, or you can get a por quilo lunch at *Buffet D'Italia*, Rua Marechal Floriano Peixoto 385, opposite Praça Xavier Ferreira. For coffee and a sandwich or a late afternoon beer, *Plaza Café* is on Rua General Netto, opposite Praça Dr Pio.

Getting There & Away

Buses connect Rio Grande with all major cities in southern Brazil, but they run more regularly from Pelotas. There are two buses a day to Chuí (US$13, four hours) on the Uruguayan border at 7 am and 3 pm.

CHUÍ

• *pop 3200* ✉ *96235-000* ☎ *0532*

The small border town of Chuí is about 245km south of Rio Grande on a good sealed road. One side of the main street, Avenida Brasil, is Brazilian; the other side is the Uruguayan town of Chuy. The Brazilian side is full of Uruguayans taking care of their clothing needs for the next six months. The Uruguayan side is a good place to eat, change money and buy cheap duty-free Scotch whisky.

Visas

It's much better to get your Uruguayan visa in Porto Alegre than in Chuí. It can be done here, but you might have to wait overnight. The Uruguayan consulate (☎ 65-1151) is 50m from the rodoviária at Rua Venezuela

311. It's open Monday to Friday from 8 am to 2 pm. Visas cost a whopping US$45.

Places to Stay & Eat

If you're stuck in Chuí, the best cheapie is *Rivero Hotel* (☎ 65-1271) at Calle Colombia 163 on the Brazilian side. Bright apartamentos cost US$7 per person. On the same street at No 191, the *Hotel e Restaurante São Francisco* (☎ 65-1096) charges the same prices. In Uruguay, the *Plaza Hotel*, Rua General Artigas 553, has singles/doubles for US$22/34.

There are some good restaurants on the Uruguayan side of Avenida Brasil. Try the *Jesus* for parillada, or *Bar Restaurante Opal* for pasta. On the Brazilian side, the restaurant in the Hotel São Francisco is as good as it gets.

Getting There & Away

The rodoviária is about three blocks from Avenida Brasil. There are regular buses to Pelotas, and two daily buses to Rio Grande (US$11, four hours), at 7 am and 3.30 pm. To Porto Alegre (US$22, 7½ hours), there are two buses a day, at noon and 11 pm. You can buy tickets to Montevideo from the bus agencies on the Uruguayan side of Avenida Brasil. Eight buses leave daily for Montevideo, the first at 3.30 am and the last at 8 pm.

All buses crossing into Uruguay stop at the Polícia Federal post on Avenida Argentina, a couple of kilometres from town. You must get off the bus here to get your Brazilian exit stamp. In Uruguay, the bus will stop again for the Uruguayan officials to check your Brazilian exit stamp and Uruguayan visa.

The Central West

The Central West

Known to Brazilians as the Centro-Oeste, this region includes almost 19% of the country's land area. It's the most sparsely populated region in Brazil, containing only 6% of the total population.

Made up of the states of Mato Grosso, Mato Grosso do Sul, Goiás and the Distrito Federal of Brasília, this massive terrain was until the 1940s the last great unexplored area on earth.

Here, the Planalto Brasileiro has been greatly eroded to form the Guimarães, Parecis and Veadeiros *chapadões* (tablelands) between the river basins. In the south-west of Mato Grosso and the west of Mato Grosso do Sul is the wildlife paradise called the Pantanal Matogrossense. It's a unique geographical depression formed by a huge inland sea which dried up millions of years ago. Large portions are covered by water during the rainy season.

As well as the Pantanal, which is the major drawing card of the region, the Central West contains many other natural attractions. There are some spectacular national parks in the above-mentioned tablelands (Chapada dos Guimarães and Chapada dos Veadeiros); the remote Parque Nacional das Emas; and the river beaches of the Rio Araguaia, which extends into the northern state of Tocantins. The Bonito area has become popular in recent years for its crystal-clear rivers and natural springs surrounded by lush forest.

There are also interesting colonial towns (Pirenópolis and Goiás Velho) and large, planned cities (Goiânia and Brasília) that are worth a look.

HIGHLIGHTS

- Driving around Brasília looking at its unique architecture and town planning (Distrito Federal)
- The weird and wonderful religious sects around Brasília (Distrito Federal)
- The colonial towns of Goiás Velho and Pirenópolis (Goiás)
- Wildlife spotting in the Pantanal (Mato Grosso and Mato Grosso do Sul)
- The train ride from Corumbá to Campo Grande across the Pantanal (Mato Grosso and Mato Grosso do Sul)
- Piranha fishing in the Pantanal (Mato Grosso do Sul)
- Parque Nacional da Chapada dos Guimarães (Mato Grosso)

THE CENTRAL WEST

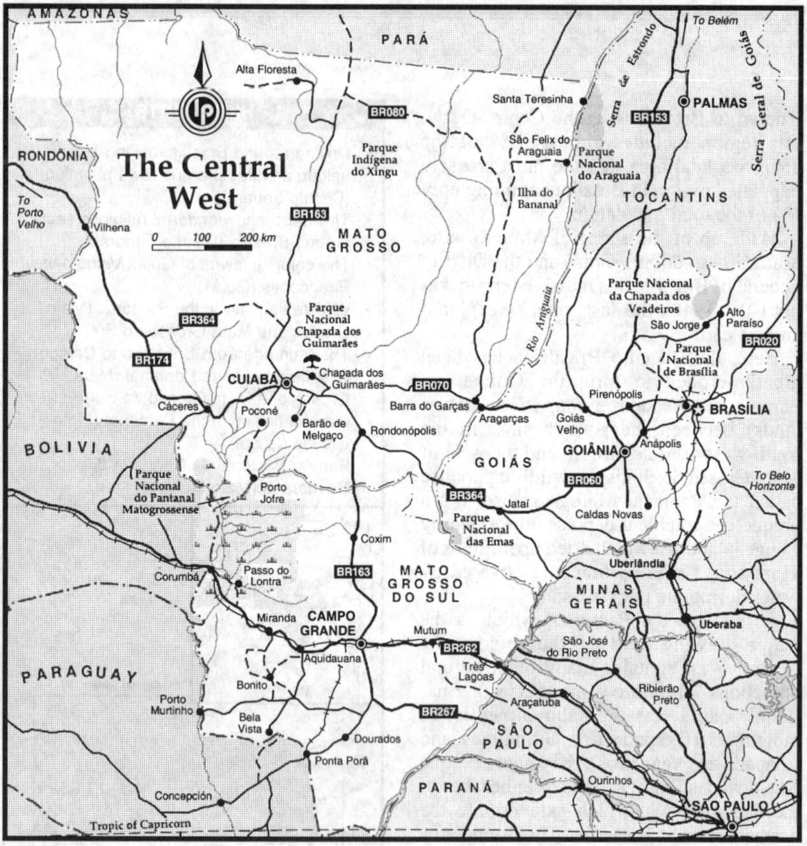

The Central West

0 100 200 km

AMAZONAS
PARÁ
RONDÔNIA
MATO GROSSO
TOCANTINS
GOIÁS
MATO GROSSO DO SUL
MINAS GERAIS
SÃO PAULO
PARANÁ
BOLIVIA
PARAGUAY
To Belém
To Porto Velho
To Belo Horizonte
Serra de Estrondo
Serra Geral de Goiás
Rio Araguaia
Alta Floresta
Santa Teresinha
PALMAS
São Felix do Araguaia
Parque Nacional do Araguaia
Ilha do Bananal
Parque Indígena do Xingu
Vilhena
Parque Nacional da Chapada dos Veadeiros
Alto Paraíso
São Jorge
Parque Nacional de Brasília
Parque Nacional Chapada dos Guimarães
Chapada dos Guimarães
CUIABÁ
Cáceres
Poconé
Barão de Melgaço
Rondonópolis
Barra do Garças
Aragarças
Goiás Velho
Pirenópolis
BRASÍLIA
Anápolis
GOIÂNIA
Caldas Novas
Jataí
Parque Nacional das Emas
Parque Nacional do Pantanal Matogrossense
Porto Jofre
Coxim
Corumbá
Passo do Lontra
Miranda
CAMPO GRANDE
Aquidauana
Bonito
Mutum
Três Lagoas
Uberlândia
Uberaba
São José do Rio Preto
Ribierão Preto
Araçatuba
Porto Murtinho
Bela Vista
Dourados
Ponta Porã
Concepción
Ourinhos
SÃO PAULO
Tropic of Capricorn
BR080
BR153
BR163
BR364
BR174
BR070
BR020
BR060
BR262
BR267

Distrito Federal

BRASÍLIA

• *pop 1.7 million* ✉ *70000-000* ☎ *061*

I sought the curved and sensual line. The curve that I see in the Brazilian hills, in the body of a loved one, in the clouds in the sky and in the ocean waves.

Oscar Niemeyer, Brasília architect

Brasília is a utopian horror. It should be a symbol of power, but instead it's a museum of architectural ideas.

Robert Hughes, art critic

The impression I have is that I'm arriving on a different planet.

Yuri Gagarin, cosmonaut

Brasília must have looked good on paper, and it still does in photos. In 1987 it was added to the UNESCO list of World Heritage Sites, being considered one of the major examples of this century's modern movement in architecture and urban planning.

But the world's great planned city of the 20th century is built for automobiles and air-conditioners, not people. Distances are enormous and no one walks. The sun blazes, but there are few trees for shelter.

Bureaucrats and politicians, who live in the model 'pilot plan' part of the city, were lured to Brasília by 100% salary hikes and big apartments in the 1960s. Even today, as soon as the weekend comes, they get out of the city – to Rio, to São Paulo, to their private clubs in the country – anywhere that's less sterile. Brasília is also one of the most expensive cities in Brazil.

The poor have to get out – they have no choice. Mostly from the Northeast, these *candangos* (pioneers) work in the construction and service industries. They live in *favelas* (slums), which they call 'anti-Brasílias', as far as 30km from the centre. This physical gulf between the haves and have-nots is reminiscent of South Africa's townships.

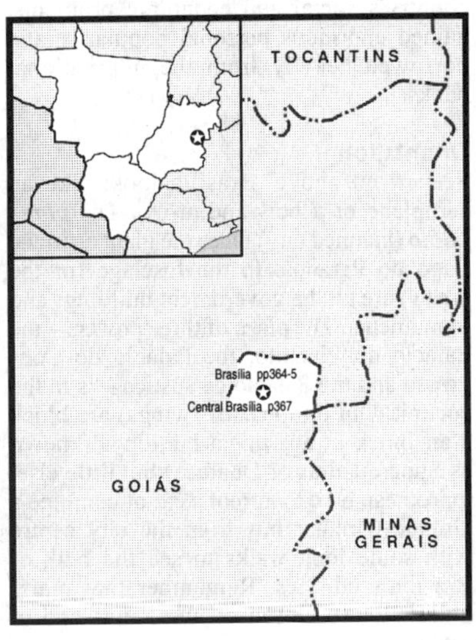

All this is the doing of three famous Brazilians: an urban planner (Lucio Costa), an architect (Oscar Niemeyer) and a landscape architect (Burle Marx), each the leading figure in his field. They were commissioned by President Juscelino Kubitschek to plan a new inland capital, a city that would catalyse the economic development of Brazil's vast interior. With millions of dirt-poor peasants from the Northeast working around the clock, Brasília was built in an incredible three years – it wasn't exactly finished but it was ready to be the capital (Niemeyer later admitted that it was all done too quickly). The capital was officially moved from Rio to Brasília on 21 April 1960.

The old Brazilian dream of an inland capital had always been dismissed as expensive folly. What possessed Kubitschek to actually do it? Politics. He made the building of Brasília a symbol of the country's determination and ability to become a great economic power. Kubitschek successfully appealed to all Brazilians to put aside their differences and rally to the cause. In doing so, he distracted attention from the country's social and economic problems, gained enormous personal popularity and borrowed heavily from the international banks.

Orientation

Seen from above, Brasília looks like an aeroplane or a bow and arrow. The *plano piloto* (planned city) faces the giant artificial Lago do Paranoá. In the fuselage (or the arrow) are all the government buildings and monuments. The plaza of three powers – the Palácio do Planalto, the Palácio do Congresso and the Palácio da Justiça – is in the cockpit. Out on the *asas* (wings) are block after block of apartment buildings (known as Superquadras or Quadras) but little else.

You can do a tour, rent a car or combine a Grande Circular bus from the city centre with some long walks to see the bulk of Brasília's edifices. Remember that many buildings are closed on weekends and at night.

Information

Tourist Office Setur (☎ 225-1914) is the government tourist information service. Its office, inconveniently located on the 3rd floor of the Centro de Convenções, is open from 9 am to 7 pm Monday to Friday. Staff are helpful and there's a useful touchscreen computer database. To get there, take bus No 131, which runs between the *rodoferroviária* (train and bus station) and the more central *rodoviária* (bus station).

Setur also operates a tourist desk at the airport, which is open from 8 am to 1 pm and 2 to 6 pm Monday to Friday (from 10 am to 1 pm and 4.30 to 7.30 pm on weekends).

If all you need is a map or a list of attractions, simply pick up a brochure from the front desk of any of the large hotels or from a travel agency.

Foreign Embassies This being the national capital you would expect them all to be here. SES stands for Setor de Embaixadas Sul.

Australia
SHIS, Q I-9, cj 16, casa 1 (☎ 248-5569; fax 248-1066)
Canada
SES, Avenida das Nações, Q 803, lote 16, sl 130 (☎ 321-2171; fax 321-4529)
France
SES, Avenida das Nações, lote 4 (☎ 312-9100; fax 312-9108)
Germany
SES, Avenida das Nações, lote 25 (☎ 224-7273; fax 244-6063)
Israel
SES, Avenida das Nações, Q 809, lote 38 (☎ 244-7675; fax 244-6129)
Sweden
SES, Avenida das Nações, lote 29 (☎ 243-1444; fax 243-1187)
Switzerland
SES, Avenida das Nações, lote 41 (☎ 244-5500; fax 244-5711)
UK
SES, Avenida das Nações, Q 801, cj K lote 8 (☎ 225-2710; fax 225-1777)
USA
SES, Avenida das Nações, Q 801, lote 3 (☎ 321-7272; fax 225-9136)

Money There are plenty of banks with money changing facilities in the Setor Bancário Sul (SBS or Banking Sector South) and Setor Bancário Norte (SBN or Banking Sector North). Both sectors are close to the rodoviária. The Banco do Brasil in the Commercial Sector South has a Visa ATM, and the travel agencies will change cash dollars.

Post & Telephone The post office is in the Setor Hoteleiro Sul (SHS – Hotel Sector South). There's a long-distance telephone office in the rodoviária.

Memorial JK

Along with the tomb of JK (President Kubitschek) (☎ 225-9451) on Praça do Cruzeiro, the memorial features several exhibits relating to the construction of the city. It's open Tuesday to Sunday from 9 am to 6 pm. Entry is US$2.

TV Tower

The 75m observation deck of the TV tower (☎ 226-2172), on the Eixo Monumental, is open Tuesday to Sunday from 9 am to 9 pm and Monday from 2 to 9 pm. At the base of the tower, on weekends, there's a handicrafts fair.

Catedral Metropolitana

With its 16 curved columns and its stained-glass interior, the cathedral is worth seeing. At the entrance are the haunting ***Four Disciples*** statues carved by Ceschiatti, who also made the aluminium angels hanging inside. It's located on the Eixo Monumental and is open daily from 8 am to 7.30 pm.

Government Buildings

Down by the tip of the arrow you'll find the most interesting government buildings. The Palácio do Itamaraty (open Monday, Wednesday and Friday from 3 to 5 pm and on weekends from 10 am to 2 pm) is one of the best [illegible] a series of arches surrounded by a reflecting pool and landscaped by Burle Marx. There's also the Palácio da Justiça; the Supreme Court (open Monday to Friday from noon to 7 pm), with water cascading between its arches; and the Palácio do Congresso (open Monday to Friday from 10 am to noon and 2 to 5 pm) with the 'dishes' and twin towers. The presidential Palácio da Alvorada is not open to visitors.

Santuário Dom Bosco

As impressive as the cathedral, the Santuário Dom Bosco (Dom Bosco's Shrine) is made of concrete columns, with blue stained-glass windows. Located at Quadra 702 Sul along Via W3 Sul, it's open from 8 am to 6.30 pm daily.

Parks

The **Parque Nacional de Brasília** is a good place to relax if you're stuck in the city. This ecological reserve is open from 8 am to 4 pm Tuesday to Sunday, and is very popular on weekends. Apart from the attraction of its natural swimming pools, it is home to a number of endangered animals, including deer, banded anteaters, giant armadillos and maned wolves. The Grande do Torto bus, No 112.1 from the city rodoviária, goes past the front gate.

Another good park is the **Parque Recreativo de Brasília Rogério Pithon Farias** in the city, where you'll find a swimming pool, and small lunch places where you can grab a snack.

Organised Tours

If you want to save your feet, half-day guided tours of the city start at around US$25. The Hotel Nacional and the Hotel Garvey-Park both house several travel agencies offering sightseeing tours. You can also book bus tours at the airport.

Places to Stay – Budget

Camping is possible not far from the city in the Setor de Garagens Oficiais. To get there, take the No 109 or 143 Buriti bus from the rodoviária. Camp sites cost US$5.

There are no cheap hotels in Brasília, but there are a few cheap pensions, mostly in W3 Sul; to get there from the rodoviária, catch any bus going along W3 Sul. Many of them are used by people getting treatment at nearby hospitals, and the rooms aren't much more than cubicles. *Pousada 47* (☎ 224-4894) is a clean, well-kept place that charges US$15 per person with breakfast. It's at Quadra 703, Bloco A, Casa 41/47. *Pousada da Nilza*, next door at Casa 54, was inexplicably asking US$40 for a room. A few blocks back off the main drag, *Pousada do Sol* (☎ 223-1754) is clean and quiet. It's in the third row of houses off the street at Quadra 703, Bloco C, Casa 47.

Cury's Solar (☎ 243-6252), run by Neusa Batista, is a friendly place in which guests are encouraged to make themselves at home. French and German are spoken. Prices per person vary according to room size, from US$15 to $20 per person. Get off at the stop between Quadras 707 and 708. Walk up through the park and turn right at the third row of houses. The address is Quadra 707 Sul, Bloco I, Casa 15. There's no sign, so watch for the numbers.

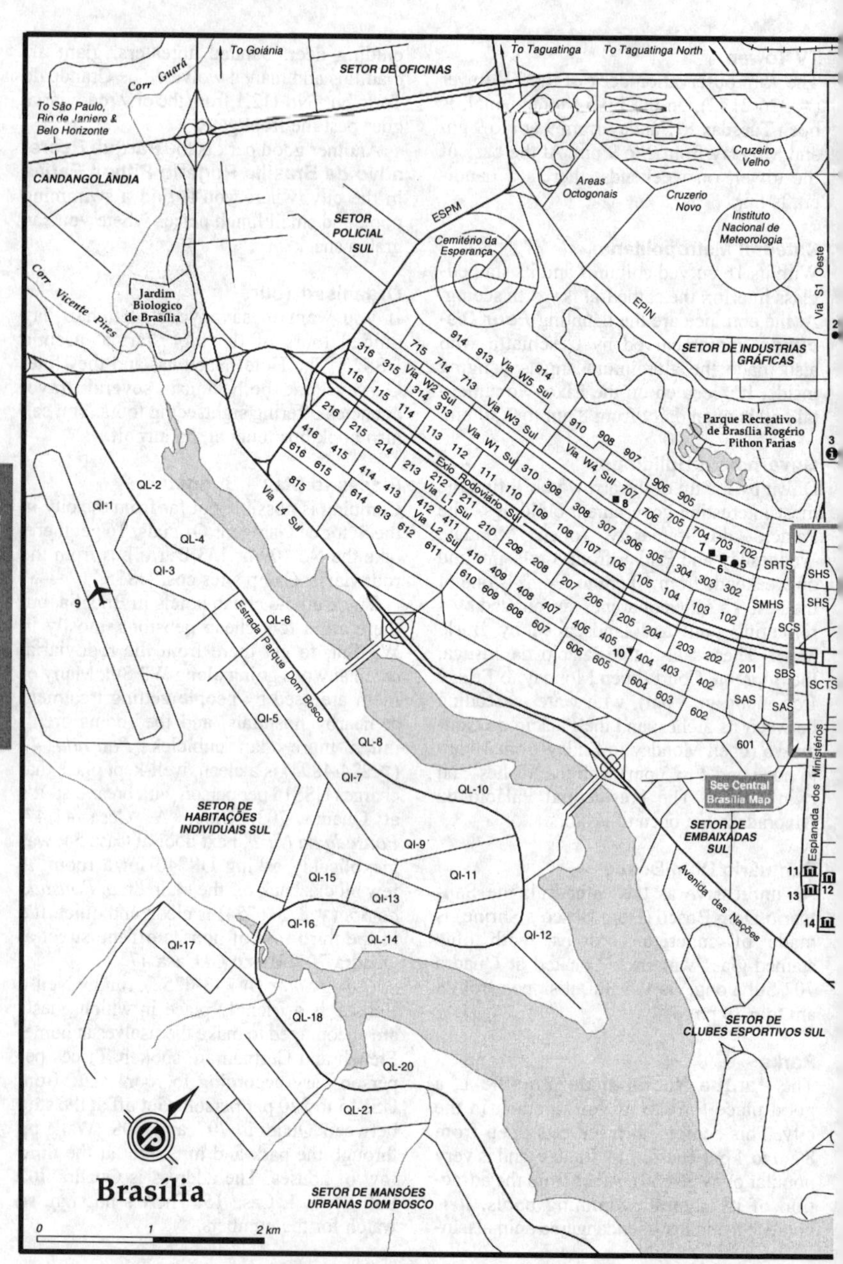
To Goiânia
SETOR DE OFICINAS
To Taguatinga
To Taguatinga North
Corr Guará
To São Paulo, Rio de Janiere & Belo Horizonte
CANDANGOLÂNDIA
Cruzeiro Velho
Areas Octogonais
Cruzerio Novo
Instituto Nacional de Meteorologia
SETOR POLICIAL SUL
ESPM
Cemitério da Esperança
Via S1 Oeste
Corr Vicente Pires
Jardim Biologico de Brasília
EPIN
SETOR DE INDUSTRIAS GRÁFICAS
Parque Recreativo de Brasília Rogério Pithon Farias
Via W5 Sul
Via W3 Sul
Via W2 Sul
Via W1 Sul
Via W4 Sul
Exio Rodoviário Sul
Via L1 Sul
Via L2 Sul
Via L4 Sul
QL-2
QI-1
QL-4
QI-3
QL-6
Estrada Parque Dom Bosco
QI-5
QL-8
QI-7
QL-10
SRTS
SHS
SMHS
SCS
SBS
SCTS
SAS
See Central Brasília Map
Esplanada dos Ministérios
SETOR DE HABITAÇÕES INDIVIDUAIS SUL
QI-9
QI-11
QI-15
QI-13
QI-16
QL-14
QI-12
QI-17
SETOR DE EMBAIXADAS SUL
Avenida das Nações
SETOR DE CLUBES ESPORTIVOS SUL
QL-18
QL-20
QL-21
Brasília
SETOR DE MANSÕES URBANAS DOM BOSCO
0
1
2 km

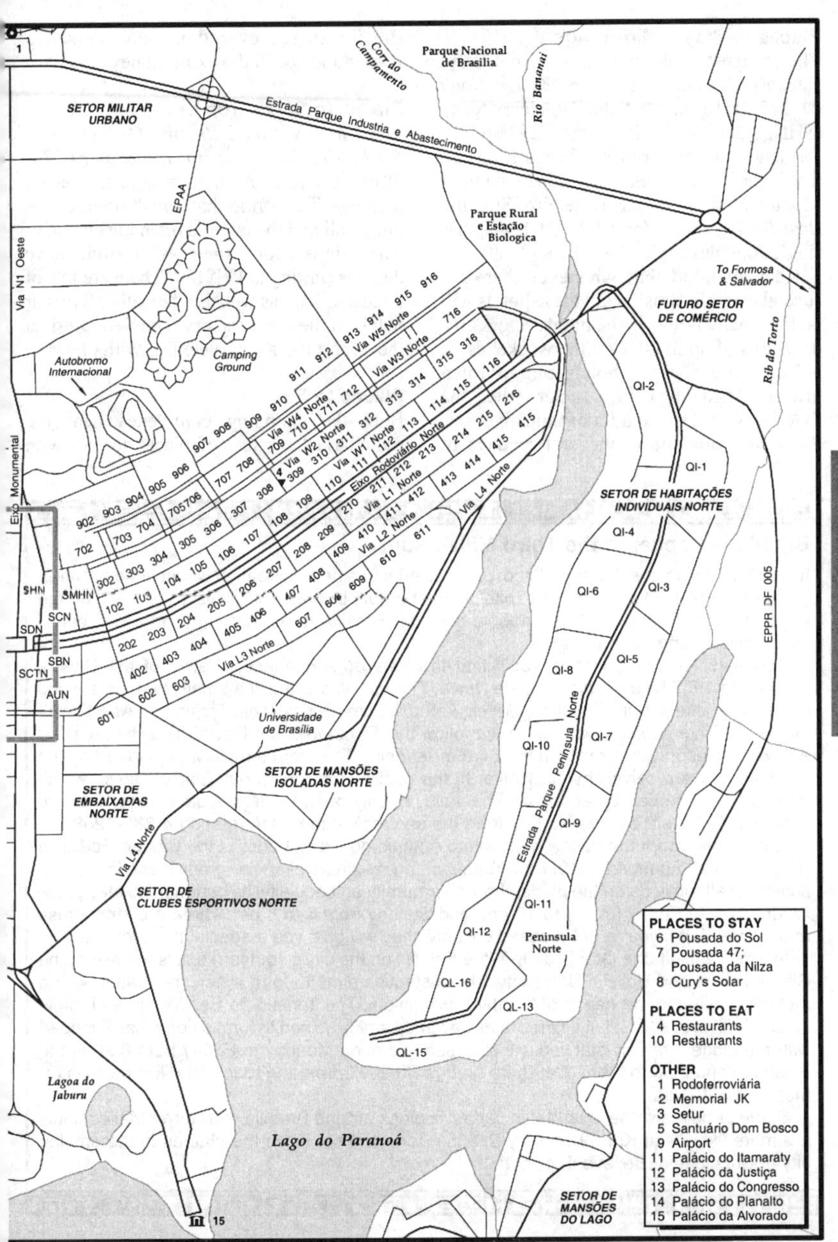

Parque Nacional de Brasilia
Corr do Campamento
Rio Bananal
SETOR MILITAR URBANO
Estrada Parque Industria e Abastecimento
EPAA
Parque Rural e Estação Biologica
Via N1 Oeste
Camping Ground
Autobromo Internacional
To Formosa & Salvador
FUTURO SETOR DE COMÉRCIO
Rib do Torto
Eixo Monumental
Via W5 Norte
Via W3 Norte
Via W4 Norte
Via W2 Norte
Via W1 Norte
Eixo Rodoviário Norte
Via L1 Norte
Via L2 Norte
Via L4 Norte
Via L3 Norte
SETOR DE HABITAÇÕES INDIVIDUAIS NORTE
EPPR DF 005
SHN
SMHN
SCN
SDN
SBN
SCTN
AUN
Universidade de Brasília
SETOR DE MANSÕES ISOLADAS NORTE
SETOR DE EMBAIXADAS NORTE
Estrada Parque Peninsula Norte
SETOR DE CLUBES ESPORTIVOS NORTE
Peninsula Norte
Lagoa do Jaburu
Lago do Paranoá
SETOR DE MANSÕES DO LAGO
PLACES TO STAY
6 Pousada do Sol
7 Pousada 47; Pousada da Nilza
8 Cury's Solar
PLACES TO EAT
4 Restaurants
10 Restaurants
OTHER
1 Rodoferroviária
2 Memorial JK
3 Setur
5 Santuário Dom Bosco
9 Airport
11 Palácio do Itamaraty
12 Palácio da Justiça
13 Palácio do Congresso
14 Palácio do Planalto
15 Palácio da Alvorado

Places to Stay – Mid-Range

The cheapest hotels fall into the mid-range category. A good one is the *Mirage Hotel* (☎ 225-7150), in the Setor Hoteleiro Norte (SHN, Q 2, Bloco N). It charges US$38/62/79 for singles/doubles/triples. There's a restaurant in the hotel. On the other side of the Eixo Monumental, in Setor Hoteleiro Sul, the *Brasília Imperial Hotel* (☎ 321-8747) has singles/doubles/triples for US$60/70/80.

Keep in mind that whenever there's a special event in Brasília, all these hotels will be full. Many hotels in the hotel sectors give discounts of up to 40% on the weekends.

There are cheaper hotels out of town towards Taguatinga, in a sector called the SIA, but you'll spend a lot of time on buses. Since you only need one or two days in Brasília to see everything, do yourself a favour and spend the extra money.

Places to Stay – Top End

The *Hotel Nacional Brasília* (☎ 321-7575; fax 223-9213) and the *Hotel Carlton* (☎ 224-8819; fax 226-8109) are two popular five-star lodgings. The former has an adjoining shopping mall and the latter is often the choice of delegations from the USA. Both have doubles starting at US$150. There are lots of three and four, as well as a few other five-star hotels in the hotel sectors. The Setur desk at the airport has a complete list, with prices.

Places to Eat

Both the shopping complexes near the rodoviária have lots of places to eat, with

Brasília – Capital of the Third Millennium

In 1883 an Italian priest, João Bosco, prophesied that a new civilisation would arise between parallels 15 and 20 and that its capital would be built between parallels 15 and 16, on the edge of an artificial lake. Many people consider Brasília to be that city, and a number of cults have sprung up in the area.

About 45 km from Brasília you'll find the Vale do Amanhecer (Valley of the Dawn), founded in 1959 by a clairvoyant, Tia Neiva. The valley is actually a small town, where you can see (or take part in) Egyptian, Greek, Aztec, Indian, Gypsy, Inca, Trojan and Afro-Brazilian rituals. The mediums who live there follow the 'Doctrine of the Dawn'. They believe that a new civilisation will come with the third millennium. The main temple was inspired by the spiritual advice received by Tia Neiva. In the centre is an enormous Star of David, which forms a lake, pierced by an arrow. The valley is only open to visitors daily from 10 pm to midnight. Get there by Bus No 617 from the centre. For more information ☎ 389-1258.

About 80km from the valley, near Santo Antônio do Descoberto, is the Cidade Ecléctica (Eclectic City). Founded in 1956 by Yokanam, an ex-airline pilot, the group's aim is the unification of all religions on the planet through fraternity and equality. Its ceremonies take place Wednesday to Friday from 8 to 10 pm, and Sunday from 3 to 6 pm. There are strict dress regulations, but if you're not dressed suitably, they will give you a special tunic to wear.

In Brasília itself, the Granja do Ipê (Ipê Estate) on the city's southern exit is the site of the City of Peace and Holistic University. This institution aims to form a new generation with a mentality suited to the needs of the third millennium. The Templo da Boa Vontade (Temple of Goodwill) is at 915 Sul. It incorporates seven pyramids, joined to form a cone that is topped with the biggest raw crystal you will ever see. It's open Monday to Friday from 8.30 am to 11.30 am and 2.30 to 6 pm. Get there on bus No 209.2 from the rodoviária. For more information ☎ 380-1202.

Some people also believe that in certain regions around Brasília extraterrestrial contacts are more likely – at Km 69 on Hwy BR-351, for instance, or on the plateau in the smaller city of Brasilândia. Believe it, or not!

many offering lunch specials. Conjunto Nacional on the northern side has the best selection. The flash new Pátio Brasil shopping complex also has a food hall on the third level with various fast-food outlets.

A good selection of restaurants and bars are clustered in two strips between Quadras 405 and 404 Sul and between Quadras 308 and 309 Norte. You can get to both of these areas on the Grande Circular bus.

There are also good restaurants scattered around. In the following addresses, SCL means Setor Comércio Local, which is the space provided in the quadras for shops, restaurants etc. The letter N or S immediately after SCL means Norte (North) or Sul (South), and is followed by the quadra number, the block number and the shop number.

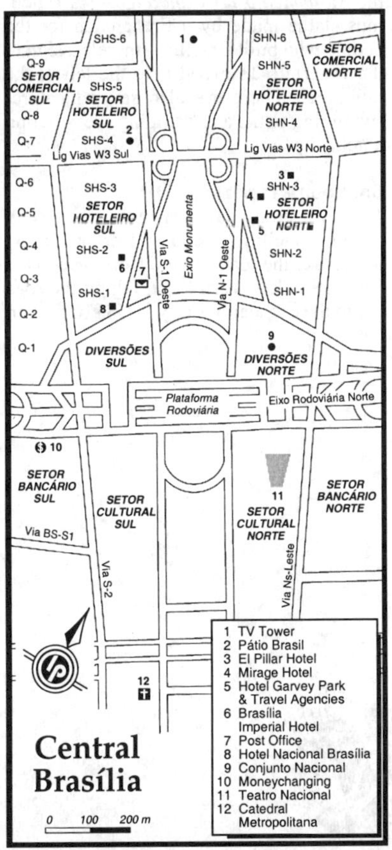

For nordestino cuisine, the *Xique-Xique* has carne de sol and feijão verde with manteiga da terra. It's at SCLS 107, Bloco A, loja 1. *Bar Beruth* is one of the city's longest established bar/restaurants and has outdoor tables under trees. It's at SCLS 109, Bloco A, loja 2/4. Another popular place is the *Bar Academia*, at SCLN 308, Bloco D, loja 11/19.

Vegetarians needn't feel left out. For some good natural food, there's *Cheiro Verde*, SCLN 313, Bloco C, loja 20. It's open Monday to Friday from 9 am to 8 pm. *Coisas da Terra*, at SCLN 703, Bloco D, loja 41, is open weekdays from 11.30 am to 2.30 pm and 5.30 to 8 pm, and weekends from noon to 6 pm.

Getting There & Away

Air With so many domestic flights making a stopover in Brasília, it's easy to catch a plane out of the city to almost anywhere in Brazil. Flying time to Rio is 1½ hours and to São Paulo, 80 minutes. Major domestic airlines with offices in Brasília include Transbrasil (☎ 243-6133), Varig/Cruzeiro (☎ 225-2883) and VASP (☎ 321-3636).

International airlines with offices in Brasília include Air France (☎ 223-4152), Swissair (☎ 223-4382), Lufthansa (☎ 223-8202) and British Airways (☎ 226-4164). All these airlines and several others are located in the Hotel Nacional.

Bus From the giant rodoferroviária (☎ 233-7200), due west of the city centre, there are buses to places you've never heard of. Destinations include Goiânia (US$9, three hours), Anápolis (US$7, 2½ hours), Belém (US$94, 34 hours), Belo Horizonte (US$33, 11 hours), Rio (US$67, 17 hours), São Paulo (US$46, 14 hours) and Salvador (US$68, 24 hours). To Pirenópolis (US$6, 2½ hours) there are five buses a day. There are also buses to Cuiabá (US$49, 19 hours), and Porto Velho (US$126, 44 hours) where you can make a connection to Manaus.

Getting Around

To/From the Airport The international airport (☎ 365-1941) is 12km south of the centre. There are two buses marked Aeroporto that go from the city rodoviária to the airport every 15 minutes. The fare is US$1.75 and the trip takes 35 minutes. A taxi between the airport and the city centre costs US$20.

Bus To get from the city rodoviária to the rodoferroviária (for long-distance buses), take the local bus No 131 (you can also flag it down along the main drag).

Car There are car rental agencies at the airport, at the Hotel Nacional and at the Hotel Garvey-Park.

AROUND BRASÍLIA

Estância de Agua de Itiquira

Itiquira is a Tupi-Guaraní Indian word meaning 'water that falls'. From the viewpoint at this 170m-high free-fall waterfall, you can see the valley of the Paranãs to the south. There's forest, several crystal-clear streams with natural pools for a swim, and the requisite restaurants and bars.

Itiquira is 110km from Brasília; you need a car to get there. Leave through the satellite cities of Sobradinho and Planaltina and the town of Formosa. The road is dirt for the next 35km.

Cachoeira Saia Velha

This is a pleasant swimming hang-out not too far from the city. Take the road to Belo Horizonte for about 20km. When you reach the *Monumento do Candango* – a ridiculous statue made by a Frenchman for the people who built Brasília – there's a sign to the waterfall. The road is to the left of the monument.There are also several natural swimming pools and camping areas but no hotel.

Cachoeira Topázio

This is a pretty fazenda with a waterfall, camping facilities, food and drink. To get there, take the road to Belo Horizonte to the Km 93 marker. Turn right, taking the road out to the cachoeira. Entry is US$10 per car.

Goiás

GOIÂNIA

• *pop 960,000* ✉ *74000-000* ☎ *062*

The capital of the state of Goiás, Goiânia is 200km south-west of Brasília and 900km from both Cuiabá and São Paulo. Planned by urbanist Armando de Godói and founded in 1933, it's a reasonably pleasant place, with lots of open spaces laid out around circular streets. There are three main zones – housing is in the south, administration is in the centre, and industry and commerce are in the north. Goiânia's economy is based on the commercialisation of the region's cattle.

Information

Tourist Office Goiastur is on the 3rd floor, Serra Dourada stadium, in the suburb of Jardim Goiás, but it is not worth the effort required to reach it. Everything you need to know about Goiânia is in the *Mini Guia de Goiânia*, available in hotels. It includes a map of the city and useful listings.

Turisplan Turismo (☎ 224-1941) is at No 388 Rua 8. This central travel agency sells airline and bus tickets and is helpful with information (in Portuguese).

Money The main branch of the Banco do Brasil is at Avenida Goiás 980. If you're going to Goiás Velho or Pirenópolis, change money here.

Post & Telephone The post office is right in the centre of town, at Praça Civica 11. Long-distance telephone calls can be made from the telephone centre on the corner of Rua 3 and Rua 7.

Things to See & Do

There's not much for the visitor in Goiânia. Our advice is to get out to one of the nearby colonial towns as quickly as you can. If you have some time to kill, try the **Parque Educativo**, on Avenida Anhanguera in Setor Oeste. It has a zoo, a zoological museum and an anthropology museum. Readers have recommended the **mercado** (market) at Praça Tamandaré on Saturday afternoon and Praça do Sol on Sunday afternoon.

Excursions within a 200km radius of Goiânia include the **Caldas Novas** hot springs, **Lake Pirapitinga**, **Pousada do Rio Quente** and the interesting rock formations of **Parauna**.

Places to Stay

There are a couple of cheap places near the rodoviária, but the centre of town is so close that it's worth staying there instead.

The *Hotel Del Rey* (☎ 224-0035), No 321 in the Rua 8 pedestrian mall, has the cheapest rooms in town, but it's pretty dingy. Shabby apartamentos cost US$15 per person. *Lord Hotel* (☎ 224-0385), Avenida Anhanguera 4999, is better value. Comfortable apartamentos with fan and fridge go for US$23/34 for singles/doubles. Ask for a room with a balcony. Another cheapie nearby on Avenida Anhanguera is the

Goiânia Palace (☎ 224-4874) which charges US$18/30 for basic quartos. The *Principe Hotel* (☎ 224-0085), Avenida Anhanguera 2936, has quartos for US$23/34 but is much more pleasant.

In the mid-range, the *Vila Rica Hotel* (☎ 223-2733), Avenida Anhanguera 3456, and the *Cabiúna Palace* (☎ 224-4355), Avenida Paranaíba 698, each charge US$55/80 for singles/doubles, but give discounts of up to 30% on weekends.

There are plenty of top-end alternatives. In the centre, *Hotel Karajás* (☎ 224-9666; fax 229-1153), No 860 Rua 3, charges US$83/100 and *Hotel Bandeirantes* (☎ 212-0066), Avenida Anhanguera 5106, charges US$86/96.

Places to Eat

Since they are surrounded by cattle, the locals eat lots of meat. They also like to munch on pamonha, a very tasty green-corn concoction sold at pamonharia stands all over town. Try it.

If you want to taste some typical Goiânian dishes, such as arroz com pequi, arroz com guariroba or peixe na telha, head for *Fogão Caipira*, No 570 Rua 83, Setor Sul, or *Tacho de Cobre* in the Serra Dourada stadium, Jardim Goiás. Our favourite dish is the empadão de Goiás, a tasty meat, vegetable and olive pie.

Vegetarian food is available at *Reserva Natural*, upstairs at No 485, Rua 7. It's open for lunch Monday to Friday. *Micky's* on Rua 4 near the Parthenon Centre is a popular place for a drink and snack.

Praça Tamandaré, a short ride on the Eixo T-7 bus or a long walk from the centre, is the pizza capital of Goiânia: *Ze Colmeia* and *Aquarela* are a couple of good places. For meat, beer and music, try *Churrascaria e Chopparia do Gaúcho* or just wander around and see what takes your fancy.

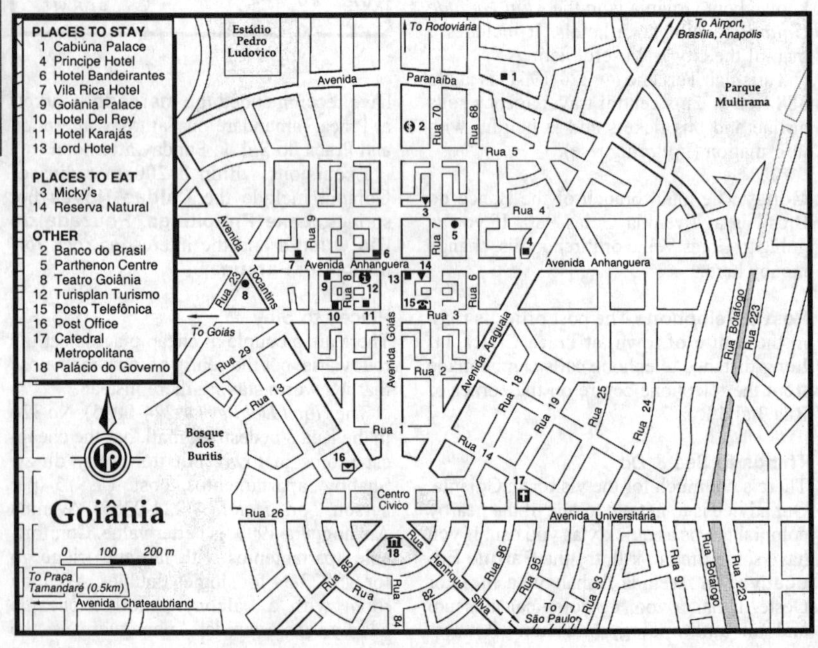

Getting There & Away

Air In addition to the regular domestic carriers, there are several air-taxi companies that go anywhere and everywhere in the Mato Grosso and Amazon, but they're expensive. If you're interested in hiring an air-taxi, call Sete Taxi Aereo (☎ 207-1519) or União (☎ 207-1600).

Major airlines include Varig (☎ 224-5049), VASP (☎ 224-6389) and Transbrasil (☎ 225-0033).

Bus The huge rodoviária (☎ 224-8466) may have lost its grip on the record for the most TV sets on poles – there are only 10 now, down from 14 and 22 on the last two research trips! Regular buses go to Brasília (US$10, three hours), Cuiabá (US$41, 13 hours) and Goiás Velho (US$10, 2½ hours). Three buses a day run to Caldas Novas (US$11, three hours) and one goes to Pirenópolis (US$9, two hours) at 4 pm. There's a daily bus to Foz do Iguaçu (US$50, 20 hours) at 11 am.

Getting Around

Aeroporto Santo Genoveva (☎ 207-1288) is 6km from the city centre – US$8 by taxi.

You can walk from the rodoviária into town – it takes 15 minutes to get to the corner of Avenida Anhanguera and Avenida Goiás, but you might melt along the way. From outside the rodoviária, take a No 163 Vila União – Centro or No 404 Rodoviária – Centro bus to town. To get to Praça Tamandare, catch the Vila União bus.

GOIÁS VELHO

• *pop 29,000* ✉ *76600-000* ☎ *062*

The historic colonial city of Goiás Velho (or simply Goiás) was formerly known as Vila Boa. Once the state capital, it is 144km from Goiânia and is linked to Cuiabá by dirt road. The city and its baroque churches shine during Semana Santa (Holy Week).

History

On the heels of the gold discoveries in Minas Gerais, *bandeirantes* (bands of Paulistas who explored the interior) pushed further into the interior in search of more precious stones and, as always, Indian slaves. In 1682, a bandeira headed by the old Paulista Bartolomeu Bueno da Silva visited the area. The Goyaz Indians gave him the nickname *anhanguera* (old devil) when, after burning some *cachaça* (Brazil's national drink, a sugar-cane rum) – which the Indians believed to be water – on a plate, he threatened to set fire to all the rivers if they didn't show him where their gold mines were. Three years later, having been given up for dead, the old devil returned to São Paulo with a few survivors and gold and Indian slaves from Goiás.

In 1722, his son, who had been on the first trip, organised another bandeira. The gold rush was on. It followed a pattern similar to that in Minas Gerais. First came the Paulistas, then the Portuguese Emboadas and soon the black slaves. With everything imported from so far away, prices were even higher than in Minas Gerais, and many suffered and died, particularly the slaves. The boom ended quickly.

Information

There is no tourist office or money exchange facility in Goiás Velho.

Things to See

Walking through Goiás Velho, the former state capital, you quickly notice the main legacies of the gold rush: 18th century colonial architecture, and a large mulatto and mestizo population. The streets are narrow, with low houses, and there are seven churches. The most impressive is the oldest, the **Igreja da Paula** (1761), at Praça Zaqueu Alves de Castro.

The **Museu das Bandeiras** is well worth a visit. It's in the old town council building (1766), at Praça Brasil Caiado. Other interesting museums are the **Museu de Arte Sacra** (in the old Igreja da Boa Morte dating from 1779, on Praça Castelo Branco), with lots of 19th century works by local Goiânian Viega Vale, and the **Palácio Conde dos Arcos** (the old governor's residence). All museums are open from 8 am to 5 pm Tuesday to Saturday and from 8 am to noon on Sunday.

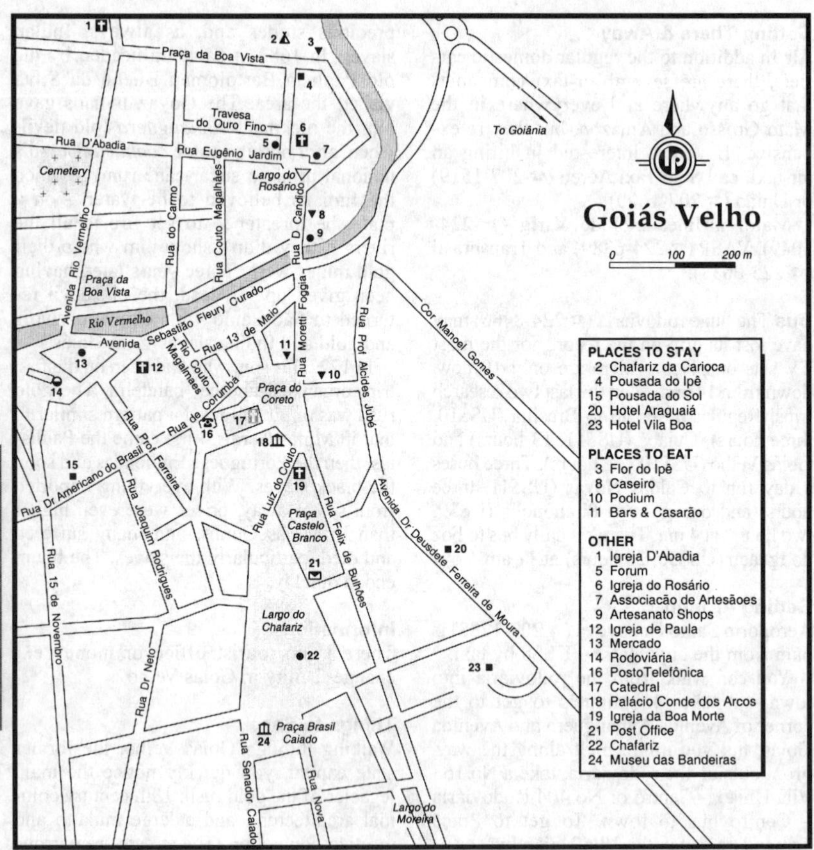

Special Events

The big occasion in Goiás Velho is Semana Santa (Holy Week). The main streets of town are lit by hundreds of torches carried by the townsfolk and by dozens of hooded figures in a procession which re-enacts the removal of Christ from the cross and his burial.

Places to Stay

You can camp in town at the *Chafariz da Carioca*, just behind the Pousada do Ipê.

The best low-budget place is the *Pousada do Ipê* (☎ 371-2065), a colonial house on Praça da Boa Vista with rooms set around a shady courtyard. Apartamentos start at US$20/30 for singles/doubles, with a healthy breakfast included. Another good option is the *Pousada do Sol* (☎ 371-1717), Rua Dr Americano do Brasil 17, with apartamentos at the same prices. Cheaper, but not as pleasant, is the *Hotel Araguaiá* (☎ 371-1462), Avenida Dr Deusdete Ferreira de Moura. It's a bit of a hike from the bus station – about 15 minutes – but has clean apartamentos for US$10/15.

The *Hotel Vila Boa* (☎ 371-1000) is up on a hill, with a view and a swimming pool. Singles/doubles go for US$80/105.

Places to Eat

The empadão reigns in Goiás Velho and the tasty savoury pie filled with meat, vegetables, olives and egg is served just about everywhere.

Flor do Ipê on Praça da Boa Vista offers very good regional food in a garden setting overlooking the river for around US$6 per person. It gets crowded on weekends, so get in early. *Caseiro*, at Rua D Candido 31, and *Pôdium*, just off Praça do Coreto, also offer regional food and churrascaria. *Casarão*, a run-down place upstairs near the corner of the praça and Rua Moretti Foggia, serves great empadãos for US$3. The praça is also the place to go for music, drinks and snacks at night.

Getting There & Away

Buses to Goiás Velho stop at the new rodoviária first, then continue on to the old rodoviária in the centre of town (see map). There are frequent buses running between Goiás Velho to Goiânia (US$9, 2½ hours). Try to get on a direct bus; the local buses stop everywhere and, consequently, take much longer.

PIRENÓPOLIS

• *pop 21,000* ✉ *72980-000* ☎ *062*

Pirenópolis, another historic colonial gold city, is 128km from Goiânia and 165km from Brasília, on the Rio das Almas. It's a laid-back, picturesque town that has since become a popular weekend retreat for Goiânians.

Founded in 1727 by a bandeira of Paulistas in search of gold, Pirenópolis was originally called Minas da NS do Rosário da Meia Ponte. In 1989 it was placed on the Patrimonio Nacional (National Heritage) register. The city's colonial buildings sit on striking red earth under big skies.

Information

There is no official tourist information office or money exchange facility in Pirenópolis. You might, though, find some brochures at the Secretária Municipal de Cultura e Tourismo on Rua do Bontim.

Cerrado Ecoturismo (☎ 331-1240), Rua do Bonfim 46, is run by Rogério de Souza Dias who speaks English and is a good source of information. He can organise historic tours of the town, including the old gold mine (Museu das Lavras de Ouro), mountain bike rides and hikes to Bon Successo waterfalls and up the Morro do Frota.

Festa do Divino Espírito Santo

Pirenópolis is famous for performing the story of Festa do Divino Espírito Santo (45 days after Easter) a tradition begun in 1819.

For three days, the town looks like a scene from the Middle Ages. *Cavalhadas, congadas, mascardos, tapirios* and *pastorinhos* perform a series of medieval tournaments, dances and festivities, including a mock battle between the Moors and Christians in distant Iberia. Riding richly decorated horses, the combatants wear bright costumes and bull-headed masks. The Moors are defeated on the battlefield and convert to Christianity, proving that heresy doesn't pay in the end.

The festival is a happy one, and more folkloric than religious. The town's population swells several-fold during the festival.

If you're in the neighbourhood, make a point of seeing this stunning and curious spectacle, one of the most fascinating in Brazil.

Chris McAsey

Churches

The **Igreja NS do Rosário Matriz** (1732) is the oldest sacred monument in the state. The **Igreja NS do Bonfim**, (1750), with its beautiful altars, contains an image of the Senhor de Bonfim brought here from Portugal in 1755. The **Igreja NS do Carmo** (1750) was built by the Portuguese and today houses the Museu das Artes Sacras.

Santuário de Vida Silvestre – Fazenda Vagafogo

Six kilometres from town, the Vagafogo Farm Wildlife Sanctuary is well worth a visit. Landowners Evandro Engel Ayer and Catarina Schiffer have set aside 23 hectares of *cerrado* (grassy plain dotted with trees) and gallery forests on the margins of the Rio Vagafogo as a nature reserve. Fauna includes brown capuchin and black howler monkeys, armadillos, pampas deer, agouti and many bird species. The forest is impressive, with a canopy top averaging 25m.

Entry is US$3. There's a café for lunch at the visitors centre.

Parque Estadual da Serra dos Pirineus

The park contains the 1385m Pico dos Pirineus, 18km from town on a well-used dirt road. Along the way there are waterfalls and interesting rock formations.

Cachoeiras de Bonsuccesso

These waterfalls 5km north of town are a good place to cool off in clear pools. Be prepared to jump some cliffs, and take your snorkel. Entry costs US$4.

Places to Stay

Pirenópolis is crowded on weekends, and during the Cavalhadas festival and Carnaval, prices are almost double those

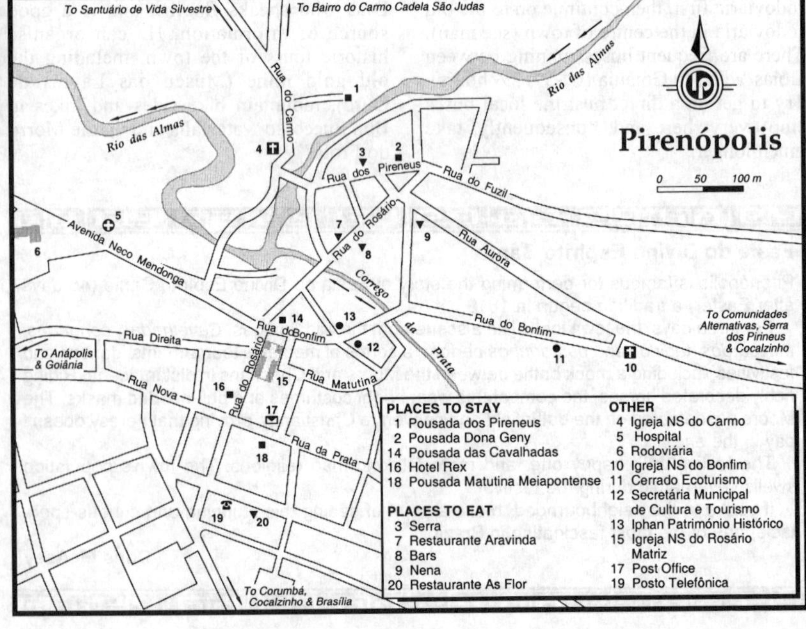

quoted here. When the pousadas fill up, most visitors camp out near the Rio das Almas or rent a room from a local.

There is a good range of pousadas in town, starting with the charming *Pousada Dona Geny* (☎ 331-1128), Rua dos Pireneus 29, at US$8 a head. The *Hotel Rex* (☎ 331-1121), Emmanoel Lopes 15, is basic but clean, with quartos for US$10 per person. The *Pousada das Cavalhadas* (☎ 331-1261), Praça da Matriz 1, has double apartamentos with air-conditioning for US$30.

The pink-and-white *Pousada Matutina Meiapontense* (☎ 331-1101) is a friendly, comfortable place with a swimming pool. Apartamentos with fan go for US$20 per person.

A couple of expensive top-end places have sprung up in the last few years, including the *Pousada dos Pireneus* (☎ 331-1028), in Bairro de Carmo (cross the bridge and follow the signs). This place has got the works – including water aerobics and donkey rides for the kids! Prices start at US$95/120 for singles/doubles.

Places to Eat

The *Restaurante As Flor* on Avenida São Jayme serves good regional cuisine. Don't fill up on your main course – there's an assortment of 18 different desserts, each sweeter than the last. *Serra* on Rua dos Pireneus, is also recommended for regional food and *Nena*, Rua Aurora 4, has an excellent por quilo lunch. The *Restaurante Aravinda* on Rua do Rosário has an extensive menu with some vegetarian dishes. Nearby, *Varanda* and *Tarsia* are good bars for a snack and a drink.

Things to Buy

Pirenópolis is considered the national silver capital, with more than 80 silversmithing studios scattered around town.

At Piretur, on Avenida Comandante Joaquim Alves, you'll find a good selection of other local craft items made from ceramic, leather, wood, straw and soapstone.

Getting There & Away

There are three buses a day to Brasília, and one direct bus to Goiânia at 6 pm. There are more frequent local buses to Anápolis, where you can catch a connection to Goiânia.

CALDAS NOVAS

• *pop 40,000 ✉ 75690-000 ☎ 062*

Caldas Novas, 187km from Goiânia and 393km from Brasília, has more than 30 hot springs, with average temperatures of 42°C (107°F). Now a fairly upmarket resort, the region has dozens of hotels. Studies have shown that the healing waters are beneficial for people suffering from high blood pressure, poor digestion, weak endocrine glands or impotence.

Information

There's a tourist information booth (☎ 453-1868) on Praça Mestre Orlando. It has information about the various springs you can dip into, most of which are out of town. The Banco do Brasil is at Rua Santos Dumond 55.

Places to Stay

Six kilometres from the city, on the road to Pires do Rio, *Camping Lagoa Quente* has two thermal swimming pools. The cost is US$10 a head.

A couple of relatively cheap places in the centre are *Serra Dourada* (☎ 453-1300), Rua Orozimbo Correia Neto 200, with simple apartamentos costing US$35 a double; and *Santa Clara* (☎ 453-1764), Rua America 109, which charges US$30/40 for singles/doubles.

There is no shortage of top-end places, with over a dozen hotels in town costing more than US$100 per night.

Places to Eat

For lunch, *Real* has a por quilo buffet at Avenida Orcalino Santos 40, or try *Agua na Boca*, on Rua Machado de Assis, for snack foods like empadão and sandwiches. *Palhoça do Ziu* on Rua do Tourismo and *Papas* at Praça Mestre Orlando 12 both have regional fish and meat dinner dishes for around US$15 for two people.

Getting There & Away

The rodoviária is at the end of Rua Antônio Coelho de Godoy. Frequent buses go to Brasília (US$30, six hours) and Goiânia (US$11, three hours), as well as to Rio de Janeiro and São Paulo.

PARQUE NACIONAL DA CHAPADA DOS VEADEIROS

Just over 220km north of Brasília and 420km from Goiânia, this scenic park is in the highest area of the Central West. With high waterfalls, natural swimming pools and oasis-like stands of wine palms, it's a popular destination for ecotourists.

Mammals include maned wolves, banded anteaters, giant armadillos, capybaras and tapirs. Birds include rheas, toucans and vultures. The best time to visit the park is between May and October, before the rivers flood during the rainy season. Entry is US$3.

Apart from the national park, there is a place that absolutely has to be seen: the Vale da Lua (Moon Valley), with its moon-like rocky geography and chilly crystal river and pools. It's about 5km from São Jorge and the admission fee is US$3.

Andreá Vannucchi, São Paulo, Brazil

Information

Visitors must enter the park with an IBAMA guide. Guides cost US$30 per group (up to 15 people) and give a rundown of the local flora and fauna. Take lunch and water with you, as there are no facilities inside the park.

Places to Stay

You can camp at *Parada Obrigatória*, 400m from the entrance to the park, for US$6 a night. There are a couple of cabins for around US$15 per person. In the small town of São Jorge, a couple of kilometres from the park, *Pousada Trilha Violeta* (☎ (061) 646-1109 in Brasília) is a friendly family-run place with apartamentos for US$25 per person. A big breakfast is included. *Pousada das Flores* (☎ (061) 234-7493) has two-storey cabanas for up to six people. A wider range of accommodation can be found at Alto Paraíso, 36km from São Jorge.

The blue macaw one of the species threatened by deforestation and the illegal wildlife trade.

Getting There & Away

From Goiânia, there's a daily bus to Alto Paraíso at 10 pm (US$20, 5½ hours). You can get a local bus from there to São Jorge. There are two buses a day from Brasília to Alto Paraíso, at 10 am and 10.30 pm.

PARQUE NACIONAL DAS EMAS

Emas is a relatively small (1300 sq km) park in the corner of the state of Goiás, where it meets the states of Mato Grosso and Mato Grosso do Sul. The park lies along the Brazilian great divide, between the Amazon and Paraná river basins, at the headwaters of the Araguaia, Formoso and Taquari rivers.

The three rivers take divergent paths to the Atlantic. The Araguaia courses north to the equator via the Tocantins and the mighty Amazon. The Rio Taquari travels westward to flood the Pantanal, then flows south via the Paraguai. The Rio Formoso changes name midstream to Corrientes, and flows into the Parnaiba and then the Paraná.

The Paraguai and the Paraná flow on either side of Paraguay, meet at Argentina, and enter the Atlantic a few hundred kilometres east of Buenos Aires and some 35° latitude south of the mouth of the Rio Amazonas.

Surrounded by farmlands, the Parque Nacional das Emas is on a high plateau covered by grassy plains and open woodlands. There's little foliage to obstruct the sighting of wildlife, which includes tapirs, anteaters, deer, capybaras, foxes,peccaries, armadillos, and blue and yellow macaws. It's the home of endangered wolves, and is the exclusive sanctuary of the jacamari (species of wolf) and other rare species. Another interesting spectacle in the park is the large number of termite mounds that 'glow' in the dark at certain times of the year (the result of fluorescence produced by the termite larvae).

During the dry season (July to October), the area is dry enough for fires to ignite spontaneously. In 1988, a fire raged for five days, burning 65% of the park. Be careful with sparks!

Places to Stay

Basic accommodation inside the park costs about US$6 per person. You'll need to take your own food, but there is a kitchen. It's also possible to camp in the park, and this costs around US$3 per person per night.

Getting There & Away

Access to the park is tough: even though it's surrounded by farmland, there are no sealed roads or regular bus routes. Visitors must arrange with private companies for 4WD vehicles or air-taxis from as far away as Cuiabá, Goiânia and Campo Grande.

Adventurous types may consider taking Hwy BR-364 to Alto do Araguaia/Santa Rita do Araguaia (531km from Goiânia, 423km from Cuiabá), then hitching 63km to Plaça dos Mineiros, and 40 to 60km further along dirt roads to the park.

RIO ARAGUAIA

For information on this park, refer to the section on the Rio Araguaia in the Pará, Amapá & Tocantins chapter.

Mato Grosso & Mato Grosso do Sul

Mato Grosso and Mato Grosso do Sul are separate states, although until the late 1970s this region was all Mato Grosso state. This chapter contains a separate section on the Pantanal, the vast wetlands which extend across parts of both states.

Mato Grosso

There's a well-known story about a naturalist in the Mato Grosso. Disoriented by the sameness of the forest, the naturalist asked his Indian guide – who had killed a bird, put it in a tree and, incredibly, knew where to return for it at the end of the day – how he knew where the tree was. 'It was in the same place' the Indian replied.

To begin to appreciate the Mato Grosso's inaccessibility and vastness, read the classic *Brazilian Adventure* by Peter Fleming. It also happens to be one of the funniest travel books ever written. Fleming tells the story of his quest to find the famous British explorer Colonel Fawcett, who disappeared in the Mato Grosso in 1925 while searching for the hidden city of gold. *The Pantanal* by Vic Banks, a more recent account of travel through the Pantanal, is also an entertaining read. For a more scientific report on the region, see *Mato Grosso: Last Virgin Land* by Anthony Smith.

Mato Grosso means bundu, savanna, bush, outback; an undeveloped thick scrub. Part of the highland plain that runs through Brazil's interior, the Mato Grosso is a dusty land of rolling hills and some of the best fishing rivers in the world, such as the Araguaia.

This is also the land where many of Brazil's remaining Indians live. They are being threatened by rapid agricultural development (which is bringing in poor peasants from the South and Northeast who are desperate for land) and by a government which is less than fully committed to guaranteeing them their rights.

There's a saying in Brazil that 'progress is roads'. Key routes such as the roads from Belém to Brasília and Cuiabá to Santarém have catalysed the opening of vast stretches of the Mato Grosso to cattle, rice, cotton, soya bean, corn and manioc, as well as to mining.

This is Brazil's Wild West, where an often-desperate struggle for land between peasants, Indians, miners, rich landowners and hired guns leads to frequent killings and illegal land expropriation.

CUIABÁ

• *pop 450,000* ✉ *78000-000* ☎ *065*

Cuiabá is a frontier boom town. New roads have opened the lands of the Mato Grosso and southern Amazon, bringing to the area peasants desperate for land, and increasing exports of agricultural products. For many years, Cuiabá's population grew at 14% annually, a national record. The population explosion has tailed off in recent years, but Cuiabá is still one of Brazil's boom towns. It has been named the *boca de sertão* (mouth of the backlands).

Founded in 1719 by gold and slave-seeking *bandeirantes* (bands of Paulistas who explored the interior), Cuiabá has little historic or cultural heritage to interest travellers. However, it's a lively place and a good base for excursions into the Pantanal and Chapada dos Guimarães, as well as a useful rest stop on the way to the Amazon and Bolivia.

The city is actually two sister cities separated by the Rio Cuiabá: old Cuiabá and Várzea Grande (where the airport is located, by the Rio Cuiabá). We found the people here friendly and gracious.

History

A Paulista, Pascoal Moreira Cabral, was hunting Indians along the Rio Cuiabá when he found gold in 1719. A gold rush followed, but many of those seeking gold never reached Cuiabá. Travelling over 3000km from São Paulo by river took five months; along the way there was little food, many mosquitoes, dangerous rapids, lengthy portages, disease and incredible heat.

There was usually one flotilla of canoes each year, bringing supplies, slaves and miners and returning with gold. Although there were several hundred people in a flotilla, including many soldiers to protect the canoes against Indian attacks, the expeditions often failed.

With the end of the gold boom and the decay of the mines, Cuiabá would have disappeared, except that the gold was never completely exhausted *(garimpeiros* – prospectors still seek their fortunes today); also, the soil along the Rio Cuiabá allowed subsistence agriculture, while the river itself provided fish.

As in many mining towns, there was tension here between Paulistas and recent Portuguese immigrants. In 1834, the small town was torn apart by the Rusga (Brawl),

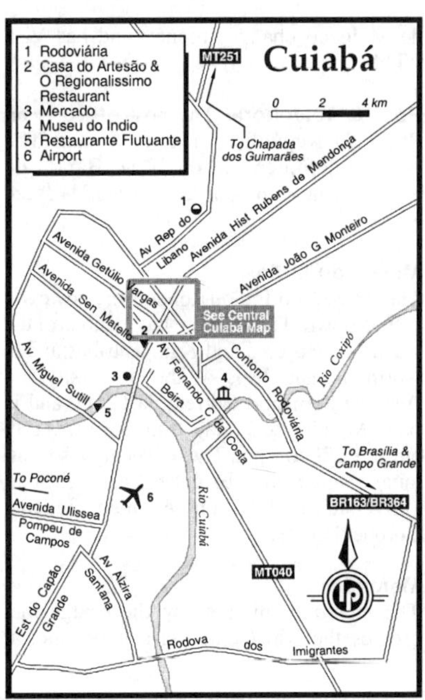

in which a nativist movement of Paulistas, inspired by wild rumours following Brazilian independence, slaughtered many of the Portuguese on the pretext that their victims wanted to return Brazil to Portuguese rule.

Information

Tourist Office Sedtur (☎ 624-9060), the Mato Grosso tourist authority, is in the city centre, on the Praça da República. The staff are helpful and speak English. The office is open Monday to Friday from 8.30 to 11.30 am and from 2 to 6 pm.

Foreign Consulate The Bolivian consulate (☎ 623-5094) is in the Cunjunto Nacional building, 5th floor, Avenida Isaac Povoas 1177.

Money The Banco do Brasil on the corner of Avenida Getúlio Vargas and Rua Barão de Melgaço changes money and has Visa ATMs.

Post & Telephone The post office is on Praça da República, next to Sedtur. The posto telefônico is on Rua Barão de Melgaço, near the corner of Avenida Isaac Póvoas.

Museu do Indio

This Museu do Indio (Rondon) is, however, played down. The museum has exhibits of the Xavantes, Bororos and Karajas tribes and is worth a visit. It is at the university, on Avenida Fernando Correia da Costa, and is open Monday to Friday from 8.30 to 11.30 am and 2.30 to 5 pm. The university also contains a small zoo. To get there, catch a Jd Universitário bus, on Avenida Tenente Coronel Duarte.

Mercado

The *mercado* (market) by the bridge that crosses the Rio Cuiabá is a good one, at least before the heat of the day. It's interesting not so much as a place to shop but as a venue to look at the people and their products. The old fish mercado nearby is being transformed into the Museu do Rio Cuiabá.

Santo Antônio de Leverger

Santo Antônio de Leverger, the site of Mato Grosso's best Carnaval, is where Cuiabános go for river-beaching from June to October. It's on the Rio Cuiabá, 28km south of Cuiabá in the direction of Barão de Melgaço.

Organised Tours

For details about excursions from Cuiabá into the Pantanal, see Organised Tours in the Pantanal section.

The travel agencies and guides in town can arrange day trips to Chapada dos Guimarães, and can help with the logistics of more ambitious trips to the Parque Nacional das Emas. Anaconda (☎ 624-6242) at

The Indians of Mato Grosso

To reach Cuiabá, the Portuguese had to cross the lands of several groups of Indians, many of whom were formidable warriors. They included the Caiapó (who even attacked the settlement at Goiás), the Bororo of the Pantanal, the Parecis (who were enslaved to mine gold), the Paiaguá (who defeated several large Portuguese flotillas and caused periodic panic in Cuiabá) and the Guaicuru (skilled riders and warriors with many years experience fighting the Europeans).

In response to the pressures imposed by a nomadic lifestyle in a region without abundant food, the Guaicuru women performed their own abortions, refusing to have children until they were near menopause. On longer journeys, when the women stayed behind, the Guaicuru men took male transvestites with them as sexual partners. Both women and men could divorce easily, and often did, several times a year.

Despite important victories, many Indians had been killed or enslaved by the time the gold boom began to fade, in the mid-1700s. Today, however, several tribes remain in northern Mato Grosso, living as they have for centuries. The Erikbatsa, noted for their fine featherwork, live near Fontanilles and Juima; the Nhambikuraa are near Padroal; and the Cayabi live near Juara. There are also the Indians of Aripuana Parque and, of course, the tribes under the care of FUNAI at Xingu park. The only tribe left in the Pantanal still to subsist by hunting and fishing is the Bororo.

You probably won't be able to overcome the many obstacles to visiting the Indians, but if you want to try, contact FUNAI (☎ (065) 644-1850) in Cuiabá.

Chris McAsey

Rua Comandante Costa 649, and Pantanal Tours (☎ 323-1557) at Rua Joaquim Murtinho 956 both run tours to Chapada.

Some of the freelance guides in town also organise trips to Chapada. Recommended guides include Joel Souza (☎ toll free 9065-983-3552), at Avenida Getúlio Vargas 155A, Munir Nasr and Laercio Sá.

Special Events

The Festa de São Benedito takes place during the first week of July, at the Igreja NS do Rosário and the Capela de São Benedito. The holiday has a more Umbanda than Catholic flavour; it's celebrated with traditional foods such as *bolo de queijo* (cheese balls) and *bolo de arroz*, (rice balls) and regional dances such as O Cururu, O Siriri, Danças do Congo and dos Mascarados.

Places to Stay

There's a shortage of good-value budget accommodation in Cuiabá, however, local guide Joel Souza has just opened a pousada. *Pousada Ecoverde* (☎ 623-4696), Rua Pedro Celestino 391, is two blocks from the VASP office in the old part of town. Rooms cost US$10 per person with breakfast included and Joel is a great source of local information. One of the better cheapies is the *Hotel Samara* (☎ 322-6001), Rua Joaquim Murtinho 270, with basic quartos for US$10 per person and boxy apartamentos at US$15/20 for singles/doubles.

Hotel Panorama (☎ 322-0072), Travessa Terreira Mendes 10, has more airy apartamentos with fan at US$18/28/33 for singles/doubles/triples. A bit dingy, but in a quiet spot on Rua Galdino Pimentel near the old town, is the *Hotel São Marcos* (☎ 624-2300). Clean apartamentos cost US$15/30. The *Hotel Presidente* (☎ 321-6162), on a busy corner at Avenida Getúlio Vargas 345, has run-down single/double quartos for US$16/26 and apartamentos for US$21/29. *Hotel Plaza* (☎ 323-2018), Rua Antônio Maria 428, is a bit sleazy, but apartamentos with air-conditioning aren't bad value at US$20/30. Bargaining is worth a try here.

Of the mid-range options, *Hotel Mato Grosso* (☎ 321-9121), Rua Comandante Costa 2522, is a travellers' favourite. It has US$28/33 apartamentos, and a good breakfast as well. *Hotel Real* (☎ 321-5375), Praça Ipiranga 102, has large apartamentos with air-conditioning and fridge for US$28/40/55 a single/double/triple. The *Jaguar Palace Hotel* (☎ 624-4404; fax 623-7798), Avenida Getúlio Vargas 600, is a three-star hotel with a pool. Singles/doubles go for US$100/130, but you can negotiate discounts of up to 50% for cash.

At the top end, the Best Western *Mato Grosso Palace* (☎ 624-7747), Rua Joaquim Murtinho 170, is a four-star job offering singles/doubles starting at US$98/118.

Places to Eat

Cuiabá offers some great fish dishes, including pacu assado com farofa de couve, piraputanga assado and pirâo de bagre – try one at the floating restaurant *Flutuante*, next to Ponte Nova bridge. Six kilometres from the centre, it's complicated to reach by public bus but from the waterfront mercado, it's a 20 minute walk. The restaurant is open daily from 11 am to 11 pm.

On Rua 13 de Junho next to the Casa do Artesão is *O Regionalissimo*, which serves excellent regional food. The cost is US$10 for buffet-style meals – lots of fish and the sweetest of sweets. It's open daily except Monday for lunch and dinner.

In the centre, a cheap, wholesome por quilo lunch spot is *Miranda's*, near the Hotel Mato Grosso on Rua Comandante Costa. Vegetarians can lunch nearby at *Tio Ari*. The centre is deserted at night, so you have to walk a bit for a good meal.

Restaurante Max, Rua Joaquim Murtinho 586, serves good value reifeições for US$3.50 and has a breezy courtyard. *Papa Gaio*, on the corner of Avenida Mato Grosso and Avenida Presidente Marcos, is a large open-air restaurant popular with locals who come to drink excellent chopp (draught beer) and dine from the varied menu. *Getulio*, Avenida Getúlio Vargas 1147, is an

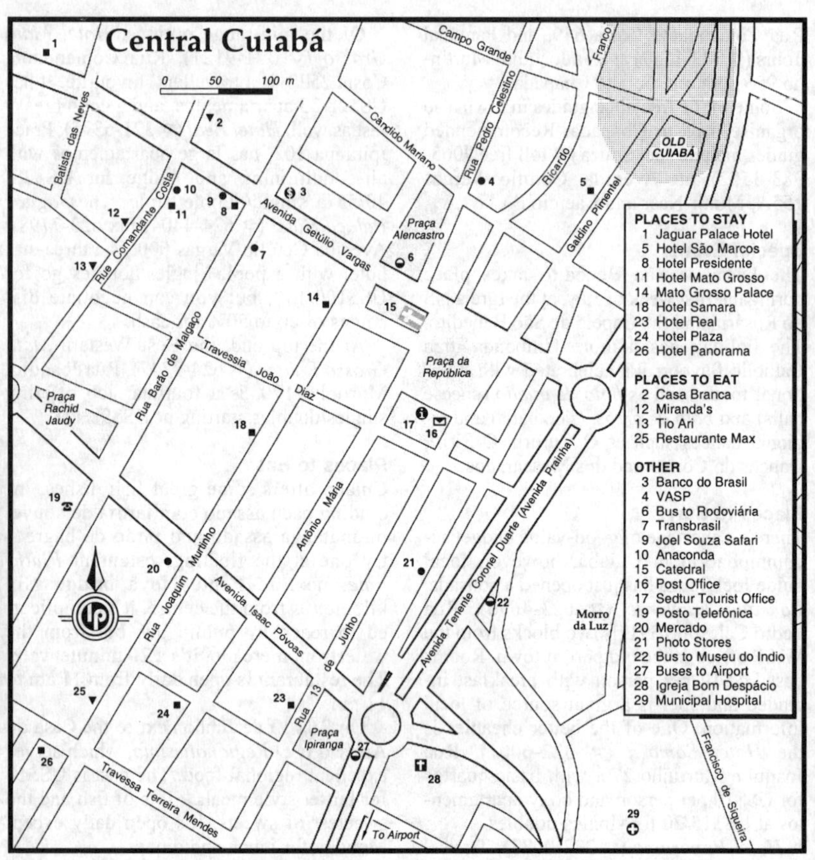

upmarket bar/restaurant popular with young Cuiabános. It's about a five minute walk past the Jaguar Palace Hotel. *Choppão*, further along Avenida Getúlio Vargas on Praça 8 de Abril, is another popular spot.

Entertainment

When the sun sets and temperatures drop a bit, the city comes to life. A great place to go, especially if you spend only one night in Cuiabá, is *Ninho's Bar*, Rua Laranjeiras 701. It has a spectacular view of the city, good chopp, and live acoustic music. *Operalight*, a band venue and dance club, is a stone's throw away if you feel like a change of pace. *Estrebaria* on Avenida Mato Grosso is a more intimate bar and a good place to meet locals. Close by on the same street, *Apoteose* is a popular dance club.

Things to Buy

The Casa do Artesão on Rua 13 de Junho has local handicrafts, including ceramics, woodcarvings, straw baskets, paintings and hammocks. The FUNAI Artindia shop, Rua Pedro Celestino 317, is open weekdays from 8.30 to 11.30 am and 2 to 6 pm. It has Indian baskets, bows and arrows, jewellery and headdresses for sale.

Getting There & Away

Air There are flights between Cuiabá and the rest of Brazil with Transbrasil (☎ 624-2000), VASP (☎ 624-2770) and Varig (☎ 624-7170). Make reservations well in advance if you're travelling in July, when many Brazilians are on holiday.

A recent introduction are flights between Cuiabá and Santa Cruz, Bolivia, leaving Cuiabá on Monday, Wednesday and Friday and cost US$170 one way, US$250 return. LAB is represented by VASP in Cuiabá.

Bus Cuiabá's rodoviária (☎ 621-3512) is situated on the highway towards Chapada dos Guimarães. To get there, catch a municipal bus from Praça Alencastro in the centre. Five buses a day make the two hour trip to Poconé (US$8, 2 hours); the first leaves at 6 am. To Barão de Melgaço (US$11, 3½ hours) there are three daily buses at 7.30 and 9 am and at 3 pm. For Chapada dos Guimarães (US$4, 2 hours) there are buses every hour or two, but take the 7 am bus if you've only got a day to spend there.

Eight buses a day go to Cáceres (US$16, 3 hours) with connections to Santa Cruz in Bolivia. Porto Velho is a hard 24 hour (US$63) ride away. There are four buses a day. To Goiânia (US$39, 13 hours), there are seven buses a day. Most of the eight buses a day to Campo Grande (US$30, 10 hours) stop at Coxim (US$21, 6 hours). To Alta Floresta (US$54, 13 hours) there are four buses a day.

Getting Around

To/From the Airport Marechal Rondon airport (☎ 682-2213) is in Varzea Grande, 7km from Cuiabá. To catch the local bus to town, walk left as you leave the airport to the Las Velas Hotel. From opposite the hotel entrance, catch a Jardim Marajoara, Cohab-canela or Imperial bus to the city centre.

Bus From inside the rodoviária, take the Rodoviária/Centro bus to Praça Alencastro. Other buses marked Centro leave from outside the rodoviária and can drop you along Avenida Isaac Povoas.

Car All the car-rental places have branches in the centre and in or near the airport. There are often promotional rates, so shop around. Central (☎ 433-4523) and Localiza (☎ 433-5866) are a couple of reliable companies. The best cars for the Pantanal are the Volkswagen Gol and the Fiat Uno.

On average, a rental car will cost around US$65 a day.

CHAPADA DOS GUIMARÃES

After the Pantanal, Chapada dos Guimarães is Mato Grosso's leading attraction. This rocky plateau is 64km north-east of Cuiabá and 800m higher, offering a cool change from the capital. It's a beautiful region reminiscent of the American south-west and surprisingly different from the typical Mato Grosso terrain.

Véu de Noiva & the Mirante Lookout

The two exceptional sights in the Chapadas are the 60m Véu de Noiva (Bridal Veil) falls, and the Mirante lookout, unofficially the geographic centre of South America. Six kilometres beyond Salgadeira you'll see the turn-off for Véu de Noiva on your right. It's well signposted. You can get off the bus from Cuiabá and walk there from the road, spend a couple of hours there, then flag down the next bus coming through.

The Mirante lookout is 8km from the town. Take the last road in Chapada on your right and go 8km; you'll see a dirt road. The rim of the canyon is a couple of hundred metres away. The view is stupendous; off to your right you can see the Cuiabá skyline.

Start walking downhill over the bluff, slightly to your right. A small trail leads to a magical lookout, perched on top of rocks with the canyon below. This is Chapada's most dazzling place.

Other Attractions

On the way to Chapada, you pass **Rio dos Peixes**, **Rio Mutaca** and **Rio Claro**, which are all popular weekend bathing spots for Cuiabanos. The sheer 80m drop called **Portão do Inferno** (Hell's Gate) is also unforgettable.

Take a waterfall shower at **Cachoeirinha** and peek into the chapel of **NS de Santãna**, a strange mixture of Portuguese and French Baroque. A hike to the top of Chapada's highest point, **Morro do São Jerônimo**, is well worthwhile.

A bit further out of town is the 1100m-long **Aroe Jari** cavern and, in another cave, the **Lagoa Azul** (Blue Lake).

Organised Tours

If you don't have a car, your best bet is to take an excursion with Jorge Mattos, who runs Ecoturismo (☎/fax 791-1393; ecotur@nutecnet.com.br) at Praça Dom Wunibaldo 57 in the nearby town of Chapada. Jorge meets the 7 and 8 am buses from Cuiabá every day. He runs four excursions: to the national park (which contains the most spectacular waterfalls); to the Blue Lake and the Aroe Jari cavern; to the stone city; and to Água Fria, a diamond-mining town 40km from Chapada. To the park and the stone city, it costs around US$20; to the lake and cavern and Água Fria it's US$30.

Unfortunately, if Jorge doesn't find at least five people, the price goes up. All tours take between four and six hours, depending on the enthusiasm of the group. If you want to spend just a day there, he can have you on the last bus back to Cuiabá at 6 pm.

An alternative is to hire a car and explore the area on your own, stopping at different rock formations, waterfalls and bathing pools at your leisure. If you do have the use of a car, drop by the Secretária de Turismo (on the left-hand side as you drive into Chapada, just before the square). A useful map is available – you'll need it!

Places to Stay

There is good camping at Salgadeira, just before the climb into Chapada, but if you want to rough it, you can basically camp anywhere.

Lodging in the area ranges from the basic *Hotel São José* (☎ 791-1454), Rua Vereador José de Souza 50, which charges US$8 per person, to the new *Pousada Penhasco* (☎ 791-1555), 2km from town, charging US$110 a double.

In between are a couple of good alternatives. The *Turismo Hotel* (☎ 791-1176; fax 791-1383), Rua Fernando Correo Costa 1065, is run by a German family. Single/double apartamentos here cost US$23/33. The *Hotel Quincó* (☎ 791-1404), Praça Dom Wunibaldo 464, has good-value apartamentos for US$13 per person.

All of these places, with the exception of the Pousada Penhasco, are close to the rodoviária.

Places to Eat

Restaurants and bars in Chapada are clustered around Praça Dom Wunibaldo. *Nivios* has excellent regional food – all you can eat for US$7. Unfortunately, it's only open for lunch. Also popular is *O Mestrinho*, Rua Quincó Caldas 119. *Nutrikilo* is a decent por quilo joint at Rua Cipriano Curvo 729. *Trapiche*, just off the main praça at Rua Cipriano Curvo 580, is good for a drink and music at night.

Getting There & Away

Buses leave Cuiabá's rodoviária for Chapada dos Guimarães every 1½ hours from 7 am to 7 pm. In the other direction, the first bus leaves Chapada dos Guimarães at 6 am and the last at 6 pm. The cost is US$4.

CÁCERES

The city of Cáceres, founded in 1778 on the left bank of the Rio Paraguai, is an access point for a number of Pantanal lodges and for Bolivia. Cáceres is 215km from Cuiabá on Hwy BR-070, close to the Ilha de Taiamã ecological reserve. In September each year, the town hosts the world's biggest river fishing competition.

Lots of travellers arrive with the misunderstanding that they'll be able to get a cement barge to Corumbá. But unless you have unlimited time to hang around, forget

JOHN MAIER, JR

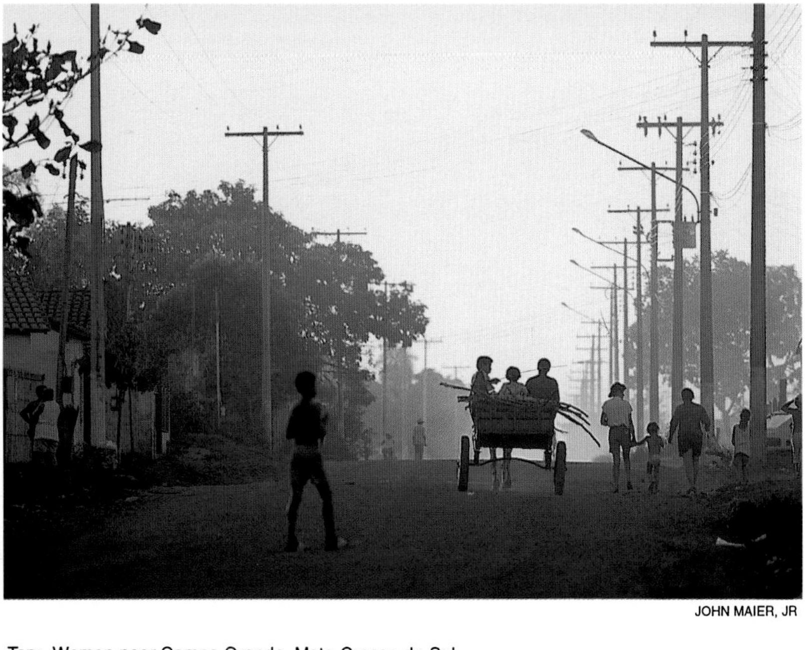

JOHN MAIER, JR

Top: Women near Campo Grande, Mato Grosso do Sul
Bottom: The town of Poconé in the Pantanal

JOHN MAIER, JR

CHRIS McASEY

Top: Capoeira show in Pelourinho, Salvador
Bottom: Lavagem do Bonfim festivities, Salvador, Bahia

it. Even the port captain has no idea when the boats are likely to arrive.

If you're going to Bolivia, get a Brazilian exit stamp from the Polícia Federal, 4km from town on Avenida Getúlio Vargas, next to the *prefeitura* (city hall). Taxis want US$10 to take you there and back.

Organised Tours

Pantanal Tours (☎ 223-1200) at Rua Coronel Faria 180, one block back from the riverfront, can organise tours into the Pantanal and boat and fishing trips along the Rio Paraguai. There are also dozens of launches and small boats along the riverfront offering fishing trips.

Places to Stay

The best place near the rodoviária is the *Capri Hotel* (☎ 223-1771), Rua Getúlio Vargas 99. Spacious, air-conditioned rooms cost US$20/30 for singles/doubles. If you're on your way to Bolivia, the *Hotel União* across the road from the rodoviária might do. Basic but clean apartamentos cost US$7/15. Closer to the river and the centre, the *Rio Hotel* (☎ 223-3084) on Praça Major João Carlos is a good option. Its quartos with fan cost US$10/18 and apartamentos are US$15/25. The hotel also has a billiard table and table tennis.

Pantanal Explorer (☎ 682-2800), at Avenida Governador Ponce de Arruda 670 in Varzea Grande, Cuiabá, can organise accommodation at isolated fishing lodges on the Rio Paraguai around Cáceres.

Places to Eat

All the action centres around the riverfront and nearby Praça Barão do Rio Branco, where there are several restaurants and bars. *Restaurant Flutuante* is a floating restaurant with an extensive menu of fish dishes costing US$12 to $15 for two people – it even has a menu in English. Nearby along the riverfront, *Corimba* is a good pizzeria and chopperia with tables set up outside overlooking the river. *Restaurant Hispano*, on Praça Barão do Rio Branco, is a por quilo restaurant with river views.

Getting There & Away

Regular buses make the journey between Cuiabá and Cáceres (US$16, three hours). To Santa Cruz (in Bolivia) there is a daily bus at 6 am (US$28, 24 hours). For more details, see the Land section of the Getting There & Away chapter. There are also bus services to Porto Velho.

BARÃO DE MELGAÇO

Along with Cáceres and Poconé, Barão de Melgaço, 135km south-east of Cuiabá, is a northern entrance into the Pantanal. Nearby, there are ruined fortresses left from the Paraguayan wars, and Sia Mariana and Chacororé, two huge bays full of fish.

Places to Stay

The *NS de Carmo Hotel* (☎ 713-1141), at Avenida A Leverger 33, is 600m from the rodoviária. Double apartamentos are US$40. The top-end place is the *Barão Tur Hotel* (☎ 713-1166, or (065) 322-1568 in Cuiabá), which charges US$90 a double.

Getting There & Away

Three buses a day make the 3 hour, US$11 trip from Cuiabá, leaving at 7.30 and 9 am and 3 pm.

POCONÉ

• *pop 30,500* ✉ *78175-000* ☎ *065*

The northern entry point to the Pantanal from Cuiabá, Poconé marks the beginning of the Transpantaneira 'highway'. In May, Poconé celebrates the week-long Semana do Fazendeiro e do Cavalo Panteiro with a cattle fair and rodeos. Most of the locals are descendants of Indians and blacks. Many have hunted the *onça* (jaguar) and have amazing stories to tell. They also play a bizarre indoor soccer game called *futeboi*. A cow is a wildcard on the field, chasing the red ball around and sometimes scoring a 'goooooooooal'!

Orientation

When you arrive at the rodoviária, you are 2km from the start of the dirt road which becomes the Transpantaneira; the centre of town is about halfway. To get there, turn left as you leave the bus station, walk two blocks down Avenida Anibol de Toledo to Rua Antônio João, then turn right. Walk up seven blocks – you'll be in the large town square (more like a rectangle). The Hotel Skala is 100m to your right. On your left, behind the church, is the road that leads to the beginning of the Transpantaneira. There are a few pousadas here.

Places to Stay & Eat

The *Dormitório Poconé* at Avenida Anibol de Toledo 1510, near the rodoviária, is a friendly place. Basic rooms with fan cost US$8 per person. Nearby on the same street, *Foi na Brasa* does a good buffet lunch for US$4. In the middle of town, the *Skala* (☎ 721-1407) at Rua Bem Rondon 64 is more comfortable, with apartamentos at US$25/30.

The best places to stay, especially if you intend to hitch on the Transpantaneira, are out of town, near the beginning of the road. The first one you'll pass is the *Pousada Pantaneira* (☎ 721-1630), on the right-hand side (and not to be confused with the Pousada O Pantaneiro much further along), which charges US$10 per person. The rooms are on the dingy side, but it's a friendly place, and serves a great rodízio for US$7. Just up the road, on the same side, the *Hotel Santa Cruz* (☎ 721-1439) is a rustic place with apartamentos for US$20/30. The rooms with air-conditioning at US$40/50 are very comfortable. A further 400m up, on the left-hand side, the *Hotel Restaurante Aurora* (☎ 721-1339) has large, basic apartamentos with fan for US$15/20 and air-conditioned rooms for US$20/30.

Getting There & Away

There are six buses a day from Cuiabá to Poconé, from 6 am to 7 pm, and six in the opposite direction, from 6 am to 7.30 pm. The 100km, two hour ride costs US$3.50. The bus is often packed, so get a seat early if you want to appreciate the vegetation typical of the Pantanal's outskirts: pequís, piúvas, babaçus, ipês and buritis.

The Pantanal

The Amazon may have all the fame and glory, but the Pantanal is a far better place to see wildlife. In the Amazon, the animals hide in the dense foliage, but in the open spaces of the Pantanal, wildlife is visible to the most casual observer. If you like to see animals in their natural state, the Pantanal – with the greatest concentration of fauna in the New World – should not be missed.

A vast wetlands in the centre of South America, the Pantanal is about half the size of France – some 230,000 sq km. Something less than 100,000 sq km of this is in Bolivia and Paraguay; the rest is in Brazil, split between the states of Mato Grosso and Mato Grosso do Sul.

The Pantanal (Terra de Ninguem, or Nobody's Land) has few people and no towns. Distances are so great and ground transport so poor that people get around in small aeroplanes or motorboats; 4WD travel is restricted by the seasons. The only road that plunges deep into the Pantanal is the Transpantaneira. This raised dirt road sectioned by 118 small, wooden bridges ends 145km from Poconé, at Porto Jofre. Only a third of the intended route from Poconé to Corumbá has been completed because of lack of funds and ecological concerns.

The road and a strip of land on either side of it comprise the Transpantanal national park. Although IBAMA is trying to expand its jurisdiction to protect the entire Pantanal region, it administers only one other park: the Parque Nacional do Pantanal Matogrossense, which encompasses the old Cará-Cará biological reserve. The rest of the Pantanal (around 90%) is privately owned.

Geography & Climate

Although *pantano* means 'swamp' in both Spanish and Portuguese, the Pantanal is not a swamp but, rather, a vast alluvial plain. In geological terms, it is a sedimentary basin of quaternary origin, the drying remains of

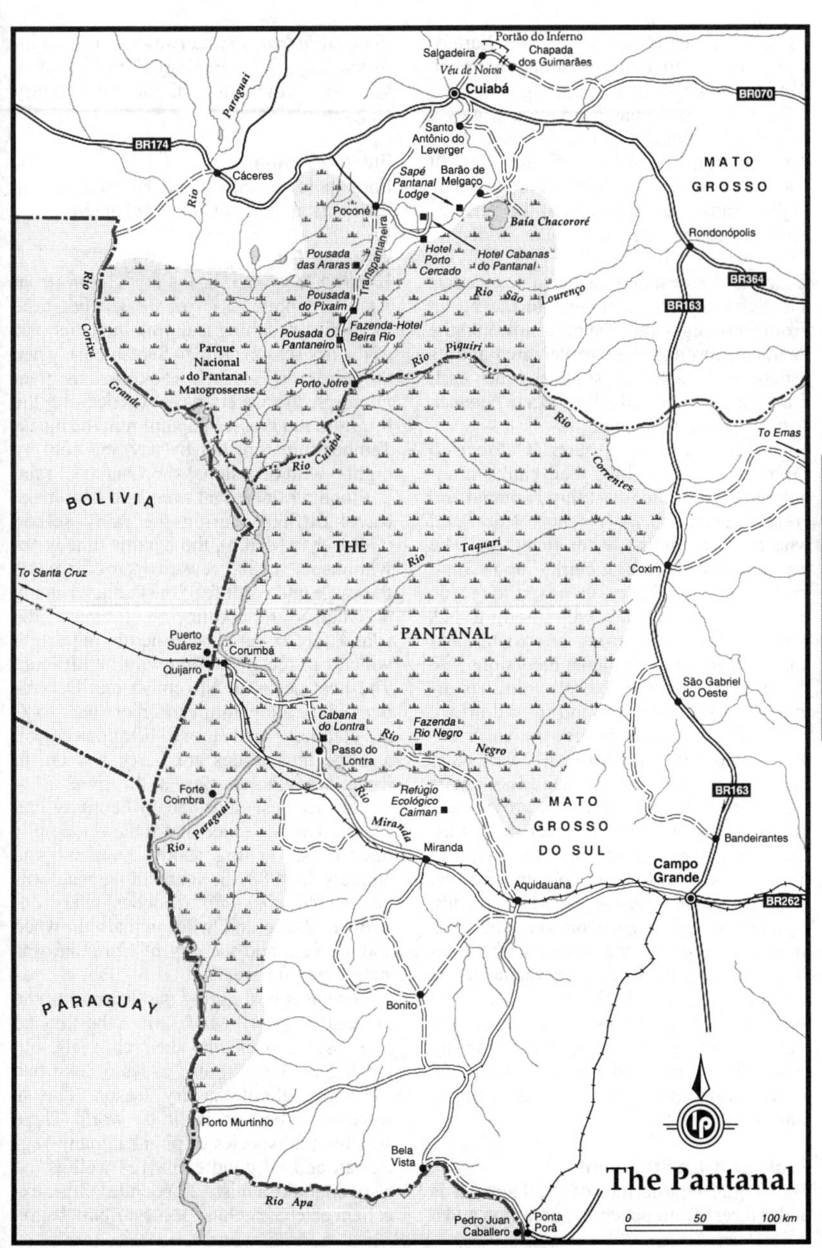

THE CENTRAL WEST

an ancient inland sea called the Xaraés, which began to dry out, along with the Amazon Sea, 65 million years ago.

First sea, then immense lake and now a periodically flooded plain, the Pantanal – 2000km from the Atlantic Ocean yet just 100 to 200m above sea level – is bounded by higher lands: the mountains of the Serra de Maracaju to the east, the Serra da Bodoquena to the south, the Paraguayan and Bolivian Chaco to the west and the Serra dos Parecis and Serra do São Geronimo to the north. From these highlands, the rains flow into the Pantanal, forming the Rio Paraguai and its tributaries (which flow south and then east, draining into the Atlantic Ocean between Argentina and Uruguay).

During the rainy season (October to March), the rivers flood their banks, inundating much of the low-lying Pantanal and creating *cordilheiras* (patches of dry land where the animals cluster together). The waters reach their high mark – up to 3m – in January or February, then start to recede in March. This seasonal flooding has made systematic farming impossible and has severely limited human incursions into the area. However, it does provide an enormously rich feeding ground for wildlife.

The floodwaters replenish the soil's nutrients, which would otherwise be very poor, due to the excessive drainage. The waters teem with fish, and the ponds provide excellent niches for many animals and plants. Enormous flocks of wading birds gather in rookeries several square kilometres in area.

Later in the dry season, the water recedes, the lagoons and marshes dry out, and fresh grasses emerge on the savanna (the Pantanal's vegetation includes savanna, forest and meadows, which blend together, often with no clear divisions). The hawks and jacaré compete for fish in the remaining ponds. As the ponds shrink and dry up, the jacarés crawl around for water, sweating it out until the rains return.

Ecology & Environment

The fragile equilibrium of the Pantanal is under threat from poaching, pollution and a planned *hidrovia* (waterway). For more information, see the Ecology & Environment section in the Facts about the Country chapter.

Flora & Fauna

For details, see the Flora & Fauna section in the Facts about the Country chapter.

When to Go

If possible, go during the dry season (from April to September/October). The best time to go bird-watching is during the latter part of the dry season (July to September), when the birds are at their rookeries in great numbers, the waters have receded and the bright-green grasses pop up from the muck. Temperatures are hot by day and cool by night – with occasional short bursts of rain.

Flooding, incessant rains and heat make travel difficult during the rainy season (October to March), though this time is not without its special rewards – this is when the cattle and wildlife of the Pantanal clump together on the cordilheiras. However, the islands are covered with dense vegetation which can make spotting wildlife difficult. The heat peaks in November and December, when temperatures higher than 40°C are common, roads turn to breakfast cereal, and the mosquitoes are fierce and out in force. Many hotels close at this time.

The heaviest rains fall in February and March. Every decade or so, the flooding is disastrous, killing both humans and animals. In 1988, the southern Pantanal was devastated: *fazendas* (ranches) were destroyed, cattle and wild animals drowned and starved, and the city of Corumbá was submerged for weeks.

Fishing is best during the first part of the dry season (April-May), when the flooded rivers settle back into their channels, but locals have been known to lasso 80kg fish right throughout the dry season. This is some of the best fishing in the world. There are about 20 species of piranha, many vegetarian and all good eating, as well as the tasty dourado, a feisty 20-pounder. Other excellent catches include pacu, suribim, bagre, giripoca, piraputanga, piapara, cachara, pintado, pirancajuva and pintado, to name but a few.

Although hunting is not allowed, fishing – with the required permits – is encouraged between February and October. It is, however, prohibited during the breeding season from November to the end of January. Fishing permits are available from the IBAMA office in Cuiabá (☎ 644-1511). Enthusiasts can study their quarry at Cuiabá's fish market, in the mercado near the bridge.

What to Bring

You can't buy anything much in the Pantanal, so come prepared. The dry season is also the cooler season. Bring attire suitable for hot days, coolish nights, rain and mosquitoes. You'll need sunscreen, sunglasses, a hat and cool clothes, sneakers or boots, light raingear, and something for the evening. Mosquito relief means long pants and long-sleeved shirts, vitamin B12 and insect repellent. Autan is the Brazilian brand recommended by eight out of 10 Pantaneiros, but some travellers claim that the mosquitoes have become so used to it that they've even started to like it!

Binoculars are your best friend in the Pantanal. Bring an alarm clock (to get up before sunrise), a tape recorder (for recording the wonderful bird calls) and a strong flashlight (to go searching for owls and anacondas after dark). Don't forget plenty of film, a camera, a tripod and a long lens (300mm is about right for wildlife).

Health

According to local tourist authorities, malaria has been eradicated from the Pantanal. There's probably only a very low risk of contracting malaria, but it's best to consult with a travel health expert for the latest information before you leave home. In Cuiabá, the municipal hospital (☎ 624-3039) is on Avenida General Valle. Hospital Modelo (☎ 623-5599), a private clinic at Rua Comandante Costa 1262, is within walking distance of the Hotel Mato Grosso.

Organised Tours

There are two main approach routes to the Pantanal: via Cuiabá in Mato Grosso and via Corumbá in Mato Grosso do Sul.

Mato Grosso From Cuiabá, the capital of Mato Grosso, travel agencies and freelance guides arrange safaris into the Pantanal. A good guide can enhance your Pantanal experience by spotting and identifying animal and bird species, explaining the diverse ecology, and taking care of any hassles along the way. But you don't actually need a guide – the Transpantaneira is the only road to follow and the wildlife is hard to miss. In Cuiabá, Anaconda (☎ (065) 624-6242), at Rua Comandante Costa 649, organises one, two and three day tours into the Pantanal for US$60/155/210. Pantanal Tours (☎ (065) 323-1557), at Rua Joaquim Murtinho 956, offers similar deals.

An alternative and good-value excursion from Cuiabá is with Joel Souza. Joel is a very enthusiastic guide who speaks English, German and Spanish. Joel's bird-watching and nature tours cost US$60 per day, including accommodation (on farms), meals, horse and boat rides. His office (☎ 9065-983-3552, toll free in Brazil ; or ☎/fax (065) 624-1386), is next to the Hotel Presidente at Avenida Getúlio Vargas 155A. Other recommended guides in Cuiabá are Laercio Sá of Faunatours (☎ (065) 321-5375), who can be contacted at the Hotel Real, Praça Ipiranga 102, and Munir Nasr.

Mato Grosso do Sul From Corumbá, many budget travellers are choosing to go on cheap three to four day tours into the southern Pantanal. Gil Tours (☎ (067) 231-8486; mobile ☎ 987-1586), run out of the Hotel Londres, and Colibri Pantanal Safari (☎/fax (067) 231-3934), run by Swiss Claudine Roth at Rua Frei Mariano 1221, both organise Pantanal excursions and offer similar deals. However, they don't come much cheaper – US$30 per day for the first three days, and US$10 per day for additional days. You can usually pay half before you leave, and the other half when you come back. In the high season, Crocodile Tourism (☎ (067) 231-7851), Rua Colombo 1047, also organises Pantanal tours.

Most of the dodgy operators have been squeezed out of Corumbá in the last few years and trips are better organised than in the past, but they can still be rough-and-ready affairs. Accommodation is at bush camps in tents or hammocks. Food is generally pretty good, though you should take extra water. Some of the guides are ex-jacaré hunters and their attitude towards animals can be less than sensitive. You'll see lots of birds, capybaras and jacarés, but mammals are harder to spot.

If you want something more comfortable, and riding around in the back of a pick-up truck doesn't grab you, you can pay a bit more and stay at a hotel-fazenda for a few days.

While the main operators are well organised, during the high season (June-August) some shonky outfits pop up to get a slice of the tourist dollar. These characters generally offer cut-price rates and bag the more reputable operators. Before signing on with one of these trips, there are a few things you should check out. Ask for a detailed itinerary, in writing if possible. Check out the truck. Does it look OK? Does it have a radio or carry a first-aid kit in case of emergency? A bite from the boca da sapo snake will kill in half an hour if left untreated.

Expect to spend at least half a day travelling into the Pantanal. But finding wildlife depends less on how far you travel and more on how well your guide knows the Pantanal. Allow at least two days for seeing wildlife at close quarters. Definitely insist on doing this on foot – vehicles should be used only for access, *not* for pursuit. Your chances of enjoying the Pantanal and its wildlife are greatly increased if you go with a reputable guide who: forsakes the 'mechanical chase' approach; accompanies small groups (preferably no more than eight people); camps out at night (away from drinking dens!); and takes you on walks at the optimum times to observe wildlife (before sunrise, at dusk and during the night). A trip along these lines will require at least four days (preferably five).

Insist on meeting your guide before you leave (or make it clear in writing that you will go only with a designated guide). A smooth-talking frontperson might sign you on, but they usually won't be your guide on the trip. How many years has your guide been in the Pantanal? Speaking English is less important than local knowledge. Someone who has spent their life in the Pantanal won't speak much English. Prior to departure, be sure to read the What to Bring part earlier in this section.

There are still some *guias piratas* (pirate guides) around in the high season. On these tours, there is a lot of *cachaça* (rum) drinking, the theory being that since cachaça is cheaper than gasoline, it costs less to convince drunk tourists that they're having a good time. Then there's no need to drive as far as promised. Tales of woe with pirate guides include abandonment in the marshes, assorted drunken mayhem and even attempted rape.

If time is a problem and money isn't, or if you'd just like one of the best guides around, write or call Doug Trent of Focus Tours (☎ 505-466-4688; focustours@aol.com), 103 Moya Rd, Santa Fe, NM 87505, USA. In Brazil, call Regina Caldeira, the fluent English and Portuguese-speaking Focus contact (☎ (031) 332-4627), in Belo Horizonte, Minas Gerais. Focus specialises in nature tours and Doug is active in trying to preserve the Pantanal. He has all the bird calls on tape, and plays them over a loudspeaker to attract the real thing. For more about Focus, see the Tours section in the Getting There & Away chapter.

Places to Stay

Pantanal accommodation is divided into four general categories: fazendas, pousadas, *pesqueiros* and *botels*. Fazendas are ranch-style hotels which usually have horses and often boats for hire. Pousadas range from simple accommodation to top-end standard. Pesqueiros are hang-outs for fishermen, and

Tripping Through the Pantanal

I stayed over a month in Corumbá, going out on four tours, so I sort of got an overview of the whole scene – and a lot of stories (good and bad) from other backpackers.

The Guides

You don't have to find a guide, they find you. They meet the buses, they come to hotels, they approach you in restaurants or outside the Banco do Brasil. The sales pitch is pretty standard: albums of photos taken on their tours, letters of recommendation from satisfied tourists, and often a bit of bad-mouthing of other guides thrown in for good measure. All offer three or four day tours, including bottled water, tents and/or hammocks.

All the guides know the Pantanal well, as the majority were born and bred in the area. Most speak only Portuguese, although quite a few are familiar with Spanish too. Some of them can say the names of some of the wildlife in the English or Hebrew they've picked up from tourists.

Generally a tour is made up of a guide, a driver, a cook and five to 10 tourists. These guys tend to freelance, alternately forming a team or competing with each other.

The Tours

We spent the first day basically driving out there. It's difficult terrain for any vehicle, but the drivers really knew what they were doing, and they were all capable mechanics who quickly and effectively fixed anything that needed repairing on the spot. They never chased animals with the truck, only pursued and caught them on foot, to give us a closer look, then released them.

The food was good, vegetarians were provided for and there was plenty of bottled water. Round the campfire at night, sometimes *caipirinhas* (drinks made from rum and citrus juice) were offered, but most of us stuck to tea or coffee. We slept in a big tent with a good mosquito net, or in hammocks strung up in an outside (mosquito-screened) room on a farm. Before we left the camp site, all the rubbish was burned, or put in bags to be taken back to Corumbá. We went on lots of lovely long walks early in the mornings, and again in the evenings. It's amazingly beautiful in the Pantanal: the landscape itself is so interesting even without all the incredible creatures that live there. The sunrises and sunsets are spectacular, and the night sky takes your breath away.

The main thing to remember is to take effective mosquito repellent and apply it liberally in the evenings. There are about one zillion mosquitoes, all extremely partial to tourists. They never seem to bother the guides – one of those intensely unfair little facts of nature.

Maryann Sewell – New Zealand

The Pantanal is a popular backpacker destination and things change fast. Help us keep up-to-date and let us know about your Pantanal trip.

boats and fishing gear can usually be rented from them. A botel (a contraction of boat and hotel) is a floating lodge.

Reservations are needed for all accommodation in July, when lots of Brazilians holiday here.

Unfortunately, nearly all accommodation is expensive. Rates will usually include transport by 4WD, boat or plane from Corumbá or Cuiabá, good food and modest lodging. More often than not, reservations are handled by a travel agent and must be paid for in advance. It's also a good idea to call ahead for weather conditions – the rainy and dry seasons are never exact, and proper conditions can make or break a trip.

Transpantaneira Accommodation on the Transpantaneira, the elevated dirt road that begins just outside Poconé and extends 145km to Porto Jofre, is plentiful.

At Km 30, the *Pousada das Araras* (☎ (065) 682-2800) has a pool, as well as boats and horses. A very informative wildlife and bird list is available. Full board is US$53/67 for singles/doubles.

Moving on down the road to the Rio Pixaim, at Km 65, you'll find two places; our advice is to check both before deciding where to stay, as their prices are similar. The *Pousada do Pixaim* (☎ (065) 721-1899) is the more rustic of the two – a classic Pantanal building (wooden, on stilts). It has air-conditioning, tasty meals (included in the accommodation price), and the last álcool and gas pump until you return to Poconé – so fill up! This hotel used to be the budget travellers' favourite, but prices have risen since the installation of air-conditioning. Prices are US$60/80 for singles/doubles. Across the bridge, the more modern *Fazenda-Hotel Beira Rio* (☎ (065) 321-9445) is also more expensive: US$82/102 a single/double. Boats and horses can be rented at both these places.

Forty kilometres further down the road is one of the cheaper pousadas on the Transpantaneira: the *Pousada O Pantaneiro* (☎ (065) 721-1545), run by Lerinho and his son Eduardo. It's a simple place, charging US$25 per person for room and board.

Porto Jofre is where the Transpantaneira meets its end, at the Rio Cuiabá. It's a one-hotel town – in fact, it's not even a town. Campers can stay at Sr Nicolino's fishing camp, near the river, for US$4 per person. He provides bathrooms and cooking facilities, and also rents boats. The only other alternative is the expensive *Hotel Porto Jofre Pantanal* (☎ (065) 321-0263), costing US$90/150 a single/double. The hotel has a swimming pool, and boats and horses for hire. It's closed from November to March.

Mato Grosso Several fazendas in the northern Pantanal are off the Transpantaneira. Accessible by car is the *Pousada Porto Cercado* (☎ (065) 721-1726), along the Rio Cuiabá, 42km from Poconé. Singles/doubles cost US$48/96, meals included. At the expensive *Hotel Cabanas do Pantanal* (☎ (065) 321-4142 in Cuiabá), 52km from Poconé, a three day package costs US$360.

One of the newer lodges is *Sapé Pantanal Lodge* (☎ (065) 322-3426) on the margins of the Rio Cuiabá, one hour by boat from the Porto Cercado. Four day packages with full board cost US$480. This one has been highly recommended by several readers so if money is no object, check it out.

Mato Grosso do Sul Southern gateways to the Pantanal are the cities of Corumbá, Aquidauana and Miranda. Most travellers head to Corumbá, while Aquidauana and Miranda are popular with Brazilian anglers.

Around Aquidauana are a number of mid-range to expensive hotel-fazendas. *Aguapé Pousada* (☎ (067) 241-2889; fax 241-2987), 57km from Aquidauana, has two, three and four day packages for US$154/232/325 per person, but you can camp there for US$6 a day and buy meals at the restaurant. The *Hotel-Fazenda Salobra* (☎/fax (067) 242-1162) is 90km from Aquidauana and costs US$60 per person a day, including meals. The *Fazenda Rio Negro* is the old Rondon homestead where the soap opera *Pantanal* was filmed. Forty minutes by plane from Aquidauana, accommodation here costs US$180 a day. For more information, go to the Panbratour office in Aquidauana.

One of the cheaper places to stay in the Miranda area is the *Hotel Beira Rio* (☎/fax (067) 242-1262), 8km from town. The hotel has air-conditioning and hot showers and is rigged out like a pesqueiro. Full board costs US$42 per person. There is cheap accommodation and boat hire available where the Campo Grande to Corumbá road crosses the Rio Miranda (15km from Miranda going toward Corumbá), but these places are geared towards fishermen, not sightseers. For more information, contact Ecoventuras (☎ (067) 242-1186) at Avenida Pedrossian 189.

The top-end place in the southern Pantanal is the *Refúgio Ecológico Caiman* (☎ (011) 246-3291 in São Paulo; (067) 725-5267 in Campo Grande, (067) 242-1102 in Corumbá), on a working cattle ranch 36km from Miranda. There are five lodges in different areas of the 53,000 hectare fazenda. Guests can stay in one of the pousadas, or move around from one pousada to another. Caiman offers 25 different programmes on foot, on

Driving down the Transpantaneira

It is, of course, impossible to know everything about travel in the vast expanses of the Pantanal, but based on several trips and conversations with literally dozens of Pantanal experts, we think the best way to visit the Pantanal, if you're in it for the wildlife and your budget is limited, is driving down the Transpantaneira.

Why the Transpantaneira? First, it's one of the best places to see wildlife, which is drawn to the roadway at all times of the year. Second, renting a car in Cuiabá and driving down the Pantanal is less expensive than most Pantanal excursions, especially if there are three or four of you in the car. (Most organised Pantanal tours require flying, boating or hiring a guide with a 4WD vehicle.) And third, if you're on a tight budget, you can take a bus to Poconé and hitch from there (it's pretty easy), if necessary returning to Poconé for cheap accommodation.

The Transpantaneira is the best place we've seen in South America for observing wildlife. During the wet season, the road is an island for wildlife driven from the floodwaters, and during the dry season, the ditches on either side of the road serve as artificial ponds, drawing birds and game towards the tourist.

Thousands of birds appear to rush out from all sides, ocelots and capybaras seem frozen by the headlights, and roadside pools are filled with hundreds of dark silhouettes and gleaming, red jacaré eyes. It's easy to approach the wildlife; you can walk within spitting distance of the jacaré, and if you're crazy enough to go cheek to cheek, you can spot the fleas which live off the lacrimal fluid of their eyeballs.

If you are driving from Cuiabá, get out early. Leave at 4 am to reach the Transpantaneira by sunrise, when the animals come to life. The official Transpantaneira highway starts 17km south of Poconé. There's a sign and a guard station (where you pay a small entrance fee).

Stopping to see wildlife and slowing down for 118 little wooden bridges and metre-wide potholes, it's possible to pass the whole day driving the Transpantaneira. Weekdays are best if you're driving, as there's less traffic kicking up dust.

Hitching down the Transpantaneira is easy enough – there aren't a lot of cars and trucks, but most will stop to give rides. The best time to hitch is on the weekend, when the locals drive down the Transpantaneira for a day's fishing. Make sure you get on the road early. We've done the entire route from Poconé to Porto Jofre several times with all sorts of folk: a rancher and his family, two American birders, a Cuiabá restaurateur, an IBAMA park ranger, a photo-safari guide, some Italian tourists, an ex-poacher and a photojournalist doing an article on jacaré poaching.

Wildlife is abundant along the length of the Transpantaneira. The birds, jacaré and families of capybaras scurry into the ponds along the road. On our last trip, we saw several toucans, dozens of luminescent-green parrots darting in and out of a huge nest, and several blue hyacinth macaws in the big trees that divide the great meadows. There are enormous flocks of birds and individual representatives of seemingly every species. For details, see the Flora & Fauna section in the Facts about the Country chapter.

Chris McAsey

horseback or by truck. All are led by one of the multilingual guides who live on the fazenda. It isn't cheap (around US$200 a day per person), but it's highly recommended.

There are a few places farther into the Pantanal, at Passo do Lontra, 120km and two hours (dry season) from Corumbá. To get there, take the dirt road leading off the road to Campo Grande. Alternatively, you can take the bus to Campo Grande and arrange for the lodge transport to pick you up from the Carandazal station. The *Cabana do Lontra* (☎ (067) 241-2121) is an excellent place, another classic Pantanal wood-on-stilt structure, with lots of wildlife around. It charges US$40 per person, including full board, but is willing to bargain out of season. It's highly recommended.

Serious fishing enthusiasts should consider the *Pesqueiro Taruma* (☎ (067) 231-4197 in Corumbá) on the Rio Paraguai 70km from Corumbá. It's small, but well equipped, with fridge, air-conditioning, hot showers and boats, and costs US$96 a day, including meals. It's closed from November to January.

Botels defy any permanent address. Most of them operate out of Corumbá and are used for fishing trips. Arara Pantaneira (☎ (067) 231-4851) and Pantanal Tour (☎ (067) 231-4683) both organise trips costing US$200 per person a day, all inclusive.

Getting There & Away

From Cuiabá, the capital of Mato Grosso, there are three 'gateways' to the Pantanal – Cáceres, Barão de Melgaço and Poconé – all of which lead to Porto Jofre, on the Transpantaneira. Corumbá is best accessed by bus from Campo Grande, capital of Mato Grosso do Sul; the route runs via Aquidauana and Miranda.

Coxim, a small town on BR-163, east of the Pantanal and accessible by bus or air-taxi from either Campo Grande or Cuiabá, is a third point of entry to the Pantanal. However, it has limited infrastructure.

Getting Around

Since the lodges are the only places to sleep, drink and eat, and public transport doesn't exist, independent travel is difficult in the Pantanal. Driving is not easy. Only a few roads reach into the periphery of the Pantanal; they are frequently closed by rains, and reconstructed yearly. Only the Transpantaneira highway goes deep into the region. See the boxed text 'Driving down the Transpantaneira'.

Hitching Hitching may be the cheapest way to go, but it doesn't allow you to stop whenever you want along the road to observe wildlife. There's quite a bit of traffic going up and down the Transpantaneira during the dry season at least, and if you make your way to one of the pousadas, you can then do walks, or rent a horse or boat.

Car In Cuiabá, there are several car rental agencies just outside the airport grounds to your right, and they're often cheaper than the agencies inside the airport. There is some competition, so shop around and ask about promotional rates. No matter what anyone tells you, you don't need a 4WD vehicle to drive the Transpantaneira. The best car is a VW Gol or a Fiat Uno. Don't forget to fill up your fuel tank in Poconé and at the Pousada do Pixaim.

Mato Grosso do Sul

CAMPO GRANDE

• *pop 600,000 ✉ 79000-000 ☎ 067*

Founded around 1875 as the village of Santo Antônio de Campo Grande, Campo Grande really began to grow when the railway came through in 1914. The city became the capital of Mato Grosso do Sul in 1977 by decree of military president Ernesto Giesel, when the new state splintered off from Mato Grosso. It is known as the Cidade Morena because of its red earth. Manganese, rice, soy and cattle are the sources of its wealth. Campo Grande lies 716km south of Cuiabá and 403km southeast of Corumbá.

There's not much for the traveller in Campo Grande, but because it's a transport hub, you might have to stay here overnight. Like all big cities, Campo Grande has plenty of hotels and restaurants, and gets pretty wild on weekends when the gaúchos come to town.

Information

Tourist Office Campo Grande has one of the best tourist offices (☎ 724-5830) in the region. It's on the corner of Avenida Afonso Pena and Avenida Noroeste, and has friendly staff who speak English and a whiz-bang computer database with loads of information about hotels, restaurants and attractions throughout the state, including the Pantanal. It's open from 9 am to 8 pm Tuesday to Saturday, and from 9 am to noon Sunday.

Money The Banco do Brasil has a câmbio at Avenida Afonso Pena 2202.

Post & Telephone The post office is on the corner of Rua Dom Aquino and Avenida Calógeras. The telefônica is near the corner of Rua Rui Barbosa and Rua Dom Aquino.

Museu Dom Bosco

The Museu Dom Bosco, Rua Barão do Rio Branco 1843, is the only museum in town that's worth a look. It has an excellent collection of over 10,000 insects, including 7000 butterflies. There are lots of stuffed animals, and interesting exhibits about the Bororo, Moro, Carajá and Xavante Indians. Reasonably priced handicrafts are also available. The museum is open daily from 8 to 11 am and 1 to 5 pm.

Places to Stay – Budget

Now that the train service between Campo Grande and Corumbá has been suspended, there's no need to worry about the dives around the train station. There are some

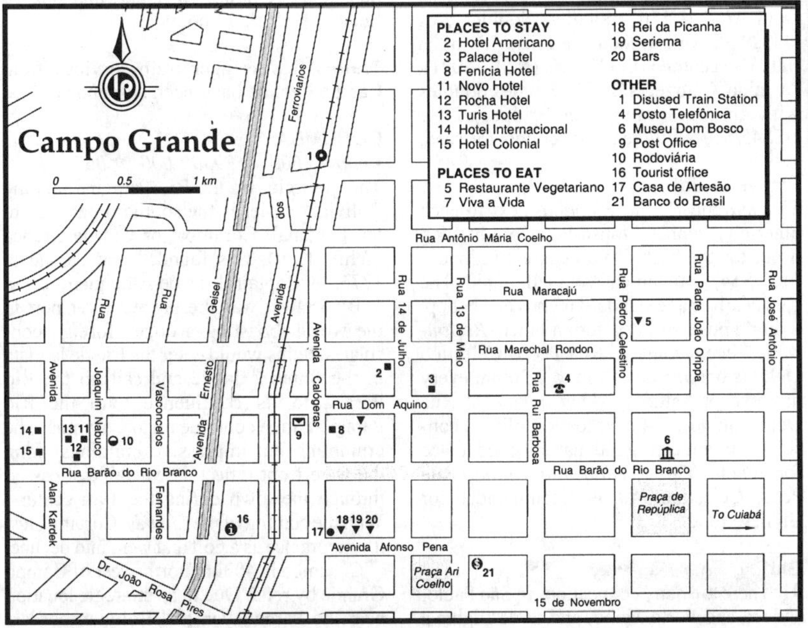

equally sleazy flophouses around the rodoviária though, that are best avoided – take care around the area at night.

The *Novo Hotel* (☎ 725-0505), Rua Joaquim Nabuco 185, is the exception. It's a friendly, clean place with apartamentos for US$15/30 singles/doubles. Just around the corner at Rua Barão do Rio Branco 343, *Rocha Hotel* (☎ 725-6874) is under the same management and offers a similar standard and price. One block west of the rodoviária on Avenida Alan Kardek is a cluster of three hotels: the *Turis Hotel* (☎ 382-7688) with basic apartamentos starting at US$9/15; *Hotel Colonial* (☎ 721-3154), offering apartamentos with fan and TV for US$22/33; and the more upmarket *Hotel Internacional* (☎ 724-6061), with apartamentos starting at US$23/44.

In the centre, a reasonable budget option is the *Hotel Americano* (☎ 721-1454), Rua 14 de Julho 2311. It has single/double quartos for US$12/24. More expensive places include the *Palace Hotel* (☎ 384-4741), Rua Dom Aquino 1501. Singles/ doubles cost US$29/36 with a good breakfast. It's often full. Also central is the *Fenícia* (☎ 383-2001), Avenida Calógeras 2262. Singles/doubles with air-conditioning and fridge go for US$45/61, but there are discounts for cash.

Places to Eat

Seriema and *Rei da Picanha*, next to each other on Avenida Afonso Pena, are battling it out for the best all-you-can-eat rodízio – for US$4, you can eat yourself stupid. The bars nearby have standard menus and chopp.

For a por quilo vegetarian lunch, *Restaurante Vegetariano*, at Rua Pedro Celestino 1696, is open from 11 am to 2.30 pm every day except Saturday. *Viva a Vida* at Rua Dom Aquino 1354 next to the Bolivian consulate, is another good natural-food place for lunch. The *Restaurante China*, Rua Pedro Celestino 750, is recommended for Chinese food.

Getting There & Away

Air There are daily connections to São Paulo, Cuiabá and Porto Velho, and three flights a week to Vilhena, Corumbá and Curitiba. For details call Varig (☎ 763-1213), VASP (☎ 763-2389) or Pantanal (☎ 763-1322).

Antônio João airport (☎ 763-2444) is 7km from town; to get there, take the Nova Campo Grande bus from the rodoviária. There are several air-taxis available for trips into remote areas of the Pantanal.

Bus The rodoviária is huge, with lots of bars, barbers and a porno movie theatre. The visiting gaúchos need never leave the bus station!

To Corumbá (US$25) there are nine buses a day, the first at 6.30 am and the last at midnight. Direct buses do the trip in around six hours; otherwise, it's about seven hours. Eight buses a day make the 10 hour trip to Cuiabá (US$30, 10 hours). There's one bus a day, at 3 pm, to Bonito (US$17.50, 5½ hours). To Ponta Porã (US$18.50, 5½ hours) there are 13 buses a day. There are also daily buses to Belo Horizonte (US$66, 22 hours), São Paulo (US$62, 13 hours) and Foz do Iguaçu (US$32, 14 hours).

Train All passenger train services from Campo Grande have been suspended.

CORUMBÁ

• *pop 90,000* ✉ *79300-000* ☎ *067*

This port city on the Rio Paraguai and the Bolivian border is the southern gateway to the Pantanal. Corumbá, or Cidade Branca (White City), was founded and named in 1776, by Captain Luis de Albuquerque.

By 1840 it was the biggest river port in the world, boasting a dozen foreign consulates. Ships would enter the Rio de la Plata in the South Atlantic and sail up the Rio Paraná to its confluence with the Rio Paraguai, then continue up to Corumbá. The crumbling but impressive buildings along the waterfront reflect the wealth that passed through the town during the 19th century. With the coming of the railway, Corumbá lost its importance as a port and went into decline.

Corumbá is 403km north-west of Campo Grande by road. Due to its strategic location near the Paraguayan and Bolivian borders

Down South on the Border

Corumbá is well known as an entry point for small-time drug runners, who bring cocaine across the border from Bolivia stashed away in all sorts of places.

While gathering information about crossing the border into Bolivia, I went to the Polícia Federal office at the Corumbá rodoviária. I was met at the door by a smartly dressed officer who asked in polite English if I would mind waiting a few minutes as he was busy. I sat down on a bench outside to wait and shortly after heard screams, shouting and whacking noises coming from inside the office.

A few minutes later, the now slightly dishevelled officer reappeared at the door and asked me to come in.

A rather sorry-looking individual was lying crumpled on the floor inside the office, wincing in pain.

'He's a drug smuggler,' the officer explained. 'I caught him carrying cocaine. Here, take a look,' he said, pointing to a package on the table.

I craned my head towards the table; a large rectangular package was lying there.

'Take a closer look,' the officer urged. I took a few steps towards the table and peered at it more closely. It was only then that he chose to tell me where he'd removed the package from!

Chris McAsey

(Puerto Suárez is only 19km away), it has a reputation for poaching and drug trafficking, but travellers are generally left alone. There are signs that the city is returning to prosperity: banks are popping up everywhere and an effort is being made to restore some of the historic buildings.

Orientation

The rodoviária is six blocks from the centre. The waterfront is three blocks away in the opposite direction.

Information

Tourist Office The tourist office at the rodoviária (☎ 231-6091) can provide information on hotels, travel agencies and boat trips. It also sells airline tickets to Bolivia. The Polícia Federal staff are also helpful, if they're not busy shaking down small-time drug runners.

Foreign Consulates The Bolivian consulate (☎ 231-5605) is at Rua Antônio Maria Coelho 881, near the intersection of Rua América. It's open from 8.30 am to 1.30 pm Monday to Friday . At the time of writing, Bolivia had waived its visa requirement for nearly all western travellers.

The Paraguayan consulate (☎ 231-1691) is at Rua Firmo de Matos 508. On the Bolivian side, the nearest Brazilian consulate is in Santa Cruz.

Money The Banco do Brasil at Rua 13 de Junho 914 has Visa ATMs and a câmbio on the 3rd floor open from 10.30 am to 3 pm Monday to Friday. When we were there, it cost US$10 to change travellers cheques or cash.

Post & Telephone The post office is in Rua Delamare, across from the Praça da República. Telems has a posto telefônica on Rua Dom Aquino.

Travel Agencies There are several travel agencies in town, most of them promoting the same things: Pantanal packages and Rio Paraguai bost and fishing trips. Some good ones are Pantur (☎ 231-4343) at Rua América 969 and Terra Tour (☎ 231-5525) at Rua 15 de Novembro 95.

Things to See & Do

Corumbá's star attraction is the Pantanal, and you can get a preview of it from **Morro Urucum** (1100m).

Tourists looking for something different might consider a two day excursion to **Forte Coimbra**, which is a seven hour boat trip south on the Rio Paraguai. In days gone by, the fort was a key to the defence of the Brazilian west. You need permission from the Brigada Mista (at Avenida General Rondon 1735) to go there, because it's still used occasionally for military training.

Daily **boat tours** of the Corumbá environs are available from all travel agencies. An all-day trip will cost US$35, including lunch. Along Rua Manoel Cavassa on the waterfront, Orlando and Urçabar can organise four hour boat trips for around US$80 (for up to four people), not including gas.

Places to Stay

There are some cheap hotels close to the rodoviária that are OK if you're just spending a night or two in Corumbá before heading out. Otherwise, there are some good

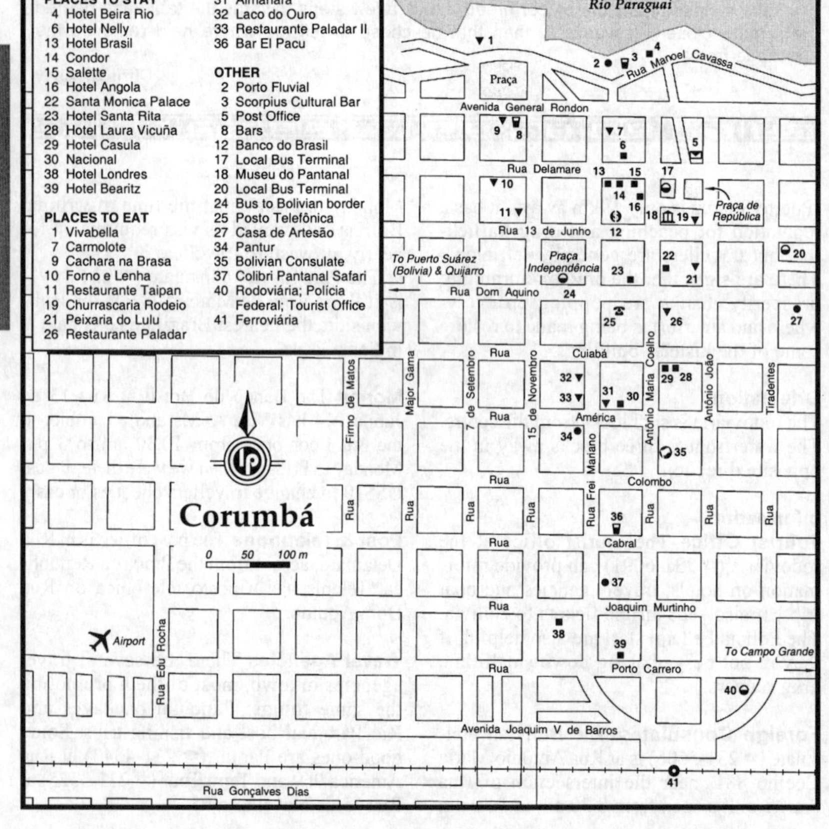

places closer to the waterfront, restaurants and bars in the centre of town. Near the rodoviária, the *Hotel Londres* (☎ 231-6717) has run-down apartamentos for US$10/20 for singles/doubles, but you'll get a 50% discount if you do a trip with Gil Tours.

Hotel Beatriz (☎ 231-8465) on Rua Porto Carrero by the rodoviária, has basic quartos at US$6/12/18 for singles/doubles/triples.

In the centre, there is a cluster of cheapies on Rua Delamare between Rua Frei Mariano and Rua Antônio Maria Coelho. The *Hotel Brasil* (☎ 231-7932) has a range of rooms, starting with quartos at US$6/12 – it's good value, as the place is clean and friendly. Next door, at the *Condor*, quartos with fan go for US$7 per person. *Salette* (☎ 231-3768) has quartos starting at US$10/18. Across the road, *Hotel Nelly* (☎ 231-6001) has clean apartamentos with fan for US$8/15.

Just around the corner at Rua Antônio Maria Coelho 124, *Hotel Angola* (☎ 231-3133) is good value. Spacious, clean apartamentos, some including a bizarre and kind of sexy round double bed, cost US$14/18. If you don't mind the stairs, ask for a room facing Rua Delamare on the 3rd floor so that you can enjoy the view of the Pantanal.

There are some good deals in the mid-range too. *Hotel Santa Rita* (☎ 231-5453), Rua Dom Aquino 860, has good, big apartamentos for US$17/28. The ones at the front have small balconies: don't lean on the railings though – they're very flimsy. The *Hotel Laura Vicuña* (☎ 231-5874), Rua Cuiabá 775, is new and comfortable. Single/double apartamentos with air-conditioning cost US$22/40. Next door, *Hotel Casula* (☎ 231-5645) has a nice atmosphere and apartamentos for US$20/35.

An interesting place to stay, though a bit out of the way, is the *Hotel Beira Rio* (☎ 231-2554), Rua Manoel Cavassa 109, on the waterfront. Popular with anglers, it charges US$10 per person.

The favourite for group tours is the two-star *Santa Monica Palace* (☎ 231-3001; fax 231-7880), Rua Antônio Maria Coelho 345. It charges US$55/75 for singles/doubles with the lot, including a pool. The *Nacional* (☎ 231-6868; fax 231-6202), Rua América 936, is the most expensive hotel in town. Singles/doubles go for US$60/80.

Places to Eat

Bar El Pacu on Rua Cabral is run by Herman the German and has good fish dishes – try a local speciality, peixe urucum (fish with cheese melted on top in a condensed milk sauce). It costs US$10, but should be enough for two. *Peixaria do Lulu* on Rua Antônio João is another good fish restaurant, and *Carmolote*, Rua Frei Mariani 33, offers fish dishes por quilo. At the other end of the scale, *Cachara na Brasa* on Rua General Rondon is a sophisticated bar/restaurant with an extensive menu of fish dishes for about US$13.

For as much meat and salad as you can eat for US$7, try *Laco do Ouro*, on Rua Frei Mariano, or *Churrascaria Rodeio*, Rua 13 de Junho 760, for tasty rodízio.

The hippest eatery in town is *Vivabella*, a small bar/restaurant tucked away near the corner of the park at the bottom of Rua 7 de Setembro. Run by Nilo, a friendly Italian who's lived in Corumbá for many years, it serves pizza, pasta, salads etc. Pasta dishes (around US$10 to $12) are enough for two. If you're *sozinho* (alone) ask for half a portion. It's also OK to go there just for a drink and to check out the great view of the Pantanal.

Forno e Lenha, Rua Delamare 1297, is a simple place that proudly serves só pizzas (just pizzas) – they're the best in town, wood-fired and very tasty. *Restaurante Paladar I* on Rua Antônio Maria Coelho, and *Restaurante Paladar II* on Rua Frei Mariano, both have pizza and pasta dishes for around US$8 to $10. For Chinese food, try *Taipan* on Rua 15 de Novembro. The *Almanara*, next to the Hotel Nacional, is recommended for Lebanese food.

Entertainment

In the evening, Avenida General Rondon is where young Corumbáns hang out to see and be seen, especially on weekends. Bars around the Praça serve chopp and snacks.

Across the road, *1054* is a dance club that gets packed on weekends. *Pagode* on Rua Santa Cruz is another hotspot on weekends. *Scorpius Cultural Bar* along the waterfront at Rua Manoel Cavassa 275 is a good place for a quiet beer on the waterfront. *Urcabar*, also along the waterfront at No 181, is a rustic little bar.

Things to Buy

The Casa de Artesão, in the old prison at Rua Dom Aquino 405, has a good selection of Indian art and artefacts, as well as the best Pantanal T-shirts in Corumbá.

Getting There & Away

Like Campo Grande, Corumbá is a transit point for travel to/from Paraguay and Bolivia. The Crossing the Border information in this section gives details on crossing the border between Corumbá and Quijarro, Bolivia.

Air The airport (☎ 231-3322) is 3km from the town centre. There are now two flights daily from Corumbá airport to Santa Cruz in Bolivia: one with Aerosur at 5 pm; and the other with LAB (Lloyd Aereo Boliviano) at 6 pm. Prices have more than halved in the last few years; tickets with both companies cost US$50 one-way (not including a US$7 airport tax). The LAB flight goes on to Cochabamba (US$54) and La Paz (US$84). TAM (Transportes Aereos Militares) has flights leaving from Puerto Suárez in Bolivia to Santa Cruz (US$38) usually on Monday, but there's no regular schedule. LAB also has a handy flight from Corumbá to Miami via Santa Cruz for US$470 one-way.

Pantur (see Travel Agencies earlier in the Corumbá section) is the agent for LAB and TAM in Corumbá.

VASP is the only major airline connecting Corumbá to Brazilian capitals, while Lineas Aéreas Pantanal flies to remote areas of the Pantanal. VASP (☎ 231-4441; fax 231-3471) has offices at Rua 15 de Novembro 392 and at the airport (☎ 231-4468). Lineas Aéreas Pantanal (☎ 231-7085) is at Rua Santos Dumont 50.

Bus From the rodoviária, buses run to Campo Grande (US$25) 11 times a day from 7 am to midnight. Direct buses do the trip in around six hours. To Aquidauana (US$16, five hours) there are five buses a day. There's also one daily bus to Bonito (US$25, seven hours) at 5.30 am.

Train Once across the Bolivian border, most people will be heading towards Santa Cruz. The train service between Quijarro, the Bolivian border town opposite Corumbá, and Santa Cruz is known as the Death Train. However, the journey is a beautiful one, passing through the steamy, sticky Pantanal area to lush jungle and chaco scrub. The many cattle ranches, agricultural projects, logging operations and Mennonite colonies along the railway are all indicators of the current developmental thrust of the Bolivian Oriente (East). Despite all the economic changes and growth in the area, there is still a diverse and abundant supply of wildlife and vegetation.

Be sure to have plenty of insect repellent on hand, since there are often long, unexplained stops in low-lying, swampy areas and the zillions of mosquitoes get voraciously hungry in those parts. Take drinking water as well.

From Quijarro to Santa Cruz, the Rapido service runs on Monday and Thursday and takes about 18 to 20 hours. Tickets cost US$22/8/6 for bracha/1st/2nd class. The Expresso Oriente leaves Quijarro on Tuesday and Saturday. It only has Pullman class; it costs US$16 and the trip takes around 16 to 18 hours.

With the onset of regular, cheap flights from Corumbá to Santa Cruz, you shouldn't have any problems buying tickets for the trains in Quijarro.

Ferrobus The luxury trip is on the ferrobus, a bus on bogies (wheels) which is considerably faster than the train. It leaves from Quijarro for Santa Cruz on Wednesday and Sunday.

Tickets cost US$40/35 for 1st/2nd class and the trip takes 12 hours. Buying tickets can be more difficult, but the taxi drivers in Quijarro may be able to help.

Boat Passenger boat services between Corumbá and Asunción (Paraguay) have been discontinued. Boat transport up through the Pantanal is infrequent – enquire at the Porto Geral.

Crossing the Bolivian Border The Bolivian border town of Quijarro is not much more than a muddy little collection of shacks. Taxis operate between the border and Quijarro station, a distance of about 4km. You may have to bargain over the unrealistic initial rates – the drivers are banking on foreigners not knowing the distance to be travelled. If you can find the oldest, most beat-up taxi in town, driven by the oldest, most cheerful taxi driver, you can pay as little as US$0.90, otherwise it's US$1.80.

Moneychangers at the frontier accept cash only and will change both reais and dollars. Have your money readily and discreetly available for a smooth transaction, unless you relish the attention of onlookers. It's impossible to quote a reliable exchange rate here; your best bet is to ask travellers going in the opposite direction.

If you're just crossing over to Bolivia for a few hours to buy train tickets, you don't need to get a Brazilian exit stamp. By the time this book is published, the new border post will be in operation, which should standardise all the procedures. All border formalities, including exit/entry stamps for your passport, will be completed there.

Entering Brazil, a taxi quoted US$10 for the ride into Corumbá – 5km from the border. For US$0.70, a city bus will take you to Rua Frei Mariano in the centre or the local bus terminal on Rua 13 do Junho.

You won't be allowed to enter Brazil without a current yellow-fever vaccination certificate, so make sure you organise your vaccination well in advance. (See the Health section in the Facts for the Visitor chapter earlier in this book)

Getting Around

A taxi from Corumbá's rodoviária to the centre costs US$7 – a rip-off, but the drivers sit around playing cards together and are all in cahoots.

From the bus stop outside the rodoviária, the Cristo Redentur bus (US$0.70) runs to the local bus terminal on Rua 13 de Junho. The Fronteira bus from Praça Independência on Rua Dom Aquino goes to the Bolivian border. It runs every 40 minutes and costs US$0.70. Cars pull up at the bus stop offering lifts to the border for US$1. Taxis want US$7. From the local bus terminal on Rua 13 do Junho, the Aeroporto bus runs (spookily) to the airport.

AQUIDAUANA

• *pop 40,000* ✉ *79200-000* ☎ *067*

Aquidauana and Anastácio are twin towns situated on the Rio Aquidauana, 138km from Campo Grande. They represent the beginning of the Pantanal and there are a number of excellent hotel-fazendas in the area. In Aquidauana there's not much to interest the traveller, but it's a friendly and relaxed place. The local government is actively promoting it as a base for Pantanal excursions.

Information

The new Fundetur office on Praça do Estudantes near the old train station has videos and information about the Pantanal. Staff are keen to help organise Pantanal tours with local operators. They also look after a growing family of friendly jacarés in the pool outside!

The Banco do Brasil, Rua Manoel Antônio Paes de Barros 535, has a Visa ATM. International telephone calls can be made from the Telems office next door.

Travel Agencies Panbratour (☎ 241-3494), Rua Estevão Alves Correa 320, specialises in the Pantanal. Staff can give you the latest information on hotel-fazendas. Buriti Viagens e Turismo (☎ 241-2718), Rua Manoel Antônio Paes de Barros 720, is another helpful agency.

Places to Stay
A good cheapie right in the centre is *Hotel Lord* (☎ 247-1857), Rua Manoel Antônio Paes de Barros 239. Quartos cost US$8/16 for singles/doubles and apartamentos US$12/24. *Hotel Fluminense* (☎ 241-2038), close by at Rua Teodoro Rondon 365, has similar prices. The *Portal Pantaneiro Hotel* (☎ 241-4328), Rua Pandía Calógeras 1067, is a reasonably priced mid-range place, with singles/doubles starting at US$25/45. This one is excellent value.

Places to Eat
O Casarão at Rua Manoel Antônio Paes Barros 533 is the top restaurant in town. Across the road at No 664, *Joinha* is good for a chopp and pizza stop. The *Churrascaria Princesa do Sul*, Rua Marechal Mallet 1047, is popular for rodízio. The best place for lunch and snacks is *Elias Lanchonete*, Rua 7 de Setembro 590.

Getting There & Away
There are frequent buses between Campo Grande and Aquidauana. There's a daily bus to Bonito (US$10.50, three hours) at 5 pm. The road turns to dirt around 30km from Aquidauana.

Getting Around
Motorcycle taxis can ferry you around town – from the rodoviária to the centre costs US$2.

COXIM
• *pop 29,000* ✉ *79400-000* ☎ *067*

Coxim is a small town about halfway between Cuiabá and Campo Grande, on the eastern border of the Pantanal. Its drawcard is the Piracema, when fish migrate up the Taquari and Coxim rivers, leaping through rapids to spawn. The Piracema usually takes place from September to December; if you're travelling this road during that period, it's worth stopping off to have a look. The fishing (for pacú, pintado, curimbatá, piracema and dourado) is good from August to November. A fishing licence is required. There are also some pretty waterfalls in the area, notably the Palmeiras falls, on the Rio Coxim.

Places to Stay
There are a number of cheap hotels in town. If you arrive late at night, the *Hotel Neves* (☎ 291-1273), Avenida Gaspar Ries Coelho 1931, is next to the bus station. Clean quartos with fan cost US$10 per person, a bit more with air-conditioning. The town is 3km away, on the banks of the river.

A reasonable hotel with a river frontage is the *Rio* (☎ 291-1295), Rua Filinto Muller 651. Singles/doubles with fan go for US$12/24.

The *Piracema* (☎ 291-1610) is a good place on the river, but it's 3km out of town. Instead of going into town from the bus station, head down the highway for another 500m. It's next to the bridge. Apartamentos with air-conditioning and frigobar cost US$30, and there's a good restaurant attached.

Getting There & Away
There are plenty of buses from both Cuiabá (US$30, six hours) and Campo Grande (US$20, four hours) to Coxim.

Getting Around
All the hotels can arrange boats, the going daily rate being around US$80.

BONITO
• *pop 15,500* ✉ *79290* ☎ *067*

Apart from the Pantanal, the small town of Bonito is the major tourist destination in Mato Grosso do Sul. The town itself has no attractions, but the natural resources of the area are spectacular. There are many caves, waterfalls and some incredibly clear rivers surrounded by lush forest, where it's possible for divers to see hundreds of fish eyeball to eyeball.

Information
Money The Banco do Brasil, at Rua Luiz da Costa Leite 2279, just off the main praça, has a Visa ATM.

Travel Agencies The main street, Rua Coronel Pilad Rebua, is lined with agencies. While their prices are the same, you might find it easier to tack onto a group that has already organised transport through the more popular agencies. Some of the better ones are Ygarapé Tour (☎/fax 255-1733) at No 1853; Muito Bonito Tourismo (☎/fax 255-1645; muitobonito@vip-cgr.com.br) at No 1448; Baia Bonito Tours (☎ 255-1193; fax 255-1750) at No 1830; and Hapakany Tur (☎ 255-1315) at No 1837.

Organised Tours

The local tourism authority has strict regulations in place for visiting the attractions, partly because many are on private land, and partly to minimise the impact on some pristine areas. Most sites have a daily limit on the number of visitors they will accept, and even these will have to be accompanied by a guide. Only local travel agencies are authorised to hire guides, so you're obliged to book tours through them. There are around 20 travel agencies in Bonito all offering the same trips at the same prices. Unfortunately, only a couple of tours are cheap and prices don't include transport, which you have to arrange yourself. See the later Getting Around section for more information.

There are around 15 attractions in the area, but only three or four are unique and essential to visit. Seven kilometres from Bonito, **Aquário Natural** has a beautiful natural spring where you can swim among 30 different varieties of fish and then float gently downstream to small waterfalls. The three hour tour costs US$28. Wetsuits and snorkels can be hired at the visitors centre for US$5. A wetsuit will take the edge off the cold water and also protect you from the sun – you aren't allowed to wear sunscreen on any of the river tours because it pollutes the water. The Aquário is managed by a Frenchman, Laurent.

Rio Sucuri, 20km from Bonito, is similar to Aquário Natural – springs, a crystal-clear river full of fish and subaquatic gardens, surrounded by lush forest – but it's further out in the wild. The cost is US$25 for three hours.

Within a fazenda 54km from Bonito, the **Rio da Prata** tour includes a short trek through rainforest and a 2km swim downstream along the river. The four hour tour costs US$28.

The bargain attractions are **Gruta do Lago Azul** (US$5 entry), a large cave with an underground lake 20km from Bonito, and the **Balneário Municipal** (US$3 entry), a natural swimming pool on the Rio Formoso 7km from town with clear water and lots of fish. You don't need a guide for the Balneário Municipal – you can spend the whole day there and have lunch at the kiosk.

Bonito is Beautiful

Bonito has become a very popular tourist destination in the last two years, not just for foreigners but for Brazilians as well. There are now around 50 guides in Bonito, some of whom speak English, French and Spanish. There are so many guides because the attractions are on private land and the owners require a guide to be present with visitors at all times. Even if you have a car, you need a guide to escort you to each attraction. Due to the volume of people, the owners have enforced limitations on the number of visitors at a time. For example, Rio da Prata will only allow 80 people per day.

The clearness of the water and the abundance of fish, birds, monkeys and other animals make the area a true rival to the Pantanal. As budget travellers, we wish that other travellers could experience what we were lucky to see. It is without doubt the experience of a lifetime.

Juanita Hamparsum, Gabrielle Ireland, Catriona Chaikin, Australia

In the high season (December to February), July and other holiday periods, many of these tours have already been booked out months ahead. If you're travelling during these times, it's a good idea to book one or two tours well advance.

Places to Stay

Accommodation in Bonito is tight and more expensive during the high season, and on weekends all year round.

You can camp at the *Balneário Municipal* for US$8, and buy meals at the canteen there.

In town, the best place to stay is *Pousada Muito Bonito* (☎/fax 255-1645), Rua Coronel Pilad Rebua 1448, which costs US$10 per person with a good breakfast included. The owner, Mario Doblack, speaks English, French, German, Spanish and Italian and is very helpful with information. He also runs a travel agency (see Information earlier) and rents houses for up to six people for US$25 per night.

Pousada Piracema (☎ 255-1641), Rua 29 de Maio 1000, is a reasonable budget option with clean rooms for US$10 per person. Better value is the *Pousada Caramachão* (☎/fax 255-1674), Rua das Flores 1203, with comfortable apartamentos for US$14/22/33 single/double/triple, including breakfast.

At the top end (Harrison Ford stayed here) is the *Resort Hotel Zagaia* (☎ 255-1777; fax 255-1710), 4.5km from town on the Rodovia Três Morros. This place has the works and costs around US$120/180 for singles/doubles.

Places to Eat

Tapera, Rua Coronel Pilad Rebua 480, has good fish, meat and chicken dishes for two people for around US$10. Just around the corner, on Rua 15 de Novembro, *Restaurante da Praça* has a reasonable prato feito for US$3.50. *Cantinho das Massas*, Rua Gen Felintro Muller 560, is a friendly place with passable pizza. *Taboa Bar*, at Rua Coronel Pilad Rebua 1841, is the place to go at night for a drink and music.

Things to Buy

Berô Can, Rua Coronel Pilad Rebua 1504, has an excellent range of indigenous artefacts from Mato Grosso and further afield.

Getting There & Away

There's a daily bus to Bonito from Campo Grande at 3 pm (US$17.50, six hours), which returns to Campo Grande at 5.30 am from Monday to Saturday and at 4 pm on Sunday. There are daily buses to Ponta Porã (US$17.50, six hours) at 12.30 pm and to Corumbá (US$25, seven hours) at 2 pm.

Getting Around

Unfortunately, most of Bonito's attractions are a fair way from town and there's no public transport. Tours booked with travel agencies in Bonito don't include transport. Your best bet is to book a tour with a busy travel agency, where you should be able to organise a ride with Brazilian tourists, most of whom are travelling by car or minibus. Otherwise, your options are to rent a dune buggy (US$60) or motorbike (US$25) from Bonito Rent-a-Car (☎ 255-1474), or use the town's new motorcycle taxi service. Prices are negotiable: two people to Rio Sucuri and back to town (40km round trip) costs around US$25. The drivers wait around for the duration of the tour.

PONTA PORÃ

• pop 58,500 ✉ 79900-000 ☎ 067

Ponta Porã is a border town divided from the Paraguayan town of Pedro Juan Caballero by Avenida Internacional. It was a centre for the yerba maté trade in the late 1800s, long before it started attracting Brazilians, who like to play in the Paraguayan casinos and shop for perfumes, electronics and musical condoms.

Information

Visas Getting exit/entry stamps involves a bit of legwork, so if you're in a hurry, grab a cab. For Brazilian entry/exit stamps, go to the Polícia Federal (☎ 431-1428) at Rua Marechal Floriano 1483. It's open on weekdays from 7.30 to 11.30 am and 2 to 5 pm.

The Paraguayan immigration office (☎ (036) 2047), where you need to go for entry/exit stamps, is at Calle Teniente Herrero 2068 in Pedro Juan Caballero. It's open Monday to Friday from 7 am to noon and 2 to 5 pm, and on Saturday from 7 am to noon.

If you need a visa, the Paraguayan consulate (☎ 431-1913) is at Avenida Presidente Vargas 120 in Ponta Porã. It's open Monday to Friday from 8 am to noon. The Brazilian consulate, on Avenida Dr Francia in Pedro Juan Caballero, is open Monday to Friday from 8 am to 2 pm and 3 to 5 pm.

Places to Stay

There are plenty of cheap places in both countries. The ones on the Paraguayan side of the border don't include breakfast.

In Brazil, the *Hotel Alvorada* (☎ 431-5866), Avenida Brasil 2977, is good value. Quartos go for US$10/15 a single/double and apartamentos for US$15/20. The *Hotel Internacional* (☎ 431-1243), Avenida Internacional 2604, is another good option. Clean and comfortable quartos cost US$10/18 and apartamentos US$16/24. At Rua Guia Lopes 63, the *Hotel Guarujá* (☎ 431-1619) is a good mid-range option. Large apartamentos with air-conditioning go for US$25/45, but this price can drop by up to 20% if it's quiet. Across the road at No 57, *Hotel Barcelona* (☎ 431-3061) has gone upmarket; comfortable apartamentos cost US$40/64.

Over the border in Paraguay there are a few cheap hotels close to each other on Calle Mariscal López. At *Hotel Acapulco* (no ☎), near the corner of Calle 14 de Mayo, basic rooms cost US$20 for up to four people. The friendly but run-down *Hotel Peralta*, at No 1257, charges US$10/20 for single/doubles.

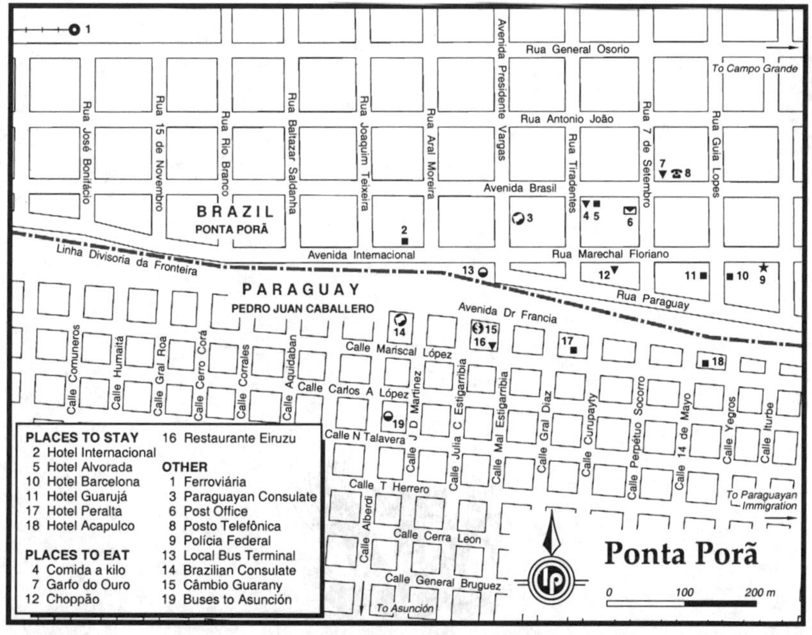

Places to Eat

Choppão, Rua Marechal Floriano 1877, is a popular spot with an extensive menu of meat, fish and pasta from US$6. *Garfo do Ouro*, next to the telephone office on Avenida Brasil, has a rodízio for US$4 and pizzas. For a cheap feed, there's a por quilo buffet restaurant next to the Hotel Alvorada. On the Paraguayan side, the restaurant in the *Hotel Peralta* serves a basic prato feito for US$2.50. The best (and most expensive) meal in town is at *Restaurante Eiruzu*, in the Eiruzu Hotel, on the corner of Calle Mal Estigarribia and Calle Mariscal Lopez.

Getting There & Away

Bus To Campo Grande (US$18, 5½ hours), there are 14 buses a day. There's a daily bus to Corumbá, via Bonito, at 6 am. From the bus station in Pedro Juan Caballero, there are frequent buses to Asunción and a daily bus to Foz do Iguaçu, (US$25, seven hours).

Getting Around

The local bus terminal is on Avenida Internacional, near the hotels. If you're coming into town from the Brazilian side, the bus can drop you here on the way in.

The Northeast

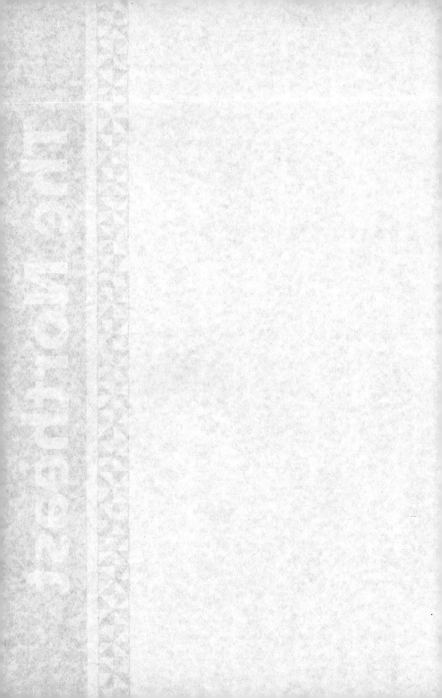

The Northeast

The Northeast region, known in Brazil as the Nordeste, covers more than 18% of the country's land area and contains 45 million inhabitants – nearly 30% of Brazil's population. The region is divided into nine states: Bahia, Sergipe, Alagoas, Pernambuco, Paraíba, Rio Grande do Norte, Ceará, Piauí and Maranhão. The archipelago of Fernando de Noronha lies over 500km east of Recife and was placed under the political administration of Pernambuco state in 1988.

The geography of the Northeast is characterised by four divisions. The *zona da mata* (forest zone) covers the fertile coastal area and extends up to 200km inland. The Atlantic rainforest, known as the Mata Atlântica, now exists only in tiny pockets – the rest was destroyed to make way for sugar-cane cultivation during the colonial period. With the exception of Teresina in Piauí state, all the major cities of the Northeast were established in this zone. Further west, the *agreste* forms a transitional strip of semifertile lands which merges into the *sertão* (backlands).

The sertão is characterised by a dry and temperate climate. Droughts, sometimes lasting for many years, have been the bane of this area for many centuries. The land is commonly referred to as *caatingas* because the landscape is dominated by vast tracts of caatinga (a scrubby shrub). The largest towns of the sertão are dotted along the Rio São Francisco, which provides irrigation.

The bleak and brutal life of the Sertanejo (inhabitant of the sertão) has received literary coverage in *Os Sertões* (published in English as *Rebellion in the Backlands*), by Euclides da Cunha, and the novel *Vidas Secas (Dry Lives)*, by Graciliano Ramos. The Cinema Novo films of Glauber Rocha depict violence, religious fanaticism, official corruption and hunger in the sertão.

The state of Maranhão and the western margin of Piauí state form the *meio norte*, a

HIGHLIGHTS

- African heritage and culture - music, dance, religion, cuisine and festivals (Bahia)
- Hikes and water slides in the Parque Nacional da Chapada Diamantina (Bahia)
- Candomblé ceremonies and festivals in Salvador and Cachoeira (Bahia)
- Pelourinho's Tuesday-night mini-Carnaval in Salvador (Bahia)
- The *roda de capoeiras*: semicircles of musicians and dancer/fighters on the streets of Bahian towns
- Diving in the Parque Nacional Marinho de Fernando de Noronha (Pernambuco) and Parque Nacional Marinho dos Abrolhos (Bahia)
- Colonial river towns along the Rio São Francisco, particularly Penedo (Alagoas)
- Colonial cities of Olinda (Pernambuco) and São Luís (Maranhão)
- Sand-dune surfing in the Parque Nacional dos Lençóis Maranhenses (Maranhão)
- Ceará's vast stretches of deserted coastline

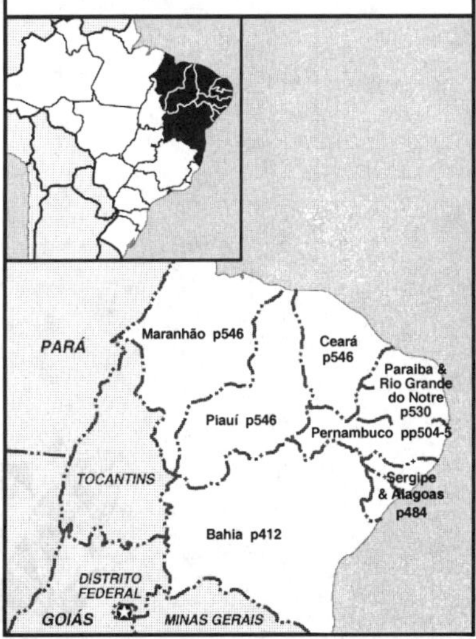

transitional zone between the arid sertão and the humid Amazon region.

The massive social problems of the Northeast include poverty, underemployment, housing shortages, a decaying education system and an absence of basic services such as sanitation. For example, many towns and villages in the state of Bahia lack basic sanitation, infant mortality rates are high and half the population is illiterate. State unemployed levels have been estimated at around 30% of the adult population.

Superintendência do Desen-Volvimento do Nordeste (SUDENE), the official government agency for development in the Northeast, has attempted to attract industry and boost the economy of the region, but these efforts have been hampered by the lack of energy sources, transport infrastructure, skilled labour and raw materials. Many Nordestinos (inhabitants of the Northeast) have emigrated to the Southeast and Central West in search of a living wage or new land for cultivation.

The economy of the zona da mata depends on the cultivation of crops such as sugar and cacao, and on the petroleum industry which is based on the coast. The inhabitants of the agreste make their living from subsistence farming, small-scale agriculture (vegetables, fruit, cotton and coffee) and cattle ranching (beef and dairy).

In the sertão, the economy is based on cattle ranching, cotton cultivation and subsistence farming, which puts the carnaubeira, a type of palm, to a multitude of uses. The meio norte is economically reliant on babaçu, another type of palm, which provides nuts and oil. The latter is converted into lubricating oil, soap, margarine and cosmetics.

Bahia

Bahia is Brazil's most historic state, and has retained strong links with the African heritage of many of its inhabitants. Its capital, Salvador da Bahia, was also once the capital of colonial Brazil, from 1549 to 1763, and was the centre of the sugar industry, which sustained the country's prosperity until the 18th century decline in international sugar prices.

The state of Bahia divides into three distinct regions: the *recôncavo*, the *sertão* and the *litoral*.

The recôncavo is a band of hot and humid lands that surrounds the Baía de Todos os Santos. The principal cities are Cachoeira, Santo Amaro, Maragojipe and Nazaré, which were once sugar and tobacco centres and the source of wealth for Salvador.

The sertão is a vast and parched land on which a suffering people eke out a meagre existence raising cattle and tilling the earth. Periodically, tremendous droughts, such as the great drought of 1877-79, sweep the land. Thousands of Sertanejos pile their belongings on their backs and migrate south or anywhere they can find jobs. But with the first hint of rain in the sertão, the Sertanejos return to renew their strong bond with this land.

The litoral south of Salvador, with beautiful, endless beaches, is a cacao-producing region and encompasses important cities like Valença, Ilhéus and Itabuna. North of Salvador the coast is only sparsely populated with a few fishing villages. The southern beaches are calm, while the northern beaches are often windy, with rough surf.

Salvador is a fascinating city loaded with colonial relics – including many richly decorated churches, one for every day of the year according to popular belief. You should also take the time to explore outside Salvador and visit the smaller cities, towns and fishing villages in Bahia, where life is unaffected by tourism and even less affected by the 20th century.

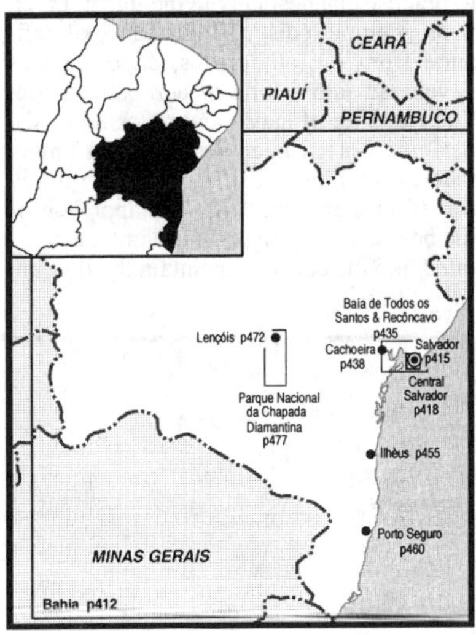

If beaches are what you want, the only difficulty is choosing. You can go to Porto Seguro for beaches with fancy hotels and restaurants or cross the river to Arraial d'Ajuda, Trancoso and Caraiva for a hipper, less developed beach scene. To really escape civilisation, you can go to the beaches up north around Mangue Seco, or to the south along the Peninsula do Maraú.

The inland regions of Bahia are less well known, but definitely worth a visit. Cachoeira and Lençóis are both interesting colonial towns and Lençóis provides a handy base for hiking trips in the Parque Nacional da Chapada Diamantina. Travellers might also like to explore the bizarre moonscapes of the sertão, where the Sertanejos have maintained a rich culture despite the poor environment.

Capoeira

Capoeira originated as an African martial art developed by slaves to fight their masters. Capoeira was prohibited by the slave owners and banished from the *senzalas* (slave barracks). The slaves were forced to practise clandestinely in the forest. Later, in an attempt to disguise this dance of defiance from the authorities, capoeira was developed into a kind of acrobatic dance. The clapping of hands and plucking of the *berimbau*, a stringed musical instrument that looks like a fishing rod, originally served to alert fighters to the approach of the boss and subsequently became incorporated into the dance to maintain the rhythm.

As recently as the 1920s, capoeira was still prohibited and Salvador's police chief organised a police cavalry squad to ban it from the streets. In the 1930s, Mestre Bimba established his academy and changed the emphasis of capoeira, from its original function as a tool of insurrection, to a form of artistic expression, which has become an institution in Bahia.

Today, there are two schools of capoeira: the Capoeira de Angola, led by Mestre Pastinha, and the more aggressive Capoeira Regional of Mestre Bimba. The former

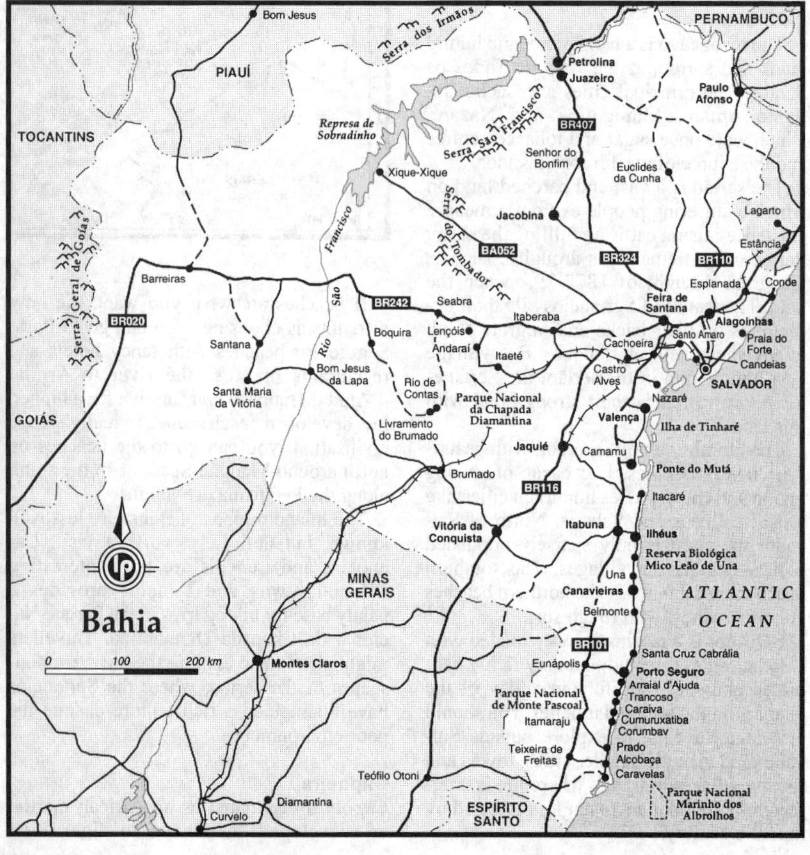

school believes capoeira came from Angola; the latter maintains it was born in the plantations of Cachoeira and other cities of the recôncavo region.

Capoeira combines the forms of the fight, the game and the dance. The movements are always fluid and circular, the fighters always playful and respectful. It has become very popular in recent years, and throughout Bahia and the rest of Brazil you will see the *roda de capoeiras* (semicircles of spectator-musicians who sing the initial *chula* before the fight and provide the percussion during the fight). In addition to the musical accompaniment from the berimbau, blows are exchanged between fighters/dancers to the beat of other instruments, such as *caxixi*, *pandeiro*, *reco-reco*, *agogô* and *atabaque*.

Folk Art

Bahia has some of Brazil's best artisans, who usually have small shops or sell in the local market. You can buy their folk art in Salvador, but the best place to see or purchase the real stuff is in the town of origin, because so much of the production is regional and specialised.

The main materials used in Bahian folk art are leather, wood, earth, metal and fibre. Feira de Santana is known for its leather work: the best examples are in the city's Casa do Sertão folklore museum. Maragojipinho, Rio Real and Cachoeira produce earthenware. Caldas do Jorro, Caldas de Cipo and Itaparica specialise in straw crafts. Rio de Contas and Muritiba have metalwork. Ilha de Maré is famous for lacework. Jequié, Valença and Feira de Santana are woodworking centres. Santo Antônio de Jesus, Rio de Contas and Monte Santo manufacture goods made of leather and silver.

Religion

Much of Bahian life revolves around the Afro-Brazilian religious cults known as Candomblé. To the Christian observer, Candomblé provides a radically different view of the world. It combines African traditions of music, dance and language into a system of worship and enjoyment of life in peace and harmony.

Much of Candomblé is secret – it was prohibited in Bahia until 1970 – but the public ceremony, conducted in the original Yoruba tongue, takes place in a *terreiro*. In Salvador, the Casa Branca, Avenida Vasco da Gama 463, in the Engenho Velho neighbourhood, is a centre for Candomblé activities.

See the Religion section of the Facts about the Country chapter for more detail about Candomblé and the Jogo dos Búzios (Casting of Shells). For suggested reading on religion, see the Books section of the Facts for the Visitor chapter.

Salvador

• *pop 2.2 million ✉ 40000-000 ☎ 071*

Salvador da Bahia, often abbreviated to Bahia by Brazilians, is the capital of Bahia state and one of Brazil's cultural highlights. This city retains its African soul, with a unique, vibrant culture. Ornate churches still stand on cobblestone streets. Festivals are spontaneous, wild, popular and frequent. Candomblé services illuminate the hillsides. Capoeira and *afoxé* (groups playing this Bahian music, which has a strong African beat) dance through the streets. The restoration of the historic centre of Salvador has revitalised areas that were previously considered dangerous and largely off limits to tourists.

However, despite the current boom in tourism, Salvador also suffers from social and economic problems, and has a great number of citizens who are jobless, homeless, hungry, abandoned and sick.

History

According to tradition, on 1 November 1501, All Saints' Day, the Italian navigator Amerigo Vespucci sailed into the bay, which was accordingly named Baía de Todos os Santos. In 1549, Tomé de Souza came from Portugal bringing city plans, a statue, 400 soldiers and 400 settlers, including priests and prostitutes. He founded the city in a defensive location: on a cliff top facing the sea. After the first year, a city of mud and straw had been erected, and by 1550 the surrounding walls were in place to protect against attacks from hostile Indians. Salvador da Bahia became the capital of the new region, and remained Brazil's most important city for the next three centuries.

During its first century of existence, the city depended upon the export of sugar cane, but tobacco cultivation was later introduced and cattle ranching proved profitable in the sertão. The export of gold and diamonds mined in the interior of Bahia (Chapada Diamantina) provided Salvador with immense wealth. The opulent baroque architecture is a testament to the prosperity of this period.

Salvador remained the seat of government until 1763 when, with the decline of the sugar-cane industry, the capital was moved to Rio. Overlooking the mouth of Baía de Todos os Santos, which is surrounded by the recôncavo, Brazil's richest sugar and tobacco lands, Bahia was colonial Brazil's economic heartland. Sugar, tobacco, sugar-cane brandy and, later, gold were shipped out, while slaves and European luxury goods were shipped in.

After Lisbon, Salvador was the second city in the Portuguese Empire: the glory of colonial Brazil, famed for its many gold-filled churches, beautiful colonial mansions and numerous festivals. It was also renowned, as early as the 17th century, for its bawdy public life, sensuality and decadence – so much so that it became known as the Bay of All Saints … and of nearly all sins!

The first black slaves were brought from Guinea in 1538, and in 1587 historian Gabriel Soares estimated that Salvador had 12,000 whites, 8000 converted Indians and 4000 black slaves. A black man was worth six times as much as a black woman in the slave market. The number of blacks eventually increased to constitute half of the population and the traditions of Africa took root so successfully that today Salvador is called the African soul of Brazil.

In Salvador, blacks preserved their African culture more than anywhere else in the New World. They maintained their religion and spirituality, within Catholicism. African food and music enriched the homes of both black and white, while capoeira developed among the slaves. *Quilombos* (runaway slave communities) terrified the landed aristocracy, and uprisings of blacks threatened the city several times.

In 1798, the city was the stage for the Conjuração dos Alfaiates (Conspiracy of the Tailors), which intended to proclaim a Bahian republic. Although this uprising was quickly quelled, the battles between those who longed for independence and those loyal to Portugal continued in the streets of Salvador for many years. It was only on 2 July 1823, with the defeat in Cabrito and Pirajá of the Portuguese troops commanded by Madeira de Melo, that the city found peace. At that time, Salvador numbered 45,000 inhabitants and was the commercial centre of a vast territory.

For most of the 19th and 20th centuries the city stagnated as the agricultural economy, based on archaic arrangements for land distribution, organisation of labour and production, went into uninterrupted decline.

Only recently has Salvador begun to move forward economically. New industries such as petroleum, chemicals and tourism are producing changes in the urban landscape, but the rapidly increasing population is faced with major social problems.

Orientation

Salvador sits at the southern tip of a V-shaped peninsula at the mouth of the Baía de Todos os Santos. The left branch of the 'V' is on Baía de Todos os Santos; the right branch faces the Atlantic Ocean; and the junction of the 'V' is the Barra district, south of the city centre.

A steep bluff divides central Salvador into two parts: Cidade Alta (Upper City) and Cidade Baixa (Lower City). These are linked by the Plano Inclinado Gonçalves (funicular railway), the Lacerda Elevator,

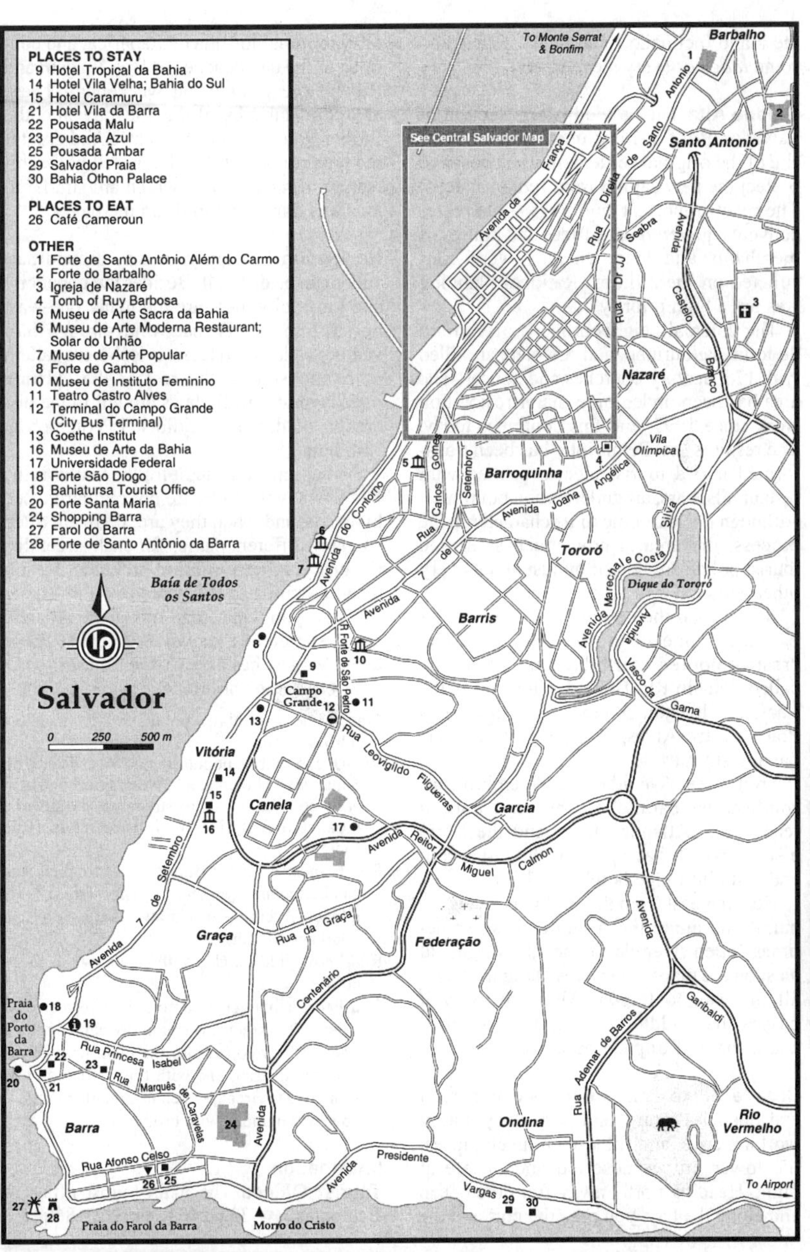
PLACES TO STAY
9 Hotel Tropical da Bahia
14 Hotel Vila Velha; Bahia do Sul
15 Hotel Caramuru
21 Hotel Vila da Barra
22 Pousada Malu
23 Pousada Azul
25 Pousada Âmbar
29 Salvador Praia
30 Bahia Othon Palace
PLACES TO EAT
26 Café Cameroun
OTHER
1 Forte de Santo Antônio Além do Carmo
2 Forte do Barbalho
3 Igreja de Nazaré
4 Tomb of Ruy Barbosa
5 Museu de Arte Sacra da Bahia
6 Museu de Arte Moderna Restaurant; Solar do Unhão
7 Museu de Arte Popular
8 Forte de Gamboa
10 Museu de Instituto Feminino
11 Teatro Castro Alves
12 Terminal do Campo Grande (City Bus Terminal)
13 Goethe Institut
16 Museu de Arte da Bahia
17 Universidade Federal
18 Forte São Diogo
19 Bahiatursa Tourist Office
20 Forte Santa Maria
24 Shopping Barra
27 Farol do Barra
28 Forte de Santo Antônio da Barra
Salvador
0 250 500 m
Baía de Todos os Santos
To Monte Serrat & Bonfim
See Central Salvador Map
Barbalho
Santo Antonio
Nazaré
Vila Olímpica
Barroquinha
Tororó
Dique do Tororó
Barris
Campo Grande
Vitória
Canela
Garcia
Graça
Federação
Ondina
Rio Vermelho
Barra
Praia do Porto da Barra
Praia do Farol da Barra
Morro do Cristo
To Airport
Avenida da França
Rua Direita de Santo Antonio
Seabra
Rua Dr JJ
Avenida Castelo Branco
Rua Carlos Gomes
Rua 7 de Setembro
Avenida Joana Angélica
Avenida do Contorno
Avenida 7
Avenida Marechal e Costa Silva
Avenida Vasco da Gama
R Forte de São Pedro
Rua Leovigildo Filgueiras
Avenida Reitor Miguel Calmon
Avenida 7 de Setembro
Rua da Graça
Centenário
Avenida
Garibaldi
Rua Ademar de Barros
Rua Princesa Isabel
Rua Marquês de Caravelas
Rua Afonso Celso
Avenida Presidente Vargas

the Plano Inclinado Liberdade/Calçada and some *ladeiras* (very steep roads).

Cidade Alta This is the historic section of Salvador. Built on hilly, uneven ground, the site of the original settlement was chosen to protect the new capital from Indian attacks. The most important buildings – churches, convents, government offices and houses of merchants and landowners – were constructed on the hilltops. Rational planning was not a high priority.

The colonial neighbourhoods of Terreiro de Jesus, Pelourinho, and Anchieta are filled with 17th century churches and houses. The area has been undergoing major restoration work since 1993, and this continues today. The result is that Pelourinho has been transformed into a tourist mecca, packed with restaurants, bars, art galleries and boutiques. Although it's lost some of its character in the process, the area is now much safer and tourist police are posted on just about every other corner.

Just around the corner from Praça da Sé is Praça Tomé de Souza and the large, cream-coloured birthday-cake building called Palácio Rio Branco. Close by is the Lacerda Elevator. A few blocks further is Praça Castro Alves, a major hub for Carnaval festivities.

From here, Avenida 7 de Setembro runs southwards (parallel to the bay) until it reaches the Atlantic Ocean and the Barra district, which has many of the city's top-end and mid-range hotels and bars.

Heading east from the Barra district is the main road along the Atlantic coast, sometimes called Avenida Presidente Vargas (at least on the maps). It snakes along the shore all the way to Itapoã. Along the way it passes the middle-class Atlantic suburbs and a chain of tropical beaches.

Cidade Baixa This is Bahia's commercial and financial centre, and port. Busy during working days, and filled with lunch places, the lower city is deserted and unsafe at night. Heading north, away from the ocean and along the bay, you pass the port and the ferry terminal for Ilha de Itaparica, and continue to the bay beaches of Boa Viagem and Ribeira (very lively on weekends). These are poor suburbs along the bay and the further you go from the centre, the greater the poverty. Watch for the incredible architecture of the *algados*, which are similar to *favelas* (slums) but built on the bay.

Navigation Finding your way around Salvador can be difficult. Besides the upper city and lower city there are too many one-way, no-left-turn streets that wind through Salvador's valleys and lack any coherent pattern or relationship to the rest of the existing paved world. Traffic laws are left to the discretion of drivers. Gridlock is common at rush hour.

Perhaps most difficult for the visitor is the fact that street names are not regularly used by locals, and when they are, there are often so many different names for each street that the one you have in mind probably doesn't mean anything to the person you're asking to assist you – the road along the Atlantic coast, sometimes known as Avenida Presidente Vargas, has at least four aliases.

Street-name variations include:

Praça 15 de Novembro – popularly known as Terreiro de Jesus

Rua Dr JJ Seabra – popularly known as Bairro do Sapateiro (Shoemaker's Neighbourhood). In early colonial days, this street was the site of a moat, the first line of defence against the Indians.

Rua Francisco Muniz Barreto – also called Rua das Laranjeiras (Street of Orange Trees)

Rua Inácio Accioli – also known as Boca do Lixo (Garbage Mouth)

Rua Leovigildo de Caravalho – known as Beco do Mota

Rua Padre Nobrega – commonly referred to as Brega. The street was originally named after a priest. It developed into the main drag of the red-light district, and with time, Nobrega was shortened to Brega, which in Brazilian usage is now synonymous with brothel!

Information

Tourist Offices The main tourist office of Bahiatursa (☎ 322-2403; fax 321-8604) is

GUY MOBERLY

GUY MOBERLY

GREG CAIRE

GREG CAIRE

Top: Beach buggy near Maceió
Middle: Dunes near Natal
Bottom Left: Old Portuguese building facade
Bottom Right: Caju fruit, São Luis

ALL PHOTOS BY ROBYN JONES

Mercado Ver-o-Peso, Belém

tucked away on the Belvedere da Sé. To find it, look for the small 'Bahiatursa' sign on the right-hand side of the Igreja da Misericórdia, close to the Praça da Sé bus terminal. Go down the alley past some barber shops until you reach the stairs leading down to the Belvedere.

The Bahiatursa office is open daily from 8 am to 6.30 pm. The staff are helpful and provide advice (in English, German, French and Spanish) on accommodation, restaurants, events, and where and when to see capoeira and Candomblé. The notice board inside the office has messages that may help you to find friends, rent houses and boats, buy guidebooks and even purchase international airline tickets.

There are also Bahiatursa offices at: Rua Francisco Muniz Barreto 12, Pelourinho (☎ 321-2463), open daily from 8 am to 10 pm; Praça Azevedo Fernandes, Largo do Barra (☎ 247-3195), open daily from 9 am to 5.30 pm; Mercado Modelo (☎ 241-0242), open Monday to Saturday from 8 am to 6 pm; the *rodoviária* (☎ 358-0871), open daily from 8 am to 10.30 pm; the airport (☎ 204-1244), open daily from 8.30 am to 10.45 pm; the Centro de Convençoes da Bahia (☎ 370-8400), open Monday to Friday from 8 am to 6.30 pm; and Shopping Iguatemi (☎ 351-4308) and Shopping Barra (☎ 332-4556), which both open Monday to Saturday from 9 am to 10 pm.

Bahiatursa operates an alternative accommodation service to locate rooms in private houses and the like during Carnaval and summer holidays. This can be an excellent way to find cheap rooms. Information on travel throughout the state of Bahia is also available, but don't expect much detail.

For general tourist information or help (in English), you can try dialling ☎ 131 for Disque Turismo (Dial Tourism).

Foreign Consulates These countries maintain consulates in Salvador:

France
  Travessa Francisco Gonçalves 1, Comércio (☎ 241-0168)
Germany
  Rua Lucaia 281, salas 204-6, Rio Vermelho (☎/fax 334-7106)
UK
  Avenida Estados Unidos 18 B, sala 800, Comércio (☎ 243-7399; fax 242-7293)
USA
  Rua Pernambuco 51, Pituba (☎ 345-1545; fax 345-1550)

Visa Extensions For visa extensions, the Polícia Federal (☎ 321-6363) is at Rua Oscar Pontes, Água de Meninos s/n (no number), Comércio. Take a Calcada bus from the Avenida da França bus stop at the base of the Lacerda Elevator, and get off at the Mercado Popular. Walk back about 100m towards the city centre and turn right. You'll see the blue and grey Polícia Federal building at the end of the street, near the docks.

Money The best places to change cash or travellers cheques are Vertur and Toursbahia, both in Pelourinho. Visa withdrawals can be made at Bradesco ATMs at the airport, the rodoviária, Shopping Barra and Shopping Iguatemi and on Largo Teresa Batista in Pelourinho.

There's an American Express/Kontik-Franstur SA office (☎ 358-6011) located in Shopping Iguatemi, loja 3 (on the ground floor next to Banco Excel), which will hold mail for travellers. It's open from 9 am to noon and 2 to 6 pm Monday to Friday. Ask for Inalda.

Post & Communications The central post office is on Praça da Inglaterra in Cidade Baixa. There are also post offices at Rua Alfredo de Brito 43, Pelourinho; at the airport; and at the rodoviária. Watch out for overcharging and make sure that items are franked.

For international long-distance calls, using a direct dial international (DDI) public telephone may be more convenient than running off to a telephone station. They work with phonecards, preferably the 90-unit ones which allow longer conversations, and are located in major hotels and tourist

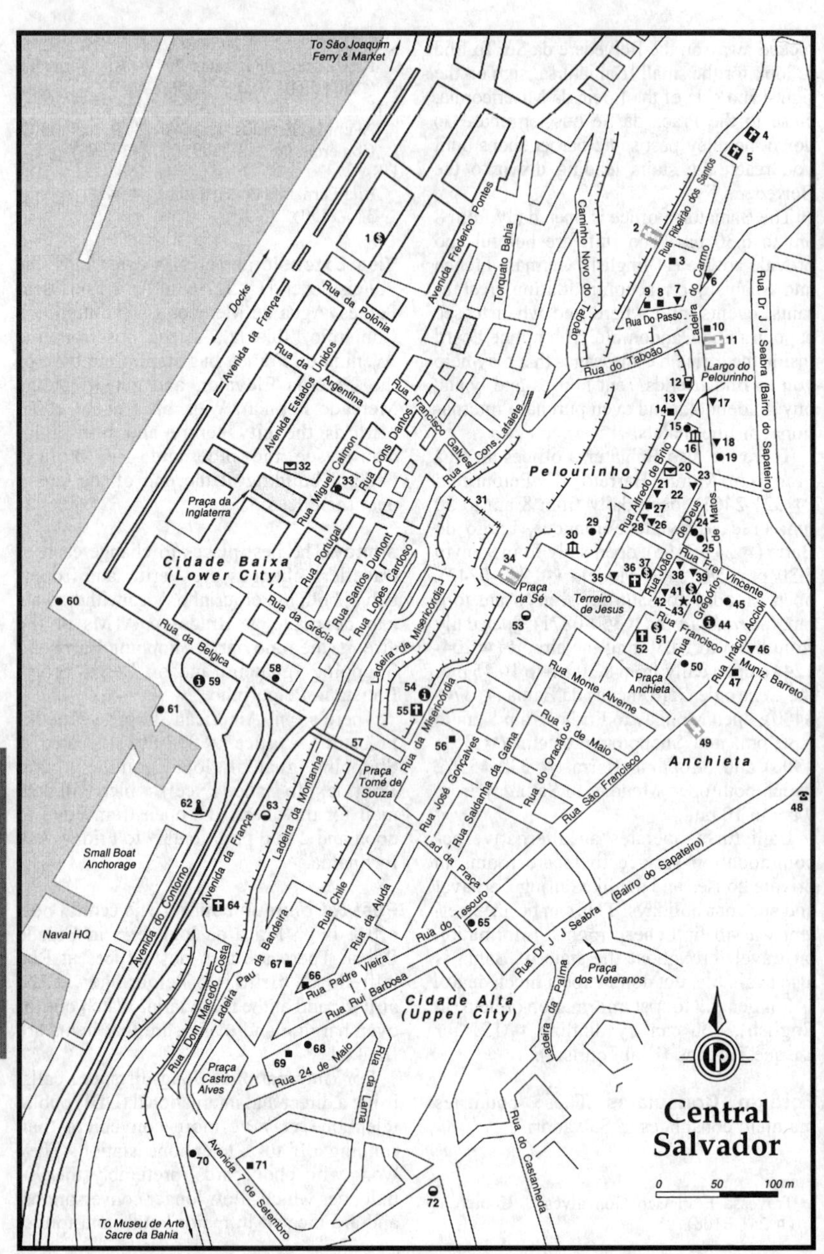
Central Salvador
To São Joaquim Ferry & Market
Pelourinho
Cidade Baixa (Lower City)
Cidade Alta (Upper City)
Anchieta
Praça da Inglaterra
Praça da Sé
Terreiro de Jesus
Praça Anchieta
Largo do Pelourinho
Praça Tomé de Souza
Praça dos Veteranos
Praça Castro Alves
Small Boat Anchorage
Naval HQ
To Museu de Arte Sacre da Bahia
Avenida da França
Docks
Avenida Estados Unidos
Rua da Polônia
Rua da Argentina
Avenida Frederico Pontes
Torquato Bahia
Caminho Novo do Taboão
Rua do Taboão
Rua Do Passo
Rua Ribeirão dos Santos
Ladeira do Carmo
Rua Dr J J Seabra (Bairro do Sapateiro)
Rua Francisco Galvão
Rua Cons Dantos
Rua Cons Lafaiete
Rua Miguel Calmon
Rua Portugal
Rua Santos Dumont
Rua Lopes Cardoso
Rua da Grécia
Rua da Bélgica
Ladeira da Misericórdia
Rua da Misericórdia
Rua Alfredo de Brito
Rua João de Deus
Rua Gregório de Matos
Rua Frei Vincente
Rua Inácio Accioli
Rua Francisco Muniz Barreto
Rua Monte Alverne
Rua 3 de Maio
Rua do Oracão
Rua São Francisco
Rua Saldanha da Gama
Rua José Gonçalves
Lad da Praça
Rua do Tesouro
Rua Dr J J Seabra (Bairro do Sapateiro)
Ladeira da Palma
Rua do Castanheda
Ladeira da Montanha
Avenida da França
Avenida do Contorno
Rua Dom Macedo Costa
Ladeira Pau da Bandeira
Rua Chile
Rua da Ajuda
Rua Padre Vieira
Rua Rui Barbosa
Rua 24 de Maio
Rua da Lama
Avenida 7 de Setembro
0
50
100 m

PLACES TO STAY
3 Albergue de Juventude Solar
8 Albergue Pousada do Passo
9 Albergue de Juventude do Pelô
10 Hotel Solara
14 Hotel Pelourinho
27 Albergue de Juventude Vagaus
47 Albergue de Juventude das Laranjeiras
56 Hotel Themis
66 Palace Hotel
67 Hotel Chile
69 Hotel Pousada da Praça
71 Hotel Maridina

PLACES TO EAT
6 Casa do Benin
7 Kilinho
13 Banzo
17 Senac
18 Restaurante da Dinha
21 Micheluccio
23 Uauá
26 Dona Chika KA
28 Mamabahia
35 Cantinho da Lua
38 Tempero da Dada
39 Yamoto
42 Senzala
46 Bargaço

OTHER
1 Banco do Brasil
2 Igreja do Santíssimo Sacramento do Passo
4 Igreja e Convento de NS do Carmo/ Museu do Carmo
5 Igreja da Ordem Teceira do Carmo
11 Igreja NS do Rosário dos Pretos
12 Bar do Reggae
15 Fundaçáo Casa de Jorge Amado
16 Museu da Cidade
19 Filhos de Ghandi
20 Post Office
22 Praça Quincas Berro d'Agua (Praça Dois M)
24 Didá Music & Dance School
25 Grupo Olodum
29 Antiga Faculdade de Medicina (Old Medical Faculty)
30 Museu Afro-Brasileiro/Museu de Arqueolgia e Etnologia
31 Plano Inclinado Gonçalves (Funicular Railway)
32 Post Office
33 VASP
34 Catedral Basílica
36 Igreja Sáo Pedro dos Clérigos
37 Toursbahia
40 Bradesco ATM
41 Largo de Tereza Batista
43 DELTUR Tourist Police
44 Bahiatursa Tourist Office
45 Largo do Pedro Arcanjo
48 Posto Telefônica
49 Igreja São Francisco
50 Mercado Artesenato
51 Vertur
52 Igreja da Ordem Teceira de Sáo Domingus
53 Praça da Sé Bus Station
54 Main Bahiatursa Tourist Office
55 Igreja da Misericórdia
57 Lacerda Elevator
58 Casa dos Azulejos
59 Mercado Modelo
60 Terminal Turístico Marítimo (Boat to Ilha de Itaparica)
61 Small Boats to Ilha de Itaparica
62 Bunda Statue
63 Avenida de França Bus Station; Buses to Mercado São Joaquim; Ferry & Igreja NS do Bonfim
64 Igreja NS da Conceiçáo
65 Casa de Ruy Barbosa
68 Livraria Brandão Bookshop
70 Varig
72 Terminal da Barroquinha

areas. If you can't find one, some of the convenient Telebahia posto telefônica posts are:

Telebahia Barra
  Avenida 7 de Setembro 533, Porto da Barra; open daily from noon to 10 pm
Telebahia Shopping Barra
  Avenida Centenário 2992, Barra; open Monday to Saturday from 9 am to 10 pm, and Sunday from 9 am to 7 pm
Telebahia Rodoviária
  Open daily from 6 am to 10 pm
Telebahia Aeroporto
  Aeroporto Internacional Dois de Julho; open daily from 7 am to 10 pm

There are also telephone stations in Iguatemi Shopping Centre, Campo da Pólvora and Centro de Convenções da Bahia.

Travel Agencies Toursbahia (☎ 322-3676; fax 242-4383), Rua João de Deus 2, 2nd floor, is operated by a young Brazilian/Swiss couple, José and Regula Iglesias. They offer a complete service for travellers, including natural and cultural history tours around Bahia. Between them, José and Regula speak English, French, German, Spanish, and Italian. They are happy to deal with groups or independent travellers, and are highly recommended.

The following travel agencies also sell bus tickets in addition to all the normal services. They can save you a trip out to the rodoviária, but check first, as some agents do not sell tickets to all available destinations.

Amaralina Viagens
  Barra (☎ 336-1099)
Itaparica Turismo
  Avenida Manoel Dias da Silva 1211, Pituba (☎ 248-3433)
Itapemirim
  Avenida ACM 1298 Casa Shopping Cidade (☎ 353-3711)

Bookshop Livraria Brandão, Rua Rui Barbosa 15B, is a huge second-hand bookshop with a large range of foreign-language books to buy or exchange.

Books & Maps Most newsagencies have maps on sale, but they lack detail and only give an overview of city layout. Bahiatursa has a free map and services guide to Pelourinho, and an essential monthly guide to cultural events, *Pelourinho Dia & Noite*. The Fundação Cultural puts out a similar, but more detailed, guide with reviews, called *Agenda Cultural*, available from Bahiatursa offices and also from most hotels. Bahiatursa also publishes a glossy, detailed guide once a year, *Guia Turístico Bahia*, which has useful listings, but it tends to sell out quickly.

Gay & Lesbian Travellers Information is available from Grupo Gay da Bahia (☎ 322-2552; fax 322-3782), Rua do Sodré 45, near the Museu de Arte Sacra da Bahia. The centre publishes an entertainment guide to Salvador's gay scene, *Guia para Gays*, which costs US$5.

Dangers & Annoyances Salvador has a reputation for theft and muggings, and tourists clearly make easy targets. Paranoia is counterproductive, but you should be aware of the dangers and understand what you can do to minimise problems. See the Dangers & Annoyances section in the Facts for the Visitor chapter for more information.

The following are some general points to remember when visiting Salvador: dress down; take only enough money with you for your outing; carry only a photocopy of your passport; and don't carry a camera outside Pelourinho.

Look at a map for basic orientation before you set out to see the sights. Although tourist police maintain a highly visible presence in the centre of Salvador, particularly Pelourinho, this does not apply in other areas. It's also difficult to see how the police in Pelourinho can control pickpockets and bag-snatchers on crowded Sunday and Tuesday nights, so don't carry valuables then. The Lacerda Elevator is renowned for crime, especially at night around the base station, and pickpocketing is common on buses and in crowded places. Don't hesitate to use taxis during the day and especially after dusk.

On the beaches, keep a close eye on juvenile thieves, often referred to as *capitões d'areia* (captains of the sand), who are quick to make off with unguarded possessions.

During Carnaval, tourist authorities highly recommend that tourists form small groups and avoid deserted places, especially narrow alleyways.

Emergency DELTUR tourist police (☎ 242-3504) operates 24 hours a day in the Pelourinho at Cruzeiro de São Francisco 14. Other useful numbers include: Disque Turismo (dial tourism) ☎ 131; Pronto Socorro (first aid) ☎ 192; and Polícia Civil (police) ☎ 197.

Business Hours In Salvador, shopkeepers often close for lunch from noon to 3 pm. Work has a different flavour: slow, relaxed and seemingly nonchalant.

The slow pace often frustrates and irritates visitors, but if you can reset your internal clock and not get uptight or unsettled, you are likely to be rewarded with many kindnesses and surprises.

Things to See & Do

Historic Salvador is easy to see on foot, and you should plan on spending a couple of days wandering among the splendid 16th and 17th century churches, homes and museums. One good approach is to ramble through the old city in the morning, head out to the beaches in the afternoon, and devote the evening to music, dance or Candomblé.

The most important sections of thecolonial quarter extend from Praça Castro Alves along Ruas Chile and da Misericórdia to Praça da Sé and Terreiro de Jesus, and then continue down through Largo do Pelourinho and up the hill to Largo do Carmo.

Catedral Basílica Starting at the Praça da Sé, walk a block to the east to the Terreiro de Jesus (Praça 15 de Novembro on many maps). The biggest church on the plaza is the Cathedral of Bahia, which served as a Jesuit centre until thethe order was expelled in 1759. The cathedral was built between 1657 and 1672, and its walls are covered with Lioz marble, which served as ballast for returning merchant ships. Many consider this the city's most beautiful church. The interior has many segmented areas and the emphasis is on verticality – raise your eyes to admire the superb ceiling. The cathedral opens from 8 am to noon and 2 to 6 pm daily.

Museu Afro-Brasileiro The Antiga Faculdade de Medicina (Old Medical Faculty) houses the Afro-Brazilian Museum (☎ 321-0383), with its small but excellent collection of *orixás* (gods; see Candomblé in the Religion section of the Facts about the Country chapter for more information) from both Africa and Bahia. There is a surprising amount of African art, ranging from pottery to woodwork, as well as superb ceremonial Candomblé apparel.

Other highlights include wooden panels representing Oxum (an orixá revered as the goddess of beauty) that were carved by Carybé, a famous Argentine artist who has lived in Salvador for many years. Entry is US$1 and the museum is open Tuesday to Saturday from 9 am to 5 pm.

In the basement of the same building is the **Museu de Arqueologia e Etnologia** (Archaeology & Ethnology Museum), open Monday to Friday from 9 am to 5 pm.

Igreja São Francisco Defying the teachings and vows of poverty of its namesake, this baroque church, east of Praça da Sé, is crammed with displays of wealth and splendour. Gold leaf is used like wallpaper. There's an 80kg silver chandelier and imported *azulejos* (Portuguese ceramic tiles).

Forced to build their masters' church and yet prohibited from practising their own religion (Candomblé *terreiros* (venues) were hidden and kept far from town), the African slave artisans responded through their work: the faces of the cherubs are distorted, some angels are endowed with huge sex organs, some appear to be pregnant. Most of these creative acts were chastely covered by 20th century sacristans. Traditionally, blacks were seated in far corners of the church without a view of the altar.

Notice the polychrome figure of São Pedro da Alcântara by Manoel Inácio da Costa. The artist, like his subject, was suffering from tuberculosis. He made one side of the saint's face more ashen than the other so that São Pedro appears more ill as you walk past him. José Joaquim da Rocha painted the hallway ceiling using perspective technique, which was considered a novelty at the time.

The poor come to Igreja São Francisco on Tuesday to venerate Santo Antônio and receive bread. The Candomblistas respect this church's saints and come to pray both here and in Igreja NS do Bonfim.

Depending on restoration work, opening hours are Monday to Saturday from 7.30 to 11.30 am and 2 to 6 pm, and Sunday from 7 am to noon.

Igreja da Ordem Terceira de São Francisco Close to the Igreja São Francisco is the 17th century Church of the Third Order of São Francisco. Notice the frontispiece, in the Spanish baroque (or plateresco) style, which remained hidden until it was accidentally discovered in the 1930s when a workman hammered off some plaster to install wiring. Opening hours are Monday to Friday from 8 to 11.30 am and 2 to 5 pm.

Igreja São Pedro dos Clérigos The Igreja São Pedro dos Clérigos is on Terreiro de Jesus, next to Cantina da Lua. This rococo church, like many others built in the 18th century, was left with one of its towers missing in order to avoid a tax on finished churches. It opens only during mass (usually from 8 to 9.30 am on Sunday), and if you visit during this time, do not disturb the service.

Pelourinho To see the city's oldest architecture, turn down Rua Alfredo de Brito, the small street that descends into the Pelourinho district.

Pelourinho means 'whipping post', and this is where the slaves were tortured and sold (whipping of slaves was legal in Brazil until 1835). The old slave-auction site on Largo do Pelourinho (also known as Praça José de Alencar) has recently been renovated and converted into the **Fundacão Casa de Jorge Amado** (Jorge Amado Museum). According to a brass plaque across the street, Amado lived in the Hotel Pelourinho when it was a student house. The exhibition is disappointing, but you can watch a free video of *Dona Flor* or one of the other films based on Amado's books. The museum is open Monday to Friday from 8 am to 6 pm and Saturday from 10 am to 6 pm.

Next door is the **Museu da Cidade**. The exhibitions on display include costumes of the orixás of Candomblé, and the personal effects of the Romantic poet Castro Alves, author of *Navio Negreiro*, and one of the first public figures to protest against slavery. The museum is open from 10 am to 6 pm Tuesday to Friday and from 1 to 5 pm on weekends.

Igreja NS do Rosário dos Pretos, across the Largo do Pelourinho, was built by and for the slaves. The 18th century church has some lovely azulejos and is beautifully lit up at night. The church is open Monday to Friday from 8 am to 5.30 pm, and Saturday and Sunday from 8 am to 2 pm.

Igreja do Santíssimo Sacramento do Passo From Pelourinho, go down the hill and then continue uphill along Ladeira do Carmo. You will reach a set of steps on the left that lead up to the church in an approach reminiscent of the Spanish Steps of Rome. The first Brazilian film to win an award at the Cannes film festival, *O Pagador de Promessa*, was filmed here.

Igreja da Ordem Terceira do Carmo This church, at the top of the hill on Ladeira do Carmo, was founded in 1636 and contains a baroque altar and an organ that dates from 1889.

Igreja e Convento de NS do Carmo & Museu do Carmo Next door, this religious complex is moderately interesting. Among the sacred and religious articles in the museum is a famous sculpture of Christ created by Francisco Chagas (also known as O Cabra). There's also a treaty declaring the expulsion of the Dutch from Salvador on 30 April 1625. The document was signed at the convent, which served as the general's quarters at the time. The museum is open Tuesday to Saturday from 8 am to noon and from 2 to 6 pm, and Sunday from 9 am to noon.

For a glimpse of old Salvador, continue walking for a few blocks past dilapidated buildings that teem with life. Also notice an odd-looking public oratory, **Oratório da Cruz do Pascoal**, plunked in the middle of Rua Joaquim Távora.

Praça Tomé de Souza While not officially recognised or protected by the Brazilian historical architecture society SPHAN, this plaza in the centre has several beautiful and important sites. The **Palácio Rio Branco** was built in 1549 to house the offices of Tomé de Souza, the first governor general of Brazil.

Elevador Lacerda The Lacerda Elevator, inaugurated in 1868, was an iron structure with clanking steam elevators until these were replaced with a new system in 1928. Today, electric elevators truck up and down a set of 85m vertical cement shafts in less than 15 seconds, and carry over 50,000 passengers daily.

Things weren't always so easy. At first, the Portuguese used slaves and mules to transport goods from the port in Cidade Baixa to Cidade Alta. By 1610, the Jesuits had installed the first elevator to negotiate the drop. A clever system of ropes and pulleys was manually operated to carry freight and a few brave souls.

You should watch out for petty crime around the elevator, particularly after dusk (see the earlier Dangers & Annoyances section).

Cidade Baixa Descending into the lower city you'll be confronted by the **Mercado Modelo**. Filled with souvenir stalls and restaurants, it's Salvador's worst concession to tourism. If you've missed capoeira, there are displays for tourists outside the building – anyone contemplating taking photos is well advised to negotiate a sensible price beforehand or risk being suckered for an absurd fee. The modernist sculpture across the street is referred to as *bunda* (arse) by the locals – which gives it a much more appealing aspect. There are many cheap *lanchonetes* (stand-up snack bars) in Cidade Baixa and the area is worth exploring.

Mercado São Joaquim To see a typical market, take either the Ribeira or the Bonfim bus heading north from the bus stop beside the elevator (base station). Get off after the Pirelli Pneus store on your left, after about 3km. Mercado São Joaquim is a small city of waterfront *barracas* (huts) open all day, every day except Sunday. It's not exactly clean (watch out for the green slime puddles) – and the meat neighbourhood can turn the unprepared into devout vegetarians. You are bound to come across spontaneous singing and dancing at barracas where *cachaça* (sugar-cane rum) is served.

Igreja NS do Bonfim Take the Bonfim bus across the road from the Mercado São Joaquim to the Igreja NS do Bonfim, further along the Itapagipe Peninsula. Built in 1745, the shrine is famous for its miraculous power to effect cures. In the Sala dos Milagres you will see votive offerings: replicas of feet, arms, heads, hearts – parts of the body devotees claim were cured.

For Candomblistas, Bonfim is the church of Oxalá and thus their most important church. In January, the Lavagem do Bonfim, one of Bahia's most important festivals, takes place here and *mães de santo* (Candomblé priestesses) lead the festivities together with Catholic priests. See the Special Events section later in this chapter for more details. There are also huge services at Bonfim on the first and last Friday of each month.

When you approach the church you'll undoubtedly be offered a *fita* (ribbon) to tie around your wrist for a small donation. With the fita you can make three wishes that will come true by the time it falls off. This usually takes over two months and you must allow it to fall off from natural wear and tear. Cutting it off is said to bring bad luck.

The church is open Tuesday to Sunday from 6 am to noon and 2 to 6 pm.

The Bay From the Igreja NS do Bonfim there is a very interesting half-hour walk to the bay, where you'll find the old **Monte Serrat lighthouse** and **church** (good crab at the barracas). Nearby is **Praia da Boa Viagem**, where one of Bahia's most popular and magnificent festivals, the Procissão do Senhor Bom Jesus dos

Navegantes, takes place on New Year's Eve. See Special Events later in this section for more details.

The beach is lined with barracas and is animated on weekends. It's a poorer part of town and quite interesting. From Boa Viagem, there are buses back to the bus stop beside the Lacerda Elevator (base station).

Museu de Arte Sacra da Bahia This museum (☎ 243-6110) Rua do Sodré 276, is housed in a beautifully restored 17th century convent. The sacred art on display includes excellent and varied sculptures and images in wood, clay and soapstone; many were shipped to Salvador from Portugal. Opening hours are Monday to Friday from 12.30 to 5.30 pm.

Museu de Arte Moderna On the bay, further down from the centre towards Campo Grande on Avenida do Contorno, is the Solar do Unhão, an old sugar estate that now houses the small Museu de Arte Moderna (☎ 243-6174), a restaurant and a ceramic workshop. Legend has it that the place is haunted by the ghosts of tortured slaves. One look at the ancient pelourinho (whipping post) and torture devices on display makes the idea credible. However, it's a lovely spot; the art exhibits are often good and the restaurant has a tranquil atmosphere and a great view.

An Evening of Candomblé

A long evening of Candomblé in Casa Branca, Salvador's oldest *terreiro*, is quite an experience. The women dress in lace and hooped skirts, dance slowly, and chant in Yoruba. The men drum complex and powerful African rhythms. The terreiro is dominated by the women: only women dance, and only they enter a trance, the principal goal of the ceremony. Men play a supporting role.

The dance is very African, with graceful hand motions, swaying hips and light steps. When a dancer enters the trance, she shakes and writhes while assistants embrace and support her. Sometimes, even spectators go into trances, although this is discouraged.

The *mãe de santo* or *pai de santo* runs the service. The *mãe pequena* is entrusted with the training of priestesses; in this case, two *filhos de santo*: one a girl over seven years of age, the other a girl under seven. The initiates are called *abian*.

On a festival morning, the celebration commences with an animal sacrifice. Only initiates may attend this service. Later in the afternoon the *padê* ceremony is held to attract the attention of Exú, and this is followed by chanting for the *orixás*, which is accompanied by *alabés* (atabaque drummers).

The festival we attended was for Ormolú, the feared and respected orixá of plague and disease. He is worshipped only on Monday and his Christian syncretic counterpart is either St Lazuras or St Roque. His costume consists of a straw belt encrusted with seashells, a straw mask and a cape and dress to cover his face and body, which have been disfigured by smallpox.

When the dancers had received the spirit of Omolú in their trance, some left the floor. They returned with a person dressed from head to toe in long straw-like strands to represent Omolú. The dancing resumed.

Although the congregants of Casa Branca are friendly and hospitable, they don't orient their practice to outsiders. Westerners may attend, and many white Brazilians are members. After the ceremony, guests are invited to the far end of the house for sweets and giant cakes – one cake decorated like the Brazilian flag.

Andrew Draffen

THE NORTHEAST

This area has a reputation for crime (especially mugging of tourists), and buses don't pass close to it, so it's better to take a taxi to and from the Solar do Unhão. Opening hours are Tuesday to Friday from 1 to 9 pm and weekends from 3 to 9 pm.

Candomblé Before doing anything in Salvador, find out about the schedule for Candomblé ceremonies so you don't miss a night in a terreiro. The Federação Baiana Do Culto Afro-Brasileiro (☎ 321-0145), Rua Alfredo do Brito 39, Pelourinho, is open Monday to Friday from 8 am to noon and provides information on Candomblé services. Go up the stairs and speak to Ari. Bahiatursa has many Candomblistas on its staff who can provide the addresses of terreiros – the *Eventos & Serviços* guide available at Bahiatursa offices lists a monthly schedule with transport details. Activities usually start around 8 or 9 pm and can be held any day of the week. For details about Candomblé, refer to the Religion section in the Facts about the Country chapter.

Capoeira School To visit a capoeira school, it's best to get the up-to-date schedule from Bahiatursa, which has a complete listing of schools and some class schedules in its monthly *Eventos & Serviços* guide. The Associação de Capoeira Mestre Bimba is an excellent school. It's at Rua Francisco Muniz Barreto 1, 1st floor, Terreiro de Jesus, and has lessons Monday to Friday, from 9 am to noon and Saturday from 3 to 9 pm. Its *roda da capoeira* is on from Tuesday to Friday at 8 pm and Saturday at 6 pm.

Beaches The beaches of **Pituba**, **Armação**, **Piatã**, **Placaford** and **Itapoã** may not be as famous as Ipanema and Copacabana, but they are just as beautiful. Although these beaches are all within 45 minutes (or more depending on traffic) of the centre by bus, Pituba, Armação and Piatã are becoming increasingly polluted and are now not recommended for swimming. It's advisable to head for Placaford, Itapoã or further north. For information on beaches north of Itapoã, see the North of Salvador section later in this chapter.

If you just want to experience Salvador's beach scene, **Barra** has the first beaches and is the liveliest – but swimming is not advisable on the Atlantic Ocean side, due to heavy pollution. Surprisingly, the water on the bay side at Barra certainly *looks* clear and inviting – locals love it, so you can make up your own mind. There are plenty of restaurants, barracas and bars along the waterfront, although it can get a bit sleazy at night. You can see Bahia's oldest fort, the polygonal **Forte de Santo Antônio da Barra**, which was built in 1598 and fell to the Dutch in 1624. The view from the fort of Ilha Itaparica is splendid.

See Getting Around earlier in this section for details about transport to these beaches.

Special Events

Salvador's Carnaval receives greatest emphasis, but it is by no means the only festival worth attending. There are many others, particularly in January and February, which attract huge crowds. Since the 17th century, religious processions have remained an integral part of the city's cultural life. Combining elements of the sacred and profane, Candomblé and Catholicism, many of these festivals are as wild as Carnaval and possibly more colourful.

Carnaval Carnaval in Salvador is justly world famous. For four nights and three days, the masses go to the streets and stay until they fall. There's nothing to buy, so all you have to do is follow your heart – or the nearest *trio elétrico* (electrified music played on the top of trucks) – and play.

Carnaval, usually held in February or March, starts on a Thursday night and continues until the following Monday. Everything, but everything, goes during these four days. In recent years, Carnaval has revolved around the trios elétricos. The trios play a distinctively upbeat music from the tops of trucks that slowly wind their way through the main Carnaval areas (Praça Castro

Capoeira

One capoeira group in Salvador is notorious for extracting money from unsuspecting tourists. Unfortunately, the group is also one of the most spectacular to watch. I should have known better, but I stopped to watch them one afternoon and was immediately asked for money 'for the school'. I handed over what I considered a reasonable sum, and having done so, thought I might as well take a photo. After taking a quick snap of the action, the '*Mestre*', a man mountain with muscles on his muscles, pulled out of the circle and approached me. He asked me for money, and I explained that I'd already given. 'Yes', he said, peering down at me with a broad smile, 'but you need to pay more for the Mestre'. I refused, but as he became more persistent (and the crowd around grew more amused at the encounter), I reached into my pocket and dropped a bunch of coins into his massive palm. He looked from the coins to me, then threw the coins onto the ground in apparent disgust. Moving closer, he took my head gently into his hands and gave me a 'friendly' headbutt!

Andrew Draffen

Alves, Campo Grande and Barra). Surrounding the trios is a sea of dancing, drinking revellers.

Carnaval brings so many tourists and so much money to Salvador that there's been an inevitable tendency towards commercialisation, although the trend here is still light years behind that in Rio. Fortunately, local residents have been very critical of this trend, and arts and community groups have now been given a greater say in the arrangements of Salvador's Carnaval. A more authentic festival has resulted from this: events have been decentralised, and freer and more impromptu expression is encouraged. Let's hope the spontaneity continues.

Take a look at the newspaper or go to Bahiatursa for a list of events. Don't miss the afoxés (Afro blocos, large groups of Carnaval revellers), such as Badauê, Ilê-Aiyê, Grupo Olodum, Timbalada, Muzenza and the most famous, Filhos de Gandhi (Sons of Gandhi). The best place to see them is in Liberdade, a couple of suburbs north of Pelourinho, Salvador's largest black district.

Also, explore Carnaval Caramuru in Rio Vermelho and the smaller happenings in Itapoã, the old fishing and whaling village that has a fascinating ocean procession on the last day of Carnaval, when a whale is delivered to the sea.

The traditional gay parade is held on Monday at Praça Castro Alves. Many of Brazil's best musicians return to Salvador for Carnaval, and the frequent rumours that so and so will be playing on the street are often true (for example, Gilberto Gil and Baby Consuelo have both taken part).

Many clubs have balls just before and during Carnaval. If you're in the city before the festivities start, you can also see some of the blocos practising. Just ask Bahiatursa.

It's most convenient to stay near the centre or in Barra. Violence can be a problem during Carnaval, and some women travellers have reported violent approaches from locals. A common problem you may encounter at Carnaval is being sucked into the crowd right behind a trio elétrico and having to dodge all the dancers with their flying elbows! See the Dangers & Annoyances earlier in this section for more details on avoiding crime.

Procissão do Senhor Bom Jesus dos Navegantes This festival, which originated in Portugal in 1750, is one of Bahia's most popular celebrations. On New Year's Eve, the image of Senhor dos Navegantes is taken to Igreja NS da Conceição, close to

Mercado Modelo in Cidade Baixa. On the morning of New Year's Day, a maritime procession, consisting of dozens of boats, transports the image along the bay and returns it to the beach at Boa Viagem, which is packed with onlookers eager to celebrate with music, food and drink.

Festas de Reis Also of Portuguese origin, this festival is held in Igreja da Lapinha on 5 and 6 January.

Lavagem do Bonfim This festival, which takes place on the second Thursday in January, is another of Salvador's most popular events and is attended by huge crowds. The festival culminates with the ritual *lavagem* (washing) of the church by mães and *filhas* (daughters) de santo. Abundant flowers and lights provide impressive decoration, and the party atmosphere continues with the Filhos de Gandhi and trios elétricos providing musical accompaniment for dancers. If you want to do the 9km walk to the church, it's best to leave early with the mães, before the trio elétricos blast into action.

Festa de São Lázaro This is a festival dedicated to the Candomblé orixá, Omulu, and culminates on the last Sunday in January with a mass, procession, festival and ritual cleansing of the church.

Festa de Iemanjá A grand maritime procession takes flowers and presents to Iemanjá, the Mãe e Rainha das Águas (Mother and Queen of the Waters). One of Candomblé's most important festivals, it's celebrated on 2 February in Rio Vermelho and accompanied by trios elétricos, afoxés and plenty of food and drink.

Lavagem da Igreja de Itapoã Celebrated in Itapoã 15 days before Carnaval, this warm-up for Carnaval is all music and dance, with blocos and afoxés.

Festa São João This festival is celebrated on 23 and 24 June with pyrotechnics and many parties on the street where *genipapo* (a local liqueur) is consumed in very liberal quantities.

Santa Bárbara The festival of Santa Bárbara is the Candomblé festa of the markets. Probably the best spot to watch the festivities which are hald from 4 to 6 December is in Rio Vermelho, at the Mercado do Peixe.

Festa de NS da Conceição This festival takes place on 8 December and features a procession in Cidade Baixa followed by Candomblé ceremonies in honour of Iemanjá.

Passagem do Ano Novo New Year's Eve is celebrated with all the zest of Carnaval – especially on the beaches.

Places to Stay

Salvador has many hotels, but they can all fill up during the Carnaval season, so reservations are a good idea. Bahiatursa can help you find lodging – just provide the staff with a general idea of your preferred price range and type of lodging. Bahiatursa also has lists of houses that take in tourists and these can be a source of excellent, cheap lodgings when hotels are full, especially during summer holidays and Carnaval. But beware: the tourist office makes selective referrals and it helps if you don't look too burnt-out or broke.

Places to Stay – Budget

Keep in mind that hostels and cheap hotels in the Pelourinho can get very noisy in the evenings, with lots of live music.

Camping On the outskirts of Itapoã is *Camping Ecológico* (☎ 374-0201), Alameda da Praia s/n (no number) at Praia do Flamengo. At Pituaçu, about 14km from the centre, there's *Camping Pituaçu* (☎ 231-7413), on Avenida Pinto d'Aguiar.

Hostels There aren't a lot of hostels throughout Brazil but in Salvador, at least, you're spoiled for choice.

City Centre There are now a couple of excellent hostels close to the city centre, mostly clustered around Pelourinho. *Albergue Pousada do Passo* (☎ 326-1954), Rua do Passo 3, is popular with backpackers. The friendly owner, Fernando, speaks English, French and Spanish. He has very clean dormitories for singles and couples for US$10/25. Another favourite is the *Albergue de Juventude das Laranjeiras* (☎/fax 321-1366), a very flash Pelourinho hostel at Rua Inácio Acciolli 13. The YHA *Albergue de Juventude do Pelô* (☎ 242-8061) is also popular and conveniently located at Rua Ribeiro Santos 5. Close by is the YHA *Albergue de Juventude Solar* (☎ 241-0055), Rua Ribeiro Santos 45. The *Albergue de Juventude Dois de Julho* (☎ 243-9513), Rua Areal de Cima 44, is just south of the city centre – very close to Praça Duque de Caxias. *Albergue de Juventude Vagaus* (☎ 321-1179; fax 371-5995) has basic dorm rooms for US$10 per person and very friendly owners Zuleide and Clarice make you feel right at home.

Beaches The following beach hostels are listed in sequence, from Barra district along the Atlantic coast towards Itapoã.

The *Albergue de Juventude Senzala* (☎ 235-4177; fax 245-9573), Rua Greenfeld 128, Barra, is close to the lighthouse. Also in Barra district, just a couple of blocks west of Shopping Barra, you'll find the *Albergue de Juventude da Barra* (☎ 247-5678; fax 247-6842) at Rua Florianópolis 134, Jardim Brasil, Barra. Close to Praia Ondina is the *Albergue de Juventude Solar* (☎ 235-2235), Rua Macapá 461. Moving further down the coast, Praia Amaralina is a couple of minutes on foot from the *Albergue de Juventude Lagash* (☎ 248-7399), Rua Visconde de Itaboraí 514. Next to Praia Pituba is the *Albergue de Juventude Casa Grande* (☎/fax 248-0527), Rua Minas Gerais 122.

Hotels The cheaper hotels in the old part of town are around Praça da Sé, Terreiro de Jesus, Praça Anchieta and Pelourinho. Prices have risen since the restoration of the area, and outside the youth hostels, good-value cheap accommodation is hard to find close to the historic centre.

The *Hotel Caramuru* (☎ 336-9951; fax 336-4553), Avenida 7 de Setembro 2125, is away from the centre in a quiet location, but offers very good value. The hotel is in a large colonial mansion with a breezy, elevated eating area. Spacious and spotless single/double quartos cost US$20/25; apartamentos cost US$25/30. The hotel also organises Candomblé excursions, and trips to Itaparica and other destinations.

The *Hotel Pelourinho* (☎/fax 243-2324), Rua Alfredo de Brito 20, right in the heart of Pelourinho, has long been a favourite with travellers but is getting pricey. It's an older, converted mansion (reputedly the setting for Jorge Amado's novel *Suor)*, and the management is reasonably security-conscious (there's a guard posted at the entrance to the building). Small apartamentos with fan cost US$20/35/50 for singles/doubles/triples. In the hotel courtyard there are handicraft shops and, right at the end, a restaurant-bar with views and regular live music.

About 20m downhill from Largo do Pelourinho is the *Hotel Solara* (☎ 321-0202), which has apartamentos starting at US$18/25/35 for singles/doubles/triples. Rooms are also used by locals for stays as short as two hours.

The *Hotel Themis* (☎ 243-1668), Praça da Sé 57, Edifício Themis, 7th floor, offers great views, but is a bit run-down. Managed by Frenchman Ivo, who can speak English when necessary, it's a popular hang-out with French travellers. There's a bar and a restaurant. Apartamentos without a view cost US$17/24/31; with view US$20/28/36. The *Hotel Pousada da Praça* (☎/fax 321-0642), close to Praça Castro Alves at Rua Rui Barbosa 5, is centrally located and offers basic, but clean, quartos at US$15/20. Apartamentos cost US$20/25

Just a short walk from Praça Tomé de Souza is the *Hotel Chile* (☎ 321-0245), at Rua Chile 7, 1st floor. Dark and beat-up quartos start at US$17/25. Apartamentos cost US$40 for a double with air-conditioning; and US$25/32 with fan. The *Palace Hotel* (☎ 322-1155; fax 243-1109), Rua Chile 20, is good value and right in the centre of the city. Comfortable apartamentos with air-conditioning start at US$25/30. Close by is the *Hotel Maridina* (☎ 242-7176), Avenida 7 de Setembro, Ladeira de São Bento 6, 1st floor. This is a friendly family-run hotel that offers good value for money. Quartos are US$15/25. Apartamentos with fan cost US$20/30, those with air-conditioning are US$25/35.

In Barra, *Pousada Azul* (☎/fax 245-9798), Rua Praguer Fróis 97, is a friendly, comfortable, highly recommended pousada. Beatriz and her helpful, all-female staff speak Spanish, English, German, and Italian. It's popular with solo women travellers. There are dorm rooms and some rooms for singles and couples. At US$15 per person with a good breakfast, it's good value and only a couple of blocks from the beach as well.

Also in Barra, *Pousada Âmbar* (☎/fax 235-6956), Rua Afonso Celso 485, is a lovely family-run pousada with a relaxed, friendly atmosphere. Paulo, Christine and their two young daughters, are excellent hosts. Christine is French and speaks English too. They charge US$10 per person without breakfast and US$13 with – it's definitely worth the extra three bucks. Right on Praia do Porto da Barra at Avenida 7 de Setembro 3801, the *Pousada Malu* (☎ 237-4461) is a relaxed place offering clean apartamentos with fan for US$18/20.

Along the beach, in Itapoã, the *Pousada Bruta Flor*, Rua Passagarda 20, is a beautiful, small pousada. It's a five minute walk from clean beaches and has a nice pool if you want to swim before breakfast. It has spotless six-bed, four-bed and two-bed quartos for US$15 or US$25 depending on the season and with or without breakfast. The bathrooms are nice too. It's highly recommended by readers.

Places to Stay – Mid-Range

Close to the Hotel Caramaru on Avenida 7 de Setembro in Vitória are two good mid-range options. At No 2009 is *Hotel Bahia do Sol* (☎ 336-7211; fax 337-7776), which has apartamentos for US$49/55/75. Almost next door at No 1971 is *Hotel Vila Velha* (☎ 336-8722; fax 336-8490), a three-star Embratur hotel with rooms for US$51/56.

If you'd rather stay opposite the beach in the Barra district, and within easy reach of the city centre, the *Hotel Villa Da Barra* (☎ 247-7908; fax 247-9667), Avenida 7 de Setembro 3959, is a very good option. It's a colourful place with a breezy courtyard and café area. Two-level apartamentos with three beds and two bathrooms cost US$25/30 in the low season. Close by at Avenida 7 de Setembro 3783, the *Hotel Porto da Barra* (☎ 247-7711; fax 245-2619) has apartamentos with fan at US$28/32, and doubles with air-conditioning at US$35.

At Rio Vermelho, the *Hotel Catarina Paraguaçu* (☎/fax 247-1488), Rua João Gomes 128, is set in an old colonial building and offers comfortable apartamentos for $US50/90.

Places to Stay – Top End

The most charming place to stay for those with no budget constraints would have to be the *Enseada das Lajes* (☎ 336-1027; fax 336-0654), Avenida Oceanica 511 in Rio Vermelho. It has large, colonial-style rooms filled with antiques. Great views and good taste combine well here. Its apartamentos start at US$200. Facing the beach at Rio Vermelho is the *Meridien Bahia* (☎ 335-8011; fax 335-8919), which has rooms starting at US$120/140.

At Praia Ondina, closer to the city, are two top-class hotels: the *Bahia Othon Palace* (☎ 247-1044; fax 245-4877), which has rooms for around US$150/200; and the *Salvador Praia* (☎ 245-5033; fax 245-5003), which has a private stretch of beach and charges US$120/140. The *Hotel Tropical da Bahia* (☎ 336-0102; fax 336-9726) is a five-star hotel between the city centre and Barra, at Praça 2 de Julho 2, Campo Grande. Room prices start at US$145/193, with a 20% discount for cash or credit card payment.

Places to Eat

Bahian cuisine is an intriguing blend of African and Brazilian cuisine based on characteristic ingredients such as coconut cream, ginger, hot peppers, coriander, shrimp and dendê oil. Dendê, an African palm oil with a terrific flavour, is used in many regional dishes (you'll also smell it everywhere). Since dendê has a reputation for stirring up trouble in travellers' bellies, you are advised to consume it in small quantities until you've become accustomed to it. For names and short descriptions of typical Bahian dishes, refer to the Food section in the Facts for the Visitor chapter.

The Pelourinho area is packed with restaurants, though many of them cater to tourists and are expensive. The best value for lunches are the popular self-serve restaurants. *Senzala*, Rua João de Deus 9, 1st floor, and *Kilinho*, close to the Pousada do Passo, are a couple of the best places.

A long-time favourite on Terreiro de Jesus is *Cantinho da Lua*, which serves good-value refeições and is a popular hangout. Nearby, at Rua Alfredo Brito 21, *Mamabahia* has a popular churrasco (barbecued meat) lunch for US$7. *Micheluccio*, Rua Alfredo Brito 33, is the place to head to for excellent pizza.

Tempero da Dada, Rua Frei Vicente 5, is a lively, casual restaurant with tasty seafood – the moqueca de caranguejo and moqueca de peixe are good. Two people can eat for around US$15. *Dona Chika Ka*, Rua João Castro Rabelo 10, continues to get rave reviews for its bobó de camarão (US$20).

If you're hanging out for some Japanese food, *Yamoto*, Rua Frei Vicente, is an elegant Japanese restaurant with superb sushi – expect to pay around US$20 per person.

In the Largo do Pelourinho there's a restaurant in the courtyard of the *Hotel Pelourinho*. The main attraction is the great view of the bay. The dishes are adequate but they tend to be overpriced, and the staff can be surly. Try the moqueca mista.

Next door to the hotel, *Banzo* is bright, animated and good value. There's a great selection of Bahian and European dishes plus all sorts of exotic drinks – expect to pay around US$15 for a main course plus a drink. When Grupo Olodum is giving one of its free Sunday evening concerts in Largo do Pelourinho, the Banzo balcony provides a good vantage point to view the gyrating crowds.

Across the street, at Praça Jose de Alencar 5, *Restaurante da Dinha* is good for a cheap feed and to meet locals – the original *Dinha*, on Largo de Santana in Rio Vermelho, is widely known as having the best acarajé in Salvador. *Novo Tempo* is in the downstairs section of Grupo Olodum on Largo do Pelourinho. It's a happening spot, with a lovely back courtyard, good music and seafood dishes from around US$15.

Also on Largo do Pelourinho is *Senac*, a cooking school that offers a huge spread of 40 regional dishes in the form of a self-service buffet. It's not the best Bahian cooking, but for US$15 you can discover which Bahian dishes you like ... and eat – till you explode! Senac is open every day except Sunday from 6 to 9 pm. Folklore shows are presented on Thursday and Saturday from 8 to 9 pm – tickets cost US$5 per person.

At the crossroads downhill from Largo do Pelourinho is *Casa do Benin* (☎ 241-6348), a superb restaurant serving excellent African food in a small courtyard complete with palm trees, a pond and thatched hut. The main dishes start around US$15 – the moqueca de peixe and frango ao gengibre (ginger chicken) are close to culinary heaven! The restaurant is open daily except Sunday from 11 am to 6 pm. Another terrific restaurant for African-influenced cuisine is the colourful *Uauá*, Rua Gregório de Matos 36, 1st floor.

Solar do Unhão (☎ 321-5551), which houses the Museu de Arte Moderna, also has a restaurant on the lower level in the old senzala (slave quarters). Ironically, the view from the restaurant is one of the best in the city, and as good a reason as any for a visit, but it's becoming a bit of a tourist trap. Dinner is usually accompanied by live music and a folklore show at 9 pm – expect to pay a cover charge. Crime is a problem in this area, so you should take a taxi.

Close to the rodoviária and adjacent to Hipermercado Paes Mendoça is *Baby Beef* (☎ 358-0811), a restaurant serving fine steaks and ribs for about US$15. In Barra, *Café Cameroun* (☎ 247-2788), Rua Afonso Celso 350, has been recommended by readers for its African food.

Excellent Bahian dishes at moderate prices are served at *Restaurante Iemanjá* (☎ 231-5770), Avenida Otávio Mangabeira s/n on Paia Armação, and *Agdá* (☎ 231-2851), Rua Orlando Moscoso 1, Boca do Rio.

Last, best and hardest to find is *Bargaço* (☎ 231-5141), Rua P, Quadra 43, Jardim Armação – it's on a small residential street near the Centro de Convenções (Convention Centre). National and international gourmets rate the seafood here as world class. The ensopada de camarão is divine, but you'll have to be prepared to splurge about US$20 – fame has set an upward trend for the prices. It's open daily from noon to midnight. There's also a branch of *Bargaço* (☎ 242-6546) in Pelourinho on the corner of Rua Francisco M Barreto and Rua Inácio Accioli.

Entertainment

Salvador is justly renowned for its music. The blending of African and Brazilian traditions produces popular styles, such as trio elétrico (which dominates Carnaval), *tropicalismo*, afoxé, *caribé*, *axé* and reggae.

Bars and clubs tend to come and go quickly in Salvador, so ask around and check the newspaper to confirm the following suggestions. If you want to plug into the arts, Fundação Cultural Estado da Bahia (☎ 320-9377; fax 320-9338) is in the Palácio Rio Branco, sala 29-C. The Fundação publishes a monthly guide, *Agenda Cultural*, which gives a comprehensive rundown of music events, theatre and dance performances, and art exhibitions. The Friday editions of local newspapers, *A Tarde* and *Correio da Bahia*, contain listings of what's on during the weekend.

Teatro Castro Alves (☎ 2[illegible] Praça Dois de Julho (Campo G[illegible] biggest music theatre in Salva[illegible] big acts play here, and they're often Brazil's best.

Pelourinho is the nightlife capital of Salvador; its cobblestone streets are lined with bars, and blocos practise almost every night. Make sure you get a copy of Bahiatursa's *Pelourinho Dia & Noite* program. Grupo Olodum play on Sunday nights in the *Largo do Pelourinho* and draw crowds of dancers into the streets. The famous *Filhos de Gandhi* has its centre close by, at Rua Gregório de Matos 53, and rehearse on Tuesday and Sunday nights. *Didá*, a music and dance school at Rua João de Deus 19, has a street practice on Friday night – a highlight is the 15-piece, all-female drum outfit.

During summer, the city sponsors free live music at several outdoor venues, including *Largo de Tereza Batista*, *Largo do Pedro Arcanjo* and *Praça Quincas Berro d'Agua* (known locally as Praça Dois M) in Pelourinho.

Praça Dois M is also home to several hip bars – *Habeus Copos* and *Kibe & CIA* are two of the popular spots. *Bar do Reggae*, right on the Pelourinho, tends to have dancers spilling out onto the street just about every night.

Tuesday night is probably the biggest night in Pelourinho. Traditionally, important religious services known as 'Tuesday's Blessing' have been held every Tuesday at the Igreja São Francisco. The services have always drawn locals to Pelourinho, and since the restoration of the area, the weekly celebrations have turned into a mini-festival. Grupo Olodum play at *Largo de Tereza Batista* (US$10 entry or US$5 later on if the show's been going for a while), on Rua Gregório de Matos, and other bands set up on Terreiro de Jesus, Largo do Pelourinho and anywhere else they can find space. Crowds pour into Pelourinho to eat, drink and dance, and the party lasts until the early hours of the morning.

Ilê Aiyê, one of the most exciting Carnaval blocos, gives free concerts every Saturday (at least during summer) in the *Forte de Santo Antônio Alèm do Carmo*, in Barbalho, from 9 pm. African culture is kept alive in Liberdade, which is a good place to see afoxé. It's best to go with someone who knows these areas.

Of the beaches, Rio Vermelho has some good nightspots, and many of the better hotels, such as the Salvador Praia, have fancy nightclubs. A few of the happening bars are *Zona Franca*, Rua João Gomes 87; *Intermezzo* at Largo da Mariquita s/n (no number), with outside tables; and *Extudo*, Rua Lidio Mesquita 4.

Barra is full of bars, discos and music. Some places are quite good, but it's more touristy and is starting to get a sleazy reputation. *Habeas Copos*, Avenida Marquês de Leão 172, is an old favourite (and attracts an older crowd); *Zimbabwe*, Rua Afonso Celso 473, has good music and specialises in *afrodisiacos* (aphrodisiac drinks)!

Praia Pituba has several bars with music, such as *Tocaia Grande*, Rua Minas Gerais 784, which specialises in Arabian appetisers.

Folklore shows, usually consisting of mini-displays of Candomblé, capoeira, samba, lambada etc, are presented in the evening at: *Senac* in Pelourinho (see Places to Eat); *Solar do Unhão*, south of the city centre (see Places to Eat); and *Moenda* (☎ 231-7915), Jardim Armação, next to the Centro de Convenções.

Things to Buy

If you're after handicrafts, browse through- Mercado Modelo, Praça da Sé, Terreiro de Jesus and numerous shops and galleries in Pelourinho – all places where articles and prices are geared to tourists. For a large, local market, try Mercado São Joaquim (also known as Feira São Joaquim), which is just north of the city centre. Dedicated shoppers should head for Shopping Iguatemi (Salvador's largest shopping centre), opposite the rodoviária, and Shopping Barra, both gigantic complexes with dozens of shops. It's easy to get lost in them.

Getting There & Away

Air The big three domestic airlines all fly to Salvador, as does Nordeste, which goes to smaller cities in the region like Ilhéus and Porto Seguro. You can fly to most cities in Brazil from Salvador, but make sure you find out how many stops the plane makes: many flights in the Northeast operate as 'milk runs', stopping at every city along the Atlantic seaboard, which makes for a long ride.

There are regular international flights between Salvador and Miami, Brussels, Frankfurt, Paris, Amsterdam, Lisbon, Madrid, Rome, Buenos Aires, Tenerife, Montevideo, Santiago, Asunción and Zürich. Following is a list of Brazilian and foreign airlines with offices in Salvador:

Aerolineas Argentinas
  Avenida Tancredo Neves 3343, sala 503, Comércio (☎ 341-0217; fax 340-6459)
Air France
  Rua Reitor Macedo Costa 134, Edifício Empresarial Itaigara, sala 208, Itaigara (☎ 351-6631; fax 351-6463)
Lanchile
  Rua Miguel Calmon 555, Edifício Citibank, sala 609, Comércio (☎ 242-8144; fax 243-9882)
Lufthansa
  Avenida Tancred Neves 805, Edifício Espaço Empresarial, sala 601, Pituba (☎ 341-5100; fax 341-4710)
Nordeste
  Avenida Tancred Neves 1672, sala 101, Pituba (☎ 341-2866)
TAP (Air Portugal)
  Avenida Estados Unidos 137, sala 401, Comércio (☎ 243-6122; fax 243-6968)
Transbrasil
  Praça General Coutinho 3, Comércio (☎ 377-2467)
Varig
  Rua Carlos Gomes 103, Centro (☎ 243-9311)
VASP
  Rua Miguel Calmon 27, Comércio (☎ 377-2495)

Bus There is a daily executivo bus to Rio leaving at 7 am (US$90, 26 hours). The cheaper standard bus leaves for Rio every Friday at 2 pm and costs US$75. A standard bus leaves for São Paulo daily at 8.15 am (US$85, 32 hours). There is also an executivo bus leaving daily at 10.30 pm (US$110) and *leitos* (super-comfortable overnight express buses) leaving Tuesday, Friday and Saturday at 10 pm (US$120). To Belo Horizonte there is a daily executivo bus leaving at 6 pm (US$65, 24 hours).

There are four standard buses departing daily to Aracaju (US$15) – buses travelling via the Linha Verde take around five hours. All stop at the rodoviária in Estância, which is on the main road. For the 13 hour trip to Recife, a standard bus departs daily at 3.30 pm (US$36), and an executivo (US$46) leaves daily at 9 pm (US$48). There is one daily departure to Fortaleza at 9 pm (US$60, 20 hours), and departures to Belém on Wednesday and Friday at 3.50 pm (US$94, 34 hours).

There are two daily departures to Lençóis, at 7.30 am and 10 pm (US$17, six hours) – the night bus is quicker because there's less traffic. There are two departures daily to Valença (US$13, four hours), at 7.50 and 11.50 am. Five buses depart daily for Ilhéus (US$28, six hours), and there is an evening departure to Porto Seguro at 9 pm (US$42, 10 hours). There are frequent departures for Cachoeira (US$4, two hours) between 5.30 am and 7 pm. Take the bus marked São Felix.

For access to beaches along the litoral north, four buses run daily to Praia do Forte (US$4, 1½ hours) and two buses daily run to Conde (US$8, three hours), at 5.40 am and 2.40 pm (more run in summer). These buses usually continue on to Sítio de Conde, but ask to make sure.

Boat Boats to points on Baía de Todos os Santos leave from the Terminal Turístico Marítimo (☎ 326-3434), on Avenida da França, one block towards the water from the Mercado Modelo. There are tours of the bay featuring Ilha Itaparica and Ilha Frade, and irregular boats to Maragojipe. See the Around Salvador and Recôncavo sections for schedules. The small dock beside the Mercado Modelo has irregular motorboats to Mar Grande and Itaparica.

During summer (December to March), there are two daily boats to Morro de São Paulo from the Terminal Turístico Marítimo. The noon boat is a large launch that makes the trip in about 1½ hours, and a second, smaller, cheaper motorboat leaves at 2 pm and takes four hours.

Getting Around

Venice has its canals and gondolas; Salvador has its bluff, elevators, hills, valleys and one-way streets. The Lacerda Elevator runs daily from 5 am to midnight, linking the low and high cities. The Plano Inclinado Gonçalves, behind the cathedral near the Praça da Sé, makes the same link and is more fun (and less claustrophobic), but only operates Monday to Saturday from 5 am to 10 pm. The city's latest addition to the lift world is the Plano Inclinado Liberdade/Calçada, which links two poor neighbourhoods north of the city centre.

To/From the Airport Dois de Julho airport (☎ 204-1010) is over 30km from the city centre, inland from Itapoã. The two taxi companies represented at the airport share a *bilheteria* (ticket office) and have the same prices. The table displayed in the office shows prices to several destinations in the city. A taxi ride from the airport to Praça da Sé costs US$30. The best way to reach the city centre is to take the green and white Ondina executivo bus marked Praça da Sé/Aeroporto. The fare is US$2.80.

There are supposed to be buses leaving Praça da Sé for the airport every half an hour between 6 am and 7 pm, but the schedule is rather flexible, so leave yourself plenty of time. The bus starts at Praça da Sé (the stop is signposted), goes down Avenida 7 de Setembro to Barra, and continues all the way along the coast before heading inland to the airport. You can flag it down along the way. In light traffic, the ride to the airport takes about an hour; with traffic allow 1¾ hours.

A municipal Aeroporto bus (fare US$0.70) follows the same route to the airport, but it gets very crowded, and isn't recommended if you're carrying a bag.

Bus The two most useful municipal bus stops in the city centre are Praça da Sé and Avenida da França.

Buses from Praça da Sé go to Campo Grande, Vitória and all the Atlantic coast beaches as far as Praia Flamengo, just past Praia Itapoã. Executivo buses marked Praça da Sé/Aeroporto also leave from here, and go along the beaches from Barra to Itapoã (US$2.80).

The Avenida da França stop is in Cidade Baixa beside the Lacerda Elevator. From here, take either the Ribeira or the Bonfim bus to the Itaparica ferry (get off after a couple of kilometres, when you see the Pirelli Pneus store on your left); the Mercado São Joaquim (get off at the stop after Pirelli Pneus); or continue to Igreja NS do Bonfim and Ribeira.

To/From the Rodoviária The rodoviária (☎ 358-0765) is 5km from the city centre, but it can be a bit messy taking a bus there – many buses marked Rodoviária drive all over the city – and can take up to an hour during rush hour.

For a quicker trip, it's advisable to take a taxi, which costs US$6 from Praça da Sé. At the rodoviária, there's a bilheteria that sells fixed-price taxi coupons, but these prices are 30% higher than regular taxis.

The most convenient way to go by bus to the rodoviária is to take the Iguatemi bus from Praça da Sé. From here, use the pedestrian footbridge to cross the highway to the rodoviária. The bus goes via Barra and Ondina and takes about 45 minutes. The fare is US$0.70. Alternatively, you can use the bus service between the rodoviária and Campo Grande and change there to a bus for the city centre.

The rodoviária is a self-contained complex with a Bahiatursa office, Telebahia office, supermarket, left-luggage service, and a couple of inexpensive eateries. For more complex requirements, you can pop across the pedestrian footbridge and visit Salvador's largest shopping complex – Shopping Iguatemi.

Around Salvador

ILHA ITAPARICA

• pop 16,000 ✉ 44600-000 ☎ 071

Many Bahians love Itaparica, the largest island in Baía de Todos os Santos. They prefer to swim in the calm waters of the bay than in the rough and tumble of the ocean. It's quite a pretty island, but not really a must-see destination. Weekends here are crowded (especially in summer), transportation can be slow without a car, and the beaches aren't as pretty as the more accessible beaches north of the city.

The island is built up with many weekend homes, but has few budget hotels. Many of the beaches are dirty and the best part of the island is owned by Club Med. Yet there still are a few clean beaches where you can just lie on the sand beneath windswept palms and gaze across the bay at the city (try Barra Grande or Aratuba for example).

Orientation

Itaparica City At the northern tip of the island is the city of Itaparica and the São Lourenço Fort. Built by the Dutch invaders in the 17th century, the fortress figured prominently in Bahia's battle for independence in 1823. The Solar Tenente Botas (Mansion of Lieutenant Botas), on the square of the same name, the Igreja Matriz do Santíssimo Sacramento, on Rua Luis Gama, and the Fonte da Bica (mineral-water fountain) complete the city sights.

Along the Coast South along the coast, between Itaparica City and Bom Despacho, is Ponta de Areia, a thin strip of sand with barracas. The water is clear and shallow, and the sandy floor slopes gently into the bay.

South of Mar Grande (perhaps the most likeable town on the island), the beaches of Barra do Gil, Barra do Pote and Coroa all have excellent views of Salvador, while on the other side of Club Med is Barra Grande, Itaparica's finest open-to-the-public beach.

The beaches further to the south up to and including Cacha Pregos are dirtier and generally less beautiful, although many Bahians consider Cacha Pregos the best beach on the island.

Tourist Office

There are two tourist information booths on the island: a tiny booth next to the rodoviária at Bom Despacho, and another on Praça de São Bento in Mar Grande, both with irregular opening hours.

Places to Stay

There's a pleasant hostel at Aratuba: the *Albergue de Juventude Enseada de Aratuba* (☎ 971-0060), Quadra H, lotes 12/1, and camping grounds at Praia de Berlinque, Praia de Barra Grande, and Praia de Cacha Pregos.

Also in Aratuba is *Zimbo Tropical*, a pleasant place owned by Philippe and Suely Kemlin. Philippe is the classic case of the French traveller who came to visit and never left. The bungalows are in a beautiful garden setting with small monkeys in the trees. They cost US$18 a single and US$30 a double. From Bom Despacho, take the bus or VW kombi to Aratuba and ask the driver to let you off at the blue and white telephone exchange on the right-hand side just before you enter Aratuba. The pousada is 200m down Rua Iemenja towards the beach, which is a further 200m away.

In Mar Grande, a good cheap option is the *Pousada Koisa Nossa* (☎ 833-1028), at Rua da Rodagam 173. As you exit the dock, walk across the square and follow the road for about 200m. It's a relaxed place, with a restaurant serving fresh, tasty refeições. Double quartos cost around US$25 with breakfast. If you want something more comfortable, have a look at the *Pousada Arco Iris* (☎/fax 833-1130), Estrada da Gamboa

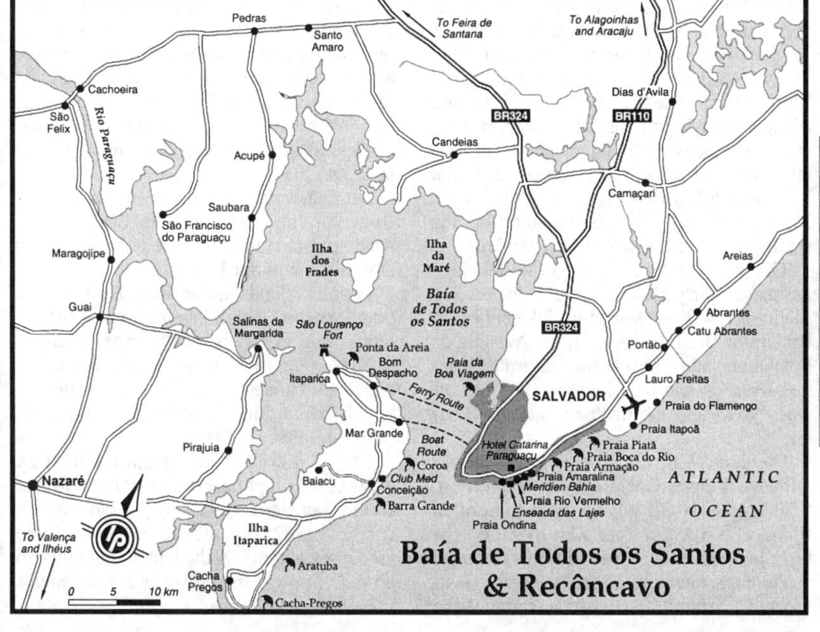

Baía de Todos os Santos & Recôncavo

102. The pousada is in the restored mansion of an old fazenda (ranch) set in spacious, shady gardens with a swimming pool and restaurant. Double quartos cost US$30; double apartamentos start at US$50. Discounts of up to 30% apply from April to November.

On the beach at Praia Conceição is Club Méditerranée (☎ 880-7141; fax 880-7165; reservations 0800-21-3782). It costs US$130/$260 single/double, all inclusive.

Places to Eat

The best eating on the island is the seafood at the beach barracas. The *Timoneiro Restaurant*, 10km from Cacha Pregos and 3km from the Bom Despacho/Cacha Pregos junction, serves expensive but tasty shrimp dishes. When in Aratuba, pay a visit to the *Wunderbar*, on the point, run by German expat Limo. It's a party on the weekends, with much drinking and craziness.

Getting There & Away

Boat There are three boats from Salvador to Itaparica. The first is a small boat that leaves from the Terminal Turístico Marítimo behind the Mercado Modelo and goes directly to Mar Grande. The trip costs US$1.45 and takes around 50 minutes. Boats depart daily every hour between 5.30 am and 10 pm. The last boat returns from Mar Grande at 5 pm. This schedule often changes. Other boats leave occasionally for Mar Grande from the small dock beside the Mercado Modelo.

The second boat is a giant car-and-passenger ferry that operates between São Joaquim and Bom Despacho. Take either the Ribeira or Bonfim bus from the Avenida da França bus stop (beside the Lacerda Elevator) for a couple of kilometres and get off when you see a Pirelli Pneus store on your left.

The fare is US$1.45 and the ride takes 45 minutes. Ferries operate every hour from 5.30 am to 10.30 pm (until midnight in summer). Expect a long wait to get on the ferry on weekends, especially in summer.

The fastest way to do the trip is in one of the new catamarans with aeroplane-like interiors, attendants and air-conditioning. It takes 20 minutes and costs US$4.50. They begin at 6.30 am and run frequently from Mar Grande until 7 pm (later in summer).

Bus Frequent buses leave from the rodoviária at Bom Despacho travelling to Valença (US$4.50, two hours) and Camamu, on the mainland.

Getting Around

Bom Despacho is the island's transportation hub. Buses, VW kombis and taxis meet the boats and will take you to any of the beaches for around US$2. Bicycles are widely available to rent for around US$10 per day and are a useful option if you want to explore under your own steam. Although the São Joaquim-Bom Despacho ferry operates until midnight during summer, island transport becomes scarce after 8 pm.

OTHER BAÍA DE TODOS OS SANTOS ISLANDS

The easiest way to cruise the lesser islands and the bay itself is to get one of the tourist boats that leave from the Terminal Turístico Marítimo (☎ 326-3434), close to Mercado Modelo in Salvador. There are various tours; most take half a day, stopping at Ilha dos Frades, Ilha da Maré and Itaparica. The cost is about US$20.

Alternatively, hire a cheap, small boat from the small port next to the Mercado Modelo. Bahiatursa's notice board often has advertisements for boat trips.

Popular islands include **Ilha Bom Jesus dos Passos**, which has traditional fishing boats and artisans; **Ilha dos Frades** (named after two monks who were killed and cannibalised there by local Indians), which has attractive waterfalls and palm trees; and **Ilha da Maré**.

Ilha da Maré has the **Igreja de NS das Neves**, the quiet beaches of **Itamoabo** and **Bacia das Neves**, and one pousada, which charges US$25 for a double quarto. There are no restaurants on the island, but you can arrange through the pousada to have meals prepared by villagers.

Getting There & Away

Boats to Ilha da Maré (US$1 – a bit more on weekends) leave from São Tomé, about one hour by bus from the Avenida da França bus station. Take a Base Naval/São Tomé bus and get off one stop before the end of the line (ask the conductor to let you know). To get to Ilha dos Frades, take an Oxalá bus to Madre de Deus (70km from Salvador) and catch a boat for Praia de Paramara for around US$0.50.

The Recôncavo

The recôncavo is the region of fertile lands spread around the Baía de Todos os Santos. Some of the earliest Brazilian encounters between Portuguese, Indian and African peoples occurred here, and the lands proved to be among Brazil's best for growing sugar and tobacco.

Along with the excellent growing conditions, the region prospered due to its relative proximity to Portuguese sugar markets, the favourable winds for sailing to Europe and the excellent harbours afforded by the Baía de Todos os Santos. By 1570 there were already 18 *engenhos* (sugar mills), while by 1584 there were 40. The sugar-plantation system was firmly entrenched by the end of the 16th century and continued to grow from the sweat of African slaves for another 250 years.

Tobacco came a bit later to the recôncavo. Traded to African slave-hunters and kings, it was the key commodity in the triangle of the slave trade. Tobacco was a more sensitive crop to grow than sugar and the estates were much smaller. But big fortunes were made growing sugar, not tobacco. On the other hand, fewer slaves were needed – about four per tobacco farm – so many poorer Portuguese settlers went into tobacco and a less rigid social hierarchy developed. Many even did some of the work!

A second subsidiary industry in the recôncavo area was cattle ranching, which provided food for the plantation hands, transport for the wood that fuelled the sugar mills, and for delivery of the processed cane to market. Cattle breeding started in the recôncavo and spread inland, radiating west into the sertão and Minas Gerais, then northwest into Piauí.

If you have time for only one side trip from Salvador, visit Cachoeira and perhaps squeeze in Santo Amaro. A suggested itinerary is to take the weekday afternoon boat to Maragojipe and then the bus along the banks of the Rio Paraguaçu to Cachoeira. You can then visit Santo Amaro on the way back to Salvador. If you're in Cachoeira on Friday or Saturday nights, you may be able to attend a terreiro de Candomblé. From Cachoeira, there are frequent buses back to Salvador.

CACHOEIRA

• *pop 28,000* ✉ *44300-000* ☎ *075*

Cachoeira, 121km from Salvador and 40km from Santo Amaro, is below a series of hills beside the Rio Paraguaçu. The river is spanned by Ponte Dom Pedro II, built by the British in 1885 as a link with its twin town, São Felix. Affectionately known as the jewel of the recôncavo, Cachoeira is at the centre of Brazil's best tobacco-growing regions. Apart from tobacco, the main crops in the area are cashews and oranges.

The town is a relaxed place, full of beautiful colonial architecture uncompromised by the presence of modern buildings and tourist hordes. As a result, it was pronounced a national monument in 1971 and the state of Bahia started paying for the restoration and preservation of historic buildings. However, these funds appear to have dried up of late and the municipal authorities of Cachoeira are attempting to continue the work on their own dwindling budget.

Cachoeira is also a renowned centre of Candomblé and the home of many traditional artists and artisans. If you get an early start, Cachoeira can be visited in a day from Salvador, but it's less hectic if you stay overnight.

History

Diego Álvares, the father of Cachoeira's founders, was the sole survivor of a ship bound for the West Indies that was wrecked in 1510 on a reef near Salvador. The Portuguese Robinson Crusoe was saved by the Tupinambá Indians of Rio Vermelho, who dubbed the strange white sea creature Caramuru, or 'Fish-Man'. Diego Álvares lived 20 years with the Indians and married Catarina do Paraguaçu, the daughter of the most powerful Tupinambá chief. Their sons João Gaspar Aderno Álvares and Rodrigues Martins Álvares killed off the local Indians, set up the first sugar-cane fazendas and founded Cachoeira.

By the 18th century, tobacco from Cachoeira was considered the world's finest, sought by rulers in China and Africa. Tobacco also became popular in Brazil. The holy herb, as it was called, was taken as snuff, smoked in a pipe or chewed.

Early in the 19th century, Cachoeira achieved fame as a centre for military operations in Bahia to oust the Portuguese rulers. On 25 June 1822, the town became

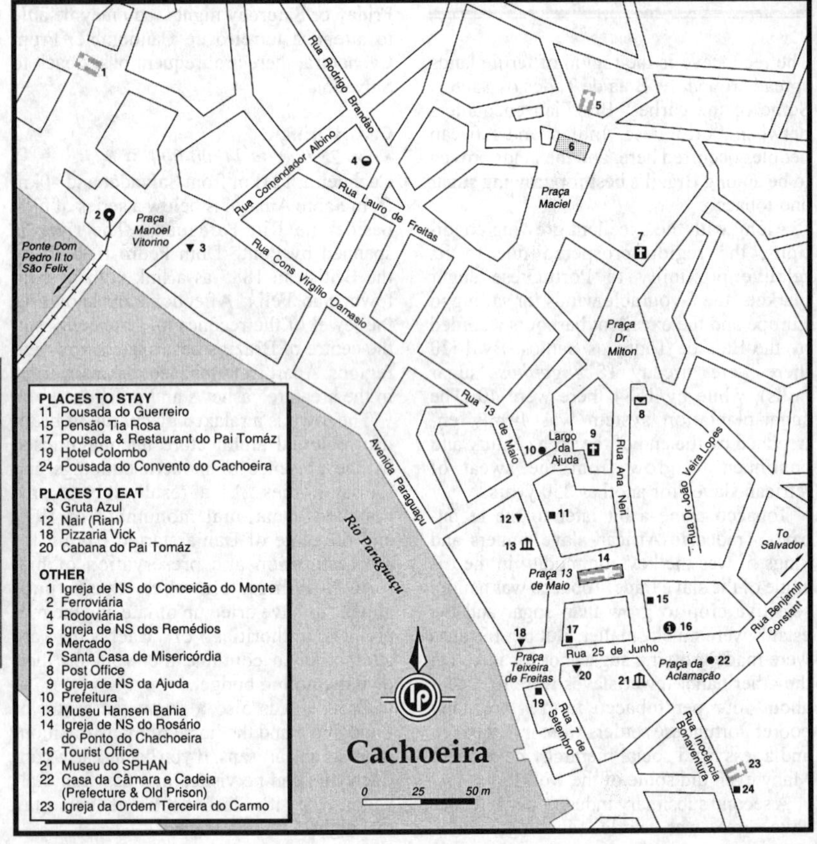

THE NORTHEAST

the first to recognise Dom Pedro I as the independent ruler of Brazil.

Orientation

Cachoeira and São Felix are best seen on foot. There's nothing that you really *have* to see, so it's best to just take it easy and explore.

Information

The tourist office on Praça da Aclamação should be able to help with accommodation and general details about the town's sights. It's usually open weekdays during working hours – a somewhat ambiguous term in Cachoeira. Other good sources of information are the helpful staff at the Museu Hansen Bahia. At some of the sights, especially churches, theft has been a problem, so you may have to phone to arrange a visit.

Igreja da Ordem Terceira do Carmo

The Church of the Third Order of Carmelites, just south of Praça da Aclamação and alongside the Pousada do Convento do Cachoeira, features a gallery of suffering polychrome Christs imported from the Portuguese colonies in Macau, and panelled ceilings. Christ's blood is made from bovine blood mixed with Chinese herbs and sparkling rubies. The church is now being promoted by the adjacent pousada as a convention centre. It's certainly a novel idea to seat delegates where there were once pews.

Opening hours are from 2 to 5 pm and Sunday from 9 to 11.30 am Tuesday to Saturday.

Casa da Câmara e Cadeia

Nearby on the same square is the yellow-with-white-trim Casa da Câmara e Cadeia, the old prefecture and prison. Organised criminals ran the show upstairs and disorganised criminals were kept behind bars downstairs. The building dates back to 1698 and served as the seat of the Bahian government in 1822. The old marble pillory in the square was destroyed after abolition.

Museu do SPHAN

Across the square, a colonial mansion houses the humble SPHAN museum, (☎ 725-1123) with squeaky bats flapping over colonial furnishings. The museum is open daily except Monday from 9 am to noon and 2 to 5 pm.

Museu Hansen Bahia

The Museu Hansen Bahia was set up in the home and birthplace of Brazilian heroine Ana Neri, who organised the nursing corps during the Paraguay War. Now the work of German (naturalised Brazilian) artist Hansen Bahia is displayed here. Among his powerful lithographs of human suffering is a series of illustrations of Castro Alves' poem *Návio Negreiro* (Slave Ship). The museum, on Rua 13 de Maio, is open Tuesday to Friday from 9 am to 5 pm and on weekends from 9 am to 2 pm. Prints and T-shirts are also on sale here.

Igreja de NS do Rosário do Porto do Cachoeira

The blue church with yellow trim, up from the Hansen Bahia museum, on the corner of Rua Ana Neri and Rua Lions Club, is the NS do Rosário do Porto do Cachoeira. The church has beautiful Portuguese tiles, and a ceiling painted by Teófilo de Jesus. Opening hours are erratic (although it's usually open in the mornings) – so it's best to phone ☎ 724-1294 and arrange a time with the custodian, who may also take you round the Museu das Alfaias, on the 1st floor. This museum contains remnants from the abandoned 17th century Convento de São Francisco do Paraguaçu.

Igreja de NS da Ajuda

On Largo da Ajuda is Cachoeira's oldest church, the tiny NS da Ajuda, built in 1595 when Cachoeira was known as Arraial d'Ajuda. Phone ☎ 724-1396 to arrange a visit to the church and the Museu da Boa Morte – an interesting museum with displays of photos and ceremonial apparel used by the exclusively female Boa Morte cult.

Santa Casa de Misericórdia
This is the municipality's oldest hospital. The complex contains a pretty chapel (founded in 1734) with a painted ceiling, gardens and an ossuary. It's open on weekdays from 2 to 5 pm.

Igreja de NS do Conceição do Monte
At the far end of town, near the bridge and the ferroviária, is the Igreja de NS do Conceição do Monte. The climb to this 18th century church is rewarded by a good view of Cachoeira and São Felix.

Praça Manoel Vitorino
Across from the ruined grand facade of the ferroviária, the wide, cobblestone Praça Manoel Vitorino feels like an Italian movie set, except for the Texaco station plonked in the middle. Try your Italian on the ice-cream seller or the pigeons, then move on to São Felix.

São Felix
When crossing the old, British-built Ponte Dom Pedro II, a narrow and dilapidated bridge where trains and cars must wait their turn, be careful where you step: loose planks have claimed the life of at least one person in recent years. When vehicles pass over the bridge it emits a wild cacophony of sounds – a bit like one of those urban/industrial/primitive percussion acts!

Apart from the view towards Cachoeira, São Felix has two other attractions: the **Casa da Cultura Américo Simas**, Rua Celestino João Severino da Luz Neto (open Tuesday to Sunday from 8 am to 5 pm), and the **Centro Cultural Dannemann** (☎ 725-2202), along the riverfront, Avenida Salvador Pinto 29 (open Tuesday to Sunday from 8 am to 5 pm).

The Centro Cultural Dannemann has displays of old machinery and the techniques used for making *charutos* (cigars). The rich tobacco smells, the beautiful wooden working tables and the sight of workers hand-rolling monster cigars will take you back in time. The art space in the front of the building has exhibitions of sculpture, painting and photography. The handmade cigars sold here make good souvenirs or presents. Admission is free.

Candomblé
Try to see Candomblé in Cachoeira. This is one of the strongest and perhaps purest spiritual and religious centres for Candomblé. Long and mysterious Candomblé ceremonies are held in small homes and shacks up in the hills, usually on Friday and Saturday nights at 8 pm.

Visitors are not common here and the tourist office is sometimes reluctant to give out this sort of information, but if you show an interest in Candomblé, and respect for its traditions, you may inspire confidence.

Other Attractions
If you have a car or like long walks, you can visit the **Pimantel Cigar Factory**, 10km out of town. **Suerdieck** is another cigar factory closer to the town.

There are also two old sugar mills near town: **Engenho da Cabonha**, 8km along the road to Santo Amaro, and **Engenho da Guaiba**, 12km along the same road.

Special Events
Festa da NS de Boa Morte falls on the Friday closest to 15 August and lasts three days. This is one of the most fascinating Candomblé festivals and it's worth a special trip to see it. Organised by the Irmandade da Boa Morte (Sisterhood of the Good Death) – a secret black religious society – the festival is celebrated by the descendants of slaves, who praise their liberation with dance and prayer and a mix of themes from Candomblé and Catholicism.

The Festa de São João, celebrated from 22 to 24 June, is the big popular festival of Bahia's interior. It's a great celebration of folklore, with music, dancing, and plenty of food and drink. Don't miss it if you're in Bahia.

Other festivals include: NS do Rosário (second half of October), which includes games, music and food; NS da Ajuda (first half of November), which features ritual cleansing of the church and a street festival; and Santa Barbara or Iansã (4 December), a Candomblé ceremony held in São Felix at Fonte de Santa Bárbara (Fountain of Santa Bárbara).

Places to Stay

The century-old *Hotel Colombo* is the cheapest in town, right on the waterfront at Praça Teixeira de Freitas. Very beat-up quartos without fans go for US$7/15 a single/double. Avoid rooms on the top floor, as there are huge holes in the roof. Much more comfortable is *Pousada do Pai Tomáz* (☎ 725-1288), Rua 25 de Junho 12, which has apartamentos for US$15/30. Across the river in São Felix, the *Pousada do Paraguaçu* (☎ 725-2550), Avenida Salvador Pinto 1, is a relaxed place along the riverfront, with a veranda overlooking the water. Apartamentos with fan cost US$15/25, or US$20/30 with air-conditioning. There's a restaurant attached.

The *Pensão Tia Rosa* (☎ 725-1792), Rua Ana Neri, has basic quartos for US$10/15 and a double apartamento for US$20, with a good breakfast included in the price. The *Pousada do Guerreiro*, Rua 13 de Maio 14, opposite Museu Hansen Bahia, has ragged but clean quartos for US$12/20 and apartamentos for US$15/25. Ask for an upstairs room.

The best place in town is the *Pousada do Convento de Cachoeira* (☎/fax 725-1716), a lovely old hotel with a courtyard and swimming pool. The dark-wood rooms of the old convent now have air-conditioning, frigobar and hot showers, and cost US$46/52 a single/double – including a major spread for breakfast. An extra bed costs US$20, or you can splurge on the suite for US$70.

Places to Eat

The *Gruta Azul* (☎ 725-1295), Praça Manoel Vitorino 2, is Cachoeira's best restaurant for lunch. The place has character: special recipes for seafood and batidas and a delightful shaded courtyard. Try the shrimp dishes for US$10 or maniçoba, the spicy local dish composed of manioc and various meats. If you're adventurous ask for the boa morte (good death) drink. Opening hours are 11 am to 5 pm on weekdays and 11 am to 2 pm on weekends.

On Rua 25 de Junho, there's more good food at *Cabana do Pai Tomáz* (the restaurant is across the road from the pousada) – check out the sensational scrap-yard roof decorations and the carved wooden panels and furniture. *Pizzaria Vick* (open daily in the evenings) is close by.

Just up from the Museu Hansen Bahia is the *Nair* restaurant, named after the owner, but locals delight in turning things around and calling it Rian. The menu includes moqueca dishes and local specialities.

Espaço ll, behind the Igreja NS do Rosário, has a decent, cheap, por quilo (buffet) lunch spread.

In São Felix, try the restaurant in the Pousada do Paraguaçu, which is open from 11 am to 11 pm.

Entertainment

Cruise the riverfront for beer drinking and *forró* dancing (dancing to the traditional music of the Northeast) at the riverside bars. On Wednesday and Saturday, there's an open *mercado* on Praça Maciel – a good place to pick up handicrafts and observe local life. Praça Teixeira de Freitas has a few bars. It's the Times Square of Cachoeira – if you sit around a while, most of the locals will pass by.

Things to Buy

Cachoeira has a wealth of wood sculptors, some of whom do very fine work, and you will see plenty of studios as you walk through town. This is some of the best traditional art still available in Brazil. Two of the best sculptors are Doidão and Loucou, who carve beautiful, heavy pieces.

Getting There & Away

Bus There are hourly departures to Salvador and Feira de Santana between 4.30 am and 6.30 pm (US$5, two hours). The rodoviária (☎ 725-1214) is tiny and easy to miss – it's a small green building with white trim. Buses to Maragojipe leave from São Felix at 7.50 and 10 am, noon and 5 pm (US$1, half an hour).

Buses to and from Valença run via Santo Antônio. From São Felix, take either the 7.50 am or 12.40 pm to Santo Antônio and catch a connection from there to Valença.

Train There are no passenger services – only the occasional freight train.

Boat After Rio Paraguaçu was blocked by Pedra do Cavalo Barragem dam, Cachoeira no longer had the waterfalls for which it was named. The river has since silted up, making boat passage up from Maragojipe and Salvador difficult and irregular. You should check the latest information with the Vapor do Cachoeira boat service at the Companhia de Navegação Bahiano (Mercado Modelo docks, Salvador). Apparently, during the festival of São João there is an attempt at operating a regular boat service to Salvador.

Getting Around

Cachoeira is just the right size to cover on foot. If you want to cross the river to São Felix by canoe, rather than crossing the bridge on foot, you can hire one for a couple of dollars at the waterfront.

SANTO AMARO

• *pop 58,000 ✉ 44200-000 ☎ 075*

Santo Amaro is an old, run-down sugar town that sees very few tourists and has an unpretentious charm. If you're passing through on your way from Cachoeira, think about stopping for a few hours, especially if it's a market Saturday, when the town comes to life. If you decide to stay the night, there's often very good local music. *Pousada Amaro's* (☎ 241-1202), Rua Conselhor Saraiva 27, is a good accommodation option, with apartamentos for US$10/12 a single/double.

In colonial days, Santo Amaro made its fortune from sugar. Today, the major industry is paper production; the paper mill is on the road to Cachoeira. The mill has spoiled the Rio Subaé and bamboo has replaced sugar cane on the hillsides.

Reminders of Santo Amaro's sugar legacy are the decrepit pastel mansions of the sugar barons, and the many churches. The plantation owners lived on Rua General Câmara, the old commercial street, and an effort is being made to restore some of these buildings.

Many of the churches have been closed since a gang of thieves stole most of the holy images and exported them to France. The largest church, Santo Amaro da Purificação, is still open.

The Festa de Santo Amaro (24 January to 2 February) is celebrated by the ritual *lavagem* (washing) of the church steps. Santo Amaro is the birthplace of two of Brazil's most popular singers: Caetano Veloso and his sister Maria Betânia. During Carnaval, they've been known to put in an appearance between trios elétricos.

Step out to the square across from the church for an evening's promenade. Despite active flirting, the sexes circle separately.

Getting There & Away

There are frequent bus services between Salvador and Santo Amaro (US$2.50, 70 minutes), and most of these continue the 32km to Cachoeira/São Felix.

MARAGOJIPE

Circled by Baía de Todos os Santos and rich green fields patched with crops, Maragojipe is a pleasantly decaying tobacco-exporting port, 32km from Nazaré and 24km from Cachoeira. The port is surrounded by mangrove swamps, and locals push off from the pier in *saveiros* (home-made fishing boats) and dugout canoes.

For information, speak to Ronald at the Fundação Suerdieck Casa da Cultura, on Praça da Matriz. He will be delighted to tell you about local sights.

Things to See

The **Suerdieck & Company Cigar Factory** (established in 1920) is open for tours

Monday to Friday from 8 am to 5 pm, and on Saturday morning.

On weekend nights head down to the dockside bars for local music. Swimming off the cement pier is popular.

Strolling through town, look out for the wrought-iron grille and sculpted façade of the pale-blue building on Rua D Macedo Costa.

Places to Stay & Eat

The *Oxumaré Hotel* (☎ 726-1104), Rua Heretiano Jorge de Souza 3, has cramped single/double quartos that cost US$15/20.

Jumbo shrimp is the local delicacy. Otherwise, go to *Pizzaria Recreio do Porto* for pizza, at the port, and to *City Bar*, Praça da Matriz, for sucos and snacks.

Getting There & Away

Bus Buses from Salvador to Maragojipe go via Santo Amaro and Cachoeira. There are six buses daily, the first departing at 7.10 am, the last at 4 pm. The trip takes three hours and costs US$6. There are no buses via Itaparica. We recommend going by boat if possible.

Boat Boats from Salvador to Maragojipe are infrequent, so call the Terminal Turístico Marítimo (☎ 326-3434) or get Bahiatursa to do it for you. Stops are made at São Roque, Barra do Paraguaçu and Enseada. There are no boats from Maragojipe to Cachoeira since the Rio Paraguaçu silted up, but there are frequent buses.

NAZARÉ

• pop 26,000 ✉ 44400-000 ☎ 075

Nazaré is an 18th century city with some colonial buildings and churches, and a good market known for its *caxixis* (small ceramic figures).

The big festivals here are the folkloric NS de Nazaré (24 January to 2 February), and Feira dos Caxixis (Holy Week), which features a large mercado on Holy Thursday and Good Friday, followed by the holiday of Micareta.

For accommodation, try the *Pousada da Fonte* (☎ 736-1287), where single/double apartamentos cost US$28/33 with fan and US$35/45 with air-conditioning.

For transport between Nazaré and Salvador, you can either take the bus or the ferry.

North of Salvador

The coastal road north from Salvador is called the Rodovia do Côco (Coconut Hwy). The excellent sealed road runs a few kilometres from the ocean, as far as the entrance to Praia do Forte, 80km north of Salvador. From Praia do Forte, the new Linha Verde (Green Line) road spans 142km to Itanhi, on the border with Sergipe. The Linha Verde, constructed in 1993 and hailed as Brazil's first 'ecologically planned' road, runs between three and 12km from the coast. The 'ecological planning' runs to a restriction on the construction of petrol stations and roadside restaurants, and to the fact that the road doesn't hug the coast, as was originally planned.

There are access roads off the Linha Verde to several small towns and fishing villages, many of which are now developing into popular weekend destinations for people from Salvador. Regular buses run along the Linha Verde from Salvador to Praia do Forte, Conde and Sitio do Conde, and enter a few coastal towns on the way. See the separate sections for each town for access details.

Municipal buses from Salvador go along the coast as far as Itapoã and then turn inland towards the airport. Buses to points further north along the Linha Verde – Praia do Forte and beyond – leave from the main rodoviária in Salvador.

The map 'Beaches of North Bahia, Sergipe & Alagoas' (in the Sergipe & Alagoas chapter) should be consulted in conjunction with the North of Salvador text.

AREMBEPE

Arembepe was one of Brazil's first hip beaches in the 1960s. Mick Jagger and

Janis Joplin got the joint rolling and many local and foreign hippies followed. It is no longer a particularly attractive or popular retreat. Exclusive private homes and pollution from the giant Tibras chemical plant have tainted the rocky coast.

If you want to head to the sea for a day from Salvador, there are prettier beaches than Arembepe, and if you're getting out of Salvador, there are less spoiled fishing villages along the Bahian litoral.

Places to Stay

If you do end up in Arembepe, you can head for the camping ground, or try the *Pousada da Fazenda* (☎ 824-1030), which looks like one of the few leftovers from the hippie days. Doubles cost US$30. The *Praias de Arembepe Hotel* (☎ 824-1415), across from the praça, has single/double apartamentos for around US$20/25.

PRAIA DO FORTE

Praia do Forte, 3km from the meeting point of the Rodovia do Côco and the Linha Verde, has fantastic beaches, a beautiful castle fortress and a sea-turtle reserve. Until recently a fishing village, Praia do Forte has been developed as an ecologically sensitive upmarket beach resort. The development has so far been held in check, but the beaches get very crowded on weekends and in summer. If you can, time your visit for the full moon and walk along the beach past the resort at sunset, when the sun turns the waters of the Rio Timeantube red as the moon rises over the sea. It's an unforgettable sight.

Praia do Forte is the seat of one of the original 12 captaincies established by the Portuguese. The huge estate extended inland all the way to Maranhão.

TAMAR Turtle Reserve

The TAMAR (Tartaruga Marinha) turtle reserve is on the beach right next to the lighthouse. The reserve is open from 8 am to 7 pm daily. Entry is US$2, or free after 6 pm.

Castelo do Garcia d'Ávila

Desperate to colonise as a means to contain his new territory, the king of Portugal set about granting lands to merchants, soldiers and aristocrats. For no apparent reason Garcia d'Ávila, a poor 12-cow farmer, was endowed with this huge tract of land.

Garcia chose a prime piece of real estate – an aquamarine ocean-view plot studded with palm trees on Morro Tatuapaçu – and built his home, Castelo do Garcia d'Ávila, there. Dating from 1552, the castle is an impressive ruin awaiting restoration. It made a fine tropical setting for director Márcio Meyrelle's production of *Macbeth*. The Castelo is open daily from 8 am to 6 pm. Entry is US$2. The Castelo – the first great Portuguese edifice in Brazil – is a 3km walk from town.

Places to Stay

Budget travellers should time their visits during the week, out of season, when there are heavy discounts on accommodation. One cheap place to stay is at the camping ground, which is just 10 minutes on foot from the beach, has cold-water showers, shady, sandy sites, and basins for washing clothes. There's also a new YHA *Albergue Praia do Forte* (☎/fax 876-1094) near the beach. One of the cheaper pousadas is the *João Sol* (☎ 876-1054), Rua da Corvina, with apartamentos for US$25/30 a single/double. Some other reasonable options are: the *Pousada Dos Coquieros* (☎ 876-1037), with comfortable single/double apartamentos for US$15/25; or the more upmarket *Pousada dos Artistas* (☎ 876-1147), on Praça dos Artistas, with friendly management, and double apartamentos with fridge and hot water for US$50. Also recommended is the friendly *Pousada Ogum Marinho* (☎/fax 876-1165), which has lovely double apartamentos with fan for US$40 a double and US$50 with air-conditioning.

The top place to stay is the renowned *Praia do Forte Resort* (☎ 876-1111; fax 876-1112), an excellent resort hotel with fabulous food. Room rates start at US$250 a double, all inclusive.

The TAMAR Project to Save Sea Turtles

ANDREW DRAFFEN

TAMAR is an abbreviation of the Portuguese name for sea turtles, TArtaruga MARinha. The highly successful TAMAR project was created in 1980 by IBAMA (the Brazilian Environment Agency) and as it quickly expanded, a nonprofit foundation (Fundação Pró TAMAR) was created to support, raise money and co-administer TAMAR with the government. Its goal is to revert the process of extinction of the five species of sea turtles in Brazil: loggerhead, hawksbill, olive ridley, green and leatherback.

At the Praia do Forte station you can see several small exhibiting pools with marine turtles of various sizes and species. If you visit during the turtle's nesting season (September to March) you will see the hatcheries functioning. There is a museum with videos and multimedia programmes showing the life of marine turtles and shops selling T-shirts and other souvenirs.

TAMAR researchers protect around 550 nests a year, along 50km of coast close to Praia do Forte. The eggs – moist, leathery, ping-pong size balls – are buried in the sand and either left on the beach or brought to the hatcheries for incubation. When they hatch, the baby turtles are immediately released into the sea.

TAMAR has another 18 stations along the coast and two stations on oceanic islands. The Comboios station (Espírito Santo state, north of Vitória and near Linhares) protects the loggerhead and leatherback turtles. The Fernando de Noronha station protects green and hawksbill turtles. Praia do Forte station protects loggerhead, hawksbill, olive ridley and green turtles. Of the 60km of beach under the jurisdiction of the TAMAR project in Bahia, 13km of coastline are patrolled by the scientists alone; the remainder is protected by a cooperative effort in which fishermen – the very same who used to collect the eggs for food – are contracted to collect eggs for the scientists.

Nowadays, commerce in endangered turtle species is illegal, but shells are still sold in Salvador's Mercado Modelo, and in Sergipe, turtle eggs are still popular hors d'oeuvres.

Andrew Draffen

Places to Eat

The barracas along the beach serve local seafood and snack food.

Brasa da Praia is seafood restaurant that sometimes has live music in the evenings. It's very expensive, but might be worth a splurge.

Getting There & Away

Buses to Praia do Forte run from just outside the rodoviária in Salvador. It takes 1½ hours and costs US$3.50, and the service operates daily between 7.30 am and 6 pm. The last bus back to Salvador leaves at 5 pm. More bus services are planned.

PRAIA DO FORTE TO CONDE

With the opening of the Linha Verde, access to the small towns and fishing communities along the Bahian north coast is easier, at least as far as the Conde area. All through this region there are fenced-off tracts of land and small real-estate offices selling beachfront property.

Imbassaí is a fine beach with choppy, rough surf. The small Rio Barroso runs parallel to the beach and is good for swimming. It's 1km off the Linha Verde. The beach towns of **Porto Suipé**, **Subaúma** and **Baixio** are 4km, 9km and 8km respectively off the Linha Verde, with sealed-road access to all of them. Porto Suipé itself is not very appealing, but there are some nice beaches to the south with calm water for swimming. Sabaúma is already quite developed, with lots of weekend beach homes, and land being bought up to construct more. There's a decent beach with strong surf, and a couple of hotels. Baixio is a pretty, clean town, but the beach is rocky and not great for swimming. There's one pousada in the town.

JOHN MAIER, JR

Jangadas, the beautiful sailboats of the Northeast, are usually built by the fishermen theselves

CONDE

• *pop 20,000 ✉ 48300-000 ☎ 075*

On the Rio Itapicuru, Conde is 3km off the Linha Verde and 6km from the sea. It's the little 'big town' of the area, and the jumping-off point for several beaches, the closest being Sítio. On Saturday, Conde hosts a large mercado where fishermen and artisans come to peddle their goods. In October, a series of rodeos takes place, when cowboys from the inland regions hit town to strut their stuff.

Getting There & Away

The town has regular bus services to Esplanada, Alagoinhas, Feira de Santana and Salvador, and local shuttle services to Sítio. There's plenty of river traffic on mercado days, which makes it easy to get a ride down the river to the ocean. During summer, however, the river is often too low for boats to make the passage.

North of Conde, there are only direct buses along the Linha Verde to Aracaju, with some making a stop in Estância (for access to Mangue Seco). You should be able to get off the bus at other points along the road, but local transport is scarce and you'll need to hitch or walk to get to beaches.

SÍTIO

From Conde it's a 6km drive to Sítio (also known as Sítio do Conde), which has a decent beach, although it's often windy with choppy surf. From Sítio you can walk north or south along the coast to some beautiful, isolated beaches. **Seribinha** is a quiet fishing community about 14km north of Sítio along a dirt road (no buses), which passes through picturesque coconut-palm forest. The village is set on a thin strip of land between the Rio Itapicuru and the coast, close to where the river meets the ocean. Jangadas will take you across the river; from here it's about a half-hour walk to Cavalho Russo, a red-water lake. There's one pousada in Seribinha.

Places to Stay & Eat

The cheapest options are the camping grounds. Ask for discounts during the low season (April to November) at all the pousadas.

Close to the beach, the *Pousada Beira Mar* (☎ 429-1286) has single/double apartamentos for US$20/25. The *Pousada Laia* is a bit more upmarket, but reasonably good value, with apartamentos for US$25/35.

There are a couple of good restaurants in town. *Zecas & Zecos*, on the main plaza, is the best place for seafood. *Sabor d'Italia* is run by an Italian and serves excellent pizzas and pastas. A note on the menu claims 'Não servimos katchup nem maionese' (we don't serve ketchup or mayonnaise). The *Restaurant Panela de Barro* serves tasty home-style cooking and has charmingly off-hand service.

Getting There & Away

Most buses from Salvador to Conde go on to Sítio and Barra de Itariri. If you get stuck in Conde, there are buses to Sítio at 8.10 and 11.20 am and 4 and 6 pm.

BARRA DE ITARIRI

Barra is a 14km drive along a dirt road south from Sítio. The road is never more than a few hundred metres from the sea, which is hidden behind a running dune spotted with coconut palms. Barra has become more popular since the construction of the Linha Verde, but it is still a charming spot, set along the banks of the Rio Itariri. The river can be waded or swum across, and the southern bank leads to an endless stretch of deserted beach. To the north are more deserted beaches; this stretch is known as 'Corre Nu' (run naked). Barra has a couple of restaurants and simple pousadas along the beachfront.

Getting There & Away

Buses run from Sítio to Barra at 9 am and noon, and return from Barra to Sítio at 2 and 5 pm. Be prepared to push-start the bus, but don't get the position closest to the exhaust pipe!

MANGUE SECO

• *pop 1000 ✉ 48325-000 ☎ 075*

Mangue Seco is a remote and tiny town on the northern border of Bahia, at the tip of a peninsula formed by the Rio Real. The town was the setting for the Jorge Amado novel *Tieta do Agreste*, and a soap opera based on the novel, filmed in the village, captured the imagination of millions of Brazilians. Access to the town is still limited, but it is receiving more tourists since the opening of the Linha Verde. The lovely setting by the river is topped off by fine, white-sand ocean beaches 1.5km away.

Places to Stay & Eat

There is a camping ground by the river close to town. Cheap pousadas in town include the *Aconchego da Telma* and the *Grão de Areia* (☎ 224-7401), with quartos for around US$10/15. The backpackers' favourite is *Pousada O Forte* (☎ 985-1217), 500m from town. It's a friendly place with a good bar/restaurant attached. Run by Argentines Fernando and Gabriela, who speak English, French, Italian and Spanish between them, it has comfortable apartamentos for US$18/25 a single/double during the low season and US$25/35 during the high season. The *Village Mangue Seco* (☎ 625-9130) is the most upmarket place, with a swimming pool, around 1km from town along the road to the beaches. Double apartamentos cost US$40 in the low season.

There are a couple of good seafood restaurants in town with great riverfront locations – try *Bafo do Bode*, *Restaurant Frutas do Mar* or *Suruby*. *Restaurant Dunasmar* is the town action spot, with forró and dance music on weekends.

Getting There & Away

The easiest access to Mangue Seco is from Pontal, in Sergipe. From Pontal there are frequent boats during summer across the Rio Real to Mangue Seco (US$1 per person, 20 minutes) until around 6.30 pm. If you are coming from the north, a daily bus runs to Pontal from Estância at 4 pm. The bus runs via Indiaroba, near the border with

Bahia, then doubles back to Pontal. If you are coming from Salvador, you can pick up the bus in Indiaroba at around 4.30 pm. The last 10km or so to Pontal over a roller-coaster dirt road is entertaining, with locals egging on the driver to get airborne over the bumps! If the bus doesn't make the last boat, or you arrive outside of summer, you'll have to bargain for a ride across – most boats want US$15 to make the crossing. The bus returns from Pontal to Estância via Indiaroba daily, at 5.30 pm.

SACO

Saco, actually across the border in the state of Sergipe, gets weekender visitors from Estância, but is quiet during the week. It's a fine beach with good swimming. There is no accommodation, but bars and restaurants open on weekends.

ABAÍS

This is another weekend spot, but with a pousada. The beach, however, is not as good as the others in the area.

South of Salvador

VALENÇA

• *pop 69,000 ✉ 45400-000 ☎ 075*

For most travellers, Valença is simply a stepping stone to the beaches of Morro de São Paulo, but it's also a small, friendly city worth a visit en route.

After routing the local Tupininquin Indians, the Portuguese settled here along the Rio Una in the 1560s, but were in turn expelled by the Aimores tribes. In 1799 the Portuguese returned to resettle and founded Vila de Nova Valença do Santíssimo Coração de Jesus.

Today, everything centres around the busy port and large mercado beside the Rio Una, where there are boats, historic buildings, and food and lodging facilities. The town is populated by a varied and interesting assortment of shipbuilders, *vaqueiros* (cowboys), artisans, fishermen and peasants.

Information

To obtain maps and information about Valença, boat schedules and pousadas, visit the helpful tourist office (☎ 741-3311), Rua Comandante Madureira, close to the port. It's open Monday to Friday from 8 am to 6 pm and Saturday from 8 am to noon. Lúcia, who works there, speaks English. If you need money, there is a Banco do Brasil branch on Rua Governador Gonçalves and a Bradesco ATM at Rua Governador Gonçalves 178.

Things to See & Do

In the centre of town, wander around the port, the central plaza and the market. At the far end of the port, the timbered ribbing of boat hulls resembles dinosaur skeletons. The *saveiros* (wooden sailing boats) are used by the local fishermen, who pull out of port early in the morning and return by mid-afternoon with the catch of the day. The smell of sap and sawdust, old fish and sea salt mingles with the wonderful smell of nutmeg. Picked from nearby groves, the nutmegs are set on a cloth and left to dry in the sun.

For a good trek, follow the left bank of the Rio Una upstream towards the **Igreja NS de Amparo**, on the hill. At the base of the hill there's a trail straight up to the church that commands a beautiful view.

Special Events

In addition to the traditional festivals of Bahia, Valença also celebrates Sagrado Coração de Jesus. A mass is held for the patron of the city in June, and a festival in honour of the patron saint of workers, NS do Amparo, on 8 November.

Boi Estrela is a folklore festival where men and women dressed as cowhands accompany Catarina the Baiana while they play tambourines and chant. Zabiapunga, another folklore festival, features musical groups playing weird instruments and running through the city streets on New Year's Eve.

There's a good Carnaval, with trios elétricos and the Carnaval-like Micareta festival held 15 days after the end of Lent. Other festivals include Festa de Reis (6 January), São João (23 June), NS do Rosário (24 September to 3 October), São Benedito, on Cairu Island (26 December to 6 January) and Iemanjá (2 February).

Places to Stay & Eat

The following prices are for the low season – prices rise by around 30% in the high season. The *Hotel Valença* (☎ 741-3807), Rua Dr Heitor Guedes Melo 15, has single quartos for US$16 and double apartamentos for US$40. The *Hotel Guaibim* (☎ 741-1114; fax 741-5108), Praça da Independência 74, is one block in from the port. Single/double/triple apartamentos cost US$15/21/37. Next door, the *Pousada Rafa* has slightly cheaper apartamentos for US$10/15, but the price doesn't include breakfast.

A good mid-range option is *Hotel Rio Mar* (☎ 741-3408; fax 741-2714), on Avenida Dendezeiros. It has a pool, and comfortable apartamentos for US$30/45.

The *Hotel Portal Rio Una* (☎ 741-5050; fax 741-2387), on Rua Maestro Barrinhão on the riverside, has more comforts and is accordingly more expensive – double apartamentos with air-conditioning, fridge and TV start at around US$90.

There's a good self-serve restaurant, *Restaurante Carvalho* at Rua Conselhor Cunha Lopes 33, near the Hotel Guaibim. The Hotel Guaibim itself has a decent self-serve lunch buffet as well. *Restaurant Capixaba*, along the riverfront at Rua Comandante Madureira 88, has a wide range of seafood dishes for around US$10 and is popular with locals. The *Recanto do Luís* in Cajaíba is also recommended for seafood, and the Hotel Rio Una has its own restaurant, the *Panorama*.

Getting There & Away

There is a small airport just outside town serviced by air-taxi companies, but there are plans for a bigger airport at Praia Guaibim.

Bus The rodoviária is on Rua da Água, about 1.5km from the port. There are frequent bus services operating daily to Salvador. The shortest route is via Ilha Itaparica (190km, US$4.50, 2½ hours), where the bus drops you off at Bom Despacho for the 45 minute ferry ride to Salvador; other buses go all the way around Baía de Todos os Santos (290km, US$9) into Salvador. There are also regular buses to Camamu (US$3.50, 2 hours).

Boat There are daily boat trips to Morro de São Paulo, Gamboa and Boipeba on Ilha de Tinharé, the large island facing Valença. Although Salvador is only 110km away by sea, the boat service is irregular.

AROUND VALENÇA

The best mainland beach in the vicinity is 16km north of town, at **Guaibim**, which is rapidly developing into a popular resort. There are local buses, and the beach gets packed at weekends. The *Pousada São Paulo* (☎ 782-1044) and the *Santa Maria Praia*, both on Avenida Beira Mar, have single/double apartamentos for around US$15/20. If you need anything on the beach, check out barraca *Cabana Nativa*. The owner, Horácio, speaks good English and is happy to give you information about local attractions and activities.

The islands of **Boipeba** and **Cairu** have colonial buildings and churches – their beaches aren't quite as good as Morro de São Paulo, but Boipeba in particular has started to attract travellers looking to escape the crowds of Morro and now has a few simple pousadas.

VALENÇA TO ILHÉUS

Morro de São Paulo

Morro de São Paulo was an isolated fishing village that was 'discovered' by Brazilian and international tourists 15 years ago. Morro is on everyone's lips and has even made it on to the best-beach lists of several Brazilian magazines. The beaches are wonderful and the village is loaded with pousadas, restaurants and bars. Outside summer, it's still quite a relaxing place.

Information There's a small information booth as you come off the pier – opening hours are very erratic. The shops in town sell a map of the island, *O Mapa da Alegria* (The Map of Happiness), for US$1, which is cute but not very detailed.

The Banco do Brasil on Caminho da Praia (Morro's main drag) changes cash and travellers cheques, but it's only open in summer. Many pousadas and restaurants accept Visa and MasterCard.

Things to See & Do At the northern tip of Ilha de Tinharé, Morro de São Paulo has sandy streets where only beach bums, mules and horses tread – there are no roads and no cars. The clear waters around the island are ideal for scuba diving and for lobster, squid and fish. The settlement comprises three hills – Morro de Mangaba, Morro de Galeão and Morro de Farol. Climb from the harbour through the 17th century **fortress gate** and up to the **lighthouse** (1835). From the top you can survey the island and its beaches. The western side of the island – the river or Gamboa side – is mostly bordered by mangroves, while the eastern side is sandy.

There are four beaches in Morro de São Paulo: **primeiro praia**, the rather dirty village beach; **segunda praia**, the 'action' beach with nightclubs, barracas and 24 hour snack huts; **terceira praia** with some good pousadas and less development; and **quarta praia**. This fourth beach is by far the best – a long, lovely stretch of sand graced by tall, swaying palms bordering the eastern half of the island, and only one barraca in sight!

Garapua is a small settlement in the south-western corner of the island with a couple of pousadas. The walk there along the beach takes about four hours, and is best done at low tide.

Boat Trip There are daily sailing boat trips to Boipeba on the *Natureza 2* (☎ 783-1070), if there are sufficient passengers, leaving at around 8 am and returning by 6 pm. The trip takes around two hours each way and costs US$15. The captain, Kako, sets up on Caminho da Praia most nights to recruit passengers; otherwise, ask at Forno a Lenha Pizzaria.

Places to Stay Without a doubt, the best deal for longer stays is to rent a house. Outside summer, it's possible to rent large, comfortable houses with cooking facilities and beds for seven or eight people for around US$100 to $150 a month. Ask the touts when you arrive at the port, or check out *Morro Imoveis* (☎/fax 783-1116), a rental agency at Caminho da Praia 40. Touts also jump on the boat at Gamboa, the stop before Morro, and swarm the tourists. Many try to take first-timers to the pousadas along the second beach. It gets very noisy at night here because of the disco, so avoid it if you are looking for peace and quiet.

The accommodation scene changes quickly and can be tight during the summer. There are now more than 100 pousadas in Morro de São Paulo, so it's definitely worth hunting around before you commit yourself.

If you want to stay right among the action, the *Pousada Gaucho* (☎ 783-1115) and the *Pousada Giras Sol*, both on Caminho da Praia, are two good, cheap options, with quartos for around US$10 per person in the low season. *Pousada Ilha do Sol* (☎ 783-1118), next to the steep concrete ramp at the beach end of Caminho da Praia, has spacious apartamentos with hammocks and beach views from the top rooms. It charges US$13/25 a single/double in the low season and US$20/40 in the high.

If you want something a bit quieter in the wooded hills behind the village, head up Rua da Fonte, the street off Praça Aureliano Lima, to *Pousada Casarão* (☎ 783-1022), which offers great views from the pool and apartamentos for US$35/40 in the low season and US$70/80 in the high. The street splits three ways when you come to Fonte Grande, a lovely spot where locals do their washing. Off to the left you'll find the *Pousada Cairu*, which has clean quartos for US$10 per person, or US$13 with breakfast. The street running straight ahead (Caminho da Lagoa) leads to the *Pousada Bugainville*, a breezy, quiet place with double apartamentos with fan for US$30. Take the right fork along Rua Porto de Cima and go to the top of the hill to *Pousada Colibri* (☎/fax 783-1056), run by a friendly German family. Bungalows for two to four people all have private bathrooms and verandas. The views are sensational, it's in a quiet location and breakfast is excellent. Low season rates are US$15/25, while high season costs US$35/45.

Along terceira praia, the *Pousada Govinda* is a tiny pousada with a rustic beach bar out the front. Mini-quartos cost US$15 per person in the low season. Also on terceira praia is *Paraiso do Morro* (☎ 981-1026), a comfortable pousada/bar/restaurant with very good food and apartamentos for US$40 a double. Near the far end of the beach, the *Pousada Fazenda Caeira* (☎ 741-4272; fax 783-1042) has spacious grounds and a resort look, but offers reasonable deals on a variety of accommodation. *La Tartaruga*, a house with two bedrooms and veranda, costs around US$70 per day.

Places to Eat The main street of Morro, Caminho da Praia, is a regular restaurant strip. New places spring up every summer but the good ones tend to remain. *Ponte de Econtro* offers a wide range of excellent, tasty por quilo vegetarian food. *Canto do Mar* and *Sabor da Terra* both have good-value seafood prato feito for around US$6. *La Strega* is a tiny restaurant with excellent pasta; across the road, at *Bella Donna*, you can eat spaghetti and watch the passing parade from the balcony. *Forno a Lenha Pizzaria* is the place to head to for pizza – they're wood-fired and good value. If you're renting a house behind town, buy your daily bread and yoghurt at *Padaria Seu Bonzinho* in front of the fountain. It's run by Adolfo, a friendly Argentine who's lived in Morro for many years. There's a notice board with housing options for rent and other useful information.

Getting There & Away Take the *Brisa Biônica* (Bionic Breeze) or *Brisa Triônica* between Morro de São Paulo and Valença for a relaxed 1½ hour boat ride (US$2). You'll pass mangroves, yachts, double-masted, square-rigged Brazilian 'junks', and palm-lined beaches that rival the Caribbean and South Pacific in beauty.

If you're in a hurry (don't be!), there are fast boats called *lanchas rapidas*, which do the trip in 25 minutes for US$8.

During the summer the schedule is : seven boats per day from Valença to Morro de São Paulo between 7.30 am and 5 pm. If you arrive later than, you should still be able to find someone at the port in Valença to take you, but expect to pay double the price. Five boats depart daily from Morro for Valença between 6 am and 5 pm.

During the rest of the year boats travel less often, except on weekends. The ever-increasing popularity of Morro de São Paulo will undoubtedly cause frequent schedule changes – if you're coming from Salvador you can confirm these times at Bahiatursa.

During summer there are also daily direct boats to and from Salvador. One is a large launch that leaves Morro at 8 am, takes about 1½ hours and costs US$40. The other boat is a smaller motorboat that leaves Morro at 6 am, takes four hours and costs US$15.

Camamu

On the mainland, further down the coast towards Ilhéus, Camamu is a quiet, picturesque town that sits on a hill above a maze of mangrove-filled islets and narrow channels (no beaches). The town is the port of call for the many tiny fishing villages in the region, and has access by boat to stunning beaches along the Peninsula de Maraú. There's a lively dock-side morning mercado with fish, fruit and drying nutmeg.

Saveiro fishing boats are built and repaired right outside the port. The **Açaraí Waterfalls** are 5km away by bus or taxi and are worth a visit.

Places to Stay & Eat The *Pousada Green House* (☎ 255-2178), near the port at Rua Djalma Dutra 61, is friendly, family-run and great value, with spotless single/double quartos for US$10 per person and larger apartamentos for US$25/30. The downstairs restaurant serves good seafood prato feito for US$4. *Rio Açaraí* (☎ 255-2312) is on Praça Dr Francisco Xavier Borges, in the cidade alta. However, after a tough walk up the very steep road from the port, what you find is a garish, modern hotel with apartamentos from US$35/45.

Getting There & Away Buses depart for Valença and Salvador almost hourly, and five buses run daily to Ubaitaba on Hwy BR-101 via Travessão (US$3, 1½ hours). If you are coming from the south, buses run to Camamu via Ubaitaba and Travessão.

Peninsula de Maraú

If you want to get off the beaten path, this is the place. The peninsula that goes out to Ponta do Mutá and the village of Barra Grande has one long, dirt road (often impassable after rain), infrequent buses and a handful of very small fishing villages (you won't find many of them on most maps). It's an unspoilt area with some breathtaking beaches, but they are hard to get to without a car. In most of the villages, you'll be able to buy a beer but little else, so you might have to work at finding food and lodging.

Barra Grande is a tranquil, slow-paced fishing village at the tip of the peninsula – a great place to stop for a while. The village is bordered by the calm beaches of Camamu Bay on one side and the surf beaches of the Atlantic Ocean on the other. It's the most easily accessible village on the peninsula, and has a handful of pousadas and a couple of restaurants.

Places to Stay & Eat All the accommodation choices and eateries are spread between Barra Grande and the beaches.

Barra Grande For reservations at these pousadas, call the Telebahia office (☎ 258-2131). Prices quoted here are for the low season.

There is a good pousada, *Lagosta Azul*, 1km from the village on a small bay. There is a restaurant and bar attached. Apartamentos go for US$20 a double. The *Pousada Entrada do Sol* is about a 10 minute walk from the village, with a lovely beachfront location. Comfortable apartamentos cost US$15/30 for singles/doubles. There's a small seafood restaurant next to the pousada.

In the village, the *Pousada Meu Sossego* (follow the signs) is a very friendly budget option, with bright apartamentos with fan and mosquito nets for US$15/30. Another good budget option near the pier is the *Pousada Maria de Firmino*, with pretty gardens and apartamentos for US$15 per person (breakfast included). The *Pousada Tubarão* is a more upmarket place, with attractive apartamentos for US$30 per person, and a restaurant attached.

Restaurant A Tapera is a tiny tropical-style restaurant with seafood refeições and pizzas.

Beaches On Praia de Três Coqueiros, 3km from Barra Grande, the *Três Coqueiros Praia Hotel* has a wide variety of accommodation, from small cabanas at US$20 per person to large double apartamentos at US$60. It's not a particularly attractive area, and the beach is not a patch on most other beaches in the area.

Praia Bela is a gorgeous, wide beach around 6km from Barra Grande. There are a couple of bars and restaurants; *Bar Frances*, run by a Frenchman, serves good seafood and very cold beer.

Praia de Saquaria has the most upmarket pousadas with facilities and prices to match, including the *Pousada Bahia Boa* (☎/fax 258-2129) and the *Pousada Maraú* (☎ 258-2113). Expect to pay around US$50 for a double apartamento.

Getting There & Away During summer, the motorboat *Sid Narref* makes two trips daily from Camamu to Barra Grande and back. This is a delightful two hour voyage (US$3) weaving through several small, isolated islands, including Ilha Pedra Furada, Ilha Grande and Ilha de Campinhas. During summer the boat leaves Camamu at 9 am and 6 pm, and returns from Barra Grande at 7 am and 3.30 pm. During the rest of the year, it runs only on weekends, but there are often boats taking locals to market at Camamu – you should be able to organise a ride by asking around at the pier in Camamu.

There is an irregular bus service from Ubaitaba on Hwy BR-101 along 80km of rough dirt road to Barra Grande. The road is impassable after rain.

Getting Around A variety of vehicles serve as 'taxis' in Barra Grande and can ferry you to beaches along the peninsula nearby – prices are always negotiable.

Itacaré

Itacaré is a quiet colonial fishing town at the mouth of the Rio de Contas, and has some of the best surf south of Salvador. In the past, distance and bad roads have shielded Itacaré from a rapid growth in tourism, but with the new coastal road cutting the trip from Ilhéus from four to 1½ hours, the tourist boom has only just begun. **Ribeira**, **Concha**, **Tiririca** and **Resende** beaches, to the south of town, are recommended for a swim and surf.

To get to the deserted beaches north of Itacaré, cross the river by long dugout canoe. If you feel energetic and are travelling light, you may consider walking 40km north to Barra Grande along stretches of coconut-palm-lined beaches. There are also surfboards for rent at Ombak Trek, on Rua Dedão Longo, for US$10 a day.

Places to Stay *Camping Estrela do Mar* (☎ 251-2119) has a good location and facilities, right on the point near the lighthouse. It gets a bit damp, so don't forget the insect repellent. Sites cost US$5 (US$7 in summer). New pousadas are springing up all over the place in Itacaré. The best place to stay, especially if you surf, is *Sage Point* (☎/fax 251-2030), 1km from town on Praia Tiririca. It's run by Ana, a friendly Cuban-American who serves a huge, healthy breakfast. Her beautiful wooden chalets are booked up quickly during the summer, but if you can get one, you'll be tempted to stay a while. Low season prices are US$15/35 a single/double, while in the high season a double costs US$50. Closer to town is a new, cheap option, *Pousada do Costinho* (☎ 251-2005), Rua Pituba 2 (which runs parallel to the main road). This pousada has clean apartamentos with balconies and hammock for US$8/16 in the low season and US$20/35 in the high season. *Pousada Swell* has rooms with all the basics for US$5/10 in the low season. It's on Rua Dedão Longo, opposite *Pousada Estrela*, another reasonable cheapie. *Pousada do Portuga*, right on the Praça containing the small dog statue, is another recommended budget pousada. Portuga, the owner, is a real character.

If you're after more comfort, *Papa Terra Pousada and Restaurante* (☎/fax 251-2137) has new, well-appointed apartamentos for US$28/40 during the low season. Its prices double in summer.

Places to Eat *Boca do Forno*, on Beco das Flores, serves excellent pizzas in a beautiful floral outdoor setting. The pizzas cost between US$8 and $13, but they're worth it. *O Restaurante*, on Rua Dedão Longo out toward the beaches, serves a good seafood and salad prato feito for US$5. *Mistura Fina*, across the road, is also a good feed. For health foods, stop in at the *Almazen Alimentos Integral*, also on Rua Dedão Longo but closer to the centre of town.

Getting There & Away There is a new coastal road southwards from Itacaré to Ilhéus and the bus trip takes about 1½ hours. An alternative, longer scenic route is to go via Uruçuca for a slice of the real Bahia. The bus passes the occasional cacao plantation, stopping every few kilometres to pick up another couple of locals, whose features are an intriguing blend of black, Indian and white.

For the first two hours, the bus travels at a snail's pace from Itacaré to Uruçuca along a bad dirt road. Uruçuca is a tiny, secluded village surrounded by lush valleys of cacao trees, and worth exploring if you have the time.

From here the road heads down through groves of cacao, coconut and enormous bamboo, to reach the coast shortly before Ilhéus.

Getting Around Boys with wheelbarrows meet every bus if you need help with your luggage, but the town centre is only a few minutes walk away.

ILHÉUS

• *pop 239,000* ✉ *45600-000* ☎ *073*

Ilhéus, the town that Jorge Amado (Brazil's best-known novelist) lived in and described with his novel *Gabriela, Cravo e Canela* (Gabriela, Clove and Cinnamon), retains some of the charm and lunacy that Amado fans know well. The colonial centre is small and distinctive, with its strange layout and odd buildings; the people are affable; the city beaches are broad and beautiful; and a short walk beyond these, there are even better beaches.

The best thing to do in Ilhéus is just wander. The centre is lively, with several old, gargoyled buildings such as the Prefeitura. If you walk up the hill to the Convento NS da Piedade, there's a good view of the city and litoral. Wherever you end up, it won't be more than a stone's throw from the beach. The Praia da Avenida, close to the city centre, is always active, but has been polluted by the port.

History

Ilhéus was a sleepy town until cacao was introduced into the region from Belém, in 1881. At the time, Brazil's many uncompetitive sugar estates, which had not followed the lead of other countries and introduced new production techniques to increase sugar output, were reeling from a drop in world sugar prices. Simultaneously, the slave system was finally coming to an end, with many slaves escaping and others being freed. With the sugar plantations in the doldrums, impoverished agricultural workers from the Northeast – black and white – flocked to the hills surrounding Ilhéus to farm the new boom crop: cacao, the *ouro branco* (white gold) of Brazil.

Sudden, lawless and violent, the scramble for the white cacao fruit displayed all the characteristics of a gold rush. When the dust settled, the land and power belonged to a few ruthless *coroneis* (rural landowners) and their hired guns. The landless were left to work, and usually live, on the fazendas, where they were subjected to a harsh and paternalistic labour system. This history is graphically told by Amado, who grew up on a cacao plantation, in his book *Terras do Sem Fim* (published in English as *The Violent Land*).

Cacao still rules in Ilhéus. The lush tropical hills are covered with the skinny cacao trees with large, pod-shaped fruit dangling. If you take a drive you will still see cacao fazendas and rural workers like those Amado wrote about. You can also visit the small Regional Museu do Cacao, the port and, with a bit of effort and luck, a fazenda.

Orientation

The city is sandwiched between hills, beach and a small harbour at the mouth of the Rio Cachoeira. The airport and the road to the Olivença beaches are in the southern part of town, beyond the circular harbour.

Information

Tourist Office Ilhéustur (☎ 634-3510) has a handy information booth on Praça do Teatro, open daily from 9 am to noon and 2 to 6 pm. The information booth at the rodoviária is only open from December to February.

Money Emcamtur Turismo, in the centre, changes cash and travellers cheques. It's open weekdays from 9 am to 5 pm and Saturday from 9 am to noon. Banco do Brasil is at Rua Marques de Paranâgua 112.

Travel Agency Emcamtur Tourismo can also book bus and airline tickets. Grou Viagens (☎ 634-8741), Avenida Soares Lopes 528, has reasonable prices and a flexible attitude to

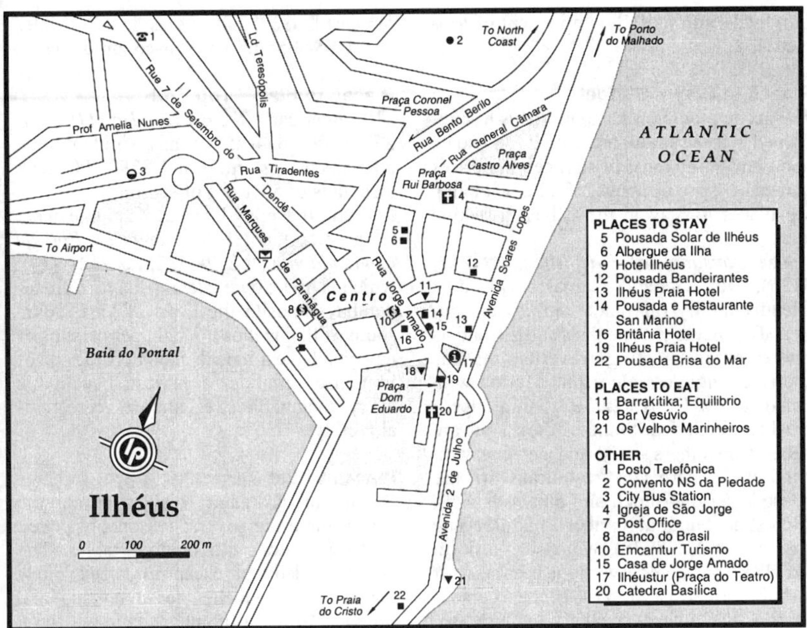

planning. Trips to Rio Almada and Rio Santana are worthwhile (for further information, see the Around Ilhéus section). Another recommended trip is to Primavera Fazenda, where you'll be taken through the process of cacao production.

Casa de Jorge Amado

The house at Rua Jorge Amado 21, where the great writer lived with his parents while working on his first novel, *O Pais do Carnaval*, has been restored and turned into a *casa de cultura*, with an interesting display about the man himself. Not many writers can boast this sort of recognition while still alive, but Amado is a national treasure.

Churches

The **Igreja de São Jorge** (1534), Praça Rui Barbosa, is the city's oldest church and houses a small sacred-art museum. It's open Tuesday to Sunday from 8 to 11 am and 2 to 5.30 pm. The Catedral de São Sebastião (Basílica) is on Praça Dom Eduardo.

Museu Regional do Cacao

The restored and upgraded Museu Regional do Cacao displays cacao artefacts and modern painting by local artists. It's at Rua AL Lemos 126, and is open Tuesday to Friday from 2 to 6 pm, and Saturday and Sunday from 3 to 6 pm. During the holiday season, from December to March, it's also open from 9 am to noon.

Special Events

As any knowledgeable Jorge Amado fan would guess, Ilhéus has highly spirited festivals. The best are: the Gincana da Pesca in early January; Festa de São Sebastião (much samba and capoeira) from 11 to 20 January; Festa de São Jorge (featuring Candomblé) on 23 April; Festa das Águas (Candomblé) in December; and, of course,

Carnaval, with its full complement of trios elétricos.

Places to Stay – Budget

The accommodation scene in Ilhéus has improved – there's now more of it, and some good budget options. In summer, the prices quoted here rise by about 25%. For camping, see Places to Stay in the Olivença section later.

The *Pousada Solar de Ilhéus* (☎ 231-5125), Rua General Camârca 50, is a friendly family-run place with good security. The manager speaks English and is interested in meeting travellers. It has spotless single/double/triple quartos with fan that cost US$15/22/30, with a superb breakfast included. Some of the rooms are better than others – try and get one with windows. There's a restaurant in the pousada serving lunch and dinner as well. Almost next door at number 31 is *Albergue da Ilha* (☎ 231-8938), which has a dorm for US$7 per person without breakfast. It also has quartos for US$10 per person. Murilo, the owner, speaks good English. Another good deal is *Pousada Bandeirantes* (☎ 231-5760), Rua Cintório Lavigne de Lemar 69, which has decent quartos for US$10/15 in the low season and US$15/20 in the high season.

The *Pousada e Restaurante San Marino* (☎ 231-6511), Rua Jorge Amado 29, is central and has four-bed quartos for US$10 per person – ask for a room at the front of the building. Double apartamentos start at US$30.

The *Britânia Hotel* (☎ 634-1722), Rua Jorge Amado 16, is a pleasant old-style hotel with quartos for US$15/25 and apartamentos for US$20/30.

THE NORTHEAST

Places to Stay – Mid-Range

The *Pousada Brisa do Mar* (☎ 231-2644), on the beachfront at Avenida 2 de Julho 136, is an Art Deco building with large, comfortable apartamentos starting at US$30/40. The *Hotel Ilhéus* (☎ 634-4242), Rua Eustáquio Bastos 44, in the centre, has a fading grandeur about it. Double apartamentos with fan cost US$30, and singles/doubles/triples cost US$44/55/65 with air-conditioning.

Places to Stay – Top End

The rather dark *Ilhéus Praia Hotel* (☎ 634-2533; fax 634-2550) has single/double apartamentos starting at US$90/100, with discounts of 50% out of season.

If you're feeling like a total splurge, there is the resort hotel *Transamérica Ilha de Comandatuba* (☎ 212-1122; fax 212-1114), which is on its own island (Ilha de Comandatuba) opposite the town of Una, 80km south of Ilhéus. For US$300 per person per day, you have all meals included, the run of immense grounds, a private beach and every imaginable (well almost) recreational facility.

Places to Eat

Behind the Catedral Basílica, along the beach, there are several reasonably priced *seafood stands* with outdoor tables. The centre is filled with cheap *restaurants* offering self-serve lunches for a few dollars. *Barrakitika* is a popular hang-out with outdoor tables, seafood and pizza. There's good live music here on Thursday, Friday and Saturday. *Equilibrio*, next door, has a varied self-serve lunch spread.

For seafood and great views of the beach, try *Os Velhos Marinheiros*, on Avenida 2 de Julho, with dishes for around US$15 to $30 for two. *Bar Vesúvio*, Praça Dom Eduardo, has been described in Amado's books and is consequently a popular spot for tourists, and for good reason – it hasn't changed since the old cocoa barons used to chew the fat there.

Getting There & Away

Air There is a small airport, serviced by Nordeste, VASP, Varig/Cruzeiro and air-taxis. You can fly to several major cities including Rio, Salvador, Recife and Belo Horizonte.

VASP (☎ 231-3412) is at Brigadeiro E Gomes, Centro, and Varig (☎ 231-5904) is at Rua Coronel Paiva 56. If you're returning to Rio, the flight stops at Salvador but is still cheaper than flying directly from Salvador.

Bus Ilhéus is 460km south of Salvador and 315km north of Porto Seguro. From Hwy BR-101 at Itabuna, it's a beautiful 30km descent through cacao plantations to Ilhéus and the sea. For most major destinations, buses leave more frequently from Itabuna than Ilhéus, so it's usually quicker to go to Itabuna first, and then shuttle down to Ilhéus. To get to Itabuna from Ilhéus, take the collective bus that leaves from out the front of the rodoviária every 30 minutes and costs US$1.50.

Buses to Salvador use two different approach routes. The regular route follows the long sweep around the recôncavo, and is recommended if you want to stop at Cachoeira on the way to Salvador. The other route runs via Nazaré and Ilha de Itaparica, where you change to the ferry for a stunning 45 minute ferry ride into Salvador.

From Ilhéus there are several buses a day to Salvador (US$28, 7 hours) and two a day to Porto Seguro (US$12, 5 hours). Buses travelling to Canavieiras (US$4, 2 hours) leave every 2 hours from 6.30 am to 10 pm. To get to Valença, you'll to go to Itabuna.

Getting Around

To/From the Airport The airport (☎ 231-7629) is at Praia do Pontal, 4km from the centre.

Bus The rodoviária (☎ 231-4221) in Ilhéus is a 15 minute bus ride from the centre. Take a local T Vilela/N Costa bus to the centre from the stop in front of the rodoviária for US$0.50. The city bus station is on Praça Cairu, on the edge of the centre. From here, there are bus services to Itabuna, Olivença, the rodoviária and the airport.

AROUND ILHÉUS

Centro de Pesquisa do Cacao (CEPLAC)

You don't have to be a chocaholic to enjoy CEPLAC's model cacao plantation and research station at Itabuna. CEPLAC (☎ 634-1418), the government cacao agency, gives tours of the facility, demonstrating the cultivation and processing of the fruit. Opening hours are Monday to Friday from 8.30 to 11.30 am and 2.30 to 3.30 pm.

Buses for Itabuna leave around every half an hour from the city bus station in Ilhéus and also stop outside the rodoviária. Ask the bus driver to let you off at CEPLAC, 8km before Itabuna.

Olivença

There are good, clean beaches, many with barracas, all the way from Ilhéus to Olivença, a spa town 16km south. You can also continue south of Olivença to yet more remote beaches. The beaches in Olivença are busy on weekends and there's some good surfing at **Batuba** and **Backdoor**, both a couple of kilometres from town.

Places to Stay A good camping ground en route to Olivença is *Camping Estância das Fontes* (☎ 212-2505), 15km from Ilhéus. It's close to the beach and charges US$8 per person for a camp site.

In Olivença, the *Albergue Juventude Fazenda Tororomba* (☎ 269-1139), on Rua Eduardo Magalhães, is set on a large property with a swimming pool, bar and restaurant. Otherwise, try the *Repousada* (☎ 231-1362), Rua Amor Perfeito 168, which is a bit out of town in a quiet location. Single/double apartamentos start at around US$25/30. The more expensive *Pousada Olivença* (☎ 269-1107) is on Praça Claudio Magalhães.

Getting There & Away To get to Olivença take one of the frequent Olivença buses from the central bus station in Ilhéus. The bus travels close to the beaches, so you can pick one to your liking and quickly hop off.

Reserva Biológica Mico Leão de Una

This small (50 sq km) biological reserve was established in 1980 to protect the *mico leão* (lion monkey) in its natural habitat of coastal forest and attempt to save the species from extinction – less than 100

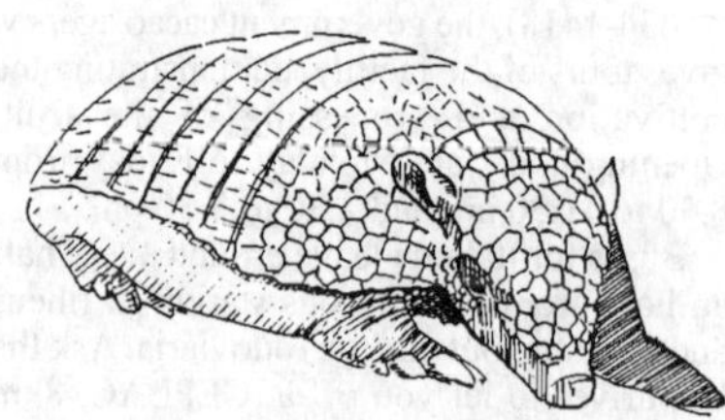

Armadillos were named by the Spanish conquistadors – their name means 'little armoured things'

remain in this reserve. It's not a park and it does not cater to visitors. Dr Saturnino Neto Souza, the director of the reserve, has been facing tourist pressure and consequent hostility from farmers and bureaucrats who are opposed to his conservation aims. At present, visits are discouraged.

If you are keen to visit, we suggest you make contact in advance with Dr Saturnino, either by phoning him at home in Una (☎ 236-2166, from 7 to 8 am or after 5.30 pm) or by writing to him at the following address: Rebio de Una, U5690, Una, Bahia. Alternatively, try calling IBAMA in Salvador (☎ 240-7322) for information.

The monkeys *(Leontopithecus rosalia chrysomelas)* have the look and proud gaze of miniature lions: a blazing yellow, orange and brown striped coat, a Tina Turner mane and a long, scruffy tail. The mico leões are hard to spot in the wild, but behind the biologist's quarters there is one monkey in captivity and one monkey-boarder who comes in from the forest every evening for milk, cheese, bananas and some shut-eye. If you're lucky you'll also see *tatus* (armadillos), *pacas* (agoutis), capybaras and *veados* (deer) that are also native to the area.

Getting There & Away Getting to the reserve is a bit difficult without a car. Take a Canavieiras bus from the rodoviária in Ilhéus and travel 35km south of Olivença along the coastal highway, until an IBAMA sign marks the turn-off to the reserve.

From here you have to hitch, which is difficult, or hike. Follow the turn-off for 5km on a pitted dirt track over the Rio Mariu and past a fazenda. Turn right at the marker; the working station is 3km further, within the park.

Canavieiras

Canavieiras is a small colonial town at the mouth of the Rio Pardo, in a cacao-producing region 118km south of Ilhéus. There is some colonial architecture in the town, including the **Igreja Matriz de São Boaventura** (1718), and long stretches of lonely beach.

Places to Stay & Eat The *Pousada Gabriela* (☎ 284-1155), Rua Augusto Severo 1056, Centro, has small single/double apartamentos with fan for US$15/20. On Praia de Costa, try *Pousada Canto da Sereia*, which has a small restaurant attached, or the more comfortable *Pousada Farol da Ilha*.

Getting There & Away Buses run to Canavieiras from the rodoviária in Ilhéus every two hours between 6.30 am and 9.30 pm. The trip takes about two hours and costs US$4. There is no road south along the coast from Canavieiras, but a daily boat makes the 2½ hour passage (US$4) to Belmonte, on the southern bank of the large Rio Jequitinhonha, where there are river beaches and a couple of pousadas. Sailing times vary with the tides – the tourist office in Ilhéus can give you the schedule. From Belmonte there are two daily buses, at 10.30 am and 1.30 pm to Eunápolis (US$8, four hours) on Hwy BR-101. There are also a couple of daily buses from Belmonte going south along the coast to Santa Cruz Cabrália and Porto Seguro.

PORTO SEGURO

• *pop 66,000* ✉ *45810-000* ☎ *073*

Porto Seguro, once a settlement of pioneers, is now a refuge for swarms of Brazilian and international tourists who come to party and take in some mesmerising beaches. Tourism is the number-one industry in Porto Seguro – at last count there were more than 570 hotels and pousadas in Porto Seguro, Arraial d'Ajuda and Trancoso! Mercifully, local building regulations limit construction to two storeys, so there are no multistorey eyesores to spoil the landscape. Other regional industries are lumber, fishing, beans, sugar cane, manioc and livestock.

History

After sighting land off Monte Pascoal in April 1500, Cabral and his men sailed for three days up the coast to find a safe port. The Portuguese landed not at Porto Seguro (literally Safe Port), but 16km further north, at Coroa Vermelha. The sailors celebrated their first mass in the New Land, stocked up on wood and fresh water, and set sail after only 10 days on shore. Three years later the Gonçalvo Coelho expedition arrived and planted a marker in what is now Porto Seguro's Cidade Alta (Upper Town). Jesuits on the same expedition built a church in Outeiro da Glória, to minister to the early colonists and convert the Tupiniquin Indians. The church is now in ruins. In 1526, a naval outpost was built in Cidade Alta, and once again, the men from the Companhia de Jesus built a chapel and convent, the Igreja NS da Misericórdia.

In 1534, when the colonies were divided into hereditary captaincies, Porto Seguro was given to Pero de Campos Tourinhos. In the following year Tourinhos founded a village at the falls of the Rio Buranhém, Porto Seguro, and seven other villages, each with a church. Despite the churches, Tourinhos was denounced to the Holy Inquisition as an atheist – apparently the captain didn't keep the holidays and, worse, he forced the colonists to work on Sunday, a blasphemy against God (and an abuse of cheap labour). Tourinhos was imprisoned, and shipped off to Portugal and the Inquisition. His son Fernando then inherited the captaincy.

Information recently unearthed at the Federal University of Bahia has revised some ideas about the history of the Indians during the colonial period. The Tupiniquin, not the Pataxó, were the indigenous tribe when the Portuguese landed. They were rapidly conquered and enslaved by the colonists, but the Aimoré, Pataxó, Cataxó and other inland tribes resisted Portuguese colonisation and constantly threatened Porto Seguro. Military outposts along the coast, in Belmonte, Vila Viçosa, Prado and Alcobaça, were built to defend the Portuguese from European attacks by sea and Indian attacks by land.

The Indians still managed to take Porto Seguro on two occasions, and according to documents sent by colonial judges to the Portuguese Crown, attacks reduced Porto Seguro to rubble in 1612 (thus undermining Porto Seguro's claims of having 16th century buildings).

It is now believed that the Jesuit College in Cidade Alta was rebuilt after 1620. In 1759, the captaincy of Porto Seguro passed to the Crown and was incorporated into the province of Bahia.

Orientation

Porto Seguro is connected by an asphalt road to Hwy BR-101 at Eunápolis, a little over 660km south-west of Salvador. The town itself has no beaches, but it's the largest town in the area, with the most facilities for tourists, and there are plenty of beaches nearby. Porto Seguro's coastline is protected by reefs; the ocean is clear, shallow, and calm. Swimming is safe.

Information

Tourist Office There is a small hotel information booth at the rodoviária, but it's only open in summer. Travel agencies can provide information if you really need it.

Money The best place to change cash and travellers cheques is Adeltur Turismo & Câmbio, loja 53 on the 2nd floor on the rear right-hand side in Shopping Avenida, Avenida 22 de Abril 100. It's open daily from 9 am to 10 pm. By the time you read this it will also have a branch at the airport. Banco do Brasil, also on Avenida 22 de

Porto Seguro
0
200
400 m
Airport
To Santa Cruz da Cabrália
Cicade Alta
Praia do Rio da Vila
Praia do Cruzeiro
Rua Guava do Moço
Avenida Biera Mar
Avenida Dos Navagantes
Avenida 22 de Abril
Stadium
ATLANTIC OCEAN
Rua da Vala
Rua do Cajueiro
Rua Pero Vaz de Caminha
Rua 2 de Julho
Rua Oscar Oliveira
Rua P A Cabral
Avenida Getúlio Vargas
Av Portugal
Passarala de Alcoól
O Beco (Bars)
Praça dos Pataxós
Sea Wall
Ferry Route
Rio Buranhém
To Arraial d'Ajuda, Trancoso & Caraiva
PLACES TO STAY
6 Pousada Oasis de Pacatá
9 Hotel Tropical
24 Pousada do Cais
27 Pousada Aquarius
30 Pousada Brisa do Mar
31 Raízes Pousada
PLACES TO EAT
11 A Taberna
17 Tia Nenezinha
18 Bar-Restaurant Tres Vintens
19 Amoarês
23 Café da Manhá
25 Atobá
32 Sambuca Pizzaria
33 Restaurante do Japonês
OTHER
1 Rodoviária
2 Igreja NS da Pena
3 Igreja NS da Misericórida
4 Museu Antigo Paço Municipal
5 Igreja NS do Rosário dos Jesuitas
7 Banco do Brasil
8 Shopping Avenida (Adeltur)
10 Curuípe Viagems & Turismo - Bus Tickets
12 Apollo Turismo
13 Posto Telefônica
14 Fish Mercado
15 Igreja NS do Brasil
16 Nirvana Turismo Marítimo
20 Bradesco ATM
21 Delegacia de Polícia
22 Post Office
26 Studio Bar
28 Buses to Santa Cruz Cabrália
29 Capitânia dos Portos

Abril, is open Monday to Friday from 8 am to 1 pm. Bradesco has an ATM on Avenida Getúlio Vargas.

Travel Agencies Many agencies offer city tours and schooner trips to Trancoso, Coroa Alta, Recife da Fora or Monte Pascoal. Prices are competitive, and all seem to be around US$15 per person. Apollo Turismo (☎ 288-2157), Avenida 22 de Abril 260, offers all the above and more, as does Nirvana Turismo Marítimo, Avenida Portugal 90. If you are in a group, these agencies can also arrange trips to Parque Nacional Marinho dos Abrolhos, but trips are much easier to organise in Caravelas (see the Caravelas section).

To buy bus tickets without having to go up to the rodoviária, go to the helpful Curuípe Viagems and Turismo (☎/fax 288-2403), Rua do Golfo 10. To buy or change plane tickets, try Adeltur Turismo & Câmbio.

Cidade Alta

If not the first, then among the first settlements in Brazil, Cidade Alta is marked with a stone (now fenced off and encased in glass) placed in 1503 by Gonçalvo Coelho. Walk north along Avenida 22 de Abril about 1km. Once you've arrived at the roundabout, don't follow the sign that points left to the historic city, unless you're driving, but take the stairs up the hill. The attractions of this part of the city include superb views of the beaches and the opportunity to see very old buildings such as **Igreja NS da Misericórdia** (perhaps the oldest church in Brazil), the small **Museu Antigo Paço Municipal** (1772), **Igreja NS da Pena** (1535, rebuilt 1773), **Igreja NS do Rosário dos Jesuitas** (1549) and the **old fort** (1503).

Reserva Biológica do Pau Brasil

This 10 sq km reserve, 15km from town, was set aside principally to preserve the *pau brasil* (brazil wood tree), which was almost completely wiped out along the coast during the early years of colonisation. For details about visiting this reserve, ask at the travel agencies.

Special Events

Porto Seguro's Carnaval is acquiring a reputation throughout Brazil as a hell of a party, although it is not at all traditional. Locals fondly remember the Carnaval in 1984 when the theme was the Adam and Eve story. Costumes were pretty skimpy to start with, then everyone stripped off as if on cue. The police were called in the following year.

Many of Brazil's favourite musicians have beach homes nearby, and often perform during Carnaval. On the Sunday before Carnaval a beauty pageant is held at the Praia Hotel.

Municipal holidays celebrated include:

3 January until February
: *Bumba Meu Boi* is celebrated with a musical parade (for details about this festival, see the São Luís section in the Maranhão chapter).

5-6 January
: *Terno de Reis* is celebrated in the streets and at the churches. Women and children carrying lanterns and *pandeiros* (tambourines) sing *O Reis* and worship the Reis Magos (Three Wise Men).

20 January
: *Puxada de Mastro* features a group of men who parade a *mastro* (sysmbolic figure) to the door of Igreja NS da Pena. Decorated with flowers, the mastro is hung in front of the church, with the flag and image of São Sebastião, and women then sing to the saint.

19-22 April
: *Discovery of Brazil* is commemorated with an outdoor mass and Indian celebrations. This seems a rather baffling celebration, since the Indians were here first, and, later, fared badly at the hands of their 'discoverers'.

15 August
: *Festa de NS d'Ajuda* is the culmination of a pilgrimage starting on 9 April. A mass procession, organised in homage to the miraculous saint, is followed by food, drink and live music.

8 September
: *Festa de NS da Pena* is the same as Festa de NS d'Ajuda except for the additional enlivenment of fireworks.

25-27 December
: *Festa de São Benedito* is held on 27 December at the door of the church of NS do Rosário. Boys and girls from Cidade Alta blacken their faces and perform African dances, such as *congo da alma*, *ole* or *lalá*, to the music of drums, *cuica atabaque* and *xeque-xeque*.

31 December
New Year's Eve is when everyone rushes around shouting '*Feliz ano novo Baiana!*' (Happy New Year), strangers kiss and serious partying ensues.

Places to Stay – Budget

Accommodation in Porto Seguro is generally more expensive and there is more of it than further south at Arraial d'Ajuda. During the low season there must be at least 20 vacant rooms for every tourist and prices go down by as much as 50%. On the other hand, during the high season accommodation can be hard to find.

If you intend to camp, try *Mundaí Praia* (☎ 879-2287), 5km north of town on the road to Santa Cruz da Cabrália, or *Tabapiri Country* (☎ 288-2269), 1.5km outside town on the way to Eunápolis. The latter only opens in summer.

The *Pousada do Cais* (☎ 288-2112; fax 288-2540), Avenida Portugal 382, is an arty, rustic place with individually decorated single/double rooms for US$12 per person in the low season and US$24/48 in the high. The friendly German owner, Jochen Heckhausen, speaks English and is always delighted to meet fellow travellers. He also owns the *Jocotoka Village* resort in Corumbau (see the later Corumbau section).

Other cheapies close to the action and the ferry south include: *Raízes Pousada* (☎ 288-4717), Praça dos Pataxós 196, which has clean, basic apartamentos for US$8 per person (US$15 in summer) without breakfast; and *Pousada Brisa do Mar* (☎ 288-2943), Praça Dr Manoel Ribeiro Coelho 188, which charges US$15 per person (US$25 in summer) with breakfast.

Places to Stay – Mid-Range

Many of the mid-range pousadas are charming hotels that reflect the character of their owners. The *Pousada Aquarius* (☎ 288-2738), Rua P A Cabral 174, is a friendly, quiet place with single/double apartamentos for around US$35/40. A pleasant option at Rua Marechal Deodoro 286 is *Pousada Oasis de Pacatá* (☎/fax 288-2221), under Swedish management. It's spacious and quiet, with double apartamentos for around US$50. The *Hotel Tropical* (☎/fax 288-2502), at Rua do Cajueiro, is a modern hotel, with double apartamentos with fridge and fan for US$40.

Places to Stay – Top End

The poshest hotel in the area, the *Porto Seguro Praia* (☎ 288-2321; fax 288-2069), about 4km north of town, is set back from the coastal road on Praia de Curuípe. Apartamentos start at US$100 a double. In the old city, the *Vela Branca* (☎/fax 288-2318) has a pool and great views for US$150 a double.

Places to Eat

Restaurants in Porto Seguro are becoming expensive – at least in summer, when many places have a minimum charge per table. The cheapest option is to eat at the stalls set up along Avenida Portugal (better known as the Passarela de Álcoól), where you can get a good chicken or meat, salad and farofa plate for US$4.

The *Bar-Restaurant Tres Vintens*, Avenida Portugal 246, serves a delicious bobó de camarão for US$20. With a side dish, this is a meal for two. For good sushi, sashimi and hot shrimp dishes (US$10 to $15), try *Restaurante do Japonês*, on Praça dos Pataxós. Another good sushi bar is *A Taberna*, Avenida 22 de Abril 222. On Friday nights you can get all you can eat for US$18. *Atobá*, O Beco, is the place for pasta. For the best pizza in town, head for *Sambuca Pizzaria*, on the corner next to Praça dos Pataxós.

Café da Manhá, on Avenida Getúlio Vargas, is the place to go for breakfast. Try cacao juice – it's not at all like chocolate, but it is very good. *Amoarés*, Avenida Getúlio Vargas No 245, serves a good, cheap, por quilo lunch. *Tia Nenezinha*, Avenida Portugal 170, has excellent Bahian cuisine.

Entertainment

Even during the low season, Porto Seguro has lots of budget package tourists taking advantage of the low prices, and most party very late.

For live music and booze go to Passarela de Álcool (the equivalent of a 'booze alley'), otherwise known as Avenida Portugal. The street is lined with bars and restaurants and the beautiful fruit displays of stalls selling killer batidas.

There's usually live music in O Beco from early on. If you want to find out what's happening on any particular evening, drop in to the *Studio Bar*, Rua do Cais 23, next to O Beco, facing the sea. It's a meeting place for the local arty types, and doesn't start to get crowded until after 10 pm. They always know which big lambada shows are on – there is a different hot spot for every night of the week in Porto Seguro. It's usually one of the beach clubs along the northern beaches close to town. They charge between US$5 an $10 admission – don't buy tickets in town as they will cost you more there, and it's easy to get tickets at the door.

Things to Buy

Porto Seguro is loaded with shops selling '5 for $10' T-shirts and '6 for $10' baseball caps. Despite this, there are some talented artisans in town. Check out the galleries on O Beco for some high-quality stuff. There's also a daily hippie mercado close to Avenida Portugal (Passarela de Álcool).

The Pataxó north of Porto Seguro sell trinkets (overpriced coloured feathers, pieces of coral, fibre wristbands with beads) to tourists at Coroa Vermelha. This make-believe village is simply a sad little collection of thatched-roof huts and dugout canoes by the beach. Porto Seguro also has souvenir shops that sell Pataxó jewellery, basketware and earthenware ceramics.

Please *don't* buy items made of turtle shell or consume turtles or their eggs! Most of the species of turtle found in Brazil are threatened with extinction. For more information about turtle conservation projects in Bahia, see the section on Praia do Forte and the TAMAR turtle reserve boxed text earlier in this chapter.

Getting There & Away

Air Nordeste (☎ 288-1888) has a daily 'milk run' to Porto Seguro, originating in Rio (Santos Dumont airport), with stops in São Paulo and Brasi. There are also daily services to Rio, Brasília and Salvador, and flights on Saturday and Sunday to Belo Horizonte. VASP has weekend flights to Belo Horizonte, Rio, São Paulo, Brasília and Salvador.

Bus The rodoviária (☎ 288-1039) is 2km outside town on the road to Eunápolis. São Geraldo runs a daily bus to São Paulo at 10.45 am (US$79, 24 hours) and an executivo bus to Rio at 5.45 pm (US$58, 18 hours). Aguia Branca has four daily buses to Salvador (US$42; leito US$73, 11 hours). There are two daily buses to Ilhéus (US$14, five hours) and five to Itabuna.

Between 5.20 am and 9.30 pm, buses depart almost hourly to Eunápolis (US$3, one hour) – some are direct buses, others make several stops along the way. Eunápolis is a large transport hub with more frequent bus departures than Porto Seguro. Buses to Santa Cruz Cabrália (40 minutes away) run about every hour between 6.20 am and 7 pm. You can also pick this bus up on Avenida Getúlio Vargas in the centre. Two daily buses run north to Belmonte at 8.10 am and 12.40 pm.

Getting Around

The ferry across the Rio Buranhém provides access to the road towards Arraial d'Ajuda, Trancoso and Caraiva. The pedestrian ferry charges US$0.50 and seems to operate every 15 minutes from dawn until late in the evening, but the car ferry charges US$5 per car (plus US$0.50 per passenger) and operates every half an hour between 7 am and 9 pm. The tired barges converted for use as ferries make the 10 minute crossing past the rotting and listing hulks of beached fishing boats.

NORTH OF PORTO SEGURO

North of Porto Seguro, next to the sealed coastal road, are several attractive beaches easily accessible by bus and, consequently, not as pristine as those to the south. The nicest are **Mundaí**, 5km north of town, and **Coroa Vermelha**, with Pataxó's craft stands and a monument to the discovery of Brazil.

At Km 25, the town of **Santa Cruz Cabrália**, with its terracotta roofs and palm trees, is pleasant enough, but not worth staying in. Climb up to the bluff for the view overlooking the town and to visit Igreja NS da Imaculada Conçeição, the lonely white church built by the Jesuits in 1630. The elderly caretaker will tell you the history of the region, as well as the inside story on Cabral's expedition. Fried shrimp and a batida de côco at the barracas by the church enhance the view of the offshore reef, the boats and the palm trees in and about the bay of Cabrália.

If you continue north and cross the Rio Joã de Tiba, you'll come to **Vila de Santo André**, a pretty fishing village that is just starting to feel the effects of tourism. It's a lovely spot.

Places to Stay

Highly recommended is *Victor Hugo* (☎ 985-5292), a relaxing pousada in Santo André, with very comfortable doubles for US$60.

SOUTH OF PORTO SEGURO

After taking the ferry across the Rio Buranhém, you rejoin the road, which continues along a long stretch of dreamlike beaches, with a bluff backdrop. Up on the bluff, a short walk from the beach, are the rapidly expanding villages of Arraial d'Ajuda (also known as NS da Ajuda) and Trancoso, which are 4.5km and 26km, respectively, from the ferry crossing. The rush to develop the region south of Porto Seguro continues in full swing in Arraial d'Ajuda and Trancoso, both town's facilities are being developed along similar lines to those of Porto Seguro: sealed roads, electricity, pousadas, and, of course, *chopp* (draught beer) on tap. South of Trancoso, the recently upgraded, unsealed road continues for 42km to the small village of Caraiva.

Arraial d'Ajuda

Twenty years ago, before the arrival of electricity or the road from Porto Seguro, Arraial was a poor fishing village removed from the world. Since then, the international tourist set has discovered Arraial and its desolate beaches, and a time-honoured way of life has all but vanished. The village has become too hip too fast: along Arraial's maze of dirt streets, barefoot jet-set trippers eat the dust of trendy package tourists in dune buggies, and slick shopping galleries sit awkwardly alongside rustic reggae cafés. The increasingly littered main beach is lined with barracas and the beach-lounge set, while further south, hippies let it all hang out along the nude beach at Pitinga.

Yet, for some, Arraial d'Ajuda is the place to be. Younger and wilder than Porto Seguro, Arraial d'Ajuda is a wonderful place to tan and slough off excess brain cells. Newcomers soon fall into the routine: going crazy every evening, recovering the following morning and crawling back onto the beach for more surf, sun and samba.

Orientation Arraial d'Ajuda is built on a little hill-top by the sea. The main street running from the church to the cemetery is called Broadway. Many of the restaurants and bars, plus a couple of cheap pousadas, are here. Most of Arraial d'Ajuda's pousadas are tucked away on the ocean side of this hill-top, along the dirt streets (now being sealed). Mucugê is the name of the beach below the maze.

From the ferry landing, the dusty 4.5km road to Arraial d'Ajuda runs about 100m inland of Praia do Arraial and passes several pousadas. Heading south from Arraial d'Ajuda towards Trancoso, the road passes a series of beaches – Pitinga, Taipe, and Rio da Barra – before reaching Trancoso.

Travel Agency Arraial Tourismo (☎ 875-1418), on Broadway, organises schooner trips to Trancoso and Caraiva. Three day catamaran trips to Parque Nacional Marinho dos Abrolhos can be arranged (minimum four people) for US$300 per person, including food and lodging (bunks on board).

Warning There's now a police post in Arraial d'Ajuda and the attitude of the police to drug-taking is less tolerant than in the past.

Beaches Praia Mucugê is good until 3 or 4 pm when the sun hides behind the hill. Many of the beach barracas are venues for do-it-yourself samba and guitar music. The barraca facing the ocean on the far right has great music and a fantastic *batida de abacaxí* (vodka and pineapple). The barracas have good fried shrimp for a few dollars.

Praia Pitinga, the river beach closest to Arraial d'Ajuda, has red and green striped sandstone cliffs, sparkling water and large-grained sand.

It's acceptable for women to go topless anywhere. Nude sunbathing is OK for both men and women on Pitinga beach and points further south.

Places to Stay Out of season, pousadas discount heavily, making some of the mid-range options quite good deals. Make sure your room has a properly fitting mosquito net over the bed or, preferably, a fan.

For cheap deals check out Rua Jotobá, which runs parallel to Broadway one block closer to the beach. At the end of the street, the *Pousada Mir a Mar* has clean apartamentos with hammocks slung outside for US$10 per person. Next door, the *Pousada Jatobá* is more basic, and has small apartamentos for the same price. Just off the main square, on Broadway, the *Pousada Lua Cheia* (☎ 875-1059) is a shady, relaxed place with apartamentos at US$15 per person.

Off Caminho do Mar (the street running to the beach), follow the signs to the *Pousada Erva Doce* (☎ 875-1113; fax 875-1071), with large, comfortable apartamentos for US$25/40 in the low season.

Tucked away on Rua das Amandoeiras, the *Pousada Céu Azul* (☎ 875-1312) has a tropical flavour, lovely gardens and a very friendly owner. Small, clean apartamentos cost US$15 per person in the low season and US$30/40 in summer. The *Pousada O Sole Mio*, about 1km from the balsa (ferry) on the road to Arraial, has been recommended by readers for its spacious, shady gardens and good Italian food.

Places to Eat If you like to eat by the kilogram, you'll do well in Arraial. *Restaurant Nóna Madeira*, on Caminho do Mar, is the best by far. A doorway on Broadway near the church leads to *Restaurant São João*, which has good-value seafood prato feito for US$5, and an extensive menu of more expensive seafood dishes. It's a friendly family-run place – you have to walk through the living room of the house to get in.

Behind the church on the edge of the bluff, *Mão na Massa* serves pasta and fish dishes. There's a great view as you eat. *Manguti*, on Rua Caminho da Praia, is recommended. Try its filé manguti for US$8. *Vale Verde* has good, cheap home cooking. *Rosa das Ventas* is not cheap but its creative mix of Austrian/Bahian cuisine is definitely worth a try. *Restaurant Champs Elysees*, on Broadway, is the place for crêpes. The barracas down at the beach have excellent fried shrimp and other seafood.

Entertainment Arraial d'Ajuda is pretty lively in the evenings. Every summer new bars compete to become the happening place for the season. Cruise Broadway for drinking and lambada or forró dancing – *Chega Mais* is a popular bar. The small shopping lanes off Caminho do Mar, A Galeria d'Ajuda and Beco dos Cores have some slick bars for more cashed-up travellers. *Cine Bar* is an open-air cinema with good movies every night for US$5. Arraial d'Ajuda's pousadas host open festas with musicians every evening. Once a month people gather on Praia de Mucugê to sing, dance and howl at the moon.

Getting There & Away For ferry details, see the Getting Around section for Porto Seguro. From the ferry landing there are four approaches to Arraial d'Ajuda: a lovely 4km hike along the beach, a taxi to town, a VW kombi to Mucugê beach or a bus to town.

Getting Around VW kombis congregate in front of the church on Broadway to ferry passengers to the beaches around Arraial. Bicycles can be hired at several shops on Broadway.

Trancoso

Trancoso lies on a grassy bluff overlooking the ocean and fantastic beaches. The central praça, known as Quadrado, is lined with small, colourful colonial buildings and casual bars and restaurants nestling under shady trees. Horse riding is popular around the area, and there are some lovely walks in the surrounding rainforest.

Places to Stay Your best bet if you are planning a long stay is to rent a house on the beach. Negotiate sizeable reductions during the low season.

Next to the school on Rua Itabela is the *Pousada Quarto Cresente* (☎/fax 868-1014), which is highly recommended. This is a quiet location, and the pousada has comfortable apartamentos, a well-stocked library, a swimming pool and superb breakfast. Friendly hosts, Eunice and Pedro, speak English, German, Dutch and Spanish. Double quartos with fan start at US$22 (US$33 in the high season), double apartamentos at around US$25 (US$45 in the high season). They also have a couple of houses for rent.

The colourful *Pousada Soloamanha* (☎ 868-1003), on the Quadrado, is a rustic place with clean collective rooms for US$20 per person during summer. Also in the Quadrado is *Pousada Seis e Meia* (☎ 868-1027), a tranquil little pousada with single/double rooms with mosquito nets for US$15 per person, with breakfast included. Out of season, it charges US$5 per person without breakfast.

The *Pousada Hibisco* (☎/fax 868-1117) is more upmarket, with large grounds and views over the forest and ocean. Double apartamentos start at US$40 (US$60 in the high season). *Pousada Capim Santo* (☎/fax 868-1122), in the Quadrado very close to the bus stop, is a highly recommended pousada/restaurant. It has comfortable apartamentos for US$40 a double (US$60 in the high season).

Places to Eat *Maré Cheia*, on the Quadrado, has a good self-serve por quilo for US$6 and prato feito for US$4. *Primavera*, close by, serves excellent home-made ice cream. *Local Bar/Retaurante* specialises in food with an Asian flavour. For good natural food, head for *Capim Santo*. Sandra is the best cook in town – her dishes are a bit more expensive (between US$10 and $35), but definitely worth it. The lobster with pineapple is delicious. On the beach, head for barraca *Raios do Sol*, where Hulysses prepares peixe amendoeira – fish wrapped in the leaves of the large Amendoeira tree behind the barraca. É uma delícia.

Entertainment *Para-Raio* is an ambient restaurant and dancing bar with outdoor tables under massive trees. *Black White Danceteria* is a large dance club open on weekends. Occasionally, raves are organised at secluded locations along the beach out of town, complete with bars, sophisticated sound and lighting systems and all-night dancing. The walking bridge across the river is missing several planks, so watch your step in the dark!

Getting There & Away Trancoso is 22km from Arraial d'Ajuda on a good dirt road, or 13km on foot along the beach. The bus from Arraial d'Ajuda to Trancoso leaves every two hours from 8 am until 7.40 pm. It originates at the ferry landing opposite Porto Seguro and stops at the bus depot in Arraial d'Ajuda, behind the main praça. Buses are less frequent during the low season. When the bus reaches Trancoso, it stops at the beach first – if you are looking for accommodation, stay on the bus until it reaches the village. Buses from Trancoso to Porto Seguro leave almost every hour from 7 am to 6 pm.

The 13km walk from Trancoso to Arraial d'Ajuda along the beach is beautiful. Hikers must ford two rivers that, according to the tides and season, are either ankle or arm-pit deep.

Caraiva

Without electricity, cars or throngs of tourists, the hamlet of Caraiva is primitive and beautiful. The village is strung out along the eastern bank of the mangrove-lined Rio Caraiva. The bus stops on the far side of the river (which is becoming rapidly developed), where small dugout canoes ferry passengers across to the village for US$0.50. The beaches are long and deserted and dashed by churning surf. A warning: the black-sand streets of the village get incredibly hot – take footwear with you at all times.

Boat trips up the Rio Caraiva and to the Parque Nacional de Monte Pascoal are easily organised in the village. The tiny fishing village of Curuípe, 9km north, has no electricity or regular accommodation, but it's possible to stay with villagers – speak to Edivaldo.

Places to Stay & Eat The *Pousada da Terra* is a rustic establishment right on the beach, with a natural-food restaurant attached. Simple quartos cost US$15 per person, with breakfast included. The *Pousada da Lagoa* (☎/fax 985-6862) is more comfortable and has a generator and a bar. Single/double apartamentos cost US$20/40 in the low season.

Dendê is a sweet, simple restaurant serving typical Bahian food – the bobó de camarão and seafood moquecas (US$10) are recommended.

Getting There & Away Buses leave Trancoso daily at 8 am and 3 pm for the 42km trip (US$5, two hours) along a reasonable dirt road to Caraiva. Buses return to Trancoso twice daily. There is a daily bus, at 7 pm, to Itabela, on Hwy BR-101, for connections north and south.

There is no road south along the coast from Caraiva – the options are to hire a boat or walk. It's a beautiful 40km walk along the beach to Cumuruxatiba, passing through the Parque Nacional de Monte Pascoal and the village of Corumbau (12km south), where there is accommodation. The walk is best done over two days, and it's only necessary to cut inland once.

Corumbau

Corumbau, on the southern side of the national park, is not as primitive as Caraiva, but it's a beautiful spot, with lots of things to do. You can go canoeing through the mangroves or on the Rio Corumbau, snorkel on offshore reefs, visit the Pataxó Indian village, or just wander along trails through the rainforest.

Places to Stay *Jocotoka Village* (☎ 288-2291; fax 288-2540) is not your usual Brazilian resort hotel – there's not a TV in sight. Run by German expat Jochen Heckhausen, the resort is geared toward taking maximum advantage of the natural beauty of the area, and has all the equipment for you to enjoy it, like kayaks and diving gear. Bungalows go for US$35/50 a single/double in the low season (US$60/80 in the high season) and apartamentos for US$25/40 (US$40/60). Prices include breakfast and dinner by candlelight. If you're in Porto Seguro, drop in and see Jochen at the Pousada dos Cais for more details. It's definitely worthwhile, especially if you're trying to get away from the tourist hordes in summer. If you're looking for something a bit cheaper, there are a couple of simple pousadas in the village.

Getting There & Away One bus leaves the large town of Itamaraju on Hwy BR-101 for Corumbau daily at 2 pm. The trip takes about three hours and costs US$5.

PARQUE NACIONAL DE MONTE PASCOAL

On 22 April 1500 the Portuguese, sailing under the command of Pedro Álvares Cabral, sighted the broad, 536m-high hump of Monte Pascoal (Mt Easter), their first glimpse of the New World. They called the land Terra da Vera Cruz (Land of the True Cross).

The park, 690km from Salvador and 479km from Vitória, contains a variety of ecosystems: Atlantic rainforest, secondary forests, swamplands and shallows, mangroves, beaches and reefs. The variety of the landscape is matched by the diversity in flora and fauna. There are several monkey species, including the endangered spider monkey, two types of sloths, anteaters, rare porcupines, capybaras, deer, jaguars, cougars and numerous species of bird.

There is a visitor centre, 14km from the western (Hwy BR-101) end of the park. It's open daily from 8 am to 4 pm, and you can pick up a guide who can accompany you on the trails or a climb of the mountain itself. The coastal side is accessible by boat or on foot from Caraiva in the north and Corumbau to the south. The north-eastern corner of the park, below Caraiva, is home to a small number of Pataxó Indians.

The spider monkey's fur is black for its first six months before adult colouring is acquired

CUMURUXATIBA

• *pop 5000* ✉ *45980-000* ☎ *073*

Sandwiched between a bluff and the ocean, this two-street beach town (pronounced koo-moo-rush-a-tee-bar) is quiet and slow-paced. There's not much to it, apart from a long beach lined with amendoeira trees, a handful of pousadas and a surprising number of good restaurants.

Boat trips to Corumbau, Caraiva and Parque Nacional de Monte Pascoal can be arranged with Leo de Escuna on his schooner *Santa Cruz de Cabralia*. Contact him at Aquamar, a barraca along the beach.

Places to Stay & Eat

If you intend to camp, try *Camping Aldeia da Lua*, Praia da Cumuruxatiba. For longer stays, houses for rent are advertised on the notice board at the Telebahia office on the main square, on Rua 13 de Maio. The *Albergue da Juventude Praia de Cumuruxatiba* (☎ 873-1020) is next to the beach on Avenida Beira Mar. The *Pousada Luana* (☎/fax 873-1090) is perched on the bluff overlooking the town and the ocean – it's worth the walk up the hill. Comfortable apartamentos with balconies and hammocks are good value at US$40 a double – discounts apply in the low season.

La Naveva is under French management and serves delicious crêpes. *Restaurant da Isabel* is a rustic place with seafood refeições, and *Falesias* is a family-run pizza restaurant with a pleasant outdoor setting. Along the beachfront, there are some great barracas, such as *Estação do Cais*, which has good music and seafood.

Getting There & Away

Cumuruxatiba is 32km north of Prado over a smooth dirt road. Buses run daily from the large town of Itamaraju on Hwy BR-101 to Cumuruxatiba, via Prado, at 6 am and 2.30 pm. Buses return to Prado daily at 5.30 and 9 am and 4 pm.

Prado & Alcobaça

These little 'big' towns on the coast south of Cumuruxatiba don't have much to offer travellers – their beaches are built up and not especially pretty. If you are heading to Cumuruxatiba to the north or Caravelas to the south, you'll have to either pass through or connect in one of them. Both towns have basic services and accommodation. Excursions to Parque Nacional Marinho dos Abrolhos are best organised in Caravelas.

On a dirt track 12km north of Prado are the semi-deserted beaches of **Paixão** and **Tororão**. The dirt road continues 22km to Cumuruxatiba. North of Cumuruxatiba, past the ocean border of Parque Nacional de Monte Pascoal, the village of Caraiva and all the way to Trancoso is a 60km stretch of relatively undeveloped coastline. Judging by the interest currently being shown by developers, it is unlikely to stay that way.

CARAVELAS

• *pop 19,000* ✉ *45900-000* ☎ *073*

Caravelas, 74km from Teixeira de Freitas on Hwy BR-101, is not only a gateway to Parque Nacional Marinho dos Abrolhos (see the next section for access details) it's also an interesting town in its own right, with a large fishing community and good beaches nearby.

Information

The Instituto Baleia Jubarte (Humpback Whale Institute), Rua 7 de Setembro 214, operates a visitor centre from 8 am to 6 pm weekdays. It also shows videos about whales and has useful information about the Parque Nacional dos Marinho Abrolhos. Abrolhos Tourismo (☎ 297-1149; fax 297-1109), on Praça Dr Imbassahi, is a private travel agency, but it also acts as a kind of unofficial tourist office. Staff speak English, French, German and Spanish. There is also a small tourist information office at the rodoviária open during summer.

Abrolhos Embarcações (☎ 297-1172), Avenida das Palmeiras 2, organises trips to Parque Nacional Marinho dos Abrolhos (see the Abrolhos section later in this chapter).

Visa card cash withdrawals can be made at the Banco do Brasil on Praça Dr Imbassahi.

A reader who spent four weeks in the area as a volunteer for a whale research project writes about Caravelas:

Caravelas is a small city with hardly any tourist facilities, which makes it a very quiet and original place. You can hardly buy a T-shirt there, and few people speak English. What also makes Caravelas special is that it lies in a delta area with mangroves and Atlantic jungle. Opposite the village is the big island of Caçumba (100 sq km), which is surrounded by the big 'arms' of the delta. Along the coast grows the mangrove and, inland, the forest. There are about 200 families living there, who cultivate the land for their own support. Some of their produce they sell on the mainland. There are three species of mangrove – red, black and white – and they all grow there. What makes the mangrove special is the extreme height of the trees (20m plus), probably the highest in the world. Enormous crabs take care of oxygen in the soil – the soil is clay and without crabs it would be too hard. In the jungle grows a variety of tropical fruits. There are lots of different species of birds and in the swamp near the shore, crocodiles live.

The second speciality of Caravelas is the harbour from where you can go to the protected marine National Park of the Abrolhos Archipelago. In wintertime (end of June to October) it is an area for humpback whales who mate and give birth there. Their population is increasing and is estimated now at about 400 to 700. A nature protection organisation is doing research into their social behaviour and is making photos for identification.

Bettina van Elk, The Netherlands

Things to See & Do

To get a feel for the town's thriving fishing industry, check out the **Cooperativa Mista dos Pescadores**, Rua da Cooperativa opposite the hospital, or wander along the riverfront to **Praça dos Pescadores**, where the fishermen hang out after coming in with the day's catch. For beaches, head for **Praia Grauçá** (8km north of town on a dirt track) and **Pontal do Sul** (across the Rio Caravelas). In addition, there are the island beaches of **Coroa da Barra** (half an hour by boat) and **Coroa Vermelha** (1½ hours by boat).

It's possible to go by boat along the mangrove-lined Rio Caravelas to the next beach town to the south, **Nova Viçosa**. Ask at the tourist office at the rodoviária, Abrolhos Tourismo or Abrolhos Embarcações (see Information earlier in this section). A snorkelling day trip to the island of Coroa Vermelho costs US$40 per person with lunch.

Places to Stay

Note that all prices in Caravelas rise at least 20% during its Carnaval, considered by locals to be the third best in the state after those of Salvador and Porto Seguro. Similar price rises can also be expected during summer.

There's a basic camping ground, *Camping Ubaitá*, at the entrance to Caravelas, but it's a long walk from the centre. In town, *Posada Shangi-Lá* (☎ 297-1059), Rua Barão do Rio Branco 219, is a friendly, cheap place to stay. Quartos cost US$7/13 a single/double and apartamentos go for US$9/17. The *Pousada Caravalense* (☎/fax 297-1182) is across the road from the bus station. Its apartamentos are US$10/20.

Across the river, on Ilha da Caçumba, the *Pousada da Ilha* is a real retreat, with a bar and a vegetarian restaurant. You can also get a massage here. Rooms cost around US$15 per person. To get there, go to Abrolhos Tourismo and ask them to call the pousada by radio. The pousada will send someone across in a boat to pick you up from the pier.

At Praia Grauçá, the budget option is the *Pousada do Juqita* (☎ 874-1038), close to the final bus stop. Clean apartamentos cost US$10 per person. Also on Praia Grauçá is Caravelas' top-end option, the four-star *Hotel Marina Porto Abrolhos* (☎ 874-1060; fax 874-1082) with chalets starting at US$64/80.

Places to Eat

The best places are out at Praia Grauçá. Seafood enthusiasts should head for *Museu da Baleia* and *Chalé Barra*. *Perplexo Creperia* is also recommended. In town try *Gaiola Aberta*, Rua 7 de Setembro 178, for home cooking, or *Encontro dos Amigos*, Rua das Palmeiras 370, for seafood specials.

Getting There & Away

Air Pantanal Linhas Aéras flies to Caravelas from São Paulo.

Bus The rodoviária is in the centre of town on Praça Teófilo Ofon. The Expresso Brasileiro bus company runs five buses daily from Teixeira de Freitas on Hwy BR-101 to Caravelas via Alcobaça, the first at 6.50 am and the last at 6.20 pm. The trip takes about two hours and costs US$5.

If you're heading north from Caravelas, catch the 11.45 am bus to Alcobaça to connect with the 12.20 pm bus to Prado. If you're lucky, you can then connect with the 1.20 pm bus to Cumuruxatiba, about an hour from Prado.

Getting Around

Regular local buses to Barra (for Praia Grauçá) leave hourly from 7.30 am until 10 pm from the rodoviária. The fare is US$0.50.

PARQUE NACIONAL MARINHO DOS ABROLHOS

Abrolhos, Brazil's first marine park, covers part of an archipelago 80km offshore from Caravelas. In 1832, Charles Darwin visited here while voyaging with HMS *Beagle*. The archipelago consists of five islands, but the only inhabited one is Santa Bárbara, which has a lighthouse, built in 1861, and a handful of buildings. Abrolhos is being preserved because of its coral reefs and crystal-clear waters. Underwater fishing within the park is prohibited. The only approach is by boat, and staying on the islands is prohibited. The Brazilian navy considers the area strategic, therefore only underwater photography is permitted.

From June to October the park is home to a large number of humpback whales, who come to give birth in the warm waters. Whale-watching is becoming very popular.

Getting There & Away

Caravelas Caravelas is the most popular gateway to the park, with several operators offering a wide range of options, from day trips to five day cruises. Abrolhos Tourismo (☎ 297-1149) runs a popular two day schooner trip, with an overnight stay on board, for US$170 per person. The price includes park entrance fees, all meals, soft drinks and water. Snorkel hire costs an extra US$10. They also offer day trips for US$99 and week-long treks from Cumuruxatiba to Trancoso for US$250. Abrolhos Embarcações (☎ 297-1172), Avenida das Palmeiras 2, offers a similar two day trip, or day trips by launch for US$95, including snacks and drinks.

Arraial d'Ajuda From Arraial d'Ajuda, Arraial Tourismo on Broadway organises three day catamaran trips that cruise south along the Bahian coast, then on to Abrolhos. The fare of US$300 per person includes food, lodging (bunks on the boat), transport and visitor's licence from the Capitânia of Porto Seguro. A minimum of four passengers is needed.

West of Salvador

FEIRA DE SANTANA

• *pop 450,000* ✉ *44000-000* ☎ *075*

At the crossroads of Hwys BR-101, BR-116 and BR-124, Feira de Santana is the main city of Bahia's interior, and a great cattle centre. There's not much to see here except the **Feira de Gado**, the big Monday cattle market (lots of tough leather) – which is great fun, but don't expect to buy much – and the **Mercado de Arte Popular** (open daily except Sunday). The **Casa do Sertão**, a folklore museum, and **Museu Regional** might also be worth a look.

Special Events

Two months after Carnaval, Feira de Santana is the scene of the Micareta – a 60-year-old local version of Carnaval that brings together the best trios elétricos of Salvador, with local blocos, samba schools and folklore groups.

The main action of the Micareta takes place on Avenida Getúlio Vargas, the city's main street, where 20 trios bop along for five days. The festivities begin on Thursday with a boisterous dance and opening ceremony. For those who missed out on Carnaval in Salvador, the Micareta could be the next best thing.

Places to Stay

There are several cheap hotels near the rodoviária, such as the *Hotel Samburá* (☎ 221-8511), Praça Dr Jackson do Amauri 132, which charges US$15/25 for singles/doubles. In the top price range, there's the *Feira Palace* (☎ 221-5011; fax 221-5409), Avenida Maria Quitéria 1572. It's a four-star affair with apartamentos starting at US$80/100.

Getting There & Away

Frequent buses make the two hour journey from Salvador for US$4. The rodoviária features an eye-catching mural painted by Lénio Braga in 1967.

SALVADOR TO LENÇÓIS

The 6 hour bus odyssey from Salvador to Lençóis first goes through Feira de Santana and then continues through typical sertão countryside: patches of low scrub and cactus where scrawny cattle graze and hawks circle above.

The bus stops for lunch at Itaberaba, where the rodoviária restaurant serves two typical sertão dishes: *carne de sol com pirão de leite* (dried salted beef with served with a manioc and milk sauce to take the edge off the salt) and *sopa de feijão* (bean soup with floating UPO – unidentified pigs' organs).

LENÇÓIS

• *pop 8000* ✉ *46960-000* ☎ *075*

Lençóis (pronunced leng-sow-iss) lies in a gorgeous, wooded mountain region – the Chapada Diamantina – an oasis of green in the dusty sertão. You'll find solitude, small towns steeped in the history and superstition of the *garimpeiros* (prospectors), and great hiking to peaks, waterfalls and rivers. If you want to see something different in Brazil, and have time for only one excursion into the Northeastern interior, this is the one.

The natural beauty of the region and the tranquillity of the small, colonial towns has attracted a steady trickle of travellers for several years; some have never left. These new residents have spearheaded an active environmental movement that successfully lobbied the government to declare the region a national park.

History

The history of Lençóis epitomises the story of the diamond boom and subsequent bust. After earlier expeditions by *bandeirantes* (bands of Paulistas who explored the Brazilian interior while searching for gold and Indians to enslave) proved fruitless, the first diamonds were found in Chapada Velha in 1822. After large strikes in the Rio Mucujê in 1844, a motley collection of prospectors, roughnecks and adventurers arrived from all over Brazil to seek their fortunes.

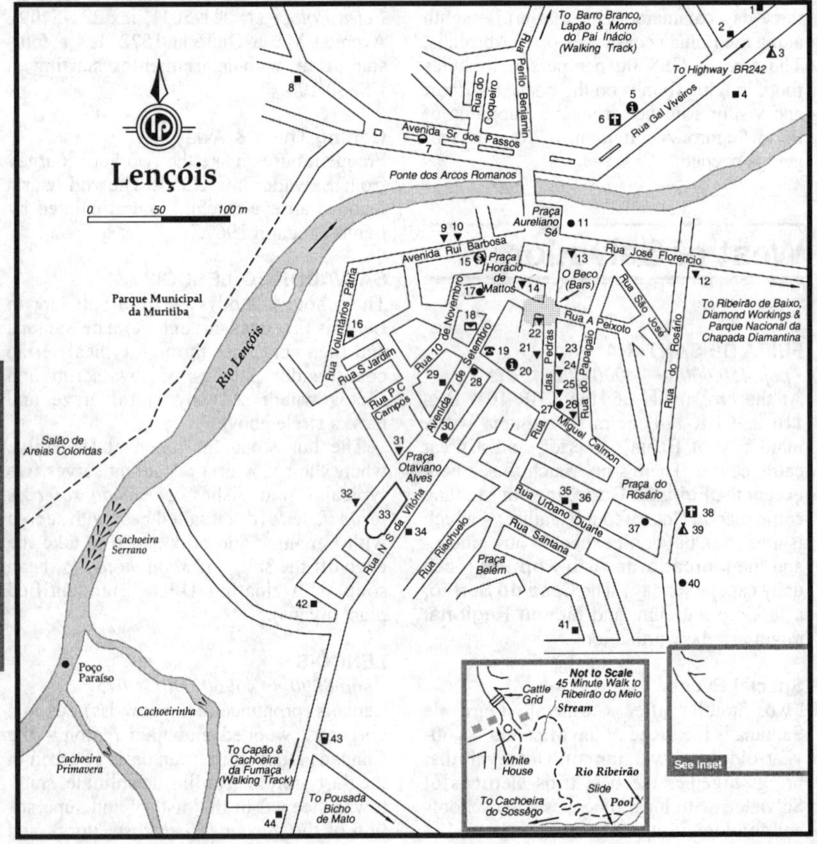

Garimpeiros began to work the mines, searching for diamonds in alluvial deposits. They settled in makeshift tents which, from the hills above, looked like sheets of laundry drying in the wind – hence the name of Lençóis (Portuguese for sheets). The tents of these diamond prospectors grew into cities: Vila Velha de Palmeiras, Andaraí, Piatã, Igatú and the most attractive of them all, the stone city of Lençóis. Exaggerated stories of endless riches in the Diamantina mines precipitated mass migrations, but the area was rich in dirty industrial stones, not display-quality gems.

At the height of the diamond boom, the French – who purchased diamonds and used them to drill the Panama Canal (1881-89), St Gothard Tunnel, and London Underground – built a vice consulate in Lençóis. French fashions and bons mots made their way into town, but with the depletion of diamonds, the fall-off in French demand (and subsequently the fall in diamond prices on the international market), the abolition of slavery, and the newly discovered South. African mines, the boom went bust at the beginning of the 20th century.

The town's economy has long since turned to coffee and manioc cultivation, and to tourism. But diamonds are what the locals still dream of. Powerful and destructive water pumps were banned in 1995, so the last few garimpeiros have returned to traditional methods to extract diamonds from the riverbeds.

Geology

According to geologists, the diamonds in Chapada Diamantina were formed millions of years ago near present-day Namibia. Interestingly, Bahia was contiguous with Africa before the continental drift. The diamonds were mixed with pebbles, swept into the depths of the sea – which covered what is now inland Brazil – and imprisoned when the seabed turned to stone. This layer of conglomerate stone was elevated, and the forces of erosion released the trapped diamonds, which were then came to rest in the riverbeds.

Information

The Secretária de Tourismo Lençóis has a tourist office on Avenida Senor dos Passos. The office has photographs of the main attractions in the Chapada Diamantina.

For any information about Lençóis or the Chapada Diamantina, seek out Olivia Taylor, a very helpful young Englishwoman who

PLACES TO STAY

1 Casa da Geléia
2 Pousada Alcino
3 Camping Alquimia
4 Pousada Canto das Águas
8 Pousada Casa da Hélia
16 Pousada Diangela
29 Nossa Casa
34 Hotel Colonial
35 Pousalegre
36 Re Pousada
39 Camping Lumiar
41 Pousada dos Duendes
42 Pousada de Lençóis
44 Portal Lençóis

PLACES TO EAT

9 Grisante
10 Pizzarela Pizza House
12 Beco da Coruja
13 Restaurant Amigo da Onça
14 Museu do Garimpo & Lanchonete Zacáo
21 Salon Mistura Fina
22 Arte Lanches
23 Doceria Vai Quem Quer
24 Dona Joaninha
25 Brilhante
26 Restaurant Os Artistas Damassa
31 Picanha na Praça
32 O Kilo

OTHER

5 Tourist Office
6 Igreja Senhor dos Passos
7 Rodoviária
11 Mercado Municipal
15 Banco do Brasil
17 Old French Vice Consulate
18 Post Office
19 Posto Telefônica
20 Cirtur
27 Saturno Informações
28 Lentur
30 Prefeitura Municipal
33 Open Air Theatre
37 Casa de Afrânio Peixoto
38 Igreja Rosário
40 Sr Dazim Horse Rental
43 Zion Bar

has made Lençóis her home. Olivia speaks English, Spanish, some French, and Portuguese with a Lençóis accent. She can be contacted through Saturno Informações or at Pousada das Duendes. She guides all-day trips on foot and is the only native English speaker guiding the three day hikes through the park.

Money Banco do Brasil charges a US$10 fee to change cash and US$20 for travellers cheques (any amount). It doesn't charge for Visa withdrawals.

Travel Agencies Lentur (☎/fax 334-1271), on Avenida 7 de Setembro, runs day trips by car to several destinations within the park for US$20 per person (a guide, admission fees and torches are included in the price). Cirtur (☎ 334-1133), Rua da Baderna 41, offers similar deals. Saturno Informações (☎/fax 334-1229), Rua da Baderna 95, arranges tours by foot or by car, and also operates a housing rental service. At the same address, Pé de Trilha (☎/fax 334-1124) also organises car and walking trips.

Things to See

The city is pretty and easily seen on foot, although, unfortunately, most of the buildings are closed to the public. See the 19th century **French vice-consulate**, a beige building where diamond commerce was negotiated, and **Casa de Afrânio Peixoto** (House & Museum of Afrânio Peixoto), with the personal effects and works of the writer Afrânio Peixoto. The **Prefeitura Municipal**, at Praça Otaviano Alves 8, is a pretty building with interesting B&W photos of old Lenço. Also worth a visit is **Lanchonete Zacão**, run by local historian Mestre Oswaldo, which displays various mining relics and artefacts.

Special Events

The principal holidays take place in January and September. Festa de Senhor dos Passos starts on 24 January, and culminates on 2 February with the Noite dos Garimpeiros (Prospectors' Night). Semana de Afrânio Peixoto, a week dedicated to the author, is held from 11 to 18 December and coincides with the municipality's emancipation from slavery. Lamentação das Almas is a mystic festival held during Lent. Lençóis is also noted for Jarê, the regional variation of Candomblé.

Another important celebration is the Festa da São João, from 23 to 25 June. There's a huge street party, bonfires outside every house, and traditional dancing.

Places to Stay

Lençóis has plenty of places to stay, but you should still try to reserve at weekends – and definitely book in advance during the high seasons: January/February and June/July. Most of the cheaper places have collective rooms and charge on a per-person basis. For longer stays, think about renting a house.

Places to Stay – Budget

Camping Lumiar, on Praça do Rosário, has shady camp sites, passable bathrooms, a bar and a restaurant – but watch out for Pablito and his marauding chickens. The cost is US$4 per person. Another good camping option is *Alquimia*, opposite Pousada Alcino. It also has some cheap rooms to rent.

The *Pousalegre* (☎/fax 334-1124) is a favourite with travellers. The rooms are certainly basic (there's a lack of windows and furniture), but the friendly staff and good breakfast (and other meals) more than compensate. Quartos cost US$5 per person without breakfast or US$8 per person with. Close by, the *Re Pousada* is also a good option, and charges the same rates.

The *Pousada dos Duendes* (☎/fax 334-1229), at Rua do Pires, is a small pousada with a relaxed atmosphere. Run by Olivia and Rao, it's a short walk from the centre, in a quiet location. Collective rooms cost US$5 per person, or US$8 with breakfast. The *Pousada Diangela* (☎ 334-1192) is a large, bright building with a pleasant eating area and quartos for US$8 per person (US$10 with breakfast). Apartamentos cost US$15 per person with breakfast.

Pousada Nossa Casa (☎ 334-1258), in the centre of town, is a friendly place run by Ana and Ze Henrique. An excellent budget option, quartos are US$15 per person with breakfast, a bit less in the low season. The *Pousada Alcino* (☎/fax 334-1171), Rua Tomba Surrão 139, is in a beautifully converted colonial building. Quartos cost US$15 per person, including a highly recommended breakfast. Alcino speaks a bit of English and French. The *Pousada Casa da Hélia* (☎ 334-1143), on Rua da Muritiba, is in a quiet area and is a short walk from the rodoviária. Quartos cost US$10 per person, with the pousada's famous breakfast included.

Places to Stay – Mid-Range

The *Hotel Colonial* (☎/fax 334-1114), Praça Otaviano Alves 750, has pleasant single/double/triple apartamentos for US$20/40/55. Discounts of up to 20% apply in the low season. Highly recommended for solo, mature travellers, *Casa da Geléia* (☎/fax 334-1151), Rua Gal Viveiros 36, has two apartamentos for rent. Hosts Zé Carlos and Lia are very friendly. Zé Carlos is a lawyer in town, and speaks good English. He is also a keen birder. The cost is US$25 a double in the low season and US$35 in the high. The range of home-made jams here is unbelievable, and even if you don't choose to stay here, come along and have a taste! You won't be able to resist taking some trekking with you.

Places to Stay – Top End

Discounts of up to 30% apply at all these hotels in the low season. The *Pousada Canto das Águas* (☎/fax 334-1154), on Avenida Sr dos Passos, has a great position, in a landscaped garden beside the river. Facilities include a restaurant, bar and swimming pool. The apartamentos overlook the cascades, which provide the pousada's background music – hence the name, which translates as Song of the Waters. Prices start at US$56/63/78 for singles/doubles/triples, including an enormous breakfast. The presidential suite with spa goes for US$125. Book well in advance during summer. At night, dinner-plate-sized toads guard the front gate!

At the top end of town is the attractive *Pousada de Lençóis* (☎ 334-1102; fax 334-1180), Rua Altina Alves 747, with gardens, swimming pool, restaurant and bar. Single/double/triple apartamentos with air-conditioning start at US$72/80/100. Books about the region are sold at the reception desk.

The new luxury five-star hotel in town is the *Portal Lençóis* (☎/fax 334-1233), on Rua Chacára Grota. Suites are US$117/130 a single/double and bungalows are US$158/176. There are great views of Lençóis from the poolside.

Places to Eat

If you like breakfast, you'll never want to leave Lençóis, where it's included in the room price of numerous lodgings, which seem to be competing for the coveted 'BBB' (Best Breakfast in Brazil) title. A local breakfast staple is baje (a warm, buttered manioc pancake with the consistency of a very chewy Styrofoam polymer). After breakfast, you've only got a few hours until you're faced with equally magnificent culinary options for the other meals of the day!

If you're camping or not eating breakfast at a pousada, *Dona Joaninha*, in Rua das Pedras, serves an excellent spread, as does *Doceria Vai Quem Quer*, also in Rua das Pedras. They also serve cakes, mousses and other sweet, delicious things.

The vegetarian restaurant *Beco da Coruja*, on Rua do Rosário, offers tasty soups, pizza and other vegetarian specialities. Carnivores should head for *Picanha na Praça* for a highly recommended churrasco. Also in the main square *Pizzarela Pizza House* and *Grisante* serve good, cheap meals and snacks – try Grisante's carne do sol with aipim frito (salted meat and fried manioc). *Lanchonete Zacão* serves great fruit juices and amazing bolinho de queijo (hot fried balls of dough filled with melted cheese) a must during cold weather. It also sells natural yoghurt and treacle.

Brilhante is a colourful natural-food store and café with healthy sandwiches, snacks and juices. The *Pousalegre* (see Places to Stay earlier in this section) serves inexpensive meals – Rosa's moqueca is justly famous. For the best self-serve in town, try *O Kilo*. *Restaurant Os Artistas Damassa* has good, cheap Italian food, and for a real taste of Europe, visit *Salon Mistura Fina*, where you can sip tea while listening to classical music. It also serves good, cheap breakfasts, lunches and dinners. Other popular restaurants in town worth visiting are *Arte Lanches*, for great sandwiches, and *Restaurant Amigo da Onça*, for home cooking and old-time dancing on weekends.

Entertainment

The bars around the Beco and *Zion Bar*, a bit further away, are popular evening hangouts.

Things to Buy

There are night stalls on Praça Horácio de Mattos selling crochet, lacework, trinkets and bottles of coloured sand collected at nearby Salão de Areias Coloridas. There are many craft stores on Rua das Pedras and Rua Miguel Calmon selling similar stuff. For jams, you can't go past the Casa da Geleia (see Places to Stay earlier in this section).

If you've been doing a lot of walking and need a massage, call Deiter (☎ 334-1200), a German who lives in town. He has magic hands, and charges US$20 for an hour – it's well worth it!

Getting There & Away

Air There's a new airport in Lençóis, inaugurated just as we were researching this edition. For flight details, check with travel agents in Salvador.

Bus The rodoviária is on the edge of town, beside the river. Buses to Salvador leave daily at 8 am and 11.30 pm. Buses to Lençóis leave Salvador at 7.30 am and 11.30 pm. The six hour trip costs US$20. If you arrive in Lençóis in the early hours, there will always be tour reps and pousada owners waiting to greet you. Most allow you to stay in their pousada the rest of the night and will only charge for breakfast. If you want to change pousadas next day, there's usually no problem. Tour company reps are also happy to drop you off at the pousada of your choice if you've already organised one.

Car If you are driving in Lençóis, there is a fuel station some 22km east of town on Hwy BR-242, in Tanquinho. The nearest station to the west is around 30km away. It's not a good idea to rely on the improvised fuel station in Lençóis, which may or may not be open, have fuel or want to sell it.

Getting Around

The town is easily covered on foot. For transport further afield, see the following section on Parque Nacional da Chapada Diamantina.

PARQUE NACIONAL DA CHAPADA DIAMANTINA

Many of the foreigners and Brazilians who came to visit have settled permanently in Lençóis. They have been the backbone of a strong ecological movement, which is in direct opposition to the extractive mentality of the garimpeiros and many of the locals. Riverbeds have been dug up, waters poisoned and game hunted for food and sport. Much of the land has been ravaged by forest fires, while the hunting and depletion of habitat has thinned the animal population severely.

After six years of bureaucratic battles, biologist Roy Funch helped convince the government to create the Parque Nacional da Chapada Diamantina to protect the natural beauty of the area. Signed into law in 1985, the park roughly spans the quadrangle formed by the cities of Lençóis and Mucujê, Palmeiras and Andaraí. The park, 1520 sq km of the Sincora Range of the Diamantina Plateau, has several species of monkey, beautiful views, clean waterfalls, rivers and streams, and an endless network of trails. Although bromeliads, velosiaceas, philodendrons and strawflowers are protected by law, these plants have been

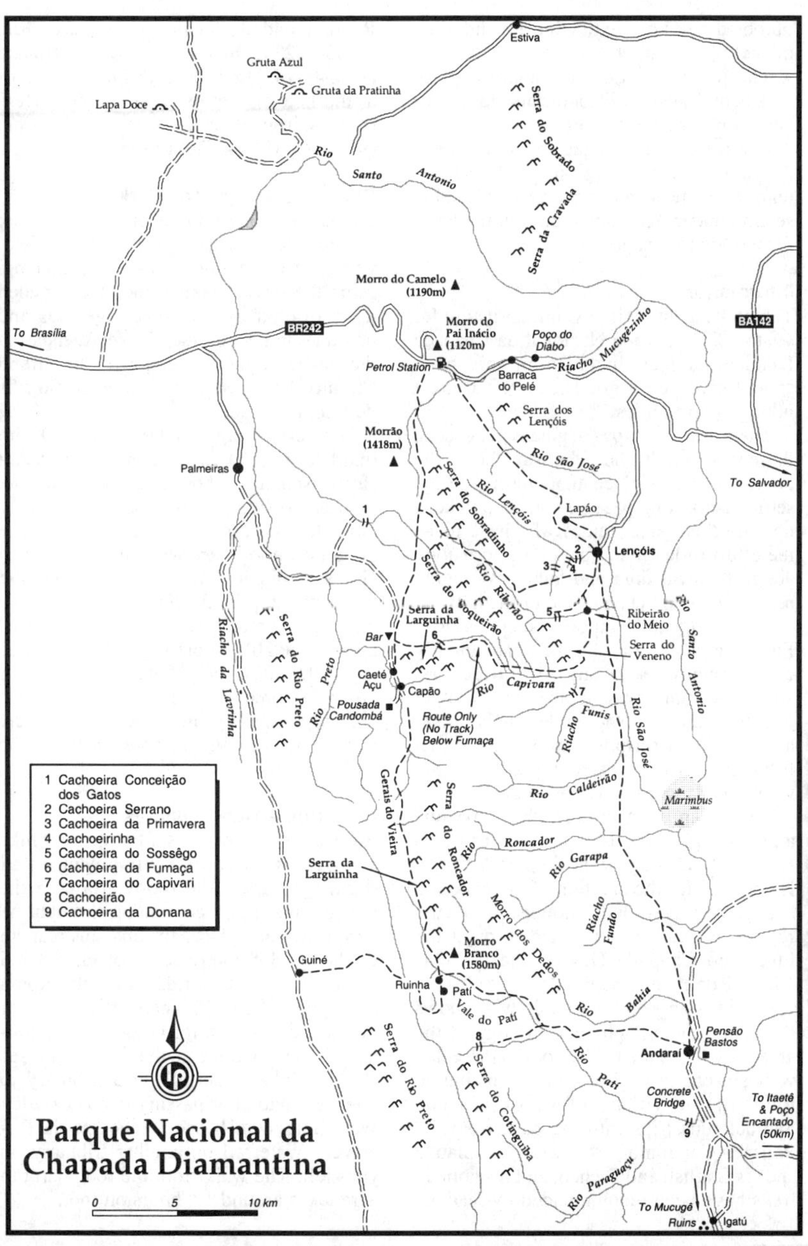

THE NORTHEAST

uprooted nearly to extinction for the ornamental plant market.

The park is particularly interesting for rock hounds, who will appreciate the curious geomorphology of the region.

For information regarding minimising the impact of camping on fragile ecosystems, see the Minimum Impact Camping section under Accommodation in the Facts for the Visitor chapter.

Information

The park has little, if any, infrastructure for visitors. The Parque Nacional da Chapada Diamantina map included in this book should give you a good idea of the great hiking opportunities.

There are three types of guides in Lençóis: those who simply show the way, those who go to the same place that you're going, setting a cracking pace so you need to keep up with them, and guides who have made the effort to learn and pass on information about the local flora and fauna. We highly recommend you choose one of the latter.

Knowledgeable guides, such as Roy Funch and Olivia Taylor, can greatly enhance enjoyment of any trip into the park, and we recommend you take one. Whether you do or not, you should definitely not go alone. In the descriptions of park hikes that follow, we've indicated those trips that would be dangerous without a guide.

Funch, an ex-American from Arizona and now a naturalised citizen, came to Brazil 20 years ago with the Peace Corps. He pushed for the creation of the park and has a very detailed knowledge of the region. He can be contacted through the Fundação Chapada Diamantina (☎ 334-1305), Rua Pé de Ladeira 212.

Olivia is an excellent guide who knows the history, geography and biology of the area, as well as the trails. For the three day walk she charges US$20 per day, including food. In the village of Capão, Claude Samuel runs trips into the park from the Pousada Candombá (☎ 332-2176). Claude speaks English and French, and his donkey treks have been recommended by readers. Recommended local guides are Rao (☎ 334-1229), João (☎ 334-1221), Trajano (☎ 334-1143), Zoi (ask for him in town or at the hotels), Carlos (☎ 334-1331), Henrique Gironha (ask in town), Virginia (☎ 334-1331) and Rosa from Pousalegre.

Day Trips Around the Park

For day trips around Lençóis, you can walk or hire a horse. For day trips further afield, you have the option of walking, hitching, using the bus, or taking one of the guided tours offered by the travel agencies and pousadas in Lençóis (see Travel Agencies in the earlier Lençóis section). The Grand Circuit, described later in this section, is best done on foot.

For horse rental, contact Senhor Dazim (marked on the Lençóis map as 'Sr Dazim Horse Rental'), who has horses available. There's no sign on his house, so you may have to ask around – everyone in the neighbourhood knows him. You can choose from his list of horse rides and treks, which are all accompanied. Sample prices per person are: one hour (US$3); half a day (US$20); whole day (US$26); three days (US$60). Negotiate discounts for groups of three or more.

Bus services are infrequent and scarce, particularly to the remote parts of the park.

Day Trips Around Lençóis

Rio Lençóis You can start a pleasant hike along the Rio Lençóis by following a trail south-west from the rodoviária (see the Lençóis map) and continuing through the Parque Municipal da Muritiba, upstream to Cachoeira Serrano (a series of rapids) and Salão de Areias Coloridas (literally 'Room of Coloured Sands'), where artisans gather their matéria prima for bottled sand paintings. If you continue up the river, you'll see Cachoeirinha Waterfall on a tributary to your left, and after passing Poço O'Halley Waterhole, you'll see Cachoeira da Primavera Waterfall on another tributary on your left. The walk from the rodoviária to here takes around 1½ hours on foot.

Ribeirão do Meio & Cachoeira do Sossêgo This hike (45 minutes) from Lençóis to Ribeirão do Meio is also relaxing. Take the road uphill from Camping Lumiar, ignoring the left turning you'll see after about 100m, and continue until the road ends at a white house. After continuing for a short distance, take the left fork of a trail that descends and crosses a stream. Keep following the track until you reach a ridge overlooking Rio Ribeirão, a tributary of Rio São José.

At the foot of the ridge, you'll find Ribeirão do Meio, a series of swimming holes with a natural waterslide (bring old clothes or borrow a burlap sack). It is *very* important not to walk up the slide: several bathers who have done so have met with nasty accidents. Instead, swim across to the far side of the pool and climb the dry rocks at the side of the slide before launching off.

Upstream from Ribeirão do Meio, a trail leads to Cachoeira do Sossêgo waterfall. The hike involves a great deal of stone-hopping along the riverbed. Don't attempt this hike without a guide, as there have been several fatal accidents recently. On *no* account should you attempt this trail during high water or rain: the river stones are covered with lichen, which becomes impossibly slippery. To walk from Lençóis to Cahoeira do Sossêgo and back takes around five hours.

Gruta do Lapão This is probably the largest sandstone cave in South America. Access is tricky and it's necessary to take a guide. The walk takes around four hours.

Day Trips Further Afield

Lapa Doce, Gruta da Pratinha & Gruta Azul These three sights are best visited by car – the guided day trips offered by travel agents and other operators in Lençóis usually take in all of these sights. Lapa Doce (70km from Lençóis, then a 25 minute hike to the entrance) is a huge cave formed by a subterranean river. Access to the cave is via an immense sinkhole; inside there's an impressive assortment of stalagmites and stalactites that prompt erotic comparisons. Entry is US$1.

About 12km from this cave are Gruta da Pratinha and Gruta Azul, two more interesting caves that can also be visited for US$1.

Rio Mucugêzinho This river, 25km from Lençóis, is a super day trip. Take the 7 am bus, and ask the driver to let you off at Mucugêzinho Bar – the bus passes this place again at around 4 pm on its return trip to Lençóis. Pick your way about 2km downstream to **Poço do Diabo** (Devil's Well), a swimming hole with a 30m waterfall. Further upstream, you'll find Rita and Marco, who have set up house in a cave, and run a snack bar outside.

Morro do Pai Inácio & Barro Branco Morro do Pai Inácio (1120m) is the most prominent peak in the immediate area. It's 27km from Lençóis and easily accessible from the highway. An easy but steep trail takes you to the summit (200m above the highway) for a beautiful view.

Hikers may want to take the trail along Barro Branco between Lençóis and Morro do Pai Inácio – allow four or five hours one way for the hike.

Palmeiras, Capão & Cachoeira da Fumaça Palmeiras, 56km from Lençóis, is a drowsy little town with a slow, slow pace and a scenic riverside position. The streets are lined with colourful houses. There is one pousada in the town and a couple of cheap places to stay.

The hamlet of Capão is 20km from Palmeiras by road (see the later Grand Circuit section for a description of the hiking trail connecting Capão with Lençóis). From here, there's a 6km trail (two hours on foot) to the top of Cachoeira da Fumaça, also known as the Glass Waterfall, after missionary George Glass, which plummets 420m – the longest waterfall in Brazil. Although marked on the map, the route to the bottom of the waterfall is very difficult, and isn't recommended without a guide.

The Three Day Walk

To go to the bottom of Cachoeira da Fumaça is a tiring three day walk, but much easier than the Inca Trail. The walk itself is extremely beautiful, passing other waterfalls on the way and enabling you to sleep in caves. You leave Lençóis in the morning of the first day and arrive in Capão on the third day. An extra day can be added walking back to Lençóis or you can continue with the Grand Circuit.

The Grand Circuit

The grand circuit of the park covers around 100km and is best done on foot in an anticlockwise direction. It takes about five days, but you should allow eight days if you include highly recommended side trips, such as Igatú and Cachoeira da Fumaça.

Lençóis to Capão You'll need a full day to hike this section. From Lençóis, follow the main trail west, crossing the river several times, and when you reach the 'bar', take the track to the left. When you reach Caeté Açu, follow the road to Capão.

Capão to Vale do Patí This section, which crosses the beautiful plains region of Gerais do Vieira, is best covered in two comfortable days, although it's possible to do it in one very long day.

The tiny settlement of Capão serves as a base for the highly recommended hike to Cachoeira da Fumaça (see the description in the earlier Day Trips Further Afield section). In Capão, you can camp or stay at the *Pousada Candombá* for US$5 per person, with breakfast an additional US$2.

Vale do Patí to Andaraí & Ruinha This section takes a day, but you should allow an extra day to potter around the valley: for example, doing a side trip to Cachoeirão (a delightful waterfall) or enjoying the atmosphere in the tiny ghost settlement of Ruinha.

Poço Encantado & Igatú These side trips are highly recommended. Poço Encantado, 56km from Andaraí, is an underground lake that is clear blue and stunningly beautiful. You'll need a car to get there; hitching is difficult because there is very little traffic.

Igatú, 12km from Andaraí, is a small community with an intriguing set of ruins (highly recommended). Either walk or drive to Igatú. In Andaraí, either camp or stay at the basic *Pensão Bastos*.

Andaraí to Lençóis This is not a very interesting walk. It's along a dirt road, not a trail, and the scenery is the destruction caused by machine mining. Many choose to bus this section, but if you decide to walk, allow two days. On the first night, camp at a site near Rio Roncador. After the Rio Roncador, you pass Marimbus, a micro-region with characteristics similar to the Pantanal. Sandro and Diana (☎ 334-1292) organise excellent canoe trips that pass the Cachoeira do Roncador.

RIO SÃO FRANCISCO

For the Brazilian, particularly the Nordestino, it's impossible to speak about the Rio São Francisco without a dose of pride and emotion. The third most important river in Brazil, after the Rio Amazonas and Rio Paraguai, there is no river that is anthropomorphised like the São Francisco. Those who live along its banks speak of it as a friend – hence the affectionate nickname *velho chico* or *chicão* (chico is short for Francisco).

The geographical situation of the São Francisco gave it a prominence in the colonial history of Brazil that surpassed the Amazon. Born in the Serra da Canastra, 1500m high in Minas Gerais, the Rio São Francisco descends from south to north, crossing the greater part of the Northeast sertão, and completing its 3160km journey in the Atlantic Ocean after slicing through the states of Minas Gerais and Bahia, and delineating the borders of the states of Bahia, Pernambuco, Sergipe and Alagoas.

For three centuries the São Francisco, also called the 'river of national unity', represented the only connection between the

Sex & the Single Spix Macaw

There's a spix macaw (*Cyanopsitta spixxi*) out west in Bahia they call the *professore* (teacher). That's because he's the last of his species in the wild – the only one who can pass on the knowledge of how to survive in the sparse, dry *caatinga* (bushland). News of his movements travels fast among the locals, who watch for the blue flash of his broad wings and long tail feathers. Every night he returns to the same tree, where locals remember large numbers of the birds used to gather.

There are only 31 females in captivity, and one of these is now part of a programme to mate the professore with one of his own. Brazilian biologist Marcos da Re, head of the BirdLife International project attempting to regenerate the species in the wild, has taught the female to eat the local seeds, and worked at strengthening her wing muscles for long flights in search of food.

There's been a slight hitch, however, in that the professore has mated with a smaller blue-winged macaw, flying around with her for most of the day before returning to his solitary roost. Aviculturists support the idea of capturing the professore, killing or otherwise removing the blue-winged, and trying to mate the two spix macaws before releasing them. Conservationists agree in getting rid of the blue-winged, but are against the captive raising theory. They are concerned that if the professore is held captive, he may lose the knowledge that makes him the professore.

'We like it when we see him fly past,' say the locals. 'It us brings luck.' They tell myths and stories about the professore to their children, and watch for poachers who may try to capture him: a breeding pair of spix macaws is worth $50,000 on the black market.

Andrew Draffen

small towns at the extremes of the sertão and the coast. 'Discovered' in the 17th century, the river was the best of the few routes available to penetrate the semi-arid Northeastern interior. Thus the frontier grew along the margins of the river. The economy of these settlements was based on cattle, to provide desperately needed food for the gold miners in Minas Gerais in the 18th century and, later, to feed workers in the cacao plantations in southern Bahia.

Although the inhabitants of the region were often separated by enormous distances, cattle ranching proved a common bond and produced a culture that can be seen today in the region's folklore, music and art.

The history of this area is legendary in Brazil: the tough *vaqueiros* (cowboys of the Northeast) who drove the cattle; the commerce in salt (to fatten the cows); the cultivation of rice; the rise in banditry; the battles between the big landowners; and the religious fanaticism of Canudos. For more information, see the History section in the Facts about the Country chapter.

The slow waters of the São Francisco have been so vital to Brazil because in a region with devastating periodic droughts, the river provides one of the only guaranteed sources of water. The people who live there know this, and thus, over the centuries, they have created hundreds of stories, fairy tales and myths about the river.

One example is the *bicho da água* (beast of the water). It is a creature, part animal and part man, that walks on the bottom of the river and snores. The crews on the riverboats throw tobacco to the bicho da água for protection.

The river's width varies from two handspans at its source in the Serra da Canastre, an empty, uninhabitable region where nothing grows, to 40km at the Lagoa do Sobradinho, the biggest artificial lake in the world. As a result, Nordestinos believe that São Francisco is a gift of God to the people of the sertão to recompense all their suffering in the drought-plagued land.

River Travel

People have always travelled along the São Francisco. In the beginning there were sailing boats and rowing boats, then came the motorboats, which became famous because of the personalities of the *barqueiros* who drove the boats and put *carrancas* on the front of them. Carrancas are wooden sculptures that represent an animal-like face – part dog, part wolf – with big teeth and open mouth. These sculptures are now popular as folk art, and are sold in Salvador and at fairs along the river.

Today, with the river cities linked by roads, river traffic has decreased drastically, but it shouldn't prove too hard to find boats for short trips on local market days (usually Saturday). See the section on Penedo in the Alagoas chapter for details of trips on the lower Rio São Francisco.

Bom Jesus da Lapa, on the São Francisco in the interior of Bahia, is the site of one of the most important religious festivals and processions in the sertão. The festival is held on 6 August.

It may be possible to hire a local boat from Juazeiro, on the Pernambuco-Bahia border, to Xique-Xique, 200km downstream in Bahia.

A reader wrote to us with the following assessment of river travel along the Rio São Francisco:

> The river appears dead as a means of commercial travel, and only a small amount of transport by local narrow boat continues between the villages. The river has become sluggish as a result of construction of a hydroelectric plant on the seaward side of Lagoa do Sobradinho, and silting is so severe in some places that the shallow-draught local boats touch bottom.
>
> Xique-Xique, at the southern end of Lagoa do Sobradinho, appears to have a mainly school-age population, most of whom are learning English and are keen to use it. A couple of islands close to the town have been declared a reserve for the protection of anteaters, which are said to be the only ones in the area.

Sergipe & Alagoas

Sergipe

Sergipe is Brazil's smallest state. It has all three zones typical of the Northeast: litoral, zona da mata and sertão. The coastal zone is wide and sectioned with valleys, with many towns dotted along the rivers.

What is there to see? There are a couple of interesting historical towns – Laranjeiras in particular is well worth a visit – and the towns along the Rio São Francisco have a unique, captivating culture – principally Propriá and Neópolis. The beaches, with their shallow, muddy waters, are not up to snuff, and the capital, Aracaju, is as memorable as last Monday's newspaper.

ARACAJU

• pop 428,000 ✉ 49000-000 ☎ 079

Aracaju just may be the Cleveland of the Northeast. The city has little to offer the visitor – there is no colonial inheritance – and it is visually quite unattractive. Even the beaches are below the prevailing high standard of the Brazilian Northeast.

Aracaju, 367km north of Salvador and 307km south of Maceió, was Brazil's first planned city. The modest requirements of the original plan called for a grid-pattern intersected by two perpendicular roads less than 2km long. The city outgrew the plan in no time, and the Brazilian norm of sprawl and chaotic development returned to the fore.

History

Some of its lack of appeal stems from the fact that Aracaju was not the most important city in the state during the colonial era. In fact, when it was chosen as the new capital in 1855, Santo Antônio de Aracaju was a small settlement with nothing but a good deep harbour – badly needed at the time to handle the ships transporting sugar to Europe.

With residents of the old capital of São Cristóvão on the verge of armed revolt, the new capital was placed on a hill 5km from the mouth of the Rio Sergipe. Within a year an epidemic broke out that decimated the population of the city. All the residents of São Cristóvão naturally saw this as an omen that Aracaju was destined to be a poor capital.

Information

Tourist Office Emsetur, the state tourist organisation in Sergipe, is trying hard to grab a slice of the rich tourist cake that its adjacent states, Bahia and Alagoas, have been enjoying in recent years. The Centro do Tourismo in Aracaju was revamped in 1994, and houses the Emsetur tourist office (☎ 224-5168) in Praça Olímpio Campos which sells useful maps of Aracaju and São Cristóvão for US$0.10 each. It also offers a small guide (in Portuguese) to Sergipe for US$1.30. It's open from 8 am to 8 pm daily.

The complex also backs onto an *artesanato mercado* (arts and crafts market), Rua 24 Horas (a shopping arcade), bars and cafés.

Money There is a branch of Banco do Brasil at Praça General Valadão 341 in the centre. Bradesco has an ATM at Praça Almirante Barroso for Visa withdrawals.

Post & Communications The central post office is at Rua Laranjeiras 229. The telephone office is on the other side of the road at No 296, opposite Rua 24 Horas, and is open daily from 7 am to 7 pm.

Beaches
On the sandy barrier island of Santa Luzia, at the mouth of the Rio Sergipe, **Praia Atalaia Nova** *(atalaia* is Portuguese for watchtower), is a popular weekend beach.

Praia das Artistas, **Praia Atalaia Velha** and **Praia Aruana** are the closest beaches to the city. They are crowded (with traffic jams on weekends) and heavily developed with hotels and motels, restaurants, bars and barracas, the latter of which are a source of inexpensive seafood.

Further south on the road to Mosqueiro, **Praia Refúgio** is the prettiest and most secluded beach close to Aracaju. It's 15km from the city. There are a few bars and one pousada.

Special Events
The maritime procession of Bom Jesus dos Navegantes, held on 1 January, is probably the best event. Festa de Iemanjá is celebrated on 8 December at Praia Atalaia Velha.

Places to Stay
Most of the hotels are in the centre or out at Praia Atalaia Velha on Avenida Atlântica. For a short stay, hotels in the centre are much more convenient and generally less

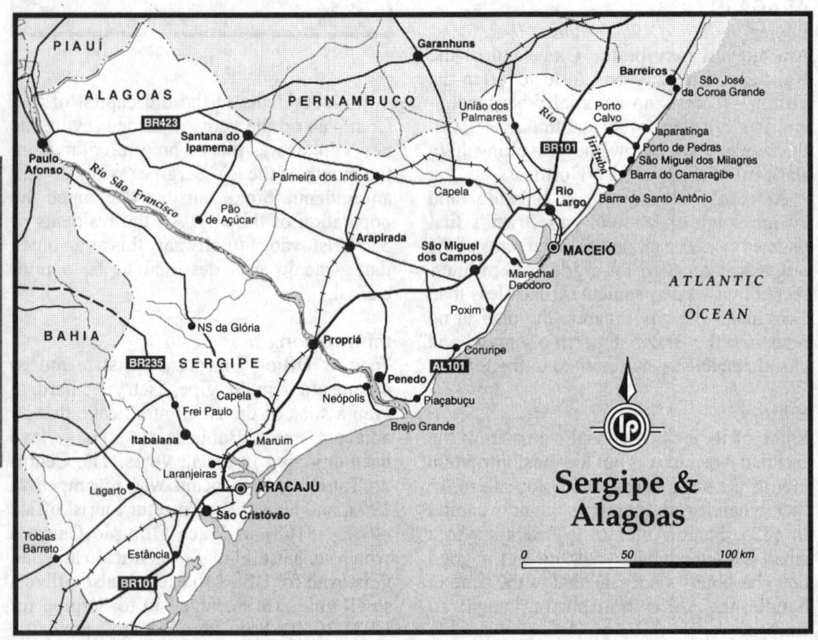

expensive. Many hotels in Aracaju seem to prefer cash – don't we all!

Budget If you intend to camp, try *Camping Clube do Brasil* (☎ 243-1413) on Atalaia Velha. It charges US$9 per person for camp sites.

The best budget option in town is the *Hotel Amado* (☎/fax 211-9937), Rua Laranjeiras 532. It has clean quartos for US$12/18. Apartamentos cost US$16/22 a single/double with fan or US$20/30 with air-conditioning. A rock-bottom choice in the centre of town is the *Hotel Sergipe* (☎ 222-7898), where quartos are US$6 per person and apartamentos US$10/15. You should also be aware that this hotel is favoured by local clientele as a short-time joint.

For much better value, try the *Hotel Oasis* (☎ 224-1181; fax 222-5288), which has bright apartamentos starting at US$22/ 30. The *Hotel Brasília* (☎ 224-8020; fax 224-8023) has apartamentos at US$25/38, with a 10% discount for cash payment.

Mid-Range A popular mid-range hotel is the *Jangadeiro* (☎ 211-1350), Rua Santa Luzia 269, in the city centre. It provides clean apartamentos at US$30/35. The *Serigy* (☎ 211-1008; fax 224-6928), Rua Santo Amaro 269, has upgraded its apartamentos, which now cost US$47/55. Just around the corner is the *Hotel Aperipé* (☎ 211-1880; fax 224-6928), Rua São Cristóvão 418, which offers apartamentos at US$45/51. Both hotels have the same owner and both offer a 30% discount for cash payment.

There's also the three-star *Grande Hotel* (☎/fax 211-1383), Rua Itabaiana 371, which provides good-value apartamentos with air-conditioning and fridge for US$51/60/78 for singles/doubles/ riples, with a 15% discount for cash.

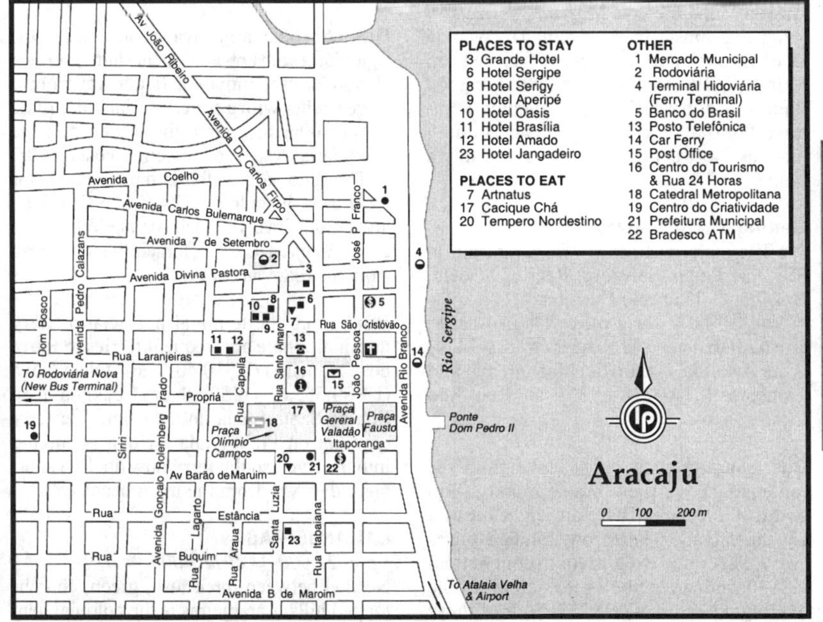

The mid-range *Pousada Do Sol* (☎/fax 255-1074) at Rua Atalaia 43, Praia Atalaia Velha, is recommended by locals. It charges US$40/50.

Top End If you want a five-star hotel in Aracaju, the *Parque dos Coqueiros* (☎/fax 243-1511), Rua Francisco Rabelo Leite Neto 1075, Praia Atalaia Velha, is the place. Doubles cost US$90, with a 30% discount for cash payment.

Places to Eat

Tempero Nordestino, Rua Santa Luzia 59, has a good self-serve lunch. It's open daily from 11 am to 3 pm. *Cacique Chá* (closed on Sunday) is a garden restaurant on Praça Olímpio Campos and a popular meeting place for the 'in' crowd. *Artnatus* at Rua Santo Amaro 282 is a well-stocked health-food store which serves vegetarian lunch meals. The cafés in Rua 24 Horas are good for snacks and drinks.

Recommended seafood restaurants at Atalaia Velha include *Taberna do Tropeiro* (with live music in the evening), Avenida Oceânica 6; and *O Miguel* (closed on Monday), Rua Antônio Alves 340. For good Italian food, try *Villa Vietri*, Avenida Francisco Porto 896, in Bairro Salgado Filho – midway between the centre and Atalaia Velha.

Getting There & Away

Air The major airlines fly from Aracaju to Rio, São Paulo, Salvador, Recife, Maceió, Brasília, Goiânia and Curitiba.

You'll find a Varig office (☎ 224-8128) at Rua Itabaiana 378, VASP (☎ 211-7474) is at Avenida Barão de Maruim 67 and Transbrasil (☎ 211-1233) at Rua São Cristóvão 14.

Bus Long-distance buses leave from the rodoviária nova (new bus terminal), 4km east of the centre. There are eight buses a day to Salvador. Fares on standard buses are US$8, on executivos (couchettes) US$20 and on leitos (super-comfortable overnight expresses) US$33. Four of these buses take the Linha Verde route along the coast (4½ hours), and the rest go inland via Entre Rios (6 hours). There are four departures a day for the 5 hour trip (US$12) to Maceió; some sections of the road are heavily potholed, so it can be slow going. Two departures a day to Recife take nearly 9 hours and cost US$21. There's one direct bus a day to Penedo (US$5, 3 hours), and seven buses a day to Neópolis, where there is access to Penedo by a short ferry ride across the Rio São Francisco.

For transport details on São Cristóvão and Laranjeiras, see their respective Getting There & Away sections. Note that bus services for these two towns operate from both the rodoviária velha (old bus terminal, in the centre on Avenida Divina Pastora) and the rodoviária nova.

Getting Around

To/From the Airport The airport is 11km south, just past Atalaia Velha. From the rodoviária velha, take the Aeroporto bus.

Bus The rodoviária nova is connected to the rodoviária velha by a frequent shuttle service (US$0.70, 15 minutes). It departs from a large shelter with a series of triangular roofs about 100m to your right as you exit the rodoviária. A taxi to the centre costs US$5.

The rodoviária velha is the terminal for local trips, including visits to São Cristóvão and Laranjeiras. To reach Atalaia Velha, take a bus marked Caroa Domeio/Santa Tereza from the rodoviária velha.

Boat From the terminal hidroviário (ferry terminal), there are frequent ferries to Barra dos Coqueiros (US$0.40) and Atalaia Nova (US$0.55, or US$0.80 on weekends) on Ilha de Santa Luzia until 11 pm. The ferry terminal on Praia Atalaia Nova is sinking into the river, so the ferry now docks a short bus ride away from the main beach.

LARANJEIRAS

• *pop 22,000* ✉ *49170-000* ☎ *079*

Nestled between three lush, green, church-topped hills, Laranjeiras is the colonial gem of Sergipe. Filled with ruins of old sugar mills, terracotta roofs, colourful colonial façades and stone roads, the town is relatively unblemished by modern development. There are several churches and museums worth visiting and the surrounding hills offer picturesque walks with good views. It's a charming little town, easy to get to and well worth a few hours sightseeing or a day or two exploring the town, the nearby sugar mill and the countryside. The town centre has recently been renovated.

History

Laranjeiras was first settled in 1605. During the 18th and 19th centuries it became the commercial centre for the rich sugar and cotton region along the zona mata west of Aracaju. At one point there were over 60 sugar mills in and around Laranjeiras. The sugar was sent on the Rio Cotinguiba about 20km downstream to Aracaju and on to the ports of Europe. The large number of churches is a reminder of past prosperity.

Information

There is a city tourism office inside the Trapiche building in the Centro de Tradições on Praça Samuel de Oliveira where you can obtain brochures and information about guides for hire. It's open from 8 am to 5 pm Tuesday to Sunday.

Engenho

This old, partly restored sugar mill a few kilometres from town is in a lovely setting. It's now privately owned, and not generally open to the public, but it may be possible to arrange a visit from the tourist office. You can walk, or hire a guide and a car.

Igreja de Camandaroba

Out at the Engenho Boa Sorte, 2km from town along the river, is the Baroque Igreja de Camandaroba, the second building that the Jesuits constructed back in 1731.

Igreja do Bonfim

At the top of the hill called Alto do Bonfim, this church has recently been restored. If the door is closed, go around to the back and ask to be let in. The short walk is rewarded with a fine view, but keep an eye out for snakes.

Trapiche

The Trapiche houses the tourism office. It's a large, impressive structure that was built in the 19th century to house the cargo waiting to be shipped downriver.

Gruta da Pedra Furada

This is a 1km tunnel built by the Jesuits to escape their persecutors. The tunnel has been closed due to cave-ins, but there are plans to restore it. Ask at the tourist office to make sure it's open. The *gruta* (tunnel) is 3km out of town on the road leading to the small village of Machado.

Museums

The small **Museu Afro-Brasileiro** (no ☎) is on Rua José do Prado Franco s/n (no number); Laranjeiras is considered to be the stronghold of African culture in Sergipe. It's open from 8 am to 5 pm Tuesday to Sunday.

Also recommended is the **Museu de Arte Sacra** (Sacred Art Museum) in Igreja NS da Conceição, Rua Dr Francisco Bragança s/n.

Special Events

During the first week of January, the Encontro Cultural folklore festival is held in the town.

Places to Stay

The only pousada in town is the *Pousada Vale dos Outeiros* (☎ 281-1027) at Rua José do Prado Franco 124. Some readers have complained about surly management, but what can you expect from a monopoly? There are good views of the surrounding hills from the back rooms. Double quartos and apartamentos with air-conditioning cost US$20 and US$30 respectively.

Getting There & Away

Laranjeiras is 21km from Aracaju and 4km off Hwy BR-101. Buses leave from and return to the rodoviária velha in Aracaju about every half hour. It's a 35 minute ride (US$1) – the first bus leaves for Laranjeiras at 6 am and the last one returns at 9 pm. Any bus travelling on Hwy BR-101 can let you off at the turn-off for Laranjeiras. There's a restaurant at the turn-off, so you can have a drink and snack while you wait to flag down a bus from Aracaju. Otherwise, you can walk or hitch to town.

SÃO CRISTÓVÃO

• *pop 58,000* ✉ *491000-000* ☎ *079*

Founded in 1590, São Cristóvão is reputedly Brazil's fourth oldest town, and was the capital of Sergipe until 1855. With the decline of the sugar industry, the town has long been in the economic doldrums and is currently trying to become a tourist attraction to bring in some cash.

Things to See

The old part of town, up a steep hill, has a surprising number of 17th and 18th century colonial buildings along its narrow stone roads. Of particular distinction are the **Igreja e Convento de São Francisco**, Praça São Francisco, which has a good sacred-art museum; the **Igreja de Senhor dos Passos**, Praça Senhor dos Passos; the **Antiga Assembléia Legislativa**; and the **Antigo Palácio do Governo**.

Special Events

Every year the town comes alive for a weekend with the Festival de Arte de São Cristóvão. The festival has both fine and popular arts, with lots of music and dance. The festival is held during the last 15 days of October.

Places to Stay & Eat

There is no real accommodation in São Cristóvão, although there is a camping ground 2km from town.

If you've got a sweet tooth, São Cristóvão is renowned for its sweet-makers, who produce a wide variety of doces caseiros (tempting home-made confectionary and cakes).

Getting There & Away

Bus São Cristóvão is 25km south of Aracaju on a good sealed road, and 7km off Hwy BR-101. The rodoviária is down the hill below the historic district, on Praça Dr Lauro de Freitas. Frequent buses running to São Cristóvão (US$0.70, 45 minutes) leave from the rodoviária velha in Aracaju. If you are travelling south to Estância, note that buses do not run there from São Cristóvão. You can take a bus back to the junction of Hwy BR-101 and try to flag down a bus to Estância, or return to the rodoviária nova in Aracaju and take one from there.

ESTÂNCIA

• *pop 57,000* ✉ *49200-000* ☎ *079*

Estância, 68km south of Aracaju, is one of the oldest towns in the state. The city has a certain amount of character, and a few historic buildings in the centre, but there's little reason to stop in Estância unless you want to head to the nearby beaches (see the Mangue Seco section in the Bahia chapter) or want to avoid spending the night in Aracaju.

Information

Estância has all basic services, including a large supermarket. The São João festivals in June are the big events.

Places to Stay & Eat

The town has a couple of hotels facing the main square, Praça Barão do Rio Branco. The *Hotel Turismo Estanciano* (☎/fax 522-1404), Praça Bar do Rio Branco, is spotless and comfortable, and has a restaurant attached. Single/double quartos with fan cost US$10/20, while single/double apartamentos with fan go for US$18/30 and double apartamentos with air-conditioning cost US$40. Some of the cheaper rooms have high ceilings – so high that even the walls don't actually reach them! Try to get a room away from the restaurant.

The *Hotel Bosco* (☎ 522-1887), 30m away, has quartos for US$10 per person and apartamentos for US$13/20.

The *Hotel Continenti*, tucked behind the rodoviária, has reasonably clean quartos at US$5/10. *Pizzaria São Geraldo* does excellent pizzas.

Getting There & Away

The town is actually a bit off Hwy BR-101, but most long-distance buses still stop at the bus station in Estância, which is on the main highway. There are buses directly from Salvador, Aracaju, Propriá and Maceió to the north.

If you are travelling south from Estância along the Linha Verde and want to visit the beach towns north of Salvador, the Bonfim bus company, which runs the Aracaju-Salvador route, makes you pay the full fare from Estância to Salvador (US$11.50) no matter where you get off along the way. There are four buses a day from Estância to Salvador, but two leave around 1 am and are impractical if you want to stop before Salvador. Daytime buses leave at 8.30 am and 1.45 pm.

For access to Mangue Seco in Bahia, a bus leaves the rodoviária in Estância daily at 4 pm for Pontal, where there are boats across the river to Mangue Seco. The 42km trip to Pontal via Indiaroba takes about two hours.

PROPRIÁ

• *pop 26,000* ✉ *49900-000* ☎ *tel 079*

Propriá is 81km north of Aracaju, where Hwy BR-101 crosses the mighty Rio São Francisco. While the town is less interesting than the cities of Penedo and Neópolis further downstream, it has the same combination of colonial charm and river culture. Thursday and Friday are the weekly mercado days in Propriá, when goods are traded from communities up and down the São Francisco.

Boat Trips

In recent years there has been a steady decline in long-distance boat travel along the Rio São Francisco. You should still be able to find boats going upriver as far as Pão de Açúcar, about a seven hour ride by

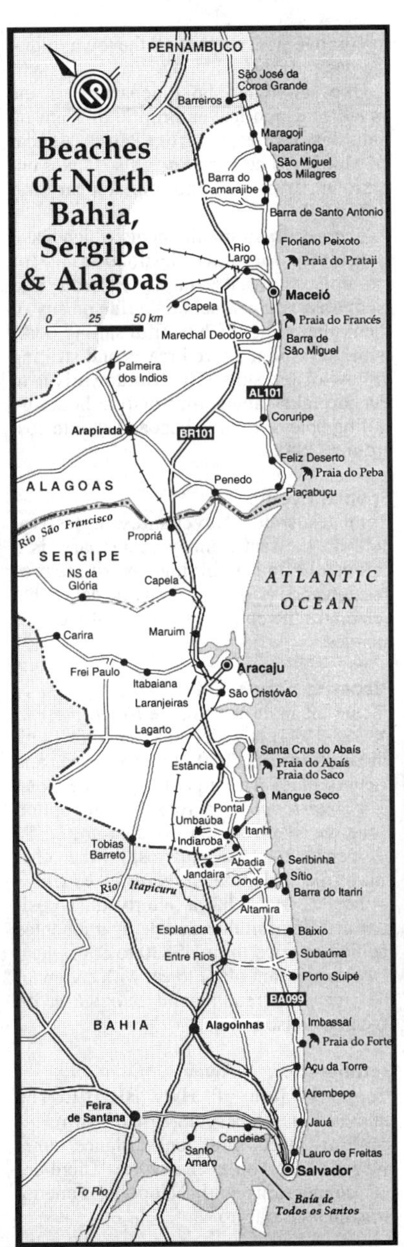

motorboat, with stops at all the towns along the way.

One scheduled boat departure is the *Oriente*, which leaves Propriá at 7 am on Saturday and returns from Pão de Açúcar on Monday. The *Vaza Baris* also makes occasional trips to Pão de Açúcar and Penedo.

There are also smaller boats which leave irregularly for other destinations – for example, downstream to Penedo and Neópolis. You can bargain a ride on any of them, including the beautiful sailing boats with their long, curved masts and striking yellow or red sails. The trip downriver to Penedo takes about four or five hours by sailing boat or rowing boat and should cost around US$7.

Special Events

Bom Jesus dos Navegantes, a festival held on the last Sunday in January, is a colourful affair involving a maritime procession and *reisado* – a dramatic dance that celebrates the epiphany. It is highly recommended.

Places to Stay & Eat

Facing the main church, the *Hotel Imperial* (☎ 322-1294) has nice apartamentos (with fan) costing US$13/20. It's a very clean and friendly place with a pool table. The *Hotel Pan Americano* is a rock-bottom option along the riverfront in town charging US$6 per person for basic quartos. At the other end of the scale, the *Hotel do Velho Chico* (☎/fax 322-1941) has a fine riverside position and comfortable double apartamentos ranging in price from US$30 to $60.

For a pleasant place to eat with a view of the river, we recommend *Beira Rio*, on Avenida Nelson Melo.

Getting There & Away

Propriá is 1km off Hwy BR-101. The rodoviária is 2km south-east of town – a local bus meets most long-distance buses and will drop you in the centre. There are bus connections with Neópolis, Penedo, Aracaju and Maceió.

Alagoas

The small state of Alagoas is one of the pleasant surprises of the Northeast. The capital, Maceió, is a relaxed, modern city, and its beaches are enchanting, with calm, emerald waters. Penedo is the colonial masterpiece of the state, with a fascinating river culture on the Rio São Francisco.

Along the coast, there are many fishing villages with fabulous beaches shaded by rows of coconut trees. Buses run along the coastal roads to the north and south of Maceió connecting the villages which are beginning to be discovered by tourists and property developers.

History

The mighty republic of runaway slaves – Palmares – was in present-day Alagoas. During the invasion by the Dutch in 1630, many slaves escaped to the forest in the mountains between Garanhuns and Palmares. Today, where the towns of Viçosa, Capela, Atalaia, Porto Calvo and União dos Palmares stand, there were once virgin forests with thick growth and plenty of animals. Alagoas today has the highest population density in the Northeast.

MACEIÓ

• *pop 725,000* ✉ *57000-000* ☎ *082*

Maceió, the capital of Alagoas, is 292km north of Aracaju and 259km south of Recife. A manageable place for the visitor, the city has a modern feeling, apart from a small historical area in the commercial centre, and offers endless sun and sea. Maceió has experienced a tourist boom over recent years, and the city beaches are being developed at a fast pace, particularly between Ponta Verde and Praia de Jatiúca.

Orientation

The rodoviária is 4km north of the city centre, which has inexpensive hotels and the bustle of commerce. On the eastern side of the city are Praia de Pajuçara and Praia dos Sete Coqueiros, which are 3km and 4km respectively from the centre.

Information

Tourist Office Maceió has well-developed tourist information facilities. The head office of Ematur (☎ 221-9393), the state tourism organisation, is at Avenida da Paz 2004, but there's no real need to visit. Emturma (☎ 223-4016), the municipal tourism body, has many useful, conveniently located information booths.

There are combined Emturma information booths/Telasa phone offices along the beachfront at Praia Pajuçara, Ponta Verde and Praia Jatiúca. These booths have loads of information on hotels, restaurants and transport tucked away in folders – including where to have your tarot read or your dog washed! There are also information booths at the airport and rodoviária.

Foreign Consulate There is a French consulate (☎ 327-2555) at Lagoa da Anta 220 in the Hotel Jatiúca.

Money There's a branch of Banco do Brasil at Rua do Livramento 120. Aero Tourismo also changes money at the same rate as the banks. It has a branch at Rua Barão do Penedo 61, in the centre, and one in the Iguatemi shopping centre. Bradesco has an ATM on Avenida Senador Robert Kennedy at Praia dos Sete Coqueiros.

Post & Communications There is a post office at Rua do Sol, in the city centre. Telasa, the state phone company, has offices in the centre at Rua Cons Lourenço de Albuquerque 369; along the beachfront at Praia Pajuçara, Ponta Verde and Praia Jatiúca; and at the airport and rodoviária.

Museums

In the centre, **Museu do Instituto Histórico** (open Monday to Friday from 8 to 11.30 am and 2 to 5 pm) has exhibits about regional history. **Museu Theo Brandão** in an attractive colonial building on the seafront, has some interesting folkloric exhibitions. It's open Monday to Thursday from 8 am to noon and 2 to 5 pm. On Friday it's open from 8 am to noon.

Beaches

Just a short walk from the centre, the beaches of Praia do Sobral and Avenida are polluted. **Praia de Pajuçara** and **Praia dos Sete Coqueiros** sometimes suffer from pollution as well. Your best bet is to head further north for some of the best beaches in the Northeast. Protected by a coral reef, the ocean is calm and a deep-emerald colour. On shore there are loads of barracas, *jangadas* (local sailing boats) and plenty of beach action.

The beaches to the north are **Ponta Verde** (5km), **Jatiúca** (6km), **Jacarecica** (9km), **Guaxuma** (12km), **Garça Torta** (14km), **Riacho Doce** (16km) and **Pratagi** (17km).

You won't go wrong with any of these tropical paradises, but they do get busy on weekends and throughout the summer, when there are many local buses cruising the beaches. On Pajuçara, you'll find jangadas that will take you out about 1km to the reef, where you can swim in the *piscina natural* (natural swimming pool), and observe the marine life (best done at low tide). The cost is US$7 per person.

Boat Trips

Many schooners depart daily from Pontal da Barra for a five hour cruise to islands and beaches. The price per person is usually US$30 with lunch, or US$20 without lunch. Atlântico Turismo (☎ 983-3695) charges US$25 for its trips. Small motorboats such as the *Turis Gomes* (☎ 221-0458) make similar cruises from Pontal da Barra for US$15 per person, or US$25 with lunch included.

Flora & Fauna

A reader provided the following information about the wildlife in Maceió:

If you are seriously interested in fauna and flora in Alagoas, the person to speak to is the biologist Gininho Britzky, Rua Augusta 251, in the city centre of Maceió (☎ 221-1987). With his long hair and beard he looks more like Jesus than the respected ecologist that he is. He has been fighting for years to protect the environment in Alagoas which is under constant attack, and he is well known locally. He speaks very little English, but will be happy to point you in the right direction, and may even be willing to go on trips with you to the few remaining pockets of forest and mangrove swamp. He won't ask for anything in return, but I think it would be polite to offer a donation to the environmental group that he heads: Brigada Ecológica de Alagoas, one of the environmental organisations mentioned in the excellent, but high priced ($35) environmental guide book, Guia Do Meia Ambiente – Litoral De Alagoas, which can be found in some Maceió bookshops and from the Instituto Brasileiro do Meio Ambiente (IBAMA) (☎ 241-1600).

W J (Bill) Hill, Cheshire, England

Special Events
Maceió is reported to have a lively Carnaval that is still considerably calmer and safer than Rio's, and features active samba clubs. Locals reckon Barra de São Miguel has the best Carnaval in the area. Festa do Mar takes place in December.

Places to Stay
Budget For camping try *Camping Jatiúca* (☎ 235-1251) on Praia Cruz das Almas, 6km from the centre.

Most hostels in Maceió have closed. The last remaining is *Albergue de Juventude Nossa Casa* (☎ 231-2246), Rua Prefeito Abdon Arroxelas 327, on Praia de Ponta Verde. It's a French-run place – call before arriving to make sure it's still open.

City Centre The *Hotel dos Palmares* (☎ 223-7024), Praça dos Palmares 253, has quartos at US$8 per person (breakfast not

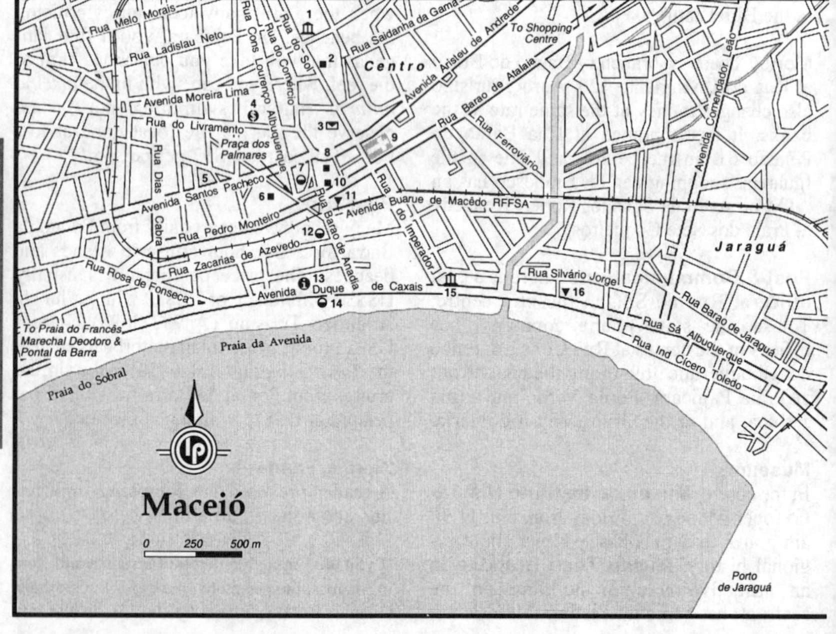

included), or US$15/28/42 for apartamentos with breakfast. There's a nice, elevated eating area which catches the breeze. Nearby, the *Hotel Maceió* (☎ 221-1883), Rua Dr Pontas de Miranda 146, offers clean, cell-like quartos for US$10 per person and single/double apartamentos for US$15/30. It's secure and friendly.

Although conveniently central at Rua Dom Pedro Segundo 73, the *Hotel Parque* (☎/fax 223-4247) is rather institutional and drab, and doesn't merit its two stars. Apartamentos cost US$15/25.

Beaches Praia de Pajuçara is the best place to base yourself, as it's midway between the city centre and the better beaches, and has more budget accommodation than the beaches further north. The cheapies are all one block from the beach on Rua Dr Antônio Pedro de Mendonça. Prices quoted here are for the low season – expect hikes of 20% to 30% in summer. *Pousada Rex* (☎ 231-4358), No 311, is a family-run place with apartamentos starting at US$10/20. It can also arrange boat trips. Next door at No 315, *Hotel Pousada Zeide* (☎ 231-1008) is another family-run place, with clean apartamentos for US$15/25. Close by is *Mar Amar* (☎ 231-1551), No 343, with air-conditioned apartamentos with TV for US$15/20.

The *Pousada da Praia* (☎ 231-6843), Rua Jangadeiros Alagoanos 545, has basic apartamentos for US$15/20. The *Pousada Saveiro* (☎ 231-9831), up the road at Rua Jangadeiros Alagoanos 905, is friendly and better value. Apartamentos (with fan) cost US$30 a double. The *Pousada Shangri La* (☎ 231-3773), Rua Jangadeiros Alagoanos 1089, is a bit dingy – apartamentos cost US$15/25. Next door, the *Pousada Amazônia* (no ☎) is brighter and cleaner, and has similar prices. Across the road, above the padaria (bakery) is *Pousada*

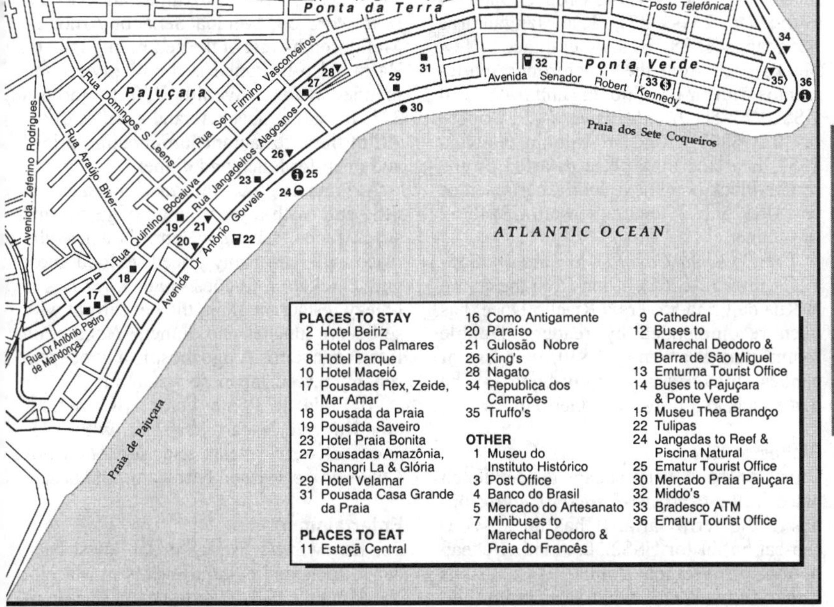

Glória (☎ 231-3261), with reasonable apartamentos for US$20/25.

Places to Stay – Mid-Range

City Centre If you want a good hotel in the centre, try the *Hotel Beiriz* (☎ 221-1080; fax 336-6282) on Rua do Sol. It's a large three-star hotel with a pool and restaurant. Rooms with air-conditioning, fridge and TV cost US$32/36.

Beaches The more reasonably priced mid-range options are the older hotels along Praia de Pajuçara. The newer hotels further north on Ponta Verde and Praia Jatiúca are generally more expensive. There are some very good out-of-season prices at the mid-range beach hotels, as you can see from the low-season prices quoted below.

The *Hotel Praia Bonita* (☎/fax 231-2565), Avenida Dr Antônio Gouveia 943, Praia de Pajuçara, has clean single/double apartamentos with air-conditioning for US$25/30. Its jangada reception desk is a nice touch. The *Pousada Casa Grande da Praia* (☎ 231-3332), Rua Jangadeiros Alagoanos 1528, is a quiet place a few blocks back from the beachfront. Apartamentos with air-conditioning and fridge cost US$20/25. The *Hotel Velamar* (☎ 327-5488; fax 231-6849), Rua Dr Antônio Gouveia 1359, is a cute little place dwarfed by the square-block hotel next door. Apartamentos cost US$25/35 in the low season, US$48/52 in summer.

The *Pousada Cavalo Marinho* (☎ 355-1247; fax 355-1265), 17km from the centre at Rua da Praia 55, Praia Riacho Doce, has been recommended by readers. Double rooms start at around US$30, with use of canoes, bicycles and body-boards. The owner speaks English and German.

Places to Eat

City Centre A very cheap, decent lunch place in the centre is *Estação Centro*, opposite the ferroviária. It has an all-you-can-eat buffet for US$2.50. Another cheap option, on Avenida Duque de Caxias, is *Como Antigamente*, which does prato feito for US$5 and has seating in a courtyard at the back of the restaurant, away from the street noise.

Beaches Most of the beaches offer a wide choice of food, with barracas and snack bars serving seafood and local dishes along the beachfront.

Local seafood specialities worth trying are sururu (a small mussel) and maçunim (shellfish) cooked in coconut sauce, served as dishes on their own, or in a caldinho (cup of sauce) which can be eaten or drunk. Other tasty local seafood dishes include peixe agulha (deep-fried needle fish) and siri na casca com coral (crab in the shell with roe). Beachside food stalls serve some delicious snacks which should be tried: acarajé (a bean paste deep fried in dendê oil and filled with shrimp and potato) and tapioca pancakes filled with grated coconut or queijo coalhado (compressed bean curd).

Other good places for seafood are *Bem* (☎ 325-1520), Rua João Canuto da Silva 21, Praia de Cruz das Almas, and *Restaurant Maré* on Avenida Senador Arnor de Mello, south-west of the centre in Pontal da Barra. Also in Pontal is the highly recommended *Alípio*, Avenida Alípio Barbosa 321. It's got atmosphere and great seafood. All of these restaurants are medium priced and open for lunch and dinner.

At Praia de Pajuçara, *Paraíso* is a casual little café with a great range of juices and snack foods. *Gulosão Nobre* is a friendly place with reasonably priced seafood, meat and chicken refeições, and *King's* is a breezy restaurant along the beachfront with self-serve lunches and dinners. *Nagato*, on Rua Jangadeiros Alagoanos, is a good, reasonably priced Japanese restaurant.

At Praia de Ponta Verde, two recommended eateries are *Truffo's*, with very good self-serve meals and *Republica dos Camarões*, a seafood barraca on the beach.

Entertainment

For reviews and listings of the latest bars, dance spots and cultural events in Maceió, check out the daily entertainment section of

O Jornal, the local newspaper. A couple of places worth a look are *D'Arcos*, Rua Jangadeiros Alagoanos 1125, at Ponta Verde, for loud and sweaty dance action, or *Middo*, Avenida Senador Robert Kennedy 2167, Praia dos Sete Coqueiros, which has *pagode* (a type of samba), *forró* (regional music of the Northeast) and other dance music. Many of the sea-front barracas have live music, especially on weekends. *Tulipas*, on Praia de Pajuçara, is one of the hotspots.

Things to Buy

There is a nightly artesanato mercado on Praia Pajuçara with dozens of stalls selling figurines, lacework, hammocks and jewellery.

The fishing village of Pontal da Barra, around 8km from the centre, is also an artesanato centre. The streets are lined with shops selling fine lacework and embroidery, and prices are generally lower there than in the city. You can often see women weaving outside the shops. The Mercado do Artesanato, next to the food mercado in the city centre, is also a good place to shop for hammocks – a decent double hammock goes for around US$20.

Getting There & Away

Air Maceió is connected by air with Rio, São Paulo, Brasília and all the major centres of the Northeast. There are plans to open an international terminal in Maceió – at the moment, there are charter services to Maceió from Rome, Madrid and Amsterdam.

The major airline offices are in the centre. Varig (☎ 322-1160) is at Rua Comendador Palmeira 129; VASP (☎ 322-1414) is at Rua do Comércio 56; and Transbrasil (☎ 322-1590) is at Rua Barão de Penedo 213.

Bus There are numerous daily bus services to Recife (US$10, 4 hours) and Aracaju (US$12, 5 hours).

Buses run five times a day to Salvador (US$28, 10 hours). Some of these take the inland route while others go via the Linha Verde along the coast. If you want to make a 2256km bus trip to Rio (US$100, 36 hours), there's a daily departure at 5 pm.

Buses leave for Penedo five times a day – the route via Hwy AL-101 along the coast is much quicker if you take an expresso – 2½ hours compared to 4½ in a normal bus (see the later Penedo section for details of the slow bus route). The fare is US$5. The São Domingus bus company services the coastal towns north of Maceió, with regular buses to Barra do Camarajibe, Barra de Santo Antônio, Japaratinga and Porto de Pedras.

Walking For details of walking from Recife to Maceió, see Getting There & Away in the Recife section of the Pernambuco chapter.

Getting Around

To/From the Airport Dos Palmares airport is 20km north of the centre. Rio Largo buses to the airport can be picked up at Praça Sinibu, on Rua Imperador. A taxi to the airport costs around US$15.

To/From the Rodoviária To reach the centre, take the bus marked Ouro Prêto. A taxi to the centre costs US$8, and US$4 more to Pajuçara.

To/From the Beaches Buses marked Santuário, Jardim Vaticano or Ponta Verde run from the centre to Pajuçara. The Jatiúca bus runs from the centre to Praia Jatiúca. If you want to travel further away from the centre, the bus marked Riacho Doce runs along the beaches north of town as far as Riacho Doce, 11km away (recommended).

Buses run to Pontal da Barra from the bus stop on Rua Pedro Montero, near Praça dos Palamares.

SOUTH OF MACEIÓ

Praia do Francês

Only 22km from Maceió, this is a popular weekend beach which is being rapidly developed and beginning to suffer from the ravages of tourism. The beach is lined with barracas and the ocean is lined with reefs. At one end, the water is calm and better for wading in than swimming while at the other end there's usually surf. It's a very social beach on weekends, with plenty of drinking, seafood-scoffing, football and music.

There is a small Ematur information booth on the roadside as you come into town. It has some brochures, and its staff can direct you to accommodation.

Places to Stay & Eat There are now some cheap options in Praia do Francês. The *Pousada João* and *Pousada Nataly* are both pretty grungy, with quartos for US$10/15. The best-value cheapie is the *Hotel Pousada do Pescador*, which has clean double apartamentos for US$15. *Pousada Kanamary* (☎ 260-1213) is a good deal with singles/doubles for US$15/30, but it's only open on weekends outside of summer. The *Pousada Bougainville* (☎ 260-1141) is also close to the beach, and recommended for a splurge. The French owner has virtually submerged the pousada in bougainvillea. Apartamentos are US$32/38 a single/double.

The adjoining restaurant, *Chez Patrick*, is run by the same person and specialises in seafood. Main dishes are expensive, but you can also drop in for an appetiser and drink served in the restaurant's shady courtyard. Numerous barracas along the beach are a good source of cheap seafood, or you could try the *Restaurant do Pescador*.

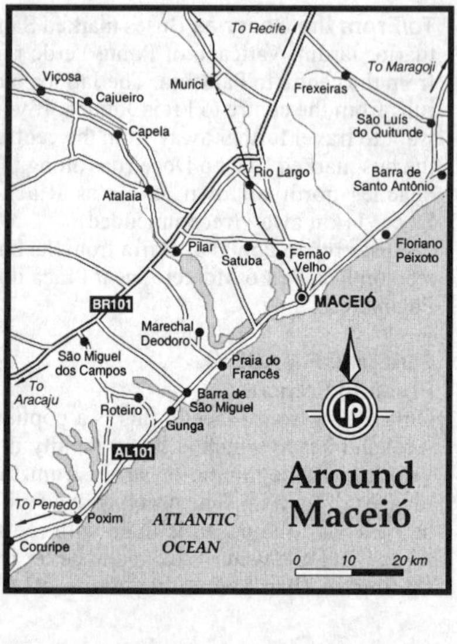

Getting There & Away From Maceió, either take the bus from the stop outside the ferroviária (hourly departure), or use the more frequent VW kombi minibus service that leaves from about 50m down the street. The same minibuses run between Praia do Francês and Marechal Deodoro.

Marechal Deodoro

Beside Lagoa Manguaba, a lagoon 21km south-west of Maceió, is the city of Marechal Deodoro, which had been the capital of Alagoas between 1823 and 1839. Small and quiet, the town is worth a visit, perhaps combined with Praia do Francês as a day trip from Maceió.

Things to See Marechal Deodoro has several churches, the most famous of which are the **Igreja e Convento São Francisco**, constructed in the 17th century, and the **Igreja de NS da Conceição**.

Inside Igreja e Convento São Francisco is the **Museu de Arte Sacra** (Museum of Sacred Art). It's open from 9 am to 1 pm, daily except on Sunday, when it's closed.

Brazilian history buffs may want to see the old governor's palace and the house where Marechal Deodoro was born. The latter has been turned into the **Museu Deodoro**, which is open from 9 am to 5 pm, daily except on Sunday, when it's closed. The exhibits give a 'deodorised' view of Manuel Deodoro da Fonseca, emphasising his role as a military hero and the first president of Brazil, but omitting to mention that he achieved this position with a military putsch in 1889, and later proved to be a poor politician. The artesanato shop next door sells the lace and home-made sweets for which the town is renowned.

The weekend mercado, held along the waterfront, is a lively, colourful event.

Place to Stay & Eat The *Hospedaria Deodorense* is a clean, very basic place to stay – usually booked solid on weekends. Quartos with fan cost US$3/5 for singles/ doubles. Breakfast is US$3. For other meals, speak to Dona Terezinho, in the house two doors up towards Praça Paulino.

There are lots of breezy bars along the lagoon.

Getting There & Away Buses to Marechal Deodoro (US$1) depart hourly from the bus stop outside the old ferroviária in Maceió. It's quicker to go by one of the VW kombi vans (US$2, half hour) – they leave every 15 minutes or so from the BR petrol station on Praça dos Palmares. Yes, the VW kombi van is definitely quicker; the demon drivers keep their accelerator foot down to the board, and your heart pressed to the roof of your mouth!

An alternative route from Maceió is to take the boat from Trapiche across Lagoa Manguaba.

Barra de São Miguel

Barra is situated 35km south of Maceió, at the mouth of the Rio São Miguel. The fine beach is protected by a huge reef and there are kayaks for rent. Barra is not too crowded midweek, but it is being built up with summer homes for Maceió's wealthy. **Praia do Gunga** is a popular beach across the river with some expensive bars. You can rent jet skis here, or go parasailing.

Places to Stay & Eat There are a couple of very expensive hotels in town. The *Pousada Sol e Mar* (☎ 272-1440), near the river, has apartamentos at US$22/30 for singles/doubles. It's overpriced but in an attractive position. If there is a group of you, better value are chalets for up to six people, with cooking facilities, for around US$60 per day. The *Condimínio Rio Mar* (☎ 272-1432; fax 272-2064) charges US$40 for a six-person chalet.

Bar do Tio has good shrimp and fish dishes for US$8 to $15. Try the super mussels.

Getting There & Away Buses run four times a day to Barra, at 7.20 and 11.30 am, and 3.20 and 7.20 pm. They leave from the bus stop at the ferroviária. The last bus leaves Barra for the return trip to at 5.30 pm.

South of Barra de São Miguel

The recent upgrading of Hwy AL-101 along the Litoral Sul has made access to the beaches and villages south of Barra de São Miguel much easier. The road runs about 1km from the coast, and regular buses travel along it from Maceió to Penedo on the Rio São Francisco. See Getting There & Away in the following Penedo section for details.

PENEDO

Penedo is best known as the *capital do baixo São Francisco* (capital of the lower São Francisco). On the shore of the mythical river, this important historic town rises imposingly on it's rock platform.

Among the attractions of the city, 42km off Hwy BR-101, are its many baroque churches and colonial buildings, and the opportunity to travel on the Rio São Francisco. Penedo bustles with people from the smaller villages up and down the river who come to buy and sell goods.

History

Penedo was founded in either 1535 or 1560 (opinions differ) by Duarte Coelho Pereira, who descended the Rio São Francisco in pursuit of Caete Indians responsible for killing a bishop. Penedo is claimed to be the river's first colonial settlement. It was also the scene of a fierce battle between the Dutch and Portuguese for control of the Northeast in the 17th century.

Tourist Office

There's a helpful tourist information office (open from 8 am to 6 pm daily) in the Casa da Aposentadoria, just up from the fort on Praça Barão de Penedo. Portuguese-speaking guides are available for a one hour walking tour of the town.

Mercado

The street mercado is held daily in Penedo, but Friday and Saturday are the big days when the city is transformed into a busy port-of-call for farmers, fishermen and artisans. The waterfront becomes a pageant as families disembark – old people with finely carved features topped by strange hats, many grasping chickens by the neck with one hand and boisterous children by the neck with the other. On the river bank, traditional musicians play accordions. The market is filled with ceramics, baskets and shrimp traps made of reeds.

Churches

Penedo has a rich collection of 17th and 18th century colonial buildings, including many churches. The **Convento de São Francisco e Igreja NS dos Anjos**, Praça Rui Barbosa, is considered the finest church in the state. Even Dom Pedro II (Brazil's second and last emperor) paid a visit. Construction began in 1660 and was completed in 1759. The rococo altar is made of gold. The saint on the left is by Aleijadinho. The church is open Tuesday to Sunday from 8 to 11 am and 2.30 to 5 pm.

Igreja da Senhora das Correntes was completed in 1764. It has some fine work done with *azulejos* (glazed blue tiles), and a rococo altar. The church is open daily from 8 am to noon and 2 to 5 pm. You'll find it at Praça 12 de Abril.

The **Igreja NS do Rosário dos Pretos**, also known as the Catedral do Penedo, was built by slaves. It's on Praça Marechal Deodoro and is open every day from 8 am to 5 pm. **Igreja de São Gonçalo Garcia** was built at the end of the 18th century and has some of the city's finest sacred-art pieces. It's on Avenida Floriano Peixoto, but is currently closed for restoration. The small **oratório** on Praça Barão de Penedo is where the condemned spent their last night praying before being hanged.

Casa do Penedo

Casa do Penedo, Rua João Pessoa 156, is a small museum with relics and photographs from Penedo's rich history. It's open daily from 8 am to 4 pm and admission is free. It sells excellent postcards.

Boat Trips

Saturday (the major market day) is the easiest day to find a boat up or down the São Francisco, but it's difficult now to find boats going upriver as far as Propriá.

The ferry between Penedo and Passagem, on the opposite side of the river, crosses every half hour, but is only of interest if you're driving. From Passagem there's a road to **Neópolis**, which is linked by another road to Hwy BR-101. A better excursion is one of the motorboat crossings direct to Neópolis, a few kilometres downriver. The 15 minute trip costs US$0.80 and boats usually depart every half hour between 5.30 am and 10 pm. Neópolis is an old colonial town on a hill overlooking the river, with some interesting buildings and good crafts for sale. For other short boat excursions, take one of the frequent boats (operating between 6 am and 6 pm) to Carrapicho, a small town 4km upriver noted for its ceramics.

A large motorboat for up to 30 people cruises to Carrapicho, Neópolis and river islands, with stops for swimming. The cost is US$15 per hour per boatload. A sailing boat makes a similar trip, depending on the wind and tides, for US$10 per hour. Ask at the tourist office for departure times.

Special Events

The Festa do Senhor Bom Jesus dos Navegantes, held over four days from the second Sunday of January, features an elaborate procession of boats.

Places to Stay

Penedo has some interesting hotels. Most are down by the waterfront, on or near Avenida Floriano Peixoto.

The *Pousada Colonial* (☎ 551-2677), Praça 12 de Abril, is a romantic place to stay. It's a beautiful converted colonial home on the waterfront with spacious apartamentos featuring stained-wood floors and antique furniture. Make sure you get one with a view of the river. Prices start at US$25/35 for single/double apartamentos.

The *Hotel São Francisco* (☎ 551-2273; fax 551-2274), Avenida Floriano Peixoto, is a 1960s-style hotel that's been in the time warp for the last 30 years. It's clean, quiet and has comfortable apartamentos with balconies and great hot showers starting at US$42/61. It usually gives a 30% discount.

For a budget option, try the *Pousada Familiar* (☎ 551-3194), Rua Siqueira 77, with quartos for US$8 with a basic breakfast (coffee, bread and an egg) or US$10 with a better breakfast. If you prefer a place where the walls reach the ceiling, walk a bit further up the same street to the *Hotel Turista* (☎ 551-2237) at No 143 which offers clean, basic apartamentos with ceiling fans for US$15/20 with breakfast.

Places to Eat

There are plenty of bars and lanchonetes where locals eat. We recommend *Forte da Rocheira*, which is open for lunch and dinner (until 11 pm) and serves abundant portions of seafood and meat for US$10 to $20. The restaurant is in an old replica fort overlooking the river. Just follow the signs to get there. The restaurant in the *Pousada Colonial* also serves good fish and meat dishes.

Getting There & Away

Bus The rodoviária is on Avenida Duque de Caxias. There are seven buses a day to Maceió (US$5). Express executivo buses leave at 6 am and 4.30 pm daily and the standard bus *pinga litoral* (literally, 'dripping along the coast') leaves at 1 pm. These three buses take the coastal route along Hwy AL-101, which is much quicker than the inland route via São Miguel.

The express buses take around 2½ hours and the pinga litoral takes 4½ hours. There is one bus, at 11 am, to Propriá (US$3, 1½ hours), which continues on to Aracaju (US$6.50, three hours). A quicker and more convenient way to get to Aracaju is to take the ferry across the river to Neópolis, where there are frequent buses to Aracaju.

The pinga litoral bus, which leaves Penedo daily at 1 pm, is the best to take if you want to look at the coast and the people who live there. The ride takes 4½ hours, compared to 2½ hours on the express bus. The extra two hours are worth it if you don't mind buses which stop at the roadside for anyone who wants to get on or off anytime.

After leaving Penedo, the bus travels along the river toward the coast, passing the mud and thatch huts of the fishermen who live in **Piaçabuçu**, then swings in from the coast to head north to **Pontal do Peba**, where it does a U-turn on the beach. From there it passes through **Feliz Deserto**, which has lots of cowboys and coconuts, one pousada and lots of seafood.

The bus turns off Hwy AL-101 a bit further north at **Miaí de Cima**, where there are no pousadas, but lots of locals on the beach at weekends. The next time the bus turns off the main road is into **Barreiras**, with good beaches but no pousadas. It then arrives in **Coruripe** just after 3 pm, before continuing to **Pontal do Coruripe** with its lighthouse and fine beaches.

Pontal just may become a backpackers' stopover. It has a couple of pousadas – one at which English is spoken (Pousada da Ada).

Next stop is **Lagoa da Pau**, with lots of shrimp and a few weekend houses. Then it's on to **Poxim**, past cane fields and coconut palms. Close to Maceió, the bus doesn't enter **Barra da São Miguel** or **Praia do Francês** but only stops at the turn-offs. Passing the huge estuaries of the **Mundaú** and **Manguaba** lagoons, it's not long before the bus reaches the capital.

If you plan on staying at Pajuçara or beaches further north, get off the bus just before it turns off the coast road into the centre of Maceió. This will save you going all the way to the rodoviária. Just cross the road and catch a local bus going along the beaches. Destinations are written on signs near the back door. As the local bus travels through Pajuçara, it doesn't follow the beach but goes along the first road parallel. For the cheap pousadas, get out at the first petrol station and walk across the road.

Car If you are driving to Penedo, there is a 41km sealed road from Hwy BR-101 in Sergipe to Neópolis, on the Sergipe side of the river, and then a short drive from Neópolis to Passagem, where a ferry makes the 10 minute river crossing to Penedo every half hour (US$6 for a car).

NORTH OF MACEIÓ

The Alagoas coast north of Maceió is ideal for independent travellers. The beaches are mostly undisturbed and tropically perfect, and the sea is calm and warm. There are several fishing villages with little tourism apart from a simple hotel or two – although the state government's Costa Dourada (Golden Coast) development plans are bringing about rapid changes, and they aren't pretty.

The coastal road, which is unsealed and slow going along the most secluded stretches, runs within a few hundred metres of the ocean, a rare occurrence along the Brazilian litoral. If you want to follow it, head to Barra de Santo Antônio. The road from here to Barra do Camaragibe is often in disarray and you have to cross some small rivers on local ferries, so check road conditions before departing.

Alternatively, from Maceió, Hwy AL-101 heads north and then divides outside Barra de Santo Antônio. The main road and most through-traffic heads inland on Hwy AL-413. It's a stunning drive (try to stop at Porto Calvo) through rolling hills covered in sugar cane, though there's the odd hill topped with virgin forest that escaped land clearing. A good road runs off Hwy AL-413 from the town of São Luiz do Quitunde, hitting the coast at Barra do Camarajibe. From Barra do Camarajibe, the coast road is sealed as far as Porto de Pedras, about 16km before Japaratinga.

Hwy AL-413 passes a large sugar-cane plant that processes the sugar-cane alcohol that fuels Brazil's cars. The Empresa de Santo Antônio employs about 800 workers in the factory and 4000 in the fields. Tours are possible and worthwhile, but hard to arrange.

A few buses from Maceió go all the way along the coast, but they are less frequent than those that run via Hwy AL-413. Ask for a bus that goes to Porto de Pedras or São Miguel dos Milagres.

Barra de Santo Antônio & Ilha da Croa

Barra is built along the mouth of the Rio Jirituba, below a small bluff. It is a relaxed fishing village only 40km from Maceió and is now attracting tourists and people constructing beach homes. Consequently, it can get busy on weekends and in summer.

The best beaches are out on the Ilha da Croa (narrow peninsula), on the other side of Rio Jirituba. You can catch a small boat across the river (US$0.50) and walk around 2km across the peninsula to the beaches, or take a motorboat all the way (US$2). *Balsas* (ferries) take cars across the river for US$5.

Tabuba beach is a quiet, pretty beach with a few bars, 3km south of Barra de Santo Antônio. There is a piscina natural off the beach – ask at the bars about a ride there by jangada.

Places to Stay & Eat In town, the *Pousada Brisa E Sonhos* is a very friendly place on the river with quartos for US$15/25 for singles/doubles with a good breakfast included. The Honeymoon suite, a room featuring a huge double bed with built-in stereo and velvet bedspreads, costs US$40. The pousada also serves good meals. The *Pousada Tabuba* is a small pousada close to Tabuba beach, with apartamentos at US$15/25. At Paripueira beach, 7km from town, *House of Leia* (☎ 293-1362), Rua Eugênio Costa 1162, has good-value apartamentos for US$25/30.

The *Peixada da Rita*, along the river in Barra de Santo Antônio, serves sensational seafood.

Getting There & Away Direct buses and VW kombi vans to Maceió (US$4, one hour) operate from 4.30 am to 10.30 pm. You can also walk for 20 minutes or hire a local cab to the main road, where you can flag down those buses which bypass the town.

Barra do Camarajibe

This idyllic fishing village, 33km further up the coast, offers fish, beer and a beautiful beach. Buses run to Barra do Camaragibe from Maceió via São Luís do Quintude.

São Miguel dos Milagres

A bit bigger than its neighbours, São Miguel's soft beaches are protected by offshore reefs and the sea is warm and shallow. There's one pousada and a petrol station in town.

Porto de Pedras

You've got to catch the local ferry to cross the river here. Porto de Pedras is a lively little fishing village with a road that connects with Hwy AL-413 at Porto Calvo. In the village there are bars, restaurants and the cheap and dingy *Hotel São Geraldo*.

Japaratinga

Japaratinga's shallow waters are protected by coral reefs and the beaches are backed by coconut trees and fishing huts. Under the moonlight you can walk a couple of kilometres into the sea. The town has a petrol station, a few pousadas and a telephone post.

Maragoji

Slightly more developed, Maragoji has some weekend homes for Pernambucanos and a couple of cheap hotels – try the *Pousada Olho D'Agua* (☎/fax 269-1263). Singles/doubles with verandas and views go for US$35/40, while those without views cost US$25/30. The sea is protected by reefs and is ideal for swimming.

Pernambuco

One of the major tourist destinations in the country, Pernambuco has a lot to offer. There's the colonial architecture of Olinda (a UNESCO World Heritage Site), interesting architectural remnants of the Dutch administration in Recife, good beaches and the beautiful Parque Nacional Marinho de Fernando da Noronha. The Pernambucanos preserve a rich cultural tradition, from the lively Carnaval in Olinda to the marketplace of Caruaru. The passion play in Nova Jerusalem is the largest in the world, drawing crowds of 80,000. Sugar cane still dominates the economy, and Recife's industrial centre is the second largest in the Northeast after Bahia's.

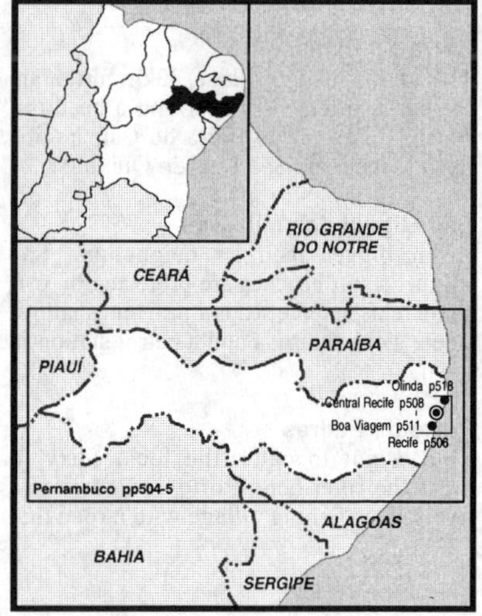

RECIFE

• *pop 1.4 million* ✉ *50000-000* ☎ *081*

Recife ('ress-eef-ay') is the country's fourth biggest city and the capital of Pernambuco. The 'Venice of Brazil' (a rather hopeful comparison), Recife is a city of water and bridges with *arrecifes* (reefs) offshore. Its sister city of Olinda is a beautiful enclave of colonial buildings filled with artists, students and bohemians.

Amid all the recent development, Recife retains a rich traditional side, with some of Brazil's best folk art, including painting and sculpture, dance, music and festivals. It takes time to discover this side of the city, but it's well worth the effort.

Recife is the port of entry for many flights from Europe and has recently been trying to broaden its tourist appeal. The main beneficiary of these developments has been Boa Viagem, the Copacabana of Pernambuco. Site of the well-to-do nightclubs, restaurants and most of the mid-priced to expensive hotels, Boa Viagem has wide beaches which are essential for escaping Recife's muggy heat, although the water is not always very clean.

Unless you want to be right on the beach, stay in Olinda, which has more cheap accommodation and is a more interesting place to stay.

History

Recife developed in the 17th century as the port for the rich sugar plantations around Olinda. With several rivers and offshore reefs, Recife proved to be an excellent port and began to outgrow Olinda. By the 17th century, Recife and Olinda combined were the most prosperous cities in Brazil, with the possible exception of Salvador (Bahia). The neighbouring Indians had been subdued after brutal warfare, and the colonial aristocracy living in Olinda was raking in profits with its many sugar *engenhos* (mills). Naturally, all the work was done by slaves labour.

No other European country had managed to grab a part of Brazil from the Portuguese until 1621, when the Dutch, who were active in the sugar trade and knew the lands of Brazil well, set up the Dutch West India

Company to get their teeth into the Brazilian cake. A large fleet sailed in 1624 and captured Salvador (Bahia), but a huge Spanish-Portuguese militia of 12,000 men recaptured the city the following year. Five years later the Dutch decided to try again, this time in Pernambuco. Recife was abandoned; the Dutch took the city and by 1640 they had control of a great chunk of the Northeast, from Maranhão to the Rio São Francisco.

The Dutch had hoped the sugar planters wouldn't resist their rule, but many Brazilian planters took up arms against the non-Catholic Dutch. In 1654, after a series of battles around Recife, the Dutch finally surrendered. This was the last European challenge to Portuguese Brazil.

Recife prospered after the Dutch were expelled, but in spite of the city's growing economic power, which had eclipsed that of Olinda, political power remained with the sugar planters in Olinda, and they refused to share it. In 1710 fighting began between the *filhos da terra* (the sugar planters of Olinda) and the *mascates* (the Portuguese merchants of Recife), the more recent immigrants. The Guerra dos Mascates (War of the Mascates), as it came to be known, was a bloody rgional feud between different sections of the ruling class and native Brazilians and immigrants. In the end, with the help of the Portuguese Crown and their superior economic resources, the mascates of Recife gained considerable political clout at the expense of Olinda, which began its long, slow decline.

More dependent on the sugar economy than Rio or São Paulo, Recife was eclipsed by these two centres as the sugar economy floundered throughout the 19th century.

Orientation

Recife is large, modern and more difficult to negotiate than most cities in the Northeast. The city centre is a confusing mixture of high-rise offices, colonial churches and popular mercados. During the day, traffic and tourists get lost in the maze of winding, one-way streets.

The heart of Recife, containing the old section of town, ranges along the waterfront in Boa Vista district, across the Rio Capibaribe to Santo Antônio district and then across to Ilha do Recife. All are connected by bridges. Olinda is 6km to the north over swamps and rivers, while Boa Viagem is 6km to the south.

Information

Tourist Office The headquarters of Empetur (☎ 241-2111; fax 241-9011), the state tourism bureau, is in the monolithic Centro de Convenções (Complexo Rodoviária de Salgadinho), between the city centre and Olinda. To get there from the centre, take a Rio Doce/Conde da Boa Vista, Jardim Brasil/Estrada de Belém, Santa Casa or Aguazinha bus. Its information desk at the airport has English-speaking attendants, sells maps and can book hotels.

Useful publications available from tourist offices include the *Recife & Olinda Tourism map – Rota do Sol,* with a map of the beaches around Recife, and *Informativo Pro Lazer*a, a bi-monthly mini-guide to Recife. All are in Portuguese. *Jornal do Commércio*, one of the local newspapers, has cultural listings (museums, art galleries, cinemas) in its daily Caderno C section.

Foreign Consulates These countries have consulates in Recife:

France
  Avenida Conselheiro Aguiar 2333, 6th floor, Boa Viagem (☎ 465-3290)
Germany
  Avenida Dantas Barreto 191, 4th floor, Santo Antônio (☎ 424-3488)
Italy
  Avenida Dantas Barreto 1200, 9th floor, Santo Antônio (☎ 224-0638)
Switzerland
  Avenida Conselheiro Aguiar 4880, Boa Viagem (☎ 326-3144)
UK
  Avenida Engenheiro Domingos Ferreira 4150, Boa Viagem (☎ 465-7744)
USA
  Rua Gonçalves Maia 163, Boa Vista (☎ 421-2441)

Visas If you need to renew a visa, go to the Polícia Federal building on Rua Cais do Apolo in Ilha do Recife.

Money Convenient casas de câmbio in the centre include Mônaco Câmbio, Praça Joaquim Nabuco 159, and Norte Câmbio Turismo, Rua Mathias de Albuquerque 223, sala 508. In Boa Viagem, Norte Câmbio Turismo has a branch at Rua dos Navegantes 691, loja 10. Close by on the same street is Colmeia Câmbio & Turismo at No 784, loja 4. There are branches of Banco do Brasil at the airport, in the centre at Avenida Dantas Barreto 541 (Santo Antônio), and in Boa Viagem at Avenida Conselheiro Aguiar 3600. Bradesco has lots of ATMs in the centre of the city and Boa Viagem.

Post & Communication The main post office is at Avenida Guararapes 250. The posta restante (postcode 50001-970) counter is in the basement. There are also post offices at the airport and the Terminal Integrado de Passageiros (TIP), the combined metrô station and rodoviária.

Telpe has telephone stations with international service at TIP, at the airport, and in the centre at Rua do Hospício 148.

Travel Agencies Andratur (☎ 465-8588), Avenida Conselheiro Aguiar 3150, loja 7 in Boa Viagem, provides national and international tickets at discounted prices. It also sells packaged trips for Fernando de Noronha.

Bookshops There are several bookstalls along Rua do Infante Dom Henrique. The airport bookshop and the Livro 7 de Setembro are the best bets if you're looking for foreign-language books. For lots of used books in French and English, try Livraria Brandão, Rua da Matriz 22.

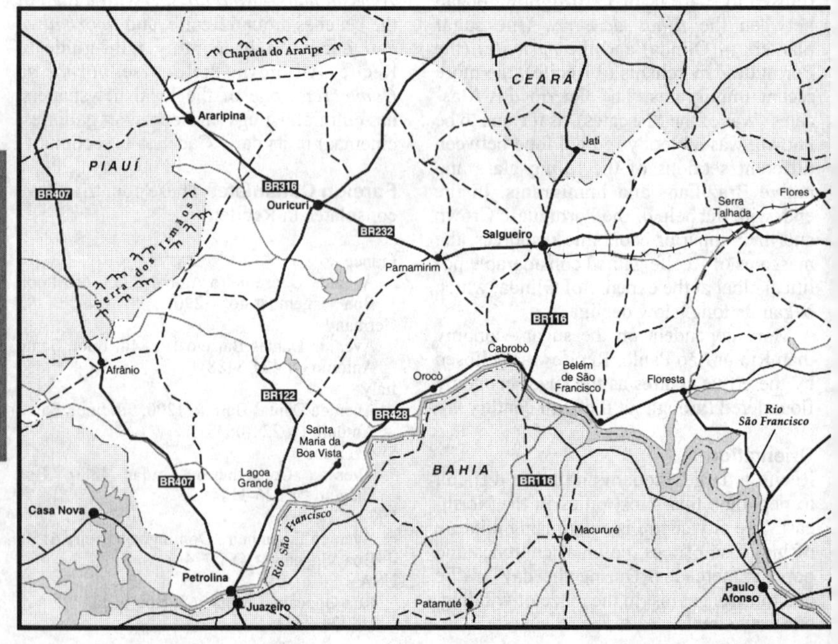

Museums & Galleries

With such a long and important history, it's not surprising that Recife is loaded with churches and museums, but few of them are must-sees.

The best museum, **Museu do Homem do Nordeste**, is east of the city centre along Avenida 17 de Agosto. Catch the Dois Irmãos bus from Parque 13 de Maio (in the city centre) and ask the driver to let you off at the right spot. The museum is divided into three sections: an anthropology section about the people of the Northeast; a popular-art section with some superb ceramic figurines; and a pharmacutical exhibit about the region's herbal/indigenous medicine. It's open from 11 am to 5 pm on Tuesday, Wednesday and Friday, from 8 am to 5 pm on Thursday, and from 1 to 5 pm on weekends.

The **Horto Zoobotânico**, a zoo and botanical garden combined (both renovated in 1990), is in the same neighbourhood as the Museu do Homem do Nordeste. Opening hours are 8 am to 5 pm Tuesday to Sunday.

Train enthusiasts might like to visit the **Museu do Trem** (Train Museum) (☎ 424-2022 ext 452) which is adjacent to Recife metrô station – formerly known as Estação Central (central train station). It's open from 9 am to noon and 2 to 5 pm Tuesday to Friday, from 9 am to noon on Saturday and from 2 to 5 pm on Sunday.

For a look at some paintings by renowned artists of Pernambuco you can visit the **Galeria de Arte Metropolitana**, Rua da Aurora 265. It's open from noon to 6 pm Tuesday to Saturday.

Archaeology buffs will want to find time to browse around through the **Museu Archeológico** (☎ 222-4952) at Rua do Hospício 130. It's open Tuesday and Wednesday from 2 to 4 pm.

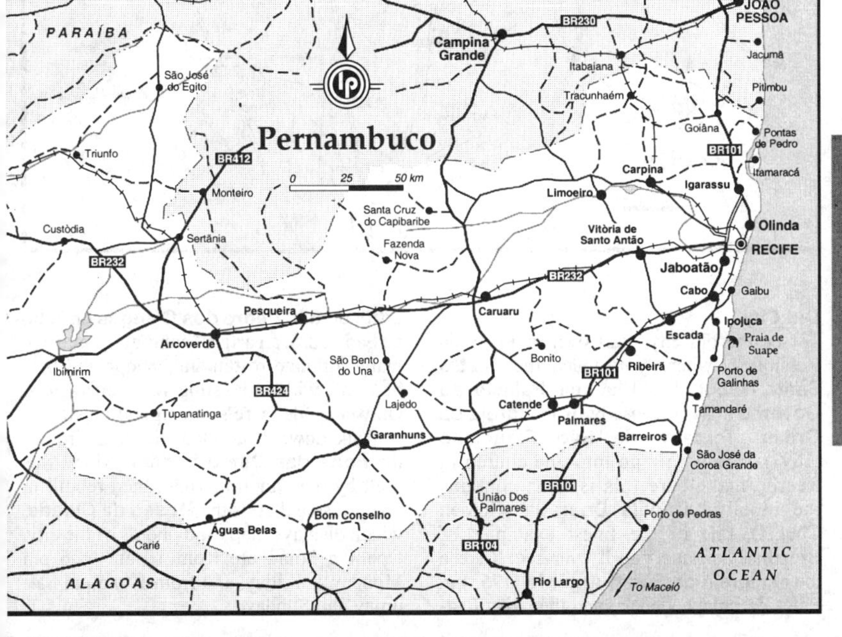

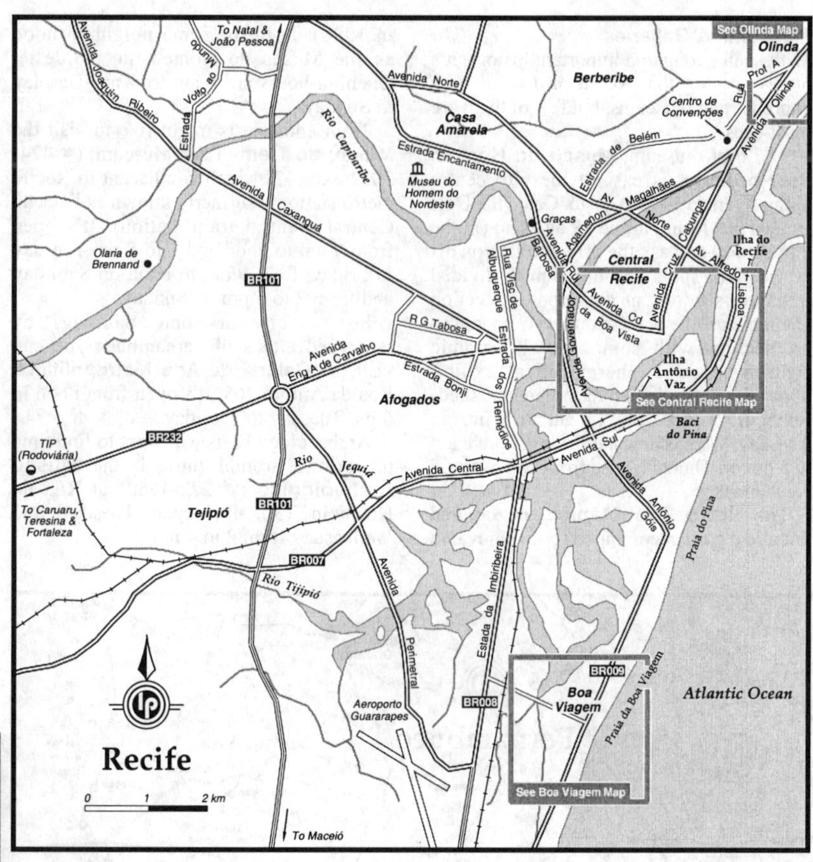

Old City

To see the old city, start over at Praça da República, where you'll see the **Teatro Santa Isabel** (1850) and the **Palácio do Governo** (1841). Close by is the **Igreja da Ordem Terceira de São Francisco** (1697). If you only go into one church in Recife, make sure this is it. It contains the beautiful **Capela Dourada** (Golden Chapel), one of the finest examples of Brazilian baroque you'll ever see. Take a look at **Igreja de Santo Antônio** (1753) in Praça da Independência, and then visit **Catedral de São Pedro dos Clérigos** on Pátio de São Pedro, an artists' hang-out. There are many intimate restaurants, shops and bars here, all with interesting local characters. On weekends there's often good music.

Walk down Rua Vidal de Negreiros to the **Forte das Cinco Pontas**, which was built by the Dutch in 1630, then rebuilt in 1677. Inside there's the **Museu da Cidade**, which displays maps and photos of the city. Opening hours are from 10 am to 6 pm Monday to Friday, and from 1 to 5 pm Saturday and Sunday.

Nearby at Praça Dom Vital is the daily **Mercado do São José** and the **Basílica de NS da Penha**. The market used to be a major centre for food and crafts from throughout Pernambuco, but now you'll find mostly manufactured goods here.

Casa da Cultura de Recife

The Casa da Cultura de Recife, across the street from the metrô station, once served as a huge, colonial-style prison, but was decommissioned and renovated in 1975. It's now home to many craft and souvenir shops. Good traditional music and dance shows are often performed outside the building. It's open from 9 am to 7 pm Monday to Saturday.

Olaria de Brennand

The Olaria, a ceramics factory and exhibition hall, is set in thickly forested surroundings, a rare landscape for suburban Recife and an even rarer chance for travellers in the Northeast to see what the Mata Atlântica looked like several centuries ago. The buildings and exhibits in Olaria de Brennand are perhaps the most bizarre highlight of the Northeast – they are highly recommended.

History The Irish forebears of the present owner, Francisco Brennand, arrived in Brazil in 1823 to work as peasant farmers. The unmarried daughter of a sugar magnate took a liking to Brennand's father, who was employed by her father. She later inherited her father's property and, when she died, willed her entire estate and immense wealth to Brennand Senior.

The house in which Francisco Brennand was born, in 1927, was imported from England in prefabricated form. Brennand's father founded a brickworks in 1917 and continued this business until 1945. Francisco left for France, where he studied art and was influenced by Picasso, Miró, Léger and Gaudi. The property in Recife remained abandoned from 1945 until 1971, when Brennand returned from France and set about restoring the dilapidated buildings.

The Gallery/Museum This contains a permanent exhibition of around 2000 pieces which are *not* for sale (see the end of this section for the address of the sales outlet in Boa Viagem).

Wander around sculptured collages of cubes, spheres and rectangles absorbed into animal shapes: worms with balaclava hats; blunt-headed lizards bursting out of parapets; cuboid geckos straddling paths; geese with flying helmets; birds of prey hatching from half-shells lodged in the walls; pigs formed from giant nails; and vistas of busts, buttocks, breasts, and phalluses ... meanwhile, black swans glide over shoals of goldfish in ponds dotted with vulvas shaped like tortoises. Kooky, but fun!

The gallery/museum is open from 8 am to 5 pm Monday to Friday. For information, contact Oficina Ceramica Francisco Brennand (☎ 271-2466).

Getting There & Away From the centre of Recife, take the bus marked Caxangá for the 11km ride to the Caxangá bus station. Continue walking about 100m away from the city and over the bridge. Then take the first road on the left – easily recognised by the roadside statue of Padre Cicero. Walk about 2km, past a couple of stray hotels, until you reach a gaudy housing development. Take the road to the left at the T-junction and continue for about 3km through dense forest to the office. Shady characters hang out in the area, so it's best if you are in a group. The walk takes about 1¼ hours.

Otherwise, you can take a taxi from the bus terminal or the bridge to the Olaria – and walk back after your visit. Tour companies and taxi companies will also do the trip from the centre of Recife or Olinda, but it's expensive unless you can form a small group to share the costs. For a recommended taxi company, see Getting Around in the later Olinda section.

Special Events

The Recife-Olinda combination may be the best Carnaval in Brazil, but even if you decide to Carnaval in Rio or Salvador,

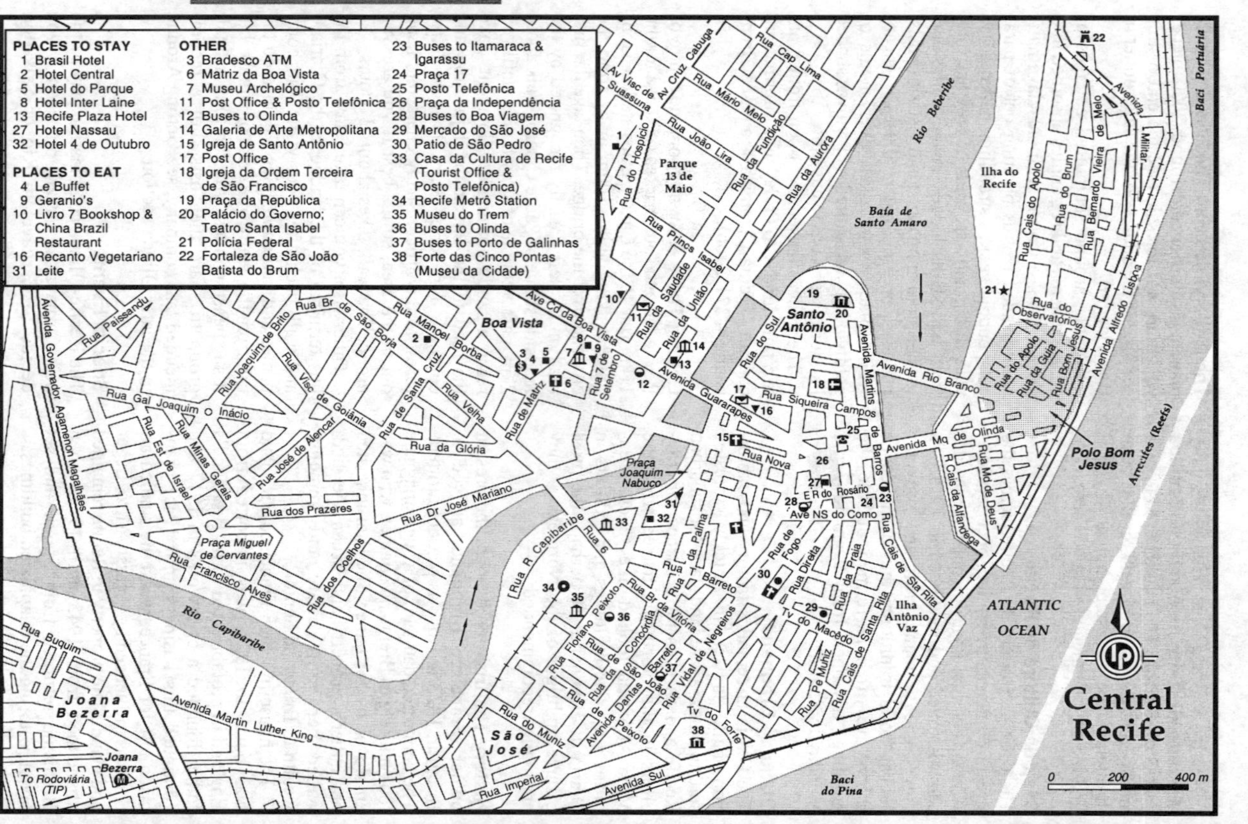
PLACES TO STAY
1 Brasil Hotel
2 Hotel Central
5 Hotel do Parque
8 Hotel Inter Laine
13 Recife Plaza Hotel
27 Hotel Nassau
32 Hotel 4 de Outubro
PLACES TO EAT
4 Le Buffet
9 Geranio's
10 Livro 7 Bookshop & China Brazil Restaurant
16 Recanto Vegetariano
31 Leite
OTHER
3 Bradesco ATM
6 Matriz da Boa Vista
7 Museu Archelógico
11 Post Office & Posto Telefônica
12 Buses to Olinda
14 Galeria de Arte Metropolitana
15 Igreja de Santo Antônio
17 Post Office
18 Igreja da Ordem Terceira de São Francisco
19 Praça da República
20 Palácio do Governo; Teatro Santa Isabel
21 Polícia Federal
22 Fortaleza de São João Batista do Brum
23 Buses to Itamaraca & Igarassu
24 Praça 17
25 Posto Telefônica
26 Praça da Independência
28 Buses to Boa Viagem
29 Mercado do São José
30 Patio de São Pedro
33 Casa da Cultura de Recife (Tourist Office & Posto Telefônica)
34 Recife Metrô Station
35 Museu do Trem
36 Buses to Olinda
37 Buses to Porto de Galinhas
38 Forte das Cinco Pontas (Museu da Cidade)
Central
Recife
0
200
400 m
ATLANTIC OCEAN
Arrecifes (Reefs)
Baci Portuária
Baci do Pina
Polo Bom Jesus
Ilha do Recife
Ilha Antônio Vaz
Baía de Santo Amaro
Rio Beberibe
Rio Capibaribe
Santo Antônio
Boa Vista
São José
Joana Bezerra
Parque 13 de Maio
Praça Joaquim Nabuco
Praça Miguel de Cervantes
To Rodoviária (TIP)
Avenida Alfredo Lisboa
Avenida Militar
Rua Cais do Apolo
Rua do Brum
Rua Bernardo Vieira de Melo
Rua do Observatório
Rua Bom Jesus
Rua da Guia
Rua do Apolo
Rua Md de Deus
R Cais da Alfandega
Avenida Mq de Olinda
Avenida Rio Branco
Avenida Martins de Barros
Rua Cais de Sta Rita
Rua Cais de Santa Rita
Rua da Praia
Rua Direita
Rua de Fogo
Tv do Macedo
Rua Pe Muniz
E R do Rosário
Ave NS do Como
Rua Siqueira Campos
Rua Nova
Rua do Sol
Avenida Guararapes
Rua da Palma
Rua T Barreto
Rua Br da Vitória
Rua Vidal de Negreiros
Rua Dantas Barreto
Rua Concordia
Rua de São João
Rua Floriano Peixoto
Avenida Dantas Barreto
Tv do Forte
Avenida Sul
Rua do Muniz
Rua Imperial
Rua 6
Rua R Capibaribe
Rua Dr José Mariano
Rua da Glória
Rua dos Coelhos
Rua dos Prazeres
Rua Francisco Alves
Avenida Martin Luther King
Rua Buquim
Avenida Governador Agamenon Magalhães
Rua Paissandu
Rua Gal Joaquim O Inácio
Rua Est de Israel
Rua Minas Gerais
Rua Joaquim de Brito
Rua Visc de Goiânia
Rua José de Alencar
Rua Br de São Borja
Rua Manoel Borba
Rua de Santa Cruz
Rua Velha
Rua de Matriz
Rua 7 de Setembro
Ave Cd da Boa Vista
Rua da Saudade
Rua da União
Rua Princs Isabel
Rua do Hospício
Av Visc de Suassuna
Av Cruz Cabuga
Rua João Lira
Rua Mário Melo
Rua Cap Lima
Rua da Fundição
Rua da Aurora

Recife starts celebrating so early that you can enjoy festivities there and then go somewhere else for Carnaval proper. Two months before the start of Carnaval, there are *bailes* (dances) in the clubs and Carnaval blocos practising on the streets, with *frevo* (fast-paced music that originated in Pernambuco) dancing everywhere. Galo da Madrugada, Recife's largest bloco, has been known to bring 20,000 people in costume onto the beaches at Boa Viagem to dance.

There are supposedly 500 different Carnaval blocos in the Recife area, and they come in all 'shakes' and colours. There are the traditional and well organised, and the modern and anarchical. There are samba schools, afoxés (music of Bahia), Indian tribes and *maracatus* (African processions accompanied by percussion musicians), but the main dance of Carnaval in Pernambuco is the frenetic frevo. The Fundação da Cultura do Recife, which runs Carnaval, has on occasion organised public frevo lessons for the uninitiated at the Pátio de São Pedro.

Along Praia Boa Viagem, Carnaval groups practice on weekends, and as Carnaval approaches they add *trios elétricos* (electrified frevo played on top of trucks) to the tomfoolery. The week before Carnaval Sunday, the unofficial Carnaval really starts. Several groups march through the city centre each day and at least one baile kicks off each evening – time to practice that frevo.

Big-time Carnaval takes place from Saturday to Tuesday, nonstop. The big Carnaval groups parade in wonderful costumes, singing and dancing. For the parade route and schedule, check the local papers or the tourism office. Along Avenida Guararapes there's a popular frevo dance that starts on Friday night and goes on and on.

Places to Stay – Budget

Although we've included details here for accommodation in Recife, most budget travellers prefer staying in Olinda: it's cheap and beautiful, there's lots happening and you can walk everywhere. If you want the beach, head to Boa Viagem, where there is a hostel and a few reasonably priced pousadas.

City Centre There are a couple of cheap places in central Recife near Parque 13 de Maio, but they are only good if you're on the tightest budget. The *Brasil Hotel* (☎ 222-3534) at Rua do Hospício 687 has grungy quartos at US$8/11 for singles/doubles and apartamentos with fan for US$10/15. Down the road is the quaint but rather run-down *Hotel do Parque* (☎ 222-5427) at Rua do Hospício 51. It has quartos with fan that cost US$10 per person. Most of the occupants are long-term. Much better value is the friendly family-run *Hotel Inter Laine* (☎ 423-2942), Rua do Hospício 186. It has clean apartamentos at US$20/25/35 for singles/doubles/triples. The owner, José Carlos, speaks English and French, and gives discounts for longer stays. Closer to the nightlife in the old city, *Hotel Nassau* (☎ 224-3977), Rua Largo do Rosário, has large, clean rooms with good-sized bathrooms. Located in a pedestrian mall, it's good value, with apartamentos for US$20/30.

Boa Viagem The *Albergue de Juventude Maracatus do Recife* (☎ 326-1221), Rua Dona Maria Carolina 185, is well located, clean, and has a swimming pool. Four-bed dormitory rooms cost US$12 per person with breakfast. Sheet and towel hire is US$4.

Places to Stay – Mid-Range

City Centre The *Central* (☎ 221-1472), Rua Manoel Borba 209, is a 30s hotel with a pleasant, rambling design and classic antique elevator. Quartos are reasonable value at US$18/20, while apartamentos start at US$25/29. You can negotiate a discount for longer stays.

The *Hotel 4 de Outubro* (☎ 424-4477; fax 424-2598), Rua Floriano Peixoto 141, is a modern, functional hotel near the metrô station. Apartamentos start at around US$35/40. The *Recife Plaza Hotel* (☎/fax 231-1200), Rua da Aurora 225, overlooks the Rio Capibaribe in the centre of town. Its apartamentos start at US$64/72, but it often gives a 20% discount.

Boa Viagem The moderately priced hotels here fill up during summer. Generally, prices drop in inverse proportion to the distance from the seafront, so the further back you go, the cheaper it gets. Prices quoted here are for the low season – expect an increase of around 30% during summer.

The *Navegantes Praia Hotel* (☎ 326-9609; fax 325-2689) is a small, well-located two-star hotel one block from the beach at Rua dos Navegantes 1997. Apartamentos start at US$33/36. *Hotel Portal de Arrecifes* (☎/fax 326-5921) is a small beachfront place at Rua Boa Viagem 864. Apartamentos here are US$28/38.

Three hotels are clustered close together along Rua Felix de Brito Melo. The *Hotel Pousada Aconchego* (☎ 326-2989; fax 326-8059), No 382, features a swimming pool, a 24-hour-a-day restaurant and some interesting original art in the foyer and halls. It also changes cash and travellers cheques at a decent rate. Apartamentos go for US$38/46. The *Hotel Pedro do Mar* (☎ 325-5340), No 604, is a friendly establishment and the manager speaks both English and German. Apartamentos cost US$26/30. The *Hotel Alameda Jasmins* (☎/fax 325-1591), No 370, also has a swimming pool but is looking a bit tired. Air-conditioned apartamentos will cost you US$30/35.

Places to Stay – Top End

On the beachfront at Avenida Boa Viagem are the five-star *Recife Palace* (☎ 465-6688; fax 465-6767), No 4070, with double rooms starting at US$150, and the *Hotel International Palace* (☎ 465-5022; fax 326-7661), No 3722, where room prices start at US$100.

Places to Eat

The city centre is loaded with self-serve lunch places – try *Le Buffet*, Rua do Hospício 147, or *Geranio's*, nearby on Rua 7 de Setembro. At night in the centre it should be easy to find something to your liking around the lively Pátio de São Pedro or at the Polo Bom Jesus in the old city. Both areas offer a surprising variety of prices and styles. *Leite* is a famous traditional lunch place on Praça Joaquim Nabuco, near the Casa da Cultura de Recife. *Recanto Vegetariano*, Avenida Guararapes 210, on the 2nd floor, is open Monday to Friday from 11 am to 3 pm.

Mangue Beat

'Os pés em Pernambuco, a cabeça no infinito'
(Feet in Pernambuco, head in the infinite) – mangue beat motto

Recife is the centre of a new music in Brazil known as 'mangue beat' – a mixture of international and local rhythms. 'Brazilian music has a new address: Recife in Pernambuco', wrote Jon Pareles in the *New York Times*.

Mestre Ambrósio combines guitar with *rabeca* (a type of rustic violin), electric base with *zabumba* (a big drum) and bases its choreography on regional folkloric dances. O Faces do Subúrbio combines American hip-hop with Northeastern traditional music. Internationally known exponents of mangue beat are Chico Science e Nação Zumbi (tragically, Chico Science was killed in an auto accident in February 1997), Mestre Ambrósio and Mundo Livre S/A.

If you want to see one of the mangue beat bands, it's best to check newspapers and cultural magazines to find out where the shows are. You won't find them on the tourist circuit – not yet anyway.

Andrew Draffen

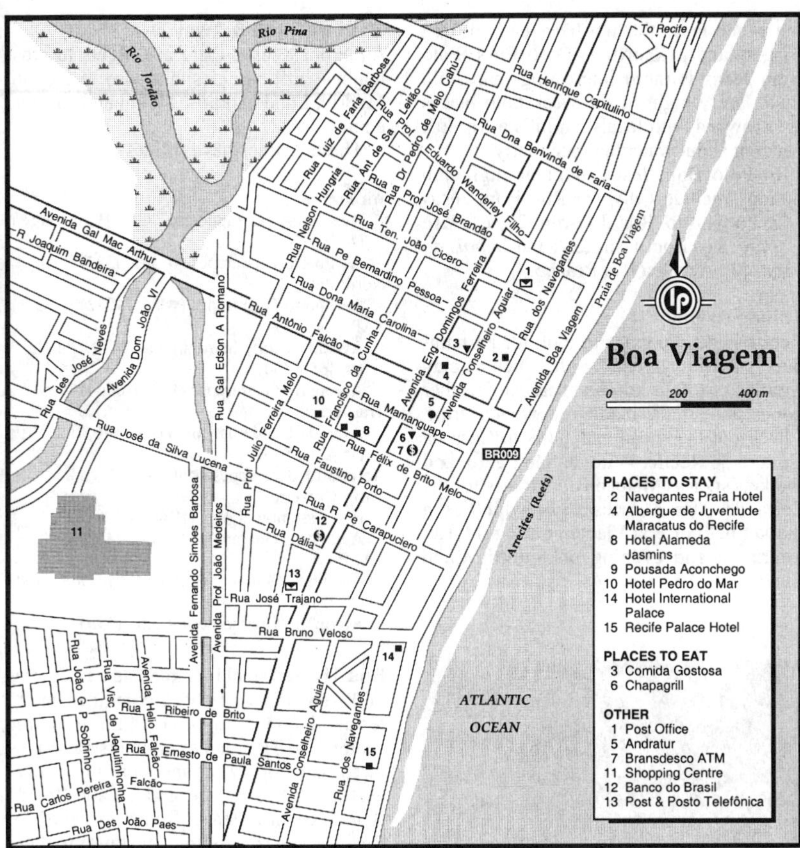

Boa Viagem has many restaurants, but apart from those in the Polo Pina (see the following Entertainment section), which has a concentrated assortment of bars and restaurants, they're widely scattered. *Comida Gostosa*, Avenida Conselheiro Aguiar, is a classy self-serve lunch place that's very popular with locals. *Chapagrill*, Rua Mamanguape 157, is a self-serve place with stacks of different salads and cold cuts. The *Lobster*, Avenida Rui Barbosa 1649, is good if you want to splurge on lobster. It provides live music at dinner and opens daily from noon to midnight. In Polo Pina *Maxime* (☎ 326-5314), Avenida Boa Viagem 21, serves traditional seafood dishes; it's not cheap, but try the lobster (US$30) or one of the local fish, such as cavala (mackerel).

Entertainment

After a trip to Europe, the mayor of Recife decided the restaurants and nightclubs of the city were too scattered, and successfully created two major leisure areas. One is in the old city and is called **Polo Bom Jesus**;

the other is at the northern end of Boa Viagem and is known as **Polo Pina**. Polo Bom Jesus is more interesting than Polo Pina. Every night of the week both places are crowded with locals, and it's a trip just hanging about watching them party.

In Polo Bom Jesus, popular nightclub options include *Calypso*, Rua Bom Jesus 147; Purgatório, Rua do Brum 27; *El Paso Cabaré*, Rua Bom Jesus 237; and *Depois do Escuro* in Avenida Rio Branco.

Things to Buy

Recife is a good place to look for Pernambuco's traditional handicrafts, such as clay figurines, wood sculptures, carpets, leather goods, and articles made from woven straw. Check out the shops and stalls in Casa da Cultura de Recife, Pátio de São Pedro, and markets such as Mercado do São José or the Feira de Arte e Artesanato, which is a market held in Boa Viagem during the late afternoon and evening on Saturday and Sunday.

JOHN MAIER, JR

Boa Viagem beach, a major attraction of Recife

Getting There & Away

Air From Recife, there are flights to most major Brazilian cities, and also to Lisbon, Madrid, London, Paris, Miami and Amsterdam.

These airlines have offices in Recife:

Air France
  Rua Padre Carapuceiro 733, Boa Viagem (☎ 465-4416)
  Aeroporto Guararapes (☎ 341-0333)
Nordeste
  Aeroporto Guararapes (☎ 341-4222)
TAP
  Avenida Conselheiro Aguiar 1472, sala 155, (☎ 465-8800)
  Aeroporto Guararapes (☎ 341-0654)
Transbrasil
  Avenida Conde da Boa Vista 1546, Boa Vista (☎ 423-2566)
Aeroporto Guararapes (☎ 465-0333)
Varig-Cruzeiro
  Rua Assembleia 456, (☎ 464-4400)
  Aeroporto Guararapes (☎ 341-4411)
VASP
  Avenida Manoel Borba 488, Boa Vista (☎ 421-3611)
  Aeroporto Guararapes (☎ 326-1699)

Bus The Terminal Integrado de Passageiros (TIP) (☎ 452-1999) is a combined metrô terminal and rodoviária 14km from the centre. The TIP handles all interstate departures and many connections for local destinations. Buses to Igarassu and Ilha do Itamaracá now leave from the centre of Recife – you can also pick up buses to these destinations from the Mercado Santo Amaro between the city centre and Olinda.

There are frequent departures to Maceió (US$11, four hours), at least five departures a day to Salvador (US$37, 12 to 14 hours), and daily departures to Rio (US$108, about 36 hours).

Heading north, it is two hours to João Pessoa (US$5), five hours to Natal (US$13), 12 hours to Fortaleza (US$41), 24 hours to São Luís (US$85) and 32 hours to Belém (US$90). There are frequent services to Caruaru (US$6, 2 hours), Garanhuns (US$10, 3½ hours), and Triunfo (US$22, 8 hours).

Getting Around

To/From the Airport Guararapes airport (☎ 464-4180) is 10km south of the city centre. Taxis cost about US$12 to the centre; catch a regular taxi – not a special airport taxi, which is almost twice as expensive.

From the airport there are regular buses and microbuses (more expensive). The Aeroporto bus runs to Avenida Dantas Barreto in the centre of Recife, stopping in Boa Viagem on the way. To Olinda, take the Aeroporto bus to Avenida Nossa Senhora do Carmo in Recife and pick up a Casa Caiada bus from there. Another option is to get off in Boa Viagem and take a Piedade/Rio Doce bus from there to Olinda.

To/From the TIP (Metrô/Rodoviária) The shiny metrô system is very useful for the 25 minute trip (US$0.50) between the TIP and the metrô terminus at the Recife metrô station, in the centre. Travellers who want to go straight to Boa Viagem from the TIP should get off at metrô stop Joana Bezerra and catch a bus from there to Boa Viagem. To Olinda, you can catch the metrô into the centre, then take a Rio Doce/Princesa Isabel bus from the stop outside the metrô station.

Bus & Taxi Buses generally have signs which show the origin of the bus followed by its destination. To telephone a taxi, dial ☎ 224-8441.

Olinda From the city centre to Olinda, catch any bus marked Rio Doce. From outside the central metrô station, catch a Rio Doce/Princesa Isabel bus. The main bus stop in Olinda is Praça do Carmo. Ask the conductor to let you know when you get there, as it's easy to miss. The Piedade/Rio Doce and Barra de Jangada/Casa Caiada buses run between Olinda and Boa Viagem. Taxis from the centre of Recife to Olinda cost US$6 and take 20 minutes. A taxi from the airport to Olinda will cost US$15.

Boa Viagem From the centre to Boa Viagem, take any bus from Avenida NS do Carmo marked Aeroporto, Shopping Center, Candeias or Piedade. To return to the centre, take any bus marked Dantas Barreto. Buses run along Avenida Engenheiro Domingos Ferreira in Boa Viagem, three blocks from the beach. A taxi from the centre to Boa Viagem costs around US$5.

BEACHES SOUTH OF RECIFE

This is excellent beach territory protected by coral reefs. The sea is calm, the waters are crystal clear and the beaches are lined with coconut palms and white sand dunes. The coastal Hwy PE-060 doesn't hug the ocean like the road in northern Alagoas, so you have to drive a dozen or so kilometres on an access road to see what each beach is like. There are frequent bus services to all these beach towns from Recife. Many of the towns have one or two simple hotels and, being away from Recife, all have excellent camping.

Gaibu & Cabo de Santo Agostinho

Although Gaibu is the larger town, beach bums should head only as far as Cabo de Santo Agostinho, one of the state's finest beaches. There are facilities for snorkelling and spear fishing. Take a walk to the ruins of the **Forte Castelo do Mar**, next to the church.

On a hill between Gaibu and Calhetas (you have to ask around for directions) there's a small freshwater stream that's used for nude bathing.

Suape & Ilha do Paiva

Ilha do Paiva, nicknamed the island of lovers, is popular for its nude beaches. Take a boat from Barra dos Jangandas – it's worth a visit.

The mainland beaches here – **Candeias**, **Venda Grande**, **Piedade** – are semi-urban beaches with many barracas, hotels, and crowds on weekends. But they are still good beaches, with clean water and sometimes strong surf. Suape has been developed as an industrial port and is worth avoiding.

Porto de Galinhas

Seventy kilometres south of Recife is Porto de Galinhas (Port of Chickens). The name

Walking from Recife to Maceió

Two Swedish travellers wrote to tell us about their walk from Recife to Maceió:

We started from Olinda, where we left most of our luggage at our pousada. From the centre of Recife we took the train (hourly departures) to Cabo, and then walked to the beach at Gaibu. The reason we started outside Recife was that we had been warned about walking around in the suburbs.

Sun protection is a must. If you walk from Maceió to Recife, the sun is in your face the whole time. We're happy we did it the other way round because the sun can really burn. You should carry a portable stove and always have at least one litre of water per person. Many villages can provide water and food. A big knife is useful as it's easy to pick coconuts along the way. A tent isn't strictly necessary, but it's good to have the option. You don't really need a mosquito net either.

After three hours of walking from Gaibu, we reached a little village and the first river. Don't try to cross it. We made this mistake and found ourselves in the Complexo Portuário e Industrial de Suape, a large oil refinery, where we had a terrible time finding a way out. It's far better to wait for a bus to NS do Ó, and walk from there to Porto de Galinhas; continue past the beautiful Praia de Galinhas until you come to a small river which you can wade across (waist level) at low tide.

At Barra de Sirinhaém, boats take you across the river free of charge. Unfortunately there is a lot of garbage along the beaches; people throw many things in the river, and you can even find needles and other things from hospitals.

At Rio Formoso, boats cross the river, but you may have to wait a while before one arrives. We got a free lift right away. After about 4km more we came to Tamandaré, a village with shops, bars, hotels and boat-rental facilities.

At the next river, Rio Una, once again we got a free ride across. Varza do Una is a very different village, and it can be difficult to find a place to stay, but ask around.

From here we had to hitchhike around a swamp to São José da Coroa Grande. From there we continued into Alagoas state where Hwy AL-101 runs not further than 100m from the beach. This makes it easy to walk up to the road to get around rivers.

Maragoji is a big beach with many bars, boat-rental and other facilities. Japaratinga was the first place we slept at a pousada (*Rei dos Peixes*). Our next stop was at the Rio Manguaba, where we were taken across by boat for US$1. It's also possible to walk to the highway and take a ferry. On the other side is a small town, Porto de Pedras, which is a nice, colourful place with good, cheap restaurants and pousadas.

From here we started to follow the main road which was hot and boring until São Miguel dos Milagres (13km from Porto de Pedras), where there is one pousada.

The following day we crossed the Rio Camarajibe by boat (fare US$0.50) and came to the nicest beach we found along this part of the coast. From there we walked 3km to Barra de Santo Antônio.

Barra de Santo Antônio is nothing special. Ilha da Croa is a peninsula. Take a boat across the river, then walk along the beach to your right and cross to the other side of the peninsula. This only takes about 20 minutes.

This walk took us 11 days. We only walked in the morning and late afternoon, and we often stopped for hours and sometimes for days. We found enormous hospitality – fishing families were very generous and they adore the company of foreigners. People invited us to stay with them. It's possible to do this route in seven days, or even five days if you're in a hurry.

With blisters on our feet and red faces, we took a bus from here to Maceió – locals said the last 40km to Maceió were nothing special. It was a great adventure and we loved every minute – almost!

Suzanne Gabrielsson & Leif Örnestrand

THE NORTHEAST

came as a result of the slave trade, which secretly continued after abolition. Upon hearing that the chickens from Angola had arrived, the masters of Recife knew to expect another load of slaves.

Porto de Galinhas has one of Pernambuco's most famous beaches, which curves along a pretty bay lined with coconut palms, mangroves and cashew trees. Unfortunately, there are some new housing estates creeping towards the town of Porto de Galinhas and it gets very crowded on weekends, even in the off season. Most of the beach, 3km from town, is sheltered by a reef, but there are some waves for surfers. The water is warm and clear – you can see the colourful fish playing around your feet. There are plenty of jangadas for rent (US$5 per person per hour). Other boats can take you out to Ilha de Santo Alexio for US$15 per person.

Should you tire of Praia de Porto de Galinhas, head for Praia de Maracaípe, a more secluded beach 3km away, which also has accommodation.

Places to Stay Many of the visitors here either own homes (the celebrities and politicos of Pernambuco), rent for the season or camp (there's a camping ground at Praia de Maracaípe). If you want to stay a few days, several houses are available to rent. There are several cheap pousadas along Rua da Esperança, all within 100m of the beach, including *Pousada da Benedita*, *Pousada da Braz*, *Pousada Litoral* and *Pousada Meninão*. During the low season, competition is keen and apartamentos go for around US$10/15 for singles/doubles, but expect to pay nearly double these prices in the high season. Chalets sleeping up to six people, with cooking facilities, are a good cheap option for groups – try *Chales Recanto Veraneio* (☎ 241-4919), which rents chalets for US$38 in the low season. *Pousada Beira Mar* (☎/fax 552-1052), Avenida Beira Mar 16, is run by Chris and Rolf, two Swiss guys. They have doubles for US$50 in the low season.

On the road to Porto de Galinhas, in Ipojuca, is *Pousada Flor de Manhã* (☎ 972-7307; fax 429-2941), Alto da Boa Vista. Under Brazilian/German management, this place is highly recommended. Reinhard organises trips to Olinda, Recife and Itamaracá, as well as to the beaches, waterfalls, caves and extinct volcanoes in the surrounding area. Portuguese language classes and natural therapy courses are also available.

Places to Eat Famed for its seafood, Porto de Galinhas has several eateries, but the town's most renowned is *Beijupirá*. Don't miss the lobster, cooked in coconut or tomato sauce or just plain grilled. Other fine restaurants in town include *Peixe na Telha*, on the beachfront, and *Brisa Maritima*. All these restaurants serve lobster, squid, shrimp and local fish cooked with coconut milk, pepper and cumin sauces. Try the barracas along the beach for fresh crabs. The locally made genipapo liqueur is worth tasting, too.

Getting There & Away Five buses a day run to Porto de Galinhas (US$3.50, 1½ hours) from the intersection of Avenida Dantas Barreto and Rua de São João (on the right-hand side of Dantas Barreto facing north) in Recife. VW kombi vans make the trip for US$6.

Getting Around Minibuses and VW kombis service local destinations.

Other Beaches

The road going south along the coast to Tamandaré heads to **Barra de Sirinhaém**, where there is a 10km access road back to the main road. It will then take you to the beaches of **Camela**, **Guadalupe** and **Ponta dos Manguinhos**.

The only lodging in these towns is with the local fishermen. During the week the beaches are practically deserted. Off the coast is Ilha de Santo Aleixo.

Tamandaré

The next access road south goes 10km to the beach at Tamandaré. There is a small fishing village here with a few restaurants and a couple of cheap hotels. The beach is idyllic and you can see the 17th century Forte Santo Inácio.

São José da Coroa Grande

The first beach town you reach after crossing into Pernambuco from Alagoas is São José da Coroa Grande. It's 120km from Recife on coastal Hwy PE-060. This fishing town now has many weekend homes. There are a few restaurants and bars and two hotels: the *Hotel Valeiro* on the beach, or the more comfortable *Hotel do Frances*, 200m back from the main beach.

OLINDA

• *pop 350,000* ✉ *53000-000* ☎ *081*

Beautiful Olinda, placed on a hill overlooking Recife and the Atlantic, is one of the largest and best-preserved colonial cities in Brazil. Although many of the buildings in Olinda were originally constructed in the 16th century, the Dutch burnt virtually everything in 1631. Consequently, most of what you now see has been reconstructed at a later date. For an account of Olinda's history, refer to History in the introduction to the Recife section.

While Recife plays the role of an administrative and economic centre, Olinda is recognised as its cultural counterpart: a living city with bohemian quarters, art galleries, museums, music in the streets and always some kind of celebration in the works.

Orientation

Olinda is 6km north of Recife. The historical district, which constitutes about 10% of the city, is concentrated around the upper streets of the hill and is easily visited on foot. The beaches immediately adjacent to the city, **Milagres** for example, suffer from pollution and swimming is not recommended. **Casa Caiada**, the district at the foot of the hill, has several restaurants.

Information

Tourist Office Whatever services you don't find in Olinda you can secure in Recife (eg airline offices and car-rental agencies). Sepactur, the main tourist office (☎ 429 1927), Rua São Bento 160, has maps, walking-tour brochures and information about art exhibitions and music performances. The office is open from 8 am to 1.30 pm Monday to Friday.

Throughout Olinda you'll no doubt hear the cry *guia* (guide). If you're carrying this book, they'll be of little use, although using one guide means the others won't be hassling you all the time. Yellow-shirted young apprentice guides are available free from the tourist office. Freelance guides, who charge between US$5 and US$10 for a three hour tour (fix the price before starting) may be more informative. One good one is Edmilson, who speaks a little French. He hangs out daily in front of the Igreja da Misericórdia.

Money Banco do Brasil is on Avenida Getúlio Vargas. Take a bus marked Ouro Prêto from Praça do Carmo to the Bank Itau stop, then walk about 100m further north.

Post & Communications The main post office, on Praça do Carmo, offers a posta restante service (postcode 53001-970). International telephone calls can be made at the Telpe office nearby.

Dangers & Annoyances Police are fairly scarce in Olinda, and there are a lot of poor people. Take the precaution of not carrying valuables in the street at night. Burglaries are common during Carnaval.

Walking Tour

Starting at Praça do Carmo, visit the recently restored **Igreja NS do Carmo** (1580). Then follow Rua de São Francisco to **Convento São Francisco** (1585), which is a large structure containing three elements: the convent, the **Capela de São Roque** (chapel) and the **Igreja de NS das Neves** (church) – approximate daily opening hours for these are 8 to 11.30 am and 2 to 4.30 pm.

At the end of the street, turn left onto Rua Frei Afonso Maria and you'll see the

Seminário de Olinda and **Igreja NS da Graça** (1549) on the hill above. Open between 8 to 11.30 am and from 3 to 5 pm.

Continue up the street and then onto Rua Bispo Coutinho. Climb up to **Alto da Sé** (Cathedral Heights), which is a good spot to enjoy the superb views of Olinda and Recife. There are outdoor restaurants, and a small craft mercado with woodcarvings, figurines and jewellery. The imposing **Igreja da Sé** (1537) is open from 8 am to noon on Saturday and Sunday.

Continue a short distance along Rua Bispo Coutinho until you see the **Museu de Arte Sacra de Pernambuco** (MASPE; ☎ 429-0032) on your right. MASPE is housed in a building, constructed in 1696, that once functioned as Olinda's Episcopal Palace & Camara (Government Council). The museum contains a good collection of sacred art and a photographic homage to the city. It's open from 8 am to 2 pm Tuesday to Saturday.

About 75m further, turn right into a pátio to visit **Igreja NS da Conceição** (1585).

Retrace your steps and continue down the street, now named Ladeira da Misericórdia, to **Igreja da Misericórdia** (1540), which has fine *azulejos* (Portuguese ceramic tiles) and gilded carvings inside. It's open daily from 8 to 11.30 am and 2 to 5 pm.

From here, turn right onto Rua Saldanha Marinho to see **Igreja NS do Amparo** (1613), which is currently under renovation.

Further along is the **Casa de Bonecos**, which houses the *Bonecos Gigantes de Olinda*, giant papier-mâché puppets used in Carnaval. Go in and have a look.

Go back along Rua do Amparo to join Rua 13 de Maio to see the **Museu de Arte Contemporânea** (MAC). This museum of contemporary art is recommended for its permanent and temporary exhibits. The museum is housed in an 18th century *ajube* (a jail used by the Catholic Church during the Inquisition). It's open Tuesday to Friday from 9 am to noon and 2 to 5 pm, and weekends from 2 to 5 pm.

Rua 13 de Maio continues in a tight curve to a junction with Rua Bernardo Veira de Melo and Rua São Bento. If you turn left here up Rua Bernardo de Melo, you'll come to **Mercado da Ribeira**, an 18th century structure that is now home to art galleries and souvenir shops. If you retrace your steps down to Rua São Bento, you'll reach the huge **Mosteiro de São Bento** (1582), which has some exceptional woodcarving in the chapel. Brazil's first law school was housed here for 24 years (it's difficult to say what lawyers actually did in colonial Brazil, but it had little to do with justice). The monastery is open daily from 8 to 11 am and 2 to 5 pm, and celebrates mass every afternoon at 5.30 pm, complete with Gregorian chant. Delicious home-made liqueurs are sold here too.

JOHN MAIER, JR

One of the quiet streets in the historic district.

Beaches
The city beaches are polluted, and not recommended for swimming. However, there are many excellent beaches north of Olinda, which are described later in this chapter.

Special Events
Olinda's Carnaval has been very popular with Brazilians and travellers for several years (see also Special Events in the Recife

section earlier in this chapter). The historic setting combined with the fact that so many residents know each other provides an intimacy and security that you don't get in the big-city Carnavals. It's a participatory festival – costumed blocos parade through the city dancing to frevo music and everyone else follows.

In recent years, there have been complaints of commercialisation creeping into Olinda's Carnaval. On the other hand, Recife's Carnaval has been getting better reviews lately. Since the two cities are so close, you could try out both of them. Publications with full information on Carnaval schedules and events are supplied by the tourist office in Olinda.

Carnaval in Olinda lasts a full 11 days. There are organised Carnaval events, including balls (of course), a night of samba and a night of afoxé, but everything else happens in impromptu fashion on the streets. The official opening events – with the pomp and ceremony of the Olympic Games – commence with a bloco of more than 400 'virgins' (men in drag), and awards

PLACES TO STAY	OTHER	
4 Pousada do Amparo	1 Casa da Boneco	17 Museu do Mamulenco
22 Pousada dos Quatro Cantos	2 Igreja NS do Amparo	18 Igreja da Boa Hora
23 Pousada Saude	5 Igreja da Misericórdia	19 Museu de Arte Comtemporânea
24 Pousada d'Olinda	6 Igreja NS da Conçeicão	20 Senado Ruins
30 Albergue de Olinda	7 Observatorio Astronômico	21 Mercado da Ribeira
28 Hotel Pousada São Francisco	8 Samba do Preto Velho (live music)	27 Posto Telefônica
PLACES TO EAT	9 Museu de Arte Sacra de Pernambuco	29 Pub Poco Loco
3 Oficina do Sabor	10 Seminário de Olinda; Igreja NS da Graça	32 Post Office
15 Restaurant Cantinho da Sé	11 Farol de Olinda	33 Atlântico
25 Maison do Bonfim	12 Praça Dantas Barrêto	34 Praça do Carmo & Buses to Recife
26 Sabor da Terra	13 Convento São Francisco	35 Igreja NS do Carmo
31 Donana	14 Igreja da Sé	39 Igreja São Pedro
36 Mourisco	16 Igreja NS do Bonfim	40 Tourist Office
37 Café Adega		41 Palácio dos Governadores
38 Viva Zapata		42 Mosteiro de São Bento
		43 Mercado Popular (Market)

for the most beautiful, the most risqué and the biggest prude.

Everyone dresses for the Carnaval, so you'll want some sort of costume. The Carnaval groups of thousands dance the frevo through the narrow streets. It's playful and very lewd. Five separate areas have orchestras playing nonstop from 8 pm to 6 am nightly.

Apart from Carnaval, we also highly recommend the festival known as Folclore Nordestino, held at the end of August, which features dance, music and folklore from many parts of the Northeast.

Places to Stay

If you want to stay in Olinda during Carnaval, book several months in advance and be prepared for massive price hikes. During summer, prices are up to 30% higher as well. At the budget end there are several pousadas and hostels. Lots of quasi-official pousadas crop up before Carnaval, which can be good deals.

If you don't mind dorm-style sleeping, the YHA *Albergue de Olinda* (☎ 429-1592), Rua do Sol 233, has clean collective rooms that sleep two to six people for US$15 per person (US$13 for members), including sheet rental and breakfast. Apartamentos are also available at US$15/28 for singles/doubles. The *Pousada Saude*, Rua 7 de Setembro 8, is not exactly plush, but it's run by a large, chirpy family and has quartos at US$10/20 for singles/doubles.

Moving up in price range, the *Pousada dos Quatro Cantos* (☎ 429-0220; fax 429-1845), Rua Prudente de Morais 441, is housed in a fine colonial building with a leafy courtyard. Quartos in the old mansion and apartamentos outside cost around US$36/42, though they will discount the quartos for longer stays or outside the high season. The splurge option is the suite (with two rooms plus a veranda), which costs US$75/85 for singles/doubles. English is spoken.

The *Pousada d'Olinda* (☎ 439-1163), Praça João Alfredo 178, is a friendly place with a swimming pool and garden. It has a variety of options: dorm rooms for US$15 per person, quartos with fan for US$25/30, apartamentos with fan for US$30/40 and apartamentos with air-conditioning for US$45/50. English, French and German are spoken.

The new *Pousada do Amparo* (☎/fax 439-1749), Rua do Amparo 191, is a charming place with a lovely garden, pool and views. Very tasteful air-conditioned suites range from US$30/35 a single/double to US$40 a double (20% more in the high season). English, German and Spanish are spoken.

At Rua do Sol 127, the *Hotel Pousada São Francisco* (☎ 429-2109; fax 429-4057) is a modern hotel that mostly caters for groups. Apartamentos cost US$45/50.

Places to Eat

The old city has a variety of restaurants tucked away in its cobblestone streets – some are pricey, but there are usually a few reasonably priced dishes on the menu.

Cantinho da Sé has a great view from Alto da Sé, but it's a bit of a trap. *Mourisco*, in a lush garden setting, has an excellent self-serve lunch from noon to 3 pm. In the evening it's one of Olinda's best fish restaurants – the servings are large and enough for two. A few doors away at Rua 27 de Janeiro 65 *Viva Zapata* is a stylish Mexican restaurant open Thursday to Sunday from 7 pm to midnight. Next door is *Café Adega*, a stylish little cafeteria and wine bar that plays classical music instead of frevo. *Oficina do Sabor*, Rua do Amparo 329, is an elegant place with views – it could be worth a splurge. For the flavours of France, there's a cute creperie on Rua Prudente de Morais and the *Maison do Bonfim* on Rua do Bonfim.

Down on Praça do Carmo, *Sabor da Terra* is a cheap self-serve lunch place crowded with locals. Along the beachfront opposite the post office, try *Donana*, Praça João Pessoa 55, for Bahian food. It's closed on Wednesday.

Entertainment

There are several music bars and a live-music venue in the old town near Pousada dos Quatro Cantos that are busy on the weekends. Alto da Sé has bars/restaurants that open late with live music – but remember to ask the price of drinks before you indulge. Try *Samba do Prêto Velho* on Sunday night.

Closer to the beach, *Atlântico* on Praça do Carmo has live frevo and samba music and dancing until daylight over the weekend, or there's *Pub Poco Loco*, Rua do Sol 225.

On Friday and Saturday night the beach restaurants/bars north of town come to life. The *Ciranda de Dona Duda*, on Janga beach, is famous for its participatory *ciranda* (round dance). The mercado at Milagres beach has a folk-music show on Tuesday night.

Getting Around

Viagens Sob O Sol (☎ 429-3303), opposite Pousada dos Quatro Cantos, has a variety of vehicles for hire, with or without guide/driver. This is an interesting option if you can form a group of four or more. Trips can be arranged to Porto de Galinhas, Itamaracá, Fazenda Nova (Nova Jerusalém), Caruaru, Olaria Brennand and various art and handicraft showrooms. Sample prices for a minibus (maximum eight passengers) are US$15 per person (minimum four) for trips along the coast to Itamaracá or Porto de Galinhas. A good deal is offered for transport to the airport – US$20 for up to five people. The company is run by two affable 'ghostbuster' lookalikes, Mauro and Felipe, who are always keen to embark on 'night sorties', trips to remote beaches or any other wild schemes!

Recife The main bus stop in Olinda is on Praça do Carmo. Buses marked Rio Doce/Conde da Boa Vista and Casa Caiada go to the centre of Recife. The Rio Doce/Princesa Isabel bus stops outside the metrô station. Taxis cost about US$6. From Recife, take any Rio Doce, Casa Caiada or Jardim Atlantico bus to Olinda.

Boa Viagem Buses marked Rio Doce/Piedade go to Boa Viagem (US$0.80).

BEACHES NORTH OF OLINDA

You've got to get out of town for a fine, clean beach. Head north to **Janga** beach (8km) or at least **Rio Doce** (6km), and beyond to **Praia do Ó** (12km), **Praia do**

Pau Amarelo (14km), **Praia da Conceição** (17km) and **Praia da Maria Farinha** (23km). The road goes along close to the beach, but don't be deterred by the ugly development beside the road; the beaches are generally undisturbed except for barracas and crowds on weekends. Enjoy the local siri (small crab) and caranguejo (big crab) at the barracas. There are local buses to these beaches from Praça do Carmo.

IGARASSU

• *pop 78,000* ✉ *53600-000* ☎ *081*

One of the oldest cities in Brazil, Igarassu is 35km north of Recife and 20km from Ilha de Itamaracá. Igarassu is small, reasonably free of tourists and full of colonial buildings.

History

The day of Saints Cosme and Damião, 27 September 1535, was a busy day for town hero Duarte Coelho and his men. They managed to fight off both the Potigar Indians at the mouth of the Rio Igarassu and the French pirates offshore. Later in the afternoon, after a big meal, Duarte Coelho founded the village, naming it São Cosme e Damião in honour of the saints. It later came to be known as Igarassu.

Information

Igarassu's tourist office (☎ 543-0435), at Praça da Bandeira 42, has brochures and (sometimes) beautiful free posters. It's open daily from 9 am to 6 pm.

Historic Section

Walking up the hill to the historic section, you'll find **Igreja Dos Santos Cosme e Damião**, which dates back to the foundation of Igarassu and is the oldest church still standing in Pernambuco state. Next door, on Largo São Cosme e São Damião, the **Museu Histórico de Igarassu** (city museum) displays sacred art, weapons and furniture from noble families. It's open from 8 am to 2 pm Tuesday to Sunday.

The **Convento de Santo Antônio** (1588), Avenida Hermes, contains the **Museu Pinacoteca** (art museum), which has paintings depicting folk tales and popular legends. The convent and museum have been superbly restored and are well worth a visit. Both are open from 8 am to 2 pm Tuesday to Sunday.

Special Events

On 27 September, the Festa dos Santos Cosme e Damião celebrates the founding of Igarassu and honours its patron saints with Bumba Meu Boi and the ciranda dance (which actually originated in Itamaracá). The Festa do Côco is held during the last week of November.

Places to Stay & Eat

There are no cheap pousadas or hotels in town, so budget travellers should only come for a day trip or keep moving on to Itamaracá.

The *Pousada Porto Canoas* (☎ 436-2220; fax 341-4382), Estrada da Gavoa 230 (Nova Cruz), has large bungalows sleeping up to five people. For singles or doubles, the price is US$50 including breakfast; for five people the cost is US$65 (breakfast not included).

In the old town, try *Ubá Refeições*, on Praça de Bandeira, or *Caminho da Ilha*, Rua do Pe 35, for regional food and seafood.

Getting There & Away

Buses leave every 15 minutes for the 45 minute trip to Recife. The buses also stop at the Mercado Santo Amaro, between Recife and Olinda, where you can grab a bus to Olinda.

AROUND IGARASSU

Engenho Mojope

The area surrounding the town also has a few treasures. The Engenho Mojope, an old sugar estate built in 1750, has ruins of a mill, *casa grande* (plantation owner's mansion), chapel and slave quarters. It's now a camping ground belonging to Camping Clube do Brasil, and worth a stop if you're going by car: take Hwy BR-101

3.5km south from the Igarassu turn-off and turn right at the Camping Club sign. The former plantation is 1km further down the road.

ILHA ITAMARACÁ

• *pop 14,000* ✉ *53900-000* ☎ *081*

Only 50km from Recife, the island of Itamaracá is a pleasant and popular weekend beach scene. During the week it's usually empty. There is a regular bus service to the island, but getting to its many beaches takes time if you don't have a car.

Beaches

Itamaracá has a long history and a lot of beach. The better beaches are north and south of **Pilar**, Itamaracá's town beach. Two kilometres north of town is **Jaguaribe**, a white-sand beach with barracas and reclining chairs for weekend sun worshippers. For more isolated beaches, hike 5km further north along the coast to **Praia Lance dos Cações** and **Fortinho**. Immediately south of town is **Praia Baixa Verde**, and every 3km south are more beaches: **Praia Rio Ambo**, **Praia Forno de Cal**, **Praia de São Paulo** and finally **Praia de Vila Velha**, which also is an historic old port near Forte Orange.

Forte Orange

This fort was built in 1630 by the Dutch and served as a base in a series of battles against the Portuguese colonies in Recife and Olinda. It's an impressive bastion, right on the water. There's now a four-star hotel nearby and souvenir shops rearing their ugly little heads, but during the week it's still very quiet.

Centro Peixe-Boi

Close to the fort, this IBAMA-run centre for studying the endangered peixe-boi (manatee or sea cow) is open Tuesday to Sunday from 10 am to 4 pm. There is a tank containing some live specimens, but keep your voice down or they'll dive down to the bottom where they're hard to see. They also customarily nap after lunch, and you're asked not to wake them.

Other Attractions

Engenho Amparo, an 18th century sugar plantation, is just past **Penitenciária Agricola** (the island's agricultural. Further from town is **Vila Velha** (1526), the first port in the Northeast, and its church, **NS da Conceição** (1526), the second oldest in Brazil. Take a VW kombi to get to these and other distant points from the town of Itamaracá.

Places to Stay & Eat

The good news is that there is some inexpensive accommodation on the island. In Pilar, *Albergue Ciranda da Itamaracá* (☎ 544-1810) has dorm rooms for US$15 per person. The *Pousada Santa Inês* is a friendly place with quartos for US$15 a single or double. In Jaguaribe, the *Pousada Rancho Ecológico*, Avenida Rios 355 (follow the sign to Pousada Jaguaribe), is a fairly rustic place also costing US$15, single or double. *Pousada Bar do Alemão* (☎ 544-1810) is another cheapie, with double apartamentos for US$20. Back in Pilar, the *Hotel do Marujo* (☎ 544-1157), Rua Padre Merchado 85, has comfortable apartamentos for US$25/30.

The *Hotel Pousada Itamaracá* (☎ 544-1152), Rua Fernando Lopes 210 (near the centre of town), is a modern hotel with a swimming pool and apartamentos at US$50 a double.

There are lots of seafood restaurants around. *Kasa Blanka* and *Pedra Furada* are both recommended. If you get tired of food with fins, have some goulash at the *Bar do Alemão*, or some Indian (subcontinental Indian, that is) food at *Khalid Indus* in Vila Velha.

Things to Buy

At Engenho São João, about 10km in the direction of Igarassu, inmates from the agricultural penitentiary sell their products, which include lithographs and *carrancas* (carved figureheads).

Getting There & Away

There are 12 buses a day to the centre of Recife, also stopping at the Mercado Santo Amaro between Recife and Olinda.

CARUARU

• *pop 232,000* ✉ *55000-000* ☎ *081*

If you like folk art and you wake up in Recife on a Wednesday or Saturday feeling like a day trip, you're in luck. Caruaru, South America's capital for ceramic-figurine art, is only a couple of hours away.

Feira Livre

The Feira Livre (Grand Open Fair), held in the centre of Caruaru on Wednesday and Saturday, is a hot, noisy crush of Nordestinos: vendors, poets, singers, rural and town folk, tourists, artisans and musicians. *Zabumba* (drum) bands are accompanied by the music of *pífanos* (vertical flutes), and *sulanqueiros* (rag merchants) hawk their scraps of clothing.

The fair has become a popular tourist attraction, and many items on sale are produced for tourists. Alongside pots, leather bags and straw baskets are representations of strange beasts and mythical monsters crafted by artists as famous as Caruaru's master, Mestre Vitalino. To see the artists at work, visit Alto do Moura (described later in this section). If you want to buy some figurines, wait until you see what is offered in Alto do Moura before buying at the fair.

In addition to ceramic artwork, you can hear singers and poets perform the *literatura de cordel* (literally 'string literature'), poetry by and for the people, sold in little brochures which hang from the fair stands by string (hence the name). The poems tell of political events (the death of Tancredo Neves is likened to a mother giving birth to a nation and then expiring before she can suckle her infant), national figures (Getúlio Vargas, José Sarney and Fernando Collor), miracles and festivals, as well as traditional comedies and tragedies (eg about a woman who lost her honour to Satan). Although its role in diffusing popular culture is threatened by TV, literatura de cordel is still written, sold and performed in public by Caruaru's poets.

In a separate section of the main fair, there's the *feira do troca-troca* (barter fair), where junk and treasure are traded.

Feira de Artesanato

This handicraft fair on Parque 18 de Maio is open daily from 6 am to 5 pm.

Feira da Sulanca

This textile and clothing fair, the largest in the Northeast, is set up on Parque 18 de Maio on Tuesday and Thursday.

Casa da Cultura José Condé

This cultural centre on Parque 18 de Maio contains a couple of museums. The most interesting is Museu do Forró, containing exhibits about forró, including records and musical instruments. It's open Tuesday to Friday from 9 am to noon and 2 to 5 pm, and on Saturday from 9 am to 1 pm.

Museu do Barro

This museum, containing displays of pottery produced by famous local artists, is inside the Espaça Cultural Tancredo Neves, Praça José Vasconcelos 100. It's open Tuesday to Saturday from 9 am to 5 pm.

Alto de Moura

Alto de Moura, 6km from Caruaru, is a small community of potters which specialises in producing *figurinhas* (figurines). Many of the potters are descendants of Mestre Vitalino, the most famous artist, who brought fame to Alto de Moura. Other noted artists are Zé Caboclo, Manuel Eudocio and Cunhado de Zé Caboclo. Museu Mestre Vitalino (Master Vitalino Museum), housed in the simple home of the master, contains his tools and personal effects. It's open Monday to Saturday from 9 am to noon and 2 to 5 pm, and Sunday from 9 am to noon.

You can wander the streets and browse through dozens of workshops and galleries. If you want to purchase figurines, you're better off buying here than in Caruaru.

Places to Stay

Caruaru is a long day trip from Recife, but there's no real need to stay here overnight. If you decide to stay, the *Hotel Centenário* (☎ 722-4011), Rua 7 de Setembro 84, has apartamentos starting at US$32 a double.

Places to Eat

Fortunately, there's plenty of cachaça (sugar-cane rum) and sugar-cane broth to quench your thirst, and local foods like dobradinhas (tripe stew), chambaril and sarapatel (a bloody goulash of pork guts) to appease your appetite. Spartan, inexpensive places for this type of food are *Bar do Biu*, Rua Sanharó 8, and *Bar da Linguiça*, Rua Nunes Machado 278.

If the appeal of these local foods fades, try *Barrilândia*, Rua Silva Jardim 71. It's a good pizzeria with the feel of a Wild West saloon. On the flip side, for excellent regional cuisine in a tasteful setting, pull into the highly recommended *Estação Central*, Avenida Magalhães 398.

Getting There & Away

Caruaru is linked by shuttle buses to Recife every half hour. The trip takes two hours and costs US$6. There is a daily bus service (US$3, one hour) to Fazenda Nova.

TRACUNHAÉM

• *pop 13,000* ✉ *55805-000* ☎ *081*

If you've missed the fair at Caruaru, the next best thing – some say better – is to be in Tracunhaém for the Sunday fair. The village of Tracunhaém, 40km from Recife in the direction of Carpina, is Pernambuco's number-two craft centre. Look for the ceramic work of master artisans Zezinho de Tracunhaém, Severina Batista and Antônio Leão.

FAZENDA NOVA & NOVA JERUSALÉM

• *pop 4000* ✉ *55175-000* ☎ *081*

The small town of Fazenda Nova, 50km from Caruaru, is famous for its theatre-city reconstruction of Jerusalem, known as Nova Jerusalém. Surrounded by a 3m-high wall with seven gateways, 70 towers and 12 granite stages, the reconstruction occupies an area equivalent to one-third of the walled city of Jerusalem as it stood in the time of Jesus.

The time to visit is during Semana Santa (Holy Week, held in March or April – dates vary), when several hundred of the inhabitants of Fazenda Nova perform the Paixão de Cristo (Passion Play).

Places to Stay

There's a camping ground, *Camping Fazenda Nova*, at Nova Jerusalém. In the centre of Fazenda Nova, you can stay at the *Grande Hotel* (☎ 732-1137), Avenida Poeta Carlos Pena Filho, s/n (no number), which has apartamentos costing US$20/25 for singles/doubles.

Getting There & Away

During Holy Week, there are frequent bus services direct from Recife, and travel agencies sell package tours to see the spectacle. During the rest of the year, there are daily bus connections between Fazenda Nova and Caruaru.

GARANHUNS

• *pop 111,000* ✉ *55290-000* ☎ *081*

Garanhuns, 100km from Caruaru and 241km from Recife, is popular as a holiday resort because of its relatively high altitude (900m). It's not exactly the 'Suiça Pernambucana' (Switzerland of Pernambuco) that it is touted to be in the tourist brochures, but it does have pleasant parks and gardens, and cool air – all of which are a respite from the oppressive heat of the interior of the state.

Places to Stay & Eat

There's a camping ground, *Camping 13*, at Km 105 on Hwy BR-423. The *Hotel Permanente* (☎/fax 761-1096), Avenida Santo Antônio, has apartamentos for around US$19/30 for singles/doubles. On the same street *Hotel Village* (☎ 761-3624) at No 149 has apartamentos for US$17/30.

For an inexpensive self-service buffet lunch, try *Jardim*, Praça Jardim 22. Fondue-lovers prepared to pay a bit extra should visit *Chez Pascal*, Avenida Rui Barbosa 891.

Getting There & Away

There are several bus departures a day to Recife (3½ hours; US$10).

TRIUNFO

• *pop 15,000* ✉ *56870-000* ☎ *081*

This small town 448km west of Recife lies at an altitude of 1000m. The cool climate and abundant vegetation have earned it the nickname *cidade jardim* (garden city).

Things to See & Do

The **Museu do Cangaço** displays a collection of weaponry and assorted personal items used by *cangaçeiros*, or brigands, whose most famous and fearsome leader was Lampião (described in the History section of the Facts about the Country chapter). The museum is open daily from 8 am to 6 pm.

The town also has some fine examples of architecture. **Cine Teatro Guarany** (1922), Praça Carolina Campos, is a stunning neoclassical piece. It's open daily from 8 am to noon.

For excursions in the region around the town, you could visit **Pico do Papagaio**, the state's highest peak (1230m) with a great view, 10km from town; **Cachoeira do Grito**, with a waterfall and swimming hole 6km from town on the road to Flores, then 2km on foot; or the pictographs at **Sítio Santo Antônio**, 3km from town.

Places to Stay & Eat

The *Pousada Baixa Verde* (☎/fax 846-1103), Rua Manoel Paiva dos Santos 114, has single/double apartamentos for US$30/40. The *Pousada Brisa da Serra*, Rua Manoel Pereira Lima 185, has similar accommodation. It's also possible to order meals here; or try *Bar Guarany* at Rua Manoel Pereira Lima, s/n (no number).

Getting There & Away

There are daily bus departures for Recife (US$22, eight hours).

Fernando de Noronha

• *pop 1800* ✉ *53990-000* ☎ *081*

The archipelago of Fernando de Noronha, with a population of 1800, lies 145km from Atol das Rocas, 525km from Recife and 350km from Natal. The 21 islands of the archipelago cover a total area of only 26 sq km. In 1989, Fernando de Noronha was incorporated into the state of Pernambuco.

With its crystal-clear water (average water temperature 24°C) and rich marine life, the archipelago is a heavenly retreat for underwater pleasures. The main island is sparsely populated and tourism has become the main source of income for locals. It's now easier for independent travellers to visit, but it is possible that organised tours will be made compulsory again if numbers of visitors prove detrimental to the environment. Even though Fernando de Noronha is now protected as a national marine park, the effects of tourism on its fragile ecosystem need to be monitored carefully (see the following History section).

When to Go & What to Bring

The rainy season is from February to July and the islands' time zone is one hour ahead of Brazilian Standard Time. Bring everything you'll need for your stay (eg sunscreen, insect repellent, magazines and snorkelling gear) as prices are high due to the cost of transporting goods from the mainland. Take sufficient Brazilian money with you. Don't rely on changing money on Fernando de Noronha, where the exchange facilities are virtually nil and the exchange rates are low.

History

Several hundred kilometres off the coast of Natal, the archipelago was discovered by the Spanish adventurer and cartographer Juan de la Cosa. The islands first appeared on the maps by the name of Quaresma (Lent). A Portuguese aristocrat, Fernan de Loronha was awarded the islands by his friend King Dom Manoel in 1504. He never set foot on the islands, forgot about them, and had them taken back by the Crown years later.

The islands, with their strategic position between Europe and the New World, were occupied by the French and the Dutch. But by 1737 the Portuguese managed to reclaim Fernando de Noronha and built 10 forts. All that remains today are the ruins of the fortresses of NS dos Remédios and São Pedro do Boldró, and a few sunken shipwrecks.

Over the years, the islands have been used as a military base by the USA (during WWII), a prison, a weather station, an air base and, most recently, a tourist resort.

There has already been some misguided tampering with the island ecology. The teju, a black-and-white lizard, was introduced to eat the island rats which had come ashore with the Europeans in colonial days. Unfortunately, the teju prefers small birds and crabs to rat.

A struggle between developers and environmentalists over the future of the islands was resolved in 1988 when most of the archipelago was declared a parque nacional marinho (marine national park) in order that its natural treasures should be protected. These treasures include 24 different species of marine bird; two species of marine tortoise, one of which – tartaruga-de-pente *(Eretmochelys imbricata)* – is in danger of extinction; sharks; stingrays; dolphins; whales; and a vast number of fish species.

Tourism has proved a blessing for the economy and a bane for the ecosystem of the archipelago. In 1996 there were 24,500 visitors or 67 a day, so IBAMA keeps tight control on access to some beaches. It has 12 guards on the islands, and plenty of signs.

Orientation

On the largest and only inhabited island, the population is concentrated in Vila dos Remé-

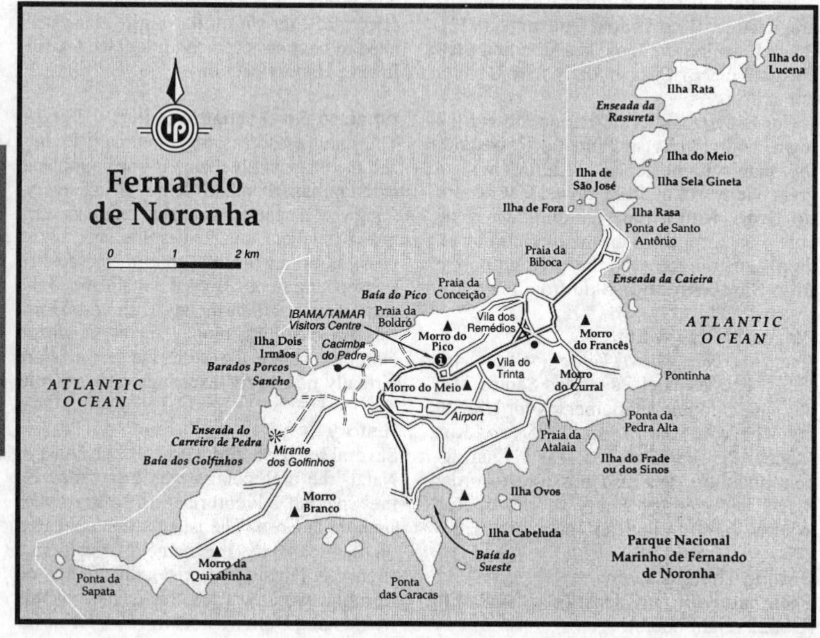

dios. Although Morro do Pico, the highest point on the island, is only 321m above sea level, it is well over 4300m above the ocean floor, as the island is an extinct volcanic cone. The island-mountain is part of the mid-Atlantic ridge, an underwater mountain chain which is over 15,000km long.

Information

Tourist Office Information is available from the Divisão de Tourismo (☎ 619-1352) in the Palácio São Miguel in Vila dos Remédios. There are great views from here. The PARNAMAR/IBAMA (☎ 619-1210) office is on Alameda do Boldró.

Money The island's one and only bank is Banco Real in Vila dos Remédios. Visa withdrawals are possible.

Post & Communications The post office is in Vila dos Remédios. The Telpe office is in the Hotel Esmeralda do Atlântico, on Alameda do Boldró.

Travel Agencies Two of the island's better travel agencies are Dolphin Travel (☎ 619-1170), and Mubatur (☎ 619-1266), both on Alameda do Boldró.

Emergency The Hospital São Lucas (☎ 619-1344), Parque Flamboyant, looks after medical emergencies. The Polícia Civil (☎ 619-1432) has its headquarters at Vila do Trinta.

Island Rules

Tourism has already effected the ecosystem. As a result visitors are expected to obey the following rules:

- Don't dump rubbish or food on the ground, in the sea or on the beach
- Don't remove coral, shells or marine creatures
- Don't use spear guns or traps
- Don't take any plants or animals to or from the archipelago
- Respect ecological protection areas
- Don't swim with the dolphins
- Don't hunt underwater

Visitors' Tax

The state government now imposes a daily tax on visitors to the island. For the first week, it's US$13 a day. After that, it increases. Two weeks costs US$240 and a month is US$1300. A week is long enough to see the sights.

Beaches

Inside the boundaries of the park, IBAMA allows bathing at certain beaches, but restricts access to others to protect marine life.

The 26 island beaches are clean, beautiful and almost deserted. The beaches facing the mainland – **Conceiçao**, **Boldró**, **do Americano**, **Quixaba** and **Cacimba do Padre** – are the surfers favourites. Cacimba do Padre is the only one with freshwater. Facing the Atlantic are the beaches of **Atalaia**, **Caiera** and **do Leão**, considered by many to be the most beautiful on the island. **Baía do Sueste** is the site of the TAMAR station, where it's possible to swim with the turtles.

Baía dos Golfinhos (Dolphin Bay) is strictly off limits to swimmers, but access is permitted to **Mirante dos Golfinhos**, a viewpoint where you can watch hundreds of dolphins cavorting in the water every morning. It's a real spectacle.

You can get to **Baía do Sancho** either by boat or by following a trail which leads through bramble and bush, past almond trees and over sharp rocks.

Diving

Diving is the island's major attraction. Its transparent waters have a 40m visibility, 230 fish species, 15 coral varieties and five types of (harmless) shark. Snorkelling is best at Baía dos Porcos, Ponta das Caracas, Baía de Sueste and Atalaia, where there is a large pool at low tide. Scuba divers prefer Ilha Rata, Morro de Fora, Rasuretas and Ponta da Sapata.

Águas Claras and Noronha Divers both organise scuba-diving excursions with instructors and both rent diving equipment. Noronha Divers is a bit cheaper. You can ask if diving is still permitted in Baía de Santo Antônio, the site of the wreck of the Greek ship *Asturia*, sunk in 1940.

Organised Tours

Organised tours sold by travel agencies in Recife usually include your airfare to and from Fernando de Noronha, lodging (apartamento, including full board) and guided tours of the island by land and sea. Higher prices apply during the high season and for apartamentos with air-conditioning (which isn't really necessary).

Independent travellers can buy airline tickets directly from Nordeste, and should have little difficulty negotiating lower prices for lodging and board on the island. This independent approach also allows travellers to pick and choose their accommodation. The accommodation included in most of the package tours is overpriced.

In Recife, Fernando de Noronha tours are packaged by three agencies: Andratur (☎ (081) 465-8588) and Dolphin (☎ (081) 465-7855), with four-day/three-night packages for US$650; and Massangana, with six-day/five-night packages (including four scuba dives) for US$870. For Massangana packages contact Quadratur in Rio (☎ (021) 262-8011), and in São Paulo, contact Vista (☎ (011) 257-6933).

Places to Stay & Eat

The only classified hotel, the *Esmeralda do Atlântico* (☎/fax 619-1255), Alameda do Boldró, is very expensive (US$90 per person) and usually fully booked with package tours. There are over 70 pousadas and *pensões* (pensions), and many of the islanders let quartos in their private homes. Some of the recommended pousadas include the very friendly *Pousada Tia Zéte* (☎ 619-1242), 500m from Vila dos Remédios; the *Pousada Da Rita* (☎ 619-1324), Floresta Velha; the *Pousada Da Helena* (☎ 619-1223), Vila dos Remédios; and the *Pousada Monsieur Rocha* (☎ 619-1227), Vila do Trinta. Rates for apartamentos start at around US$40 per head and include breakfast, lunch and dinner. Quartos are about US$5 less per person.

Since accommodation prices usually include full board, restaurants are virtually nonexistent. There's a restaurant in Esmeralda do Atlântico Hotel, or you could try *Ekologicus*, with seafood platters for US$30, or *Natalicius*, which serves barbecued lamb for US$20. Bars on the island include *O Mirante*, Alameda do Boldró; *Bar do Meio*, Praia do Meio; *Bar da Angélica* Vila do Trinta; and *Bar da Vila*, Vila dos Remédios.

Getting There & Away

Air Rio Sul/Nordeste flies daily between Recife and Fernando de Noronha. The flight takes 1½ hours and a return ticket costs around US$400. A return flight from Natal to Fernando de Noronha costs around US$300.

Nordeste (☎ 619-1144) is on Alameda do Boldró. The airport (☎ 619-1182) is a couple of kilometres from the centre of Vila dos Remédios.

Boat From Natal, José Martino (☎/fax (084) 221-4732) charters his four-berth yacht *Delícia* for US$400 a day. The trip out takes around 48 hours and the return trip 38 hours.

Getting Around

Buggies, cars, small motorcycles and bicycles are available from several operators, including Eduardo Galvão de Brito Lira (☎ 619-1355) at the Esmeralda do Atlântico Hotel. The average cost of buggies and cars is US$30 per person per day with a driver. Motorcycles are US$80 a day. Bicycles are US$15 a day. Boats are available at Vila Porto de Santo Antônio.

Paraíba & Rio Grande do Norte

Paraíba

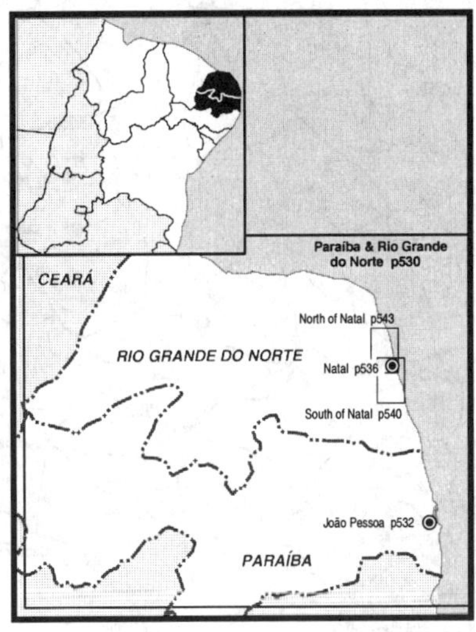

Sandwiched between Pernambuco and Rio Grande do Norte, the small, sunny state of Paraíba contains the easternmost point of the continent, Pontal de Seixas. The coastal strip is this small state's most important economic region, fuelled by tourism, sugar cane and pineapples. The interior is severely affected by drought, and those Paraíbanos who haven't already moved away live in poverty and misery.

For most travellers, Paraíba means coloured coastal cliffs, coconut palms and the only official nude beach in Brazil – Praia de Tambaba.

JOÃO PESSOA

• *pop 550,000* ✉ *58000-000* ☎ *083*

Founded in 1585, the coastal city of João Pessoa is the capital of Paraíba. It lies 120km north of Recife, 688km south of Fortaleza and 185km south of Natal. The city centre has a few interesting churches and other buildings, and Praia de Tambaú, 7km east, is a pleasant place to hang out for a few days.

The city is named after João Pessoa, the governor of Paraíba who formed an alliance with Getúlio Vargas to run for the presidency of Brazil in 1929. In response to advances from other political parties attempting to gain his support, João Pessoa uttered a pithy *'nego'* (I refuse), which is now given prominence in all Brazilian history books, and is emblazoned in bold letters on the state flag of Paraíba.

João Pessoa's aspirations to the vice presidency were short-lived: in July 1930 he was assassinated by João Dantas, an event that sparked a revolutionary backlash that eventually swept Getúlio Vargas to power (with considerable help from the military) in October 1930.

Orientation

The rodoviária is on the western edge of the city. The main hotel and shopping district, known as Praça, is further east; and close by is Parque Solon de Lucena, a large lake circled by trees, which locals simply call Lagoa. There are numerous bus stops here, which are convenient for local transport (see the Getting Around section), for example, to travel to the beach district of Tambaú or further up the coast to Cabo Branco.

Information

Tourist Offices PBTUR (☎ 226-7078), Avenida Almirante Tamandaré 100, in Tambaú, is a good source of maps and leaflets. You'll find it inside the Centro Turístico, diagonally opposite Tropical Hotel Tambaú. There are also helpful tourist information stands at the rodoviária and the airport. All are (supposedly) open daily from 8 am to 8 pm.

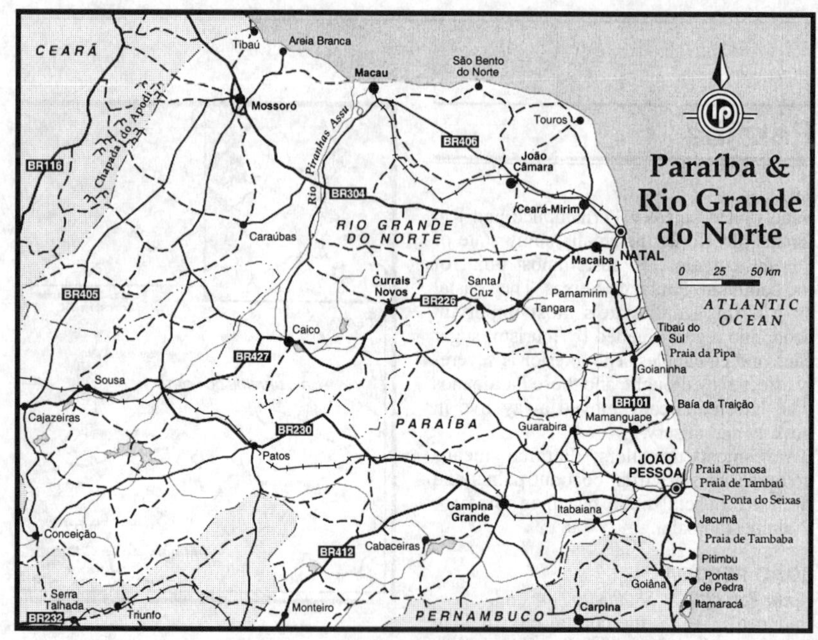

Money Banco do Brasil is on Praça João Pessoa – a couple of doors down from Hotel Aurora. It's open Monday to Friday from 10 am to 4 pm. In Tambaú, the branch in the Centro Turístico is open the same hours. There are Bradesco ATMs in the centre on Rua Duque de Caxias and on the beachfront in Tambaú.

Post & Communications The main post office in the centre of town is on Avenida Guedes Pereira. The main office of Telpa, the state telephone company, is on Rua Visconde de Pelotas 259. Both have branches in the rodoviária.

Igreja São Francisco

The principal tourist attraction is the Igreja São Francisco in Praça São Francisco, considered one of Brazil's finest churches. Construction was interrupted by successive battles with the Dutch and French, resulting in a beautiful but architecturally confused complex built over three centuries. The façade, church towers and monastery (of Santo Antônio) display a hotchpotch of styles. Portuguese tiled walls lead up to the church's carved jacaranda-wood doors. The church is open from 8 to 11 am and 2 to 5 pm Tuesday to Saturday.

Museu Fotográfico Walfredo Rodrigues

The Walfredo Rodrigues Photographic Museum in the old Casa da Pólvora (Powder House), Ladeira de São Francisco, has an interesting collection of pictures of the old city. It's open Monday to Friday from 8 am to noon and 1.30 to 5.30 pm.

Beaches

Aside from the rusty remains of battles against the French and Dutch, the beaches are clean. **Praia de Tambaú**, 7km directly east of the centre, is rather built up, but nice. There are bars, restaurants, coconut palms and fig trees along Avenida João Maurício (north) and Avenida Almirante Tamandaré (south).

South of Tambaú is **Praia Cabo Branco**. From here it's a glorious 15km walk along **Praia da Penha** – a beautiful stretch of sand, surf, palm groves and creeks – to **Ponta de Seixas**, the easternmost tip of South America. Clear water and coral make it a good spot for diving.

Immediately north of Tambaú there are good urban beaches: **Manaíra**, **Praia do Bessa**, **Praia do Macaco** (a surf beach) and **Praia do Poço**.

About 20km north of Tambaú are the **Forte Santa Catarina**, **Costinha** (once a whale-hunting centre) and **Camboinha** beaches.

Praia Cabedelo has a couple of pousadas, restaurants and bars. Boats to **Ilha de Areia Vermelha**, an island of red sand that emerges from the Atlantic at low tide, also leave from here. In summer, dozens of boats park around the island and the party lasts until the tide comes in.

Boat & Buggy Trips

Navegar Turismo (☎ 246-2191), Rua Artur Monteiro de Paiva 99, Praia de Bessa, sells buggy trips from João Pessoa to Jacumã for US$25 per person. Sun Marine Turismo (☎ 228-1219) operates excursions on a motor schooner to Areia Vermelha for US$8. Preocuação Zero (☎ 226-4859), Avenida Cabo 2566, operates schooner trips to Picãozinho for US$15.

Places to Stay – Budget

João Pessoa's main attraction is Praia de Tambaú, and that's where many of the hotels are. Although there are cheaper hotels in the centre, it's worth spending a bit extra to stay near the beach.

City Centre The *Hotel Aurora* (☎ 241-3238), Praça João Pessoa 51, has adequate quartos at US$7/12 for singles/doubles. Apartamentos with fans cost US$16/22. Avoid the rooms overlooking the street, which can be noisy. The *Rio Verde* (☎ 222-4369), Rua Duque de Caxias 111, has clean, basic, windowless apartamentos for US$10/13 with fan or US$13/17 with air-condtioning. The price includes a surprisingly decent breakfast.

Tambaú The best deal in Tambaú is the *Hotel Pousada Mar Azul* (☎ 226-2660), Avenida João Maurício 315. Huge apartamentos with a kitchen and refrigerator cost US$15 (US$20 in the high season), single or double. Breakfast is not included.

The *Hotel Gameleira* (☎ 226-1576), Avenida João Maurício 157, has standard apartamentos (with fan) for US$15/18 and apartamentos with air-conditioning for US$18/20; it charges 30% more in summer. Both these hotels are opposite the beach.

Praia de Seixas If you fancy camping at the easternmost tip of Brazil, there's a Camping Clube do Brasil camping ground, *Camping-PB-01*, at Praia de Seixas, 16km from the centre of João Pessoa.

Places to Stay – Mid-Range

City Centre The *Hotel Guarany* (☎ 241-2308), Rua Marechal Almeida Barreto 181, is a clean, functional business hotel. Apartamentos with fan start at US$25/40, while those with air-conditioning start at US$31/45.

The *Lagoa Park Hotel* (☎ 241-1414; fax 241-1404), next to the Lagoa at Parque Solon de Lucena 19, is a modern hotel with well-appointed rooms at US$43/50 in the high season. In the low season, it gives a 40% discount.

Tambaú The *Hotel dos Navegantes* (☎ 226-4018; fax 226-4592), Avenida NS dos Navegantes 602, has apartamentos costing US$58/72 in the high season. It's two blocks from the beach and has a swimming pool.

Places to Stay – Top End

The five-star *Tropical Hotel Tambaú* (☎ 247-3660; fax 247-1070), Avenida Almirante Tamandaré 229, on Praia de Tambaú,

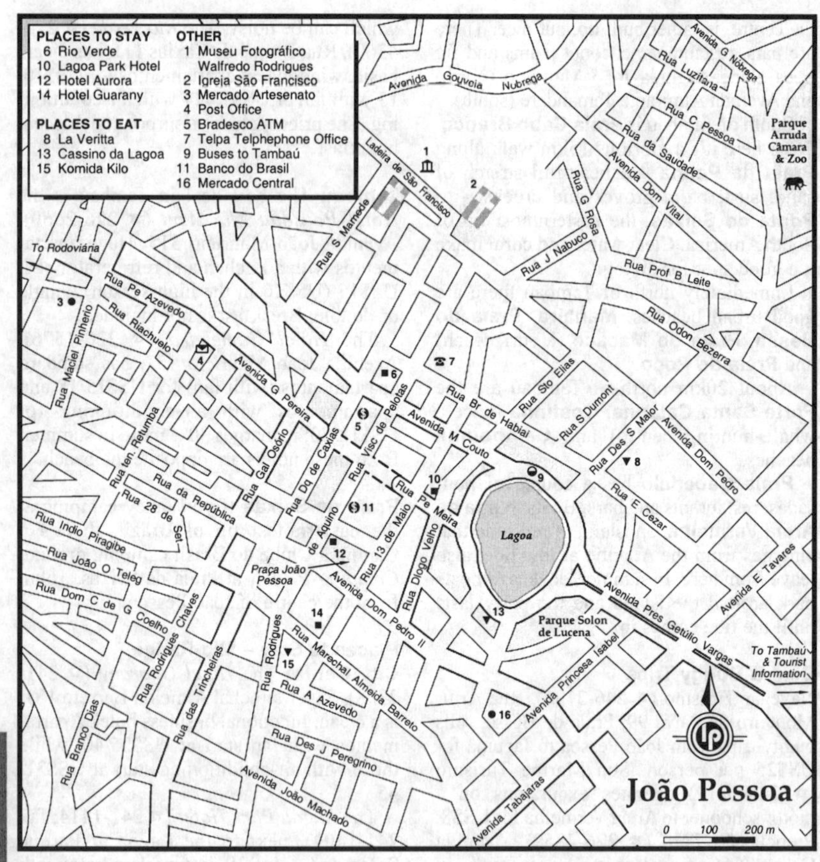

is the city's entry into the world of modern architecture. From a distance this immense edifice (part of the Varig hotel group) bears a close resemblance to a rocket launching pad. The hotel has standard rooms for US$123/141, and luxury ones for US$170/197. It may offer a 20% discount.

Places to Eat

City Centre *Cassino da Lagoa* has an open patio and a fine position beside the Lagoa. Seafood and chicken dishes are recommended. *La Veritta*, Rua Desembargador Souto Maior 331, does good Italian food. *Sorveteria Tropical* is close to Hotel Guarany and serves ice cream in exotic flavours. Vegetarians can head for *Komida Kilo*, Rua Rodrigues de Aquino 177, but it only serves lunch.

Tambaú Rua Coração, a block back from the beachfront, near the Tropical Hotel Tambaú, is a compact restaurant strip with a variety of styles. Rua Coração de Jesus, one block from the beach and close to the Tropical Hotel Tambaú, has lots of good places. *Adega do Alfredo*, at No 22, specialises in Portuguese dishes, but it's a bit of a tourist trap. *Nova China*, at No 100, is an inexpensive option for Chinese food. At No 144 is *Meio Ambiente*, which has live music and cheap Bahian food. For seafood, there's *Peixada do Duda* at No 147. The ensopado de caranguejo (crab stew) here is superb.

O Cariri, opposite the Tropical Hotel Tambaú on the corner of Avenida Olinda, is a good lunch spot with cold meats, salads and hot food priced by the kilogram.

Entertainment

Nightlife in Tambaú centres around the beachfront along Rua João Maurício and Avenida Olinda, which runs off the beachfront near the Tropical Hotel Tambaú.

Bahamas Chopp, on Rua João Maurício next to the pier, is a popular meeting place and has live music on the weekend. Along Avenida Olinda there's usually some live music on weekends. On the corner of Avenida Almirante and Avenida Olinda there's a small outdoor bar that caters to João Pessoa's alternative crowd – grunge types, surf rats, metal heads and punks all thrown together in the one place!

Things to Buy

Avenida Rui Carneiro on Praia de Tambaú has ceramic, wicker, straw and leather goods for sale. On weekends, craft stalls set up in front of Tropical Hotel Tambaú. In the city centre, Casa do Artesão Paraibano, Rua Maciel Pinheiro 670, also has crafts for sale.

Getting There & Away

Air Presidente Castro Pinto airport (☎ 232-1200) is 11km from the city centre. Flights operate to Rio, São Paulo and the major cities of the Northeast and the North.

The addresses for Brazilian airlines are:

Transbrasil
  Rua General Osório 177, sala 1 (☎ 241-2822)
Varig/Cruzeiro
  Avenida Getúlio Vargas 183 (☎ 221-1140)
VASP
  Parque Solon de Lucena 530, Edifício Lago Center (☎ 221-3434)

Bus The rodoviária (☎ 221-9611) is on Avenida Francisco Londres. There are frequent services to Recife (US$6, two hours), Natal (US$8, 2½ hours) and Fortaleza (US$22, 10 hours). There are nine departures a day direct to (or via) Sousa (US$20, seven hours).

Getting Around

Bus Local buses can be boarded at the rodoviária; at the bus stop next to the main post office; and at the bus stops next to the Lagoa. Bus Nos 510 and 511 run frequently to Tambaú (US$0.55, 25 minutes) from outside the rodoviária. If you catch them from the Lagoa they will loop back through the city, pass the rodoviária and continue to Tambaú. Bus No 507 runs to Cabo Branco.

Taxi *Taxistas* (taxi drivers) on short hauls may try to charge Tariff 2 (generally applicable at night and on Sunday) instead of Tariff 1, which applies during the day. Take a careful look at the price table, and work out your position on the map and point out obvious 'detours'.

A taxi to the airport costs around US$18; from the rodoviária to the centre costs around US$3. To telephone a taxi, call Teletaxi (☎ 222-3765).

SOUTH OF JOÃO PESSOA

Jacumã & Praia do Sol

Thirty-five kilometres south of João Pessoa is Praia Jacumã, a long, thin strip of beach featuring coloured sand bars, natural pools, mineral water springs and barracas.

The town's pousada, the *Valhall* (☎ (083) 290-1015), perched on a hill overlooking the ocean, is run by a group of young Swedes led by Leif, who has travelled widely in Brazil. Comfortable apartamentos cost US$25, with a huge Swedish/Brazilian breakfast included. The attached bar/restaurant serves excellent local dishes with a Swedish touch and in summer there's live music.

Halfway between Jacumã and João Pessoa is Praia do Sol, which is similar to Jacumã and an equally good place to relax – swaying in a hammock and sipping coconut milk in the shade.

The **Buraquinho Forest Reserve**, operated by IBAMA, is 10km before João Pessoa on Hwy BR-230.

Getting There & Away There are direct buses to Jacumã from the stop in front of the petrol station 50m to the left as you leave the rodoviária. Travelling north from Pernambuco state on Hwy BR-101, ask to be dropped off at the Conde/Jacumã turn-off, and take a local bus from there to Jacumã.

Tambaba

About 10km south of Jacumã is Praia de Tambaba, the only official nudist beach in the Northeast. The beach, rated by Brazilians as among the top 10 in Brazil, is divided into two parts: one section is reserved exclusively for nudists, and the other is open to clothed bathers. To prevent problems, the nude section has public relations officers who explain the rules to bathers. There are two barracas along the beach. When the beach is crowded, men are not allowed in the nude section unless accompanied by a woman.

Pousada Valhall may be able to arrange transport to Tambaba; otherwise it's a 1½ hour walk along the beach from Jacumã.

Pitimbu

Praia Pitimbu, 75km south of João Pessoa, has a long, broad beach, a coconut grove, some thatched-roof houses, and a couple of bars frequented by sugar-cane farmers, fisher and *jangada* (beautiful sailing boats of the Northeast) sailmakers. There are no hotels, but if you look friendly and bring a hammock, someone will put you up for a nominal fee.

Travelling north on Hwy BR-101 from Pernambuco state into Paraíba state, there's a turn-off just after the border that leads 35km down a rough road to Praia Pitimbu.

BAÍA DA TRAIÇÃO

Despite its peaceful, reef-sheltered waters, coconut palms and gentle breezes, Baía da Traição has a bloody past. In 1501, the first Portuguese exploratory expedition was slaughtered here by the Tabajara Indians. In 1625 the Portuguese had it out with the Dutch, claimed victory and left some rusty cannons and the ruins of a fortress in their wake.

This fishing village, 85km north of João Pessoa, has only one pousada, your alternative is to sling a hammock in a fisherman's house. The beach is better than the one at Barra do Cunhaú, which is further north along the coast, in the state of Rio Grande do Norte.

Places to Stay & Eat

Pousada Ponto do Sol Nascente (☎ 296-1050), Rua Dom Pedro 537, is a friendly place with double apartamentos starting at US$25. Ask for a room upstairs to catch the sea breeze. They also serve local dishes.

Getting There & Away

There's a partially sealed turn-off to the beach on Hwy BR-101 at Mamanguape. The Rio Tinto bus company operates buses twice daily, at 5.30 am and 3 pm, from João Pessoa's rodoviária (US$3, 2 hours).

SOUSA

• *pop 80,000* ✉ *58800-000* ☎ *083*

Sousa, 434km west of João Pessoa, is known for an offbeat tourist attraction: dinosaur tracks. The tracks were discovered in 1920 by a geologist who was researching drought – a major preoccupation in the *sertão* (drought-stricken region of the Northeast). Later discoveries of tracks at over 13 different sites along the Rio do Peixe showed that the whole region had once been a *vale dos dinossauros* (valley of dinosaurs). There are at least three sites in the proximity of Sousa. The best is 4km from town, at **Passagem das Pedras da Fazenda Ilha**, on the banks of the Rio do Peixe, where at least 50 prints have been left by dinosaurs, which, judging by the depth and size of the imprints, weighed between three and four tonnes.

This site is subject to flooding during the rainy season and is best visited with a guide.

Transport options are limited to either hiring a taxi at the rodoviária in Sousa or asking the staff at the Hotel Gadelha Palace to arrange transport and a guide.

Travellers interested in handicrafts should make a side trip to the town of Aparecida, 14km east of Sousa, which is famed as a centre for the production of superb hammocks, textiles, and goods made from leather and straw.

Places to Stay & Eat

The *Hotel Gadelha Palace* (☎ 521-1880), Rua Presidente João Pessoa 2, has apartamentos for US$25/35 for singles/doubles. There's a restaurant in the hotel, or if you hanker for pizza, try *Diagonal*, Rua Getúlio Vargas 2.

Getting There & Away

There are six bus departures a day that run via Patos and Campina Grande to João Pessoa (US$20, seven hours). Buses also depart four times a day to Juazeiro do Norte (described in the Ceará chapter).

Rio Grande do Norte

Pure air, sun, fine beaches and sand dunes symbolise this small state in the extreme north-east of Brazil. From here, the coast changes direction from north/south to north-west/south-east, and the strong, dry ocean winds pile sand in huge dunes – the most famous being the 50m-tall dunes at Genipabu. The Potiguenses, as locals are known, are a friendly bunch and delight in their favourite dish, *carne do sol*. Like Paraíba, the interior of the state is drought-stricken, and many former inhabitants have already migrated to other parts of Brazil.

NATAL

• *pop 657,000* ✉ *59000-000* ☎ *084*

Natal, the capital of Rio Grande do Norte, is a clean, bright city that is being developed at top speed into the beach capital of the Northeast. There is very little to see of cultural or historical interest: the main attractions are beaches, buggy rides and nightlife.

History

In 1535, a Portuguese armada left Recife for the falls of the Rio Ceará-Mirim (12km north of present-day Natal) to drive out the French, who had set up trading posts in the area. Although the territory had been proclaimed by King João III of Portugal in 1534 as one of the 12 coastal captaincies, the Portuguese then abandoned the area for 60 years, until the French again began to use it as a base for attacks on the south. The Portuguese organised a huge flotilla from Paraíba and Pernambuco that met at the mouth of the Rio Potengi on Christmas Day 1597 to battle the French.

On 6 January, the day of Os Reis Magos (The Three Wise Kings), the Portuguese began to work on the fortress, which they used as their base in the war against the French. The Brazilian coastline was hotly contested, and in 1633 the fortress was taken by the Dutch, who rebuilt it in stone but retained the five-point star shape. First under Dutch and thereafter Portuguese occupation, Natal grew from the fortress, which was named the Forte dos Reis Magos.

With the construction of a railway and a port, Natal continued to develop as a small and relatively unimportant city until WWII. Recognising Natal's strategic location on the eastern bulge of Brazil, Getúlio Vargas and Franklin D Roosevelt decided to turn the sleepy city into the Allied military base for operations in North Africa.

Orientation

Natal is on a peninsula flanked to the north-west by the Rio Potengi and the south-east by Atlantic reefs and beaches. The peninsula tapers, ending at the Forte dos Reis Magos, the oldest part of the city. The city centre, Cidade Alta, was developed around the river port, which was built in 1892.

Information

Tourist Office Setur's headquarters in the Centro Convenções de Natal is a bit out of the way. More convenient and useful are the information booths at Praia das Artistas and the airport. They have maps and tour pamphlets and touchscreen multimedia, multi-lingual information terminals. If you're lucky they may be functioning. The Centro de Turismo in the Casa de Detenção (old prison) on Rua Aderbal Figueiredo is not very useful, though there's a fine view from the heights of this renovated prison.

Another source of information is at the rodoviária nova, which has a private information booth open daily from 8 am to 6 pm. It has maps and brochures and can book hotels. Francisco Assis de Oliveira, a hyperactive lawyer fighting part time for truth and justice (and his commission) in Natal's tourist industry, is on duty there a couple of days a week. On other days his niece carries on the good work.

Money Change money before heading to the beaches. Banco do Brasil, Avenida Rio Branco 510, is open Monday to Friday from 10 am to 4 pm. Bradesco has an ATM on the other side of the road.

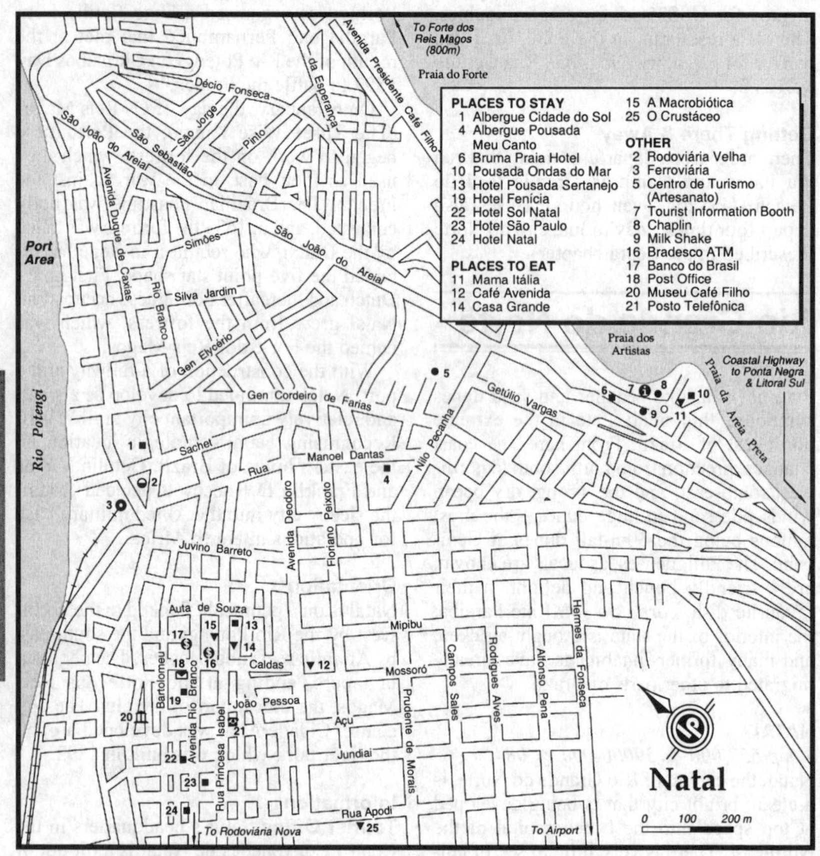

Post & Communications The main post office is at Avenida Rio Branco 538. The telephone office is at Rua Princesa Isabel 687. Both have branches at the rodoviária nova.

Dangers & Annoyances The dramatic increase in visitors to the beaches has attracted petty thieves. There's no cause for paranoia, but you should take the usual precautions – refer to the Dangers & Annoyances section in the Facts for the Visitor chapter for general advice on beach security. Praia das Artistas has a prostitute scene, and it can get a bit sleazy at night.

Things to See

The principal nonbeach attractions of Natal are the pentagonal **Forte dos Reis Magos** (open Tuesday to Sunday from 8 am to 4.30 pm) at the tip of the peninsula, and the **Museu da Câmara Cascudo** (☎ 222-0923), Avenida Hermes da Fonseca 1398. This museum of folklore and anthropology features a collection of Amazon Indian artefacts. It's open on Tuesday to Friday from 8 to 11 am and 2 to 5 pm, and Saturday from 10 am to 4 pm.

The **Museu Café Filho**, Rua da Conceição 601, will probably only appeal to history buffs. This museum is housed in the mansion that once belonged to João Café Filho, and now displays his personal effects. It's open Monday to Friday from 8 am to 5 pm and Saturday from 8 am to 2 pm.

In 1954, the military presented President Getúlio Vargas with an ultimatum to resign from the presidency, whereupon Vargas left a patriotic note and then shot himself through the heart. Café Filho, who had been vice president, assumed the presidency, and muddled through political crises until he suffered a major heart attack in 1955 and gave way to Carlos Luz. Although Café Filho recovered quickly and tried hard to be reinstated, he'd missed his turn on the political carousel and had to be content with his brief moment of fame as the first person from the state of Rio Grande do Norte to become a president.

Beaches

Natal's city beaches – **Praia do Meio**, **Praia dos Artistas**, **Praia da Areia Preta**, **Praia do Pinto** and **Praia Mãe Luiza** – stretch well over 9km, from the fort to the Farol de Mãe Luiza lighthouse. These are mostly city beaches, with bars, nightlife and big surf. The ones closest to the fort are rocky and closed in by an offshore reef.

Buggy Rides

Beach-buggy excursions are offered by a host of *bugeiros* (buggy drivers), mostly in Brazilian-built vehicles with brand names such as Bird, Baby, Praya or Malibuggy. An excursion lasting from 8 am to 4 pm costs US$15 per person with four passengers in the buggy (a tight squeeze). The price includes transport and driver/guide, but excludes food and ferry fees (minimal). Take sunscreen, a tight-fitting hat and swimwear; and keep all photo gear in a bag as protection from sand.

Bugeiros seem to be a crazy bunch of wannabe racing drivers (check out the dragstrip traffic lights in the centre) intent on demonstrating a variety of buggy tricks and spins on the dunes. You may be treated to some or all of the following: Wall-of-Death, Devil's Cauldron, Vertical Descent, Roller-Coaster, and something best described as Racing the Incoming Tide – if you lose, the surf claims the buggy and the passengers scramble for high ground.

There are pirate bugeiros and accredited bugeiros, and the latter are represented by the Associação de Bugeiros (☎ 225-2077). You can usually arrange a deal through your hotel, and hostels may be able to negotiate a discount. A recommended driver is Celio Barreto, who works for Top Buggy (☎ 235-1430).

Although Brazilians and foreigners clearly have a fun time zooming around in buggies, the more remote beaches don't exactly benefit from the commotion and erosion. The coastline close to Natal has been claimed by bugeiros, but there are moves to protect beaches further afield from their impact.

Places to Stay

Natal's hotel district are around Cidade Alta (in the city centre) and along the city beaches. Ponta Negra, 14km south of the city, also has some low-budget options. See the Places to Stay section in Ponta Negra.

City Centre *Albergue Pousada Meu Canto* (☎ 212-2811), Rua Manoel Dantas 424, in a beautiful garden setting, offers quartos for US$10 per person (US$8 for YHA members) with a good breakfast. Tia Helena is a delightful host who will treat you as a member of her family. It's highly recommended. There's another good central hostel, the *Albergue Cidade do Sol* (☎ 211-3233; fax 211-4151), near the rodoviária velha at Avenida Duque de Caxais 190. It also has quartos for US$10 per person for YHA members. Double apartamentos are US$20 with fan and US$30 with air-conditioning.

The *Hotel Pousada Sertanejo* (☎ 221-5396), Rua Princesa Isabel, is stylish and moderately priced, with spotless apartamentos with fan at US$15/25 for singles/doubles. The *Hotel Natal* (☎ 222-2792; fax 222-0232), on Avenida Rio Branco, has standard apartamentos at US$12/16, but better value are its apartamentos with air-conditioning at US$14/18. Another budget option is the *Hotel Fenícia* (☎ 211-4378), Avenida Rio Branco 586, although it's looking a bit the worse for wear. Its apartamentos cost US$15/20 without breakfast. The *Hotel São Paulo* (☎ 211-4130), Avenida Rio Branco 697, has apartamentos with fan for US$10 per person without breakfast.

The two-star *Hotel Sol Natal* (☎ 221-1154; fax 221-1157), Rua Heitor Carrilo 107, has nice double apartamentos for US$50 but often offers huge discounts.

City Beaches On Praia dos Artistas, *Pousada Ondas do Mar* (☎ 211-3481), on Rua Valentim de Almeida, has adequate apartamentos with fan for US$12/20. The *Bruma Praia Hotel* (☎/fax 211-4947) has doubles for US$35 (US$55 in summer).

Places to Eat

For natural food, you can head for *A Macrobiótica*, on Rua Princesa Isabel, where the healthy atmosphere is accentuated by staff running around in white coats!

O Crustáceo, Rua Apodi 414, specialises in seafood. The ambience is enhanced by a large tree poking through the roof in the centre of the restaurant. Coffee enthusiasts should get their caffeine fix at *Café Avenida* on Avenida Deodoro. It also serves a delicious selection of pastries and cakes. The *Casa Grande*, Rua Princesa Isabel 529, is a stylish place with regional food.

Mama Itália, Rua Silvio Pedrosa 43, has a wide range of excellent pastas and pizzas. The spaghetti fruta do mar (US$10) is chock full of seafood and is delicious.

Rio Grande do Norte boasts a few good brands of cachaça (sugar-cane rum). Try a shot of Ohlo d'Água, Murim or Caranguejo with a bite of cashew fruit.

Entertainment

Chaplin is a pricey and popular bar on Praia dos Artistas. Across the road, *Milk Shake* may look like a McDonald's outlet, but there's good live music most nights and a lively dance floor.

For folkloric shows and dancing, try *Zás-Trás*, Rua Apodi 500, in the Tirol district. It has a restaurant section and the shows start at around 8 pm. After the show, the dancers will teach guests dances such as forró, *ciranda de roda* (round dancing) and something called *aeroreggae*. From 11 pm onwards, the dance floor gets crowded and the action hots up. Forró com Turista, on Thursday nights from 10 pm in the *Casa do Turismo*, sounds corny but it's a lot of fun.

Things to Buy

The Centro de Turismo has lots of stalls selling bottles of coloured sand, ceramics and other local handicrafts. Chacal, in Alecrim mercado, has the best pirate tapes in Brazil.

Getting There & Away

Air There are flights to all major cities in the Northeast and the North, and to Rio and São Paulo.

Airline offices in the Cidade Alta are:

VASP
Avenida João Pessoa 220 (☎ 211-4374)
Varig/Cruzeiro
Rua Vigário Bartolomeu 635 (☎ 221-1537)
Transbrasil
Avenida Deodoro 363 (☎ 221-1806)

Nordeste (☎ 743-1212) has an office at the airport.

Bus There is a daily departure to Salvador at noon (US$60, 18 hours); six buses a day to Recife (US$12, 4½ hours); and frequent services to João Pessoa (US$8.50, 2½ hours). Five regular buses (US$29, eight hours) and one *leito* (US$48) depart daily for Fortaleza. Two executivo buses a day depart for Rio (US$90, 44 hours), at 3.30 and 3.45 pm. There are eight departures a day for Mossoró (US$11, 4½ hours) and one a day for Juazeiro do Norte (US$14, nine hours), which leaves at 7 pm.

Getting Around

To/From the Airport Natal's Augusto Severo airport (☎ 272-2811) is 15km south of town on Hwy BR-101. Bus A-Aeroporto runs between the airport and the rodoviária velha (old bus station), in the city centre. The taxi fare to the city centre is US$23.

To/From the Rodoviária The rodoviária nova (☎ 205-4377), the new bus station for long-distance buses, is 6km south of the city centre. Bus Nos 38 and 20 connect the rodoviária nova with the rodoviária velha on Praça Augusto Severo, in the city centre. The taxi fare to the centre is US$7. Bus Nos 21 and 38 are useful for getting to Praia dos Artistas.

To/From the Beaches The rodoviária velha is the hub for bus services to the airport (Bus A), the rodoviária nova, city beaches such as Praia dos Artistas, beaches further south such as Ponta Negra (Nos 46 and 54) and Pirangi, and beaches as far to the north as Genipabu.

A taxi from the centre to Praia dos Artistas costs around US$6, while to Ponta Negra it's US$15.

SOUTH OF NATAL

Ponta Negra

Ponta Negra is 14km south of Natal. The beach is nearly 3km long and full of hotels, pousadas, restaurants, barracas and sailing boats – at weekends the place really jumps. The water is calm towards the end of the bay and safe for weak swimmers. At the far end of the beach is **Morro da Careca**, a monstrous sand dune. Its face is inclined at 50° and drops straight into the sea. The slope is now closed off to save the dune from ending up in the sea.

Evening activities consist of beer drinking and snacking at the barracas, and gazing for shooting stars and straying rockets (from the nearby air force base).

Places to Stay There are two hostels close together: the *Albergue de Juventude Lua Cheia* (☎ 236-3696), Rua Estrela do Mar 2215, and the *Albergue de Juventude Verdes Mares* (☎ 236-2872), Rua das Algas 2166.

There are dozens of pousadas and hotels. Some of the cheaper ones along the beachfront include the *Pousada Bella Napoli Praia* (☎ 219-2667; fax 211-2821), Avenida Beira Mar 3188, with apartamentos for US$20/30 in the low season, US$35/45 in the high season; and *Londres Pousada* (☎ 236-2107; fax 222-1514), Avenida Erivan Franca 11, with quartos with a sea view for US$15 per person and apartamentos for US$25/35.

An excellent mid-range option is *Hotel Tubarão* (☎/fax 741-1029), Rua Manoel Coringa Lemos 333, a beautiful hotel with a sea view, swimming pool and very comfortable apartamentos for US$35/40 in the low season and US$50/60 in summer. The manager, Rogério, speaks fluent English, and is very helpful.

Barreira do Inferno

Barreira do Inferno (Hell's Gate), 20km from Natal, is the Brazilian air force (FAB) rocket base. The base is open to visitors on Wednesday. The tour is pretty lame, and will only appeal to real enthusiasts. It includes a half-hour talk with slides and films. Intending visitors must call ☎ 211-4799, ext 205 (after 1.30 pm), at least one day in advance to reserve a place on the tour.

Pirangi do Sul & Pirangi do Norte

The pretty twin beach towns of Pirangi do Sul and Pirangi do Norte are split by a river which weaves through palm-crested dunes on its way to the ocean. It's a quiet area where wealthy folk from Natal have put up their beach bungalows. There are a few pousadas in the palm grove where the road crosses the river.

The *Pousada Esquina do Sol* (☎ 238-2078) is a friendly place with apartamentos at US$30/35 for singles/doubles with air-conditioning and US$20/25 with fan. Nearby is the world's largest cashew tree: its rambling sprawl of branches is over half a kilometre in circumference, and still growing!

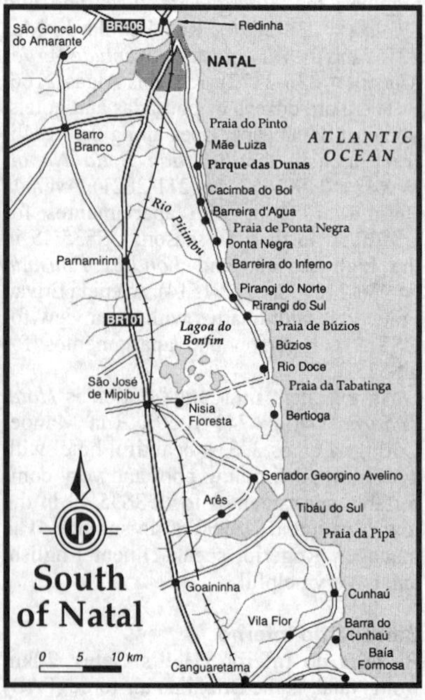

Búzios to Senador Georgino Alevino

This stretch of coast has some of the best beaches in Rio Grande do Norte, a state with so many great beaches it's difficult to find one that's not worth raving about.

Búzios is a beach town 40km south of Natal. The beach is nice, but the area is a bit dry and barren. A couple of hotels here cater to weekenders. The *Varandas de Búzios* (☎ 239-2121) has large chalets on the beach for US$25/40 for singles/doubles.

Resist the temptation to get off the bus at Búzios. After Búzios, the road crosses a stream and follows the coast – there's nothing here but small waves crashing against the beach, white dunes, coconut palms, uncut jungle and pretty little farms. The place is idyllic.

Getting There & Away From Natal there are two buses a day, at 7.30 am and 4.30 pm, that go directly to Senador Georgino Alevino, but it's more fun to take a bus along the winding, cobblestone coastal road. From Natal take a Tabatinga bus as far as Búzios (one hour). Just to confuse you some more, from Monday to Saturday buses for Senador Georgino Alevino leave from the rodoviária nova at 6, 6.30, 7.30 and 9.30 am and 5.50 pm, while other buses leave from the rodoviária velha at 10.30 am and 12.30, 1.30 and 4 pm; on Sunday, however, all the buses leave from the rodoviária nova, except for the two that leave from the rodoviária velha at 7.30 am and 5.30 pm.

Tibaú do Sul

The small and rocky beaches of Tibaú do Sul – **Praia da Madeira, Praia da Cancela** and Praia da Pipa (see the following section) are said to be among the finest in Rio Grande de Norte. From Goaininha, 75km south of Natal on Hwy BR-101, there's a 20km sealed road to the coast.

Pria da Pipa

Pipa is the main attraction of Tibaú do Sul and has developed into a small, laid-back resort with lots of pousadas, a hostel and some good restaurants and bars. Many of these are run by foreigners, which perhaps explains the greater sense of hygiene and sanitation here than in most other Northeastern beach resorts. The main beach is lovely, but it can get crowded on weekends. North and south of town, there are plenty of isolated beaches. Apart from beaches, there's the **Sanctuário Ecológico** 1km north of town, a flora and fauna reserve on 14 hectares in which an attempt is being made to recreate the natural environment of the area.

Places to Stay *Espaço Verde* (☎ 981-0765) offers basic camp sites for US$2.50 (US$4 in the high season), but the ground isn't very flat.

The *Albergue Enseada Dos Golfinhos* (☎ 502-2303), Rua do Barreiro, just north of town, is a friendly place run by two Pedros from Portugal. They speak English, French, German, Italian and Spanish as well as their native tongue. The bus can drop you there. Dormitory beds go for US$10 (US$12.50 in the high season) including breakfast. *Pousada do Golfinho*, on Rua Principal (the main street), is run by a friendly Italian family. Some rooms have a sea view. The family also serves good, cheap Italian food. Apartamentos cost US$10/15 (US$25/35 in the high season). *Pousada Aconchego*, just up from the main street opposite Pousada do Golfinho, has comfortable, spacious chalets with individual verandas and hammocks for US$10/15 (US$15/25 in the high season). The best chalet is No 5, with a view of the sunset and Mata Atlântica.

Other good options include *Oásis* (☎ 502-2340), on Rua Principal, with apartamentos for US$35 (US$50 in the high season) and *Pousada da Pipa* (☎ 982-2753), Rua do Cruzeiro, in a small cul de sac off the main road opposite the Oásis. Apartamentos are US$15 (US$20 in the high season) and Rudolph, an Austrian, speaks English and German.

Places to Eat There are some very good restaurants in Pipa. *A Vivenda*, on Rua Principal, serves pasta, grilled meat and seafood in an ambient setting. *Creperia da Pipa*, also on Rua Principal, is a good option if you're sick of prato feito and pizza. *Cruzeiro do Pescador*, near Pousada da Pipa, has great seafood. Two French restaurants in town are *La Provence*, run by Jean Louis from Maxime, and *Chez Liz*, run by Patrick. Both offer excellent food. *Casarão* has great views overlooking the beach and serves regional and seafood dishes. *Espaço Verde* has the cheapest self-serve lunch in Pipa.

Getting There & Away From the rodoviária nova in Natal, there are two buses a day to Pipa (US$4, two hours) from Monday to Saturday at 8 am and 3.15 pm. On Sunday, there's one bus, at 8 am. If you come from the south, get out at Goaininha (1½ hours from João Pessoa) and head toward the church. Follow the road behind the church for about five minutes until you get to the bus stop (there's no sign but it's quite obvious where it is). VW kombis to Tibaú do Sul and Pipa pass frequently. There's also a daily bus from Goaininha to Pipa at 11 am. From Pipa, buses leave for Natal daily at 5 am and 4 pm. There's another bus that goes to Goaininha daily at 7.30 am.

Another option is to go to Canguaretama and cross on the ferry at Sibauma. It's also possible to take a boat from Tibaú across to Senador Georgino Alevino. Ask around at the port in Tibaú.

Barra do Cunhaú

Barra do Cunhaú, 10km from Canguaretama on a dirt track, is a hybrid fishing village/resort town. You can camp in the coconut grove.

There are four buses a week from Natal, on Monday, Thursday, Friday and Saturday at 3.45 pm (US$4, 2½ hours).

Baía Formosa

The fishing village of Baía Formosa has lovely beaches, a couple of cheap pousadas and little tourism.

Backed by dunes, Baía Formosa sweeps from the end of the village (on the southern part of the bay) to an isolated point to the north. Parts of the beach have dark volcanic rocks eroded into weird shapes by the surf. The beaches further south of town are spectacular and usually deserted. There's a couple of decent point breaks for surfers.

Getting There & Away Around 17km off Hwy BR-101 and 10km from the Rio Grande do Norte-Paraíba border, Baía Formosa is serviced by two daily buses. The buses leave town for Natal at 5.30 am and 2.20 pm Monday to Saturday, and at 5 am and 4 pm on Sunday. Heading north, you should be able to meet the early bus at the junction of Hwy BR-101 at around 1 pm on its return to Baía Formosa. Otherwise, hitching is possible. Direct buses from Natal's rodoviária leave at 7.15 and 11.30 am and 6 pm (US$4, 2 hours).

NORTH OF NATAL

The beaches immediately north of Natal, where sand dunes plunge into the surf, are beautiful, but not quite as spectacular as the southern beaches.

Praia Redinha

Praia Redinha, 25km by road north of Natal, features 40m dunes, a good view of Natal, lots of bars and *capongas* (freshwater lagoons).

Getting There & Away Catch a ferry from the waterfront close to the rodoviária velha in Natal for the 20 minute trip to Redinha. It's more relaxing than the bus.

Genipabu

About 5km further north is Genipabu, where golden sand dunes, palm trees and dune buggies converge on a beach lined with numerous barracas, pousadas and restaurants.

It's a popular, crowded place where you can swim, toboggan down the dunes, or take a half-hour jangada trip.

Places to Stay Among the cheapest of the area's pousadas are the *Casa de Genipabu* (☎ 225-2141), which charges US$20/30 for apartamentos with a sea view, and the *Pousada Marazul* (☎ 225-2065), similarly priced. The *Pousada Villa do Sol* (☎ 225-2132) is a more upmarket place with a swimming pool, but it will discount heavily during the week. Lon, the American owner, has lived here for over eight years.

Getting There & Away Buses to Genipabu and Redinha leave Natal regularly from the rodoviária velha.

Praia Jacumã to Praia Maxaranguape

There is a coastal road that heads north from Genipabu towards praias **Jacumã**, **Muríu**, **Prainha** and **Maxaranguape**. These are little, palm-graced bay beaches separated from one another by rivers and hills. The beaches are readily accessible, but off the beaten track. Muriú and Prainha (still undeveloped) are especially nice.

Getting There & Away Viação Rio Grandense buses from Natal's rodoviária nova service the area. Five buses a day leave for Maxaranguape between 7.30 am and 6.30 pm (US$3, 1½ hours), while others leave for Jacumã at 7.30 am and 3 pm (US$2.50, 1½ hours). Local buses to Pitangui leave every half an hour from the rodoviária velha.

Touros

Eighty-three kilometres north of Natal is Touros, a fishing village which has several beaches, bars and a couple of cheap pousadas. It's a convenient base from which to explore isolated beaches to the north, such as São Miguel do Gostoso and Praia do Cajueiro.

Places to Stay & Eat The *Pousada do Atlântic* (☎ 263-2218), on the waterfront at Avenida

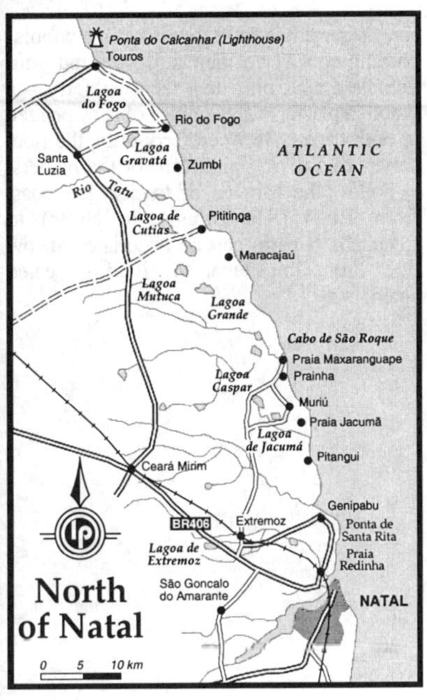

Atlântica 4, has friendly management and apartamentos at US$25 a double. The *Pousada Rio do Fogo* (☎ 221-5872), on Praia Rio do Fogo, offers similar accommodation. *O Castelo*, on Avenida Atlântica, serves tasty local seafood.

Getting There & Away Seven buses a day leave from the rodoviária nova in Natal for Touros from 6.30 am to 5.30 pm (US$3, 1½ hours).

AREIA BRANCA

The town of Areia Branca, 50km from Mossoró and Hwy BR-304, is a small fishing port. It's possible to visit the supermodern salt docks 25km away, but only with advance notice.

The hotel *Pousada Porto do Sal* (☎ 332-2386) is in the centre of town. It's basic but clean and charges US$12 per person with breakfast.

MOSSORÓ

To break the trip between Natal and Fortaleza, you might want to visit this town on the fringe of the sertão. About 4.5km out of town there are hot springs at the Hotel Termas de Mossoró. The hotel is expensive, but you can pay a small fee just to use the springs.

The **Museu Histórico** (☎ 321-2304), Praça Antônio Gomes 514, has all sorts of personal effects, weapons and documents connected with Lampião and his bandit colleagues, who attacked Mossoró in 1924. It's open Tuesday to Friday from 8 am to 8 pm; Saturday from 8 to 11 am and 1 to 5 pm; and Sunday from 8 to 11 am. See the 'Lampião' boxed text in the Facts about the Country chapter.

Information

Money Banco do Brasil, on Praça Vigário Antônio Joaquim, changes money. Bradesco has an ATM on the corner of Rua Santos Dumont and Rua Coronel Vincente Saboi.

Places to Stay

For rock-bottom prices, try the cowboys' favourite, the *Hotel Zinelandia* (☎ 321-2949), at Praça São Merchado 89. Quartos are US$7 per person and apartamentos with ceiling fan are US$9 without breakfast. For more upmarket lodgings, the *Hotel Imperial* (☎ 316-2210; fax 317-3524), Rua Santos Dumont 237, has comfortable apartamentos for US$33/42. If you fancy staying at the *Hotel Termas de Mossoró* (☎ 321-1200; fax 321-5060), 4.5km from town, double rooms start at US$100.

Getting There & Away

The rodoviária is 3km out of town on Rua Felipe Camarão. Mossoró has frequent bus services to Natal (US$11, four hours) and Fortaleza (US$16 in an executivo with air-conditioning and videos, 3½ hours). Buses run daily at 5 and 8 am and noon to Aracati, in Ceará (for access to Canoa Quebrada). There are also local bus services between Mossoró and Areia Branca.

TIBAÚ

Tibaú, 25km from Hwy BR-304, is a bustling resort beach on the border between Ceará and Rio Grande do Norte. Truck caravans roll past the surf into Ceará, saving a few kilometres and giving the place a frontier-town flavour. Locals sell bottles filled with sand in many different colours, which they collect from the beach.

Another 4km west on the coast you come to a river and a friendly outdoor bar. The river's current is swift, but it's still a popular bathing spot. Two men pull you and your vehicle across on a low-tech car ferry – a wooden platform and a piece of rope pegged to both banks. Between ferry duty, the float serves as a diving platform for the bathers.

Follow the caravan of trucks. The coast from Tibaú (Rio Grande do Norte) to Ibicuitaba (Ceará) can be negotiated at low tide. From Ibicuitaba, the road is sealed again.

THE NORTHEAST

Ceará, Piauí & Maranhão

Ceará

Ceará's pride and glory is its coastline – nearly 600km of glorious beaches. The beach in this part of the Northeast engenders a special way of life. In nearly all of the small beach towns, the people of Ceará continue to live out their unique folklore every day of the year. They make old-fashioned lacework and handicrafts, cook according to traditional recipes, sleep in hammocks, sail out on *jangadas* (the beautiful traditional sailing boats of the Northeast) to catch fish and live in thatch-roofed homes.

Should you stray inland into the sertão, you will see a rugged, drought-plagued land, a bleak landscape of dust and caatinga, peopled by *vaqueiros* (cowboys) who still rely on their cattle for almost everything. The dried meat serves as food, tools are fashioned from the bones, and the hides provide clothing – nothing is of a cow wasted.

For a complete contrast, visit the Serra de Baturité, a small chain of hills southwest of Fortaleza, which features an agreeable climate and coffee and banana plantations.

For all its size and wealth of culture, much of Ceará is poor and undeveloped. Almost half of the state's seven million inhabitants live in absolute poverty.

FORTALEZA

• *pop 2,000,000 ✉ 60000-000 ☎ 085*

Fortaleza is a major fishing port and commercial centre in the Northeast. The tourist attractions of the city include a small historical section, a large selection of regional handicrafts, and an active nightlife scene along Praia de Iracema and Praia do Meireles. There are some super beaches beyond the city limits in either direction.

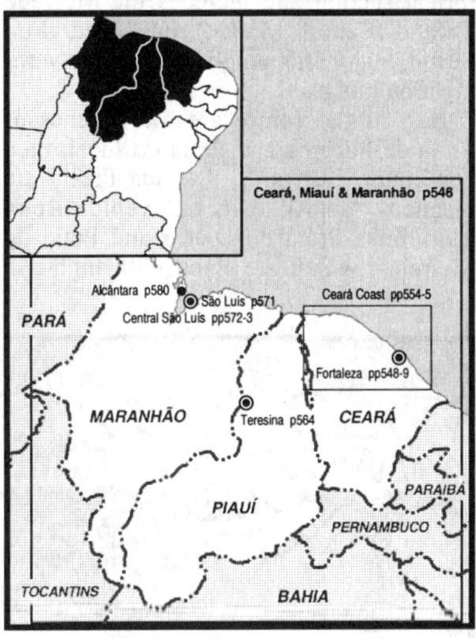

History

According to some revisionist Cearense historians, the Spanish navigator Vicente Yanez was supposed to have landed on Praia Mucuripe on 2 February 1500, two months before Pedro Álvares Cabral sighted Monte Pascoal, in Bahia. Despite this early claim to fame, it was only in 1612 that the first colonisers sailed from the Azores to settle on the banks of the Rio Ceará.

The settlement at present-day Fortaleza was hotly contested: it was taken over by the Dutch in 1635, then, in turn, lost to the Tabajara Indians. In 1639, the Dutch under the command of Matias Beck landed once again, fought off the Indians and constructed a fortress. In 1654 the Portuguese captured the fortress and reclaimed the site. A town grew around the fortress, which was given the name of Fortaleza de NS da Assunção (Fortress of Our Lady of Assumption). Fierce battles with the local Indians continued to delay colonisation for many years.

Orientation

The city is laid out in a convenient grid pattern. The centre lies above the old historical section and includes the Mercado Central (Central Market), the Catedral do Séand, major shopping streets and government buildings.

East of the centre are the beaches of Praia de Iracema and Praia do Ideal; then continuing eastwards, Avenida Presidente Kennedy (also known as Avenida Beira Mar) links Praia do Diário and Praia do Meireles, which are lined with high-rise hotels and restaurants. Beyond here are Porto do Mucuripe (the port) and the Farol Velha (Old Lighthouse). Praia do Futuro begins at the lighthouse and extends 5km southwards along Avenida Dioguinho to the Clube Caça e Pesca (Hunting and Fishing Club).

Information

Tourist Office Setur, the state tourism organisation, has a convenient branch office in the Centro de Turismo (☎ 231-3566), Rua Senador Pompeu 350, inside a reno-

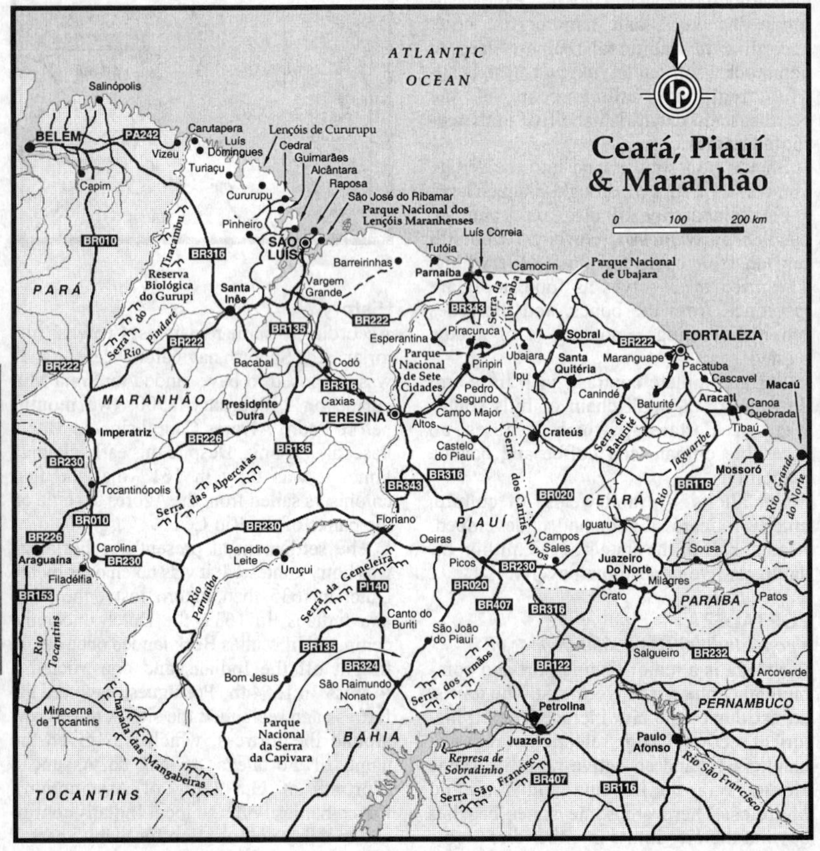

vated prison. It has English-speaking attendants, stacks of information and can help with booking accommodation, tours to the beaches and details on bus transport. The Centro de Turismo is open every day from 7 am to 6 pm.

There is also a Setur booth at the airport, open 24 hours a day, and another at the rodoviária, open daily from 6 am to 10 pm.

Fortur, the municipal tourism organisation, has an information booth in the centre on Praça da Ferreira and one on Praia Meireles.

A tourist information telephone service, Disque Turismo (English spoken), is also available from Monday to Friday from 8 am to 6 pm – just dial ☎ 516.

Money Banco do Brasil has a convenient branch in the city centre on Rua Floriano Peixoto open Monday to Friday from 10 am to 3 pm. In Meireles, there's a branch on Avenida Abolicão, open the same hours. Bradesco has ATMs in the centre and in Iracema. There are lots of *casas de câmbio* (money-exchange houses) in Meireles, and large hotels there will also change cash at a lower rate.

Post & Communications The main post office in the centre is on Rua Floriano Peixoto. Teleceará, the state telephone company, has a convenient office in the city centre, at the intersection of Rua Floriano Peixoto and Rua Dr João Moreira. Other useful phone stations are at the airport (open 24 hours a day), the rodoviária, Praia Iracema and Praia Meireles.

Travel Agency Hoje Turismo (☎ 226-8293), Rua Major Facundo 52, has friendly staff and competitive prices for national and international ticketing.

Dangers & Annoyances Travellers have reported pickpocketing in the city centre and petty theft on the beaches.

We've also heard reports about solicitous females on the city beaches who cuddle up to travellers, drug them (in their drinks) and relieve them of their valuables.

Museums

The **Centro de Turismo** contains a folk museum, tourist information office and shops. It's open Monday to Friday from 8 am to 6 pm and Saturday from 8 am to noon. The **Museu de Arte e Cultura Popular** houses a variety of interesting displays of local handicrafts, art and sculpture. Its opening hours are the same. Entry is US$0.50.

The **Museu do Ceará**, a museum devoted to the history and anthropology of Ceará, is in the old provincial assembly building on Rua São Paulo in the centre. It opens weekdays from 8.30 am to 5.30 pm and Saturday from 8.30 am to 2 pm.

Car enthusiasts will want to visit the **Museu do Automóvel**, Avenida Desembargador Manoel Sales de Andrade 70, in the Água Fria district on the southern edge of the city. The museum displays a variety of veteran cars including Buicks, Pontiacs, Cadillacs and Citroens. It's open Tuesday to Saturday from 9 am to noon and 2 to 5 pm and Sunday from 9 am to 1 pm. Entry is US$1.

Teatro José de Alencar

The José Alencar Theatre (1910) is an impressive building – a pastel-coloured hybrid of classical and Art-Nouveau architecture which was constructed with cast-iron sections imported from Scotland. It is now used for cultural events.

Beaches

Fortaleza's city beaches are generally less than clean, with the exception of Praia do Futuro, but the locals don't seem to worry about it, so you can make up your own mind. The best beaches all lie further away from Fortaleza.

Near Ponte Metálica, the old port, **Praia de Iracema** was a source of inspiration to Luís Assunção and Milton Dias, Ceará's bohemian poets of the 1950s, and some of this atmosphere lives on in a few bars and restaurants around Rua Dos Tabajaras. Ponte Metálica has been restored recently, and includes, a space for cultural exhibitions and an outdoor music stage which has occasional free concerts. There's a lovely promenade along the waterfront, and a capoeira school often practises here in the evenings.

Praia do Meireles fronts Avenida Presidente Kennedy, and is the upmarket hotel and restaurant strip. It's also a popular place to hang out in the evening.

Praia do Futuro is a clean length of sand that stretches 5km towards the south along Avenida Dioguinho to the Clube Caça e Pesca. It is the best city beach. Like Rio de Janeiro's Barra de Tijuca, it's being built up at an alarming rate. There are *barracas* (stalls) here which serve fried fish and shrimp. On Thursday night, there's live *forró* (traditional music of the Northeast) along the beach and comedy shows in some of the bars.

The beaches immediately north of Fortaleza, **Cumbuco** and **Iparana**, are both pleasantly tranquil. Harried travellers can relax, string up a hammock in the shade of the palm trees, sip coconut milk and rock themselves to sleep.

Parque Ecológico do Côco

This park, opposite Shopping Center Iguatemi, is the city's main recreational park. It was set up in 1991 after local ecological groups pressed for protection of the mangrove swamps from encroaching highways and the industrial zone. Entrances to the park, which is 7km from the centre, are on Avenida Engenheiro Santana and Rua Vicente Leite. From the centre, take the bus marked Edison Quieroz to Shopping Center Iguatemi.

Organised Tours

There are several tours available from Fortaleza, mostly to beach destinations such as Beach Park, Lagoinha, Jericoacoara, Canoa Quebrada, Morro Branco, Iguape and

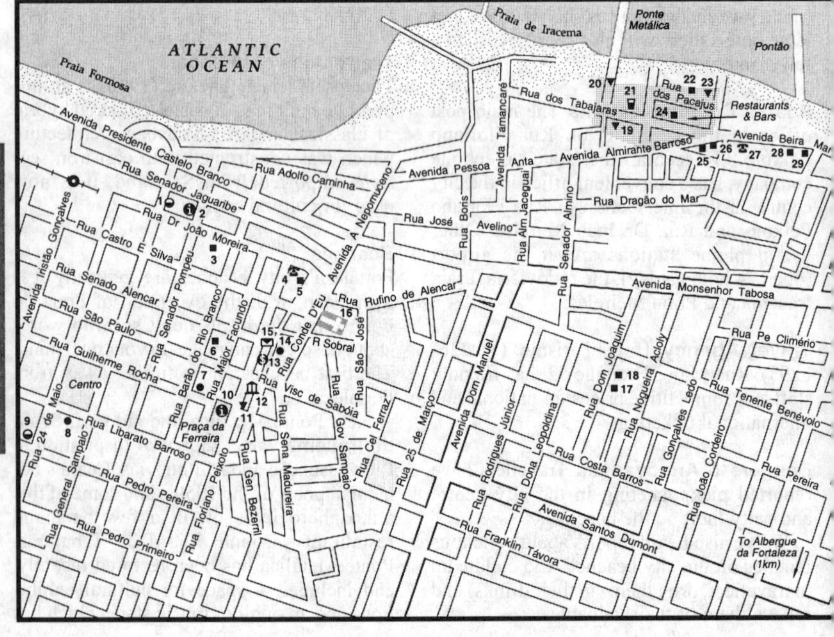

Prainha. Although there are regular bus services to all these places, the tours can be a good idea if you don't have time to arrange your own transport or don't want to stay overnight at the beach towns.

The tour prices include transportation only. Some sample per-person prices are: Beach Park, US$15; Morro Branco, US$20; Iguape, US$20; Lagoinha, US$25; Canoa Quebrada, US$25; and Jericoacoara, US$60.

Setur can give up-to-date advice on reliable agencies. Recommended operators include:

Ernanitur
  Avenida Barão de Studart 1165 (☎ 244-9363)
Valtur
  Avenida Monsenhor Tabosa 1078, Praia de Iracema (☎ 231-9157)
Egotur
  Rua M Rocha 700 (☎ 224-6778)
Petritur
  Avenida Desembargador Moreira 2033 (☎ 261-8999)

Special Events
The Regata de Jangadas, a jangada regatta between Praia do Meireles and Praia Mucuripe, is held in the second half of July. The Iemanjá festival is held on 15 August at Praia do Futuro. The Semana do Folclore, the town's folklore week, takes place from 22 to 29 August. Fortal, Fortaleza's lively 'out-of-season' Carnaval, is held in the last week of July.

Places to Stay – Budget
City Centre There are lots of dives in the centre – shop around for cleanliness not price, and check that you're not paying by the hour. The *Hotel Passeio* (☎/fax 252-2104), Rua Dr João Moreira 221, has reasonable apartamentos with fan at US$20/28 for singles/doubles.

A good budget option between the centre and the beaches is the friendly and clean *Pousada do Tourísta* (☎ 226-5662), Rua

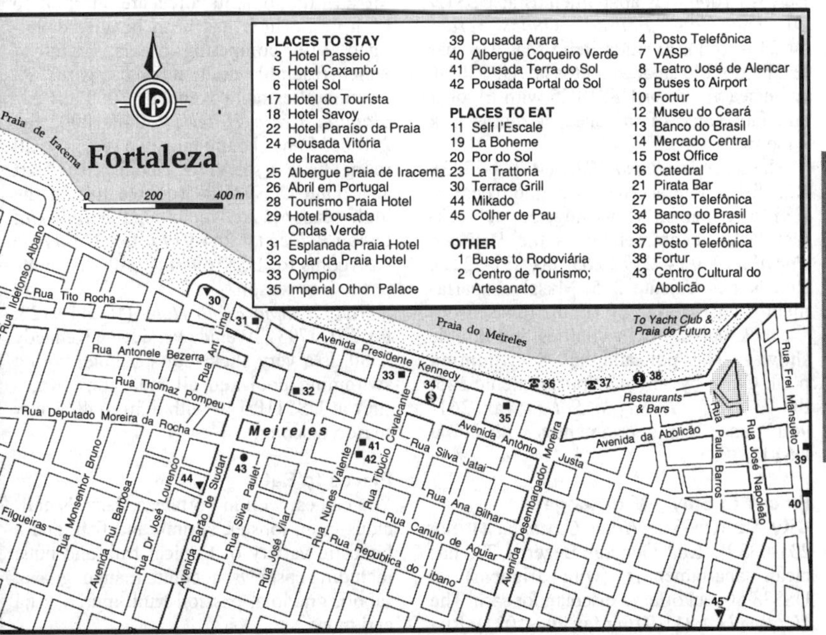

Dom Joaquim 351, with quartos at US$12/23/27 for singles/doubles/triples. Nearby, the *Hotel Savoy* (☎ 226-8426), Rua Dom Joaquim 321, has apartamentos (with fan) at US$15/25.

City Beaches Praia de Iracema is generally less expensive for accommodation than Praia do Meireles, and a more interesting area to explore. The YHA *Albergue de Juventude Praia de Iracema* (☎ 219-3267), Avenida Almeida Barroso 998, on Praia de Iracema, is a convenient distance from the centre. The YHA *Albergue de Juventude Coqueiro Verde* (☎ 267-1998), Rua Frei Mansueto 531, is a friendly, comfortable hostel close to the glitz of Praia do Meireles. It charges US$15 (US$10 for members).

The *Pousada Vitória de Iracema* (no ☎), Rua dos Tabajaras 673, is a friendly place with clean, basic quartos at US$10/18. It also has a kitchen you can use. The *Abril em Portugal* (☎ 219-9509), Avenida Almirante Barroso 1006, has apartamentos at US$12/20. The *Hotel Pousada Ondas Verdes* (☎ 219-0871), Avenida Beira Mar 934, has bright double apartamentos at US$20/30 (with sea view), or US$18/25 with frigobar and fan (some of the cheaper rooms lack windows).

The *Solar da Praia Hotel* (☎ 224-7323), Rua Silva Paulet 205, is a good deal at US$15 per person, with a huge buffet breakfast. Also recommended is the *Pousada Portal do Sol* (☎ 219-6265; fax 231-5221), Rua Nunes Valente 275. Massive apartamentos cost US$25/30 (in the low season) – check out the twin vanities and double shower. The pousada has a swimming pool. Close by, at Rua Nunes Valente 245, the *Pousada Terra do Sol* (☎/fax 261-9509) has clean apartamentos with fan at US$15/30.

Places to Stay – Mid-Range

City Centre The *Hotel Caxambú* (☎/fax 231-0339), Rua General Bezerril 22, has clean apartamentos (with frigobar) at US$38/50, but offers a discount for cash. The *Hotel Sol* (☎ 211-9166; fax 262-1021), Rua Barão do Rio Branco 829, has a pool and charges US$54/60 for standard apartamentos. It also offers a discount for cash payment.

City Beaches At Praia de Iracema, the *Hotel Paraíso da Praia* (☎ 219-3387; fax 226-1964), Rua dos Pacajus 109, has a swimming pool and good standard apartamentos at US$37/44 (US$74/88 in the high season). The *Turismo Praia Hotel* (☎ 219-2204; fax 219-1638), Avenida Beira Mar, has apartamentos at US$30/36 (US$40/55 in the high season). Not far from the beach at Praia Meireles, *Pousada Arara* (☎ 263-2277; fax 263-6096), Rua Frei Mansueto 343, has colourful, comfortable air-conditioned apartamentos for US$35/45. The French owner, Gilbert, is friendly and helpful. He speaks English, German and Spanish.

Places to Stay – Top End

Most of the top-end hotels are on Praia do Meireles, which has been heavily developed with competing hotels, many of which resemble multistorey car parks. At Avenida Presidente Kennedy 2000, the *Esplanada Praia Hotel* (☎ 248-1000; fax 248-8555) has been renovated recently; all rooms have a sea view. Room prices start at around US$98/108 (double this in the high season). At No 2500, the *Imperial Othon Palace* (☎ 244-9177; fax 224-7777) has rooms for US$169/188, with discounts in the low season.

The *Olympio Praia Hotel* (☎ 244-9122; fax 261-2793), Avenida Presidente Kennedy 2380, is a very slick four-star hotel with a swimming pool and all mod cons. Rates start at US$110/140 with a 30 to 40% low season discount.

Places to Eat

You can eat well in Fortaleza. There's delicious crab, lobster, shrimp and fish, and a fantastic variety of tropical fruit and nuts, including cashews, coconut, mango, guava, sapoti, graviola, passion fruit, murici, cajá and more.

There are several local dishes worth tasting. Peixe a delícia is a highly recommended favourite. Try paçoca, a typical Cearense dish made of sun-dried meat, ground with a mortar and pestle, mixed with manioc and then roasted. The tortured meat is usually accompanied by baião de dois, which is a mixture of rice, cheese, beans and butter.

City Centre The centre has lots of eateries which offer self-serve por quilo lunches. A good one is *Self L'Escale*, just off Praça da Ferreira. In the evening, you have a much wider choice at the city beaches.

City Beaches There are some excellent restaurants along Rua Tabajaras and Praia de Iracema, near the Ponte Metálica. For Italian food, try *La Trattoria*, Rua dos Pacujus 125, where the owner proudly claims 'cutting spaghetti is a crime, ketchup is forbidden; and no one will be served beans and rice'! *La Boheme*, Rua dos Tabajaras 380, is a sophisticated, arty restaurant with a gallery attached – even the chairs are individually painted works of art. If you are feeling like a major splurge, try the seafood dishes that are recommended.

Praia do Meireles is packed with restaurants. *Terrace Grill* is a churrascaria on the beach, with tables set out in the open to catch the breeze. The Japanese restaurant *Mikado*, Avenida Barão de Studart 600, specialises in teppanyaki.

Colher de Pau, Rua Frederico Borges 204 (Varjota district), serves excellent regional dishes and is very popular with locals. It's closed on Monday.

Entertainment

Pirata Bar, Rua dos Tabajaras 325, Praia de Iracema, is clearly the place to go, at least on Monday when it claims *a segunda feira mais louca do planeta* (the craziest Monday on the planet). The action includes live music for avid forró or lambada fans, who can dance until they drop. Admission is US$10. The surrounding bars also get very lively.

On Tuesdays the hot spot is *Oásis*, Avenida Santos Dumont 5779, a gigantic dance hall with room for several thousand people. On Wednesday and Friday, *Clube de Vaqueiro*, Anel Contôrno, between Hwys BR-116 and CE-04, is a huge forró club, a long way from the centre and best reached by taxi. On Friday, there's a rodeo before 11 pm when the forró dancing kicks off. During the holiday season, the barracas along the beaches are a constant source of entertainment in the evenings.

Things to Buy

Fortaleza is one of the most important centres in the Northeast for crafts. Artisans work with carnaúba palm fronds, bamboo, vines, leather and lace. Much of the production is geared to the tourist, but there are also goods for urban and sertanejo customers. The mercados and fairs are the places to look for clothing, hammocks, carvings, saddles, bridles, harnesses and images of saints. Mercados are held about town (usually from 4 pm onwards) from Tuesday to Sunday. Setur has a complete listing.

There is a craft fair every night on Praia Meireles, where you can purchase sand paintings, watch the artists work and have them customise your design.

Lacework, embroidery, raw leather goods, ceramics, and articles made of straw are also available from: the Central de Artesanato Luiza Távora (Handicrafts Centre), at Avenida Santos Dumont 1589, in Aldeota district; the Centro do Turismo, at Rua Senador Pompeu 350; the Mercado Central (which has cheaper prices) on Rua General Bezerril; and tourist boutiques (clothing, jewellery, fashion) along Avenida Monsenhor Tabosa. Cashew nuts are also excellent value in Fortaleza.

Getting There & Away

Air Pinto Martins airport (☎ 272-6166) is 6km south of the city centre. Flights operate to Rio, São Paulo and major cities in the Northeast and the North.

Following are the addresses for Brazilian and foreign airlines:

Air France
Rua E Garcia 909 (☎ 264-1500)
Transbrasil
Rua Barão do Rio Branco 1251 (☎ 254-4261)
Varig
Avenida Santos Dumont 2727, Aldeota (☎ 244-8111)
VASP
Avenida Santos Dumont 3060, Aldeota (☎ 244-2244)

Bus The rodoviária (☎ 186 for information or ☎ 272-1566) is 6km south of the centre.

Buses run daily to Salvador (US$60, 22 hours) and Rio de Janeiro (US$145, 48 hours); seven times a day to Natal (US$22, eight hours), Teresina (US$26, 10 hours) and São Luís (US$46, 16 hours); and three times a day to Recife (US$42, 12 hours) and Belém (US$66, 22 hours).

The Redencão bus company runs buses at 9 am and 9 pm each day to Jericoacoara (US$15, 6½ hours) and 10 times a day to Quixada (US$8, 3½ hours). The Empresa São Benedito bus company runs three a day to Canoa Quebrada (US$7, 3½ hours). The Empresa Redentora bus company runs 10 buses a day to Baturité (US$4, 2½ hours). The Ipu Brasileira bus company runs services to Ubajara six times a day (US$14, 6 hours) and four times a day to Camocim via Sobral (US$15, 7½ hours). Six buses a day run to Juazeiro de Norte (US$24, 9 hours).

Getting Around

To/From the Airport Pinto Martins airport is just a couple of kilometres from the rodoviária. From the airport there are buses (No 404 Aeroporto/Benfica) to Praça José Alencar in the centre. A fixed-price taxi to the centre costs around US$17, a normal one US$10.

To/From the Rodoviária To reach the city centre, take any bus marked 13 de Maio or Aguanambi (passes the Centro de Turismo). A taxi to the centre costs around US$6.

Highly recommended if you're coming or going to the rodoviária or airport is the air-conditioned Guanabara Top Bus, which loops from the airport and rodoviária through the centre and on to Praias Iracema and Meireles. It passes the local bus stop outside the rodoviária every 30 minutes from 7 am to 10 pm daily. The fare is US$2.

To/From City Beaches From outside the Centro de Turismo, on Rua Dr João Moreira, take the bus marked Circular along the beachfront to Praia de Iracema and Praia do Meireles. Meireles buses also go to Praia do Meireles. A taxi from the centre to Praia de Iracema costs US$4.

From Avenida Castro E Silva (close to the Centro de Tourismo), Praia do Futuro and Serviluz buses run to Praia do Futuro.

To/From Beaches West of the City For beaches west of the city, such as Icaraí and Cumbuco, you can take a Cumbuco bus from Praça Capistrano Abreu, on Avenida Tristão Gonçalves. You can also pick up the Cumbuco bus along Avenida Presidente Kennedy.

BEACHES SOUTH-EAST OF FORTALEZA

The coastal road from Fortaleza south to Aracati, Hwy CE-004, runs about 10km inland. It's mostly a flat, dry landscape of shrubs, stunted trees and some lakes. The towns are small, with good beaches, jangadas and dunescapes.

Beach Park

This full-blown beach resort, 22km from Fortaleza, is one of the most modern in Brazil, with facilities such as ultralights, surfboards and dune buggies. It also has an Aqua Park, which features a huge swimming pool complex with the highest water-toboggan run in Brazil (24m, and speeds up to 80km/h). It's quite expensive and would probably appeal more to tourists in search of structured fun. Entry is US$30, but children under 1m tall get in free.

Getting There & Away From Praça Tristão Gonçalvez in Fortaleza, take a Beach Park bus to Beach Park. This bus also runs along Avenida Presidente Kennedy.

Iguape

Iguape, 5km south of Prainha, has a long stretch of white-sand beach with jangadas, a few lonely palm trees and sand dunes breaking the clean line of the horizon. The kids from town ski down the dunes on planks of wood.

In Iguape, women and children make wonderful lacework. Four or more wooden bobs are held in each hand and clicked rapidly and rhythmically. The bobs lay string around metal pins which are stuck in burlap cushions. Using this process, beautiful and intricate lace flowers are crafted.

Save your purchases for Centro das Rendeiras, 6km inland, where the lacework is just as fine and cheaper. Also on sale are sweet cakes made from raw sugar-cane broth which is boiled into a thick mass, pressed and reboiled in vats.

Places to Stay & Eat There are two hotels in town, but you can easily rent rooms or houses. The *Pousada Dunas do Iguape* (☎ 370-1294) is close to the beach and charges US$20 a double. *Hotel Soleste* (☎ 243-5123) has a pool and charges US$45 a double. Recommended restaurants are *Peixado do Iguape* and *João do Camarão*.

Getting There & Away São Benedito buses to Iguape leave every hour until 8 pm from Terminal Domingos Olympio in Fortaleza.

Morro Branco

Bounded on the coast by the Rio Choro and Rio Piranji and inland by red cliffs, Morro Branco is 4km south of the town of Beberibe. Recent development is quite ugly. There are several barracas along the beach for sipping and sunning. If you're feeling active, take a jangada ride to the caves, or hike to the cliffs of coloured sands and the natural springs at Praia das Fontes.

The big festival here, dedicated to São Francisco, is held on 3 and 4 September and features a grand procession.

Places to Stay & Eat Along the beachfront, there's the *Pousada Sereia* (no ☎), a friendly place with basic apartamentos at US$15/20 for singles/doubles, or the more upmarket but fading *Pousada do Morro Branco* (☎ 223-3433), with apartamentos at US$20/25. In the village, the *Pousada Labrinito* (☎ 330-1121), Rua Luiz Gama 120, has quartos at US$20 a single or double.

Bar o Claudio is a relaxed little restaurant just off the beach, with a good range of local seafood dishes.

Getting There & Away Beberibe is 78km south of Fortaleza on Hwys BR-116 and CE-004. There are four buses each day travelling to São Benedito running via Beberibe to Morro Branco from Fortaleza. The first leaves at 6.30 am and the last leaves at 7.20 pm (US$3, 2½ hours). There are also several buses running daily from Beberibe to Aracati.

ARACATI

• *pop 57,000* ✉ *62800-000* ☎ *088*

Aracati is a large town by the Rio Jaguaribe, which provided transport for sugarcane, and thus wealth, in the 18th century.

Things to See & Do

Although Aracati is not in the best of shape architecturally, some of its historical buildings are worth visiting. The **Igreja Matriz de NS do Rosário**, on Rua Dragão do Mar, dates from the late 18th century and is a fine example of colonial architecture. The attractive **Sobrado do Barão de Aracati** houses the **Museu Jaguaribano**, which contains sacred art and local handicrafts. For a look at more colonial houses, some of which have retained their *azulejo* (ceramic tile) façades, wander down Rua do Comércio (Rua Grande).

The town is also known for its handicrafts, and the best time to see them is at the **Feira do Artesão** (Artisan Market) held on Saturday. Aracati's street Carnaval is the liveliest in the state.

Places to Stay & Eat

There are a few inexpensive hotels near the rodoviária. The *Pousada Litorânea* (☎ 421-1001), Rua Cel Alexandrino 1251, is the best, with apartamentos costing US$10/15 for singles/doubles. There's also a restaurant downstairs. The *Brisa Rio* (☎ 421-1881), Rua Cel Alexandrino 1179, is similarly priced. *Pousada Restaurante Canteiros* (☎ 421-1757), Rua Alexandrino 1559 next to the rodoviária is another good option. *Churrascaria Raimundo do Caranguejo*, Rua Hilton Gondim Bandeira 505, serves good crab dishes.

Getting There & Away

From Fortaleza's rodoviária, take one of the seven buses a day to Aracati. The 2½ to four hour (depending on stops) trip costs US$5. There are frequent services to Fortaleza and Natal from Aracati. There are sharks waiting at Aracati's rodoviária to whisk you off to Canoa Quebrada in taxis for US$10 – walk 800m down to Rua Dragão do Mar and take a bus, passenger truck or VW kombi from the stop across from the Igreja Matriz. The fare is US$1. There are also regular buses from Aracati to Majorlândia and Beberibe.

CANOA QUEBRADA

Once a tiny fishing village cut off from the world by its huge, pink sand dunes, Canoa Quebrada, 13km from Aracati, is still small and pretty, but it is no longer the Shangri-la it was in the past. The road to town is sealed and there is electricity and *chopp* (draught beer). There are lots of gringos running about, and on weekends it's a party town, when tourist buses roll in and dwarf the village. Other than the beach, the main attractions are watching the sunset from the dunes, tearing round in buggies and dancing forró or reggae. If you still have energy remaining after a night of dancing, the beautiful 70km walk south to Tibaú is well worthwhile – take a hammock. Buggy rides to Ponta Grossa, Redonda and Cumbe

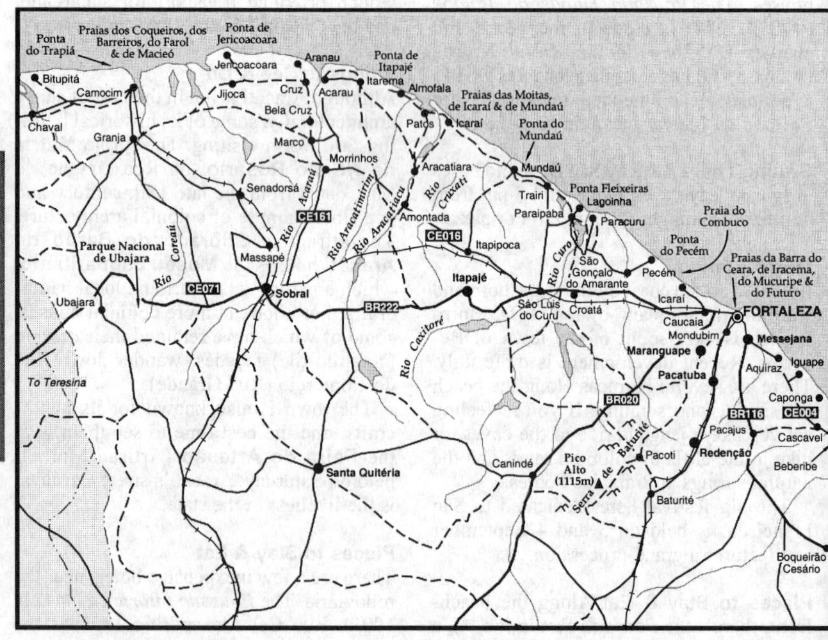

are also available at US$10 per person per day.

Take care, as *bichos de pé* (small parasites) are underfoot. Wear shoes all around town and wherever pigs and dogs roam freely.

Places to Stay

Individual phone lines were due for installation a couple of months after our visit. We suggest you get hold of a recent phone book if you feel the need to make a reservation. Outside summer this shouldn't be necessary. Prices quoted here are for the low season; expect a stiff price hike in summer.

The *Albergue Lua Estrela* is a hostel, but looks more like a resort hotel – there are great views from the attached restaurant. The *Pousada Holandes* is a friendly place and good value at US$5 without breakfast. Highly recommended is *Pousada do Toby*, Rua Nascer do Sol, which has a pool on the roof with a great view; it also provides a good breakfast. Doubles go for around US$30 – cheaper if you stay a while. *Pousada Oásis do Rei* is a very nice pousada with lots of greenery. Doubles go for US$30 and its restaurant serves Austrian and German dishes. Other good options include *Pousada Quebra Mar*, with large, airy rooms with sea views for US$10/15, and the similarly priced *Pousada Lua Morena*, at the end of the main street towards the beach. *Tranquilandia* (☎ 941-1187) is a more upmarket place with a grassy courtyard (a rare sight among the sandy streets of the village) and pool. Apartamentos are US$35/40 (US$60 in the high season).

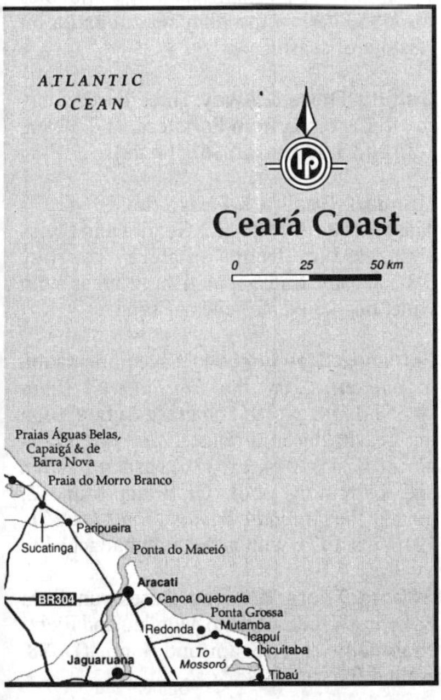

Places to Eat

The main street of Canoa Quebrada, known as Broadway, is the restaurant and bar strip. Recommended eateries include *Casa Verde*, *Restaurant da Lurdinha* for cheap prato feito and *Restaurant Dali* with good pizzas and other Italian dishes. Broadway also hosts a few lively bars, including the stylish *Todo Mundo*, run by Toby from Denmark, and *Boi Mamão*, the local chopparia. *Eu Quero Mais*, opposite Todo Mundo, is the town dancetaria.

Getting There & Away

There are three buses daily to Canoa Quebrada from Fortaleza's rodoviária, at 8.30 am, and 1.40 and 3.30 pm (US$5, 4½ hours).

SOUTH TO RIO GRANDE DO NORTE

Access by road to this stretch of coast is limited, so there are some great deserted beaches and small fishing villages. Buggies zoom along, but the rest of the time it's pretty quiet. The first town after Canoa Quebrada is **Majorlândia**, 7km south, a popular resort which gets crowded on weekends. There are places to stay, but it's best to keep moving. Four kilometres south of Majorlândia on a sandy track are the distinctive, chalky-white sandstone bluffs of

Quixaba. From the bluffs, cut by gullies between cacti and palms, you can see the pink hills of Canoa Quebrada. You can rent a jangada and visit the neighbouring beaches.

The 60km south-east from Quixaba to the border with Rio Grande do Norte is just a series of primitive little beaches and towns mostly off the maps and definitely out of the guidebooks: **Lagoa do Mato**, **Fontainha**, **Retirinho** and **Retiro Grande Mutamba**, **Ponta Grossa**, **Redonda** and **Retiro** (a waterfall), **Peroba**, **Picos**, **Barreiras** and **Barrinha** and finally, **Icapuí**, which has a couple of pousadas.

A road continues to **Ibicuitaba** and **Barra do Ceará** beach. It's possible to drive from there to Tibaú, in Rio Grande do Norte, at low tide.

BEACHES NORTH-WEST OF FORTALEZA

Paracuru

About 100km from Fortaleza on BR-222 and CE-135, Paracuru is a Cearense version of Rio de Janeiro's Búzios. It's a clean, relaxed and fairly affluent town, popular with local surfers. Coconut palms, natural freshwater springs and jangadas complete a tranquil beach picture. Although the beach attracts crowds from Fortaleza at weekends, it's quiet during the rest of the week. In recent years, Carnaval in Paracuru has become a byword amongst Cearenses for hot beach action.

Places to Stay & Eat A good budget option is the *Pousada da Praça* (☎ 344-1271), on Praça da Matriz. Bright apartamentos cost US$15/20 for singles/ doubles (breakfast not included). The *Pousada Villa Verde* (☎ 344-1181), on Rua Professora Maria Luiza, is set in lovely gardens with huge, shady trees. Basic apartamentos cost US$10/12 (breakfast not included). The *Pousada da Gaviota* (☎ 344-1352), Rua Coroneu Meireles, has apartamentos for US$20/30.

Restaurant Don Carlo, Rua Saturnino de Carvalho, has a wide range of pastas, pizzas and seafood dishes. *Formula 1* is a pleasant restaurant run by Frenchman Michel. There are loads of self-serve ice-cream places in town.

Getting There & Away Ten buses a day run to Paracuru from Fortaleza (US$4, 2½ hours), the first at 5.45 am, the last at 7 pm.

Praia da Lagoinha

Praia da Lagoinha, a short distance up the coast from Paracuru, has lots of coconut palms, good camping and a small but deep lagoon near the sand dunes. The beach is considered by Cearenes to be in the top three in the state, and its relative isolation has so far kept crowds down.

Places to Stay & Eat The *Pousada O Milton* (☎ 363-1232, ext 102) is right on the beachfront and has a popular restaurant – try the delicious fish stew. Other options are *Lagoinha Praia Hotel* (☎ 363-1232, ext 122) and *Pousada Ondas do Mar* (☎ 363-1232, ext 135) which has singles/doubles for US$30/50 in the high season and a bit less out of season.

Getting There & Away Three buses a day run to Lagoinha from Fortaleza, at 7.30 am, 1.30 and 3.30 pm (US$5, 3hours).

Mundaú, Guajira & Fleixeiras

The beaches of Mundaú, Guajira and Fleixeiras, 155km from Fortaleza via Hwy BR-222, are traditional fishing areas with wide, unspoiled stretches of sand.

Places to Stay For budget accommodation in Fleixeiras, try the *Pousada da Célia* (☎ 351-1134, ext 105) on Praça da Igreja. On the beach, the mid-range *Solar das Fleixeiras* (☎ 344-1044, ext 136) has a restaurant and swimming pool. On Praia Mundaú, there's the *Mundaú Dunas Hotel* (☎ 351-1210, ext 197), with a restaurant attached.

Getting There & Away Buses run from Fortaleza's rodoviária to Mundaú and Fleixeiras daily at 6.15 am and 4 pm (US$8, around four hours).

Itapipoca

The city of Itapipoca, 120km west of Fortaleza, can be used as a starting point for exploring the beaches of Baleia, Pracianos, Inferno and Marinheiros.

Places to Stay The *Hotel Municipal* (☎/fax 631-1001) is on Rua Anastácio Braga, in Itapipoca. Single/double apartamentos are US$15/25. Right on Praia Baleia is the *Pousada Maresia* (☎ 631-1844, ext 23), which has simple apartamentos for US$20/30.

JERICOACOARA

• pop 1500 ✉ 62598-000 ☎ 088

The small fishing village of Jericoacoara another remote 'in' beach, popular among backpackers and hip Brazilians. It's a long haul to get there, so you might as well stay a while – in fact, it may be harder to leave. It's a beautiful spot where dozens of palms drowning in sand dunes face jangadas stuck on a broad grey beach. Pigs, goats, horses, cows, bulls and dogs roam the sandy streets at will.

It's best to avoid bichos de pé and other parasites by not walking the streets barefoot. If you stay bicho-free, you can practise your steps at the forró held in an outdoor courtyard every Wednesday and Saturday – just follow the music. You can also climb the sand dunes (watching the sunset from the top is mandatory, but dune-surfing down is only for crazies), go for a ride on a jangada, or walk to **Pedra Furada**, a rock 3km east along the beach. At low tide the beach route is easier than the hill route. You can also hire horses and gallop along the beach.

Organised Tours

Fortaleza tour operators and upmarket pousadas in Jericoacoara offer tour packages for Jericoacoara. Two day trips cost around US$60, including accommodation. Extra days cost around US$25 each.

Places to Stay

There is plenty of cheap accommodation in Jericoacoara and also several upmarket options – the latter have generators. For longer stays, ask about renting a local house – you should be able to get something for about US$5 per night. Words to the wise: bring a large cotton hammock or bedroll with sleeping sack.

Reservations can be made by calling the village telephone office (☎ 621-0544). An excellent inexpensive option is the *Pousada da Renata*, 500m from town along the beach. It's quiet, and has a nice patio. Staff speak English, Italian and German, and charge US$10 per person (US$5 extra if you want dinner). Also recommended is *Pousada Casa do Turismo* (☎/fax 621-0211), on Rua Das Dunas. The pousada also serves as the village post office and agent for the Fortaleza bus. Another good budget option is the *Pousada Isalana*, Rua Principal, with apartamentos for US$10 per person.

More upmarket lodgings include the *Pousada Matusa*, Rua São Francisco; *Pousada do Avalon*, Rua Principal; the *Pousada Hippopotamus* (☎ 603-1616); and the *Jericoacoara Praia Hotel* (☎ 603-1602). The last two are both on Rua Forró. Package deals from Fortaleza usually include accommodation at one of these four pousadas.

Places to Eat

The best place in town to eat is *Isabel*, on the beach at the end of Rua do Forró. Set on a large seafront patio, Dona Isabel prepares fantastic seafood dishes. Try her peixada. On Rua Principal, *Mama na Égua* also serves good-value seafood; *Restaurant Avalon* has a wide range of salads and crêpes; and *Alexandre Bar* is the prime location along the beach for afternoon drinks, sunset-gazing and seafood dishes. Most of the budget places to stay also serve food.

Entertainment

Later in the evening, everyone goes to *Bar do Forró*.

Getting There & Away

Two buses a day leave Fortaleza's rodoviária for Jericoacoara (US$15, around 7 hours), at

9 am and 9 pm. In Jijoca, you are transferred to a passenger truck (included in the ticket price) for the 24km rodeo ride to Jericoacoara. Of the two options, the night bus is quicker and cooler, but you arrive in Jericoacoara at around 3.30 am. Someone from one of the pousadas will meet the bus, and you can always move to another pousada later in the day.

If you have come by car, leave it parked in Jijoca, where some of the pousada owners can keep an eye on it. The ride over and around sweeping dunes, lagoons, bogs and flat scrub terrain is beautiful, but very hard on people and machines. Transport leaves Jericoacoara for Fortaleza at 6 am and 10.30 pm.

To get to Jericoacoara from Sobral, a Vale do Acaraú bus runs from Sobral at noon over an abysmal road to Jijoca (US$6, three hours), and should connect with the Fortaleza bus there – if not, you should be able to collectively bargain to get a fare of about US$3 per person for a jeep. To get to Sobral, you will have to catch a bus leaving Jijoca at 2 am – take the 10.30 pm truck out of Jericoacoara and think up new and interesting ways to amuse yourself in Jijoca for three hours.

For details about access from Camocim, see Getting There & Away in the Camocim section.

TATAJUBA

Tatajuba, about 30km west of Jericoacoara, is a tiny, isolated fishing village at the mouth of a tidal river. The beach is broad and lonely, and there's a lagoon surrounded by extensive dunes about 2km from the village. The only restaurant and pousada, the *Verde Folha*, is run by Marcus and Valéria, refugees from the 'big smoke' of Jericoacoara. They have a couple of rooms with beds and hammocks. Full board, including great home cooking, costs US$15 per person.

There is no regular transport to Tatajuba. The walk along the beach from Jericoacoara takes about five hours; leave early in the morning and take water. At Guriú, a little less than half way, there's a river to cross – canoes will take you over for about US$2. The river at Tatajuba can be waded at low tide. Don't try to cross it if the water is high, as the current is very strong.

Alternatively, you should be able to rent a boat in Jericoacoara to take you there; ask around at the beach.

CAMOCIM

Camocim is a lively fishing port and market town at the mouth of the Rio Coreaú, in north-western Ceará, near the Piauí border. The town's economy revolves around the saltworks, lobster fishing and a busy daily mercado.

On **Praia dos Barreiros** and **Praia do Farol**, 2km and 4km from town respectively, you can sip coconut milk while tanning.

Places to Stay & Eat

The *Pousada Ponta Pora* (☎ 621-0505), the colourful *Pousada Beira Mar* (☎ 621-0048), and the *Municipal Hotel* (☎/fax 621-0165), are all along the riverfront, on Avenida Beira Mar. All have cheap quartos and apartamentos. River-bank restaurants serve local seafood and typical Cearense dishes.

Getting There & Away

Four buses a day run to Camocim via Sobral from Fortaleza's rodoviária (US$15, 7½ hours), the first at 7.30 am and the last at 6.30 pm.

A jeep leaves the central mercado in Camocim for Jijoca at around 10.30 am daily, and if there are enough people, it will carry on to Jericoacoara.

During the high season there are boats sailing from Camocim to Jericoacoara – the trip takes four hours. Half the adventure is getting there.

SOBRAL

• *pop 140,000* ✉ *62000-000* ☎ *088*

Sobral has two minor sights – faded glories from a time before everything was changed by the construction of Hwy BR-222. The **Museu Diocesano Dom José** (a museum of sacred art), on Avenida Dom José, houses an eclectic collection of images of saints. It's from 2 to 5 pm open Monday to Saturday. The **Teatro Municipal São João**, on Praça Dr Antônio Ibiapina, is an impressive neoclassical theatre, built in (1880).

Places to Stay

Hotel Beira Rio (☎/fax 613-1040), Rua Consuleiro Rodrigues Jr 400, has apartamentos at US$30 a double.

Getting There & Away

There are two buses a day to Camocim from Sobral. The earliest bus to make the 3½ hour trip leaves at 3.30 am, the second at 10.30 pm. One bus leaves Sobral daily, at noon, to Jijoca via Cruz, for access to Jericoacoara.

SERRA DE BATURITÉ

Ceará's interior is not limited to the harsh landscapes of the sertão. There are also ranges of hills which break up the monotony of the sun-scorched land. The Serra de Baturité is the range of hills closest to Fortaleza. A natural watershed, it is an oasis of green where coffee and bananas are cultivated around the cliffs and jagged spines of the hills. The climate is tempered by rain, the evenings are cool and morning fog obscures Pico Alto (1115m), the highest point in the state.

Baturité

Founded in 1745, the town of Baturité (95km west of Fortaleza) was once at the forefront of the fight against slavery, and is now the economic and commercial centre of the region. Most of the town's attractions are grouped around the Praça Matriz and include the *pelourinho* (whipping post), the baroque church of Matriz NS de Palma (1764), the Palácio Entre-Rios, and the Museu Comendador Ananias Arruda, which contains exhibits from the town's past (though surprisingly little on the struggle to abolish slavery). There are also a few *termas* (resorts with mineral pools) clustered around the town. There are local handicrafts on sale in Baturité that include embroidery, tapestry and straw goods.

Places to Stay Apart from staying in the nearby villages of Guaramiranga and Pacoti, lodgings are also available in Baturité at the *Hotel Canuto*, on Praça Santo Luiza, and the *Balneário Itamaracá Club* (☎ 347-0113), at Sítio Itamaracá.

Getting There & Away Four buses leave Fortaleza's rodoviária daily for Baturité (US$4, 2½ hours).

Guaramiranga & Pacoti

The two prettiest villages on the heights of Serra de Baturité are Guaramiranga and Pacoti, 19km and 26km respectively from Baturité.

Places to Stay & Eat The hills are a popular weekend retreat from Fortaleza, so prices rise about 20% on weekends. The *Hotel Escola de Guaramiranga* (☎ 321-1106), a training centre for hotel staff in Guaramiranga, has spotless apartamentos, a

Brazil is the world's largest producer of coffee

bar, a swimming pool and table-tennis tables. The single/double rooms cost US$33/40. It's unmarked and tricky to find (no sign), but it's a good deal.

The *Remanso Hotel da Serra* (☎ 325-1222) is 5km from Guaramiranga on the beautiful road to Pacoti. It has pleasant apartamentos at around US$32/48, a restaurant and a swimming pool. Slightly more expensive, and closer to Pacoti, is the *Estância Vale das Flores* (☎ 325-1233), at Sítio São Francisco. It's set in a park with a swimming pool, sports facilities, horse rental and mini-zoo. Chalets cost US$30/58 including breakfast and lunch.

Getting There & Away The Empresa Redentora bus company runs a daily bus direct to Guaramiranga from Fortaleza's rodoviária, at 3 pm (US$6, three hours). From Baturité, there's one bus, at 10 am, running to Guaramiranga and Pacoti, and another bus, at 5.30 pm, to Guaramiranga only.

CANINDÉ

Canindé, only 110km south-west from Fortaleza on Hwy BR-020, is the site of one of the Northeast's great religious pilgrimages, O Santuário de São Francisco das Chagas. Since 1775 pilgrims have been coming to Canindé to offer promises to and ask favours of São Francisco de Assis. Nowadays around 250,000 fervent believers arrive each year, most from the sertão, almost all dirt poor. For westerners the festival is both colourful and bizarre, and laced with superstition. You'll see many votive offerings and evidence of miracle cures. It's a scene right out of a Glauber Rocha film.

The festival begins on 2 September at 4 am and continues until 4 October. On 30 September, the climax of the festival begins with the celebration for the *lavradores* (farm workers), which is followed in turn by celebrations for the vaqueiros (cowboys) on 1 October, and for the *violeiros* (guitarists and luthiers) on 2 October.

The culmination of all the festivities begins at 3 am on 4 October, when the first of nine masses commences. These are followed by a 70,000-strong procession through the town.

PARQUE NACIONAL DE UBAJARA

The Parque Nacional de Ubajara is just a few kilometres from the small town of Ubajara, 200km west of Fortaleza on Hwy BR-222. The main attractions are the cable-car rides down to the caves and the caves themselves.

The park, with its beautiful vistas, forest, waterfalls and 3km trail to the caves is well worth a visit. At 850m above sea level, temperatures in the surrounding area are cool and provide a welcome respite from the searing heat of the sertão.

Information

The IBAMA office, 5km from Ubajara proper, at the entrance to the park, provides guides for the tour, but the information centre has been abandoned. If you fancy a strenuous hike take the 3km *trilha* (trail) down to the cave. Allow at least half a day for the round trip. Start in the cool of the early morning, wear sturdy footwear and take enough to drink. Alternatively, you can walk down to the caves and take the cable car back up.

Cable Car & Caves

In 1987 the lower station of the *teleférico* (cable car) was wiped out by boulders which fell after winter rains. The cable-car system has been replaced, and now operates every day from 10 am to 4 pm. The ride costs US$4. Guides accompany you on the one hour tour through the caves.

Nine chambers with strange limestone formations extend over half a kilometre into the side of a mountain. The main formations seen inside the caves are: **Pedra do Sino** (Bell Stone), **Salas da Rosa** (Rose Rooms), **Sala do Cavalo** (Horse Room) and **Sala dos Retratos** (Portrait Room).

Places to Stay & Eat

The *Sítio do Alemão*, set in a shady coffee plantation about 1.5km from the entrance to the park, is run by a German/Brazilian couple who can provide walking maps for the park and loads of information about local attractions. There are wonderful vistas over the sertão from the property. Day trips to Parque Nacional de Sete Cidades (140km away on a good road) can also be arranged. Spotless chalets cost US$10 per person, with a generous breakfast.

There are two pousadas near the park entrance: the *Pousada da Neblina* (☎ 634-1270) has apartamentos at US$28/35 for singles/doubles and a swimming pool; and the *Pousada Gruta de Ubajaras* (☎ 634-1375) has apartamentos for US$10/20. Both of these pousadas also have restaurants.

The *Churrascaria Hotel Ubajara* (☎ 634-1261), Rua Juvêncio Luís Pereira 370, in Ubajara, has quartos that cost US$10/18.

Getting There & Away

Empresa Ipu-Brasília has four buses a day from Fortaleza to Ubajara (US$14, six hours). The first bus leaves at 6.30 am, the last one at 9 pm. There are also bus connections to Teresina (US$11, 6 hours), the capital of Piauí state.

To reach the park entrance from the town of Ubajara, either walk the 3km or take a taxi (US$6).

SERRA DA IBIAPABA

The Serra da Ibiapaba is a range of hills running along the undefined border with the state of Piauí which forms a rugged terrain of buttes, bluffs and cliffs overlooking distant plains.

The town of **Ipu** lies 75km south-east of Ubajara, in the Serra da Ibiapaba. The main attraction of Ipu (the name means 'waterfall' in the Tabajara Indian language) is the **Bico do Ipu**, a powerful waterfall that jets 100m downwards and fans out into sheets of mist and spray. A few kilometres out of town are some strange stone stairs built by the Tabajara.

There is a sleazy restaurant under the falls, but no hotels in town. Ipu is worth a visit if it happens to be on your route, but it's not worth a special detour.

JUAZEIRO DO NORTE

• *pop 190,000* ✉ *63000-000* ☎ *088*

Juazeiro do Norte, 528km from Fortaleza, is a magnet for believers in Padre Cícero, who lived in this town and became a controversial figure of the sertão. Not only was he a curate, with several miracles to his credit, he also exercised a strong political influence. His astonishing rise to fame was started when an elderly woman received the host from him at mass and claimed that it had miraculously turned to blood. Soon he was being credited with all kinds of miracles, and later became drawn into a leading role in the social and political upheavals in the Northeast. Padre Cícero died in 1934, but despite attempts by the Catholic Church to deny his sainthood, the claims and adoration of his followers seem to be as strong as ever.

The best time to see this magnetic attraction and devotion is during the festivals and pilgrimages in honour of Padre Cícero. On 24 March, the Aniversário do Padre Cícero celebrates Padre Cícero in legend and song. The *romaria* (pilgrimage) to Juazeiro do Norte in honour of Padre Cícero takes place on 1 and 2 November and is known as the Dia do Romeiro e Festa do Padre Cícero.

The city of Padre Cícero is rich in wood and ceramic sculpture. Look for the work of Expedito Batista, Nino, Cizinho, José Celestino, Luís Quirino, Maria de Lourdes, Maria Cândida, Francisca, Daniel, José Ferreira and Maria das Dores.

Logradouro do Horto

On the hill above the town, accessible either by road or via a path laid out with the stations of the cross, is the colossal statue of **Padre Cícero** (25m), which was built in 1969 and now ranks as the fourth-tallest statue in the record books. Those taller are Cristo Rey (Cochabamba, Bolivia), Cristo Redentor on Corcovado (Rio) and the Statue of Liberty (New York). Nearby is a small chapel and a building filled with votive offerings which represent the diseases, afflictions and problems from which the worshippers have been freed: wooden or wax replicas of every conceivable body part, and graphic representations of survival from accidents.

Túmulo do Padre Cícero

Padre Cícero's tomb is beside the Capela NS do Perpétua Socorro, on Praça do Socorro.

Gráfica de Literatura de Cordel

If you are interested in *literatura de cordel* (literally, 'string literature'), visit this workshop on Rua Santa Luzia, where you can see the pamphlets being produced for sale on the premises. It's open from 7 to 11 am and 1 to 5 pm Monday to Friday. It's closed on Saturday afternoon.

Places to Stay

Since this town is a pilgrimage centre, there is no lack of accommodation, except during the main festivals. For inexpensive apartamentos, try the *Pousada Portal do Cariri* (☎ 571-2399), Avenida Leão Sampaio, or the *Panorama* (☎ 512-3100), Rua Santo Agostinho 58, US$15/30 for singles/doubles.

Getting There & Away

There are four departures a day for Fortaleza (US$24, nine hours), and regular buses to all the major cities in the Northeast.

Piauí

Piauí, one of the largest states in the Northeast, is also one of the poorest in Brazil, due to the oppressively hot and arid climate in its eastern and southern regions. The odd shape of the state – broad in the south, tapered at the coast – is due to a unique pattern of settlement which started from the sertão in the south and gradually moved towards the coast.

The climate on the Litoral Piauiense (Piauí coast) is kept cool(er) by sea breezes. If you're heading into the interior of the state, the best time for festivals and cool breezes is during July and August. The worst time, unless you want to be sunbaked to a frazzle, is between September and December.

Although Piauí is usually bypassed by travellers, it offers superb beaches along its short coast, the Delta do Parnaíba, interesting rock formations and hikes in the Parque Nacional de Sete Cidades, prehistoric sites and rock paintings in the Parque Nacional da Serra da Capivara (which ranks as one of the top prehistoric sites in South America), and the chance for rock hounds to visit Pedro Segundo – the only place in South America where opals are mined.

TERESINA

• *pop 660,000 ✉ 64000-000 ☎ 086*

Teresina, the capital of Piauí, is famed as the hottest city in Brazil. Promotional literature stresses heat, heat and yet more heat, with blurb bites such as 'Even the Wind Here isn't Cool' and 'Teresina – as Hot as its People'.

It's an interesting, quirky place which seems addicted to giving a Middle Eastern slant to the names of its streets, hotels and sights. The city itself is a Mesopotamia of sorts, sandwiched between the Rio Poty and Rio Parnaíba. Teresina is unpretentious and tourists are still reasonably rare, and the inhabitants will stop you on the street to ask, 'Where are *you* from?'. Like the British, residents of Teresina instantly warm to discussion of the weather, and especially of their favourite topic: *o calor* (the heat).

We recommend a visit if you yearn for attention or would like to feel famous for a day or so. And there's got to be something good going for a city that hosts an annual festival of humour!

Information

Tourist Offices Piemtur (☎ 223-4417), the state tourism organisation, has its head office at the Centro do Convenções, close to the Rio Poty. Its helpful staff happily dole out literature and advice. More convenient is the booth inside the Centro Artesanal, on

Watch out for Bowl-Head!

Any virgins named Mary need to be very careful when travelling in Teresina. Locals tell the story of Crispim, a young man who lived with his old, sick mother and fished along the banks of the Rio Parnaíba, close to its junction with the Rio Poty.

One day, after fishing without success, he returned home angry and frustrated. When he asked his mother what there was to eat, she could only offer a thin bone-soup. Irritated, Crispim screamed that it was only fit for a dog, grabbed the bone out of the soup and started beating his mother with it.

Revolted by what he had done, Crispim ran out and threw himself into the river. As his mother died in agony, she laid a curse on Crispim which turned him into a terrible monster – *cabeça-de-cuia* (bowl-head). The only way he can break the curse is to deflower seven virgins named Mary.

So far, this hasn't happened, so cabeça-de-cuia rises from the depths to scare women washing clothes on the riverbank and threaten those who take more fish from the river than they need. During nights of the full moon, cabeça-de-cuia transforms himself into an old man and wanders the streets of Teresina.

Andrew Draffen

Praça Dom Pedro II. Both are open from 8 am to 6 pm Monday to Friday.

Travel Agencies For tours to sights in Piauí, contact Servitur Turismo (☎ 223-2065), Rua Eliseu Martins 1136, or Aldatur (☎ 221-3932), Rua Lizandro Nogueira 1384.

Museu Histórico do Piauí

This state museum (☎ 221-6027) is divided into a series of exhibition rooms devoted to the history of the state; religious art; popular art; archaeology; fauna, flora and minerals; and an eclectic assortment of antique radios, projectors and other ancient wonders. Hidden in the corner of one room is a pathetic cabinet containing a flag, kerchief and some scribbled notes from *comunistas*, a flexible term used here to describe a group of independent thinkers, who were wiped out by the government in 1937.

The museum is on Praça Marechal Deodoro and opens from 8 to 11 am and 3 to 6 pm Tuesday to Friday, and from 8 am to noon on weekends. Admission is US$1.

Palácio de Karnak

This neo-classical structure on Avenida Antônio Freire was once the governor's residence and contained valuable works of art and antiques. In the late 1980s, the outgoing governor made a quick exit, together with much of the valuable contents.

Centro Artesanal

This is a centre for artesanato from all over Piauí. It is pleasant to come here and browse among the shops that sell leather articles, furniture, extremely intricate lacework, colourful hammocks, opals and soapstone (from Pedro Segundo), and liqueurs and confectionery made from genipapo, cajú, burití and maracujá.

Mercado Troca-Troca

In an attempt to perpetuate the old traditions of *troca troca* (barter), the government has made a permanent structure out of what was once an impromptu barter market. Unless you are curious to see the river, it's not worth a visit.

Potycabana

If you hanker after aquatic frolics and games as a respite from the searing heat, visit the Potycabana, an aquatic entertainment centre with water tobogganing and a surf pool, close to the Rio Poty.

Special Events

The main festivals, with typical dancing, music and cuisine of the Northeast, are held between June and August. The Salão Internacional de Humor do Piauí (Piauí Festival of Humour) is held during October or November and features comedy shows, exhibitions of cartoons, comedy routines and lots of live music.

Places to Stay – Budget

Camping Club do Nordeste (☎ 222-6202) is 12km out of the city on Estrada da Socopo, the road running east towards União.

The best cheapie is *Hotel São Benedito* (no ☎), Rua Senador Teodoro Pachêco 1199, a friendly place with quartos at US$9/14 for singles/doubles, and apartamentos at US$15. The *Hotel Fortaleza* (☎ 222-2984), Rua Coelho Rodrigues 1476, is another option with quartos (with fan) at US$15/25. Apartamentos with air-conditioning cost US$25/40. It seems a bit overpriced. The two-star *Teresina Palace Hotel* (☎ 221-2770; fax 221-4476), Rua Paissandu 1219, is good value and worth considering. It has a swimming pool, and its apartamentos (with air-conditioning) start at US$23/30 (this price includes its usual 20% discount).

Places to Stay – Mid-Range

The *Novo Hotel Sambaiba* (☎ 222-6711), Rua Gabriel Ferreira 230, has apartamentos at US$40/50. The *Royal Palace Hotel* (☎/fax 221-7707), Rua 13 de Maio 233, has apartamentos (with air-conditioning) starting at US$64/71, but usually offers a 25% discount.

Places to Stay – Top End

Shaped like a pyramid, the five-star *Rio Poty Hotel* (☎ 223-1500; fax 222-6671), Avenida Marechal Castelo Branco 555, is the poshest place in town. Double rooms start at US$180.

Another luxury pad with very smooth service is the *Hotel Luxor Palace* (☎ 222-4911; fax 222-4171), Praça da Bandeira 310, which has rooms costing US$112/125 (this price includes its standard discount of up to 30% for payment by cash or credit card).

Places to Eat

Gustavo's, on the corner of Rua David Caldas and Rua Alvaro Mendes, is an excellent por quilo lunch place, with a great variety of salads and an air-conditioned dining room upstairs.

If you feel like seafood, try *Camarão do Elias*, Avenida Pedro Almeida 457, or *O Pesqueirinho*, which is at Avenida Jorge Velho 6889, several kilometres outside town on the riverside. It serves crab and shrimp stew. For a splurge, visit the *Forno e Fogão*, inside the Hotel Luxor Palace, which charges US$12 per person for a gigantic buffet lunch. There's also a good restaurant inside the Teresina Palace Hotel serving regional food.

Getting There & Away

Air The airport is on Avenida Centenário, 6km north of the centre. There are flights between Teresina and Brasília, Rio, São Paulo, and the major cities in the Northeast and North.

Varig (☎ 223-4940) has an office at Rua Frei Serafim 1932, and VASP (☎ 223-3223) is at No 1826.

Bus Teresina has regular bus connections with Sobral (US$17, 6 hours), Fortaleza (US$28, or US$54 for leito, 10 hours), São Luís (US$20 for numerous daily services, 7 hours) and Belém six times a day (US$34, 15 hours).

To Parnaíba there are two executivo buses (US$22, 5 hours) and several standard buses (US$17, six hours) each day. There are bus connections twice a day to São Raimundo Nonato (US$25, 10 hours). Buses run hourly between 5.45 am and 7 pm for Piripiri (US$5, 3 hours), and there are several buses a day to Pedro Segundo (US$9, 4 hours).

Getting Around

To/From the Airport A taxi to the airport from the centre is US$5.

To/From the Rodoviária The cheapest option is to take the bus from the stop across the road from the rodoviária – it's OK if you arrive at night, when it's cooler, but during the day it's a frying pan on wheels.

Although the rodoviária has a *bilheteria* (ticket office) with a mandatory price table posted on the window, the ticket price for a taxi ride to the city centre is calculated at US$9 – almost twice what you pay if you walk out to the road and hail one there.

PARNAÍBA

• *pop 125,000* ✉ *64200-000* ☎ *086*

Parnaíba, once a major port at the mouth of the Rio Parnaíba, is a peaceful, charming town. It's well worth a trip from Teresina, and onward travel to Maranhão state is possible for adventurous travellers.

Information

Tourist Office The Piemtur office (☎ 321-1532) is in Porto das Barcas. It is supposed to open Monday to Friday from 8 am to 7 pm. It can provide limited information about the boat trip around the Delta do Parnaíba and buses to local destinations. The municipal tourist office, also in Porto das Barcas, is more helpful.

Money The Banco do Brasil on Praça da Graça changes money. Bradesco has an ATM opposite the telephone office on Avenida Presidente Vargas.

Post & Communications The main post office is on Praça da Graça, next to the Banco do Brasil. The telephone office is at Avenida Presidente Vargas 390.

Travel Agencies Igaratur (☎ 322-2141), Porto das Barcas, runs boat trips into the Delta for US$15 including lunch. During the off season, it only goes on weekends, leaving at 8 am and returning at 4 pm. Clip (☎ 322-3129; fax 322-1781), Avenida Presidente Vargas 274, organises similar trips. A knowledgeable independent guide is Mara (☎ 322-1645). She speaks a bit of English and is very lively.

Porto das Barcas

Porto das Barcas, the old warehouse section along the riverfront, has been restored, and contains a maritime museum, an artesanato centre, art galleries, bars and restaurants.

Beaches & Lagoons

Piauí's 66km coastline is the result of a land swap with Ceará late last century. There are some fine beaches, many of which are fast being developed. **Praia Pedra do Sal**, 15km north-east of the centre, on Ilha Grande Santa Isabel, is a good beach divided by rocks into a calm section suitable for swimming, and a rough section preferred by surfers. **Lagoa do Portinho** is a lagoon surrounded by dunes about 14km east of Parnaíba on the road to the small town of Luís Correia. It's a popular spot for swimming, boating, sailing and fishing.

The prime beaches closer to Luís Correia are **Praia do Coqueiro** and **Praia de Atalaia**. The latter is very popular at weekends and has plenty of barracas selling drinks and seafood. The nearby lagoon, **Lagoa do Sobradinho**, is renowned for its shifting sands which bury surrounding trees. **Macapá** is a small fishing village which only recently received electricity. It's a good base for exploring the deserted beaches further east – **Barra Grande**, (considered by many to be the pick of the bunch), **Barrinha**, **Sardi**, **Morro Branco** and **Cajueiro da Praia**. Adventurous travellers should bring their hammocks if they want to stay at these beaches. In Macapa, stay at the *Macapa Praia Hotel* (☎ 983-1635). The owner, Lopes, is a real character, and cooks a great fish dish called peixada macapense. Simple, comfortable rooms are US$25 a double.

Delta do Parnaíba

The Delta do Parnaíba, the only delta in the Americas facing the open sea, is a 2700 sq km expanse of islands, beaches, lagoons, sand dunes and mangrove forest, with abundant wildlife, which straddles the border of Piauí and Maranhão. Sixty-five per cent of its area is in Maranhão state, but the easiest access is from Parnaíba. Day trips by boat around the delta run from Porto das Barcas on weekends, with a stop on Ilha do Caju; the cost is around US$40. Ilha do Caju has been owned for several generations by an English family who have established an ecological reserve there.

There is one pousada on the island. For more details, contact its office at Avenida Presidente Vargas 235 (☎ 322-2380; fax 321-1308). Three-day/two-night packages cost around US$300.

Places to Stay

The *Pousada Porto das Barcas* (☎ 321-1856) is a friendly hostel in a restored warehouse right in Porto das Barcas. Dormitory rooms cost US$10 per person with breakfast. Ricarte, the owner, also has an interesting gemstone workshop on the premises. The *Hotel Cívico* (☎ 322-2470; fax 322-2028), Avenida Governor Chagas Rodrigues 474, in the centre of town, has a swimming pool and apartamentos starting at US$20/30 for singles/doubles with a huge buffet breakfast.

At Luís Correira, there's the three-star *Rio Poty Hotel* (☎/fax 367-1277) on the beach, or the *Hotel Central*, a cheaper, family-run place. On the beach at Pedra do Sol, the *Pousada do Sol* has been recommended by readers.

Places to Eat

Zé Grosso, on the river bank on Ilha Grande, is a very friendly place with great, cheap regional dishes. It's 3km from town, over the bridge, but well worth the effort it takes to get there. *Lulu* is the best place on the Beira Rio restaurant strip. The fish dishes are outstanding. *Sabor e Arte*, on Rua Almirante Gervasio Sampaio, is a relaxed little place with cheap home-cooked meals and interesting original art on the walls. In Porto das Barcas, *Restaurant Portas das Barcas* has a great riverfront patio and local seafood dishes. Across the street, *Comilão* has good pizzas.

Getting There & Away

For bus services between Parnaíba and Teresina, see the Getting There & Away section for Teresina. Agencia Empresa São Francisco runs two buses daily from Praça Santa Cruz to Tutóia (Maranhão state), at noon and 5 pm. The trip takes about four hours over a brain-rattling dirt road. From Tutóia there are trucks running via Rio Novo to Barreirinhas, for acce ss to the Parque Nacional dos Lençóis Maranhenses (see Tutóia in the Maranhão section later in this chapter).

A small wooden boat plies a route daily through the Delta do Parnaíba to Tutóia (US$5, about six hours). This is a good way to check out some of the Delta do Parnaíba – if you have a hammock (cheap ones at the market cost US$8), you can sling it on the top deck, relax and enjoy the voyage. The boat leaves from Porto Salgado, on the riverfront close to Porto das Barcas, between 10 am and noon – check at the port in the morning for departure times. Take some food and water along.

PARQUE NACIONAL DE SETE CIDADES

Sete Cidades is a small national park with interesting rock formations that resemble *sete cidades* (seven cities). Various researchers have analysed nearby rock inscriptions and deduced that the formations are ruined cities from the past, estimated to be at least 190 million years old.

The Austrian historian Ludwig Schwennhagen visited the area in 1928 and thought he'd found the ruins of a Phoenician city. The French researcher Jacques de Mabieu considered Sete Cidades to be proof that the Vikings had found a more agreeable climate in South America. And Erich van Daniken, the Swiss ufologist, theorised that extraterrestrials were responsible for the cities which were ruined by a great fire some 15,000 years ago. There's clearly lots of scope here for imaginative theories. See what you think!

The road around the park's geological monuments starts 1km further down from the Abrigo do IBAMA (IBAMA office and hostel). The loop is a leisurely couple of hours' stroll – more if you go to the swimming pool at Primeira Cidade. It's best to start your hike early in the morning. Bring water because it gets hot, and watch out for the cascavelas – poisonous black-and-yellow rattlesnakes.

The park is open from 6 am to 6 pm. Entry costs US$3 for 24 hours. The IBAMA office (☎ 343-1342) can supply a useful map; guides are available at a small cost. Zé Carlos is a good one.

Sexta Cidade (Sixth City) and **Pedra do Elefante** (Elephant Rock) the first sites on the loop, are lumps of rock with strange scaly surfaces. The **Pedra do Inscrição** (Rock of Inscription) at **Quinta Cidade** (Fifth City) has red markings which some say are cryptic Indian runes. The highlight of **Quarta Cidade** (Fourth City) is the **Mapa do Brasil** (Map of Brazil), a negative image in a rock wall. The **Biblioteca** (Library), **Arco de Triunfo** (Triumphal Arch) and **Cabeça do Cachorro** (Dog's Head) are promontories with good views.

Places to Stay & Eat

Six kilometres from the park entrance, *Abrigo do IBAMA* is a good-value hostel –

apartamentos with fan cost US$20 and can sleep up to four people. There's a restaurant attached to the hostel. Designated camp sites are also available here for US$6.

The *Hotel Fazenda Sete Cidades* (☎ 276-2222), a two-star resort hotel just outside the park entrance, has attractive apartamentos for US$34/48 for singles/ doubles. Even if you don't stay overnight, it's good for lunch and a quick dip in the pool. The *Hotel Martins* (☎ 276-1273), at the intersection of Hwy BR-222 and the road into Piripiri (2km from town), has clean, simple apartamentos with fan for US$12/18 or US$20/30 with air-conditioning. It also has a quarto with two beds for US$8.

Getting There & Away

The park is 180km from Teresina and 141km from Ubajara (Ceará state). Buses leave Teresina hourly between 5.45 am and 6 pm for Piripiri (US$4.50, 3 hours). There are several daily buses from Piripiri to Fortaleza (US$11, 9 hours) and Parnaíba (US$5, 3 hours).

Getting Around

The small IBAMA courtesy bus for the 26km trip to the park leaves from Praça da Bandeira, in the centre of Piripiri, daily at 7 am. There is usually some transport returning from Abrigo do IBAMA to Piripiri in the morning between 9 and 10 am, and the bus returns at 5 pm. A taxi from Piripiri costs around US$20. A mototaxi (motorcycle) is US$8. Hitchhiking is also effective. In the park itself, you can drive on the roads or follow the trails on foot – they're well marked.

PEDRO SEGUNDO

The town of Pedro Segundo lies in the hills of the Serra dos Matões, around 50km south of Piripiri. Close to the town are several mines which are the only source of opals in South America.

The only accommodation in town is the *Hotel Rimo Pedro Segundo* (☎ 271-1543), on Avenida Itamaraty.

For bus services between Pedro Segundo and Teresina, see the Getting There & Away section for Teresina.

PARQUE NACIONAL DA SERRA DA CAPIVARA

The Parque Nacional da Serra da Capivara, in the south-west of the state, was established in 1979 to protect the many prehistoric sites and examples of rock paintings in the region. It was declared a UNESCO World Heritage Site in 1991. Archaeological sites in the park date human presence as far back as 50,000 years – much longer than was previously believed.

There are over 300 excavated sites which are opened to the public depending on the research schedule. If the staff have time, you may be lucky enough to receive a lift and be shown around. For details about access and archaeological sites, contact Doutora Niede Guidon at Fundação Museu do Homem Americano (FUMDHAM; ☎ 582-1612), Rua Abdias Neves 551, São Raimundo Nonato. There are viewing platforms at some of the sites.

Places to Stay

The closest hotel to the park is the *Serra da Capivara* (☎ 582-1389) in São Raimundo Nonato. It has a restaurant, pool and comfortable apartamentos for US$35/40 a single/double. It can also provide information about park visits.

Getting There & Away

For bus services between São Raimundo Nonato and Teresina, see Getting There & Away in the Teresina section earlier in this chapter.

Maranhão

Maranhão, with an area of 333,367 sq km and a population of over five million, is the second largest state in the Northeast, after Bahia.

For many years after their discovery of Brazil, the Portuguese showed little interest in the area which now forms the state of Maranhão. In 1612, the French arrived to construct a fort at São Luís, which later became the capital of the state. See the section on São Luís for more details about the historical and economic development of Maranhão.

Although the southern and eastern areas of Maranhão are characterised by vast expanses of babaçu palms and typical sertão landscapes, the western and north-western regions merge into humid Amazon rainforests.

The rural economy of Maranhão is dependent on the babaçu palm, which serves an amazing multitude of purposes: the nuts can be eaten straight out of the fruit or crushed to produce vegetable oil (for margarine) or industrial lubricating oils; the tips of the young palms can be eaten as 'palm hearts'; and the older trunks are used for the construction of huts, with roofing material supplied by the leaves – which can also be used for the production of cellulose and paper. The residue from the crushed nuts provides excellent fertiliser and cattle feed; and the hulls of the fruit are used in the production of acetates, tar and methyl alcohol. Finally, the hulls are turned to charcoal for use in smelting. Things go better with babaçu!

SÃO LUÍS

• *pop 740,000* ✉ *65000-000* ☎ *098*

São Luís, the capital of Maranhão, is a city with unpretentious colonial charm and a rich folkloric tradition – definitely a highlight for travellers in the Northeast. It was recently declared a World Heritage Site by UNESCO. The population is a diverse mixture of Europeans, blacks and Indians. Apart from the attractions of the restored colonial architecture in the historical centre, São Luís offers passable beaches only 10 minute by bus from the centre (with better ones further afield), as well as an opportunity to cross Baía de São Marcos to visit Alcântara, an impressive historic town slipping regally into decay.

History

São Luís was the only city in Brazil founded and settled by the French. In 1612 three French ships sailed for Maranhão to try to cut off a chunk of Brazil. They were embraced by the local Indians, the Tupinambá, who hated the Portuguese. Once settled in São Luís, named after their King Louis XIII, the French enlisted the help of the Tupinambá to expand their precarious foothold by attacking tribes around the mouth of the Rio Amazonas.

But French support for the new colony was weak, and in 1614 the Portuguese set sail for Maranhão. A year later the French fled, and the Tupinambá were 'pacified' by the Portuguese.

Except for a brief Dutch occupation between 1641 and 1644, São Luís developed slowly as a port for the export of sugar, and later cotton. As elsewhere, the plantation system was established with slaves and Indian labour, despite the relatively poor lands. When demand for these crops slackened in the 19th century, São Luís went into a long and slow decline.

In recent years the economy of São Luís has been stimulated by several mega-projects. A modern port complex has been built to export the mineral riches of the Serra dos Carajás, a range of hills in the Amazon which has the world's largest deposits of iron ore. In the 1980s, Alcoa Aluminium built an enormous factory for aluminium processing – you'll see it along the highway south of the city. The US$1.5 billion price tag for this project was the largest private investment in Brazil's history. A missile station has been built near Alcântara, and oil has been found in the bay.

Orientation

Perched on a hill overlooking the Baía de São Marcos, São Luís is actually on an island of the same name. The historic core of São Luís, now known as Projeto Reviver (Project Renovation), lies below the hill. Going north from the old town, the Ponte José Sarney bridge will take you across to São Francisco, where there is the new and affluent district with several hotels, restaurants and trendy nightspots.

It's easy to get around on foot – despite the hills and confusing street layout – because everything is so close. In fact, as long as you're in the old part of town, a bus is rarely needed.

The most confusing thing about getting around São Luís is the existence of several different names for the same streets. There are the new official names that are on street signs and the historical names or nicknames that the locals use. No two city maps seem to be the same.

Alternative Street Names The following is a short list of streets with their common alternative names in brackets:

28 de Julho	(Rua do Giz)
Rua da Estrêla	(Rua Candido Mendes)
Rua Afonso Pena	(Rua Formosa)
Rua do Sol	(Rua Nina Rodrigues)
Rua do Egito	(Rua Tarquinho Lopes)
Rua do Veado	(Rua Celso Magalhães)
Rua dos Afogados	(Rua José Bonifácio)
Rua de Nazaré	(Rua de Nazaré e Odilo)
Rua das Barrocas	(Beco dos Barracas; Rua Isaacs Martins)
Rua Jacinto Maia	(Rua da Cascata)
Rua Portugal	(Rua Trapiche)
Rua da Alfândega	(Rua Marcelino de Almeida)
Praça Dom Pedro II	(Avenida Dom Pedro II)

Information

Tourist Office São Luís has recently upgraded its tourist information facilities. The most useful office is run by Funtur (☎ 222-5281), on Praça Dom Pedro II. It has brochures and maps in English and French, as well as helpful English-speaking attendants. The office hours are weekdays from 8 am to 7 pm and Saturday from 9 am to 6 pm. Maratur, the state tourism organisation, has its head office just off Praça Dom Pedro II, and opens weekdays from 1 to 6 pm. Other Maratur information booths are on Rua da Estrêla, in the historic centre; at the rodoviária; and at the Centro de Artesanato (CEPRAMA), Rua de São Panteleão 1232.

Money Banco do Brasil has a *casa de câmbio* (money-exchange house) at Avenida Gomes de Castro 46. Banco da Amazonia, Avenida Pedro Segundo II 140, also changes money. Bradesco has an ATM near the Mercado Central. There are also moneychangers hanging about outside Funtur who change cash and travellers cheques at good rates.

Post & Communications The main post office and Telma, the state telephone company, are in the same building on Praça João Lisboa.

Foreign Consulates The following countries are represented in São Luís:

Denmark
  Rua do Sol 141 (☎ 222-4075)
France
  Rua Santo Antônio 259, Colégio Franco Maranhense (☎ 231-4459)
Germany
  Praça Gonçalves Dias 301 (☎ 221-2294)
Italy
  Avenida do Vale 9 (☎ 227-2387)
Portugal
  Rua de Nazaré 258 (☎ 221-4264)
Spain
  Praça Duque de Caxias 3 (☎ 223-2846)

Travel Agencies Highly recommended is Giltur (☎/fax 232-6041), Rua do Giz 46. It offers organised tours of the historic centre, Alcântara, Parque Nacional dos Lençóis Maranheses and other destinations in the state, at very reasonable prices. In the shopping gallery at Rua do Sol 141, there are several travel agencies offering package tours, and they also sell bus tickets at the same price as at the rodoviária. An efficient travel agency in the shopping gallery is Taguatur (☎ 232-0906) at loja 14.

Bookshop Poem-se, a second-hand bookshop on Rua Humberto de Campos, has many books in English, French and German. It also has a large collection of used CDs and magazines.

Catedral da Sé

Constructed by the Jesuits in 1629 as the Igreja NS da Boa Morte, this building in Praça Dom Pedro II, became the official

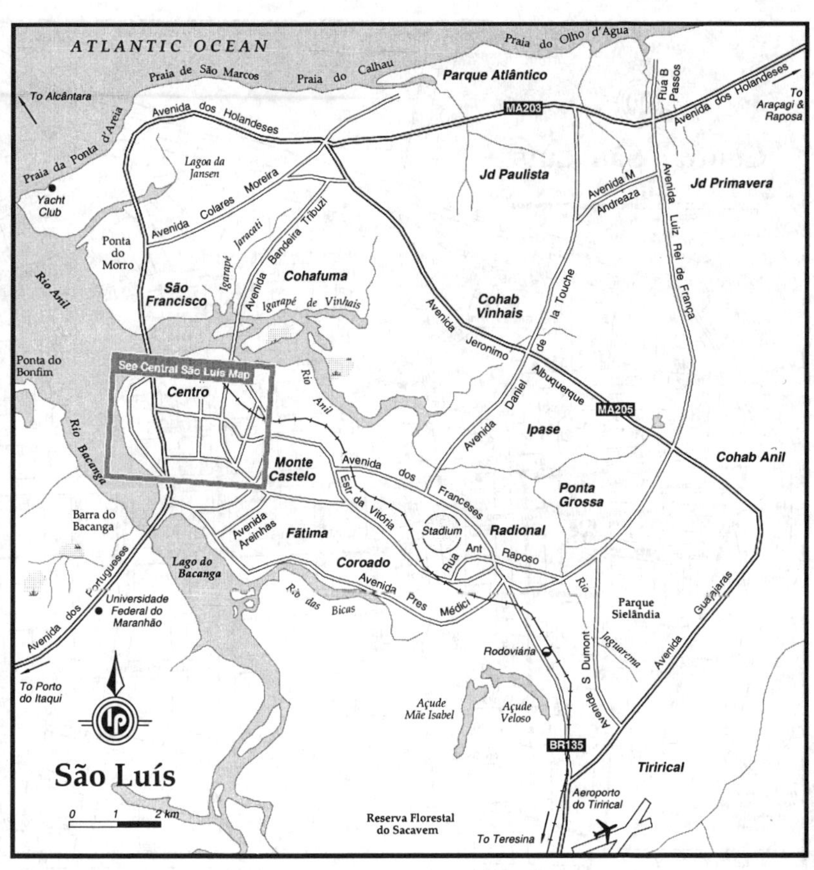

cathedral in 1762. Inside, there's a fine baroque altar and ceiling frescoes decorated with babaçu motifs.

Palácio dos Leões

Originally a French fortress built in 1612 by Daniel de la Touche, during the reign of Louis XIII, this is now the Palácio do Governo, the state governor's residence and office. The interior reflects the pomp of Versailles and French architectural tastes. Visiting hours are from 3 to 6 pm Monday, Wednesday and Friday.

Teatro Artur Azvedo

Dating from 1815, this is one of the most beautiful theatres in Brazil and has been lovingly restored. If you can, go to a show there. Guided tours are available for US$1 Monday to Friday at 10 am and 3 pm.

Projeto Reviver

During the late 1980s, the state authorities finally agreed to restore the historical district, which had been neglected and decaying for many decades. The initial restoration project was completed in 1990,

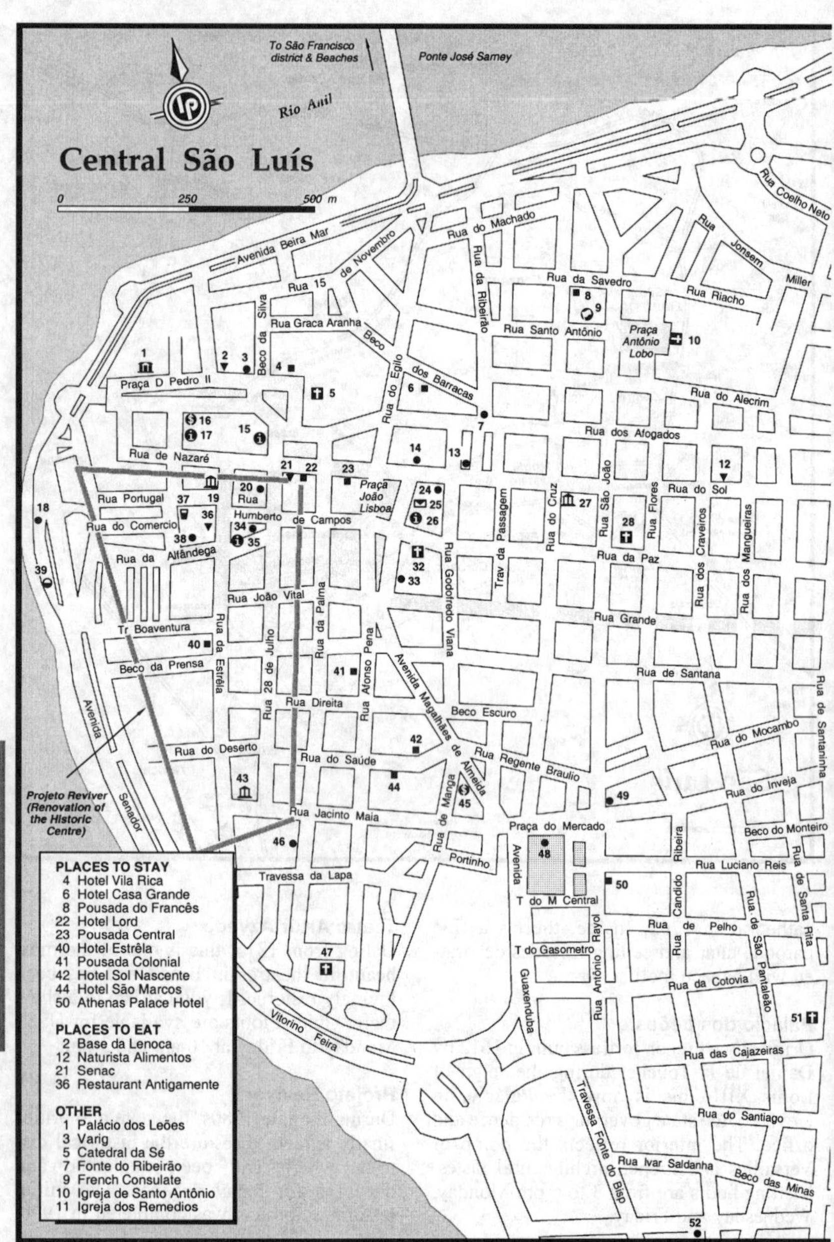

THE NORTHEAST

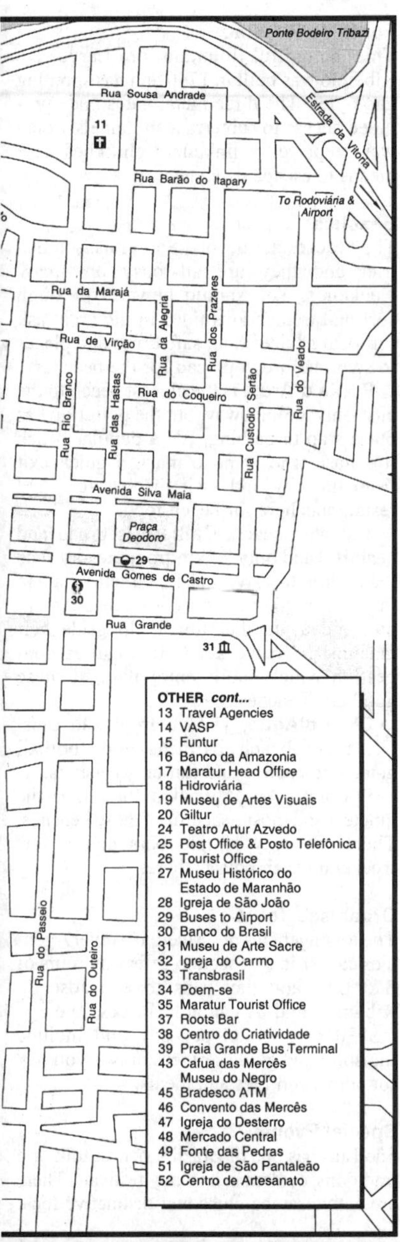

and the city's new UNESCO status should ensure funds for ongoing work.

Over 200 buildings have already been restored and the district has been turned into one of the architectural highlights of Brazil. To appreciate the superb colonial mansions and the many designs and colours of their azulejo façades, just wander around the district. Azulejos were first produced in Portugal and later became a popular product in France, Belgium and Germany. Since azulejos provided a durable means of protecting outside walls from the humidity and heat in São Luís, their use became standard practice during colonial times.

Museu de Artes Visuais

This museum (no ☎) at Rua Portugal 273, has a fine collection of old azulejos, engravings, prints and paintings. It's open from 9 am to 6 pm Tuesday to Saturday.

Opposite the museum is the old round mercado, where you can shop with the locals for dried salted shrimp (eaten with shell and all), *cachaça* (sugar-cane rum), dried goods and basketwork, or visit the lunch counters for cheap local cooking.

Cafua das Mercês & Museu do Negro

This museum is housed in the old slave market building where slaves were kept after their arrival from Africa and until they were sold – notice the absence of windows. A small and striking series of displays documents the history of slavery in Maranhão. The museum is open from 1 to 5.30 pm Tuesday to Saturday.

The African slaves brought to Maranhão were Bantus from Africa who were used primarily on the sugar plantations, and to a lesser extent for the cultivation of rice and cotton. They brought their own type of Candomblé, which is called Tambor de Mina in this part of Brazil. The museum director, Jorge Babalaou, is an expert on Candomblé and Bantu/Maranhense folklore. He may be able to indicate where you can visit a ceremony, but the major houses – the Casa das Minas, Casa de Nagô and Casa Fanti-Ashanti-Nagô – don't welcome visitors.

Museu do Centro de Cultura Popular

This museum is at Rua 28 de Julho 221, just a few minutes on foot from the Cafua das Mercês. The displays include a good collection of handicrafts from the state of Maranhão, and Bumba Meu Boi costumes and masks (see the boxed text 'Bumba Meu Boi' in this chapter). It's open from 3 to 6 pm Monday to Friday, and from 10 am to 1 pm on Saturday and Sunday.

Centro do Criatividade

This exhibition and performance space (☎ 231-4058) at Rua da Alfândega 200, in the heart of Projeto Reviver, is for culture vultures interested in the local art scene. There's a theatre for local plays and dance productions, an art gallery and a cinema showing arthouse films. It's open from 8 am to 10 pm Tuesday to Friday .

Igreja do Desterro

This church on Largo do Desterro, notable for its façade, was built between 1618 and 1641 and is the only Byzantine church in Brazil. There's a small adjoining museum, the Museu de Paramentos Eclesiásticos, containing a display of ecclesiastical apparel.

Fonte das Pedras

This fountain, built by the Dutch during their brief occupation of São Luís, marks the spot where, on 31 October 1615, Jerônimo de Albuquerque and his troops camped before expelling the French. The fountain at Rua Antônio Rayol 363 is inside a small, shady park.

Museu Histórico e Artístico do Estado de Maranhão

This museum, housed in a restored mansion built in 1836, provides an insight into daily life in the 18th century, with an attractive display of artefacts from wealthy Maranhão families. There are furnishings, family photographs, religious articles, coins, sacred art – not to mention President José Sarney's bassinet. Opening hours are from 10 am to 5 pm Tuesday to Saturday.

Fonte do Ribeirão

This delightful fountain on Largo Do Ribeirão was built in 1796 and has spouting gargoyles. The three metal gates once provided access to subterranean tunnels which were reportedly linked to churches as a means to escape danger.

Beaches

The beaches are beyond São Francisco district and they are all busy on sunny weekends. You should beware of rough surf and tremendous tides in the area: ask for local advice about safe times and places to swim before you head for the beaches.

Ponta d'Areia is the closest beach to the city, only 3.5km away, but the pollution has put a stop to bathing. It's a popular beach for those who want to make a quick exit from the city and visit the barracas and restaurants here for beach food.

The next beach, **Calhau**, is broad and beautiful and only 7.5km from the city. The locals like to drive their cars onto Calhau (as well as the next beach, Olho d'Agua), park and lay out their towels alongside their machines. On weekends this causes congestion which spoils enjoyment of these good city beaches.

Olho d'Agua, 11.5km from São Luís, has more beach barracas and football games. It's active and fun on weekends.

Praia do Araçagi, 4km further, is the quietest and most peaceful of these beaches. There are only simple bars and a few weekend beach houses there.

Organised Tours

The tour agencies described in Travel Agencies earlier in this section offer city tours of São Luís and day trips to São José do Ribamar and Alcântara. Prices average US$30 per person per day and include transport and guide services only – you pay for admission fees and meals.

Special Events

São Luís has one of Brazil's richest folkloric traditions, evident in its many festivals. There are active samba clubs and distinctive local dances and music. Most Carnaval activity is out on the streets and the tourist influence is minimal. Marafolia, the out-of-season Carnaval, is held in mid-October, and is reputed to be more lively than the main one.

The Tambor de Mina festivals, held in July, are important events for followers of the Afro-Brazilian religions in São Luís, and São Luís' famous Bumba Meu Boi festival commences in the second half of June, continuing until the second week of August. The Festa do Divino, celebrated on Pentecost (between May and June), is especially spectacular in Alcântara.

Places to Stay – Budget

City Centre A good budget option is the *Hotel Casa Grande* (☎ 232-2432), at Beco das Barracas 98. Large, basic apartamentos cost US$15/17/20 for singles/doubles/triples, with a bread and coffee breakfast included. Some of the rooms on the 3rd floor have views over the river.

There are several very cheap places right in the heart of town, but the area is not too safe at night. The *Hotel Estrêla* (☎/fax 232-7172), Rua da Estrêla 370, is a popular cheapie in the heart of the historic district. Quartos (with fan) cost US$8/13. Don't leave valuables in your room – there's a safe at reception. The *Pousada Central* (☎ 221-1649), Rua Nazaré 350, offers clean quartos for US$15 a single and apartamentos for US$18/28.

The *Hotel Sol Nascente* (☎ 221-2655), Rua da Saúde 221, offers good-value apartamentos for US$12/20 and extremely basic quartos for US$6 without breakfast. The *Hotel São Marcos* (☎/fax 232-3763), Rua do Saúde 178, has recently been renovated. Smallish apartamentos cost US$19/25. There's a swimming pool and restaurant. It also provides off-street parking.

A good deal is the *Hotel Lord* (☎ 222-5544), Rua de Nazaré 258. It's a large, time-worn hotel with comfortable quartos at US$18/24, and apartamentos at US$26/33.

Places to Stay – Mid-Range

City Centre The *Pousada do Francês* (☎ 231-4844; fax 232-0879), Rua 7 de Setembro 121, is housed in a beautifully restored

Bumba Meu Boi

São Luís is famous for its Bumba Meu Boi – a fascinating, wild folkloric festival with a Carnavalesque atmosphere in which participants dance, sing and tell the story of the death and resurrection of the bull – with plenty of room for improvisation. Parade groups spend the year in preparation, costumes are lavish and new songs and poetry are invented. There are three forms of Bumba Meu Boi in Maranhão: *bois de matraca*; *bois de zabumba*; and *bois de orquestra*.

The story and its portrayal differ throughout the Northeast, but the general plot is as follows:

Catrina, goddaughter of the local farm owner, is pregnant and feels a craving to eat the tongue of the best *boi* (bull) on the farm. She cajoles her husband, Chico, into killing the beast. Once the dead bull is discovered, several characters (caricatures drawn from all levels of society) do some detective work and finally track down the perpetrator of the crime. Chico is brought to trial, but the bull is resuscitated by various magic incantations and tunes. A pardon is granted and the story reaches its happy ending when Chico is reunited with Catrina.

The festivals start in the second half of June and continue into the second week of August. Give the tourist office a call to get the exact date.

Andrew Draffen

colonial building. Apartamentos with air-conditioning, fridge and TV cost US$40/50, and some of the higher rooms have views. There's also a swish bar/restaurant in the hotel. It's excellent value. The *Pousada Colonial* (☎ 232-2834), Rua Afonso Pena 112, is in a restored colonial mansion and offers good value. Comfortable apartamentos cost US$42/50, but there's often a 20% discount.

Beaches At Praia do Araçagi there's one medium-priced hotel, the *Chalé da Lagoa* (☎ 226-4916), a relaxing place surrounded by gardens. Doubles are US$32 with fan and US$40 with air-conditioning.

Places to Stay – Top End

City Centre The five-star *Vila Rica* (☎ 232-3535; fax 232-7245) is very central, at Praça Dom Pedro II 299, with a view overlooking the bay. Apartamentos cost a whopping US$165/184 – but there's a 40% discount for cash payment. The presidential suite is US$590.

São Francisco There are several upmarket hotels in the São Francisco district – north of town, on the other side of the Rio Anil. These are not recommended unless you have a car or prefer to stay outside the city centre.

The *Hotel São Francisco* (☎ 235-5544; fax 235-2138), Rua Luís Serson 77, has apartamentos for US$66/82. The *Panorama Palace Hotel* (☎ 235-4242; fax 227-4736), at Rua dos Pinheiros Q-16, 15, has apartamentos for US$60/70.

Beaches The five-star *Sofitel Quatro Rodas* (☎ 235-4545; fax 235-4921) is at Praia do Calhau, a 15 minute drive from town. It has rooms for US$150/180, but may offer a 20% discount.

Places to Eat

The best Maranhense food comes from the sea. In São Luís you'll find many of the familiar dishes of the Northeast, and regional specialities such as torta de sururu (mussel pie), casquinha de caranguejo (stuffed crab), caldeirada de camarão (shrimp stew) and the city's special rice dish – arroz de cuxá (rice with vinegar, local vegetables and shrimp).

City Centre There are plenty of *lanchonetes* (stand-up snack bars) serving cheap food. Across from the Fonte do Ribeirão, you'll find a couple of decent self-serve lunch spots. *Fonte de Sabor* is a good one.

The *Base da Lenoca*, Praça Dom Pedro II, is a popular restaurant with a great position overlooking the Rio Anil – order a beer and a snack and enjoy the breeze. In the heart of the historic district, on Rua da Estrêla, there's the *Restaurante Antigamente*, which has tables on the street and seafood and meat dishes. There's live music here in the evening on weekends. *Senac*, Rua de Nazaré 244, offers fine dining in a lovely colonial building. *Naturista Alimentos*, Rua do Sol 517, has the best vegetarian food in the city.

São Francisco The main drag through São Francisco has many new restaurants, particularly pizzerias and bars. The *Oriental*, Avenida Presidente Castelo Branco 47, has a nice view and serves Chinese food. It's right next to the bridge. *Galetão* is a good, cheap roast chicken joint a bit further up on the right-hand side.

Outside City Centre The seafood is highly recommended at *Base do Edilson* (☎ 222-7210), Rua Alencar Campos 31, in the Vila Bessa district. It's a 10 minute drive from the city centre. The restaurant starts serving lunch at 11.30 am and dinner at 7 pm. The portions are not big for what you pay, but we'd suggest ensopado de camarão com molho pirão and peixada com pirão, for US$20.

Beaches At Ponte d'Areia, *Tia Maria* has good seafood, and it's also a fine place to watch the sunset while enjoying a cool drink. This is also the closest beach to the city with barracas serving food.

Entertainment

São Luís is currently the reggae centre of the Northeast, and many of the nightspots cater to *reggeiros* (reggae fans). The tourist office has a list of places to check out – some of them can be a bit dangerous, although this also seemed to be a prerequisite for a happening place! It's worth asking locals for recommendations. *Roots Bar* in the historic city is big on Wednesday and Friday nights.

For dancing, try *Boate Génesis*, Avenida dos Holandeses Qd-28, 4, at Praia do Calhau; *Boate Tucanos*, at Avenida Jerônimo Albuquerque, Curva do 90, in the Vinhais district, north-east of the city centre; or *Le Maison*, Rua Haroldo Paiva 110, São Crisóvão.

The beaches at Ponta d'Areia and Calhau are very active on weekends, with lots of live music and revelry.

Things to Buy

São Luís is the place for the traditional handicrafts of Maranhão, such as woodcarving, basketry, lacework, ceramics, leatherwork, and woven goods made from linen. Also on sale are featherwork, and items made from straw or plant fibres (from baskets to bracelets) by the Urubus-Caapor Indians and the Guajajara Indians, both from the interior of Maranhão state.

Centro de Artesanato (CEPRAMA), Rua de São Pantaleão 1232, is housed in a renovated factory and functions as an exhibition hall and sales outlet for handicrafts. It's open Sunday and Monday from 3 to 9 pm, and Tuesday to Saturday from 9 am to 9 pm. Also worth visiting are the Centro Artesanal do Maranhão, Avenida Marechal Castelo Branco 605, and the Mercado Central. The Mercado Central is open Monday to Saturday from 7 am to 4 pm, and the Centro Artesanal do Maranhão is open Monday to Friday from 8 am to 8 pm and Saturday from 8 am to 1 pm.

Getting There & Away

Air The new international airport was close to completion on our last visit. Currently, domestic air services connect São Luís with Rio, São Paulo and the major cities in the Northeast and the North.

These are the addresses for Brazilian and foreign airlines:

Air France
  Praça Gonçalves Dias 301(☎ 221-2416)
Transbrasil
  Praça João Lisboa 432 (☎ 232-1414)
Varig/Cruzeiro
  Avenida Dom Pedro Segundo 221 (☎ 231-5066)
VASP
  Rua do Sol 43 (☎ 231-4422)

Bus The rodoviária (☎ 243-1253) is 8km south-east of the city centre on Avenida dos Franceses. Bus tickets can be booked and purchased in the city centre at several travel agencies listed under Information earlier in this section.

There are frequent daily buses to Teresina (US$20, seven hours); Belém (US$38, 12 hours, twice a day); Carolina (US$30, 12 hours, once a day via Imperatriz); Guimarães (US$24, 10 hours, once a day); Fortaleza (US$46, 18 hours); and Recife (US$50, 24 hours, twice a day).

Boat The *hidroviária* (boat terminal) is on the quayside, just beyond the western end of Rua Portugal. From here, it's possible to take passage on boats sailing along the coast. Sailing times are always approximate and depend on the tides. The regular daily service to Alcântara is described in the Getting There & Away section for Alcântara. There are regular local services to Pinheiro, Porto de Itaúna and São Bento.

There are also departures at least once a week to Guimarães, a major centre for boatbuilding and fishing, and infrequent departures from there to destinations further along the western coast, such as Turiaçu, Luís Domingues and Carutapera (on the Pará border).

Getting Around

To/From the Airport Do Tirirical airport (☎ 245-1688) is 15km south-east of the city.

The bus marked São Cristóvâo runs from the bus stop opposite Banco do Brasil on Praça Deodoro to the airport in 35 minutes. There's a bilheteria system for taxis at the airport – a taxi to the centre costs around US$14.

To/From the Rodoviária Several buses go to the rodoviária from Praça Deodoro, and you can also pick one up at the Praia Grande bus terminal on Avenida Beira Mar. There's a bilheteria system for taxis – from the rodoviária to the city centre costs US$8.

To/From the Beaches Buses run to Ponta d'Areia and Calhau from Praça Deodoro – take buses marked Ponta d'Areia or Calhau. For buses to Araçagi, Raposa and São José do Ribamar, there's a bus stop beside the Mercado Central. To get to Olho d'Agua, take a bus marked Olho d'Agua from Praça Deodoro.

ILHA DE SÃO LUÍS

Praia da Raposa

Out at the tip of the Ilha de São Luís, 30km from the city, is the interesting and very dirty fishing centre of Raposa, also known for its lacework. It's a poor town, built on stilts above mangrove swamps, which gives it an unusual appearance. The bulk of the town's population is descended from Cearense immigrants. There are no tourist facilities but the ocean here is pretty and very shallow. There are lots of small fishing boats and it's not too hard to negotiate a ride. Bathing at the beach is dangerous due to extreme tidal variations. The water recedes up to 1km at low tide.

Getting There & Away There are frequent buses from to São Luís – a convenient bus stop is the one beside the Mercado Central. The trip takes 45 minutes.

São José do Ribamar

This fishing town is on the east coast of the island, 30km from the city. There's a busy little waterfront with boats leaving for small towns along the coast. This is a good way to explore some of the more out-of-the-way villages on the island. On Sunday buses go from São José to nearby Ponta de Panaquatira, a popular weekend beach.

The São José do Ribamar Miracle

The origins of the town date back to the early 18th century when a Portuguese sailing ship went astray and started to flounder on the sandbanks of the Baía de São José. The desperate crew begged for mercy from São José das Botas and promised to procure the finest statue of the saint and construct a chapel for it if they were spared.

The ship and its crew were miraculously saved and several years later the promise was kept and a fine statue of the saint was installed in a chapel at the tip of the cape where the disaster was narrowly avoided. The settlement on this site later received the name São José do Ribamar: a fusion of the saint's name and the local Indian name for the rock formation at the cape.

According to local legend, the statue was moved away from its site beside the shore, but miraculously reappeared in its original position the next day, without any signs of human intervention. This miracle was repeated a couple more times until the locals decided the statue should be left in its preferred place. During its trek, the statue left deep footprints along the rocky coastline which are now venerated by the townsfolk, who host the annual Festa do Pedroeiro (held in September) in honour of the saint.

Andrew Draffen

Places to Stay & Eat There are two hotels: the *Hotel Mar e Sol* and the *Hotel Tropical*. Both offer simple quartos for about US$10 per person, and both have restaurants. Beach camping is permitted at Praia Panaquatira. The 7m tide is very fast, so don't camp close to the water.

Getting There & Away Frequent buses leave from São Luís (convenient bus stop beside the Mercado Central) for the 45 minute trip to São José do Ribamar. The last bus back to São Luís leaves at 10.30 pm.

ALCÂNTARA

• *pop 20,000* ✉ *65250-000* ☎ *098*

Across the Baía de São Marcos from São Luís is the colonial town of Alcântara. Founded in the early 1600s with extensive slave labour, the town was the hub of the region's sugar and cotton economy. The beneficiaries of this wealth, Maranhão's rich landowners, preferred living in Alcântara to São Luís.

While the town has been in decline since the latter half of the 19th century, it is still considered an architectural treasure, and some experts claim that it is the most homogeneous group of colonial buildings and ruins from the 17th and 18th centuries in Brazil.

Construction of the Centro do Lançamento de Alcântara (CLA), a nearby rocket-launching facility, caused mutterings amongst residents, who disagreed with the forceful resettlement policy undertaken to clear the construction site. There couldn't be a greater contrast with this slumbering colonial town than a space-age launching pad!

Information

The tourist office in São Luís has brochures about Alcântara.

Things to See & Do

The town is very poor and decaying, but don't miss the following: the beautiful row of two-storey houses on **Rua Grande**; the **Igreja de NS do Carmo** (1665); and the best preserved **pelourinho** (whipping post) in Brazil, on Praça da Matriz.

The **Museu Histórico**, on the Praça da Matriz, displays a collection of sacred art, festival regalia and colonial furniture. Each room has its own guardian – a source of employment for the locals. Opening hours for the museum are Tuesday to Saturday from 8 am to 2 pm, and Sunday from 8 am to 1 pm.

Once you've seen the main sights, you can walk to the beaches or take a boat trip out to nearby islands.

Special Events

The Festa do Divino is held on the first Sunday after Ascension Day. Check the date for the festival (usually held in May) with the tourist office in São Luís.

This is considered one of the most colourful annual festivals in Maranhão, a fusion of African and Catholic elements with two children dressed as the emperor and empress paraded through the town and accompanied by musicians.

Places to Stay & Eat

Alcântara has simple camp sites close to Praça da Matriz and near the *farol* (lighthouse). There are also several inexpensive pousadas. The *Pousada Pelourinho* (☎ 337-1150), Praça da Matriz, has spacious quartos for US$15/25 – check out the Egyptian-style dance space out the back. *Pousada do Mordomo Régio* (☎ 337-1221) has quartos for US$20/25 a single/double and apartamentos for US$30. The *Pousada do Imperador*, Rua Grande, charges US$10 per person. It only has single beds. *Chale da Baronesa* (☎ 337-1339) is right on the beachfront at Praia da Baronesa. It's a quiet, relaxing place to stay – simple chalets cost US$10 per person and there's a restaurant/bar as well. Keep an eye out for the guará, a beautiful red bird threatened with extinction in other parts of Brazil.

All the hotels have restaurants, and there are also two restaurants close together on Rua Direito – *Restaurante Copos e Bocas* and *Restaurante da Josefa*.

Getting There & Away

Boats from São Luís to Alcântara depart from the hidroviária (boat terminal) on the quayside, just beyond the western end of Rua Portugal. It's a good idea to book your ticket the day before departure, and check the departure times, which vary according to the tide.

Three types of boats make the trip to Alcântara. The *Batevento* is a large motorboat which leaves twice a day, at 7 and 9.30 am. The trip takes about one hour. The boat returns from Alcântara at around 4 pm. Early risers are rewarded with a significant discount – the early boat to Alcântara costs US$3, while the later boat costs US$6. As a result, the early boat is crowded: the best positions are the seats at the back of the boat.

For the more adventurous, there are two sailing boats straight out of pirate tales – the *Newton Belle* and the *Mensageiro da Fé* – which also ply the route. Both leave from the hidroviária twice a day at around 6.30 am and 4 pm. Pandemonium reigns as the last passengers and cargo get stuffed below

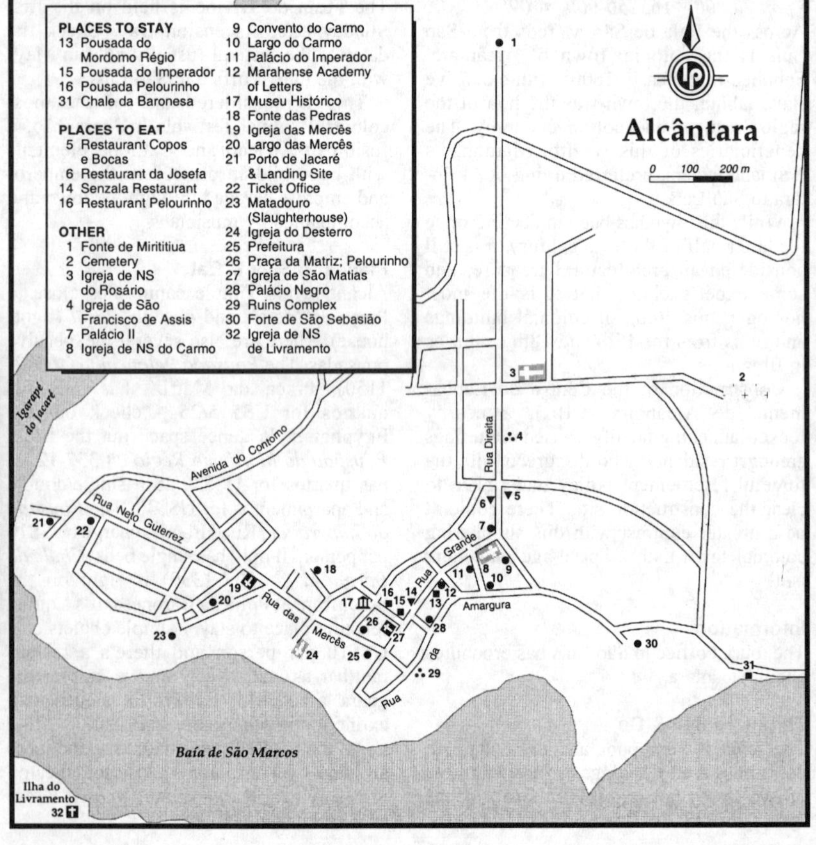

at sailing time. Try to avoid the crush by sitting outside at the front of the boat. The trip takes about 1½ hours. These boats cost US$3.

The third option is to go by catamaran. These boats are probably more suited to travellers able to cope with rough seas. Make sure you protect cameras etc with plastic. They don't run to any particular schedule, so ask at the port for departure times.

PARQUE NACIONAL DOS LENÇÓIS MARANHENSES

The natural attractions of this national park include 1550 sq km of beaches, mangroves, lagoons, dunes and local fauna (turtles and migratory birds). The park's name refers to the immense dunes which look like *lençóis* (bedsheets) strewn across the landscape. Since 1981 this parcel of land has been set aside as a protected ecological zone, staving off the ruinous effects of land speculation. The best time to visit is between March and September, when rain which has filtered through the dunes forms crystal-clear pools between the dunes.

The park has minimal tourist infrastructure, but it's currently possible to arrange a visit from the town of Barreirinhas, two hours by boat from the dunes.

Information

As you go downriver, the boat passes the tiny fishing villages of **Mandacaru**, with its lighthouse, and **Caburé**, where the very basic *Pousada e Restaurante Lençoes de Areia* charges US$8 per person for a quarto or US$5 to sling a hammock. Further downriver, close to the park, is the small village of **Atins**, where you should contact Lavio, a recommended local guide who can arrange simple accommodation and visits inside the park.

Organised Tours Giltur (☎ (098) 231-6041), in São Luis runs tours to the park. A three day tour costs around US$195, including accommodation in Barreirinhas, bus and boat transport. Funnily enough, a two day package where you fly instead of taking a bus, costs US$210 per person. The road to the park is a shocker, so it's probably worth the extra fifteen bucks, plus you get an aerial view of the park.

BARREIRINHAS

Barreirinhas, the jumping-off point for visiting the Parque Nacional dos Lençóis Maranhenses, is also a pretty little town on the banks of the Rio Preguiça. There is a river beach with sand dunes near the centre of town, and a couple of good pousadas and restaurants.

Pousada Lins organises tours of the park – the day trip by boat up the Rio Preguiça costs US$90 for up to five people. Otherwise, ask around for Edivaldo, a friendly and honest young guide, who can organise transport for day trips. If you want to do it yourself, it's possible to get a ride on a boat going downriver to the beginning of the park for a few dollars. Get to the riverfront early and ask around.

Places to Stay & Eat

The *Pousada Lins* (☎ 349-1203), Avenida Joaquim Soeiro de Cavalho 550, is the nicest place to stay. Quartos with fan cost US$10 per person, and spotless apartamentos with air-conditioning go for US$25/30 for singles/doubles. The *Pousada dos Viajante* (☎ 349-1106), Rua Clarence Ramos, has basic quartos at US$8/12 and apartamentos for US$10/15. *Pousada Giltur* (☎ 349-1177), Avenida Brasília 259, has comfortable apartamentos for US$10 per person.

Restaurant Porta do Sol, Avenida Joaquim Soeiro de Cavalho 583, is a friendly place serving local seafood and chicken dishes. *Restaurant Lins*, under the same management as Pousada Lins, offers a similar menu.

Getting There & Away

There are two bus services a day to Barreirinhas, leaving at 9.30 am and 9.45 pm from the rodoviária in São Luís (US$21, around 8 hours). The trip is bad news – the first half is along a road with major potholes, and the second half along a rutted dirt road – a bit like driving on corrugated iron. The return service fom Barreirinhas departs daily at 6 am (10 am on Sunday). The bus fills up quickly, so you should book tickets in advance at Taguatur on Rua Inaçio Lins.

To Tutóia, there's a couple of ruts through the sand passable only by 4WD vehicles. You'll need to go via Rio Novo, about halfway to Tutóia, where there is one pousada. The 'road' passes by (and over) some superb dunescapes and very isolated, traditional fishing communities of straw huts. From Rio Novo, there are regular (though not that frequent) jeeps to Tutóia.

RIO NOVO

A small fishing and farming community between Barreirinhas and Tutóia, Rio Novo is a tranquil little place with one main attraction. Its coastal dunes are almost an extension of those in the park to the west, and they're much more easily accessible – a short walk from the village itself.

Information

You should contact English-speaking Genário Peixoto (☎ (086) 983-2269), a dynamic guide who also runs an ecological education programme for the children of the village. Genário is a visionary, and it's a pity there aren't more like him. He runs his programme on a shoestring budget, and would certainly appreciate any assistance you could offer.

Places to Stay & Eat

The only pousada in town is *Pousada Oásis dos Lençõis* (☎ (098) 529-1003). It's very comfortable and has the river running past the back gate. Dona Mazé oozes tranquillity and cooks a fabulous moqueca. She charges US$8 per person for quartos and US$10 for apartamentos with breakfast. The only entertainment in Rio Novo is at the bar next to the bridge, where you may be able to persuade the proprietor, Seu Zézico, to pull out his mandolin.

Getting There & Away

There are 4WD Toyotas leaving for Tutóia (US$5, 1½ hours) and Barreirinhas (US$6, two hours) each morning. For the rest of the day, there's usually someone coming or going, but there's no set timetable.

TUTÓIA

Tutóia is a fishing port and beach town on the edge the Delta do Parnaíba, the 2700-sq-km expanse of rivers, dunes, beaches and mangrove forest which straddles the borders of Maranhão and Piauí.

Places to Stay & Eat

The best budget option is *Pousada Tremembes* (☎ 479-1109), Praça Tremembes 49. The owner, Cacau, is a very helpful gentle giant. He can arrange for the 4WD to Rio Novo to pick you up in the morning. Simple quartos are US$8 per person with breakfast. The restaurant in the pousada serves a good, cheap prato feito.

On the beachfront, the *Pousada Embarcação* (☎ 479-1219) is a beach shack with a bar decorated with shark's jaws and snake skins. Apartamentos cost US$10/15 a single/double. The most upmarket place in town is the *Tutóia Palace Hotel* (☎/fax 479-1247), near the waterfront, to the left as you get off the boat. Apartamentos cost US$20/36.

Getting There & Away

Two buses a day run over a rough dirt road to Parnaíba (Piauí). The trip takes about four hours. A small motorboat cruises through the delta daily to Parnaíba (US$5, about seven hours). To Rio Novo, there's a truck leaving daily at around 10 am from Praça Getúlio Vargas. You can pick up another truck or jeep there to Barreirinhas, but you should be prepared to stay overnight.

THE NORTH COAST

The town of Guimarães is a centre for boat-building and fishing. Further north is Cururupu, a small town which is the gateway to the Lençóis de Cururupu – a huge expanse of coastal dunes similar to, but not to be confused with, those in the Parque Nacional dos Lençóis Maranhenses.

About 80km offshore is Parcel de Manoel Luís, a coral reef named after the *Manoel Luís*, the first ship to be lost there. According to experts, this reef, extending over 288 sq km, is the largest in South America, and there are plans to turn it into a marine park. There are also plans to develop and exploit it as one of the world's top attractions for divers, especially those with nice fat wallets tucked into their wet suits.

RESERVA BIOLÓGICA DO GURUPI

This biological reserve in the Serra do Tiracambu, on the western border of the state, is not open to the public. This news does not seem to have reached the sawmill owners, loggers and assorted industrialists clustered on the fringe of the reserve, who are plundering it at top speed.

IMPERATRIZ

• *pop 297,000* ✉ *65900-000* ☎ *098*

Imperatriz, 636km from São Luís, is a rapidly expanding city on the border with Pará. The expansion is due to the rabid logging and mining of the surrounding region, which is turning the forests into ecological nightmares and attracting plenty of low-life characters to make a quick killing. The only possible reason to visit would be to change buses – otherwise, just keep going. The airports at Imperatriz and nearby Açailândia are frequently closed for days on end because of the huge clouds of smoke from forest fires.

CAROLINA

• *pop 26,000* ✉ *65980-000* ☎ *098*

The town of Carolina, 242km south of Imperatriz, lies beside the Rio Tocantins, and provides a handy base for visiting nearby natural attractions.

Pedra Caída, 35km from town towards Estreito, is a dramatic combination of rock canyons and waterfalls. Some of the other spectacular waterfalls in the region are: **Cachoeira do Itapecuruzinho**, 27km from town on the road that goes toward Riachão; **Cachoeira de São Simão**, at Fazenda São Jorge, about 10km from Carolina; and **Cachoeira da Barra da Cabeceira**. There are rock paintings and inscriptions at **Morro das Figuras**, close to Fazenda Recanto; and bat enthusiasts will want to visit the colony of bats in **Passagem Funda**, a large cave 70km from Carolina.

Places to Stay

The *Pousada do Lajes* (☎ 731-1499), 3km outside town towards Riachão, has chalets for US$40. The *Recanto Pedra Caída* (☎ 731-1318) is a tourist complex with chalets and sports facilities at the Pedra Caída waterfalls. Apartamentos are US$25/30.

Getting There & Away

There's a daily bus service from São Luís (US$30, 12 hours); and four services daily from Imperatriz (four hours).

Getting Around

A frequent ferry service (15 minute ride) operates across the Rio Tocantins to the town of Filadélfia, which is in the state of Tocantins.

CAROLINA

[illegible] the town of Carolina, 34 km [illegible] of the [illegible] outskirts, lies inside the [illegible] [illegible] previous [illegible] nearby natural attractions.

Pedra Caída [illegible] from [illegible] [illegible] [illegible] canyons and waterfalls, [illegible] [illegible] Cachoeira [illegible] [illegible] [illegible] [illegible] Cachoeira [illegible] [illegible] about [illegible] [illegible] [illegible] [illegible] Cachoeira [illegible] [illegible] paintings [illegible] [illegible] [illegible] and [illegible] will want to visit the [illegible] in [illegible] [illegible] large cave [illegible] from Carolina.

Places to Stay

[illegible] [illegible] [illegible] [illegible] [illegible] [illegible] [illegible] [illegible] [illegible] [illegible] [illegible] [illegible] [illegible] [illegible] [illegible] [illegible] [illegible] [illegible]

Getting There & Away

There are daily bus [illegible] [illegible] [illegible] [illegible] [illegible] [illegible] [illegible]

Getting Around

[illegible] [illegible] [illegible] [illegible] [illegible] [illegible] [illegible] to the town of [illegible] [illegible] in the [illegible]

huge expanse of cerrado plains similar to [illegible] [illegible] be confused with those in the [illegible] [illegible] Lençóis Maranhenses. [illegible] [illegible] [illegible] [illegible] [illegible] [illegible] [illegible] [illegible] [illegible] [illegible] [illegible] [illegible] [illegible] over [illegible] [illegible] [illegible] South America [illegible] [illegible] park [illegible] [illegible] [illegible] [illegible] [illegible] [illegible] [illegible] [illegible]

RESERVA BIOLÓGICA DO GURUPI

This [illegible] [illegible] reserve in the Serra do Gurupi [illegible] [illegible] of the state [illegible] [illegible] the [illegible] [illegible] [illegible] [illegible] [illegible] [illegible] [illegible]

IMPERATRIZ

[illegible] [illegible] [illegible]

Imperatriz [illegible] [illegible] [illegible] [illegible] border with [illegible] [illegible] [illegible] [illegible] [illegible] region [illegible] [illegible] [illegible] [illegible] [illegible] [illegible] [illegible] [illegible] [illegible] [illegible] [illegible] [illegible] [illegible] [illegible] [illegible] [illegible] [illegible] smoke [illegible]

The North

The North

The North of Brazil is made up of seven states: Pará, Amapá, Tocantins, Amazonas, Roraima, Rondônia and Acre.

In 1541, the Gonzalvo Pizarro expedition ran short of food supplies while searching for El Dorado, the mythical kingdom of gold. Captain Francisco de Orellana, who had joined the expedition earlier, offered to take a small group of soldiers and forage for supplies.

From Peru, Orellana floated down the Rio Napo all the way to the Amazon, which was so named after the group reported attacks by female warriors (prompting comparisons in the west with the Amazons of Greek mythology). Although Orellana had disobeyed orders, his exploits found favour with the Spanish king, who sent him back on a second expedition, during which Orellana died from malaria.

Despite this foray into the region, the Spanish were not interested in claiming the territory, which had been assigned to the Portuguese under the terms of the Treaty of Tordesillas (signed in 1494).

The Amazon Basin, six million sq km of river and jungle, is the world's largest river basin in terms of volume and drainage area. Its flow is 12 times that of the Mississippi, with 12 billion litres of fresh water flowing down the river every minute – enough to supply New York City for 60 years! The Rio Amazonas reaches depths of up to 120m. There are 80,000km of navigable rivers in the Amazon system. Ocean-going vessels can sail deep into South America: from the mouth of the Amazon (300km east of Belém) to the Solimões and Marañon rivers, and all the way to Iquitos in Peru.

Although the Rio Amazonas dominates the record books, many of its tributaries are also enormous: the Rio Juruá is a 3280km tributary of the Solimões, the Rio Madeira-Mamoré flows for 3240km, the Rio Purus/Pauini is 3210km (1667km of which is navigable) and the Rio Tocantins

HIGHLIGHTS

- The village of Alter do Chão near Santarém with its clear-water beaches and the Centro da Preservação a Arte Indígena (Pará)
- The exotic range of fruit, vegetables, fish and medicinal herbs at Mercado Ver-o-Peso in Belém (Pará)
- Ilha do Marajó beaches, buffalo and birdlife (Pará)
- The white sands of Praia do Algodoal on a full-moon night (Pará)
- Fresh regional fish in the traditional restaurants of Belém or Manaus (Pará)
- The remote Parque Nacional da Ilha do Bananal (Tocantins)
- A jungle trip outside Manaus, including canoeing on lakes, birdwatching and sighting fresh-water dolphins (Amazonas)
- The *pororoca*, the collision between the Atlantic tide and the Rio Amazonas (Pará and Amapá)
- Colonial and rubber-boom architecture of the Amazon such as the opera houses and palácios

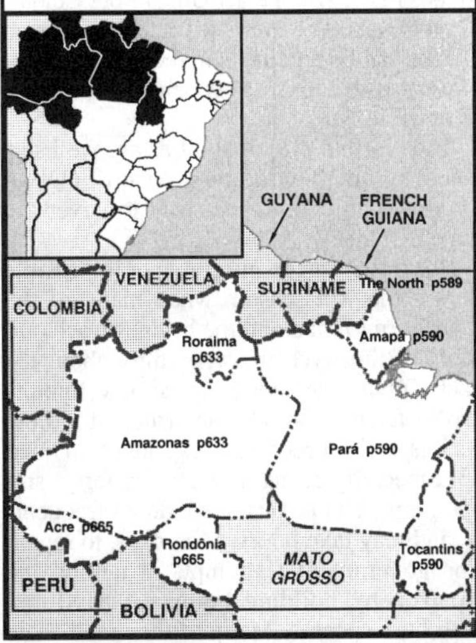

is a respectable 2640km long. The Rio Negro runs 1550km (only the lower half is navigable and fully explored).

The best time to visit the Amazon if you are interested in making a jungle trip is when the water level is high – March to July. On the other hand, August to February is the low water period when the river beaches are uncovered.

Most of the rivers are so wide you won't see much flora and fauna from the boats. To see the wildlife of the Amazon – *jacaré* (yacare caiman), monkeys, hawks, anacondas, toucans and pink *botos* (freshwater dolphins) – you must leave the major rivers and explore the *igarapés* (channels cutting through the jungle, so narrow that the forest brushes your face). A glimpse of life at the level of the jungle canopy is far richer than the view from the jungle floor. If you opt for a jungle trip with an independent guide, part of your agreement should include a tour of igarapé by canoe or small boat, since noisy motorboats scare the wildlife away.

Many travellers enter the Brazilian Amazon via the overland route from Venezuela. Good roads provide access between Manaus and the Caribbean. It is easy to cruise downriver from Iquitos in Peru or to enter Brazil from Colombia at Leticia. The overland route from French Guiana can be unreliable in the wet season. It is also possible to cross overland from Guyana or from Bolivia.

The North's principal cities are well serviced by air. If you are short on time, an airpass is an economical way to cover the huge distances.

Bus travel can be miserable or impossible during the wet season, when many of the roads turn to mud and the bridges wash out. Most of the river crossings throughout the back country are made on simple, motor-driven ferries that take one truck at a time. As it is a slow process, trucks are often lined up, especially at night, when the ferry isn't operating. The ferries break down frequently, and may take hours, even days, to repair. The government's attempts at taming the Amazon by building highways have met with little success. Many of the grand-scale megaprojects such as the Transamazônica highway (BR-230) which links Amazonas and Rondônia to Pará are now semi-abandoned. It is only possible to travel by bus on Hwy BR-230 from Santarém to Belém (via Marabá and Imperatriz) in the dry season. No buses run between Porto Velho and Manaus, or between Santarém and Cuiabá, as the unsealed roads (Hwys BR-319 and BR-163, respectively) are in disrepair.

However, buses are a good way to cover a lot of ground in the states of Pará, Roraima, Rondônia, Acre and Amapá. Hwy BR-174 links Manaus with Boa Vista and on to Venezuela, and Rio Branco and Porto Velho are linked to the eastern states by Hwy BR-364.

For the majority of the people who live in the Amazon interior, the rivers are their roads. If time is on your side, boats are a great way to experience the North. River travel is the obvious way to travel in the Amazon, it's cheap and easy; sling up your hammock and join the locals.

Things can get very wet, so bring along a hooded poncho or windbreaker to keep yourself dry, and use ziplock plastic storage bags to compartmentalise tickets, travellers cheques and other valuables (unless you prefer to entrust them to a hotel safe). You'll also need a hammock (fabric is preferable to net), a sheet, a blanket and some rope. To keep your possessions dry, your backpack should be waterproofed, wrapped in a groundcloth or a large plastic bag, then suspended above the floor of the boat.

Long-sleeved cotton shirts and light cotton trousers with elastic drawstrings at the ankles keep some of the bugs from nipping. Cloth or rubber flip-flops and sneakers are also comfortable boat/jungle gear. Bring a day pack containing toiletries, a torch, pocket knife, water bottle, a thick novel and plenty of insect repellent. Don't forget a camera, binoculars and a good bird-watching guide. For suggested reading and reference material, see the Books and Maps sections in the Facts for the Visitor chapter. Finally, antimalarials and purifying your drinking water should prevent most medical problems.

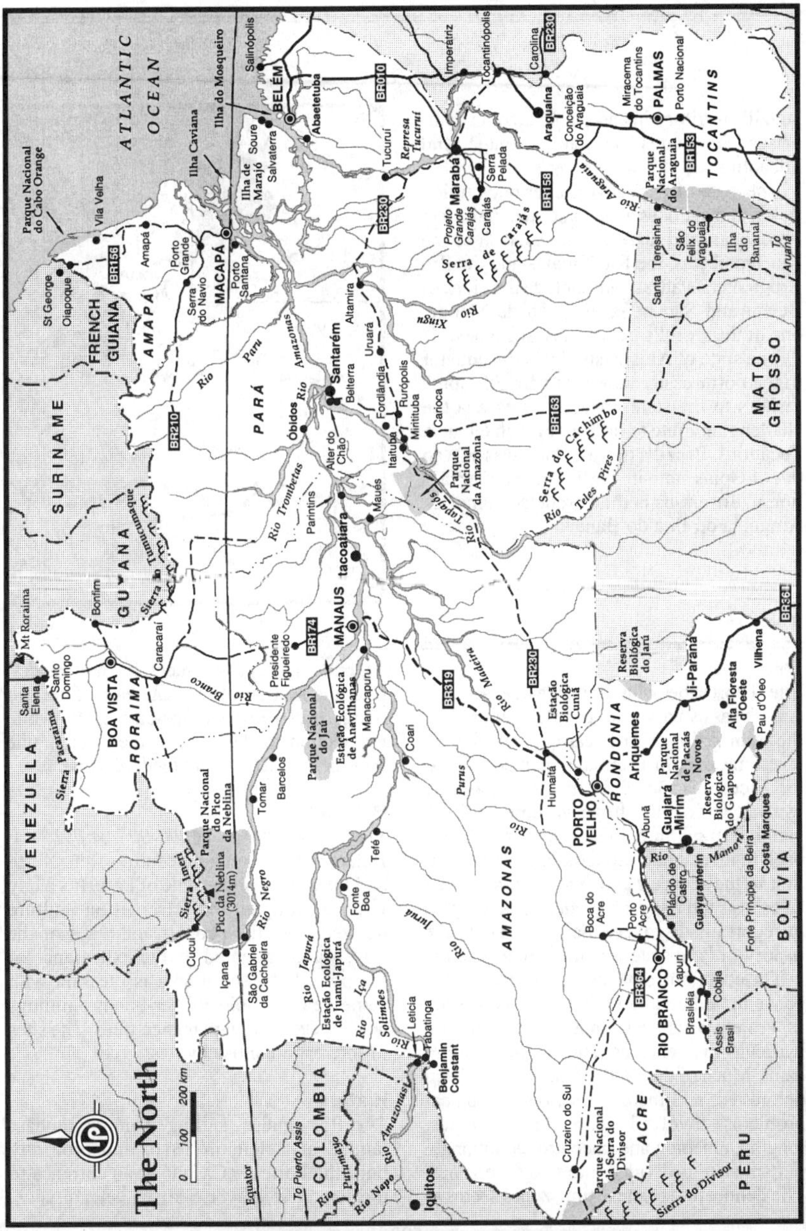

The North

0 100 200 km

Pará, Amapá & Tocantins

Brazil's territory in eastern Amazonia comprises the states of Pará, Amapá and Tocantins.

The state of Pará covers over one million sq km and includes a major stretch of the Rio Amazonas, and huge tributaries such as the Rio Trombetas, the Rio Tapajós and the Rio Xingu. Pará's attractions include the cities of Belém and Santarém, and Ilha de Marajó, one of the world's largest fluvial islands.

The state of Amapá straddles the equator in the north-eastern corner of Brazil. Some visitors to the state arrive or leave via the challenging route to or from French Guiana. Tocantins, Brazil's newest state, was carved out of Goiás state in 1989. The main attraction in Tocantins is the Parque Nacional do Araguaia on Ilha do Bananal.

Pará

The Tupi tribe who lived beside the Rio Amazonas estuary prior to colonisation used the term *pa'ra* (vast ocean) to describe its awesome size. In 1500, the Spanish navigator Vicente Yáñez Pinzón sailed past the estuary noting the huge volume of fresh water issuing into the ocean, and turned back to investigate. Concluding that navigation to the source of such a gigantic 'ocean river' was too risky, he headed back to Spain to report his discovery. For more about the history of Pará state, see the Belém section.

The economic development of the state is concentrated on giant mining projects (such as Projeto Grande Carajás) and grandiose hydroelectric schemes (such as the Tucuruí dam). Much of the south of the state has been deforested, and there are serious ecological problems involved with land disputes, logging, ranching and uncontrolled mining.

Pará state is divided into two time zones. The delineation of these time zones seems to depend on local assessment, but as a general rule, the section of the state east of the Rio Xingu uses Brazilian Standard Time, while the section to the west of the river is one hour behind Brazilian Standard Time.

BELÉM

• *pop 1,144,000* ✉ *66000-000* ☎ *091*

Belém is the economic centre of the North and the capital of the state of Pará. It's a city with a unique and fascinating culture derived from the peoples and ways of the forest, and animated by the exuberance of the port. The central area is pleasant with some beautiful old rubber-boom buildings and streets lined with mango trees. The sites of interest are close by.

History

The Portuguese, sailing from Maranhão, landed at Belém in 1616, and promptly built the Forte do Castelo at an entrance to the Rio Mar (River Sea) to deter French,

Logging The Amazon

JOHN MAIER, JR

Since the end of the 1960s, deforestation of the Amazon has been happening at a frightening pace. Currently, the Amazon forest is disappearing at a rate of more than two million hectares per year, due to clearing of land for agriculture and logging. This is the highest rate in the world, 30% more intense than in Indonesia, the second country in ranking of environmental destruction.

Now that the primary forests of southeast Asia are becoming scarce, multinational logging companies are investing heavily in the Amazon, at the invitation and encouragement of the state governments. The government of Pará, in the name of jobs and development, has sold vast tracts of land to Malaysian and other multinational logging companies which together already own vast areas of forest (equivalent to the size of Belgium).

The logging industry is the third largest employer in the Amazon after agriculture and fishing. However, because of rudimentary techniques and lack of logging management, the activity is very inefficient, generating a large amount of wastage and low profitability. It has been estimated that for every 27 trees felled in Pará only one actually arrives at a timber mill. Paradoxically, the potential for ecotourism activities in the Amazon is underdeveloped.

English, Spanish and Dutch boats from sailing up the Rio Amazonas and claiming territory. By 1626, the area encompassed by the present-day states of Pará and Maranhão was set up as a colony separate from the rest of Brazil. It had its own governor, who reported directly to the Portuguese king, and its own capital (in São Luís do Maranhão). This colony remained officially separate from the rest of Brazil until 1775.

Creating a separate administration for the territory stretching from Belém to São Luís made geo-political sense: the prevailing winds and ocean currents along the coast of Brazil made it extremely difficult for ships to leave Belém and reach Salvador, and the inland route was long and perilous. The trip from Belém to Lisbon lasted just six weeks, whereas the journey to Salvador took considerably longer.

Belém's economy relied on *drogas do sertão* (the spices of the backlands). The white settlers (predominantly poor farmers who had emigrated from the islands of the Azores, off the coast of Portugal) were entirely dependent on the labour of the *filhos do mato* (sons of the forest), native Indians who knew the ways of the Amazon and who could find cacao, vanilla, cassia and cinnamon for export to Europe. These riches, and the enslavement and destruction of the Indians, made Belém a relatively prosperous settlement. For hundreds of years, the settlement survived by striking further and further into the Amazon, destroying tribes of Indians in one slaving expedition after another.

As elsewhere in Brazil, the Jesuits came to the Amazon to 'save' the Indians and to install them in *aldeias* (mission villages) throughout the region. Terrible epidemics killed many Indians, while Catholicism killed their culture. Indians who chose to escape this fate fled further into the Amazon, along smaller tributaries.

With the depletion of the Indian labour force, by the late 18th century Belém's economy began to decline and the 1820s and 1830s saw a period of intense civil war (see the boxed text 'The Cabanagem Rebellion' in this chapter).

Decades later, the regional economy was revitalised by the rubber boom. A vast number of poor peasants fled the drought-plagued Northeast, particularly Ceará, to tap the Amazon's rubber trees. Most of the *seringueiros* (rubber gatherers) arrived and then died in debt.

By 1910 rubber constituted 39% of the nation's total exports. Belém's population grew from 40,000 in 1875 to over 100,000 in 1900. The town had electricity, telephones, streetcars and a distinctly European feel, in the midst of the tropical heat. The rubber boom provided the money for the city to erect a few beautiful monuments, such as the Teatro da Paz and the Palácio Antônio Lemos.

Climate

Belém is one of the rainiest cities in the world. There is no dry season – October has the least rain – but it rains more often and with greater abundance from December to June. This is not as bad as it sounds: the rain is often a brief, welcome relief from the heat. It is not unusual for the locals to arrange appointments according to daily rainfall time, saying 'I will meet you tomorrow after the rain'! The humidity is very high, but unlike Manaus, Belém gets breezes from the Atlantic Ocean, which makes the heat more bearable.

Orientation

As it approaches the Atlantic, the Rio Amazonas splinters into many branches and forms countless channels, numerous fluvial islands and, finally, two great estuaries. These estuaries separate the Ilha de Marajó, the 'island continent', from the mainland. The southern estuary is joined by the mighty Rio Tocantins and is known as the Baía de Marajó before it enters the Atlantic.

Belém is 120km from the Atlantic, at the point where the Rio Guamá turns north and becomes the Baía do Guajará, which soon feeds into the massive Baía de Marajó. It's the biggest port on the Rio Amazonas and from here you can set sail for any navigable port of the river and its tributaries. Distances are great, river travel is slow and often dull, and you may have to change ships along the way, but it is cheap.

The heart of town lies along Avenida Presidente Vargas, from the bay to the Teatro da Paz (in Praça da República). Here, you'll find the largest concentration of hotels. Praça da República, a large central park, is a good place to relax and socialise in the early evening.

Just west of Avenida Presidente Vargas are several narrow shopping streets. Continue a few blocks to the Cidade Velho (Old Town), with its colonial architecture, or turn right to see the Mercado Ver-o-Peso and the waterfront.

The area between the centre and the Praça Justo Chermont, with its wide streets lined with mango trees, has hotels and some good restaurants. Avenida Visconde de Souza Franco, running down to the Porto de Belém, has many bars and restaurants which get busy at night.

Information

Tourist Offices Belémtur (☎/fax 241-3194; belemtur@cinbesa.com.br), Avenida Governador José Malcher 592 (the municipal tourism agency) is now actively promoting tourism in Belém. It has a wide range of brochures and information about things to do in the city. Belémtur also has an information booth at the airport.

Paratur (☎ 223-6198; fax 223-6198; www.prodepa.gov.br/turismo), the state tourism agency, has its main office at the Feira de Artesanato do Estado, Praça Kennedy. The staff are helpful and provide free maps. It's open weekdays from 8 am to 6 pm.

Money The main branch of Banco do Brasil in Belém is at Avenida Presidente Vargas 248; there's another branch at the airport. Other more convenient places for currency and travellers cheque exchange are Casa do Cruzeiro Câmbio (☎ 241-5558), Rua 28 de Setembro 62; Casa Francesa de Câmbio (☎ 241-2716), Travessa Padre Prudencio 40; and Turvicam Turismo Viagens e Câmbio (☎ 241-5465), Avenida Presidente Vargas 640, loja 3. The American Express agent is Colombo Turismo (☎ 225 0696), Avenida Governador José Malcher 815.

Post & Communications The central post office is at Avenida Presidente Vargas 498. The head office of Telepará, the state telephone company, is two blocks away on the corner of Avenida Presidente Vargas and Rua Oswaldo Cruz.

Foreign Consulates The following countries have diplomatic representation in Belém:

France
: Rua Presidente Pernambuco 269, Batista Campos (☎ 224-6818; fax 225-4106)

Germany
: Travessa Campos Sales 63, sala 404, Comercio (☎ 222-5634)

Japan
: Avenida Magalhães Barata 651 (Edifício Officer Center, 7th floor) São Braz (☎ 249-3344; fax 249-3655)

Netherlands
: Rua José Marcelina de Oliveira 304, Ananindeua (☎ 255-3339)

Peru
: Honorary Consulate, Avenida José Bonifácio 2432 (☎ 229-7278; fax 249-3809)

Sweden
: Avenida Senador Lemos 529, Umarizal (☎ 222-0148; fax 224-4306)

UK
: Avenida Governador José Malcher 815, salas 401/411 (☎ 223-0990)

USA
: Travessa Padre Eutiquio 1309 (CCBEU), Batista Campos (☎ 223-0613; fax 223-0413)

Venezuela
: Avenida Presidente Pernambuco 270 (☎ 222-6396; fax 222 6396)

Travel Agencies Belém has a range of travel agencies offering city tours, river tours, and excursions to Ilha de Marajó. It's worth comparing prices.

Amazon Star Turismo, Rua Henrique Gurjão 236 (☎/fax 224-6244)
Mururé Turismo, Avenida Presidente Vargas 134 (☎ 241-0891; fax 241-2082)
Amazon Incoming Services, Avenida Gentil Bittencourt 3552 (☎ 249-4904)
Carimbó Viagens e Turismo, Travessa Piedade 186 (☎/fax 223-6464)
Neytour Turismo, Rua Carlos Gomes 300 (☎ 241-0777; fax 241-5669)
Lusotour, Avenida Braz de Aguiar 471 (☎ 241-1011; fax 223-5222)

Bookshops For a reasonable selection of English-language books try Ponto e Vírgula at Avenida Conselheiro Furtado 1142 and in the Iguatemi Shopping Centre, Travessa Padre Eutíquio 1078, loja 313. Livraria O Arqueólogo at Avenida Presidente Vargas 762, has a variety of second-hand books.

Dangers & Annoyances Many readers have written to warn about the pickpockets who operate alone or in gangs at Mercado Ver-o-Peso. Don't take anything of value to this market, and avoid hanging around there after 5 pm or on Sunday afternoons. If you feel insecure about going around the market by yourself contact Geptur (the tourist police) and ask for one of their officers to accompany you. Their office is in the Solar da Beira building at the market, almost opposite the Hotel Ver-o-Peso. You can also contact Geptur (☎ 212-0948) at the Paratur tourist office (see the Information section for the address).

Theft at the rock-bottom hotels is commonplace – see Places to Stay. If alone, avoid walking around the backstreets of the commercial and dock areas at night. If you intend to travel by boat from Belém, watch your gear carefully.

For more advice, see the Dangers & Annoyances section in the Facts for the Visitor chapter, which also contains a salutary tale about a bogus official at the boat dock in Belém.

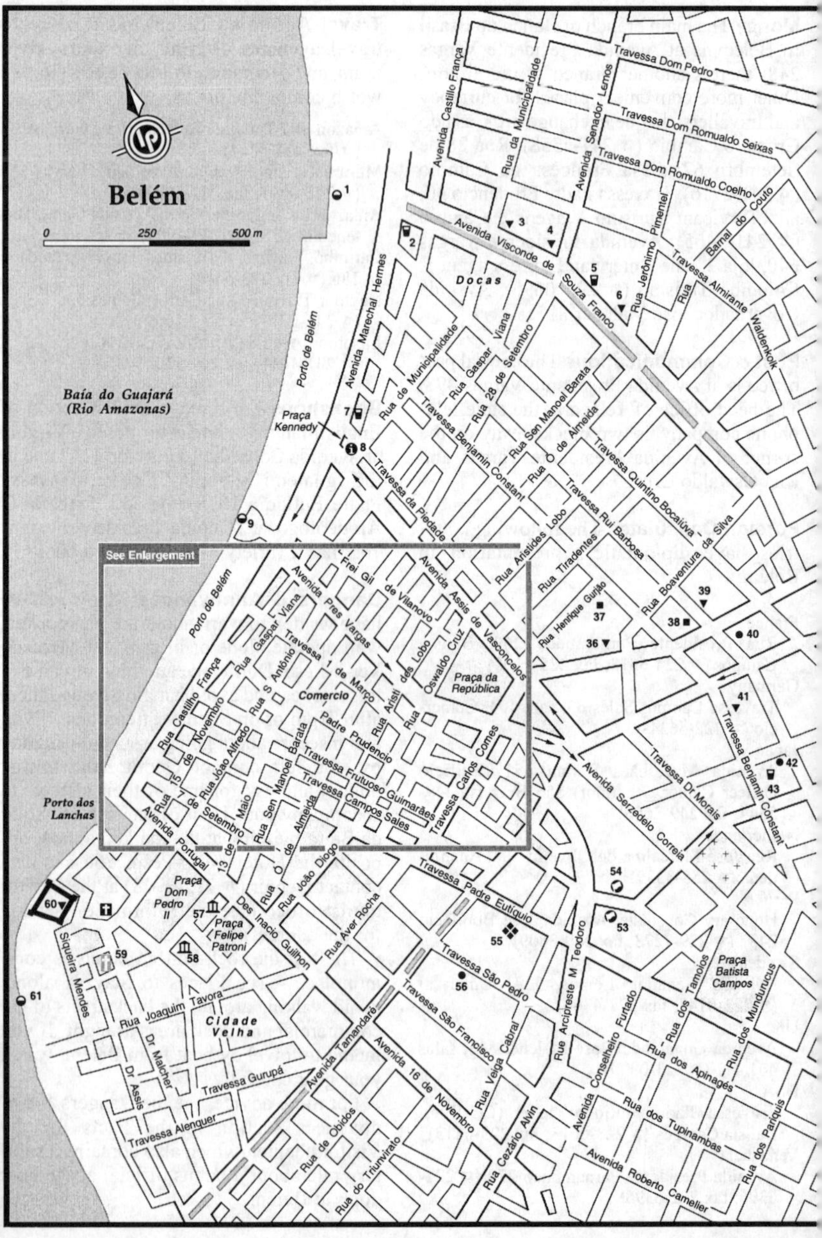

Belém

0 250 500 m

Baía do Guajará
(Rio Amazonas)

Porto de Belém

Porto dos Lanchas

Docas

Comercio

Cidade Velha

See Enlargement

Praça Kennedy

Praça da República

Praça Dom Pedro II

Praça Felipe Patroni

Praça Batista Campos

Avenida Castillo França
Rua da Municipalidade
Avenida Senador Lemos
Travessa Dom Pedro
Travessa Dom Romualdo Seixas
Travessa Dom Romualdo Coelho
Rua Jerônimo Pimentel
Rua Bamal do Couto
Travessa Almirante Waldenkolk
Avenida Visconde de Souza Franco
Avenida Marechal Hermes
Rua de Municipalidade
Rua Gaspar Viana
Rua 28 de Setembro
Travessa Benjamin Constant
Rua Sen Manoel Barata
Rua O de Almeida
Travessa Quintino Bocaiúva
Travessa Rui Barbosa
Rua Boaventura da Silva
Travessa da Piedade
Rua Aristides Lobo
Rua Tiradentes
Rua Henrique Gurjão
Avenida Assis de Vasconcelos
Frei Gil de Vilanovo
Avenida Pres Vargas
Travessa 1 de Marco
Rua S Antônio
Rua Gaspar Viana
Rua Castilho França
Rua 15 de Novembro
Rua João Alfredo
Rua Aristi des Lobo
Rua Oswaldo Cruz
Padre Prudencio
Travessa Frutuoso Guimarães
Travessa Campos Sales
Travessa Carlos Gomes
Rua Sen Manoel Barata
Rua 13 de Maio
Rua 7 de Setembro
Avenida Portugal
Rua O de Almeida
Rua João Diogo
Des Inacio Guilhon
Rua Aver Rocha
Travessa Padre Eutíquio
Travessa São Pedro
Travessa São Francisco
Avenida Serzedelo Correia
Travessa Dr Morais
Travessa Benjamin Constant
Rua Arcipreste M Teodoro
Siqueira Mendes
Rua Joaquim Tavora
Dr Malcher
Dr Assis
Travessa Gurupá
Travessa Alenquer
Avenida Tamandaré
Avenida 16 de Novembro
Rua de Obidos
Rua do Triunvirato
Rua Veiga Cabral
Rua Cezário Alvin
Avenida Conselheiro Furtado
Rua dos Tamoios
Rua dos Mundurucus
Rua dos Apinagés
Rua dos Tupinambas
Rua dos Pariquis
Avenida Roberto Camelier

1 2 3 4 5 6 7 8 9 36 37 38 39 40 41 42 43 53 54 55 56 57 58 59 60 61

THE NORTH

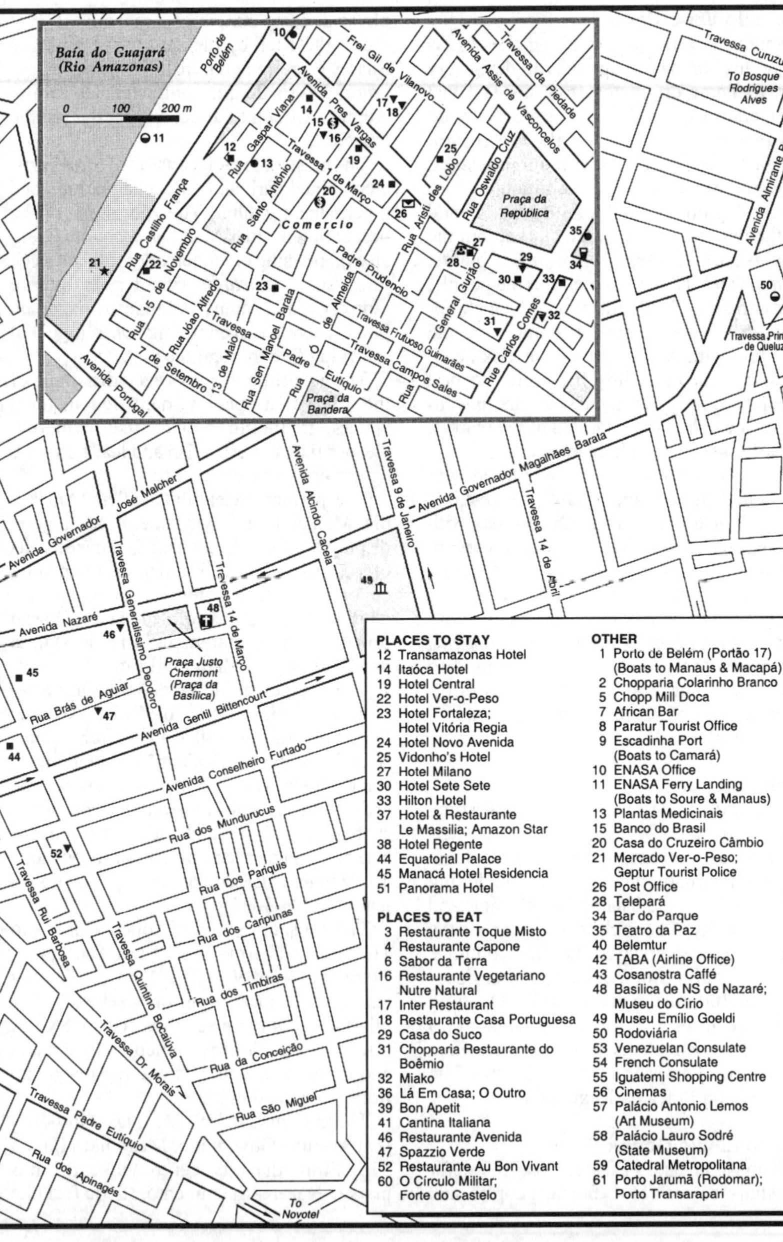
Baía do Guajará
(Rio Amazonas)
0 100 200 m
Porto de Belém
Frei Gil de Vilanova
Avenida Assis de Vasconcelos
Travessa da Piedade
Avenida Pres Vargas
Rua Gaspar Viana
Travessa 1 de Março
Rua Santo Antônio
Rua Castilho França
Rua 15 de Novembro
Comercio
Rua Aristi des Lobo
Rua Oswaldo Cruz
Praça da República
Padre Prudencio
Rua General Gurjão
Rua Carlos Gomes
Rua João Alfredo
Travessa Padre Eutíquio
Rua 13 de Maio
Rua Sen Manoel Barata
Rua O de Almeida
Travessa Frutuoso Guimarães
Travessa Campos Sales
Praça da Bandera
Avenida Portugal
7 de Setembro
Travessa Curuzu
To Bosque Rodrigues Alves
Avenida Almirante Barroso
Travessa Primeira de Queluz
Avenida Governador Magalhães Barata
Avenida Governador José Malcher
Avenida Alcindo Cacela
Travessa 9 de Janeiro
Travessa 14 de Abril
Travessa 14 de Março
Travessa Generalíssimo Deodoro
Avenida Nazaré
Praça Justo Chermont (Praça da Basílica)
Rua Brás de Aguiar
Avenida Gentil Bittencourt
Avenida Conselheiro Furtado
Rua dos Mundurucus
Rua Dos Pariquis
Rua dos Caripunas
Rua dos Timbiras
Rua da Conceição
Rua São Miguel
Travessa Rui Barbosa
Travessa Quintino Bocaiúva
Travessa Dr Morais
Travessa Padre Eutíquio
Rua dos Apinagés
To Novotel
PLACES TO STAY
12 Transamazonas Hotel
14 Itaóca Hotel
19 Hotel Central
22 Hotel Ver-o-Peso
23 Hotel Fortaleza; Hotel Vitória Regia
24 Hotel Novo Avenida
25 Vidonho's Hotel
27 Hotel Milano
30 Hotel Sete Sete
33 Hilton Hotel
37 Hotel & Restaurante Le Massilia; Amazon Star
38 Hotel Regente
44 Equatorial Palace
45 Manacá Hotel Residencia
51 Panorama Hotel
PLACES TO EAT
3 Restaurante Toque Misto
4 Restaurante Capone
6 Sabor da Terra
16 Restaurante Vegetariano Nutre Natural
17 Inter Restaurant
18 Restaurante Casa Portuguesa
29 Casa do Suco
31 Chopparia Restaurante do Boêmio
32 Miako
36 Lá Em Casa; O Outro
39 Bon Apetit
41 Cantina Italiana
46 Restaurante Avenida
47 Spazzio Verde
52 Restaurante Au Bon Vivant
60 O Círculo Militar; Forte do Castelo
OTHER
1 Porto de Belém (Portão 17) (Boats to Manaus & Macapá)
2 Chopparia Colarinho Branco
5 Chopp Mill Doca
7 African Bar
8 Paratur Tourist Office
9 Escadinha Port (Boats to Camará)
10 ENASA Office
11 ENASA Ferry Landing (Boats to Soure & Manaus)
13 Plantas Medicinais
15 Banco do Brasil
20 Casa do Cruzeiro Câmbio
21 Mercado Ver-o-Peso; Geptur Tourist Police
26 Post Office
28 Telepará
34 Bar do Parque
35 Teatro da Paz
40 Belemtur
42 TABA (Airline Office)
43 Cosanostra Caffé
48 Basílica de NS de Nazaré; Museu do Círio
49 Museu Emílio Goeldi
50 Rodoviária
53 Venezuelan Consulate
54 French Consulate
55 Iguatemi Shopping Centre
56 Cinemas
57 Palácio Antonio Lemos (Art Museum)
58 Palácio Lauro Sodré (State Museum)
59 Catedral Metropolitana
61 Porto Jarumã (Rodomar); Porto Transarapari

THE NORTH

Mercado Ver-o-Peso

Spanning several blocks along the waterfront, this big market operates all day, every day. Its name originated from the fact that the market was established as a checkpoint where the Portuguese would *ver o peso* (watch the weight) in order to impose taxes.

Many readers have commented unfavourably on the smell of putrefaction and on the rampant crime in the market, but the display of fruits, vegetables, plants, animals and fish, not to mention the people, is fascinating. While this would be a photographer's paradise, don't wander around dreamily with your camera – you risk being accosted with a big, dirty fish knife! It's best to get there early, when the boats are unloading their catches at the far end of the market. Look for the *mura*, a human-size fish.

The most intriguing section is filled with medicinal herbs and roots, snakeskins, *jacaré* (yacare caiman) teeth, amulets with mysterious powers, and potions for every possible occasion. There are shops selling weird and wonderful religious objects used for *macumba* ceremonies, such as incense to counter *mau olho* (evil eye), and *guias* (necklaces that, when blessed, are used to provide a connection with the spirit world). There are also restaurants and food stalls for good, cheap meals.

Teatro da Paz

Constructed in 1874 in neoclassical style, this theatre (☎ 224-7355) has hosted performances by numerous Brazilian stars and various international favourites, including Anna Pavlova, the Vienna Boys' Choir and the Cossacks. The architecture has all the sumptuous trappings of the era: columns, busts, crystal mirrors, and an interior decorated in Italian theatrical style. Opening hours are from 8 am to 6 pm Monday to Friday (weekend visits need to be booked in advance). Admission is US$1.20. The theatre is on Praça da República.

Museu Emílio Goeldi

This museum is a research institution for the study of the flora, fauna, peoples and physical environment of Amazonia. It was created in 1866 by the naturalist Domingos Soares Ferreira Pena. In 1894 the state governor, Lauro Sodré, contracted Dr Emílio Augusto Goeldi to direct and reorganise the museum.

The museum's park consists of three parts: a combined park and zoo, an aquarium, and a permanent exhibit. The zoo is one of the best in South America. It has *peixe-boi* (manatees) browsing on underwater foliage, sleek jungle cats, *ariranha* (giant river otters), monkeys and many strange Amazonian birds. There are even roving *cotias* (agoutis) scurrying free through the park.

The aquarium displays a small sample of the 1500 fish species identified in local waters, including hoover fish, window-cleaner fish, butterfly fish and leaf fish – the names are self-explanatory.

The permanent exhibit, called 'Amazonia: Man and the Environment', has a good display of minerals, utensils and handicrafts of various Indian tribes, and an interesting collection of archaeological specimens, including intricately decorated ceramic burial urns from the Santarém and Ilha de Marajó pre-Colombian Indian civilisations.

The Museu Emílio Goeldi also has a research campus (☎ 246-9777), Avenida Perimetral 766, as well as the Ferreira Penna scientific station at Caxiuanã National Forest some 350km west of Belém. It is a preserved area, with typical Amazonian ecosystems such as upland, wetland and flooded forests. The station has accommodation for visitors. To arrange a visit contact the station coordinator (☎ 226-3824).

The museum's park is open from 9 to 11.45 am and from 2 to 5 pm Tuesday to Thursday, from 9 am to noon on Fridays and from 9 am to 5 pm on weekends. Admission to all three sections costs US$3. A gift shop sells T-shirts, minerals, Indian arts and crafts, and booklets about Amazonian flora, fauna and culture.

The museum (☎ 249-1233; fax 249-0466) is at Avenida Governador Magalhães Barata 376. From the city centre, take the bus marked Nazare- Sacramento. If you feel like

Bio-piracy in Amazonia

Biopirataria or bio-piracy, is a new term but an old occupation. In 1876 Henry Wickham stole rubber seeds from the Amazon and ruined the Brazilian rubber boom. He was committing bio-piracy.

Natural products are the basis of some of the pharmaceutical industry's most profitable formulations, and tropical forests and indigenous knowledge are a hothouse for new products. The incredible biodiversity of the Amazon forest is a formidable source for potential new drugs. In some five million sq km of forest it is estimated that there are up to 30 million different plant species. Within just a small area of forest, equivalent to a few hours walk, there is a higher diversity of plants than one finds in the whole of Europe. It also has the world's largest variety of birds, mammals, rodents, alligators, lizards, frogs, insects and freshwater fish.

Several cases of bio-piracy in the Amazon have been reported recently. One notorious case was that of DNA samples extracted from Indian blood being sold via the Internet. Another company patented a substance obtained from seeds of an Amazon tree, traditionally used as a contraceptive by the Wapixana. Another is being sued for advertising and selling medicinal plants and traditional Indian cures in Europe. A foreigner was imprisoned for smuggling beetles from São Gabriel da Cachoeira in the upper reaches of Rio Negro (Amazonas state).

While the Brazilian government has begun to take the issue more seriously, the bureaucracy is slow to act with neither the Federal Police or the scientific institutions keen to take responsibility. Meanwhile the bio-pirates find easy ground to carry on their job.

walking from the centre, it takes about 35 minutes and you can include a couple of sights en route. Starting from the Teatro da Paz, walk down Avenida Nazaré, which becomes Avenida Governador Magalhães Barata, and continue past the Basílica de NS de Nazaré, which is close to the museum.

Basílica de NS de Nazaré

The basílica is visited annually by over one million worshippers during the Círio de Nazaré (see the boxed text 'Our Lady of Nazaré' in this chapter). It was built in 1909, in Roman architectural style inspired by the Basilica of St Paul in Rome. The artisans as well as much of the material were imported from Europe, and the interior is lined with fine marble. The elaborate altar piece frames a tiny statue of the Virgin, while the façade has a mural depicting the arrival of the Portuguese colonisers in Brazil. Included among Indians, soldiers and priests are a couple of men dressed in suits and ties! They are the figures of the wealthy patrons who sponsored the basílica's construction.

Downstairs is a sacred-art museum, Museu do Círio (☎ 224-9614) which is open Tuesday to Friday from 9 am to 6 pm. Admission is free. Here you can buy the traditional *briquedos de abaetetuba* (toys made of balsa wood, which are sold in the streets during the Círio festival). The church is on Praça Justo Chermont – a short walk from the Museu Emílio Goeldi – and it's open daily from 6.30 to 11.30 am and 3 to 9 pm.

Bosque Rodrigues Alves

This 16 hectare park at Avenida Almirante Barroso 1622 contains a lake, and a zoo with turtles and jacaré. Apart from the Museu Emílio Goeldi, this is the only large patch of greenery close to the city centre. Frequented by couples kissing in the grottoes, it's a pleasant place to relax. Avoid it on Sunday, though, when little brats torment the turtles and jacaré by throwing plastic bags filled with water at their heads – one reader felt like feeding the perpetrators to the victims!

Opening hours are Tuesday to Sunday from 7 am to 5 pm. To get there take the bus marked Aeroclube from the city centre.

Cidade Velha

The old part of Belém is mostly run-down, but authentic. It's a good area in which to walk, drink and explore. There are colonial buildings notable for their fine *azulejos* (blue Portuguese tiles).

Palácio Antônio Lemos (Art Museum)

This former palace (☎ 224-3322) which had almost been condemned and had animals roaming around inside, was renovated in 1993, and now houses the Belém Museum of Art (MABE) and the municipal government headquarters.

It was built during the second half of the 19th century, when Belém was the largest city in the region and the main beneficiary of the rubber trade. At this time Belém was considered to be 'the tropical Paris', because its opulent architecture and customs were similar to those of the French capital. Built in the Brazilian imperial style, the symmetrical building has a grand central staircase made of Portuguese marble. Its vast rooms have a selection of opulent imported furniture, including a Louis XVI setting. The mayor's office is one of these grandiose rooms.

The Palácio Antônio Lemos is the blue building between Praça Dom Pedro II and Praça Felipe Patroni and is open Tuesday to Friday from 9 am to noon and 2 to 6 pm, and weekends 8 am to noon. Admission is free.

Palácio Lauro Sodré (State Museum)

The former government house has recently been renovated and turned into the state museum (☎ 225-2414). It was built during the 18th century to house the Portuguese crown's representatives in Belém. Early this century, in response to the French influence on Belém's bourgeois culture, the main rooms were redecorated, each in a different style. The service areas at the rear are just as interesting. There is a small chapel (stripped of its religious decoration during

The Cabanagem Rebellion

By the end of the 18th century, as its Indian labour force became depleted, the economy of Belém began to decline. In the 1820s, a split between the white ruling classes led to civil war. It quickly spread to the dominated Indians, mestizos, blacks and mulattos, and after years of fighting, developed into a popular revolutionary movement that swept through Pará like wildfire. The Cabanagem rebellion was a guerrilla war fought by the wretched of the Amazon.

In 1835 the guerrilla fighters marched on Belém, taking the city after nine days of bloody fighting. They installed a popular government, which expropriated the wealth of the merchants, distributed food to all the people and declared Belém's independence. But the revolutionary experiment was immediately strangled by a British naval blockade, Britain being the principal beneficiary of trade with Brazil in the 1800s.

A year later, a large Brazilian force recaptured Belém. The vast majority of the city's population fled to the interior to resist again. Over the next four years, the military hunted down, fought and slaughtered two-thirds of the men in the state of Pará – they killed anyone who was black or brown – 40,000 out of a total population of some 100,000. The Cabanagem massacre was one of the bloodiest and most savage of Brazil's many military campaigns against its own people.

the time of the military junta) stables and a slaves' dungeon. In 1835 the Cabanagem invaded the palace, killing the president on the front steps. (See the boxed text 'The Cabanagem Rebellion'.)

The state museum is next door to the Palácio Antônio Lemos, facing Praça Dom Pedro II, and is open Tuesday to Friday from 12.15 to 5.30 pm. There are guided tours and admission is free.

Special Events

Every year on the morning of the second Sunday of October, the city of Belém explodes with the sound of hymns, bells and fireworks. Started in 1793 as a tribute to the Virgin of Nazaré, the Círio de Nazaré is Brazil's biggest religious festival. People from all over Brazil flock to Belém, and even camp in the streets, to participate in the grand event. A crowd of 300,000 fills

Our Lady of Nazaré

The origins of the image of Our Lady of Nazaré, the devotion to the Virgin and how she came to Belém are shrouded in myth and misunderstanding, but many people accept the following account to be the true version of events.

According to the Portuguese, the holy image was sculpted in Nazareth (in Galilee). The image of the Virgin made its way through many European monasteries before arriving at the monastery of Gauliana, in Spain. In 711, the forces of King Roderick, the last Visigoth king, were routed by the Moors at the battle of Gaudelette. Retreating to the only remaining patch of Christian soil in Iberia, at Asturias, the king took refuge at the monastery of Gauliana. Still pursued by the Moors, Roderick fled to Portugal with Abbot Romano, who had the presence of mind to bring the Virgin with him. Before his capture and execution, the abbot hid the Virgin from the iconoclastic Muslims, while King Roderick escaped unharmed. Historians disagree as to the fate of the king.

Over 400 years later, shepherds in the mountains of Siano (now São Bartoloomeu) found the Virgin of Nazaré, and the statue became known as a source of protection. The first miracle occurred on 9 October 1182. Dom Fuas Roupinho was riding in pursuit of a stag when he was miraculously saved from falling off a cliff. According to local belief, his horse stopped so suddenly that bits of iron from the horseshoes were embedded into the stones underfoot. The miracle was attributed to the Virgin of Nazaré, as he had called upon her help in his moment of danger.

In the 17th century, Jesuits brought the cult and the image to north-eastern Brazil and somehow the Virgin made her way to Vigia, in Pará, where she was worshipped. An attempt was made to bring the Virgin to Belém but the image was lost in the jungle and forgotten. In October of 1700, Placido José de Souza, a humble rancher, led his cattle to drink from Murucutu Igarapé and rediscovered the Virgin. Placido placed the statue on a rough altar in his hut. News spread and many of the faithful gathered from miles around. Before long, Placido's hut became the sanctuary of NS de Nazaré. In 1721 Bishop Dom Bartolomeu do Pilar confirmed that the image was the true Virgin of Nazaré. In 1793 Belém had its first Círio (see the section on Special Events above) and the city has staged an annual celebration ever since.

the streets to march from the Catedral Metropolitana (also known as the Igreja da Sé) to the Basílica de NS de Nazaré.

The image of the Virgin, centrepiece of the procession, is placed on a flower-bedecked carriage. While the faithful pray, sing hymns, give thanks to or ask favours of the Virgin, the pious (often barefoot) bear heavy crosses and miniature wax houses, and thousands squirm and grope in the emotional frenzy of their efforts to get hold of the 300m cord for an opportunity to pull the carriage of the Virgin. Five hours and just 2.5km later, the Virgin reaches the basílica, where she remains for the duration of the festivities.

After the parade, there is the traditional feast of *pato no tucupi* (duck cooked in manioc extract). Círio de Nazaré without this dish is akin to a US Thanksgiving without turkey. From the basílica, the multitudes head to the fairgrounds for mayhem of the more secular kind: food, drink, music and dancing. The party continues unabated for a fortnight. On the Monday, 15 days after the first procession, the crowd reassembles for the Recírio parade, in which the Virgin is returned to her proper niche and the festivities are concluded.

Organised Tours

The travel agencies mentioned in the Information section, offer various tours. City tours and cultural tours can be good if you are short on time, as they give a quick overview of Belém. For information about excursions to Ilha de Marajó and Ilha de Cotijuba, see the requisite section later in this chapter.

Prices are around US$50 per person for a standard full-day river tour. The Rio Guamá tours are heavily promoted, but not particularly exciting. You are going to cruise the river, go down a channel, get out on an island, and walk down a path where many have travelled before to see the local flora (rubber trees, mahogany trees, *açaí* palms, *sumauma*, mangoes and cacao trees). This voyage into the known is recommended only if you have no time to really see the jungle and rivers. The early bird half-day tour offered by Amazon Star is an interesting alternative. It starts at 4 am, before sunrise, when you can see parrots and other birds leaving Ilha dos Papagaios (Parrot Island) at daybreak. This tour costs US$50, including breakfast.

Places to Stay

Despite the overall price increases in Brazil, Belém, with its abundance of two-star hotels, still has some of the best accommodation deals in the Amazon region. Several places with mid-range facilities charge reasonable rates. Consequently, even travellers on a tight budget may want to consider a minor splurge on the mid-range hotels described. Most of these hotels are central – along or close to Avenida Presidente Vargas (an ideal location). There are also cheap dives and opulent, old hotels. If you're just passing through, there are hotels near the rodoviária.

Places to Stay – Budget

There are rock-bottom cheap dives along the waterfront, on Avenida Castilho França, but you may have to compromise on security and cleanliness. The *Transamazonas Hotel*, on Travessa de Indústria, charges US$8/12 for singles/doubles, but like many others, it also rents by the hour for prostitutes and their clients.

For the same price or just a little more, there are better options, with cleaner, safer and more comfortable rooms. The *Hotel Fortaleza* at Travessa Frutuoso Guimarães 276, is in an old house with wonky stairs and a cute sitting area upstairs. Rooms are small and the shared bathroom is very basic. It costs US$8/13 for singles/doubles without breakfast; or US$10/16 with breakfast (eggs, fruit juice, bread and coffee).

Hotel Vitória Régia (☎ 212-2077) on the same street, at No 260, has less of a traveller's atmosphere but rooms are clean and more private. Standard rooms here with fan, TV, fridge and shared bathroom cost US$16/20/25 for singles/doubles/triples; air-conditioned shared bath versions are US$22/24/30. Special apartamentos with air-conditioning and bathroom cost US$27/30/38 for singles/doubles/triples.

Hotel Sete Sete (☎ 222-7730), Travessa Primeiro de Março 673, is near Praça da Republica. The street is in an area where prostitutes hang out. It offers small rooms with basic bathroom facilities for US$17/19.

The *Panorama Hotel* (☎ 226-9724), Travessa Primeira de Queluz 81, is a good budget option near the rodoviária. It offers simple and clean fan cooled rooms for US$17/20.

Places to Stay – Mid-Range

The *Hotel Central* (☎ 242-3011; fax 241-7177), Avenida Presidente Vargas 290, is a large, classic Art-Deco hotel popular with foreign travellers. It charges US$18/23 for single/double rooms with fan and shared bath; US$30/35 for air-conditioned apartamentos. Rooms are relatively spacious with high ceilings and good windows. Those facing Avenida Presidente Vargas can be noisy. Rates include a nice breakfast in a spacious area on the rooftop. *Hotel Novo Avenida*, Avenida Presidente Vargas 404 is just as convenient but does not have as much character. Nevertheless, it offers simple and clean fan-cooled rooms for US$20/26 a single/double; air-conditioned versions for US$30/35.

Vidonho's Hotel (☎ 242-1444; fax 224-7499), Rua Ó de Almeida 476, is a modern, spic-and-span place with all the amenities of an expensive hotel including air-conditioning, colour TV and refrigerator-bar. Apartamentos cost US$30/37 for singles/doubles. The *Hotel Milano* (☎ 224-7045), Avenida Presidente Vargas 640, faces the Praça da República. It offers standard apartamentos with air-conditioning for US$32; versions with a park view cost US$36.

If you like the atmosphere of the waterfront and market, try *Hotel Ver-o-Peso* (☎/fax 241-1093), Avenida Castilho França 208. It offers standard single apartamentos for US$22 and plusher versions for US$30/35 a single/double. All rooms have air-conditioning, TV, fridge and phone. The rooftop restaurant has good views of the river and the market. However, one reader complained that his sleep was constantly interrupted by prostitutes knocking on the door.

There are more upmarket options for a similar price. The *Manacá Hotel Residencia* (☎ 222-6227; fax 222-5665) at Travessa Quintio Bocaiúva 1645, offers good-value deals. It is well located, secure and in a stylishly renovated old house. Apartamentos with fan cost US$31/37. Optional extras include breakfast (US$7 per person) and air-conditioning (US$7 per room). The French-run *Hotel Le Massilia* (☎ 224-7147), Rua Henrique Gurjão 236, is close to Belém's centre and also has a guesthouse atmosphere. It has a cute French restaurant at the front. Modern new rooms with air-conditioning, hot shower, TV and fridge cost US$40/55. Discounts are available if you are staying for a few days.

The *Itaóca Hotel* (☎ 241-3434; fax 241-2082), Avenida Presidente Vargas 132, (near the waterfront) has comfortable apartamentos for US$79/89, with off-peak discounts of 25%. The *Hotel Regente* (☎ 241-1222), Avenida Governador José Malcher 485, also has business-type rooms from US$74/83 a single/double.

Places to Stay – Top End

These top-end hotels will often give a 20 to 35% discount for advance bookings or low season. Belém's most upmarket option is the *Hilton Hotel* (☎ 242-6500; fax 225-2942), Avenida Presidente Vargas 882. Standard singles/doubles cost US$235/260 and a night in the presidential suite is a mere US$865!

The *Equatorial Palace* (☎ 241-2000; fax 223-5222), Avenida Brás de Aguiar 612, is in a boring high-rise building with slow lifts. Singles/doubles here cost US$135/150 and its rooftop restaurant offers a good buffet lunch and dinner for US$13. The *Novotel* (☎ 229-8011; fax 229-8709) at Avenida Bernardo Sayão 4804, is about 5km from the city centre. However, it is right on the riverbank and some tour agencies use the hotel's port for their river tour departures.

Standard rooms cost US$100/120. *Hotel Vila Rica* (☎ 257-1522; fax 257-0222), Avenida Júlio César 1777, is close to the airport. It is a bit old and lacking in maintenance, but does have a nice swimming pool, garden and OK services. Singles/doubles here cost US$93/114.

Places to Eat

Belém's cuisine features a bewildering variety of fish and fruit, and a distinct regional cuisine that includes several delicious dishes. Pato no tucupi is a lean duck cooked in tucupi sauce (a yellow liquid extract from manioc or cassava root, poisonous in its raw form). Maniçoba (a stew of maniva and meats) takes a week to prepare – shoots of maniva (a variety of manioc) are ground, cooked for at least four days, then combined with jerked beef, calves' hooves, bacon, pork and sausages. If you enjoy feijoada, Brazil's national dish, you will appreciate maniçoba. Also try the local unhas de caranguejo (crab claws) and casquinha de caranguejo (stuffed crab).

Three of the best local fish are filhote, pescada amarela and dourada – great eating. Açai, acerola, uxi, murici, bacuri and sapoti, just a few of the luscious Amazonian fruits which make fantastic juice and ice cream.

For cheap victuals, snack bars throughout the city offer sandwiches and regional juices. Mercado Ver-o-Peso has a thousand and one food stalls serving big lunches for small prices. It's also a good place to try the local fish.

Another way to eat cheaply is self-serve. Get to these restaurants early for the best choice and the freshest food. Both *Spazzio Verde*, Avenida Brás de Aguiar 824, and *Bon Apetit*, Travessa Rui Barbosa 1059, have excellent self-service for US$12 por quilo. There are good options closer to downtown for around US$7 por quilo. Try *Inter Restaurant*, Rua 28 de Setembro 304, for typical Brazilian fare or for vegetarian meals *Restaurante Vegetariano Nutre Natural*, upstairs at Rua Santo Antônio 264. *Casa do Suco* Avenida Presidente Vargas 794, facing Praça da República, has heavenly fruit juices. It also has a section upstairs which opens for self-service lunch. Try *Sorveteria Cairu* at the food court in Iguatemi Shopping Centre for the best ice cream in town.

There aren't many budget options for dinner close to downtown. Try *Chopperia Restaurante do Boêmio* which has refeições for around US$10 for two to share; *prato feitos* cost US$4. *Restaurante Casa Portuguesa*, Rua Senador Manoel Barata 897, has mains and soups from US$5 to $9 and OK seafood dishes (up to US$22).

There are, however, some very good restaurants just a short walk east of the city. *Cantina Italiana* (☎ 225-2278), Travessa Benjamin Constant 140, has quality pasta dishes for around US$10. For French-style cuisine try *Restaurante Le Massilia* (☎ 224-7147), Rua Henrique Gurjão 236. Dishes are between US$12 and US$20.

Belém also has several excellent restaurants where you can enjoy fine dining for US$10 to $24. *Lá Em Casa* and *O Outro* (☎ 223-1212), Avenida Governador José Malcher 247, are two restaurants on the same site close to downtown. They serve all the best regional dishes. Nearby *Restaurant Au Bon Vivant* (☎ 225-0019), Travessa Quintino Bocaiuva 2084, has a fine and creative menu with pasta, meat and seafood and a good selection of drinks. *O Círculo Militar* (☎ 223-4374), at the old Forte do Castelo in Cidade Velha, has a great bay view and good regional cooking. *Restaurante Lacuticho* (☎ 224-8884), Rua Bernal Couto 40, Umarizal, has been highly recommended by locals for comida mineira (food typical of Minas state).

The *Miako* (☎ 242-4485), Travessa Primeiro de Março 766 (behind the Hilton Hotel), serves Japanese food for around US$15. If you are down near the Docas try *Restaurante Toque Misto* (☎ 223-2732), Avenida Visconde de Souza Franco 1415, for Japanese-style dishes, or *Restaurante Capone* for Italian-style food in designer surroundings. *Restaurante Avenida* (☎ 223-4015), Avenida Nazaré 1086, near Praça da

Basílica, has a varied menu, including regional food and exotic meat such as alligator, capybara and wild boar!

Entertainment

Bar do Parque, a 24 hour outdoor bar at Praça da Republica, is a popular meeting place. *Cosanostra Caffé* (☎ 241-1068) just east of downtown at Travessa Benjamim Constant 1499, is a hang-out for intellectual types. It has a bar and restaurant with live instrumental music at night – jazz, blues and Brazilian pop. Happy hour is from 6 to 8 pm Monday to Friday.

The upgraded Docas area along Avenida Visconde de Souza Franco has Belém's busiest late afternoon and night scene. There you will find some good bars such as the *Copperia Colarinho Branco* on the corner of Avenida Visconde de Souza Franco and Avenida Marechal Hermes. It is an interesting barn-like space with tables inside and outside and live bands on Friday and Saturday.

Another popular joint nearby is the outdoor bar *Chopp Mill Doca*, Avenida Visconde de Souza Franco 589 near Avenida Senador Lemos. It has live music Wednesday to Sunday and serves delicious appetisers. Try picanha argentina fatiada (barbecue meat slices) or caldinho de feijão com torresmo (black bean soup).

Belém has many nightclubs offering music, dance and shows. Check what's on at the *Bora-Bora* (☎ 241-5848), Rua Bernal do Couto just off Avenida Visconde de Souza Franco down at the Docas area; *African Bar* (☎ 241-1085) at Praça Kennedy near Paratur; *Escápole* (☎ 248-2217), Rodovia Montenegro, Km 7, No 400; *Boite Olé-Olá* (☎ 243-0119), Avenida Tavares Bastos 1234; and *Lapinha* (☎ 249-2290), Travessa Padre Eutíquio 3901.

Samba clubs include *Rancho Não Posso me Amofiná* (☎ 225-0918), Travessa Honório José dos Santos 764, in the Jurunas district and, closer to the city, *Quem São Eles* (☎ 225-1133), Avenida Almirante Wandenkolk 680, in the Umarizal district. The clubs operate on weekends all year round, but the best time to go is around Carnaval (February).

The region has some great traditional music and dance which is hard to find in Belém. Performances are occasionally arranged for tour groups and it's worth doing anything to see and hear the old dances and music. Call the tourism office and tell them you want to see *carimbó*, which is a dance named after the drum used for the performance. Other dances include the *lundú*, the origin of which goes back to the Bantu slaves from Africa, and the *siriá*, the dance whose movements imitate the siri (a type of crab). *Sabor da Terra* (☎ 241-5377) at Avenida Visconde de Souza Franco 685, is a combined restaurant and club which presents an interesting carimbó dance show; it's open Monday to Saturday from 8.30 pm.

There are cinemas on Avenida Nazaré near the basilíca and on Travessa São Pedro behind the Iguatemi Shopping Centre.

Things to Buy

If you have a cassette player, pick up a recording by local musician Pinduca, who is a carimbó maestro. Other popular local musicians and groups to look out for are Nilson Chaves, Marcos Monteiro, Grupo Oficina, Vital Nima and Banda Nova. The music style *brega* is also popular in Belém and the country areas of Pará, especially on Ilha do Marajó. It's a bit daggy to listen to, but great fun for dancing.

Belém has a strong tradition in ceramics. It is possible to buy replicas of the Marajoara pre-Colombian style artefacts as well as beautiful modern pieces. There are superb huge pots, unfortunately a bit ungainly in your backpack! Although the souvenir shops sell pottery, the best place to buy it is direct from the makers, in the township of Icoaraci. Refer to the Icoaraci section in this chapter for further information.

There are two really interesting shops on Rua Gaspar Viana. Raízes e Plantas Medicinais and Plantas Medicinais da Amazonia (☎/fax 224-8911). Fantastic aromas waft among the leaves, roots, herbs, bark and powders. There are treatments for just about any illness from diabetes to cancer. Try *pega pinto* for rheumatism, *umbigo da castanha* for hepatitis, *casca de copaiba* for bronchitis or *cabeca de negro* for impotence! Since it will probably be impossible to get any of these things through customs, try the more industrialised items for sale at pharmacies or souvenir shops.

The market also has many stalls selling medicinal plants, perfumes, balms, trinkets and items made from the scented *pacholi* root. Rua João Alfredo is good for cheap clothes and hammocks. Liqueurs made from *açai* or *cupuaçu* are also a good buy.

The FUNAI shop, Loja Artíndia (☎ 223-6248) is in the arcade, Avenida Presidente Vargas 762, loja 2, is the best place to buy authentic Indian handicrafts.

Getting There & Away

Air Air services connect Belém with the major Brazilian cities. There are daily flights to Macapá (Amapá state), Santarém and Manaus. International destinations serviced from Belém include Cayenne (French Guiana), Paramaribo (Suriname), and Miami (USA).

The following national and international airlines have offices in Belém:

Alitalia
  Rua dos Mundurucus 1451 (☎ 241-7610; fax 225-0566)
American Airlines
  Avenida Governador José Malcher 815, sobre loja 9 (☎ 241-7320; fax 222-7401)
Japan Airlines
  Avenida Nazaré 272, 12th floor 205 (☎ 241-3766)
LAB Airlines
  Avenida Presidente Vargas 762 loja 7 (☎ 223-6234)
Singapore Airlines
  Avenida Alcindo Cacela 104 (☎ 241-2799; fax 212-4333)
Suriname Airways
  Rua Gaspar Viana 48 8 (☎ 212-7144; fax 224-7879)
United Airlines
  Avenida Presidente Vargas 620 (☎ 241-6451; fax 223-9332)
Varig
  Avenida Presidente Vargas 768 (☎ 212-4222; fax 224-0245)
VASP
  Avenida Presidente Vargas 354 (☎ 224-5588; fax 224-2676)

Air-Taxi In Belém, air-taxis fly from Aeroporto Júlio César (☎ 233-3868) at Avenida Senador Lemos 4700. There are a few different carriers, such as Kovacs (☎ 233-2786), Soure Taxi Aéreo (☎ 233-3099) and Jet News (☎ 257-1366).

Bus There are regular bus services to São Luís (US$38, 12 hours), Fortaleza (US$70, 25 hours), Recife (US$95, 34 hours) and Rio de Janeiro (US$146, 52 hours). There also direct buses from Belo Horizonte (US$85, 30 hours), São Paulo (US$137, 46 hours) and Brasília (US$94, 36 hours). During the dry season, there are bus services to Santarém via Imperatriz and Marabá and along the semi-abandoned Transamazônica highway (BR-230). It is a much better option to go by river!

Boat The government-operated Empresa de Navegação da Amazônia, or ENASA (☎ 242-5870), Avenida Presidente Vargas 41, has significantly reduced its passenger-boat services. The private companies have improved the standard of their boats, and virtually superseded ENASA for passenger transportation.

Food is usually included in ticket prices, and includes lots of rice, beans and some meat. Downriver travel is considerably faster than up, but the upriver trip goes closer to the shore and is consequently more scenic.

To select a boat, go down to the docks and ask on board for information – most boats will take a day or two to load up before they depart. The best place to look is Portão 17 (Armazém 9) at the Porto de Belém. The entrance is where Avenida Visconde de Souza Franco meets Avenida Marechal Hermes. You can also get information from the boat company agents who have booths at Escadinha Port (at the beginning of Avenida Presidente Vargas). Boats also depart from the Porto Jarumã (Rodomar) and Porto Transarapari, both in Cidade Velho and the Porto das Lanchas, between Mercado Ver-o-Peso and the Forte do Castelo. ENASA has its own ferry landing just north-east of Mercado Ver-o-Peso.

Beware of theft on boats – a common complaint. Also, do not entrust baggage to a boat official or allow it to be stored in a locker unless you are quite certain about the identity of the official. Bogus officials and related locker thefts have been reported by readers. For more tips, see the Dangers & Annoyances section in the Facts for the Visitor chapter.

Santarém & Manaus ENASA operates a monthly ferry-catamaran Cruzeiro Pelo Rio Amazonas (Amazon Cruise) service to Manaus and back. This is not a good way to see the Amazon because the boat usually stays too far out in the middle of the wide river for passengers to see the forested riverbanks. It's also expensive because you pay for 'love boat' distractions such as a swimming pool. The cruise from Belém to Manaus takes five days, with prices starting at US$540 per person for cabin accommodation. The catamaran (138 passenger capacity) departs from the dock on Rua Castilho França, near Mercado Ver-o-Peso.

ENASA also has a weekly service leaving Belém every Wednesday at 8 pm, arriving in Santarém by noon on Saturday and in Manaus on Tuesday morning, and stopping at several towns along the way. The fare to Santarém is US$61 and to Manaus it's US$87 *classe regional* with hammock accommodation and food included. The boat's capacity is 600 passengers, but several readers have advised that these regular ENASA services are very crowded, serve poor food and are prone to theft. Arrive early on the day of departure, and take your own snacks and water.

The smaller operators' prices are often more competitive and the quality of their service is generally much better. The return service leaves Manaus on Thursday night, reaching Santarém on Saturday and Belém a couple of days later.

Apart from ENASA, there are various boat companies' booths at Escadinha Port. Empresa de Navegação Alves e Rodrigues (☎ 224-1225) is one of the largest passenger services for the Belém-Santarém-Manaus route. Expect to pay around US$75 per person in hammock space to Manaus and about US$45 per person for tickets to Santarém.

For more information on services between Manaus and Belém, see the Getting There & Away section for Manaus.

Soure & Camará The ENASA ferry to Soure departs on Friday at 8 pm and on Saturday at 2 pm. The return service leaves Soure on Sunday at 3 pm. The five hour trip costs US$9/15 in economy/1st class (the only difference is a separate cabin in 1st class with more comfortable chairs).

The Arapari boat service to Camará Port (on Ilha de Marajó) takes three hours, and from Camará you can catch a bus for the 30km ride to Salvaterra. Soure is a short ferryboat ride across the Rio Paracauari. It sounds like a logistical hassle, but is quite an enjoyable trip. Boats to Camará leave Escadinha port Monday to Saturday at 7 am returning at 10 am. Tickets cost US$9. The Paraense boats do the same route for the same price also leaving Escadinha port Monday to Saturday at 7.30 and 11 am, and 2 pm returning a couple of hours after arrival. For returning on Sundays catch the ENASA boat from Soure at 3 pm, or the Balsa da Setran, a large ferryboat which departs from Salvaterra port at 4 pm.

Macapá Souzamar agency (☎ 212-5851) has boats departing from Belém to Macapá Tuesdays and Thursdays at 10 am. Tickets cost US$30 and the trip takes about 24 hours.

Getting Around

To/From the Airport The main airport for Belém's, Aeroporto Internacional Val de

Cans (☎ 257-0522) is on Avenida Júlio César, north of the centre. Airport facilities include a Belémtur tourist information booth, a branch of the Banco do Brasil (open from 10 am to 2 pm) a newsagency, a post office and a restaurant.

Take the bus marked Marex – F Patroni to the city centre or the bus terminal – it's quick (half an hour) and, of course, cheap. A taxi trip from the airport to the city centre costs about US$14.

Remember, air-taxis leave from a different airport: Aeroporto Júlio César (☎ 223-3986), Avenida Senador Lemos 4700.

To/From the Rodoviária The rodoviária (☎ 228-0500) is on the corner of Avenida Almirante Barroso and Avenida Ceará – about a 15 minute bus ride from the city. To reach the city centre from the rodoviária, take any bus marked Aeroclube; Cidade Nova 6; or Universidade (Presidente Vargas). All buses that are marked Cidade Nova 5 or Souza run via Mercado Ver-o-Peso.

Bus You can catch the bus marked Sacramenta – Nazaré from the city centre (Avenida Presidente Vargas) and head out along Avenida Gentil Bittencourt which runs parallel to Avenida Nazaré. Near here are the Basílica de NS de Nazaré and the Museu Emílio Goeldi. The Aeroclube bus runs from the city centre past the rodoviária and the Bosque Rodrigues Alves.

There are frequent buses to the beaches of Ilha do Mosqueiro. For details, see the Getting There & Away section for Ilha do Mosqueiro.

ILHA DO MOSQUEIRO

• *pop 18,300 ✉ 660000-000 ☎ 091*

Mosqueiro is the weekend beach for Belenenses (inhabitants of Belém) who attempt to beat the heat by flocking to the island's 19 freshwater beaches on the east side of the Baía de Marajó. It's close enough to Belém for plenty of weekend beach houses, and some well-to-do Belenenses even commute to the city. The island is particularly crowded between July and October. The beaches are not nearly as nice as those on Ilha de Marajó or the Atlantic coast, but if you want to get out of Belém for just a day, they're not bad.

Beaches

The best beaches are Praia do Farol, Praia Chapéu Virado, Praia do Murubira, Praia do Paraíso and the more remote Baía do Sol.

The Legend of Muiraquitã

In the mountains of Serra Yacy-taperé, there is a lake that the Indians called 'Yacy-uaruá' (mirror of the moon). Annually, by the light of a full moon, the all-female Ikambiadas Indian tribe would celebrate the moon, and the mother Muyrakitan, who lived in the depths of the lake. They would invite the men from local tribes to the party to have sexual relations with them. During the party, the women would dive into the lake to receive from Mother Muyrakitan an amulet in the form of a small frog. These amulets were then presented to the lucky men participating in the party.

Robyn Jones & Leonardo Pinheiro

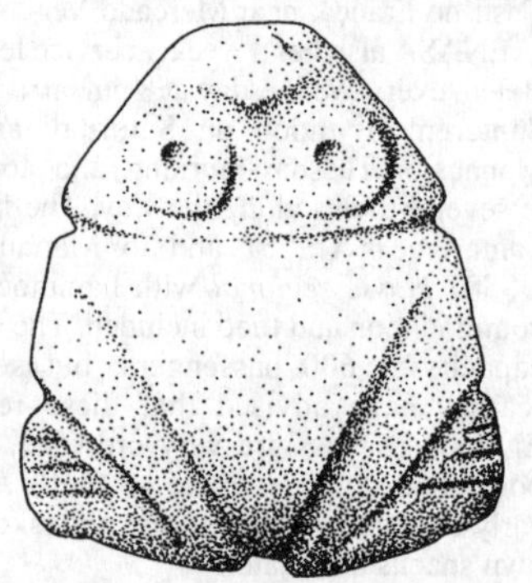

THE NORTH

Special Events

Mosqueiro's traditional folklore festival, held in June, features the dance and music of carimbó and *bois-bumbas*. In July, during the Festival de Verão, the island shows off some of its art and music. The Círio de NS do Ó, the principal religious event on the island, is celebrated on the second Sunday of December. Like Belém's Círio, this is a very beautiful and joyous event, and well worth seeing if you're in Belém at the time.

Places to Stay & Eat

During the dry season, you can use the camp sites on the island. There are also a handful of hotels. *Hotel Farol* (☎ 771-1219), Praça Princesa Isabel 3295, Praia do Farol, offers quartos with shared bathroom for US$25 and apartamentos for US$45/50 with fan/air-conditioning. There's a weekday discount of up to 20%, except during the July and January high seasons. The hotel is in a pleasant old building facing the water. The owner is interested in the island history and organises river tours to igarapés. The *Elite Hotel* (☎ 771-2402) at the main praça near the bus terminal, is an interesting budget option. It offers clean, simple singles/doubles for US$10/20 upstairs in an old building with balconies facing the plaza and market. The *Ilha Bela* (☎ 771-3197), Avenida 16 de Novembro 409-463, has air-conditioned apartamentos at the back of its restaurant for US$20/30 singles/doubles, the double rooms upstairs are better value for US$35.

Hotel e Restaurante Murubira (☎ 772-1256) is part of a residential condominium at Praia do Murubira. It offers uninteresting old apartamentos for US$60/70. *Hotel Fazenda Paraíso* (☎ 228-2925) at Praia do Paraíso offers nice timber chalets for US$60 a double and US$40 for double apartamentos. It also has a restaurant across the road serving seafood meals (US$10 to $18 – enough for two). This is one of the best beaches on the island, but gets really busy during the weekends.

Maresias, on Praia Chapéu Virado, serves the best seafood on the island with dishes from US$10 to $16 (try peixe com molho de castanha). The owner Senhor Carlos is a friendly local guide who organises river tours (US$25, four hours). There are cheap food stalls at the market on the plaza (try tapioca com recheio de queijo).

Getting There & Away

Ilha do Mosqueiro is a 1½ hour bus ride (84km) from Belém. The island is linked to the mainland by good sealed roads and a bridge. Buses to Ilha do Mosqueiro leave from the rodoviária in Belém every half hour (US$2.70). There are also daily boats from the Porto Jarumã (Rodomar) in the Cidade Velha. They leave at 6 pm weekdays (US$0.55) and at 8.30 am weekends (US$1.10).

ILHA DE COTIJUBA

This island, about 30km from Belém, is part of the Marajó bay archipelago. The island has the **ruins** of an old prison (previously a correctional boarding school), nice **beaches**, fruit trees and hardwood forests. The 2000 or so inhabitants live mostly by subsistence fishing and farming.

The best place to stay in Cotijuba is the *Pousada Trillha Dourada* (☎ 266-2277) just across the road from the beach on Praia Funda. It has rustic huts with mosquito nets, one double or two single beds, and shared outside toilet facilities. A two-night (Friday and Saturday) package including breakfast and lunch is US$45 per person. There is also a cute restaurant serving refeições for US$6.

Getting There & Away

Boats depart from the Porto Rodomar, at Rua Siqueira Mendes, at noon on weekdays, returning at 5 pm. On weekends, the first boat departs at 8 am. Tickets cost US$0.50 on weekdays and US$1 on weekends (the trip takes 1½ hours one way). Alternatively and more conveniently you can go by local bus from Avenida Presidente Vargas in Belém to Icoaraci and from there catch a regular local boat to Cotijuba.

ICOARACI & OUTEIRO

The district of Icoaraci is 23km north of Belém. Its main attraction is the **pottery village** whose talented potters produce replicas of Marajoara pre-Colombian pottery as well as beautiful original designs. It is well worth visiting. Here you can see the whole process, including collecting the clay from the river, throwing huge pots, and carving intricate designs. It's the best place to buy the pottery especially since you know the money is going directly to the craftspeople. The township of Icoaraci has nothing of interest apart from the riverfront restaurants.

The large island of Outeiro, also known as Ilha de Caratateu, is linked by a bridge to Icoaraci. Hordes of Belenenses flock here on weekends for its beach and rustic restaurants. For those interested in schooling, consider a visit to the **Escola Bosque** which follows an alternative curriculum with an emphasis on local culture and environmental education.

Getting There & Away

There are regular local buses from Belém to Icoaraci from Avenida Presidente Vargas and to Outeiro from the bus stop opposite the rodoviária. The Belém travel agencies offer guided tours to the village but you can also reach the pottery village by bus from Icoaraci and ask one of the locals to show you around.

PRAIA DO ALGODOAL

• pop 800 ✉ 68710-000 ☎ 091

The small fishing village of Algodoal attracts younger Belenenses and a handful of foreign travellers. This beautiful and remote area has windswept beaches and a sometimes turbulent sea. But all this may change, hopefully not too radically, because Algodoal is in the process of being 'discovered'.

The name Algodoal comes from the Portuguese word *algodão*, which means cotton (the sand dunes when viewed from a distance resemble hills of cotton). It is on Ilha de Maiandeua, the Indian term for *mãe terra* (motherland).

There are a few things to see around the island. **Praia da Princesa**, across the inlet from the village, is the best beach. **Lagoa da Princesa** is a freshwater lake about an hour's walk inland from Algodoal. The dark water of the lake is surrounded by white sand and native vegetation. The tropical forest reserve of **Rio Centenário**, the largest igarapé on the island, has a forest of *miritizeiros* (the Amazonian royal palm) and other native species. **Ilha do Marco** (Praia da Marieta) is about 10km by boat from Algodoal, and has a petrified-tree

The Legend of Praia da Princesa

Long ago an enchanting blonde, green-eyed, princess lived in a white sand-dune castle on Praia da Princesa. At that time, turtles used to lay their eggs on the beaches and dolphins would frolic with the big fish.

The princess was shy and would only appear to others on the night of a full moon. Concerned about how the people were neglecting the island, she resolved to appear before a young fisherman to give him some advice. However, he had heard about the big snakes which defended her castle and was afraid of crossing the inlet, so he ran away. The princess cried, swearing that if they did not stop destroying the island, she would have to relocate to another beach. Ever since that incident, the turtles have stopped laying eggs on the beaches, and the dolphins and big fish have all gone away.

Several men have drowned at Praia da Princesa. It is said they were lured into the water by a beautiful woman.

Robyn Jones & Leonardo Pinheiro

ROBYN JONES

ROBYN JONES

GUY MOBERLY

ROBYN JONES

Top: Fish trap, Ilha de Pará
Left: Santarém, Pará

Middle Right: Santarém beach market
Bottom Right: Curiaú, Amapá

LEONARDO PINHEIRO

ROBYN JONES

Top : Praia da Atalaia, Salinopolis
Bottom: Butcher's shop in Careiro

cemetery, interesting rock formations and a natural swimming pool.

Algodoal village is poor but very picturesque with sand streets and no vehicles except for horse or donkey drawn carts. There is a Telepara telephone exchange on Travessa 4.

Places to Stay

The village has quite a few places to stay; all are pretty rustic. Prices double in the month of July, at Carnaval time, during Holy Week and on long weekends.

Hotel Bela Mar (☎ 968-4144) on Avenida Beira Mar, is the closest accommodation to the boat drop-off point. Double rooms cost US$30 with shared bath and US$35 with shower, including breakfast. A bit further along the beach is *Caldeirão* (☎ 227-0984 in Belém). It is less clean but cheaper. Apartamentos with mosquito net are US$10/15. Rooms facing the back garden are better ventilated and have hammocks on the veranda.

Pousada ABC near Praia da Vila offers simple rooms with bath and breakfast for US$20/25. *Cabanas Hotel* on Rua Magalhães Barata, at the far end of the village, has rustic fan-cooled apartamentos for US$10/15, including breakfast. It also has a cute double-storey room; US$20/35 for a single/double. *Paraiso do Sol* (☎ 233-8470) is a bit further along on the inlet. It has chalets (with double beds and mosquito nets) for US$18.

Places to Eat

Cabanas Hotel serves meals for US$8. *Hotel Bela Mar* on Avenida Beira Mar has set menus offering a fish or meat refeição for US$10 (enough for two). *Restaurant Prato Cheio*, Praia da Vila, has good views and a more varied menu, dishes cost around US$10. *Lua Cheia* restaurant, also at Praia da Vila, is a hang-out for local youth.

Across the inlet at Praia da Princesa there are bars for beers, peixe-frito (fried fish) and caranguejo toc-toc (whole crab): *Bar do Gil*, *Julia* and *Porquinho*. These also serve cheap meals. For cakes and sweets (afternoons only) there's *Dona Guiomar* on Rua Bragantina.

Getting There & Away

Algodoal is north-east of Belém, on the island of Maiandeua off the tip of a cape jutting into the Atlantic Ocean. Access is via the mainland fishing village of **Marudá** which has a couple of cheap hotels and an OK beach, so it's no problem if you're stuck there overnight. Cars cannot make the journey to Algodoal and will have to be left at Marudá. The road linking Belém to the town of Marudá is now fully sealed and the bus trip should take about three hours, depending how often it stops for passengers. From there it is half an hour by small boat (US$3). You'll have to lug your gear along the sand to the village or take the donkey cart taxi for a couple of dollars.

Rápido Excelsior buses leave the rodoviária in Belém for Marudá five times daily; the first at 6 am and the last at 4.30 pm (US$7.50). The last bus leaves Marudá for Belém at 5 pm.

SALINÓPOLIS

• *pop 28,400* ✉ *6872-0001* ☎ *091*

Salinópolis is Pará's major Atlantic coastal resort, with good beaches and some mineral spas. This is where the well-to-do of Belém have their summer homes, and during the July holiday month, the town becomes very crowded. If you want beautiful, deserted beaches, this is not the place to go. The best beach is **Praia do Atalaia**, about 14km from Salinopólis, and its quite a scene. If you haven't got wheels you'll feel left out! Everyone drives to the beach and the wide extent of hard sand becomes the car park. There are lots of outdoor bars and restaurants and the water is great for swimming.

Places to Stay

If you are keen to visit Salinopólis consider hiring a car in Belém. If you are not driving it's probably best to stay at Praia do Atalaia and enjoy the nice beach. However, if you stay in Salinópolis you'll have more to do at night.

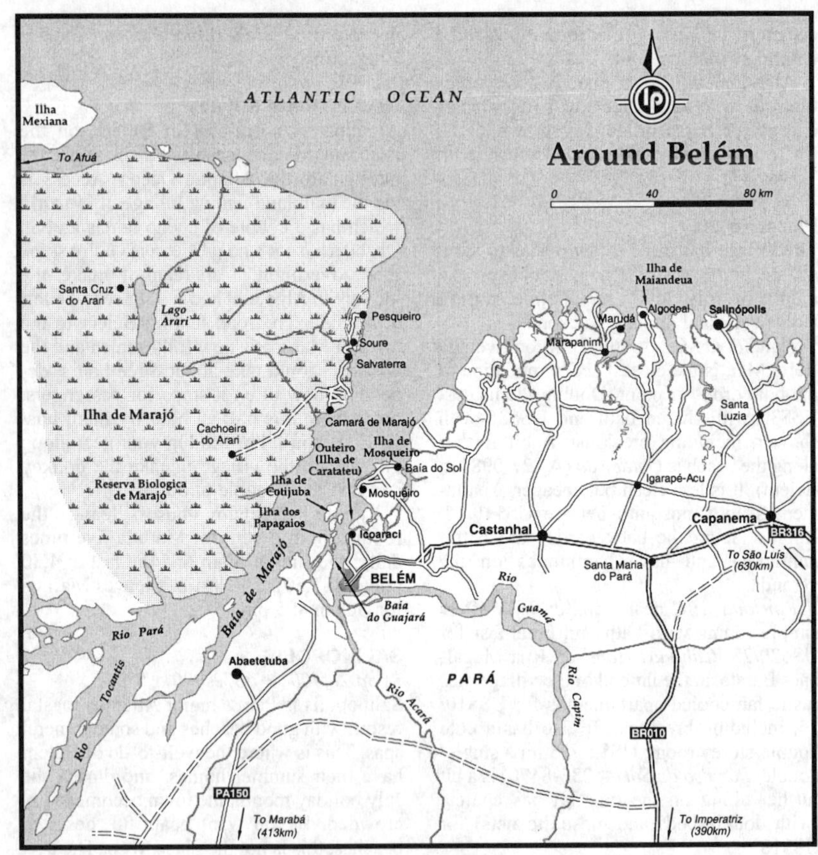

Hotel accommodation is generally expensive but there are a couple of budget options between the rodoviária and the town centre. *Pousada Ipanema* (☎ 823-3799) on Travessa Balduino Borges (near restaurante Bife de Ouro) offers very basic rooms with fan but no windows for US$15/20 a single/double. *Pousada Dona Lindalva* (☎ 823-2764) is a much better option. It's further up the same street, on the corner of Travessa 2 de Julho. Rooms with fan and bathroom are US$20/30. The upstairs apartamento with cooking facilities costs US$60 (during July and long weekends places get booked out and prices go up).

Hotel Joana D'arc (☎/fax 823-1422) is in the town centre at Rua João Pessoa 555. It offers good air-conditioned rooms for US$50/70. Rates include an excellent breakfast. *Hotel Salinópolis* (☎ 823-1230; fax 823-2452) is in a good spot on the waterfront, at Avenida Beira Mar 26. Air-conditioned rooms here are US$68/75. It has a restaurant and swimming pool.

The most upmarket place to stay in Salinópolis is the new *Valerry Dreams Hotel*

(☎ 823-2550), Balneário do Atalaia, Q-23 l-15. It has all the amenities of a luxury hotel including nice gardens, two swimming pools, pier, restaurant and bar. It charges US$120 for double rooms.

There are also a few hotels at Praia do Atalaia. *Hotel Marissol* (☎ 824-1097) on Estrada do Atalaia near the main access to the beach, has clean, good-value rooms for US$50 for up to four people. The *Atalaia Inn* (☎ 824-1122), Caminho das Dunas, Beira Mar, is right on the beach. Double rooms are US$65 (low season) or US$75 (high season).

Places to Eat

Restaurante do Nicolau (☎ 823-3037), Avenida Almirante Barroso 594, Porto Grande is one of the best restaurants in Salinopólis. The deck overhanging the water has a great view and is very pleasant in the evenings. Try the delicious sopa de caranguejo (US$7) or some of the fish or prawn dishes (US$10 to $18). For good-quality meat meals under US$10 go to *Restaurante Bife de Ouro*, Avenida Miguel Santa Brigida 1776 (the main road to the town centre, a short walk from the rodoviária). Downtown near the praça *Cantina Italiana* has good-quality pasta dishes for around US$10 and *Sorvetaria Cairu* has ice cream and juices. *Pizzaria Caiçara* at the end of Praia do Maçarico, has pizza and pasta. This area gets busy late at night.

Getting There & Away

There is a regular bus service from Belém's rodoviária to Salinópolis (US$5, 3 hours). Alternatively, a shared taxi costs US$15. The Salinópolis rodoviária is a couple of kilometres from the town centre. Taxis to anywhere within the town cost US$3.

ILHA DE MARAJÓ

Ilha de Marajó, one of the largest fluvial islands in the world, lies at the mouths of the Amazon and Tocantins rivers. The island's 250,000 inhabitants live in 13 municipalities and on the many *fazendas* spread across the island. Although visiting Marajó is fairly straightforward for independent travellers, many travel agencies in Belém offer package tours to the main town (Soure) and to remote fazendas. See the Soure section for details.

History

Researchers have discovered that the island was inhabited between 1000 BC and 1300 AD by successive Indian civilisations. The first of these, known as the Ananatuba civilisation, was followed by the Mangueiras, the Formiga Marajoara and, finally, the Aruã. The ceramics produced by these civilisations were ornamented with intricate designs in black, red and white. The best examples of these ceramics are displayed at the Museu Emílio Goeldi in Belém.

The resemblance of these designs to those found in Andean civilisations prompted the theory that the inhabitants of Ilha de Marajó had originally floated down the Rio Amazonas from the Andes. However, in 1991 a team of international archaeologists reported the discovery of pottery fragments near Santarém which were estimated to be between 7000 and 8000 years old which predate what was previously considered the oldest pottery in the Americas.

Geography

Ilha de Marajó, slightly larger in size than Switzerland, has close to 50,000 sq km of land, which divides into two geographical regions of almost equal size. The eastern half of the island is called the *região dos campos*. This area is characterised by low-lying fields with savanna-type flora, and sectioned by strips of remaining forest. Palms and dense mangrove forests line the coast. The island's western half, the *região da mata*, is primarily forest.

Climate

Marajó has two seasons: the very rainy, from January to June, and the dry (less rainy!) from July to December. During the rainy season, much of the island turns into swamp and the região dos campos becomes completely submerged under a metre or more of water. The island's few roads are elevated by 3m but are nonetheless often impassable during the rainy season.

Fauna

The herds of buffalo which wander the fields provide Marajó's sustenance, being well adapted to the swampy terrain. Legend has it that a French ship was sailing to French Guiana with a load of buffalo that it had picked up in India. The boat sank near Ilha de Marajó and the buffalo swam to shore. The island also has many snakes, most notably large boas. There are hoards of birds, especially during the dry season, including the *guará*, a graceful flamingo with a long, curved beak. The sight of a flock of deep-pink guarás flying against Marajó's green backdrop is truly spectacular.

Soure

Soure, the island's principal town, is on the Rio Paracauari, a few kilometres inland from the Baía de Marajó. Here the tide along the shore oscillates a remarkable 3m. With regular boat services from Belém and easy access to several of the best beaches and fazendas, Soure is probably still the most convenient place to stay on the island, although since the introduction of the ferry to Camará, Salvaterra with its beachfront accommodation and restaurants, is becoming more popular.

Like all the island's coastal towns, Soure is primarily a fishing village, but it's also the commercial centre for the island's buffalo business, and these animals rule the place like kings. The townsfolk work around the buffalo, or sometimes with or on them, but never obstruct their passage: right of way in town belongs indisputably to the buffalo!

The best way to get around is by bicycle. You can hire them for US$10 per hour (negotiate a daily rate) at Bike Tur, on the corner of Rua Terceira and Travessa 14.

Information There is no money-exchange service in Soure, but you can get cash advances on your Visa card at the Banco do Brasil. The Telepará telephone office is at Travessa 16 in between Segunda and Terceira Ruas.

Warning *Bichos de pé* (unpleasant bugs that burrow into human feet) are found in and around the towns, and the island has many other nasty parasites. Keep your head on your shoulders and shoes on your feet.

Beaches The bay beaches near Soure are excellent. They are often covered with fantastic seeds washed down from the Amazon forests. Praia do Araruna, the most beautiful beach, is also the closest, just a 10 minute taxi ride from town. To return, ask the driver to pick you up at a set hour … and pay then. You can also walk the 5km to the beach; ask for directions in town. The road passes through farmland where you might spot a flock of guará, then follow the pedestrian bridge over the lagoon to the beach. The bay here, 30km from the ocean, is a mixture of fresh and salt water. At low tide, you can walk about 5km in either direction along the beach. It is practically deserted during the week, and could scarcely be called crowded on weekends.

Praia do Pesqueiro, 13km from town (a 25 minute drive) is also a very nice beach, popular on weekends. Ask about buses at Soure. There are barracas serving great caranguejo (crab) and casquinha de caranguejo (stuffed crab) but lousy shrimp.

O Curtume About a 10 minute walk from town (upriver) is a small tannery which sells sandals, belts and saddles made from buffalo leather. The merchandise on sale isn't very good, but it's illuminating to see the production line from raw materials to the finished product. The tannery is next door to the slaughterhouse.

Special Events On the second Sunday of November, Soure has its own Círio de Nazaré. The festival features a beautiful procession, and the town bursts with communal spirit. Just about everyone in the region comes to Soure for the festival, so accommodation can be difficult to find. The festival of São Pedro, on 29 June, is a very colourful celebration and includes a maritime procession. The Agro-Pecuária fair, held during the third week of September, revolves around buffalo breeding. On weekends try brega dancing at Badalaué on Travessa 14 near Hotel Araruna.

Places to Stay Although travel agencies in Belém are keen to promote their package tours to Ilha de Marajó, with accommodation booked in Soure, independent travel on the island is really no more difficult than anywhere else in the Amazon region. Providing you have a flexible schedule, it's easy to set out on your own.

The *Soure Hotel* (☎ 741-1202), Terceira Rua, is in the centre of town and has simple apartamentos for US$17 (with fan) or US$25 (air-conditioning). It has little atmosphere and lots of mosquitoes. *Hotel Araruna* (☎ 741-1347) at Travessa 14, next to the Cosampa water towers, is better value. It has simple, private and clean rooms with air-conditioning and hot showers for US$25/40 a single/double, including a simple breakfast. *Pousada Marajoara* (☎/fax 246-8369), built some 20 years ago, was Marajó's first pousada. It lacks maintenance but still has nice hexagonal brick huts around a garden, swimming pool and lake on the riverfront. The air-conditioned rooms here cost US$30/40 a double/triple.

On the other side of town, *Hotel Marajó* (☎ 741-1396) at Praça Inhangaíba 351 has a swimming pool and simple but small, air-conditioned apartamentos for US$25/40 singles/doubles. *Hotel Ilha do Marajó* (☎ 741-1315) at Travessa 2 is Soure's most upmarket hotel. It is nicely set up in a couple of double-storey blocks linked by suspended walkways and has disabled access, swimming pool, tennis court, games room and restaurant. It's spotlessly clean rooms are good value for US$50/60.

Places to Eat *Restaurante O Canecão*, Terceira Rua (facing the market plaza) serves prato feito (fish or meat, rice and salad) for US$3. *Restaurante Minha Deusa* is in a cute spot at Travessa 14 near Praia do Araruna and serves excellent fish for about US$7. Meals at the restaurant at Pousada Marajoara (including buffalo meat) are US$6, while the restaurant at Hotel Marajó has a varied menu (refeições for two for US$10).

Salvaterra

Salvaterra is separated from Soure by a short boat ride across the river. Shuttle boats leave every hour during the day and cost US$1. A 10 minute walk from town, **Praia Grande de Salvaterra** is a long, picturesque beach on the Baía de Marajó. It's popular on weekends, when the barracas open, but often windy. This is a good place to see the beautiful **fish corrals** which dot Marajó's coastline (from the air, they appear as a string of heart shapes). The corrals are pole fences that use the falling tide to capture fish.

Places to Stay & Eat Spread along Praia Grande are a range of accommodation options and restaurants where you can eat well for about US$6. *Pousada Anastácia* has basic singles/doubles for US$8/15 and a rustic restaurant. *Pousada Tropical* (☎ 765-1155) on Avenida Beira Mar, next to the inlet Córrego da Praia Grande, has apartamentos with mosquito nets, bathroom and fan for US$12/20. It has a popular restaurant. *Pousada Bosque dos Aruãs* (☎ 765-1115) at Segunda Rua, along the waterfront has comfortable wooden huts with bathroom, fan and view over the bay, but no beach, for US$28/30 including breakfast. The restaurant here is good value. For a more upmarket place try *Pousada dos Guarás* (☎ 242-6273 in Belém for reservations). It offers three-day packages with local transport, meals and guided tours included for around US$230 per person.

Remote Fazendas

The fazendas where the buffalo roam are enormous estates occupying most of the island's eastern half. They are also beautiful, rustic refuges filled with birds and monkeys. Most of the fazendas have dorms with an extra bunk or a place to hitch a hammock, but not all will welcome outsiders.

Places to Stay & Eat *Fazenda Carmo Camará* (☎ 223-5696) is well organised for tourist visits, and charges about US$100 per person per day. Alternatively, Amazon Star (address under Belém tour agencies) offers three-day (two-night) tour packages including transport, meals and activities for US$220. These depart Monday through Saturday; book at least 36 hours in advance.

Fazenda Bom Jardim (☎ 241-6675) is a three hour boat ride, or a slightly shorter taxi ride, from Soure. Air-taxis take half an hour from Belém. The fazendeiro, Eduardo Ribeiro, often comes to Soure, so if you want to stay at Bom Jardim, you may be able to track him down in town and organise transport with him.

Fazenda Jilva (☎ 225-0432) 40km from Soure, is reported to be one of the most beautiful fazendas. It has accommodation for about 10 people, and charges around US$100 per person per day. It's a 45 minute flight from Belém to the fazenda.

For information about other fazendas, contact Paratur in Belém, or the travel agencies described under information in Belém.

Around Ilha de Marajó

From Salvaterra, a dirt road goes to Camará (24km) and then continues to Cachoeira do Arari (51km) a very pretty, rustic town which reportedly has a pousada.

To the north, accessible only by plane, is the town of **Santa Cruz do Arari**, on the immense Lagoa Arari. This town is completely submerged during the rainy season, and is famous for its fishing.

The western half of the island is less populated and less interesting for travellers. There are boat services to the city of **Breves**, which has a pousada. **Afuá**, on the northern shore, is built on water and also has a pousada. It is accessible by fishing boat from Macapá. Both of these cities are linked to Belém by air-taxi.

Ilha Caviana, an island lying off the north coast of Ilha de Marajó, is an excellent base from which to observe the **pororoca** (the thunderous collision between the Atlantic tide and the Rio Amazonas). The best time to see this phenomenon is in March, either when the moon is full or when there's a new moon. It happens in September also but is not as big. Marcelo Morelio (☎ 223-5794) is a local pilot/guide who shuttles between Belém and Ilha de Marajó. He charges US$200 per person or US$1000 per group (a maximum of six people) for an excursion to Ilha Caviana to see the pororoca.

Getting There & Away

Air Air-taxis fly regularly between Belém and Soure, and to other towns on the island. It's a beautiful 25 minute flight over the immense river and thick forests. A five seater from Belém to Soure costs US$400. For details about air-taxi companies, see the Getting There & Away section under Belém.

Boat For details about boat services between Belém and Ilha de Marajó, see the Getting There & Away section for Belém.

From Macapá (Amapá state), there are boats to Afuá, the northern most tip of Ilha de Marajó. Local fishing boats sail the high seas, and it's possible to use them to get all the way around the island and to some of the fazendas.

SANTARÉM

• *pop 24,2750* ✉ *68000-000* ☎ *091*

Santarém is a pleasant city with a mild climate (22 to 36°C), Atlantic breezes, calm waters and beautiful forests. The region around Santarém was originally inhabited by the Tapuiçu Indians. In 1661, over three decades after Captain Pedro Teixeira's expedition first contacted the Tapuiçu, a Jesuit mission was established at the meeting of the Tapajós and Amazon rivers. In 1758 the village that grew around the mission was named Santarém, after the city of that name in Portugal.

In 1867, a group of 110 Confederates from the breakaway Southern states of the

USA emigrated to Santarém, where they attempted to start new lives as farmers or artisans. Only a handful of these settlers managed to prosper; the rest drifted away from Santarém, were killed off by disease, or accepted the offer of a free return passage on an American boat to the USA.

Later developments in Santarém's history included the boom-and-bust cycle of the rubber plantations (for the story of the bust, see the boxed text 'Henry Wickham – Executioner of Amazonas' in the History section of the Facts about the Country chapter), and a series of gold rushes which started in the 1950s and have continued to this day. The construction of the Transamazônica highway (in 1970) and the Santarém-Cuiabá highway (completed six years later) attracted hordes of immigrants from the Northeast, few of whom were able to establish more than a brief foothold before abandoning the region for the favelas of Manaus or Belém.

The economy is based on rubber, hardwoods, brazil nuts, black pepper, mangoes, soybeans, jute and fish. There has been rapid development over the past 20 years, with the discovery of gold and bauxite and the construction of the Curuá-Una hydroelectric dam. With the deterioration of the road links to Santarém, the area is suffering from its isolation from the rest of Pará. There is a popular movement to form a new state of Tapajòs, to guarantee that government funding reaches the area.

Orientation

Santarém lies 2½° south of the equator, at the junction of the Tapajós and Amazon rivers, about halfway between Manaus and Belém, and only 30m above sea level. Although it's the third largest city on the Rio Amazonas, Santarém is merely a sleepy backwater in comparison to Manaus and Belém.

The city layout is simple: the Cuiabá-Santarém highway runs directly to the Docas do Pará, dividing the city into old (eastern) and new (western) halves. East from the Docas do Pará, where the large boats dock, is Avenida Tapajós, which runs along the waterfront and leads to the marketplace and commercial district.

Information

Tourist Office There is no tourist office, but you can get information from the friendly staff at Santarém Tur (☎ 522-4847; fax 522-3141; santaremtur@gregonet.com.br), Rua Adriano Pimentel 44. A good person to speak to is Steve Alexander, an expatriate American who runs Amazon Tours (☎ 522-1928; fax 522-1098; alexander@gregonet.com.br;www.amazonriver.com), Travessa Turiano Meira 1084.

Money To change cash dollars or travellers cheques go to Casa de Câmbio Ourominas, Travessa dos Mártires 198, or Santarém Tur travel agency, Rua Adriano Pimentel 44. Cash dollars can be exchanged at the Hotel Tropical, or try airline offices and chemists. The Santarém Banco do Brasil has no exchange services but you can get Visa cash advance.

Post & Communications Both Telepará (the Posto Telefônico) and the central post office are on Rua Siqueira Campos between the church and the market.

Waterfront

Walk along the waterfront of Avenida Tapajós between the Docas do Pará and Rua Adriano Pimentel. This is where drifters, loners and fishermen congregate. Include a stop at the Mercado de Peixes (Fish Market) and the floating market.

Centro Cultural João Fona

The Centro Cultural, at Praça Barão de Santarém, features a collection of pre-Columbian pottery. The building dates from 1867.

River Beaches

Santarém's natural river beaches are magnificent. As elsewhere in the Amazon, the seasonal rise and fall of the waters uncovers lovely white river beaches, and sweeps them clean of debris at the end of the beach season.

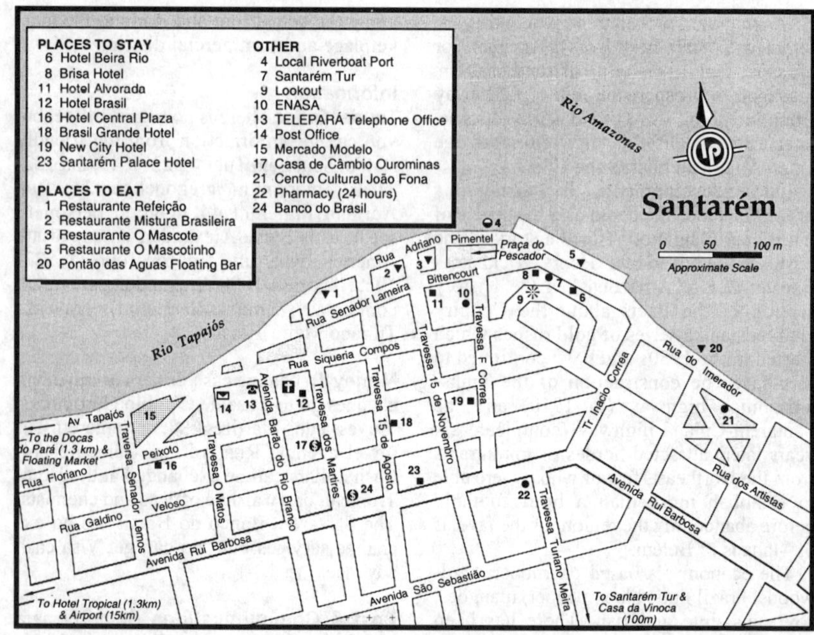

Special Events

The Indian Festa do Çairé and the Christian ceremony of NS da Saúde are traditionally celebrated since 1880 in Alter do Chão. It happens during September. The Çairé is a standard which is held aloft to lead a flower-bedecked procession. This is perhaps a re-enactment of the historic meeting between the Tapuiçus and the Portuguese, or a ritual which originated when the Jesuits introduced Christianity. The patron saint of fishermen, São Pedro, is honoured with a river procession on 29 June, when boats decorated with flags and flowers sail before the city.

Fishing enthusiasts should note that October and November are the best months to fish for pirarucu and tucunaré in the Rio Itaqui and Lago Grande de Curuaí.

Places to Stay – Budget

The *Brisa Hotel* (☎ 522-1296), Rua Senador Lameira Bittencourt 5, is in a renovated old house which faces the waterfront. It has clean but small windowless rooms with shared bathroom for US$10/15 a single/double; air-conditioned rooms with bathroom cost US$28/38. Try to get the room upstairs at the back which has three single beds and large windows for US$25 a triple. *Hotel Beira Rio* (☎ 522-2519), Rua Adriano Pimentel 90, is just around the corner. It has simple rooms with shared bath for US$10/15. *Hotel Brasil* (☎ 522-4719), Travessa dos Mártires 30, is in a large old building in the commercial area, and offers basic rooms for US$10/15. *Hotel Alvorada* (☎ 522-5340), Rua Senador Lameira Bittencourt 179, opposite the Restaurante O Mascote, has small rooms with fan for US$10/15 and US$15/25 with air-conditioning.

Hotel Central Plaza (☎ 522-3814), Rua Floriano Peixoto 887, opposite the market, has not-so-clean apartamentos with fan at

US$10/15 for singles/doubles; air-conditioned versions are slightly better value for US$15/20. The *Brasil Grande Hotel* (☎ 522-5660), Travessa 15 de Agosto 213, has clean, fan-cooled rooms for US$15/26 with shared bathroom. Good rooms with front-facing windows cost US$20/30 singles/doubles. It also offers apartamentos with TV, air-conditioning and refrigerator for US$35/46.

Places to Stay – Mid-Range & Top End

The *Santarém Palace Hotel* (☎ 522-1285), Avenida Rui Barbosa 726, has spacious (if a bit grungy) apartamentos for US$40/50. The *New City Hotel* (☎ 522-3764; fax 522-4719), Travessa Francisco Correia 200, offers free transport from the airport and organises tours. Standard apartamentos cost US$37/52 for singles/doubles (rooms upstairs are better).

The *Hotel Tropical* (☎ 522-1533; fax 522-2631), Avenida Mendonça Furtado 4120, is the only luxury (or once luxury) hotel in Santarém. Despite the amenities, such as swimming pool, restaurant and bar, it's definitely a bit frayed around the architectural edges. Nevertheless, it is good value. Fan-cooled singles/doubles are US$39/46; US$66/77 for air-conditioning.

Places to Eat

Succulent species of local fish include curimatá, jaraqui, surubim, tucunaré and pirarucu. Local dishes use cassava: maniçoba is made from pork and cassava, while pato no tucupi is a duck-and-cassava-root concoction.

Casa da Vinoca isn't quite a restaurant but a few tables in the front yard of a house on Travessa Turiano Meira, on the third block up from Avenida Rui Barbosa. It is open from 4.30 to 9 pm and serves cheap and excellent regional dishes. Try the delicious vatapá. *Restaurante O Mascote* on Praça do Pescador has good-quality fish meals from US$8 (enough for two); try the tucunaré recheado or caldeirada de peixe for around US$15. There's live music on Friday evenings. For good cheap meals (US$2.50) go to *Restaurante Refeição* on Avenida Tapajós, next door to Lobrás shop. It's popular with locals. Another good-value eatery nearby is the *Restaurante Mistura Brasileira*, on the corner of Avenida Tapajós and Travessa 15 de Novembro. It has self-serve for US$7/kg.

Restaurante Lumi, on Avenida Cuiabá, not far from the Hotel Tropical, has OK Japanese-style food. *Restaurante Tapaiu*, in the lobby of the Hotel Tropical, has a pleasing menu.

Restaurante O Mascotinho, on Rua Adriano Pimentel, is an outdoor bar where you can enjoy a beer, pizza and snacks and overlook the river. A bit further along the waterfront there is a floating bar, *Pontão das Águas*, which has burgers for US$3.

Things to Buy

Artesanato Dica Frazão, Rua Floriano Peixoto 281, is a clothing and craft shop. The proprietor, local character Dona Dica, creates women's clothing from natural fibres, and makes patchwork-decorated hammocks. Now in her late 70s, she has received a government grant to reproduce a selection of her works such as the dress made for a Belgian Queen and a tablecloth made for the Pope. Loja Regional Muiraquitã and Souvenir Artesanatos, both on Rua Senador Lameira Bittencourt, sell local handicrafts.

Getting There & Away

Air Varig (☎ 522-4328) has an office at the airport and has daily flight connections to other major cities in Brazil (via Manaus and Belém). Ticket to Manaus cost US$157, and to Belém US$175. Varig offers Santarém as a free stop on its Brazil Airpass. Penta (☎ 522-4021), Travessa 15 de Novembro 183, also has flights to Manaus (US$142) and Belém (US$113) using 30 passenger Brasília aircraft.

Bus The rodoviária (☎ 522-1342) is 5km from the Docas do Pará, on Avenida Cuiabá. There are regular bus services to Itaituba (370km) and during the dry season, there are buses on the Transamazônica highway

(Hwy BR-230) to Marabá (1087km) from where you can continue to Belém (1369km) via Imperatriz. Tickets to Belém cost US$118. Bus services to Cuiabá have been discontinued due to poor road conditions on the Santarém-Cuia bá highway (BR-163). Bus travel can be miserable and/or impossible during the wet season. Most travellers still rely on river transport.

Boat For details about boat services to Manaus, Santarém and Belém, see the respective Getting There & Away sections for Belém and Manaus. Anticipate three days upstream to Manaus or downstream to Belém. Cabins are normally already taken in Manaus or Belém.

Most of the boats to Belém and Manaus depart from the Docas do Pará, the deepwater pier. The private companies have booths in front of the main gate to the Docas, where you can check schedules and buy tickets. Ticket prices with Agencia Tarcisio Lopes (☎ 522-2034) are US$100/61 per person for cabin/hammock to Belém, US$140/45 to Manaus. An air-conditioned cabin is about US$20 extra. The ENASA office (☎ 522-1934) is at the Eletrocenter shop, Travessa Francisco Correa 34, and is open Monday to Friday from 7.30 to 11.30 am and 2 to 6 pm, and on Saturday from 8 am to noon. ENASA boats come past on Saturdays: Manaus (US$38) or Belém (US$46).

The river trip between Santarém and Belém includes an interesting section downstream from Monte Alegre; a relatively narrow section where the boat passes closer to jungle. It's a breezy ride; the endless view of long, thin, green strips of forest and wider bands of river and sky is OK for the first day, but after a while, you'll start talking to your hammock and chewing on the life belts.

There is also a twice-weekly boat service (Mondays and Saturdays; US$48) between Santarém and Porto Santana, Amapá's major port, 20km from Macapá (see also the Getting There & Away section under Macapá).

Getting Around

To/From the Airport The airport is 15km from the city centre; there are hourly buses to the centre from 6 am to 7 pm. Alternatively, you may be able to use the courtesy shuttle bus which runs between the Hotel Tropical and the airport. The New City Hotel also runs a free shuttle bus for its clients. The taxi fare is about US$22.

AROUND SANTARÉM

Alter do Chão

The village of Alter do Chão, a weekend resort for the people of Santarém, is upstream on the Rio Tapajós. It has good fishing, a beautiful turquoise lagoon, white-sand beaches and an interesting museum. It was once a sacred site for the Tapajós Indians. It's easy to get there by bus and many travellers find it a more attractive option than staying in Santarém.

Centro de Preservação da Arte Indígena Cultura e Ciências This excellent and comprehensive exhibit of Indian art and artefacts, on Rua Dom Macedo, far surpasses any such collections in Manaus or Belém. It is quite a bizarre find in such a tiny village. Admission is US$3. The museum has an excellent shop, though the items are generally more expensive than FUNAI shops elsewhere.

Beaches Alter do Chão's Lago Verde (green lake) and the Rio Tapajós have good beaches for swimming and walking.

Places to Stay & Eat *Pousada Alter-do-Chão* (☎ 522-3411), Rua Lauro Sodré 74, has simple fan-cooled apartamentos for US$25 a double (negotiable for single) and US$40 for a five bed room. It has a restaurant and a great view of the beach from the veranda. *Pousada Vila da Praia* (☎ 522-1161) a block away from Pousada Alter-do-Chão, offers simple chalets with four beds for US$40.

Tia Marilda (☎ 522-3629), Travessa Antônio Agostinho 599, has doubles with shower and fan for US$20; air-conditioned rooms cost US$25. *Pousada Tupaiulândia* (☎ 522-2980), Rua Pedro Teixeira 300, offers the most comfortable accommodation in Alter do Chão. It has two blocks each with four units of reasonably comfortable apartamentos with air-conditioning, TV, and fridge for US$35/30 a single/double, or US$15 per person for a group of five.

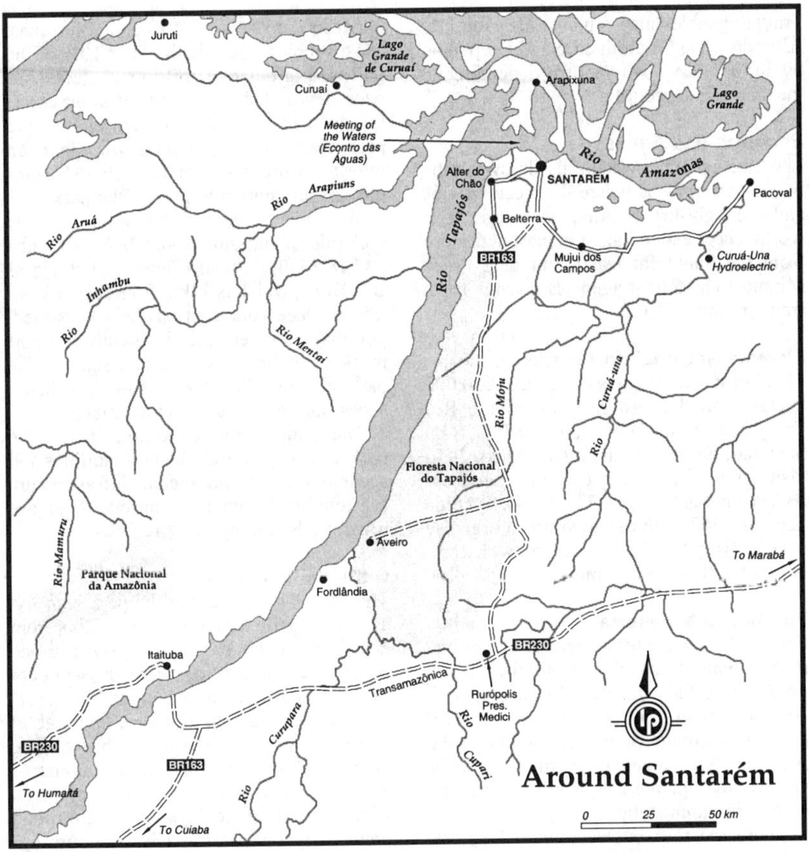

For a good, simple fish or meat dish, try one of the restaurants on Praça 7 de Setembro, such as *Alter Nativo*, *Lago Verde*, or *Toca da Jô*. Prices for a refeição average US$10 (normally big enough to share) or prato feito for US$3. The restaurant at Pousada Alter-do-Chão is similarly priced and is recommended.

Getting There & Away It is 35km from Santarém to Alter do Chão on a sealed road. There are regular local buses (between 7 am and 5.30 pm) from any bus stop on Avenida Rui Barbosa (US$1.50 one way). There are six buses on weekdays, five on Saturday and an hourly service on Sunday.

Alternatively, you may be able to hitch a boat ride from the town docks (3 hours).

Travel agencies also organise day tours to Alter do Chão for around US$40 per person by bus or US$90 by boat (less depending on the size of the group).

Encontro das Águas

The Meeting of the Waters, also known as the *águas barrentas*, is where the clear Tapajós and the light-brown Amazon merge. It is worth a boat excursion, or at least a glimpse from the Santarém waterfront near Praça Mirante. The tourist agencies arrange trips, from around US$30.

Floresta Nacional do Tapajós

This forest reserve covers an area of 650,000 hectares on the eastern bank of the Rio Tapajós. The entrance is about 83km from Santarém on the Santarém-Cuiabá road. To visit, you must first get permission from IBAMA in Santarém (☎ 523-2964), Avenida Tapajós 2267. You can then try to organise a visit, with their assistance or with Santarém-Tur (US$55 minimum of six people).

Fordlândia & Belterra

Fordlândia and Belterra, Henry Ford's huge rubber plantations, date from the 1920s. Ford successfully managed to transplant an American town, but his Yankee ingenuity failed to cultivate rubber efficiently in the Amazon. Abandoned by Ford, the rubber groves now operate as a Ministry of Agriculture research station.

There are four buses daily to Belterra, 67km south of Santarém. Fordlândia is reached by boat, about 16 hours from Santarém. Amazon Tours and Santarém Tours (see the Information section for Santarém) can arrange trips to Belterra and to Fordlândia. Day trips to Belterra cost US$45 per person in groups of two. The three day boat excursion to Fordlândia with stops at Alter do Chão and Aramaní rubber plantations (food and boat accommodation included) costs US$360 per person for a group of six.

Parque Nacional da Amazônia

This national park lies close to the town of Itaituba, extending to the western boundary between the states of Pará and Amazonas. Most sources agree that at least 10% of the park's original one million hectares has been devastated as a result of *depredação* (predatory behaviour) by garimpeiros and prospective land-grabbers, who face an utterly absurd force of four IBAMA employees attempting to protect the park.

To arrange a visit to the park, you must seek prior permission from IBAMA/Itaituba (☎ 518-1530), Posto do Fomento, Estrada 53 Bis, Km 2, which is 73km from the park entrance. Once your visit has been approved, you may be given assistance with transport up the Rio Tapajós to the park station. The park administration operates on less than a shoestring, so don't expect too much.

The administrative station inside the park, at Uruá, has rudimentary facilities and a camp site, but no special infrastructure for tourists. From this station, there are rough trails leading into the forest.

Getting There & Away

The easiest way to get to the park is to fly. There are daily Penta Air Taxi flights from Belém or Santarém to Itaituba (US$86 one way). The bus service between Santarém and Itaituba takes about eight hours (assuming the road conditions are favourable) and costs around US$10. The bus service between Belém and Itaituba is unreliable and only recommended if you're prepared to spend up to three days slogging through delays. By boat Itaituba is 12 hours upstream from Santarém the Rio Tapajós.

Amapá

Three-quarters of the state's 289,000 inhabitants live in Macapá, leaving almost the whole state (142,358 sq km, extending north to the French Guiana border) to the remaining quarter of the population. Only 0.2% of the Brazilian population live in Amapá, which is the second least populated state of Brazil, after Roraima.

During the 18th century, the Portuguese built a fort at Macapá to protect access to the Amazon. The discovery of gold in the region prompted several attempts by the French to invade from French Guiana and claim Amapá. At the turn of this century, after international arbitration had snubbed the French and definitively awarded Amapá to Brazil, the area was promptly annexed by Pará. This annexation greatly displeased the Amapaenses, who relentlessly pursued autonomy until it was finally granted by the Brazilian government in 1943. Today, the state's economy is based on lumber and the mining of manganese, gold and tin ore.

MACAPÁ

• *pop 22,000* ✉ *68900-000* ☎ *096*

Officially founded in 1815, Macapá, capital of the state of Amapá, lies on the equator, in a strategic position on the Rio Amazonas estuary. It is inhabited mostly by public servants and apart from its 18th century fort, the town has few attractions. From Macapá it is possible to take an excursion to see the pororoca (a thunderous collision between the Atlantic tide and the Rio Amazonas).

Information

Tourist Office The DETUR/AP tourist office (☎/fax 241-1136; segovl@nutecnet.com.br), Rodovia JK, Km 2, is underneath the Monumento Marco Zero do Equador – which marks where the equator crosses Macapá, about 5km from the fort at the southern end of town. The office has brochures with general information about the area (mostly in Portuguese); one of the staff also speaks French. The office is open weekdays from 8 am to noon and 2 to 6 pm. To get to the office catch a Universidade or Fortaleza bus from the municipal bus terminal near the fort.

Money Banco do Brasil, Rua Independência, will exchange US dollars and travellers cheques.

Post & Communications The central post office is on Avenida Coriolano Jucá, and the TELEAMAPÁ telephone office is on Rua São José.

Foreign Consulate Citizens of the USA, Canada, New Zealand and the EU do not require visas, however, Australians do. The French consulate (☎ 222-4378; fax 223-7554) is at Rua Jovino Dinoá, 1693. It takes around 30 days to get a visa to French Guyana from Macapá because applications go to Belém, Cayenne and Paris. First you will need your passport, proof of funds and income, hotel bookings, airline tickets, four photos and US$7. Then if your application is accepted you will need your passport, onward or return tickets, a US$38 visa fee, plus US$14 post fee. There are also French Consulates in Belém, Manaus, Recife, Salvador, Rio de Janeiro, São Paulo and Brasília where applications may be processed more quickly.

Forte São José de Macapá

The Portuguese built this impressive stone fort in 1782 to defend against French invasions from the Guianas. It is Macapá's most interesting sight and is still in good condition. It has a square plan with four pentagonal bastions at the corners. Protected inside the massive stone walls are the buildings which served as soldiers' quarters, a hospital, jail cells, gunpowder and rations stores, a chapel and the commandant's house. More than 800 labourers were involved in the construction, mostly Indians, blacks and caboclo. Many died during the laying of the foundations from accidents in the wet and difficult building conditions on the riverbank. Many others died at the hands of the extremely repressive and violent administration. Escape attempts were common and contributed to the appearance of Afro-Brazilian communities in the region.

Museu de Plantas Medicinais Waldemiro de Oliveira Gomes

This museum (☎ 223-1951), on Avenida Feliciano Coelho 1509, has a display of medicinal plants, a caboclo's house, Indian

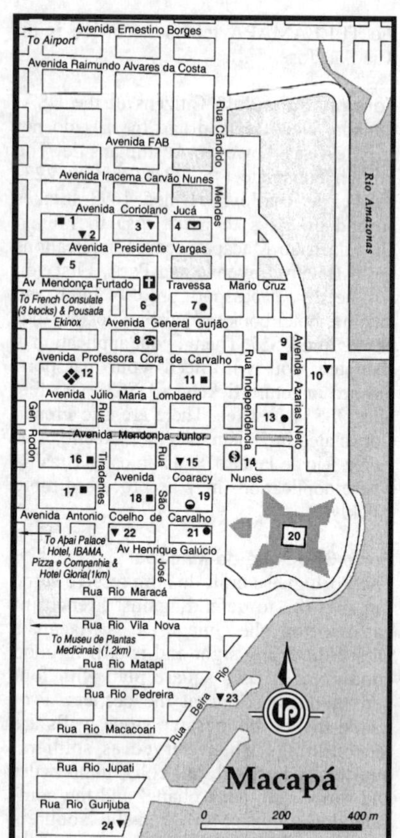

PLACES TO STAY
1 Hotel Santo Antonio
9 Novotel
11 Mercurio Hotel
16 Frota Palace Hotel
17 Emerick Hotel
18 Mara Hotel

PLACES TO EAT
2 Bom Paladar Kilos
3 Sorveteria Macapá
5 Chalé Restaurante
10 Kiosks
15 Restaurante Kilão
22 Só Assados
23 Peixaria Amazonas
24 Martinho's Peixaria

OTHER
4 Post Office
6 Biblioteca
7 Teatro das Bacabeiras
8 TELEAMAPÁ Telefone Office
12 Shopping Araras
13 Casa do Artesão
14 Banco do Brasil
19 Rodoviária
20 Forte São José de Macapá
21 Mercado

artefacts and a moth-eaten collection of stuffed birds and animals. It's open weekdays from 9 am to noon and 2 to 5 pm. There is no entry fee.

Casa do Artesão

This artists' workshop on Avenida Azarias Neto was set up to foster local arts and handicrafts, and to attract some tourist dollars.

Organised Tours The helpful Topaza turismo (☎ 217-2407; fax 217-2406), Avenida Padre Júlio Maria Lombaerd 545, in the Araras Shopping Centre, organises weekend excursions to Serra do Navio, Cachoeira Grande in Calçoene and Pousada Sonho Meu near Ferreira Gomes and Rio Araguari. Trips can also be arranged to see the phenomenon of the pororoca (see the entry under Around Macapá later in this chapter). Other agencies include Amapátur (☎/fax 222-2553) at the Novotel hotel, and Martinica (☎ 222-1671), Rua Jovino Dinoá 2010, near the French consulate.

Special Events

O Marabaixo is an Afro-Brazilian holiday celebrated 40 days after Semana Santa (Holy Week). The Festa de Joaquim, celebrated in the village of Curiaú, is another Afro-Brazilian party held during the month of August, with *ladainha* (praying), *batuque* (drumming) and *folia* (dancing in colourful costumes).

The Festa da Piedade Batuque is celebrated during the last week of June in Igarapé do Lago, a village 85km from Macapá. The people from this village are strongly devoted to Nossa Senhora da Piedade, and celebrate their devotion through various religious rituals, including a river procession. The party's main performance is the batuque. Forty dancing women in costume depict the *bailantes escravas devotas* (devoted slave dancers). You can get festival programmes from the DETUR tourist office (for the address, see the earlier Information section for Macapá).

Places to Stay

Hotel Santo Antonio (☎ 222-0226), Avenida Coriolando Jucá 485, is probably the best budget option in Macapá. It has communal rooms for US$9 per person and single rooms with shared bath for US$10. Fan cooled apartamentos cost US$15/23 a single/double and US$21/28 with air-conditioning.

The *Emerick Hotel* (☎ 223-2819), Avenida Coaracy Nunes 333, has small rooms with shared bath and fan for US$12/20. The rooms at the front are the best. Fan-cooled apartamentos with bathroom are US$20/25, while air-conditioned apartamentos cost US$30/36.

The *Mercurio Hotel* (☎ 223-1699), Rua Cândido Mendes 1300, has large air-conditioned rooms for US$32/48. The *Mara Hotel* (☎ 222-0859) at Rua São José 2390 doesn't offer such a good deal, charging US$28/39 for ordinary quartos with fan, and air-conditioned versions for US$39/54. The *Açai Palace Hotel* (☎ 223-4899), Avenida Antônio Coelho de Carvalho 1399, offers OK single/double apartamentos for US$15/31 with fan; US$26/37 with air-conditioning. Nearby at *Hotel Glória* (☎ 222-0984), Rua Leopoldo Machado 2085, the rooms are better value. Neat, air-conditioned singles/doubles with hot shower go for US$25/23.

The finest accommodation in Macapá is the *Pousada Ekinox* (☎ 222-4378; fax 223-7554), Rua Jovino Dinoá 1693, at the rear of the French consulate. It has a fitness area, video and book library, original prints depicting Amazonian flora and fauna, and a cosy courtyard area and restaurant. The 14 pleasant rooms with air-conditioning, hot shower, fridge, TV and VCR cost US$70/90 with breakfast; US$100/130 full board. Advance booking is preferred. The *Frota Palace Hotel* (☎ 223-3999; fax 222-4488), Rua Tiradentes 1104, has spacious single/double apartamentos for US$55/65. Also known as the Amazonas, the *Novotel* (☎ 223-1144; fax 223-1115) at Avenida Azarias Neto 17 (on the waterfront) falls far short of its luxury hotel rating. Singles/doubles here cost US$120/145.

Places to Eat

Macapá has two good fish restaurants on the waterfront, south of the fort. *Peixaria Amazonas* on Avenida Beira Rio, a few hundred metres from the fort, serves an excellent prato feito for US$5. Try tucunaré na manteiga (US$15), enough for two to share. *Martinhos Peixaria*, Avenida Beira Rio 140, has fish dishes for around US$16 for two and camarão rosa (local saltwater prawns) for US$19.

For good por quilo meals, try *Bom Paladar Kilos*, Avenida Presidente Getúlio Vargas 456. Cheaper options are *Só Assados*, Avenida Henrique Galúcio 290 and *Restaurante Kilão* on the corner of Avenida Coaracy Nunes and Rua São José. The *Chalé Restaurant*, Avenida Presidente Vargas 499, has a finer ambience, a large variety of dishes and wines and good service. Fish or meat dishes here cost between US$9 and US$22 and regional dishes are around US$12. *Pizza & Companhia*, Avenida Henrique Galúcio 1634-A, is a bit far from the centre but has OK pizza. *Sorvetaria Macapá*, Rua São José 1676, has the best ice cream in town. There are kiosks lining the waterfront to the north of the fort which are popular for evening snacks.

Entertainment

Amapá's nightlife is virtually nonexistent, but if you're desperate for a dance, try the *Planet Plane* (☎ 971- 4929) on Avenida

Almirante Barroso or, on Tuesdays nights, *SESC Araxá*, Rua Jovino Dinoá. The *Cinema Imperator* is in the Araras Shopping Centre.

Getting There & Away

Air The airport is about 3.5km north-west of the centre. Varig and VASP both have daily flights from Macapá to most other capitals in Brazil, but tickets are generally expensive. Return airfares cost US$798 to Rio de Janeiro, US$974 to Salvador, US$534 to Manaus and US$190 to Belém. A cheaper alternative is to fly by small plane. Penta Air Taxis has one daily flight (except Sunday) to Belém (US$97) Santarém (US$162) and Manaus (US$256).

It's possible to fly with Air France from Paris to Cayenne, French Guiana, and then continue overland to Amapá; however, travellers who want to avoid overland hassles may prefer to fly from Cayenne to Macapá. Suriname Airways flies three times a week to Cayenne from Macapá (US$131/176 one way/return) and three times a week to Georgetown (US$197/310).

Bus Macapá is linked by Hwy BR-156 to Oiapoque, the Brazilian border town beside the Rio Oiapoque, on the border with French Guiana. The first 170km of the road is sealed but later it degenerates into an unsealed track. In the wet season it's frequently washed out, and you should be prepared to hire vehicles or hitch on an impromptu basis. There are buses direct to Oiapoque, departing from Macapá on Monday, Wednesday and Friday. Tickets are sold at Viação Catani booth, Rua Candido Mendes next to municipal bus terminal (US$35). The trip takes a minimum of 12 hours.

Boat Souza Mar boat agency has an office two doors from the church opposite the plaza. It has boats from Macapá to Belém twice weekly (US$30, 24 hours). Note that boats to Santarém and Belém depart from Porto Santana, the main port, 20km down the coast from Macapá. If you need to stay overnight in this archetypal Amazon port, the *Hotel Muller* (☎ 281-2018), Rua Felinto Muller 373, charges about US$5 per person for a fan-cooled apartamento. There are regular buses between Porto Santana and the bus terminal in Macapá.

Crossing the Border The remote Brazilian border town of Oiapoque, 560km north of Macapá, is the main crossing point for overland travellers between Brazil and French Guiana. Be careful here as it's not a safe town. Smuggling and illegal immigration are rife on this border.

It is a long and rugged bus trip from Macapá to the border. It may also be possible to arrange a private boat from the Macapá docks to Oiapoque, but waters can be treacherous. Unless you have a great deal of time and patience or absolutely *must* do the trip overland, you may prefer to avoid all the hassles and hop on a plane. This also makes visa requirements (for onward or return tickets) easier to comply with. For specific details, see the respective air, bus and boat descriptions in this Getting There & Away section. For more information, see the French Guiana section about land routes in the Getting There & Away chapter.

There are a few cheap dives in Oiapoque. *Hotel do Governo* and *Hotel Kayama* are probably the best options.

Get your Brazilian exit stamp from the Polícia Federal in Oiapoque, and your French Guianese entry stamp at the *gendarmerie* in St Georges (French Guiana), reached by a 20 minute motorboat ride (US$5) from Oiapoque. There's a casa de câmbio at the harbour in Oiapoque but it has poor rates; it's best to change money in Macapá or Belém.

AROUND MACAPÁ

Curiaú

This African village 8km from Macapá was founded by escaped African slaves. They chose this area for its natural pastures, perfect for raising buffalo. The main street (lined with distinctive timber houses) and the flooding valley are very picturesque.

Parque Zoobotânico
This zoo has a small sample of local fauna. It has tapirs, deer, monkeys, alligators and birds, as well as some jaguars which definitely fancied us for their next meal. Take the Fazendinha bus from the local bus terminal and ask the driver where you should get off.

Praia da Fazendinha
Buses run to Praia da Fazendinha, the local beach, 19km south of town. There are various beachside bars and restaurants – *Julião* and *Naira* are recommended for good seafood.

Cachoeira de Santo Antônio
This is a waterfall in the municipality of **Mazagão**, an 18th century Portuguese town which is accessible by ferry from Porto Santana.

Rio Araguari & The Pororoca
At the mouth of the Rio Araguari, about 100km north-east of Macapá, you can observe (and hear!) the pororoca (a thunderous collision between the Atlantic tide and the Rio Amazonas). The best time to see this phenomenon is between January and April, at either the full or new moon. Excursions by boat (18 hours from Porto Santana) to see the pororoca can be organised by the local tour agencies (for addresses, see the Information section for Macapá).

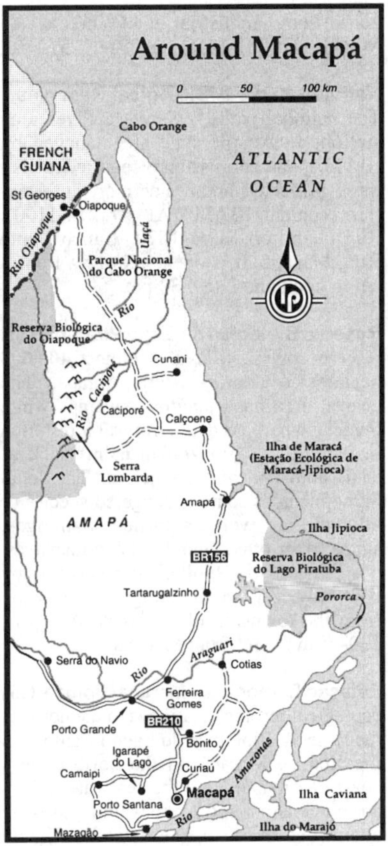

Serra do Navio
The mining town Serra do Navio is 200km north-west of Macapá. To prevent it becoming a ghost town when manganese exploration ceases in 2003, Serra do Navio is being used as a research base for ecology, meteorology, hydrology and anthropology. The University of São Paulo has a small facility here. Research is being carried out into the industrialisation of the area's forest products (medicinal plants, natural dyes and insecticides, resins, essences and oils) for pharmaceutical use. Collection areas and processing bases are planned, with the objective of improving the Amazonian per capita income (currently just 10% of the Brazilian average).

Getting There & Away Serra do Navio is connected to Porto Santana by a railway which crosses 200km of savanna and native forest. The train departs from Porto Santana on Friday and Sunday (five hours). Alternatively, you can drive to Serra do Navio (about four hours on Hwy BR-210). The road passes through beautiful forests. For more information, contact the mining consortium Indústria e Comércio de Minérios (☎ 281-1415; fax 281-1175).

National Parks & Biological Reserves

The national parks, reserves and research stations in Amapá state are managed by IBAMA, and permission is required to visit these protected areas. For more information, contact IBAMA/AP (☎ 214-1100), Rua Hamilton Silva 1570, Bairro Santa Rita, Macapá. It is open weekdays from 8 am to noon and 2 to 4.30 pm.

Reserva Biológica do Lago Piratuba This reserve covers an area of almost 400,000 hectares of north-eastern Amapá. The coastal area has mangrove swamps while the inland part has dense tropical forest, rich in varieties of Amazonian palms such as açaí, andiroba and palmeiras. The local fauna includes some endangered species of alligator, as well as turtles, flamingos, sloths, river otters, monkeys and manatees.

Access to the biological reserve is by boat only, via the Rio Araguari, departing from the township of Cutias do Araguari, 130km overland from Macapá.

Estação Ecológica – Maracá-Jipioca This ecological research station is to the north of the Reserva Biológica do Lago Piratuba, on the Ilha de Maracá on the north-eastern coast of Amapá. Here the sea water enters an immense mangrove swamp covering about one-third of the island's 72,000 hectares, habitat for large numbers of various species of aquatic birds. The clay-coloured water indicates it is actually an extension of the Rio Amazonas mixed with sea water. Access to the island is by local boats from the township of Amapá, 308km overland north of Macapá.

Parque Nacional do Cabo Orange This national park is at the extreme north of Amapá state, covering an area of 619,000 hectares of the districts of Calçoene and Oiapoque. Most of the park's area is covered by mangrove swamps and sandbanks within 10km of the Atlantic coast, with the rivers Cassiporé and Uaçá crossing it to the ocean.

It has diverse fauna due to the variety of environments. There are manatees in the slow river waters, crab-eating racoons, birds such as flamingos and guarás in the mangrove swamps, endangered species of armadillos, anteaters, and jaguars in the forest, and turtles laying eggs on the beaches.

Access to the park isn't easy – a rugged overland trip up to the town of Calçoene, 380km from Macapá, then a boat ride out to sea and into the Rio Cassiporé. The park has an airstrip for small aircraft.

Tocantins

The new state of Tocantins, which was created on 1 January 1989, encompasses what was previously the northern half of the state of Goiás. Until the Belém-Brasília highway was built, there was no road link between southern and northern Goiás and each area developed with a different cultural history. The new highway served mostly as an expressway from the north to the south of Brazil, and consequently, each region maintained its own character. Southern Goiás had mostly been colonised by people from the southern states of Brazil, who traditionally didn't mix with the local Indians or black slaves. Colonisation of the northern part of Goiás was mostly by people from the northern parts of Brazil, with strong interracial pairing between Indians, blacks, and those of European descent, creating a new ethnic group with different physical characteristics and a distinctive culture. The separatist movements in what is now Tocantins started as far back as the early 19th century, with the most significant one, headed by Joquim Segurado, in 1821.

The state was supposedly created to give the Indians of the region greater autonomy; however, they appear to have been conveniently shuffled aside to make way for grandiose plans and lavish use of statistics and slogans, such as '20 anos em 2' (20 years of progress in two).

Tocantins currently has over 1.2 million inhabitants in 123 municipalities over its area of 286,706 sq km. Technically, it belongs to the northern region of Brazil, with Pará and Mato Grosso states to the west, Maranhão and Bahia to the east and Goiás to the south.

Geographically, the state has three defined regions: Amazon rainforest in the north; median (Araguaia), an area of transition; and central south-east, which is mostly savanna, with sections of deciduous forest on the borders with Bahia and Goiás. The state's climate is humid, with average temperatures between 25 and 36°C.

PALMAS

• *pop 86,000 ✉ 77000-000 ☎ 063*

The state capital is a planned city strategically placed in the centre of Tocantins. It is 973km from Brasília and 1271km from Belém.

In 1991, Palmas had 2000 inhabitants, mostly public officials and construction workers. In 1995 its population was 25,000 and by 1997 the town already had over 86,000 inhabitants. The original plan of organised growth seems to be getting out of control, with migrants from other states arriving every day seeking new opportunities.

Apart from the grandiose **Palácio Araguaia**, and other government buildings, there isn't much of interest in Palmas. The vast, sparse scale of the city is typical of the megalomania rampant in the state. Unless you have a specific reason to visit, give it a miss.

During the months of June, July and August, the beach of **Graciosa** (in the town of Canela, 12km west of Palmas) and the **Taquarassú** (in Serra do Carmo, about 26km south-east of Palmas) are where locals go for relief from the heat.

Information

Money At this stage, there are no official money-exchange facilities in Tocantins.

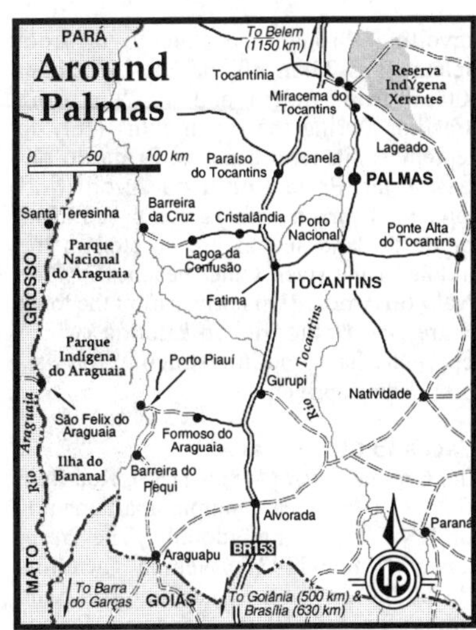

Places to Stay

Accommodation in Palmas is generally expensive. Try the *Hotel Casa Grande* (☎ 215-1813) on Avenida Joaquin Teotônio Segurado (US$40/50 for single/ double) or the *Pousada dos Girassois* (☎ 215-1187; fax 215-2321) at ACSO I, Conj 3, lt 43 for US$40/93.

Getting There & Away

Air From Palmas airport (☎ 216-1237) accessed via Avenida Teotônio Segurado, Km 2, there are interstate flights to Belém and Brasília, as well as for Araguaína, Redenção and Tucuruí with TAM (☎ 216-1969) and Air Taxi Nobre (☎ 216-1500).

Bus There are daily buses from the Palmas rodoviária (☎ 216-1603), Avenida Teotonio Segurado, to Belém, Brasília, Teresinha, Belo Horizonte, Rio and São Paulo. There are also regular buses to most towns in Tocantins.

MIRACEMA DO TOCANTINS

• *pop 17,483 ✉ 77650-000 ☎ 063*

This small town on the Rio Tocantins is as good a place as any for a stopover if you are travelling through the state to or from Belém. It is 23km off the BR-153, about 800km from Belém and 1032km from Brasília. During the dry months (July to September) its river beaches, **Praia do Mirassol** and **Praia Ponte de Apoio** (just opposite the main street) are exposed. Huts for drinks and snacks are erected in the middle of the river. Other beaches include **Praia do Amor**, 3km upriver from the town centre, and **Balneário do Lucena** (which reportedly has good infrastructure for visitors), 17km upriver.

Places to Stay & Eat

The *Grande Hotel* (☎ 866-1155), Rua Bela Vista 771, has clean, simple apartamentos for US$7/13 a single/double. The *Hotel Zezito* (☎ 866-1142), Avenida Tocantins 258 on the way to the riverfront, has basic rooms for US$7/13. *Miracema Palace* (☎ 866-1161) is a bit further out of town on Avenida Tocantins on the road to Miranorte. It has apartamentos for US$25/30.

Restaurante Gaúcho on the corner of Avenida Tocantins and Avenida Getúlio Vargas, has all-you-can-eat for US$3.50. The *Restaurante Bom Paladar*, Rua Primero de Janeiro 318, has good, self-service meals. You could also try the *Restauant Palace*, at the Miracema Palace.

Getting There & Away

From the rodoviária (☎ 866-1281), Avenida Tocantins 1376, there are daily buses to Belém, Brasília, Conceição do Araguaia, Goiânia, Imperatriz and Marabá, and at least two buses daily to Palmas. Vans shuttle between Miranorte and Miracema (US$1, 20km).

AROUND MIRACEMA

Tocantínia

Tocantínia is on the opposite bank of the Rio Tocantins, a short ferryboat crossing from Miracema. It is now compulsory to exit your vehicle, since a bus rolled off the ferry into the river! There are huts at both sides of the ferry port that sell inexpensive local Indian handicrafts.

Wooly monkeys live in the rainforest canopy and rarely come down to ground level.

Tocantínia is 89km from Palmas, on the edge of the **Reserva Indígena Xerente**. One of the state government's development strategies is to build a highway linking Palmas to the Northeast. Pacifying the Xerente by saying that a small bridge was going to be built over the Rio do Sono, they promptly began construction of a massive structure. Recognising that a substantial highway was intended to cut straight through their reserve, the Xerente set up an *aldeia* (village) at the site to halt the work.

The Xerente we spoke to said that if necessary, they would fight to the death to protect their land, for if the highway proceeded, their culture would be destroyed.

The hydroelectric dam of Lageado will flood an area near the Indian reserve and affect all the beaches downriver from Miracema. Construction has begun and certainly during the works alcohol and prostitution will affect the reserve. To visit an aldeia, you will need permission from FUNAI in Gurupi (see the Gurupi Information section following).

Lageado

This very small town has a picturesque, rocky river beach and a waterfall. There are no hotels, but you can stay at Miracema (50km away) or camp by the river.

GURUPI

• *pop 64,725* ✉ *77400-000* ☎ *063*

Gurupi is one of the largest towns in the state and one of Tocantins' most important agro-industrial areas. It is 712km north of Brasília on the Belém-Brasília highway. June and July is beach season. There are good beaches on the margins of Rio Tocantins, in the municipality of Peixe about 80km from Gurupi, with regular buses during these months. Festejos de Santo Antônio and the state's largest agricultural show are both held in June.

Information

Money You can exchange cash dollars at Urutur Turismo.

Post & Communications The telephone office, Telegoais, is at Rua 07 near the corner of Avenida Saõ Paulo. The post office is also on Rua 07, on the corner of Avenida Pará.

Travel Agency Urutur Viagens e Turismo (☎ 851-3398), Rua Antônio Lisboa da Cruz 1695, sala 5, is one the few travel agencies in Tocantins. It can provide information about places of interest around the state, including Ilha do Bananal.

Visiting Indian Reserves

To visit the Karajá and Javaés Indian reserves (on Ilha do Bananal) or the Xerente Indian village (near Tocantínia), you need permission from the FUNAI office in Gurupi (☎/fax 712-3988), Rua Presidente Castelo Branco 1363. It takes a minimum of 10 days to get formal permission, so you may want to fax your request in advance (read the Visiting a Reservation section in Facts about the Country chapter).

Places to Stay & Eat

There are two small hotels in front of the bus terminal – try the *Hotel Vila Rica* (☎ 851-2910) which is friendly and has clean quartos for US$8/12 a single/double. Another budget option is the *Hotel Castelo*, Avenida Mato Grosso 1640. It's in good area opposite a plaza and near the town centre. It has clean basic rooms with shared bath for US$6/12, or US$8/14 for apartamentos with private bath. The *Veneza Plaza* (☎ 712-3500), Avenida Pará 1823, is the best hotel in Gurupi. It has a swimming pool, air-conditioned restaurant, good service and charges US$49/64 for singles/doubles apartamentos (up to 30% discount for cash payments). *Grande Hotel* (☎ 851-1065) is around the corner on Avenida Goiás. It offers good fan-cooled rooms with bath for US$13/20. The best rooms are upstairs.

Restaurante Mama Pizza, on the corner of Rua 07 and Avenida Saõ Paulo, serves large pizzas for US$12 and good fish. Try their moqueca de peixe (US$15) which is enough for two. *Minas Restaurante*, Rua Mato Grosso, between Rua 07 and Rua 08, has home-style por quilo. There are also good-value self-service meals at *Restaurante e Churrascaria Parolle*, Rua 05, 1373.

Getting There & Away

From Gurupi airport (☎ 851-2468) on Avenida Sergipe there are daily flights to São Félix do Araguaia (Mato Grosso) for US$148. There are also daily flights to Brasília (US$262) and Goiania (US$287).

The bus terminal (☎ 851-1544) is on Rua 19. There are daily interstate buses from

Gurupi to Belém, Brasília and Imperatriz, and at least twice-daily bus services to the main towns within the state.

LAGOA DA CONFUSÃO

This small town, with just over 2000 inhabitants, is 87km west of the Belém-Brasília highway. It's one of the main tourist destinations in Tocantins and serves as a good base for visiting Ilha do Bananal. The area is picturesque, with flat-topped hills and miles of green savanna. The town is on a lake about 4.5km in diameter, which has a protruding boulder in the middle. Its name, which means 'Lake of Confusion', comes from the disagreement over whether the rock moves around the lake!

The Secretaria Municipal de Turismo (☎/fax 864-1148) has an information shed opposite the pier. It can help with arrangements to visit Ilha do Bananal.

Places to Stay & Eat

Pousada Ilha do Bananal (☎ 864-1146), Rua Vicente Pereira de Sá, has clean, new fan-cooled rooms with bathroom for US$15/20 a single/double (US$5 for an extra person on a mattress on the floor). They can help you organise a trip to Ilha do Bananal. *Hotel Lagoa da Ilha Praia Clube* (☎ 864-1110) has a large swimming pool. Simple but comfortable double rooms here cost US$80/90 for fan/air-conditioning. There is a also camping ground on the lake's edge, with basic toilet and shower facilities. Camping is free year-round, but it can get crowded during Carnaval and the July holidays.

Restaurante do Filó on the lakefront serves refeições for US$4, while next door the *Kabana Bar e Restaurante* has the best por quilo meals in town. *Bar do Tin Tin* opposite the pier serves beer and snacks.

Getting There & Away

There are daily buses to Lagoa da Confusão from Palmas. The road is now fully sealed.

AROUND LAGOA DA CONFUSÃO

You can access the Parque Nacional da Ilha do Bananal from Barreira da Cruz, a small fishing village on the margin of Rio Javaés, 52km from Lagoa da Confusão. Lagoa dos Pássaros, 45km from Lagoa da Confusão via Rodovia Lagoa-Fazenda Conag, is reportedly good for birdwatching from June to September.

RIO ARAGUAIA

The Rio Araguaia begins in the Serra dos Caiapós and flows 2600km northwards, forming the borders of Mato Grosso, Goiás, Tocantins and Pará before joining the Rio Tocantins where the states of Tocantins, Maranhão and Pará meet, near Marabá. About 500km from its source, the Araguaia bifurcates into the greater and lesser Araguaia rivers, which course west and east respectively and then rejoin, having formed the largest river island in the world, Ilha do Bananal.

The river is not easily accessible, so tours are a good idea. The best access from Mato Grosso is via Barra do Garças, about 500km from Cuiabá. Barra do Garças has the Parque de Águas Quentes (hot springs). Camping facilities are open from May to October. It's a rapidly growing agricultural boom town of 30,000 people and there are four simple hotels.

The stretch of the Rio Araguaia from the town of Aruanã up to Ilha do Bananal is considered one of the best freshwater fishing areas in the world. The region attracts Brazilian holiday-makers during the dry season (June to September) when the receding waters uncover white beaches along the riverbank. Many camp on the banks of the river. During the May to October fishing season, pintado, pirarucu, pacu, tucunaré, suribim and matrinchã are there for the taking.

Organised Tours

If you're serious about fishing and have the money, there are tours, arranged in Brasília and Goiânia (in Goiás state), where you meet a boat-hotel in Aruanã and sail around the island. If you want to explore the river without a tour, catch a boat in Aruanã or Barra do Garças (in Mato Grosso state);

however, a cheaper way to get as far north as Ilha do Bananal is to take a bus up to São Felix do Araguaia (in Mato Grosso state) and hire a boat from there.

Ilha do Bananal

Formed by the splitting of the Rio Araguaia, Ilha do Bananal is the world's largest river island, covering 20,000 sq km. The northern section is the Parque Nacional do Araguaia, but most of the island is an Indian reserve inhabited by Karajás and Javaés Indians. Farmers use the island's lush pastures for grazing their cattle. In 1994 the federal government declared that all trespassers were to vacate the island. Since many of the 900 families have lived on the island for generations, this has caused a lot of ill feeling in the community. At the time of writing, compensation (in the form of relocation) was being arranged. The Indians were becoming impatient with the bureaucracy, and threatening to take their own action.

Much of the island is covered with forest and there is plenty of wildlife, but only birds are visible in abundance. At sunset and sunrise you can reel in all sorts of fish, including dogfish with teeth so large that the Indians used them for shaving. There are tucunaré with colourful moustaches, ferocious tabarana, pirarucu (2m, 100kg monsters) and several other slimy critters. The river also harbours *botos* (freshwater dolphins), jacaré, *soias* (rare, one-eyed fish) and *poraquê* (electric fish).

Peter Fleming describes an excursion in this region in his excellent travelogue *Brazilian Adventure* (see the Books section in the Facts for the Visitor chapter). Fleming's route took him down the Araguaia to São Felix do Araguaia, where his group prepared for an expedition up the Rio Tapirapé in an attempt to discover what had happened to Colonel Fawcett, an English explorer who disappeared there in 1925.

Permission to visit the park can be obtained from IBAMA in Brasília or Palmas (☎ 215-1873, 215-1865). Of course, if you just show up, you may save a lot of time and hassle and get in just the same. There is simple accommodation on the island, but no food.

São Felix do Araguaia

São Felix, with a population of around 8500, is in Mato Grosso state, on the Rio das Mortes. There are a couple of upmarket hotels along the river catering for fishing tours; the cheap option is *Hotel Xavante* (☎ 522-1305) at Avenida Severiano Neves 391. Rooms cost around US$20/30 for singles/doubles. The best restaurant in town in *Botu's* along the river on Avenida Araguaia. It's open for lunch and dinner.

You can arrange boat trips along the river and to Ilha do Bananal with fishermen and locals along the waterfront on Avenida Araguaia. In July, the town may well be flooded with local tourists looking to catch some rays.

Air-taxi companies in Brasiléia fly to São Felix. Contact BASEI or Baú at the airport in Brasiléia. Buses run to São Felix from Barra do Garças in Mato Grosso state and Goiânia in Goiás.

Santa Teresinha

Another access point for Ilha do Bananal is the small town of Santa Teresinha (in Mato Grosso state). A small hotel on the water's edge is popular with foreign naturalists, who use it as a base for visits to the Parque Nacional do Araguaia.

For other accommodation options, see the Places to Stay sections for Lagoa da Confusão earlier in this chapter.

Aruanã

Aruanã, 318km from Goiânia in Goiás state, has camping grounds and several mid-range hotels. Try the *Recanto Sonhado* (☎ 376-1294) at the end of Avenida Altamiro Caio Pacheco or the *Araguaia* (☎ 376-1251) at Praça Couto Magalhães 53. Both places charge around $US30/60 for singles/doubles. The *Columbia* at Rua João Artiaga serves good home-style cooking.

Boat trips along the river can be organised at Avenida Altamiro Caio Pacheco 377.

For fishing trips between May and June and September-October, contact the Associaçao dos Barqueiros de Aruanã on Praça Couto Magalhães. You can apply for a fishing licence at any Banco do Brasil.

It's easier to reach Aruanã from the state of Goiás (Goiânia in particular) than from Mato Grosso. For those without a 4WD vehicle, Aruanã is accessible by bus from Goiânia (310km) and Goiás Velho.

Barra do Garças

The long, dry road to Ilha do Bananal begins 400km west of Goiânia, at Barra do Garças (in Mato Grosso state). Buses leave early in Mato Grosso, in an unsuccessful attempt to beat the heat – the bus from Barra do Garças to São Felix do Araguaia leaves daily at 5 am.

If you don't want to take the bus, air-taxis cover the distance in one hour.

Barreira da Cruz

It's possible to reach the Parque Nacional da Araguaia on Ilha do Bananal from this small fishing village on the margin of Rio Javaés, 52km from Lagoa da Confusão, in Tocantins state.

Amazonas & Roraima

The state of Amazonas covers most of the western Amazonian river basin, an area of over 1.5 million sq km, and is Brazil's largest state. It's possible to travel downstream to Brazil, via the triple frontier, from neighbouring Peru and Colombia. Pico da Neblina (3014m), one of the country's highest peaks, is on Amazonas' northern border with Venezuela. The state of Roraima lies to the north-east, bordering Venezuela and Guyana. The only reliable road link out of Manaus is Hwy BR-174 which cuts the equator, linking the Brazilian Amazon with the Caribbean Sea

Amazonas

Approximately 75% of Amazonas' two million inhabitants live in the metropolis of Manaus or in the much smaller cities of Manacapuru, Itacoatiara, Parintins and Coari.

For more information on the Amazon region, including Amazonas state, see the Facts about the Country chapter (Flora & Fauna; Ecology & Environment; National Parks). For information on getting around the Amazon region, see the introductory section of The North chapter.

Amazonas state is one hour behind Brazilian Standard Time.

MANAUS

• pop 1,160,000 ✉ 69000-000 ☎ 092

Manaus lies beside the Rio Negro – 10km upstream from the confluence of the Solimões and Negro rivers (which join to form the Rio Amazonas). In 1669 the fortress of São José da Barra was built here by Portuguese colonisers, who later named the place 'Manaus' after a tribe of Indians who inhabited the region. The village which grew from the fort was little more than a minor trading outpost populated by traders, black slaves, Indians and soldiers, until the rubber boom pumped up the town.

Although Manaus continues to be vaunted in countless glossy advertising brochures as an 'Amazon wonderland', the city itself has few attractions. The flora and fauna have been systematically despoiled for hundreds of kilometres around the city. Many travellers now only use the city for a brief stopover before making excursions far beyond Manaus, where it is still possible to experience the rainforest wonders that Manaus promises but cannot deliver.

History

In 1839 Charles Goodyear developed the vulcanisation process which made natural rubber durable, and in 1888 John Dunlop patented pneumatic rubber tyres. Soon there was an unquenchable demand for rubber in the recently industrialised USA and Europe, and the price of rubber on international markets soared.

In 1884, the same year that Manaus abolished slavery, a feudal production system was established that locked the *seringueiros* (rubber-tappers) into a cruel serfdom. Driven from the sertão by drought, and lured into the Amazon with the false promise of prosperity, they signed away their freedom to the *seringalistas* (owners of rubber plantations).

The seringalistas sold goods to the seringueiro on credit – fishing line, knives, manioc flour, hammocks – and purchased the seringueiros' balls of latex. The illiteracy of the seringueiros, the brutality of *pistoleiros* (the hired guns of the seringalistas), deliberately rigged scales, and the monopoly of sales and purchases all combined to perpetuate the seringueiro's debt and misery. The seringueiros also had to contend with loneliness, jungle fevers, hostile Indian attacks and all manner of deprivation. Seringueiros who attempted to escape their serfdom were hunted down and tortured by the pistoleiros.

The plantation owners, the rubber traders and the bankers prospered, and built palaces with their wealth. Gentlemen had their shirts sent to London to be laundered, while ladies sported the latest French fashions. Manaus became Brazil's second city after Rio de Janeiro to get electricity, and an opera house was built in the heart of the jungle.

Despite Brazilian efforts to protect their world rubber monopoly, Henry Wickham managed to smuggle rubber seeds out of the Amazon. (For details about this episode, see the History section in the Facts about the Country chapter.) Botanists in Kew Gardens (London) grew the rubber-tree seedlings and exported them to the British colonies of Ceylon and Malaysia, where they were transplanted and cultivated in neat groves. The efficient Asian production was far superior to the haphazard Brazilian techniques, and the Brazilian rubber monopoly eroded. As more Asian rubber was produced, the price of latex on the world market plummeted. By the 1920s the boom was over, and Manaus declined in importance.

During WWII, when Malaysia was occupied by the Japanese, Allied demand created a new rubber boom. The seringueiros became known as the 'rubber soldiers', and 150,000 Nordestinos were once again recruited to gather rubber.

In many ways the international port of Manaus is still the capital of a land far removed from the rest of Brazil, and there has always been a fear of foreign domination of the Amazon. One of the official slogans of the military government of the 1970s was *Integrar para não entregar* (integrate or give it away). As a result, the government has made a determined attempt to consolidate Brazilian control of the Amazon by creating roads through the jungle and colonising the interior. It has also made Manaus an industrial city. In 1967 Brazil established a *zona franca* (free-trade zone) in Manaus, and multinational industries, drawn to the area by tax and tariff benefits, have set up manufacturing plants. Although the Manaus free-trade zone has not spawned Brazilian industry – Brazilian entrepreneurs have not successfully competed with multinationals in the Amazon – the infusion of money has invigorated Manaus. However, since the Brazilian government relaxed restrictions on imports, the Zona Franca has become less effective.

Climate

Manaus is hot and humid. During the rainy season (January to June), count on a brief but hard shower nearly every day – the area gets over 2m of rainfall per year. During the rainy season, temperatures range from 23 to 30°C. Dry-season weather (July to December) is usually between 26 and 37°C. The river level varies 10m to 14m between the high-water level (March to July) and the low-water period (August to February). Manaus is 40.33m above sea level.

Orientation

The city of Manaus lies 3° south of the equator, on the northern bank of the Rio Negro, 10km west of the confluence of the Rio Negro and the Rio Solimões, which form the mighty Rio Amazonas. Iquitos (Peru) and Leticia (Colombia) are 1900km and 1500km upriver, and Santarém and Belém are 700km and 1500km downriver.

The most interesting parts of Manaus as far as the traveller is concerned are close to the waterfront: the Mercado Municipal, the customs house and the floating docks. The opera house is an impressive reminder of Manaus' past opulence.

Maps Refer to the local phone book for maps covering Manaus' outer suburbs. If you are travelling off the beaten track detailed maps of the province (scale 1:250,000; US$10) can be obtained from the military: DIPEQ/Amazonas (☎ 232-0152), Avenida Airão 667.

Information

Tourist Offices FUMTUR (☎ 622-4948; fax 232-7025; fumtur@internext.com.br), Rua Bernardo Ramos 173, is Manaus' municipal tourist office. It has helpful staff (you need some Portuguese here) and various brochures and booklets for sale. A Manaus city guide is US$6. For those particularly interested in buildings and the history of the town, *Caminhando por Manaus* (English and French also) describes several walking tours. It costs US$5. There is an information booth at Praia da Ponta Negra. FUMTUR's Web site is at www.internext.com.br/fumtur.

For information about jungle lodges and operators contact EMAMTUR (☎ 633-2983; fax 233-9973), the state tourism organisation. The office is near the Palaçio Rio Negro, at Avenida 7 de Setembro 1456 and is open Monday to Friday from 7.30 am to 1.30 pm. Both EMAMTUR and FUMTUR also have information booths at Manaus international airport Eduardo Gomes.

For details about national parks in Amazonas, contact IBAMA (☎ 237-3710; fax 237-5177) at Rua Ministro João Gonçalves de Souza, Hwy BR-319, Km 01, Distrito Industrial.

Foreign Consulates Expect a delay of a few weeks for visas for French Guiana as applications are sent to Brasília. Countries represented in Manaus include:

Bolivia
: Avenida Eduardo Ribeiro 520, sala 1410, Centro (☎ 234-6661)

Chile
: Rua Marques de Caravelas Q/B15, casa 8, Parque das Laranjeiras (☎/fax 236-1621)

Colombia
: Rua Dona Libânia 62, Centro (☎ 234-6777; fax 622-6078)

Ecuador
: Rua 6, casa 16, Jardim Belo Horizonte, Parque Dez (☎ 236-3698; fax 622-3679)

France
: Avenida Joaquim Nabuco 1846, Bl A, sala 02, Centro (☎ 233-6583)

Germany
: Rua Barroso 355, 1 Andar, sala A, Centro (☎ 232-0890)

Peru
: Conj. Morada do Sol, Rua KL c/6, Aleixo (☎ 642-1646; fax 642-1089)

UK
: Rua Poraquê 240, Distrito Industrial (☎ 237-7869; fax 237-6437)

USA
: Rua Recife 1010, Adrianópolis (☎ 234-4546; fax 234-4546)

Venezuela
: Rua Ferreira Pena 179, Centro (☎ 233-6004; fax 233-0481)

Money Casa de Câmbio Cortez on Rua Guilherme Moreira and also at Avenida Sete de Setembro 1199, are convenient places to exchange money. They are open weekdays from 9 am to 5.30 pm, and Saturday from 9 am to 12.30 pm. The main branch of Banco do Brasil, Rua Guilherme Moreira 315, is open for exchange weekdays from 9 am to 3 pm. Visa is the most accepted credit card in Manaus, and you can get cash advances from the Banco do Brasil. The American Express representative in Manaus is Selvatur at Praça Adalberto Vale; for American Express cash advances, go to the Banco Economico (on Rua Saldanha Marinho). For MasterCard cash advances try Banorte, at Avenida 7 de Setembro 727.

Post & Communications Manaus has a few postal agencies in the centre. The main post office, on Rua Marechal Deodoro, is

Manaus

0 150 300 m

PLACES TO STAY
3 Hospedaria de Turismo 10 de Julho
4 Taj Mahal Continental Hotel
9 Hotel Imperial
13 Hotel Krystal
22 Best Western
31 Hotel Central
34 Hotel Sol
37 Hotel Rei Salomão
42 Ana Cassia Palace Hotel
43 Hotel Continental
44 Pensao Sulista
46 Hotel Jangada & Hotel Ideal
47 Hotel Dona Joana
50 Hotel Rio Branco

PLACES TO EAT
6 Mandarim
8 Restaurante La Veneza
10 Skina dos Sucos
14 Sorveteria Glacial
20 Restaurant Fiorantina
21 Mister Pizza
24 O Naturalista
33 Churrascaria Búfalo
35 Big Frango
45 Você Decide
49 Galo Carijó

OTHER
1 Porto de São Raimundo (Low Water Port)
2 Bar do Armando
5 Teatro Amazonas (Opera House)
7 Colombian Consulate
11 Fumtur (Municipal Tourist Office)
12 Biblioteca
15 Casa de Cambio Cortez
16 Museu do Homem do Norte
17 Palácio Rio Negro
18 Emamtur (State Tourist Office)
19 Praça da Policia (Praça Roosevelt)
23 Banco do Brasil
25 Praça da Matriz; Cathedral
26 Museu do Porto
27 Local Bus Station
28 Relógio Municipal (Town Clock)
29 Post Office
30 Teleamazon (National Calls)
32 Bus to Hotel Tropical & Praia da Ponta Negra
36 Choparia São Marcos
38 Rodomar; Porto Flutuante
39 British Customs House (Alfândega)
40 Praça Adalberto Vale & Artíndia
41 Selvatur
48 Arts Centre Chiminé
51 Mercado Municipal; Escadaria dos Remedios Port
52 Educandos Port Area

open Monday to Saturday from 8 am to 6 pm and Sunday from 8 am to 2 pm. For international calls go to Teleamazon, Avenida Getúlio Vargas 950, which is open daily from 8 am to 11 pm. National calls can also be made at the Teleamazon office on Rua Guilherme Moreira.

Emergency Emergency numbers include: Police (☎ 190) and Ambulance (☎ 192).

Dangers & Annoyances Theft at rock-bottom hotels is common – duplicate keys are sometimes used to gain access to your room. When travelling by boat, watch your gear very carefully. Taxi drivers in Manaus are expensive and have a poor reputation: avoid them whenever possible! Watch out for blatant rip-off attempts: spurious 'extra charges', slack use of meters and cosy 'deals' whereby hotel clerks are paid a fat commission by taxi drivers who are willing to pay for the privilege of being able to rip off foreign tourists.

After 11 pm it's best to avoid some places such as the port area, Praça Pedro II and Praça da Matriz.

For more tips, see the security advice in the Dangers & Annoyances section of the Facts for the Visitor chapter.

Teatro Amazonas

Teatro Amazonas, the famous opera house of Manaus, was designed by Doménico de Angelis in eclectic neoclassical style at the height of the rubber boom, in 1896. The materials and artists were imported from Europe, and more than any other building associated with the administration of Mayor Eduardo Ribeiro, this opera house is symbolic of the opulence that was Manaus. It's open daily from 9 am to 4 pm. Admission costs US$5 and includes a compulsory guided tour. Opera and ballet performances

Meeting of the Waters

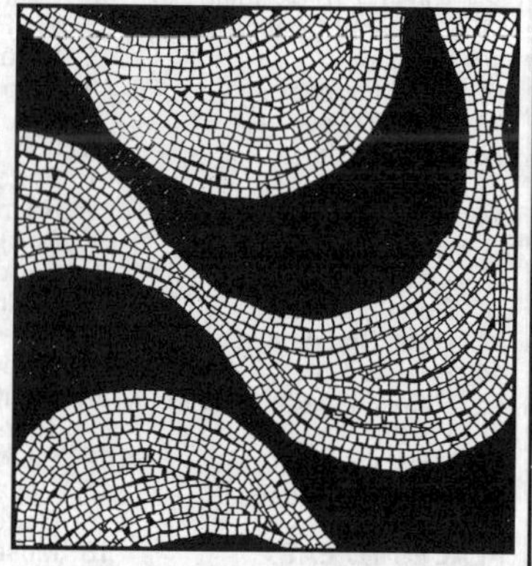

Take note of the curvaceous design of the pavement of the Praça São Sebastião, the plaza in front of Teatro Amazonas. The black and white stone mosaic is a traditional Portuguese effect, but the flowing pattern is said to be symbolic of the Meeting of the Waters: of the black Rio Negro and the light-coloured Rio Solimões.

Rio de Janeiro's famous Copacabana beachfront promenades, designed by landscape architect Roberto Burle Marx in the late 1960s, were inspired by this design. He chose the fluid serpentine pattern to echo the waves breaking on the shore. The motif was also used in his huge rectangular garden near Rio's Museum of Modern Art in Flamengo Park, where the lawn is planted in alternating colours of grass.

Leonardo Pinheiro & Robyn Jones

are held here throughout the year. Ask the guide about the schedule or check the entertainment section in the local newspaper.

British Customs House & the Porto Flutuante

The British customs house (alfândega) dates back to 1906. It was imported from the UK in prefabricated blocks. The Porto Flutuante (floating docks), also installed in 1906, were considered a technical marvel because of their ability to rise and fall as the water level of the river changed with the seasons (10m to 14m). It's quite a scene and well worth a visit – you can watch the boats being loaded with produce, and the swarms of people using river transport.

Mercado Municipal

The imposing cast-iron structure of the Mercado Municipal was designed in 1882 by Adolfo Lisboa after the Parisian Les Halles. Although the Art-Nouveau ironwork was imported from Europe, the place has acquired Amazonian character. In and around the market, you can purchase provisions for jungle trips: strange fruits, old vegetables, several varieties of biscuits, sacks of beans and rice, lanterns, rope, straw hats, perhaps some powders and incense. Most food produce however, is now sold at the new market further along the waterfront.

At the back end of the mercado, there's a grimy cafeteria where you can have lunch and contemplate Manaus' complete ignorance regarding sanitation. The water which keeps enormous fish and fly-covered meats cool, drains from the stalls, mingles with meat, fish and urine, flows underfoot, runs off into the river and mixes with discarded meats and produce and all the sewage of Manaus. Vultures swarm around the refuse and roost in the rusty ironwork of the cafeteria. Take the tables at either end for the best view.

Palácio Rio Negro

This imposing colonial building was built last century as a home for an eccentric German rubber baron, Waldemar Scholz. It was bought by the state in 1918 and named Palácio Rio Negro to serve as the government seat. The building has recently been restored and now serves as an interesting cultural centre with space for music and art exhibitions, a bookshop, video room, handicraft shop and coffee shop. The restaurant here is open Thursday to Saturday and there are often music performances on Sunday afternoons. The Palácio Rio Negro (☎ 622-2840), Avenida 7 de Setembro 1546, is beside the bridge over Igarapé do Manaus.

Arts Centre Chaminé

This old water-treatment plant off Rua Isabel, facing the Igarapé dos Educandos, has been converted into an art gallery (☎ 234-7877). It often has some interesting art exhibitions and is open daily from 9 am to 6 pm.

Museu do Homem do Norte

The Museum of Northern Man (☎ 232-5373), at Avenida 7 de Setembro 1385, is an ethnology and anthropology museum dedicated to the lifestyle of the river-dwelling Caboclos. It has an interesting display of Indian weapons, including the vicious *furador de olhos* (eye piercer). It's open Monday to Thursday from 9 am to noon and 1 to 5 pm, and Friday from 1 to 5 pm. Admission is US$1, free for students.

Museu do Índio

This museum (☎ 234-1422), run by the Salesian nuns, has displays of ceramics, featherwork, weaving, hunting and ritual objects of the Indian tribes of the upper Rio Negro and Rio Amazonas, where the nuns operate as missionaries. Bad luck though if you can't read Portuguese! There is also a small shop which sells Indian handicrafts. The museum is open weekdays from 8.30 to 11.30 am and 2 to 4.30 pm, and Saturday from 8.30 to 11.30 am. Admission is US$2.50. The museum is at Avenida Duque de Caxias 356. It's a bit of a walk from the centre along Avenida 7 de Setembro, but there are a few interesting examples of rubber-boom architecture and views from the bridges of the precarious and resourceful houses on stilts along the river inlets.

Museu de Ciencias Naturais da Amazônia

Operated by the Associação Naturalista da Amazonia, this natural-science museum (☎ 644-2799), at Estrada Belém, Colônia Cachoeira Grande, has an comprehensive exhibit of fish, insects and butterflies from the Amazon region, with descriptions in English and Japanese. The aquarium has 2m long pirarucú fish. The museum shop sells Indian crafts. Open Tuesday to Sunday from 9 am to 5 pm, the museum is somewhat out of the way, but it's worth the trip. Take the São José bus to INPA, then catch a taxi.

Instituto Nacional de Pesquisa da Amazônia (INPA) & Bosque da Ciência

This research institute manages natural reserves and experimental areas in the jungle. One of their many projects is a joint study with the Smithsonian Institute to determine the 'minimal critical size of ecosystems' – the smallest chunk of land that can support a self-sustaining jungle forest and all its attendant creatures. Various-sized parcels of jungle are studied, first in their virgin state, then later, after the surrounding land has been cleared to create islands of jungle. Changes in plant and animal populations are carefully scrutinised. Results are suggesting that the complex interdependence of plants and animals and the heterogeneity of species pose a barrier to maintaining an isolated patch of jungle.

INPA scientists are also studying *jacaré* (yacare caiman), freshwater manatee, river otter and porpoises. These animals are on display in the botanical garden and zoo, the Bosque da Ciência. The garden has samples of medicinal plants and raised walkways through tree canopies. Avoid feeding time at the jacaré enclosure if you don't want to see live mice sacrificed.

The Casa da Ciência has a permanent exhibition of the institute's activities, including other INPA projects such as: the environmental impact of deforestation and of hydroelectric dams; mercury poisoning of the rivers by gold mining; kit housing for impoverished locals; stingless bees; and the study of medicinal orchids and bromeliads. There is a giant leaf on display, measuring about 2m high. The Bosque da Ciência is open Tuesday to Friday from 9 am to noon and 2 to 4 pm; Saturday and Sunday from 9 am to 4 pm. Admission is US$4.

INPA (☎ 643-3300; fax 643-3095; inpa@inpa.gov.br; www.inpa.gov.br), Alameda Cosme Ferreira 1756, Km 4 Bairro Aleixo, is open Monday to Friday from 8 am to noon and 2 to 6 pm. Call ahead (☎ 643-3135) to find out the topic (and language) of Tuesday's seminar series. To reach INPA, either take the bus marked São José from the city centre or use a taxi.

Parque Municipal do Mindu

Mindu Municipal Park (☎/fax 236-7702), Avenida Perimetral, Parque 10, occupies 33 hectares of forest within the urban area of Manaus. The area is considered one of the last refuges of the pied bare-face tamarin, a monkey threatened with extinction. The park has trails and elevated walkways, herb and orchid gardens, a library, and a cute amphitheatre which serves as a venue for outdoor shows. Admission is US$2. Take the bus Parque Dez from the centre.

Amazon Ecopark & Amazon Monkey Jungle

The Amazon Ecopark, a private nature reserve with a tourist centre, is half an hour by boat from Manaus. The park runs survival courses in the tropical rainforest, with a local rainforest ranger. Next to the Ecopark is the Amazon Monkey Jungle, set up by the Living Rainforest Foundation for the rehabilitation of orphan animals. For information about tours, contact the Amazon Ecopark office (☎/fax 234-0939), Praça Auxiliadora 04, grupo 103, Centro, Manaus.

Praia da Ponta Negra

This strip of river beach on the outskirts of Manaus, with its many restaurants and bars, is a popular weekend hang-out. The best time to go is between September and December (and sometimes as early as July), when the waters recede, and locals sunbake or play soccer on the beach. After March the high waters flood the sand and cleanse the beach for the following season. From the city centre, take the bus marked Praia da Ponta Negra (US$0.70, 30 minutes). A more expensive (but quicker) option to reach Ponta Negra is the Tropical Hotel shuttle bus. See the Getting Around section for details. On the was you will see the contrast of *favelas* with fenced residential compounds, and the beginnings of high-rise, beachfront development.

Encontro das Águas

An interesting phenomenon is the Encontro das Águas (meeting of the waters), the point where the inky-black waters of the Rio Negro meet the clay-yellow waters of the Rio Solimões. It's not absolutely necessary to take a tour – it can be seen just as well from the *balsa* (ferry) which shuttles between Carreiro and the Porto Velho highway (BR-319). If you do include the meeting of the waters in your tour, you may lose time that could be better spent exploring the more interesting sights further along the rivers.

Jungle Tours

The top priority for most foreign visitors to Manaus is a jungle tour. From here, it's possible to arrange anything from standard day trips and overnight excursions to months of travel in the hinterland.

It is common for travellers to be greeted at the airport by a tour-agency representative keen to sign them up for trips. These representatives can be useful sources of information, and may even offer transport into the city centre to a budget hotel, from which they gain a commission. It's best to take the local bus to the city and hold off booking a tour until you've had time to shop around for the right deal. There are dozens of agencies vying for your custom, with trendy names ('Eco' and 'Green' have quickly become standard prefixes) and glossy brochures, touting all sorts of encounters with wildlife and Indians just a few kilometres from the city.

GUY MOBERLY

ROBYN JONES

ROBYN JONES

Top: Fish at Manaus market
Bottom Left: Favela, Manaus
Bottom Right: Loading bananas, Manaus

LEONARDO PINHEIRO

JOHN MAIER, JR

GUY MOBERLY

Top Left: Small boats, Porto Flutuante, Manaus
Top Right: Amazon girl
Bottom: Amazon tributary

What you *can* expect on day trips or tours by boat lasting three or four days is a close-up experience of the jungle flora, with abundant bird life and a few jacaré (more easily located at night by guides using powerful torches) and, if you're lucky, porpoises. It is also a chance to see what life is like for the Caboclos in the vicinity of Manaus.

You *cannot* expect to meet remote Indian tribes or dozens of free-ranging beasts, because the former have sensibly fled from contact (after centuries of annihilation or forced assimilation) and the latter have been systematically hunted to the brink of extinction. In both cases, access has become synonymous with destruction.

This does not mean that the tours are not worthwhile, merely that prospective tour participants should ignore flowery propaganda and instead ask the tour operators for exact details. Does the tour include extended travel in small boats (without use of motor) along *igarapés*? How much time is spent getting to and from your destination? What is the cost breakdown (food, drinks, lodging, fuel and guides)? You may want to pay some of these expenses en route, thereby avoiding fanciful mark-ups, and should insist on paying only a portion of the costs at the beginning of the trip, settling the rest at the end. This payment schedule helps to maintain the interest of tour operators and guides in defining and abiding by a tour schedule. It also provides some leverage if promises are not kept.

If you are trying out jungle tours for the first time and intending to do extended trips in the Amazon region, it's useful to take a short trip from Manaus as a taster. This will allow you to assess the idea in practice and give you the confidence to do longer trips either from Manaus or from other parts of the Amazon. The latter option is becoming increasingly popular among travellers disenchanted with Manaus.

We have received lots of enthusiastic letters from readers who thoroughly enjoyed their tours, and just as many complaint letters from readers who felt the tours were a complete rip-off (see the boxed text 'Jungle Trips – Readers' Experiences' in this chapter).

What you get out of your trip depends on several factors: expectations, experience, the competence and breadth of knowledge of tour operators and guides, and the ability to accept life in the Amazon at face value – one enterprising tour operator advertises 'Selva sem Sofrimento' (the Jungle without Suffering!). Although the 'jungle' is often described in exaggerated terms as a 'Green Hell', it seems rather odd to want to turn a jungle tour into a luxury outing with all mod cons, thereby distancing yourself from the 'wild' characteristics that are the hallmark of such an experience.

Larger Operators Organised tours cost US$85 to $200 per person per day. These tours usually use larger boats than those of the independent operators – too big to negotiate the narrow igarapés where the wildlife roams – though they may include canoe trips. There are advantages to the organised tours; they are relatively hassle-free, there is nothing to arrange and English-speaking guides are often available. A 'Meeting of the Waters' day tour is a standard excursion, which often includes en route igarapé sighting, a visit to Lago Januário reserve (15km from Manaus), a jungle walk to see lily pads, a motorised canoe ride to *igapós* and lunch. A three day (two night) trip to Lago Mamori is good when the waters are high, when boats can float through the tree tops. A longer tour is to head 100km up the Rio Negro to the Arquipélago das Anavilhanas (best between July and December).

Travel agencies which organise excursions for large tour groups include Fontur (☎ 658-3052; fax 658-3512), Hotel Tropical, Estrada da Ponta Negra, Km 18; and Selvatur (☎ 622-2088; fax 622-2177), Praça Adalberto Valle.

Smaller Operators If you speak Portuguese and don't mind travelling a bit rough, there are plenty of smaller operators and freelance guides offering tours. If they are registered with EMAMTUR you may

The Amazon Circuit

It seems odd that in the millions of sq km that make up the Amazon, everyone seems to congregate upon such a small spot during the pre-Carnaval season, but Lago Janauário draws hordes of visitors at this time of year. One thing that cheapens the jungle experience here is the feeling of being pumped through a tourist circuit: everyone bangs on the flying buttresses of the same sambaiaba tree, cuts the same rubber tree for latex sap, then pulls over to an authentic jungle house where a monkey, a sloth, a snake and a jacaré are tied up to amuse visitors.

After a quick bite at a jungle restaurant, take the elevated walk to the Vitória Regia water lilies, beyond the make-believe Indian craft stalls (10 stores operated by one athletic Indian, who follows alongside the group and pushes feathered novelty-shop junk). At this point, one disregards the water lilies and the Kodak boxes floating alongside and compares notes with one's neighbour about respective tour costs, boat sizes and whether or not a flush toilet has been provided.

The water lilies, 1m floating rimmed dishes adorned with flowers above and protected by sharp spikes below, are lovely, despite it all.

Robyn Jones & Leonardo Pinhiero

have more recourse if you have any complaints. It is quite possible to end up feeling totally confused as you sift through the countless brochures.

Often the choice simply comes down to luck. We met one group who had spent three whole days pondering which trip to take. Then on their carefully chosen tour, they spent a sleepless night in hammocks camped across an ant path, several ended up with mild food poisoning and the inebriated guide became a little too flirtatious. Try to meet the actual guide prior to committing to a trip.

It takes time to hammer out a deal, change money, arrange supplies and buy provisions – allow at least a day for this. When serious haggling is called for, ask the tour operator to itemise expenses. Disproportionately inflated estimates can work in your favour. If the food budget seems unreasonable, buy provisions at the Mercado Municipal. If the fuel budget seems too high, offer to pay at the floating gas stations. Subtract the items from your original quote. As a rough rule of thumb, expect prices to start at about US$80 per person per day (not much cheaper than the larger operators), for two people on a two day (one night) trip, including boat transport, guide, food and hammock lodging. If you are solo, try to join a group to make the trip more economical. In the low season, a lack of travellers can be a problem.

Remind your guide to bring fishing gear, straps and cords (to suspend packs), and of course cachaça, sugar and lemons for *caipirinhas* at the end of the day. Shop for food with your guide so that you can inflict your tastes on them, rather than vice versa. Don't scrimp on water – carry at least four litres of bottled water per person per day. It's nice to have two styrofoam coolers on board, one to keep perishables from spoiling and the second to keep valuables dry when the weather becomes wet and wild. Last, but definitely not least, insist on life jackets.

Swallows and Amazons (☎/fax 622-1246), Rua Quintino Bocaiuva 189, Andar 1, Sala 13, is a reliable small operator. It offers various trips including camping or accommodation at its Over Look Lodge.

Amazonas Indian Turismo (☎ 233-3104), Rua dos Andrades 335, has been recommended. It takes trips up the Rio Urubu, staying overnight in rustic cabanas. Christophor Gomes (☎ 645-4101) is a good person to talk to about jungle trips. He books trips with two guides, Gerry Hardy and Elmo de Morais Lopes. He can also be contacted through the Hotel Rio Branco (☎ 233-4019).

Moaçir Fortes (☎ 671-2866) speaks English, and operates his own boat from the Porto Flutuante. He runs a small, first class operation, charging US$80 to $100 per person per day, depending on the number of passengers on board (a maximum of 14, minimum of four). Everyone sleeps in a clean cabin that has hot showers. The boat is fitted out with canoes and a small outboard, and has a well-stocked bar, a library full of wildlife guidebooks, binoculars and even a telescope on board.

The canoe guides have their own association, Associação dos Canoeiros (☎ 238-8880). While a trip with one of their members may be less predictable than the organised tours, it may be more authentic. Usually you stay with Caboclo families from the surrounding river settlements. Ask at the Porto Flutuante for Bacuri or Samuel. A trip to the Encontro das Águas (minimum four people) will cost US$20 per person. Overnight jungle trips

Jungle Trips: Readers' Experiences

You are clearly warned that in Manaus you won't see wild Indios running around. Although our indio guide, on showing us how to get up a tree was busy not to loose his pager, it was still a strong experience hard to get into the brain of an Irian-Jaya-experienced traveller.

Rainer Knyrim, Austria

I made an eight day jungle tour. I bargained and paid US$525 including all food, water and accommodation. My guide, Luiz Alberto Motta (☎ 651-1028), was the best you could ever find, even if he only spoke Portuguese. We bought food for the trip in the market. We went by boat for seven hours on the Rio Solimões and after that about three hours by small canoe which was our vehicle for the rest of the week. We stayed with Caboclo families in their small wood houses and slept in hammocks.

We saw a lot of animals for example: monkeys; crocodiles; anacondas; armadillos; pink river dolphins; manatees; big green lizards; sloths; birds like toucans, hawks, parrots and hummingbirds. I was lucky to see all these animals, but somebody told me if I wanted to see animals to follow Rio Solimões and if I wanted to see flowers to follow Rio Negro.

Helena Ahlund, Sweden

We were told it's a must to go on a jungle tour if you visit Manaus. Unfortunately it was very disappointing. We didn't see many animals on our two day tour and it was also very expensive, especially if you compare it to Ecuador where you can go on similar tours. The one day tour is not good: you spend 10 hours on the boat!

Going on a canoe trip is one way of getting out of the claws of the tour operators. Buy all food and equipment in Manaus. Get decent maps from the office of the military.

Buying a canoe for two persons was impossible. Small one-person canoes (US$50) were available in Barcelos. We ended up renting one for US$30 a week. We had a great time, went into the flooded forest, camped in hammocks over the water and watched river dolphins. The crocodiles found our canoe quite interesting! The river was still near its highest level in July. Don't forget a mosquito net that is designed for use over a hammock. They are available in Manaus.

Burkhard Militzer, USA

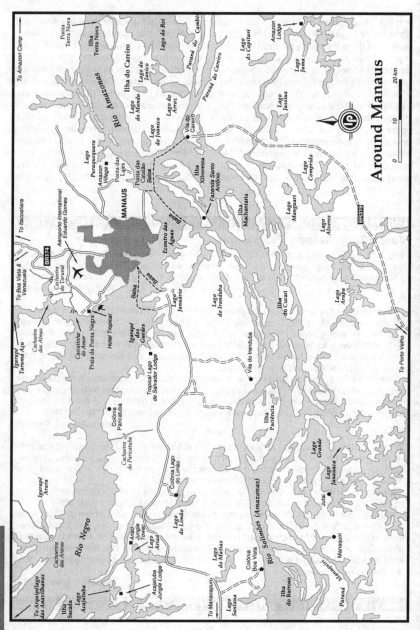

Around Manaus

involving transport by boat will cost US$40 to $80 per day; and by bus, you may negotiate as low as US$30 to $40 per day.

Jungle Tours The upmarket packaged tours based at the many jungle lodges can be a good option for a comfortable, safe and not-too-adventurous way to experience the Amazon jungle environment. Most packages include the standard jacaré-spotting, piranha-fishing, canoeing and visits to a Caboclo house. Prices average US$300 to $400 for a three day package. There is usually a surcharge for singles. See Places to Stay – Jungle Lodges for more information.

Special Events

A folklore festival held during the second half of June coincides with a number of saints' days and culminates in the Procissão Fluvial de São Pedro (São Pedro River Procession) when hundreds of regional boats parade on the river before Manaus to honour São Pedro, the patron saint of fishermen.

During the month of June, Manaus has a variety of regional folklore performances, including the party of the *bumbás* (stylised bulls), tribal dances and square dances. It represents a mixture of indigenous Amazonian culture with influences from the Northeastern and Portuguese cultures.

Places to Stay – Jungle Lodges

Manaus' largest jungle lodge, *Ariaú Jungle Tower*, on Lago do Ariaú near the Arquipélago das Anavilhanas, is three hours by boat from Manaus up the Rio Negro. The complex for up to 300 guests has towers linked by walkways through the treetops, a 50m high observatory, a convention centre and helipad. An all-inclusive three day package starts at US$312 or US$370 for the *Tarzan House*. A day trip to the hotel with lunch is US$90. Rio Amazonas Turismo (☎ 234-7308; fax 233-5615) Rua Silva Ramos 20, can arrange bookings.

In contrast, *Amazon Lodge*, a cute small-scale floating lodge on Lago Juma, caters for a mere 28 guests. It is about five hours by ferry, bus and speedboat from Manaus. A three day package costs US$414 per person. *King's Island Lodge* is 1600km from Manaus, in São Gabriel da Cachoeira, close to the frontiers with Venezuela and Colombia. It was closed for renovation in 1998. A six day (minimum) package costs around US$900; the cost of the trip from Manaus (five to six days by boat or three hours by air) is not included. You can make reservations for both of these lodges through Nature Safaris in Manaus (☎ 622-4144; fax 622-1420) or Rio (☎/fax (021) 502-2208).

Amazon Village, on the edge of Lago Puraquequara, is two hours by boat from Manaus. It is within the municipality of Manaus, a bit too close to civilisation. Reserve through Grand Amazon Turismo (☎ 633-1444; fax 633-3217).

A three day package at the *Acajatuba Jungle Lodge*, Lago Acajatuba, 60km (four hours by boat) north-west of Manaus, costs US$290. Reserve through Anaconda Turismo (☎/fax 233-7642) or Ecotéis (☎/fax 233-7642) Rua Doutor Alminio 36.

Pousada dos Guanavenas is on Ilha de Silves, 300km east of Manaus (about five hours by car). Make reservations through Guanavenas Turismo (☎ 656-3656; fax 656-5027), at Rua Constantino Nery 2486.

The *Tropical Lago de Salvador* is a small hotel on Igarapé dos Guedes, about 30km from Manaus – a 35 minute boat trip from the Hotel Tropical at Ponta Negra (see Places to Stay – Top End). Book through Amazonia Expeditions (☎/fax 671-2731), Hotel Tropical.

Places to Stay – Budget

As in most of Brazil, since the introduction of the Plano Real, accommodation prices have increased. However, there's still plenty of cheap lodging in Manaus, ranging from grungy to decent. A reader wrote 'if you want to save some money the observation deck at the airport is a great place to lay out a sleeping bag and spend the night before an early morning flight'.

The *Hotel Rio Branco* (☎ 233-4019), Rua dos Andradas 484, is a good budget option. Single beds in the dormitory rooms cost

US$7.50/10 for fan/air-conditioning. Apartamentos with fan cost US$9/15 for singles/doubles, while apartamentos with air-conditioning are US$15/20. A 15% discount is given for payment in advance. Prices include a simple breakfast. At the *Hotel Ideal* (☎ 233-9423) just across the road, you'll pay US$12/18 for single/double apartamentos with fan (US$18/29 with air-conditioning). The *Pensão Sulista* (☎ 234-5814), Avenida Joaquim Nabuco 347, is also recommended. It has clean quartos with fan and shared bath for US$10/15 a single/double, while doubles with bathroom, air-conditioning, and TV are US$25. Rooms upstairs are better, downstairs rooms are small with no windows. Breakfast is included and there are washing tubs and clotheslines for your laundry.

The *Hotel Jangada* (☎ 232-2248), a few doors up from Hotel Ideal on Rua dos Andradas, offers basic dormitory beds with fan for US$9 and double rooms for US$15. There are other cheapies nearby on Rua José Paranaguá. Most of them double as short-stay hotels. *Hotel Sol* (☎ 232-8165), Rua Josè Paranaguá, should be OK and offers rooms for US$10.

At the *Hotel Dona Joana* (☎ 233-7553), Rua dos Andradas 553, double apartamentos (with air-conditioning) start at around US$20, and the suite with TV and fridge costs US$27. The rooms at the top have good views across the river. Patrons of the rooftop restaurant are able to wander through the hotel, so don't expect much security.

The *Hotel Continental* (☎ 233-3342), at Rua Coronel Sergio Pessoa 198 (Praça dos Remédios), has air-conditioned apartamentos for US$25/33, some with good views.

The *Hospedaria de Turismo 10 de Julho* (☎ 232-6280; fax 232-9416), Rua 10 De Julho 679, is recommended. It's in a convenient location near the opera house, and has value single/double apartamentos with air-conditioning and breakfast for US$20/25.

Places to Stay – Mid-Range

There is a significant difference in quality between the top and mid-range hotels, many of which appear to cater to Brazilians making a flying visit to Manaus to shop like crazy for duty-free goods. Check your rooms for working air-conditioners and showers before paying, and always check whether there is any discount available. Most places have a 10% service charge. The mid-range hotels in the centre are mostly clustered along Rua Dr Moreira within the Zona Franca, where it is hectic during the day and dead at night.

The *Hotel Rei Salomão* (☎ 234-7374; fax 633-2180), Rua Dr Moreira 119, has single/double apartamentos for US$43/53. The *Hotel Central* (☎ 622-2600; fax 622-2609) at Rua Dr Moreira 202 offers apartamentos for US$55/66. The *Ana Cassia Palace Hotel* (☎ 622-3637; fax 622-4812), Rua dos Andradas 14, has apartamentos at US$99/132. Discounts are available for cash payment. *Hotel Krystal* (☎ 233-7305; fax 633-3393), opposite the library at Rua Barroso 54, is in a better location. It has clean apartamentos for US$66/82. The *Imperial Hotel* (☎ 622-3112; fax 622-4857), Avenida Getúlio Vargas 227, has apartamentos for US$88/99 with just breakfast or US$120/130 including lunch and dinner.

Places to Stay – Top End

For details about jungle tours and package tours based on upmarket jungle lodges, pousadas and safari camps, refer to the Jungle Lodges section in this chapter.

The *Taj Mahal Continental Hotel* (☎/fax 633-1010), Avenida Getúlio Vargas 741, offers high-rise apartments and a view of the opera house for US$126/140 a single/double. The *Best Western* (☎ 622-2844; fax 622-2576), Rua Marcílio Dias 215, in the Zona Franca, offers single/double apartamentos for US$137/159.

The 601 room *Hotel Tropical* (☎ 658-5000; fax 658-5026), Manaus' premier luxury hotel, is a self-contained resort 16km out of Manaus, at Ponta Negra. Singles/doubles start at US$231/266, and suites are available from US$532. It belongs to Varig's chain of hotels, so Varig passengers can get a 30% discount.

Even if you don't stay here, you may want to visit this huge complex, which has a well-arranged mini-zoo, a superb giant pool with waves, a coffee shop, and a staff of 1000 to keep guests happy.

The hotel also provides a shuttle service to and from the centre of Manaus (see the Getting Around section for details).

Places to Eat

Before taking a long riverboat ride or foray into the jungle, you should splurge on a few good meals in Manaus. The local fish specialities are tucunaré, tambaqui, dourada and pirarucu, served grilled (na brasa), pickled (escabeche) or stewed (caldeirada). Locals recommend the *Paramazon Restaurant* (☎ 233-6374), at Rua Santa Isabel 1176, Cachoeirinha, for good regional dishes. More conveniently located and also recommended for fish (US$5 to $8) is *Galo Carijó*, opposite the Hotel Dona Joana on Rua dos Andradas. The restaurant is favoured by locals, who drop in for uma cerveja estupidamente gelada (an idiotically cold beer). If you are visiting Praia da Ponta Negra try *Restaurante Brazeiro*, Estrada da Ponta Negra 112.

Restaurante Fiorentina (☎ 232-1295), Praça da Polícia 44, has Manaus' best pizza and pasta dishes. Lunch here is pricey at US$15/kg, but the quality is good. Pasta is normally around US$9, but there is a 30% discount on Sunday. For somewhere more low-key try *Mister Pizza*, a few doors away also on Praça da Polícia, or *Restaurante La Veneza*, Avenida Getúlio Vargas 257. *Mandarim*, Avenida Eduardo Ribeiro 650, serves reasonable Chinese style dishes for around US$6. The *Taj Mahal Continental Hotel* has an international menu and a disconcertingly squeaky revolving restaurant which overlooks the opera house.

Churrascaria Búfalo, Avenida Joaquim Nabuco 628, is a decidedly non-vegetarian place; in addition to serving massive steaks, it has an interesting buffet lunch for US$11/kg.

Avenida Joaquim Nabuco also has several cheap eateries. The *Big Frango* (on the corner of Rua José Paranagua) offers serves of barbecue chicken, pork or beef for around US$3 and *Você Decide*, opposite Pensão Sulista has prato feito for the same price and good-value soup for US$1. Vegetarians should head for *O Naturalista* upstairs at Avenida Sete de Setembro 752. It offers good vegetarian food for US$10/kg.

Adventurous palates will venture to the street stalls and sample tacacá, a gummy soup made from lethal-if-not-well-boiled manioc root, lip-numbing jambu leaves and relatively innocuous dried shrimp. The best tacacá stall in town is on Avenida Getúlio Vargas, next to the Hotel Imperial. Tip: tacacá sem goma (without the gooey stuff) is less off-putting.

For dessert, there's always strange fruit to taste, including pupunha, bacaba and buriti. *Sorveteria Glacial* are the most popular ice-cream parlours in town. There are two on opposite sides of Avenida Getúlio Vargas at the intersection of Rua H Martins; one sells por quilo which is a good way to taste a bit of each flavour. Since your body will be craving liquids, try *Skina dos Sucos* on Avenida Eduardo Ribeiro, diagonally opposite Mandarin restaurant. It has great juices of those exotic fruits (US$2 for a large glass). Try guaraná, acerola, cupuaçú or graviola.

Entertainment

Bars and restaurants lie along Avenida Eduardo Ribeiro, Avenida 7 de Setembro and Avenida Getúlio Vargas. *Bar do Armando* on Rua 10 de Julho near the opera house, is known for its ice-cold beer and is a traditional rendezvous for Manaus' intellectual types; it's open from noon to midnight. *Choparia São Marcos*, on the noisy corner of Rua Floriano Peixoto and Rua Quintino Bocaiúva, is another traditional bar recommended for the best chopp and bolinhos de bacahau (fish balls) in town. It's open from 8 am to 8 pm. *Você Decide* is an open-air bar on Avenida Joaquim Nabuco opposite Pensão Sulista which can get a bit sleazy late at night but is popular with travellers.

The dancing establishments are all clustered in the Cachoeirinha district, north-east of the centre. *Nostalgia* (☎ 233-9460), at Avenida Ajuricaba 800, is a hot spot for forró.

There is a small cinema on Avenida 10 de Julho and six cinemas at Amazonas Shopping (take a bus from the centre).

Things to Buy

The best place to buy Indian crafts is Artíndia (☎/fax 232-4890), at Praça Adalberto Vale, housed in the Pavilhão Universal, a prefabricated cast-iron building built by the English during the rubber boom period. It is open weekdays from 7.30 am to noon and 1.30 to 5 pm, Saturdays 7.30 am to noon. The shop at the Museu do Indio sells crafts of the Wai-wai and Tikuna tribes. It is open weekdays from 8.30 to 11.30 am and 2.30 to 5 pm, and Saturdays from 8.30 to 11.30 am. The shop at the Paláçio Rio Negro also sells Indian crafts.

There are many souvenir shops near the Opera House, including Artesanato da Amazônia, at Rua José Clemente 500. For hammocks try Casa das Redes on Rua Floriano Peixoto or the street vendors around Praça Adalberto Vale. For some local music, try the group *Carrapicho*.

Getting There & Away

Air The Aeroporto Internacional Eduardo Gomes (☎ 652-1337) is on Avenida Santos Dumont, 14km north of the city centre.

From Manaus, it's a five hour flight to Miami with Lloyd Aereo Boliviano (LAB) or Varig, and a four hour flight to Rio de Janeiro. There are international flights to Caracas (Venezuela), Iquitos (Peru), Georgetown (Guyana), Bogotá (Colombia) and La Paz (Bolivia). In general, it's cheaper to purchase the ticket abroad and have it sent to Brazil by registered mail.

Varig, VASP and Transbrasil serve all major cities in Brazil, and air-taxis such as Meta, Tavaj and Rico fly to smaller Amazonian settlements. Varig has regular flights to Tabatinga (see Getting There & Away for the Triple Frontier later in this chapter). Varig (☎ 622-3090) is at Rua Marcílio Dias 284; VASP (☎ 622 3470) is at Avenida 7 de Setembro 993; and Transbrasil (☎ 622-3738) is nearby, at Rua Guilherme Moreira 150.

Bus The rodoviária (☎ 236-2732) is 7km north of the town centre at the junction of Rua Recife and Avenida Constantino Nery. Phone for information on road conditions. All road travel from Manaus involves ferry transport.

Overland travel southwards from Manaus to Porto Velho on Hwy BR-319 has been suspended since 1991. River travel along the Rio Madeira is an alternative.

Hwy BR-174, the 770km road north from Manaus to Boa Vista, crosses the equator, which means that travellers must contend with two rainy seasons. However, most of it is now sealed. União Cascavel buses (☎ 236-3409) depart three times daily (US$63, about 13 hours).

There are regular buses to the townships of Manacapuru, 85km south-west of Manaus (US$6.50, 2½ hours) and Presidente Figueiredo, 128km north of Manaus on the way to Boa Vista (US$7). Presidente Figueiredo has various waterfalls, caves and grottoes which are worth visiting. Both towns have a couple of hotels.

Boat Three major ports in Manaus function according to high and low-water levels. Bairro Educandos is the port for sailing to Porto Velho. For sailing as far as Caracaraí, on the Rio Branco via the Rio Negro, the requisite high-water port is Ponte de São Raimundo; during low water, the port is Bairro de São Raimundo, about 2.5km away. The Porto Flutuante serves mainstream Amazon destinations – Belém, Santarém, Tefé and Benjamin Constant – and is the port used by ENASA.

For information, go to the Porto Flutuante entrance opposite the Praça da Matriz, where the various boat companies display destinations and fares and have booths for ticket sales. The local newspaper *Jornal do Comércio* publishes a daily list of boats, destinations, departure times and fares. The

ENASA ticket office (☎ 633-3280) is at Rua Marechal Deodoro 61.

Remember that the waters drop 10m to 14m during the dry season, and this restricts river traffic, particularly in the upper Amazon tributaries. Ports of call are marked on the boats, and fares are pretty much standardised according to distance. If you are going on a long trip, it's advisable to get to your boat early on the morning of departure to secure a good spot. Some even camp on the boat overnight.

Although food and drink are included in the fare, it's a good idea to bring bottled water and snacks as a supplement. Unless you have cabin space, you will need a hammock, as well as rope to string it up. It can get windy and cool at night, so a sleeping bag is also recommended. Hang your hammock in the cooler upper deck, preferably towards the bow.

Beware of theft on boats – a very common complaint. For more advice, see the security section under Dangers & Annoyances in the Facts for the Visitor chapter.

Santarém & Belém Heading downriver, the big boats go in the faster central currents several kilometres from shore. Travelling upriver, they stay in the slow currents by the riverbanks, though not as close as the smaller boats, which hug the shore. You won't miss much as there's not much to be seen, anyway. If viewing wildlife is a priority, this is not the way to go.

ENASA's ferry-catamaran takes two days to Santarém and four days downstream to Belém. Cabin accommodation for the five day tourist cruise from Manaus to Belém starts at US$430 per person. ENASA also has a weekly boat to Belém, departing on Thursdays (US$65).

Apart from the ENASA (☎ 633-3280) services, there are now various companies operating passenger boats between Manaus, Santarém and Belém. Prices for hammock space average US$45 to Santarém (24 to 30 hours) and US$90 to Belém (3½ days). You can get discounts on those prices if you shop around.

For details of regular ENASA services and other companies operating to Santarém and Belém see the Getting There & Away sections for those destinations.

The Triple Frontier From Manaus, it's a five day trip (if all goes well) to the Brazilian border towns of Benjamin Constant and Tabatinga, or longer if the boat makes many stops. Various boats make the trip, departing Manaus on Wednesday, Friday and Saturday. Ticket prices average US$260/80 for double cabin/hammock accommodation. Downstream the trip takes three to six days. From the Colombian border town of Leticia there are regular fast-boat services upstream on the Rio Amazonas to Iquitos (Peru) (US$50, eight to 10 hours); irregular cargo boats upstream on the Rio Putumayo to Puerto Asís (Colombia); and flights to Bogotá. Refer to the Triple Frontier, Getting There & Away section later in this chapter for details of these services.

Porto Velho Another long river journey can be taken from Manaus up the Rio Madeira to Porto Velho. The trip takes a minimum of 3½ days and costs US$220/70 double cabin/hammock including meals. For more details, see the Getting There & Away section for Porto Velho.

São Gabriel da Cachoeira It is possible to sail up the Rio Negro to São Gabriel da Cachoeira near the Colombian and Venezuelan border (US$70, five to six days).

Getting Around

To/From the Airport Aeroporto Internacional Eduardo Gomes (☎ 621-1212) is 14km north of the city centre on Avenida Santos Dumont. The bus marked Aeroporto runs every half hour between the airport and the local downtown bus terminus and from 6 am to midnight (US$0.70, 40 minutes). Taxis between the airport and the centre can cost up to US$28, which is the Brazilian minimum weekly wage! See Dangers & Annoyances in the introduction to the Manaus section.

The Origin of Guaraná

Long ago in the beginning of all things, two brothers and a sister lived at Noçoquem, on the banks of the Rio Tapajós. The girl, Uniai, also known as Ohiamuaçabe, was so beautiful and wise that every animal desired her. Of all the animals, the snake was the first to express his desire and act upon it. With a magic perfume, the snake enchanted Uniai and made her pregnant.

Her brothers were none too pleased, and kicked Uniai out of Noçoquem. The child was born far from Noçoquem, but Uniai often told her son about their place of origin and of the brazil-nut tree which grew there. Although the brothers had a parakeet and a macaw on guard at the brazil-nut tree, the child wanted to taste the delicious nuts, and as he grew stronger and more beautiful, his desire to taste the nuts also grew. Finally, he convinced his mother to accompany him to the tree.

The birds spotted the ashes of a fire in which mother and child had roasted the delicious brazil nuts. After the birds reported the incident, the brothers replaced the inept guard birds with a reliable monkey guard. Now that the boy knew the path to Noçoquem, he returned alone to the tree the following day. The monkey spied the boy, drew his bow and shot the child full of arrows.

Uniai found her dead child beneath the tree. As she buried him, she vowed: 'You will be great; the most powerful tree will grow from you; you will cure sickness, provide strength in war and in love'. From the boy's left eye grew the false guaraná *uaraná-hop*, while from his right eye grew the true guaraná *uaraná-cécé*. This is why the berries of the guaraná look like eyes.

Days later, a child was born from the guaraná tree and emerged from the earth. The child was Uniai's, and he was the first Maûé Indian.

To this day, the Maûé call themselves sons of guaraná, and because of this plant, their favourite decorative colours are red and green. The ritual drink of the Sateré-Maûé Indians is *çapo* of guaraná, which is prepared from the eye-like berries. The berries, collected before the fruit opens, are dried, washed in running water and cooked in earth ovens. Water is added, and the guaraná is moulded into black sticks, which are then dried in a smokehouse. The Maûé shave guaraná flakes from the black sticks, using either the raspy tongue of the pirarucu or a rough stone. The flakes are then mixed into water to make the çapo.

The Maûé drink çapo of guaraná on important occasions, to affirm the life force, to cure all illness, to bring strength in times of war and to bring fertility in times of peace.

Originally the Saterê-Maûé lands encompassed the vast stretch of jungle between the Madeira and Tapajós rivers. Today the Maûe live in a small tribal reservation. In late November or early December, the Festa do Guaraná is celebrated in the town of Maués (about 200km east of Manaus), the largest cultivator of guaraná.

Most Brazilians take their guaraná in the form of a tasty sweetened and carbonated soft drink. Coca Cola bottles one of the most popular brands of guaraná soda: Taí Guarana. Like Coke, guaraná is a mild stimulant, but unlike Coke, guaraná is said to have aphrodisiac powers. Brazilians take guaraná to keep themselves up for Carnaval. Pharmacies and herbal medicine shops also sell guaraná, in the form of syrups, capsules and powders.

Leonardo Pinhiero & Robyn Jones

To/From the Rodoviária The rodoviária (☎ 236-2732) is 6km north of the centre of town. Buses marked Ileia, Santos Dumont or Aeroporto run from the centre via the rodoviária. A taxi to the centre costs around US$12.

Bus The local bus terminus is on Praça da Matriz, near the cathedral. Beware of child pickpockets here. From here you can catch buses to Praia da Ponta Negra and the sights in town (details provided under the individual sights). A more expensive (but quicker) option to travel between the centre and Ponta Negra is the Hotel Tropical shuttle bus (US$6). Buses leave every few hours between 9 am and 5 pm. The requisite bus stop in the centre of Manaus is on Rua Dr Moreira. The Fontur travel agency at the Hotel Tropical has timetables.

PARINTINS

• *pop 71,575* ✉ *69150-000* ☎ *092*

Parintins is 420km east of Manaus, on the island of Tupinambarana, on the Rio Amazonas, near the border of Pará state.

The Parintins Folk Festival, the largest cultural festival of the northern region of Brazil, is held over three days during the last week of June. A competition is held between two rival bulls – Caprichoso (the blue bull) and Garantido (the red bull). Dressed in outlandish costumes, the 10,000 or so participants parade into the *bumbódromo* (stadium). The *boi-bumbás* (people dressed in bull costumes) dance to the beat of drums and the chanting of their team. Each team is judged on its music, dance performance and costumes. The competition is intense, every citizen barracks for either red or blue and the over-the-top spectacle rivals that of Rio's Carnaval.

Places to Stay

The town's hotels are quickly booked during the festival and many people take package tours which include boat accommodation. The *Uyrapurú Hotel* (☎ 533-1834) and *Hotel Ilha Bela* (☎/fax 533-2737) both have suites with air-conditioning, TV and frigobar. Other options are the *Hotel Avenida*, *Hotel Palace*, *Hotel Martins*, *Hospedaria Siridó* and the *Torres de Melo*.

Getting There & Away

Air There are daily TABA flights from Manaus to Parintins. Air-taxis also make daily trips, more often during the festival.

Boat There are daily boats from Manaus' floating dock (around US$25, 15 hours). The trip upstream to Manaus takes about 27 hours. Boats downstream take 10 hours more to Santarém and three days to Belém. Upstream from Santarém to Parintins takes 15 hours and from Belém, four days.

THE TRIPLE FRONTIER

The two Brazilian ports of Tabatinga and Benjamin Constant are about 20km apart on opposite sides of the Rio Solimões (Amazonas) at the border between Brazil, Colombia and Peru. Neither port is particularly attractive, and most travellers view them as transit points. If you have to wait a few days for a boat, the Colombian border town of Leticia is a more interesting place to hang out or take a jungle tour. Tabatinga and Leticia are practically the same town, just separated by a border post. You can get your Brazilian entry/exit stamp from the Polícia Federal in either Benjamin Constant or Tabatinga. The Peruvian village of Santa Rosa is on the opposite side of the river to Tabatinga/Leticia.

Getting There & Away

Manaus From Tabatinga airport (☎ 412-2179), there are four weekly Varig flights to Manaus (US$222). There are also irregular cargo planes.

Boats down the Rio Amazonas to Manaus leave from Benjamin Constant, but usually go up to Tabatinga to load/unload. Regular boats depart from Tabatinga (theoretically) on Wednesday and Saturday mornings, departing Benjamin Constant the same night. The journey takes three to six days, and costs around US$80 for hammock space or US$260 for a double cabin. Many

other irregular cargo boats take passengers on deck. Prices and journey times are similar. In the opposite direction, upstream from Manaus to Benjamin Constant, the trip takes a minimum of five days. For more advice on boat travel see the Manaus Getting There & Away section.

Peru Military transport planes operate irregularly from Ramón Castilla (Peru) to Iquitos (Peru). Upstream to Iquitos (Peru) from Leticia (Colombia), there are four companies operating rápido (fast-boat) passenger services, each with two to three boats per week (US$50, 8 hours). The boats call at the Peruvian immigration post at Santa Rosa, across the river from Tabatinga, which has replaced the old port of Ramón Castilla. Alternatively, there are irregular cargo boats between Santa Rosa and Iquitos: upstream (US$40, about 3 days), and downstream (US$20, if you bargain; about 36 hours), food included. Iquitos has a Brazilian consulate (☎ (094) 23-2081), Sargento Lores 363 and a Colombian consulate (☎ (094) 23-1461) at Putumayo 247.

Colombia Air Avianca has daily flights to Bogotá (US$170). Aerosucre runs several cargo flights a week to Bogotá, and usually take passengers (about US$75). Enquire at the airport. Satena flies to/from Bogotá on Sunday, in light planes (US$96). It is difficult to get on these flights unless you book in advance.

Irregular cargo boats to Puerto Asís (Colombia), on the upper reaches of the Rio Putumayo, can take 12 to 20 days, and the price varies substantially – from US$60 to $120, food usually included. From Puerto Asís, you can continue by road to Pasto, or head to Ecuador via San Miguel. It's much better to do this route in reverse, (downstream) as it is faster and cheaper.

Getting Around

There is a ferry service, with two boats sailing daily between Tabatinga and Benjamin Constant (US$3, two hours). There are also *deslizadores* (small boats) (US$5, 40 minutes). Both services depart from Porto da Feira in Tabatinga.

TABATINGA

Tabatinga and Leticia (Colombia) are practically the same town. Tabatinga's main thoroughfare, Avenida da Amizade, runs north-south, parallel to the river. The airport and military base are at the southern end of town and the border is a couple of kilometres to the north, where the road becomes Leticia's Avenida Internacional. Motorbikes, the main form of transport in both towns, scurry along the roads, and fuel is sold in bottles by the roadside.

Information

Money CNM Cambio e Turismo, Avenida da Amizade, 2217, will change cash and Visa and American Express travellers cheques but usually pays less than you can get in Leticia.

It is open Monday to Friday from 8 am to 1 pm and 2.30 to 5 pm, and Saturday 8 am to noon.

Immigration There is no border checkpoint at the frontier and locals and foreigners can cross without visas. If you plan to travel further into either country however, you must complete immigration formalities. You can get your Brazilian entry/exit stamps at the Polícia Federal towards the southern end of Avenida da Amizade near the hospital (away from the border). The office is open daily from 8 am to noon and 2 to 6 pm. A yellow fever vaccination certificate may be required by officials when entering Brazil.

Places to Stay & Eat

Tabatinga has a couple of hotels, including *Hotel Central* (☎ 412-2346) on Avenida da Amizade near Banco do Brazil, but Leticia has much better options. Surprisingly, Tabatinga has the best value eatery of the two border towns: *Restaurante Tres Fronteiras* (☎ 412-2858), Rua Rui Barbosa, where you can have caipirinha and an excellent quality meal for two to share for US$12. It is about 100m south-west of Avenida da Amizade towards the river. Nearby on Avenida da Amizade near CNN, *Panificadora Dipan* has delicious pudim and pão de queijo.

LETICIA (COLOMBIA)

• *pop 23,000 ☎ 9819*

On the Rio Amazonas where the borders of Colombia, Brazil and Peru meet, Leticia is the most popular place in Colombian Amazonia, mostly due to its well-developed tourist facilities and good flight connections with the rest of the country. Leticia has become the leading tourist centre for Colombians thirsty to see primitive tribes, buy their handicrafts, and to get a taste of the real jungle. The influx has upset the natural balance, and today, the Indians work hard on their crafts to keep up with tourist demand.

For travellers, Leticia is interesting because it is linked via the Amazon to Manaus and Iquitos, and therefore offers reasonably easy travel between Brazil, Colombia and Peru. The best time to visit the region is in July or August, which are the only relatively dry months.

Information

Tourist Office The Oficina de Turismo (☎ 27505), No 11-35 Carrera 11, is open weekdays from 7 am to noon and 2 to 6 pm. The Polícia de Turismo can be contacted here.

Money Banks in Leticia will not exchange travellers cheques or cash dollars. However, there are several casas de câmbio near the corner of Calle 8 and Carrera 11 which convert to or from Colombian pesos, Brazilian reais and Peruvian nuevos soles or US dollars. The Banco Ganadero, Carrera 11, does cash advances on Visa cards only. There are also casas de câmbio in Tabatinga, but these usually pay less than you can get in Leticia. You can change Visa and American Express travellers cheques in Tabatinga (see the Tabatinga section earlier in this chapter).

Post & Communications The post office is on Calle 8 and the Telecom office is on Carrera 11 near the corner of Calle 9.

Immigration The Departamento Administrativo de Seguridad or DAS (☎ 27189), the security police office on Calle 9, is open 24 hours. This is where you get your passport stamped when leaving or entering Colombia, free for all nationalities.

Foreign Consulates The Brazilian consulate (☎ 27530) is on Calle 13, and is open Monday to Friday from 8 am to 2 pm. Check if your nationality requires a visa; prices vary from country to country. Visas are issued on the spot: you will need to present a valid passport, a photo and an onward ticket out of Brazil or out of South America. The Peruvian consulate, Calle 10, 9-82, is open from 8 am to 2 pm Monday to Friday. If you need a visa, it will usually be issued on the spot.

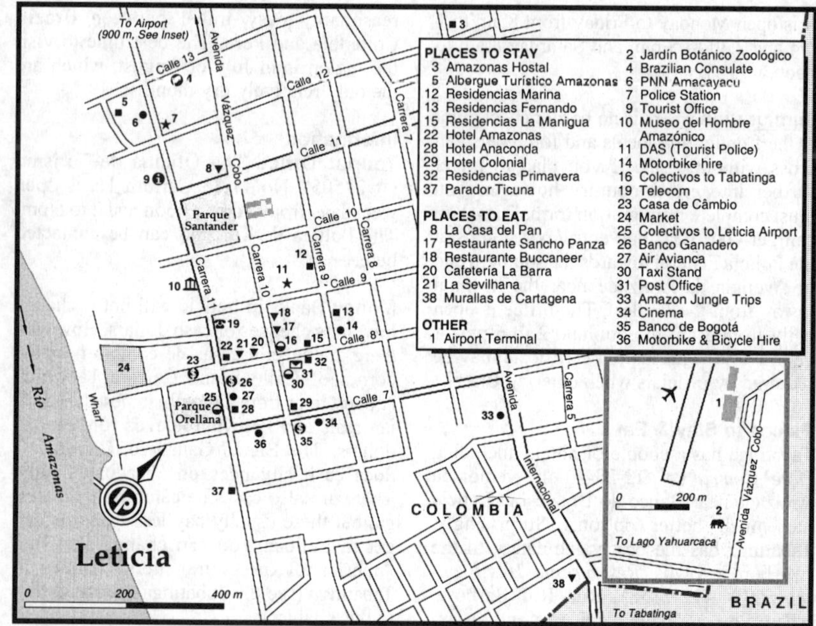

Things to See & Do

The **Jardín Botánico Zoológico**, near the airport, has a poor sample of the local flora and some monkeys, crocodiles, anteaters and anacondas; it's open daily from 7 am to 6 pm. Entry cost US$1. The **Museo del Hombre Amazónico** on Carrera 11, has a small collection of Indian artefacts and implements; it's open Monday to Thursday from 8 am to noon and from 2 to 6 pm. Admission is US$0.50.

Leticia has become a tourist town not for what the town itself offers, but for the surrounding region. However, as almost all transport is by river and there are no regular passenger boats, it's difficult to get around cheaply on your own. For a cheap trip into the countryside take the *coletivo* (minibus) from in front of Parque Orellana which goes past the zoo and airport and continues on past small villages and fenced estates.

Parque Nacional Amacayacu This is a national park covering 293,500 hectares of jungle to the north of Puerto Nariño. A spacious visitors centre with food and accommodation facilities has been built beside the Rio Amazonas. Accommodation in bed/hammock costs US$18/14 per person, and the three meals will cost US$11.50; add US$10 for the park entry fee. From the centre you can explore the park by marked paths or by boat especially during the high-water period (May to July).

Two small boat companies, Tres Fronteras and Expresso Amazonas (both with offices near the waterfront in Leticia), operate fast passenger boats to Puerto Nariño daily leaving at 11.45 am and returning at 9 am the next day. They will drop you off at the visitors centre (US$8, 1½ hours).

The main Indian tribes living in the region are the Ticunas and Yaguas. The major settlement of the Ticunas is **Arara**, but the village is on the route taken by almost every tour, so it's become something of a theatre, with Indians as the actors. The Yaguas are ethnically different and are noted for their *achiote*, a red face.

For information on the national park, telephone Leticia (☎/fax 27124) or Bogotá (☎/fax (91) 243-3004) or go to PNN Amacayacu, near the police station in Leticia.

Jungle Trips

There are lots of travel agencies in Leticia offering jungle trips. The two major travel agencies, Turamazonas (in the Parador Ticuna) and Anaconda Tours (☎ 27119; fax 27005) in the Hotel Anaconda, offer packaged excursions. The one-day excursions are well-organised standard tours, but don't offer anything too adventurous and are not worthwhile unless you have only a day to spend in the region.

It is better value to contract an independent operator and negotiate. Make sure you clearly delineate the conditions of the trip, the places you want to visit and the prices. Pay only part of the tour price on departure and the balance at the end. A three to five day tour is the best idea. Normally in those excursions you will sleep in locals' huts or in camps. Count on spending around US$60 per person per day for a group of four, or US$45 if you are in a bigger group. Excursions are better during high-water period (May to July). Try to choose an operator who pays the local Indian tribes properly for their services. It's a good idea to bring some food (rice, coffee, powdered milk, salt and sugar) or useful presents (pencils and pens, paper pads, dental paste and toothbrushes) for the Indian tribes you visit.

Tony (Mowgli) Vargas and his French partner Sophie (mobile ☎/fax 93281-3301), Calle 9, 8-63 in Leticia run tours to visit local Indian groups as well as trips to more remote areas along Rio Yavarí and Rio Kixito where you may see tapir if you're lucky. Sophie is a member of Association Curupira (22 Rue Vrenguy, 56450 Le Hezo, France) and her jungle exploits have been the subject of articles published in the Journal Concorde de L'Ambassade and several French magazines. You can also contact Club Aventure (☎ (01) 44 32 09 30; fax (01) 44 32 09 59), 18 rue Séguier 75006, Paris.

Other agents offering jungle trips include Amazon Expedition, on the corner of Calle 7 and Carrera 11, and Amazon Jungle Trips (☎ 27377), Avenida Internacional 6-25, which runs a jungle lodge on a tributary of the Río Yavarí (in Peru).

Places to Stay

Accommodation in Leticia is not cheap, but there is a reasonably good range of options. The best budget places to stay are a bit of a walk from the town centre. One of them is the *Amazonas Hostal* (☎/fax 27069), Avenida Internacional 11-84. It has good, clean facilities and even a swimming pool. Dormitory rooms here have TV and air-conditioning and cost US$20 per head, while fan-cooled rooms with private bath and TV cost US$30 a double; breakfast is included in the price and cards are accepted. Another good budget option is the *Albergue Turístico Amazonas* (☎ 27291), Carrera 11A, 12-74. It has small dormitory rooms with air-conditioning and TV for US$12 per person, and rooms with bathroom cost US$23 a double; breakfast is included.

Other budget places include *Residencias La Manigua* (☎ 27121), Calle 8, 9-22, which has a courtyard and OK rooms with fan and bath for US$15/20 a single/double or the *Residencias Marina* (☎ 27309), Carrera 9, 9-29, offering rooms with fan, TV and fridge for US$18/22. The *Residencias Primavera* is across the street from La Manigua and has triple rooms for US$25 and singles/doubles for US$10/15. It's not bad, but its bar with music at full volume can be quite irritating.

At the pleasant *Residencias Fernando* (☎ 27362) at Carrera 9, 8-80, where all rooms have air-conditioning, TV and fridge, you will pay US$20/30 for singles/doubles.

If you want something flashier, check out the *Hotel Anaconda* (☎ 27119), Carrera 11,

7-34, but get a room on the top floor with nice views over the Amazon to make it worth the US$78/106 for singles/doubles. The *Parador Ticuna*, (☎ 27241), Carrera 11, 6-11, appeared abandoned when we came past, but it has spacious rooms with a veranda overlooking a nice tropical garden. Accommodation costs US$69/89 for singles/doubles. The *Hotel Colonial*, (☎ 27164), on the corner of Carrera 10 and Calle 7, is faded but has atmosphere and OK rooms for US$40/52 a single/double. The *Hotel Amazonas* (☎ 28026), Calle 8, 10-32, has modern, clean rooms for US$55/70; try to negotiate a discount if the hotel isn't busy.

Places to Eat

The food is not bad in Leticia, though the standard cheap meals including the obligatory banana pisada (fried 'stepped-on' banana) can get a bit repetitive. Obviously, the local speciality is fish; don't miss the delicious gamitana. Also try copoasú juice, known to Brazilians as cupuaçu, which is a local fruit somewhat similar in taste to guanábana.

The best value restaurant in the area is actually in Tabatinga (see the Tabatinga section earlier in this chapter). *Restaurante Sancho Panza*, Carrera 10, is one of Leticia's cheapest and has a menu with set dishes for US$2. Next door at the *Buccaneer* you can have tastier meals for around US$7. On Calle 8 is *Cafetería La Barra*, a popular place for fruit juices. The restaurant at *Hotel Colonial* has a nice atmosphere and good meals for US$2.50. *La Casa del Pan*, in the Parque Santander, is a good place for afternoon coffee and fresh bread, and to watch the hoards of screeching parrots return to their nests at dusk. *La Sevilhana* next to Hotel Amazonas is good for a simple and cheap breakfast. *Murallas de Cartagena* on Avenida Internacional, next to the border, is open until late at night.

If you want to eat in a more upmarket restaurant, try the *Hotel Anaconda* or the *Parador Ticuna*, though you might get a bit lonely.

There are also lots of bars along Calle 8, also known as Calle Coca Cola.

Getting There & Away

For details of plane and boat connections see the Getting There & Away section for the Triple Frontier.

Getting Around

Tabatinga's airport is on the southern edge of town, some 2km from what could be called the town centre. From here you can catch a colectivo along Avenida da Amizade to Leticia (US$0.75); taxis to Tabatinga cost US$10 and to Leticia US$15. There are also frequent colectivos between the Leticia and Tabatinga ports (US$0.75); otherwise, it's a 30 minute walk. A taxi will cost about US$5. You probably won't be stopped at the border but in Tabatinga you should get an entry/exit stamp in your passport from Brazilian officials at Polícia Federal on Avenida da Amizade.

Leticia's airport is also close to the town's centre and is served by regular local colectivos which depart from in front of Parque Orellana.

There are a couple of places which hire motorbikes (US$5 per hour) or bicycles (US$1 per hour).

Roraima

The remote and beautiful mountain region straddling the Venezuelan border to the north of Roraima is perhaps the ultimate Amazon frontier. Roraima is the least populated state in Brazil. This rugged land is home to the Yanomami, who represent about one-third of the remaining tribal Indians of the Amazon. Because the Indian lands are sitting on huge deposits of iron, cassiterite and gold, the Yanomami are threatened by the building of roads, and encroachment from garimpeiros and others seeking to expropriate these lands. Although the Brazilian government has declared the area a special

Cutting through an Indian Reserve

The Manaus-Boa Vista highway (BR-174) has a violent history. A 132km section cuts through the 2.5 million hectare Uaimiri Indian reserve. The Uaimiri fiercely defended their land against the construction of the road, combating the forces of the Brazilian army in the 1970s. During the confrontations more than 200 soldiers were killed by poison arrow. Casualties on the Indian side however, were a lot higher. From a population of 1500 in 1974, their numbers were reduced to a mere 374 in 1986, when finally they agreed to negotiate with the government. Today the population is increasing, with around 700 people living in 14 aldeias. The road though Uaimiri land as yet remains unpaved and it is prohibited for outsiders to enter the forest.

Robyn Jones & Leonardo Pinhiero

Indian reserve, this declaration will be worthless unless the government is prepared to enforce it and eject trespassers from Yanomami lands. For a description of the Yanomami, see the section on Indians under Population & People in the Facts about the Country chapter.

In early 1998 the Yanomami were also threatened by natural disaster when huge fires reached the outskirts of their reserve. Drought resulting from the El Niño phenomenon had left Roraima's savanna and rainforests exceptionally dry and fires lit by farmers to clear land blazed out of control for months. Firefighters were flown in from Rio de Janeiro, Brasilia and Argentina but their efforts were hindered by difficult access and lack of water. Witch doctors were also flown in from Mato Grosso to pray for rain. Over 600,000 hectares of savanna, farmland and forest were burnt before the fires were eventually doused by heavy rains.

Roraima state is one hour behind Brazilian Standard Time.

BOA VISTA

• pop 154,000 ✉ 69300-000 ☎ 095

A planned city on the banks of the Rio Branco, Boa Vista, the capital of Roraima, is home to more than half of the state's population. Most residents are public servants lured to the frontier by government incentives.

Although there is now a sealed road between Boa Vista and Venezuela, and many locals take holidays to the Caribbean, the city feels very remote and isolated from the rest of Brazil. With the improvements on Hwy BR-174 to Manaus this may be set to change. Boa Vista is growing at a bounding pace, but while lots of money has been pumped into the construction of an aquatic park, concert grounds and various sporting facilities, there is still much poverty. Most travellers consider this city 'the ultimate bore', 'one of the armpits of the universe', bereft of any interest, and nothing more than a transit point between Brazil and Venezuela. However, there are some intriguing sights in the vicinity of Boa Vista which are becoming increasingly accessible.

Orientation

The city is shaped like an arch, with the base on the Rio Branco and the arch itself formed by Avenida Major Williams and Avenida Terencio Lima. Avenidas radiate from the top, dividing the outskirts into wedges. The city planners were clearly a race of giants: the scale of the place is totally unsuited to pedestrians who could quite easily spend a whole day trying to do a couple of errands.

The government buildings are located right in the centre, at the intersection of Avenida Ville Roy and Avenida Capitan Ene Garcez, while the commercial district runs

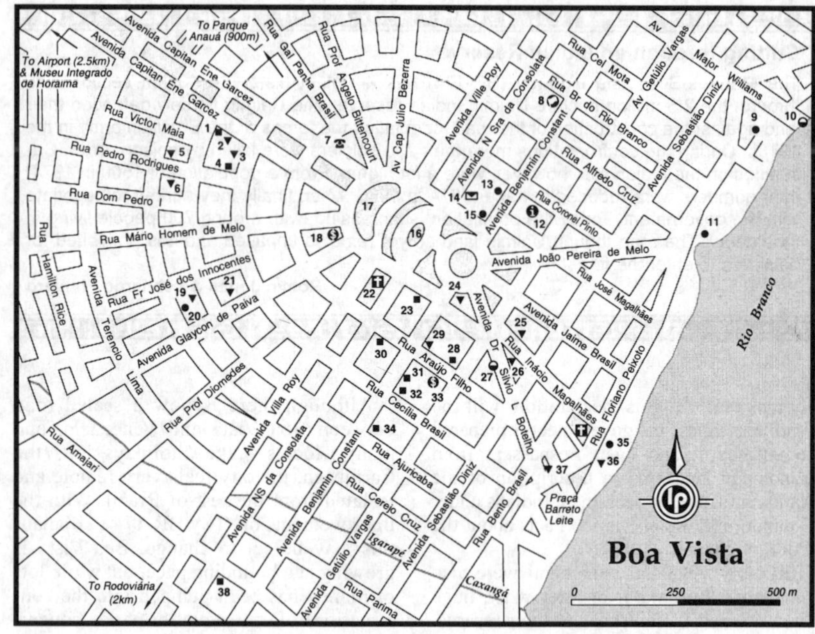

from the centre of town along Avenida Jaime Brasil to Rua Floriano Peixoto, on the waterfront.

Information

Tourist Office The information booth at the rodoviária (☎ 623-1238) can supply you with a map, a weekend entertainment program, and help with booking accommodation. It's open Monday to Friday from 8 am to noon and from 2 to 7 pm. There is also an information desk at the airport open from 7 to 11 pm.

The office of CODETUR (☎/fax 623-1230), the state tourism administration, at Rua Coronel Pinto 241 has brochures with general tourist information. Apparently, the state administration is interested in developing tourism, and advertises the state as an 'Ecological Sanctuary – a beautiful wilderness for the adventurer', but so far, there is very little tourist infrastructure in the region.

Money There is a branch of Banco do Brasil (☎ 623-2646) is at Avenida Glaycon de Paiva 56, close to Praça do Centro Cívico. It's open for câmbio from 10 am to 2 pm Monday to Friday. Other useful moneychangers, with longer opening hours include: Casa de Câmbio Pedro José (☎ 224-9797) at Rua Araújo Filho 287, which is open Monday to Friday from 8 am to noon and 1.30 to 5.30 pm. It exchanges travellers cheques and US, Bolivian, German, Italian and Guianense currency. Another is Timbó Viagens e Turismo at Avenida Benjamin Constant 170; it's open Monday to Friday from 8 am to 6 pm, and Saturday from 8 am to noon, and also exchanges the previously mentioned currencies and French francs.

Post & Telephone The post office (☎ 224-0699) is on the north side of the Praça do Centro Cívico. The telephone office Posto

PLACES TO STAY
1 Uiramutan Palace
4 Hotel Euzebio's
23 Aipana Plaza
28 Hotel Barrudada
30 Hotel Ideal
31 Hotel Monte Libano
32 Hotel Brasil
34 Hotel Imperial
38 Pousada Beija Flor (Beija Flor Tours)

PLACES TO EAT
2 Pigalle
3 Restaurante Euzebio's
5 Peixada Tropical
6 La Carreta
19 Banana Paçoca Restaurante
21 Só Caldos
24 La Gondola
25 Mister Kilo
26 Pik Nik Ice Cream
29 Margô Pizzaria
36 Restaurante Peixada Panorama
37 Black & White

OTHER
7 Posto Telefônica
8 Venezuelan Consulate
9 Iguana Tours
10 Porto do Babá
11 Toca Tour
12 CODETUR Tourist Office
13 Prefeitura
14 Post Office
15 Biblioteca e Palácio da Cultura
16 Praça do Centro Cívico
17 Palácio do Governo
18 Banco do Brasil
20 Palácio da Micro Empresa
22 Catedral
27 Municipal Bus Terminal
33 Casa de Cambio Pedro José
35 Centro de Artesanato

de Serviço TELAIMA (☎ 623-1001) is at Avenida Capitan Ene Garcez 100.

Foreign Consulates The Venezuelan consulate (☎ 224-2182) is on Avenida Benjamin Constant and is open from 8 am to noon Monday to Friday. Free tourist cards are issued for most nationalities who intend to stay in Venezuela for less than 90 days and only enter once. Multiple-entry visas valid for over 90 days are US$30.

If you arrive early in the morning, you may be able to pick up your visa at noon. You'll need one photo, a photocopy of your passport and a completed application form. However, it's best to get your visa beforehand and avoid the delay in Boa Vista. More visa details for Venezuela can be found in the Visas for Adjoining Countries section in the Facts for the Visitor chapter.

Parque Anauá

The park at Avenida Brigadeiro Eduardo Gomes is quite a hike from the centre on the way to the airport. Within the vast grounds are gardens, a lake, a museum, an amphitheatre and various sporting facilities including an aquatic park and a public swimming pool. The **Museu do Parque** is quite interesting with burial urns, archaeological artefacts and a section on garimpos. Nearby is the grand *forródromo* especially built for forró concerts (typical music and dance enjoyed by immigrants from the Northeast). There is also a bar on the edge of the lake where you can have a late afternoon beer.

Beaches

The main beach is **Praia Grande**, opposite Boa Vista on the Rio Branco. To get there, walk down from the city centre to the waterfront and look for Porto do Babá, at Avenida Major Williams. Cross on a small boat (US$2). Babá is a local who organises the Festa do Luau, a party on the beach under a *lua* (full moon) with an open fire, and drinks and fruit provided.

Other beaches include **Água Boa** (on the Rio Branco, 15km from the city centre), and **Caçari**, **Curupira** and **Cauamé** (on the Rio Cauamé).

Organised Tours

Iguana Tours (☎ 971-7006; iguana@technet.com.br) is at Rua Floriano Peixoto 505. Eliezer, a local artist and tour operator who speaks English, organises a variety of boat trips, such as a day excursion to Fazenda São Marcos (a cattle ranch) and Forte São Joaquim (the ruins of a colonial fort), upstream on the Rio Branco, or trips to

Serra Grande, beaches and creeks downriver. Day tours cost US$50. A two hour tour to Ponte dos Macuxí, Paraná do Surrão and Ilha da Praia Grande, including a walk through the forest to an inland lake, costs US$15. Overnight stays in the jungle (in hammocks) cost US$120 per person, including meals and drinks; negotiate discounts for groups. Eliezer also provides transport to the beach opposite Boa Vista (US$2) and to camp sites on the Rio Branco.

Beija Flor Tours (☎ 224-8241; fax 224-6536) at Avenida NS da Consolata 939, run by Belgian Jean-Luc Félix and his Brazilian wife Néa, is good for adventure excursions. Jean organises camps and hikes to Serra Grande. A three day trip costs US$35 per person per day for a group of four. He also takes excursion to Ilha de Maracá northwest of Boa Vista. It is possible to visit more remote areas with the help of local Indian guides. For a three day trip expect to pay US$55 each for a group of four to six.

The Barco do Toca Tour (☎ 623-2597) is a pleasant and cute floating deck with a bar and one table where beer, appetisers and meals are served. It can be hired for short-distance, full-day excursions along the Rio Branco; US$200 for a maximum of 10 people, but is ideal for four to six. The excursion can include a small hike to a waterfall.

Places to Stay

The *Pousada Beija Flor* (☎ 224-8241), Avenida NS da Consolata 939, Bairro São Vicente, is nearly halfway between the centre and the rodoviária. It's run by a friendly couple, Jean and Néa, who offer basic rooms at the rear of their house. Dormitory rooms with hammocks, veranda and shared outdoor bathroom, cost US$10 per person; negotiable for groups. *Hotel Brasil*, Avenida Benjamin Constant 331, is definitely a rock-bottom cheapie, with quartos at US$8/10 for singles/doubles. *Hotel Ideal* (☎ 224-6342), Rua Araújo Filho 467, has small, old and grubby apartamentos with air-conditioning, TV and fridge for US$25/32. Better apartamentos are currently being built next door and will cost US$25/35 for singles/doubles.

The *Hotel Monte Libano* (☎ 224-7232), Avenida Benjamin Constant 319, has rooms with fan and shared bathroom for US$13/18; apartamentos upstairs are better value for US$17/23. The *Hotel Imperial* (☎ 224-5592), Avenida Benjamin Constant 433, has been partially renovated and now offers OK apartamentos with fan for US$16/18. Double air-conditioned apartamentos are not bad value for US$20. The *Hotel Tres Nações* (☎ 224-3439), Avenida Ville Roy 188W, São Vicente (near the bus terminal), charges US$15/20 for its air-conditioned rooms.

The *Hotel Barrudada* (☎ 623-9335), Rua Araújo Filho 228 near the municipal bus terminal, is one of newest and best value hotels in town. It has spotlessly clean apartamentos with air-conditioning, TV, fridge, and phone for US$40/45 a single/double and includes an excellent breakfast. *Hotel Euzebio's* (☎ 623-0300; fax 623-9131), Rua Cecília Brasil 1107, has a tacky foyer and small but reasonably clean apartamentos for US$27/33. The rooms upstairs are better.

Boa Vista's more upmarket hotels include the *Uiramutan Palace* (☎ 224-9912; fax 224-9221), Avenida Capitan Ene Garcez 427, at US$50/72; and the *Aipana Plaza* (☎ 224-4800; fax 224-4116), Praça do Centro Cívico, Joaquim Nabuco 53, with rooms for US$88/110.

Places to Eat

Pigalle, Avenida Capitan Ene Garcez 153, does good pizza, and hosts live music at weekends. *Margô Pizzaria*, Rua Benjamin Constant 193, also has pizza but pasta dishes are a better choice.

La Gondola, at Avenida Benjamin Constant 35W, is a good place for por quilo. Another self-serve place is *Mister Kilo*, at Rua Inácio Magalhães 346.

If you are a meat lover, try the US$7 all-you-can-eat meat and salads at *La Carreta*, Rua Pedro Rodrigues 185. Nearby, the *Peixada Tropical* serves fish dishes for US$17 which are large enough for two.

Down near the river at Praça Barreto Leite, *Black & White* has good local fish dishes. *Restaurante Peixada Panorama* at Rua Floriano Peixoto opposite the church overlooks the river. It's owned by the local fishermen's association and despite the low overall maintenance is friendly and serves excellent fish dishes for around US$16. Try the peixe na telha US$20 – it's enough for two to three people.

You'll find excellent regional food at *Banana Paçoca Restaurante* in the grounds of Palácio da Micro Empresa, Avenida Glaycon de Paiva. Dishes such as paçoca, carne de sol or linguiça caseira cost US$6 to $12, and it has live music on Thursday nights. The *Bistro Restaurante* at the front of Pousada Beija Flor also has regional dishes and a pleasant atmosphere. Carne de sol desfiada is US$15 for two.

For thick nutritious soups for US$4 head for *Só Caldos* at Avenida Glaycon de Paiva 348 near the government building. Open 24 hours, it has many different kinds of caldos (including fish, vegetables, eggs or meat). Caldo de feijão com mocotó (a gelatinous black bean soup) is recommended. It's an interesting spot, popular with locals.

The hotel restaurants, such as the *Aipana Plaza*, and the *Uiramutan Palace* are also worth a look. The *Restaurante do Hotel Euzebio's* has air-conditioning and meat fillets for US$12. The Saturday special of feijoada carioca costs US$15. *Pik Nik*, Rua Inácio Magalhães 325, is the best place for ice cream.

Entertainment

The Complexo Poliesportivo Ayrton Senna, close to the Parque Anauá, runs along the median strip of the wide Avenida Capitan Ene Garcez. During the day the grounds are used for sports activities and at night it's a popular entertainment spot with its many bars, live music and stalls selling regional food. Forró concerts are held occasionally at the forródromo at Parque Anauá.

Things to Buy

The small Centro de Artesanato, Rua Floriano Peixoto 158, has some handicrafts. It's open everyday from 8 am to 6 pm. The Palácio da Micro Empresa, Avenida Glaycon de Paiva 510, has regional handicrafts, woodwork, pottery and clothing. It's open Monday to Friday, 8 am to 6 pm.

Getting There & Away

Air Varig (☎ 224-2351) at Rua Araújo Filho 91, operates daily flights between Boa Vista and most capitals in Brazil. Meta Mesquita Taxi Aéreo (☎ 224-7677) at the Boa Vista international airport also has weekday flights to Manaus.

Bus Boa Vista to Manaus is a 13 hour bus ride on a mostly sealed road with a 132km section through Uaimiri territory (see the boxed text 'Cutting Through an Indian Reserve' earlier in this chapter) and one ferry crossing along the way. There are three daily departures at 8.30 am and 2.30 and 4 pm; tickets cost US$63. Hitching can be difficult, as the traffic – mostly gravel trucks – is usually local.

If you're not limited by time, another option is to take the bus from Boa Vista to Caracaraí (US$5, two hours). From there, you may be able to catch a ride on a cargo boat to Manaus (a seven to 10 day trip).

For details of bus services to the Venezuelan and Guyanese borders, see the following Crossing the Border sections.

Crossing the Venezuelan Border The road linking Boa Vista to Santa Elena (Venezuela) is fully sealed. There are four buses daily from the Boa Vista rodoviária: 6.30 and 7 am and 1 and 5.30 pm (US$13, about 3½ hours). For more details about the border crossing, see the Getting There & Away section for Santa Elena later in this chapter.

Crossing the Guyanese Border Buses travel the 125km from Boa Vista to Bonfim twice daily at 7.30 am and 3 pm (US$7, two hours). It's best to take the early bus to avoid staying the night in Bonfim, however, if you do get stuck, there are places to stay. A reader recommended Carlos Amazonas' place, a local teacher who has a couple of rooms near the bus station. Ask the driver where to get off. There is a Brazilian checkpoint before Bonfim, where you can get an exit stamp from the Polícia Federal. A taxi for the 5km to the border at the Rio Tacutu costs US$3. There you can hire a small boat across to Lethem (Guyana). Once in Lethem go to the police station to have your passport stamped. Be aware that Guyanese officials worry about illegal immigration from Brazil, and tend to scrutinise travellers fairly carefully.

There is a road from Lethem to Georgetown, but it can become impassable in the wet.

Every few days there is a truck that goes from Lethem to Georgetown. The ride takes one day and night and is truly an epic ride. The trucks are huge all-terrain vehicles, and you sit at the back with a bunch of people and animals – the back isn't covered, the sun is very strong. Part of the ride is on a newly created unsealed road through the rainforest. You can see parrots, anteaters, jaguars; it's incredible.

Parts of the ride are through places that look as if no one has ever been there before. At one point we reached a collapsed bridge across a small canal and had to place two logs and carefully drive on top of them! This truck ride is extremely bumpy, extremely rough and not everyone would enjoy it. The way I see it, every adventurous traveller should do this, but nobody should have to do it more than once. We paid US$20 per person, to go one way, to Georgetown.

Danko Taborosi

Guyana Airways flies to and from Georgetown and Lethem four times a week (US$55). Trans Air has daily flights, which groups can charter. At the time of writing, direct flights from Boa Vista to Georgetown had been suspended.

Getting Around

Whoever planned Boa Vista on such a vast scale clearly didn't think about pedestrians – getting around on foot is really difficult. Bicycles are a better option – to find out about renting one, ask Eliezer (Iguana Tours), or at Porto do Babá.

The airport (☎ 224-3680) is 4km from the city centre. To get there, take a bus marked Aeroporto from the municipal bus terminal. Most flights, however, arrive late at night. The taxi fare from the airport to the centre is about US$15.

The rodoviária (☎ 224-6168), Avenida das Guianas, Bairro São Vicente, is 3km from the centre – about 40 minutes by foot. Take a bus marked Jockey or 13 de Setembro' from the municipal bus terminal. A taxi from the centre to the rodoviária costs about US$6.

AROUND BOA VISTA

Mt Roraima This mountain is one of Brazil's highest peaks at 2875m and straddles the Brazilian-Venezuelan-Guyanese borders. The easiest access for climbers is from the Venezuelan side (see Mt Roraima and Gran Sábana later in this chapter for more details).

The archaeological site of **Pedra Pintada** (Painted Rock) is 140km north of Boa Vista, next to the Rio Parimé. The large mushroom-shaped granite boulder is about 60m across by 35m high, with painted inscriptions on its external face and caves at its base. There are no buses to the area – consider hiring a car or negotiating a tour with one of the local travel agents or guides.

Lago Caracaranã, a large lake 180km from Boa Vista, is a popular weekend destination for locals. A bus departs for the lake from the rodoviária in Boa Vista on Saturday morning and returns at noon on Sunday. There's a camp site and a basic hotel at the lake.

The **Estação Ecológica da Ilha de Maracá** (an ecological reserve) is an island 120km from Boa Vista, on the Rio Uraricuera. The reserve can only be visited with permission from IBAMA (☎ 623-9513; fax 623-9161) in Boa Vista.

The municipality of **Caracaraí** is 142km south of Boa Vista, on the west margin of the Rio Branco. The region has a number of river rapids and waterfalls, the most popular being the Bemquerer waterfall. The area also has rock paintings.

SANTA ELENA (VENEZUELA)

• *pop 10,000* ☎ *088*

Santa Elena is on the only land-border crossing between Venezuela and Brazil. It's a pleasant and relaxed border town, and being higher and cooler it's a nice change from the heat of Boa Vista.

Information

There's no tourist office in Santa Elena; try the travel agencies for information.

Money Various shops, travel agencies and hotels will change US dollars and occasionally travellers cheques (but at rates lower than the official bank rate). Banco del Orinoco is the only bank which may change your money and it's not possible to get cash advances from credit cards in Santa Elena.

Immigration If you're heading for Brazil, pick up an exit stamp from the DIEX office, right at the border. It's open daily from 8 am to 5 pm. Across the border, just metres away, is the Brazilian Polícia Federal where you must have your passport stamped to enter Brazil.

Foreign Consulates The Brazilian consulate is on Avenida Gran Mariscal, at the northern end of town, near the *prefeitura* (town hall). It's open weekdays, 8 am to noon.

Tour Operators Santa Elena has various tour operators offering standard two or three day jeep tours around La Gran Sábana. Count on roughly US$25 to $35 per person per day for a group of three or four. Some operators will drop off or pick up from Paraitepui (the starting point for the Roraima trek) for around US$80 each way per jeep for up to six or seven people.

Ivan Artal from Ruta Salvaje Tours (☎/fax 951667), Calle Kukenán 1-5, Urb Akurimá, offers the standard tours but also specialises in river rafting. A two day rafting or canoeing trip (including equipment and activities) costs US$70 per person, or US$100 with food included. Miguel Angel (☎ 951171), Calle Urdaneta 187 (La Casa de Gladys), offers standard Gran Sábana trips, excursions to gold and diamond mines as well as some longer and more adventurous trips.

Places to Stay & Eat

There is no shortage of places to stay and eat in Santa Elena. The best budget option, popular among travellers, is the friendly, family-run *La Casa de Gladys* (☎ 951171), Calle Urdaneta 187, formerly Pousada Alfonso. It offers basic clean rooms with three beds and shared bathroom (outside) for US$9; a room with one double bed for US$6 or rooms with two single beds for US$7. You can do your own cooking and laundry and there is camping gear for rent.

The new and clean *Posada La Aventura* (☎/fax 951371), Avenida Perimetral, offers good double rooms for US$7 (shared bathroom) or US$10 (with bathroom). It has hot showers and laundry facilities.

Other cheap lodging includes *Hotel Panayma*, *Hotel Gabriela* and *Hotel Luz*. The more basic *Hotel Yarima* is not recommended, and the *Hospedaje Turi Uairén* has gone downhill.

A nice place to eat in Santa Elena is the *Chirikayen* on Calle Perimetral. It has good burgers for around US$3 and regional specialities for around US$6. Try one of the delicious banana pisada burgers. For good-value chicken go to *Restaurante La Dorada* near the Hotel Yarima. *Panaderia Trigo Pan* on Calle Bolivar has good coffee and bread and cakes for US$1.

Getting There & Away

Santa Elena's airport is about 5km south of town. There is no public transport and taxis cost about US$4. Servivensa has regular flights to the Venezuelan towns of Puerto Ordaz and Canaima. The bus terminal is 2.5km from town. There are eight buses daily along the Cuidad Guayana highway to Ciudad Bolívar (US$15, 10 hours) and one air-conditioned bus directly to Isla de Margarita on the Caribbean (US$22, 18 hours). There are irregular por puestos (shared taxis) to San Francisco de Yuruaní. See also the Getting There & Away section for Mt Roraima & the Gran Sábana.

Crossing the Venezuelan Border A sealed road links Boa Vista with the Caribbean and the Venezuelan capital Caracas. The border is about 15km south of Santa Elena and the buses stop here at the Venezuelan and Brazilian immigration posts. There are four bus departures daily from Santa Elena to Boa Vista (US$13, 3½ hours).

For details aboutobtaining Venezuelan visas in Boa Vista, refer to the Boa Vista section in this chapter.

MT RORAIMA & THE GRAN SÁBANA

From the Indian village of San Francisco de Yuruaní, 69km north of Santa Elena, you can hire a guide to take you to the geographically spectacular and botanically unique area around Mt Roraima, which straddles the Brazilian-Venezuelan-Guyanese borders.

From there, it's 22km to Paraitepui, a small Indian village and the entrance to the Parque Nacional do Roraima Monte. You can also hire a guide here. From Paraitepui, the trail is easy to follow, although it quickly deteriorates after rain. There's the odd rattlesnake, but no other large wildlife.

Although you must bring food from Santa Elena, good water can be found in streams every 4 or 5km along the way. The trail has spectacular waterfalls. The top of Mt Roraima is a moonscape; it would be very easy to get lost, so don't wander far. You might consider spending an extra day on top of the mountain, but be prepared for cool drizzle and fog.

The return trip from Santa Elena will take five days, but some people allow up to two weeks in the area.

The Gran Sábana has been described as 'beautiful open rolling grassland with pockets of cool jungle, all eerily deserted and silent'. It's best to visit the area in the dry season (December to April), but even then you will still be wet much of the time.

Getting There & Away

You can travel by shared taxi from Santa Elena to the small village of San Francisco de Yuruaní (on the main road 69km north of Santa Elena). Hike for six to eight hours to Paraitepui, or hire a jeep from Santa Elena (US$80). If you want to try your luck hitching, the best chance of finding a lift will be at the petrol station at the northern end of Santa Elena, but it is possible that the driver will charge you for the lift.

Getting around the Gran Sábana can be difficult if you want to rely on public transport – an organised tour from Santa Elena is a better option.

Rondônia & Acre

The states of Rondônia and Acre, previously undeveloped frontier regions, have undergone rapid development, mainly as a result of the construction of Hwy BR-364. The highway, already sealed from Cuiabá (Mato Grosso) through Porto Velho to Rio Branco, extends as far as Boqueirão da Esperança on the Peruvian border. The two states are of intense interest to environmentalists studying the effects of deforestation, which has left vast tracts of land looking like the aftermath of a holocaust.

Many travellers will simply pass through these states en route to or from neighbouring Peru or Bolivia, but all should be aware that both states, especially Rondônia, are major distribution centres for the Peruvian and Bolivian cocaine trade. Travellers are generally left alone, providing they mind their own business.

Guajará-Mirim is an entry point for the *rota formiguinha* (ant route), favoured by the small-scale smugglers – hence the reference to ants – who arrive from Bolivia with the white stuff hidden within their baggage or concealed in their vehicles. Large-scale smugglers use *aviãozinhos* (light aircraft) to pick up the cocaine in Bolivia and then fly it to the secret landing strips in Rondônia – for example, in the vicinity of Cacoal, Ji-Paraná and Rolim Moura. From there, the goods are distributed to Rio, São Paulo and *fazendas* in Mato Grosso state.

Another of the so-called *Transcoca Highway* runs is from San Joaquim (in Bolivia) to the Rio Guaporé, where the cocaine is ferried across to the Brazilian town of Costa Marques for distribution in Brazil. Most is ultimately exported to the USA and Europe.

Rondônia

In 1943 Getúlio Vargas created the Territory of Guaporé from chunks of Amazonas and Mato Grosso. In 1981 the Territory of Guaporé became the state of Rondônia, named in honour of Marechal Cândido Mariano da Silva Rondon, the soldier who 'tamed' the region in the 1920s. A legendary figure, Rondon was honoured by the Indians he helped subdue. He linked Cuiabá, Porto Velho and Rio Branco by telegraph to the rest of Brazil.

In recent years improved roads and a gold rush attracted *Nordestinos* from the drought-stricken areas and Indians from the jungles to the frontier towns. The population increased tenfold in the 1980s with the waves of poor but hopeful migrants. In the same period, 23% of the state's forests were cleared.

Rondônia state is one hour behind Brazilian Standard Time.

National Parks & Biological Reserves

Contact IBAMA in Porto Velho for details about national parks and ecological reserves in Rondônia.

Parque Nacional de Pacaás Novas This park has a great diversity of ecosystems: dense tropical forests; savanna; grasslands and highland plateaus. The latter have canyons and caves and the **Pico do Tracoá**, the state's highest peak at 1230m. It is possible to see monkeys, jaguars, tapirs, deer, anteaters, armadillos, wild pigs, toucans, parrots and a large variety of small birds. IBAMA intends to set up visitor infrastructure in 1998. To visit, seek permission from the IBAMA office in Porto Velho. Access is via Hwy BR-364 for 200km to Ariquemes, and another 140km on unsealed road to the park entrance.

Estação Biológica Cuniã Lago do Cuniã, a biological reserve 150km north of Porto Velho, on the Rio Madeira, contains the state's largest spawning area for fish and is renowned for its abundant bird life. It is in the process of being officially recognised as a *reserva extravista* and IBAMA intend to open the area for tourism. The intention is to offer an alternative income for the 48 families living in the area. The reserve is accessible only by boat.

Reserva Biológica do Guaporé This reserve's main attractions are its flora and fauna, similar to that found in the Pantanal – hence the reserve's nickname: 'Pantanal de Rondônia'. Access is by boat from Costa Marques (756km from Porto Velho) to Pau d'Óleo (about six hours; 160km). There is a government fazenda with accommodation (cabanas), transport into the reserve is also provided here.

PORTO VELHO

• *pop 320,000* ✉ *78900-000* ☎ *069*

Now the capital of the young state of Rondônia, Porto Velho is rapidly losing its frontier feel. The streets have been sealed, most of the Indians are dead and the forests are rapidly being felled. Nevertheless, 20th century Porto Velho retains elements of the American Wild West: land-hungry cattle ranchers, fierce Indians, gold prospectors and desperados of all kinds. The newspaper headlines tell the story, with articles ranging from the gold strike to border cocaine-trafficking, from poaching to conflicting land claims settled at gunpoint.

History

During the 17th and 18th centuries, Portuguese *bandeirantes* in pursuit of gold and Indian slaves crossed the lines drawn by the Treaty of Tordesillas and entered what is now known as Rondônia, to roam the Guaporé and Madeira river valleys. Since the Spanish were incapable of defending themselves from these incursions, the occupation was officially sanctioned in lofty Latin terms, which meant that it was ignored. The Portuguese secured their new possessions by building the Forte Príncipe da Beira, a fortress at the confluence of the Mamoré and Guaporé rivers.

The Treaty of Tordesillas was kept more in the breach than the observance; the Portuguese continued to push west and occupy Bolivian lands. The Brazil-Bolivia Treaty of Friendship (1867) and the Treaty of Petrópolis (1901) addressed Bolivian grievances. The Bolivians ceded the region – known today as the state of Acre – in return for £2 million and the construction of a railway along the upper reaches of the Rio Madeira to give landlocked Bolivia access to world rubber markets via the Amazon. For more on the construction of the railway see the boxed text 'The Madeira-Mamoré Railway' in this chapter.

Since the railway did not go as far as intended (above the rapids of Rio Mamoré at Riberalta) and the price of rubber had plummeted on the world market, the project was effectively useless. However, the towns of Guajará-Mirim and Porto Velho were founded at either end of the completed railway, which functioned sporadically until it was officially closed in 1972.

Today the line is used only as a tourist novelty, from the Porto Velho end. Marcio Souza chronicles the whole brutal story in his book *Mad Maria* (published by Avalon in an English-language paperback edition), which is mandatory reading for anyone interested in how a small parcel of the 'Green Hell' was briefly conquered.

During WWII, when the Japanese occupation of Malaysia cut Allied rubber supplies, rubber production in the Amazon briefly picked up once again. In 1958 cassiterite (tin ore) was discovered. Mining of cassiterite, other minerals (gold, iron, manganese) and precious stones together with timber extraction became Rondônia's principal source of wealth. Now mining is slowing down, but a new cycle is starting for granite and ornamental stones. Timber is still important and accounts for up to 30% of the state's industry figures.

Agriculture has also become an important activity in Rondônia. The state produces grains but almost all vegetables are imported from São Paulo. Land clearing for cattle ranching is rampant and the government is proud of the state herd which is approaching five million head.

In fact, Porto Velho is riding out the tail end of a gold rush. There are still a few gold shops along Avenida 7 de Setembro, all empty save for the old-fashioned powder scales in glass cases. The prospectors haven't seen much gold lately, but they're still dredging, dumping mercury as they go.

Orientation

Porto Velho sits on the eastern bank of the Rio Madeira, almost contiguous with the state of Amazonas. The Rio Madeira, a 3240km tributary of the Rio Amazonas, is formed by the Mamoré and Abunã rivers.

Porto Velho's main street is Avenida 7 de Setembro, which stretches almost 2km, from the riverfront docks and Madeira Mamoré train station to Avenida Jorge Teixeira.

Information

Tourist Offices Fundação Cultural e Turística do Estado de Rondônia or FUNCETUR (☎ 221-1881) is at Avenida 7 Setembro 237, 1st floor, above the Museu Estadual. It was created recently as part of a government move to promote the state's culture and tourism and can provide helpful information if you speak some Portuguese.

SEBRAE (☎ 224-1380; fax 224-3326) Avenida Campos Sales 3421, Bairro Olaria, is an agency providing services for small business, including tourism. The state of Rondônia has a Portuguese-only Web site at www.ronet.com.br/~rondonia/estado.htm.

The state office of IBAMA (☎ 223-3607), Avenida Jorge Teixeira 3477, Bairro Costa e Silva (take the Aeroporto bus from

The Madeira-Mamoré Railway

The Public Works Construction Company of London started work on a Madeira-Mamoré railway in 1872, but abandoned the project after two years, due to rampant disease and Indian attacks. These swampy jungle lands came to be known as the most hostile in the world.

In 1907, the North American company Jeckyll & Randolph began work on a 364km railway from the vicinity of Vila do Santo Antônio do Rio Madeira to the Bolivian border town of Riberalta, on the Rio Mamoré. German, Jamaican and Cuban workers, and old Panama Canal hands, were brought in as labourers to do the job. The track was completed in 1912; however, this achievement claimed the lives of over 6000 workers, who perished from malaria, yellow fever and gunfights – 'one death for every railway sleeper' was the expression of the day.

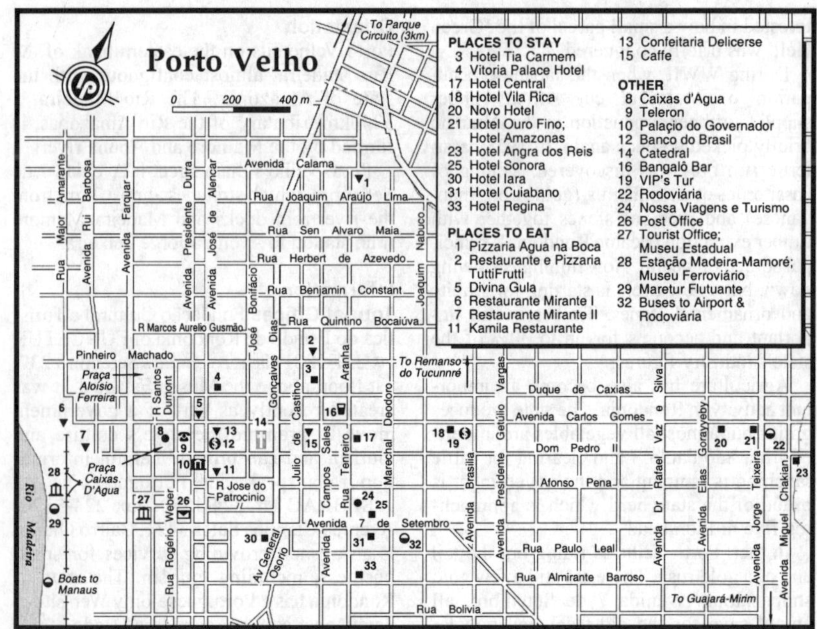

the centre and ask the conductor to tell you when to get off), gives details about national parks and ecological reserves in Rondônia. Only Portuguese is spoken, and while the office is clearly overworked and restricted in its powers and facilities, if you're a genuinely interested traveller, they may be able to help you with introductions to park staff and details about access options.

Money The main branch of Banco do Brasil, Avenida José de Alencar, has câmbio from 10 am to 2 pm. It changes Visa and American Express travellers cheques charging a minimum commission of US$10 or 4% of the transaction value. You can also change US cash dollars at VIP's Tur (☎ 224-7850), Avenida Carlos Gomes 1700, and at the reception of Hotel Vila Rica.

Post & Communications The main post office is on Rua Rogério Weber. TELERON, the state telephone company, is on Avenida Presidente Dutra. Porto Velho's rodoviária has a *posto telefônico* open from 6 am to 11 pm and there's also a branch post office just across the street.

Estação Madeira-Mamoré & Museu Ferroviário

The original terminal of the Madeira-Mamoré railway is Porto Velho's main tourist attraction. For details about the history of this railway, see the boxed text 'The Madeira-Mamoré Railway' in this chapter.

Housed in a huge train shed, the museum displays train relics, memorabilia, and photographs charting the construction of the railway and the history of the Madeira-Mamoré line. Completed in 1912, the railway quickly fell into disuse. By 1931 the private railway had been nationalised, and was abandoned in 1966. Railway buffs will also get a kick out of the *Colonel*

THE NORTH

Church. Built in 1872, this dinosaur was the first locomotive in the Amazon. The museum is open daily from 8 am to 5 pm and entry is free.

In 1979, as a tribute to its historical origins, the new state government reinstated 25km of the famous Madeira-Mamoré railway. Currently the Maria Fumaça (Smoking Mary) steam locomotive chugs to and from Santo Antônio (7km from Porto Velho) on Sunday between 9 am and 6 pm. A return ticket for this excursion costs US$2.

Caixas d'Água

The symbol of Porto Velho, these three water towers date from the time of the Madeira-Mamoré railway's construction.

Museu Estadual

The state museum (☎ 221-1881), at the intersection of Avenida 7 de Setembro and Avenida Farquar, houses modest exhibits on the state's archaeology, mineralogy, ethnology and natural history. It has a display of stuffed animals (including an alligator, anteater and anaconda), a big buffalo skull, ancient pottery, and various human skulls found at old mining sites. The museum is open on weekdays from 8 am to 6 pm and admission is free.

River Beaches

During the low-water season (July to September), several river beaches are uncovered near the city centre: ask at the tourist office for directions to **Areia Branca** (on the opposite banks of the river from the railway station), and **Candeias** (20km off Hwy BR-364; take the Linha Novo Brasil bus). The fishing village of **Belmont**, 20km from Porto Velho, is a calm place to swim or fish.

Organised Tours

Nossa Viagens e Turismo (☎ 221-1567; fax 224-3660), Rua Terneiro Aranha 2125, offers tours to Hotel Flutuante Maici, near the border of Rondônia and Amazonas state, 235km north of Porto Velho, on the Rio Maici tributary of the Rio Madeira. A weekend package, including land and boat transport, accommodation, food and guided tours, costs US$300 for two. Alternatively, if you have a tent, a weekend package for two will cost US$190. This agency is also involved with IBAMA's tourism project for the Estação Ecológica Lago do Cuniã (see National Parks & Biological Reserves earlier in this chapter).

Maretur Flutuante runs one hour booze cruises, using the Manaus-Porto Velho boats on Sunday only between 2 and 6 pm (US$3, excluding drinks). It also runs excursions to the Santo Antônio rapids.

Special Events

Indian legends and traditions were so corrupted by Jesuit missionaries that the Indians circulated stories of the Virgin Mary visiting the Amazon. However, theatrical interpretations of authentic Amerindian legends, ritual dances and ceremonies are becoming popular among students in Porto Velho. They organise the FEMUTE theatre festival during the second half of September. For information contact the Departamento de Cultura at FUNCETUR.

Places to Stay – Budget

The *Hotel Cuiabano* (☎ 221-4084), Avenida 7 de Setembro 1180, has quartos with shared bathroom for US$10 a single or double. Apartamentos with bath and fan cost US$15. Rooms are small and can be a bit grotty, but they open on to a courtyard. The cheap and grungy *Hotel Sonora* (no ☎) has coffin-sized quartos at US$10 a double, and apartamentos for US$15. The five front rooms (US$12 a double) have a strange piped air-conditioning system. There's an on-and-off price war between these hotels; shop around before deciding on one, and check doors and windows for security. Generally, breakfast isn't included.

In a quieter and better location is the *Hotel Tia Carmem* (☎ 221-7910), Rua Campos Sales 2895. It offers good-value, basic quartos with fan and shared bathroom for US$10/15 a single/double; better quartos with air-conditioning and shared bathroom cost US$17/25; apartamentos with fridge, bathroom, air-conditioning and TV cost US$20/30. Prices include a simple breakfast. If Tia Carmem is full another option for the same budget is the *Vitoria Palace Hotel* (☎ 221-9232), Rua Duque de Caxias 745. It has simple, fan-cooled rooms for US$15/20; rooms with air-conditioning and TV cost US$20/30.

It is best to stay downtown but if you want to stay close to the rodoviária (2km east of downtown) there are a few cheap hotels. The *Hotel Angra dos Reis* (☎ 225-2976) on Avenida Dom Pedro II is the best budget option. It has a friendly atmosphere and small but clean rooms with fan and bath for US$13/15. Rooms with air-conditioning cost US$20. *Hotel Ouro Fino* (☎ 223-1101), Avenida Carlos Gomes 2844, near the rodoviária, has dark, musty quartos at US$10/15. Next door, the *Hotel Amazonas* (☎ 221-7735) has slightly better and cleaner single quartos (shared bathroom) for US$7 and apartamentos for US$10/15.

Places to Stay – Mid-Range

The *Hotel Iara* (☎ 221-2127), Rua General Osorio 255, has fairly ordinary single/double apartamentos with air-conditioning for US$20/25. Apartamentos with fridge, air-conditioning, TV and phone cost US$25/35. Better value, and more secure, is the *Hotel Regina* (☎ 224-3411), Rua Almirante Barroso 1127. Clean apartamentos with air-conditioning, fridge and TV cost US$25/40. Close to the rodoviária is the *Novo Hotel* (☎/fax 224-6555), Avenida Carlos Gomes 2776. It has average apartamentos with air-conditioning, TV, phone and fridge for US$32/48, breakfast included.

Places to Stay – Top End

The *Hotel Vila Rica* (☎ 224-3433), Avenida Carlos Gomes 1616, is Porto Velho's finest hotel and one of the few tall buildings in the city. It has an impressive foyer, good swimming pool, nice bar and coffee shop. Comfortable singles/doubles here cost US$115/137, but with the 30% discount for cash payments it costs US$93/111 – good value for what you get. The *Hotel Central* (☎ 224-2099; fax 223-2302), Rua Terneiro Aranha 2472, is frequented by less affluent businesspeople. Apartamentos with air-conditioning, TV, fridge and phone cost US$43/58, with a very good breakfast included.

Places to Eat

Porto Velho is not known for its haute cuisine, but does have a few decent restaurants. One of the best places for fish is *Remanso do Tucunaré* (☎ 221-2353) on Avenida Brasília 1506. This classic restaurant has a simple atmosphere with river fishing decor and funny portraits of Anthony Quinn and Cindy Crawford painted on the entrance to the toilets. It offers excellent value dishes for around US$12 for two. Try the caldeirada of tucunaré or tambaqui (big chunks of fish fillets boiled with onion and tomatoes in a soup-like sauce). Accompanied by rice and pirão (manioc flour cooked in the sauce) it's really delicious! *Caravelas do Madeira* (☎ 221-6641), Rua Jose Camacho 104, is expensive but reportedly also has very good fish dishes.

Restaurante Mirante I, on the hill overlooking the Rio Madeira at the end of Avenida Carlos Gomes, has a great river view and both indoor and outdoor tables. Fish dishes here cost between US$10 and $18, pizzas US$12, and meat dishes around US$13. A block away on Avenida Rui Barbosa is *Restaurante Mirante II* which also has an outdoor patio and view. It's a bit more low-key, serving fish dishes for US$7 to $16 and sandwiches for US$2 to $5; there's cheaper beer on Tuesday nights. Both restaurants have live music on weekends.

The *Pizzaria Agua na Boca* on the corner of Rua Terneiro Aranha and Rua Calama, has Porto Velho's best pizza and excellent service. It is a large but pleasant restaurant with outdoor tables and a large TV screen so you don't escape the Brazilian soapies. Large pizzas cost US$8 to $15, pasta US$8, meat or fish dishes US$13. Another large, open-air restaurant, also with a big TV screen and varied menu, is the *Restaurante e Pizzaria TuttiFrutti* on the corner of Avenida Pinheiro Machado and Rua

Campos Sales. Here you can get a good meat or fish dish for two for about US$12, pasta for US$7 and excellent large juices for US$1.50. Lunch is US$9/kg.

Many other restaurants also have por quilo lunches. *Kamila Restaurante*, Rua José Patrocínio 673, is recommended for its friendly atmosphere and good-value meals for US$6.50/kg. If you are desperate for air-conditioning try *Caffe*, Rua Carlos Gomes 1097, which has good-quality meals for US$9/kg. *Divina Gula*, on the corner of Avenida Carlos Gomes and José de Alencar, also has good, similarly priced self-serve. *Confeitaria Delicerse*, Rua José de Alencar 3050, has excellent quality *salgadinhos* (savoury snacks) for US$1.30, and delicious juices for US$1.50. Burger lovers should head for *Sanduba's* on Rua Carlos Gomes two doors from Hotel Tia Carmem. Hamburgers cost around US$2.50.

Entertainment

The *Bangalô Bar*, Rua Terneiro Aranha 2613, is a traditional bar with a good atmosphere and live music Thursday to Saturday nights. It serves snacks and meat dishes (dinner only; US$10). *Maretur Flutuante* is a popular floating bar at the docks – if you're looking for beer and sweaty dancing, this is the place to go. It can get a bit seedy late at night – check to see if police security is around. The *Mirante* restaurants also have live music on weekends.

Getting There & Away

Air There are flights from Porto Velho to all major Brazilian cities. The major airlines with offices in Porto Velho are Varig (☎ 224-2282), Rua Campos Sales 2666 and VASP (☎ 223-3755), Rua Tenreiro Aranha 2326.

Bus Porto Velho has bus connections to Rio Branco, Guajará-Mirim, Cuiabá, Humaitá and Costa Marques – services to Manaus have been suspended indefinitely. Driving conditions are generally poor (roads to the interior are often impassable during the wet season), so you should view schedules and trip times as optimistic approximations.

Viação Rondônia (☎ 225-2891) has four daily departures for Rio Branco (US$25, around eight hours). It's best to travel overnight (leaving at 11.30 pm) to avoid the heat. There are five buses a day from Porto Velho to Guajará-Mirim (US$15.50, around five hours), two of which (2 pm and 1 am) are direct services. Alternatively you can catch a shared cab for US$25. União Cascavel (☎ 222-2233) has daily bus connections to São Paulo (US$126, 46 hours) and Rio de Janeiro (US$155, 52 hours).

Boat Boat services run between Porto Velho and Manaus three times per week. The US$60/100 fare for hammock/cabin accommodation on the three day trip includes three meals a day but take bottled water. The trip can sometimes take longer than scheduled. It is advisable to check out the boat and fellow passengers for unsavoury characters before committing yourself. The *Alfredo Zani III* is reportedly a good boat. Most boats go directly to Manaus; others require transfers halfway down the Rio Madeira, at Manicoré. The trip takes anywhere from three days to a week, depending on the level of the water, the number of breakdowns and the availability of onward connections. One reader recommended taking a bus to Humaitá (203km from Porto Velho) and then catching a boat to Manaus – this shaves about 24 hours off the normal trip time.

Getting Around

To/From the Airport Aeroporto Belmont (☎ 221-3935) is 7km out of town. You can catch a bus to the city centre via the rodoviária from outside the airport. A convenient place to catch the bus to the airport is on Avenida 7 de Setembro, near the budget hotels – buses leave from here hourly, on the half hour. The set price for a taxi from the airport to the city centre is US$15, but it's only about US$10 from the centre to the airport by the meter.

To/From the Rodoviária The rodoviária (☎ 222-2223) is about 2km from the centre, on Avenida Jorge Teixeira. The Hospital de

Base bus runs to the rodoviária from Avenida 7 de Setembro, in the city centre.

AROUND PORTO VELHO

Santo Antônio

This small riverside settlement, 7km south-west of Porto Velho, is popular with the residents of Porto Velho who come to fish and swim. You can get here by boat (see the Organised Tours information under Porto Velho).

Teotônio

This little fishing village (Km 23 off Hwy BR-364, 38km south-west of Porto Velho), situated by the longest waterfall on the upper Rio Madeira, is the site of an annual fishing championship held in August and September.

Waterfalls

Salto do Jirau is an impressive waterfall on the Rio Madeira, 132km south-west of Porto Velho on Hwy BR-364. About 215km down Hwy BR-364, south-west of Porto Velho and near the town of Abunã, is the Cachoeira Três Esses. Near this spectacular waterfall on the Rio Abunã are some Indian rock inscriptions.

FORTE PRÍNCIPE DA BEIRA & COSTA MARQUES

Remote and little-visited Forte Príncipe da Beira, 170km south of Guajará-Mirim by river, was constructed between 1776 and 1783 on the eastern bank of the Rio Guaporé. The fort has 10m walls and four towers, each holding 14 cannons (which took five years to carry from Pará). The fortress walls, nearly 1km around, are surrounded by a moat and enclose a chapel, an armoury, officers' quarters, and prison cells in which bored convicts have scrawled poetic graffiti. Underground passageways lead from the fortress directly to the river. Nearby, there's a mini meeting of the waters, where the clear, dark Rio Baures flows into the murky, brown Rio Guaporé.

The region around Costa Marques has many Indian **archaeological sites**, inscriptions and cemeteries. Notable sites here are Pedras Negras and Ilha das Flores. For details about the Reserva Biológica do Guaporé, see the section on National Parks & Biological Reserves in this chapter.

Getting There & Away

Air There are no direct flights from Porto Velho to Costa Marques. Take a bus or shared taxi to Guajará-Mirim and from there catch the TAVAJ (☎ 225-2999 in Porto Velho) flights to Costa Marques (US$150 return, three times weekly).

Bus It's a long haul to the fort! To get the bus connections right, you should go on the daily 10.30 pm bus from Porto Velho's rodoviária to Presidente Medici (around seven hours). The next morning at 7 am, a bus leaves Presidente Medici for Costa Marques (US$60, around 12 hours). This is as far as you can go by bus, and from there it's still 25km to Forte Príncipe da Beira. West of Presidente Medici is a wild stretch of road, and the environmental destruction is heartbreaking.

Boat An alternative to the bus may be to travel by boat up the Mamoré and Guaporé rivers from Guajará-Mirim. Boats ply this stretch of the river, making the trip from Guajará-Mirim to the military post at Forte Príncipe da Beira in two to three days. They then continue to Costa Marques, where food and accommodation are available. Enquire about schedules at the Capitânia dos Portos in Guajará-Mirim, but don't expect much help.

GUAJARÁ-MIRIM

• *pop 36,542* ✉ *78957-000* ☎ *069*

Guajará-Mirim, on the Brazilian-Bolivian border, and its Bolivian counterpart, Guayaramerín, have gone through a reversal of roles in recent years. While the Brazilian town is now quiet and subdued by Brazilian standards, the Bolivian town is experiencing a boom since the upgrading of the roads from Porto Velho (on the Brazilian side) and Riberalta (on the Bolivian side). It's become popular with crowds of Brazilians, who pop over the border for shopping. For more information see the History section for Porto Velho.

Information

Tourist Office There is no tourist office in Guajará-Mirim. Cristours (☎/fax 541-3485) on Avenida Presidente Dutra, next to Banco Beron, may help you with information.

Bolivian Consulate If you require a visa, there is a Bolivian Consulate (☎ 541-2862) in Guajará-Mirim, at Avenida Costa Marques 495. It's open on weekday mornings. Have two photographs ready.

Money There is a Banco do Brasil branch on Avenida Mendonça Lima, for exchange of US cash dollars and Visa and American Express travellers cheques.

Museu Municipal

With an old steam locomotive parked outside, this marginally interesting museum, housed in the old train station on Avenida 15 de Novembro, focuses on the history of the region and contains a few stuffed examples of Rondônia's threatened wildlife. There is a huge anaconda which stretches the length of the main salon. The museum's collection of photographs has an especially intriguing portrayal of an Indian attack (or defence) taken in the 1960s. Opening hours are 8 am to noon and 2.30 to 6 pm. Admission is free.

Places to Stay

Guajará-Mirim is quite popular as a weekend destination, so it's worth ringing ahead to book a hotel if you're arriving on a weekend. One cheap and good-value place to stay in town is the *Hotel Pousada Tropical* (☎ 541-3308) on Avenida Leopoldo de Matos that offers small but clean singles/doubles for US$10/20 with fan or US$15/30 with air-conditioning. All rooms have bathrooms and breakfast is included.

Another budget option is the *Hotel Chile* (☎ 541-3846) on Avenida Quintino Bocaiúva. Quartos with fan and shared bath cost US$10/15 and the musty apartamentos with air-conditioning cost US$20/25; breakfast is extra. The *Fenix Palace Hotel* (☎ 541-2326) is right in the town's centre at Avenida 15 de Novembro 459. It has good-value quartos

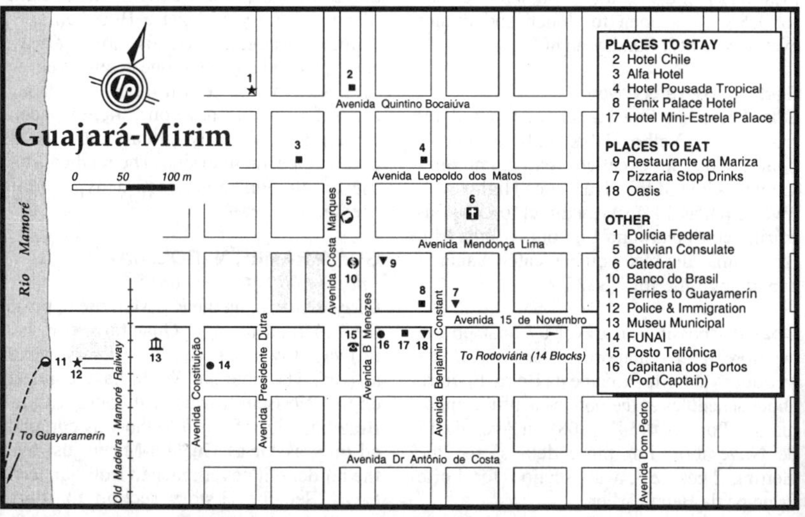

with fan at US$10/18 and air-conditioned apartamentos for US$18/30; both prices include breakfast. Across the road, the popular *Hotel Mini-Estrela Palace* (☎ 541-4798) has a friendly atmosphere. Single/double apartamentos with fan are US$15/25, or US$25/35 with air-conditioning. Apartamentos upstairs are better.

More upmarket, the *Alfa Hotel* (☎ 541-3121) on Avenida Leopoldo de Matos, charges US$30/45 for single/double air-conditioned apartamentos with TV, fridge and hot shower, breakfast included.

Places to Eat

The *Oasis*, on Avenida Benjamin Constant next door to the Hotel Mini-Estrela Palace, is universally recommended as Guajará-Mirim's best restaurant. It has a good all-you-can-eat buffet for US$8 per head at lunch time (11 am to 3 pm) and for dinner only on Friday and Saturday. Across the road, *Pizzaria Stop Drinks*, Avenida 15 de Novembro, has large pizzas for US$12 and is popular at night – in fact, some of the clientele stop and drink all night! Another option for good value meals is the *Restaurante da Mariza* on Avenida Mendoça Lima. It has a varied menu with meat and fish dishes for US$8 and *refeições* for US$5. It's open for lunch and dinner everyday except Sunday night.

Getting There & Away

Bus There are five bus connections daily from Porto Velho (US$15.50, around 5 hours), along an excellent road, commonly known as one of the 'Transcoca Highways'. Two (2 pm and 1 am) run direct to Guajará-Mirim, cutting around 1½ hours off the trip. If you miss the bus, you can catch a shared cab at any time for US$25.

Boat It's possible to travel by boat up the Mamoré and Guaporé rivers to Costa Marques via Forte Príncipe da Beira. Enquire about schedules at the not-so-helpful Capitânia dos Portos (☎ 541-2208) on Avenida 15 de Novembro. For more details, see the Getting There & Away section for Forte Príncipe da Beira earlier.

Crossing the Bolivian Border If you're not planning to travel further into Bolivia, you can pop across the Rio Mamoré to visit Guayaramerín, which has cheaper accommodation than Guajará-Mirim. Between early morning and 6.30 pm, small motorised canoes and larger motor ferries cross the river from Guajará-Mirim every few minutes (US$1.50). After hours, there are only express motorboats (US$4 to $5.50 per boat). You are permitted to travel back and forth across the river at will, but those travelling beyond the frontier area will have to complete border formalities.

There is a Bolivian consulate in Guajará-Mirim, however, citizens of most countries do not require a visa to travel to Bolivia. If you are leaving Brazil to travel further into Bolivia, you need to get a Brazilian exit stamp at the Polícia Federal (☎ 541-2437), three blocks from the port in Guajará-Mirim on Avenida Presidente Dutra. Once across the Rio Mamoré, pick up an entrance stamp at Migración (Bolivian immigration) at the ferry terminal.

If you are planning to leave Bolivia from Guayaramerín, you must have your passport stamped at Bolivian Migración, and again at the Brazilian Polícia Federal in Guajará-Mirim, where you'll get a Brazilian entry stamp. Although officials don't always check, technically everyone needs a yellow-fever vaccination certificate to enter Brazil here. If you don't have one, there is a convenient and relatively sanitary clinic at the port on the Brazilian side. The medical staff use an air gun rather than a hypodermic needle.

GUAYARAMERÍN (BOLIVIA)

• *pop 14,000* ☎ *(591) 0855*

Guayaramerín, on the Rio Mamoré opposite the Brazilian town of Guajará-Mirim, is a railway town where the railway never arrived. The line that would have connected the Rio Beni town of Riberalta with the Brazilian city of Porto Velho was completed only as far as Guajará-Mirim just over the border – it never reached Bolivian territory! (See the History section for Porto

Velho for more information about the railway).

Guayaramerín retains a frontier atmosphere, but is growing quickly – a constant stream of motorbikes buzz around the streets, and the shops are overflowing with electronic goods from Japan, China and Taiwan. The town serves as a river port and an entry point to or from Brazil; it is also the terminus of the road linking it and Riberalta, 90km away, with Santa Ana, Rurrenabaque and La Paz.

Information

Tourist Office There's a tourist information office (of sorts) at the port – it has no literature, but staff will gladly help with some general information about transport and accommodation. Cristours (☎ 3620; fax 3610) on the corner of Avenida 24 de Septiembre and Plaza Principal, can help with information about tours in the area and around Bolivia.

Brazilian Consulate There is a Brazilian Consulate in Guayaramerín, on Avenida 24 de Septiembre, one block east of Plaza Principal. Open Monday to Friday from 9 am to 1 pm, it will issue visas on the same day.

Money US dollars can be changed at the Hotel San Carlos, at a good rate. Alternatively, exchange US dollars, Bolivian bolivianos or Brazilian reais with the cambistas who hang around the port area. In 1998, the going rate was approximately US$1 = B$5.

Places to Stay

The mellowest budget place to stay in Guayaramerín is undoubtedly the *Hotel Litoral* (☎ 2016) near the airport. Private baths, refreshingly tepid showers and clean rooms are offered here for only US$4 per person. Across the street, the quiet and shady *Hotel Santa Ana* (☎ 2206) offers similar amenities for the same price.

The *Hotel Central* (☎ 2042) on Calle Oruro Santa Cruz costs US$3. It's a low-budget option, with shared baths and no double beds. The *Hotel Plaza Anexo* (☎ 2086) on Calle Oruro Santa Cruz has clean rooms with bath and good atmosphere for US$5.

The *Hotel San Carlos* (☎ 2419) on Calle 6 de Agosto is the upmarket place in town, with a restaurant, TV, sauna, air-conditioning, billiards room and 24 hour hot water. Singles/doubles cost US$20/30.

Places to Eat

Patujú Churrasqueria at Calle 6 de Agosto has good-value tasty meals. Another recommended place for lunch and dinner is the *Ricon* on Calle Frederico Roman near the Plaza Principal. It offers good but not so cheap Brazilian-style meals.

Sujal Churrasqueria is a good restaurant out of town. Motorbike taxis will get you there for B$1.50. On the plaza on Calle Federico Roman, *Los Bibosis* is a popular place for drinks and snacks.

Getting There & Away

Air Guayaramerín's airport is at the southern edge of town. AeroSur (☎ 3731) has a daily flight at 9.15 am to Trinidad, with same-day connections to Santa Cruz, La Paz and Cobija. LAB (☎ 2130) flies twice weekly to Santa Cruz (on Thursday and Sunday) and twice a week to La Paz (on Tuesday and Saturday). The LAB office in Guayaramerín is not yet computerised, so book flights out of Guayaramerín elsewhere or risk not getting a seat.

Bus Most bus services to and from Guayaramerín (with the exception of services to Riberalta) operate only during the dry season – roughly from May to October. Trans Guaya Tours has two buses daily, at 7 am and 3 pm, to Riberalta (US$2, two hours), a once-weekly (Wednesday) service to Cobija (US$16, 14 hours) and three buses a week, on Wednesday, Friday and Sunday, to Trinidad (US$22, 35 hours). Flota Yungueña has Wednesday, Friday and Sunday departures for Riberalta, Rurrenabaque and La Paz (US$28, 36 hours).

Boat From the port, ships leave frequently for Trinidad, five to seven days up the Rio

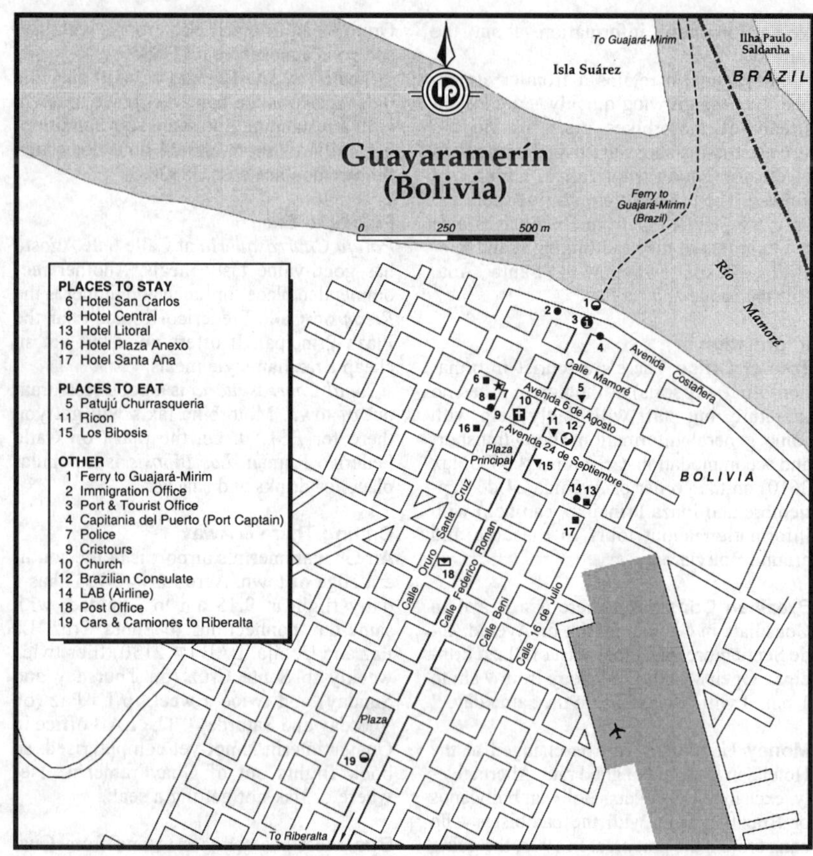

Mamoré. For information regarding departures, the port captain's office has a notice board which lists any activity into or out of town.

Hitching Camiones (trucks) to Riberalta leave from the main street, 2½ blocks west of the market, near the park. They charge the same as buses, and make the trip in less time. If you'd like to travel a bit more comfortably, cars (US$6) spare you exposure to the choking red dust that seems to get into everything. To Cobija, YPFB petrol trucks and a white Volvo freight carrier occasionally depart from the same place.

Crossing the Brazilian Border For information about onward travel into Brazil, see the Getting There & Away section for Guajará-Mirim.

Getting Around

You'll quickly discover that there are no automobile taxis in Guayaramerín, but then the town is so small that you can walk just about anywhere you'd like to go. There are motorbike taxis, which cost B$1.50 anywhere around town. Those who want to do some exploring of the surrounding area can hire a motorbike from the Plaza Principal for US$2 per hour (negotiate a discount for daily rentals). Don't be tempted to take a swig of the stuff sold in Coke bottles on the street: it's motorbike petrol!

Acre

The state of Acre has become a favoured destination for developers and settlers, who have followed Hwy BR-364 and started claiming lands, clearing forest and setting up ranches. The issues of land ownership and sustainable forest use have caused major conflicts between the developers and the indigenous tribes and rural workers, mostly rubber-tappers, who are descended from settlers who arrived many decades ago. This conflict received massive national and international attention in 1988, with the assassination of Chico Mendes, a rubber-tapper and an opponent of rainforest destruction (see the boxed text 'Chico Mendes' in this chapter). For information about the history of Acre, refer to the History section for Porto Velho.

The state is two hours behind Brazilian Standard Time.

RIO BRANCO

• *pop 229 000 ✉ 69900-000 ☎ 068*

Rio Branco, the capital of Acre, was founded in 1882 on the banks of the Rio Acre, which is navigable via the Rio Purus to the Amazon. There's a relaxed and surprisingly cosmopolitan feel to this city, which has a few attractions close to the centre, and other points of interest, including intriguing religious communities, further afield.

Information

Tourist Office The Departamento de Turismo (☎ 229 2134), Estrada Dias Martins, Km 5, Distrito Industrial, is a bit far out of town. It is open from 8 am to 1 pm on weekdays. In the city centre you can try SEBRAE (☎ 223 2100; fax 224 9514) at Rua Rio Grande do Sul, 109.

Money The main branch of the Banco do Brasil is at Rua Arlindo Porto Leal 85. The exchange counter is open from 9 am to noon Monday to Friday.

Post & Communications The central post office is on Rua Epaminondas Jacome 447. TELEACRE, the state telephone company, is on Avenida Brasil 378 and is open 6 am to 10 pm.

Casa do Seringueiro

This museum has a collection of photos, paintings and replicas of housing and utensils that portray the life of a typical *seringueiro* (rubber-tapper). There is also a small area devoted to Chico Mendes.

The museum is on the corner of Avenida Getúlio Vargas and Avenida Brasil and is open Monday to Friday from 7 am to 1 pm and 2 to 5 pm. Entry is free.

Museu da Borracha

The collection in this museum is divided into sections relating to the archaeology, palaeontology, ethnology and recent history of Acre. It's well organised, housed in a cute building, and well worth a visit. The museum is at Avenida Ceará 1177. It is open Monday to Friday from 9 am to noon and 2 to 5 pm. Entry is free.

Colônia Cinco Mil

The Colônia Cinco Mil (literally 'Colony of the 5000') is a religious community which follows the doctrine of Santo Daime, introduced in 1930 by Raimundo Irineu Serra, also known as Mestre Irineu. The cult's practices revolve around the sacred hallucinogenic drink called *ayahuasca*. For more details see the Religion section in the Facts about the Country chapter.

If you wish to visit Colônia Cinco Mil try to find somebody from the community to

Chico Mendes

Chico Mendes was born in 1944 at Seringal Cachoeira, in Acre, into a family descended from a rubber-tapper. At an early age, he became interested in asserting the rights of rubber-tappers to their lands. In the 1970s the Plano de Integração Nacional (PNI), an ambitious government plan to tame the Amazon, attracted developers, ranchers, logging companies and settlers into Acre. In 1975, Chico Mendes organised a rural workers' union to defy the tactics of violent intimidation and dispossession practised by the newcomers, who were destroying the forest and robbing the rural workers of their livelihood.

Mendes organised large groups of rural workers to form nonviolent human blockades around forest areas threatened with clearance, and soon attracted the wrath of developers, who were used to getting their way either through corrupt officials or by hiring pistoleiros to clear human impediments. These *empates*, or 'confrontational standoffs', proved effective in saving thousands of hectares of forest, which were set aside as *reservas extrativistas* where rural workers could continue to tap rubber and gather fruits, nuts and fibres.

International interest focused on Mendes as a defender of the forests, but his role as a leader also made him a natural target for frustrated and infuriated opponents. Early in December 1988, he moved to establish his birthplace, Seringal Cachoeira, as a reserva extrativista, defying the local landowner and rancher, Darly Alves da Silva, who disputed ownership of the land.

On 22 December, Chico Mendes, who had received numerous death threats, momentarily left his bodyguards inside his house and stepped out onto the back porch. He was hit at close range by shots fired from the bushes, and died shortly afterwards.

For almost two years, there was much speculation about the murderers; although they were well known, the men were considered out of legal reach because of their connections with the influential landowners and corrupt officials of the region – a common arrangement in the frontier lands of Brazil. Intense national and international pressure finally brought the case to trial. In December 1990, Darly Alves da Silva received a 19-year prison term for ordering the assassination; his son, Darci, was given an identical sentence for pulling the trigger.

organise your visit. Ask around Rio Branco or at the Fundação Cultural do Acre on Avenida Getúlio Vargas, Palácio das Secretarias, 2nd floor. If you stay overnight, no fee will be charged, but you will be expected to share the cost of transport and food. It's possible to arrive at the community independently; you can get there by local bus from the city centre. A taxi from Rio Branco will cost around US$15.

Praia do Amapá

While this beach is not fantastic, during weekends from the second half of August until the first half of September it comes alive for the Festival de Artes da Praia do Amapá, with sports, folk music and dance and stalls selling regional food.

The beach is out of town, near Colonia do Amapá, 10km from Rio Branco upstream on the Rio Acre. It takes about an hour to get there by boat, less than half an hour by car along the sealed Hwy AC-40, and then along a small stretch of gravel road.

Parque Ambiental Chico Mendes

This is Rio Branco's most interesting park. About half of its 52 hectares is covered with native forest and there is some local fauna. The other half is regenerating.

There is a memorial to Chico Mendes near the entrance, with pictures and samples of his writing (in Portuguese). The park also has a picnic area, toilets, a funny cast-iron treetop lookout, bike paths and a small zoo. There are walking paths with

The verdict pleased rural workers, world opinion and the Brazilian government, which badly needed to demonstrate to Brazilians and foreigners a modicum of control in the Amazon region. But while the media spotlight moved on to other sensations, the murders continued. Documentation shows that this exhibition of justice was a rare flash in the media pan – of the hundreds of murders of union leaders and land-rights campaigners since the late 1970s, the only one that was thoroughly investigated and prosecuted was that of Chico Mendes.

Itamar Mendes, Chico's wife, was courted by 10 Hollywood producers to sell the film rights to her husband's story (*The Burning Season* was released in late 1994, directed by David Puttnam). International organisations made posthumous awards to Chico Mendes, and several parks in Brazil were named after him. In Xapuri, his house has been made into a commemorative museum. The rubber-tappers and rural workers of the region are keen to keep up the pressure, not only to establish more extractive reserves throughout the Amazon region, but most importantly, to force the Brazilian government to enforce the laws governing the establishment of such reserves and to punish those who violate them.

In February 1992 the state appeals court in Rio Branco annulled the conviction of Darly Alves da Silva. For those who had hoped to see a glimmer of justice in Brazil, it was just another nail in the coffin.

theme huts representing different aspects of life in the region including rubber-tappers, an Indian *maloca* (dwelling) and myths and legends.

The park (☎ 220 2894) is on Hwy AC-40, Km 3, near Vila Acre, about 10km south of Rio Branco. To get there catch one of the regular Rio Branco-Vila Acre buses.

Parque Ecológico Plácido de Castro

In the municipality of Plácido de Castro, 95km east of Rio Branco, on the Brazilian-Bolivian border, the 44 hectares of native forest offers good swimming at river beaches, and it's possible to follow forest paths that were originally used by rubber-tappers.

There are four buses daily from Rio Branco to Plácido de Castro. As well as the *Hotel Carioca* (☎ 237-1064) on Rua Juvenal Antunes, the town has various inexpensive *pensões* and restaurants.

Organised Tours

Currently, the only agency in Rio Branco offering tour packages was Senhor Carlos at Biotur Eco-Turismo (☎ 985-2272). Enquire at the reception of Hotel Rio Branco. He organises tours for groups of four to seven people, using a 4WD vehicle and local boats. A Rio Branco city tour costs US$28 per head; excursions to Parque Ecológico Plácido de Castro US$30 and to Guajará-Mirim US$50.

Places to Stay

If you're just passing through or have an early bus departure, the *Hotel Flor da Mata*

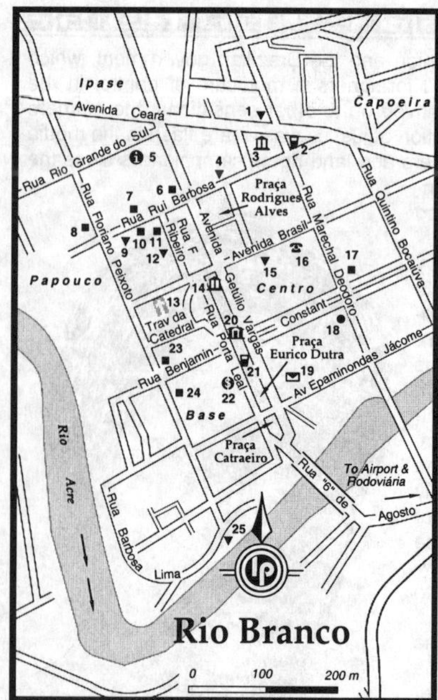

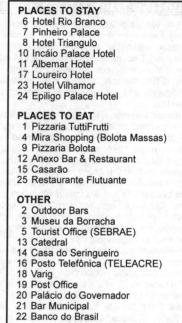

PLACES TO STAY

6 Hotel Rio Branco
7 Pinheiro Palace
8 Hotel Triangulo
10 Incáio Palace Hotel
11 Albemar Hotel
17 Loureiro Hotel
23 Hotel Vilhamor
24 Epiligo Palace Hotel

PLACES TO EAT

1 Pizzaria TuttiFrutti
4 Mira Shopping (Bolota Massas)
9 Pizzaria Bolota
12 Anexo Bar & Restaurant
15 Casarão
25 Restaurante Flutuante

OTHER

2 Outdoor Bars
3 Museu da Borracha
5 Tourist Office (SEBRAE)
13 Catedral
14 Casa do Seringueiro
16 Posto Telefônica (TELEACRE)
18 Varig
19 Post Office
20 Palácio do Governador
21 Bar Municipal
22 Banco do Brasil

(☎ 224-0087), Avenida Uirapuru 533 next to the rodoviária, has clean single/double apartamentos for US$18/23.

The *Albemar Hotel* (☎ 224-1938; fax 224 8965), Rua Franco Ribeiro 99, has clean, small apartamentos with air-conditioning and bathroom for US$20/25. The manager speaks English.

The *Loureiro Hotel* (☎ 223-1560), Rua Marechal Deodoro 196, has clean but musty apartamentos for US$24/35. The rooms have air-conditioning, TV, phone, fridge and a good breakfast is included.

One of the best value deals in town is the *Hotel Triangulo* (☎ 224-4117), Rua Floriano Peixoto 227. The entrance is rather like a parking lot (convenient for most of its interstate clientele) but it has good-value simple and clean rooms with bathroom, TV and air-conditioning for US$20/26, with breakfast. It also has more expensive versions, with fridge and phone, for US$30/40.

The *Epilogo Palace Hotel* (☎ 223-1886), Rua Floriano Peixoto 308, has clean and neatly presented fan-cooled apartamentos for US$20/29, including breakfast. *Hotel Vilhamor* (☎ 223-2399), Rua Floriano Peixoto 317, offers clean, comfortable apartamentos for US$36/50, plus a 10% surcharge if paying by credit card.

The *Hotel Rio Branco* (☎ 224-1785; fax 224-2681), Rua Rui Barbosa 193, is a classic Acreano lodging with good service, breakfast and dated decor. Apartamentos cost US$30/40/60 for singles/doubles/triples. The *Inácio Palace Hotel* (☎ 224-6397; fax 224-5726), Rua Rui Barbosa 72, is a bit old and tacky but offers reasonably clean and comfortable apartamentos for US$30/40 a single/double (cash) or US$42/63 (credit card). The *Pinheiro Palace* (☎ 224-7191; fax 224-5726), just across the street and under the same management, has a pool and good apartments for US$60/85/110 singles/doubles/triples (cash) and US$73/ 110/140 (credit card).

Places to Eat

Italian food seems to be the rage in Rio Branco. The *Anexo Bar & Restaurant* on Rua F Ribeiro serves tasty Italian food for US$9, meat dishes for US$13 and self-service por quilo for lunch. *Pizzaria Bolota*, Rua Rui Barbosa 325, has tables set out on a terrace and serves average pizza and pasta. *Bolota Massas* in the Mira Shopping food court on Rua Rui Barbosa opposite Praça Plácido de Castro, has pizza for US$5, pasta dishes for US$8 and beer on tap for US$1.30.

Mira Shopping, an air-conditioned oasis in Rio Branco's heat, also has *Big Food* with self-serve until 3 pm or grilled meat and rice during the evenings for US$5; or *Café do Ponto,* good for coffee, pastries and ice cream.

Pizzaria TuttiFrutti, Avenida Ceará 1132, has pizza and ice cream. The *Casarão*, Avenida Brasil 310, has good value por quilo food at lunch and is popular with locals.

Meat-eaters should try *Churrascaria Triangulo* at the Hotel Triangulo on Rua Floriano Peixoto. A refeição comercial for lunch or dinner is US$5. A good value rodizio costs U$8 for as much meat as you like. Also recommended is the air-conditioned *Inacio's Restaurante*, on Rua Rui Barbosa 82, next door to Inácios Palace Hotel. It has à la carte grilled fish and steaks from US$14.

The *Restaurante Flutuante* (☎ 224-7248) at the end of Rua Floriano Peixoto is a pleasant floating restaurant with a good view along the Rio Acre. During the wet season (February through April) the water level raises the restaurant by 10m; they'll show photos if you doubt it! Fish dishes are from US$15, meat dishes from US$11.

Entertainment

The *Bar Municipal* at Praça Eurico Dutra, near the government building, is an interesting spot for a beer and snack.

The small square sandwiched between Avenida Ceará, Rua Marechal Deodoro and Rua Rui Barbosa, has several outdoor bars that can get crowded at night. The *Imperador Galvez* at Bairro Tropical is reportedly a good nightclub with an open-air bar and music for dancing.

Getting There & Away

Access to Rio Branco has improved and now you can get there year-round along sealed roads from Brazil's eastern states. However, between October and June, when the rivers are at their highest, the roads to the more isolated towns (off Hwy BR-364) are precarious and often impassable, leaving plane or boat the only viable transport options. From July to September, when the rivers are at their lowest levels, the roads are passable but river traffic is restricted.

Air There are flights between Rio Branco and Cruzeiro do Sul, Manaus, Porto Velho, Cuiabá, Rio and São Paulo. Varig (☎ 224-2226) at Rua Marechal Deodoro 115, is the main airline operating interstate flights. There are various air-taxi companies at the airport such as TACEZUL (☎ 224-3242) and TAVAJ (☎ 223-2701). At the time of writing regular flights to Puerto Maldonado (in Peru) had been discontinued, but it is possible to hire an air-taxi to Puerto Maldonado (US$1400 for a maximum of six passengers).

Bus The Açilandia bus company (☎/fax 224-2746) services the interstate capitals: four departures daily to Porto Velho (US$24, about 10 hours); twice weekly (Wednesday and Friday) to Belém (US$220, four days); weekly (Saturday) to Fortaleza (US$250, four days); and daily to Goiania (US$130, 48 hours). Services to Manaus have been suspended indefinitely.

Interior destinations are covered by Acreana buses: five departures daily to Brasiléia (US$6, six hours); twice daily to Xapuri (US$17, four hours); four times daily to Plácido de Castro (US$5.50, 2½ hours);

and twice daily to Boca do Acre in Amazonas state (US$8.50, four hours).

Boat Enquire about boats at the port at the eastern end of Avenida Epaminondas Jácome. You might score a ride at the port; if there's a group of you, prices quoted for a 1½ day trip to Boca do Acre (Amazonas) are around US$65. From Boca do Acre, there is river traffic along the Rio Purus as far as the Amazon, and even to Manaus.

Getting Around

To/From the Airport Aeroporto Internacional Presidente Medici (☎ 224-6833), is about 2km east of town on Hwy AC-40, at Km 1. The rodoviária (☎ 224-2746) is also a couple of kilometres east, on Avenida Uirapuru in the Cidade Nova district.

From the airport, the bus marked Norte/Sul runs via the rodoviária to the city centre. A taxi from the airport to the city centre costs an exorbitant US$15 (flat rate), but from the centre to the airport or to the rodoviária it's only about US$5 (by the meter).

BRASILÉIA

The small town of Brasiléia lies on the Brazilian border with Bolivia, separated from Cobija (its Bolivian counterpart) by the Rio Abunã and the Rio Acre. Brasiléia has nothing to interest travellers except an immigration stamp into or out of Brazil. The Polícia Federal is 2km north-east of the centre; dress nicely. The office is open daily from 8 am to noon and 2 to 5 pm.

There is a Bolivian Consulate in Brasiléia, at Rua Major Salinas 205. It's open Monday to Friday from 8 to 11 am.

Places to Stay & Eat

If you're stuck in Brasiléia, try the *Hotel Fronteiras* (☎ 546-3045), near the church in the centre. Apartamentos cost US$12/15 for singles/doubles. *Restaurant Carioca*, beside the hotel, serves typical Brazilian fare.

Hotel Brasiléia (☎ 546-3562) on Rua A Matos, also near the church, has simple rooms with breakfast for US$9/16. *Pousada las Palmeras* (☎ 546-3284), also in the centre, has fan-cooled rooms for US$11/20 and air-conditioned apartamentos for US$18/ 25. Alternatively, there's the *Hotel Kador* (☎ 546-3283), at Avenida Santos Dumont 25, on the road between the international bridge and the Polícia Federal. Apartamentos here cost US$12/18 for singles/ doubles. *Pizzaria Ribeira* is just across the road.

Getting There & Away

From the rodoviária, five buses run daily to Rio Branco (US$16, six hours). Buses go to Assis Brasil in the dry season (roughly June to October); during the rainy season, you may be able to organise a ride with a truck; contact Transport Acreana (☎ 546-3057) in Brasiléia on Avenida Santos Dumont.

Crossing the Bolivian Border If you're crossing to or from Bolivia, you'll have to get entry/exit stamps from migración (immigration) in Cobija and from the Polícia Federal just outside Brasiléia. A yellow-fever vaccination certificate is technically required to enter Brazil from Cobija, but there doesn't seem to be much checking done. There's no vaccination clinic in Brasiléia, so you'll have to track down a private physician if your health records aren't in order.

Since it's a rather long up-and-down slog from Cobija across the bridge to Brasiléia, you may want to take a taxi, but negotiate the route and the fare in advance. For about US$3.50 the driver will take you from Cobija to the Polícia Federal in Brasiléia, wait while you complete immigration formalities and then take you to the city centre or to the rodoviária. Going the other way, from the centre of Brasiléia, taxis try to charge double the price.

Alternatively, you can take the rowboat ferry (US$0.50 per person) across the Rio Acre to the landing in the centre of Brasiléia. From here it's about 1km to the rodoviária and another 1.5km to the Polícia Federal.

COBIJA (BOLIVIA)

• *pop 15000* ☎ *0842*

The border town of Cobija is linked to its Brazilian counterpart, Brasiléia, by the International Bridge. Founded in 1906 as Bahia, Cobija experienced a boom as a rubber-producing centre during the 1940s. When the rubber industry declined, so did Cobija's fortunes, and the town was reduced to a forgotten hamlet of 5000 people. Today, the population has doubled, and the town has at least one claim to fame: with 1770mm of precipitation falling annually, it is the wettest spot in Bolivia.

There are a few interesting things to see, including rubber and brazil-nut plantations, a number of lakes and places to observe wildlife, but transport is difficult and the hinterlands are not easily accessible.

There are buses from Cobija to La Paz via Riberalta. Cobija has an international airport, with connections for the popular La Paz-Santa Cruz-Panama City-Miami flights.

Information

Brazilian Consulate There is a Brazilian consulate (☎ 2110) on the corner of Calle Beni and Fernandez Molina. It's open from 8.30 am to 12.30 pm Monday to Friday.

Immigration Bolivian immigration is in the prefectural building on the main plaza. It's open weekdays from 9 am to 5 pm.

Money Casa Horacio changes Brazilian *real*, Bolivian bolivianos and US cash dollars at official rates (in 1998, about US$1 = B$5). There is a 10% commission charged for cashing travellers cheques.

Places to Stay

The friendly, Spanish-run *Hotel Prefectural* (☎ 2230), also known as the Hotel Pando, is near the market and has nice breezy rooms with fan and private bath for US$11 per person (US$13 for a room with a double bed). Breakfast is included in the price.

The *Residencial Frontera* (☎ 2740) on Calle 9 de Feberero is clean, but a bit overpriced, with quartos at US$5 per person and apartamentos at US$8/10 for singles/doubles. It's pleasant if you can get a room with a window onto the patio. Another option is the *Residencial Cocodrilo* (☎ 2215) on Avenida Fernandez Molina near the Brazilian consulate, which charges US$3/8 for clean (but far from opulent) singles/doubles.

Places to Eat

In the early morning, the market sells chicken empanadas, fresh fruits and vegetables and lots of tinned Brazilian products.

The *Restaurant La Esquina de La Abuela*, on Avenida Fernandez Molina, is Cobija's nicest restaurant, with outdoor tables. Chicken and meat dishes cost US$3. If you really want to pig out, finish with an ice-cream sundae at *Heladeria Y Licoreria El Tucáno*, across the road. On the same street, about a five minute walk from thecentre, is *Churrasqueria La Cabaína del Momo* (long names seem to be in vogue in Cobija). Here you can eat churrasco (US$2) on a raised balcony.

Getting There & Away

Air AeroSur flies daily from Cobija to Trinidad, with same-day connections to La

Paz and Santa Cruz. Next-day connections are available from Trinidad to Guayaramerín, Riberalta and San Borja. From La Paz, there are daily flights to Trinidad, with connections to Cobija. AeroSur (☎ 2562) has an office in the Hotel Prefectural.

LAB (☎ 2170), the Bolivian national airline, has an office on Avenida Fernandez Molina, near the Polícia Nacional base. LAB has two direct flights a week to and from La Paz, and another two flights weekly with stops in Riberalta, Guayaramerín, Trinidad and Cochabamba.

Bus There is a bus to Riberalta (US$10, 12 hours). Connections can be made there for the 24 hour ride to La Paz. Purchase tickets at Trans Guaya Tours, near the Hotel Prefectural. Details about bus connections from Brasiléia (Brazil) are given in the Getting There & Away section for Brasiléia.

Crossing the Brazilian Border For information about crossing the border between Brasiléia (Brazil) and Cobija, see Crossing the Bolivian Border in the Getting There & Away section for Brasiléia.

ASSIS BRASIL & IÑAPARI (PERU)

Although we haven't tried the route described here, locals reckon that access from Assis Brasil to Iñapari (Peru) is possible for the adventurous traveller. Unfortunately, Peru's Madre de Dios region has been a centre of operations for the Sendero Luminoso (Shining Path) guerrillas, drug-running, lawless gold digging and other renegade activities. If you do manage to get through, please write and let us know how it went!

Places to Stay & Eat

There's one hotel in Assis Brasil: the *Assis Brasil Palace Hotel* (☎ 548-1045), on Rua Eneide Batista. For places to eat in the town centre, try *Restaurante Seridó*, at Rua Valério Magalhães 62, or the *Bar & Restaurante Petisco*, on Rua Raimundo Chaar.

Getting There & Away

Crossing the Peruvian Border Take a bus or a jeep from Brasiléia to Assis Brasil, 110km west of Brasiléia. It may be simpler to complete Brazilian immigration procedures in Brasiléia.

Across the Rio Acre from Assis Brasil is the muddy little Peruvian settlement of Iñapari, where you must register your arrival with the police. From Iñapari, there is a road (of sorts) to Puerto Maldonado, which is accessible to Cuzco on the Peruvian road system but which is, for practical purposes, impassable to all but pedestrians or motorbikes. You may be able to fly from Iñapari – there is an airport S7km from the village – to Puerto Maldonado on a Grupo Ocho cargo flight, but you shouldn't count on it.

CRUZEIRO DO SUL

Another option to reach Peru – and a decidedly bad idea, due to drug-running and Sendero Luminoso activity in the area – is to fly, or hitch on a truck (654km along Hwy BR-364), from Rio Branco to Cruzeiro do Sul (in western Acre), and then fly from there to the Peruvian Amazon city of Pucallpa.

Places to Stay & Eat

In Cruzeiro do Sul, there are a couple of hotels: the *Plínio Hotel* (☎ 322-3445) at Boulevard Thaumaturgo 155, and *Sandra's Hotel* (☎ 322-2481) at Avenida Coronel Mâncio Lima 241. For places to eat in the town centre, try the *Restaurante Popular* on Rua Joaquim Távora, or the *Zanzibar Bar & Restaurante*, at Avenida Getúlio Vargas 19.

Language Guide

Viajando na maionese
'I'm travelling through the mayonnaise'
(colloquial for 'I'm totally spaced out')

Portuguese is similar to Spanish on paper but sounds completely different. Brazilians will understand what you say if you speak Spanish but you won't get much of what they say. So don't think studying Portuguese is a waste of time. Listen to language tapes and develop an ear for Portuguese – it's a beautiful-sounding language.

When they settled Brazil in the 16th century, the Portuguese encountered the diverse languages of the Indians. These, together with the various idioms and dialects spoken by the Africans brought in as slaves, extensively changed the Portuguese spoken by the early settlers.

Along with Portuguese, Tupi-Guaraní (language), written down and simplified by the Jesuits, became a common language which was understood by the majority of the population. It was spoken by the general public until the middle of the 18th century, but its usage diminished with the great number of Portuguese gold-rush immigrants and a royal proclamation in 1757 prohibiting its use. With the expulsion of the Jesuits in 1759, Portuguese was established as the national language.

Still, many words remain from the Indian and African languages. From Tupi-Guaraní come lots of place names (eg Guanabara, Carioca, Tijuca and Niterói), animal names (eg *piranha*, *capivara* and *urubu*) and plant names (eg *mandioca*, *abacaxí*, *caju* and *jacarandá*). Words from the African dialects, mainly those from Nigeria and Angola, are used in Afro-Brazilian religious ceremonies (eg *Orixá*, *Exú* and *Iansã*), cooking (eg *vatapá*, *acarajé* and *abará*) and in general conversation (eg *samba*, *mocambo* and *moleque*).

Brazilians are easy to befriend, but unfortunately the vast majority of them speak little or no English. This is changing, however, as practically all Brazilians in school are learning English. All the same, don't count on finding an English speaker, especially out of the cities. The more Portuguese you speak, the more you will get out of your trip.

Portuguese has masculine and feminine forms of nouns and adjectives. Alternative gender endings to words appear separated by a slash, the masculine form first. Generally, 'o' indicates masculine and 'a' indicates feminine.

Books

Most phrasebooks are not very helpful. Their vocabulary is often dated and they contain the Portuguese spoken in Portugal, not Brazil. Notable exceptions are Lonely Planet's *Brazilian phrasebook*, and a Berlitz phrasebook for travel in Brazil. Make sure any English-Portuguese dictionary is a Brazilian Portuguese one. Wordsworth Reference publishes a handy one. If you're determined not to learn, get a copy of Jonathan Maeder's *The Wordless Travel Book* (Ten Speed Press), a collection of drawings of just about everything you'd need on a trip – point to what you want!

If you're more intent on learning the language, try the US Foreign Service Institute (FSI) tape series. It comes in two volumes. Volume 1 includes 23 cassettes and accompanying text, costs US$188 in the US, Canada and Mexico and US$219.60 elsewhere and covers pronunciation, verb tenses and essential nouns and adjectives. Then slightly cheaper Volume 2 includes 22 tapes with text and includes some useful phrases and a travel vocabulary. The tapes are sold through National Technical Information Service (NTIS; ☎ (703) 605-6000), 5285 Port Royal Rd, Springfield, VA 22161.

For fluent Spanish speakers, NTIS has 'Portuguese – From Spanish to Portuguese', which consists of two tapes and a text explaining similarities and differences between these languages. This one costs US$59/71.25.

In Australia, most foreign-language and travel bookstores stock a wide range of material. The Foreign Language Bookshop (☎ (03) 9654-2883), 259 Collins St, Melbourne, Victoria, 3000, carries three types of learning kits: *Language 30: Portuguese* (booklet and cassette, A$35.95); Berlitz' *Portuguese for Travellers* (booklet and cassette, A$30.95 or A$39.95 with CD) and HUGO's *Portuguese Travel Kit* (booklet and cassette, A$19.95).

Combine these with a few Brazilian samba tapes and some Jorge Amado novels and you're ready to begin the next level of instruction on the streets of Brazil.

Pronunciation

The big shocker is that generally, an 'r' is pronounced like an 'h': Rio becomes 'Hee-oh', the currency (the *real)* is pronounced 'hee-ow' etc.

In the same spirit of fun, a 't' (or 'd') followed by a vowel becomes a 'ch' (or 'dj'), so the word 'restaurante' is pronounced approximately 'hess-to-ROCH'. But wait … there's more! An 'lh' combination generally produces a 'ly-' sound, so 'Ilha Grande' sounds like 'eel-ya grunge'.

The 'ç' is pronounced like an English 's'; the letter 'x' as the 'sh' as in 'ship'. So 'Iguaçu' is 'ig-WA-soo' and 'Caxambu' 'ka-SHAM-boo'.

You'll know you've mastered Brazilian Portuguese pronunciation when you've successfully ordered one of the country's more popular beers, Antarctica (that's right, you say 'ant-OKT-chee-kah'!).

Accents

Within Brazil, accents, dialects and slang *(gíria)* vary regionally. A Carioca inserts the 'sh' sound in place of 's'. A *gaúcho* speaks a Spanish-sounding Portuguese, a Baiano (from Bahia) speaks slowly and the accents of a Cearense (from Ceará) is often incomprehensible to outsiders.

Greetings & Civilities

Hello.	*Oi.*
Goodbye.	*Tchau.*
Good morning.	*Bom dia.*
Good afternoon.	*Boa tarde.*
Good evening.	*Boa noite.*
Please.	*Por favor.*
Thank you (very much).	*(Muita/o) obrigado/a.*
Yes.	*Sim.*
No.	*Não.*
Maybe.	*Talvez.*
Excuse me.	*Com licença.*
I'm sorry.	*Desculpe (me perdoe).* (lit: forgive me)
How are you?	*Como vai você?/ Tudo bem?*
I'm fine thanks.	*Vou bem, obrigado/a. Tudo bem, obrigado/a.*

Language Difficulties

Do you speak English?	*Você fala inglês?*
Does anyone speak English?	*Alguem fala inglês?*
I (don't) speak Portuguese.	*Eu (não) falo português.*
I (don't) understand.	*Eu (não) entendo.*
Please write it down.	*Escreva por favor.*
Please show me (on the map).	*Por favor, me mostre (no mapa).*
How do you say … in Portuguese?	*Como você fala ... em Português?*

Paperwork

I have a visa/ permit.	*Eu tenho um visto/ uma licença.*
Passport	*Passaporte*
Surname	*Sobrenome*
Given name	*Nome*
Date of birth	*Data de nascimento*
Place of birth	*Local de nascimento*
Nationality	*Nacionalidade*
Male/Female	*Masculino/Feminino*

Small Talk

What's your name?	*Qual é seu nome?*
My name is …	*Meu nome é ...*
I'm a tourist/ student.	*Eu sou um turista/ estudante.*

What country are you from?	*Da onde você é?*
I'm from …	*Eu sou ...*
How old are you?	*Quantos anos você tem?*
I'm … years old.	*Eu tenho ... anos.*
Are you married?	*Você é casado/a?*
Do you like … ?	*Você gosta de ... ?*
I (don't) like …	*Eu (não) gosta de ...*
I like it very much.	*Eu gosto muito.*
May I?	*Posso?*
It's all right/ No problem.	*Está tudo bem/ Não há problema.*

Getting Around

I want to go to …	*Eu quero ir para ...*
I want to book a seat for …	*Eu quero reservar um assento para ...*
What time does the … leave/arrive?	*A que horas ... sai/ chega?*
Where does the … leave from?	*Da onde o/a ... sai?*
aeroplane	*avião*
boat	*barco*
bus	*onibus*
ferry	*ferry/balsa*
train	*trem*
tram	*bonde*
How long does the trip take?	*Quanto tempo a viagem demora?*
Do I need to change (trains)?	*Eu precisa trocar de (trem)?*
You must change (platform).	*Você precisa trocar de (plataforma).*
one-way (ticket)	*passagem de ida*
return (ticket)	*passagem de volta*
station	*estação*
ticket	*passagem*
ticket office	*bilheteria*
timetable	*horário*
The (train) is …	*O (trem) está ...*
delayed	*atrasado*
cancelled	*cancelado*
on time	*na hora*
early	*adiantado*
I'd like to hire a …	*Eu gostaria de alugar um/uma ...*
bicycle	*bicicleta*
car	*carro*
guide	*guia*
horse	*cavalo*
motorcycle	*moto*

Directions

How do I get to … ?	*Como eu chego a ... ?*
Where is … ?	*Aonde é ... ?*
Is it near/far?	*É perto/longe?*
What … is this?	*O que é ... isto?*
house number	*numero da casa*
street/road	*rua/estrada*
suburb	*bairro*
town	*cidade*
Go straight ahead.	*Vá em frente.*
Turn left.	*Vire a esquerda.*
Turn right.	*Vire a direita.*
at the traffic lights	*no farol*
at the next corner	*na próxima esquina*
up/down	*acima/abaixo*
behind/opposite	*atrás/em frente*
here/there	*aqui/lá*
east/west	*leste/oeste*
north/south	*norte/sul*

Accommodation

I'm looking for the …	*Eu estou procurando o/a ...*
camping ground	*camping*
guesthouse	*pousada*
hotel	*hotel*
manager	*gerente*
owner	*dono*
youth hostel	*albergue da juventude*
What is the address?	*Qual é o endereço?*
Do you have a … available?	*Você tem um/uma ... para alugar?*
cheap room	*quarto barato*
single room	*quarto de solteiro*
double room	*quarto de casado*
room with two beds	*quarto com duas camas*

How much is it ...? *Quanto é ...?*
per night *por noite*
per person *por pessoa*

It's very ... *É muito ...*
dirty *sujo*
noisy *barulhento*
expensive *caro*

Do you have ... ? *Você tem ... ?*
a clean sheet *um lençol limpo*
hot water *água quente*
a key *uma chave*
a shower *um chuveiro*

Is breakfast included? *O café de manha está incluído?*
Can I see the room? *Posso ver o quarto?*

I'm/We're leaving now. *Eu estou/Nós estamos saindo agora.*
Where is the toilet? *Aonde é o banheiro?*

Signs

CAMPING	CAMPING GROUND
ENTRADA	ENTRANCE
SAIDA	EXIT
CHEIO	FULL
ABERTO	OPEN
FECHADO	CLOSED
HOMENS	GENTS'
MULHERES	LADIES'
POUSADA	GUESTHOUSE
HOTEL	HOTEL
INFORMAÇÃO	INFORMATION
POLÌCIA	POLICE
DELEGACIA	POLICE STATION
PROIBIDO	PROHIBITED
QUARTOS PARA ALUGAR	ROOMS AVAILABLE
BANHEIROS	TOILETS
ESTAÇÃO DE TREM	TRAIN STATION
ALBERGUE DA JUVENTUDE	YOUTH HOSTEL

Around Town

Where is the/a ... ? *Aonde é o/a ... ?*
city centre *centro da cidade*
embassy *embaixada*
hospital *hospital*
market *mercado/feira*
post office *correio*
public toilet *banheiro público*
restaurant *restaurante*
telephone centre *telefônica*
tourist information office *posto de informações turísticas*
bridge *ponte*
cathedral *catedral*
church *igreja*
fort *forte*
lake *lago*
main square *praça principal*
old city *cidade velha*
palace *palácio*
ruins *ruínas*
square *praça*
bank *banco*
exchange office *casa de câmbio*

I'd like to change some money/travellers cheques. *Eu gostaria de trocar de dineiro/cheques de viagem.*

Food

breakfast *café da manhá*
lunch *almoço*
dinner *jantar*
set menu *refeição*
food stall *barraca de comida*
grocery store *mercearia*
delicatessen *confeitaria*
restaurant *restaurante*

I'm hungry/thirsty. *Eu estou com fome/sede.*
I'd like the set lunch please. *Eu gostaria do prato feito por favor.*
Is service included in the bill? *O serviço esta incluído na conta?*
I'm a vegetarian. *Eu sou vegetariano/a.*
I don't eat ... *Eu não como ...*
I'd like some ... *Eu gostaria de ...*
Another ..., please. *Outro/a ..., por favor.*

beer	*cerveja*
bread	*pão*
chicken	*frango*
coffee	*café*
eggs	*ovos*
fish	*peixe*
food	*comida*
fruit	*frutas*
meat	*carne*
milk	*leite*
mineral water	*água mineral*
pepper	*pimenta*
salt	*sal*
soup	*sopa*
sugar	*açucar*
tea	*chá*
vegetables	*verduras*
wine	*vinho*

Shopping

I'm looking for …	*Estou procurando …*
a chemist	*uma farmácia*
clothing	*roupas*
souvenirs	*lembanças*
I'd like to buy ...	*Queria comprar ...*
How much is it?	*Quanto custa?*
It's too expensive.	*É muito caro.*
Can I look at it?	*Posso ver?*
I'm just looking.	*Só estou olhando.*
big/bigger	*grande/maior*
small/smaller	*pequeno/menor*
more/less	*mais/menos*
cheap/cheaper	*barato/mais barato*
Do you have ...?	*Você tem ...?*
another colour	*outra cor*
another size	*outra tamanho*
Do you take ...?	*Você aceita ...?*
credit cards	*cartões de crédito*
travellers'cheques	*cheques de viagem*

Times & Dates

What time is it?	*Que horas são?*
It's …	*São ...*
1.15	*uma e quinze*
1.30	*uma e meia*
1.40	*uma e quarenta*
o'clock	*horas*
in the morning	*da manhã*
in the evening	*da noite*
When?	*Quando?*
today	*hoje*
tonight	*hoje de noite*
tomorrow	*amanhã*
day after tomorrow	*depois de amanhã*
yesterday	*ontem*
morning	*a manhã*
afternoon	*a tarde*
night	*a noite*
all day	*todos o dia*
every day	*todos os dias*
Sunday	*domingo*
Monday	*segunda-feira*
Tuesday	*terça-feira*
Wednesday	*quarta-feira*
Thursday	*quinta-feira*
Friday	*sexta-feira*
Saturday	*sábado*
January	*janeiro*
February	*fevereiro*
March	*março*
April	*abril*
May	*maio*
June	*junho*
July	*julho*
August	*agosto*
September	*setembro*
October	*outubro*
November	*novembro*
December	*dezembro*

Numbers

0	*zero*
1	*um/uma*
2	*dois/duas*
3	*três*
4	*quatro*
5	*cinco*
6	*seis*

(quoting telephone or house numbers, Brazilians often say *meia* instead of *seis*)

7	*sete*
8	*oito*
9	*nove*
10	*dez*

11	*onze*
12	*doze*
13	*treze*
14	*catorze*
15	*quinze*
16	*dezesseis*
17	*dezessete*
18	*dezoito*
19	*dezenove*
20	*vinte*
30	*trinta*
40	*quarenta*
50	*cinqüenta*
60	*sessenta*
70	*setenta*
80	*oitenta*
90	*noventa*
100	*cem*
1000	*mil*
one million	*um milhão*

first	*primeiro*
last	*último*

Slang

Brazilians pepper their language with strange oaths and odd expressions. Literal translations are in brackets:

Hello!	*Oi!*
Everything OK?	*Tudo bem?*
Everything's OK	*Tudo bom.*
That's great/Cool!	*Chocante!*
That's bad/Shit!	*Merda!*
Great/Cool/OK!	*'ta lógico/'ta ótimo/'ta legal!*
My God!	*Meu deus!*
You're crazy!	*'ta louco!*
Damn! (curse word)	*Palavrão!*
Gosh!	*Nossa!* (Our Lady!)
Whoops!	*Opa!*
Wow!	*Oba!*
You said it!	*Falou!*
I'm mad at ...	*Eu estou chateado com ...*
Is there a way?	*Tem jeito?*
There's always a way.	*Sempre tem jeito.*
shooting the breeze	*batendo um papo*
bald	*careca*
Brazilian bikini	*fio dental* (dental floss)
bum	*bum-bum/bunda*
a fix/problem	*abacaxí*
girl	*garota*
guy	*cara*
marijuana	*fumo* (smoke)
money	*grana*
a mess	*bagunça*

Beach Words

I can't swim.	*Eu não sei nadar.*
Can I swim here?	*Posso nadar aqui?*
Is it safe to swim here?	*É seguro nadar aqui?*
What time is high/low tide?	*A que horas será a maré alta/baixa?*
How's the surf?	*Como estão as ondas?*
Where's a good place to surf?	*Onde existe um bom lugar para surfar?*

beach	*praia*
beach towel	*toalha de praia*
coast	*costa*
lifesaver	*salva-vidas*
rock	*pedra*
sand	*areia*
sea	*mar*
sunblock	*protetor solar*
wave	*onda*

Jungle Words

Does the tour include ...?	*A excursão inclui ...?*
Will we sleep in hammocks?	*Iremos dormir em redes?*
What is the breakdown of costs?	*Como é dividido o custo?*
Is the water level high or low?	*O nível das águas esta alto ou baixo?*
Does the boat have lifejackets?	*O barco tem coletes salva-vidas?*
How long does it take to get there?	*Quanto tempo leva para chegar lá?*
Can we shop for food together?	*Podemos ir comprar comida juntos?*
Do you have fishing gear?	*Voce tem equipamento de pesca?*
Is it safe to go there?	*É seguro ir lá?*

Will we see animals?	*Iremos ver animais?*
Are there ...?	*Existem lá ...?*
dangerous animals	*animais perigosos*
spiders	*aranhas*
lots of mosquitoes	*muitos mosquitos*

accommodation	*alojamento*
canoe	*canoa*
food/drinks	*comida/bebida*
fuel	*combustível*
guides	*guias*
jungle	*selva; mata; floresta*
tree	*arvore*

Body Language

Brazilians accompany their speech with a rich body language, a sort of parallel dialogue. The thumbs up of *tudo bem* is used as a greeting, or to signify 'OK' or 'Thank you'. The authoritative *não, não* finger-wagging is most intimidating when done right under someone's nose, but it's not a threat.

The sign of the *figa*, a thumb inserted between the first and second fingers of a clenched fist, is a symbol of good luck that has been derived from an African sexual charm. It's more commonly used as jewellery than in body language.

To indicate *rápido* (speed and haste), thumb and middle finger snap while rapidly shaking the wrist – a gesture it would seem only Brazilians can make.

If you don't want something (*não quero*), slap the back of your hands as if ridding yourself of the entire affair.

Touching a finger to the lateral corner of the eye means 'I'm wise to you'.

Health

I'm ...	*Eu sou ...*
diabetic	*diabético/a*
epileptic	*epilético/a*
asthmatic	*asmático/a*

I'm allergic ...	*Eu sou allergico/a ...*
to penicillin	*a penicilina*
to antibiotics	*a antibiôticos*

antiseptic	*antiséptico*
aspirin	*aspirina*
condoms	*camisinhas*
contraceptive	*contraceptivo*
diarrhoea	*diarréia*
medicine	*remédio*
nausea	*nausea*
sunblock cream	*creme de proteção solar*
tampons	*absorventes internos*

Emergencies

Help!	*Socorro!*
Call a doctor!	*Chame o médico!*
Call the police!	*Chame a polícia!*
Where is the toilet?	*Aonde é o banheiro?*
Go away!	*Va embora!*

Glossary

ABCD cities – refers to Brazil's industrial heartland; the cities of São André, São Bernardo, São Caetano and Diadema, which flank the city of São Paulo
abandonados – abandoned children
abertura – opening; refers to the process, begun in the early 1980s, of returning to a civilian, democratic government
afoxé – music of Bahia with strong African rhythms and close ties to the Candomblé religion
aguardente – firewater, rotgut; any strong drink, but usually *cachaça*
albergue – lodging house or hostel
albergues de juventude – youth hostels
álcool – car fuel made from sugar cane; about half the cars, and all new cars, in Brazil run on *álcool*
aldeia – originally a mission village built by Jesuits to 'save' the Indians, but now any small village of peasants or fishermen
andar – the verb 'to walk'; also used to denote the floor number in a multistorey building
apartamento – hotel room with a bathroom
arara – macaw
artesanato – art and crafts
autódromo – racetrack; the one near Barra in Rio is the location of the Brazilian Grand Prix
automotriz – tourist train
avelã – hazelnut
ayahuasca – hallucinogenic drink
azulejos – Portuguese ceramic tiles with a distinctive blue glaze. You'll often see them in churches.

bandeirantes – bands of *Paulistas* who explored the vast Brazilian interior while searching for gold and Indians to enslave. The bandeirantes were typically born of an Indian mother and a Portuguese father.
banzo – a slave's profound longing for the African homeland, which often resulted in a 'slow withering away' and death
barraca – any stall or hut, including those omnipresent food and drink stands at the beach, park etc
bateria – any rhythm section, including the enormous ones in samba parades
beija-flor – hummingbird; beija-flor is also the name of Rio's most famous samba school
berimbau – fishing rod-like musical instrument used to accompany the martial art/dance of capoeira
bicho de pé – parasite that burrows into the bottom of the foot and then grows until it is cut out. It's found near the beach and in some jungle areas.
bloco – a large group, usually numbering in the hundreds, of singing Carnaval revellers in costume. Most *blocos* are organised around a neighbourhood or theme.
boate or **boîte** – nightclub; refers to both the expensive joint and the strip joint
bogó – leather water-pouch typical of the sertão
bonde – cable car; tram/trolley
bossa nova – music that mixes North American jazz with Brazilian influences
boto – freshwater dolphin of the Amazon. Indians believe the *boto* has magical powers, most notably the ability to impregnate unmarried women.
Brazilian Empire – the period from 1822 to 1889, when Brazil was independent of Portugal but was governed by monarchy
Bumba Meu Boi – the most important festival in Maranhão; a rich folkloric event that revolves around a Carnavalesque dance/procession
bunda – an African word for buttocks

caatinga – scrub vegetation of the Northeast sertão
Cabanagem – the popular revolt that swept through Pará state in the 1830s it was suppressed by until a large government force which then massacred 40,000 of the state's population of 100,000

caboclo – literally, copper-coloured; a person of mixed Caucasian and Indian ancestry
cachaça – Brazil's national drink: a sugarcane spirit also called *pinga* and *aguardente*. Hundreds of small distilleries produce *cachaça* throughout the country.
cachoeira – waterfall
café – *café da manha* (breakfast) or just plain coffee
caipirinha – drink made from *cachaça* and crushed citrus fruit such as lemon, orange or maracujá
câmara – town council during colonial days
camisa-de-Vênus, camisinha – literally, cover or shirt of Venus; a condom
Candomblé – Afro-Brazilian religion of Bahia
canga – wrap-around fabric worn when going to and from the beach and for sitting on at the beach
cangaceiro – legendary bandits of the *sertão*
capanga – hired gunman, usually employed by rich landowners in the Northeast
capitania hereditária – hereditary province or estate. To settle Brazil at minimum cost to the crown, in 1531 the king of Portugal divided the colony into 12 capitanias hereditárias.
capivara (capybara) – the world's largest rodent; it looks like a large guinea pig and lives in the waters of the Pantanal
capoeira – martial art/dance performed to the rhythms of an instrument called the berimbau. Capoeira was developed by the slaves of Bahia.
capongas – a freshwater lagoon
Carioca – a native of Rio de Janeiro
casa grande – big house or plantation owner's mansion
casa de câmbio – money-exchange house
casal – married couple; also a double bed
castanha – brazil nut
catamarãs – typical boats of the Amazon
cerveja – beer
chapadões – tablelands or plateaux which divide river basins
chopp – draught beer
churrascaria – restaurant featuring meat, which should be *churrasco* (barbecued)
Círio de Nazaré – Brazil's largest religious pilgrimage; takes place in Belém
cobra – any snake
collectivá – bed in a shared room or dorm-style accommodation
comida caseira – home-style cooking
comida mineira – typical cuisine of Minas Gerais state
comida por kilo – pay-by-weight buffet
comunidades de base – neighbourhood organisations of the poor led by the progressive Catholic Church and inspired by liberation theology. They are involved in many struggles for social justice.
congelamento – freeze, as in a price freeze
coronel – rural landowner who typically controlled the local political, judicial and police systems; any powerful person
correios – post offices
couvert – appetiser
cruzeiro – former unit of national currency

delegacia – police station
dendê – palm oil; the main ingredient in the cuisine of Bahia
drogas do sertão – plants of the *sertão* such as cacao and cinnamon

Economic Miracle – period of double-digit economic growth while the military was in power during the late 1960s and early 1970s; now mentioned sarcastically to point to the failures of the military regime
embalagem – doggie bag
Embolada – kind of Brazilian rap, where singers trade off, performing verbal jests, teasing and joking with the audience; most common in Northeastern fairs
EMBRATUR – federal government tourism agency
Empire – see Brazilian Empire
ENASA – a government-run passenger-shipping line of the Amazon
engenho – sugar mill or sugar plantation
escolas de samba – these aren't schools, but large samba clubs. In Rio the escolas

have thousands of members and compete in the annual Carnaval parade. Weekend rehearsals begin around November and continue until Carnaval; they are open to the public.
Estado Novo – literally, New State; dictator Getúlio Vargas' quasi-fascist state, which lasted from 1937 until the end of WW II
estações ecológicas – ecological stations
estância hidromineral – spa, hot springs
exús – spirits that serve as messengers between the gods and humans in Afro-Brazilian religions

facão – large knife or machete
fantasia – Carnavalesque costume
farinha – flour made from the root of the manioc plant. It was the staple food of Brazil's Indians before colonisation and is the staple for many Brazilians today, especially in the Northeast and Amazon.
favela – slum, shantytown
fazenda – ranch or farm, usually a large landholding; also cloth, fabric
fazendeiros – estate owners
ferroviária – railway station
ficha – token; due to inflation, machines (eg telephones) take tokens, not coins
fidalgos – gentry
figa – good-luck charm formed by a clenched fist with the thumb between the index and middle fingers. The *figa* originated with Afro-Brazilian cults but is now popular with all Brazilians.
Filhos de Gandhi – Bahia's most famous Carnaval *bloco*
fio dental – literally, dental floss. This is what Brazilians call their famous skimpy bikinis.
Flamengo – Rio's most popular football team; also one of Rio's most populated areas
Fluminense – native of Rio state; also the football team that is Flamengo's main rival
forró – the music of the Northeast, which combines the influences of Mexico and the Brazilian frontier. The characteristic instruments used are the accordion, harmonica and drums.
frevo – fast-paced, popular music that originated in Pernambuco
frigobar – refrigerator
FUNAI – government Indian agency (Fundação Nacional do Indio)
Fusca – a Volkswagen beetle, long Brazil's most popular car; they stopped making them in 1986
futvolei – foot volleyball

garimpeiro – a prospector or miner; originally an illegal diamond prospector
gaúcho – pronounced 'gaoooshoo'; a cowboy of southern Brazil
gíria – slang
gringo – you don't have to be from the USA: any foreigner or person with light hair and complexion, including Brazilians, qualifies. (Not necessarily derogatory.)
Gruta – grotto or cavern
guaraná – an Amazonian shrub whose berry is believed to have magical and medicinal powers; also a popular soft drink

hospedagem – cheap boarding house used by locals
hidrovia – aquatic freeway
hidroviária – boat terminal

igapó – flooded Amazon forest
igarapés – pools formed by the changing paths of the rivers of the Amazon
ilha – island
INPA – national agency for research on the Amazon

jaburú – giant white stork of the Pantanal with black head and red band on neck
jacaré – yacaré caiman, a reptile similar to an alligator
jagunço – the tough man of the *sertão*
jangada – beautiful sailboat of the Northeast, usually made by the fishermen themselves with building techniques passed from generation to generation
jangadeiros – fishermen who use jangadas
jeito (dar um jeito or jeitinho) – possibly the most Brazilian expression; *jeito* means finding a way to get something done, no matter how seemingly impossible. It may not

be an orthodox or legal way but is nonetheless effective in the Brazilian context. *Jeito* is both a feeling and a form of action.
jogo de bicho – a popular lottery, technically illegal but played on every street corner by all Brazilians, with each number represented by an animal. The *banqueiros de bicho* who control the game, have become a virtual mafia and traditionally help to fund the *escolas de samba*. Many consider the *jogo de bicho* the most honest and trustworthy institution in the country.
Jogo dos Búzios – type of fortune-telling performed by a *pai* or *maê de Santo* throwing shells

Labour Code – legislation, modelled on Mussolini's system, designed to maintain government control over labour unions
ladrão – thief
lanchonete – stand-up snack bar. They are found all over Brazil.
lavrador – peasant, small farmer or landless farm worker
leito – super-comfortable overnight express bus
lemanjá – the Afro-Brazilian goddess of the sea
liberation theology – movement within the Catholic Church that believes the struggle for social justice is part of Christ's teachings
Literatura de Cordel – literally, 'Literature of String'. Popular literature of the Northeast, where pamphlets are typically hung on strings. Sold at markets where authors read their stories and poems.
litoral – coastal region

maconha – type of marijuana
machista – male chauvinist
mãe de Santo – female Afro-Brazilian spiritual leader
maharajás – pejorative term for government employees getting rich from the public coffers; usually refers to army and police officers
malandro do morro – vagabond; scoundrel from the hills; a popular figure in Rio's mythology
maloca – Indian dwelling
mameluco – offspring of a white father and an Indian mother
manatee or **peixe-boi** – literally, 'cow fish'; an endangered aquatic mammal that grows to 1.5 metres in length
Manchete – number-two national TV station and a popular photo magazine
Maracanã – football stadium in Rio; supposedly the world's largest, the stadium allegedly holds 200,000 but looks full with 100,000
maté – popular tea of southern Brazil
mato grosso – thick forest
mercado – market
mestiço – a person of mixed Indian and European parentage
mineiro – miner; also a person from the state of Minas Gerais
miúdo – change
mocambo – community of runaway slaves; small version of a *quilombo*
moço – waiter or other service industry worker
morro – hill; also used to indicate a person or culture of the *favelas*
motel – sex hotel with rooms to rent by the hour
mulatto – person of mixed black and European parentage

novela – soap opera. They are the most popular TV shows in Brazil and are funnier and have more insights than their American counterparts. From directors to actors to composers, many of Brazil's most talented and famous artists work on novelas.
NS – *Nosso Senhor* (Our Lord), or *Nossa Senhora* (Our Lady)

O Globo – Brazil's number-one media empire. O Globo owns the prime national TV station and several newspapers and magazines.
Old Republic – period from the end of the Brazilian Empire in 1889 until the coup that put Getúlio Vargas in power in 1930. There were regular elections but only a tiny percentage of the population was eligible to vote.

Orixás – the deities of the Afro-Brazilian religions

pagode – today's most popular samba music
pai de Santo – male spiritual leader in Afro-Brazilian religions
pajé – shaman, witch doctor
palácio – palace or large government building
palafitas – houses built on sticks above water, as in Manaus
pampas – grassy plains of the interior of southern Brazil
papelaria – stationery shop
paralelo – the parallel, semi-official exchange rate that reflects the currency's market value, not the government's regulated official value
paroara – Amazon resident who came from the Northeast
parques nacionais – national parks
pau brasil – brazil-wood tree. It produces a red dye that was the colony's first commodity. The trees are scarce today.
Paulista – native of São Paulo State
Paulistano – native of São Paulo city
PCB – Communist Party of Brazil
pelourinho – stone pillar used as a whipping-post for punishing slaves
pensão – guesthouse
Petrobrás – the government-owned oil company. Brazil's largest corporation is so powerful that it's referred to as a 'government within a government'.
pinga – another name for *cachaça*, the sugar cane spirit
pistoleiro – gun-toting henchman
Planalto – enormous plateau that covers a part of almost every state in Brazil
Plano Real – financial plan introduced by Franco's Finance Minister Fernando Henrique Cardoso in 1994
PMDB – the governing party, a loose coalition that encompasses a wide variety of ideologies and interests from far right to centre
por quilo – per kilo
posseiro – squatter
pousada – guesthouse
praça – plaza or town square
praia – beach
prato feito, prato do dia – literally, 'made plate', 'plate of the day'; typically, an enormous and incredibly cheap meal
prefeitura – city or town hall
PT – Worker's Party. Brazil's newest and most radical political party. It came out of the massive strike waves of the early 1980s and is led by Luís Inácio 'Lula' da Silva. The PT's support is strongest in São Paulo and among industrial workers and the Catholic base communities.
PTD – Democratic Workers' Party; a social democratic party dominated by the charismatic populist leader Leonel Brizola
puxar – means pull, not push

quarto – hotel room without a bathroom
quilombo – community of runaway slaves. They posed a serious threat to the slave system as hundreds of *quilombos* dotted the coastal mountains. The Republic of Palmares was the most famous: it survived for most of the 17th century and had a population of as many as 20,000.

rápido – speed, haste
real – Brazil's unit of currency since 1994
rede – hammock
refeição – meal
refeição comercial – meal/serving of various dishes normally enough for two to share
reserva extravista – a reserve where the local inhabitants have the exclusive right to collect forest products such as fruit, rubber and fish
reservas biológicas – biological reserves
Revolution of '64 – the military takeover in 1964
rodízio – a smorgasbord with lots of meat (similar to a *churrascaria*)
rodoferroviária – bus and train station
rodoviária – bus station
salgadinhos – savoury snacks
sambista – samba composer or dancer
sambódromo – the road and bleachers where the samba parade takes place on Rio's north side

senzala – slave quarters
serrá – mountain range
sertanejo – inhabitant of the *sertão*
sertão – drought-stricken region of the Northeast, known as the backlands. It has a dry, temperate climate, and the land is covered by thorny shrubs.
shiita – term derived from the Shiite Muslims of Iran, used to describe any zealot or radical, no matter their cause
suco – juice bar or juice

Terra de Vera Cruz – Land of the True Cross. This was the original but short-lived Portuguese name for Brazil. Generations of Portuguese believed Brazil was the work of the devil (who, according to common wisdom, was active in the sinful colony).
terreiro – Afro-Brazilian house of worship
travesti – transvestite; a popular figure throughout Brazil and considered by some to be the national symbol
Treaty of Tordesillas – agreement signed in 1494 between Spain and Portugal, dividing Latin America
trio elétrico – literally, a three-pronged electrical outlet; also a musical style that is a sort of electrified *frevo* played on top of trucks, especially during Carnaval in Bahia
troco – change
tropicalismo – important cultural movement centred in Bahia in the late 1960s
Tupi – the Indian people and language that predominated along the Brazilian coast at the time of the European invasion. Most animals and places in Brazil have Tupi names.

Umbanda – Rio's version of the principal Afro-Brazilian religion

vaqueiro – cowboy of the Northeast
várzea – Amazonian flood plain
Velho Chico – literally, Old Chico; the affectionate nickname for the great Rio São Francisco
violeiros – guitarists and guitar makers

zona da mata – bushland just inside the litoral in the Northeastern states

Index

ABBREVIATIONS

Acr	– Acre	Mar	– Maranhão	RGN	– Rio Grande do Norte
Ala	– Alagoas	MG	– Mato Grosso	RGS	– Rio Grande do Sul
Ama	– Amapá	MGS	– Mato Grosso do Sul	RJ	– Rio de Janeiro State
Amz	– Amazonas	Min	– Minas Gerais	Ron	– Rondônia
Bah	– Bahia	Pab	– Paríba	Ror	– Roraima
Cea	– Ceará	Pan	– Paraná	SC	– Santa Caterina
DF	– Distrito Federal	Par	– Pará	Ser	– Sergipe
ES	– Espirito Santo	Per	– Pernambuco	SP	– São Paulo
Goi	– Goiás	Pia	– Piauí	Toc	– Tocantins

MAPS

TEXT

Map references are in **bold** type

A

B

BOXED TEXT

Thanks

Thanks to the travellers who wrote to us about their experiences in Brazil. They include:

Philip Agre, Helena Åhlund, Greg Allen, Brian Ambrosio, Ron Anderson, Fernando Andrade, Ram Avni, Michael Ayling, Christine Badre, Don & Joan Bailey, Neil Bailey, James Baker, Harry Baker, Tim Barrett, Friedrich Bellermann, John Beswetherick, Rene Beuchle, Maarten Biesheuvel, Fabio Biserna, Bonnie Bloch, Alistair Bool, Claudia Bozzone, Peter Brichzin, Sue Brooklyn, Linda Broschofsky, Heather Brown, Olivier Brunel, Michi Camenzind, George Candler, Kacie Chang, Catriona Charkin, Pierre Chaux, Claire Collings, Jeremy Coon, Theo Cooney, Aaron Corcoran, Catherine Correa, O de Corta, David Cosgrove, Pedro Moura Costa, Maria Courtney, Maralo Crew, Antoinette B d'Oronzio, Wojciech Dabrowski, Phillip A Dale, Jamie Dalrymple, João-Geraldo Damasceno, Salee & David M Davis, Ric Delaney, Francois Desmeules, Monique Dodinet, Rafael Dreyfus, Rose Dryden, Audrey & Jack Duchesne, Fedor Dullaert, Oliva V Eeghem, Eric Eidsmoe, Herodotos Ellinas, Sally Elvin, Cynthia Esteban, Guy Eysseric, Peter Felix Feneberg, Antonio Ferrada, Chris Fields, Douglas W Fischer, Peter Fischl, Dairne Fitzpatrick & Cherie Anderson, Marilyn Flax, Richard Fogel, Johannes & Roswitha Fresner, Erik Futtrup, Jeremy Gage, Ramona Gallo, Nisha Gambhir, Wil & Joyce Gesler, Tessa Gibbs & David Smith, J Kenneth Glass, C Gomes, Cecilia Graber, David P Grill, Mark Groves, Daniel Guerrera C, Anna Carin Gustafson, Robert Hackman, Susanna Hagman, Juanita Hamparsum, Vagn Asbjørn Hansen, Debbie Harris, Colin Harvey, Boris Hasselblatt, Arthur Hawley, Michelle Hecht, Siegmar & Gerfried Hein, A Henderson, Clive Henman, Boris Henn, B Henn, Kirsten Heuschen, Mark Hewitt, Sally Hill, Dieter Hloop, Richard Hoath, Chuck Hollenbeck, Koosje van der Horst, S D Huet, Ashley Huggins, Maria Shiguemi Ichiyama, Richard Lite de Ingunza, Gabrielle Ireland, Mirko Ivandic, Ken Johannesson, Power Johnson, Ripton Johnson, David Morris Johnston, Kath Jones, Marilyn Jones-Gotman, N Jrik, Kristine Jürs, Michael K Gshwind, Jane Kelly, Jarrod & Cathy Kelly, Devin Kelso, Herbert Josef Klein, Birgit Kleymann, Jennifer Klinec, Paul Knøbel, Rainer Knyrim, Steven Koenig, Thilo Kopp, André H Korenhof, Adrie & Jopie Kouwenberg, Ben Kraijnbrink, Dale & Adrienne de Kretser, Dr D Kumar, Lucy Kunkel, Peter Kunkel, Steven Kusters, Fernando Lara, Ludovic N Leforestier, Matthew Lehmann, Andrew Leyland & Ian Collins, Yannick Liogier, G Lloyd, E Lloyd, Ovo Loyola, Gill Lobel, Ivo Loyola, Andrew Ludasi, Jean Luis, Francesco Lulli, Mari Tomine Lunden, Dikrán P Lutufyan, Gary McCall, Denise & Malcolm McDonough, Twid McGrath, Rachel McGregor, Helen Mader, Jay Mappus, Harry Marieke, Riamon Markoeski, Steven & De Meiers, Osman K Mian, Paola Marinoni Morgado, Don McNeill, Osman Mian, Burkhard Militzer, Mike Miller, Peter Milton, Adrian Mitu, Dick Momsen, Mark Monsma, Rody Moore, Rohan Morton, Benjamin Moser, Robin Moss, Claudia Mueller, Lori Murphy, Annette Murphy, Danielle Nadeau, Bruce & Maria Nesbitt, Olivia Nickel, Jan Nielsen, Eric Noble, Dennis Nolan, Pedro Novak, Ota Novotny, Betty Odell, Birgit Oehmichen, Felicia Oeystaa, Z Oliveira, Isaias Ortiz R, Neil Orvay, Marcel Ott, Margrit de Marez Oyens, Pierluigi Palmonari, Julie & Spiros Pappas, Joseph Parkhurst, Elton-Jon Passini, Louise Pabe, Siegrun Päßler, Audrey Patterson, Theon Pearce, Mick Pease, Karlos Pena, Denise Pendexter, RJ Penlington, Hilde Perdok & Dirk van Ostveen, Paulode Sousa Pinto, Joaquina Pires-O'Brien, Julianne Power, Monica Pranzl, Hans Chr Rasmussen, Hans R Roth, Rodney Ramos, Phillipe Raoul, Hans Rasmussen, Brigette Rauch, Bob Redlinger, Judith Rhodes, Thomas Ribisel, Cynthia Rickett, Randy Riddell, Gunther Riebel, Daniel Filipe Rios, Roman Ritter, Gerry & Janine Rodgers, Willem Roemer, David Rogan & Anna Austin, Ilana Rosenfeld, Valentina Salapura, Matt Salmon, Volker Sauer, Sigrid Schapitz, Ron Scharis, Mareike Schaube, James Schmidt, Johanne Schulz, Linda Scott, Jerome Sgard, Shaun Shaver, Ondrej Simetke, Duncan Smith, David Smith, Heather Smith & Friends, Charlotte Snowden, Hans Stangerl, Raffa Stefano & Deborah Prhafo, Christine Stolpmann, Jesse R Struson, Erik Svane, Danko Taborosi, Olivia Taylor, Michael Tille, Sara Tizard & Pat Coleman, Giovanni Tosatti, Helen A Tsefuhl, Marisel Traverzo, Helen Tsefuch, Ingeborg Uitentuis, Bonnie Valentine, Andrea Vannucchi, Jean-Marie Verniers, Rodrigo Fernandes Vieira, Manuel Candéa Viana, Pam Wadworth, Hans Wagner, Stefani Warren, Dalma Whang, Rob Williams, Anne Wilshin, Anne Winchester, Emanuel & Helgard Wirfel, Joan Wood, Alta Zyl.

Phrasebooks

Lonely Planet phrasebooks are packed with essential words and phrases to help travellers communicate with the locals. With colour tabs for quick reference, an extensive vocabulary and use of script, these handy pocket-sized language guides cover day-to-day travel situations.

- handy pocket-sized books
- easy to understand Pronunciation chapter
- clear & comprehensive Grammar chapter
- romanisation alongside script to allow ease of pronunciation
- script throughout so users can point to phrases for every situation
- full of cultural information and tips for the traveller

'...vital for a real DIY spirit and attitude in language learning'
– Backpacker

'the phrasebooks have good cultural backgrounders and offer solid advice for challenging situations in remote locations'
– San Francisco Examiner

Arabic (Egyptian) • Arabic (Moroccan) • Australian *(Australian English, Aboriginal and Torres Strait languages)* • Baltic States *(Estonian, Latvian, Lithuanian)* • Bengali • Brazilian • British • Burmese • Cantonese • Central Asia • Central Europe *(Czech, French, German, Hungarian, Italian, Slovak)* • Eastern Europe *(Bulgarian, Czech, Hungarian, Polish, Romanian, Slovak)* • Ethiopian (Amharic) • Fijian • French • German • Greek • Hill Tribes • Hindi/Urdu • Indonesian • Italian • Japanese • Korean • Lao • Latin American Spanish • Malay • Mandarin • Mediterranean Europe *(Albanian, Croatian, Greek, Italian, Macedonian, Maltese, Serbian, Slovene)* • Mongolian • Nepali • Papua New Guinea • Pilipino (Tagalog) • Quechua • Russian • Scandinavian Europe *(Danish, Finnish, Icelandic, Norwegian, Swedish)* • South-East Asia *(Burmese, Indonesian, Khmer, Lao, Malay, Tagalog Pilipino, Thai, Vietnamese)* • Spanish (Castilian) *(also includes Catalan, Galician and Basque)* • Sri Lanka • Swahili • Thai • Tibetan • Turkish • Ukrainian • USA *(US English, Vernacular, Native American languages, Hawaiian)* • Vietnamese • Western Europe *(Basque, Catalan, Dutch, French, German, Greek, Irish)*

LONELY PLANET JOURNEYS

JOURNEYS is a unique collection of travel writing – published by the company that understands travel better than anyone else. It is a series for anyone who has ever experienced – or dreamed of – the magical moment when they encountered a strange culture or saw a place for the first time. They are tales to read while you're planning a trip, while you're on the road or while you're in an armchair, in front of a fire.

JOURNEYS books catch the spirit of a place, illuminate a culture, recount a crazy adventure, or introduce a fascinating way of life. They always entertain, and always enrich the experience of travel.

'Idiosyncratic, entertainingly diverse and unexpected . . . from an international writership'
– The Australian

'Books which offer a closer look at the people and culture of a destination, and enrich travel experiences'
– American Bookseller

FULL CIRCLE
A South American Journey
Luis Sepúlveda

Translated by Chris Andrews

Full Circle invites us to accompany Chilean writer Luis Sepúlveda on 'a journey without a fixed itinerary'. Whatever his subject – brutalities suffered under Pinochet's dictatorship, sleepy tropical towns visited in exile, or the landscapes of legendary Patagonia – Sepúlveda is an unflinchingly honest yet lyrical storyteller. Extravagant characters and extraordinary situations are memorably evoked: gauchos organising a tournament of lies, a scheming heiress on the lookout for a husband, a pilot with a corpse on board his plane . . . Part autobiography, part travel memoir, *Full Circle* brings us the distinctive voice of one of South America's most compelling writers.

Luis Sepúlveda was born in Chile in 1949. Imprisoned by the Pinochet dictatorship for his socialist beliefs, he was for many years a political exile. He has written novels, short stories, plays and essays. His work has attracted many awards and has been translated into numerous languages.

'Detachment, humour and vibrant prose' **– El País**

'an absolute cracker' **– The Bookseller**

This project has been assisted by the Commonwealth Government through the Australia Council, its arts funding and advisory body.

LONELY PLANET TRAVEL ATLASES

Lonely Planet has long been famous for the number and quality of its guidebook maps. Now we've gone one step further and produced a handy companion series: Lonely Planet travel atlases – maps of a country produced in book form.

Unlike other maps, which look good but lead travellers astray, our travel atlases have been researched on the road by Lonely Planet's experienced team of writers. All details are carefully checked to ensure the atlas corresponds with the equivalent Lonely Planet guidebook.

The handy atlas format means no holes, wrinkles, torn sections or constant folding and unfolding. These atlases can survive long periods on the road, unlike cumbersome fold-out maps. The comprehensive index ensures easy reference.

- full-colour throughout
- maps researched and checked by Lonely Planet authors
- place names correspond with Lonely Planet guidebooks – no confusing spelling differences
- legend and travelling information in English, French, German, Japanese and Spanish
- size: 230 x 160 mm

Available now:
Chile & Easter Island • Egypt • India & Bangladesh • Israel & the Palestinian Territories • Jordan, Syria & Lebanon • Kenya • Laos • Portugal • South Africa, Lesotho & Swaziland • Thailand • Turkey • Vietnam • Zimbabwe, Botswana & Namibia

---

LONELY PLANET TV SERIES & VIDEOS

Lonely Planet travel guides have been brought to life on television screens around the world. Like our guides, the programmes are based on the joy of independent travel, and look honestly at some of the most exciting, picturesque and frustrating places in the world. Each show is presented by one of three travellers from Australia, England or the USA and combines an innovative mixture of video, Super-8 film, atmospheric soundscapes and original music.

Videos of each episode – containing additional footage not shown on television – are available from good book and video shops, but the availability of individual videos varies with regional screening schedules.

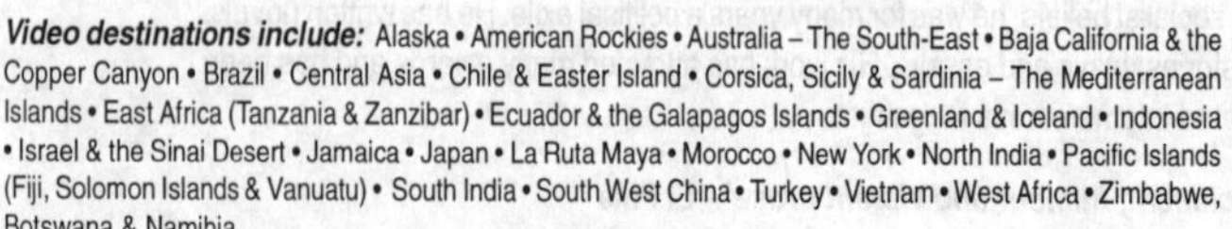

Video destinations include: Alaska • American Rockies • Australia – The South-East • Baja California & the Copper Canyon • Brazil • Central Asia • Chile & Easter Island • Corsica, Sicily & Sardinia – The Mediterranean Islands • East Africa (Tanzania & Zanzibar) • Ecuador & the Galapagos Islands • Greenland & Iceland • Indonesia • Israel & the Sinai Desert • Jamaica • Japan • La Ruta Maya • Morocco • New York • North India • Pacific Islands (Fiji, Solomon Islands & Vanuatu) • South India • South West China • Turkey • Vietnam • West Africa • Zimbabwe, Botswana & Namibia

The Lonely Planet TV series is produced by:
Pilot Productions
The Old Studio
18 Middle Row
London W10 5AT UK

For video availability and ordering information contact your nearest Lonely Planet office.

Music from the TV series is available on CD & cassette.

PLANET TALK

Lonely Planet's FREE quarterly newsletter

We love hearing from you and think you'd like to hear from us.

PLANET TALK

Slovenia:
River Deep, Mountain High

When... is the right time to see reindeer in Finland?
Where... can you hear the best palm-wine music in Ghana?
How... do you get from Asunción to Areguá by steam train?
What... is the best way to see India?

For the answer to these and many other questions read PLANET TALK.

Every issue is packed with up-to-date travel news and advice including:

- a letter from Lonely Planet co-founders Tony and Maureen Wheeler
- go behind the scenes on the road with a Lonely Planet author
- feature article on an important and topical travel issue
- a selection of recent letters from travellers
- details on forthcoming Lonely Planet promotions
- complete list of Lonely Planet products

To join our mailing list contact any Lonely Planet office.

Also available: Lonely Planet T-shirts. 100% heavyweight cotton.

LONELY PLANET ONLINE

Get the latest travel information before you leave or while you're on the road

Whether you've just begun planning your next trip, or you're chasing down specific info on currency regulations or visa requirements, check out Lonely Planet Online for up-to-the minute travel information.

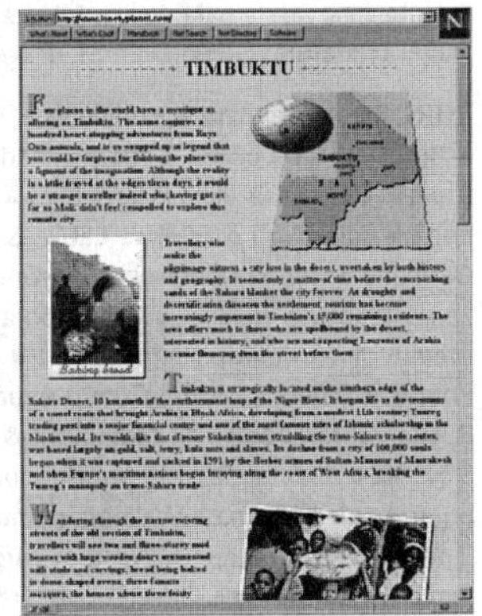
TIMBUKTU

As well as travel profiles of your favourite destinations (including maps and photos), you'll find current reports from our researchers and other travellers, updates on health and visas, travel advisories, and discussion of the ecological and political issues you need to be aware of as you travel.

There's also an online travellers' forum where you can share your experience of life on the road, meet travel companions and ask other travellers for their recommendations and advice. We also have plenty of links to other online sites useful to independent travellers.

And of course we have a complete and up-to-date list of all Lonely Planet travel products including guides, phrasebooks, atlases, Journeys and videos and a simple online ordering facility if you can't find the book you want elsewhere.

www.lonelyplanet.com
or
AOL keyword: lp

LONELY PLANET

Guides by Region

Lonely Planet is known worldwide for publishing practical, reliable and no-nonsense travel information in our guides and on our Web site. The Lonely Planet list covers just about every accessible part of the world. Currently there are nine series: travel guides, shoestring guides, walking guides, city guides, phrasebooks, audio packs, travel atlases, diving and snorkeling guides and travel literature.

AFRICA Africa – the South • Africa on a shoestring • Arabic (Egyptian) phrasebook • Arabic (Moroccan) phrasebook • Cairo • Cape Town • Central Africa • East Africa • Egypt • Egypt travel atlas • Ethiopian (Amharic) phrasebook • The Gambia & Senegal • Kenya • Kenya travel atlas • Malawi, Mozambique & Zambia • Morocco • North Africa • South Africa, Lesotho & Swaziland • South Africa, Lesotho & Swaziland travel atlas • Swahili phrasebook • Tanzania, Zanzibar & Pemba • Trekking in East Africa • Tunisia • West Africa • Zimbabwe, Botswana & Namibia • Zimbabwe, Botswana & Namibia travel atlas
Travel Literature: The Rainbird: A Central African Journey • Songs to an African Sunset: A Zimbabwean Story • Mali Blues: Traveling to an African Beat

AUSTRALIA & THE PACIFIC Australia • Australian phrasebook • Bushwalking in Australia • Bushwalking in Papua New Guinea • Fiji • Fijian phrasebook • Islands of Australia's Great Barrier Reef • Melbourne • Micronesia • New Caledonia • New South Wales & the ACT • New Zealand • Northern Territory • Outback Australia • Papua New Guinea • Papua New Guinea (Pidgin) phrasebook • Queensland • Rarotonga & the Cook Islands • Samoa • Solomon Islands • South Australia • Sydney • Tahiti & French Polynesia • Tasmania • Tonga • Tramping in New Zealand • Vanuatu • Victoria • Western Australia
Travel Literature: Islands in the Clouds • Sean & David's Long Drive

CENTRAL AMERICA & THE CARIBBEAN Bahamas and Turks & Caicos • Barcelona • Bermuda • Central America on a shoestring • Costa Rica • Cuba • Dominican Republic & Haiti • Eastern Caribbean • Guatemala, Belize & Yucatán: La Ruta Maya • Jamaica • Mexico • Mexico City • Panama
Travel Literature: Green Dreams: Travels in Central America

EUROPE Amsterdam • Andalucía • Austria • Baltic States phrasebook • Barcelona • Berlin • Britain • British phrasebook • Canary Islands • Central Europe • Central Europe phrasebook • Corsica • Croatia • Czech & Slovak Republics • Denmark • Dublin • Eastern Europe • Eastern Europe phrasebook • Edinburgh • Estonia, Latvia & Lithuania • Europe • Finland • France • French phrasebook • Germany • German phrasebook • Greece • Greek phrasebook • Hungary • Iceland, Greenland & the Faroe Islands • Ireland • Italian phrasebook • Italy • Lisbon • London • Mediterranean Europe • Mediterranean Europe phrasebook • Norway • Paris • Poland • Portugal • Portugal travel atlas • Prague • Provence & the Côte d'Azur • Romania & Moldova • Rome • Russia, Ukraine & Belarus • Russian phrasebook • Scandinavian & Baltic Europe • Scandinavian Europe phrasebook • Scotland • Slovenia • Spain • Spanish phrasebook • St Petersburg • Switzerland • Trekking in Spain • Ukrainian phrasebook • Vienna • Walking in Britain • Walking in Italy • Walking in Ireland • Walking in Switzerland • Western Europe • Western Europe phrasebook
Travel Literature: The Olive Grove: Travels in Greece

INDIAN SUBCONTINENT Bangladesh • Bengali phrasebook • Bhutan • Delhi • Goa • Hindi/Urdu phrasebook • India • India & Bangladesh travel atlas • Indian Himalaya • Karakoram Highway • Nepal • Nepali phrasebook • Pakistan • Rajasthan • South India • Sri Lanka • Sri Lanka phrasebook • Trekking in the Indian Himalaya • Trekking in the Karakoram & Hindukush • Trekking in the Nepal Himalaya
Travel Literature: In Rajasthan • Shopping for Buddhas

LONELY PLANET

Mail Order

Lonely Planet products are distributed worldwide. They are also available by mail order from Lonely Planet, so if you have difficulty finding a title please write to us. North and South American residents should write to 150 Linden St, Oakland, CA 94607, USA; European and African residents should write to 10a Spring Place, London NW5 3BH, UK; and residents of other countries to PO Box 617, Hawthorn, Victoria 3122, Australia.

ISLANDS OF THE INDIAN OCEAN Madagascar & Comoros • Maldives • Mauritius, Réunion & Seychelles

MIDDLE EAST & CENTRAL ASIA Arab Gulf States • Central Asia • Central Asia phrasebook • Iran • Israel & the Palestinian Territories • Israel & the Palestinian Territories travel atlas • Istanbul • Jerusalem • Jordan & Syria • Jordan, Syria & Lebanon travel atlas • Lebanon • Middle East on a shoestring • Turkey • Turkish phrasebook • Turkey travel atlas • Yemen
Travel Literature: The Gates of Damascus • Kingdom of the Film Stars: Journey into Jordan

NORTH AMERICA Alaska • Backpacking in Alaska • Baja California • California & Nevada • Canada • Chicago • Florida • Hawaii • Honolulu • Los Angeles • Louisiana • Miami • New England USA • New Orleans • New York City • New York, New Jersey & Pennsylvania • Pacific Northwest USA • Rocky Mountain States • San Francisco • Seattle • Southwest USA • USA • USA phrasebook • Vancouver • Washington, DC & the Capital Region
Travel Literature: Drive Thru America

NORTH-EAST ASIA Beijing • Cantonese phrasebook • China • Hong Kong • Hong Kong, Macau & Guangzhou • Japan • Japanese phrasebook • Japanese audio pack • Korea • Korean phrasebook • Kyoto • Mandarin phrasebook • Mongolia • Mongolian phrasebook • North-East Asia on a shoestring • Seoul • South-West China • Taiwan • Tibet • Tibetan phrasebook • Tokyo
Travel Literature: Lost Japan

SOUTH AMERICA Argentina, Uruguay & Paraguay • Bolivia • Brazil • Brazilian phrasebook • Buenos Aires • Chile & Easter Island • Chile & Easter Island travel atlas • Colombia • Ecuador & the Galapagos Islands • Latin American Spanish phrasebook • Peru • Quechua phrasebook • Rio de Janeiro • South America on a shoestring • Trekking in the Patagonian Andes • Venezuela
Travel Literature: Full Circle: A South American Journey

SOUTH-EAST ASIA Bali & Lombok • Bangkok • Burmese phrasebook • Cambodia • Hill Tribes phrasebook • Ho Chi Minh City • Indonesia • Indonesia's Eastern Islands • Indonesian phrasebook • Indonesian audio pack • Jakarta • Java • Laos • Lao phrasebook • Laos travel atlas • Malay phrasebook • Malaysia, Singapore & Brunei • Myanmar (Burma) • Philippines • Pilipino (Tagalog) phrasebook • Singapore • South-East Asia on a shoestring • South-East Asia phrasebook • Thailand • Thailand's Islands & Beaches • Thailand travel atlas • Thai phrasebook • Thai audio pack • Vietnam • Vietnamese phrasebook • Vietnam travel atlas

ALSO AVAILABLE: Antarctica • Brief Encounters: Stories of Love, Sex & Travel • Chasing Rickshaws • Not the Only Planet: Travel Stories from Science Fiction • Travel with Children • Traveller's Tales

THE LONELY PLANET STORY

Lonely Planet published its first book in 1973 in response to the numerous 'How did you do it?' questions Maureen and Tony Wheeler were asked after driving, busing, hitching, sailing and railing their way from England to Australia.

Written at a kitchen table and hand collated, trimmed and stapled, *Across Asia on the Cheap* became an instant local bestseller, inspiring thoughts of another book.

Eighteen months in South-East Asia resulted in their second guide, *South-East Asia on a shoestring*, which they put together in a backstreet Chinese hotel in Singapore in 1975. The 'yellow bible', as it quickly became known to backpackers around the world, soon became *the* guide to the region. It has sold well over half a million copies and is now in its 9th edition, still retaining its familiar yellow cover.

Today there are over 350 titles, including travel guides, walking guides, language kits & phrasebooks, travel atlases and travel literature. The company is the largest independent travel publisher in the world. Although Lonely Planet initially specialised in guides to Asia, today there are few corners of the globe that have not been covered.

The emphasis continues to be on travel for independent travellers. Tony and Maureen still travel for several months of each year and play an active part in the writing, updating and quality control of Lonely Planet's guides.

They have been joined by over 80 authors and 200 staff at our offices in Melbourne (Australia), Oakland (USA), London (UK) and Paris (France). Travellers themselves also make a valuable contribution to the guides through the feedback we receive in thousands of letters each year and on our web site.

The people at Lonely Planet strongly believe that travellers can make a positive contribution to the countries they visit, both through their appreciation of the countries' culture, wildlife and natural features, and through the money they spend. In addition, the company makes a direct contribution to the countries and regions it covers. Since 1986 a percentage of the income from each book has been donated to ventures such as famine relief in Africa; aid projects in India; agricultural projects in Central America; Greenpeace's efforts to halt French nuclear testing in the Pacific; and Amnesty International.

'I hope we send people out with the right attitude about travel. You realise when you travel that there are so many different perspectives about the world, so we hope these books will make people more interested in what they see. Guidebooks can't really guide people. All you can do is point them in the right direction.'

– Tony Wheeler

LONELY PLANET PUBLICATIONS

Australia
PO Box 617, Hawthorn 3122, Victoria
tel: (03) 9819 1877 fax: (03) 9819 6459
e-mail: talk2us@lonelyplanet.com.au

USA
150 Linden St
Oakland, CA 94607
tel: (510) 893 8555 TOLL FREE: 800 275-8555
fax: (510) 893 8572
e-mail: info@lonelyplanet.com

UK
10a Spring Place,
London NW5 3BH
tel: (0171) 428 4800 fax: (0171) 428 4828
e-mail: go@lonelyplanet.co.uk

France:
1 rue du Dahomey, 75011 Paris
tel: 01 55 25 33 00 fax: 01 55 25 33 01
e-mail: bip@lonelyplanet.fr

World Wide Web: http://www.lonelyplanet.com
or *AOL keyword: lp*